Economics of Land Degradation and Improvement – A Global Assessment for Sustainable Development

Ephraim Nkonya · Alisher Mirzabaev
Joachim von Braun
Editors

Economics of Land Degradation and Improvement – A Global Assessment for Sustainable Development

Springer Open

Editors
Ephraim Nkonya
International Food Policy Research Institute (IFPRI)
Washington, DC
USA

Joachim von Braun
Center for Development Research (ZEF)
University of Bonn
Bonn
Germany

Alisher Mirzabaev
Center for Development Research (ZEF)
University of Bonn
Bonn
Germany

ISBN 978-3-319-36426-1 ISBN 978-3-319-19168-3 (eBook)
DOI 10.1007/978-3-319-19168-3

Springer Cham Heidelberg New York Dordrecht London

Softcover re-print of the Hardcover 1st edition 2016

Printed on acid-free paper

Springer International Publishing AG Switzerland is part of Springer Science+Business Media (www.springer.com)

Foreword

Fertile soils are an essential building block for human existence on Earth. The degradation of soils and land, in this regard, poses significant challenges for the well-being and food security of all the people around the world. Moreover, soils provide not only food, fiber, and many types of biomass we use, but also a wide range of other essential ecosystem services, such as carbon sequestration, water purification, cultural, and esthetic values. Unfortunately, in the Anthropocene, our age of mankind, the degradation of natural ecosystems, including land and soils, has rapidly increased, posing daunting challenges to achieving sustainable development and poverty reduction. Degradation of ecosystems is posing environmental challenges and is leading to the loss of land productivity—which in turn leads to conversion of high-value biomes—such as forests—to low-value biomes—especially in low-income countries, where majority of the rural poor heavily depend on natural resources. The resulting scarcities are often exacerbated by prohibiting and dispossessing people from access to land and fertile soils. Hence, sustainable soil management and responsible land governance have a great potential for being one of the corner stones of achieving the sustainable development goals (SDGs). Specifically, sustainable land management contributes to achieving several of the SDGs, such as land degradation neutrality and an ambitious climate and biodiversity agenda, as highlighted in the series of Global Soil Week events in Berlin in recent years.

This book on *Economics of Land Degradation and Improvement* provides with valuable knowledge and information both at the global, regional, and national levels on the costs of land degradation and benefits of taking action against land degradation. A key advantage of this book is that it goes beyond the conventional market values of only crop and livestock products lost due to land degradation, but seeks to capture all major terrestrial losses of ecosystem services. Twelve carefully selected national case studies provide rich information about various local contexts of cost of land degradation as evaluated by local communities, drivers of land degradation, and amenable strategies for sustainable land management.

The research presented in the book shows that investments to address land degradation have significant economic payoffs. Next to investments, we have to address the question of adoption of sustainable land management practices and policies. To implement land restoration, we need to understand obstacles within the social, economic, and the political context. The results of this study show that particular attention needs to be paid to tangible local incentives for taking action against land degradation. This requires secure land rights, enhancing extension services, and empowering local communities to manage their natural resources. The identification of implementation pathways through multi-stakeholder processes assumes a particular importance in this regard. This book can serve as a highly valuable resource and reference for policymakers, civil society, researchers, and practitioners.

Klaus Töpfer
Executive Director, Institute for Advanced
Sustainability Studies (IASS) and former Under
Secretary General of the United Nations, Executive
Director of the United Nations Environment Programme

Acknowledgments

The relationships between human well-being and land and soils are still not getting appropriate policy attention. Over the past few years, however, the research and action community concerned with the consequences of degradation of land and soils, and the need for sustainable land management, has grown rapidly. The global reach of this volume is testimony to that. We hope that interdisciplinary research with an emphasis on economics and social science in combination with biophysical research on land and soils may help trigger public and private action. A central perspective provided with this volume is that the costs of inaction on land degradation are much higher than that of the costs of taking action against degradation.

The joint research teams at Center for Development Research (ZEF) and International Food Policy Research Institute (IFPRI) are grateful for the many partnerships we were able to build around this topic, which is so fundamental for sustainable development. The research presented in this book is the outcome of collaborative efforts by numerous individuals and institutions. Up front we thank them all, although inadvertently not all may have been mentioned here.

This book would not have been possible without the time and efforts of thousands of households who participated in the surveys and community focus group discussions contributing to the individual case studies and sharing their knowledge and experiences for addressing land degradation.

Each of the studies benefited from the advice of external reviewers, individual researchers, and development and policy practitioners. We would like to express our heartfelt appreciation to Professor Rattan Lal for serving as the leading external reviewer of this volume and for sharing his tremendous experience and advice with us throughout the background research for this volume. We are also highly indebted to Zhanguo Bai, Edward Barbier, Rashid Hassan, Jane Kabubo-Mariara, Tobias Landmann, Erik Nelson, Martin Petrick, and Paul Reich for their highly insightful comments and suggestions during the review of individual studies. The interim results of the chapters were presented in several workshops and conferences, including the Global Soil Weeks in Berlin, where they received valuable comments and suggestions. We thank the experts who shared with us their wisdom during these presentations of early findings from the studies.

We are very grateful to the collaborating institutions and their staff in the case study countries who provided both technical and logistic support. Particularly, we thank the Argentinian National University Arturo Jauretche, Bhutanese National Soil Services Center, Center for Chinese Agricultural Policy of the Chinese Academy of Sciences, Ethiopian Economic Association, Indira Gandhi Institute of Development Research, Kenyan Agricultural and Livestock Research Institute, Institut National de la Recherche Agronomique du Niger, Eurasian Center for Food Security, Tanzanian office of the International Institute of Tropical Agriculture, Institut National de Pédologie du Sénégal, Central Asian and Caucasian office of the International Center for Agricultural Research in the Dry Areas. We are also highly thankful to many international partner institutions for promoting and facilitating this research, specifically, Economics of Land Degradation Initiative Secretariat, European Commission, GIZ, and UNCCD.

Each of the studies has also benefited from research guidance and strong encouragements from policymakers in a number of ministries and departments in the study countries, and many colleagues and friends. We are particularly grateful for these inputs to Tahirou Abdoulaye, Assefa Admassie, Jamal Annagylyjova, Mahendra Dev, Georg Deichert, Marlene Diekmann, Nicolas Gerber, Zhe Guo, Jikun Huang, Issoufou Issaka, Eliud Kereger, Pavel Krasilnikov, Adam Mamadou, Mame Ndéné Lo, Alfred Tine, Talla Gueye, Mamadou Maiga, Papa Nekhou Diagne, Ephraim Mukisira, Nandan Nawn, Vijaylaxmi Pandey, Mark Schauer, Kamil Shideed, Abasse Tougiani, Timothy Thomas, Josef Turok, and Rebecca Wahome.

We would also like to thank all the colleagues who provided us with logistic support and also worked with us on the ground, especially Muzaffar Aliev, Moussa Boureima, Silvana Builes, Zakir Khalikulov, Marlen Krause, Karin Hagedorn-Mensah, Aziz Nurbekov, Subashin Mesipam, Milo Mitchell, Arpita Nehra, Evelyne Odiambo, Clemens Olbrich, Andrea Pedolsky, Rebecka Ridder, and Alma van der Veen.

We would like to gratefully thank German Federal Ministry for Economic Cooperation and Development (BMZ), for providing the financial support for this research. BMZ's wise decision to make economics of land degradation a development policy theme augmented the development agenda, and the continued support for research and action on Economics of Land Degradation has been crucial in making this volume possible. The chapter on Bhutan also received funding from the World Bank-Netherlands Partnership Program. Similarly, the chapter on Russia received funding from the Russian Research Fund.

The mission of this volume is to trigger more appropriate care for earth. We hope the research and methodologies described in this volume will stimulate further interdisciplinary research on land degradation and land improvement, especially locally.

Ephraim Nkonya
Alisher Mirzabaev
Joachim von Braun

Contents

Abbreviations

AEZ	Agro-ecological zone
AF	Atmospheric fertilization
AFSIS	Africa Soil Information Service
AHL	Annual harvest limit
AIC	Agro-industrial complex
AISP	Agricultural Input Subsidy Program
APDM	Area percentage data model
ARPU	Agro-climatic regional planning unit
ASAL	Arid and semiarid lands
ASDSP	Agricultural Sector Development Support Program
AVHRR	Advanced very high-resolution radiometer
AVNIR	Advanced land observation satellite
AWM	Agriculture water management
BAU	Business as usual
BBS	Broad-based surveys
BMZ	German Federal Ministry for Economic Cooperation and Development
BRDF	Bidirectional reflectance distribution function
CA	Conservation agriculture
CAC	Central American and Caribbean
CACP	Commission for agricultural costs and prices
CBD	Convention on biological diversity
CBFM	Community-based forest management
CBPA	Community-based protected areas
CCS	Cost of cultivation survey
CF	Community-managed forests
CGIAR-CSI	Consultative Group for International Agricultural Research—Consortium for Spatial Information
CIESIN CIAT	Center for International Earth Science Information Network—Centro Internacional de Agricultura Tropical

CIESIN	Center for International Earth Science Information Network, Columbia
CIP	Crop Intensification Program
CRILAR	Centro Regional de Investigaciones La Rioja
CRILAR-CONICET	The National Observatory of Desertification and Land Degradation, coordinated by the Regional Centre for Scientific and Technological Research of La Rioja
CRU	Climate Research Unit, University of East Anglia
CSA	Central Statistical Agency, Ethiopia
CT	Conventional tillage
dbh	Diameter at breast height or drashing size trees
DEM	Digital elevation model
DFID	Department for International Development, UK
DM	Dry matter
DMI	Dry matter intake
DOS	Strategic orientation document
DSSAT-CENTURY	Decision support system for agro-technology transfer crop simulation model
ECOWAS	Economic community of West African States
EKC	Environment Kuznets curve
ELD	Economics of land degradation
EPI	Environmental performance index
ERSS	Ethiopia Rural Socioeconomic Survey
ES	Ecosystem services
ETIP	Extended targeted input program
ETM	Enhanced thematic mapper
EU	European Union
FAO	Food and Agriculture Organization of the United Nations
FAOSTAT	Food and Agriculture Organization Corporate Statistical Database
FD	Federal district
FE	Fixed effect
FGD	Focus group discussion
FMNR	Farmer management natural regeneration
FMSP	Federal Market Stabilization Program
FRA	Forest resource assessment
FYM	Farm yard manure
GADM	Database of global administrative areas
GDP	Gross domestic product
GE	Government effectives
GEF	Global environment facility
GEI	Government effectiveness index
GHG	Greenhouse gas
GHI	Global Hunger index
GIMMS	Global inventory modeling and mapping studies

GIS	Geographic information system
GLADA	Global assessment of land degradation and improvement
GLADIS	Global land degradation information system
GLASS	Global land surface characteristic parameters product and applications study
GLCF	Global land cover facility
GLS	Global land survey
GLW	Gridded livestock of the world
GM	Genetically modified
GMO	Genetically modified organism
GNI	Gross national income
GOANA	Grande Offensive Agricole pour la Nourriture et l'Abondance
GoK	Government of Kenya
GRP	Gross regional product
GRUMP	Global rural–urban mapping project
GTP	Growth and transformation plan, Ethiopia
HANPP	Human appropriation of net primary production
HDI	Human development index
HEP	Hydroelectric power
HRU	Hydrologic response unit
HYV	High yielding varieties
ICAR	Indian Council of Agricultural Research
ICARDA	International Center for Agricultural Research in the Dry Areas
IFPRI	International Center for Food Policy Research
IGBP	International Geosphere–Biosphere Program
IHS	Integrated Household Survey, Ethiopia
IIASA	International Institute for Applied Systems Analysis
IISD	International Institute for Sustainable Development
IMT	Irrigation management transfer
IMR	Infant mortality rate
INTA	National Institute of Agricultural Technology
IRR	Internal rate of return
IRWR	Internal renewable water resources
ISFM	Integrated soil fertility management
ISRIC	International Soil Reference and Information Center
ITU	International Telecommunication Union
IV-LPM	Instrumental variable linear probability model
KALRO	Kenya Agricultural and Livestock Research Organization
KARI	Kenya Agricultural Research Institute
KIHBS	Kenya Integrated Household Budget Survey
KLA	Kenya Land Alliance
LAC	Latin America and Caribbean
LADA	Land degradation assessment in drylands

LCA	Life cycle analysis
LD	Land degradation
LPI	Logistics performance index
LSMS-ISA	Living standards measurement study—integrated surveys on agriculture
LUCC	Land use and cover change
LUP	Land use planning
LUPP	Land use planning processes
MEA	Millennium Ecosystem Assessment
MoAF	Ministry of Agriculture and Forests
MODIS	Moderate resolution imaging spectroradiometer
MoFED	Ministry of Finance and Economic Development, Ethiopia
MRR	Marginal rate of return
MSS	Multispectral scanner
NAAIP	National Accelerated Agricultural Input Program
NAIVS	National agricultural input voucher system
NALEP	National Agricultural and Livestock Extension Program
NAM	North America
NAP	National action plan
NAPA	National adaptation program of action
NASA	National Aeronautics and Space Administration
NBS	National Bureau of Statistics, Tanzania
NBSS	National Bureau of Soil Survey
NDVI	Normalized difference vegetation index
NENA	Near East and North Africa
NFP	National Forest Policy
NGO	Non-Governmental Organization
NLP	National land policy
NOAA	US National Oceanic and Atmospheric Association
NPP	Net primary productivity
NPV	Net present value
NRM	Natural resource management
NRSA	National Remote Sensing Agency
NSE	Nash-Sutcliffe model efficiency
NSO	National Statistics Office, Ethiopia
NSSC	National Soil Services Center
NT	No tillage
NTFP	Non-timber forest products
ODA	Official development assistance
PAE	Public agricultural expenditure
PBIAS	Percent bias
PBL	Netherlands Environmental Assessment Agency
PES	Payment for Ecosystem Services
PEV	Post-election violence
PG	Planted pasture

PI	Soil productivity index
PIK	Projet Intégré Keita
PIECAS-DP	Plan for Integral Strategic Planning for Conservation and Sustainable Development of the Paraná Delta Region
PN	Natural regeneration pasture
POP	Population
PRM	Poisson regression model
PROSAP	Program of Agricultural Services in Provinces
PUG	Proportion of unpalatable grasses
R&D	Research and Development
RDS	Rural development strategy
RF	Rainfall
RGoB	Royal Government of Bhutan
RNR	Renewable natural resource
ROSSTAT	Federal state statistics service
RS	Remote sensing
RUB	Russian rubles
SayDS	Secretariat of Environment and Sustainable Development
SDG	Sustainable development goal
SDI	Steppe degradation index
SE	South–East
SFA	State forestry administration
SFM	Sustainable forest management
SFSR	Soviet Federative Socialist Republic
SIAD	National strategy for sustainable input supply to farmers
SLCP	Sloping Land Conversion Program
SLM	Sustainable land management
SLWM	Sustainable land and water management
SOM	Soil organic matter
SRTM	Shuttle radar topography mission
SSA	Sub-Saharan Africa
SWAT	Soil and water assessment tool
SWC	Soil and water conservation
TAP	Total agricultural product
TEEB	The economics of ecosystems and biodiversity
TERI	The Energy and Resources Institute
TEV	Total economic value
TIP	Targeted Input Program
TLU	Tropical livestock unit
TM	Thematic mapper
TME	Tecnología de Manejo Extensivo
TNC	Transnational corporations
TNPS	Tanzania National Panel Survey
UMEOA	West African Monetary and Economic Union
UNCCD	United Nations Convention to Combat Desertification

UNDP	United Nations Development Program
UNEP	United Nations Environmental Program
UNFCCC	United Nations framework convention on climate change
UON	University of Nairobi
URT	United Republic of Tanzania
US	United States
USD	United States Dollar
USDA-NRCS	US Department of Agriculture, Natural Resources Conservation Service
UTM	Universal Transverse Mercator
VFC	Vegetation fractional coverage
VP	Vertical plowing (Vertical Chisel)
WB	The World Bank
WEF	Water–energy–food
WER	Wind erosion risk
WFP	Wood forest product
WHO	World Health Organization
WOCAT	World overview of conservation approaches and technologies
WRI	World Resources Institute
YCEO	Yale Center for Earth Observation
ZEF	Center for Development Research, University of Bonn

Chapter 1
Economics of Land Degradation and Improvement: An Introduction and Overview

Ephraim Nkonya, Alisher Mirzabaev and Joachim von Braun

Abstract Land degradation is occurring in almost all terrestrial biomes and agro-ecologies, in both low and high income countries. However its impact is especially severe on the livelihoods of the poor who heavily depend on natural resources. Despite the severe impact of land degradation on the poor and the crucial role that land plays in human welfare and development, investments in sustainable land management (SLM) are low, especially in developing countries. This chapter summarizes the results from global and regional levels as well as 12 case study countries. The chapter also draws conclusions and implications for taking action against land degradation. Land degradation stretches to about 30 % of the total global land area and about three billion people reside in degraded lands. The annual global cost of land degradation due to land use/cover change (LUCC) and using land degrading management practices on static cropland and grazing land is about 300 billion USD. Sub-Saharan Africa (SSA) accounts for the largest share (22 %) of the total global cost of land degradation. Only about 46 % of the cost of land degradation due to LUCC—which accounts for 78 % of the US$300 billion loss is borne by land users and the remaining share (54 %) is borne by consumers of ecosystem services off the farm. This further illustrates that land degradation is a global problem even though its impact is much greater on poor land users. The cost of taking action against land degradation is much lower than the cost of inaction and the returns to taking action are high. On average, one US dollar investment into restoration of degraded land returns five US dollars. This provides a strong incentive for taking action against land degradation. This study shows that simul-

E. Nkonya (✉)
International Food Policy Research Institute, 2033 K Street NW, Washington, DC 20006, USA
e-mail: e.nkonya@cgiar.org

A. Mirzabaev · J. von Braun
Center for Development Research (ZEF), University of Bonn, Walter Flex Str 3, Bonn 53113, Germany
e-mail: almir@uni-bonn.de

J. von Braun
e-mail: jvonbraun@uni-bonn.de

E. Nkonya et al. (eds.), *Economics of Land Degradation and Improvement – A Global Assessment for Sustainable Development*,
DOI 10.1007/978-3-319-19168-3_1

taneously enhancing local and national level governments, land tenure security, and improving market access is the most effective strategy for addressing land degradation. Given that LUCC accounts for the largest share of cost of land degradation, there is a need for developing land use planning that will ensure that forests and other high value biomes are effectively protected. Empirical evidence has shown that involvement of local communities in managing forests and other high value biomes and creating mechanisms for them to directly benefit from their conservation efforts lead to more effective protection than is the case with centralized protection. The assessment in this volume is being conducted at a time when there is an elevated interest in private land investments and when global efforts to achieve sustainable development objectives have intensified. This means, results of this volume will contribute significantly to the ongoing policy debate and efforts to design strategies for achieving sustainable development goals and other efforts to address land degradation and halt biodiversity loss.

Keywords Economics of land degradation and improvement · Sustainable land management · Cost of action · Ecosystem services

Land Degradation: A Global Problem

Sustainable land use and protection of soils play a key role in food, climate, and human security (Lal 2005, 2014; von Braun 2013; Lal et al. 2014; Amundson et al. 2015). In spite of this, land degradation has become a global problem occurring in most terrestrial biomes and agro-ecologies, in both low income and highly industrialized countries (Le et al. 2014; Chap. 4). On the other hand, fertile soils are a non-renewable resource by human time spans as their formation and renewal could take hundreds, if not thousands, of years (Lal 1994). For this reason, the human management of soil resources will have wide-ranging consequences on human security for generations to come.

Already, sharp acceleration in environmental pollution and natural resource degradation over the past century has led to a higher recognition of the importance of sustainable development, including the first global landmark event—the Human Environment Conference in Stockholm in 1972 (World Bank 2010). Continuing on this path towards sustainability, the United Nations have set 17 Sustainable Development Goals (SDGs) to guide the future global development agenda. One of the 17 targets aims to "protect, restore and promote sustainable use of terrestrial ecosystems, sustainably manage forests, combat desertification, and halt and reverse land degradation and halt biodiversity loss" (UNDP 2015). Thus, SDGs envision providing a global commitment to address land degradation and achieve a land and soil degradation-neutral world (Lal et al. 2012).

Crucially in this context, the livelihoods of the majority of the rural poor depend on land (Nachtergaele et al. 2010). Additionally, food, fiber and other terrestrial ecosystem goods for the global population are drawn from land, the degradation of which has both direct and indirect impacts on overall human welfare. Addressing land degradation can, therefore, provide with cross-cutting contributions to achieving many of the other SDGs as well. Despite the crucial role that land plays in human welfare and development, investments in sustainable land management (SLM) are low, especially in developing countries. For example, public investments per worker in the agricultural sector in Sub-Saharan Africa (SSA) declined to one third from 152 USD in 1980–1989 to only 42 USD in 2005–2007 (FAO 2012). In particular, investments and incentives for sustainable land use and for prevention of land and soil degradation are presently inadequate and would need to be substantially increased in order to eradicate poverty and enhance food security in the world.

Why Economics of Land Degradation and Improvement

Given the above, the research presented in this book has been conducted with the objective to strengthen the foundations of ecological and economic knowledge that may stimulate putting sustainability of land and soils appropriately on the political agendas. These studies at global, regional and national levels evaluate the costs of land degradation and benefits of sustainable land management. They also identify the drivers of land degradation in order to devise polices to address them. Using case studies helps analyze in more detail the aspects of land degradation that cannot be captured using global or regional-level data, especially due to the diverse nature and process of land degradation under different biophysical and socio-economic characteristics at the local levels. A total of 12 country-level case studies were conducted for more detailed analyses of the costs and drivers of land degradation. The case study countries were carefully selected to be globally representative for major biophysical and socio-economic characteristics. They account for 43 % of the global population and 28 % of the land area.

The second objective of the volume is to provide empirical evidence and information to help the global community to take action against land degradation and its impacts on human wellbeing. The third objective of the study is to develop analytical approaches and generate data that could be used to conduct regular assessment of land degradation and improvement at global, regional, country and local levels.

The analytical methods are presented in a manner to allow their applications across disciplines and by researchers and practitioners with varying needs and capacities. The study covers two major categories of land degradation: namely, long-term loss of value of land ecosystem services due to land use and cover change (LUCC) and the use of land degrading management practices on cropland and grazing lands that do not experience LUCC. The six major biomes covered include forest, shrublands, grasslands, cropland, barren land, and woodlands and they accounted for about 86 % of global land area in 2001 (NASA 2014).

The broad research questions covered in this book include:

1. What are the appropriate and practical methods for global assessment of land degradation and improvement?
2. What are the global and regional extent and severity of land degradation and opportunities for improvement?
3. What are the key drivers of land degradation across typical socio-ecological regions of the world?
4. What are the economic, social and environmental costs of land degradation and net benefits resulting from taking actions against degradation compared to inaction?
5. What are the feasible policy and development strategies that enable and catalyze sustainable land management (SLM) actions?

The book makes two major new contributions. Firstly, it develops a conceptual framework to guide economic assessments of land degradation using the Millennium Ecosystem Assessment (MEA 2005), which defines land degradation as a long-term loss of ecosystem services (Chap. 2). Most previous studies on economics of land degradation concentrated on the impacts of land degradation on loss of provisioning services of croplandand grazing land and have ignored the loss of other ecosystem services (e.g. carbon sequestration and nutrient cycling) on agricultural land and other biomes. Secondly, this conceptual framework and the corresponding methodological approaches developed (Chaps. 2, 6 and 7) are consistently applied through comparable national case studies. Implementation of such harmonized case studies allows drawing more generalizable conclusions about the costs and drivers of land degradation. Most previous studies on economics of land degradation—while insightful locally—are much less comparable since they use different methods and approaches, and thus do not add up to a global picture.

Additionally, each chapter seeks to make more specific new contributions to the existing methodological, thematic or region-specific knowledge. Below we summarize major empirical findings of the chapters.

Scale of Global Land Degradation

Using remote sensing data, Chap. 4 identifies global hotspots of land degradation by correcting for biases found in previous mapping exercises, thus improving on the previous efforts on global land degradation mapping. The results show that land degradation stretches to about 30 % of the total global land area and is occurring across all agro-ecologies. In total, there are about 3 billion people who reside in the areas with land degradation hotspots. However, the true number of people affected by land degradation is likely to be higher, because even those people residing outside degrading areas may be dependent on the continued flow of ecosystem goods and services from the degrading areas. One third of the area of land degradation hotspots is directly identifiable from a statistically significant declining trend in normalized difference vegetation index (NDVI), which is an index that measures the density of greenness of plants on a patch of land. However, the remaining two thirds of land degradation are concealed by rainfall dynamics, atmospheric fertilization and application of chemical fertilizers. Globally, human-induced biomass productivity decline is found in 25 % of croplands and vegetation-crop mosaics, 29 % of mosaics of forests with shrub- and grasslands, 25 % of shrublands, and 33 % of grasslands, as well as 23 % of areas with sparse vegetation. The share of degrading croplands is likely to increase further when we take into account the croplands where intensive fertilizer application may be masking land degradation. Although this study does find land degradation to be a major problem in croplands, it also emphasizes, in contrast to most previous studies, the extent of degradation in areas used for livestock grazing by pastoral communities, including grasslands, shrublands, their mosaics, and areas with sparse vegetation. In most countries, livestock production and its value chains produce a comparable economic product and incomes for rural populations as crop production.

The results of this land degradation mapping were also groundtruthed in several dozen locations in six case study countries (Chap. 5). This evaluation showed an intermediate agreement between the mapping based on remotely sensed data and field results collected from focus group discussions with communities in six countries (Ethiopia, India, Niger, Senegal, Tanzania and Uzbekistan). In general, there was a higher agreement between the corrected NDVI results (Chap. 4) and focus group discussions (FGDs) on degraded lands than on lands which experienced improvement. The FGDs and field observations indicate that the results of the land degradation mapping are robust. This approach and its findings suggest that there may be ample opportunities for more "citizen research" and monitoring by communities on land degradation.

Costs of Action and Inaction

The annual costs of land degradation at the global level were found to equal about 300 billion USD[1] (Chap. 6). Sub-Saharan Africa (SSA) accounts for the largest share (22 %) of the total global cost of land degradation. The analysis of the cost of land degradation across the type of ecosystem services shows that 54 % of the cost is due to the losses in regulating, supporting and cultural services (for example, carbon sequestration), which are considered as global public goods. Thus, the major share of the costs of land degradation affects the entire global community. The cost of taking action against land degradation is much lower than the cost of inaction. The benefits from investments into sustainable land management were found to exceed their costs by at least two times over a 30-year planning horizon globally. In many case study countries and sub-regions, the returns from each dollar of

[1]Unless otherwise stated, all values used in the cost of land degradation are in constant 2007 USD.

investments into land rehabilitation were found to reach up to 5 dollars over the same period (Chaps. 11–21).

Policies for Global and Regional Consideration

In order to help in formulating policies and strategies for taking action against land degradation, Chap. 7 discusses the drivers of land degradation and improvement. The major factors affecting land degradation at the global level include land tenure security, population density, market access and rule of law. Better rule of law was found to positively influence sustainable land management in most cases, especially in sub-Saharan Africa. The areas with high population densities were found to manage their land resources more sustainably when they have a dynamic non-farm sector which facilitates cross-sector labor, technological and capital spillovers. Secure land tenure may provide additional benefits and opportunities for sustainable land management (SLM). With relatively well-functioning markets, including output, input and financial markets, land degradation also declines. Where markets do not function well or are very thin, secure land tenure may have much less effect on SLM. The findings further illustrate the key role played by governance and incentives for wider adoption of SLM practices.

Rangelands used by pastoral feeding systems account for 45 % of ice-free land area (Asner et al. 2004) and 70 % of the world agricultural land area (FAO 2008). Additionally, the demand for livestock products is rapidly increasing in both medium and low income countries. This underscores the importance of understanding the cost of land degradation on grazing lands. Therefore, Chap. 8 focuses on the analysis of the impacts of degradation on grazing lands that did not undergo LUCC—an area that accounts for 10 % of the grasslands and about 6 % of the total livestock population. The results show that the annual global cost of losses in milk and meat production due to grassland degradation is about 7 billion USD. Addressing grassland degradation could lead to win-win outcomes both in terms of lower poverty and higher carbon sequestration rates in grasslands.

Sub-Saharan Africa (SSA) experienced the most severe land degradation over the last decade and is also the region with the highest rates of poverty in the world. Chapter 9 analyzes the policies and land investments, the cost of land degradation and the drivers of land degradation and cropland expansion in the region. SSA has a large potential to become a global food breadbasket but presently faces daunting challenges. The analysis shows that the conversion of grassland to cropland and deforestation account for the largest share of the cost of land degradation in the region. The major driver of conversion of grassland to cropland is the low livestock productivity. Addressing this challenge requires an increase in the public allocations to livestock production and research, which currently represent only about 5 % of the public budgets in the region. Efforts to improve grasslands through controlled grazing, planting legume crops, and other sustainable practices will increase both livestock productivity and carbon sequestration. The econometric results show tenure security, access to markets and government effectiveness are major factors for enhancing crop and livestock productivity and reducing land degradation. The analysis of cropland degradation shows an inverse relationship between profitability and adoption rates of sustainable land management practices. This is largely due to poor access to markets and credit, as well as low capacity of agricultural extension services to provide advisory services on SLM practices.

Chapter 10 analyzes land degradation in **Central Asia**—a region that has experienced a combination of extensive land degradation and fundamental institutional and economic transformations over the last three decades. This and other challenges have led to abandonment of large rainfed croplands, mainly in Kazakhstan, the continued desiccation of the Aral Sea, and wide-spread secondary salinization in the irrigated areas of the region, especially in the downstream of the region's two major rivers, Amudarya and Syrdarya. The annual costs of land degradation in Central Asia due to LUCC are about 6 billion USD. About 4.6 billion USD of the cost of land degradation are related with shifts from grasslands to lower value shrublands and barren lands. A total of about 14 million ha of grasslands have shifted to shrublands and barren lands in the region between 2001 and 2009, highlighting the massive problem of rangeland degradation. Another 0.75 billion USD were due to shifts from shrublands to barren lands, especially in the parts of the region near the Aral Sea, highlighting the growing problem of desertification. The loss of ecosystem services due to deforestation is about 0.32 billion USD, whereas the abandonment of croplands and their conversion to barren lands has resulted in about 110 million USD of losses, annually. The costs of taking action against land degradation are found to be 5 times lower than the cost of inaction over a 30-year period. Better access to markets, extension services, secure land tenure, and livestock ownership among smallholder crop producers are found to be major drivers of SLM adoptions. This further underlines the importance of tenure security and access to rural services in achieving sustainable land management.

There have been numerous but isolated attempts in the past to assess the causes and costs of land degradation at the national level. However, the differences in concepts and methodologies do not allow for their meaningful comparison, and quite often have led to contradicting policy conclusions. The series of country case studies included in this volume have been conducted in Asia, Europe, South America and sub-Saharan Africa using a standardized method, thus allowing for comparability of the results and drawing more generalizable conclusions (Chaps. 11–21). In the following section, we synthesize the major lessons learnt and the so-called "low hanging fruits" to address land degradation based on the global, regional and country case studies. The findings below are divided into individual strategies but an integrated approach involving several actions taken simultaneously is essential and could lead to bigger impacts and lower costs in addressing land degradation.

Lessons Learnt and Implications

Taking Action Against Land Degradation Due to Land Use/Cover Change (LUCC)

The cost of land degradation due to LUCC accounts for 78 % of the total global cost of land degradation of about 300 billion USD, suggesting that high priority should be given to addressing land degrading land use and cover change. There is a need for developing land use policies and planning that will ensure that forests and other high value biomes are protected and continue to provide ecosystem services both to local communities and to the global community (Chap. 6). The global efforts towards increasing protected areas have been successful, especially in the temperate areas. The deforestation rates in the tropical areas of the developing countries have also decreased significantly, but continue posing a big challenge (CBD 2014). There are still substantial deforestation and other forms of LUCC that need particular attention in the tropics and temperate regions. The conversion of forests into grazing lands was the major driver of deforestation in the Amazon region. In Central Asia, conversion of grassland to barren lands and shrublands was the major type of land degradation (Chap. 10), while in the SSA, the conversion of grassland to cropland was the leading cause of land degradation due to LUCC (Chap. 9). One of the major reasons for the conversion of grassland to cropland in SSA is the low livestock productivity. Strategies for addressing the conversion of grassland to cropland involve increasing livestock productivity, which may be more effective than enforcement of land use policies aimed at preventing LUCC. In general, the findings suggest that LUCC involving grasslands need to be given much higher attention than it has been the case so far. Empirical evidence has also shown that deforestation and sustainable forest management has been more likely in forests managed by local communities (Poteete and Ostrom 2004). Likewise, protected areas that involve local communities in management and who, in return, receive direct benefits have been more successful (Coad et al. 2008). This suggests strengthening community participation—a topic discussed in detail in the next section—is key to addressing degradation due to LUCC.

Strengthening Community Participation for SLM

Involving local communities and using their traditional knowledge and innovations are crucial to achieving effective conservation efforts. This is also consistent with the Aichi biodiversity target 18, which aims to respect and use traditional knowledge, innovations and practices of indigenous people and involve local communities in implementing conservation efforts (CBD 2014). Their involvement will ensure that they benefit and get rewarded for their protection efforts (Chap. 9). Such efforts could also involve *payment for ecosystem services* (PES), given that land degradation is a global "public bad", with the global community bearing a larger share of the cost of land degradation than the local community. Incentive mechanisms need to be developed to reward those who practice land management that provides significant global ecosystem services. This means that taking action against land degradation requires both local and global policies and strategies. However, experiences have shown that PES schemes did not work well in countries with poor markets and weak local institutions (Karsenty and Ongolo 2012). On the other hand, country-level PES schemes and policies that enhance incentives for investment in land improvement have also shown promising results, as illustrated in Niger (Chap. 19) and Costa Rica where the government collects a tax for PES and rewards land users who protect forests.

However, the low capacity of local communities to tackle technical issues of natural resource management is seen as a significant constraint that compromises effective SLM. This is especially the case for the relatively new paradigms such as integrated soil fertility management (ISFM), ecosystem service management and climate change (Chap. 9). This suggests the need to invest in training and awareness creation. For example, the Dankou forest program—a community-based forest management (CBFM) program in Senegal—spends about 54 % of its budget for information and awareness (Chap. 19). Dankou CBFM has been very successful since the communities have been highly sensitized about the ecosystem services provided by the forests. As emphasized above, the technical support should take on board the indigenous knowledge and experience on ecosystem services. In other words, the information sharing and awareness creation should be two-way and sensitive to the indigenous communities.

A number of studies have shown that the pastoral systems in arid and semi-arid areas of Eastern Africa are generally sustainable even in the face of large biomass productivity changes largely due to the unpredictable precipitation and other natural shocks (Chaps. 8 and 9). There is a need to take advantage of the rich ecosystem knowledge of the pastoral nomadic communities in order to address the current challenges facing pastoral communities in the dry areas. As elaborated further, this will also require securing their communal grazing lands to stem the arbitrary expropriations and to invest in improvement of livestock productivity and marketing systems.

Strong customary institutions and environment-friendly cultural values could also be used for promoting sustainable land management. The case of strong cultural values in Bhutan (Chap. 12) illustrates the role played by cultural values in the protection of ecosystem services. Mahayana Buddhism places a strong value on the peaceful co-existence of people with nature and the sanctity of life and compassion for others. This is one of the major drivers of the high share (71 %) of the land area under forests in Bhutan and of the fact that 25 % of the population lives in the protected areas.

Enhancing Government Effectiveness and Rule of Law

The results at the global and regional levels, as well as in the case study countries consistently show that improved government effectiveness and rule of law enhance the adoption of sustainable land management practices. Improved government effectiveness works especially well when it gives local communities the mandate to manage their natural resources. For example, the key driver of Nigerien success story of tree planting and protection was improved government effectiveness, which simultaneously enabled communities to independently manage their natural resources and accrue direct benefits from their investments (Chap. 17). The country also learnt hard lessons from its past mistakes that involved policies which provided disincentives to land investment and the consequences of land degradation that were amplified by a prolonged drought.

In the past 20 years, government effectiveness has generally increased due to prolonged global democratic advocacies (Lynch and Crawford 2011). For example, development aid is given to developing countries which do not exercise flagrant undemocratic policies (Chap. 9). So in countries where rule of law is improving, SLM efforts are likely to yield favorable results (Chap. 7). This means that there may be more opportunities for addressing land degradation in countries which have shown significant improvements in government effectiveness and rule of law. Additionally, given that many donor programs require good governance as a condition for receiving aid, the donor community could continue this approach to promote government effectiveness *and* indirectly improve land management.

Improving Access to Markets and Rural Services

Controlling for government effectiveness and other important variables, access to markets could reduce the costs of land degradation (Chap. 9), and was consistently found to lead to wider adoption of SLM practices in several case study countries, such as Ethiopia, Malawi, Senegal, Tanzania and Uzbekistan (Chaps. 14, 19–21). In addition to increasing incentives, access to markets could help create alternative non-farm employment that could reduce pressure on land resources (Chap. 19).

In many developing countries, the capacities of agricultural extension services to provide advisory services on new approaches on integrated soil fertility management (ISFM), ecosystem services, climate change and other new paradigms is low (Chaps. 9 and 21). Likewise, there are limited advisory services on non-production technologies such as processing and marketing—the aspects which could contribute to enhancing SLM. This suggests the need to increase the capacity of agricultural extension agents to provide advisory services on SLM covering the entire value chain. The case study country results in Chaps. 11–21 show access to agricultural extension services improves tree planting (Bhutan) and adoption of SLM in general (Bhutan, Ethiopia, Kenya, Ethiopia, Malawi). Access to credit also increases the adoption SLM practices (Ethiopia, Malawi). In general, when major mediating factors—especially government effectiveness—are in place, improvement of rural services increases the adoption rates of SLM practices. For example, successful adoption of conservation agricultural practices in Argentina was achieved through strong extension services and public-private partnerships (Chap. 11). Conservation agriculture is considered as one of the best practices for sustainable land management (Lal 2015). This suggests the need to provide short-term training to agricultural extension agents and to incorporate the new paradigms in the agricultural curricula to ensure that future agents have greater capacity to provide appropriate advisory services. A pluralistic extension services could be required to achieve this objective since different providers will give complementary advisory services to cover many aspects where the traditional extension services might be deficient.

Improving Land Tenure Security

The findings from several case study countries have also consistently shown that adoption of sustainable land management practices is often dependent on secure land tenure (Tanzania, Malawi, Uzbekistan, and Ethiopia). Abdulai and Goetz (2014) establish similar relationships based on panel date analyses in Ghana. In this context, given that land prices and shadow prices are increasing due to the growing incomes, population and demand for biofuels and other alternative uses of agricultural products, land insecurity of the poor and vulnerable is becoming more acute. The recent trends in national and foreign land acquisitions in many developing countries, especially in SSA, illustrate this since such land acquisitions were concentrated in areas held under customary tenure and/or communal land with no formal tenure (Baumgartner et al. 2015). There is a need for policies which protect customary tenure systems against arbitrary expropriation. Additionally, long-term strategies for enhancing women's access to land under customary tenure need to be taken. Studies have shown that land markets improve women's access to land (Nkonya et al. 2008). This means, establishing land markets—especially in countries where land belongs to the government and land sales are illegal—could be one of the short-term term strategies for improving women's access to land.

Going Forward

The assessment in this volume is being conducted at a time when there is an elevated interest in private land investments and when global efforts to achieve sustainable development objectives have intensified (Chap. 2). For example, one of the 17 SDGs is specifically aimed at addressing land degradation and halt biodiversity loss. There have been numerous but isolated attempts in the past to assess the causes and consequences of land degradation (a review see in Nkonya et al. 2011). This study was done using a framework that could provide a consistent conceptual basis for other ongoing or future similar research activities and case studies on economics of land degradation and improvement.

The costs of land degradation are substantial and the costs of action to address land degradation are often several times lower than those of inaction. In spite of these high returns on investments in sustainable land management, land degradation is persisting, due to inadequate levels of investments in sustainable land management. There are two reasons for this, which need to be adequately addressed to incentivize more investments into SLM.

- First, as we have seen, the global costs of land degradation are higher than local costs, whereas the investments into SLM are often required from local land users, who include only the private costs of land degradation in their action calculations.
- Secondly, even in cases when the private costs of land degradation may be higher than the costs of inaction, many land users may be constrained in their actions by lack of knowledge of sustainable land management practices, access to markets, insecure land tenure, and other barriers to SLM.

Thus, the basic issue is that while land is, of course, local, costs and benefits of land (miss-) use are partly trans-regional and even global, i.e. land degradation is partly a global and national "public bad". Therefore policies and investments are needed to minimize the negative externalities of land degradation, for instance, by subsidizing sustainable land management.

The opportunity costs of taking action are main drivers that contribute to inaction in many countries. Strategies should be developed that give incentives to better manage lands and reward those who practice sustainable land management. The payment for ecosystem services (PES) mechanisms that saw large investments in carbon markets should be given a new impetus to address the loss of ecosystem services through land use/cover change (LUCC) which accounts for the largest cost of land degradation. Allowing landusers to internalize some of the positive externalities created by sustainable land management through PES schemes may be key to achieving a "land degradation neutral" world.

There is a need for strong emphasis on addressing land degradation in international and national investment programs.

The research on economics of land degradation needs to be increasingly based on comprehensive trans-disciplinary conceptual frameworks, such as Water-Energy-Food Security Nexus. However, this also necessitates further methodological advances in the valuation of ecosystem services and the inclusion of details of soil quality changes. Finally, there is a need for more research quantifying the long run impacts of land degradation on poverty and food security.

Sustainable land management is fundamental for humanity's sustainability in general. The land degradation trends must be reversed, and that makes economic sense.

References

Abdulai, A., & Goetz, R. (2014). Time-related characteristics of tenancy contracts and investment in soil conservation practices. *Environmental & Resource Economics, 59*, 87–109.

Amundson, R., Berhe, A., Hopmans, J., Olson, C., Sztein, A. E., Sparks, D. (2015). Soil and human security in the 21st century. *Science, 348*(6235). doi:10.1126/science.1261071

Asner, G. P., Elmore, A. J., Olander, L. P., Martin, R. E., & Harris, A. T. (2004). Grazing systems, ecosystem responses, and global change. *Annual Review of Environment and Resources, 29*, 261–299.

Baumgartner, P., von Braun, J., Abebaw, D., & Müller, M. (2015). Impacts of large-scale land investments on income, prices, and employment: Empirical analyses in Ethiopia. *World Development*, 175–190.

CBD (Convention on Biological Diversity). (2014). Global biodiversity outlook 4. Montréal, 155 p.

Coad, L., Campbell, A., Miles, L., & Humphries, K. (2008). The costs and benefits of forest protected areas for local livelihoods: A review of the current literature. UNEP—World Conservation Monitoring Centre: Cambridge, UK. Commissao Pastoral da Terra (2008). Online at http://apps.unep.org/publications/pmtdocuments/Cost_benefits_protected_forests_area.pdf. Accessed 10 July 2014.

FAO. (2008). Are grasslands under threat? Brief analysis of FAO statistical data on pasture and fodder crops. Online at http://www.fao.org/ag/agp/agpc/doc/grass_stats/grass-stats.htm. Accessed 17 May 17 2015.

FAO (Food and Agriculture Organization). (2012). *State of food and agriculture. Investing in agriculture for a better future*. Rome: FAO.

Karsenty, A., & Ongolo, S. (2012). Can 'fragile states' decide to reduce their deforestation? The inappropriate use of the theory of incentives with respect to the redd mechanism. *Forest Policy and Economics, 18*, 38–45.

Lal, R. (1994). Sustainable land use systems and soil resilience, In D. J. Greenland & I. Szabolcs (Eds.), *Soil Resilience and Sustainable Land Use* (pp. 41–67). CAB-International, Wallingford, Oxon. UK.

Lal, R. (2005). *Encyclopaedia of soil science* (Vol. 1). CRC Press.

Lal, R. (2014). Societal value of soil carbon. *Journal of Soil and Water Conservation, 69*(6), 186A–192A.

Lal, R. (2015). Sequestering carbon and increasing productivity by conservation agriculture. *Journal of Soil and Water Conservation, 70*(3), 55A–62A.

Lal, R., Safriel, U., & Boer, B. (2012). Zero net land degradation: A new sustainable development goal for Rio + 20. A report prepared for the Secretariat of the United Nations Convention to Combat Desertification.

Lal, R., Singh, B. R., Mwaseba, D. L., Karybill, D., Hansen, D., & Eik, L. O. (2014). *Sustainable intensification to advance food security and enhance climate resilience in Africa*. Cham, Switzerland: Springer.

Le, Q. B., Nkonya, E., & Mirzabaev, A. (2014). Biomass productivity-based mapping of global land degradation hotspots. ZEF-Discussion Papers on Development Policy, (193). ZEF, University of Bonn, Bonn, Germany.

Lynch, G., & Crawford, G. (2011). Democratization in Africa 1990–2010: An assessment. *Democratization, 18*(2), 275–310.

MEA (Millenium Ecosystem Assessment). (2005). Dryland systems. In R. Hassan, R. Scholes, & N. Ash (Eds.), *Ecosystem and well-being: Current state and trends* (pp. 623–662). Washington, DC: Island Press.

Nachtergaele, F., Petri, M., Biancalani, R., Van Lynden, G., & Van Velthuizen, H. (2010). Global land degradation information system (GLADIS). Beta version. An information database for land degradation assessment at global level. Land degradation assessment in Drylands technical report, no. 17. FAO, Rome, Italy.

NASA (National Aeronautic Space Authority). (2014). Moderate resolution imaging spectroradiometer (MODIS) data. Online at https://lpdaac.usgs.gov/. Accessed 20 Apr 2015.

Nkonya, E., Gerber, N., Baumgartner, P., von Braun, J., de Pinto, A., Graw, V., Kato, E., Kloos, J., Walter, T. (2011). The economics of land degradation. Towards an integrated global assessment. Development economics and policy, Band 66. Peter Lang.

Nkonya, E., Pender, J., Benin, S., & Kato, E. (2008). Land rental markets and land management: Evidence from Uganda. In S. Holden, K. Otsuka, & F. Place (Eds.), *Emerging land markets in Africa—implications for poverty, equity and efficiency*. Washington, D.C.: Resources For the Future Press.

Poteete, A., & Ostrom, E. (2004). Heterogeneity, group size and collective action: The role of institutions in forest management. *Development and Change, 35*, 435–461.

UNDP (United Nations Development Program). (2015). Sustainable development goals proposals. Online at https://sustainabledevelopment.un.org/sdgsproposal. Accessed 21 Apr 2015.

von Braun, J. (2013). International co-operation for agricultural development and food and nutrition security: New institutional arrangements for related public goods (No. 2013/061). WIDER Working Paper.

World Bank. (2010). Development and climate change. World Development Report, 2010. Washington DC. 418 p.

Chapter 2
Concepts and Methods of Global Assessment of the Economics of Land Degradation and Improvement

Ephraim Nkonya, Joachim von Braun, Alisher Mirzabaev, Quang Bao Le, Ho-Young Kwon and Oliver Kirui

Abstract The Economics of Land Degradation (ELD) initiative seeks to develop a science basis for policy actions to address land degradation. The purpose of this chapter is to provide with a conceptual framework and sound and feasible methodological standards for ELD assessments at global and national levels. Only if some basic standards are identified and adhered to, comparative assessments can be conducted between countries and useful aggregation of findings, based on these case studies, can be achieved. Therefore, using the Total Economic Value (TEV) framework, the chapter identifies minimum core standards that need to be adhered to in all country case studies to generate comparable material for international assessment and ELD policy guidance.

Keywords Economics of land degradation · Case studies · Natural capital · Total economic value

Introduction

Healthy land ecosystems (hereafter referred to simply as "land") that function well and ensure their services—are essential to sustainable development, including food security and improved livelihoods. Yet, key services provided by land have habitually been taken for granted and their true value—beyond the market value—has

E. Nkonya (✉) · H.-Y. Kwon
International Food Policy Research Institute, 2033 K Street NW, Washington, DC 20006, USA
e-mail: e.nkonya@cgiar.org

J. von Braun · A. Mirzabaev · O. Kirui
Center for Development Research (ZEF), University of Bonn, Water Flex Street 3, D-53113 Bonn, Germany

Q.B. Le
CGIAR Research Program on Dryland Systems (CRP-DS), International Center for Agricultural Research in the Dry Areas (ICARDA), PO Box 950764, Amman 11195, Jordan
e-mail: q.le@cgiar.org; q.le@alumni.ethz.ch

E. Nkonya et al. (eds.), *Economics of Land Degradation and Improvement – A Global Assessment for Sustainable Development*, DOI 10.1007/978-3-319-19168-3_2

been underrated (von Braun et al. 2013). This pattern of undervaluation of lands is about to change in view of the rapidly rising land prices, which is the result of increasing shortage of land and high output prices (ibid.). Moreover, the value of land ecosystem services is gradually being better understood. Globally, it is estimated that about a quarter of land area is degraded, affecting more than a billion people all over the world (Lal et al. 2012). Land degradation is defined as the persistent reduction of land's biological and/or economic production capacity, or as the long-term loss of land ecosystem functions and services (Safriel 2007; Vogt et al. 2011). Land degradation wreaks its highest toll on the livelihoods and well-being of the poorest households in the rural areas of developing countries (Nachtergaele et al. 2010). Vicious circles of poverty and land degradation, as well as transmission effects from rural poverty and food insecurity to national economies, critically hamper their development process.

Despite the urgent need for preventing and reversing land degradation, the problem has yet to be appropriately addressed (Lal et al. 2012). Policy actions for sustainable land management (SLM) remain inconsistent and often ineffective (Nkonya et al. 2011). Such policy frameworks to combat land degradation need to be supported by evidence-based and action-oriented research (von Braun et al. 2013). The past studies on land degradation had played a useful role in highlighting land degradation as a globally critical issue. However, most of them tended to focus only on simpler relationships, such as, for example, soil erosion and its impact on crop yield, while ignoring the broader values of land ecosystem services, various off-site and indirect costs in their analytical frameworks. The losses from land degradation include not only environmental degradation cost measured directly on-site (e.g., soil loss and nutrient depletion), but also the cost of indirect and off-site environmental impacts (e.g., siltation of water bodies, water pollution, and biodiversity declines) (Foley et al. 2005).

Yet it is empirically challenging to account for all the costs of land degradation. Among major challenges are measurement and valuation of losses in ecosystem benefits due to land degradation (Barbier 2011a, b). Moreover, the double-counting of these ecosystem benefits needs to be avoided—a complex task by itself (Barbier 2010). Processes (e.g. water purification) and benefits (e.g. purified potable water) could be double counted if each is given a separate value (Balmford et al. 2008). The benefits are the end products of the beneficial processes. One approach to avoid double counting in this regard is to only take the value of potable water with different qualities and skip counting of the water purification process. However, it is equally obvious that the conceptual framework for Economic Assessment of Land Degradation and Improvement should not be limited to only more easily measurable direct on-site and off-site costs of land degradation since taking such an approach ignores the intrinsic relationship of ecosystems and will lead to undervaluing the cost of land degradation and benefits of taking action against land degradation. Hence the conceptual framework should be able to accommodate all losses due to land degradation, thus providing guidance and basis for a comprehensive evaluation, even if it means that empirical gaps will be filled not immediately but through a longer-term research.

This action-oriented focus and the definitions of land and land degradation determine the methodological approaches applied in this book. United Nations Convention to Combat Desertification (UNCCD) (1996) defines land as a terrestrial ecosystem consisting of flora, fauna, hydrological processes and other ecological services beneficial to human beings. The Millennium Ecosystem Assessment (MEA 2005) defines land degradation as long-term loss of on-site and off-site terrestrial ecosystem goods and services, which humans derive from them. These definitions lead to using a comprehensive approach which takes into account both short- and long-term direct and indirect, on-site and off-site benefits of sustainable land management versus the related costs of land degradation. Thus, to be comprehensive, this economic assessment study uses TEV approach, which assigns value to all use and non-use ecosystem services. This means the TEV approach captures the value of ecosystem goods and services and goes beyond the common monetary values of provisioning services used in many past economic studies. Consequently, this approach strives to capture all changes, both degradation and improvement, in ecosystem functions and services attributed to land ecosystems.

The action against land degradation involves preventing the degradation of currently used or usable lands or rehabilitating degraded lands. Action against land degradation is referred here as sustainable land management, which according to TerrAfrica (2006), is generally understood as the "adoption of land systems that, through appropriate management practices, enables land users to maximize the economic and social benefits from the land, while maintaining or enhancing the ecological support functions of the land resources". However, this definition is too general, lacking measurable criteria to guide policy focuses regarding SLM. In this study, "actions against land degradation" are defined as land management which leads to persistent improvement of biological productivity and biodiversity of the land. However, relevant understanding of these criteria has to be based on the usage people expect from the land (i.e., expected land use) and the baseline for assessment. With land intentionally used for agricultural or forest production, long-term soil-driven net primary productivity (NPP), i.e. the net biomass produced by the soil and other natural resources (water and sunlight) without remarkable external inputs (e.g., improved rainfall, fertilizer use, atmospheric fertilization), can be a proxy for SLM or land degradation assessment. However, the treatment of observed biomass productivity trend has to further depend on the baseline of the assessment. Where the initial productivity was already low (degraded), a long-term improvement of soil-driven productivity can reflect SLM. Where the beginning productivity was already high, at least an absence of decline (a steady state) of soil-driven productivity also may indicate SLM. On land used/planned for nature protection, soil-driven NPP is still important, but biodiversity is an additional criterion for SLM. In many cases soil quality and biodiversity support each other, but in some other cases, they may not necessarily be mutually consistent. For example, an invasion of exotic plant species can lead to high biomass productivity but dramatically reduce biodiversity, which is not desirable. Increasing of soil nutrients can reduce plant diversity in some cases (Chapin et al. 2000; Sala et al. 2000; Wassen et al. 2005). The use of soil-based biomass productivity to indicate land degradation in these areas may not be relevant to the land-use goal. To include these areas in the land degradation or SLM assessment, in addition to soil resources, other foundational aspects of forest ecosystems (e.g. flora and fauna structures and composition) have to be considered. Thus, using biomass productivity trend alone to indicate land degradation or SLM on such protected areas can give misleading results. Further, there is still a lack of data to more accurately delineate global forest cover into different use regimes.

Land improvement is generally recognized as being closely determined by the increasing of net primary productivity (NPP) of the land, under certain conditions, and the improvement of soil fertility. The NPP trend, approximated by the trend of inter-annual Normalized Difference Vegetation Index (NDVI), can be an indirect indicator of soil degradation or soil improvement if the nutrient source for vegetation/crop growth is solely, or largely, from the soils (i.e., soil-based biomass productivity). In the agricultural areas with intensive application of mineral fertilizers (i.e. fertilizer-based crop productivity), NPP trend (via NDVI trend) principally cannot be a reliable indicator of soil fertility trend (Le 2012). In this case, alternative indicators of soil fertility should be used. Moreover, the elevated levels of CO_2 and NOx in the atmosphere (Reay et al. 2008; WMO 2012) can cause a divergence between NPP trend and soil fertility change as the atmospheric fertilization effect has not been substantially mediated through the soil. The rising level of atmospheric CO_2 stimulates photosynthesis in plants' leaves, thus increasing NPP, but the soil fertility may not necessarily be proportional to the above ground biomass improvement. The wet deposition of reactive nitrogen and other nutrients may affect positively plant growths as foliate fertilization without significantly contributing to the soil nutrient pool, or compensating nutrient losses by soil leaching and accelerated erosion. The correction of the masking effect of atmospheric fertilization can be done by considering the quantum of biomass improvement in intact vegetation area, using the method proposed in Vlek et al. (2010) and Le et al. (2012). However the result must be evaluated by comparing the spatial corrected NDVI trend pattern with independent indicators, such as ground-measured NPP or soil erosion (e.g. Le et al. 2012).

The Conceptual Framework

The conceptual framework (Fig. 2.1) categorizes the causes of land degradation into proximate and underlying, which interact with each other to result in different levels of land degradation. Proximate causes of land degradation are those that have a direct effect on the terrestrial ecosystem. The proximate causes are further divided into biophysical proximate causes (natural) and unsustainable land management practices (anthropogenic). The underlying causes of land degradation are those that indirectly affect the proximate causes of land degradation, such as institutional, socio-economic and policy factors. For example, poverty could lead to the failure of land users to invest in sustainable land management practices leading to land

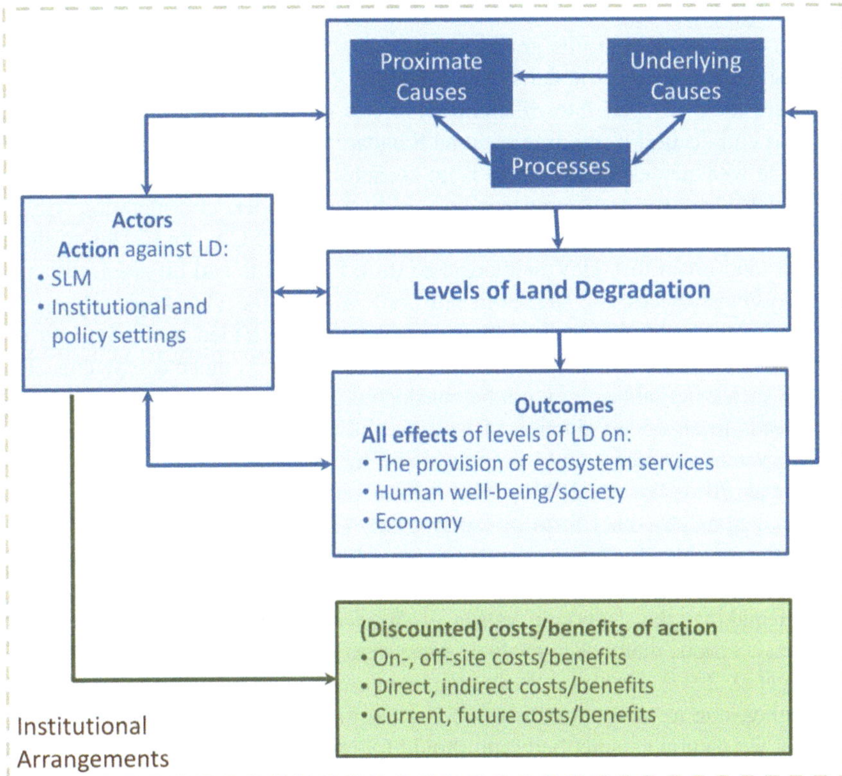

Fig. 2.1 The conceptual framework (*Source* Adapted from Nkonya et al. (2011))

degradation (Way 2006; Cleaver and Schreiber 1994; Scherr 2000). Understanding of the causes of land degradation and of their interactions is essential for identifying relevant actions for addressing land degradation. Therefore, as we will see further, the first step in the empirical ELD research involves the analysis of both proximate and underlying causes of land degradation.

Inaction against land degradation would lead to continuation, even acceleration, of land degradation and of its associated costs. However, besides its benefits, action against land degradation also involves costs—the costs of specific measures and economy-wide indirect effects—that is, opportunity costs, involving resources devoted for these actions which cannot be used elsewhere. The ultimate goal of the present conceptual framework is to compare the costs and benefits of action against land degradation versus the costs of inaction.

The level of land degradation determines its outcomes or effects—whether on-site or offsite—on the provision of ecosystem services and the benefits humans derive from those services. Other methods are also used to measure the on-site and off-site flow and stock of ecosystems services. Of particular importance is the life cycle analysis (LCA), which assesses the environmental impacts of a product during its life cycle (Rebitzer et al. 2004). In what is known as the environmental impact of products from its cradle to its grave, impact categories of a product and the corresponding indicators and model(s) are identified (Reap et al. 2008). The impact results are then grouped into different categories (Ibid). Despite its popularity of LCA and codification in the International Standardization Organization, LCA has a number of weaknesses (ibid.). There is no consensus on types of stressors, impacts, the models to use and corresponding indicators under consideration (ibid). Like TEV, double counting remains a major problem of LCA (ibid). Due to these problems and given that TEV methods also trace the on-site and off-site impacts of the ecosystem services, the studies in this book will use the TEV approach.

Many of the services provided by ecosystems are not traded in markets, so the different actors do not pay for negative or positive effects on those ecosystems. The value of such externalities may not be considered in the farmer's land use decision, which leads to an undervaluation of land and its provision of ecosystem services. The ecosystem services should be considered as capital assets, or natural capital (Daily et al. 2011; Barbier 2011c). This natural capital should be properly valuated and managed as any other form of capital assets (Daily et al. 2000). The failure to capture these values for land ecosystems could lead to undervaluing the impact of higher rates of land degradation. To adequately account for ecosystem services in decision making, the economic values of those services have to be determined. There exist various methods to evaluate ecosystem services (Barbier 2010, 2011a, b; Nkonya et al. 2011). However, attributing economic values to ecosystem services is challenging, due to many unknowns and actual measurement constraints. The valuation of the natural capital, therefore, should follow three stages (Daily et al. 2000): (i) evaluation of alternative options, for example, degrading soil ecosystem services versus their sustainable management, (ii) measurement and identification of costs and benefits for each alternative, and (iii) comparison of costs and benefits of each of the alternatives including their long-term effects (ibid.). However, identifying and aggregating individual preferences and attached values to ecosystem services, including over time, for each alternative option, is not a straightforward task (ibid.) As economic values are linked to the number of (human) beneficiaries and the socioeconomic context, these services depend on local or regional conditions. This dependence contributes to the variability of the values (TEEB 2010).

The green square box in Fig. 2.1 deals with the economic analysis to be carried out, and the green arrow shows the flow of information that is necessary to perform the different elements of the global economic analysis. Ideally, all indirect and off-site effects should be accounted for in the economic analysis to ensure that the assessment is from society's point of view and includes all existing externalities, in addition to the private costs that are usually considered when individuals decide on land use. This assessment has to be conducted at the margin, which means that costs of small changes in the level of land degradation, which may accumulate over time, have to be identified. Bringing together the different cost and value types to fully assess total costs and benefits over time and their interactions can be done within the framework of cost–benefit analysis and mathematical modeling. In doing this, care should be taken in the choice of the discount rates because the size of the discount rate, as well as the length of the considered time horizon, can radically change the results. Discount rates relate to people's time preferences, with higher discount rates indicating a strong time preference and attaching a higher value to each unit of the natural resource that is consumed now rather than in the future.

Institutional arrangements, or the "rules of the game" that determine whether actors choose to act against land degradation and whether the level or type of action undertaken will effectively reduce or halt land degradation, are represented as dotted lines encapsulating the different elements of the conceptual framework. It is crucial to identify and understand these institutional arrangements in order to devise sustainable and efficient policies to combat land degradation. For example, if farmers over-irrigate, leading to salinization of the land, it must be understood why they do so. As an illustration, it may be that institutional arrangements, also referred to as distorting incentive structures, make it economically profitable for farmers to produce as much crops as possible. Missing or very low prices of irrigation may act as such an incentive in a misleading institutional setup (Rosegrant et al. 1995).

Finally, it is also essential for the analysis to identify all the important actors of land degradation, such as land users, landowners, governmental authorities, industries, and consumers, as well as identify how institutions and policies influence those actors. Transaction costs and collective versus market and state actions are to be considered.

The Methodological Framework

The methodological approaches applied throughout the chapters of this book consist of two mutually complementary lines of research, which tackle two different aspects of the research agenda described in the conceptual framework (Fig. 2.1). This first line of research is based on descriptive and econometric analysis of causes of land degradation. Here, we seek to identify the key underlying and proximate causes of land degradation. This analysis will help to identify strategies for taking action against land degradation. However, action or non-action against land degradation will depend on its costs and benefits of taking action. This justifies and links the first part to the second part of analysis, whereas the second line of research looks specifically into the costs of land degradation and net benefits from SLM.

Analysis of Causes of Land Degradation

The causes of land degradation are numerous, interrelated and complex. Quite often, the same causal factor could lead to diverging consequences in different contexts because of its varying interactions with other proximate and underlying causes of land degradation. The results imply that targeting one underlying factor is not, in itself, sufficient to address land degradation. Rather, a number of underlying and proximate factors need to be taken into account when designing policies to prevent or mitigate land degradation. For our model specification, it is essential not to look for only into individual causes of land degradation, but rather identify the effects of various combinations and interactions of underlying and proximate causes of land degradation in a robust manner, with appropriate handling of potential issues related to endogeneity, multicollinearity, omitted variable bias and other statistical challenges.

At the start of the empirical work, an exploratory analysis is conducted for better understanding the characteristics and trends in land degradation, the interaction of proximate and underlying causes of land degradation and other relevant socio-economic data. This exploratory analysis is used for refining the hypotheses about the causes of land degradation, which is later tested using the in-depth data in each case study country. The exploratory analysis is done using simple descriptive tools, while the results are illustrated using maps, figures and tables. For example, the correlation between poverty, government effectiveness, land tenure, environmental policies and other key causes of land degradation is overlaid with a change in NDVI or other relevant land degradation indicators. This forms useful and simple patterns to be used to enrich the econometric results. For example, data on land tenure is overlaid with change in NDVI to show areas where NDVI decreased (possible land degradation) or increased (possible land improvement) while such areas had secure land tenure or insecure land tenure.

Therefore, the proximate and underlying causes of land degradation are analyzed at two levels:

- Global at pixel level. Like in Nkonya et al. (2011), a pixel-level estimation of causes of land degradation is made. However, we improve on Nkonya et al. (2011) by using more recent data and controlling for more causes of land degradation (Chap. 7 of this volume). Moreover, NDVI values used by us are corrected for the effects of fertilization that has been shown dissimulate land degradation (Chap. 4 of this volume).
- Household level analysis in the case study countries with panel (or cross-sectional, if panel is not available) household data. Using land use change, or households' reporting of their plot level land quality, or factual measurements of land quality at the household plots, or very high resolution NDVI images, or lack of application of sustainable land management practices, as available, as an indicator for land degradation.

The choice of variables for model specification is based on theoretical grounds and previous research, which has been described in detail in Nkonya et al. (2011) and von Braun et al. (2013). Additionally they follow established literature on causes of land degradation (Meyfroidt et al. 2010; Lambin 2001; Lambin and Geist 2006, Chap. 7).

Following Meyfroidt et al. (2010), Lambin (2001), Lambin and Geist (2006) and Nkonya et al. (2011), the structural first difference model estimating causes of land degradation or land improvement at global, regional/district and household levels, using annualized data is:

$$\Delta \text{NDVI} = \beta_0 + \beta_1 \Delta x_1 + \beta_2 \Delta x_2 + \beta_3 \Delta x_3 + \beta_4 \Delta x_4 + \beta_5 \Delta z_i + \varepsilon_i \quad (2.1)$$

where,

Δ NDVI—change in the values of the NDVI between the baseline and endline periods;
x_1—a vector of biophysical causes of land degradation (e.g. climate conditions, topography, soil constraints);
x_2—a vector of policy-related, institutional, demographic and socio-economic causes of land degradation (e.g. population density and growth rate, urban growth, GDP per capita, agricultural intensification and growth, national, international policies directly affecting land management, government effectiveness, land tenure, etc.);
x_3—a vector of variables representing access to rural services (e.g. links to extension services, road proximity or density, access to information, assess to rural credits);
x_4—vector of variables representing rural household level capital endowment, level of education, poverty level, physical capital, social capital;
z_i—vector of fixed effect variables, including administrative divisions (region, NDVI prior to the baseline period, etc.).

Alternatively, this model could be estimated using fixed effects approach instead of the first difference approach. The choice between first difference and fixed effects estimations usually depends on the characteristics of the panel data and specifically those of the error term. We expect the error terms to follow random walk, requiring first difference estimation rather than being serially uncorrelated when fixed effects is better. However, the ultimate choice between first difference and fixed effects should be made based on the characteristics of the actual data used. Various appropriate interactions and nonlinear relationships among specific variables are also tested following theoretical expectations. The results of this model are triangulated whenever possible using alternative measures of land degradation as dependent variable (such as actual soil quality measurements, etc.).

The use of NDVI or other satellite-derived measures as proxies of land degradation may, in some cases, lead to less accurate results as NDVI or other satellite-derived indicators may not be fully collinear with land degradation processes on the ground. For example, NDVI cannot easily differentiate between composition changes in vegetation, hence can lead to misleading conclusions when secondary salinization leads to abandonment of previously agricultural areas and replacement of agricultural crops by halophytic weeds. To minimize such inaccuracies, ground-truthing of satellite-derived data is conducted. More specifically, sub-national ground-truthing studies are conducted in some case study countries to assess land degradation using local-specific data to triangulate the results with the global satellite-based analysis.

However, NDVI pixels could be too big to make any meaningful conclusions at the household level. To address this problem, the above equation, which is more suited to global level analyses, is modified taking alternative household-level indicators of land quality as the dependent variable, such as land use change, or households' reporting of their plot level land quality, or the lack of application of 3 practices, factual measurements of land quality at the household plots, or very high resolution NDVI data, as available. The explanatory variables are also at the household level:

$$\Delta H = \beta_0 + \beta_1 \Delta x_1 + \beta_2 \Delta x_2 + \beta_3 \Delta x_3 + \beta_4 \Delta x_4 + \beta_5 \Delta z_i + \varepsilon_i \qquad (2.2)$$

where,

H = household land quality indicator;
x_1 = a vector of biophysical causes of land degradation (e.g. climate conditions, topography, soil constraints) at household plots;
x_2 = a vector of policy-related, institutional, demographic and socio-economic causes of land degradation (e.g. household income per capita, family labor availability, fertilizer/manure application rates, land tenure, etc.);
x_3 = a vector of variables representing access to rural services (e.g. links to extension services, road proximity or density, access to information, assess to rural credits);
x_4 = vector of variables representing household level asset endowments, level of education, poverty level, physical capital, social capital;
z_i = vector of fixed effect variables, including administrative divisions, household fixed effects, etc.

Similarly, here as well, an alternative fixed effects model will also be considered. In case of cross-sectional data, the panel estimation approach will be replaced by methods suitable for cross-sectional data. Various appropriate interactions and nonlinear relationships among specific variables will be tested following theoretical expectations.

Cost and Benefits of Action Versus Inaction Against Land Degradation

The TEV approach is required to comprehensively capture the costs of land degradation. It consists of use and non-use values (Remoundou et al. 2009). The use value is further divided into direct and indirect use. The direct use includes marketed outputs involving priced consumption (e.g. crop production, fisheries, tourism, etc.) as well as un-priced benefits such as local culture and recreation. The indirect use value consists of un-priced ecosystem functions such as water purification, carbon sequestration, etc. Non-use value is divided into bequest, altruistic and existence values, all of which represent the un-priced benefits. In between these two major categories, there is the option value, which includes both marketable outputs and ecosystem services for future direct or indirect use. It is usually challenging to measure the non-use and indirect use values as mostly they are not traded in markets. An additional challenge of measuring TEV is the potential of double-counting of benefits from ecosystems services (Barbier 2010). Following Balmford et al. (2008) and others, care is taken to avoid double counting, by partitioning the broad but closely related benefits and process and traced their links such that they avoided double-counting (ibid).

Since we follow the broad definition of land degradation which captures the on-site and off-site effects of land management, we use social costs and benefits of land degradation. The social cost and benefit of action against land degradation and inaction is given by the net present value (NPV) for taking action against land degradation in year t for the land users planning horizon T:

$$\pi_t^c = \frac{1}{\rho^t}\sum_{t=0}^{T}\left(PY_t^c + IV_t + NU_t + b_t^c - lm_t^c - c_t^c - \tau_t^c\right) \quad (2.3)$$

where, π_t^c = net present value (NPV) for taking action against land degradation in year t for the land users planning horizon T; Y_t^c = production of direct use provisioning services when using SLM practices; P = unit price of Y_t^c; IVt = indirect use value; NUt = on-site non-use value; b_t^c = off-site positive benefit of SLM practices; ρt = 1 + r, r = land user's discount rate; lm_t^c = cost of SLM practices; c_t^c = direct costs of production other than land management; τ_t^c = off-site costs of SLM—including use and non-use costs. The term τ_t^c implies that even SLM could produce negative off-site costs. For example, application of chemical fertilizer leads to greenhouse gas emission. 1 kg of nitrogen requires about 3 kg of CO_2-equivalent (Vlek et al. 2004) because of the high energy requirement for the manufacture and transport of fertilizer.

If land user does not take action against land degradation, the corresponding NPV is given by

$$\pi_t^d = \frac{1}{\rho^t}\sum_{t=0}^{T}\left(PY_t^d + IV_t + NU_t + b_t^d - lm_t^d - c_t^d - \tau_t^d\right) \quad (2.4)$$

where π_t^d = NPV when land user uses land degrading practices. All other variables are as defined in above but with superscript d indicating land degrading practices.

The benefit of taking action against land degradation is given by $BA = \pi_t^c - \pi_t^d$.

The difference $\pi_t^c - \pi_t^d$ plays an important role in land users' decision making during their planning horizon T. Table 2.1 summarizes the actions of land users when returns to SLM are smaller, greater or equal to the corresponding returns to SLM. If the returns to land management for the SLM are smaller than the corresponding returns for land degrading practices, the land user is likely to use land degrading practices.

However, given that prevention of land degradation is expected to be cheaper than rehabilitation of degraded lands, it is always prudent to prevent land degradation. The

Table 2.1 Action versus inaction decisions at different levels

$\pi_t^c - \pi_t^d$	Logical action/inaction
>0	Take action against LD
<0	Don't take action. Alternatively provide incentives to take action against land degradation (e.g. PES[a])
=0	Indifferent, hence provide incentives to take action against land degradation (e.g. PES)

Note Taking action against land degradation include: prevention of land degradation or rehabilitation of degraded lands. [a]Payment for Ecosystem Services. *Source* The authors

challenge is internalization of SLM benefits and enhancing adoption of SLM practices for low income farmers who may not have paid to adopt SLM. For example, payment for ecosystem services (PES) could be used when BA ≤ 0 (see Table 2.1).

Sampling Framework for Case Studies

Proximate and underlying causes of land degradation are intricately embedded in their specific local contexts (Nkonya et al. 2011; von Braun et al. 2013), and hence, only through comprehensive analysis of these local heterogeneous interactions that meaningful insights could be derived about causes and necessary actions against land degradation. On the other hand, needless to say that these insights should not be exclusively limited only to some specific local settings, but should have a global relevance. In this regard, case study methodology is a preferred choice of method when the phenomenon being studied is indistinguishable from its context (Yin 2003)—which enables to achieve the first objective of local thoroughness. The second objective of global relevance is achieved by designing a rigorous sampling framework with theoretically sound case study selection strategy.

Extrapolation of case study findings beyond these case studies themselves is possible only when the case study design has been based on theoretical grounds: where specific research questions are asked to test the validity of rival explanations of cause-and-effect relationships in land degradation. Carefully selected multiple case studies are the means to provide a more convincing test of a theory and specify conditions under which different, perhaps even opposing, theories could be valid (De Vaus 2001). Moreover, the external validity of a case study depends on its capacity for theoretical generalization, rather than statistical generalization which is conducted through probability-based random sampling techniques. In that sense, case studies are like experiments with replications: if the theoretical insights gained from case studies conducted in multiple settings coincide, then the potential of external validity of these results is higher. To achieve such external validity, case studies are selected not statistically, but "strategically" (ibid.), which necessitates selecting those cases which will enable to rigorously test the causal relationships in different contexts (ibid.). Moreover, random probability based selection of countries is also practically infeasible within realistic time and budget constraints. Finally, it is essential that the core research methodologies and protocols in each of the case studies should be similar for ensuring comparability of their results.

For conducting this global economic analysis of land degradation, case study countries have been carefully selected based on purposive sampling framework and maximum variation approach, where it was sought to comprehensively capture a wide spectrum of heterogeneous contexts of land degradation in order to test rival cause-and-effect hypotheses about land degradation. Thus, the main objective in the sampling was to ensure the external validity and global relevance of the selected case study countries for a big heterogeneity of land degradation, institutional and socio-economic situations around the world.

The sampling strategy consisted of three steps:

First, earlier analyses of causes of land degradation have identified such key socio-economic and institutional underlying factors of land degradation as per capita GDP, population density, government effectiveness and agricultural intensification (Nkonya et al. 2011). Based on these characteristics, the countries of the world have been clustered using K-means clustering technique into seven clusters with more homogenous within-cluster characteristics (Table 2.2). The decision on the optimal number of clusters was guided both by the results of the formal statistical Calinski-Harabasz stopping rule (Calinski and Harabasz 1974),[1] and graphical and numerical exploratory analysis of the data. **Second**, the selected clusters were formally validated against several key socio-economic and biophysical variables, which were not part of the initial clustering, such as long-term changes in remotely-sensed NDVI values (Tucker et al. 2004), which can be used as a potential proxy for land degradation, share of rural population in the total, share of agriculture in GDP, average cereal yields per hectare. The identified clusters showed significant differences for each of these variables, thus providing a strong evidence for the validity of the clustering approach employed (Table 2.2 and Fig. 2.2). **Third**, once the countries have been put through these selection filters to ensure their representativeness of global heterogeneity in terms of socio-economic, institutional and land degradation characteristics, countries were selected from each cluster for in-depth case studies, based on such additional criteria as i) regional representativeness, ii) the selected countries have collected or are collecting the data required for the assessment.

This selection of countries is highly and sufficiently heterogeneous in terms of both biophysical, socio-economic and institutional characteristics to enable rigorous ground-level testing of various causal hypotheses about land degradation, and for specifying which causal relationships could be prevailing under each of these different interactions of factors. The representativeness of the case study countries is also demonstrated by their good coverage of the world biomes (Fig. 2.2). Moreover, these globally representative case studies also allow for achieving the objective of

---

[1]Milligan and Cooper (1985) conclude, using a Monte Carlo simulation, that Calinsky-Harabasz stopping rule provides the best results among the 30 stopping rules they have compared.

Table 2.2 Clustering and validation results

Clusters	GDP per capita	Government effectiveness	Population density	Agricultural Intensification	Maximum changes in NDVI values between the baseline (1982–1984) and endline (2003–2006)[a]	Cereal yields	Share of agriculture in GDP	Share of rural population in total
1	Lower	Lower	Higher	Lower	Highest dispersion, both biggest decreases and increases	Lower	Higher	Higher
2	Mid	Mid	Higher	Higher	Smaller decreases	Mid	Mid	Higher
3	Mid	Mid	Higher	Mid	Smaller decreases	Mid	Mid	Mid
4	Mid	Mid	Lower	Mid	Larger decreases	Mid	Mid	Lower
5	Mid	Mid	Lower	Lower	Smaller decreases	Lower	Mid	Mid
6	Higher	Higher	Mid	Higher	Larger decreases	Mid	Mid	Lower
7	Higher	Higher	Higher	Higher	Smaller decreases	Higher	Lower	Lower

Source The authors
Notes The NDVI time-series comes from GIMMS dataset, which is driven from NOAA AVHRR satellite data (http://glcf.umd.edu/). The NDVI changes here have not been corrected for the effects of inter-annual rainfall variation, atmospheric fertilization and human application of mineral fertilizer

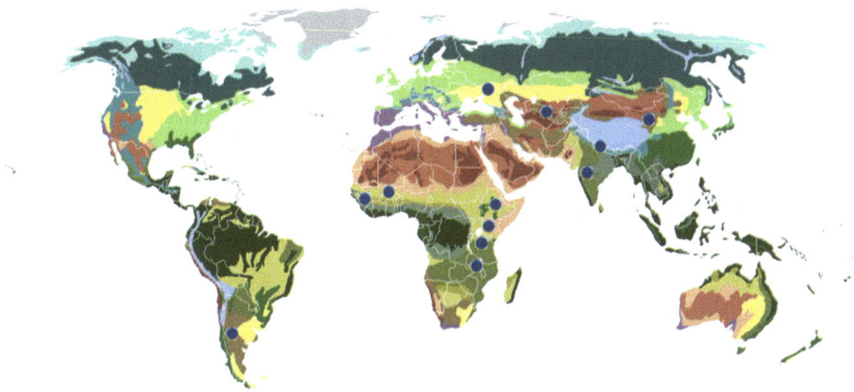

Fig. 2.2 Global Map showing the correspondence of case study countries to major global biomes (*Source* Modified from Wikipedia Commons, from http://commons.wikimedia.org/wiki/File:Vegetation-no-legend.PNG, accessed on 08 October 2013. Selected case study countries are identified by *blue circles*, and include: Argentina, Bhutan, China, Ethiopia, India, Kenya, Malawi, Niger, Tanzania, Russia, Senegal and Uzbekistan.)

providing national and global-level estimates of costs of land degradation and net benefits of taking action against it through SLM investments and policies. The 12 selected case study countries account for 43 % of the global population and 28 % of the land area.

Given higher levels of development challenges and opportunities posed by land degradation impacts, Cluster 1 countries, mostly from sub-Saharan Africa, are given higher weight in this particular selection. Naturally, the more is the number of case study countries, the higher is the accuracy of generalizations.

Following this sampling framework, and using the European Joint Research Center (JRC) guidelines (Toth et al. 2012), the data collected from the case study countries will be interpolated across the corresponding farming systems within the same cluster or the same region. No interpolation will be made across regions. For example, no data from sub-Saharan Africa will be interpolated to Latin America or Asia. This is because the interpolation within a region increases the accuracy of results as there are unobservable characteristics that could play an important role in causing land degradation. Interpolating within a region minimizes such omitted variable effects.

Conclusions and Reflections

There have been numerous but isolated attempts in the past to assess the causes and consequences of land degradation. However, the differences in concepts and methodologies did not allow for their meaningful comparison, and quite often have led to contradicting policy conclusions. Only if some basic standards are identified and adhered to, comparative assessments can be conducted between countries and useful aggregation of findings, based on these case studies, can be achieved. This is quite important for making impact on policy for investment and land use, and for getting land degradation problems out of their current obscurity. The proposed framework can provide a consistent conceptual basis for other ongoing or future similar research activities on economics of land degradation and improvement.

Certainly, causes, consequences and solutions for land degradation problems are not limited to agriculture alone. Reducing poverty, enhancing food security, promoting rural development through addressing land degradation, require that the applied methodologies need to involve all the relevant sectors, institutions, and policies. It is also true that one needs to start somewhere—without any doubt, agriculture is at the heart of land degradation problems, and while the other sectors need to be included too. It is also crucial to incorporate ecosystem values in assessing the costs of land degradation, in addition to direct costs. Many of the services provided by ecosystems are not traded in markets, so the different actors do not pay for negative or positive effects on those ecosystems. The value of such externalities may not be considered in the farmer's land use decision, which leads to an undervaluation of land and its provision of ecosystem services.

What is proposed here is a comprehensive conceptual framework for conducting the ELD assessment, concentrating on two core analytical methods demonstrating the use of methodological standards to guide other ELD case studies: (1) identification of causes of land degradation, (2) economic modeling of action versus inaction against land degradation. However, the conceptual framework represents a forward-looking agenda which can guide future research to fill the other elements of this comprehensive framework. Therefore, building national and international capacities, mobilizing bottom-up national research and action against land degradation is one of the key expectations from this research work.

References

Balmford, A., Rodrigues, A., Walpole, M., Ten Brink, P., Kettunen, M., Braat, L., & De Groot, R. (2008). *Review on the economics of biodiversity loss: scoping the science*. Cambridge, UK: European Commission.

Barbier, E. B. (2011a). *Capitalizing on nature: Ecosystems as natural assets*. Cambridge and New York: Cambridge University Press. 321 pp.

Barbier, E. B. (2011b). Pricing nature. *Annual Review of Resource Economics, 3*, 337–353.

Barbier, E. (2011c). Capitalizing on nature: Ecosystems as natural assets. Cambridge, UK; New York: Cambridge University Press.

Barbier, E. B., Hacker, S. D., Kennedy, C., Koch, E. W., Stier, A. C., & Silliman, B. R. (2010). The value of estuarine and coastal ecosystem services. *Ecological Monographs, 81*(2), 169–193. doi:10.1890/10-1510.1.

Caliński, T., & Harabasz, J. (1974). A dendrite method for cluster analysis. *Communications in Statistics-theory and Methods, 3*(1), 1–27.
Chapin, F. S. I., Zavaleta, E. S., Eviner, V. T., Naylor, R. L., Vitousek, P. M., Reynolds, H. L., et al. (2000). Consequences of changing biodiversity. *Nature, 405*, 234–242.
Cleaver, K. M., & Schreiber, G. A. (1994). *Reversing the Spiral: The Population, Agriculture, and Environment Nexus in Sub-Saharan Africa*. Washington, DC: The World Bank.
Daily, G. C., Kareiva, P. M., Polasky, S., Ricketts, T. H., & Tallis, H. (2011). Mainstreaming natural capital into decisions. *Natural Capital: Theory and Practice of Mapping Ecosystem Services*, 3–14.
Daily, G. C., Söderqvist, T., Aniyar, S., Arrow, K., Dasgupta, P., Ehrlich, P. R., et al. (2000). The value of nature and the nature of value. *Science, 289*(5478), 395–396. doi:10.1126/science.289.5478.395.
De Vaus, D. A. (2001). *Research design in social research*. London: SAGE.
Foley, J. A., DeFries, R., Asner, G. P., Barford, C., Bonan, G., Carpenter, S. R., et al. (2005). Global consequences of land use. *Science, 309*, 570–574.
Lal, R., Safriel, U., & Boer, B. (2012). Zero net land degradation: A new sustainable development goal for Rio + 20. A report prepared for the Secretariat of the United Nations Convention to Combat Desertification.
Lambin, E. (2001). Predicting land-use change. *Agriculture, Ecosystems & Environment, 85*(1–3), 1–6.
Lambin, E. F., & Geist, H. (Eds). (2006). *Land-use and land-cover change local processes and global impacts*. Berlin: Springer.
Le, Q. B. (2012) Indicators of global soils and land degradation. Slides of oral presentation at the first global soil week, 18–22 Nov 2012, Berlin, Germany. The First Global Soil Week, Berlin.
Le, Q. B., Tamene, L., & Vlek, P. L. G. (2012). Multi-pronged assessment of land degradation in West Africa to assess the importance of atmospheric fertilization in masking the processes involved. *Global and Planetary Change, 92–93*, 71–81.
MEA (Millenium Ecosystem Assessment). (2005). Dryland Systems. In R. Hassan, R. Scholes, & N. Ash (Eds.), *Ecosystem and well-being: Current state and trends* (pp. 623–662). Washington, DC: Island Press.
Meyfroidt, P., Rudel, T. K., Lambin, E. (2010). Forest transitions, trade, and the global displacement of land use. *Proceedings of the National Academy of Sciences, 107*(49), 20917–20922. www.pnas.org/cgi/doi/10.1073/pnas.1014773107
Milligan, G., & Cooper, M. (1985). An examination of procedures for determining the number of clusters in a data set. *Psychometrika, 50*(2), 159–179. doi:10.1007/bf02294245.
Nachtergaele, F., Petri, M., Biancalani, R., Van Lynden, G., & Van Velthuizen, H. (2010). Global land degradation information system (GLADIS). Beta version. An information database for land degradation assessment at global level. Land degradation assessment in drylands technical report, no. 17. FAO, Rome, Italy.
Nkonya, E., Gerber, N., Baumgartner, P., von Braun, J., De Pinto, A., Graw, V., et al. (2011). The economics of desertification, land degradation, and drought—toward an integrated global assessment. ZEF-Discussion Papers on Development Policy No. 150, Center for Development Research (ZEF), Bonn, Germany.
Reap, R., Roman, F., Duncan, S., & Bras, B. (2008). A survey of unresolved problems in life cycle assessment. *The International Journal of Life Cycle Assessment., 3*(5), 374–388.
Reay, D. S., Dentener, F., Smith, P., Grace, J., & Feely, R. (2008). Global nitrogen deposition and carbon sinks. *Nature Geoscience, 1*, 430–437.
Rebitzer, G., Ekvall, T., Frischknecht, R., Hunkeler, D., Norris, G., Rydberg, T., et al. (2004). Life cycle assessment part 1: Framework, goal and scope definition, inventory analysis, and applications. *Environment International, 30*, 701–720.
Remoundou, K., Koundouri, P., Kontogianni, A., Nunes, P. A. L. D., & Skourtos, M. (2009). Valuation of natural marine ecosystems: an economic perspective. *Environmental Science & Policy, 12*(7), 1040–1051. doi:10.1016/j.envsci.2009.06.006.

Rosegrant, M. W., Schleyer, R. G., & Yadav, S. N. (1995). Water policy for efficient agricultural diversification: market-based approaches. *Food Policy, 20*(3), 203–223. doi:10.1016/0306-9192(95)00014-6.

Safriel, U. N. (2007). The assessment of global trends in land degradation. In: M. V. K. Sivakumar & N. Ndiang'ui. (Eds.), *Climate and land degradation* (pp. 1–38). Berlin: Springer.

Sala, O. E., Chapin, F. S. I., Armesto, J. J., Berlow, E., Bloomfield, J., Dirzo, R., et al. (2000). Global biodiversity scenarios for the year 2100. *Science, 287*, 1770–1774.

Scherr, S. (2000). Downward spiral? Research evidence on the relationship between poverty and natural resource degradation. *Food Policy, 25*(4), 479–498.

TEEB (The Economics of Ecosystems and Biodiversity). (2010). Mainstreaming the economics of nature: A synthesis of the approach, conclusions and recommendations of TEEB. Malta.

TerrAfrica. (2006). Assessment of the nature and extent of barriers and bottlenecks to scaling sustainable land management investments throughout sub-Saharan Africa. Unpublished TerrAfrica report.

Toth, K., Portele, C., Illert, A., Lutz, M., & Nunes de Lima, V. (2012). A conceptual model for developing interoperability specifications in spatial data infrastructures. JRC Reference Reports. Online at http://ec.europa.eu/dgs/jrc/index.cfm?id=2540

Tucker, C. J., Pinzon, J. E., & Brown, M. E. (2004) Global inventory modeling and mapping studies. NA94apr15b.n11-VIg, 2.0, Global Land Cover Facility, University of Maryland, College Park, Maryland, USA.

UNCCD (United Nations Convention to Combat Desertification). (1996). *United Nations convention to combat desertification in countries experiencing serious drought and/or desertification*. Germany: Bonn.

Vlek, P., Le, Q. B., & Tamene, L. (2010). Assessment of land degradation, its possible causes and threat to food security in Sub-Saharan Africa. In R. Lal & B. A. Stewart (Eds.), *Food security and soil quality* (pp. 57–86). Boca Raton, Florida: CRC Press.

Vlek, P., Rodriguez-Kuhl, G., & Sommer, R. (2004). Energy use and CO_2 production in tropical agriculture and means and strategies for Reduction or mitigation Environment. *Development and Sustainability, 6*, 213–233.

Vogt, J. V., Safriel, U. N., Von Maltitz, G., Sokona, Y., Zougmore, R., Bastin, G., & Hill, J. (2011). Monitoring and assessment of land degradation and desertification: Towards new conceptual and integrated approaches. *Land Degradation & Development, 22*, 150–165.

von Braun, J., Gerber, N., Mirzabaev, A., & Nkonya, E. (2013). The economics of land degradation. (ZEF Working Papers 109). Bonn, Germany.

Wassen, M. J., Olde Venterink, H., Lapshina, E. D., & Tanneberger, F. (2005). Endangered plants persist under phosphorus limitation. *Nature, 437*, 547–550.

Way, S. A. (2006). Examining the Links between poverty and land degradation: From blaming the poor toward recognizing the rights of the poor. In P. Johnson, K. Mayrand, & M. Paquin (Eds.), *Governing Global Desertification: Linking Environmental Degradation, Poverty, and Participation* (pp. 27–41). VT: Ashgate, Burlington.

World Meteorological Organization. (2012). *WMO greenhouse gases bulletin: the state of greenhouse gases in the atmosphere using global observations through 2011*. Switzerland: WMO Greenhouse Gas Bulletin.

Yin, R. K. (2003). *Applications of case study research*. Thousand Oaks, California: Sage Publications.

Chapter 3
Institutional Framework of (In)Action Against Land Degradation

Philipp Baumgartner and Jan Cherlet

Abstract While econometric and spatial data are increasingly helpful to quantify and locate the extent and costs of land degradation, there is still little understanding of the contextual factors that determine or influence the land users' practices that aggravate or counteract land degradation. In this chapter, we take an institutional economic approach to analyse the persistence of degrading practices, the low adoption of sustainable land management (SLM), or the eventual organisational reaction to land degradation. The chapter reviews four examples of land degradation in different contexts to reveal the multiple driving forces and contextual factors. We then propose a conceptual framework to better understand the incentive structure and factors determining the land users' decision making. A layered analysis of the social phenomena is applied, following Williamson (2000). The chapter shows how actions at different layers can help improve land management. The chapter concludes with practical recommendations for the institutional economic analysis of land degradation.

Keywords Land degradation · Institutional economics · Economics of land degradation · Mixed method analysis · Sustainable land management

---

The chapter builds on earlier work with, and significant contributions of, Ephraim Nkonya and Julia Kloos, which is highly appreciated by the two authors.

P. Baumgartner (✉)
Center for Development Research, University of Bonn, Bonn, Germany
e-mail: ph.baumgartner@gmail.com

P. Baumgartner
International Fund for Agricultural Development, Rome, Italy

J. Cherlet
Secretariat of the International Land Coalition, Rome, Italy

E. Nkonya et al. (eds.), *Economics of Land Degradation and Improvement – A Global Assessment for Sustainable Development*,
DOI 10.1007/978-3-319-19168-3_3

Introduction

Land degradation as a global phenomenon occurs in many countries and in very different ecological, socioeconomic and climatic contexts. Estimations suggest that between 20 and 30 % of the global land surface is already degraded (Imeson 2012; Stavi and Lal 2014; Le et al. 2014). Anthropogenic as well as natural drivers of land degradation continue to exist and some even accelerate (see Chap. 7), mainly due to climate change and population growth. Sustainable land management (SLM) and mitigating measures are widely known, but adoption rates remain low. Two explanations for action and inaction prevail: (i) actor-oriented explanations that focus on socio-economic characteristics of the land user, suggesting that resource-poor households do not have the capacity, incentives or resources to invest in land improvement, and (ii) institutional economic explanations that underline the importance of constraining and enabling environments within which the land users take their land-use decisions.

This chapter presents a framework that combines and links both perspectives, demonstrating their complementarity. The framework includes the different layers of the institutional environment within which land users take their decisions. It builds on the works of Williamson (2000) and his analytical framework for institutional analysis as well as relevant sections in Nkonya et al. (2011).[1]

The chapter starts with a review of the existing literature on the action/inaction against land degradation and identifies, by means of four instructive case studies, the knowledge gap in the institutional understanding of this action/inaction. A structured analysis of the four cases reveals that the drivers of land degradation and the actors' behaviour related to land degradation are regulated and modified through different institutional layers.[2] In the second half of the chapter, we list a number of possible institutional responses to land degradation, showing how multiple entry paths can address the issue sustainably. The chapter concludes with policy recommendations and indications for future research.

Review of Institutional Causes of Land Degradation

About 3.2 billion people are affected by land degradation globally (Chap. 4). Population pressure, poverty, and market and institutional failures are commonly identified as the main drivers of land degradation (Kirui and Mirzabaev 2014). However, the link between the drivers on the one hand and land degradation on the

[1]We expand on discussions in Nkonya et al. (2011) by adding examples to underline the implication of applying a layered approach to economic analysis of land degradation.

[2]These different institutional layers are understood as different sets of economic/social rules that act upon individuals/society at different speeds, with different purposes, and with different degrees of formality. Therefore, these different layers need to be analysed separately.

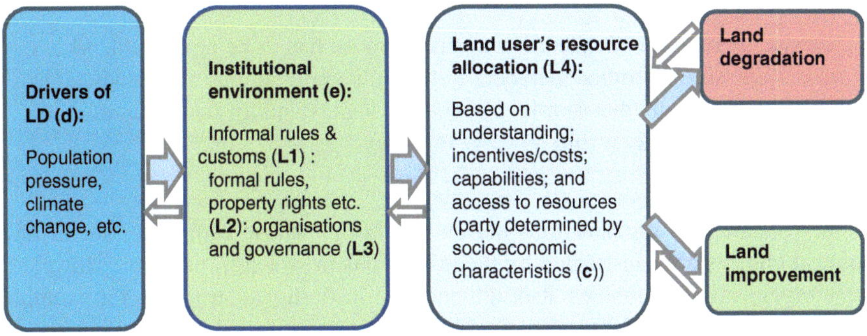

Fig. 3.1 *Conceptual framework* The mediating role of institutions in land degradation and land improvement (*Note* The links are not necessarily uni-directional; there are feed-back loops. However, to understand the behaviour of the land-user, the simplified scheme shows how his or her decisions "filter" through a number of institutional levels (e))

other hand is not direct. The drivers of land degradation ('d' in Fig. 3.1) are mediated and altered by the institutional environment ('e' in Fig. 3.1). Land improvement and mitigation of land degradation can come about through behavioural change of land users and following their re-allocation of resources (money, time, etc.) to land-improving practices. The land users' decision regarding their resource allocation will depend on contextual factors such as incentives, knowledge, capabilities or access to resources. These are partly a function of their socio-economic characteristics ('c' in Fig. 3.1), and partly the outcome of the institutional environment which enables and constrains their actions.[3] Analysis of land degradation and measures against it should thus consider these three dimensions.

Text box 3.1: Definitions

Institutions, defined here as "the formal and informal rules governing economic production and exchange" (North 1990), play a mediating role between the society and socio-economic and environmental drivers of land degradation and land improvement (Fig. 3.1).

Organisations are the groups of people bound by a common purpose to achieve objectives. They include political bodies such as city councils or ministries, economic bodies such as firms or trade unions, and social bodies such as associations or churches (North 1990). To reach this common

[3]Some socio-economic characteristics of a land user, as well as some plot-level characteristics can be considered exogenous (such as age of the user or slope of the plot), while others can be considered the result of the surrounding institutional environment or endogenous. Depending on the focus and time span of analysis, some characteristics can be considered exogenous or endogenous. For instance the level of education of a land user is not likely to change in the short term, but its changes throughout generations can be considered the outcome of education policies.

purpose, a mutual understanding of this purpose has to be developed, which makes decision by other members not only acceptable but also predictable (Ostrom 1976). In that sense, perception, understanding and aspiration of group members play a role.

We assume that organisations act as one body, whose economic, social and political choices are constrained by the institutions in which it functions. However, these organizations or bodies also influence the institutional structure, for example by issuing laws or regulation (political bodies), community rules (social bodies) or contractual arrangements between business partners (economic bodies).

Analyses of land degradation often focus exclusively on characteristics at household level (indicated as 'c' in Fig. 3.1), including the socio-economic characteristics of the farmers (age, gender, level of education, etc.), characteristics of the plot and the natural conditions (farm size, plot size, slope), farm management practices, and institutional aspects (support programs, access to credits, etc.) to explain land degradation (Tenge et al. 2004; Bravo-Ureta et al. 2006). Following a quantitative logic, data is often obtained through surveys and objectified in econometric analyses.

However, the socio-economic characteristics obtained at household level do not always fully explain land degradation. For instance, age or level of education are ambiguous characteristics and their role in the adoption of SLM practices is not straightforward. Pender and Kerr (1998) and Tenge et al. (2004) identified a positive influence of education on investment in indigenous conservation measures. To the contrary, Scherr and Hazell (1994) found a negative link between education and the adoption of labour-intensive land management practices, due to the higher opportunity cost of labour for farmers with a higher education. Asfaw and Ademassie (2004) found that education was positively related to the application of fertiliser. The inverse farm-size-productivity relationship (Lamb 2003; Lipton 2009) has shown that small-scale farmers invest more in labour intensive land management than large-scale farmers. However, the adoption of SLM measures increases with an increasing farm size (Norris and Batie 1987; Pender 1992; Bravo-Ureta et al. 2006; Amsalu and de Graaf 2007). This positive relationship is due to the ability of large-scale farmers to purchase inputs such as fertilizer or use labour-saving technologies. Some land management practices, such as tree planting, could take away some land area and are therefore less desirable to small-scale farmers (Bekele and Drake 2003). Livelihood strategies and the mix of income sources matter as well: Hopkins et al. (1999) and Pender and Kerr (1998) showed that non-farm income has a positive effect on the adoption of SLM, whereas Amsalu and de Graaf (2007) found that non-farm income had a significantly negative impact on the continued use of stone terraces.

However, all the studies referred to above have found that the impacts of these biophysical and socio-economic factors are context-specific. In other words, the household level characteristics ('c') explain part of the story, but the broader institutional environment ('e') plays a major role, too. To understand the role of institutions it might be helpful to see that similar drivers of land degradations ('d'), such as population growth, can lead to opposite outcomes, depending on the surrounding context (Fig. 3.1). We give four case studies of the adoption or non-adoption of sustainable land management practices from around the world, with a focus on the institutional environment ('e' in Fig. 3.1). The subsequent analysis of the four examples will illustrate the multiple dimensions of these two broad categories.

Case 1: Different factors explain adoption of organic fertilizer in China (Xu et al. 2014)

Soil salinity is a severe problem in China, as in many other parts of the world. Application of organic fertiliser, especially in combination with chemical fertiliser can reduce the negative impact of saline soils on crop land's productivity in a cost efficient way (Liu et al. 2010). While for the last half century the use of chemical fertilizer has risen dramatically, the use of organic fertiliser[4] decreased, which led to augmented risk of secondary soil salinization. In that regard, farmers' fertiliser choice impacts strongly on saline soil farmland's productivity. Xu et al. (2014) made a comparative study of eight villages in three saline soil areas in China, exploring the relative importance of household characteristics, land policy measures and contextual elements in mitigating soil salinity. The three locations (Kenli, Jilin; Zhenlai, Shandong; and Chabuacher, Xinjiang) are characterised by different levels of socio-economic development, different types of agricultural land use and different soil conditions. In each village 20–50 farm households were interviewed to gather information on household and plot characteristics, the tenure of the saline farmland, and agricultural policy and social service system. Monoculture prevailed and farming was the main income for most of the households. Education levels were low and the labour force was middle-aged. Income structures were similar across the three areas and comparable to other areas of rural China. Overall, organic fertiliser application was higher in the poorer areas and decreased with raising average income of the area. However, an econometric analysis revealed that the decision to apply organic fertiliser—which has high input cost in the form of labour and shows results only in the medium term—depends much on the land tenure arrangement. Farmers were much more likely to apply organic fertiliser on land they had directly contracted, rather than subcontracted with shorter lease duration. Also the stability of the tenure arrangement and the willingness of farmers to mortgage the land played a role. Farmers mortgaged their land to get additional funding, which they then invested to increase the plot's productivity and to expand the scale of agricultural production. Finally, policies had an effect as well: subsidies

[4]Organic fertiliser use is understood as returning crop residue and crashed stalks to the ground, mulching, application of biogas slurry, livestock manure as well as oil cake and green manure (Xu et al. 2014).

for organic fertiliser and the level of technological extension services affected farmers response.

The most interesting aspect of the study by Xu et al. (2014) is that across the three Chinese counties, different variables seemed to explain the farmers' decision to apply organic fertiliser or not. In the most developed of the three locations (KenLi), on the eastern coastal area, land tenure (i.e. institutions) played the biggest role in the households' decisions. In the north-western county (Zhenlai), with average household incomes, the household characteristics were most significant. In the western location (Chabuachaer), which is the poorest of the three locations, subsidies for organic fertilisers explained the high rates of adoption.

Case 2: Political context drives land degradation in Jocotán, Guatemala (Warren 2005; as cited in FAO 2006)

The Jocotán municipality, located in southeast Guatemala, is dominated by five rivers and has a very hilly landscape whose altitude ranges from 300 to 1800 m. The natural vegetation is subtropical rain forest in the valleys, acacia forest on the hillsides, and pinewoods in the dryer and chillier highlands. When the Spanish colonisers arrived in Jocotán in the 16th century, they started exploiting the fertile valley for the intensive cultivation of cocoa, tobacco, sugarcane, sarsaparilla, indigo and cattle. The indigenous Ch'orti' communities of the area were not employed on these colonial farms and were forced to move uphill and continue their subsistence farming—based on maize—on the dryer and more fragile hillsides. As this land was poorer, it required more frequent rotation, which induced them to clear part of the acacia forests. In the 19th century, the Spanish colonists took further control of the arable land by transferring all communal land titles of the indigenous communities' territories to the municipality while coffee plantations were created in the highlands. As the plantations in the valleys and the highlands attracted migrant workers to the municipality, the pressure on the land further increased and the Ch'orti' moved further towards less accessible and less productive land. Their subsistence farming on the shrinking and increasingly poor land was no longer sustainable and needed to be complemented with the sale of handicrafts or wage labour on the plantations. This situation persisted throughout the 20th century. As of the 1970s, adverse conditions on the global food market, local population growth and further fragmentation of the arable plots have plummeted the small-holder farmers into deeper poverty, making it impossible to invest in soil conservation or water harvesting. The few remaining patches of pinewood on highlands are being used for small-scale timber activities and the collection of firewood. The vegetation cover in the municipality is now completely insufficient to retain rainfall, humidity and soil—aggravating even further the land degradation in the area. The story of the Jocotán shows how a changing political context at global and national level can cause land degradation at local level. Today the local people and institutions realise the need to identify sustainable development alternatives in order to combat land degradation.

Case 3: Fragmentation of tenure contributes to land degradation in Nyando River basin, Kenya
(Swallow et al. 2005; as cited in FAO 2006)

The Nyando River basin, which covers around 3500 km^2 in western Kenya, is one of the poorest and most degraded areas of the country. The basin is home to about 750,000 people from principally two ethnic groups: the Luo in the lower and middle parts of the basin and the Kalenjin upstream. The land uses vary considerably along the river. The Kalenjin area is covered by protected forests, by small-scale farms in zones that over the past 40 years have been "degazzetted" as forests, and large-scale commercial tea plantations in the highlands. The middle part presents a mixture of land uses, including both smallholder farms (maize and beans and some cash crops as coffee and banana) and large-scale commercial farms (mostly sugar cane). The flood-prone shores of lake Victoria, in which the river drains, are used by the Luo for subsistence farming of maize, beans and sorghum, and by commercial farmers for the production of sugar cane and rice. The tenure systems that regulate the access to land and water equally vary along the river. There are three types of private tenure on government land (former 'crown land')—large agricultural leaseholds, subdivided agricultural leaseholds and non-agricultural leaseholds—and four types of private tenure on trust land—freehold land in adjudication areas,[5] freehold land in settlement schemes, non-agricultural leaseholds, and group ranches. There are also five types of public land in the Nyando basis, including native reserves. Land degradation and soil erosion in the Nyando river basin varies according to the tenure system that governs the land and water resources in the different areas. It is most severe in the subdivided agricultural leaseholds and in freehold land in adjudication areas, due to poor land-use planning during the 1960s and early 1970s when large farms were subdivided and sold to communities or smaller companies. Also the native reserves on public land suffer from severe land degradation, due to the natural growth of the populations living in these reserves and the fragmentation of the plots.

Case 4: Participatory land conservation policies reduce land degradation in Tunisia
(De Graaff et al. 2013)

Tunisia is a country strongly affected by land degradation and desertification. Measures to conserve soil and water sources were already undertaken before the Roman period. After independence, the government put a strong focus on tree planting, contour ploughing and limited grazing in erosion prone zones. In the 1960s, focus was put on large scale conservation efforts, mainly through the construction of huge earth bunds (banquettes). An area of about 700,000 ha was covered and costs for these measure reached USD55 million. However, in 1976 only 23 % of these bunds were still intact. While technicians indicated that the

[5]Adjudication is the process of authoritatively ascertaining existing land rights. This process is used in the conversion of land held under customary tenure into individual holdings.

measures had not been effective for the given conditions, others indicated that a lack of farmer involvement in planning of the bunds resulted in low acceptance. Especially since in the 1960s a land reform and policy of collectivisation had created high resistance among farmers and scepticism with regard to central level land policies. In the 1970s not much policy effort focused on soil and water conservation or sustainable land management. However, the Institute for Arid Regions (IRA) was established in the Southern part of the country in 1976, which since then played a major role in improving rangeland management, as well as water harvesting practices in the arid hillside area. In addition, the construction of new dams in Central Tunisia led to increased focus on reduction of sedimentation further upstream. In the 1980s, contour-ridged terraces on an area of 25,000 ha were built. Large-scale dam building programmes in the 1970s and 1980s did not alter the farmers' cropping or herding practices in the hillside areas (De Graaf et al. 2013). In the mid-1980s a Soil and Water Conservation department was established in the Ministry of agriculture and policy formulation became more participatory. The first 10 year National Soil and Water Conservation Strategy was launched in 1990, and a second followed in 2001. Indigenous measures have increasingly received more attention (De Graaff and Ouessar 2002). Finally, in the 2000s, community based approaches and Conservation Agriculture, especially direct seeding, were promoted by donors and the government, with so far very positive results (De Graaff et al. 2013).

Analysis of the Cases

In all four cases the drivers of land degradation are the same: anthropogenic drivers such as population growth and poverty combined with natural drivers such as background soil erosion and climate change. However, the characteristics of the land users alone do not explain the action/inaction to combat the drivers. A whole set of structural—or 'institutional'—layers modify, alter, or even determine how the drivers translate in actual land degradation. The case of China shows that every context has different determinants, which can be situated at household, institutional, or governmental level. The Guatemala case highlights that historical events, such as the settlement of colonisers in the fertile areas, and economic structures, such as the need for labour force, have triggered or aggravated the process of land degradation. In the Kenya case it is the type of land and water tenure, and especially the fragmentation of land and water tenure, that explain how drivers such as population growth and failing institutions determine where land degradation is more or less severe. The Tunisian case show that well-conceived policies can be effective in changing the land users' behaviour, but the case also shows that the participatory policies of the 1990s were much more effective than the top-down policies of the 1970s and 1980s.

These many different institutional layers can help explain why some land user undertake action against land degradation and invest in soil productivity, while others do not. Household and plot characteristics ('c' in Fig. 3.1) partly explain this, but other environmental factors ('e' in Fig. 3.1) play the role of modifying interface between drivers ('d' in Fig. 3.1), farm level characteristics ('c' in Fig. 3.1) and action/inaction. In the next section we make a fine-grained analysis of this institutional interface ('e' in Fig. 3.1).

Analytical Framework: Layered Approach of Institutional Economic Analysis

Institutions define the structure within which (economic) actors make decisions and shape their choices for action and exchange. Williamson (2000) distinguished four levels of institutional analysis (see Fig. 3.2) depending on their velocity of change. The top level is the level of *social embeddedness*, which comprises customs, traditions and social norms (L1). This level is taken as a given by most institutional

	Level of social analysis	**Frequency of change** (years)	**Purpose** of change
L1	Embeddedness: informal institutions, customs, traditions, norms, religion	10^2 to 10^3	Often non-calculative: spontaneous
L2	Institutional environment: formal rules of the game – esp. property (polity, judiciary, bureaucracy)	10 to 10^2	Get the institutional environment right: 1st order economizing
L3	Governance: play of the game – esp. contract (aligning governance structures with transactions)	1 to 10	Get the governance structures right: 2nd order economizing
L4	Resource allocation and employment (prices and quantities; incentive alignment	Continuous	Get the marginal conditions right: 3rd order economizing

Theoretical approach
L1: social theory
L2: economics of property rights
L3: transactions costs economics
L4: neoclassical economics/ agency theory

Fig. 3.2 *Analytical framework* Layered approach to institutional economic analysis of land degradation. *Source* Adopted from Williamson (2000)

economists, because changes in this layer are extremely slow and are the result of a collective, social process rather than of an orchestrated action by a group of actors. Translated in terms of land use, this level includes the norms and traditions that govern people's attitude towards their natural environment and the use of natural resources.

The second level is the *institutional* level. The social-institutional structures at this level are in part the product of evolutionary processes and in part designed (L2). Influenced by both old and recent history, this layer includes the judicative, legislative, and executive structures of government, as well as their share of power (for example, the degree of federalism). The structure and enforcement of property rights are part and parcel of this level.[6] The importance of this level is shown in the example of Kenya, where the type of land tenure played an important role in land degradation.

At the third level are the institutions of *governance* located (L3). The focus of this level lies on the contractual arrangements between interacting parties—that is, to the organization of economic transaction. Every time a contract is renewed, a reorganisation of the governance structures is possible (for example in firms). The frequency of rearrangements at this level is somewhere between one and ten years. The importance of this level is shown by the Guatemalan and Tunisian example, where respectively colonial powers and governmental policies periodically changed the rules of economic transactions.

These three levels of discrete analysis of governance structures must be distinguished from the fourth layer, which is the level where *neoclassical* economic analysis and *agency* theory explain the allocation of resources (such as wages, employment, or prices). At this level, firms and farms are typically depicted as production functions and analysed as an "optimality apparatus," whereby prices and outputs are adjusted continuously. The example from China showed how the characteristics of the farms and land users themselves determined the adoption or non-adoption of sustainable land practices. The four levels of institutions are illustrated in Fig. 3.2. The conclusion is that the root drivers of land degradation—to wit, population growth and poverty—have different effects in different places in the world, because they are mediated, altered or aggravated by a number of institutional layers.

It should be noted that depending on the time span considered in the analysis, some of the levels are taken as exogenous or given. Most economists, for example, consider L1 as exogenous, given slow rate of change and difficulty to attribute this change. The shorter the time period considered for analysis the more dimensions of the institutional environment are taken as exogenous, and hence switch to the category of "drivers" in above conceptual figure ('d' in Fig. 3.1). However, to

[6]These first-order choices are, without doubt, important for the outcome of an economy (Coase 1992; Olson 1996). Still, cumulative change of such structures is very difficult to orchestrate, though it occasionally takes place when sudden events introduce a sharp rupture in the established procedures.

understand today's behaviour of land users (L4) it remains important to see this behaviour as framed in an institutional environment (L2 and L3).

Institutional Framework of Action Against Land Degradation

Action against land degradation necessarily depends on a behavioural change of the land users, who should adopt sustainable land management practices. In other words, when policy makers devise policies or programs to prevent or revert land degradation, whether at local, national or regional level, they are actually adjusting the institutional environment ('e' in Fig. 3.1) in order to provoke the desired behavioural change at individual level.

In the rest of this section we analyse in a more systematic way the different actions that can be taken at each of the institutional layers (L1–L4), to adjust the institutional environment in such a way that land users adopt sustainable land management practices.[7] Remark, however, that adjustments are usually made at several institutional layers (L1–L4) at the time.

Building on Customs/Traditions, or "L1 Actions"

The cultural embeddedness of norms, customs and traditional institutions makes them very resistant to changes. However, history shows numerous examples of colonial or totalitarian regimes that have tried to alter traditional institutions. Actions at the L1 level often impinge on people's cultural freedom and identity, making these actions extremely controversial.

Yet, this layer of the institutional environment can also be an enabler of sustainable resource management and the reversion of land degradation. We give two examples: one of the artificial creation of new cultural values, and the other of the formal recognition of existing cultural values. In Niger, in 1970, the government relabeled the Independence day as National Tree Day. This helped raise awareness among farmers and land-users to invest in reforestation (Gerber et al. 2014). In Mongolia, the government is experimenting with an innovative form of co-management of pasture land in 54 pastoralist communities, in which the communities sign a contract with the local government for the sustainable use and rotation of the pastures and for the sustainable management of the land (Ykhanbai and Boroowa 2014). This contract is a formalisation of an existing, traditional institution.

---

[7]The presented examples of actions are a selection of measures that worked in the given contexts. They serve as illustrations. Nothing guarantees that they would equally work in other contexts.

In general, it is impossible to engineer culturally embedded institutions, but interventions can build on these culturally embedded institutions. Such bottom-up approach in policy design and implementation is also discussed at the following two layers.

Reforms of the Institutional Environment, or "L2 Actions"

The level L2 is the institutional environment. It is the level at which the executive, legislative, judicial and bureaucratic functions of the government are organised. This includes the horizontal distribution of power across different agencies (such as different ministries), the vertical distribution across levels (decentralisation), or the set of rules that determine access to and ownership of productive resources (tenure). The L2 provides the infrastructure and the playing field in which actors interact and take decisions. The L2 is often shaped by historic events, such as regime changes, crises or major intervention with large political support. While it is mostly the product of historical processes, opportunities for design exist.

Horizontal linkages across ministries At the national level, countries responded to natural resource and environmental degradation by forming ministries of environment to address degradation. One of the weaknesses of such ministries was their limited interaction with other ministries and departments (Volkery et al. 2006). Initially, responsibility for the promotion of soil and water conservation measures lay with the forestry ministries. This often led to coordination failure and little outreach to farmers and private land user (De Graaff et al. 2013). Promoting sustainable land management beyond boundaries of ministries might be an important pre-condition to reduce conflicting regulations and harmonise national efforts to fight land degradation.

Decentralisation The lack of involvement of local communities in managing natural resources is often identified as one of the major reasons for the failure of centralised governments to effectively manage land resources (Gibson et al. 2005; Robinson et al. 2011). The exclusion of local communities alienates them, which in turn leads to poor cooperation between local communities and natural resource managers. Ostrom and Nagendra (2006) found that locally-managed forests are usually managed more effectively than centrally-managed forests. FAO estimates that around one-quarter of forests in developing countries are in some way managed by local communities (FAO 2011). The share of community-managed forests is increasing, thanks to the promotion of decentralisation and community-based management by non-governmental organisations (NGOs) and international organisations (FAO 2011).

Payment for Ecosystem Services (PES) Somewhere between policy making, the involvement of local users, and the creation of innovative institutions floats the concept of *Payment for Ecosystem Services* (PES). PES is an economic, market-based approach for sustainability: PES schemes try to change the structural economic conditions in a certain area in such a way that the local resources users are incentivised to alter their resource use to maintain or restore certain ecosystem services. PES schemes are increasingly used in developing countries for the conservation of standing forests or wildlife habitat, but they are still in their infancy when it comes to combating land degradation.

The most notorious example of PES to combat land degradation is China's Sloping Land Conversion Program (SLCP). It was initiated by the central government in 1999 with the goal of reducing water and soil erosion, by converting agricultural land on steeply sloping and marginal lands into forest. Set to reforest or afforest 16 million hectares of sloping land, the SLCP is one of the largest PES schemes in the world (Li et al. 2011). The program is a public scheme, as the compensation of farmers is fully paid for by the central government. However, the economic incentives of PES schemes need to be well designed in order to ensure sustainability and to avoid 'leakage' of the negative effects to other regions. Therefore, besides direct compensation of the farmers, the Chinese government has also created favourable tax conditions for forest products, in order to make the conversion of farmland to forested land economically sustainable.

Tenure Property rights regimes prescribe access to productive resources. For our purpose, access to and control over land is key. Especially in rural societies they are crucial for most people's livelihoods, equity and also productivity of farmland (Deininger 2003; Lipton 2009). The change of a property right regime requires either a change in the political regime, or a high political effort by the existing regime.

Ethiopia constitutes an interesting example. In 1991 the military regime of the *derg* was overthrown and the current political system installed. Initially, tenure security was low, causing low level investments in soil conservation measures despite high degrees of land degradation (Shiferaw and Holden 1998). Poor households even removed soil conservation structures to increase short term yields at the risk of long-term damage on land productivity. Increased tenure security following a land policy reform in the early 2000s led to a behavioural change among smallholders in the densely populated highland. Initially, the tenure reform led to perceived lower security of tenure which caused a decline of land conservation measures (Holden and Otsuka 2014). However, once the new policy was accepted and understood, higher levels of investments were reached. Studies in Amhara and Tigray indicate that a strengthened feeling of tenure security was accompanied by increasing investment in soil conservation (Holden et al. 2009; Deininger et al. 2011).

Reforms of Governance, or "L3 Actions"

The focus of the third layer of social analysis (L3) lies on the governance of transactions between actors. Transactions can involve goods, services and rights over assets (e.g. property rights to land). An important feature of governance is that it should be capable to maintain order and mitigate conflict in the transactions. This can be enforced by means of institutional incentives, such as property rights, or self-imposed, which is often the case in organisations or communities. One important way of influencing or reforming the governance of transactions is through the formulation and enforcement of policies. Another way is by creating or changing the internal structure or organisation of the groups involved in the transactions. Changes of the internal structure can be the outcome of events at a higher level, or result from bottom-up feedback in the group.

Policy measures The Brazilian forest legislation has shown that well-designed policy interventions, such as the certification of sustainable production, can improve sustainable resource use and reduce forest degradation (vertical integration). In the 1990s and early 2000s, deforestation rates were high despite national laws protecting the forests. In 2005 deforestation rates started to decrease from its highest annual rate of 72,000 km^2 in 2003–04 to only over 7000 km^2 in 2008–09. Such a huge decrease was largely due to factors previously unaccounted for, namely international demand. Producers of soy bean and beef received special certifications and economic incentives if they signed and adhered to moratoriums on deforestation. This, as well as international funds for community-based conservation, triggered what may be "the end to deforestation" (Nepstad et al. 2010).

While the sustainability of this policy intervention in Brazil has still to be proven, it has shown that relatively simple measures in a related field (in this case: international marketing of agricultural products) directly led to changes in the contracting between buyers and producers, and indirectly to positive changes in land use.

Creation of local management structures As Robinson et al. (2011) discuss in their review of sustainable forest management, there is increasing evidence that indigenous groups and other communities can be successful at managing forest resources, provided that their land tenure is secured (Nepstad et al. 2006; Sandbrook et al. 2010; Wynberg and Laird 2007; Stevens et al. 2014). Policies that foster and build the capacity of local government and user groups generally enhance the sustainable land management at local level.

A study covering four African countries compared the number of bylaws related to natural resource management and observed a clear relationship between the number of enacted bylaws and the effectiveness of decentralisation (Ndegwa and Levy 2004). In other words, they found a correlation between enforcement of bylaws and *de facto* decentralisation. Ostrom and Nagendra (2006) demonstrated that communities manage better their forest resources than the central government manages protected forests. Similarly, a number of studies showed that timber and firewood theft and poaching were reduced when surrounding communities were involved in managing and sharing the benefits of forests and wildlife (Magrath et al. 2007; Cooke et al. 2008). The government in Senegal took measures to invest in community-based forest planning, especially through awareness campaigns.[8] In addition, local communities were incentivised through access to forest products. The results are very positive—area under forest cover quadrupled in the past decade, though from a very low initial base (see Chap. 19).

The pattern emerges that where local organizations are given the mandate to manage natural resources they are better at preventing and/or mitigating than their central governments (Blaikie 2006; Heltberg 2001; Ostrom 1990). However, an extensive review by Blaikie (2006) showed that strong local organisations are a necessary but not a sufficient condition for sustainable natural resource management. Participatory approaches to natural resources governance usually imply active engagement of local communities and agencies that goes beyond opinion sharing, but extends their engagement to interactive dialogue, collective learning, and joint action. This type of approach values local knowledge—not only scientific and technical knowledge.

Bottom-up organisation Higher degrees of internal organisation can help a group of individuals to pool their resources or knowledge. This can enable the individuals or the group to effectively act against land degradation. For most households in developing countries labour is a major constraint to productivity and has to be allocated across different activities. Especially for labour-intensive conservation measures, membership of a local organization with labour-exchange arrangements can lead to more effective action against land degradation (Lapar and Pandey 1999). Similarly, groups of farmers might pool resources to gain access to new technologies and spread innovations—technical as well as organisational—among them (Fischer and Qaim 2012). Availability of new technologies, such as mechanical mulching of straws, have a strong impact on the adoption of SLM, as the Chinese example indicated (Xu et al. 2014).

Improving Resource Allocation, or "L4 Actions"

A rational farmer may let land degradation happen to the point that the costs of additional degradation equals or exceeds the cost of adopting SLM practices. Each farmer determines her or his own *optimal private rate of land degradation*. Depending on the circumstances, it may be rational for local users to deplete their land up to a certain degree. It may also be rational for farmers to use land degrading practices,

[8]The government initially had to spend substantial amounts in equipment to be distributed to the communities. Eventually the expenditure for maintenance and awareness overtook the expenditures, but led to an overall sharp decrease of expenditure necessary to maintain good adoption rates.

which have high short-term returns in order to finance higher paying enterprises (e.g. non-farm activities) or services (e.g. children' education or health services). This optimal private rate mainly depends on the farmer's perception of costs and benefits—usually the balance between short-term and long-term yield gains or losses. Hence, only those ecosystem services that result in higher or lower production levels are considered in the decision, whereas those services that are not immediately measurable in terms of lost production (off-site effects) are neglected in the decision.

From an economic perspective it may be optimal for farmers to make production choices in which rates of soil depletion exceed what would be socially optimal. As a consequence, the private rate of degradation is not likely to reflect the optimal rate of degradation from society's viewpoint that includes impacts not covered by market forces ("externalities").[9] The optimal private rate of degradation is also determined by time preference and risk behaviour (Nkonya et al. 2011). If farmers are risk averse, they are less likely to adopt practices with high returns but with high risks. Policies for addressing time preference and "high" private optimal rate of land degradation require similar policies and strategies as those discussed above. Additionally sensitisation on the importance of SLM and moral suasion could enhance other incentive-based strategies (e.g. PES). The Senegalese example in this book (Chap. 19) also illustrates this phenomenon: the interviewed communities had partly agreed to improve their natural resource management. Most succeeded with regard to forest and grazing land management. However, the degradation of agricultural land continued, despite significant on-site and off-site costs.

Explaining Actors' Land Use Decision—Actor Oriented Approach

As described above, analyses at the L4 level often consider farms as profit functions (Fig. 3.2; Williamson 2000). Action and inaction regarding land degradation is thus reduced to cost-effectiveness, which is not likely to explain the phenomenon adequately. Farmers and their organisation are not only constrained and incentivised by their institutional environment but can also act as agents and influence the structure. In line with this, Jones (2002) actor-oriented approach can explain different behaviour within similar circumstances, while avoiding deterministic frameworks.[10] Jones identifies four broad variables or a combination which drive decision-makers to invest in maintaining or improving productivity of their land:

[9]This includes environmental impacts such as changes in the value of ecosystem services, sedimentation as well as indirect effects on the economy, government policies and other institutional factors can lead to socially and privately non-optimal rates of land degradation (see Nkonya et al. 2011).

[10]This underlines that the process of a reform might be as important as the content of the reform itself, as the capacity created and linkages touched will be of major importance for the sustainability of the reform.

1. **Perception of the problem**: Land users will only take action to protect or invest into their land if they perceive[11] a threat to its productivity or are aware of broader economic, social or environmental costs of the phenomenon.
2. **Knowledge** about potential mitigation strategies and how to apply them: Understanding or knowledge of techniques to remedy the loss of productivity is prerequisite for actions to be taken to prevent further loss. Boserup (1965) described that in many cases populations faced with increasing density were without any knowledge of fertilization techniques. However, though soil and water conservation are often key component of indigenous farming, non-indigenous observers might not "see" those techniques (Pawluk et al. 1992). In many cases, local users may be aware of certain new technologies, e.g. water harvesting or mulching, but might lack incentives or the financial means necessary to apply them.
3. **Incentives to invest** in productivity of land (or lack thereof): Without the perspective to get some future return from investing in the land, owners/users are not likely to bear the accompanied costs and will not take action. The most notable factors affecting incentives might be the security of tenure. Those may take the form of private land titles but also informal institutions such as customary or communal titles can meet this requirement (Ostrom 1990; Migot-Adholla et al. 1991; Besley 1995; Gavian and Ehui 1999). Other factors also matter: relative priority accorded to land productivity maintenance compared with, for example, off-farm activities that might yield higher returns to labor can play a big role (Jones 2002; Woelcke 2006).[12] Thus, the more off-farm activities contribute to the livelihood, the less incentives to maintain land productivity. Disincentives may include feelings of exploitation, e.g. through extraction of surplus from landlords or the state, high production risk through price volatility, or other external factors. This already indicates that several reasons for unsustainable land management might be found off-farm and corrections will have to tackle those in order to reach lasting improvements.
4. **Capability to invest**: This can be seen as a function of available resources (conservation or improvement often requires additional land, labour or capital) and the social relations determining access and control (Jones 2002). For example, the capability to manage common property resources without degradation signifies an effective system of social organisation (Ostrom 1990). At the individual and household level, capability implies the power to make decisions and effect action (*ibid.*). Access to economic resources (capital, credit, labour and land) play an important role, but institutional settings strongly matter as well.

[11]Interpretation of environmental changes is culturally constructed and need to be appreciated for thoroughly understanding of farmers' behaviour.

[12]The application of manure is another example for conflicting use of limited resources. While most farmers in arid and semi-arid areas are aware that manure will increase fertility of their plots, they are using dried manure for cooking and do not have adequate substitutes for this use. Again, policies might have to address this problem from a rather indirect side—maybe subsidizing stoves or other sources of energy, will keep manure on the field.

Conclusions

In this chapter, it is argued that neither the root drivers of land degradation nor farm characteristics can entirely explain land users' action or inaction with respect to land degradation. We argue that a meaningful analysis of action/inaction has to unwrap the black box of institutions and understand how they influence the impacts of the root drivers. By means of four examples of land degradation from around the world, the reader is made aware of the many forces at work. The chapter then proposes an analytical framework, consisting of four different institutional layers, to explain the action/inaction of land users against land degradation.

The analytical framework is as follows. At individual level (level L4), the way actors allocate resources depending on farm characteristics but also on the incentives created by the institutional surrounding. The institutional surrounding is the ensemble of cultural values regarding natural resources management (level L1), formal institutions for natural resources management (level L2), and policies and governance structures for natural resources management (level L3). The second half of the chapter shows how actors and organisation can shape the different layers of the institutional environment, in order to create the right incentives for the adoption of sustainable land management methods, through interventions at any of the four institutional layers.

Implications for policy making Not one institutional measure is the silver bullet to mitigate land degradation. However, some measures stand out as generally more effective. Decentralisation of competencies and the involvement of local communities are often associated with improvements in management of natural resources, in particular pastures and forests. Nonetheless, participatory or community action alone is not sufficient to revert back land degradation; public policies and public investment that support land management are also needed (Koning and Smaling 2005). Policies could target the poor through investments that increase their off-farm employment opportunities and thus reduce dependency on natural resources (Barbier 2010). While this is likely to reduce pressure on collectively owned or managed natural resources, such as forest, watersheds or range land, it is not clear if it will increase investment in protection of agricultural land against soil/land degradation. Several authors indicate that decreasing dependence on agricultural land also came about with decreasing investment in land conservation (Holden et al. 2004; Woelcke 2006). Policy actions have to take into consideration at which level of the institutional environment they are aiming to change the setting and how those are interlinked with other levels (Fig. 3.2). The probability of successful policy implementation and related costs depend on such analysis as well as on the consideration of actors involved and how they are positioned with regard to the new design (Norton et al. 2008).

Implications for data generation and analysis Institutions are complex and diverse. Analysis of institutions should therefore adopt a certain pluralism of approaches (Williamson 2000). One approach is to look for similarities and differences in institutional environments, in order to understand how similar drivers can have different outcomes, depending on the institutional setting. The example of the study in China (Xu et al. 2014) applied such a strategy. Another approach is to look at institutional change over time and see how different institutional arrangements and governance affected outcomes. The discussion on land conservation policies since the 1960s in De Graaff et al. (2013) illustrates this. When gathering and analysing data, it is important to conceptualise the institutional environment together with the speed and purpose of its changes and to think beyond the household or plot-level characteristics, in order to capture all dimensions of action/inaction against land degradation.

References

Amsalu, A., & de Graaf, J. (2007). Determinants of adoption and continued use of stone terraces for soil and water conservation in an Ethiopian highland. *Ecological Economics, 61*, 294–302.

Asfaw, A., & Admassie, A. (2004). The role of education on the adoption of chemical fertilizer under different socioeconomic environments in Ethiopia. *Agricultural Economics, 30*(3), 215–228.

Barbier, E. B. (2010). Poverty, development, and environment. *Environment and Development Economics, 15*(06), 635–660.

Bekele, W., & Drake, L. (2003). Soil and water conservation decision behavior of subsistence farmers in the eastern highlands of Ethiopia: A case study of the hunde-lafto area. *Ecological Economics, 46*, 437–451.

Besley (1995). Property rights and investment incentives: Theory and evidence from Ghana. *Journal of Political Economy, 103*(5), 903.

Blaikie, P. (2006). Is small really beautiful? Community-based natural resource management in Malawi and Botswana. *World Development, 34*(11), 1942–1957.

Boserup, E. (1965). *The conditions of agricultural growth: The economics of agrarian change under population pressure*. London: Allen and Unwin.

Bravo-Ureta, B. E., Solis, D., Cocchi, H., & Quiroga, R. E. (2006). The Impact of Soil Conservation and Output Diversification on Farm Income in Central American Hillside Farming. *Agricultural Economics, 35*, 267–276.

Coase, R. (1992). The institutional structure of production. *American Review, 82*(4), 713–719.

Cooke, P., Köhlin, G., & Hyde, W. (2008). Fuelwood, forests and community management—evidence from household studies. *Environment and Development Economics, 13*(01), 103–135.

De Graaff, J., Aklilu, A., Ouessar, M., Asins-Velis, S., & Kessler, A. (2013). The development of soil and water conservation policies and practices in five selected countries from 1960 to 2010. *Land Use Policy, 32*, 165–174.

De Graaff, J., & Ouessar, M. (2002). Water harvesting in Mediterranean zones: an impact assessment and economic evaluation. In *Proceedings from EU Wahia Project Final Seminar in Lanzarote*. Tropical Resource Management Paper No. 40, Wageningen.

Deininger, K. (2003). *Land policies for growth and poverty reduction: Key issues and challenges ahead*. Washington D.C: World Bank.

Deininger, K., Ali, D. A., & Alemu, T. (2011). Impacts of land certification on tenure security, investment, and land market participation: Evidence from Ethiopia. *Land Economics, 87*(2), 312–334.

FAO. (2006). The new generation of watershed management programmes and projects (p. 137). FAO Forestry Paper 150. Rome: FAO.

FAO. (2011). *State of the world's forests* (p. 179). Rome: FAO.

Fischer, E., & Qaim, M. (2012). Linking smallholders to markets: Determinants and impacts of farmer collective action in Kenya. World Development.

Gavian, S., & Ehui, S. (1999). Measuring the production efficiency of alternative land tenure contracts in a mixed crop-livestock system in Ethiopia. *Agricultural Economics, 20*(1), 37–49.

Gerber, N., Nkonya, E., & von Braun, J. (2014). Land degradation, poverty and marginality. In J. von Braun & F. W. Gatzweiler (Eds.), *Marginality: Addressing the nexus of poverty, exclusion and ecology* (pp. 181–203). Netherlands: Springer.

Gibson, C., Williams, J., & Ostrom, E. (2005). Local enforcement and better forests. *World Development, 33*(2), 273–284.

Heltberg, R. (2001). Determinants and impact of local institutions for common resource management. *Environment and Development Economics, 6*, 183–208.

Holden, S. T., Deininger, K., & Ghebru, H. (2009). Impacts of low-cost land certification on investment and productivity. *American Journal of Agricultural Economics, 91*(2), 359–373.

Holden, S., Shiferaw, B., & Pender, J. (2004). Non-farm income, household welfare, and sustainable land management in a less-favoured area in the Ethiopian highlands. *Food Policy, 29*, 369–392.

Holden, S. T., & Otsuka, K. (2014). The roles of land tenure reforms and land markets in the context of population growth and land use intensification in Africa. *Food Policy, 48*, 88–97.

Hopkins, J., Southgate, D., & Gonzalez-Vega, C. (1999). Rural poverty and land degradation in El Salvador. Paper Presented at the Agricultural and Applied Economics Associations Annual Meeting. Abstract in American Journal Agricultural Economics 81 (December 1999).

Imeson, A. (2012). *Desertification, land degradation and sustainability*. Chichester: Wiley.

Jones, S. (2002). A framework for understanding on-farm environmental degradation and constraints to the adoption of soil conservation measures: case studies from highland Tanzania and Thailand. *World Development, 30*(9), 1607–1620.

Kirui, O., & Mirzabaev, A. (2014). Economics of Land Degradation in Eastern Africa. ZEF Working Paper Series (128).

Koning, N., & Smaling, E. (2005). Environmental crisis or "lie of the land"? The debate on soil degradation in Africa. *Land Use Policy, 22*(1), 3–11.

Lamb, R. L. (2003). Inverse productivity. Land quality, labor markets, and measurement errors. *Journal of Development Economics, 71*(1), 71–96.

Lapar, M., & Pandey, S. (1999). Adoption of soil conservation: The case of the Philippine uplands. *Agricultural Economics, 21*(3), 241–256.

Le, Q. B., Nkonya, E., & Mirzabaev, A. (2014). Biomass productivity-based mapping of global land degradation hotspots. ZEF-Discussion Papers on Development Policy (193).

Li, J., Feldman, M. W., Li, S., & Daily, G. (2011). Rural household income and inequality under the sloping land conversion program in western China. *PNAS, 108*(19), 7721–7726.

Lipton, M. (2009). Land reform in developing countries—property rights and property wrongs (p. 456). Routledge: Oxon.

Liu, E. K., Zhao, B. Q., Mei, X. R., Li, X. Y., & Li, J. (2010). Distribution of water-stable aggregates and organic carbon of arable soils affected by different fertilizer application. *Acta Ecologica Sinica, 30*(4), 1035–1041.

Magrath, W., Grandalski, R., Stuckey, G., Vikanes, G., & Wilkinson, G. (2007). *Timber theft prevention: Introduction to security for forest managers* (p. 128). Washington, D.C.: World Bank.

Migot-Adholla, S., Hazell, P., Blarel, B., & Place, F. (1991). Indigenous land rights systems in Sub-Saharan Africa: A constraint on productivity? *The World Bank Economic Review, 5*, 155–175.

Ndegwa, S., & Levy, B. (2004). *The politics of decentralization in Africa, Chapter, 9* (pp. 283–321). World Bank: Washington D.C.

Nepstad, D., Soares-Filho, B., Merry, F., Lima, A., Moutinho, P., Carter, J., et al. (2010). The end of deforestation in the Brazilian Amazon. *Science, 326*, 1350–1351.

Nepstad, D. C., Stickler, C. M., & Almeida, O. T. (2006). Globalization of the Amazon soy and beef industries: Opportunities for conservation. *Conservation Biology, 20*, 1595–1603.

Nkonya, E., Gerber, N., Baumgartner, P., von Braun, J., De Pinto, A., Graw, J., et al. (2011). *The economics of land degradation: Toward an integrated global assessment*. Development Economics and Policy. Frankfurt a.M.: Peter Lang.

Norris, E., & Batie, S. (1987). Virginia farmers' soil conservation decisions: An application of tobit analysis. *Southern Journal of Agricultural Economics, 19*(1), 88–97.

North, D. C. (1990). *Institutions, institutional change and economic performance*. Political Economy of Institutions and Decisions (p. 159). Cambridge, UK: Cambridge University Press.

Norton, A., Beddies, S., Holland, J., Garbarino, S., Gamper, C., Ruckstuhl, S., & Sjorslev, J. (2008). *The political economy of policy reform: Issues and implications for policy dialogue and development operations* (p. 116). Washington, D.C.: World Bank Publications.

Olson, M. (1996). Distinguished lecture on economics in government: Big bills left on the sidewalk: why some nations are rich, and others poor. *The Journal of Economic Perspectives, 10*(2), 3–24.

Ostrom, E. (1990). *Governing the commons: The evolution of institutions for collective action*. Cambridge, UK: Cambridge University Press.

Ostrom, V. (1976). John R. common's foundations for policy analysis. *Journal of Economic Issues, 10*(4), 839–857.

Ostrom, E., & Nagendra, H. (2006). Insights on linking forests, trees, and people from the air, on the ground, and in the laboratory. *Proceedings of the National Academy of Sciences of the United States of America, 103*(51), 19224–19231.

Pawluk, R., Sandor, J., & Tabor, J. (1992). The role of indigenous soil knowledge in agricultural development. *Journal of Soil and Water Conservation, 47*(4), 298–302.

Pender, J. (1992). *Credit rationing and farmers' irrigation investments in south India*. Ph.D. thesis, Department of Economics, Stanford University, Stanford, California, USA.

Pender, J., & Kerr, J. (1998). Determinants of farmers' indigenous soil and water conservation investments in semiarid India. *Agricultural Economics, 19*, 113–125.

Robinson, B., Holland, M. B., & Naughton-Treves, L. (2011). Does secure land tenure save forests? A review of the relationship between land tenure and tropical deforestation. CCAFS Working Paper No. 7.

Sandbrook, C., Nelson, F., Adams, W. M., & Agrawal, A. (2010). Carbon, forests and the REDD paradox. *Oryx, 44*(03), 330–334.

Shiferaw, B., & Holden, S. T. (1998). Resource degradation and adoption of land conservation technologies in the Ethiopian highlands: A case study in Andit Tid, North Shewa. *Agricultural Economics, 18*, 233–247.

Scherr, S., & Hazell, P. (1994). Sustainable agricultural development strategies in fragile lands. IFPRI Discussion Paper.

Stavi, I., Lal, R. (2014). Achieving zero net land degradation: Challenges and opportunities. Journal of Arid Environments (in press).

Stevens, C., Winterbottom, R., Springer, J., & Reytar, K. (2014). *Securing rights, combating climate change. How strengthening community forest rights mitigates climate change*. Washington: World Resources Institute.

Swallow, B., Onyango, L., & Meinzen-Dick, R. (2005). Catchment property rights and the case of Kenya's Nyando basin. In B. Swallow, N. Okono, M. Achouri, & L. Tennyson (Eds.), *Preparing for the next generation of watershed management programmes and projects. Proceedings of the African Workshop, Nairobi, 8 to 10 October 2003*. Watershed Management and Sustainable Mountain Development Working Paper No. 8. Rome, FAO, FORC.

Tenge, A. J., De Graaff, J., & Hella, J. P. (2004). Social and economic factors affecting the adoption of soil and water conservation in west Usambara highlands, Tanzania. *Land Degradation and Development, 15*, 99–114.

Volkery, A., Swanson, D., Jacob, K., Bregha, F., & Pintér, L. (2006). Coordination, challenges, and innovations in 19 national sustainable development strategies. *World Development, 34*(12), 2047–2063.

Warren, P. (2005). Between the household and the market. A livelihoods analysis of SPFS-promoted seed multiplication in Eastern Guatemala. Livelihoods Support Programme Working Paper No. 20. Rome, FAO.

Williamson, O. E. (2000). The new institutional economics—taking stock, looking ahead. *Journal of Economic Literature, 38*(3), 595–613.

Woelcke, J. (2006). Technological and policy options for sustainable agricultural intensification in eastern Uganda. *Agricultural Economics, 34*(2), 129–139.

Wynberg, R., & Laird, S. (2007). Less is often more: Governance of a non-timber forest product, marula (Sclerocarya birrea subsp. caffra) in southern Africa. *International Forestry Review, 9* (1), 475–491.

Ykhanbai, H., & Boroowa, K. (2014). Community-based co-management of pasture land, Mongolia. Case study of the ILC Database of Good Practices for People-Centred Land Governance. Rome: ILC.

Xu, H., Huang, X., Zhong, T., Chen, Z., & Yu, J. (2014). Chinese land policies and farmers' adoption of organic fertilizer for saline soils. *Land Use Policy, 38*, 541–549.

Chapter 4
Biomass Productivity-Based Mapping of Global Land Degradation Hotspots

Quang Bao Le, Ephraim Nkonya and Alisher Mirzabaev

Abstract Land degradation affects negatively the livelihoods and food security of global population. There have been recurring efforts by the international community to identify the global extent and severity of land degradation. Using the long-term trend of biomass productivity as a proxy of land degradation at global scale, we identify the degradation hotspots in the world across major land cover types. We correct factors confounding the relationship between the remotely sensed vegetation index and land-based biomass productivity, including the effects of inter-annual rainfall variation, atmospheric fertilization and intensive use of chemical fertilizers. Our findings show that land degradation hotpots cover about 29 % of global land area and are happening in all agro-ecologies and land cover types. This figure does not include all areas of degraded lands, it refers to areas where land degradation is most acute and requires priority actions in both in-depth research and management measures to combat land degradation. About 3.2 billion people reside in these degrading areas. However, the number of people affected by land degradation is likely to be higher as more people depend on the continuous flow of ecosystem goods and services from these affected areas. Land improvement has occurred in about 2.7 % of global land area during the last three decades, suggesting that with appropriate actions land degradation trend could be reversed. We also identify concrete aspects in which these results should be interpreted with cautions, the limitations of this work and the key areas for future research.

Q.B. Le (✉)
CGIAR Research Program on Dryland Systems (CRP-DS),
International Center for Agricultural Research in the Dry Areas (ICARDA),
PO Box 950764, Amman 11195, Jordan
e-mail: q.le@cgiar.org; q.le@alumni.ethz.ch

E. Nkonya
International Food Policy Research Institute (IFPRI), 2033 K Street NW,
Washington, DC 20006, USA

A. Mirzabaev
Center for Development Research (ZEF), University of Bonn, Walter Flex Str 3,
53113 Bonn, Germany

E. Nkonya et al. (eds.), *Economics of Land Degradation and Improvement – A Global Assessment for Sustainable Development*,
DOI 10.1007/978-3-319-19168-3_4

Keywords Land degradation · Land improvement · NDVI · Rainfall variation · Fertilization

Introduction

Land degradation is a global problem affecting at least a quarter of the global land area (Lal et al. 2012) and seriously undermining the livelihoods, especially of the poor, in all agro-ecologies across the world (Nkonya et al. 2011). Although land degradation has been critical problem throughout the history (Diamond 2005), it has attained its current global scales, becoming a major global issue especially since the second half of the 20th century (Nkonya et al. 2011). Since the first global mapping of desertification in 1977 (Dregne 1977), there have been numerous efforts at global mapping of land degradation (Oldeman et al. 1990; USDA-NRCS 1998; Eswaran et al. 2001). The earlier generation of these studies had been constrained by lack of global level quantitative data which could be used for mapping soil and land degradation, and therefore were based on expert opinions. The developments in the remote sensing and satellite technologies allowed the later studies to be based on quantitative satellite data, such as Global Inventory Modelling and Mapping Studies (GIMMS) dataset of 64 km^2-resolution of Normalized Difference Vegetation Index (NDVI) data, however, several methodological challenges still exist on more accurately estimating the land degradation hotspots (Vlek et al. 2010; Le et al. 2012).

In this context, addressing land degradation may require channeling substantial amounts of scarce resources and making long-term investments. These investments are likely to yield high levels of social returns and welfare improvements. However, all countries in the world have budgetary constraints, necessitating the prioritization of such investments. To combat land degradation, both on the international and national levels, policy makers often need information about areas of severe degradation in order to prioritize national budgets and plan strategic interventions (Vlek et al. 2010; Vogt et al. 2011; Le et al. 2012). To achieve this, accurate maps of land degradation hotspots—where land degradation is most acute, are needed. This study seeks to meet that objective at the global level.

As indicated above, there have been several efforts in the past to map land degradation at the global scale. The major objective of this global study is the identification of regions where degradation magnitude and extent are relatively high, i.e. geographic degradation hotspots, for prioritizing both preventive investments for the restoration or reclamation of degraded land, and subsequent focal ground-based studies. Consequently, this mapping of degradation hotspots is different from, indeed not as contentious as, the production of an accurate map of all degraded areas.

Literature Review

Land degradation is a major global problem. There have been many efforts to map land degradation at global and regional scales (Dregne 1977; Oldeman et al. 1990; USDA-NRCS 1998; Eswaran et al. 2001; Herrmann et al. 2005; Wessels et al. 2007; Bai et al. 2008b, 2013; Hellden and Tottrup 2008; Hill et al. 2008; Vlek et al. 2008, 2010; Le et al. 2012; Conijn et al. 2013; Dubovyk et al. 2013). However, despite these efforts, the existing global maps of land degradation are weakened by serious shortcomings. The earlier mapping exercises used subjective expert opinion surveys as the basis for the maps, with unknown direction and magnitudes of measurement errors. The more recent of these studies are making use of now globally available remotely-sensed NDVI data (Tucker et al. 2005), but NDVI also has its own shortcomings as a proxy for land degradation, such as various confounding effects (Pettorelli et al. 2005). These include: (1) remnant cloud-cover effects in humid tropics, (2) soil moisture in sparse vegetative areas, which reduces the NDVI signal, (3) seasonal variations in vegetation phenology (proportional with weather seasonality) and time-series autocorrelation, (4) site-specific effects of vegetation structure and site conditions (e.g. topography and altitude). These confounding effects can be mitigated at some degree, but not completely removed. As a consequence, NDVI trend is always affected by unexpected noise, thus bearing considerable uncertainty in a way that where there are small magnitudes of NDVI trend, the risk that errors/noises in the NDVI data are larger than the trend itself is much higher (Tucker et al. 2005).

Moreover, there are major factors confounding the relationship between NDVI (NPP) trend and human-induced land degradation. These confounding effects include: (1) the effect of inter-annual rainfall variation on NDVI (NPP) (Herrmann et al. 2005), (2) the effect of atmospheric fertilization on vegetation greenness and growth (Boisvenue and Running 2006; Reay et al. 2008; Lewis et al. 2009; Buitenwerf et al. 2012; Le et al. 2012), and (3) intensive uses of chemical fertilizers in intensified croplands (Vlek et al. 1997; Potter et al. 2010; MacDonald et al. 2011). The biomass productivity of the land is often a low priority service in many urbanized areas, where space provision is usually the most expected service of the land.

To isolate human-induced biomass production decline from the one driven by rainfall, currently, there are different methods: residual trend analysis method (*ResTrend*) (Evans and Geerken 2004; Herrmann et al. 2005) (Wessels et al. 2007), the trend-correlation stepwise method (*Trend-Correlation*) (Le et al. 2012; Vlek et al. 2010; Vu et al. 2014a), or trend-correlation with the additional use of rain-use efficiency (RUE) (Bai et al. 2008a; Fensholt et al. 2013). The first two methods use the correlation between inter-annual NDVI and rainfall data for isolating pixels with biomass production decline not caused by rainfall inter-annual variation. If there is no other natural drivers of biomass production decline besides the reduction of annual rainfall, the biomass production decline in these pixels is likely caused by human activities. The comparisons between the uses of two methods at global level (Dent et al. 2009) and national level (Vu et al. 2014a) showed similar results. While rain-use efficiency has been recently used in some land degradation assessments in dry lands (Wessels et al. 2007; Fensholt et al. 2013), there are concerns about the use of rain-use efficiency for continental and global scale (Dent et al. 2009), especially in the humid tropics where rainfall is generally not a limited factor of primary productivity.

The effect of atmospheric fertilization caused by elevated levels of CO_2 and NO_x in the atmosphere (Dentener 2006; Reay et al. 2008) complicates the global assessment of land degradation using the NDVI-based approach. Increased atmospheric fertilization (AF) can cause a divergence between greenness trend and soil fertility change as the fertilization effect has not been substantially mediated through the soil. The rising level of atmospheric CO_2 stimulates photosynthesis in plants' leaves, thus increasing NPP, but the soil fertility may not necessarily be proportional with the above ground biomass improvement. The wet deposition of reactive nitrogen and other nutrients may affect positively plant growths as foliate fertilization without significantly contributing to the soil nutrient pool, or compensating nutrient losses by soil leaching and erosion. Global observations, both field measurements (Boisvenue and Running 2006; Lewis et al. 2009; Buitenwerf et al. 2012) and remotely sensed data analyses (Vlek et al. 2010; Fensholt et al. 2012; Le et al. 2012) show long-term improvement of biomass productivity in large areas that cannot be attributed to either human interventions or rainfall improvement. In Africa, the biomass increased at a rate of 0.63 ± 0.31 mg ha^{-1} $year^{-1}$ over the past 4 decades for closed-canopy tropical forest sites with ample rain and free of human interventions (Lewis et al. 2009).

As NDVI values can be affected by several site- and land cover-specific factors (Pinter et al. 1985; Markon et al. 1995; Thomas 1997; Mbow et al. 2013), different locations with the same NDVI value are not necessarily have the same biomass productivity. Thus, comparison of biomass productivity between pixels using NDVI is a pitfall that should be avoided (Pettorelli et al. 2005). Recent studies suggested interpreting the NDVI trend results for each spatial stratum of social-ecological conditions in order to gain more insights about likely degradation processes and affecting factors in the delineated hotspots (Vlek et al. 2010; Sommer et al. 2011; Le et al. 2012; Vu et al. 2014b). Because land use/cover refers to ecosystem exploitation (Nachtergaele and Petri 2008) and is conditioned by several anthropogenic factors that define the social and ecological contexts for interpreting causalities from statistical results, broad land-use classes have been recommended for stratifying causal analyses and interpretations of land degradation (Vlek et al. 2010; Sommer et al. 2011; Vu et al. 2014b).

The Conceptual Framework

In this study, "land degradation" is understood in a broad sense. From internationally authoritative concepts of United Nations Convention to Combat Desertification (UNCCD 2004) and Millennium Ecosystem Assessment (MEA 2005), land degradation is defined as the persistent reduction or loss of land ecosystem services, notably the primary production service (Safriel 2007; Vogt et al. 2011). The aspects emphasized in this definition of land degradation include:

1. "Land" is understood as a terrestrial ecosystem that includes not only soil resources, but also vegetation, water, other biota, landscape setting, climate attributes, and ecological processes (MEA 2005) that operate within the system, ensuring its functions and services.
2. The definition focuses on the ecological services of the land: land degradation makes sense to our society only in the context of human benefits derived from land ecosystems uses (Safriel 2007). Negative changes in soil component (e.g. soil erosion, deteriorations of physical, chemical, and biological soil properties) are concerned as much as how serious these changes result in reductions of supporting (e.g. primary production), provisioning (e.g. biological products including foods) and regulating (e.g. carbon sequestration) services of the land (i.e. land ecosystem).

As a consequence, the definition emphasizes the pivotal role of primary production among a wide range of land's services. The crucial reason for this emphasis is that primary production generates products of biological origin, on which much of other ecosystem services depend (Safriel 2007). The primary production is the basis of food production, regulates water, energy, and nutrient flows in land ecosystems, sequestrates carbon dioxide from the atmosphere and generally provides habitats for diverse species (MEA 2005).

Methodology and Data

The methodological approaches applied in this study build on this previous literature and, in fact, seek to address some of the shortcomings of the previous research on global land degradation hotspots mapping.

Proxy Indicator Approach to Mapping of Degradation Hotspots

In the context of land degradation hotspots mapping, land degradation proxies (i.e. key indicators that approximate relevant processes of land degradation) are often used to delineate degradation hotspots. Although using proxies of land degradation is always prone to considerable uncertainties, the proxy method is relevant for mapping global, continental and national degradation hotspots due to the following reasons:

1. The main target is the areas with high magnitude and extent of degradation, i.e. where temporal and spatial variations of the used proxies are high and observable. This helps mitigate the adverse effects of the inherently high

uncertainty of the used proxies (Vu et al. 2014a). The lower is the temporal and spatial variation of the used proxies, the lower is the relevance of the proxy method.
2. The considered scale is global, or continental or national and the related need is to delineate degradation hotspot at coarse resolution (e.g. 1–10 km) (Vogt et al. 2011).
3. There are no other data alternatives for long-term (>2 decades), large scale (global or continental) assessments (Vlek et al. 2010; Fensholt et al. 2012).
4. Efforts to improve global/continental land degradation assessment require the first version of a global land degradation map to guide where and what needed to be verified in the next steps.

Long-Term Trend of Annual NDVI as the Proxy of Long-Term Biomass Productivity Decline

Given the global scale and long-term perspectives of the study, we used the long-term trend of inter-annual mean Normalized Difference Vegetation Index (NDVI) over the period 1982–2006 as a proxy for a persistent decline or improvement in the Net Primary Productivity (NPP) of the land, thereby delineating past land degradation hotspots. This NDVI-based assessment of land degradation has been used by many studies (Bai et al. 2008b; Hellden and Tottrup 2008; Vlek et al. 2010; Le et al. 2012). However, as we highlighted in the literature review, NDVI as a proxy for land degradation has several caveats. Our strategy to address these caveats in this NDVI-based mapping of land degradation hotspots is summarized in Table 4.1.

GIMMSg-NDVI Data

The employed dataset of vegetation index Global Inventory Modeling and Mapping Studies (GIMMS) Satellite Drift Corrected and NOAA-16 incorporated Normalized Difference Vegetation Index (NDVI), Monthly 1981–2006, is called GIMMSg-NDVI dataset. This dataset is available for free at the Global Land Cover Facility (GLCF), the University of Maryland (GLCF—http://glcf.umiacs.umd.edu/data/gimms/—accessed in 01 May 2013).

This GIMMSg-NDVI version is selected for analysis because of several reasons. For global land degradation assessment over long terms, there may be no other alternative data. At present the GIMMS-NDVI data archive is the only global coverage dataset spanning 1982 to recent time. The NDVI dataset was calibrated and corrected for view geometry, volcanic aerosols, and other effects not related to vegetation change (Pinzon et al. 2005; Tucker et al. 2005). As a result, this new

Table 4.1 Measures for mitigating or correcting confounding effects in the presented NDVI-based mapping of land degradation hotspots

Confounding factors	Affected relationship or process	Mitigating/correcting measure used in this study	Done/advised by other studies
Remnant cloud-cover effect in humid tropics	NDVI versus NPP weakened	Only non-flagged pixels used (2)[a]	Tucker et al. (2005), Brown et al. (2006)
Effect of soil moisture in sparse vegetative areas	NDVI versus NPP weakened	Eliminating pixel with NDVI < 0.05, arid zone, cautions in sparse vegetation areas (2)[a]	de Jong et al. (2012), Fensholt et al. (2012), Le et al. (2012)
Seasonal variations in vegetation phenology and time-series autocorrelation	Inter-annual NDVI (NPP) trend confounded	Use annually average NDVIs instead of bi-weekly or monthly NDVIs (1)[a]	Bai et al. (2008b), Hellden and Tottrup (2008), de Jong et al. (2011, 2012)
Site-specific effects of vegetation/crop structure and site conditions	NDVI versus NPP weakened	No spatial trend of NDVI used (3)[a] Land-use/cover-specific interpretation (6)[a] Eliminate/cautious with area having LAI > 4 (6)[a]	Pettorelli et al. (2005), Vu et al. (2014a), Carlson and Ripley (1997), Vu et al. (2014a)
Larger errors/noises in the NDVI data compared to the small NDVI trend itself	Not reliable Inter-annual NDVI (NPP) trend	Not consider pixels with no statistical significance or very small magnitude of NDVI trend (e.g. <10 %/25 years) (3)[a]	Le et al. (2012), Vu et al. (2014a)
Effect of inter-annual rainfall variation on NDVI (NPP)	Mixture between climate-driven and human-induced NPP trend	Correct partly rainfall effect by consider NDVI-rainfall correlation (4)[a]	Herrmann et al. (2005), Bai et al. (2008b), Le et al. (2012)
Effect of atmospheric fertilization (AF) on NDVI (NPP)	Mixture between climate-driven and human-induced NPP trend	Correct partly AF effect by consider NPP growth in pristine areas (5)	Le et al. (2012)
Effect of intensive fertilizer uses on NDVI (NPP)	Mixture between fertilizer-driven NPP soil-based NPP	Masking areas with high fertilizer use for follow-up study (7)	
Irrelevance of considering NPP in urbanized areas	NPP is not relevant indicator	Masking urban areas from the consideration (2)	Le et al. (2012), Vu et al. (2014a)

[a]Number within parentheses indicates the related step in Fig. 4.1

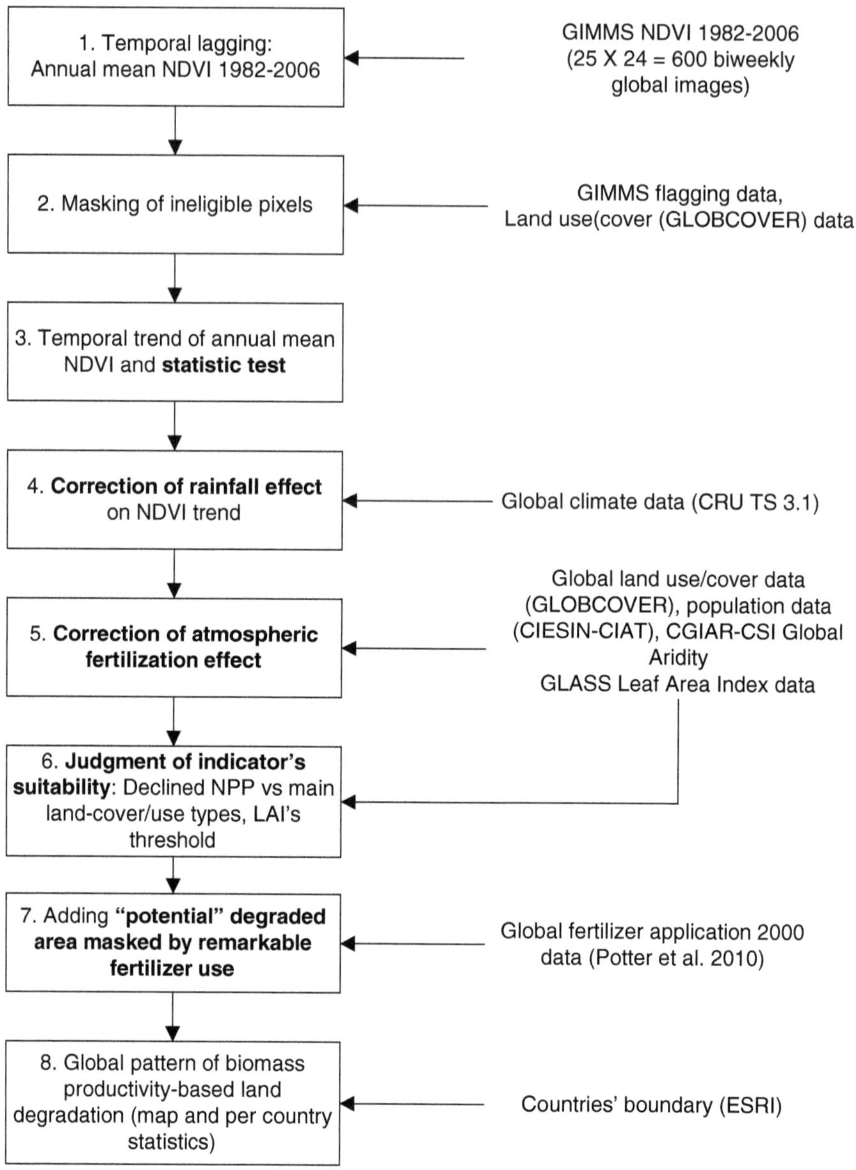

Fig. 4.1 Procedure of biomass productivity-based assessment of NDVI. *Note* The *bold text* indicates relatively new features compared to previous studies

GIMMS NDVI dataset, used in this study, is relatively consistent over time and is of higher quality compared to the previous versions produced by the GIMMS group (Brown et al. 2006). Using Terra MODIS NDVI as a reference (Fensholt et al. 2009) in Sahel region found that the GIMMS NDVI data set is well-suited for long term vegetation studies of the Sahel–Sudanian areas. The GIMMSg-NDVI archive "should provide a large improvement over previously used NDVI data sets, because the data are collected by one series of instruments, and they give a more realistic representation of the spatial and temporal variability of vegetation patterns over the globe" (GLCF accessed in 01 May 2013).

Validity of the GIMMS dataset has been discussed in previous studies (Tucker et al. 2005; Brown et al. 2006), and is subjected to ongoing validation (Fensholt et al. 2012; GLCF accessed in 01 May 2013). The procedure of the analytical flow is shown in Fig. 4.1. The detailed explanations of major analysis steps are given in the corresponding results sections for better contextual understanding.

Results

Aggregating Annual Mean NDVI Time-Series (1982–2006) (Step 1 in Fig. 4.1)

To minimize the confounding effects of seasonal variations and time-series autocorrelation, we used annual average NDVI instead of the original bi-weekly GIMMS NDVI time-series, which is similar to Hellden and Tottrup (2008) and Vlek et al. (2010). This treatment is supported by the recent findings of de Jong et al. (2011). They found that inconsistencies between the linear trends of annually aggregated GIMMS NDVI and the seasonality-corrected, non-parametric trends of the original GIMMS NDVI time-series (biweekly) were mainly on areas with weak or non-significant NDVI trends, which are not central in our hotspot approach. The year 1981 was excluded because it has only data for the later 6 months (July–December). As a result, there are 25 annual mean NDVI images calculated from 600 original GIMMSg images.

Masking Ineligible Pixels (Step 2 in Fig. 4.1)

As explained in Table 4.1, pixels with the following statuses were masked from the course of the analyses. To partly avoid the effect of cloud cover or cloud shade, flagged GIMMS pixels, i.e. flag > 0 indicates a not good value of NDVI, were masked. As NDVI is not a suitable indicator of NPP in bare, or very sparse vegetation, pixels with NDVI < 0.05 were masked. Pixels with bare surface, urban and industrial areas, based on GLOBCOVER version 2.2 data (Bicheron et al. 2008), were masked. Figure 4.2 depicts the resulting global pattern of the average annual mean NDVI over 1982–2006 on the eligible (non-grey) areas.

Significant Trend of Annual Mean NDVI Over 1982–2006 (25 Years) (Step 4 in Fig. 4.1)

Temporal Slope Metrics and Statistical Test

For each pixel i, the long-term trend of annual NPP (via vegetation index) can be formalized by the slope coefficient (Ai) in the simple linear regression relationship

$$V_i = A_i \times t + B_i \tag{4.1}$$

where V_i = annual mean NDVI, A_i = long-term trend of NDVI, t = year (elapsing from 1982 to 2006), B_i = intercept (an indicator for a possible delay in the onset of degradation). The computed slope coefficient A_i for each pixel was tested for statistical significance at different confidence levels at 90 % ($p < 0.1$), which is sufficient for long-term trend analyses of noisy parameters like NDVI (Le et al. 2012; Vlek et al. 2010).

Figure 4.3 shows the significant trend in a statistical manner only. A statistically significant trend can be with a too small magnitude that can be either not significant in practice, or lower than errors/noises in NDVI time-series. Both cases should not be meaningful for consideration. Thus, it is much more meaningful to look at the relative change in inter-annual NDVI compared to the period mean (see Fig. 4.2).

Significant Biomass Productivity Decline

Significant biomass productivity (annual mean NDVI) decline is defined by the following criteria: negative NDVI slope with a statistical significance ($p < 0.1$), and Meaningful magnitude of the NDVI decline: relative NDVI annual reduction ≥ 10 %/25 years (or ≥0.4 %/year) (Vlek et al. 2010; Le et al. 2012; Vu et al. 2014a). There are two reasons for selecting this cut-off threshold.

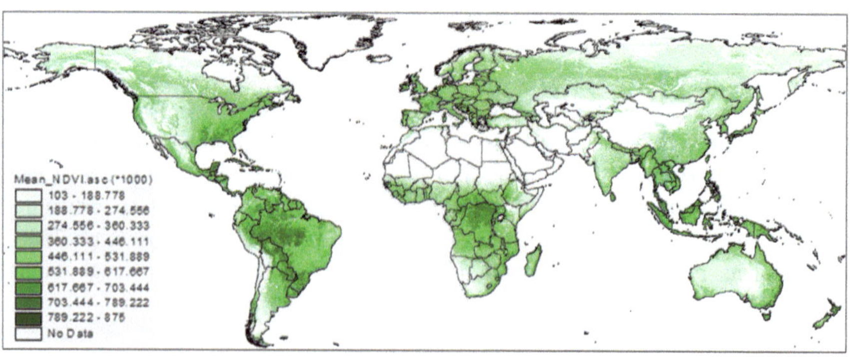

Fig. 4.2 Average annual mean NDVI (scale factor = 1000) of the period 1982–2006

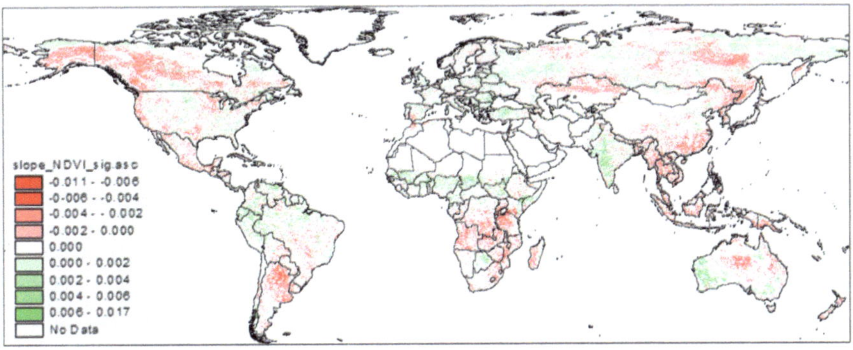

Fig. 4.3 Significant ($p < 0.1$) slope of inter-annual NDVI over 1982–2006. *Notes White areas* are with either no data, or statistically non-significant trend. There has been no minimal threshold of NDVI slope applied yet

First, from a common sense, a reduction rate of less than 0.4–0.5 % per year can be considered to be insignificant in practice. Second, with these very small magnitudes of NDVI trend, the risk that inherent errors/noises in the NDVI data are larger than the trend itself is high, making the NDVI trend less reliable (Tucker et al. 2005). This cut-off value helps avoid that risk.

Figure 4.4 shows spatial pattern of annual decline of biomass productivity in percentages of the period mean of NDV (Fig. 4.4a) and in the dummy scale (i.e. 1 = significant productivity decline, 0 = otherwise) (Fig. 4.4b).

Correction of Rainfall Variation Effect

The significant decline of inter-annual NDVI shown in Fig. 4.4 can be attributed to either temporal variation in rainfall or human activities (e.g. land cover/use conversion and/or change in land use intensity). The annual rainfall data for the period 1982–2006, which was extracted from the TS 3.1 dataset of the Climatic Research Unit (CRU) at the University of East Anglia (UK), were used for the isolating purpose. The original data include grids of monthly rainfall data at a spatial resolution of 0.5°, covering the 1901–2006 period (Jones and Harris 2008). To match the spatial resolution of AVHRR-NDVI data for later analysis, the grid cells of rainfall data were re-sampled to match with the 8-km resolution of NDVI data, using nearest neighbor statistics. The *Trend-Correlation* method is used to account for rainfall variation effect. The procedure of *Trend-Correlation* method (Vlek et al. 2010) involves: For each pixel, Pearson's correlation coefficient between inter-annual NDVI and rainfall over the 1982–2006 period (R_i) is calculated. The statistical significance for pixel-based correlation coefficients at a confidence level of 95 % ($p < 0.05$) is tested. A pixel was considered to have a strong correlation between its inter-annual NDVI and rainfall if the correlation coefficient was

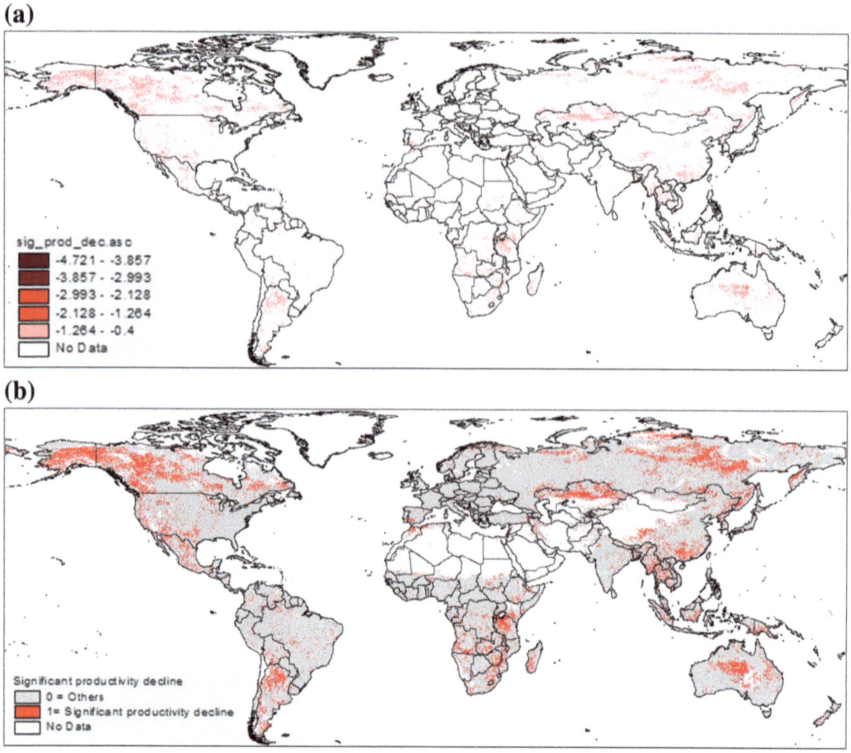

Fig. 4.4 Significant ($p < 0.1$ and reduction rate ≥ 10 %/25 years) biomass productivity decline over 1982–2006. **a** Annual reduction rate (% of period mean), **b** dummy scale (area of significant productivity decline = 15,336,128 km^2)

significant ($p < 0.05$) and greater than 0.5 or lower than −0.5. If the pixel has a significantly negative NDVI trend (negative A_i, $p < 0.1$) and a strongly positive vegetation–climate correlation ($R_i > 0.5$, $p < 0.05$), the NDVI decline at the location was determined by the rainfall factor. Otherwise, the NDVI decline was likely caused by non-climate factors. The limitation of the method is that in the pixels with significantly negative NDVI trend and positive vegetation–rainfall correlation (or non-significant residue trend in *ResTrend* method), both rainfall and human effects can be mutually exclusive. The elimination of these pixels may also exclude some human-induced degradation areas. The long-term response of inter-annual NDVI to rainfall variation is shown in Fig. 4.5. Then, the NDVI decline pattern from which rainfall-driven pixels were masked is given in Fig. 4.6.

(a)

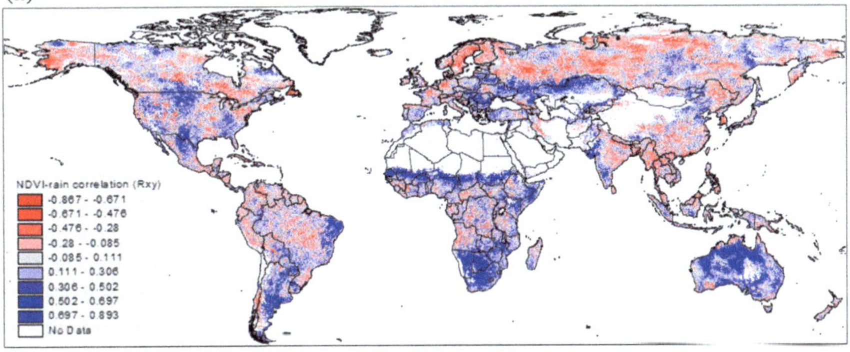

(b)

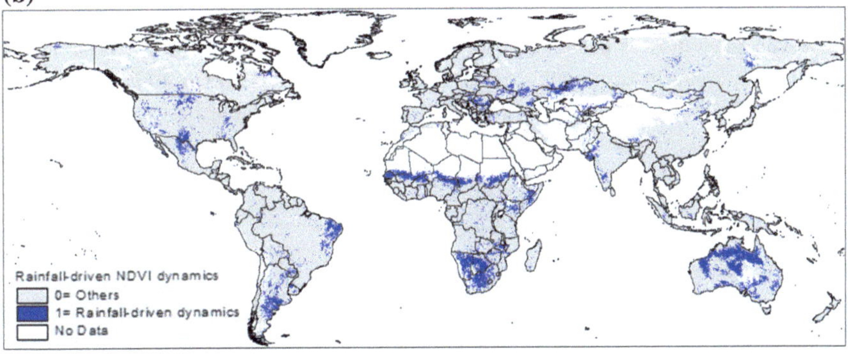

Fig. 4.5 Long-term response of inter-annual NDVI to rainfall variation (1982–2006): **a** correlation coefficient (R_{xy}) between inter-annual NDVI and rainfall, **b** area of rainfall-driven NDVI dynamics ($p < 0.05$ and $R_{xy} \geq 0.5$) that was masked from further analysis (masked area in *blue* = 10,654,464 km^2)

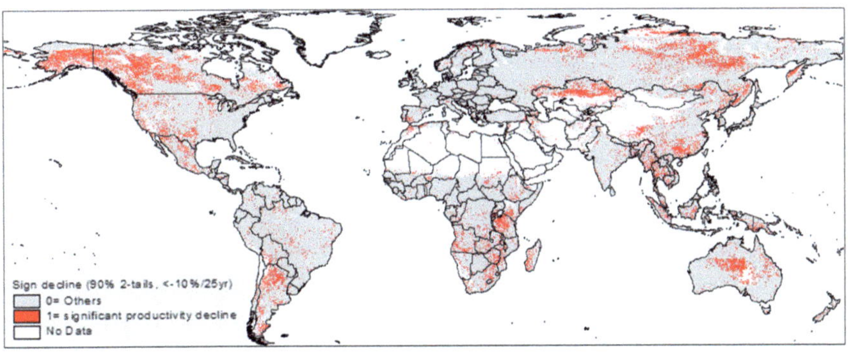

Fig. 4.6 Significant ($p < 0.1$ and reduction rate ≥ 10 %/25 years) biomass production (NDVI) decline corrected for rainfall effect (area in *red* = 14,525,952 km^2)

Correction of Atmospheric Fertilization Effect (Step 5 in Fig. 4.1)

Calculate the Sub-component of AF-Driven Growth

The actual change in vegetation productivity can be considered the net balance between the partial changes caused by human activities and those caused by natural processes (i.e. effects of rainfall and/or AF). In pristine vegetative areas, actual vegetation dynamics can be driven by only natural drivers as the human-induced component of biomass dynamics can be assumed to be zero. If these areas, in addition, have no correlation between biomass productivity and weather parameters, weather effects can be neglected and the actual growth can be assumed to be caused by atmospheric fertilization (Vlek et al. 2010). Thus, the quantum of AF-driven growth of a particular vegetation type can be found in the pristine (no significant human disturbance) areas of that type with no NDVI-rainfall correlation.

Based on the map in Fig. 4.6, the total land with significant biomass production decline ($p < 0.1$, reduction rate ≥ 10 %/25 years) corrected for rainfall effect is about 14.5 million km^2, or about 10 % of the total global land area (i.e. 226,968 pixels, or 14,525,952 km^2). We defined the above-mentioned areas by applying an overlaying scheme as shown in Fig. 4.7.

As a result, we identified 246,159 pixels (i.e. 15,754,176 km^2) belonging to 85 'pristine' (no significant human disturbance) Cover-Climate types that are all with no significant NDVI-rainfall correlation (see Fig. 4.8). As explained, vegetation biomass dynamics in these areas are likely driven by atmospheric fertilization (AF) effect.

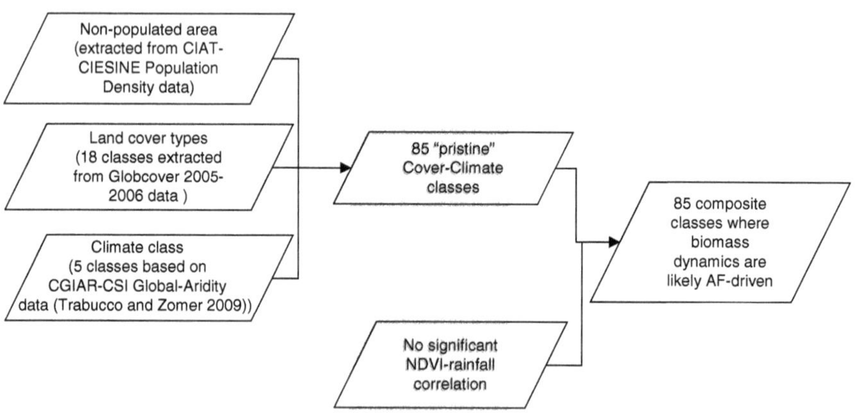

Fig. 4.7 Overlaying scheme for defining areas of pristine (no significant human disturbance) vegetation with no NDVI-rainfall correlation, where biomass dynamics are likely AF-driven

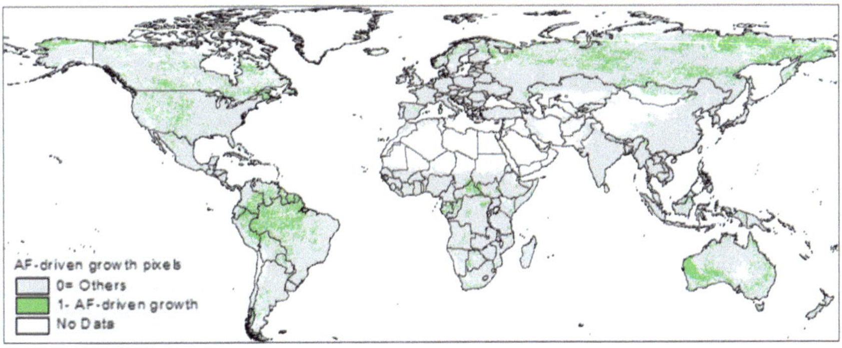

Fig. 4.8 Spatial pattern of pristine vegetation with no NDVI-rainfall correlation where biomass dynamics are likely AF-driven (area in *green* = 15,754,176 km^2)

The correction of AF effect was then done by three steps:

1. Calculate means of NDVI slope for each Cover-Climate-No Correlation types: $dNDVI_{AF,k}/dt$ where k indexes the Cover-Climate type.
2. Re-calculation of AF-adjusted inter-annual NDVI time-series through subtracting the NDVI data by quantum $dNDVI_{AF,k}/dt$. This re-calculation of NDVI time-series was specific for each Cover-Climate class k, i.e. AF-driven NDVI accrual for each class was used for recalculation of NDVI time-series on elsewhere with the same class

$$\begin{aligned}
NDVI_{AF-adjusted,1983,k} &= NDVI_{1982,k} - 1^{*}\ dNDVI_{AF,k}/dt \\
NDVI_{AF-adjusted,1984,k} &= NDVI_{1982,k} - 2^{*}\ dNDVI_{AF,k}/dt \\
NDVI_{AF-adjusted,1985,k} &= NDVI_{1982,k} - 3^{*}\ dNDVI_{AF,k}/dt \\
\ldots \\
NDVI_{AF-adjusted,2006,k} &= NDVI_{1982,k} - 24^{*}\ dNDVI_{AF,k}/dt
\end{aligned}$$

3. Re-calculate the trend of inter-annual AF-adjusted NDVIs, test the statistical significance of the trend, and calculate $NDVI_{AF\text{-}adjusted}$—Rainfall correlation.

The AF-corrected significant biomass productivity decline is showed in Fig. 4.9a (in % of period-mean $NDVI_{AF\text{-}adjusted}$) and Fig. 4.9b (in dummy scale). There are 633,443 pixels, i.e. 40,540,352 km^2 of global land (i.e. 27 %) likely to have experienced significant biomass productivity decline given that the effects of rainfall and atmospheric fertilization are taken into account.

Identification of Areas with Saturated NDVI and Relation to Land-Use/Cover Strata (Step 6 in Fig. 4.1)

The NDVI-vegetation productivity relationship can be saturated, thus biased in areas with dense vegetation canopies (Pettorelli et al. 2005). In the areas having

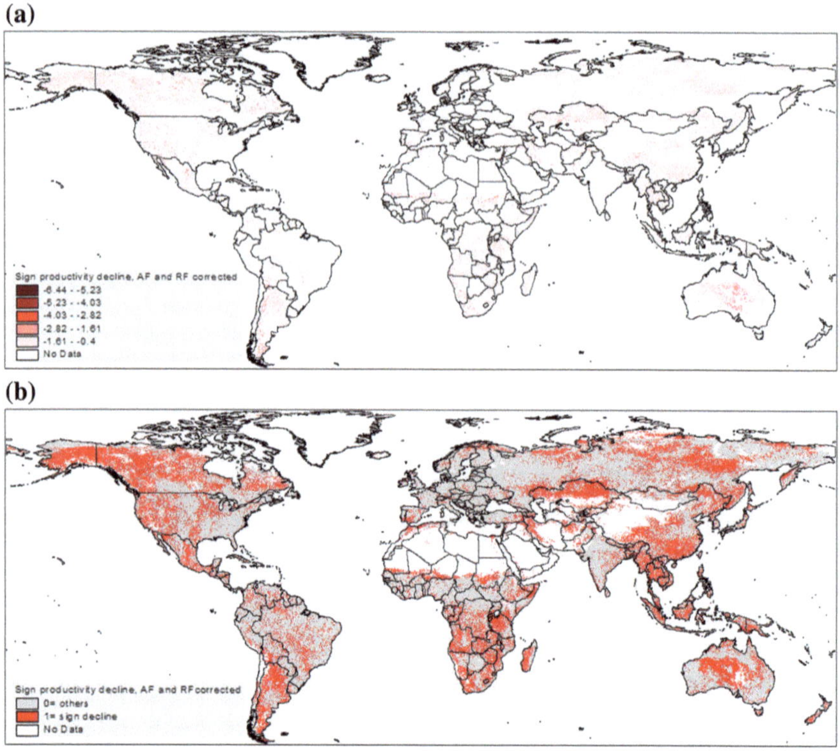

Fig. 4.9 Significant productivity decline with correction for both atmospheric and rainfall effects: **a** relative annual rate, **b** dummy scale (area in *red* = 40,540,352 km^2)

dense vegetation with Leaf Area Index (LAI) more than 4, the relationship between NDVI and the vegetation biomass tends to be saturated (i.e. NDVI is less sensitive to actual biomass change), thus should be used with special cautions (Carlson and Ripley 1997).

We calculated the mean annual LAI of the period 1982–2006 by using the GLASS LAI dataset (Liang and Xiao 2012; Xiao et al. 2014). To avoid the computational abundance (each year has 46 8-day LAI images), we calculated the mean of 8-day LAI in representative years 1985, 1990, 1995 and 2000 (i.e. $n = 46 \times 4 = 184$ global images taken into account).

As a result, of 633,443 declined pixels in Fig. 4.9 there are 71,755 pixels (11 %) with LAI > 4 possibly making their NDVI trend not reliable for indicating vegetation biomass productivity. Land degradation in these NDVI-saturated pixels should be considered with other indicators, rather than NDVI signals. Given the NDVI-saturated pixels masked, the area of biomass productivity decline is about 36 million km^2, i.e. 24 % of global land area. These areas are shown in Fig. 4.10a (in % of period-mean NDVIAF-adjusted) and Fig. 4.10b (in dummy scale). The map in Fig. 4.10a shows that most of NDVI degrading areas have small annual

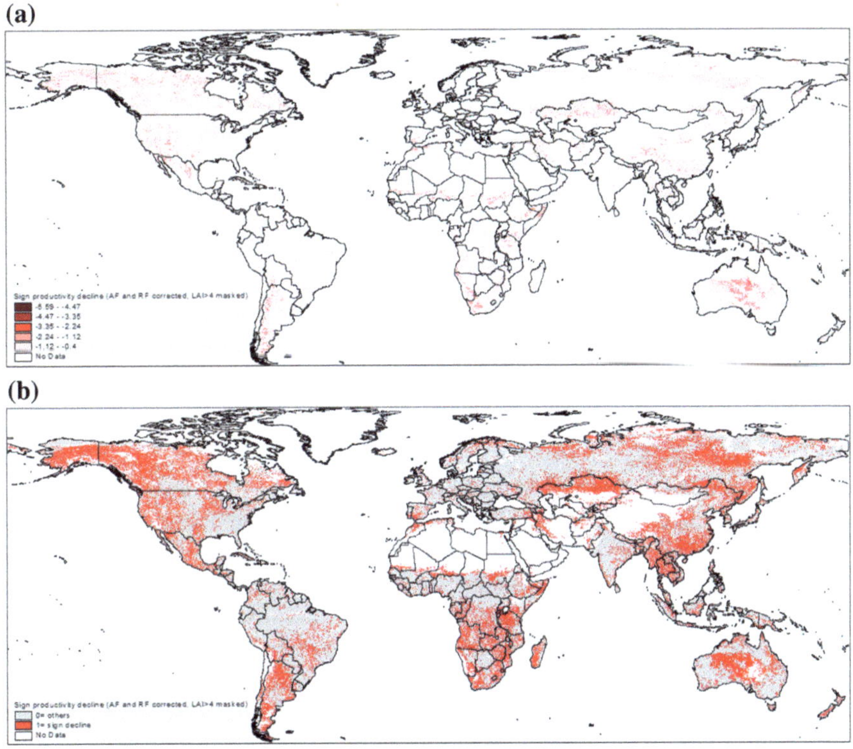

Fig. 4.10 Significant productivity decline with correction for rainfall and atmospheric fertilization effects and masking of NDVI-saturated pixels. **a** Relative annual rate, **b** dummy scale (area in *red* = 35,948,032 km^2)

reduction magnitude (i.e. less than 1 %/year, as showed in the area in pink). Given the inherently high noise of NDVI signal, uncertainty of the calculated degrading trend in these pink areas can be higher than the pixels with higher annual NDVI reduction rate, i.e. the red to dark red pixels in Fig. 4.10a.

Relation to Land Cover Strata

At the resolution of this global study (i.e. 8-km pixel), many sub-classes of scattered land cover/use (e.g. slash-and-burn field, mountain paddy rice terraces and fruit plantations) will be dissimulated. Thus, we used 7 broad land use/cover classes (see Fig. 4.11) aggregated from 23 classes of the Globcover 2005–2006 data (Bicheron et al. 2008). The spatial pattern of long-term (1982–2006) NDVI decline with correction of RF and AF effects and masking of saturated NDVI zone versus main land cover/use types is shown in Fig. 4.11. The related statistics for regions in the

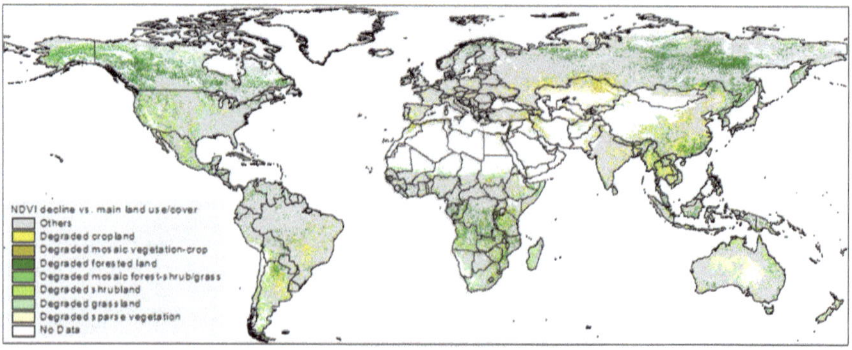

Fig. 4.11 Areas of long-term (1982–2006) NDVI decline (with correction of RF and AF effects and masking saturated NDVI zone) versus main land cover/use types

world are summarized by major world regions in Table 4.2. Table 4.2 shows at varying magnitudes of land degradation according to land use/cover types and geographic regions. One of the key highlights of this summary is the substantial shares of degradation in grasslands and shrublands, especially in North Africa and Near East (52 %) and Sub-Saharan Africa (40 %), which negatively affects the livelihoods of especially the pastoralist communities. In a related note, about 43 % of the areas with sparse vegetation are degraded in Asia. Quite often, these areas also serve as grazing grounds for ruminants, for example in Central Asia (Pender et al. 2009). The share of cropland degradation seems especially high in Asia (30 %), North Africa and Near East (45 %), the regions with extensive irrigated agriculture.

These results in Fig. 4.11 and Table 4.2 should be treated with special cautions regarding the following aspects:

1. Although pixels of saturated greenness (LAI > 4) are masked out, the indication of biomass production dynamics using inter-annual NDVI trend in the forested areas (data in 2005–2006) may not be reliable compared to those of herbaceous vegetation types. The reason would be that most biomass of closed forest is in the woody component whose annual dynamics (rather relatively slow or steady) may not be necessary well-related to annual greenness of the forest canopy (rather rapidly variable). Moreover, with forest ecosystems, especially those used for nature protection, biodiversity is often a prioritized task in the ecosystem assessments. However, increases of biomass production and/or soil nutrients may not necessarily be correlative with biodiversity maintenance. For example, invasion of exotic plant species can lead to high biomass productivity but dramatically reduce biodiversity, which is not desirable regarding the land-use purpose (Nkonya et al. 2013). Increasing of soil nutrients can reduce plant diversity in some cases (Chapin et al. 2000; Sala et al. 2000; Wassen et al. 2005).

Table 4.2 The share of degrading area in each type of land cover by continental regions and world (unit: % of total area of a land cover type across a continental region)

Continents	Crop land (%)	Mosaic vegetation-crop (%)	Forested land (%)	Mosaic forest-shrub/grass (%)	Shrub land (%)	Grass land (%)	Sparse vegetation (%)
Asia	30	31	30	36	33	24	43
Europe	19	21	21	20	6	17	17
North Africa and Near East	45	42	30	36	39	52	18
Sub-Saharan Africa	12	26	26	26	28	40	29
Latin America and Caribbean	25	16	10	29	29	24	34
North America and Australasia	17	16	32	36	27	40	22
World	25	25	23	29	25	33	23

Note The results for forested land and sparse vegetation should be treated with caution, see explanation in the next page

2. NDVI signal may not be a suitable indicator of degradation of sparse vegetation areas. When wet exposed soils tend to darken, i.e. soils' reflectance is a direct function of water content. If the spectral response to moistening is not exactly the same in the two spectral bands (IR and NIR), the NDVI of sparsely vegetative areas can appear to change as a result of soil moisture changes (precipitation or evaporation) rather than because of vegetation changes.[1] Although soil-adjusted vegetation index (SAVIs) (Huete 1988) can help improve the correlation between the index and the actual vegetation status, vegetation biomass itself may be not so crucial for indicating the status of the exposed soil.
3. The attribution of "human-induced" degradation to the "rainfall- and atmospheric fertilization-corrected" NDVI decline makes sense in areas where there is no other natural drivers of biomass production decline besides the reduction of annual rainfall and atmospheric fertilization. Event-based wild fires which may be a factor that has likely reduced biomass production in remote, unpopulated regions like Alaska (Boles and Verbyla 2000) or the inland of the Australian continent (Kasischke and Penner 2004). Thus, the term "human-induced degradation" may be less applicable in these areas. Furthermore, the use of mean annual NDVI can reduce partly, but not eliminate completely the effects of change in the seasonality of weather parameters that are important in many climate change scenarios.

Potential Soil Degradation Masked by Fertilizer Application

The trend of above ground biomass productivity can be an indirect indicator of soil degradation or soil improvement if the nutrient source for vegetation/crop growth is solely, or largely, from the soils (i.e. soil-based biomass productivity). In the agricultural areas with intensive application of mineral fertilizers (i.e. fertilizer-based crop productivity), the net primary productivity principally cannot be a reliable indicator of soil fertility trend (Le 2012). In this case, alternative indicators of soil fertility should be used. Global patterns of fertilizer applications, based on data reported in around 2000 (Potter et al. 2010; MacDonald et al. 2011), are shown in Fig. 4.12. The amount of fertilizers used in East Asia (e.g. China and Vietnam), Northern India, Europe and in considerable areas in North America is equal to 18–20 times of those in sub-Saharan Africa (see Fig. 4.12 and Table 4.3), which has been only around 1 kg/ha/year (Vlek et al. 1997). Although the global spatial data of fertilizer use is available for year 2000 or around, the estimated regional averages and trends (Table 4.4) show that the 2000 fertilizer use maps can be used to depict the relative global patterns of the study period. Pixels with remarkable fertilizer

---

[1] http://en.wikipedia.org/wiki/Normalized_Difference_Vegetation_Index.

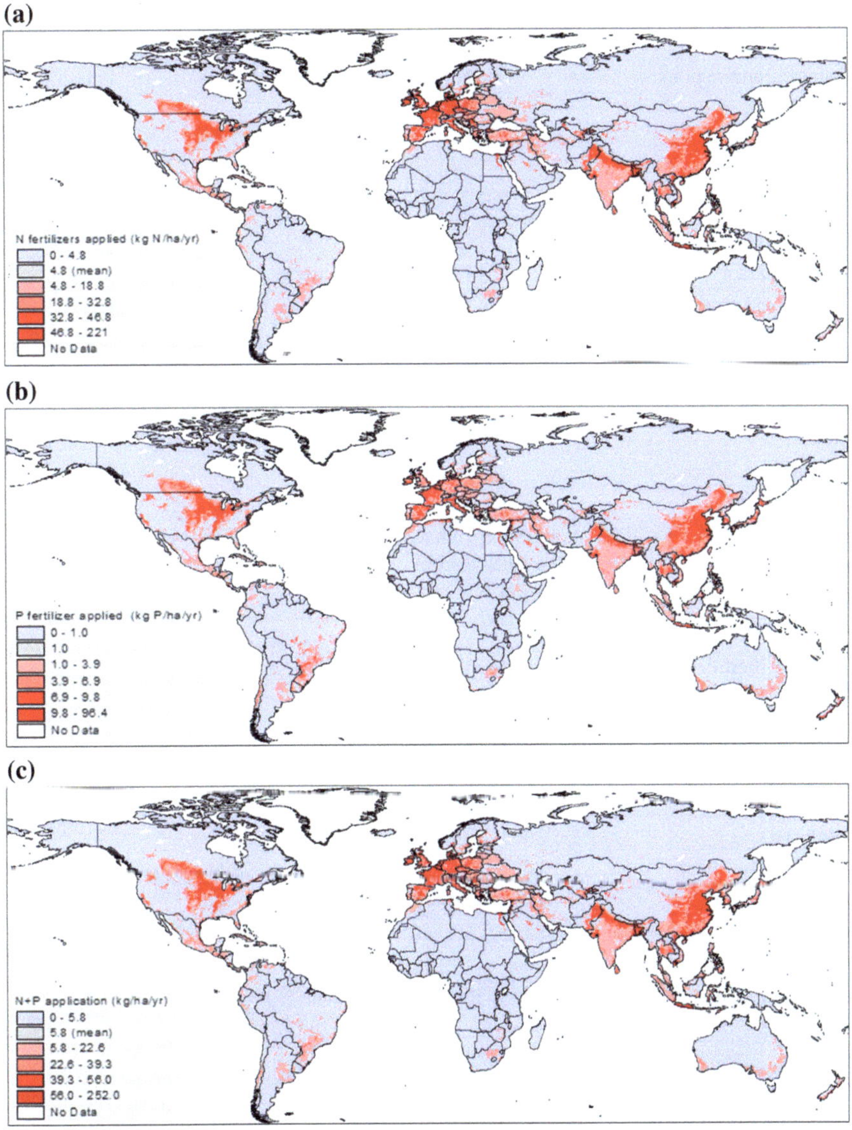

Fig. 4.12 Global patterns of N and P fertilizers application for major crops in 2000. *Data sources* Potter et al. (2010), MacDonald et al. (2011). **a** Application of nitrogen fertilizer, **b** application of phosphorus fertilizer, **c** combination of nitrogen and phosphorus application

application (e.g. >5.8 kg/ha/year, i.e. the global mean) and neutral biomass productivity trend, may have a potential risk of soil degradation that cannot be detected by NDVI-based analysis. These areas are shown in Fig. 4.13, accounting for about 7 million km^2, or 4.8 % of global land area.

Table 4.3 Fertilizer consumptions in different regions of the world in 2011 (in million metric tons)

Countries and regions	Nitrogen	Phosphorous	Potash
China	33.8	11.5	5.2
India	17.4	8.0	2.6
United States	12.1	4.0	4.3
East Asia	41.7	14.1	9.5
South Asia	22.0	9.2	3.0
North America	14.4	4.8	4.6
Western and Central Europe	10.3	2.4	2.7
Latin America and the Caribbean	7.4	5.7	5.6
Eastern Europe and Central Asia	4.4	1.2	1.3
West Asia	2.9	1.1	0.3
Africa	3.3	1.0	0.5
Sub-Saharan Africa	1.7	0.6	0.4
World	108	41	28

Source International Fertilizer Association (www.ifa.org, accessed on 06 February 2014). The figures for Sub-Saharan Africa were calculated by the authors' based on country fertilizer consumption statistics for Africa given by IFA

Table 4.4 Fertilizer uses (in million tons) and average annual growth rates (in %) in different periods

Regions	Fertilizer use			Annual growth	
	1959/60	1989/90	2020	1960–90	1990–2020
East Asia	1.2	31.4	55.7	10.9	1.9
South Asia	0.4	14.8	33.8	12	2.8
West Asia and North Africa	0.3	6.7	11.7	10.4	1.9
Latin America	0.7	8.2	16.2	8.2	2.3
Sub-Saharan Africa	0.1	1.2	4.2	5.5	1.2
World	27.4	143.6	208	5.5	1.2

Data source FAO and the calculations by Bumb and Baanante (1996)

Areas of Soil Improvement

In addition to the areas with land degradation, we have also identified that there has been NDVI improvement in about 2.7 % of global land area. The analysis identifies the areas of land improvement ("bright spots") by the increasing slope of inter-annual mean NDVIs: more by 10 % or more over 25 years and at 90 % statistical significance. This is also adjusted/corrected for rainfall and atmospheric fertilization effects, LAI < 4), (Fig. 4.14).

The major "bright spots" of land improvement are located in the Sahelian belt in Africa, Central parts of India, western and eastern coasts of Australia, central Turkey, areas of North-Eastern Siberia in Russia, and north-western parts of Alaska in the US.

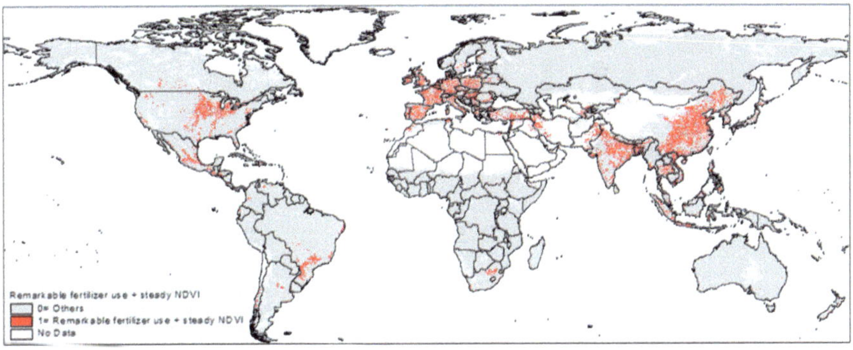

Fig. 4.13 Pixels with remarkable fertilizer application (e.g. ≥12 kg N + P/ha/year = twice of the global mean) but with neutral trend of biomass productivity, may have a potential risk of soil degradation

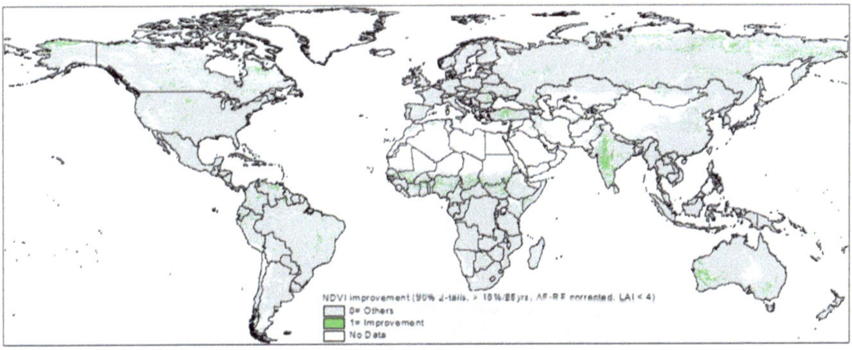

Fig. 4.14 The areas of NDVI improvement, with slope of inter-annual mean NDVIs ≥ 10 % over 25 year and 90 % statistically significant, adjusted/corrected for RF and AF effects, LAI < 4

Overlaying land degradation (Figs. 4.10 and 4.13) with population density projections for 2010 (CIESIN-CIAT 2005) shows that about 3.2 billion people are currently residing in degrading areas. Of this total number, about 0.6 billion people live in areas where land degradation is directly observed in the remotely sensed data, another 1.2 billion people live in areas where land degradation is likely masked by rainfall dynamics and atmospheric fertilization effects, finally, another 1.3 billion people reside in areas where chemical fertilization may be masking soil and land degradation. The regional breakdown of the population residing in degrading areas is given in Table 4.5. The biggest number of people residing in degrading areas is found in Asia, followed Europe, Middle East and North Africa, Latin America and Caribbean, Sub-Saharan Africa and finally, North America and Australasia. In terms of the share of people residing in degrading areas, the most

Table 4.5 The number of people residing in degrading areas by region, the number in millions and the share in percentages

Regions	Visible degradation	Degradation masked by rainfall and atmospheric fertilization	Degradation masked by chemical fertilization	Total population in degrading areas	Total population in 2010	Share of population in degrading areas (%)	Share of population in degrading areas, excluding areas with masking effect of chemical fertilization (%)
Asia	434	834	1055	2324	4184	56	30
Europe	11	48	143	203	575	35	10
Latin America and Caribbean	45	98	57	200	583	34	25
Middle East and North Africa	48	133	22	202	272	74	66
North America and Australasia	22	55	29	107	372	29	21
Sub-Saharan Africa	64	113	4	180	800	22	22
World	624	1282	1310	3216	6787	47	28

affected are Middle East and North Africa, and Asia. In Asia and Europe, the higher shares of land degradation and of people residing in degrading areas are found in areas where land degradation might be masked by chemical fertilizer application. Whereas in other regions, visible decline and masking effects of rainfall and atmospheric fertilization seem to dominate. One caveat, these are still somewhat conservative estimates of the livelihoods which have potentially been affected by land degradation, because the number of people affected by land degradation is likely to be higher due to off-site and indirect externalities of land degradation.

Conclusions

In this study, we advance our knowledge by making the following relatively new contributions. Firstly, the major contribution of this global study is the identification of regions where degradation magnitude and extent are relatively high for prioritizing both preventive investments for the restoration or reclamation of degraded land, and subsequent focal ground-based studies. The map of degradation hotspots is different from the production of an accurate map of all degraded areas that seems impractical at global level due to lacking data on many aspects of land degradation. Secondly, we account for masking effects of rainfall dynamics, atmospheric and anthropogenic fertilizations. To our knowledge, there has been no previous published study at global level accounting for all these masking factors. Moreover, we also identify the areas where land improvement has occurred.

The results show that land degradation hotspots stretch to about 29 % of the total global land area and are occurring across all agro-ecologies. One third of this degradation is directly identifiable from a statistically significant declining trend in NDVI. However, the remaining two thirds of this degradation are concealed by rainfall dynamics, atmospheric fertilization and application of chemical fertilizers. Globally, human-induced biomass productivity decline are found in 25 % of croplands and vegetation-crop mosaics, 29 % of mosaics of forests with shrub- and grasslands, 25 % of shrublands, and 33 % of grasslands, as well as 23 % of areas with sparse vegetation. The share of degrading croplands is likely to increase further when we take into account the croplands where intensive fertilizer application may be masking land degradation. Although this study does find land degradation to be a massive problem in croplands, it also emphasizes, in contrast to most previous similar studies, the extent of degradation in areas used for livestock grazing by pastoral communities, including grasslands, shrublands, their mosaics, and areas with sparse vegetation. In most countries, livestock production and its value chains produce comparable economic product and incomes for rural populations as crop production. In total, there are about 3.2 billion people who reside in these degrading areas. However, the true number of people affected by land degradation is likely to be higher, because even those people residing outside these degrading areas may be dependent on the continued flow of ecosystem goods and services from the degrading areas.

It is quite encouraging that about 2.7 % of the global land mass has experienced significant improvement of biomass productivity over the last 25 years. However, the improving figure is modest as being 10 times smaller than the extent of areas with degrading lands, resulting extremely high net land degradation over the globe. Achieving the goal of Zero Net Land Degradation (Lal et al. 2012) would, therefore, require considerable multiplication of efforts to rehabilitate degraded lands and also prevent further increasing rates of land degradation.

Despite being an advancement to the past studies on global land degradation mapping, the current work has several limitations. First, conceptually and practically the present study capture only the "primary productivity" aspect of land degradation. The other important aspects of land degradation such as soil/water pollution and biodiversity, which do not necessarily correlate with primary productivity, are still out of the scope of this study. Secondly, some degraded areas may not be captured by the NDVI-based assessment employed here, such as: the areas facing both human-induced and climate-driven declines, and areas facing biodiversity decline in natural vegetation. Thirdly, robustness of some key parametric procedures needs to be further evaluated. Moreover, the delineated degradation hotspots need to be validated by ground-level studies. This ground-level verification work is planned as the next step of our research activities. Further research is also required for evaluating the robustness and uncertainties of the presented results. The reported results (Figs. 4.11, 4.13 and Table 4.2) should be used as rough guides for geographic focus/prioritization in regional/national studies. The first activity of follow-up regional/national studies is to conduct activities for validating the "potential" hotspots. These may include the use of independent data, e.g. finer NDVI time-series like MODIS, accurate land cover change over the study period, soil degradation assessment (modeled erosion, leaching, change in key soil properties) (e.g. Le et al. 2012), change in species composition (e.g. Mbow et al. 2013), fertilizer/water uses and yields.

The drivers of land degradation are numerous, complex and interrelated (Nkonya et al. 2011; Pender et al. 2009; Chap. 7). In most cases, the effects of different land degradation drivers are modulated by context-specific factors (Nkonya et al. 2013), necessitating local level in depth studies to identify the role of various factors on land degradation and improvement. The results of global level correlative studies comparing several factors, such as population pressure, income per capita, poverty rates, governance (Vlek et al. 2010; Nkonya et al. 2011; Vu et al. 2014a, b) with land degradation provide with broadly useful estimates, but remain equivocal, due to difficulty of appropriately accounting for various omitted variables and endogeneity issues at such a broad scale. The results of this study are planned to be validated at the local level, and also would serve as a basis for the in-depth analysis of land degradation drivers through country case studies.

References

Bai, Z., Dent, D., Yu, Y., & de Jong, R. (2013). Land degradation and ecosystem services. In R. Lal, L. Lorenz, R. F. Hűttle, B. U. Schneider, & J. Von Braun (Eds.), *Ecosystem services and carbon sequestration in the biosphere* (pp. 357–381). Dordrecht: Springer.

Bai, Z. G., Dent, D. L., Olsson, L., & Schaepman, M. E. (2008a). *Global assessment of land degradation and improvement 1. Identification by remote sensing*. Report 2008/01. Wageningen: ISRIC—World Soil Information.

Bai, Z. G., Dent, D. L., Olsson, L., & Schaepman, M. E. (2008b). Proxy global assessment of land degradation. *Soil Use and Management, 24*, 223–234.

Bicheron, P., Defourny, P., Brockmann, C., Schouten, L., Vancutsem, C., Huc, M., et al. (2008). *GLOBCOVER: Products Description and Validation Report*. http://due.esrin.esa.int/globcover/LandCover_V2.2/GLOBCOVER_Products Description_Validation_Report_I2.1.pdf. ESA Globcover Project, led by MEDIAS-France/POSTEL.

Boisvenue, C., & Running, S. W. (2006). Impacts of climate change on natural forest productivity —Evidence since the middle of the 20th century. *Global Change Biology, 12*, 862–882.

Boles, S. H., & Verbyla, D. B. (2000). Comparison of three AVHRR-based fire detection algorithms for interior Alaska. *Remote Sensing of Environment, 72*, 1–16.

Brown, M. E., Pinzon, J. E., Didan, K., Morisette, J. T., & Tucker, C. J. (2006). Evaluation of the consistency of long-term NDVI time series derived from AVHRR, SPOT-Vegetation, SeaWIFS, MODIS and LandSAT ETM+. *IEEE Transactions Geoscience and Remote Sensing, 44*, 1787–1793.

Buitenwerf, R., Bond, W. J., Stevens, N., & Trollope, W. S. W. (2012). Increased tree densities in South African savannas: >50 years of data suggests CO_2 as a driver. *Global Change Biology, 18*, 675–684.

Bumb, B. L., & Baanante, C. A. (1996). World trends in fertilizers use and projections to 2020. In *2020 BRIEF—A 2020 Vision for Food, Agriculture, and the Environment* 38 (October 1996), 1–2.

Carlson, T. N., & Ripley, D. A. (1997). On the relation between NDVI, fractional vegetation cover, and leaf area index. *Remote Sensing of Environment, 62*, 241–252.

Center for International Earth Science Information Network (CIESIN), Centro Internacional de Agricultura Tropical (CIAT). 2005. Gridded Population of the World Version 3 (GPWv3): Population Density Grids. http://sedac.ciesin.columbia.edu/gpw (Accessed on May 01 2013). Socio-economic Data and Applications Center (SEDAC), Columbia University, Palisades, NY.

Chapin, F. S. I., Zavaleta, E. S., Eviner, V. T., Naylor, R. L., Vitousek, P. M., Reynolds, H. L., et al. (2000). Consequences of changing biodiversity. *Nature, 405*, 234–242.

Conijn, J. G., Bai, Z. G., Bindraban, P. S., & Rutgers, B. (2013). *Global changes of net primary productivity, affected by climate and abrupt land use changes since 1981—Towards mapping global soil degradation*. Report 2013/01. Wageningen: ISRIC—World Soil Information.

de Jong, R., de Bruin, S., de Wit, A., Schaepman, M. E., & Dent, D. L. (2011). Analysis of monotonic greening and browning trends from global NDVI time-series. *Remote Sensing of Environment, 115*, 692–702.

de Jong, R., Verbesselt, J., Schaepman, M. E., & de Bruin, S. (2012). Trend changes in global greening and browning: Contribution of short-term trends to longer-term change. *Global Change Biology, 18*, 642–655.

Dent, D., Bai, Z., Schaepman, M. E., & Olsson, L. (2009). Letter to the editor—Response to wessels: Comments on 'Proxy global assessment of land degradation'. *Soil Use and Management, 25*, 93–97.

Dentener, F. J. (2006). Global maps of atmospheric nitrogen deposition, 1860, 1993 and 2050—Data set. Oak Ridge National Laboratory, Distributed Active Archive Center, Oak Ridge, Tennessee, USA.

Diamond, J. (2005). *Collapse: How societies choose to fail or succeed*. New York, NY: Viking.

Dregne, H. E. (1977). Generalized map of the status of desertification of arid lands. Report presented in the 1977 United Nations conference on desertification. FAO, UNESCO and WMO.

Dubovyk, O., Menz, G., Conrad, C., Kan, E., Machwitz, M., & Khamzina, A. (2013). Spatio-temporal analyses of cropland degradation in the irrigated lowlands of Uzbekistan using remote-sensing and logistic regression modeling. *Environmental Monitoring and Assessment, 185*, 4775–4790.

Eswaran, H., Lal, R., & Reich, P. (2001). Land degradation: An overview. In E. Bridges, I. Hannam, L. Oldeman, F. Penning de Vries, S. Scherr, S. Sompatpanit (Eds.), In *Responses to Land Degradation. Proceedings of 2nd International Conference on Land Degradation and Desertification in Khon Kaen, Thailand.* New Delhi: Oxford Press.

Evans, J., & Geerken, R. (2004). Discrimination between climate and human-induced dryland degradation. *Journal of Arid Environments, 57*, 535–554.

Fensholt, R., Langanke, T., Rasmussen, K., Reenberg, A., Prince, S. D., Tucker, C., et al. (2012). Greenness in semi-arid areas across the globe 1981–2007 — an Earth Observing Satellite based analysis of trends and drivers. *Remote Sensing of Environment, 121*, 144–158.

Fensholt, R., Rasmussen, K., Kaspersen, P., Huber, S., Horion, S., & Swinnen, E. (2013). Assessing Land Degradation/Recovery in the African Sahel from Long-Term Earth Observation Based Primary Productivity and Precipitation Relationships. *Remote Sensing, 5*, 664–686.

Fensholt, R., Rasmussen, K., Nielsen, T. T., & Mbow, C. (2009). Evaluation of earth observation based long term vegetation trends: Intercomparing NDVI time series trend analysis consistency of Sahel from AVHRR GIMMS, Terra MODIS and SPOT VGT data. *Remote Sensing of Environment, 113*, 1886–1898.

GLCF, accessed in 01 May (2013). Global Inventory Modeling and Mapping Studies (GIMMS) AVHRR 8 km Normalized Difference Vegetation Index (NDVI), Bimonthly 1981–2006. *Product Guide.* http://glcf.umd.edu/library/guide/GIMMSdocumentation_NDVIg_GLCF.pdf. Global Land Cover Facility (GLCF), the University of Maryland.

Hellden, U., & Tottrup, C. (2008). Regional desertification: A global synthesis. *Global and Planetary Change, 64*, 169–176.

Herrmann, S., Assaf, A., & Compton, J. T. (2005). Recent trends in vegetation dynamics in the African Sahel and their relationship to climate. *Global Environmental Change, 15*, 394–404.

Hill, J., Stellmes, M., Udelhoven, T., Roder, A., & Sommer, S. (2008). Mediterranean desertification and land degradation: Mapping related land use change syndromes based on satellite observations. *Global and Planetary Change, 64*, 146–157.

Huete, A. R. (1988). A soil-adjusted vegetation index (SAVI). *Remote Sensing of Environment, 25*, 295–309.

Jones, P., & Harris, I. (2008). CRU Time-Series (TS) High Resolution Gridded Datasets. http://badc.nerc.ac.uk/view/badc.nerc.ac.uk__ATOM__dataent_1256223773328276 (Accessed on May 01 2013). NCAS British Atmospheric Data Centre Climate Research Unit (CRU), University of East Anglia.

Kasischke, E. S., & Penner, J. E. (2004). Improving global estimates of atmospheric emissions from biomass burning. *Journal of Geophysical Research, 109*(D14S01).

Lal, R., Safriel, U., & Boer, B. (2012). *Zero net land degradation: A new sustainable development goal for Rio+ 20. Secretariat of the United Nations Convention to Combat Desertification (UNCCD)*, pp. 1–30. URL http://www.unccd.int/Lists/SiteDocumentLibrary/secretariat/2012/Zero%2020Net%2020Land%2020Degradation%2020Report%2020UNCCD%2020May%202012%202020background.pdf (Accessed 202020 August 202013).

Le, Q. B. (2012). Indicators of global soils and land degradation. Slides of Oral Presentation at the First Flobal Soil Week, November 18–22 2012, Berlin, Germany. The First Global Soil Week, Berlin.

Le, Q. B., Tamene, L., & Vlek, P. L. G. (2012). Multi-pronged assessment of land degradation in West Africa to assess the importance of atmospheric fertilization in masking the processes involved. *Global and Planetary Change, 92–93*, 71–81.

Lewis, S. L., Lopez-Gonzalez, G., Sonké, B., Affum-Baffoe, K., & Baker, T. R. (2009). Increasing carbon storage in intact African tropical forests. *Nature, 457*, 1003–1006.

Liang, S., & Xiao, Z. (2012). *Global land surface products: Leaf area index product data collection (1985–2010)*. Beijing: Beijing Normal University.

MacDonald, G. K., Bennett, E. M., Potter, P. A., & Ramankutty, N. (2011). Agronomic phosphorus imbalances across the world's croplands. *Proceedings of the National Academy of Sciences of the United States of America, 108*, 3086–3091.

Markon, C. J., Fleming, M. D., & Binnian, E. F. (1995). Characteristics of vegetation phenology over the Alaskan landscape using AVHRR time-series data. *Polar Record, 31*, 179–190.

Mbow, C., Fensholt, R., Rasmussen, K., & Diop, D. (2013). Can vegetation productivity be derived from greenness in a semi-arid environment? Evidence from ground-based measurements. *Journal of Arid Environments, 97*, 56–65.

MEA. (2005). *Ecosystems and Human Well-being: Synthesis*. Washington DC: Millennium Ecosystem Assessment.

Nachtergaele, F., & Petri, M. (2008). *Mapping land use systems at global and regional scales for land degradation assessment analysis*. Rome: FAO.

Nkonya, E., Braun, Jv, A, Mirzabaev, Le, Q. B., Kwon, H. Y., & Kirui, O. (2013). Economics of Land Degradation Initiative: Methods and Approach for Global and National Assessments. *ZEF—Discussion Papers on Development Policy, 183*, 1–41.

Nkonya, E., Gerber, N., Baumgartner, P., von Braun, J., De Pinto, A., & Graw, V., et al. (2011). The economics of desertification, land degradation, and drought—Toward an integrated global assessment. ZEF-Discussion Papers on Development Policy No. 150, Center for Development Research (ZEF).

Oldeman, L. R., Hakkeling, R. T. A., & Sombroek, W. G. (1990). *World map of the status of human-induced soil degradation: An explanatory note* (2nd ed.). Wageningen, The Netherlands: International Soil Reference and Information Centre.

Pender, J., Mirzabaev, A., & Kato, E. (2009). Economic Analysis of Sustainable Land Management Options in Central Asia. *Final Report for the ADB. IFPRI/ICARDA, 168*.

Pettorelli, N., Vik, J. O., Mysterud, A., Gaillard, J.-M., Tucker, C. J., & Stenseth, N. C. (2005). Using the satellite-derived NDVI to assess ecological responses to environmental change. *Trends in Ecology & Evolution, 20*, 503–510.

Pinter, P. J., Jackson, R. D., Elaine Ezra, C., & Gausman, H. W. (1985). Sun-angle and canopy-architecture effects on the spectral reflectance of six wheat cultivars. *International Journal of Remote Sensing, 6*, 1813–1825.

Pinzon, J., Brown, M. E., & Tucker, C. J. (2005). Satellite time series correction of orbital drift artifacts using empirical mode decomposition. In N. E. Huang & S. S. P. Shen (Eds.), *Hilbert-Huang transform and its applications* (pp. 167–186). Singapore: World Scientific Publishing.

Potter, P., Ramankutty, N., Bennett, E. M., & Donner, S. D. (2010). Characterizing the spatial patterns of global fertilizer application and manure production. Earth Interactions 14. Paper No. 2, 22 p. doi:210.1175/2009ei1288.1171.

Reay, D. S., Dentener, F., Smith, P., Grace, J., & Feely, R. (2008). Global nitrogen deposition and carbon sinks. *Nature Geoscience, 1*, 430–437.

Safriel, U. N. (2007). The assessment of global trends in land degradation. In M. V. K. Sivakumar, & Ndiang'ui, N. (Eds.), *Climate and land degradation* (pp. 1–38). Berlin: Springer.

Sala, O. E., Chapin, F. S. I., Armesto, J. J., Berlow, E., Bloomfield, J., Dirzo, R., et al. (2000). Global biodiversity scenarios for the year 2100. *Science, 287*, 1770–1774.

Sommer, S., Zucca, C., Grainger, A., Cherlet, M., Zougmore, R., Sokona, Y., et al. (2011). Application of indicator systems for monitoring and assessment of desertification from national to global scales. *Land Degradation and Development, 22*, 184–197.

Thomas, W. (1997). A three-dimensional model for calculating reflection functions of inhomogeneous and orographically structured natural landscapes. *Remote Sensing of Environment, 59*, 44–63.

Trabucco, A., & Zomer, R. J. (2009). Global Aridity Index (Global-Aridity) and Global Potential Evapo-Transpiration (Global-PET) Geospatial Database. CGIAR Consortium for Spatial Information, CGIAR-CSI GeoPortal: http://www.csi.cgiar.org.

Tucker, C. J., Pinzon, J. E., Brown, M. E., Slayback, D. A., Pak, E. W., Mahoney, R., et al. (2005). An extended AVHRR 8-km NDVI data set compatible with MODIS and SPOT Vegetation NDVI data. *International Journal of Remote Sensing, 26*, 4485–4498.

UNCCD. (2004). UNCCD Ten Years On. Secretariat of the United Nations Convention to Combat Desertification (UNCCD), Bonn, Germany.

USDA-NRCS. (1998). *Global Desertification Vulnerability Map. U.S. Department of Agriculture, Natural Resources Conservation Science (USDA-NRCS).* http://www.nrcs.usda.gov/wps/portal/nrcs/detail/national/nedc/training/soil/?cid=nrcs142p2_054003 (Accessed on May 31 2014).

Vlek, P., Le, Q. B., & Tamene, L. (2010). Assessment of land degradation, its possible causes and threat to food security in Sub-Saharan Africa. In R. Lal & B. A. Stewart (Eds.), *Food security and soil quality* (pp. 57–86). Boca Raton, Florida: CRC Press.

Vlek, P. L. G., Kühne, R. F., & Denich, M. (1997). Nutrient resources for crop production in the tropics. *Philosophical Transactions of the Royal Society of London. Series B, Biological sciences, 352*, 975–985.

Vlek, P. L. G., Le, Q. B., & Tamene, L. (2008). *Land decline in land-rich Africa: A creeping disaster in the making*. Rome, Italy: CGIAR Science Council Secretariat.

Vogt, J. V., Safriel, U., Maltitz, G. V., Sokona, Y., Zougmore, R., Bastin, G., & Hill, J. (2011). Monitoring and assessment of land degradation and desertification: Towards new conceptual and integrated approaches. *Land Degradation and Development, 22*, 150–165.

Vu, Q. M., Le, Q. B., & Vlek, P. L. G. (2014a). Hotspots of human-induced biomass productivity decline and their social-ecological types towards support national policy and local studies on land degradation. *Global and Planetary Change, 121*, 64–77.

Vu, Q. M., Le, Q. B., Frossard, E., & Vlek, P. L. G. (2014b). Socio-economic and biophysical determinants of land degradation in Vietnam: An integrated causal analysis at the national level. *Land Use Policy, 36*, 605–617.

Wassen, M. J., Olde Venterink, H., Lapshina, E. D., & Tanneberger, F. (2005). Endangered plants persist under phosphorus limitation. *Nature, 437*, 547–550.

Wessels, K. J., Prince, S. D., Malherbe, J., Small, J., Frost, P. E., & VanZyl, D. (2007). Can human-induced land degradation be distinguished from the effects of rainfall variability? A case study in South Africa. *Journal of Arid Environments, 68*, 271–297.

Xiao, Z., Liang, S., Wang, J., Chen, P., Yin, X., Zhang, L., & Song, J. (2014). Use of general regression neural networks for generating the GLASS leaf area index product from time-series MODIS surface reflectance. *IEEE Transactions on Geoscience and Remote Sensing, 52*, 209–223.

Chapter 5
Evaluating Global Land Degradation Using Ground-Based Measurements and Remote Sensing

Weston Anderson and Timothy Johnson

Abstract Understanding the impacts of land degradation is, at least in part, limited by our ability to accurately characterize those impacts in space and time. While in recent decades remote sensing has offered unprecedented coverage of the land surface, the evaluation of remote sensing products is often limited or lacking altogether. In this chapter we use a survey-based approach to evaluate how well already existing remotely sensed datasets depict areas of land degradation. Ground-based surveys are compared to existing maps of land degradation and independent remote sensing datasets. This provides a metric of evaluation by using the commonly understood confusion-matrix. A representative set of case study countries was chosen after all countries were grouped using a k-means clustering approach (see Chap. 2). Survey sites within each country were sampled according to the intersection of agro-ecological zones, land cover, and the dataset to be evaluated. This two-tiered approach to sampling ensured a diversity of ground-truth surveys and therefore a robustness of results. Although ground-based surveys are resource and time-intensive, they provide information on both the evolution of the land cover and the drivers of land-cover change. Land degradation is a very complex process where diverse data are often needed for interpretation.

Keywords Remote sensing · Land degradation · NDVI · Landsat · MODIS

W. Anderson (✉)
Department of Earth and Environmental Sciences, Columbia University, New York, NY, USA
e-mail: weston@ldeo.columbia.edu

T. Johnson
Environment and Production Technology Division, International Food Policy Research Institute, 2033 K Street, NW, Washington, DC 20006-1002, USA

E. Nkonya et al. (eds.), *Economics of Land Degradation and Improvement – A Global Assessment for Sustainable Development*,
DOI 10.1007/978-3-319-19168-3_5

Introduction

Sustaining the biological or economic production capacity of land is vital to ensuring the well-being of all that depends on that land. Although it may seem to be a problem affecting only those with a vested interest in a relatively confined plot of land—such as subsistence farmers—land degradation also affects large swaths of land over longer timescales. Land degradation has been defined as the persistent reduction of the production capacity of a land, which may be manifest through any combination of a number of interrelated processes, such as: soil erosion, deterioration of soil nutrients, loss of biodiversity, deforestation or declining vegetative health (Le et al. 2012). These various processes are considered as leading to land degradation assuming that ecosystem services are lost. Some processes such as deforestation act as enabling processes for degradation, such as soil fertility decline and biodiversity loss (Chap. 6). Land degradation may be either anthropogenic or natural, although this analysis is primarily focused on anthropogenic degradation. Furthermore, although a reduction of biodiversity is considered land degradation, the global scale of this analysis precluded the evaluation of such losses. As such, the working definition of land degradation used in the land degradation dataset produced by Le et al. (2014) focuses on primary production, such as changes in the productivity of the soil and biomass. Owing to the focus on terrestrial ecosystems, changes in quantity or quality of water resources is beyond the scope of this analysis.

Without proper monitoring and evaluation of land degradation, not only is it difficult to assess the losses attributable to such degradation, but also it is difficult to develop practices and policies aimed at improving livelihoods. Monitoring land degradation, however, is more complex than it may seem as many degradation-inducing processes act on local scales but have regional to global implications. Monitoring and evaluation, therefore, cannot be limited to local evaluations if effective policies directed at reducing land degradation are to be developed. A global analysis identifying the extent and intensity of land degradation would be an invaluable tool for policy makers, and as such has been an active topic of research for nearly a decade. In this chapter we explore how global land degradation maps are formulated and evaluated using remote sensing and field-based observations.

The need to monitor land degradation at regional to global scales in a consistent manner makes remote sensing an invaluable tool for doing so, however, products derived from remote sensing datasets may have systematic or structural errors that should be acknowledged and explored. Failure to do so will likely lead to overconfidence or misuse of remote sensing-based estimates of land degradation. These structural errors may be conceptualized as falling into one of three related categories: errors arising from the type of sensor used, errors arising from the spatial and temporal resolution of the analysis, and errors arising from the derived data used (i.e. indices, land cover/land use classifications, etc.).

Most global-scale analyses have used the Normalized Difference Vegetation Index (NDVI), which is a measure of vegetative health derived from the difference in the intensity of near-infrared wavelengths and that of visible wavelengths (Huete et al. 1999). In effect, NDVI quantifies the photosynthetic capacity of a given pixel. The type of sensor used to gather measurements is important because it dictates the type of information returned, and under what conditions that information is returned. Sensors used to measure NDVI, for example, require clear-sky conditions as they are not cloud penetrating. This has serious implications for available sampling frequency during the rainy season in habitually cloudy environments. Most curated datasets will screen out cloud cover or systematically sample for clear-sky images, but this means that seasonal consistency is difficult to maintain when comparing images from different years. The specific sensor chosen will ultimately dictate the temporal frequency and spatial resolution of the data. Already compiled NDVI datasets are available at a broad range of time scales (1975-present) and resolutions (30 m–8 km). Issues of differing timeframes and resolutions pose a serious challenge to analyses attempting to combine or compare datasets, although past studies have shown that these challenges are not insurmountable. After comparing five different NDVI datasets—including products derived from the Moderate Resolution Imaging Spectroradiometer (MODIS), Advanced Very High Resolution Radiometer (AVHRR), and Landsat satellite sensors—over 13 sample sites, Brown et al. (2006) noted that although the sensors differed significantly, "the NDVI anomalies exhibited similar variances". The authors concluded that despite differences in the absolute values or time series of each product, comparisons of anomalies/trends between datasets is still valuable. More recently, Fensholt and Proud (2012) found that when NDVI data from MODIS is resampled to the resolution of AVHRR, the two datasets compare favorably over the global land surface. Similarly, Beck et al. (2011) compared Landsat NDVI measurements to those from four separate AVHRR-derived products, and to MODIS NDVI. The resulting correlations compare favorably, ranging from 0.87 to 0.90 (Beck et al. 2011).

While challenges posed by specific NDVI products may be overcome using a combination of datasets, the index as a whole has noted limitations in its use for measuring land degradation. Most notably, NDVI asymptotically saturates in high biomass areas when compared to indices such as the Enhanced Vegetation Index, and may therefore be a poor indicator of vegetative health over dense canopies (Huete et al. 2002). The high-biomass saturation of NDVI makes it a poor indicator of thinning in forests, meaning that as an index of land degradation NDVI may overlook certain forms of deforestation. Furthermore, NDVI cannot distinguish between categories of land degradation nor can it provide information on some types of land degradation, such as loss of biodiversity or soil erosion. In fact, if invasive species grow densely, the result will be in an increase in NDVI, which is often understood as an indication of land improvement. Compounding the complexity of using NDVI as a measure of land degradation is that land degradation may be driven by either natural or anthropogenic forces, which is a distinction that is often impossible to make using NDVI alone. And while many studies are interested in anthropogenic land degradation, most changes to net primary production (a measure closely related to NDVI) over the last decade have been naturally occurring (Zhao and Running 2010). Although this adds to the complexity of developing datasets focusing on anthropogenic degradation, it does not make the task intractable.

Indeed, researchers have already developed numerous remote sensing derived datasets that identify individual components of anthropogenic land degradation: declining vegetative health (Huete et al. 2002), crop yields (Iizumi et al. 2014), deforestation (Hansen et al. 2010, 2013), declining water supplies including groundwater depletion (Voss et al. 2013), and even a partial proxy for soil salinity (Lobell et al. 2009). The Food and Agriculture Organization (FAO) attempted to move beyond individual components and produce more inclusive estimates of land degradation at a global scale, based at least in part, on remote sensing products in its Global Assessment of Land Degradation and Improvement (GLADA) project. As part of the project, Bai et al. (2008) proposed several methods of measuring land degradation at a global scale based entirely on remote sensing products. The Global Land Degradation Information System (GLADIS), which also relates to the GLADA framework, builds upon the analysis of Bai and Dent (2009) by modifying their product before incorporating it into a database that assesses the current capacity of and trends in the ecosystem services of land. While the accuracy of these products are debated, they are generally recognized as an important first step towards globally consistent estimates of land degradation (Wessels 2009).

In this chapter we use both remote sensing and survey-based datasets to analyze and evaluate an updated methodology for producing global estimates of land degradation, which was produced by Le et al. (2014). Although the coarse resolution and global coverage of the land degradation dataset precludes a complete, in-depth evaluation of the dataset, we present a robust method of evaluation that incorporates multiple regions and spatial scales by making use of a diverse collection of datasets. In the following sections we present the datasets used, the methods of analysis, and the results. We conclude with a brief discussion of the implications of these results for global land degradation mapping.

Data

Independent datasets and previous estimates both play an important role in our evaluation of the new land degradation map produced by Le et al. (2014): the former identifies potential errors associated with input data while the latter is used as an independent estimate, which provides an independent perspective arrived at using alternative methodologies. In this analysis we compare the Le et al. (2014) map to the soil and biomass components of the GLADIS database as a reference to past efforts aimed at mapping terrestrial anthropogenic land degradation. The GLADIS database as a whole contains information at a resolution of five arc minutes for six distinct categories: biomass, soil, water, biodiversity, economic, and social (Nachtergaele et al. 2010). The biomass components of GLADIS are based on the work of Bai and Dent (2009), which uses NDVI and rainfall to estimate land degradation. Bai and Dent derive trends in net primary productivity (NPP) from NDVI and establish areas of degradation by overlaying an index of rain use efficiency, which is calculated using time series information on rainfall and NDVI (Chap. 4; Le et al. 2014).

While many remote sensing datasets either lack ground-based evaluation entirely or provide few details on such analyses, the GLADIS framework conducted and documented extensive ground based evaluations over South Africa. The GLADIS evaluation is particularly relevant because the dataset being evaluated is of a similar scale as the dataset used in our analysis. In their analysis, Bai and Dent performed field evaluation of 165 sites in South Africa using point estimates and circular areas with an 8 km radius as a means of accounting for errors in geolocation. The authors found agreement between the land degradation status map and the field sites to be 33 % for the point estimates and 48 % for the area-based estimates. A number of problems pervaded the satellite based estimates. In terms of removing the climate influence, the rainfall-corrected trends still displayed a systematic relation with climatic conditions. Specific land uses proved difficult throughout the analysis. Cultivated land, for example, was often classified as degraded owing to management practices such as crop rotation or fallowing fields. Areas with sparse vegetation also proved difficult to correctly classify. These areas were often identified as improved in the satellite dataset when, in fact, they were among the most degraded lands due to over-grazing and heavy erosion (Bai and Dent 2008). Systematic errors inevitably manifest themselves as well: the presence of dense vegetation considered a weed showed up as land improvement in the remote sensing dataset. The source of some errors could not be identified, as was the case for a number of areas indicated as degraded in the remote sensing dataset but showing no indication of such from the ground. Issues of resolution also proved problematic when deforestation and heavy erosion was undetected in the remote sensing analysis due to the coarse resolution of the dataset. Ultimately, the authors concluded that the GLADIS dataset may not be used as a proxy for land degradation, but is never-the-less valuable as an indicator map to be used as a guide to further explore potentially degraded areas.

The Le et al. (2014) land degradation dataset evaluated in this analysis builds upon the GLADIS methodology and recommendations. The dataset is a global study that aims to identify "geographic degradation hotspots", meaning regions where degradation magnitude and extent is relatively large (Le, submitted). As such, this dataset is intended to be used as a guide for prioritizing investments and further in-depth studies at regional scales rather than a final map of land degradation. The dataset uses the Global Inventory Modeling and Mapping Studies (GIMMS) NDVI dataset, which is derived from data collected by AVHRR), to calculate statistically significant long-term trends in NDVI from 1982 to 2006. The effects of rainfall are removed by correlating the NDVI with precipitation estimates from CRU v3.1 (Harris et al. 2014), and masking out any areas with significant correlation from further analysis. The dataset further corrects for atmospheric fertilization-dominated dynamics in areas without significant rainfall-NDVI correlations by dividing the unpopulated land surface of the earth according to aridity class and land cover before identifying the mean NDVI trend in each class. These mean trends are considered the atmospheric fertilization driven dynamics, and are removed from each NDVI time-series within each class. The dataset also addressed some of the structural issues with NDVI by identifying areas of saturated NDVI, a common problem in densely vegetated regions. A leaf area index of four was used as the threshold at which NDVI trends were considered unreliable and were screened out. Le proposes that the remaining pixels indicate anthropogenic trends in biomass productivity excluding areas with rainfall-driven dynamics, corrected for atmospheric-fertilization and with unreliable NDVI trends removed. The dataset represents significant progress towards overcoming the many limitations to measuring anthropogenic land degradation at a global scale (Chap. 4; Le et al. 2014).

A comparison of the Le et al. (2014) dataset to the previously developed GLADIS database will prove useful, but would be incomplete due to interdependencies of the two products. Interdependencies of the two products arise due to the lack of multiple, independent datasets of NDVI on a global scale during the 1980s and 1990s. Only the AVHRR satellite sensor provides a global, continuous time-series of NDVI data dating back to the 1980s. This sensor therefore provides the foundation of nearly all long-term, continuous estimates of land degradation including those developed by Bai and Dent (2009) for the GLADIS framework and the reconstruction of historical yields by Iizumi et al. (2014). In particular, each of these analyses use the GIMMS NDVI dataset. We therefore choose to use Landsat measurements of NDVI and MODIS estimates of land cover as independent datasets to evaluate the data-specific errors while the ground-based samples from field surveys are used to assess physical processes occurring on the ground that may be missed by the remote sensing estimates. This approach allows us to separately evaluate the inconsistencies relating to datasets—an important aspect given that the GIMMS NDVI dataset has a coarse spatial resolution of approximately 8 km—and those relating to the methods of correcting for atmospheric fertilization, NDVI adjustments and rainfall-dominated dynamics.

Although AVHRR data is the only global dataset dating back to the 1980s that provides a continuous time series, the Global Land Survey (GLS) Landsat dataset provides NDVI estimates with near-global coverage for the years 1975, 1990, 2000, 2005 and 2010. Table 5.1 provides an overview of the GLS datasets used in this analysis, including the Landsat sensors used to collect the images for each dataset. In many cases multiple sensors were used since the GLS Landsat datasets provide NDVI estimates around a target year, rather than for a specific date. This is necessary because the effective return time for cloud free images—or images with minimal cloud cover—is dependent on both the season and region being observed. As may be expected, coverage is greater in the dry season and over arid areas when

Table 5.1 Summary of Landsat Global Land Survey 2005, 2000, 1990 and 1975 datasets

Categories	GLS 2005	GLS 2000	GLS 1990	GLS 1975
Level of processing	Terrain corrected	Terrain corrected	Terrain corrected	Terrain corrected
Number of bands	8	8	7	4
Resolution (m)	30.0	30.0	30.0	30.0
Projection	Universal Transverse Mercator (UTM)	Universal Transverse Mercator (UTM)	Universal Transverse Mercator (UTM)	Universal Transverse Mercator (UTM)
Datum	WGS84	WGS84	WGS84	WGS84
Instrument	Landsat 5 Thematic Mapper (TM) Landsat 7 ETM + EO-1 ALI	Landsat 7 ETM+	Landsat 4–5 Thematic Mapper (TM)	Landsat 1–3 Multispectral Scanner (MSS)

compared to the tropics or to rainy seasons. The Landsat sensors have a return interval of 16 days, meaning that they take images of the same spot every 16 days, but that data must be downloaded and stored in order for it to become available for analysis. In practice, it takes many years of available data, often spanning more than a decade, to create global coverage.

Figure 5.1 illustrates the histogram of image acquisition dates. Neither the 1975 nor the 1990 dataset provides an ideal fit to the GIMMS NDVI start date of 1981: the GLS 1975 contains only a few images after the 1980s and in fact has a skewed distribution of images towards those prior to 1975. GLS 1990 contains images nearly a full decade after the GIMMS start date, but has a more normal distribution such that the majority of images acquired for the dataset are fewer than 5 years away from the GIMMS start date. By contrast those images obtained for the 2000 and 2005 datasets were drawn from a relatively small number of years. The images for the GLS 2000 dataset came from just 4 years, with the majority drawn from 2000 or 2001. With the exception of a negligible number of images drawn from 1989, presumably to fill spatial gaps in the coverage, the GLS 2005 dataset was also drawn almost entirely from four years with the majority of images coming from 2005 and 2006.

While the GLS Landsat dataset provides information at a finer spatial resolution dating back further than would be available with the MODIS sensor, which begins coverage in 2000 at a spatial resolution of 250 m up to 1 km, the Landsat dataset is not without its problems. Owing to the variability of acquisition dates (both annual and seasonal), the observed changes in NDVI may reflect a degree of seasonality in areas where seasonal consistency could not be obtained. This problem will be particularly pronounced in transitional zones that demonstrate relatively greater variability in seasonal vegetation cover. Despite this limitation, the GLS Landsat

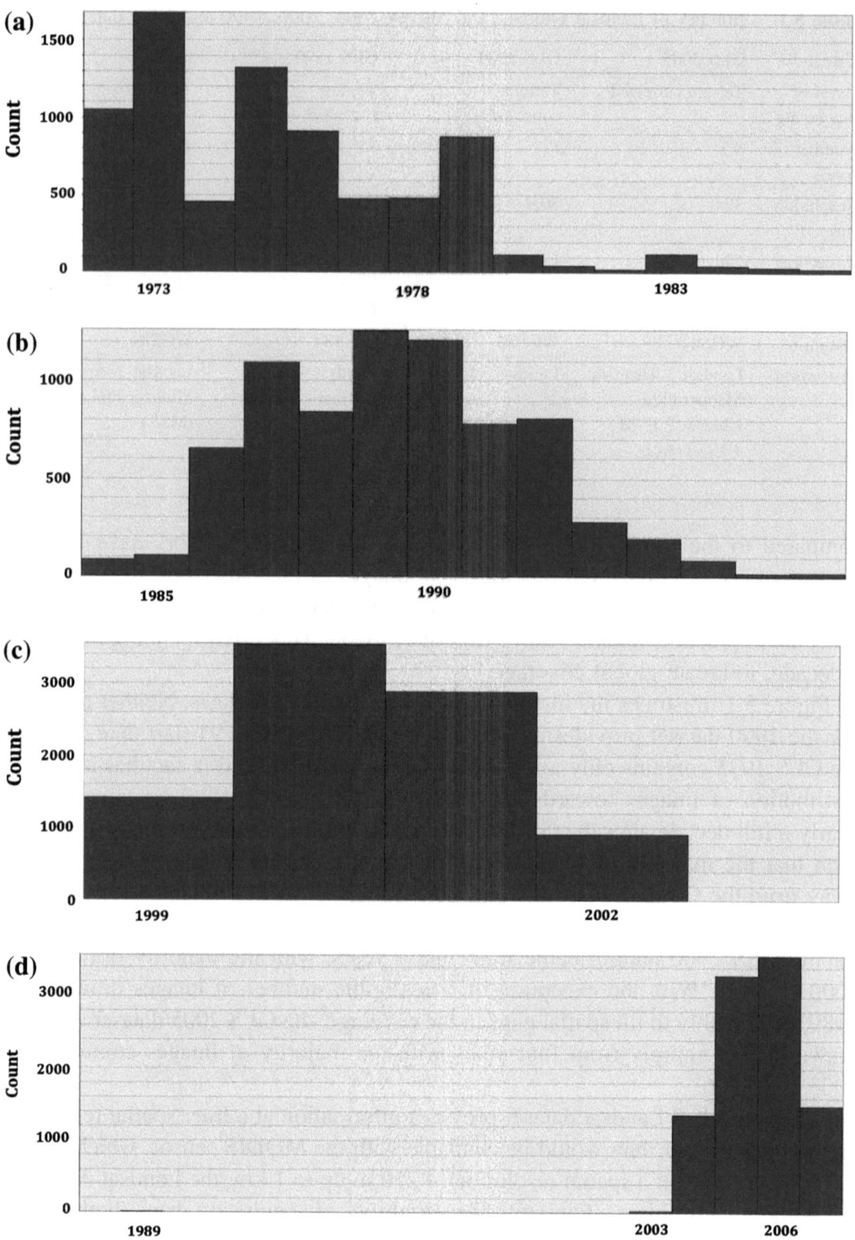

Fig. 5.1 Global Land Survey histograms of Landsat image acquisition dates for **a** 1975, **b** 1990, **c** 2000 and **d** 2005. Count equals number of images used globally

datasets have proven to be preferable to alternative data sources covering comparable time periods, such as GeoCover (Townshend 2012).

MODIS data, although only available beginning in 2001, are a valuable source of information as independent, global estimates of both land cover and NDVI. For this analysis the land cover information was chosen to provide estimates to be compared to the FGD (focus group discussion) survey results, which estimate land-cover changes from 2000 to 2006 as a measure of recent degradation trends. Collection 5 of the MODIS land cover type dataset (MCD12Q1) was used, which provided land cover information at a 500 m spatial resolution annually (Friedl et al. 2010). Input datasets used in the classification procedure include information from MODIS bands 1–7, the enhanced vegetation index, land surface temperature, and nadir BRDF-adjusted reflectance data. The data are produced using an ensemble supervised classification algorithm, which employs a decision tree model structure and uses boosting to estimate the classifications. The classification process includes techniques for stabilizing year-to-year variations in land cover labels not associated with land-cover change. As a means of evaluating the overall accuracy of the dataset, it is ground-truthed using 1860 sites distributed across Earth's land areas (see Fig. 2 in Friedl et al. 2010), sampled with reference to adequate coverage of a range of geographic and ecological variability using a layer of ecoregions. The overall accuracy of the product is about 75 %, although the performance of each class varies considerably.

FGD surveys were used as a complement to the remote-sensing based observations, which provide great volumes of information but are limited in the physical processes they can measure. These surveys provide ground-based estimates of land degradation from the perspectives of the communities involved. In Senegal and Niger, communities were selected by intersecting the Le Land Degradation map (submitted), Global Land Cover 2000 v1, and the global environmental stratification (GEnS) datasets as a means of sampling both degraded and improved pixels across a range of agro-ecological zones. Figure 5.2 depicts the datasets used to determine sampling criteria for these countries. The Le et al. (2014) dataset identifies both areas of degraded pixels as well as areas of improved pixels. Improved pixels represent areas of increased vegetation (Chap. 4; Le et al. 2014) In addition to Senegal and Niger, communities were also chosen for India, Uzbekistan, Tanzania, and Ethiopia. The study sites within these countries differ in that they were not chosen to represent degraded and improved areas of the Le et al. (2014) dataset but rather areas that were most successful for conducting interviews with local stakeholders. For all six countries, communities were chosen so people surveyed would have knowledge of a surrounding land spanning an area of 8 km × 8 km, which is the size of a single pixel in the Le et al. (2014) dataset. Individual participants were selected such that community leaders, women, cultural leaders, and a diversity of occupations as well as ages were present. These selection criteria ensured that a broad variety of land users would be present, particularly those with intimate knowledge of past land use developments. Information elicited in the survey includes estimates of the severity and drivers of many land degrading

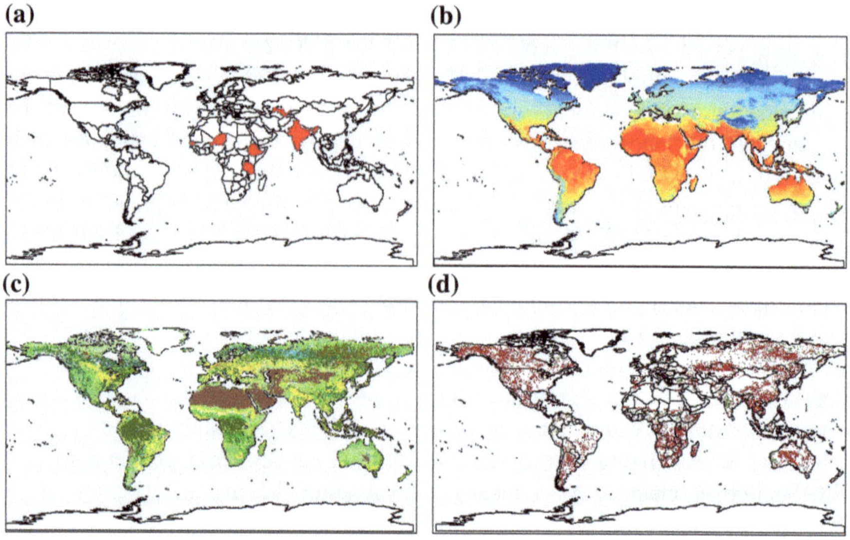

Fig. 5.2 Sample criteria and selection. *Note* **a** Case study countries, **b** GeNS climate zones, **c** GlobCover land cover (*dark greens* forest, *light greens* shrubs, *yellow* crops, *brown* barren), **d** Le Land Degradation Dataset (*red* areas of degradation, *green* improvement)

processes, such as; the land cover for the area surrounding the community in 2000 and 2006, the deforestation occurring during that time, changes in cropping intensity, and changes in crop yields. This information was elicited using a variety of techniques, including relative questions (i.e. were yields this year higher or lower than five years ago), collaborative map making, and GPS coordinates taken by the surveyor.

Methods

The design of our evaluation analysis builds upon established methods and previous studies in an effort to complement the in-depth insight from ground-based evaluation techniques with the near-ubiquitous coverage of remote sensing estimates. We first compare the new estimates of land degradation to the methods and results of previous products as a means of identifying systematic similarities and differences. In the comparative analysis we identify overlapping input datasets and methods as well as key differences. This analysis, while not an evaluation of accuracy, provides context crucial for the accuracy evaluation analysis.

As described previously in the data section, the sites used to evaluate the accuracy of the land degradation map in Senegal and Niger, are selected within a framework that maximizes selection of appropriately sized degraded and improved sites within a range of agro-ecological zones for each case study country. In India, Uzbekistan, Tanzania, and Ethiopia, these sites were chosen randomly. The processes of land degradation or improvement are identified and analyzed at each site using FGDs conducted with the communities as well as a number of remote sensing-based analyses. The FGD questions are synthesized into five major categories for this portion of our analysis: (1) changes in land cover, (2) deforestation, (3) crop intensity/yield changes, (4) community perception of trends in land degradation/improvement, and (5) processes that would be unobservable using remote sensing. Each of these categories are designed to elicit, either directly or indirectly, the presence or absence of land degradation and the associated impacts. Unfortunately surveys in India, Uzbekistan, Tanzania, and Ethiopia did not contain information relating to numbers 4 and 5 above. These surveys were conducted by independent researchers. The benefit of using survey information from these study sites is to see how randomly chosen areas agree or disagree with remote sensing datasets.

The immediately visible forms of potential land degradation—deforestation, land clearing, etc.—are relatively easy to identify using remote sensing. The strength of the field survey is in identifying attributes that may not be immediately visible using satellite sensors such as changes in forest productivity through selective logging, erosion, salinization, or nutrient depletion leading to decreased crop yields. The field surveys also provide robust information that is not confounded by complex surface processes such as invasive species acting to increase vegetative cover or systematic fallowing of crop fields, both of which would lead to erroneous remote sensing assessments. The limitation of the FGDs, however, is the time frame available. Community members cannot be expected to remember specifics of land cover, yields, or cropping intensity as far back as three decades, so those questions are limited to the years since 2000. More general questions do elicit information on land degradation dating back to 1982, but do not gather information in the same manner as the specific questions designed to identify those physical processes on which the land degradation map is based.

The first three categories of FGD questions (changes in land cover, cropping intensity and yields, and deforestation) are designed to allow direct comparison to available remote sensing estimates in our analysis. This direct comparison isolates reliability of remote sensing estimates of land degrading processes without the complication of differing time frames or unobservable processes. Building on established methods and those proposed by Bai and Dent in their evaluation of the GLADIS framework, we conduct the remote sensing analyses using a buffer radius of 8 km around each site as a means of approximating the resolution of the land degradation dataset as well as to account for errors in geo-location. Each remote sensing analysis consists of three parts: an analysis of the change in Landsat NDVI from 2000 to 2005, an accounting of changes in MODIS land cover from 2001 to 2006, and an assessment of trends in Landsat NDVI using GLS data from 1975, 1990, 2000 and 2005.

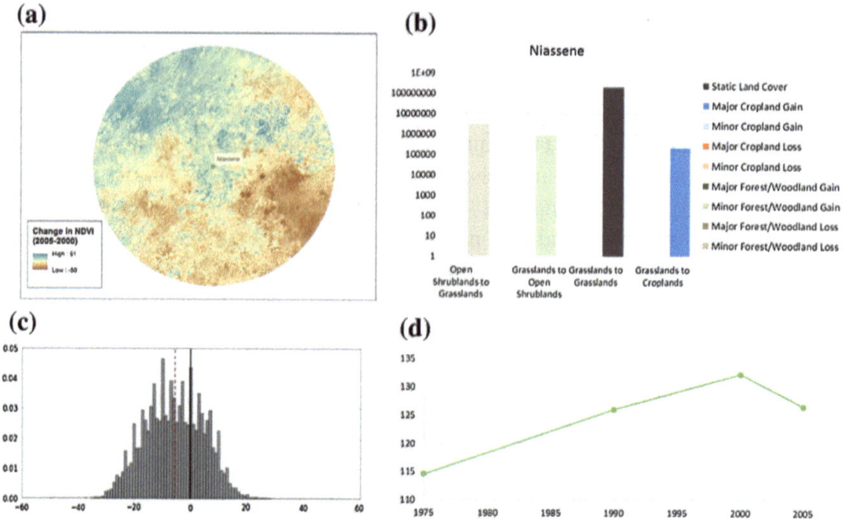

Fig. 5.3 Remote sensing analysis for the buffer area around Niassene, Senegal. *Note* This site demonstrated degradation dynamics that were largely captured accurately by the remote sensing analyses (see Table 5.3). Panels **a** and **c** illustrate changes in Landsat NDVI from 2000 to 2005. Both are shown on a relative scale where the more positive the number the greater increase in NDVI and vice versa. Panel **b** shows changes in MODIS land cover from 2001 to 2006, and **d** shows Landsat NDVI from 1975, 1990, 2000 and 2005 (scaled from 0 to 255)

The analysis of changes in NDVI from 2000 to 2005 using the Landsat GLS datasets allows for a direct comparison to the field based survey, which asks participants about deforestation, and changes in land cover over the same time period. In this case, NDVI is averaged annually and compared across a five year time period. A decrease in NDVI is considered degradation and an increase improvement. The changes in land cover from the survey can be further corroborated against the MODIS land use/cover change analysis. A qualitative ordinal ranking of total economic value was used as a guideline to assess whether observed land-cover changes constituted degradation or improvement. For example, the removal of forest or shrubland to plant crops, is recorded as degradation, since this process often leads to erosion, a loss of nutrients in the soil, and other longer term issues. The long term trends in vegetation health/cover can be assessed using the Landsat trend analysis, which has a timeframe comparable to that of the GIMMS NDVI trend analysis at the heart of the land degradation map. Improvement is recorded when, during most of the time period NDVI is increasing, degradation is recorded when the opposite occurs. In all cases, if there was both degradation and improvement, it was analyzed which influence was more widespread. See Figures 5.3 and 5.4 for examples of the data collected for two of the survey sites in Senegal used in the remote sensing analyses.

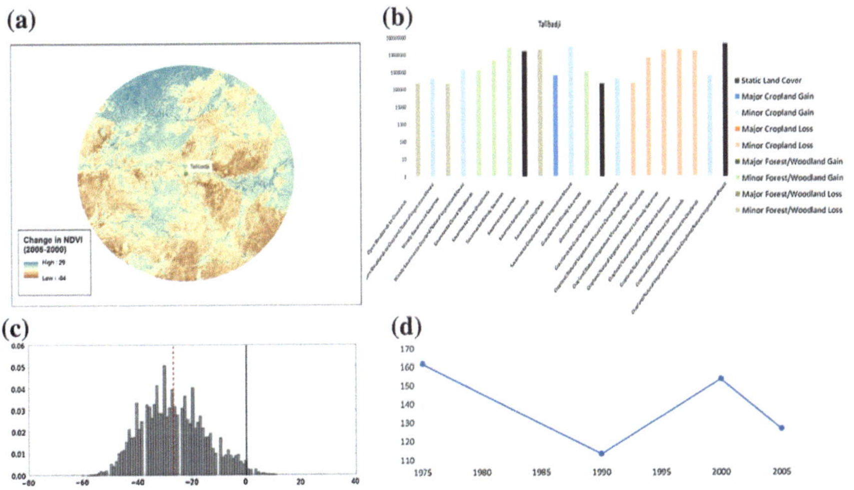

Fig. 5.4 Remote sensing analysis for the buffer area around Talibdji, Senegal. *Note* This site demonstrated dynamics that were driven by processes with little agreement in the remote sensing analyses (see Table 5.3). Panels **a** and **c** illustrate changes in Landsat NDVI from 2000 to 2005. Both are shown on a relative scale where the more positive the number the greater increase in NDVI and vice versa. Panel **b** shows changes in MODIS land cover from 2001 to 2006 (changes summarized by color on y-axis) and **d** depicts Landsat NDVI from 1975, 1990, 2000 and 2005 (scaled from 0 to 255)

Results and Discussion

Comparisons to Past Work

A comparison between the Le et al. (2014) land degradation dataset and aspects of the GLADIS land degradation database serves as a useful benchmark. While the Le et al. (2014) dataset provides only one map indicating whether areas are degraded or improved and is based entirely on terrestrial processes, the GLADIS database provides estimates for multiple categories of land degradation, including biomass, biodiversity, soil, water, economic, and social. For this comparison the biomass categories were considered most relevant. Table 5.2 illustrates the input data used in the Le et al. (2014) land degradation map as compared to the GLADIS biomass analyses. Although both land degradation maps rely on the GIMMS NDVI and CIESIN-CIAT population datasets, each incorporates independent ancillary information using different methods such that the two datasets may be considered separate, if not independent, estimates of land degradation processes.

Figure 5.5 demonstrates the comparison between the Le map and the GLADIS trends in NDVI, which are identified as being anthropogenic or natural, trends in total biomass, and trends in soil degradation or improvement. The terrestrial biomass-based datasets (panels a–c) largely agree over Canada, Northern Argentina, Democratic Republic of the Congo, Angola, Tanzania, Mozambique,

Table 5.2 Inputs for global land degradation datasets

Input dataset	GLADIS trends in NDVI	GLADIS total biomass trends	Le (2014) land degradation	Citation
GIMMS NDVI	x	x	x	Tucker et al. (2005)
MODIS NPP	x	x		Running et al. (2004)
GLASS leaf area index			x	Liang and Xiao (2012), Xiao et al. (2013)
FRA deforestation trends		x		FAO (2005)
GLC-2000 land use	x	x		JRC (2003)
GLOBCOVER land use			x	Bicheron et al. (2008)
CRU 2.1 temperature	x	x		Mitchell and Jones (2005)
CRU 3.1 precipitation			x	Jones and Harris (2008)
VASClimO station rainfall	x	x		Beck et al. (2005)
CIESIN-CIAT population	x	x	x	CIESIN and CIAT (2005)
CGIAR-CSI Global Aridity			x	Trabucco and Zomer (2009)
Carbon above ground		x		Nelson and Robertson (2008)

Malawi, India, Kazakhstan, the majority of Southeast Asia, and Australia. However, they disagree over most of the US, Europe, much of Brazil, the Sahel, South Africa, China and portions of Russia. In general, the GLADIS datasets indicates larger areas of land improvement, arising from both natural and anthropogenic influences. Without extensive ground-based measurements it is difficult to evaluate which dataset is more accurate in the areas of disagreement, but the regions of good agreement lends confidence to both datasets in these regions.

While the GLADIS estimates of soil degradation or improvement have no direct analog to the Le dataset, the comparison between the two is useful as it may elaborate the extent to which the Le dataset captures soil degradation processes (Fig. 5.5d). The GLADIS soil degradation map (panel d) shows little resemblance to the Le land degradation data. Le et al. (2014) does develop an additional dataset identifying areas in which excessive fertilizer application may mask land degradation (data not shown), which produces similar patterns to the GLADIS map over China, Northeast India and much of Europe. The comparison of soil degradation products reveals that the Le et al. (2014) data and the GLADIS data capture some

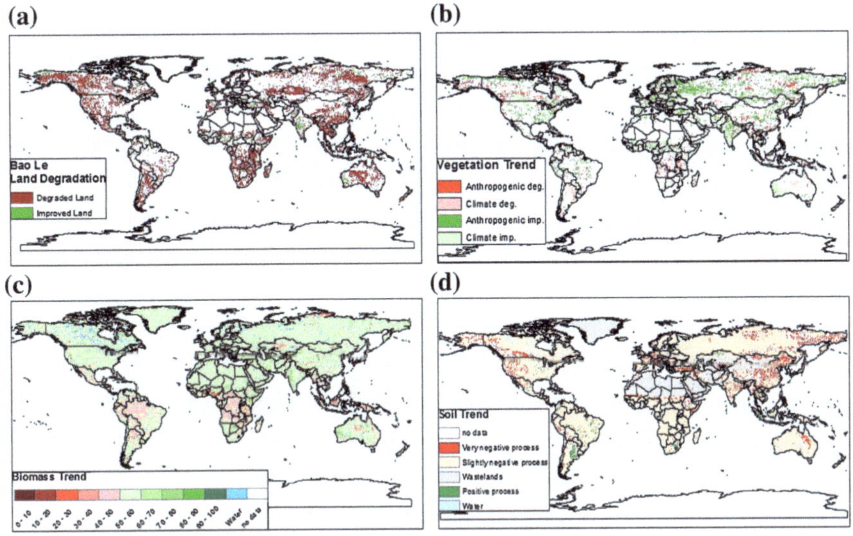

Fig. 5.5 Comparison between land degradation maps. *Note* **a** Le land degradation, **b** GLADIS trends in NDVI distinguished as being primarily anthropogenic or natural, **c** GLADIS total biomass trends, **d** GLADIS trends in soil degradation or improvement

similar soil processes in parts of Europe and Asia, but diverge widely in most other regions indicating a high level of uncertainty. These dissimilarities are to be expected provided the difficulty of measuring processes of soil degradation on global scales.

In addition to considering existing land degradation maps, it is important to use independent datasets to evaluate new estimates of land degradation. The results of the survey-based analysis and the remote sensing analyses provide useful insight into the value of the Le et al. (2014) land degradation dataset, and of the scale-dependent processes involved in the construction of the dataset. A total of 6 countries were analyzed to compare remote sensing analyses with survey results for selected sites. The sites represent a range of agro-ecological zones, and include both areas indicated as degraded and improved in the Le et al. (2014) dataset.

Senegal Sample Sites

Figure 5.6 illustrates the seven sample sites chosen for the evaluation analysis in Senegal. A comparison between the focus group discussions conducted at each site and the remote sensing analyses indicate a high level of agreement (3.5/4 or 4/4) for four sites, a moderate level of agreement (3/4 or 2.5/4) for two sites and no agreement (2/4) for one site, as indicated in Table 5.3.

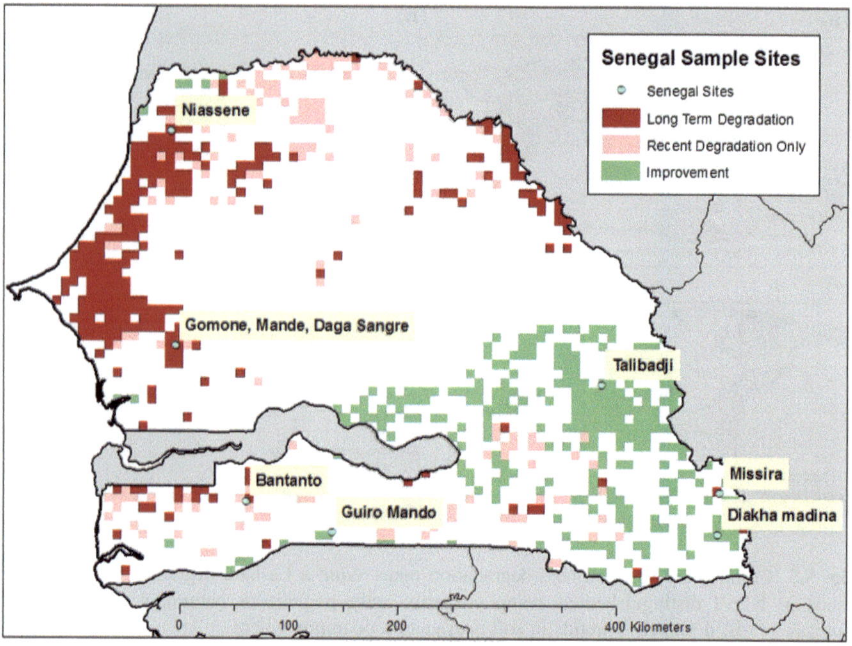

Fig. 5.6 Selected ground truthing sites in Senegal. *Note Dark red* indicates pixels that demonstrate both long-term degradation as well as degradation in recent (2000–2006) years, *green pixels* indicate sites with improved land

Table 5.3 Agreement between the Le et al. (2014) land degradation map, the focus group discussions (FGD), and the independent remote sensing analyses for each of the seven sites in Senegal

Site	Le assessment	FGD assessment	Change in Landsat NDVI	MODIS land-cover change	Agreement
Talibdji	Improved	Degraded	Degraded	Improved	2/4
Niassene	Degraded	Degraded	Degraded	Degraded	4/4
Missira	Degraded	Degraded	Improved	Mixed	2.5/4
Guiro Yoro Mandou	Improved	Degraded	Degraded	Mixed	2.5/4
Gomone	Degraded	Degraded	Degraded	Degraded	4/4
Diakha Madina	Improved	Mixed	Improved	Improved	3.5/4
Bantanto	Degraded	Degraded	Degraded	Degraded	4/4

The sites that demonstrated unanimous, or near unanimous, consensus on the state of land degradation had a number of systematic similarities. Out of the four sites with a high level of agreement, three were degraded (Bantanto, Gomone, and

Niassene) and one was improved (Diakha Madina). These sites all experienced clear areas of deforestation, or reforestation in the case of Diakha Madina, which was captured in the FGD, the Landsat analysis, and the MODIS analyses (see Table 5.4 for a summary of FGD results and Table 5.5 for a summary of the remote sensing results). While there are land degrading processes that were not captured in the remote sensing analysis—such as wind/water erosion and salinization—occurring at each of the degraded sites, the remote sensing analysis already correctly categorized these sites due to the clear decrease in vegetative health. The inability of remote sensing products to capture erosion or salinization processes, however, became relevant for the improving sample site. The results of the focus group discussion at Diakha Madina, the improved site, revealed that the narrative of land improvement is somewhat undercut by factors not captured in the remote sensing analysis, particularly a decrease in crop yields due to erosion. Figure 5.3 depicts the remote sensing analysis for Niassene as an example of the data provided by such analyses.

The sample sites that demonstrated intermediate agreement, Guiro Yoro Mandou and Missira, also contain systematic similarities in that both sites demonstrated a dynamic of cultivation that the remote sensing analysis was unable to capture (see Guiro Yoro Mandou and Missira in Tables 5.4 and 5.5). In Guiro Yoro Mandou the MODIS analysis indicates an increase in wooded cover in some areas and a loss of natural vegetation in other areas due to cropland expansion. However, the FGD results clarify that this site has seen considerable planting of mango and cashew trees. The site is therefore clearly degraded due to expanding croplands, declining yields, and loss of natural vegetation, but the remote sensing estimates have difficulty capturing these dynamics due to the tree-crops planted. In Missira, on the other hand, the MODIS and FGD analysis agree on a decrease in forested area, but show opposite trends in cropland: MODIS indicates a loss while the FGD indicates increased cropland extent. This difference is likely due to patterns of fallowing and regeneration, as indicated by the FGD. This same pattern of regenerating fallowed fields may account, at least in part, for the demonstrated increases in NDVI measured by Landsat. There may, in fact, be a number of competing processes at work as increasing cropland area is causing deforestation, but regeneration of fallowed fields is increasing natural vegetation cover. Similarly the site has experienced water erosion and a perceived decrease in crop values but also reports an increased yields in recent years.

In Talibdji, the site that demonstrated the lowest level of agreement, uncertainties in the remote sensing dataset compound with dynamic local processes to confound agreement on the status of the site (see Talibdji in Tables 5.4 and 5.5). The long-term NDVI trend for Talibdji showed no coherent pattern, although it demonstrated degradation in recent years (2000–2005). Figure 5.4 demonstrates the data derived from the remote sensing analysis for Talibdji. The GLS Landsat data showed no coherent trend for NDVI, MODIS land cover showed many shifts in

Table 5.4 Summary of the focus group discussion results for sample sites in Senegal

Site	Changes in land use	Yields and cropping intensity	Forest cover	Perception of long-term trends in degradation	Unobservable using remote sensing
Talibdji	Fairly stable land cover	Declining yields	Minor deforestation	Forests provide less value, grasslands/livestock provide greater value. Decrease in cropland value due to erosion	Wind erosion, gullies due to water erosion, laterite soil
Niassene	Grassland/shrubs replaced with crops	Declining yields	Deforestation	Livestock have become more important, erosion has decreased value of cropland, forests have declined in value	Wind erosion
Missira	Decrease in wooded cover, increase in grasslands. Increase in cropland extent	Mixed crop intensification, improved yields	Minor deforestation	Decrease in crop and livestock value, stable value for forests	Regeneration from fallowing, development of new avg areas. Water erosion
Guiro Yoro Mandou	Decreased natural vegetation, increased cropland	Decrease in cropping intensity and yields	Deforestation	Decrease in crop, livestock and forest values due to land degradation and climate	Cashew/mango fields may be considered increase in forest cover by remote sensing
Gomone	Decreased natural vegetation, increased cropland and area for residences	Decrease in yields, slight increase in cropping intensity	Deforestation	Decrease in crop and forest values due to land degradation and climate. Livestock saw an increase in importance but potential drop in overall value	Wind erosion. Livestock trampling vegetation. Laterite outcrop
Diakha Madina	Land-cover change mixed. Decrease in grassland and shrubland, increase in cropland	Increased cropping intensity but decreased yields	Forest regrowth	Decrease in cropland value due to land degradation	Water erosion, sand mining
Bantanto	Decrease in natural vegetation, increase in crop cover	Decrease in cropping intensity and yields	Minor deforestation	Perceived decreasing value of cropland, forests and livestock due to degradation	Salinization of cropland and erosion due to water

Table 5.5 Summary of remote sensing analyses for sample sites in Senegal

Site	MODIS land-cover change	Change in Landsat NDVI	Long-term trends in Landsat NDVI
Talibdji	Increases in wooded land cover. Many shifts in cropland extent in both directions (gain/loss) with a net increase in natural vegetation	Spatially coherent patterns of intensive NDVI change. Normally distributed with nearly all values negative	NDVI shows no coherent trend, increasing and decreasing over the time period
Niassene	Loss of natural vegetation to cropland	Spatially coherent patterns of intensive NDVI change. Normally distributed with a mean at a slight decrease in NDVI	Steady increase in NDVI from 1975 to 2000, but a sharp decrease in recent years
Missira	Deforestation but increase in natural vegetation due to decreased cropland cover	Scattered decreases with large spatially coherent regions of improvement. Largely distributed towards improvement	Consistently increasing NDVI during the study period
Guiro Yoro Mandou	Widespread transition towards more wooded land cover, but also significant loss of natural vegetation to cropland	Spatially coherent patterns of intensive NDVI change, largely negative distribution of changes	Fluctuating NDVI with a slight overall increase. Degraded in recent years
Gomone	Major decrease in natural vegetation due to increasing cropland	Degraded but with few spatially coherent patterns. About 1/4th of the distribution positive	Sharp increase from 1975/1990 to 2000, but a decrease in recent years
Diakha Madina	Minor loss of wooded land cover, but increase in natural vegetation	largely positive, but skewed with a negative tail due to Landsat image tiling	Consistently increasing NDVI during the study period
Bantanto	Minor increased woodland cover, but increase in cropland at expense of natural vegetation	Largely negative distribution of changes in NDVI	Fluctuating NDVI with a slight overall increase. Degraded in recent years

cropland extent in both directions, while the FGD indicated stable cropland. These discrepancies likely indicate a system of fallowing or rotating fields that is not captured well in the remote sensing analyses. The FGD and MODIS analyses also disagree on wooded cover, which is likely because the MODIS land cover classes that dominate Talibdji have poor user accuracy (many below 50 %, see Table 5.6), meaning that misclassifications are likely (Friedl et al. 2010). The FGD, meanwhile, revealed that erosion has decreased yields and therefore the value of crops, which would not have shown up in the NDVI analysis.

Table 5.6 User's accuracy for MODIS MCD12Q1 land cover classifications

Land cover class	User's accuracy (%)
Evergreen needleleaf forest	78.0
Deciduous needleleaf forest	83.1
Evergreen broadleaf forest	90.4
Deciduous broadleaf forest	75.9
Mixed forest	53.1
Closed shrubland	47.0
Open shrubland	74.1
Woody savanna	34.3
Savanna	39.0
Grasslands	55.9
Permanent wetlands	96.4
Cropland	92.8
Cropland/natural vegetation mosaic	27.5
Snow	96.8
Barren	92.7
Water	99.3

Niger Sample Sites

In addition to Senegal, six sites were chosen in Niger to compare the FGD and remote sensing results. Only two of the sites chosen have FGD results due to data collecting issues. Sites containing only remote sensing data were still analyzed to see whether agreements existed. Figure 5.7 illustrates the six sites chosen, which have a range of agro-ecological zones, and include both areas of degraded and improved land from the Le et al. (2014) dataset. Of the two sites with FGD results, Tiguey had high agreement (3.5/4) and Koné Béri had low agreement (2/4). Out of the four sites without FGD results, three showed a moderate to high level of agreement between the remote sensing datasets (2/3–3/3) and one showed a high level of disagreement (0/3), as shown in Table 5.7.

Similar to the Senegal results, sites showing a high level of agreement were mostly degraded. Tiguey for example, one of the two sites with FGD results, showed a conversion of grassland to cropland in the MODIS analysis and a recent decrease in NDVI (although historically NDVI increased from 1975 to 2000) (Table 5.9). Another change contributing to degradation was deforestation indicated by both the MODIS and FGD data (Table 5.8). Sites showing a moderate to high level of agreement without FGD results are Babaye, Bazaga, and Béla Bérim, all of which are mostly degraded. Béla Bérim showed 100 % agreement. The MODIS results indicate a decrease in wooden cover here where conversion to grassland is

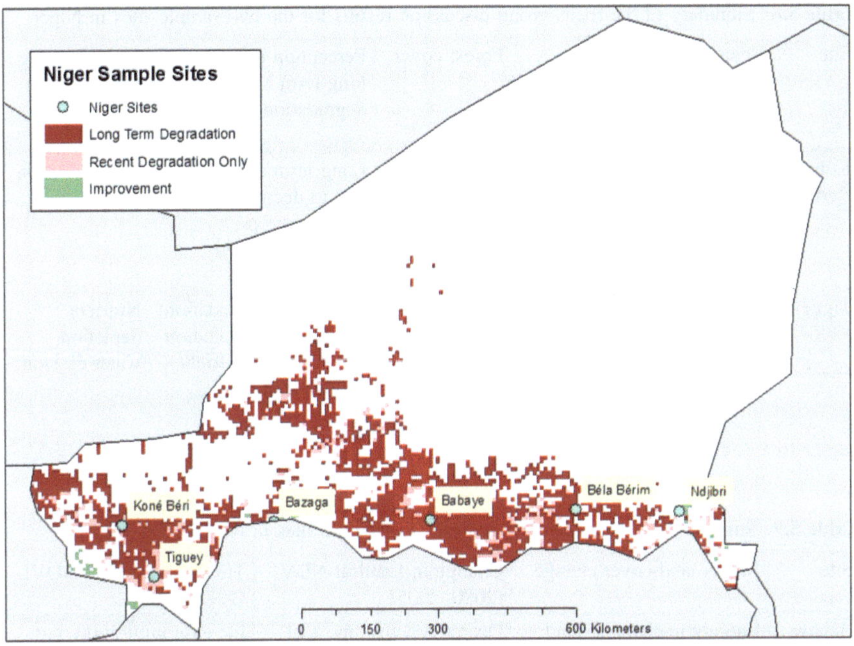

Fig. 5.7 Selected ground truthing sites in Niger. *Note Dark red* indicates pixels that demonstrate both long-term degradation as well as degradation in recent (2000–2006) years, *green pixels* indicate sites with improved land

Table 5.7 Agreement between the Le et al. (2014) land degradation map, the focus group discussions (FGD), and the independent remote sensing analyses for each of the six sites in Niger

Site	Le et al. (2014) assessment	FGD assessment	Landsat NDVI (2000–2005)	MODIS land-cover change	Agreement
Babaye	Degraded	N/A	Degraded	Improved	2/3
Bazaga	Improved	N/A	Degraded	Degraded	2/3
Béla Bérim	Degraded	N/A	Degraded	Degraded	3/3
Koné Béri	Degraded	Degraded	Improved	Improved	2/4
Ndjibri	Improved	N/A	Degraded	Mixed	0/3
Tiguey	Degraded	Degraded	Degraded	Mixed	3.5/4

occurring. Babaye and Bazaga had somewhat mixed results, and without the FGD results it is more difficult to interpret what is actually occurring.

Two sites showed less agreement, Ndjibri with 0/3 agreement and Koné Béri with 2/4 agreement. The FGD results indicate that Koné Béri had a decrease in crop

Table 5.8 Summary of the focus group discussion results for the two sample sites in Niger

Site	Changes in land use	Yields and cropping intensity	Forest cover	Perception of long-term trends in degradation	Unobservable using remote sensing
Koné Béri	Decrease in cropland. Increase in shrubland and bare soil	Increased intensity but decreased yields	Severe deforestation	Long term degradation due to decreasing value of crops, deforestation and ensuing erosion	Water erosion
Tiguey	Decrease in grasslands, increase in croplands	Static cropping intensity, decreased yields	Moderate deforestation	Long-term degradation due to overexploitation and too little nutrient recirculation. Extensive deforestation	Nutrient depletion, water erosion

Table 5.9 Summary of remote sensing analyses for sample sites in Niger

Site	Modis land-cover change	Change in Landsat NDVI (2000–2005)	Trends in Landsat NDVI (1975–2005)
Babaye	Largely unchanged land cover. Increase in wooded cover but loss of grasslands	Decrease across most of the area. Some areas have a mixed pattern of spatial change	Increase until 2000, but then degrades sharply back down to ~1990 levels
Bazaga	Changes in cropland extent both directions, net increase. Decrease in wooded cover with increases in barren and grasslands	Coherent spatial pattern of decrease. Most areas demonstrate large decreases	No coherent pattern. Decrease to 1990, increase to 2000, decrease to 2005
Béla Bérim	Largely unchanged land cover. Decrease in wooded cover but gain of grasslands	Small magnitude changes, spatially coherent and largely decreasing	Increase to 2000, decrease in recent years to 2005 only slightly above 1975 levels
Koné Béri	Both gain and loss of wooded cover, but slight net increases with additional increase from barren to grassland	Spatially coherent patterns of primarily improvement, but ravine in study area shows degradation	Static from 1975 to 1990, decrease to 2000 but increase in recent years to 2005
Ndjibri	Both gain and loss of wooded cover and grasslands. Slight net decrease in wooded cover and larger net increase in grasslands	Large spatially coherent patterns of change, largely decrease in recent years of large magnitude	Static from 1975 to 1990, increase to 2000 but decrease in recent years to 2005 down to below 1975 levels
Tiguey	Loss of grasslands to cropland. Increase in wooded cover from grasslands	Somewhat spotty spatial patterns of change, largely negative changes but some positive	Steady increase to 2000, decrease in recent years to 2005, but still above 1990 levels

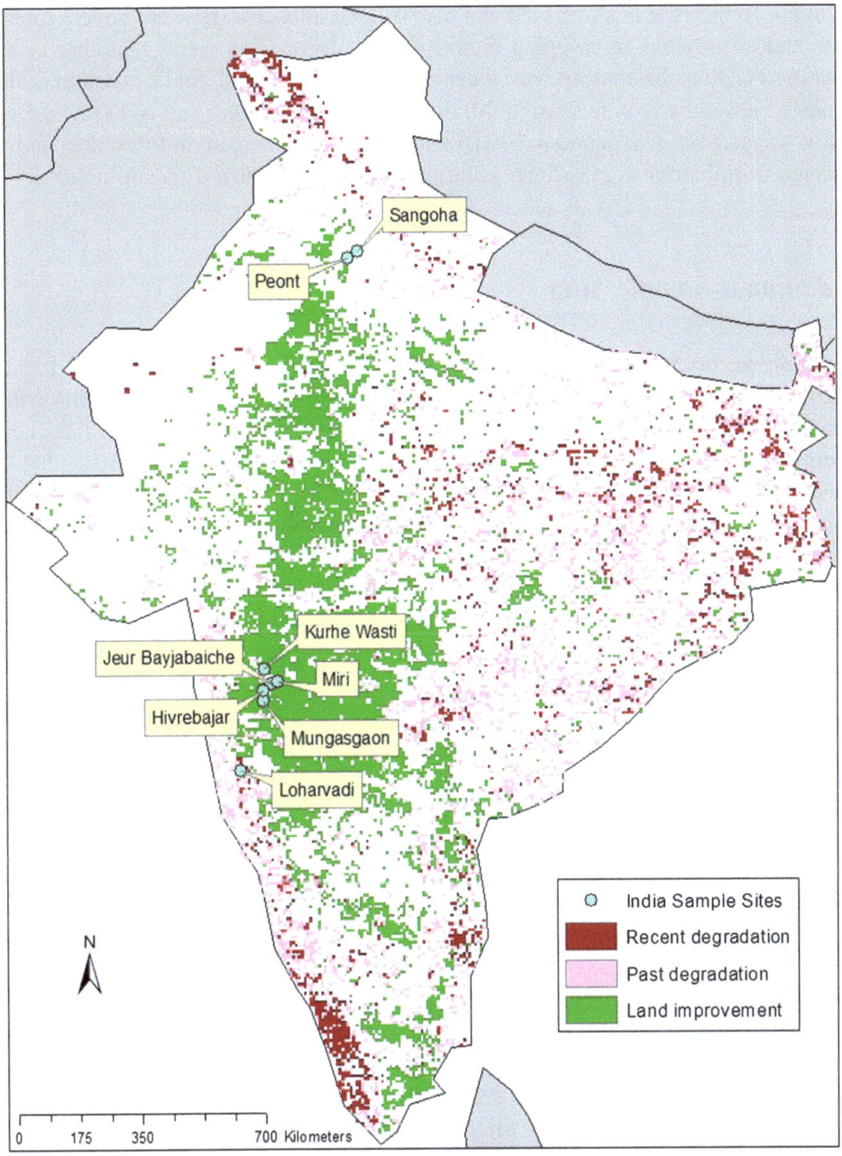

Fig. 5.8 Selected ground truthing sites in India. *Note dark red* indicates pixels that demonstrate both long-term degradation as well as degradation in recent (2000–2006) years, *green pixels* indicate sites with improved land

land but an increase in shrub land and bare soil. Results also showed a severe forest loss and an increase in cropping intensity but a decrease in yields. Another issue that the FGD results showed was water erosion, which would not be an observable change viewed by remote sensing. MODIS land-cover changes and NDVI however show an increase in vegetation. MODIS shows a slight increase in forest area and a change from barren to grassland. Landsat NDVI trends show a recent increase.

Additional Sample Sites

In addition to Niger and Senegal, study sites within the countries of India, Uzbekistan, Tanzania, and Ethiopia were chosen to compare survey results with remote sensing datasets. The study sites within these countries differ in that they were not chosen to represent degraded and improved areas of the Le et al. (2014) dataset but rather areas that were most successful for conducting interviews with local stakeholders. Study sites that did not intersect with either degraded or improved pixels of the Le et al. (2014) dataset were considered to have mixed results. A benefit to this analysis is the comparison of improved or degraded areas not identified by the Le et al. (2014) dataset with the survey and other remote sensing results. Following are comparisons of the survey results with the remote sensing datasets.

India Sample Sites

Figure 5.8 illustrates the eight sites chosen in India. The site with the highest agreement was Hivrebajar (3.5/4). Other sites with high agreement were Sangoha Jeur and Bayjabaiche both 3/4 agreement.

In general, study sites in India showed many mixed results. The highest agreement was in Hivrebajar at 3.5/4. Unlike the previous countries, this site showed both a high level of agreement and mostly improvement. Almost all sites fluctuated between improvement and degradation, with many sites showing mixed categories. The main reason for this is that many of these sites had fluctuating agriculture between years. The MODIS land cover data showed changes within cropland but the cropland area itself was mostly static. Changes in agricultural intensity and crops grown in this area could have wide ranging effects on both the Landsat NDVI and the Le et al. (2014) data. This alone can cause discrepancies between datasets. Another issue with agreement was between the FGD results and the NDVI and MODIS land cover data. In most cases the FGD results had different results than NDVI and/or MODIS land cover, although tended to agree more with the Le et al. (2014) dataset (Table 5.10).

Table 5.10 Agreement between the Le et al. (2014) land degradation map, the focus group discussions (FGD), and the independent remote sensing analyses for each of the eight sites in India

Site	Le assessment	FGD assessment	Landsat NDVI (2000–2005)	MODIS land-cover change	Agreement
Jeur Bayjabaiche	Improved	Mixed	Improved	Mixed	3/4
Miri	Improved	Degraded	Improved	Mixed	2.5/4
Loharvadi	Improved	Degraded	Improved	Mixed	2.5/4
Kurhe Wasti	Mixed	Degraded	Improved	Mixed	2/4
Mungasgaon	Improved	Improved	Degraded	Mixed	2.5/4
Hivrebajar	Improved	Improved	Improved	Mixed	3.5/4
Peont	Mixed	Mixed	Degraded	Degraded	2/4
Sangoha	Mixed	Mixed	Degraded	Mixed	3/4

Uzbekistan Sample Sites

Figure 5.9 illustrates the six sites chosen in Uzbekistan. The site with the highest agreement was Khorezm (4/4). Other sites with high agreement were Shirin KFI (3/4) and Fazli (3.5/4).

Similar to Senegal the highest agreement was in areas of degradation. Khorezm showed 4/4 agreement, followed closely by Fazli, which had 3.5/4 agreement due to the FGD data being unavailable for this village. A lot of the FGD results showed mixed degradation in Uzbekistan. Similar to India, many of the villages had rotating cropland areas. Almost all sites showed a resent decrease in Landsat NDVI, much of this decrease could be due to changing agricultural practices. In many cases the MODIS land cover showed some areas being converted to agriculture while other areas nearby were reverted to natural land. This could be due to the nature of agricultural practice rather than permanent or long-term land-cover conversion (Table 5.11).

Tanzania Sample Sites

Figure 5.10 illustrates the eight sites chosen in Tanzania. The sites with the highest agreement were Mazingara and Mamba (4/4). These sites also appeared to be the sites with the most degradation. Other sites with higher agreement that were mostly degraded were Sejeli, Maya Maya, Zuzu, and Dakawa (3/4).

Similar to Senegal the highest agreement was in areas of degradation. Mamba and Mazingara both showed 4/4 agreement. The Le et al. (2014) dataset and the

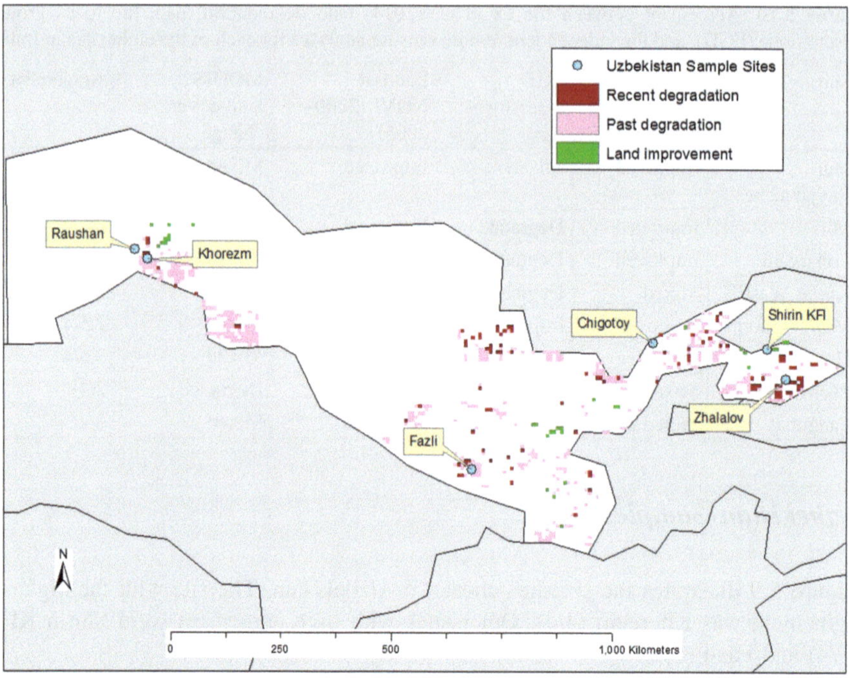

Fig. 5.9 Selected ground truthing sites in Uzbekistan. *Note Dark red* indicates pixels that demonstrate both long-term degradation as well as degradation in recent (2000–2006) years, *green pixels* indicate sites with improved land

Table 5.11 Agreement between the Le et al. (2014) land degradation map, the focus group discussions (FGD), and the independent remote sensing analyses for each of the eight sites in Uzbekistan

Site	Le assessment	FGD assessment	Landsat NDVI (2000–2005)	MODIS land-cover change	Agreement
Chigotoy	Mixed	Mixed	Degraded	Improved	2/4
Zhalalov	Mixed	Mixed	Improved	Degraded	2/4
Shirin KFI	Mixed	Mixed	Degraded	Mixed	3/4
Fazli	Degraded	Mixed	Degraded	Degraded	3.5/4
Khorezm	Degraded	Degraded	Degraded	Degraded	4/4
Raushan	Degraded	Improved	Degraded	Mixed	2.5/4

FGD results showed a near consensus. MODIS land-cover change also showed a high level of agreement. Most of the disagreement occurred with the Landsat NDVI data which showed improvement for many villages that the other datasets showed

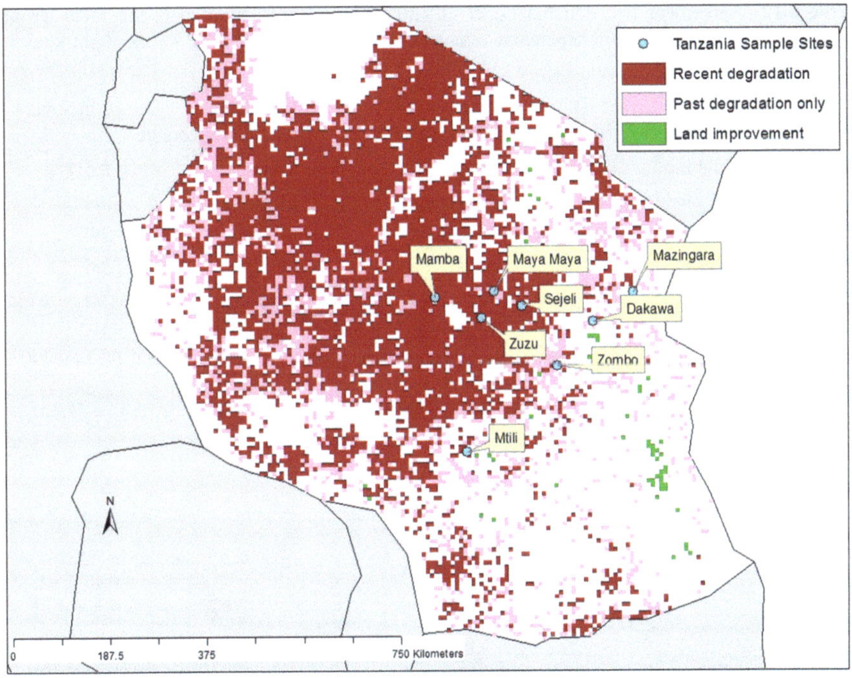

Fig. 5.10 Selected ground truthing sites in Tanzania. *Note Dark red* indicates pixels that demonstrate both long-term degradation as well as degradation in recent (2000–2006) years, *green pixels* indicate sites with improved land

degradation. Some of the sites, such as Sejeli, Zombo, and Zuzu, that showed recent Landsat NDVI improvement, had mostly declining NDVI values from 1975 to 2000 indicating degradation (Table 5.12).

Ethiopia Sample Sites

Figure 5.11 illustrates the eight sites chosen in Ethiopia. The site with the highest agreement was Kawo (4/4). The rest of the sites showed mostly poor agreement at 2/4 or less.

The highest agreement was in an area of degradation for the site Kawo. The rest of the sites in Ethiopia showed poor agreement at 2/4 or less. The Le et al. (2014) dataset and the FGD results showed either mixed or degradation results, however the Landsat NDVI and MODIS land-cover change datasets also showed some sites having improvement. One issue was that all of the sites except Kawo and Koka

Table 5.12 Agreement between the Le et al. (2014) land degradation map, the focus group discussions (FGD), and the independent remote sensing analyses for each of the eight sites in Tanzania

Site	Le assessment	FGD assessment	Landsat NDVI (2000–2005)	MODIS land-cover change	Agreement
Zombo	Degraded	Degraded	Improved	Mixed	2.5/4
Dakawa	Degraded	Degraded	Improved	Degraded	3/4
Mtili	Mixed	Improved	Degraded	Mixed	2/4
Sejeli	Degraded	Degraded	Improved	Degraded	3/4
Zuzu	Degraded	Degraded	Improved	Degraded	3/4
Maya Maya	Degraded	Degraded	Improved	Degraded	3/4
Mamba	Degraded	Degraded	Degraded	Degraded	4/4
Mazingara	Degraded	Degraded	Degraded	Degraded	4/4

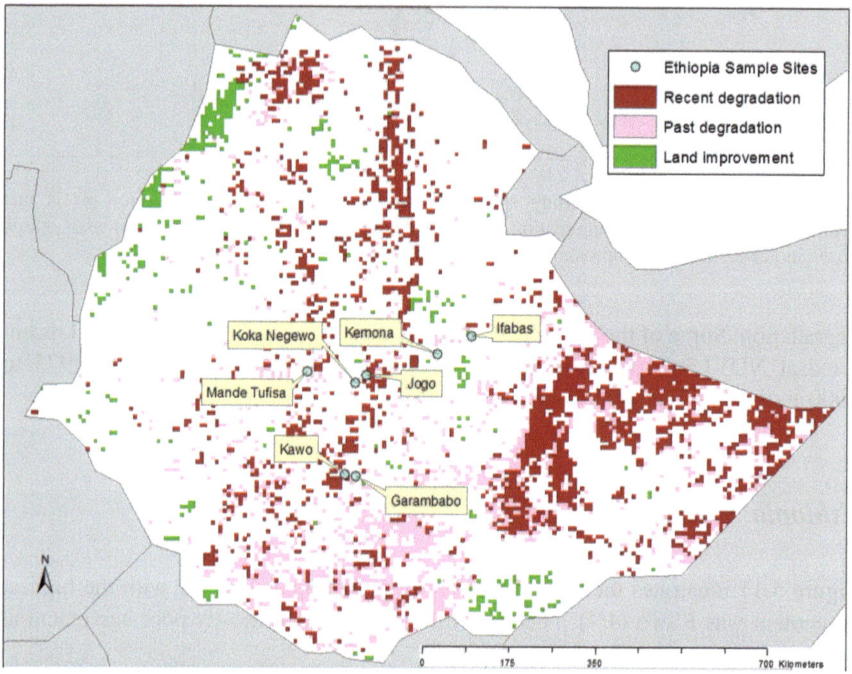

Fig. 5.11 Selected ground truthing sites in Ethiopia. *Note Dark red* indicates pixels that demonstrate both long-term degradation as well as degradation in recent (2000–2006) years, *green pixels* indicate sites with improved land

Negewo did not intersect the Le et al. (2014) data so they were given a mixed result. This was only a small part of the lower agreement between datasets since most of the sites also have confusion within the remote sensing datasets (Table 5.13).

Table 5.13 Agreement between the Le et al. (2014) land degradation map, the focus group discussions (FGD), and the independent remote sensing analyses for each of the eight sites in Ethiopia

Site	Le assessment	FGD assessment	Landsat NDVI (2000–2005)	MODIS land-cover change	Agreement
Kemona	Mixed	Mixed	Improved	Improved	2/4
Ifabas	Mixed	Degraded	Improved	Mixed	2/4
Mande Tufisa	Mixed	Degraded	Improved	Mixed	2/4
Jogo	Mixed	Degraded	Improved	Improved	1/4
Garambado	Mixed	Mixed	Degraded	Degraded	2/4
Kawo	Degraded	Degraded	Degraded	Degraded	4/4
Koka Negewo	Degraded	Mixed	Improved	Mixed	2/4

Conclusions

Land degradation is a growing issue as an expanding population with changing and increasing consumption patterns is placing a higher demand on the land. Properly identifying areas of degradation is vital in creating policies aimed at restoring the land. This study evaluated past efforts at identifying areas of land degradation hotspots by comparing these past results with field surveys, MODIS land-cover data, and Landsat NDVI data. This evaluation showed that, similar to the global analysis of GIMMS NDVI and Landsat NDVI, the final Le et al. (2014) dataset displayed intermediate agreement with the field results. Many of the same problems identified in the GLADIS field evaluation in South Africa persist in the Le et al. (2014) dataset. Discrepancies relating to processes that are unobservable using remote sensing, such as erosion and salinization, pervaded the sample sites. Dynamic farming landscapes posed an additional challenge to the NDVI and land-cover change analyses, particularly the practice of following fields and planting permanent tree crops. Finally, the coarse resolution of the global dataset was unable to disentangle coexisting processes of improvement and degradation from one-another on spatial scales finer than ~8 km.

Additional discrepancies exist, such as the data resolution gap between each of the data sets (8 km^2 AVHRR, 1 km^2 MODIS, and the 30 m^2 Landsat data). Also, although land-cover change is a good indicator of land degradation, it is not directly comparable with changes in NDVI. It can be difficult to identify whether deforestation or conversion of shrubland to cropland, will lead to land degradation in the future. Land degradation is a creeping process, often taking many years to manifest in issues such as soil fertility loss and erosion.

The Le et al. (2014) dataset makes considerable progress in that it corrects for systematic problems associated with using NDVI alone as an indicator of land degradation, and addresses the issue of atmospheric fertilization and NDVI saturation. However, the dataset does not identify or treat differently areas of forest management or other temporary land-cover/land-use changes that may not be associated with land degradation. The Le et al. (2014) dataset was developed with the intent of identifying "hot spots" of land degradation, and further progress is needed before global maps may be used as a proxy for land degradation.

References

Bai, Z., & Dent, D. (2009). Recent land degradation and improvement in China. *Ambio, 38*, 150–156.

Bai, Z. & Dent, D. (2008) Verification report on the GLADA land degradation study: Land degradation and improvement in South Africa identification by remote sensing by D J Pretorius Department of Agriculture.

Bai, Z. G., Dent, D. L., Olsson, L., & Schaepman, M. E. (2008). Proxy global assessment of land degradation. *Soil Use and Management, 24*, 223–234.

Beck, C., Grieser, J. & Rudolf, B. (2005). *A new monthly precipitation climatology for the global land areas for the period 1951–2000.* Climate Status Report 2004, pp. 181–190. German Weather Service, Offenbach.

Beck, H. E., McVicar, T. R., van Dijk, A. I. J. M., Schellekens, J., de Jeu, R. A. M., & Bruijnzeel, L. A. (2011). Global evaluation of four AVHRR–NDVI data sets: Intercomparison and assessment against Landsat imagery. *Remote Sensing of Environment, 115*, 2547–2563.

Bicheron, P., Defourny, P., Brockmann, C., Schouten, L., Vancutsem, C., & Huc, M., et al. (2008). *GLOBCOVER: Products description and validation report.* http://due.esrin.esa.int/globcover/LandCover_V2.2/GLOBCOVER_Products_Description_Validation_Report_I2.1.pdf. ESA Globcover Project, led by MEDIAS-France/POSTEL.

Brown, M. E., Pinzon, J. E., Didan, K., Morisette, J. T. & Tucker, C. J. (2006). Evaluation of the consistency of long-term NDVI time series derived from AVHRR, and LandSAT ETM+ Sensors.

Center for International Earth Science Information Network (CIESIN), Centro Internacional de Agricultura Tropical (CIAT). (2005). *Gridded population of the world version 3 (GPWv3): Population density grids.* http://sedac.ciesin.columbia.edu/gpw (Accessed on May 01 2013). Socio-economic Data and Applications Center (SEDAC), Columbia University, Palisades, NY.

FAO. (2005). *Global forest resources assessment 2005.* Progress towards sustainable forest management. Forestry Paper 147.

Fensholt, R., & Proud, S. R. (2012). Evaluation of earth observation based global long term vegetation trends—Comparing GIMMS and MODIS global NDVI time series. *Remote Sensing of Environment, 119*, 131–147.

Friedl, M. A., Sulla-Menashe, D., Tan, B., Schneider, A., Ramankutty, N., Sibley, A., & Huang, X. (2010). MODIS collection 5 global land cover: Algorithm refinements and characterization of new datasets. *Remote Sensing of Environment, 114*, 168–182.

Harris, I., Jones, P. D., Osborn, T. J., & Lister, D. H. (2014). Updated high-resolution grids of monthly climatic observations—The CRU TS3.10 dataset. *International Journal of Climatology, 34*, 623–642.

Hansen, M. C., Potapov, P. V, Moore, R., Hancher, M., Turubanova, S. A., & Tyukavina, A. et al. (2013). High-resolution global maps of 21st-century forest cover change. *Science, 342*, 850–3.

Hansen, M. C., Stehman, S. V., & Potapov, P. V. (2010). Quantification of global gross forest cover loss. *Proceedings of the National Academy of Sciences of the United States of America, 107*, 8650–8655.

Huete, A., Didan, K., Miura, T., Rodriguez, E., Gao, X., & Ferreira, L. (2002). Overview of the radiometric and biophysical performance of the MODIS vegetation indices. *Remote Sensing of Environment, 83*, 195–213.

Huete, A., Didan, K., Leeuwen, W. Van Jacobson, A., Solanos, R. & Laing, T. (1999) MODIS vegetation index (MOD 13) algorithm theoretical basis document.

Iizumi, T., Yokozawa, M., Sakurai, G., Travasso, M. I., Romanenkov, V., Oettli, P., et al. (2014). Historical changes in global yields: Major cereal and legume crops from 1982 to 2006. *Global Ecology and Biogeography, 23*, 346–357.

Jones, P., & Harris, I. (2008). *CRU Time Series (TS) high resolution gridded datasets*. http://badc.nerc.ac.uk/view/badc.nerc.ac.uk__ATOM__dataent_1256223773328276 (Accessed on May 01 2013). NCAS British Atmospheric Data Centre Climate Research Unit (CRU), University of East Anglia.

JRC. (2003). *Global Land Cover 2000 database*. European Commission, Joint Research Centre. Available at http://www-gem.jrc.it/glc2000.

Le, Q. B., Tamene, L., & Vlek, P. L. G. (2012). Multi-pronged assessment of land degradation in West Africa to assess the importance of atmospheric fertilization in masking the processes involved. *Global and Planetary Change, 92–93*, 71–81.

Le, Q. B., Nkonya, E., & Mirzabaev, A. (2014). *Biomass Productivity-Based Mapping of Global Land Degradation Hotspots*. ZEF-Discussion Papers on Development Policy No. 193. University of Bonn.

Liang, S., & Xiao, Z. (2012). *Global land surface products: Leaf area index product data collection (1985–2010)*. Beijing Normal University.

Lobell, D. B., Lesch, S. M., Corwin, D. L., Ulmer, M. G., Anderson, K. A., Potts, D. J., et al. (2009). Regional-scale assessment of soil salinity in the red river valley using multi-year MODIS EVI and NDVI. *Journal of Environmental Quality, 39*, 35–41.

Mitchell, T. D., & Jones, P. D. (2005). An improved method of constructing a database of monthly climate observations and associated high-resolution grids. *International Journal of Climate, 25*, 693–712.

Nachtergaele, F., Petri, M., Biancalani, R., Van Lynden, G., & Van Velthuizen, H. (2010). Global Land Degradation Information System (GLADIS). Beta Version. An Information Database for Land Degradation Assessment at Global Level. *Land Degradation Assessment in Drylands Technical Report,* no. 17. FAO, Rome, Italy.

Nelson, G. C., & Robertson, R. D. (2008). Green gold or green wash: Environmental consequences of biofuels in the developing world. *Review of Agricultural Economics, 2008, 30*(3), 517–529.

Running, S. W., Heinsch, F. A., Zhao, M., Reeves, M., & Hashimoto, H. (2004). A continuous satellite-derived measure of global terrestrial production. *BioScience, 54*, 547–560.

Townshend, J. R., Masek, J. G., Huang, C., Vermote, E. F., Gao, F., Channan, S., et al. (2012). Global characterization and monitoring of forest cover using Landsat data: opportunities and challenges. *International Journal of Digital Earth, 5*, 373–397.

Trabucco, A., & Zomer, R. J. (2009). *Global Aridity Index (Global-Aridity) and Global Potential Evapo-Transpiration (Global-PET) Geospatial Database*. CGIAR Consortium for Spatial Information, CGIAR-CSI GeoPortal http://www.csi.cgiar.org.

Tucker, C. J., Pinzon, J. E., Brown, M. E., Slayback, D. A., Pak, E. W., Mahoney, R., et al. (2005). An extended AVHRR 8-km NDVI data set compatible with MODIS and SPOT vegetation NDVI data. *International Journal of Remote Sensing, 26*, 4485–4498.

Voss, K. A., Famiglietti, J. S., Lo, M., Linage, C., Rodell, M., & Swenson, S. C. (2013). Groundwater depletion in the Middle East from GRACE with implications for transboundary water management in the Tigris-Euphrates-Western Iran region. *Water Resources Research, 49*, 904–914.

Wessels, K. J. (2009). Letter to the editor. *Soil Use and Management, 25*, 91–92.

Xiao, Z., Liang, S,. Wang, J,. et al. (2013). Use of General Regression Neural Networks for Generating the GLASS Leaf Area Index Product from Time Series MODIS Surface Reflectance. *IEEE Transactions on Geoscience and Remote Sensing*, doi:10.1109/TGRS.2013.2237780.

Zhao, M., & Running, S. W. (2010). Drought-induced reduction in global terrestrial net primary production from 2000 through 2009. *Science, 329*, 940–943.

Chapter 6
Global Cost of Land Degradation

Ephraim Nkonya, Weston Anderson, Edward Kato, Jawoo Koo, Alisher Mirzabaev, Joachim von Braun and Stefan Meyer

Abstract Land degradation—defined by the Millennium Ecosystem Assessment report as the long-term loss of ecosystems services—is a global problem, negatively affecting the livelihoods and food security of billions of people. Intensifying efforts, mobilizing more investments and strengthening the policy commitment for addressing land degradation at the global level needs to be supported by a careful evaluation of the costs and benefits of action versus costs of inaction against land degradation. Consistent with the definition of land degradation, we adopt the Total Economic Value (TEV) approach to determine the costs of land degradation and use remote sensing data and global statistical databases in our analysis. The results show that the annual costs of land degradation due to land use and land cover change (LUCC) are about US$231 billion per year or about 0.41 % of the global GDP of US$56.49 trillion in 2007. Contrary to past global land degradation assessment studies, land degradation is severe in both tropical and temperate countries. However, the losses from LUCC are especially high in Sub-Saharan Africa, which accounts for 26 % of the total global costs of land degradation due to LUCC. However, the local tangible losses (mainly provisioning services) account only for 46 % of the total cost of land degradation and the rest of the cost is due to the losses of ecosystem services (ES) accruable largely to beneficiaries other than the local land users. These external ES losses include carbon sequestration, biodiversity, genetic information and cultural services. This implies that the global

E. Nkonya (✉) · E. Kato · J. Koo
International Food Policy Research Institute, 2033 K Street NW, Washington, D.C. 20006, USA
e-mail: e.nkonya@cgiar.org

W. Anderson
Department of Earth & Environmental ScienceLamont-Doherty Earth Observatory, Columbia University, 61 Route 9W, Palisades 10964, NY

A. Mirzabaev · J. von Braun
Center for Development Research (ZEF), University of Bonn, Water Flex Street 3, Bonn D-53113, Germany

S. Meyer
International Food Policy Research Institute, IFPRI Malawi office, Lilongwe 3, Malawi

E. Nkonya et al. (eds.), *Economics of Land Degradation and Improvement – A Global Assessment for Sustainable Development*,
DOI 10.1007/978-3-319-19168-3_6

community bears the largest cost of land degradation, which suggests that efforts to address land degradation should be done bearing in mind that the global community, as a whole, incurs larger losses than the local communities experiencing land degradation. The cost of soil fertility mining due to using land degrading management practices on maize, rice and wheat is estimated to be about US$15 billion per year or 0.07 % of the global GDP. Though these results are based on a crop simulation approach that underestimates the impact of land degradation and covers only three crops, they reveal the high cost of land degradation for the production of the major food crops of the world. Our simulations also show that returns to investment in action against land degradation are twice larger than the cost of inaction in the first six years alone. Moreover, when one takes a 30-year planning horizon, the returns are five dollars per each dollar invested in action against land degradation. The opportunity cost accounts for the largest share of the cost of action against land degradation. This explains why land users, often basing their decisions in very short-time horizons, could degrade their lands even when they are aware of bigger longer-term losses that are incurred in the process.

Keywords Land degradation · Total economic value · Land use/cover change · Ecosystem services · Global cost

Introduction

Land degradation—defined as persistent or long-term loss of ecosystem services, has recently gained a more prominent attention in national and international agendas, especially after the food crisis in 2008 with spiking food and land prices (von Braun 2013) and higher demands for biofuels. The rising concern for sustainable development and poverty reduction has also contributed to increased attention to sustainable land management. Land degradation affects the poor the most since they heavily depend on natural resources. Despite the increasing need for addressing land degradation, investments in sustainable land management remain limited—especially in low income countries. An FAO study on agricultural investment showed a declining public investment in agricultural sector in Sub-Saharan Africa (SSA) over the past three decades (FAO 2012), with the public expenditure per worker declining from US$152 in 1980–89 to only US$42 in 2005–07 (ibid).

As part of efforts to raise awareness of the cost of inaction against land degradation, this study is conducted to determine the cost of land degradation across regions and globally. The study makes new contributions to literature by adopting the Millennium Ecosystem Assessment (MEA 2005) definition of land degradation and, therefore, using the Total Economic Value (TEV) approach to determine the value of land degradation (see Nkonya et al. 2013).

This study contributes to literature significantly as it develops analytical methods that use TEV approaches and data that are easily available to allow regular economic assessment of land degradation and improvement. The analytical methods are presented in a simplified language to allow application across disciplines and different analytical skill levels of economics and ecology. The study also covers two major forms of land degradation—namely loss of value of ecosystem services due to land use change/cover (LUCC) of six major biomes and use of land degrading management practices on cropland and grazing lands that do not experience LUCC. The six major biomes include forest, shrublands, grasslands, cropland, bare land, and woodlands and they accounted for about 86 % of land area in 2001 (NASA 2014).

Even though this study uses TEV to reflect the broader concept of land degradation and includes six biomes, it does not comprehensively cover all forms of land degradation. We do not cover some forms of environmental degradation—such as over-application of fertilizers or agrochemicals that lead to eutrophication. We also do not cover degradation of forests, grasslands, shrublands and woodlands that did not experience LUCC. Additionally our study does not consider loss of wetlands—a biome that covers 550 million ha (Spiers 2001), which is about 4 % of global land area. This is due to lack of proper data to analyze loss of wetlands.

Our study does not analyze the impact land degradation on consumers of food, feed, etc. Our study also does not analyze indirect impacts of land degradation such as the increasing prices of land, migration, etc. These omissions are necessary to make the study tractable. Other studies could be commissioned to cover these gaps.

This paper is organized as follows. The next section discusses past studies on the costs of land degradation at regional or global levels. This is followed by a description of the analytical methods and data used in this study. The results section follows and the last concludes with policy implications.

Previous Global Studies on the Costs of Land Degradation

A number of studies have estimated the costs of land degradation at the global level. It is not our aim to conduct a comprehensive review of such studies, rather our objective is to highlight the different estimation methods and consequent wide variation of findings on the global costs of land degradation. The 12 studies reviewed are summarized in Table 6.1. The costs of land degradation range from US$17.58 billion to as high as US$9.4 trillion (both at 2007 values). Two major reasons explain the large variation of these estimates. First, the studies use different methodological approaches. Secondly, some studies evaluate only few biomes while others are more comprehensive and cover all major biomes. Dregne and Chou (1992) were among the earliest to evaluate the global costs of land degradation. Using a loss of productivity approach, they estimated that the global cost of cropland and grassland degradation in 1990 at US$43 billion. A more recent study, based on literature review, estimated the cost of land degradation to be about US $450 billion per year (UNCCD 2013). Using loss of carbon sink as an indicator of

Table 6.1 Global costs of land degradation of past studies

Author(s)	Annual cost reported (US$ billion)	Equiv. annual cost in 2007 US$ billion	Comments
FAO (2007)	40	40.00	Methods not reported
UNCCD (2013)	490	685.40	Review of literature
Trivedi et al. (2008)	43–65	41.4–62.6	Loss of carbon sink due to deforestation of tropical rainforests
Dregne and Chou (1992)	43	54.69	Loss of productivity of cropland and grassland
Basson (2010)	21	20.27	Off-site cost of soil erosion: (i) reduced water storage structures, with the replacement costs of silted-up reservoirs (ii) loss of hydroelectric power (HEP) and damage to HEP infrastructure (iii) reduction of irrigation reservoir
Myers et al. (2000)	300	361.15	Cost of protection of biodiversity loss
Costanza et al. (2014)	9400	9400.00	Benefit transfer approach to estimate the Total economic (TEV) of ecosystem services. Cost of terrestrial land degradation computed as net loss/gain of value of ecosystem services of terrestrial biomes
Trutcost (2014)	6900	6900.00	Literature review and government studies and stylized environmental evaluation methods of environmental pollution
Dodds et al. (2013)	900	800.73	Anthropogenic degradation of freshwater ecosystem services
Chiabai et al. (2011)	261[a]	277.07	Simulation using IMAGE 2.4 model of net present value of forest ecosystem services, 2000–2050

[a]Lower bound of the estimate increase in value of ecosystem services equal to US$61

land degradation, Trivedi et al. (2008) estimated the global cost of deforestation of tropical forests and rainforests was about US$43–65 billion. The cost of avoiding degradation could also be used to measure the cost of land degradation (Requier-Desjardins et al. 2011). Accordingly, Myers et al. (2000) estimated the cost of avoiding the loss of biodiversity to be about US$300 billion. Using replacement costs of silted up reservoirs, loss of hydroelectric power and reduction in irrigated production, Basson (2010) estimated the annual global cost of siltation of water reservoirs to be about $18.5 billion.

A more recent study by Costanza et al. (2014) uses the total economic value approach and estimated the net cost of terrestrial ecosystem services to be about US $9.9 trillion. As shown in Fig. 6.1, a large share of the loss of terrestrial ecosystems in this study came from wetlands degradation.

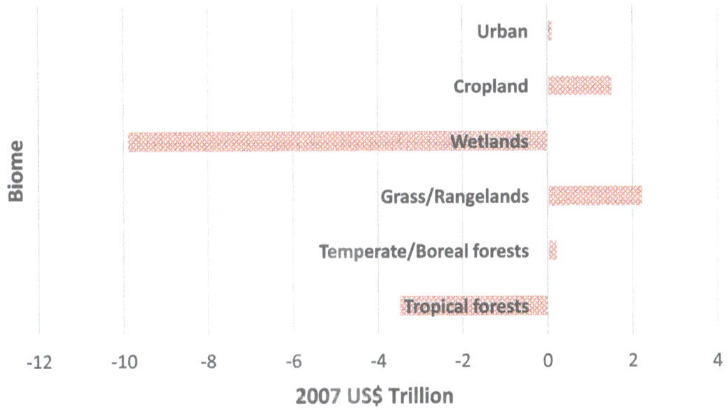

Fig. 6.1 Global value of change of ecosystem services, 1997–2007. *Source* Computed from Costanza et al. (2014)

The net loss of terrestrial ecosystem services is about US$9.4 trillion but the gross loss is US$13.4 of which wetlands loss accounts for 74 % and the remaining loss is accounted for by tropical forests. The other terrestrial biomes included in the study registered gains.

Unlike Costanza et al. (2014), Trucost (2014) directly estimated the environmental impacts of economic activities. Specifically, the environmental impacts were measured by the cost of land use, greenhouse gas emission, water consumption and air pollution. The direct measurement of environmental pollution by companies is a significant contribution of the Trucost (2014) study.

The review above shows that the costs of land degradation include a wide range of costs, an aspect which implies the difficulty of achieving a consensus on one specific costs estimate. As argued by Nkonya et al. (2013), this study approach bears in mind the data availability at the global level and the key elements that need to be taken into account in any global ELD assessment. A standardized procedure could, thus, allow the comparison of ELD values across studies.

To lay ground for the methodological approaches used in this study, the following section discusses the land use types and their major characteristics.

Land Use Types and Their Characteristics

We discuss the terrestrial land use types used in this analysis, highlighting their extent and importance across regions. We focus on seven major terrestrial land use types, namely forests, shrublands, grasslands, cropland, woodlands, urban and bare or barren lands.

Definition and Classification of Terrestrial Biomes and Land Use/Cover Types

There is a number of definition and classification of biomes that reflect the scientists' area of emphasis (McGinley 2014). For example, FAO defines forest as an area with a minimum coverage of 1 ha, with at least 10 % crown cover and with mature trees at least 2 m tall (FAO 2011). The definition explicitly includes open woodlands, such as those found in the African Sahel. This differs from the International Geosphere-biosphere Programme (IGBP) definition, in which a forest is an area with 60 % tree canopy coverage (Table 6.2). Miller (1990) includes shrublands in grasslands while IGBP assigns shrublands a separate biome. In this study we use the IGBP definitions since the MODIS data used are defined according to IGPBP.

The seven major terrestrial biomes covered in study account for about 86 % of the global land area in 2001. The rest of the area was covered by inland water bodies and wetlands. Wetlands cover less than 5 % of Earth's ice-free land surface (NASA 2014), but they play a key role in carbon and water cycles. For example, Costanza et al. (2014) estimated the cost of wetlands degradation to be about 2007 US$9.4 trillion/year or 50 % of the total annual cost of loss of terrestrial and marine ecosystem services estimated at 2007 US$20.2 trillion. However, we focus our analysis on the seven major biomes mentioned above.

Table 6.2 defines each biome while Fig. 6.2 reports the global extent of each biome in 2001 at the global level. The table below Fig. 6.2 reports the corresponding extent of each biome at region level. We use the Moderate Resolution

Table 6.2 Definition of biomes used in the study

Biome	IGBP definition
Forests	Woody vegetation with height >2 m and covering at least 60 % of land area. Forest trees divided into three categories: (i) Deciduous Broadleaf—broadleaf trees that shed leaves in annual cycles. (ii) Deciduous Needleleaf—as deciduous broadleaf but with narrow leaves. (iii) Evergreen Broadleaf Forests—broadleaf trees that remain green foliage throughout the year. (iv) needleleaf evergreen—like evergreen broadleaf but with narrow leaves
Grassland	Lands with herbaceous types of cover. Tree and shrub cover is less than 10 %
Cropland	Lands covered with temporary crops followed by harvest and a bare soil period (e.g., single and multiple cropping systems). Note, perennial woody crops are classified as forest or shrubland
Bare	Barren or Sparsely Vegetated (Bare Soil and Rocks). Lands with exposed soil, sand or rocks, with less than 10 % vegetated cover throughout the year
Shrublands	Vegetation with mainly shrubs or short trees (shrubs) of less than 2 m. Canopy of shrublands is fairly open and allows grasses and other short plants grow between the shrubs
Woodland	Biome with tree cover of 5–10 %, with trees reaching a height of 5 m at maturity

For more definitions, please see http://earthobservatory.nasa.gov/Experiments/Biome/vocabulary.php

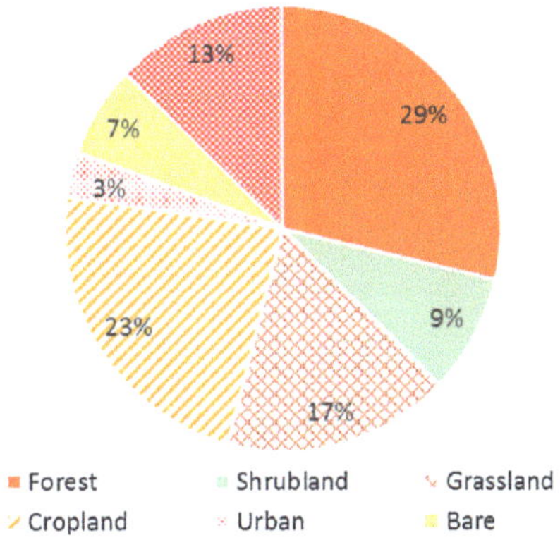

Region	Forest	Shrubland	Grassland	Cropland	Urban	Bare	Woodlands
	Area as percent of total land area						
SSA	21.88	11.21	20.21	18.1	2.58	11.41	14.6
LAC	37.36	8.79	22.48	14.66	5.46	3.16	8.11
NAM	39.16	5.94	8.37	36.11	2.61	0.93	6.89
East Asia	35.7	5.28	9.54	18.37	9.65	4.31	17.14
Oceania	37.4	15.9	17.96	15.19	0.19	3.72	9.65
South Asia	48.51	4.15	5.9	23.08	2.59	2.88	12.9
SE Asia	46.82	0.99	5.22	27.84	2.34	0.95	15.83
East Europe	28.83	4.45	7.85	50.31	2.88	0.63	5.06
West Europe	26	6	21.78	27.44	4.65	1.28	12.85
Global	28.72	8.62	16.75	23.22	3.26	6.69	12.74

Fig. 6.2 Extent of the major terrestrial biomes, 2001. *Note SSA* Sub-Saharan Africa; *LAC* Latin American Countries; *NAM* North America; *SE* South-east. See Appendix for countries in each region. *Source* Calculated from MODIS data

Imaging Spectroradiometer (MODIS) landcover data to analyze the land use and land cover change (LUCC). MODIS data are collected by NASA's two satellites (Terra (EOS AM) and Aqua (EOS PM)) and have three levels of resolutions (250, 500, and 1000 m) (NASA 2014) and were launched in December 1999. For our study we use the 1-km resolution that matches the International Geosphere-Biosphere Program (IGBP) land cover classification. The data include a much greater number of inputs (7 wavelengths, or "bands") as well as the enhanced minimum and maximum annual values of vegetation index, land surface temperature. The MODIS data are quality controlled and ground-truthed (Friedl et al. 2010). The overall accuracy of land use classification is about 75 % (Friedl et al. 2010). As will be discussed below, LUCC will be used as one form of land degradation or improvement.

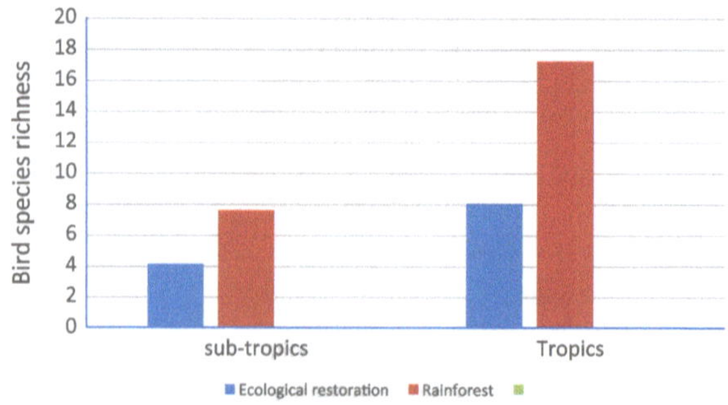

Fig. 6.3 Species bird richness in ecological restoration 10-year trees versus primary rainforest. *Source* Computed from Cateral et al. (2004)

Forest

The forests serve as the biggest terrestrial carbon sink as they store about 861 petragrams of Carbon (PgC) (Pan et al. 2011), which is about half the global terrestrial global carbon stock (FAO 2013). However, due to different definitions of forest by FAO and IGBP, the extent and land use change reported in this study could differ from those reported by FAO. Our analysis will look at the change in forest extent as land degradation/improvement even though other forms of land degradation or improvement may happen through changes of forest density. In the past two decades (1990–2010), global forest density—tree density per hectare—increased (Rautiainen et al. 2011). The increase was most pronounced in North America and Europe and the increase in Africa and South America was only modest. In Asia, forest density increased in 1990–2000 but decreased in 2000–2010 (ibid).

Loss and gain in biodiversity is another important aspect that changes as forest LUCC occurs. Unfortunately, biodiversity builds over many years and cannot be fully restored through reforestation and afforestation programs (CBD 2010). Newly planted forests have fewer tree species and lower fauna and flora biodiversity (Ibid). For example, a study of ecological restoration through replanting of rainforest in Australia showed that birds richness in planted rainforest was only about half of their reference rainforest (Fig. 6.3).

Grassland

According to the MODIS data, grassland covers 17 % of the land area (Fig. 6.2), but grassland could also include shrublands (Miller 1990; FAO 2010). Using the broader definition of grassland, including subtropical deserts,[1] grasslands, tundra,

[1]Subtropical deserts differ from bare deserts since they have vegetation with strong moisture and water conservation mechanisms, which are well-adapted to the low precipitation.

Table 6.3 Land area of grassland (million km^2)

Regions	Savanna	Shrublands	Non-wood grassland	Tundra	Global
Asia (excl NENA)	0.9	3.76	4.03	0.21	8.89
Europe	1.83	0.49	0.7	3.93	6.96
NENA	0.17	2.11	0.57	0.02	2.87
SSA	10.33	2.35	1.79	0	14.46
NAM	0.32	2.02	1.22	3.02	6.58
CAC	0.3	0.44	0.3	0	1.05
South-America	1.57	1.4	1.63	0.26	4.87
Oceania	2.45	3.91	0.5	0	6.86
World	17.87	16.48	10.74	7.44	52.53

Note CAC Central American and Caribbean; *NENA* Near East and North Africa. *Source* White et al. (2000)

woodlands and shrublands (Miller 1990), it is estimated that the biome cover 5 billion ha or 40 % of global land area and store about 30 % of carbon stock (Tennigkeit and Wilkies 2008) Grasslands, account for 70 % of the global agricultural area, and about 20 % of the soil carbon stocks (Ramankutty et al. 2008). However, not all grasslands are used for livestock production. FAO (2012) estimates that 26 % of the ice-free land area is used for livestock production, supporting about one billion people, mostly pastoralists in South Asia and SSA. Livestock provides about a quarter of protein intake and 15 % of dietary energy by global human population (Ibid). Table 6.3 reports the distribution of grassland across regions in 2000.

Shrublands and Woodlands

We discuss shrublands and woodlands together, similarly to previous literature (e.g. see MEA 2005). The major difference between them is the tree height. Shrublands are covered by shorter trees (shrubs) and woodland is a biome with tree cover of 5–10 %—with trees reaching 5 meters height at maturity (FAO 2010). Shrublands account for 9 % of the global land area while woodlands cover about 13 % of the land area (Fig. 6.2). Shrublands and woodlands serve as pasture and provide many other forms of ecosystem services (MEA 2005).

Cropland

According to the MODIS data used in this study, cropland is the second largest biome as it covers 23 % of land area (Fig. 6.2). Extent of cropland area in 1992–2009 decreased by 0.3 % but increased by 4 % in SSA—the largest increase in the world (FAOSTAT 2014; Foley et al. 2011). Consequently SSA experienced the highest deforestation rate in the world (Gibbs et al. 2010). Cropland mainly provide provisioning services though it also provides regulating and cultural services, supporting services, regulation of water and climate systems and aesthetic services (Swinton et al. 2007).

Bare Lands

Covering about 7 % of the land area, bare land has exposed soil, sand or rocks, with less than 10 % vegetative cover throughout the year. This includes the deserts and degraded lands. This also includes the Polar Regions permanently covered with snow or ice. In our LUCC analysis, the bare biome analysis will focus on bare land that could have been affected by anthropogenic changes and will exclude Polar Regions and other uninhabited areas.

Urban

The urban areas have been expanding rapidly in the past few decades, covering 3 % of the global land area in 2001 (Foley et al. 2005). For the first time, the urban population surpassed the rural population in 2009 (UN 2010). We do not include the urban areas in ecosystem services valuation due to their complex nature.

Analytical Approach

We use the Total Economic Value (TEV) approach, which assigns value to both tradable and non-tradable ecosystem services. There is a considerable debate on the usefulness of the TEV approach (e.g. see a review by Nijkamp et al. 2008; Seppelt et al. 2011). Given the complex nature of ecosystem services, double-counting is a major problem of TEV approach (Balmford et al. 2008). Another problem is assigning value to non-tradable ecosystem services. For example an attempt to assign value to some of the ecosystem services—e.g. the air we breathe—could be futile as such resources may not be amenable to valuation and could put unnecessary cost burden on producers. For example, Trucost (2014) evaluated the global social cost of loss of ecosystem services to be about US$4.7 trillion per year and concluded that the top 20 production sectors that lead in ecosystem services degradation would not make profit if they took into account the lost ecosystem services.[2] Despite this, there is a strong realization of the importance of using the broader MEA (2005) definition of land degradation and this justifies the use of the TEV approach to determine the cost of land degradation. Our approach uses methods that avoid double counting or assigning values that may be contestable.

We divide the causes of land degradation into two major groups and evaluate the cost for each:

1. Loss of ecosystem services can be due to LUCC that replaces biomes that have higher ecosystem value with those that have lower value. For example, change from one hectare of forest to one hectare of cropland could lead to loss of ecosystem services since the TEV of a forest is usually higher than the value of cropland. We focus on five major land use types: cropland, grassland, forest, woodland, shrublands and barren land. Even though Costanza et al. (2014) report that wetlands degradation accounts for about 50 % of total annual land degradation, we do not include wetlands because of their small extent (5 %) and limited data availability.
2. Using land degrading management practices on a static land use, i.e. land use did not change from the baseline to endline period. Due to lack of data and other constraints, we focus on cropland and livestock only.

We focus on anthropogenic land degradation, but due to the lack of relevant TEV data, we use a value transfer approach, which assigns ES values from existing case studies to ES valuation in other areas with comparable ES (Desvousges et al. 1998; Troy and Wilson 2006). The value transfer approach has its weaknesses (e.g. see Defra 2010), but lack of data makes it the only feasible approach for global or regional studies.

Land Degradation Due to LUCC

The cost of land degradation due to LUCC is given by

$$C_{LUCC} = \sum_{i}^{K} (\Delta a_1 * p_1 - \Delta a_1 * p_2) \tag{6.1}$$

---

[2]Coal power generation (Eastern Asia); Cattle ranching (South America); coal power generation (North America); Wheat farming (Southern Asia); Rice farming (Southern Asia); Iron and steel mills (Eastern Asia); Cattle ranching (Southern Asia); Water supply (Southern Asia); Wheat farming (North Africa); Rice farming (Eastern Asia); Water supply (western Asia); Fishing (global); Rice farming (Northern Africa); Maize farming (Northern Africa); Rice farming (SE Asia); Water supply (Northern Africa); Sugar (Southern Asia); Natural gas extraction (Eastern Europe); and Natural gas generation (Northern America).

where CLUCC = cost of land degradation due to LUCC; a_1 = land area of biome 1 being replaced by biome 2; P_1 and P_2 are TEV biome 1 and 2, respectively, per unit of area.

By definition of land degradation, $P_1 > P_2$.

This means, LUCC that does not lead to lower TEV is not regarded as land degradation but rather as land improvement or restoration. To obtain the net loss of ecosystem value, the second term in the equation nets out the value of the biome 1 replacing the high value. i = biome i, i == 1, 2, … k.

The ecosystem services included in the TEV and their corresponding value are reported in Table 6.4. Discussion on how data were processed to avoid double-counting is done in the data section below.

Land Degradation Due to Use of Land Degrading Management Practices on a Static Cropland

The provisioning services of crops are well known and directly affect rural households. What is less known are the ecosystem services provided by cropland. One such service is carbon sequestration, which we measure in this study by comparing sequestration due to sustainable land management (SLM) with that arising from land degrading practices.

We use DSSAT-CENTURY (Decision Support System for Agrotechnology Transfer) crop simulation model (Gijsman et al. 2002) to determine the impact of SLM practices on crop yield and soil carbon. Among the most widely used crop models globally, DSSAT employs a process-based approach to model the growth of crops and their interaction with soils, climate, and management practices. DSSAT combines crop, soil, and weather databases for access by a suite of crop models enclosed under one system. When calibrated to local environmental conditions, crop models can help understand the current status of farming systems and test hypothetical scenarios. DSSAT model was modified by incorporating a soil organic matter and residue module from the CENTURY model. The combined DSSAT-CENTURY model used in this study was designed to be more suitable for simulating low-input cropping systems and conducting long-term sustainability analyses.

DSSAT has been calibrated using many experiments around the world. However, the DSSAT and other process-based models have a number of disadvantages as reported by Lobell and Burke (2010). Process-based crop models give point estimates and do not include all relevant biological processes. For example DSSAT cannot simulate the effect of salinity, soil erosion, phosphorus, potassium, intercropping and other processes that could affect yield. As a part of efforts to address these disadvantages, we also estimate empirical models that are based on previous studies. The empirical models incorporate the effect of salinity and soil

Table 6.4 Terrestrial ecosystem services and their global average value (2007 US$/ha/year)

Ecosystem services	Inland wetlands	Tropical forest	Temperate forest	Woodlands	Grasslands
Provisioning services	1659	1828	671	253	1305
Food	614	200	299	52	1192
Water	408	27	191		60
Raw materials	425	84	181	170	53
Genetic resources		13			
Medicinal resources	99	1504			1
Ornamental resources	114			32	
Regulating services	17,364	2529	491	51	159
Air quality regulation		12			
Climate regulation	488	2044	152	7	40
Disturbance moderation	2986	66			
Regulation of water flows	5606	342			
Waste treatment	3015	6	7		75
Erosion prevention	2607	15	5	13	44
Nutrient cycling	1713	3	93		
Pollination		30		31	
Biological control	948	11	235		
Habitat services	2455	39	862	1277	1214
Nursery service	1287	16		1273	
Genetic diversity	1168	23	862	3	1214
Cultural services	4203	867	990	7	193
Esthetic information	1292				167
Recreation	2211	867	989	7	26
Inspiration	700				
Cognitive development			1		
Total economic value	25,682	5264	3013	1588	2871

Extracted from Groote et al. (2012)

erosion (Nkonya et al. 2013). To capture the long-term impacts of land management practices, the DSSAT model will be run for 40 years.

We use two crop simulation scenarios:

1. SLM practices are the combination of organic inputs and inorganic fertilizer. Integrated soil fertility management (ISFM)—combined use of organic inputs, judicious amount of chemical fertilizer and improved seeds (Vanlauwe and

Giller 2006) is considered an SLM practice. Long-term soil fertility experiments have shown that ISFM performs better than the use of fertilizer or organic input alone (Vanlauwe and Giller 2006; Nandwa and Bekunda 1998).

2. Business as usual (BAU). The BAU scenario reflects the current management practices practiced by majority of farmers. These could be land degrading management practices or those which are not significantly different from the performance of ISFM.

Long-term soil fertility experiments have shown that even when using ISFM at recommended levels, yields decline due to decrease of soil organic matter (Nandwa and Bekunda 1998). This is also an indication of land degradation that will be taken into account as shown below.

$$\mathrm{CLD} = \left(y^c - y^d\right)P * \left(A - A^c\right) + \left(y^c_{t=1} - y^c_{t=40}\right) * A^c\big)P - \tau\Delta \mathrm{CO}_2 \qquad (6.2)$$

where CLD = cost of land degradation on cropland, y_c = average yield with ISFM in the 10 years, y_d = average yield with BAU in the last 10 years, A = total area that remained under in baseline and endline periods, A_c = cropland area under ISFM. P = price of crop i; $y^c_{t=1}, y^c_{t=40}$ are average yield under ISFM in in the first 10 years and last 10 years respectively; ΔCO_2 = change in the amount of carbon sequestered under SLM and BAU and τ = price of CO_2 in the global carbon market.

We compute the net carbon sequestration after considering the amount of CO_2 emission from nitrogen fertilization and from manure application. One kilogram of nutrient nitrogen requires about 77.5 MJ for its production using the Haber-Bosch process, packaging, transportation, distribution, and application (Stout 1990). Of the 3553 PJ energy used in agriculture in 1998, nitrogen alone accounted for 64 % of the energy. The remaining energy in agriculture was used by (with their percent contribution in brackets) farm machinery (26 %), irrigation pumps (3 %) and pesticides (1 %) (Vlek et al. 2004).

We focus on three major crops: maize, rice and wheat, which cover about 42 % of cropland in the world (FAOSTAT 2014). The three crops also consume the largest share of fertilizer use in all regions (Table 6.5).

Table 6.5 Fertilizer use by the three most important crops in the world

Region	Maize	Rice	Wheat	Total
	% of total consumption of N, P and K			
SSA	26	8	7	41
LAC	25	6	8	39
South Asia	2	32	23	56
SE Asia	8	51	0	58
NENA	7	3	37	46
Global	17	17	22	55

Notes: *SSA* Sub-Saharan Africa; *LAC* Latin America, *SE* South-east, *NENA* Near East and North Africa
Source FAO (2006)

DSSAT will simulate maize, rice and wheat yields at a half degree resolution, i.e., about 60 km.

Land Degradation on Static Grazing Land

We use methods discussed in Chap. 8 and for brevity, we only summarize the discussion in this chapter. The models used to determine cost of land degradation is:

$$\begin{aligned} CLD_m &= \sum_{i=1}^{I} [DMI_{t=2001} - DMI_{t=2010}]\theta_m x_i P_m \\ DMI_t &= biom_t \gamma \kappa \end{aligned} \tag{6.3}$$

where DMI_t = dry matter intake (tons) in year t in pixel i; $\boldsymbol{\theta_m}$ = Conversion factor of grass DMI to the fresh weight of milk; P_m = price of milk per ton; biomt = grass biomass production (DM) in year t; γ = contribution of grass to total feed intake; xt = number of milking cows in pixel i; and $\boldsymbol{\kappa}$ = share of above ground grass biomass actually consumed by livestock.

Likewise, the loss of meat production due to land degradation (CLD_b) is given by

$$CLD_b = [DMI_{t=2001} - DMI_{t=2010}]\theta_b x_t \tau_t P_b, \tag{6.4}$$

where P_b – price of meat per ton; θ_b = conversion factor of grass DMI to the fresh weight of meat; τ_t = off-take rate; other variables are as defined above.

The total cost of static grassland degradation (LLD) is given by:

$$\mathrm{LLD} = \mathrm{CLD_m} + \mathrm{CLD_b}. \tag{6.5}$$

We only consider on-farm losses including milk production and off-take rate for meat and ignore the loss of live weight of livestock not slaughtered or sold since such loss is not liquidated and eventually affects human welfare. Due to lack of data, we also ignore the impact of degradation on livestock health, parturition, and mortality rates as well as loss of carbon sequestration and other environmental and ecological services provided by grasslands. This results in conservative estimates.

Total Cost of Land Degradation

We combine the total cost of land degradation from LUCC and from static land use as follows:

$$TCLD = \sum_{i}^{H} [CLD + LLD] + C_{LUCC}, \tag{6.6}$$

where TCLD = total cost of land degradation; CLUCC is cost of land degradation from LUCC; H = number of crops considered, H = 1, 2, 3, 4 (see Table 6.5).

Other variables are as defined in equation in (6.1)–(6.5). We will express the total land degradation per year basis and assume that the rate of land degradation is linear. Hence the annual cost of land degradation will be expressed as:

$$TCLD_a = \frac{TCLD}{T}. \tag{6.7}$$

where $TCLD_a$ = annual cost of land degradation; T = time from baseline to endline period. It should be noted that the annual cost of land degradation increases cumulatively as extent of land degradation increases. Thus, $TCLD_a$ reflects the long-term average—as stated in the definition of land degradation.

Cost of Taking Action Against Land Degradation

The approach for determining the cost of action for degradation due to LUCC has to consider the cost of reestablishing the high value biome lost and the opportunity cost of foregoing the benefits drawn from the lower value biome that is being replaced (Torres et al. 2010). For example, if a forest were replaced with cropland, the cost of planting trees or allowing natural regeneration (if still feasible) and cost of maintaining the new plantation or protecting the trees until they reach maturity has to be taken into account. Additionally, the opportunity cost of the crops being foregone to replant trees or allow natural regeneration has to be taken into account. This means the cost of taking action against land degradation due to LUCC is given by

$$CTA_i = A_i \frac{1}{\rho^t} \left\{ z_i + \sum_{t=1}^{T} (x_i + p_j x_j) \right\}. \tag{6.8}$$

where CTAi = cost of restoring high value biome i; ρt = land user's discount factor; Ai = area of high value biome i that was replaced by low value biome j; z_i = cost of establishing high value biome i per ha; xi = maintenance cost of high value biome i per ha until it reaches biological maturity—i.e., the age at which biome is capable of reproducing and bearing seeds (hereafter referred to as maturity); x_j = productivity of low value biome j per hectare; p_j = price of low value biome j per unit (e.g. ton); t = time in years and T = Land user's planning horizon. The term $p_j x_j$

represents the opportunity cost of foregoing production of the low value biome j being replaced.

The cost of inaction will be the sum of annual losses due to land degradation

$$CI_i = \sum_{t=1}^{T} C^i_{LUCC}, \tag{6.9}$$

where CI_i = cost of not taking action against degradation of biome i; C^i_{LUCC} is the cost of land degradation due to LUCC for biome i. Other variables are as defined in Eq. (6.1). As Nkonya et al. (2013) note, land users will take action against land degradation if $CTA_i < CI_i$.

The cost of action given in Eqs. 6.8 and 6.9 assumes all degradation effects are fully reversible but as discussed earlier, such assumption does not hold. For example, Fig. 6.3 shows that biodiversity of restored forests is lower than that of the natural forests. This is due to the loss of species habitat and biomes that take centuries to be restored. Given that the benefit of restoring degraded land goes beyond the maturity period of biome i, we have to use the land user's planning horizon to fully capture the entailing costs and benefits. Poor farmers tend to have shorter planning horizon while better off farmers tend to have longer planning horizon (Pannell et al. 2014). The planning horizon also depends on the type of investment. For example, tree planting requires longer planning horizon than annual cropland. For brevity however, we will assume a 30 year planning horizon for all the biomes considered.[3] Our assumption implies that during this time, farmers will not change their baseline production strategies dramatically. It is important to consider the biome establishment period since it has important implications on decision making. Poor land users are less likely to invest in restoration of high value biomes that take long time to mature. For example, trees take about 4–6 years to reach maturity (Wheelwright and Logan 2004). Given this we assume a 6 year maturity for trees. For grasslands, we assume a 2 year maturity age for natural regeneration or planting. The assumption is based on perennial grass like Rhodes grass (Chloris gayana), which reach full maturity after 2 years (Heuzé et al. 2015). Replanting is necessary if the LUCC involved excessive weeding of grass. Natural regeneration may take longer than 3 years but for simplicity we assume a three natural regeneration period.

As expected both the cost of action and inaction differ significantly across space and time. For example, reforestation costs are lower in low income regions than in high income countries (Benítez et al. 2007). However low government effectiveness and other challenges exist in low income countries and these could lead to even higher costs to maintain improvement. Our analysis will take into account such differences by using actual costs that have been observed in projects/programs in two major economic groups—high and low income countries.

[3]The 30 year planning period for land degradation due to LUCC should not be confused with the 40 year used in the crop simulation.

We also take into account the cost of land degradation across agroecological zones. For example, establishing a biome in a semi-arid area is more difficult than would be the case in humid and subhumid regions. Pender (2009) illustrate this using the survival rate of planted trees in the Niger, which was only 50 %. Other challenges also face farmers in arid and semi-arid areas (with annual average rainfall below 700 mm) when compared to land users in humid and subhumid areas (with annual precipitation above 700 mm) (IISD 1996). Hence for any given region, we assume that the cost of establishing any biome in arid and semi-arid areas is twice the corresponding cost in the humid and subhumid regions in the same economic group.

There are alternative land rehabilitation strategies available to land users. For example, action against deforestation could be taken using the traditional tree planting approach, which unfortunately is expensive but could achieve faster results. Assisted natural regeneration is also used and is cheaper than the conventional tree planting. For example, Bagong Pagasa Foundation (2011) found that the cost of the traditional replanting trees on deforested area was US$1079/ha compared to only US$579 for assisted natural regeneration. We will use the most common strategy in any given region and economic group.

Data

LUCC

Table 6.6 reports the extent of each biome in 2001 and the corresponding change in 2009. Figures 6.4 and 6.5 spatially report the corresponding changes. Extent of forest biome increased by almost 6 % globally with much of the increase occurring in temperate regions while almost all tropical regions experienced deforestation (Fig. 6.3). During the same period (2000–10), FAO (2011) reported an annual global deforestation rate of 0.1 %. As observed above, the disagreement between the MODIS land cover and FAO (2011) could be due to the differences in definition of forests.

While the extent of shrublands and cropland increased, the changes are quite different across different regions. The extent of cropland increased by 32 % in Oceania and by 12 % in SSA, but decreased in the Americas, Europe and SE Asia. Forest accounted for over 30 % of cropland expansion in Oceania and South Asia (Table 6.7). The source of cropland expansion in SSA was mainly shrublands and woodlands while forests accounted for only 19 % of cropland expansion (Table 6.7). This is contrary to Gibbs et al. (2010) who observed that forests contributed the largest share of crop expansion in SSA. Again, the difference could be explained by inclusion of woodlands and shrublands in the forest biome. MODIS data used in this study treats forest, shrublands and woodlands as separate biomes (Tables 6.2 and 6.6; Fig. 6.5).

Table 6.6 Land area of terrestrial biomes 2001 and change in 2009

Region	Forest	Shrubland	Grassland	Cropland	Bare	Woodlands
	Area of biome in 2001 (million ha)					
SSA	493.41	640.63	1402.09	300.99	2761.62	821.59
LAC	854.43	180.1	465.77	131.7	51.22	143.83
NAM	717.83	444.38	323.88	559.81	100.64	276.62
East Asia	442.56	137.32	305.29	327.95	302.69	547.9
Oceania	313.63	3230	2570.83	87.46	14.98	2044.14
South Asia	191.96	22.82	21.72	194.52	20.65	81.97
SE Asia	182.61	3.13	12.21	60.2	1.03	72.9
East Europe	586.77	510.75	165.96	310.86	15.89	268.3
West Europe	141.7	57	96.82	156.19	202.2	103
Total	3924.9	5226.12	5364.59	2129.69	3470.92	4360.23
	Change in area in 2009 as % of area in 2011					
SSA	1.15	−6.30	−2.08	−12.08	2.26	4.37
LAC	5.15	−2.41	−18.80	8.18	0.98	24.74
NAM	−18.79	1.56	4.38	13.50	1.12	11.82
East Asia	−5.27	45.97	−5.11	−12.14	7.99	−2.85
Oceania	8.17	−3.03	8.50	−32.67	−120.69	−5.00
South Asia	1.81	−6.35	−16.71	−2.18	15.98	3.11
SE Asia	7.65	−44.41	−4.34	9.52	63.11	−25.69
East Europe	−23.19	−7.43	42.44	2.60	−22.28	35.47
West Europe	−14.34	5.86	7.51	5.22	0.82	−1.59
Total	−5.65	−2.10	3.24	−0.03	2.08	1.46

Notes 1 % change in area = $\frac{a_1 - a_2}{a_1} * 100$

SSA Sub-Saharan Africa; *LAC* Latina American countries; *NAM* North America; *NENA* Near East and North Africa; *SE* South East

See Appendix for countries in each region

Source MODIS data

Total Economic Value Data

We derive the TEV from the economics of ecosystems and biodiversity (TEEB) database, which is based on more than 300 case studies—reporting more than 1350 ES values (de Groot et al. 2012). The spatial distribution of the terrestrial biome studies is shown in Fig. 6.6. Studies on coastal, coastal and inland wetlands, coral reefs, freshwater, and marine are excluded in accordance to our study's focus on the seven major terrestrial biomes. It is clear that the studies are well-distributed even in SSA. Areas with limited coverage include Russia, central Asia and NENA. However, there are few studies conducted in these regions that will serve as representative of the regions. Due to a large variation of the data source and methods used, data were standardized to ensure that the reported values are comparable. The criteria used for including studies were: the study has to be original, i.e., not based on literature review; reported value of ES value per ha for specific biome and

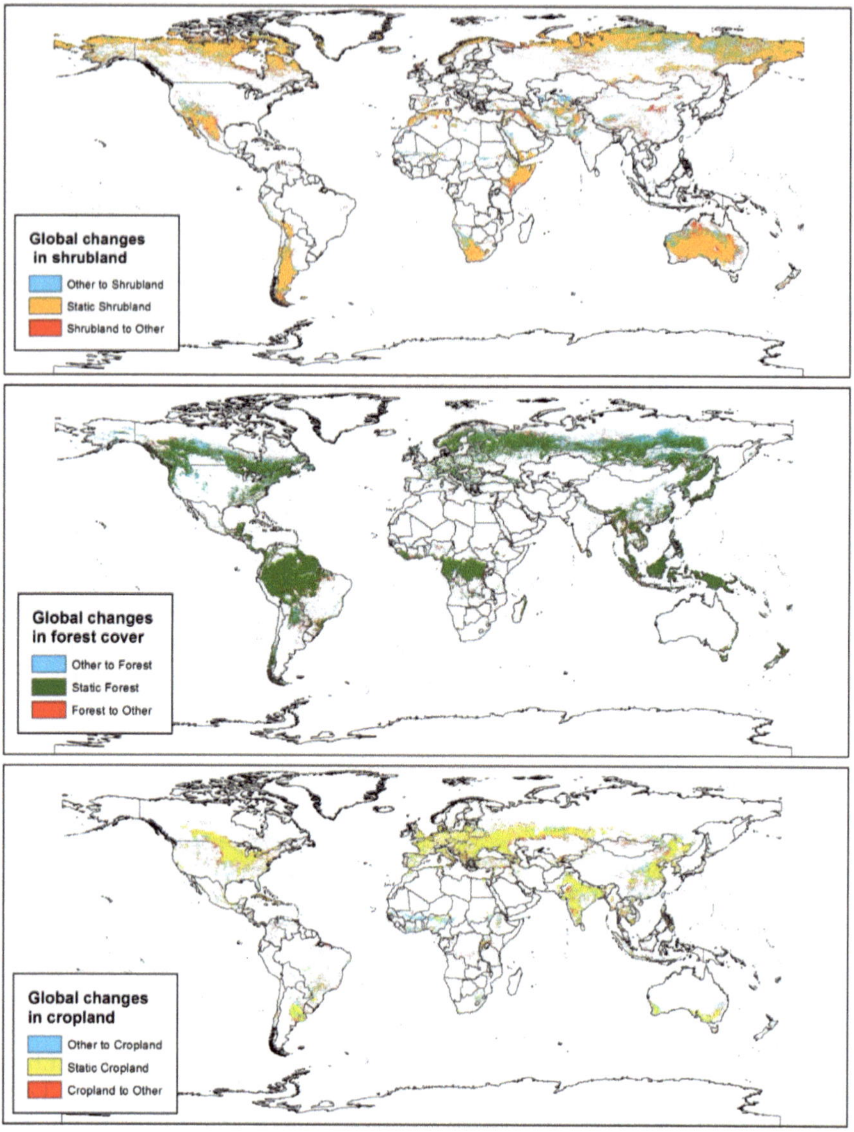

Fig. 6.4 Change of extent of shrubland, forest and cropland, 2001–09. *Source* Calculated from MODIS land cover data

specific time period, valuation method is included, and surface area studied is reported (de Groot et al. 2012). Only 665 of the 1350 case studies met these conditions (de Groot et al. 2012).

The data were converted to 2007 US$ to allow value comparison across time. One of the major weaknesses of the ES values included in the database was the

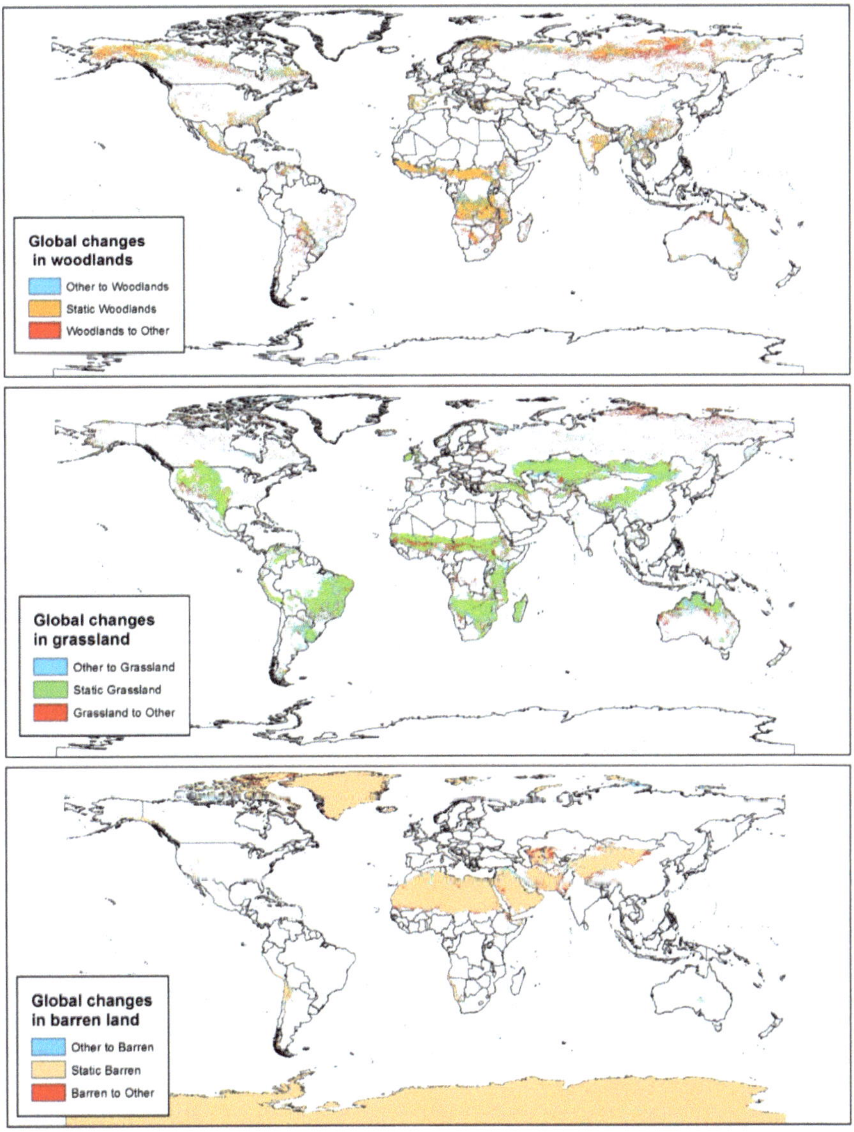

Fig. 6.5 Change of extent of woodlands, grassland and barren land, 2001–09. *Source* Calculated from MODIS land cover

wide variation of the ES values. For example value of tropical forests ranges from less than US$1 to US$9412/ha/year. Likewise, the value of grasslands varies from less than US$1 to US$ 6415/ha/year. De Groot et al. (2012) attribute the wide variation to five major reasons (i) locations attach different values to different biome ES (ii) different valuation methods were used but over 60 % used annual TEV

Table 6.7 Sources of cropland expansion

Source	SSA	East Asia	Oceania	South Asia
	Percent contribution			
Forest	19	17	36	36
Grassland	18	20	18	11
Shrubland	37	19	29	20
Bare	4	1	1	1
Woodlands	22	43	16	33

Note Includes regions that experienced cropland area expansion reported in Table 6.6

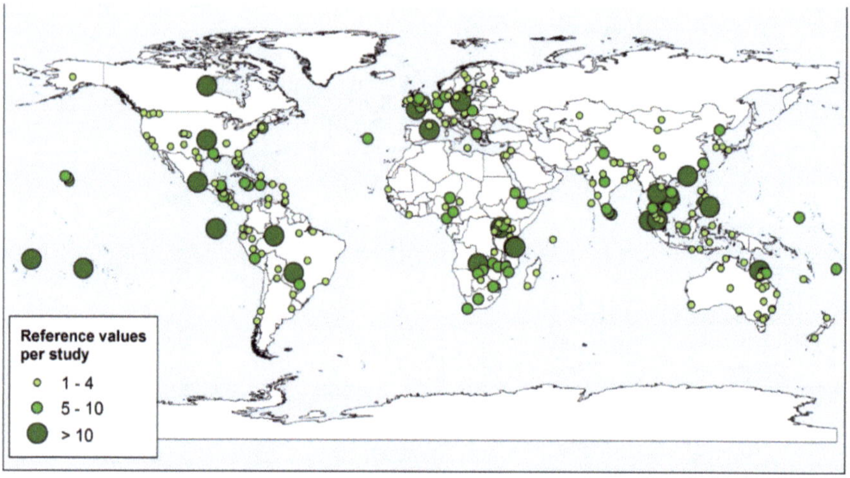

Fig. 6.6 Location of TEEB database of terrestrial ecosystem service valuation studies. *Source* Derived from TEEB database, the TEV of the five major biomes is shown below

(Table 6.8) (iii) different sub-biomes were considered in different studies (iv) attribution of ES values to different services, which could lead to double-counting when ES are aggregated and (v) ES values are time specific (e.g. see Costanza et al. 2014).

Additionally, most studies used did not exhaustively cover all ES and therefore the average values reported are conservative estimates of the total value (Ibid). To address this problem, we only included studies that used TEV.

TEV and Double-Counting Challenge

Double counting—i.e., assigning value of an ecosystem service at two different stages of the same process providing human welfare is a common problem in ecosystem valuation using TEV approaches. The potential for double-counting is

Table 6.8 Analytical methods of terrestrial biome ES evaluation

Analytical method	# of studies	%
Annual	827	63.5
Benefit Transfer	165	12.7
Direct market pricing	100	7.7
Net Present Value	56	4.3
Total Economic Value	46	3.5
Contingent Valuation	25	1.9
Avoided Cost	21	1.6
Replacement Cost	20	1.5
Others	42	3.2
Total	1302	100.0

Others include: Capital/stock value, factor income/production function, group valuation, hedonic pricing, marginal value, mitigation and restoration cost, one time payment/WTP, PES and present value

Source Compiled from TEEB database

hard to completely rule out due to the complex interlinkages of ecosystem services and processes (Fu et al. 2011). For instance if there are pollination services value of forest (or other biomes) these are certainly reflected in the value of crop harvests and hence adding them up is a double counting. The same applies to nutrient cycling, disease and climate regulation, flood and erosion regulation, etc. The potential for double-counting leads to overestimation of the cost of land degradation.

de Groot et al. (2012) use different standardization methods to address these issues. These include assigning value to final products of regulating and supporting services (Fisher et al. 2008). Other measures used to avoid and/or reduce double-counting include: Use case studies with consistent ES classification systems and selecting annual TEV valuation methods which are widely used in the ES literature (Fu et al. 2011).

Comparison of TEV of Biomes Across Studies and with Conventional GDP

Comparison of the TEEB average ES values with Chiabai et al. (2011) and CBD (2001)—both of which are global studies—reveal that TEEB average values are lower (e.g. see Fig. 6.7). Chiabai et al. (2011) value of tropical forests is about 10,000/ha/year compared to about US$5000 for TEEB and US$6000 for CBD value (Fig. 6.7). TEEB's value for temperate forests is the highest however but comparable to the value reported by Chiabai et al. (2011). Hence even though we believe that the values used are conservative, the values should be interpreted with these differences in mind.

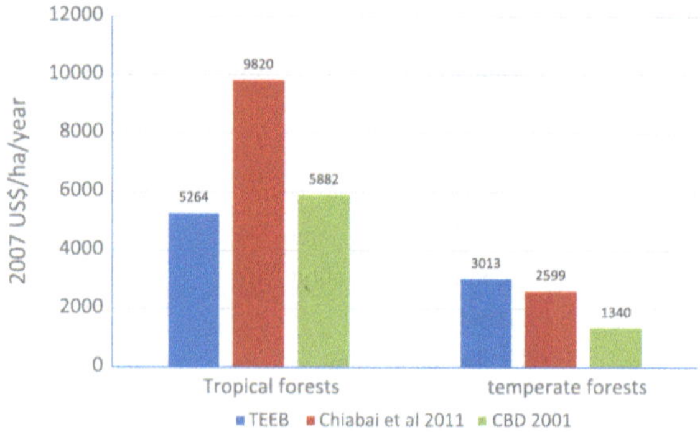

Fig. 6.7 Comparison of TEV of tropical and temperate forests across three studies. *Source* Computed from CBD (2001), Chiabai et al. (2011), de Groot et al. (2012)

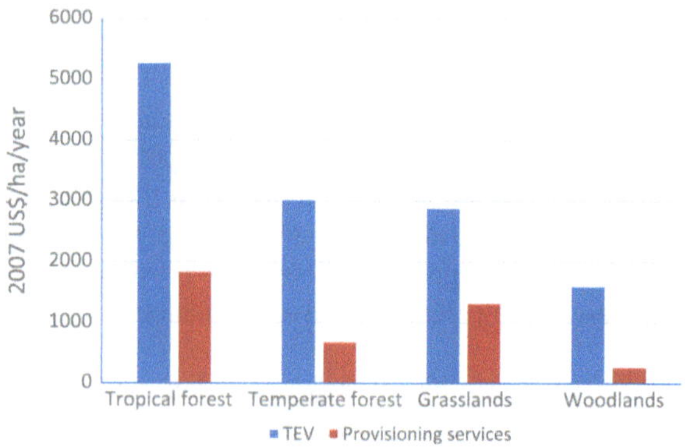

Fig. 6.8 TEV of major biomes. *Source* de Groot et al. (2012)

Figure 6.8 reports the average TEV of the major terrestrial biomes. Figure 6.8 also reports the corresponding value of provisioning services to reflect the traditional assessment of cost of land degradation that considered only provisioning services. In all cases, the TEV is more than twice the corresponding value of provisioning services.

We compare the ecosystem value endowment and the corresponding GDP per capita of each country to reflect the large differences between the traditional valuation methods that only takes into account tangible marketable services and the TEV approach. It can be easily seen that countries considered among the poorest have equivalent or greater TEV than high income countries (Figs. 6.9 and 6.10). For example, if TEV were used to group countries in three "income" groups, majority of SSA countries could be regarded as "middle-income" countries while majority of West European countries would fall in the "low-income" countries. North America, China, Russia, Australia and Brazil would fall in the "high income countries" largely due to their large land area and rich endowment of high-value biomes—

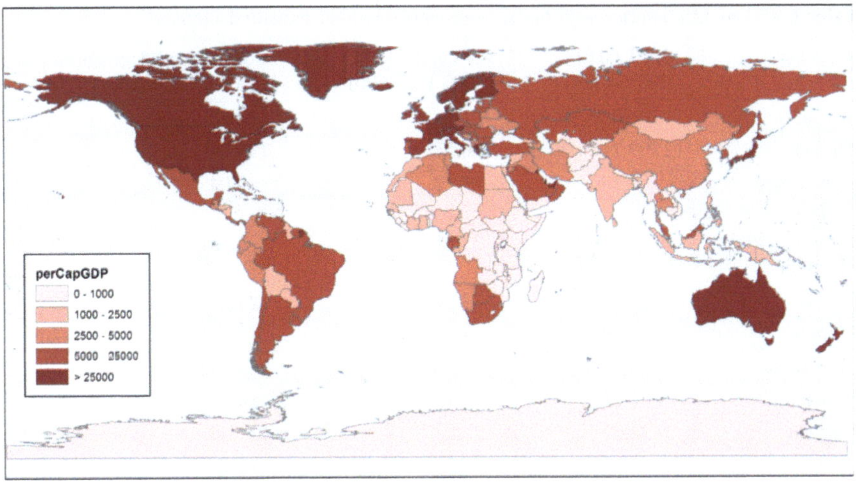

Fig. 6.9 Gross domestic product per capita, 2007 US$

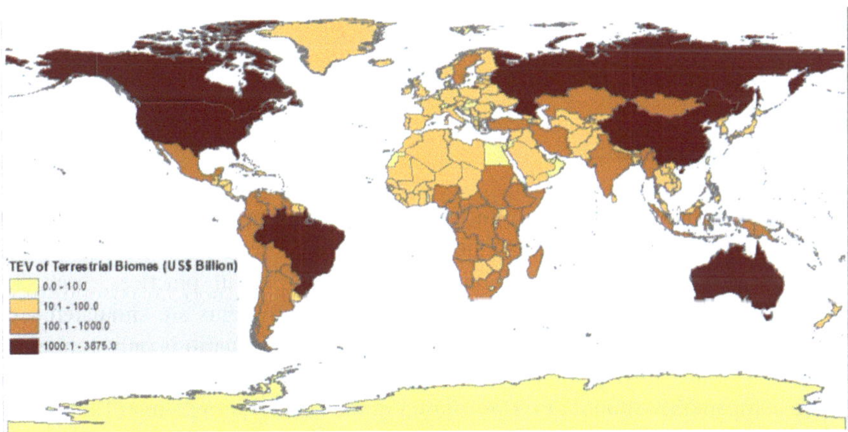

Fig. 6.10 TEV endowment at country level in 2001

namely forest or grasslands. Taking population into account but dropping countries577 with fewer than one million people, only three countries (Australia, Canada and Russia) classified as high income countries are among the top 12 countries with highest per capita TEV of terrestrial biomes and the rest in list are low income countries with sparse population (Table 6.9). However, given that a large share of the TEV benefits of ecosystems cannot be internalized in the resident country, such endowment does not reflect the welfare of the people in the country or community around the biome. Never-the-less, the spatial distribution helps to determine where the world needs to concentrate its effort to protect ecosystem services.

Table 6.9 Top 12 countries with highest per capita TEV of terrestrial biomes

Country	2007 GDP (billion US$)	Per capita TEV (2007 US$ 000)	Cost of land degradation (2007 US$ billion)
Kazakhstan	104.85	21.52	23.73
Russia	1299.71	26.57	193.98
Papua New Guinea	6.33	29.12	−0.04
Central African Republic	1.70	33.96	5.35
Bolivia	13.12	43.36	24.25
Congo	8.39	43.82	7.77
Botswana	10.94	64.70	3.15
Mongolia	4.23	64.73	18.96
Canada	1424.07	72.83	114.26
Namibia	8.81	75.26	14.72
Australia	853.86	93.93	117.97
Gabon	11.57	110.94	1.89

Notes Countries with fewer than one million people are excluded

Land Degradation on Static Cropland

DSSAT Crop Simulation

The DSSAT crop simulation baseline land management practices were based on a compilation of global dataset and literature review. Given that there is a large difference between irrigated and rainfed land management practices, both the baseline and ISFM scenarios for irrigated and rainfed systems are simulated separately. In the irrigated simulation, a water management scenario is only applied to areas where water management is practiced.

We compare the amount of nitrogen used in the DSSAT simulation (Table 6.10) and the corresponding application rate obtained from FAOSTAT data (Table 6.11 and 6.12). We also compare the simulated and actual yield under irrigated and rainfed production systems. Table 6.9 shows that the average application rates of fertilizer in most regions is much lower than rates used in the DSSAT model. For example, while average application rate in SSA is 6 kgN/ha, it is 22 kgN/ha for rainfed maize. This large difference could be due to the fact that FAOSTAT nitrogen rate was computed by assuming that all cropland received fertilizer. Calibration of DSSAT model fertilizer rate assumed application rate at crop level, rather than entire cropland. However, FAO fertilizer application rate for each crop of the three crops considered in this study (maize, rice and wheat) is much higher than the corresponding average for all crops combined in each region (Table 6.9).

Table 6.10 Fertilizer application rates on cropland across regions

Region	Maize (KgN/ha)		Rice (KgN/ha)		Wheat (KgN/ha)	
	Irrigated	Rainfed	Irrigated	Rainfed	Irrigated	Rainfed
SSA		22.7	134.5	20.5	100.0	20.4
LAC	184.5	44.7	153.6	40.9		58.5
NAM			214.5			
East Asia						59.7
SE Asia		31.2	136.0			80.0
Oceania		70.3	184.5			59.9
South Asia	147.4	40.3	154.1			55.0
East Europe		60.0		90.0		60.0
West Europe	200.0	150.0			150.0	59.6
Central Asia	147.5		147.5			
NENA	149.8	60.0	141.7	20.0	141.8	60.0
Total	155.0	37.3	151.0	37.2	123.5	42.8

Note Empty cells imply that the production system is not applicable in the corresponding region
SSA Sub-Saharan Africa; *LAC* Latina American countries; *NAM* North America; *NENA* Near East and North Africa; *SE* South East
See Appendix for countries in each region

Table 6.11 Application rate of Nitrogen used in DSSAT simulation

Region	N	P_2O_5	K_2O	NPK
	Average application (2001–10) Kg/ha			
SSA	6.04	3.00	1.83	10.86
NAM	59.6	21.1	21.1	101.8
LAC	29.7	23.9	23.0	76.6
South Asia	82.3	30.7	12.6	125.6
South-east Asia	60.2	15.5	22.3	98.1
East Asia	254.5	94.5	44.4	393.4
Central Asia	13.0	3.1	0.6	16.7
Oceania	25.0	31.0	5.5	61.6
East Europe	20.5	6.5	7.5	34.5
West Europe	95.8	26.8	29.9	152.5
NENA	42.2	14.3	3.7	60.2

Computed from FAOSTAT raw data
SSA Sub-Saharan Africa; *LAC* Latina American countries; *NAM* North America; *NENA* Near East and North Africa; *SE* South East
Note See Appendix for countries in each region

For example application rate on maize and rice in north America is respectively 257 and 184 kgNPK/ha while the equivalent average amount for all crops is only 101 kgNPK/ha. The regional average may also mask the large differences within each region (Table 6.10).

Table 6.12 Application rate of NPK by crop

Region	Wheat	Maize	Rice
	kgNPK/ha		
NAM	84	257	184
LAC	76	67	90
West Europe	213	276	279
East Europe	95	40	–
USSR	25	294	107
Africa	63	55	19
Asia	144	117	140
World	116	136	134

Notes: *NAM* North America; *LAC* Latin American countries
Source FAO (2006)

Another challenge is to determine the adoption rate of ISFM in each country. We reviewed literature and used secondary data to determine adoption rate reported in Table 6.11. We then use the DSSAT simulation results at each pixel (half degree resolution) to determine the yield under ISFM and BAU scenarios and use the realistic adoption rates to determine the cost of land degradation on static cropland.

The secondary data used to determine adoption rate of ISFM include household surveys in SSA and conservation agriculture data reported by AQUASTAT website. Conservation agriculture is the practice that has soil cover throughout the year, minimizes soil disturbance through minimum tillage and spatio-temporal diversification of crops (Kassam et al. 2009; FAO 2008). Hence in countries with high fertilizer use, conservation agriculture could effectively mean ISFM since the crop residue component and crop rotation significantly increases soil carbon and yield. However, the impact of conservation agriculture on yield and profitability is heterogeneous (Pannell et al. 2014) but some of its components have been shown to have consistent positive impact. Zero tillage has been shown to significantly increase yield over long-term period in North America (Fulton 2010) and Australia (Llewellyn et al. 2012). Likewise, maize-legume rotation has been shown to increase yield of up to 25 % higher than monoculture (Brouder and Gomez-Macpherson 2014). Based on a global literature review, Palm et al. (2014) show that it increases biodiversity, topsoil organic matter and reduces soil erosion and runoff—leading to improved water quality.

The global adoption rate of conservation agriculture is 124 million ha or 9 % of the global cropland (Friedrich et al. 2012), 87 % of which is in Argentina, Australia, Brazil, Canada, and US (Brouder and Gomez-Macpherson 2014). The adoption rate in SSA and South Asia is generally low (Pannell et al. 2014; Brouder and Gomez-Macpherson 2014).

Due to the low adoption of conservation agriculture and fertilizer in SSA, conservation agriculture may not be equivalent to ISFM in the region. Hence we use household survey data to determine the adoption rate of ISFM in SSA. The average ISFM adoption rates in each region are reported in Tables 6.13 and 6.14.

Table 6.13 Adoption rates of SLM practices across regions

Region	Management practices	Adoption rate
SSA	Low-cost, productivity enhancing land management practices	3 % or 5 million ha on 191 million ha of cropland (Pender 2009)
Global (Kassam et al. 2009)	Conservation agriculture	10.2
LAC		37
SSA		0.7
LAC		26.6
NAM		20.6
Pacific		15.1
East Europe		1.7
Central Asia		5.7
West Europe		3.4
NENA		0.1
East Asia		10.0

Note See Appendix for countries in each region

Table 6.14 Adoption rates of inorganic and organic inputs and ISFM in SSA: Household survey

Country	ISFM	Organic inputs	Fertilizer	Nothing	Institution that collected data, data type and year survey conducted
	Adoption rate (percent)				
Mali	18	39	16	27	Direction nationale de l'informatique (DNSI). Recensement general de l'agriculture, 2004/2005
Uganda	0	67.61	0.96	31.42	Uganda Bureau of Statistics. Uganda national panel survey 2009/10
					Agriculture module
Kenya	16	22.3	17.44	43.66	ASDSP/KARI/UONa
					Kenya agricultural sector household baseline survey
Nigeria	1.28	28.23	23.31	47.17	IFPRI. Fadama III household survey, 2012
Malawi	7.52	2.77	51.58	38.14	National Statistics Office. Third integrated household survey, 2010/11, agricultural module
Tanzania	0.56	2.89	0.58	95.19	National bureau of statistics. National panel survey, agriculture module
Overall adoption rate (%)	6.2	19.1	24.6	49.8	

Notes: *ASDSP* Agriculture sector development support program; *KARI* Kenya Agricultural Research Institute; *UON* University of Nairobi

Results

Table 6.15 and Fig. 6.11 report the loss of ecosystems due to LUCC. Table 6.15 shows that the global annual average cost of land degradation due to LUCC was 2007 US$230.76 billion/year or 0.4 % of the global GDP in 2007. If the cost of land degradation were a country's GDP, it would be about the 8th richest country in the world. The total value of land degradation surpasses the GDP in 2007 of all countries in SSA. Figure 6.12 shows that SSA accounted for about 26 % of the cost of land degradation—underscoring the severity of land degradation in the region. Accordingly, the cost of land degradation is about 7 % of SSA's GDP—the highest level in the world. However, measured as percent of ecosystem total economic value (1.24 %), SSA's cost of land degradation is the second highest after NENA's, which is about 1.62 %. NAM, Pacific and East and West Europe experienced the lowest TEV loss of ecosystem services. In the humid and subhumid regions—where land degradation is more pronounced than in the arid and semi-arid regions (Bai et al. 2008), the Pacific region did remarkably well (Table 6.15). The results in

Table 6.15 Terrestrial ecosystem value and cost of land degradation due to LUCC

Region	GDP	Ecosystem value	% of TEV	Cost of land degradation		Cost of LD (TEV) as % of		
				TEV	Provisioning services only			
	2007 US$ billion/year			2007 US$ billion/year		GDP	TEV of ES	Total cost of LD
SSA	879.15	4844.17	18.82	60.290	30.34	6.86	1.24	26.13
LAC	3880.41	5958.52	23.15	52.551	22.31	1.35	0.88	22.77
NAM	15904.3007	3776.08	14.67	26.443	13.48	0.17	0.70	11.46
East Asia	10182.76	1552.63	6.03	16.704	5.87	0.16	1.08	7.24
Pacific	1001.55	1982.66	7.70	13.928	8.90	1.39	0.70	6.04
South Asia	1784.75	1065.43	4.14	9.664	2.55	0.54	0.91	4.19
SE Asia	861.12	562.02	2.18	5.793	1.82	0.67	1.03	2.51
Central Asia	180.4	492.30	1.91	5.743	12.58	3.18	1.17	2.49
West Europe	17144.86	684.37	2.66	5.252	2.14	0.03	0.77	2.28
East Europe	3023.14	4180.28	16.24	23.957	2.89	0.79	0.57	10.38
NENA	2040.19	643.99	2.50	10.436	3.74	0.51	1.62	4.52
Global	56882.69	25742.44	100	230.761	106.63	0.41	0.90	100

Notes: *SSA* Sub-Saharan Africa; *LAC* Latina American countries; *NAM* North America; *NENA* Near East and North Africa; *SE* South East

See Appendix for countries in each region

Source GDP—World Bank data, TEV and land degradation—authors

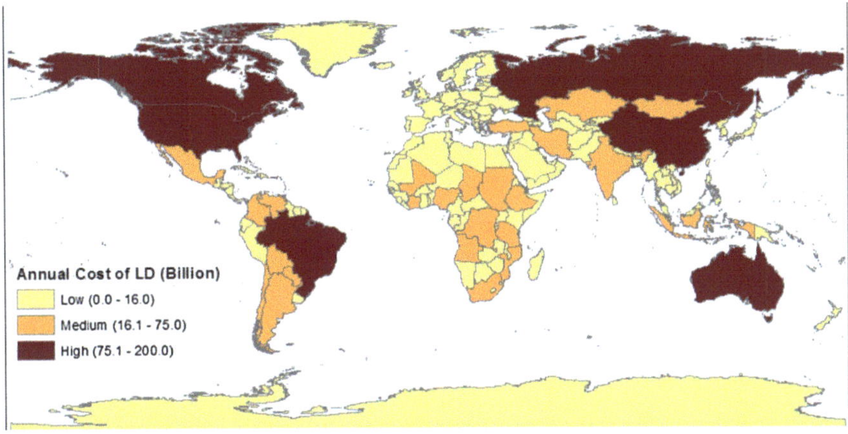

Fig. 6.11 Global cost of land degradation (2007 US$ billion), 2001–09

West Europe and NAM are consistent with Costanza et al. (2014) who reported increasing forest cover in these regions. The results in Europe are also consistent with Environmental performance index (EPI) ranking, which ranks region's performance in environmental health and ecosystem sustainability as highest in the world (EPI 2012). Nine of the countries with highest EPI ranking were European. European country with the lowest EPI ranking is Malta, which is the 87th of the total of 130 countries ranked.[4]

Who Bears the Burden of the Cost of Land Degradation?

We compare the cost of land degradation by separating the ES losses into two major components:

Provisioning services, which have direct impact on land users, and which account for the largest share of benefits that drive their decision making. This is the portion that has been used in many studies that do not use the TEV approach.

The value of the rest of ecosystem services—regulating, habitat and cultural services. These ecosystem services include both global benefits—such as carbon sequestration and biodiversity—and indirect local benefit, that land users may not assign low priority in their decision making process.

Figure 6.13 shows that loss of provisioning services account for only 38 % of the cost of land degradation—suggesting that the largest share of the cost of land degradation is borne by the global community. For example value of regulating

[4]Malta is included in the West Europe group in the EPI ranking but under NENA in this study.

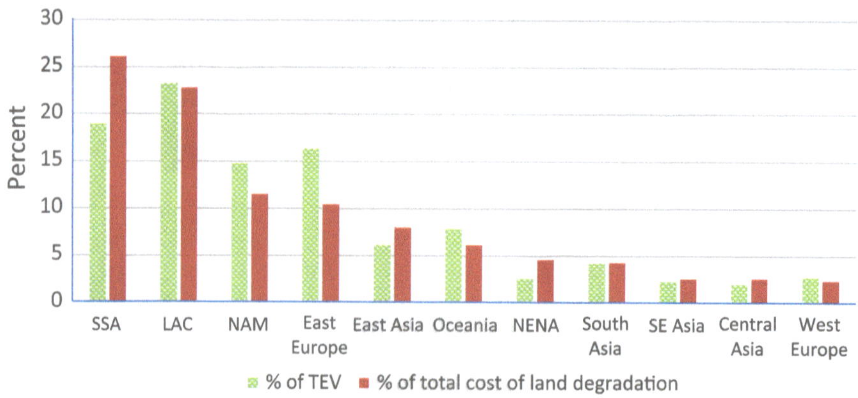

Fig. 6.12 Regional contribution of total economic value of terrestrial ecosystem services and cost of land degradation. *Note* See Appendix for countries in each region. *SSA* Sub-Saharan Africa; *LAC*

services accounts for the largest share of total economic value (TEV) of both tropical and temperate forests (Fig. 6.14). Provisioning services account for the lowest or second lowest share of TEV of both tropical and temperate forest TEV (Fig. 6.14). Thus if land holders are managing forests, the value of provisioning services will play the biggest role in decision making while regulating services will be given a low priority despite its large value. This suggests that land degradation is a global problem that requires both global and local solutions. Some studies that have compared the local benefits for protected areas showed that the benefit of converting forests to small-scale farming was greater than the benefit local communities draw from protected forests in Cameroon (Yaron 1999) or to unsustainably harvest timber in Malaysia (Shahwahid et al. 1999).

Fig. 6.13 Who bears the burden of the cost of land degradation?

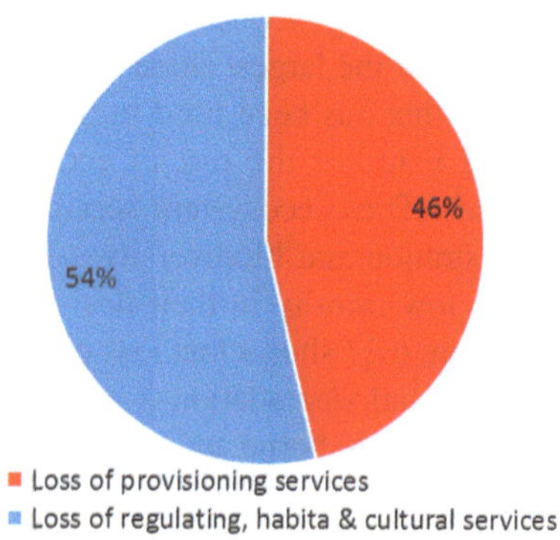

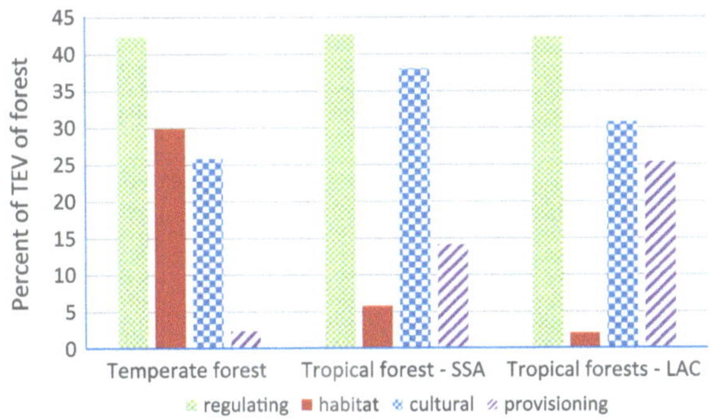

Fig. 6.14 Type of ecosystem services and their contribution to total value of forest biomes. *Notes* Average of total economic value (2007 US$) is 5264 (tropical forests) an 3013 (temperate forests). *Source* Calculated from TEEB database

Cost of Land Degradation Due to Use of Land Degrading Practices on Cropland

Table 6.16 shows that use of land degrading management practices in SSA on rainfed maize leads to a 25 % fall in yield compared to yield in the past 30 years. This is the highest loss of productivity of the cropland in the world. However, yield levels observed from the FAOSTAT shows an increase in yield in all regions for all crops in the corresponding periods simulated (Table 6.17). The reason for the inconsistency is that FAOSTAT yield includes yields from cropland expansion on forests and other virgin lands (Table 6.7) that is higher than yield on continuously cultivated cropland. Additionally, there has been an increase of fertilizer use and other inputs that mask the loss of productivity of land reflected in the simulation model (Le et al. 2014). The increase in use of fertilizer and improved technologies leads to higher yield despite the degraded lands. For example, Vlek et al. (2010) report land degradation in SSA. In NAM, East and West Europe and central Asia however, we see an increase in yield and consistent with the FAOSTAT yield trend. This could be a result of the higher use of fertilizer rates under BAU than yield under ISFM. But greater fertilizer use under BAU masks the environmental degradation due to eutrophication (enrichment of surface waters with plant nutrients) and other forms of water pollution (Glibert et al. 2006) that is not included in this study.

For irrigated rice, we see a fall in yield in all regions—as expected—except in Central Asia (Table 6.18). Surprisingly, the largest loss is experienced in NAM followed by LAC. Losses in SSA are only 20 %, the fifth largest in the world. For rainfed wheat, we see a yield decline in all regions except South Asia, central Asia and Asia and pacific (Table 6.19).

The cost of land degradation on static cropland is reported in Table 6.20 and is divided according to the components described in Eq. 6.2, i.e., loss of provisioning services and carbon sequestration under BAU and continuous cropping under ISFM.

Table 6.16 Change in rainfed maize yield under business as usual and ISFM—DSSAT results

Maize	BAU		ISFM		Yield change (%)		Change due to degradation/improvement (%)
	Baseline	Endline	Baseline	Endline	BAU	ISFM	
	Yield (tons/ha)				$\% \Delta y = \frac{y_2 - y_1}{y_1} * 100$		$\% D = \frac{y_2^c - y_2^d}{y_2^d} * 100$
SSA	2.2	1.7	2.5	2.1	−23.2	13.9	25
LAC	3.4	3.1	3.8	3.6	−10.5	−6.7	16
NAM	6.1	6.4	5.7	6.2	4.2	10.1	−2
South Asia	3.4	3.1	3.6	3.4	−9.3	−5.8	11
Asia and Pacific	4.4	4.4	4.5	4.4	1.4	−0.4	1
East Europe	3.3	3.6	2.7	3.2	7.8	19.3	−12
Central Asia	5.1	5.5	4.1	4.9	7.1	18.3	−11
West Europe	5.3	5.6	4.4	5.1	5.4	15.6	−9
NENA	4.4	4.3	4.0	4.4	−1.1	7.9	1

Note Y1 = Baseline yield (average first 10 years); Y2 = Yield endline period (average last 10 years)
y_2^c = ISFM yield in the last 10 years; y_2^d = BAU yield, last 10 years
See Appendix for countries in each region
SSA Sub-Saharan Africa; *LAC* Latina American countries; *NAM* North America; *NENA* Near East and North Africa

Table 6.17 Actual crop yield and change

Region	Maize		Rice		Wheat	
	Baseline yield (Tons/ha)	Change (%)[a]	Baseline yield (Tons/ha)	Change (%)[a]	Baseline yield (Tons/ha)	Change (%)[a]
SSA	1.28	44.28	2.38	3.67	1.88	37.62
LAC	2.1	94	2.3	93.6	1.8	43
NAM	6.8	37.9	6	28.6	2.3	22.1
East Asia	3.9	33.4	5.3	18.7	2.9	51.5
Oceania	1.5	58.35	3.3	16.5	1.4	8.2
South Asia	1.4	74.3	2.3	42.1	1.8	44.9
SE Asia	1.7	101.6	2.9	36.5	1.4	15.3
East Europe	–	–	–	–	1.9	31.1
West Europe	5.53	37.4	5.45	11.55	5	11.73
Central Asia[b]	3.33	53.2	2.45	30.6	1.11	35.1
NENA	3.47	48	4.47	40.73	1.7	40.7

Note [a]Change ($\% \Delta y$) is computed $\% \Delta y = \frac{y_2 - y_1}{y_1} * 100$
[b]Baseline period for Central Asia is 1992–2001 and 1981–90 for the rest of regions. Endline for all regions is 2001–10
See Appendix for countries in each region
SSA Sub-Saharan Africa; *LAC* Latina American countries; *NAM* North America; *NENA* Near East and North Africa; *SE* South East
Source FAOSTAT raw data

Table 6.18 Change in irrigated rice yield under business as usual and ISFM

Region	BAU		ISFM		Yield change (%)		Change due to degradation/improvement
	Yield (Tons/ha)						$\% \Delta y = \frac{y_2 - y_1}{y_1} * 100$
Baseline							$\% D = \frac{y_2^c - y_2^d}{y_2^d} * 100$
Endline	Baseline	Endline	BAU	ISFM			
SSA	4.4	3.2	4.9	3.9	−26.8	−19.9	20
LAC	7.6	5.5	8.8	7.1	−27.5	−19.2	29
NAM	4.8	5.9	6.1	7.8	22.5	28.0	33
South Asia	6.5	4.9	7.5	6.1	−24.9	−18.0	25
Asia and Pacific	3.5	6.1	4.2	7.8	75.6	86.5	27
East Europe	2.1	5.3	2.1	5.4	147.3	157.0	2
Central Asia	0.8	1.4	0.8	1.4	69.6	68.0	−1
West Europe	7.7	5.1	8.1	5.7	−33.4	−29.2	11
NENA	1.0	2.8	1.1	3.2	189.3	180.8	15

Note Y1 = Baseline yield (average first 10 years); Y2 = Yield endline period (average last 10 years)
y_2^c = ISFM yield in the last 10 years; y_2^d = BAU yield, last 10 years
See Appendix for countries in each region
SSA Sub-Saharan Africa; *LAC* Latina American countries; *NAM* North America; *NENA* Near East and North Africa

Table 6.19 Change in rainfed wheat yield under business as usual and ISFM—DSSAT results

	BAU		ISFM		Yield change (%)		Change due to degradation/improvement
	Baseline	Endline	Baseline	Endline	$\% \Delta y = \frac{y_2 - y_1}{y_1} * 100$		$\% D = \frac{y_2^c - y_2^d}{y_2^d} * 100$
SSA	1.4	1.2	1.4	1.3	−15.2	−10.7	8
LAC	1.8	1.6	1.8	1.7	−8.8	−6.7	1
NAM	2.3	2.2	2.4	2.2	−7.7	−6.3	3
South Asia	1.4	1.3	1.3	1.1	−8.8	−11.8	−12
Asia and Pacific	2.0	1.8	1.9	1.8	−6.1	−5.6	−1
East Europe	1.3	1.1	1.4	1.2	−10.9	−9.7	7
Central Asia	0.8	0.8	0.8	0.8	0.8	2.2	−7
West Europe	2.1	2.0	2.2	2.1	−7.7	−7.2	6
NENA	1.3	1.2	1.3	1.2	−7.7	−4.9	2

Note Y1 = Baseline yield (average first 10 years); Y2 = Yield endline period (average last 10 years)
y_2^c = ISFM yield in the last 10 years; y_2^d = BAU yield, last 10 years
See Appendix for countries in each region
SSA Sub-Saharan Africa; *LAC* Latina American countries; *NAM* North America; *NENA* Near East and North Africa

The global cost of land degradation for the three crops is about US$56.60 billion per year (Table 6.20), of which, East and South Asia accounted for the largest share of loss. However when the loss is expressed as percent of GDP, South Asia experiences the most severe cost of land degradation on cropland. The cost of land degradation shown is generally low than what has been reported in other studies largely due to DSSAT's assumption of much higher BAU fertilizer application rates. This reduces the actual cost of land degradation. Additionally, DSSAT assumes no salinity or soil erosion. This further demonstrates the underestimation of land degradation on static cropland. The total cost due to the loss of carbon sequestration accounts for 67 % of the total cost at global level—suggesting the cost of land degradation on static cropland is borne more heavily the global community than the farmers. The results also underscore the great potential of ISFM in carbon sequestration.

The three crops account for about 42 % of the cropland in the world. If all cropland is assumed to experience the same level of degradation, the total cost of land degradation on cropland is about 0.25 % of the global GDP.

As discussed in the introduction section, our estimates are conservative since we do not take into account other costs of land degradation. For example we do not include off-site cost of pesticide use, which are quite high. Pimental et al. (1995) estimated that the environmental and social costs were about US$8 billion per year, of which $5 billion are external social costs. The social costs considered were human health and the environmental effects were, pest resistance, loss of natural enemies, groundwater contamination, and loss of pollinating insects and other agents (Ibid).

We also do not consider the point and nonpoint pollution of inorganic fertilizer that leads to eutrophication and other forms of surface and underground water

Table 6.20 Cost of soil fertility mining on static maize, rice and wheat cropland

Region	Cost of land degradation (2007 US$) due to		Type of ecosystem loss			Total cost	Cost of LD as % of GDP
	BAU	Continuous ISFM	Provisioning services	CO_2 sequestration			
				BAU	continuous ISFM		
SSA	0.689	0.126	0.815	1.604	0.947	3.367	0.38
LAC	0.433	0.194	0.627	2.006	2.015	4.648	0.12
NAM	0.275	0.165	0.44	5.00	1.013	6.453	0.04
East Asia	4.331	0.244	4.575	7.071	1.708	13.354	0.13
Oceania	0.03	0.045	0.075	0.365	0.47	0.909	0.09
South Asia	4.724	0.5	5.224	4.541	4.093	13.858	0.78
SE Asia	1.439	0.22	1.659	0.516	1.651	3.827	0.44
East Europe	0.144	0.034	0.178	3.045	0.275	3.498	0.12
West Europe	0.16	0.027	0.187	1.872	0.161	2.219	0.01
Central Asia	0.007	0.004	0.011	0.257	0.076	0.344	0.19
NENA	0.261	0.04	0.301	3.373	0.448	4.122	0.20
Total	12.493	1.599	14.092	29.651	12.856	56.599	0.10

Note See Appendix for countries in each region
SSA Sub-Saharan Africa; *LAC* Latin American countries; *NAM* North America; *NENA* Near East and North Africa; *SE* South East
Source Authors

pollution. About 47 % of nitrogen applied is lost annually to the environment through leaching, erosion, runoff, and gaseous emissions (Roy et al. 2002). Agriculture is the leading cause of eutrophication and other forms of freshwater pollution (Ongley 1996). Pretty et al. (2003) estimated the cost of eutrophication in the United Kingdom to be about £75.0–114.3 million or 2003 US$ 127 to 193 million and 2.2 billion in US (Dodds et al. 2003). Another study estimated that water pollution costs from agriculture in the United Kingdom is US$141–300 million per year or about 1–2 % of the value of gross agricultural output (DEFRA 2010; Pretty et al. 2003). At a global level, Dodds et al. (2013) estimated the loss of freshwater ecosystems due to human activities is 2013 US$900 billion per year. In general, our estimates are conservative due to the limitation of the crop modeling used and future studies are required to take into account the gaps in this study.

Cost of Land Degradation on Grazing Biomass

The cost of land degradation on grazing land that takes into account only loss of milk and meat production is about 2007US$7.7 billion (Table 6.21). As discussed in Chap. 8, loss of milk production accounts for the largest share of total cost. NAM

Table 6.21 Cost of loss of milk and meat production due to land degradation of grazing biomass

Regions	Milk	Meat	Total	Gross total	Percent of total cost
	2007 US$ Million				
SSA	1018.02	127.26	1145.28	1489.46	15
LAC	1082.78	82.46	1165.23	1494.67	15
NAM	2633.68	283.49	2917.17	3495.73	38
East Asia	13.62	5.08	18.70	22.66	0
Oceania	336.75	190.33	527.08	565.25	7
South Asia	16.00	0.90	16.90	21.54	0
SE Asia	156.76	2.30	159.05	178.11	2
East Europe	271.44	364.11	635.55	360.92	8
West Europe	586.93	252.10	839.03	941.58	11
Central Asia	102.51	6.63	109.14	126.38	1
NENA	15.07	113.80	128.88	42.71	2
Global	6233.56	1428.45	7662.01	8739.02	

Note: *NAM* North America, *LAC* Latin American Countries, *SSA* Sub-Saharan Africa, and *NENA* Near East and North Africa

accounts for 38 % of the total cost due to the high productivity of livestock system in the region and the severe land degradation that occurred. Other regions that experienced severe grazing land degradation are SSA and LAC.

Summary of Cost of Land Degradation

Table 6.22 shows that the total cost of land degradation due to LUCC and use of land degrading management practices on static cropland and grazing land is about US$300 billion. LUCC accounts for the largest of total cost of land degradation. This is largely due to its broader coverage of biomes and ecosystems services. Likewise, SSA and West Europe respectively accounts for the largest and smallest share of the global total cost of land degradation.

We now turn to cost of action against land degradation in order to determine whether action could be justified economically. As Nkonya et al. (2013) note, an action against land degradation will be taken if the cost of inaction is greater than the cost of taking action.

Cost of Action Against land degradation

We computed the cost of taking action against land degradation using Eq. (6.5). The components of taking action against land degradation, namely the cost of establishing and maintaining degraded biome, and the opportunity cost of taking

Table 6.22 Summary of cost of land degradation

Region	Type of land degradation			Total cost of LD	Cost of LD as percent of	
	LUCC	Use of land degrading management practices on:				
		Cropland	Grazing lands			
	2007 US$ billion				GDP	Total cost
SSA	60.29	3.367	1.49	65.15	7.4	22.0
LAC	52.551	4.648	1.49	58.69	1.5	19.8
NAM	26.443	6.453	3.50	36.39	0.2	12.3
East Asia	16.704	13.354	0.02	30.08	0.3	10.2
Pacific	13.928	0.909	0.57	15.40	1.5	5.2
South Asia	9.664	13.858	0.02	23.54	1.3	8.0
SE Asia	5.793	3.827	0.18	9.80	1.1	3.3
East Europe	23.957	3.498	0.36	27.82	0.9	9.4
Central Asia	5.743	2.219	0.94	8.90	4.9	3.0
West Europe	5.252	0.344	0.13	5.72	0.0	1.9
NENA	10.436	4.122	0.04	14.60	0.7	4.9
Global	230.761	56.599	8.74	296.10	0.5	

Note: *LD* Land degradation
Sources Tables 6.15, 6.20 and 6.21

action—are explained in detail in the methods section. This section only presents the results. To completely rehabilitate land degradation due to LUCC in all regions, a total of US$4.6 trillion will be required in 6 years (Table 6.22). But if action is not taken to rehabilitated degraded lands, the world will incur a loss of US$14 trillion during the same.

During the entire 30 year planning horizon, the cost of action is at most 34 % of the cost of inaction. The opportunity cost accounts of taking action accounts for over 90 % of the total cost of action in the first 6 years in all but one region (NENA). This suggests there is a large opportunity cost of taking action against land degradation and such opportunity cost explains the economic rationale of land degradation for private land users. Over the 30 year planning horizon, the cost of action falls dramatically once the opportunity cost is dropped at the establishment period.[5] This means it is the establishment period that matters most and not the rest of the planning horizon (Table 6.23).

The returns to taking action against land degradation are quite high. In the first 6 years, land users will get at least US$2 for every dollar they spend on rehabilitating degraded lands. At the end of land user's 30-year planning horizon, the

[5]Please see discussion in the methods section on why the opportunity cost is dropped at the end of the establishment period.

Table 6.23 Cost of action and inaction against LUCC-related land degradation during the rehabilitation period and planning horizon

Region	Cost of action	Cost of inaction	Cost of action	Cost of inaction	Cost of action as % of cost of inaction[a]		Opportunity cost as % of cost of action, (1st 6 years)	Returns to action against LD		
	First 6 years		30-year planning horizon		1st 6 years	30-year planning horizon				
	2007 US$ billion							6 years	30 years	Without opportunity cost
SSA	795	2696	797	3343	29	24	96	3	4	80
LAC	752	2309	754	2977	33	25	98	3	4	167
NAM	739	2251	751	4545	33	17	93	3	6	45
East Asia	495	1278	508	2594	39	20	98	3	5	150
Oceania	399	1247	407	2442	32	17	97	3	6	105
South Asia	210	493	210	646	43	33	98	2	3	137
SE Asia	134	304	135	400	44	34	98	2	3	148
East Europe	765	2366	777	4813	32	16	92	3	6	36
West Europe	178	451	181	926	39	20	96	3	5	57
Central Asia	53	230	53	277	23	19	97	4	5	130
NENA	80	395	80	504	20	16	81	5	6	27
Total	4600	14021	4653	23465	33	20	94	3	5	50

[a]The inverse of the corresponding percent is the returns on investment
Note See Appendix for countries in each region

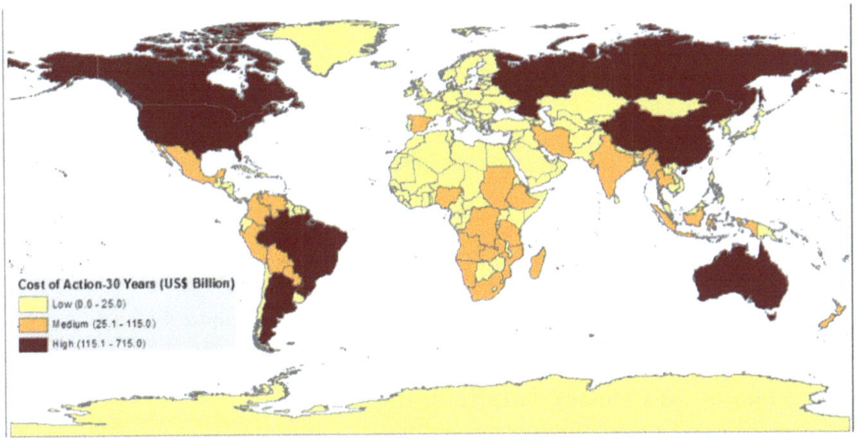

Fig. 6.15 Cost of action against land degradation, 30-year planning horizon

returns to taking action against land degradation increases to at least US$3 for each dollar invested. If we ignore the opportunity cost and consider only the actual cost incurred by land users to address land degradation, the returns are at least US$27 per dollar invested (Table 6.23). The results suggest that the large returns to investment in addressing land degradation but also raise important question as to why many land users do not take action despite the high returns. The chapter on drivers of land degradation addresses this question.

The global distribution of the cost of taking action against land degradation (Fig. 6.15) is consistent with the pattern revealed in the cost of land degradation (Fig. 6.11).

Contrary to Bai et al. (2008), land degradation is severe in both temperate and tropical regions. However the corresponding cost of taking action is highest in high income countries due to their high value of land and labor costs and other factors discussed by Benítez et al. (2007). Country-level cost of taking action against land degradation are highest in North America, Russia, China, Australia Brazil and Argentina. However, regional analysis show that SSA contributes the largest share (17 %) of cost of taking action against land degradation (Fig. 6.16) despite having the small unit cost of biome restoration (Sathaye et al. 2006). This is due to the extent and severity of land degradation in the region. East Europe, North America and LAC also contribute large shares of cost of taking action against land degradation while West Europe, NENA and Central Asia contribute smallest shares. The results underline the global nature of land degradation and the corresponding cost of taking action to address the problem and where large costs are expected to be incurred.

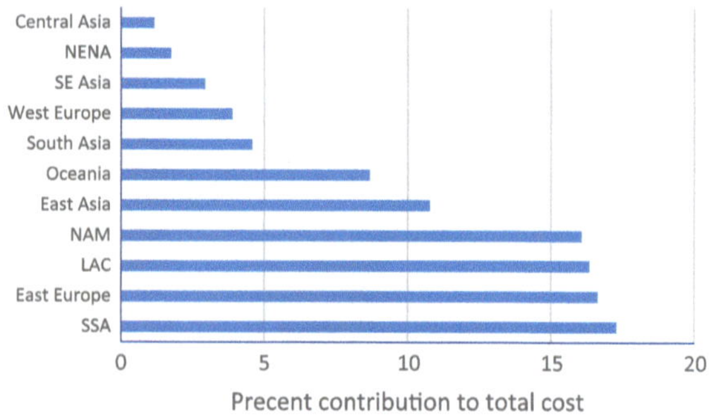

Fig. 6.16 Regional cost of taking action against land degradation

Conclusions and Policy Implications

Land degradation is a global problem that requires both local and global policies and strategies to address it. The global community bears the largest share of land degradation while the local land users where biomes are located bears a smaller share of the cost. As expected, the cost of taking action against land degradation is lower than the cost of inaction even when one considers only the first 6 years of rehabilitation. Returns to investment in action against land degradation is at least twice the cost of inaction in the first six years. But when one takes into account the 30-year planning horizon, the returns are five dollars per dollar invested in action against land degradation. The opportunity cost of taking action accounts for the largest share of the cost and this contributes to inaction in in many countries. Furthermore, the prices of land (and shadow prices) are expected to increase as the world gets wealthier and more crowded moving from 7 to 9 billion in the coming generation. Any further degradation of land and soils will increase even more with the increase of the value of the degraded resources.

Strategies should be developed that give incentives to better manage lands and reward those who practice land management that provide significant global ecosystem services. The payment for ecosystem services (PES) mechanisms that saw large investments in carbon markets should be given a new impetus to address the loss of ecosystem services through land use/cover change (LUCC) which accounts for the largest cost of land degradation.

SSA accounts for the largest share of land degradation and the corresponding cost of action. The global community needs to pay greater attention to addressing land degradation in SSA, since the region accounts for the largest share of total value of ecosystem services and that its highest level of poverty and other challenges reduces its capacity to achieve United Nations Convention to Combat desertification (UNCCD)'s target of zero net land degradation by year 2030. The new strategies need to learn from past success stories and failed projects. There are success stories that have proven that even poor farmers could practice sustainable land management practices. The case of Niger and the re-greening of the Sahel demonstrates this. The top-down programs implemented in developing countries prove that they rarely work.

The extent of land degradation high cost of taking action against land degradation in high income countries also requires greater attention. However, the large endowment of financial and human capital and greater government effectiveness give the high income a greater opportunity to achieving UNCCD's target of zero net land degradation by year 2030.

Appendix

Countries, Sub-regions and Regions

Central Africa	Caribbean countries	East Asia	East Europe	Central Asia
Cameroon	Puerto Rico	Macao	Kosovo	Kyrgyzstan
Gabon	Cayman Islands	Hong Kong	Armenia	Azerbaijan
Equatorial Guinea	Dominica	China	Ukraine	Uzbekistan
Central African Rep.	Bahamas	South Korea	Iceland	Turkmenistan
Sao Tome and Principe	Saint Vincent and the Grenadines	Mongolia	Slovakia	Tajikistan
DRC	Cuba	Taiwan	Slovenia	Kazakhstan
Congo	Turks and Caicos Islands	North Korea	Poland	**NENA**
Eastern Africa	Dominican Republic	Japan	Belarus	Lebanon
Eritrea	Guadeloupe	**Pacific/Oceania**	Croatia	Jordan
Burundi	Barbados	Niue	Hungary	Morocco
Kenya	Haiti	Tuvalu	Latvia	Malta
Ethiopia	French Guiana	Papua New Guinea	Czech Republic	Syria
Uganda	Jamaica	Tonga	Lithuania	Tunisia
Somalia	Antigua and Barbuda	New Zealand	Romania	West Bank
Sudan	Montserrat	Fiji	Albania	Algeria
Rwanda	Belize	French Polynesia	Montenegro	Libyan Arab Jamahiriya
Djibouti	Saint Helena	Guam	Czechoslovakia	Cyprus

(continued)

(continued)

Central Africa	Caribbean countries	East Asia	East Europe	Central Asia
Indian Ocean	Saint Kitts and Nevis	Micronesia	Bulgaria	Israel
Mayotte	Guyana	Marshall Islands	Yugoslavia	Western Sahara
Comoros	Anguilla	Samoa	Bosnia and Herzegovina	Egypt
Mauritius	Suriname	Cook Islands		Gibraltar
Madagascar	Grenada	Palau	Russia	UAE
Seychelles	Netherlands Antilles	Wallis and Futuna Islands	Macedonia	Turkey
Reunion	Martinique	Kiribati	Estonia	Yemen
Southern Africa	British Virgin Islands	New Caledonia	Serbia and Montenegro	Iraq
Botswana	Trinidad and Tobago	Vanuatu	Georgia	Kuwait
Malawi	Bermuda	Solomon Islands	Modova	Qatar
Zambia	Saint Lucia	Northern Mariana Islands	Serbia	Palestinian Territory
Namibia	Aruba	Pitcairn Islands	**West Europe**	Afghanistan
Zimbabwe	**Central America**	American Samoa	Isle of Man	Saudi Arabia
Angola	Honduras	Norfolk Island	Belgium	Oman
Lesotho	Costa Rica	Tokelau	Norway	Pakistan
Mozambique	Nicaragua	Pacific Islands Trust Territory	Andorra	Bahrain
South Africa	El Salvador	Australia	Saint Pierre and Miquelon	Iran
Swaziland	Guatemala	**Southern Asia**	United Kingdom	
Tanzania	Mexico	Nauru	Greece	
Western Africa	Panama	India	Liechtenstein	
Chad	**North America**	Sri Lanka	France	
Ghana	Canada	Nepal	Sweden	
Sierra Leone	US Virgin Islands	Bhutan	Ireland	
Gambia	USA	Maldives	San Marino	
Burkina Faso	Southern America	Bangladesh	MONACO	
Guinea-Bissau	Chile	Indonesia	Netherlands	
Benin	Colombia	Viet Nam	Greenland	
Côte d'Ivoire	Falkland Islands (Malvinas)	Cambodia	Portugal	
Mauritania	Uruguay	Philippines	Luxembourg	

(continued)

(continued)

Central Africa	Caribbean countries	East Asia	East Europe	Central Asia
Guinea	Argentina	Lao People's Democratic Republic	Switzerland	
Mali	Ecuador	Timor-Leste	Finland	
Togo	Brazil	Singapore	Spain	
Senegal	Bolivia	Malaysia	Denmark	
Nigeria	Peru	Brunei Darussalam	Italy	
Niger	Venezuela	Thailand	Channel Islands	
Liberia	Paraguay	Myanmar	Faroe Islands	
Cape Verde			Germany	
			Austria	

References

Bagong Pagasa Foundation. (2011). Cost comparison analysis of ANR compared to conventional reforestation. In P.B. Durst, P. Sajise, & R.N. Leslie (eds.) *Proceedings of the Regional Workshop on Advancing the Application of Assisted Natural Regeneration for Effective Low-Cost Restoration*. Bohol, Philippines. FAO, Bangkok, May 19–22, 2009

Bai, Z. G., Dent, D. L., Olsson, L., Schaepman, M. E. (2008). *Global assessment of land degradation and improvement. 1. Identification by remote sensing*. GLADA Report 5 (November). Wageningen, The Netherlands.

Balmford, A., Rodrigues, A., Walpole, M., ten Brink, P., Kettunen, M., Braat, L. (2008). *The economics of biodiversity and ecosystems: scoping the science*. Final Report. Cambridge, UK: European Commission (contract: ENV/070307/2007/486089/ETU/B2).

Basson, G. (2010). *Sedimentation and sustainable use of reservoirs and river systems*. International Commission on Large Dams (ICOLD) Bulletin. Online at http://www.icold-cigb.org/userfiles/files/CIRCULAR/CL1793Annex.pdf. Accessed Sept 23, 2014.

Benítez, P. C., McCallum, I., Obersteiner, M., & Yamagata, Y. (2007). Global potential for carbon sequestration: Geographical distribution, country risk and policy implications. *Ecological Economics, 60*(3), 572–583.

Brouder, S. M., & Gomez-Macpherson, H. (2014). The impact of conservation agriculture on smallholder agricultural yields: A scoping review of the evidence. *Agriculture, Ecosystems & Environment, 187*, 11–32.

Catterall, C. P., Kanowski, J., Wardell-Johnson, G. W., Proctor, H., Reis, R., Harrison, D., & Tucker, N. I. (2004). Quantifying the biodiversity values of reforestation: Perspectives, design issues and outcomes in Australian rainforest landscapes. In D. Lunney (Ed.), *Conservation of Australia's Forest Fauna* (pp. 359–393). Mosman: Royal Zoological Society of New South Wales.

CBD (Convention on Biological Diversity). (2001). The value of forest ecosystems. Montreal, SCBD, 67 p. (CBD Technical Series no. 4).

CBD (Secretariat of the Convention on Biological Diversity). (2010). Global biodiversity outlook 3. Montréal, 94 p.

Chiabai, A., Travisi, C. M., Markandya, A., Ding, H., & Nunes, P. A. (2011). Economic assessment of forest ecosystem services losses: Cost of policy inaction. *Environmental and Resource Econonomics., 50*(3), 405–445.

Costanza, R., de Groot, R., Sutton, P., van der Ploeg, S., Anderson, S. J., Kubiszewski, I., et al. (2014). Changes in the global value of ecosystem services. *Global Environmental Change, 26*, 152–158.

de Groot, R., Brander, L., van der Ploeg, S., Costanza, R., Bernard, F., Braat, L., et al. (2012). Global estimates of the value of ecosystems and their services in monetary units. *Ecosystem Services, 1*, 50–61.

Defra (UK Department for Environment, Food, and Rural Affairs). (2010). *Improving the use of environmental valuation in policy appraisal: A Value transfer strategy*. London: Defra.

Desvousges, W. H., Johnson, F. R., & Spencer Banzhaf, H. S. (1998). *Environmental policy analysis with limited information: Principles and application of the transfer method*. Cheltenham, UK: Edward Elgar.

Dodds, W. K., Bouska, W.W., Eitzmann, J. L., Pilger, T. J., Pitts, K. L., Riley, A. J., Schloesser, J. T., & Thornbrugh, D. J. (2003). Eutrophication of U.S. freshwaters: Analysis of potential economic damages. *Environmental Science and Technology* 43(1), 12–19 (2009).

Dodds, W. K., Perkin, J. S., & Gerken, J. E. (2013). Human impact on freshwater ecosystem services: A global perspective. *Environmental Science and Technology, 47*(16), 9061–9068.

Dregne, H. E., & Chou, N. T. (1992). Global desertification dimensions and costs. *Degradation and restoration of arid lands*, 73–92.

EPI (Environmental Performance Index). (2012). *Environmental performance index and pilot trend of environmental performance index*. Online at www.epi.yale.edu. Accessed June 4, 2014.

FAO 55, www.fao.org/docrep/w2598e/w2598e06.htm. Accessed June 20, 2014.

FAO. 2006. Fertilizer use by crop.

FAO. (2007). *State of world's forests*. FAO Rome.

FAO, 2008. Conservation Agriculture, 2008-07-08. Available at http://www.fao.org/ag/ca/index.html.

FAO. (2010). *Global Forest Resources Assessment 2010. Terms and Definitions*. Working paper 144/E.

FAO. (2010). *Challenges and opportunities for carbon sequestration in grassland systems* (Vol. 9). A technical report on grassland management and climate change mitigation. Integrated Crop Management.

FAO. (2011). State of the world's Forests 2011.

FAO. (2012a). State of food and agriculture. Paying farmers for ecosystem services.

FAO. (2012b). *Livestock and landscape*. Online at http://www.fao.org/fileadmin/templates/nr/sustainability_pathways/docs/Factsheet_LIVESTOCK_and_LANDSCAPES.pdf. Accessed on May 21, 2014.

FAO. (2013). *Climate change guidelines for forest managers*. FAO Forestry Paper No. 172. Rome, Food and Agriculture Organization of the United Nations.

FAOSTAT. (2014). Online agricultural database. http://faostat3.fao.org/faostat-gateway/go/to/home/E. Accessed April 2, 2014.

Fisher, B., Turner, K., Zylstra, M., Brouwer, R., Groot, R. D., Farber, S., et al. (2008). Ecosystem services and economic theory: Integration for policy-relevant research. *Ecological Applications, 18*(8), 2050–2067.

Foley, J. A., DeFries, R., Asner, G. P., Barford, C., Bonan, G., Carpenter, S. R., et al. (2005). Global Consequences of Land Use. *Science, 309*, 570. doi:10.1126/science.1111772.

Foley, J., Ramankutty, N., Brauman, K. A., Cassidy, E. S., Gerber, J. S., Johnston, M., et al. (2011). Solutions for a cultivated planet. *Nature, 478*, 337–342.

Friedl, M., Sulla-Menashe, D., Tan, B., Schneider, A., Ramankutty, N., Sibley, A., & Huang, X. (2010). MODIS global land cover: Algorithm refinements and characterization of new datasets. *Remote Sensing of Environment, 114*(1), 168–182.

Friedrich, T., Derpsch, R., Kassam, A. (2012). Overview of the global spread of conservation agriculture. *The Journal of Field Actions*. Field Actions Science Reports Special Issue 6, http://factsreports.revues.org/1941.

Fu, B. J., Su, C. H., Wei, Y. P., Willett, I. R., Lü, Y. H., & Liu, G. H. (2011). Double counting in ecosystem services valuation: Causes and countermeasures. *Ecological Research, 26*(1), 1–14.

Fulton, M. (2010). Foreword. In C. Lindwall, B. Sonntag, (Eds.), *Landscapes trans-formed: The history of conservation tillage and direct seeding. Knowledge impact in society, Saskatoon, Saskatchewan* (pp. ix–xiv). http://www.kis.usask.ca/ZeroTill/LandscapesTransformed_HistoryofCT_Book.pdf.

Gibbs, H. K., Ruesch, A. S., Achard, F., Clayton, M. K., Holmgren, P., Ramankutty, N., & Foley, J. A. (2010). Tropical forests were the primary sources of new agricultural land in the 1980s and 1990s. *Proceedings of the National Academy of Sciences of the United States, 107*(38), 16732–37.

Gijsman, A. J., Hoogenboom, G., Parton, W. J., & Kerridge, P. C. (2002). Modifying DSSAT crop models for low-input agricultural systems using a soil organic matter–residue module from CENTURY. *Agronomy Journal, 94*(3), 462–474.

Glibert, P., Harrison, J., Heil, C., & Seitzinger, S. (2006). Escalating worldwide use of urea—A global change contributing to coastal eutrophication. *Biogeochemistry, 77*, 441–463.

Heuzé V., Tran, G., Boudon, A., & Lebas, F. (2015). *Rhodes grass (Chloris gayana). Feedipedia. org. A programme by INRA, CIRAD, AFZ and FAO.* http://www.feedipedia.org/node/480. Accessed March 31, 2015.

IISD (international Institute for Sustainable Development). 1996. *Arid and semi-arid lands: Characteristics and importance.* Online at http://www.iisd.org/casl/asalprojectdetails/asal.htm.

Kassam, A., Friedrich, T., Shaxson, F., & Pretty, J. (2009). The spread of conservation agriculture: Justification, sustainability and uptake. *International Journal of Agricultural Sustainability, 7* (4), 292–320.

Le, Bao Q.B., Nkonya, E., Mirzabaev, A. (2014) Biomass Productivity-Based Mapping of Global Land Degradation Hotspots. ZEF-Discussion Papers on Development Policy No. 193. University of Bonn

Llewellyn, R. S., D'Emden, F. H., & Kuehne, G. (2012). Extensive use of no-tillage in grain growing regions of Australia. *Field Crops Research, 132*, 204–212.

Lobell, D. B., & Burke, M. B. (2010). On the use of statistical models to predict crop yield responses to climate change. *Agricultural and Forest Meteorology, 150*(11), 1443–1452.

McGinley, M. (2014). Biome. Retrieved from http://www.eoearth.org/view/article/150661.

MEA (Millennium Ecosystem Assessment). (2005). *Ecosystems and human well-being.* Washington, DC: Island Press.

Miller, G. T. (1990). *Resource conservation and management.* Belmont California Wadsworth Publishing Co.

Myers, N., Mittermeier, R. A., Mittermeier, C. G., da Fonseca, G. A. B., & Kent, J. (2000). Biodiversity hotspots for conservation priorities. *Nature, 403*, 853–858.

Nandwa, S., & Bekunda, M. A. (1998). Research on nutrient flows and balances in East and Southern Africa: State-of-the-art. *Agriculture, Ecosystems & Environment, 71*(1), 5–18.

NASA (National Aerospace Authority). (2014). Moderate-resolution Imaging Spectroradiometer (MODIS). Online at http://modis.gsfc.nasa.gov/about/media/modis_brochure.pdf. Accessed May 27, 2014.

Nijkamp, P., Vindigni, G., & Nunes, P. A. L. D. (2008). Economic valuation of biodiversity: A comparative study. *Ecological Economics, 67*, 217–231.

Nkonya, E., von Braun, J., Mirzabaev, A., Bao, Q., Le, H., Kwon, Y., Kirui, O. (2013). Economics of land degradation initiative: Methods and approach for global and national assessments. ZEF-Discussion Papers on Development Policy No. 183

Ongley E.D. (1996). Control of water pollution from agriculture. Fertilizers as water pollutants.

Palm, C., Blanco-Canqui, H., Declerck, F., Gatere, L., & Grace, P. (2014). Conservation agriculture and ecosystems services. An overview. *Agriculture, Ecosystems & Environment, 187*, 87–105.

Pan, Y., Birdsey, R. A., Fang, J., Houghton, R., Kauppi, P. E., Kurz, W. A., et al. (2011). A large and persistent carbon sink in the world's forests. *Science, 333*, 988–993.

Pannell, D. J., Llewellyn, R. S., & Corbeels, M. (2014). The farm-level economics of conservation agriculture for resource-poor farmers. *Agriculture, Ecosystems & Environment, 187*(1), 52–64.

Pender, J. (2009). Impacts of sustainable land management programs on land management and poverty in Niger Report No.: 48230-NE.

Pimentel, D., Harvey, C., Resosudarmo, P., Sinclair, K., Kurz, D., McNair, M., et al. (1995). Environmental and economic costs of soil erosion and conservation benefits. *Science, 267* (5201), 1117–1123.

Pretty, J. N., Mason, C. F., Nedwell, D. B., & Hine, R. E. (2003). Environmental costs of freshwater eutrophication in England and Wales. *Environmental Science and Technology, 37*, 201–208.

Ramankutty, N., Evan, A. T., Monfreda, C., & Foley, J. A. (2008). Farming the planet: 1. Geographic distribution of global agricultural lands in the year 2000. *Global Biogeochemical Cycles, 22*(1), 1–19.

Rautiainen, A., Wernick, I., Waggoner, P. E., Ausubel, J. H., & Kauppi, P. E. (2011). A national and international analysis of changing forest density. *PLoS, 259*(7), 1232–1238.

Requier-Desjardins, M., Adhikari, B., & Sperlich, S. (2011). Some notes on the economic assessment of land degradation‖. *Land Degradation and Development, 22*, 285–298.

Roy, R., Misra, R., & Montanez, A. (2002). Decreasing reliance on mineral nitrogen—yet more food. *Ambio, 31*(2), 177–183.

Sathaye, J., Makundi, W., Dale, L., Chan, P., & Andrasko, K. (2006). GHG mitigation potential, costs and benefits in global forests: A dynamic partial equilibrium approach. *The Energy Journal, 27*, 127–162.

Seppelt, R., Dormann, C. F., Eppink, F. V., Lautenbach, S., & Schmidt, S. (2011). A quantitative review of ecosystem service studies: approaches, shortcomings and the road ahead. *Journal of Applied Ecology, 48*, 630–636.

Shahwahid, M., Awang Noor, H. O., Abdul Rahman, A. G., & Shaharuddin Ahmad, M. D. (1999). Cost and earning structure of logging industry in Peninsular Malaysia. *The Malayan Forester*, 62, 107–117.

Spiers, A. G. (2001). Wetland inventory: Overview at a global scale. In Wetland inventory, assessment and monitoring: Practical techniques and identification of major issues. *Proceedings of Workshop* (Vol. 4, pp. 23–30).

Stout, B. A. (1990). *Handbook of energy for world agriculture*. London & New York: Elsevier Applied Science.

Swinton, S. M., Lupia, F., Robertson, G. P., & Hamilton, S. K. (2007). Ecosystem services and agriculture: Cultivating agricultural ecosystems for diverse benefits. *Ecological Economics, 64*, 245–252.

Tennigkeit, T. & Wilkies, A. (2008). *An assessment of the potential for carbon finance in rangelands*. ICRAF. Online at http://www.worldagroforestrycentre.org/our_products/publications/.

Torres, A. B., Marchant, R., Lovett, J. C., Smart, J. C. R., & Tipper, R. (2010). Analysis of the carbon sequestration costs of afforestation and reforestation agroforestry practices and the use of cost curves to evaluate their potential for implementation of climate change mitigation. *Ecological Economics, 69*, 469–477.

Trivedi, M., Papageorgiou, S., Moran, D. (2008). *What are rainforests worth? And why it makes economic sense to keep them standing*. Oxford, UK, pp iv + 48.

Troy, A., & Wilson, M. (2006). Mapping ecosystem services: Practical challenges and opportunities in linking GIS and value transfer. *Ecological Economics, 60*(2), 436–449.

Trustcost. (2014). *Natural capital at risk: The top 100 externalities of business*. Online at http://www.trucost.com/ accessed June 17, 2014.

UN. (2010). *World urbanization prospects: The 2009 Revision*. Online at http://www.un.org/en/development/desa/population/publications/pdf/urbanization/. Accessed May 29, 2014.

UNCCD. (2013). *Background document. The Economics of desertification, land degradation and drought: Methodologies and analysis for decision-making*. Online at http://2sc.unccd.int/fileadmin/unccd/upload/documents/Background_documents/Background_Document_web3.pdf.

Vanlauwe, B., & Giller, K. E. (2006). Popular myths around soil fertility management in sub-Saharan Africa. *Agriculture, Ecosystems & Environment, 116*(1), 34–46.

Vlek, P. L. G., Le, Q. B., & Tamene, L. (2010). Assessment of land degradation, its possible causes and threat to food security in Sub-Saharan Africa. In *Food security and soil quality. Advances in Soil Science* (pp. 57–86). Taylor & Francis, Boca Raton, FL, USA.

Vlek P., G. Rodr´iguez-Kuhl and R. Sommer. 2004. Energy use and CO2 production in tropical agriculture and means and strategies for reduction or mitigation. Environment, Development and Sustainability 6: 213–233.

von Braun, J. (2013). *International co-operation for agricultural development and food and nutrition security. New institutional arrangements for related public goods.* WIDER Working Paper No. 2013/061.

Wheelwright, N. T., & Logan, B. A. (2004). Previous-year reproduction reduces photosynthetic capacity and slows lifetime growth in females of a neotropical tree. In *Proceedings of National Academy of Sciences* (Vol. 101, No. 21).

White, R., Murray, S., & Rohweder, M. (2000). *Pilot analysis of global ecosystems grassland ecosystems*. World Resources Institute: Washington D.C.

Yaron, G. (1999). *Forest, plantation crops or small-scale agriculture? An economic analysis of alternative land use options in the mount Cameroon area.* UK Economic and Social Research Council Centre for Social and Economic Research on the Global Environment (CSERGE) Working Paper GEC 99–16. Online http://www.cepal.org/ilpes/noticias/paginas/4/31914/Yaron_1999_Mount_Cameroon.pdf.

Chapter 7
Global Drivers of Land Degradation and Improvement

Alisher Mirzabaev, Ephraim Nkonya, Jann Goedecke, Timothy Johnson and Weston Anderson

Abstract Identification of factors catalyzing sustainable land management (SLM) could provide insights for national policies and international efforts to address land degradation. Building on previous studies, and using novel datasets, this chapter identifies major drivers of land degradation at global and regional levels. The findings of this study confirm the earlier insights in the literature on the context-specific nature of the drivers of land degradation. This context-dependence explains the previous contradictions in the literature on the effects of various socio-economic and institutional factors on land degradation. It also calls for the localized diagnostic of the drivers of land degradation. The drivers of land degradation are predominantly local, so actions to address them should be based on the understanding of the local interplay of various factors and how they affect land degradation.

Keywords Drivers of land degradation · Endogeneity · Land degradation hotspots

---

A. Mirzabaev (✉) · J. Goedecke
Center for Development Research, University of Bonn, Walter Flex Str 3, 53113 Bonn, Germany
e-mail: almir@uni-bonn.de

J. Goedecke
e-mail: jann.goedecke@kuleuven.be

E. Nkonya · T. Johnson
International Food Policy Research institute, 2033 K Street NW, Washington DC 20006, USA

J. Goedecke
Faculty of Economics and Business, KU Leuven, Warmoesberg 26, Brussels1000, Belgium

W. Anderson
Department of Earth and Environmental Sciences, Columbia University, New York, USA
e-mail: weston@ldeo.columbia.edu

E. Nkonya et al. (eds.), *Economics of Land Degradation and Improvement – A Global Assessment for Sustainable Development*,
DOI 10.1007/978-3-319-19168-3_7

Introduction

Land degradation has occurred on about 30 % of global land area between 1982 and 2006 (Chap. 4), resulting in substantial economic impacts on agricultural livelihoods and national economies (Chap. 6), especially in developing lower income countries. The drivers of land degradation are numerous, complex and interrelated (Nkonya et al. 2011; von Braun et al. 2013; Pender et al. 2009), with often context-dependent characteristics. Therefore, identification of the important drivers of land degradation is crucial for national and international efforts to reduce, and optimally, prevent land degradation and promote land restoration and improvement. Based on this problem definition, this chapter seeks to answer the following research question: what are the major drivers of land degradation at the global and regional levels?

While answering this research question, the present study intends to make the following contributions. Many previous studies have used raw values of the Normalized Difference Vegetation Index (NDVI) as a proxy for land degradation (Nkonya and Anderson 2014; Nkonya et al. 2011). These raw values may be significantly biased by such factors as rainfall dynamics (Bai et al. 2008) and atmospheric or chemical fertilization (Vlek et al. 2010). This chapter uses a new global dataset of land degradation hotspots (Le et al. 2014, Chap. 4) as its dependent variable, which corrects for the above mentioned sources of potential biases. Moreover, many previous studies at the global level (cf. Nkonya et al. 2011 for a review) explore the drivers of land degradation by grouping countries within geographic regions, i.e. Sub-Saharan Africa, Asia, etc. However, the same geographic region may contain countries with very differing conditions. For example, Asia contains both Japan and North Korea, putting such very different countries together may make the results more ambiguous. A more theoretically motivated approach would be to run sub-global regressions for groupings of countries with similar socio-economic, agro-ecological and institutional features. The study makes use of such a country clustering (Table 7.8), developed in Nkonya et al. (2013) and Chap. 2, by making the sub-global regressions more easily interpretable along the major socio-economic and institutional characteristics of the countries. Furthermore, the dependent variable in the present study includes not only degraded and non-degraded categories, but also a category designating areas where land improvement has occurred. Most previous studies confound improved areas with non-degraded areas. To illustrate, land degradation is often considered under dichotomous representation whether land degradation has occurred or not (e.g. usually using a dummy variable with categories 0—land degradation, and 1—no land degradation). However, this ignores the fact that the "no land degradation" category consists of two distinct groups: one group where there has been no change in land quality, and the second group where land quality has improved. The present study disentangles "no land degradation" and "land improvement" as two distinct categories. Fourthly, we seek to further minimize potential omitted variable bias by including some relatively new global level datasets, such as night time lighting intensity series (Elvidge et al. 2001), which were found to be good proxies of institutional development and poverty (Ebener et al. 2005; Sutton et al. 2007; Michalopoulos and Papaioannou 2013). Moreover, the inclusion of regional, country, and agro-ecological zone fixed effects also minimizes the omitted variable bias. Finally, previous work is challenged by the endogeneity of some of the variables in the global models; the present study makes a step forward in addressing this issue.

Literature Review

The causes of land degradation are numerous and complex (Table 7.1). Quite often, the same causal factor could lead to diverging consequences in different contexts because of its varying interactions with other proximate and underlying causes of land degradation.

The effects of proximate drivers of land degradation—such as topography, climate, and soil characteristics—are well understood as causes of land degradation and there is a broad consensus about their causal mechanisms. For example, steeper slopes are more vulnerable to water-induced soil erosion (Wischmeier 1976; Voortman et al. 2000) and soils with high silt content are naturally more prone to degradation (Bonilla and Johnson 2012). There are also a large number of available SLM technologies developed to address soil and land degradation (Liniger and Schwilch 2002; Liniger and Critchley 2007). However, there is an on-going debate on the role of various underlying drivers of land degradation (von Braun et al. 2013; Nkonya et al. 2011) and why many existing SLM technologies are not adopted by landusers (for example, Pender et al. 2009, for Central Asia). For instance, as summarized in Mirzabaev et al. (2015), some well-known points of debate on the drivers of land degradation include: whether higher population causes land degradation (Grepperud 1996), or leads to SLM (Tiffen et al. 1994); whether poverty is a primary driver of land degradation (Way 2006; Cleaver and Schreiber 1994; Scherr 2000) or not (Nkonya et al. 2008); and whether higher market access leads to SLM (Pender et al. 2006), or to land degradation (Scherr and Hazell 1994). Table 7.1 elaborates on these underlying drivers and on the theoretical intuitions behind their cause-and-effect mechanisms.

The conclusions reached have been quite diverse and often contradicting depending on the datasets used, methodologies applied, timeframes considered, and locations studied (Mirzabaev et al. 2015). The purpose of the present analysis is not to give the final word on this debate: the nature of available datasets and of methodological challenges would not allow it. However, our objective is to bring the debate a step forward, both by using more advanced datasets which became available at this scale relatively recently and through methodological upgrades to the previous studies.

The diversity of the results implies that targeting one underlying factor is not, in itself, sufficient to address land degradation. Rather, a number of underlying and

Table 7.1 Proximate and underlying drivers related to land degradation and their potential cause-effect mechanisms (selective)

Drivers	Type	Examples of causality	References
Topography	Proximate and natural	Steep slopes are vulnerable to severe water-induced soil erosion	Wischmeier (1976), Voortman et al. (2000)
Land cover change	Proximate and natural/anthropogenic	Conversion of rangelands to irrigated farming with resulting soil salinity. Deforestation	Gao and Liu (2010), Lu et al. (2007)
Climate	Proximate and natural	Dry, hot areas are prone to naturally occurring wildfires, which, in turn, lead to soil erosion. Strong rainstorms lead to flooding and erosion. Low and infrequent rainfall and erratic and erosive rainfall (monsoon areas) lead to erosion and salinization	Safriel and Adeel (2005), Barrow (1991)
Soil erodibility	Proximate and natural	Some soils, for example those with high silt content, could be naturally more prone to erosion	Bonilla and Johnson (2012)
Pest and diseases	Proximate and natural	Pests and diseases lead to loss of biodiversity, loss of crop and livestock productivity, and other forms of land degradation	Sternberg (2008)
Unsustainable land management	Proximate and anthropogenic	Land clearing, overgrazing, cultivation on steep slopes, bush burning, pollution of land and water sources, and soil nutrient mining are among the major causes of land degradation	Nkonya et al. (2008, 2011), Pender and Kerr (1998)
Infrastructure development	Proximate and anthropogenic	Transport and earthmoving techniques, such as trucks and tractors, as well as new processing and storage technologies, could lead to increased production and foster land degradation if not properly planned	Geist and Lambin (2004)

(continued)

Table 7.1 (continued)

Drivers	Type	Examples of causality	References
Population density	Underlying	No definite answer Population density leads to land improvement	Bai et al. (2008), Tiffen et al. (1994), Boserup (1965),
		Population density leads to land degradation	Grepperud (1996)
Market access	Underlying	No definite answer Land users in areas with good market access have more incentives to invest in sustainable land management	Pender et al. (2006),
		High market access raises opportunity cost of labor, making households less likely to adopt labor-intensive sustainable land management practices	Scherr and Hazell (1994)
Land tenure	Underlying	No definite answer Insecure land tenure can lead to the adoption of unsustainable land management practices	Kabubo-Mariara (2007)
		Insecure land rights do not deter farmers from making investments in sustainable land management	Besley (1995), Brasselle et al. (2002)
Poverty	Underlying	No definite answer There is a vicious cycle between poverty and land degradation. Poverty could lead to land degradation while land degradation could lead to poverty	Way (2006), Cleaver and Schreiber (1994), Scherr (2000),
		The poor heavily depend on the land, and thus, have a strong incentive to invest their limited capital into preventing or mitigating land degradation if market conditions allow them to allocate their resources efficiently	De Janvry et al. (1991), Nkonya et al. (2008)

(continued)

Table 7.1 (continued)

Drivers	Type	Examples of causality	References
Access to agricultural extension services	Underlying	No definite answer Access to agricultural extension services enhances the adoption of land management practices	Clay et al. (1996) Paudel and Thapa (2004)
		Depending on the capacity and orientation of the extension providers, access to extension services could also lead to land-degrading practices	Benin et al. (2007), Nkonya et al. (2010)
Decentralization	Underlying	Strong local institutions with a capacity for land management are likely to enact bylaws and other regulations that could enhance sustainable land management practices	FAO (2011)
International policies	Underlying	International policies through the United Nations and other organizations have influenced policy formulation and land management	Sanwal (2004)
Non-farm employment	Underlying	Alternative livelihoods could also allow farmers to rest their lands or to use nonfarm income to invest in land improvement	Nkonya et al. (2008)

Proximate drivers are biophysical factors and unsustainable land management practices. Underlying drivers are social, economic and institutional factors that lead to unsustainable land management practices. See Chap. 2 for more detailed discussion
Source von Braun et al. (2013)

proximate factors need to be taken into account when designing policies to prevent or mitigate land degradation (ibid.). For the analysis of land degradation, it is necessary to explicitly model nonlinearities and interactions between the variables, and to address potential biases emanating from omitted variables and reverse causalities. It is likely that such diversity and contradictions will remain in future studies, since these contradictions may simply be reflecting the diverging and context-dependent causal interplays of factors affecting land management, i.e. the same factor (e.g. population pressure) may lead to land degradation or land improvement depending on its interactions with other factors (such as poverty, access to markets and extension, etc.) (ibid.).

Methods and Data

This study is guided by the ELD conceptual framework presented in Chap. 2. The ELD conceptual framework classifies the drivers of land degradation into two categories: (1) proximate and (2) underlying (Table 7.2). Biophysical factors, such as precipitation, agro-ecological zones, land use and land cover, are classified as proximate drivers. Whereas such socio-economic and institutional factors as rule of law, land tenure security, GDP per capita, and infant mortality rates, are classified as underlying drivers of land degradation. The econometric model to identify the drivers of land degradation is specified as follows:

$$
\begin{aligned}
&P(SLM = 0|x_1, x_2, z) = \Phi[\mu_1 - (\beta_1 x_1 + \beta_2 x_2 + \beta_3 z_i)] \\
&P(SLM = 1|x_1, x_2, z) = \Phi[\mu_2 - (\beta_1 x_1 + \beta_2 x_2 + \beta_3 z_i)] - \Phi[\mu_1 - (\beta_1 x_1 + \beta_2 x_2 + \beta_3 z_i)] \\
&P(SLM = 2|x_1, x_2, z) = 1 - \Phi[\mu_2 - (\beta_1 x_1 + \beta_2 x_2 + \beta_3 z_i)] = \Phi(\beta_1 x_1 + \beta_2 x_2 + \beta_3 z_i - \mu_2)
\end{aligned}
\tag{7.1}
$$

where, of land degradation (e.g. precipitation, length of growing period, land cover/use); density, GDP per capita, land tenure security, rule of law, etc.);

SLM a categorical variable, where, 0—land degradation, 1—no change, 2—land improvement, with the baseline in 1982–84 and the endline in 2004–06

x_1 a vector of proximate drivers of land degradation (e.g. precipitation, length of growing period, land cover/use);

x_2 a vector underlying drivers of land degradation (e.g. population density, GDP per capita, land tenure security, rule of law, etc.);

z_i vector of fixed effect variables, including administrative divisions (region, country, etc.);

μ_1, μ_2 model constants;

$\Phi(.)$ the standard normal cumulative distribution function.

Taking into account that the dependent variable has three ordered categories, the present study uses an ordered probit model in the estimation. The ordered probit model assumes that a latent variable (not explicitly modeled above) underlying the state of land degradation is normally distributed, while the effects of the independent variables on the ordered outcomes are restricted to be monotonous. The coefficients are then estimated via the maximum likelihood (ML) method. As can be seen from the model equations, if the independent variables have a positive average effect on the probability that "land degradation" will be the outcome, they will unambiguously reduce the probability that "land improvement" will occur. Formally, it means that if

Table 7.2 Description of the variables

Variable name	Description	Source
SLM: sustainable land management	A categorical variable, where, 0—degraded land, 1—no change, 2—improved land. The baseline 1982–84 and the endline 2004–06	Le et al. (2014), Chap. 4 of this volume
Precipitation	Total annual precipitation (mm) during the baseline period of 1982–84	Climate research unit (CRU), University of East Anglia, through Nkonya and Anderson (2014)
AEZ	Length of growing period (LGP). Categorized into six regions: LGP1: 0–59 days, LGP2: 60–119 days, LGP3: 120–179 days, LGP4: 180–239 days, LGP5: 240–299 days, and LGP6: more than 300 days	Source: Alexandros (1995), through Nkonya and Anderson (2014)
Distance to markets	Travel time to urban areas with 50,000 people or more. Most of the underlying data layers are from around baseline period or do not change over time	Uchida and Nelson (2010), through Nkonya and Anderson (2014)
Population density	The data is for 1990. The data is only for one period because using the population density data for some later period as well could have an endogeneity problem with the dependent variable	CIESIN (2010)
Infant mortality rate	Mortality of children below 5 years per 1000 of live births. Baseline: 1982–82, endline: 2005	Baseline: World development indicators, World Bank. Endline: Source: CIESIN http://sedac.ciesin.columbia.edu/povmap
GDP per capita	For the baseline period of 1982–1984	World development indicators, World Bank
DMSP-OLS nighttime lights time series	Remotely sensed intensity of night time lighting for 1992 (i.e. at the basic level shows the availability of electricity during the night time. Should not be confounded with natural day time brightness). Here used as a proxy for broad socio-economic development and availability of non-farm sector	Image and data processing by NOAA's National Geophysical Data Center. DMSP data collected by US Air Force Weather Agency. http://ngdc.noaa.gov/eog/dmsp/downloadV4composites.html
Land tenure security	Global Land Tenure Master Database. 2007. Has four categories: good—1, moderate concern over the security of land tenure—2, severe concern—3, and extremely severe concern—4. The database was developed in 2004–2006, based on subjective expert evaluations. Closeness to the endline period and	USAID and ARD, Inc. (2008)

(continued)

Table 7.2 (continued)

Variable name	Description	Source
	subjective nature of the evaluation causes potential problems, specifically, endogeneity through reverse causality and measurement error. Though, theoretical reasons for the reverse causality with the dependent variable are thin, i.e. land degradation may not have affected the way experts evaluate the security of land tenure in a specific country. Despite these shortcomings, this is a very important variable that should rather be not missed in the model. Moreover, it is likely that the land tenure situation changes, in most cases, gradually, and this dataset also depicts well the baseline period (perhaps, except for Eastern Europe and the former USSR). To check for sensitivity of the results, we run the global regression with and without this variable to see any influence on other variables	
Rule of law	"Perceptions of the extent to which agents have confidence in and abide by the rules of society, and in particular, the quality of contract enforcement" (Kaufmann et al. 2010), property rights, the police, and the courts, as well as the likelihood of crime and violence, baseline of 1996–1998, endline 2002–2004	Worldwide Governance Indicators: http://info.worldbank.org/governance/wgi/index.asp, through Nkonya and Anderson (2014)
Land use/cover	Globcover 2005–2006 data (interpretation should be only as association, not causality). The regressions are run with and without to see any biasing effects of this variable	Bicheron et al. (2008)

$$\frac{\partial P(SLM = 0)}{\partial x_j} = -\beta_j \phi(\mu_1 - \mathbf{X\beta}) < 0 \tag{7.2}$$

it follows that

$$\frac{\partial P(SLM = 2)}{\partial x_j} = \beta_j \phi(\mathbf{X\beta} - \mu_2) > 0 \tag{7.3}$$

where ϕ denotes the standard normal density and $\mathbf{X\beta} = \beta_1 x_1 + \beta_2 x_2 + \beta_3 z_i$. In contrast, it is generally not clear how the independent variables affect the probability of the "no change" state.

Data

A major shortcoming of many previous global studies is that they do not address the endogeneity between dependent and explanatory variables. For example, poverty may lead to land degradation, but at the same time, land degradation may lead to poverty. If one does not account for such a reverse causality between the dependent and independent variables the model estimates will be biased. To avoid this problem, only variables corresponding to the baseline period (1982–1984) are used as explanatory variables in the model, i.e. the NDVI changes in the future could not have any causal effect on the past values of the explanatory variables (Table 7.2).

However, not all variables are available for the period of 1982–1984, therefore some variables, such as night-time lighting intensity, are taken for the earliest year available, 1992 in this case. There is very little theoretical basis for concluding that land degradation would affect night time lighting intensity, but night time lighting intensity can serve as a proxy for some variables which affect land degradation (e.g., availability of non-farm sectors in the area). At the same time, the use of variables too close to the endline period is minimized, because then the econometric model would not make much sense, since the future cannot cause past: at best, any relationship would be associative, not causal (Table 7.2).

NDVI has well-known limitations as a proxy for land degradation (Le et al. 2014, Chap. 4). However, it can be a good estimate of global vegetation change over a long period of time. Le et al. (2014) address some of the caveats related to using raw values of NDVI by addressing potential distorting effects of rainfall dynamics, atmospheric and chemical fertilization (ibid). The comparison of land degradation results emerging from the work of Le et al. (2014) and the results of land degradation when raw NDVI values are used directly (Nkonya and Anderson 2014), shows considerable and statistically significant discrepancies (Table 7.3).

Both indicators agree on the land degradation status of 63 % of pixels (Table 7.3). However, they disagree on the remaining 37 %, especially concerning the location of degraded areas. The Le et al. (2014) database does not consider a pixel to be degraded if the NDVI value decreases by less than 10 %, as values less than 10 % are not distinguishable from expected measurement errors and noise in the NDVI dataset (Le et al. 2014). In 11 % of areas, the Le et al. (2014) dataset points at degradation, whereas the raw NDVI values do not show degradation. This is due to the fact that Le et al. (2014) also accounts for the masking effects of rainfall, atmospheric and chemical fertilization. For example, the soils may have been completely degraded, but application of chemical inputs may result in similar

Table 7.3 Comparison of land degradation by Le et al. (2014) with the one based on raw NDVI change used by Nkonya and Anderson (2014)

Land degradation categories		Nkonya and Anderson (2014)	
		Degraded (%)	Not degraded (%)
Le et al. (2014), Chap. 4	Degraded	8	11
	Not degraded	25	55

Note Pearson $chi^2(1) = 1.5e{+}04$ Pr = 0.000. The correlation coefficient 0.096

levels of NDVI as before degradation. The overall coefficient of correlation between these two sets of land degradation indicators is 0.096, indicating that these datasets are very divergent.

The descriptive statistics of the variables in the model are given in Table 7.4. All of the variables are in the pixel format (8×8 km^2). Some variables, such as rule of law, land tenure security, do not vary by pixel but vary by country. So in the case of these variables, the same value is attached to all the pixels within a single country.

Most of the descriptive statistics in Table 7.4 are self-explanatory. However, some of the variables warrant more elaboration. Specifically, night time lighting intensity measures the luminosity of night time lighting emitted from the Earth surface during the night, i.e. this measures artificial night time lighting, and can serve as a proxy for the spread and magnitude of electricity use. The potentially distorting effect of the clouds, sun and moonlight interferences are excluded from the data.[1] The higher the number the brighter is the location. Number zero signifies a dark pixel during the night. The rule of law variable is an index number from the World Bank's World Governance Indicators database.[2] The higher number means a better rule of law. Land tenure security variable varies between 1 and 4, with 1 indicating good land tenure security and 4-extremely severe concern over land tenure security.

Results

The results of the analyses are presented in Tables 7.5, 7.6 and 7.7. The theoretical intuitions behind these findings are discussed on more detail further below after the presentation of the full results.

Table 7.5 presents the global level findings. The model results are checked for robustness by testing several model specifications. The first is the full model, in which all variables described in the data section are included. The second model excludes the variables that are taken from periods closer to the endline period due to

[1]http://ngdc.noaa.gov/eog/gcv4_readme.txt.

[2]http://info.worldbank.org/governance/wgi/index.aspx#doc.

Table 7.4 Descriptive statistics of the variables used

Variable	Mean	Standard deviation	Median	Min	Max
Precipitation, baseline (in mm)	772	660	553	1	6901
Population density, baseline	37	181	2	0	35,662
Distance to market (in minutes)	1106	1522	463	0	27,584
Night time lighting intensity 1992[a]	1.19	5.35	0	0	63
GDP per capita (in USD), baseline	9365	10,228	2816	0	55,221
Rule of law, baseline	0.21	1.11	−0.24	−2.19	1.93
Rule of law, change to endline	−0.06	0.22	−0.07	−1.08	1.08
Infant mortality rate, baseline	41	37	26	6	171
Infant mortality rate, change	9	16	5	−132	146
Land tenure security	1.45	0.92	1	1	4.00

[a]The urban areas are excluded from the analysis

their unavailability for the baseline period (their interpretation being associative, not causal). The third model excludes country dummies, the fourth model is without squared terms, the fifth model is without interaction terms, and the last model is without change variables (i.e. those variables showing the change between the baseline and endline periods). The major finding of this sensitivity analysis is that the same results persist throughout the models, pointing at the robustness of the findings. This also shows that endogeneity or omitted variables are not likely to be an issue in the full model. The check for multicollinearity also shows no problem, with the overall variance inflation factor (VIF) being below 10, and even this is mostly driven by the presence of both level and squared terms. Since model 4, where the squared terms are excluded, does not give results different from the full model, it is concluded that multicollinearity is unlikely to have any tangible effects on the model results. For these reasons, below the results are interpreted based on the full model—our preferred specification.

Most of the variables in the model are statistically significant at 1 % and the overall Pseudo R^2 of the full model is equal to 28 %. The key variables that positively influenced sustainable land management are precipitation and longer distance to markets, including when it interacted with crop production. However, the relationship between distance to markets and sustainable land management is concave, meaning that after a certain distance the effect levels out. Moreover, it is found that higher population density and more intense night-time lighting (a proxy for higher socio-economic development) is positively associated with higher land degradation, though in the case of night time lighting intensity the relationship is convex. However, the interaction of night time lighting intensity and higher

Table 7.5 Global level regression

Variables	Model 1	Model 2	Model 3	Model 4	Model 5	Model 6
	Full	No endline variables	No country dummies	No squared terms	No interaction terms	No change variables
Precipitation	0.000139***	0.00024***	0.000216***	0.000151***	0.000142***	0.000144***
Population density	−0.000376***	−0.00057***	−0.000488***	−0.000508***	−0.000339***	−0.000346***
Population density, squared	1.24e−09	3.27e−09	6.03e−09*		1.40e−08***	9.84e−10
Distance to market	0.000379***	0.00045***	0.000428***	0.000197***	0.000377***	0.000379***
Distance to market, squared	−3.55e −08***	−4.51e−08***	−4.48e−08***		−3.52e−08***	−3.57e−08***
Night time lighting intensity	−0.0247***	−0.0308***	−0.0335***	−0.0134***	−0.0283***	−0.0248***
Night time lighting intensity, squared	0.000308***	0.00041***	0.000477***		0.000470***	0.000307***
GDP per capita	1.38e−07	0.0000235	9.51e−05***	9.30e−06	2.77e−06	1.24e−05
GDP per capita, squared	2.40e−10	−2.64e−10	−2.43e−09***		1.81e−10	−0
Rule of law	0.0960*	0.0481726	−0.0747***	0.0870	0.0950*	0.0699
Change in Rule of Law	0.118		0.328***	0.115	0.106	
Infant mortality rate	0.00325***	0.0050***	0.00444***	0.00345***	0.00358***	0.00430***
Change in infant mortality rate	0.00257***		0.00403***	0.00240***	0.00234***	
Distance to market with cropland	0.0446***		0.0207***	0.0665***		0.0413***
Night time lighting intensity with population density	7.78e−06***	0.000011***	8.40e−06***	1.18e−05***		7.38e−06***
Distance to market with population density	−2.93e −06***	−2.98e−06***	−4.91e−06***	−2.43e−06***		−3.05e−06***
Land use, cropland-base						
Mosaic vegetation—crop	0.662***		0.453***	0.788***	0.442***	0.637***
Forest	1.101***		0.878***	1.255***	0.886***	1.076***

(continued)

Table 7.5 (continued)

Variables	Model 1	Model 2	Model 3	Model 4	Model 5	Model 6
	Full	No endline variables	No country dummies	No squared terms	No interaction terms	No change variables
Mosaic forest—shrub	0.724***		0.450***	0.872***	0.507***	0.708***
Shrublands	0.729***		0.415***	0.882***	0.512***	0.711***
Grassland	0.694***		0.413***	0.856***	0.479***	0.664***
Sparse vegetation	0.796***		0.619***	0.937***	0.580***	0.775***
Bare surface or water	0.590***		0.549***	0.722***	0.379***	0.572***
Land tenure security, base—good						
Moderate concern	0.729***		−0.0320***	0.718***	0.723***	0.853***
Severe concern	−0.850***		−0.0444***	−0.903***	−0.920***	−0.966***
Extremely severe concern	−0.166		0.0783***	−0.218**	−0.176*	−0.256***
Missing values for land tenure	−0.404**		0.175***	−0.397**	−0.540***	−0.290*
Regional dummies, base—SSA						
LAC	1.549***	1.41***	−0.381***	1.613***	1.729***	1.450***
North America	1.574***	1.38***	0.142***	1.657***	1.762***	1.438***
NENA	1.593***	1.35***	0.426***	1.571***	1.775***	1.529***
Asia and Pacific	0.115	−0.66***	0.0954***	0.114	0.113	0.222***
Europe	0.710***	−0.74	0.427***	0.703***	0.733***	0.703***
Length of growing period—LGP1						
LGP2	−0.0454***	−0.071***	−0.0784***	0.00323	−0.0461***	−0.0468***
LGP3	−0.0766***	0.01***	−0.127***	−0.0638***	−0.0842***	−0.0655***
LGP4	−0.413***	−0.35***	−0.642***	−0.426***	−0.436***	−0.375***

(continued)

Table 7.5 (continued)

Variables	Model 1	Model 2	Model 3	Model 4	Model 5	Model 6
	Full	No endline variables	No country dummies	No squared terms	No interaction terms	No change variables
LGP5	−0.486***	−0.46***	−0.817***	−0.496***	−0.521***	−0.465***
LGP6	−0.453***	−0.39***	−0.753***	−0.460***	−0.497***	−0.437***
Country dummies	Yes	Yes	No	Yes	Yes	Yes
μ1	0.797***	0.58***	0.253***	0.901***	0.616***	0.938***
μ2	4.858***	4.57***	4.125***	4.933***	4.677***	4.981***
Observations	1,572,534	1,585,096	1,572,534	1,572,534	1,572,594	1,585,096

Notes Country dummies are also included, but not reported here due to space limits. LGP1: 0–59 days, LGP2: 60–119 days, LGP3: 120–179 days, LGP4: 180–239 days, LGP5: 240–299 days, and LGP6: more than 300 days. *,** and ***Mean associated coefficient is statistically significant, respectively, at 0.10, 0.05 and 0.01 %, respectively. *Blank cells* mean the associated variable was not reported in the corresponding region or that it had only one value. For example, rule of law and land tenure security had the same value in North America. Robust standards errors are applied.

Table 7.6 Regression by major geographic regions

Variables	SSA	LAC	North America	NENA	Asia	Europe
Precipitation	0.000592***	0.000125***	0.000347***	0.000497***	−8.21e−05***	0.000312***
Population density	−1.79e−05	−0.000517***	−0.000208	−0.000828***	−0.000658***	−8.06e−05
Population density, squared	1.13e−08	−2.70e−08***	7.80e−08***	3.07e−08	7.87e−09**	4.30e−10
Distance to market	0.00107***	0.00121***	0.000885***	0.000724***	0.000231***	0.00100***
Distance to market, squared	−2.86e−07***	−2.33e−07***	−1.12e−07***	−1.09e−07***	−8.74e−09***	−1.46e−07***
Night time lighting intensity	−0.0611***	−0.0562***	−0.0439***	−0.0160***	0.00617***	−0.0108***
Night time lighting intensity, squared	0.000998***	0.000831***	0.000624***	0.000156*	−0.000225***	0.000260***
GDP per capita	0.000327**	−0.000926	−3.18e−05	−0.000482	0.000220	3.17e−05
GDP per capita, squared	−3.06e−08**	1.21e−07		1.01e−07	−5.26e−09	5.52e−11
Rule of law	0.391***	0.449		−0.00900	2.31e−05	−0.402***
Change in rule of law	0.316**	−1.239		0.302	−0.0970	−0.623*
Infant mortality rate	0.00400*	0.00678		0.00324	0.00468***	0.00345
Change in infant mortality rate	−0.00231***	0.0141***	0.0942***	−0.00470***	0.00576***	0.00572***
Distance to market with cropland	0.115***	−0.0187	0.127***	0.192***	0.0939***	−0.240***
Night time lighting intensity with population density	4.95e−06**	1.63e−05***	1.62e−06	1.28e−05***	9.20e−06***	1.73e−06*
Distance to market with population density	−9.61e−06***	−9.99e−06***	−5.79e−06***	−5.27e−06***	−2.17e−06***	−1.50e−06***
Land use, Cropland-base						
Mosaic vegetation—crop	0.383***	0.326**	1.186***	1.448***	0.930***	−0.495***
Forest	0.654***	0.683***	1.803***	1.733***	1.352***	−0.0412
Mosaic forest—shrub	0.247**	−0.0776	1.292***	1.419***	0.802***	−0.159***
Shrublands	0.0779	−0.00660	1.437***	1.391***	0.875***	−0.290***
Grassland	0.199*	−0.0383	1.329***	1.390***	0.861***	−0.405***
Sparse vegetation	0.558***	0.694**	1.076***	1.708***	0.793***	−0.271***

(continued)

Table 7.6 (continued)

Variables	SSA	LAC	North America	NENA	Asia	Europe
Bare surface or water	1.339***	2.386***	1.014***	2.335***	0.645***	0.278*
Land tenure security, base—good						
Moderate concern	0.836***	−0.259	−1.820**			
Severe concern	0.555***	2.013**		−0.487*		
Extremely severe concern	0.512***	0.158		0.0569	0.130	−0.679
Missing values for land tenure	1.560***	0.164		−0.339		
Length of growing period—LGP1						
LGP2	−0.0267*	−0.165***	−0.116***	−0.652***	−0.00234	0.552***
LGP3	−0.0871***	−0.569***	−0.536***	−0.645***	−0.0172	0.770***
LGP4	−0.154***	−0.419***	−1.262***	−0.651***	−0.464***	0.803***
LGP5	−0.369***	−0.405***	−1.161***	−0.909***	−0.371***	0.765***
LGP6	−0.346***	−0.482***	−0.646***	−1.098***	−0.303***	1.199***
Country dummies	Yes	Yes	Yes	Yes	Yes	Yes
μ1	1.301***	−0.920	−0.854	−0.484	1.571	0.0552
μ2	4.974***	3.530*	4.283***	3.886***	4.933***	4.901***
Observations	175,919	33,631	354,118	173,015	299,334	461,666

Notes Country dummies are also included, but not reported here due to space limits. LGP1: 0–59 days, LGP2: 60–119 days, LGP3: 120–179 days, LGP4: 180–239 days, LGP5: 240–299 days, and LGP6: more than 300 days. *,** and ***Mean associated coefficient is statistically significant, respectively, at 0.10, 0.05 and 0.01 %, respectively. Blank cells mean the associated variable was not reported in the corresponding region or that it had only one value. For example, rule of law and land tenure security had the same value in North America. Robust standards errors are applied. Europe includes Russia.

population density has a positive relationship with sustainable land management.[3] Those areas which have both higher population and good socio-economic development[4] are found to be likely to manage their land resources more sustainably. Better rule of law is significant at 10 % and positively related to SLM in the full model. Another key variable found to be positively associated with SLM is secure land tenure. Those areas with serious and severe concerns over land tenure security are associated with land degradation. Among various land covers and uses, cropland was found to be more associated with land degradation. Longer length of the growing period is found to lead to more land degradation. At the same time, the results do not find a statistically significant impact of GDP per capita. Of course, a lack of statistical significance does not mean a lack in significance of GDP per capita in general. In general, it would mean that lower GDP per capita, and hence, poverty, does not have to lead to land degradation. This finding is also corroborated by the fact that those countries with higher infant mortality rates (a classic proxy for poverty) in 1982–1984 have managed their lands more sustainably than those countries with lower infant mortality rates. Infant mortality rate is a strong proxy for poverty. These results signify that poorer locations are not necessarily associated with land degradation. The causal mechanism driving this could be that since dependence on agriculture and land is higher in poorer locations, landusers in these areas are more motivated to manage land sustainably (Nkonya et al. 2011). At the same time, it should be noted that those countries which made more progress towards reducing infant mortality during the studied period, also made more progress in terms of sustainable land management.

Table 7.5 presents the results of the regression run separately for major global regions. The sub-global regressions are broadly consistent with the global model results, even though there are some region-specific divergences. Precipitation, similarly, is positively associated with land improvement in all regions, except Asia. One potential explanation for this could be that Asia has much higher reliance on irrigated agriculture, with a lower role for rainfall in crop production. Population density has negative association with sustainable land management in Asia, Near East and North Africa (NENA) and Latin America and Caribbean (LAC). However, in other regions, the regressions do not show statistically significant results for the effect of population density. The distance to markets has a concave relationship with SLM in all regions. The night time lighting intensity has convex relationship with SLM in most regions, except in Asia, where the relationship is concave. GDP per capita does not show statistical significance, but only in Sub-Saharan Africa (SSA) where it has a concave relationship with SLM. Similarly, better rule of law is positively related to SLM in SSA, but not in Europe. Those countries with higher

[3]Land degradation hotspots database by Le et al. (2014) used here excludes urban areas from its analysis, so our night time lighting intensity and population density variables are not biased by urban areas.

[4]For example, availability of non-farm sector. The night time lighting intensity variable at its basics also stands for availability of electricity, which may imply having better access to broader development opportunities.

infant mortality rates (i.e. here used as a proxy variable for poverty) in Asia and SSA were associated with less land degradation, whereas in other regions the effect is non-significant. The reductions in infant mortality rates (a proxy for poverty reduction) have led to higher land degradation in SSA and NENA, but to lower land degradation in other regions. As we said earlier, infant mortality rate is taken as a proxy for poverty. The explanation for this seemingly surprising finding can be that those areas with higher economic development achieved reductions in infant mortality rates, but also the opportunity costs of labor might have increased as a result of economic growth. Consequently, making the application of labor-intensive SLM measures more costly. Other surprising results from Table 7.5 are that less secure land tenure does not seem to be associated with higher land degradation in SSA. In most regions higher levels of land degradation occur in croplands, but not in Europe, where other land uses, such as shrublands, forests, grasslands, have experienced more land degradation. In all regions a longer period of growing days is associated with more land degradation.

The results of the analyses are further nuanced by Table 7.7, where separate regressions are run for each cluster of countries with similar socio-economic and institutional conditions. The characteristics of these clusters are explained in detail in Table 7.8, however, what needs to be borne in mind is that the higher the number of the cluster, the higher the level of economic, institutional and technological development of the countries making up that cluster. For example, Cluster 1 is made up of the least developed countries (so called, “the bottom billion”, Collier (2007)), whereas cluster 8 is comprised of the most advanced countries, mostly OECD countries. The major characteristics of the clusters are shown in Table 7.8. The results presented in Table 7.7 are also broadly consistent with global findings, but also have their specific insights. The positive association of precipitation with land improvement is present for the least developed and most developed countries, but not for those countries in the middle. Population density is negatively related to SLM in lower income countries, but positively for higher income countries. Distance to markets seems to lead to more SLM all across the clusters and higher night time lighting intensity to less SLM.

The results of these three tables are summarized in Table 7.9. The variables showing a larger consistency across all the regression models are distance to markets and the interaction of distance to markets with population density. The longer distance to markets means less land degradation (both in croplands and non-cropped areas). However, higher population densities combined with longer distance to markets seem to mean more land degradation. At first sight, it is understandable that remote areas have lower chances then areas closer to major urban centers of being deforested, overgrazed, and used in crop production (unless they are densely populated). For example, in Central Asia, it was found that most of rangeland degradation happens in areas near population settlements, as the costs of moving livestock to more remote pastures are high (Pender et al. 2009). However, as we have seen in the literature review section, higher market access could also give more incentives for sustainable land management as the opportunity cost of fertile soil is higher in areas closer to markets (Pender et al. 2006). On the other

Table 7.7 Regression by clusters

Variables	Cluster 1	Cluster 2	Cluster 3	Cluster 4	Cluster 5	Cluster 6	Cluster 7	Cluster 8
Precipitation	0.000297***	0.000132**	−0.000137***	−1.12e−05	0.000440***	−4.56e−05***	0.000570***	0.000463***
Population density	−0.000430***	−0.00893***	−0.000496***	0.000148**	−0.000835***	−0.000378***	−0.000322	0.000683***
Population density, squared	2.97e−08***	1.19e−05***	7.19e−09**	9.08e−09	−5.13e−09	6.74e−08***	2.44e−07***	−1.82e−08**
Distance to market	0.000798***	0.000650***	0.000299***	0.00123***	0.000695***	0.000763***	0.00128***	0.00170***
Distance to market, squared	−1.88e−07***	−1.75e−07***	−1.49e−08***	−3.89e−07***	−1.00e−07***	−9.91e−08***	−1.63e−07***	−3.13e−07***
Night time lighting intensity	−0.0169***	0.131**	0.00788***	−0.0139***	−0.0145***	−0.0287***	−0.0232***	−0.0191***
Night time lighting intensity, squared	0.000253**	−0.00187	−0.000232***	0.000246***	9.94e−05	0.000367***	0.000547***	0.000291***
GDP per capita	0.000184*	0.000204	0.000181**	7.98e−05	−0.00136*	0.000143	−1.67e−06	−5.84e−05
GDP per capita, squared	−1.94e−08**	−3.54e−09	−8.61e−09	−3.11e−09	2.67e−07*	−2.39e−09	1.29e−10	1.58e−09
Rule of law	0.166*	0.0138	0.154	−0.219*	0.318	−0.423**	−0.386**	−0.390
Change in rule of law	0.236*	−0.392	−0.332	−0.0343	0.807***	−0.406	−0.739**	0.228
Infant mortality rate	0.00454**	0.00260	0.00418**	−0.00130	0.00453	−0.00584*	0.0333***	−0.0343**
Change in infant mortality rate	−0.00201***	−0.0145***	0.00523***	0.00794***	−0.00660***	0.00940***	−0.113***	−0.00356
Distance to market with cropland	0.101***	−0.0906	0.0667***	−0.0866***	0.183***	−0.105***	−0.0223	−0.0469***
Night time lighting intensity with population density	5.52e−06*	−0.00314***	6.27e−06***	−3.38e−06	1.69e−05***	3.30e−06*	−1.21e−05***	−7.81e−06***

(continued)

Table 7.7 (continued)

Variables	Cluster 1	Cluster 2	Cluster 3	Cluster 4	Cluster 5	Cluster 6	Cluster 7	Cluster 8
Distance to market with population density	−5.80e−06***	−8.49e−06***	−1.87e−06***	−4.52e−06***	−7.29e−06***	−4.25e−06***	−4.76e−06***	−8.28e−06***
Land use, cropland-base								
Mosaic vegetation—crop	0.640***	−0.826*	0.759***	−0.0499	1.372***	0.0233	0.420***	0.284***
Forest	0.917***	−0.731*	1.137***	0.226***	1.644***	0.694***	0.997***	0.827***
Mosaic forest—shrub	0.458***	−1.038**	0.594***	−0.255***	1.388***	0.555***	0.462***	0.229***
Shrublands	0.226***	−1.208***	0.665***	−0.241***	1.426***	0.505***	0.384***	0.272***
Grassland	0.184**	−1.148***	0.803***	−0.00128	1.516***	0.461***	0.297**	0.141***
Sparse vegetation	0.739***	−0.414	1.107***	0.209***	1.790***	0.528***	0.359**	0.241***
Bare surface or water	1.875***	0.793*	1.784***	1.551***	2.669***	0.254***	2.168***	1.438***
Land tenure security, base—good								
Moderate concern	0.638***	1.044	−0.134	−1.240***	−1.816***		−2.981***	
Severe concern	0.0222	0.370		−1.447***	−0.865**	−0.296	−1.718***	
Extremely severe concern	0.397***	1.408*	0.0510	−0.481***	−0.504***	0.740***		
Missing values for land tenure	0.948***	0.977*		−1.290***	−0.858***	−1.045***	−0.660**	−2.032***
Length of Growing Period—LGP1								
LGP2	0.359***	0.322***	−0.0586***	−0.311***	−0.426***	0.0892***	−0.437***	−0.225***
LGP3	0.467***	1.548***	−0.0847***	−0.665***	−0.716***	0.351***	−0.612***	−0.997***
LGP4	0.560***	1.174***	−0.402***	−0.566***	−0.682***	0.417***	−1.010***	−1.347***
LGP5	0.407***	0.925***	−0.371***	−0.195***	−0.985***	0.451***	−0.782***	−1.314***

(continued)

Table 7.7 (continued)

Variables	Cluster 1	Cluster 2	Cluster 3	Cluster 4	Cluster 5	Cluster 6	Cluster 7	Cluster 8
LGP6	0.476***	0.799***	−0.278***	−0.247***	−1.102***	0.512***	−0.931***	−0.934***
Country dummies	Yes	Yes	Yes	Yes	Yes	Yes	Yes	Yes
μ1	1.846***	0.0298	1.271***	−1.109***	−2.367***	−0.222	−1.700***	−2.470**
μ2	5.226***	4.252***	3.545***	1.993***	1.999**	4.810***	2.814***	1.949**
Observations	126,716	24,677	161,004	94,401	161,812	769,961	23,508	210,455

Notes Country dummies are also included, but not reported here due to space limits. LGP1: 0–59 days, LGP2: 60–119 days, LGP3: 120–179 days, LGP4: 180–239 days, LGP5: 240–299 days, and LGP6: more than 300 days. *,** and ***Mean associated coefficient is statistically significant, respectively, at 0.10, 0.05 and 0.01 %, respectively. *Blank cells* mean the associated variable was not reported in the corresponding region or that it had only one value. For example, rule of law and land tenure security had the same value in North America. Robust standards errors are applied.

Table 7.8 The socio-economic and institutional characteristics of clusters

Clusters	GDP per capita	Government effectiveness	Population density	Agricultural intensification	Maximum changes in NDVI values between the baseline (1982–84) and endline (2003–06)*	Cereal yields	Share of agriculture in GDP	Share of rural population in total
1	Lower	Lower	Higher	Lower	Highest dispersion, both biggest decreases and increases	Lower	Higher	Higher
2	Mid	Mid	Higher	Higher	Smaller decreases	Mid	Mid	Higher
3	Mid	Mid	Higher	Mid	Smaller decreases	Mid	Mid	Mid
4	Mid	Mid	Lower	Mid	Larger decreases	Mid	Mid	Lower
5	Mid	Mid	Lower	Lower	Smaller decreases	Lower	Mid	Mid
6	Higher	Higher	Mid	Higher	Larger decreases	Mid	Mid	Lower
7	Higher	Higher	Higher	Higher	Smaller decreases	Higher	Lower	Lower

Source Chap. 2

Notes *The NDVI time-series comes from GIMMS dataset, which is driven from NOAA AVHRR satellite data (http://glcf.umd.edu/). The NDVI changes here-calculated have not been corrected for the effects of inter-annual rainfall variation, atmospheric fertilization and human application of mineral fertilizer.

hand, the opportunity cost of labor is also higher in high market access areas, thus, was suggested to be a barrier for implementing labor-intensive SLM measures in those areas (Sherr and Hazell 1994). In this regard, even the interaction of distance to markets with croplands has a negative association with SLM in a majority of the models used. It means that, in most cases, the areas closer to markets have higher chances of being degraded. The incentive effect of nearness to markets for SLM seems to be working only in more advanced economies and not in lower income countries. The reason for this might be (in addition to physical access to the area) that in lower income countries the higher opportunity cost of labor in high market access areas is preventing the application of SLM measures, which are necessarily labor-intensive as the capital-intensive measures are even less affordable. Whereas in more advanced economies, the capital may be more affordable than labor, and the capital is certainly cheaper in areas with higher market access than in remote areas, so farmers cultivating croplands closer to urban centers in advanced countries are more able to implement SLM measures through more intensive use of capital (satellite guided precise fertilization, drip irrigation, etc.).

Another more consistent finding is the lack of significance of GDP per capita in explaining SLM. As stated earlier, this lack of significance should not be considered

Table 7.9 Summary of findings in global, regional and cluster-based regressions

Variables affecting SLM	Global	Regional	Cluster	Exceptions from the dominant sign
Precipitation	+	+/−	+/−	Asia, Clusters 3 and 6
Population density	−	−	+/−	Clusters 4 and 8
Distance to market	+	+	+	
Night time lighting intensity	−	+/−	+/−	Asia, Clusters 2 and 3
GDP per capita	.	.	.	SSA(+), Clusters 1 and 3 (+), Cluster 5(−)
Rule of law	+	+/−	+/−	Clusters 4, 6, 7, Europe
Change in rule of law	.	+/−	+/−	Europe
Infant mortality rate	+	+	+/−	Clusters 6 and 8
Change in infant mortality rate	+	+/−	+/−	SSA, NENA, Clusters 1, 2, 5 and 7
Distance to market with cropland	+	+/−	+/−	Europe, Clusters 4, 5, 6 and 8
Night time lighting intensity with population density	+	+	+/−	Clusters 2, 4, 7 and 8
Distance to market with population density	−	−	−	
Land use (most degradation)	Cropland	Cropland	Cropland	Europe, Cluster 2 and 4
Land tenure insecurity	−	+/−	+/−	SSA, Clusters 1 and 2
Length of growing period	−	+/−	+/−	Clusters 1, 2 and 6

Note Plus means positively associated with SLM, minus—negatively, dot—not significant. In regional and cluster-based regressions, if there are differences between groups, more prevalent sign is depicted in bold.

unimportant except in a few isolated cases. For example higher GDP per capita seems to be positively associated with SLM in SSA, but overall these two variables are not significant in other regions. The lack of significance of GDP may also hint at the fact that the impact of GDP is already captured by other variables indicating economic performance, which are available on a smaller geographic level, such as night-time light intensity. While night lights per se may represent a cruder measure of economic development than GDP, they do not ignore its spatial variability.[5] This stresses the importance of including the variables in the analysis that contain information on a more detailed level, since land degradation may also be a highly dispersed phenomenon not limited to country borders or within-country boundaries. The conclusion we can draw is that GDP per capita is not a major factor influencing sustainable land management in many cases. Moreover, higher infant mortality rate, used as a proxy for poverty, has not prevented SLM in most regions of the world. Poorer households are expected to have higher reliance on natural resources, including land, for the livelihoods. Thus, they have more incentives to manage land sustainably. Moreover, the opportunity cost of labor in poorer locations is lower, thus allowing for its use in implementing labor-intensive SLM measures. This finding is also agrees with the results of Nkonya et al. (2008). On the other hand, those countries which have reduced infant mortality rates more than others seem to be also making more efforts toward SLM.

Higher population density is also found to be leading to more land degradation, except in the most advanced countries and some middle income countries (Clusters 4 and 8). Supporting this finding, most estimations show that night time lighting intensity interacted with population density is leading to SLM. Night-time light intensity can be used as a proxy for socio-economic development of the area, the higher prevalence of non-farm sectors, and easier access to capital. More economically dynamic areas with larger populations, thus, can provide more incentives and opportunities for SLM adoptions and innovations (a la Boserup 1965), information costs can be assumed to be lower and technology spillover effects are more likely. However, densely populated, but economically backward areas seem to be following a more Malthusian scenario, where higher population is translating to more land degradation. It is also found that in advanced economies with higher night time lighting intensity, the effect of population density on promoting SLM is decreasing. This may be due to the overall higher level of night time lighting intensity in advanced economies, where even relatively less densely populated areas have high night time lighting intensity (and also high share of non-farm sectors).

Rule of law was found to be positively associated with SLM in most cases, especially in SSA and other developing lower income countries, but not in Europe, and the countries of Clusters 4, 6 and 7. First of all, this may be due to nonlinearities in the effect of rule of law on SLM outcomes. Any increases from very low

[5]This is highlighted by the fact that night lighting and GDP have a moderate correlation on country level (0.44), but only a weak one on pixel level (0.13), which points at substantial variation of night lights within countries.

levels of rule of law to higher levels may have huge positive effects for SLM. However, further changes in already high levels of rule of law may have a marginally lower or no effect.

Land tenure, a measure of security, also shows interesting results. Insecure land tenure seems to be a deterrent for SLM in middle income and advanced economies, but not for the lowest income countries, especially in Sub-Saharan Africa. Secure land tenure may provide additional benefits and opportunities with relatively well-functioning markets, including output, input and financial markets. Credible land property rights expand the planning horizon of agricultural entrepreneurs and make costly innovations in SLM with large mid- to long term benefits more profitable in expectations. Where markets do not function well or are very thin, secure land tenure may have much less effect on SLM. It should also be noted that a credible and stable rule of law is a precondition for secure land tenure, so that the effect of rule of law on SLM supersedes the one of land right security.

Conclusions

There have been numerous studies on the drivers of land degradation in the past with often contradicting results. It is believed that the contradictions are due to differences in applied methods and the datasets. Although these differences in methods and datasets play a crucial role in explaining the diverging findings on the causal mechanisms of the factors affecting land management, these differences are also due to context-specific nature of the interactions between various drivers of land degradation, where socio-economic, institutional and technological particularities of the location shape the nature of the interactions between the drivers of land degradation. SLM is positively associated with land tenure security, especially in middle-income and advanced economies. In lower income countries a lack of secure land tenure is not associated with less SLM. Shortening the time to reach markets may have many other desirable outcomes but not necessarily a decrease in land degradation, especially in low income countries. Population pressure may lead to land degradation unless public policies provide for increases in non-farm jobs. The findings of this study call for localized diagnostic of the drivers of land degradation and for elaborating policy actions targeting the local interplay of major drivers of land degradation.

References

Alexandratos, N. (Ed.). (1995). World agriculture: Towards 2010: An FAO study. Food & Agriculture Org.

Bai, Z., Dent, D., Olsson, L., & Schaepman, M. (2008). Proxy global assessment of land degradation. *Soil Use and Management, 24*(3), 223–234.

Barrow, C. (1991). *Land degradation: Development and breakdown of terrestrial environments*. Cambridge, UK: Cambridge University Press.

Benin, S., Nkonya, E., Okecho, G., Pender, J., Nahdy, S., Mugarura, S., et al. (2007). Assessing the Impact of the National Agricultural Advisory Services (NAADS) in the Uganda rural livelihoods. IFPRI Discussion Paper 00724. Washington, DC: International Food Policy Research Institute.

Besley, T. (1995). Property rights and investment incentives: Theory and evidence from Ghana. *The Journal of Political Economy, 103*(5), 903–937.

Bicheron, P., Defourny, P., Brockmann, C., Schouten, L., Vancutsem, C., Huc, M., & Arino, O. (2008). *Globcover: Products description and validation report*. Toulouse: MEDIAS France.

Bonilla, C. A., & Johnson, O. I. (2012). Soil erodibility mapping and its correlation with soil properties in Central Chile. *Geoderma, 189*, 116–123.

Boserup, E. (1965). *The conditions of agricultural growth: The economics of Agrarian change under population pressure*. New York, USA: Aldine Press.

Brasselle, F., Brasselle, A., Gaspart, F., & Platteau, J. P. (2002). Land tenure security and investment incentives: Puzzling evidence from Burkina Faso. *Journal of Development Economics, 67*, 373–418.

CIESIN. (2010). Socioeconomic Data and Applications Center (SEDAC) Raw data. Online at http://sedac.ciesin.columbia.edu/. Accessed 21 Mar 13.

Clay, D. C., Byiringiro, F. U., Kangasniemi, J., Reardon, T., Sibomana, B., Uwamariya, L., & Tardif-Douglin, D. (1996). Promoting food security in Rwanda through sustainable agricultural productivity: Meeting the challenges of population pressure, land degradation, and poverty. Food Security International Development Policy Syntheses 11425. East Lansing: Michigan State University, Department of Agricultural, Food, and Resource Economics.

Cleaver, K. M., & Schreiber, G. A. (1994). *Reversing the spiral: The population, agriculture, and environment nexus in Sub-Saharan Africa*. Washington, USA: The World Bank.

Collier, P. (2007). The bottom billion: Why the poorest countries are failing and what can be done about it. Oxford: Oxford University Press.

De Janvry, A., Fafchamps, M., & Sadoulet, E. (1991). Peasant household behavior with missing markets: Some paradoxes explained. *The Economic Journal, 101*, 1400–1417.

Ebener, S., Murray, C., Tandon, A., & Elvidge, C. C. (2005). From wealth to health: Modelling the distribution of income per capita at the sub-national level using night-time light imagery. *International Journal of Health Geographics, 4*(1), 5.

Elvidge, C. D., Imhoff, M. L., Baugh, K. E., Hobson, V. R., Nelson, I., Safran, J., & Tuttle, B. T. (2001). Night-time lights of the world: 1994–1995. *ISPRS Journal of Photogrammetry and Remote Sensing, 56*(2), 81–99.

FAO. (2011). *State of the world's forests*. Rome, Italy: FAO.

Gao, J., & Liu, Y. (2010). Determination of land degradation causes in Tongyu County, Northeast China via land cover change detection. *International Journal of Applied Earth Observation and Geoinformation, 12*, 9–16.

Geist, H. J., & Lambin, E. F. (2004). Dynamical causal patterns of desertification. *BioScience, 54* (9), 817–829.

Grepperud, S. (1996). Population Pressure and Land Degradation: The Case of Ethiopia. Journal of Environmental Economics and Management *30* (1): 18–33.

Kabubo-Mariara, J. (2007). Land conservation and tenure security in Kenya: Boserup's hypothesis revisited. *Ecological Economics, 64*, 25–35.

Kaufmann, D., Kraay, A., & Mastruzzi, M. (2010). The worldwide governance indicators: Methodology and analytical issues. World Bank Policy Research Working Paper No. 5430. Available from http://ssrn.com/abstract=1682130

Le, Q. B., Nkonya, E., & Mirzabaev, A. (2014). Biomass productivity-based mapping of global land degradation hotspots. ZEF Discussion Papers 193.

Liniger, H., & Schwilch, G. (2002). Enhanced decision-making based on local knowledge: The WOCAT method of sustainable soil and water management. *Mountain Research and Development, 22*(1), 14–18.

Liniger, H., & Critchley, W. (2007). *Where the land is greener*. Wageningen: Technical Center for Agricultural and Rural Cooperation.

Lu, D., Batistella, M., Mausel, P., & Moran, E. (2007). Mapping and monitoring land degradation risks in the Western Brazilian Amazon using multitemporal landsat TM/ETM+ images. *Land Degradation and Development, 18*, 41–54.

Michalopoulos, S., & Papaioannou, E. (2013). Pre-colonial ethnic institutions and contemporary African development. *Econometrica, 81*(1), 113–152.

Mirzabaev, A., Nkonya, E., & von Braun, J. (2015). Economics of sustainable land management. *Current Opinion in Environmental Sustainability, 15*, 9–19.

Nkonya, E., & Anderson, W. (2014). Exploiting provisions of land economic productivity without degrading its natural capital. *Journal of Arid Environments,*. doi:10.1016/j.jaridenv.2014.05.012.

Nkonya, E., Gerber, N., Baumgartner, P., von Braun, J., De Pinto, A., Graw, V., et al. (2011). The economics of desertification, land degradation, and drought—toward an integrated global assessment. ZEF-Discussion Papers on Development Policy No. 150. Center for Development Research (ZEF), Bonn, Germany.

Nkonya, E., Pender, J., Kaizzi, K., Kato, E., Mugarura, S., Ssali, H., & Muwonge, J. (2008). Linkages between land management, land degradation, and poverty in Sub-Saharan Africa: The case of Uganda. IFPRI Research Report 159. Washington D.C., USA.

Nkonya, E., Phillip, D., Mogues, T., Pender, J., & Kato, E. (2010). *From the ground up: Impacts of a pro-poor community-driven development project in Nigeria*. Washington, DC, USA: IFPRI Research Monograph.

Nkonya, E., von Braun, J., Mirzabaev, A., Le, B., Kwon, H., Kirui, O., Gerber, N. (2013). Economics of land degradation initiative: Methods and approach for global and national assessments. ZEF-Discussion Papers on Development Policy No. 183. Center for Development Research (ZEF).

Paudel, G. S., & Thapa, G. B. (2004). Impact of social, institutional, and ecological factors on land management practices in mountain watersheds of Nepal. *Applied Geography, 24*(1), 35–55.

Pender, J., & Kerr, J. (1998). Determinants of farmers' indigenous soil and water conservation investments in semiarid India. *Agricultural Economics, 19*, 113–125.

Pender, J., Mirzabaev, A., & Kato, E. (2009). Economic analysis of sustainable land management options in Central Asia. Final report for the ADB.IFPRI/ICARDA, 168. Washington DC, USA.

Pender, J., Nkonya, E., Jagger, P., Sserunkuuma, D., & Ssali, H. (2006). Strategies to increase agricultural productivity and reduce land degradation in Uganda: An econometric analysis. In J. Pender & S. Ehui (Eds.), *Strategies for sustainable land management in the East African highlands* (pp. 165–190). Washington, DC, USA: International Food Policy Research Institute.

Safriel, U. N., & Adeel, Z. (2005). Dryland systems. In R. Hassan, R. Scholes, & N. Ash (Eds.), *Ecosystems and human well-being: Current state and trends* (Vol. 1, pp. 623–662). Washington, DC: Island Press.

Sanwal, M. (2004). Trends in global environmental governance: The emergence of a mutual supportiveness approach to achieve sustainable development. *Global Environmental Politics, 4* (4), 16–22.

Scherr, S. (2000). Downward spiral? Research evidence on the relationship between poverty and natural resource degradation. *Food Policy, 25*(4), 479–498.

Scherr, S., & Hazell, P. (1994). Sustainable agricultural development strategies in fragile lands. Environment and Production Technology Division Discussion Paper, no. 1. International Food Policy Research Institute, Washington, DC, USA.

Sternberg, T. (2008). Environmental challenges in Mongolia's dryland pastoral landscape. *Journal of Arid Environments, 72*, 1294–1304.

Sutton, P. C., Elvidge, C. D., & Ghosh, T. (2007). Estimation of gross domestic product at sub-national scales using night time satellite imagery. *International Journal of Ecological Economics & Statistics, 8*(S07), 5–21.

Tiffen, M., Mortimore, M., & Gichuki, F. (1994). *More people, less erosion: Environmental recovery in Kenya*. London, UK: Wiley and Sons.

Uchida, H., & Nelson, A. (2010). Agglomeration index: Towards a new measure of urban concentration (No. 2010, 29). Working paper//World Institute for Development Economics Research.

USAID (United States Agency for International Development), ARD, Inc. (2008). Global Land Tenure Master Database. 2007. Unpublished data. Original graphics published in USAID and ARD, Inc. 2007. "Land Tenure and Property Rights Tools and Regional Reports." Washington, DC: USAID EGAT/Natural Resources Management/Land Resources Management Team and Burlington, Vermont: ARD, Inc.

Vlek, P., Le, Q. B., & Tamene, L. (2010). Assessment of land degradation, its possible causes and threat to food security in Sub-Saharan Africa. In R. Lal & B. A. Stewart (Eds.), *Food security and soil quality* (pp. 57–86). Boca Raton, Florida: CRC Press.

von Braun, J., Gerber, N., Mirzabaev, A., & Nkonya, E. (2013). The economics of land degradation. ZEF Working Papers 109. Bonn, Germany.

Voortman, R. L., Sonneveld, B. G., & Keyzer, M. A. (2000). African land ecology: Opportunities and constraints for agricultural development. Center for International Development Working Paper 37. Harvard University, Cambridge, Mass., U.S.A.

Way, S. A. (2006). Examining the links between poverty and land degradation: From blaming the poor toward recognizing the rights of the poor. In P. Johnson, K. Mayrand, & M. Paquin (Eds.), *Governing global desertification: Linking environmental degradation, poverty, and participation* (pp. 27–41). Burlington, VT: Ashgate.

Wischmeier, W.H. (1976). Use and Misuse of the universal soil loss equation. *Journal of Soil and Water Conservation. 13* (1): 5–9.

Chapter 8
Global Estimates of the Impacts of Grassland Degradation on Livestock Productivity from 2001 to 2011

Ho-Young Kwon, Ephraim Nkonya, Timothy Johnson, Valerie Graw, Edward Kato and Evelyn Kihiu

Abstract In response to the needs for estimating the cost of grassland degradation to determine the cost of inaction and for identifying cost-effective strategies to address the consequent loss of livestock productivity, we developed a modeling framework where global statistics databases and remote sensing data/analyses coupled with empirical/statistical modeling are designed to quantify the global cost of grassland degradation. By using this framework, we identified grassland degradation hotspots over the period of 2001 to 2011 and estimated changes in livestock productivity associated with changes in grassland productivity within the hotspots. Ignoring environmental benefits and losses in live weight of livestock not slaughtered or sold, the cost of livestock productivity was estimated about 2007 US $6.8 billion. Although on-farm cost is small in Sub-Saharan Africa due to the low livestock productivity, the impact on human welfare would be much more severe in the region where majority of the population is below the poverty line. This implies that addressing grassland degradation is even more urgent in the region, given the increasing demand for livestock products and the potential contribution to poverty reduction. Taking action toward grassland degradation could simultaneously reduce poverty and promote carbon sequestration while conserving socio-economic, cultural, and ecological benefits that livestock provide.

Keywords Empirical modeling · Global cost · Grassland degradation · Grazing biomass · Livestock productivity · Remote sensing data

H.-Y. Kwon (✉) · E. Nkonya · T. Johnson · E. Kato
Environment & Production Technology Division, International Food Policy Research Institute, 2033 K Street, NW, Washington, DC 20006-1002, USA
e-mail: h.kwon@cgiar.org

V. Graw
Center for Remote Sensing of Land Surfaces (ZFL), University of Bonn, Walter Flex Str 3, D-53113 Bonn, Germany

E. Kihiu
Center for Development Research (ZEF), University of Bonn, Walter Flex Str 3, D-53113 Bonn, Germany

E. Nkonya et al. (eds.), *Economics of Land Degradation and Improvement – A Global Assessment for Sustainable Development*,
DOI 10.1007/978-3-319-19168-3_8

Introduction

Global meat and dairy consumption is projected to increase by 173 and 158 % from 2010 to 2050 and an even higher increase in meat and dairy consumption is expected for developing countries. This rapid increase in demand for livestock products would require corresponding increases in demand for animal feeds, which in turn would lead to conversion of high value biomes—such as forest to grazing lands—and overgrazing especially for grassland-based livestock production systems (Asner and Archer 2010). In fact, over the last few decades, grasslands have been degraded due to overgrazing and account for the largest extent of degradation among all major biomes considered. Steinfeld et al. (2006) estimated that about 20 % of global pasture and 73 % of the rangelands in the drylands have been degraded. About 70 % of deforestation in the Amazon was due to expansion of pasture and a large part of the remaining 30 % of cleared forests was due to feed crops expansion (ibid). Other studies also reported severe degradation in grazing biomes. Nabuurs (2004) estimated that about 5 % of soil organic carbon has been lost from overgrazed or moderately degraded temperate and/or boreal grasslands. More recently, Le et al. (2014), Chap. 4, estimated that about 40 % of grasslands experienced degradation between 1982 and 2006 by employing long-term data of remotely sensed Normalized Difference Vegetation Index (NDVI) as a proxy for global land degradation.

Degradation of grazing biomes poses a big threat to sustain and/or increase global livestock productivity, which serves multiple purposes including economic, social and ecological functions (Nabuurs 2004; Randolph et al. 2007). Livestock plays an especially important role in the livelihoods of the rural poor households, two-thirds of whom keep livestock (Livestock in Development 1999). Low-income rural households also use livestock as living “savings accounts” (Moll 2005) and insurance against risks and shocks (Hoddinott 2006). Additionally, livestock is used to strengthen social bonds (e.g. dowry) and serve as an indicator of social importance (Kitalyi et al. 2005). In Sub-Saharan Africa (SSA), animal and human power account for 80 % of total farm energy (FAO 2011a). The multiple objectives of livestock suggests that the sector has a large potential to contribute to poverty reduction efforts in developing countries. Such potential is amplified by the increasing demand for livestock products as incomes and food tastes and preferences change in middle and low income countries. Currently livestock accounts for about 13 and 28 % of the global caloric and protein intakes, respectively (FAO 2011b). Livestock also plays a vital role in maintaining soil nutrients in cropland, as livestock manure accounts for 54–64 % of total nitrogen applications and 64 % of phosphorus (Sheldrick et al. 2004; Potter and Ramankutty 2010).[1] Given the important role of livestock and the severe land degradation in grasslands, it is

[1] Sheldrick et al. (2004) estimate that global total recoverable N and P from manure is respectively 93.6 TgN $year^{-1}$ and 21.7 TgP $year^{-1}$ of the total 171.8 TgN and 34.4 TgP $year^{-1}$ consumption global of N and P. Note, one terragram (Tg) = one million tons.

necessary to estimate the cost of land degradation in grazing biomes to determine the cost of inaction and to identify cost-effective strategies to address the consequent loss of livestock productivity.

In response to these needs, we developed a modeling framework where global statistics databases and remote sensing data/analyses coupled with empirical/statistical modeling approach are designed to estimate global impacts of land degradation on spatial and temporal changes of agronomic and environmental indicators (e.g. productivity and soil carbon stock) in both croplands and grasslands. In this chapter, we focused to quantify the cost of grassland degradation on a global scale by using this framework. This type of work contributes to literature in two ways. Firstly, our modeling framework employs empirical/statistical models to estimate the loss of grassland biomass productivity. This simple approach allows estimating a complex system (Wainwright and Mulligan 2005). It also utilizes easily available remote-sensing data to estimate changes in biomass productivity so that it could allow building modeling systems for low-cost global and regional monitoring of grazing land degradation and improvement. Secondly, to the best of our knowledge, this is the first global assessment of the cost of grazing land degradation. Many past global studies have largely dwelt on biophysical assessments of grazing land degradation (e.g. Steinfeld et al. 2006). The few past global or regional studies on the cost of grassland degradation have largely been based on review of literature (e.g. Dregne 2002; Requier-Desjardins 2006) or covering a specific area (e.g. Quinlan 1995; Harris 2010).

This chapter detailed procedures included in our modeling framework such as (i) identifying land degradation hotspots where inter-annual mean NDVI over the historical period of 2001 to 2011 has a declining trend, (ii) classifying statistical models to estimate changes in biomass from NDVI based on biome, (iii) developing simple relationships between the NDVI trend and livestock productivity within the hotspots, and iv) estimating changes in livestock productivity. Finally we reported the costs of grassland degradation associated with changes in livestock productivity.

Modeling Procedures

Identifying Land Degradation Hotspots in Grasslands

The identification of land degradation hotspots within grasslands was based on time series analysis of global Moderate Resolution Imaging Spectroradiometer (MODIS) NDVI data (MYD13C1) from 2001 to 2011 with a temporal resolution of 16 days and a spatial resolution of 0.05° (5.6 × 5.6 km). MODIS was launched in February 2000 and provides a cloud-free global coverage of NDVI data (Huete et al. 2011) (Table 8.1). The time series analysis for this study used the year 2001 as a starting point and covered an equal number of 16-day datasets for each year of the analysis. The trend, depicting the slope of the linear regression, was calculated for the period of 2001 to 2011 when the datasets regarding geographic, demographic, economic, technological, institutional and cultural factors (e.g. climate and agricultural practices, population density, poverty, absence of secure land tenure, lack of market access) were available.

Mean annual values of NDVI were calculated for every year from 2001 to 2011. Based on these, the slope of the linear regression was calculated to get the NDVI trend for each pixel. The dataset was corrected for rainfall because it is the dominant causative factor having the highest impact on vegetation greenness which is represented by NDVI (Nicholson et al. 1990; Hermann et al. 2005). It is important to remove this influence, since we are only interested in anthropogenic causes of land degradation and not natural causes such as drought or natural vegetation changes, both of which can caused by fluctuations in rainfall.

The same time period used for the NDVI analysis was taken into account for the rainfall analysis based on monthly precipitation data by the University of East Anglia's Climatic Research Unit time-series data (CRU 3.1) (Jones and Harris 2008), which has a spatial resolution of 0.5° (56 × 56 km), much coarser than the one of the NDVI data (Table 8.1). Considering that (i) high resolution of historical precipitation data comparable to the resolution of the NDVI data has not been developed, (ii) the CRU data is the most reliable precipitation data on the global scale covering the time period of our study, and (iii) the minimum rainfall station density required to adequately describe annual rainfall varies from 200 to 800 km depending on latitude/longitude location (New et al. 2000), we assumed that the CRU data still works as a way of approximating rainfall effects on vegetation. To correct the NDVI dataset for rainfall, statistically significant trends between 2001 and 2011 ($P < 0.05$) were calculated. Again mean annual values were composed on which significant trends were calculated for every pixel. All significant positive and negative pixels were then masked in the final dataset. Since the rainfall data has a coarser resolution than the NDVI data, some NDVI pixels which might not be directly influenced by rainfall were masked.

A classified dataset for land cover and land use on a global level, Globcover 2004–2006 data (Bicheron et al. 2008), was used to extract all grassland areas[2] within land degradation hotspots (Table 8.1). Globcover 2004–2006 data was used because it best approximated the extent of grasslands during the study period from 2001 to 2011. Derived from remote sensing data between 2004 and 2006 this global land cover map was generated with a spatial resolution of 300 m. Since not all grasslands contain active grazing, especially when estimated from remote sensing imagery, a grazing land extent was used to further narrow down the areas of degradation that would most affect livestock. This was done by using the same grazing land extent based on the Gridded Livestock of the World (GLW) dataset (See Gathering datasets for livestock productivity). Thus, the final global extent

[2]Two classes of Globcover data—140: Closed to open (>15 %) herbaceous vegetation (grassland, savannas or lichens/mosses) and 180: Closed to open (>15 %) grassland or woody vegetation on regularly flooded or waterlogged soil—Fresh, brackish or saline)—are categorized as grassland.

Table 8.1 Datasets used for vegetation trend analysis in grasslands

Data	Source	Temporal resolution	Spatial resolution	Data record
Vegetation (MODIS-NDVI)	LP DAAC (Land Processes Distributed Active Archive Center) (2011)	16 days	0.05°	Year 2001–2011
Rainfall (CRU 3.1)	Jones and Harris (2008)	Monthly	0.5°	Year 2001–2011
Land cover/use (Globcover 2004–2006)	Bicheron et al. (2008)		300 m	Year 2004–2006

Source The authors

includes areas classified as grassland, where active grazing is occurring, within land degradation hotpots.

Deriving Grassland Productivity from Remote Sensing Imagery Data and Statistical Models

Many studies have developed statistical models to estimate grassland productivity by using remote sensing imagery data of NDVI and net primary productivity (NPP) (Table 8.2). Although there seems to be no consensus on the universally accepted model to derive absolute values of grassland productivity on a global scale, NDVI or NPP are still good proxies for grassland productivity. Accordingly, we used the linear regression model results reported in Table 8.2 to estimate grazing biomass. As far as possible, we used the regression results in regions and agro-ecological zones where it was derived.

When the regression results were compared with the actual biomass productivity reported in different agro-ecological zones (AEZ), they showed that the predictive power of the model was reasonably accurate as only 6 of the 21 AEZ-level predicted values fell outside the 95 % interval (Table 8.3).

Gathering Datasets for Livestock Productivity

FAO and the Environmental Research Group Oxford published the first version of GLW dataset in order to address important issues of the livestock sector, such as increased pressures on natural resources and the environment (2007). The GLW provides livestock densities of cattle, buffalo, sheep, goats, pigs, and poultry/chickens modeled at a spatial resolution of 0.05°, based on statistical relationships between observed densities within administrative units derived from survey and census data, and several explanatory variables (e.g. a time-series of remotely sensed satellite data relating to climate and the environment) (Robinson et al. 2014) (Table 8.4).

Table 8.2 Literature review on statistical models to predict biomass as a function of remote sensing imagery data in grasslands

Region	Relational equation	R^2	Source
China (Meadow Steppe)	$Biomass_{grass} = 1478 \times NDVI^{2.56}$	0.60	Jin et al. (2014)
China (Typical Steppe)	$Biomass_{grass} = 910 \times NDVI^{1.627}$	0.57	Jin et al. (2014)
China (Desert Steppe)	$Biomass_{grass} = 487 \times NDVI - 27.719$	0.49	Jin et al. (2014)
China (Arid-Semi arid)	$Biomass_{grass} = 896 \times NDVI - 75.5$	0.46	Ren and Zhou (2014)
Mongolia (Arid-Semi arid)	$Biomass_{grass} = 1.097 \times NPP - 4.776$	0.55	Zhao et al. (2014)
Madagascar (Humid subtropical)	$Biomass_{forage} = 867.9 \times NDVI - 329.2$	0.61	Rahetlah et al. (2014)
Madagascar (Humid subtropical)	$Biomass_{forage} = 0.143 \times e^{3.812\times NDVI}$	0.73	Rahetlah et al. (2014)
Montana-USA	$Biomass_{forage} = 25 \times NDVI - 2739$	0.63	Thoma et al. (2002)
India	Biomass estimated from linear regression of NPP	0.77	Roy and Ravan (1996)
Canada, Finland, Norway, Russia, USA, Sweden	Biomass estimated from linear regression of Advanced Very High Resolution Radiometer (AVHRR)		Dong et al. (2003)
Canada	Biomass estimated form multiple regression and artificial neutral networks as a function of SPOT Vegetation		Fraser and Li (2002)
Finland and Sweden	Biomass estimated from non-Linear regression and K-Nearest Neighbor as a function of Landsat-Tm		Tomppo et al. (2002)

*Source*The authors

Along with the GLW, we obtained the map of livestock production systems developed by FAO and the International Livestock Research Institute (Robinson et al. 2011). This map is an extension of previous classification schemes, made by Sere and Steinfeld (1996) into global coverage with better quality and higher spatial resolution input data such as land cover, length of growing period, highland and temperate areas, human population, and irrigated areas. By overlaying these two maps, we summarized livestock density in each livestock production system (Table 8.4).

Furthermore we acquired estimates of supply for animal-source foods (beef, milk, mutton, pork, poultry meat, and eggs) that are spatially disaggregated based

Table 8.3 Validation of biomass productivity model

Agro-ecological zone	Predicted biomass productivity		Observed biomass productivity
	Dry matter tons/ha		
	Predicted	Standard deviation	Predicted
Boreal	1.00	0.44	<0.5
Subtropic-cool/Semi-arid	0.95	0.61	<0.5
Subtropic-cool/arid	0.66	0.42	0.5–1
Subtropic-cool/humid	5.30	2.98	1–1.5
Subtropic-cool/sub-humid	1.85	1.58	1–1.5
Subtropic-warm/Semi-arid	3.34	3.58	−1–1.5
Subtropic-warm/arid	0.88	0.52	5.1–18
Subtropic-warm/humid	**12.18**	**4.41**	**0.5–1**
Subtropic-warm/sub-humid	6.08	4.08	5.1–18
Temperate/Semi-arid	0.94	0.49	5.1–18
Temperate/arid	0.51	0.34	<0.5
Temperate/humid	1.25	0.42	<0.5–1
Temperate/sub-humid	2.32	1.51	0.7–3.1
Tropic-cool/Semi-arid	1.50	0.68	0.7–3.1
Tropic-cool/arid	0.69	0.57	<0.5
Tropic-cool/humid	**4.24**	**2.30**	**0.5–1**
Tropic-cool/sub-humid	3.44	1.44	1–1.5
Tropic-warm/Semi-arid	**1.76**	**0.59**	**<0.5**
Tropic-warm/arid	0.90	0.63	0.5–1
Tropic-warm/humid	**4.67**	**1.72**	**1–1.5**
Tropic-warm/sub-humid	**3.98**	**1.39**	**1–1.5**

Notes Predicted outside the 95 % confidence interval are emphasized in bold

Table 8.4 Datasets for livestock productivity

Data	Source	Spatial resolution	Data record
Livestock density	Robinson et al. (2014)	0.05°	Year 2000
Livestock production system	Robinson et al. (2011)	0.05°	Year 2000
Supply and demand for animal-source foods	Robinson and Pozzi (2011)	0.05°	Year 2000

Source The authors

on information derived from the GLW and models for livestock growth and off-take (Robinson and Pozzi 2011). In the latter models, livestock production and off-take rates, varying across different agro-ecological zones and livestock production systems, are parameterized differentially for different zones or systems using the herd growth model within the Livestock Development Planning System Version 2 (Lalonde and Sukigara 1997).

Given that we dealt with grazing biomass, our analysis focused on the grassland-based (grazing) livestock production systems, in which more than 90 % of the dry matter intake is obtained from grasslands (Steinfeld et al. 2006). Accordingly, we considered only grazing livestock, namely buffalo, cattle, goat, and sheep. According to Steinfeld et al. (2006), the grazing production systems account for 28 % of the livestock population and covers 26 % of the ice-free land area (ibid.) (Table 8.5). To avoid double counting cost of land degradation considered in Chap. 6, we do not consider livestock feeding other biomes other than grasslands. This includes about 72 % of the livestock population (Table 8.5). Our study also considers degraded "static" grasslands—that is grassland area that did not undergo land use cover change from 2001 to 2011. Degraded grasslands account for 10 % of the grassland area and about 6 % of total livestock population (Table 8.6). SSA reported the largest population of livestock on degraded grassland while Central Asia reported the largest degraded grazing area as percent total grassland area (Table 8.6).

Estimating Changes in Livestock Productivity

To estimate changes in livestock productivity, we first resampled all datasets to a spatial resolution of 0.08° to link to global grids containing unique IDs for each grid cell, developed by HarvestChoice at the International Food Policy Research Institute. Grassland productivity derived from NDVI and statistical models (Table 8.2) was combined with conversion factors developed by Wirsenius et al. (2010) and Bouwman et al. (2005) to estimate the impact of grazing land degradation on livestock productivity (Eq. 8.1). As shown in Fig. 8.1, Wirsenius et al. (2010) and Bouwman et al. (2005)'s conversion factors are comparable in North America but vary widely in SSA. However, Bouwman et al. (2005)'s conversion factors are disaggregated across feeding systems—namely pastoral and mixed and landless (zero-grazed) feeding systems. Unfortunately we only used Wirsenius et al. (2010) since we do not have global data on feeding systems at the resolution used in this study.

The impact of degradation within grazing biomass on livestock productivity has to take into account two important aspects that affect animal food intake:

i. Non-grass feeds—which include: feed supplements, food crops and its by-products, crop residues and fodder crops, scavenging (road-side grazing, household wastes, feedstuffs from backyard farming, etc.), and animal products. Contribution of non-grass DMI vary widely across regions. For example in the Sahelian region of SSA, shrub, tree and crop residues contribute 33 % of livestock biomass requirements (Le Houérou and Hoste 1977; Pieri 1989) even though such feeding systems are regarded as 100 % grassland-based. To take

Table 8.5 Livestock production systems and corresponding livestock populations and production

	Grazing	Rainfed mixed	Irrigated mixed	Zero-grazed/industrial	Total
Million heads—average 2001–2003					
Cattle and buffaloes	406	641	450	29	1526
Sheep and goats	590	632	546	9	1777
Tropical livestock units (TLU)	343	512	370	21	1246
% of total	27.5	41.1	29.7	1.7	
Production (Million tons)—average 2001–2003					
Beef	14.6	29.3	12.9	3.9	60.7
Mutton	3.8	4.0	4.0	0.1	11.9
Pork	0.8	12.5	29.1	52.8	95.2
Poultry meat	1.2	8.0	11.7	52.8	73.7
Milk	71.5	319.2	203.7	–	594.4
Eggs	0.5	5.6	17.1	35.7	58.9

Notes Livestock considered include buffalo, cattle, goats and sheep. Conversion factor to *TLU* buffaloes = 0.7; cattle = 0.7; goats and sheep = 0.1. Grazing: >90 % of dry matter intake (DMI) obtained from grasslands; Rainfed mixed: >10 % of DMI come from crop residues and non-livestock farming activities and >90 % of the value of non-livestock farm production comes from rainfed land use; Irrigated mixed: >10 % of value of non-livestock farm production comes from irrigated land use; Landless (zero-grazed)/industrial: <10 % of DMI is farm produced
Source Calculated from Steinfeld et al. (2006)

this into account we net out the impact of non-grass intake using Bowman et al. (2003) data on feed composition (Fig. 8.2). However, we compute one conversion factor weighted by the contribution of each feeding system to total production of meat and milk.

ii. Grass biomass that is not all consumed by animals. Studies have shown that the consumable forage of grasses is only one-third of the above-ground biomass (Penning de Vries and Djitèye 1982; de Leeuw and Tothill 1993).

Given the above discussion, the cost of milk production loss due to land degradation (CLD_m) is given by:

$$CLD_m = \sum_{i=1}^{I} [DMI_{t=2001} - DMI_{t=2010}]\theta_m x_t P_m \tag{8.1}$$

$$DMI_t = biom_t \gamma \kappa$$

where DMI_t = dry matter intake (tons) in year t in pixel i; θ_m = conversion factor of grass DMI to the fresh weight of milk; P_m = price of milk per ton; $biom_t$ = grass biomass production (DM) in year t; γ = contribution of grass to total feed intake; x_t = number of milking cows in pixel i; and κ = share of above ground grass biomass actually consumed by livestock.

Table 8.6 Livestock population on degraded grazing lands across regions

	Degraded grazing area (million ha)	Degraded area of total grazing area (%)	Livestock population on degraded grazing area (million TLU)	Livestock population on degraded grazing area of total livestock population global (%)
SSA	339.8	18.5	23.32	14.0
LAC	157.36	8.1	14.63	6.4
NAM	129.71	7.9	12.59	12.5
East Asia	77.32	8.9	3.69	2.4
Oceania	153.15	18.3	1.35	3.6
South Asia	3.42	0.7	0.14	0.1
Southeast Asia	9.55	3.8	1.14	2.9
East Europe	26.77	1.5	0.73	1.2
West Europe	17.87	5.1	4.95	5.5
Central Asia	153.68	47.3	3.39	26.7
NENA	36.58	10.8	1.78	2.9
Global	1105.21	10.3	67.7	5.7

Notes Livestock considered include buffalo, cattle, goats and sheep. Conversion factor to *TLU* buffaloes = 0.7, cattle = 0.7, boats and sheep = 0.1. *SSA* Sub-Saharan Africa; *LAC* Latin America and Caribbean; *NAM* North America; *NENA* Near East and North Africa
Sources Livestock population—FAO 2005 livestock density: http://www.fao.org/ag/aga/glipha/index.jsp

Likewise, the loss of meat production due to land degradation (CLD_b) is given by

$$CLD_b = [DMI_{t=2001} - DMI_{t=2010}]\theta_b x_t \tau_t P_b \tag{8.2}$$

where P_b = price of meat per ton; θ_b = conversion factor of grass DMI to the fresh weight of meat; τ_t = off-take rate; other variables are as defined above.

We only consider on-farm losses including milk production and off-take rate for meat and ignore the loss of live weight of livestock not slaughtered or sold since such loss is not liquidated and eventually affects human welfare. We also ignore the impact of degradation on livestock health, parturition, and mortality rates due to lack of data as well as loss of carbon sequestration and other environmental and ecological services provided by grasslands. The ignored costs of grazing land degradation are large. For example, Chap. 17 shows that in Niger, 82 % of the total cost of degradation of grazing lands was due to loss of carbon sequestration. This means our results are conservative estimates.

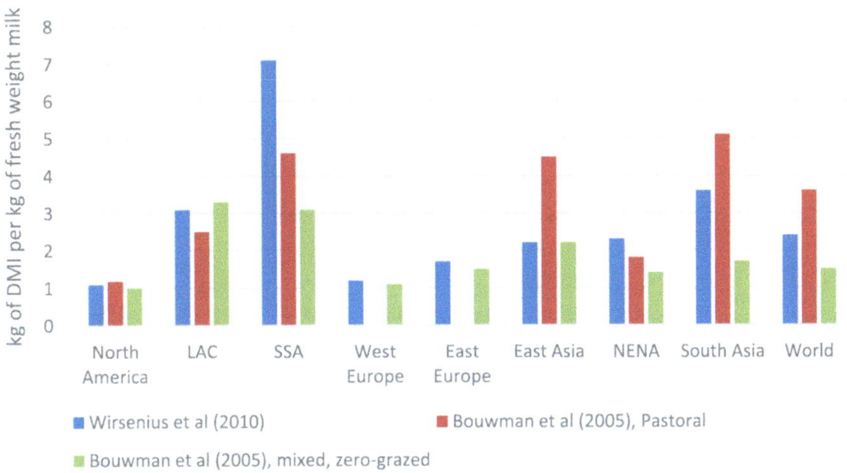

Fig. 8.1 Feed conversion factor to unit of milk and beef across regions. *Note* DMI is intake of all food categories. *LAC* Latin American Countries; *SSA* Sub-Saharan Africa; *NENA* Near East and North Africa

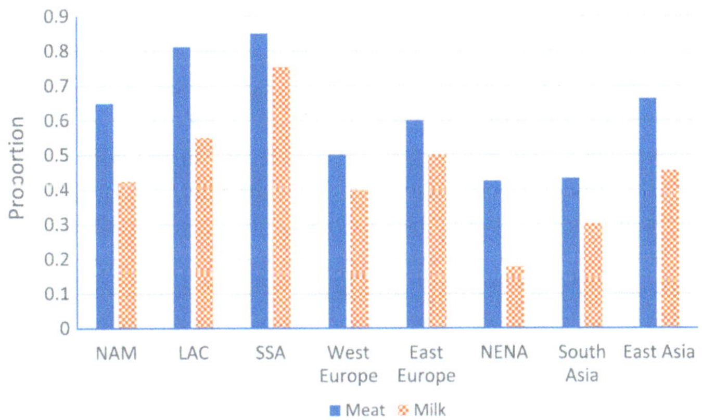

Fig. 8.2 Share of grass to total dry matter intake of meat and dairy ruminants. *Note* Meat whole carcass from all animal categories and the share of intake is weighted by the contribution pastoral and mixed and zero-grazed feeding systems to total production. *NAM* North America; *LAC* Latin American Countries; *SSA* Sub-Saharan Africa; *NENA* Near East and North Africa

Results and Discussion

Ignoring the environmental benefits of carbon sequestration and the loss in live weight of livestock that were not slaughtered or sold, the cost of livestock productivity was about 2007 US$6.8 billion (Table 8.7). North America accounts for about 55 % of the loss due to the severe land degradation in the region and the high

Table 8.7 Cost of loss of milk and meat production due to land degradation of grazing biomass

Region	Milk	Meat	Total loss	% of global loss
2007 US$ billion				
SSA	0.753	0.059	0.812	11.9
LAC	0.928	0.073	1.000	14.7
NAM	3.473	0.273	3.746	55.0
East Asia	0.094	0.051	0.145	2.1
Oceania	0.083	0.171	0.255	3.7
South Asia	0.011	0.000	0.011	0.2
Southeast Asia	0.102	0.002	0.103	1.5
East Europe	0.060	0.037	0.098	1.4
West Europe	0.402	0.125	0.527	7.7
Central Asia	0.066	0.003	0.068	1.0
NENA	0.005	0.039	0.044	0.6
Global	5.978	0.832	6.809	11.9

Note: SSA Sub-Saharan Africa; *LAC* Latin American Countries; *NAM* North America; *NENA* Near East and North Africa

livestock productivity and off take rate. For example, Table 8.8 shows that the loss of one ton of grazing biomass leads to a loss of US$98 in SSA but the same leads to a loss $514 in North America. The low off take rate in SSA also reduces the loss of meat productivity since we ignore the live weight loss of not culled animals.

Loss of milk production contributes 99 % of the total cost of grazing biomass degradation mainly due to its high sensitivity to the loss of grazing biomass. For example, loss of one DM ton of grazing biomass in North America leads to a loss of 909 kg of milk but only about 42 kg of meat respectively worth US$435 and US$79 (Table 8.8). As noted above, the low offtake rate of meat also contributes to its low contribution to the total loss.

Overall, the cost of land degradation is small compared to the area covered by grazing biomass. The low productivity of livestock in developing countries is part of the reason for the low cost. Additionally, other sources of dry matter consumption are not taken into account. These include animal feeds and crop-based DMI. And, as discussed in the methods section, it is only a third of the grassland biomass that is included in the computation of the cost of grazing biomass degradation due to the overlay of degradation and grazing areas. In addition, the loss of carbon sequestration and other ecosystem services are not considered. The livestock population in the grassland considered is also low as it accounts for only 28 % of the total livestock population (Table 8.5), though it covers 20 % of the ice-free global land area (Steinfeld et al. 2006).

Milk and beef productivity in the 2001–2011 period showed a statistically significant upward trend for all regions. A sample of the trend line is reported in Table 8.9 illustrating an upward trend of productivity for both low and high income regions.

Table 8.8 Annual cost of milk and meat productivity due to loss of 1 ton of grazing biomass

Region	Price per ton		Annual productivity loss (kg/ton of dry matter)		Cost of loss (US$)		
	Milk	Meat	Milk	Meat	Milk	Meat	Total
SSA	503	2775	140.8	9.8	71	27	98
LAC	261	1550	322.6	15.6	84	24	109
NAM	479	1907	909.1	41.7	435	79	514
East Asia	581	2590	454.5	20.4	264	53	317
Oceania	270	2812	454.5	20.4	123	57	180
South Asia	305	1696	277.8	6.8	85	12	96
Southeast Asia	746	2955	277.8	6.8	207	20	228
East Europe	368	3723	588.2	27.8	217	103	320
West Europe	476	4829	833.3	38.5	397	186	582
Central Asia	255	1676	277.8	6.8	71	11	82
NENA	413	5979	434.8	20.8	179	125	304
Global	395	2472	416.7	20.0	165	49	214

Note: SSA Sub-Saharan Africa; *LAC* Latin American Countries; *NAM* North America; *NENA* Near East and North Africa *Source* Computed from Fig. 8.1

This pattern is similar to what is reported on cropland in Chap. 6 of this volume. The seemingly conflicting results are due to farmers' efforts to compensate the loss due to land degradation by using other productivity enhancing inputs and technologies.

Figure 8.3 reports the cost of land degradation and illustrates the high cost in North America, Latin America and SSA.

Table 8.9 Trendline regression of cow milk & cattle carcass weight for selected regions for the period of 2001 to 2011

Region	Carcass weight/head	Milk yield/cow
SSA	0.004	0.014
LAC	0.0036	0.046
NAM	0.0017	0.148
South Asia	0.0009	0.019
West Europe	0.049	0.263

Note Regression trendline: $Y = \beta_1 + \beta_2 \text{ year} + \varepsilon$ where β_1 = constant, β_2 = coefficient associated with year, and ε = error term with normal distribution

SSA Sub-Saharan Africa; *LAC* Latin American countries; *NAM* North America

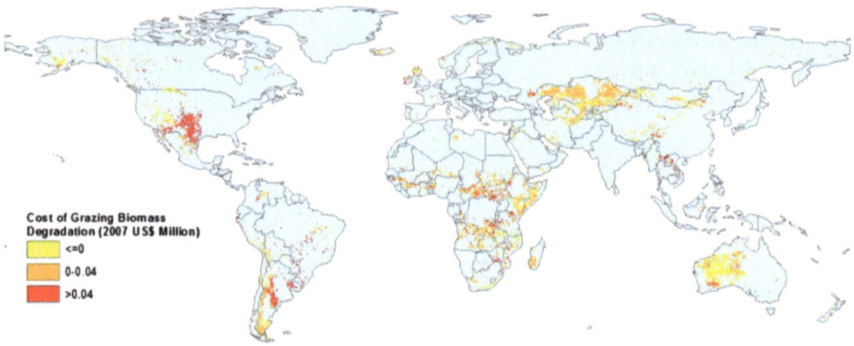

Fig. 8.3 Cost of land degradation of grazing biomass

Conclusions and Implications

This study used innovative approaches that could be used to conduct regular global assessment of grassland degradation or improvement. The approach considers only on-farm cost and ignores off-site costs—such as loss of carbon sequestration. The results reported have important implications on taking action on addressing grazing land degradation but they should be interpreted bearing in mind the weaknesses and gaps of the study.

The on-farm cost of grassland degradation is about 2007 US$6.8 billion. North America accounts for more than 50 % of the loss due to the severe land degradation and the high livestock productivity. The cost of land degradation is not reflected in the loss of productivity due to the ability of farmers in North America to use improved production technologies to maintain or increase livestock productivity. Additionally, the impact of changes in grazing land productivity on human welfare in North America is minimal given the farmers' ability to cushion such shocks using insurance, government programs, credit and other programs. Although the grazing land degradation is much more widespread in SSA, its actual cost is small due to the low livestock productivity. However, the impact on human welfare is much more severe—especially in the drylands where majority of the livestock is located and where majority of the population is below the poverty line. This implies that efforts to address grassland degradation is even more urgent in SSA. This is especially urgent given the increasing demand of livestock products and the potential to contribute to poverty reduction. Addressing grassland degradation could simultaneously reduce poverty, contribute to carbon sequestration, increase productivity of crops, provide more draft power, and other socio-economic, cultural, and ecological benefits that livestock provide. The large cost of grassland degradation, the increasing demand for livestock products, and the multiple benefits of livestock provide opportunities to take action.

Among the actions that could be taken to increase livestock productivity is to increase public budget allocation to livestock production in developing countries.

For example, in SSA public budget allocation to livestock is only about 5 %. Investments in livestock productivity need to be directed to both cost-effective and amenable pasture management practices and breeding programs. Some developing countries can serve as success stories since they have successfully increased livestock productivity, which in turn have contributed to poverty reduction. The Kenyan dairy programs and Botswana's beef production demonstrate such success stories. Both countries have developed the livestock sector due to long-term policies for livestock development, which aimed at genetic improvement, disease control, strengthening domestic and international markets to allow farmers to address highly seasonal supplies, and health and safety standards (Hazell 2007). Efforts to improve grassland through controlled grazing, planting legumes, and other amenable practices will increase both livestock productivity and carbon sequestration (Henderson et al. 2015). This means the international community has the responsibility to support livestock development programs in low income countries due to large potential of carbon sequestration for improved grasslands management. For example, Henderson et al. (2015) show that improved grassland management could sequester up to 33.3 Tg CO_2 $year^{-1}$ in SSA. Such support could be done by giving aid specifically aimed at grassland improvement.

Access to market in largely pastoral areas is low and this contributes to the low livestock productivity. Improvement of market access in grazing areas has also been shown to improve livestock productivity (Barrett 2008). Improvement of market access will have multiplier effects on rural development as it will have favorable impacts on poverty reduction, access to health and other rural services.

References

Asner, G., & Archer, R. (2010). Livestock and carbon cycle. In H. Steinfeld., H. A. Mooney, F. Schneider & L. E. Neville (Eds.), *Livestock in a changing landscape. Drivers, consequences and responses* (pp. 69–82). Scientific Committee on the Problems of the Environment (SCOPE): Island Press.

Barrett, C. B. (2008). Smallholder market participation: Concepts and evidence from eastern and southern Africa. *Food Policy, 33*, 299–317.

Bicheron, P., Defouny, P., Brockmann, C., Schouten, L., Vancutsem, C., Huc, M., et al. (2008). *GLOBCOVER: Products description and validation report*. MEDIAS-France/POSTEL: ESA Globcover Project.

Bouwman, A. F., Van der Hoek, K. W., Eickhout, B., & Soenario, I. (2005). Exploring changes in world ruminant production systems. *Agricultural Systems, 84*, 121–153.

Bowman, G. R., Beauchemin, K. A., & Shelford, J. A. (2003). Fibrolytic enzymes and parity effects on feeding behavior, salivation, and ruminal pH of lactating dairy cows. *Journal of Dairy Science, 86*(2), 565–575.

de Leeuw, P. N., & Tothill, J. C. (1993). The concept of rangeland carrying capacity in Sub-Saharan Africa—myth or reality. In R. H. Behnke Jr., I. Scoones, C. Kerven (Eds.), *Range*

Ecology at Disequilibrium. New Models of natural variability and pastoral adaptation in African Savannah (pp. 77–88). London: IIED, Overseas Development Institute.

Dong, J., Kaufmann, R. K., Myneni, R. B., Tucker, C. J., Kauppi, P. E., Liski, J., et al. (2003). Remote sensing estimates of boreal and temperate forest woody biomass: carbon pools, sources, and sinks. *Remote Sensing of Environment, 84*, 393–410.

Dregne, H. E. (2002). Land degradation in the drylands. *Arid land research and management, 16*, 99–132.

FAO. (2011a). *Energy-smart food for people and climate*. Rome: United nations food and agriculture organization.

FAO. (2011b). *World livestock 2011—livestock in food security*. Rome: United Nations Food and Agriculture Organization.

Fraser, R. H., & Li, Z. (2002). Estimating fire-related parameters in boreal forest using SPOT VEGETATION. *Remote Sensing of Environment, 82*, 95–110.

Harris, R. B. (2010). Rangeland degradation on the Qinghai-Tibetan plateau: A review of the evidence of its magnitude and causes. *Journal of Arid Environments, 74*, 1–12.

Hazell, P. (2007). All-Africa review of experiences with commercial agriculture. Case study on livestock. Background paper for the Competitive Commercial Agriculture in Sub–Saharan Africa (CCAA) Study. http://siteresources.worldbank.org/INTAFRICA/Resources/257994-1215457178567/Ch11_Livestock.pdf. Accessed Mar 2014.

Henderson, B., Gerber, P., Hilinksi, T., Falcucci, A., Ojima, D. S., & Salvatore, M. (2015). Greenhouse gas mitigation potential of the world's grazing lands: modeling soil carbon and nitrogen fluxes of mitigation practices. *Agriculture, Ecosystems & Environment, 207*, 91–100.

Hermann, S. M., Anyamba, A., & Tucker, C. J. (2005). Recent trends in vegetation dynamics in the African Sahel and their relationship to climate. *Global Environmental Change, 15*, 394–404.

Hoddinott, J. (2006). Shocks and their consequences across and within households in rural Zimbabwe. *Journal of Development Studies, 42*, 301–321.

Huete, A., Didan, K., van Leeuwen, W., Miura, T., & Glenn, E. (2011). Moderate resolution imaging spectroradiometer vegetation indices. In B. Ramachandran, C. Justice, & M. Abrams (Eds.), *Land remote sensing and global environmental change, NASA's earth observing system and the science of ASTER and MODIS*. New York: Springer.

Jin, Y., Yang, X., Qiu, J., Li, J., Gao, T., Wu, Q., et al. (2014). Remote sensing-based biomass estimation and its spatio-temporal variations in temperate grassland, Northern China. *Remote Sensing, 6*, 1496–1513.

Jones, P., & Harris, I. (2008). CRU time-series (TS) high resolution gridded datasets. NCAS British Atmospheric Data Centre Climate Research Unit (CRU), University of East Anglia. http://badc.nerc.ac.uk/view/badc.nerc.ac.uk__ATOM__dataent_1256223773328276. Accessed Mar 2014.

Kitalyi, A., Mtenga, L., Morton, J. U., McLeod, A., Thornton, P., Dorward, A., et al. (2005). Why keep livestock if you are poor? In E. Owen, A. Kitalyi, N. Jayasuriay, & T. Smith (Eds.), *Livestock and wealth creation: Improving the husbandry of animals kept by resource-poor people in developing countries* (pp. 13–27). Nottingham, UK: Nottingham University Press.

Lalonde, L. G., & Sukigara, T. (1997). *Livestock development planning system version 2 user's guide*. Rome: United Nations Food and Agriculture Organization.

Le Houérou, H. N., & Hoste, H. (1977). Rangeland production and annual rainfall relations in the mediterranean basin and in the African Sahelo-Sudanian zone. *Journal of Range Managements, 30*, 181–189.

Le, Q. B., Nkonya, E., Mirzabaev, A. (2014). Biomass productivity-based mapping of global land degradation hotspots. ZEF-Discussion Papers on Development Policy No. 193. University of Bonn.

Livestock in Development. (1999). *Livestock in poverty-focused development*. LID, Somerset, UK: Crewkerne.

LP DAAC (Land Processes Distributed Active Archive Center) (2011). MODIS/AQUA MYD13C1 Vegetation Indices 16-DAY L3 Global 0.05Deg CMG. Collection 5.

Moll, H. A. J. (2005). Costs and benefits of livestock systems and the role of market and nonmarket relationships. *Agricultural Economics, 32*, 181–193.

Nabuurs, G. J. (2004). Current consequences of past actions: how to separate direct from indirect. In C. B. Field & M. R. Raupach (Eds.), *The global carbon cycle* (pp. 317–326). Washington, DC: Island Press.

New, M., Hulme, M., & Jones, P. (2000). Representing twentieth-century space-time climate variability. Part II: development of 1901–96 monthly grids of terrestrial surface climate. *Journal of Climate, 13*, 2217–2238.

Nicholson, S. E., Davenport, M. L., & Malo, A. R. (1990). A comparison of the vegetation response to rainfall in the Sahel and East Africa, using normalized difference vegetation index from NOAA AVHRR. *Climate Change, 17*, 209–241.

Penning de Vries, F. W. T. & Djiteye, M. A. (1982). La productivite des paturages saheliens: une etude des sols, des vegetations et de l'exploitation de cette ressource naturelle.

Pieri, C. (1989). Fertilité des terres de savanes. Bilan de trente ans de recherche et de développement agricole au sud du Sahara. Ministère de la Coopération/CIRAD/IRAT, Paris.

Potter, P., & Ramankutty, N. (2010). Characterizing the spatial patterns of global fertilizer application and manure production. *Earth Interactions, 14*, 1–22.

Quinlan, T. (1995). Grassland degradation and livestock rearing in Lesotho. *Journal of Southern African Studies, 21*, 491–507.

Rahetlah, V. B., Salgado, P., Andrianarisoa, B., Tillard, E., Razafindrazaka, H., Mézo, L. L., et al. (2014). Relationship between normalized difference vegetation index (NDVI) and forage biomass yield in the Vakinankaratra region, Madagascar. *Livestock Research for Rural Development*. 26: Article #95.

Randolph, T. F., Schelling, E., Grace, E., Nicholson, C. F., Leroy, J. L., Cole, D. C., et al. (2007). Invited review: Role of livestock in human nutrition and health for poverty reduction in developing countries. *Journal of Animal Science, 85*, 2788–2800.

Ren, H., & Zhou, G. (2014). Determination of green above ground biomass in desert steppe using litter-soil-adjusted vegetation index. *European Journal of Remote sensing, 47*, 611–625.

Requier-Desjardins, M. (2006). The Economic costs of desertification: A first survey of some cases in Africa. *International Journal of Sustainable Development, 9*, 199–209.

Robinson, T. P., Thornton P. K., Franceschini, G., Kruska, R. L., Chiozza, F., Notenbaert, A., et al. (2011). Global livestock production systems. Rome, Food and Agriculture Organization of the United Nations (FAO) and International Livestock Research Institute (ILRI), 152 p.

Robinson, T. P., & Pozzi, F. (2011). Mapping supply and demand for animal-source foods to 2030, Animal Production and Health Working Paper. No. 2. Rome.

Robinson, T. P., William Wint, G. R., Conchedda, C., Van Boeckel, T. P., Ercoli, V., Palamara, E., et al. (2014). Mapping the global distribution of livestock. *Plos One*. doi:10.1371/journal.pone.0096084.

Roy, P. S., & Ravan, S. A. (1996). Biomass estimation using satellite remote sensing data-An investigation on possible approaches for natural forest. *Journal of Bioscience, 21*, 535–561.

Sere and Steinfeld, (1996). World livestock production systems: current status, issues and trends. Animal production and health paper No127. FAO. Rome.

Sheldrick, W. F., Syers, J. K., & Lingard, J. (2004). Contribution of livestock extreta to nutrient balances. *Nutrient Cycling Agroecosystems, 66*, 119–131.

Steinfeld, H., Gerber, P., Wassenaar, T., Castel, V., Rosales, M., & De Haan, C. (2006). *Livestock's long shadow: Environmental issues and options*. Rome: United Nations Food and Agriculture Organization.

Thoma, D. P., Bailey, D. W., Long, D. S., Nielsen, G. A., Henry, M. P., Breneman, M. C., et al. (2002). Short-term monitoring of rangeland forage conditions with AVHRR imagery. *Journal of Range Management, 55*, 383–389.

Tomppo, E., Nilsson, M., Rosengren, M., Aalto, P., & Kennedy, P. (2002). Simultaneous use of Landsat-TM and IRS-1C WiFS data in estimating large area tree stem volume and aboveground biomass. *Remote Sensing of Environment, 82*, 156–171.

Wainwright, J., & Mulligan, M. (2005). Modelling and model building. In J. Wainwright & M. Mulligan (Eds.), *Environmental modelling: Finding simplicity in complexity* (pp. 7–74). Chichester, England: John Wiley & Sons.

Wirsenius, S., Azar, C., & Berndes, G. (2010). How much land is needed for global food production under scenarios of dietary changes and livestock productivity increases in 2030? *Agricultural Systems, 103*, 621–638.

Zhao, F., Xu, B., Yang, X., Jin, Y., Li, J., Xia, L., et al. (2014). Remote sensing estimates of grassland aboveground biomass based on MODIS net primary productivity (NPP): A case study in the Xilingol grassland of Northern China. *International Journal of Remote Sensing, 6*, 5368–5386.

Chapter 9
Economics of Land Degradation in Sub-Saharan Africa

Ephraim Nkonya, Timothy Johnson, Ho Young Kwon and Edward Kato

Abstract Sub-Saharan Africa (SSA) has experienced the most severe land degradation in the world. Given that livelihoods of the majority of the rural poor heavily depend on natural resources, countries in the region have designed a number of policies and strategies to address land degradation and to enhance productivity. However investment from both countries and their development partners has remained low, especially for livestock, which accounts for the largest area degraded. Our results show that conversion of grassland to cropland and deforestation are the major factors driving land use/cover change (LUCC). One of the major reasons leading farmers to convert grassland to cropland is the low livestock productivity. The increasing demand for livestock products provides an ample opportunity to the value of grasslands and in turn livestock productivity. Given that donor funding accounts for the largest share of expenditure on agriculture and natural resource management in most SSA countries, econometric analysis showed that donor funding reduces the cost of land degradation. This positions donors in a position of influencing efforts to combat land degradation in SSA. The fact that SSA has poor marketing infrastructure suggests that its improvement will enhance efforts to address low productivity and land degradation. Econometric analysis showed that access to market leads to a reduction of the cost of land degradation related to LUCC. Improvement of market infrastructure will achieve a win-win benefit as it will improve natural resources and reduce poverty. Consistent with results from other regions, improvement of government effectiveness reduces cost of land degradation and cropland expansion. This illustrates the key role played by governance in mediating the drivers of land degradation. Efforts to increase adoption of integrated soil fertility management will require improvement of access to markets, advisory services and retraining of agricultural extension services. There is also need to find practical and amenable strategies for incentivizing farmers to use ISFM. For example, conditional fertilizer subsidy could provide incentives for farmers to adopt nitrogen fixing agroforestry trees and

E. Nkonya (✉) · T. Johnson · H.Y. Kwon · E. Kato
International Food Policy Research Institute, 2033 K Street NW,
Washington, DC 20006, USA
e-mail: e.nkonya@cgiar.org

E. Nkonya et al. (eds.), *Economics of Land Degradation and Improvement – A Global Assessment for Sustainable Development*,
DOI 10.1007/978-3-319-19168-3_9

improve significantly the current subsidy programs in several SSA countries. Overall, our results show that SSA has the potential to become the breadbasket of the world but it has to significantly improve its market access and government effectiveness to create incentives for land holders to invest in land improvement. The increasing demand for land, urbanization, and other global regional changes are creating a conducive condition for taking action against land degradation. These opportunities should be exploited effectively as they lead to win-win outcomes—reducing poverty and achieving sustainable land management.

Keywords Sub-Sahara Africa · Land degradation · Sustainable land management · Land tenure · Access to markets · Government effectiveness

Introduction

Sub-Saharan Africa (SSA) has ample opportunities to become the future bread-basket of the world. While crop yield gaps—the difference between potential and actual yield (Lobell et al. 2009)—in other regions are narrow and closing, SSA has the widest yield gap of maize, rice, and wheat in the world (Nkonya et al. 2013). For example, average maize yield in the tropical lowlands in SSA is only 16 % of its potential (Lobell et al. 2009). Closing such a yield gap will provide food for both the SSA population and the rest of the world. About 90 % of the remaining 1.8 billion ha of global arable land in developing countries is in Latin America (LAC) and SSA (Bruinsma 2009) and it is estimated that about 50 % of the land to be converted to agricultural use by 2050 will come from SSA (Alexandratos and Bruinsma 2012). Three of the seven countries, which account for half of the remaining suitable land in the world, are in SSA (Angola, Democratic Republic of Congo, and Sudan) (Ibid).[1]

In the past two decades (1995 and 2013), SSA's average economic growth was 4.5 % per year in real terms—a level that is about twice the economic growth of the rest of the world during the same period (World Bank 2014; Andersen and Jensen 2014). Such growth has been driven by increasing consumer spending, investment in extraction of natural resources and infrastructure, a rapidly growing services sector, and increased agricultural productivity (World Bank 2014). SSA agricultural productivity has increased in the past few decades, thanks to farmer investments which has led to increased use of improved seeds and inorganic fertilizer (Sheahan and Barrett 2014). For example, Sheahan and Barrett (2014) found that in three of the six countries with a nationally representative household survey, farmers used an average of 57 kg/ha of fertilizer—a level which is much higher than the 13 kg/ha

[1]But as it will be discussed in the cost of land degradation section, conversion of forest, grassland, and other forms of land use/cover change (LUCC) leads to land degradation.

widely cited level, which is based on Food and Agriculture organization (FAO) data. A recent study showed that SSA GDP growth originating from agriculture accounted for income growth of the 40 % poorest population—a level about three times larger than the growth originating from other sectors (De Janvry and Sadoulet 2010).

Despite these potential and economic achievements, SSA faces daunting challenges. About 28 % of the 924.7 million people in SSA (UN 2014) live in areas that have experienced degradation since the 1980s (Le et al. 2014). The most severe land degradation occurred on grasslands, 40 % of which experienced degradation (Le et al. 2014). About 26 % of forestland and 12 % of cropland also experienced land degradation (Ibid). The high land degradation rate coupled with economic development reflect the tradeoffs involved in clearing forest or other high value biomes for crop production. The two processes also suggest an environmental Kuznet curve process—i.e., initial phases of economic development are done at the expense of the environment. Even though land degradation is reducing SSA's agricultural potential, the increasing use of fertilizer and other inputs on cropland has led to greater productivity and it masks the land degradation in the region. Additionally, closing the wide agricultural yield gap requires significant investment to address constraints which lead to low agricultural productivity. One of such constraints is poor market infrastructure which increases the cost of external inputs. SSA has the lowest logistics performance index (LPI)—an index that reflects perceptions on efficiency of customs clearance process, quality of trade and transport-related infrastructure, and other marketing logistics (Arvis et al. 2012). The cost of transporting a ton for 1 km ranges from 0.04 to 0.14 USD in Africa compared to only 0.01–0.04 USD in other developing countries (Foster and Briceno-Garmendia 2010).

Government investment in natural resource development is generally low and has been declining in the past two decades (FAO 2010). Total SSA's public expenditure on agriculture, forestry, wildlife, and fisheries is only about 4 % of the total government budget even though these sectors account for about 25 % of the GDP (FAOSTAT 2012). Official development assistance (ODA) accounts for the largest share of forest investment in most SSA countries (Gondo 2010). SSA's investment in agricultural research and development (R&D) is the lowest in the world and is declining. Intensity of investment in agricultural research—investment in agricultural R&D as share of agricultural GDP—has steadily declined, from 0.59 % in 2006 to 0.51 % in 2011. The intensity is well below the recommended target of 5 % set by the United Nations' Sustainable Development (Beintema and Stads 2014). This shortcoming affects SSA's rural development since countries which invest in agricultural R&D achieve greater land productivity and are more likely to achieve sustainable land management (SLM) than those which spend less (Lobell et al. 2009).

SSA countries have been implementing a number of policies to address land degradation in line with their broad objective of poverty reduction through enhancement of productivity of natural resources upon which majority of the poor depend. These include; establishing protected area, R&D, input subsidies, agricultural water management, land tenure, and others. This chapter analyzes the cost of land degradation in SSA and identifies the drivers of cost of land use/cover change (LUCC)-related land degradation and change of cropland. Given the large amount of donor contribution to land-based development, donor support on cropland expansion and the cost of land degradation will be included in the analysis of drivers of cost of land degradation and cropland expansion. The results of this analysis will help SSA countries to design policies and strategies for taking action against land degradation. To lay ground for the analysis, the chapter first discusses the major land and natural resource management policies and the corresponding public investment. This is followed by a brief discussion of methodological approaches for analyzing the severity and cost of LUCC-related land degradation in SSA—which are discussed in detail in Chaps. 4 (extent of land degradation) and 6 (cost of land degradation). Given that cropland expansion is the major driver of land degradation (Chap. 6), we explore the drivers of cropland expansion. The last section draws policy implications on action to be taken to address land degradation.

Sustainable Land Management (SLM) Policies in SSA

We focus our discussion on policies with direct impacts on SLM—i.e., policies that have direct impacts on land management. For example, although trade policies may have large impacts on land management via their impacts on prices, these impacts are indirect and likely have mixed (positive or negative) impacts, depending on the local contexts (such as whether farmers are net buyers or sellers of tradable commodities). We also focus on policies that are amenable to change. For example, although broader monetary, fiscal, financial, and exchange rate policies may have large impacts on land management, these are unlikely to be changed in order to improve land management, although it may be important to take steps to ameliorate any negative consequences that such policies may have. The review focuses on SSA governments' commitment to achieve sustainable development enshrined in the Rio summits three major conventions (climate change, biological diversity, and land degradation). However, focus of the discussion is on land policies. Country level policies are also reviewed but summarized at regional level to reflect the countries' commitment to sustainable development. Other policies with strong potential impact on land management are also reviewed. These include input subsidies, agricultural water management, land tenure, government effectiveness, market access, and population. To determine the government commitment to implementing their SLM policies, the last section analyzes the SSA government investment in land-based sectors.

Sustainable Development Policies

On conservation of biodiversity, 46 out of 51 (90 %) of SSA countries have ratified the convention on biological diversity (CBD).[2] Accordingly, protected area has been increasing in all sub-regions (Fig. 9.1). Protected areas provide both local and international benefits—especially when policies and strategies involve communities surrounding the protected areas in managing them (Wilkie et al. 2006). For example, Mugisha and Jacobson (2004) observed that seven community-based protected areas (CBPA) management in Uganda had significantly lower bush burning, logging, and encroachment than nine other protected areas without local community involvement.

All SSA countries have ratified the United Nations Framework Convention on Climate Change (UNFCCC) and two thirds of the 51 countries have submitted their national adaptation program of action (NAPA) and 22 countries have submitted the Nationally Appropriate Mitigation Actions (NAMA) to the UNFCCC (2014a, b). Accordingly, many SSA countries are reducing their CO_2 emissions and use of ozone-depleting substances (UNECA 2014). Additionally, forest policies in SSA have increasingly incorporated sustainable forest management (SFM) and have embraced community-based forest management (FAO 2012)—an aspect which has enhanced SFM (Seymour et al. 2014). However, SSA still experiences high deforestation. Deforestation and other forms of land use accounts for 43 % of CO_2 emission in SSA (TerrAfrica 2009). Unfortunately, public investment for forest development and the environment in general remains low in SSA.

All 51 SSA countries have ratified the United Convention to Combat Desertification (UNCCD)[3] and prepared the national action plan (NAPs). Implementation of NAPs follow a bottom-up approach, an aspect regarded as one of the success stories of UNCCD (Bruyninckx 2004). According to Kellner et al. (2011) however, institutional uptake of bottom-up approach has been limited. Additionally, the NAP projects have lacked monitoring and evaluation systems (Ibid). Limited funding for combatting land degradation has generally been common across SSA countries and NAPs have been largely funded by donors. Limited funding from national governments to finance implementation of the three Rio summit conventions is a common problem across all countries.

Input Subsidies

A number of countries—including Burkina Faso, Ethiopia, Ghana, Kenya, Malawi, Mali, Nigeria, Rwanda, Senegal, Tanzania, and Zambia—have subsidized fertilizer and/or improved seeds in efforts to increase farm crop yield level fertilizer

---

[2]Source: http://www.cbd.int/information/parties.shtml.

[3]Source:http://www.unccd.int/Lists/SiteDocumentLibrary/convention/Ratification%20list%20May 2014.pdf.

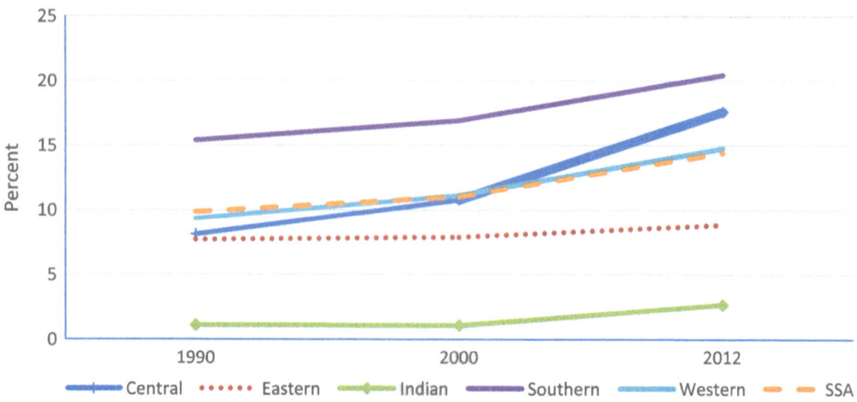

Fig. 9.1 Protected terrestrial and marine area as percent of sub-regional territorial area of SSA

application (Tables 9.1 and 9.2). In five countries (Kenya, Malawi, Rwanda, Tanzania, and Zambia), subsidies were targeted to either the poor or priority crops and reached a large proportion of farmers. For example, about 65 % of farm households in Malawi benefited from the subsidy program (Druilhe and Barreiro-Hurlé 2012). Likewise, about 95 % of the 2.7 million rural households in Kenya benefited from the subsidy program that targeted the universally grown maize crop (KNBS 2014). The number of farmers reached in the subsidies that were not targeted is unknown in most countries reported in Table 9.2. However, in cases where the number of farmers reached was known, beneficiaries of the universal subsidies was significantly smaller than the case of targeted subsidy programs (Tables 9.1 and 9.2).

Investment in input subsidies as share of agricultural budget ranged from 11 % in Burkina Faso to as high as 59 % in Malawi (Tables 9.1 and 9.2). In most cases, government budget covered the entire or largest share of subsidy budget (Druilhe and Barreiro-Hurlé 2012) due to the previous donor's negative perception towards subsidies (Kelly et al. 2011). As shown in Fig. 9.5, the large share of agricultural budget on subsidies has crowded out investment into other essential rural services—such as market infrastructure, extension services, and development of private input markets (Ricker-Gilbert et al. 2013). Jayne and Rashid (2013) also show that the cost of input subsidy is greater than its benefits and that investment into R&D and rural infrastructure would provide higher returns to agricultural growth and poverty reduction.

Agricultural Water Management Policies

Agricultural water management (AWM) includes water conservation practices, water harvesting, supplemental irrigation, ground water irrigation, surface water irrigation, and drainage (CAADP 2013). Given that water supports all forms of life,

Table 9.1 Investment in targeted subsidies and number of beneficiaries

Country	Kenya	Malawi	Rwanda	Tanzania	Zambia
Name and date[a]	NAAIP	AISP	CIP	NAIVS	FISP (ex-FSP)
	2007-on	2005-on	2007–10	2008-on	2002-on
Amount (US$ million)	54.5	171.8	–	121.8	113.2
Subsidy as % of ag budget	19.0	58.9	–	46.0	29.3
Number of beneficiaries (million)	2.5	1.5	0.7	2.5	0.5
Targeted crops	Staples	Maize and tobacco	Maize, wheat, potato	Maize, rice	Maize
Targeted farmers	Poor	Poor	Poor land >0.5 ha	Land poor (<1 ha) in high potential areas	Less poor land 1–5 ha
Allocation criteria		Farm size and need5		Female-headed HH in priority	
% subsidy and ration	100 % on 1 acre or for 2 bags	64–91 % on 1 acre or for 2 bags	75, 50 and 25 % up to 3 bags	50 % on 1 acre or for 2 bags	50–60 % on 2 acres (1 ha bef. 2009) or for 4 bags
Distribution system	Vouchers	Vouchers	Vouchers	Vouchers	Physical distribution

Notes: *NAAIP* National Accelerated Agricultural Input Programme; *AISP* Agricultural Input Subsidy Programme; *CIP* Crop intensification programme; *NAIVS* National Agricultural Input Voucher System; *FSP* Fertilizer Support Programme
Sources Druilhe and Barreiro-Hurlé (2012) and Jayne and Rashid (2013)

AWM is a major determinant of quality and quantity of ecosystem and biodiversity services (Barron 2009). This means AWM is an important component in land degradation and improvement. Of key importance is the high level of water wastage that could lead to salinity and other forms of land degradation. About 50 % of urban water in SSA is unaccounted for and about 70 % of irrigation water is lost (ECA 2014). The major driver of such loss is the poor or lack of water infrastructure which is compounded by weak local institutions and limited investment in water development, all of which significantly contribute to efficient water use efficiency (Ibid).

AWM policies include water law, rights, pricing and subsidy or taxation, allocation, user participation, and decentralization of irrigation infrastructure management or Irrigation Management Transfer (IMT) (Kuriakose and Ahlers 2008). At the regional level, the African Union has adopted the African Water Vision 2025 as

Table 9.2 Investment in universal subsidies

Country	Burkina Faso	Ghana	Mali	Nigeria	Senegal
Name and date	2008-on	2008-on	Rice initiative 2008-on	FMSP 1999-on	GOANA 2008-on
Cost of subsidy (US$ million)	21.1	73.2	21.5	152.3	40.3
# of beneficiaries (million)	0.5	0.9	Unknown	Unknown	Unknown
Targeted crops	Rice, maize, cowpea + cotton (credit)	Staples + cash crops	Rice, maize, wheat + cotton	Staples	Staples
% subsidy	≤50 % (15–30 % actual)	50 % (30–50 % actual)	25 %	25 % (federal) + 0–60 % (state)	50 %
Distribution system	Physical	Physical (vouchers piloted)	Physical (vouchers may be piloted)	Physical (vouchers piloted)	Physical local committees
Participation of agrodealers	None	Very limited	Very limited	None	Unknown

Notes: *GOANA* Grande Offensive Agricole pour la Nourriture et l'Abondance; *FMSP* Federal Market Stabilization Programme
Source Druilhe and Barreiro-Hurlé (2012)

the policy instrument for achieving sustainable water resource management and use (WWAP 2015). Africa's Water Vision 2025 is "Africa where there is an equitable and sustainable use and management of water resources for poverty alleviation, socioeconomic development, regional cooperation, and the environment" (Ibid). To achieve this, Water Vision 2025 sets ten targets and strategies that broadly aim to sustainably provide adequate potable and agricultural water to ensure food and energy security for all while also ensuring that there is enough quantity and quality of water for sustaining the ecosystems and biodiversity. Enabling environment needed to achieve this vision includes creation of strong and effective water resource management institutions, policies, financial and technical support, all of which will ensure integrated water management and cooperation at local, national, and transboundary water basin levels (Ibid).

Faced with the increasing water demand, climate change, renewed effort to achieving food security, sharp increase in food prices, and other challenges, African countries in the past 10 years have increasingly been receptive of the Water Vision 2025 and to investment in irrigation (Pinstrup-Andersen 2014; Lankford 2009). Among new directions in achieving the vision include an increasing commitment to water-policy reform, decentralization of water institutions, IMT, building water financial sustainability through treating water as an economic good rather than a free resource, and providing a safety net for the poor (Ibid).

Situation Analysis of AWM in SSA

SSA has the smallest irrigated area compared to other regions—despite its above average need for irrigation compared to other regions. Irrigated area as share of cultivated area is only 6 %—a level far lower than the corresponding share of 37 % in Asia and 14 % in Latin America (AQUASTAT 2014). Additionally only 5 % of the region's potential water resources are developed and the per capita water storage is only 200 m^3 compared to 6000 m^3 in North America (WWAP 2015). The Gulf of Guinea (coastal West Africa) and the Sudano-Sahelian zone respectively exploit only 1.3 and 35 % of their Internal Renewable Water Resources (IRWR) (Frenken 2005). The gross volume of SSA's harvestable water runoff is about 5195 km^3 and if only 15 % of the rainwater were harvested, it would be more than enough to meet all of the water needs of the region (Malesu et al. 2006). In fact, and Hatibu et al. (2000) note that rainfall variability, frequent droughts, and high intensity storms create more challenges to potential water quantities.

The rainfall variability and frequent droughts and storms renders SSA's agriculture to highly unreliable rainfed production—especially in the arid and semi-arid areas which contain 54 % of total land area (Jahnke 1982). Frequent events of drought have led to famine and loss of livestock in the region. This has prompted SSA countries to invest in mainly large-scale irrigation in the 1960s to late 1980s (AGRA 2014; Inocencio 2007; Turral et al. 2010). The need for investing in both irrigation infrastructure and local institutions cannot be emphasized enough given SSA's great irrigation potential. In fact, the amount of water in SSA is not the key limiting factor even in the semi-arid areas (Hatibu et al. 2000).

The large-scale irrigation schemes were largely centrally managed with a top-down approach as involvement of local institutions and communities in investment planning and water management was limited (Turral et al. 2010). The policies and investments in the 1990s to present have been directed towards development of smallscale irrigation (AGRA 2014). Empirical evidence shows that there is strong justification for the new direction toward small-scale irrigation. You et al. (2011) showed that the internal rate of return for small-scale irrigation investment was 28 % compared to only 7 % for large scale irrigation. Involvement of local communities and their institutions have also shown much more effective and sustainable water and natural resource management (Pahl-Wostl et al. 2008). However, recent work has shown that even small-scale irrigation in SSA is not a panacea as they fail if their local institutions are weak (Burney and Naylor 2012).

The AWM investment will lead to greater yields and reduced soil erosion. For example, it is estimated that rainfed grain yield is 1.5 metric tons per ha, compared with 3.1 metric tons per ha for irrigated yields (Rosegrant et al. 2002). AWM will also enhance adoption of new crops and varieties that may not be produced under rainfed conditions or during rainy seasons. For example, Smith et al. (2010) observe that AWM investment enhances production of much needed nutritious vegetable and horticultural crops and other high value crop production which simultaneously improves nutrition and income. Unfortunately current policies and investment strategies have not been commensurate to the region's water challenges. As stated above however, new interest in AWM gives promise that governments are getting serious to address the water challenges.

Land Tenure

Studies have shown that secure land rights and presence of land titles are often associated with greater long-term land investment and market transactions (de Soto 2000; Besley 1995; Place and Otsuka 2002; Gavian and Fafchamps 1996). Customary land tenure dominates ownership in SSA as formal tenure covers only between 2 and 10 % of the land (Deininger 2003). Conventional wisdom has postulated that customary land tenure is insecure because it does not involve legal documents. Additionally, customary land tenure puts women at a disadvantage since land is normally bequeathed to sons (Doss et al. 2013). Accordingly, concerted land registration efforts have been made in many SSA countries (Deininger 2003). However, Deininger (2003) and Otsuka and Place (2014) observed that formal tenure systems have also resulted in increased tenure insecurity in many SSA countries, because of the weak enforcement of the formal laws and the stronger customary institutions which still dominate rural communities. Additionally, claims that customary land tenure has an inherent insecurity have been challenged by research. Empirical evidence has demonstrated that customary land tenure is resilient and provides security that has led to comparable or greater long-term investment than land held under formal tenure security (Cotula 2006; Nkonya et al. 2008).

Given the recent land grabbing and interest in large-scale land investments in SSA, there is need of designing tenure systems and land policies to protect the vulnerable groups and enhance security of customary tenure that will provide incentive for land investments by farmers. Place (2009) summarizes key points on policy reforms that need to be taken into account to address the tenure security challenges related to the predominantly customary tenure:

- Tenure security needs to be well-understood and secure—especially for women and other vulnerable groups.
- Tenure security of customary land tenure is a problem—especially for women farmers. Changing customary tenure systems requires long-term strategies to

address cultural biases against women land ownership. In the short-term, improvement of land market is one approach for increasing women's access to land (Nkonya et al. 2008).

Empirical evidence shows that customary land tenure provides adequate investment security. This means efforts to protect customary tenure systems against arbitrary expropriation that occurred during the land grabbing by government or wealthy individuals requires immediate policy action. However the lack of formal titles is a constraint for farmers who need to access credit. This means the current land titling efforts should be targeted to areas where there is demand for land titling. Heterogeneity in land policies is also required to reflect the different socio-economic environments prevailing in rural SSA communities. Currently almost all land policies in SSA recognize the customary land rights and give rights to groups or communities to reflect the common communal land ownership and management. Additionally, restrictions on land markets are being relaxed in many countries but selling and buying land in countries where land belongs to the state is illegal (e.g. Rwanda).

Our study will analyze the impact of land tenure on land degradation and improvement. The study will especially look at the influence of land tenure security on change of cropland and LUCC-related cost of land degradation.

Government Effectiveness and Governance

As noted by Nkonya and Anderson (2015), government effectiveness—defined as the quality of public & civil services and their degree of independence from political pressures, the quality of policy formulation and implementation, and the credibility of the government's commitment to such policies—has a positive impact on SLM. Government effectiveness index (GEI) scale ranges from −2.5 (weak) to 2.5 (strong). Using the average GEI in 2005–07, we divided countries in three groups, weak government effectiveness, whose GEI was lower than −1.0; medium (−1.0 < GEI < 0.0), and Strong (GEI ≥ 0). SSA has the lowest government effectiveness in the world as a third of the 48 SSA countries reporting have a GEI index below −1—the world's largest share in this group (Table 9.3).

There has been significant improvement in democracies in some SSA countries and setbacks in democratization in other countries (Lynch and Crawford 2011). About 35 % of the SSA countries experienced improvement in government effectiveness in the 2007–12 period compared to the 1997–2000 period (Table 9.4). Nine of the 16 countries that experienced GEI improvement fall in the medium GEI category and two in the best GEI (Mauritius and Réunion). The remaining five fall in the worst case group (GEI smaller than −1). This suggests the difficulty in government effectiveness improvement for countries with weak GEI. Accordingly, most of the countries which experienced weakening of government effectiveness are grouped in the worst case group, i.e., a GEI smaller than average GEI.

Table 9.3 Government effectiveness index of all regions, across groups

	Weak		Medium		Strong	
	Percent[a]	$\overline{GEI}$[b]	Percent[a]	$\overline{GEI}$[b]	Percent[a]	$\overline{GEI}$[b]
SSA	31.3	−1.4	47.8	−0.5	20.9	0.5
LAC	4.9	−1.3	39.0	−0.4	56.1	0.7
NAM	0.0	–	0.0	–	100.0	1.5
East Asia	22.2	−2.0	11.1	−0.6	66.7	1.1
Oceania	6.3	−1.5	68.8	−0.7	25.0	1.0
South Asia	0.0		87.5	−0.4	12.5	0.5
SE Asia	20.0	−1.4	30.0	−0.7	50.0	0.9
East Europe	4.2	−1.1	41.7	−0.3	54.2	0.8
West Europe	0.0	–	0.0	–	100.0	1.5
Central Asia	16.7	−1.5	83.3	−0.7	0.0	–
NENA	17.4	−1.2	34.8	−0.4	47.8	0.7
World	14.8	−1.4	40.6	−0.5	44.5	0.9

Notes [a]Percent of countries in the region belonging to corresponding group
[b]$\overline{GEI}$ = Average GEI in corresponding group. GEI Scale: −2.5 weak to 2.5 Strong
Source Compiled from Kaufmann et al. (2012)

Table 9.4 SSA government effectiveness index, 1997–2012

Group	Percent of SSA countries (%)	Countries
Countries which GEI improved: Average GEI1997–2000 < GEI2007–12	35	Angola, Burkina Faso, Burundi, DRC, Congo, Djibouti, Ethiopia, Ghana, Guinea-Bissau, Liberia, Mauritius, Niger, Réunion, Rwanda, Sierra Leone, Swaziland and Zambia
Worst (GEI ≤ −1)	40	Burundi, Central African Republic, Chad, Comoros, DRC, Congo, Côte D'Ivoire, Equatorial Guinea, Eritrea, Guinea, Guinea-Bissau, Liberia, Nigeria, Sierra Leone, Somalia, South Sudan, Sudan, Togo, and Zimbabwe
Medium: −1 < GEI < 0	45	Angola, Benin, Burkina Faso, Cameroon, Djibouti, Ethiopia, Gabon, Gambia, Ghana, Kenya, Lesotho, Madagascar, Malawi, Mauritania, Mozambique, Niger, Rwanda, Senegal, Swaziland, Tanzania, Uganda and Zambia
Best: GEI ≥ 0	15	Botswana, Cape Verde, Mauritius, Namibia, Réunion, Seychelles and South Africa

Note GEI ranking as worst, medium and best based on average GEI from 2007–2012
Source Compiled from Kaufmann et al. (2012)

Access to Market Infrastructure

SSA has the second lowest LPI—a measure of market services and infrastructure performance (Table 9.5). Though there has been improvement over the past decade, the region faces a daunting challenge in improving its market infrastructure and logistics.

Studies have shown that access to market infrastructure could lead to land improvement or degradation, depending on other mediating factors (Nelson and Hellerstein 1997; Cropper et al. 2001; Laurance et al. 2009). Access to markets could either lead to an increase in land degradation through forest clearing to increase cropland extent (e.g. see Fearnside 2002; Peres 2001) or could lead to agricultural intensification and engagement in non-farm activities, which in turn could lead to a decrease of cropland extent and thus land improvement (e.g. see Haggblade et al. 2007). SSA has the worst access to markets and consequently the highest transaction costs and water and energy tariffs in the world (Table 9.6). Such high transaction costs have led to the limited use of external inputs, which in turn have contributed to SSA's fastest cropland expansion in world.

Though some studies are showing a negative impact of market access to land management, improvement of market infrastructure is necessary to achieve development objectives. However, government effectiveness needs to be improved to mediate the potential negative impact of access to market on land management.

Table 9.5 Logistics performance index

Region	Logistics performance index (LPI)		
	2011–13	2007–10	Change
SSA	2.62	2.69	0.07
LAC	2.77	2.87	0.10
NAM	3.86	3.91	0.06
East Asia	3.38	3.50	0.12
Oceania	3.73	3.68	−0.05
South Asia	2.79	2.93	0.14
SE Asia	2.91	3.02	0.11
East Europe	2.79	2.95	0.16
West Europe	3.81	3.83	0.03
Central Asia	2.42	2.43	0.01
NENA	2.82	2.92	0.10
World	3.13	3.22	0.08

Notes LPI ranges from 1 (low) to 5 (high)
Calculated from World Bank database available at http://lpi.worldbank.org/

Table 9.6 Africa's infrastructure deficit and cost

Characteristics	Africa	Other developing countries
Paved road density (km/km^2 of arable land)[a]	0.34	1.34
Population with access to electricity (%)[a]	14	41
Population with access to improved potable water (%)[a]	61	72
Power tariffs ($/kWh)	0.02–0.46	0.05–0.1
Transportation cost ($/ton/km)	0.04–0.14	0.01–0.04
Tariffs of urban potable water ($/cu m)	0.86–6.56	0.03–0.6

[a]Excludes medium income African countries (South Africa, Kenya, Botswana, Gabon, Namibia, Cape Verde, etc.) and is compared to other low income countries. The rest of the statistics refers to entire Africa and other developing countries
Source Foster and Briceno-Garmendia (2010)

Population

One of the Millennium Development Goals was to provide universal access to reproductive health by 2015. Women with no access to family planning in SSA is 25 %—about twice the level in other regions (Ibid). Given this and other confounding factors, it is not surprising that the SSA region has the fastest growing population—both in terms of number and urbanization. SSA's population growth rate in 2010–15 was 2.7 %—the fastest in the world (UNFPA 2014). About 37 % of the SSA 924.7 million people live in urban areas but by 2050, the urban population will be 55 % of the total population (UN 2014). This trend and pattern poses a concern on land and other natural resources. However, concerns of the pressure the high population puts on natural resources are not emphasized in policy design, rather, in almost all SSA countries, family planning policies to reduce high fertility are formulated and implemented with the emphasis of health and education improvement (Ezeh et al. 2012). However, there has been considerable debate on the impact of human population on land degradation. In the famous publication on population bomb, Ehrlich (1968) predicts that overpopulation and consequent over-exploitation of natural resources will result in human starvation. Ehrlich's conclusions have been heavily criticized and—just as the Malthusian doomsday theory prediction was proven wrong—Ehrlich's prediction of mass starvation in the 1970s–80s didn't happen. The Green Revolution and other improved agricultural technologies have proved wrong Malthusian's and Ehrlich's population doomsday theories (Galor and Weil 2000). Additionally, international trade has also altered the local impacts of population on local biomes and settlement patterns in arable lands (Rudel et al. 2009a; Foley et al. 2011). For example in 2001, Switzerland imported agricultural products equivalent to 150 % of cultivated land area in the country (Wuertenberger et al. 2006).

Recent analyses of overexploitation of resources have focused less on human population and more on natural resource use that lead to depletion and degradation. Concerns on greenhouse gas (GHG) emissions, use of chemicals and other pollutants are simultaneously increasing with the demand for natural resources resulting from increasing income and changing consumption and lifestyles. For example the increasing demand for livestock products in low and medium income countries is due to increasing income (Thornton 2010) and it leads to greater demand for land area and consequently deforestation and loss of biodiversity (Smith et al. 2010).

Accordingly the new measures of land degradation encompass much broader indicators of anthropogenic impacts on ecosystems than focus on population. One such measure is the recent concept of planetary boundaries that needs to be observed to prevent irreversible ecological changes (Rockstrom et al. 2009)—reflects anthropogenic impacts on ecosystems that could result from GHG emission, pollution and depletion of natural resources resulting from changing consumption patterns, demand, and natural resource harvesting and utilization. Another interesting measure of land degradation is the human appropriation of net primary production (HANPP)—which is the aggregate impact of land use on biomass available in a given area (Haberl et al. 2004). HANPP measures the alterations of photosynthetic production in ecosystems and the harvest of products that use photosynthesis. For example SSA harvested only 18 % of its net primary production compared to the global average of 22 and 63 % for Southern Asia (Ibid). This puts SSA in a category of low pressure on natural resource harvesting even though studies focusing on population growth puts the region at much more dire conditions.

The SLM review above shows significant policy commitment to achieve SLM and to improve government effectiveness and market infrastructure. To assess the SSA governments' commitment to its SLM policies, the section below discusses SLM financing.

SLM Financing

On average, public expenditure on land-based sectors (agriculture, forestry, and wildlife) and fisheries in SSA countries is only about 4 % of the total government budget even though these sectors account for about 25 % of the GDP (Table 9.7). Dividing the 28 countries reporting the public expenditure into three equal groups (high, medium, and low share of public expenditure on land-based sectors and fisheries—hereafter referred to as agricultural sectors)—shows that countries where the agricultural sector contributed the largest share of GDP, allocated the lowest share of public expenditure to agriculture (Table 9.7). Only six countries—namely Burkina Faso, Guinea, Mali, Niger, Senegal, and Ethiopia have reached the Maputo Declaration target of spending 10 % or more of the government budget on agriculture (Benin et al. 2010), which was reaffirmed and upheld by the recent Malabo Declaration (AU 2014). In fact, the agricultural orientation index—government expenditure on agriculture as share of total budget divided by the agricultural share

Table 9.7 Public expenditure on land-based sectors and fisheries and their contribution to GDP

Country	Public expenditure as percent to total government budget			Contribution to GDP (%)
	2001–05	2006–2012	2001–12	
Zimbabwe		38.4	38.4	17.8
Ethiopia	7.4	18.7	12.4	45.9
Zambia	3.9	8.6	7.7	21.6
Madagascar	7.4	6.4	7	28.1
Swaziland	4.4	6.2	5.4	8.6
Mali		5.4	5.4	37.4
Namibia	5.1	5.2	5.1	9.6
Sao Tome and Principe		4.3	4.3	19.7
Cabo Verde	4.9	4	4.1	
Average, high % of ag expenditure	5.5	10.8	10.0	23.6
Kenya	4.5	3.8	4.1	27.7
Mauritius	4	3.8	3.9	5
Uganda	3.6	3.7	3.6	25
Congo, Republic of	1.2	3.6	2	4.7
Botswana	3.9	3.3	3.6	2.7
Lesotho		3	3	9.2
Tanzania	3.6	3	3.2	30.4
Liberia	1.3	2.6	2.4	62.2
Angola	1.4	2.5	2	8.9
Average, medium % of ag expenditure	2.9	3.3	3.1	19.5
Seychelles		2.4	2.4	2.7
Central African Republic		2	2	54.8
Ghana	1.6	1.8	1.8	33.4
Nigeria	1.1	1.7	1.4	35.1
Cote d'Ivoire		1.5	1.5	24.2
South Africa	1.1	1.5	1.3	3
Benin	3.1	1.4	2.5	32.6
Sierra Leone	1.6	1.4	1.5	53.4
Burkina Faso	0.1	1.1	0.8	36.4
Equatorial Guinea		1.1	1.1	5.2
Average, low % of ag expenditure	1.4	1.6	1.6	28.1
SSA	3.3	5.1	4.8	23.9

Sources Public expenditure as percent of government (FAOSTAT—http://faostat3.fao.org/download/I/IG/E). Contribution of land-based sectors and fisheries to GDP (World Bank http://data.worldbank.org/indicator/NV.AGR.TOTL.ZS)

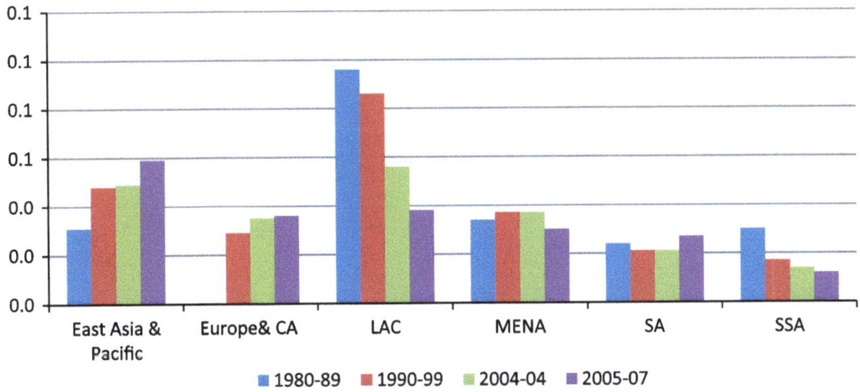

Fig. 9.2 Agricultural orientation index across regions. *Source* Computed from FAO (2012)

of GDP (FAO 2012)—for SSA is the lowest in the world and was falling between the 1980s and 2007 (Fig. 9.2).

As noted above however, the agricultural sector accounted for 40 % of the poorest populations' economic growth—a level about three times larger than the growth originating from other sectors (De Janvry and Sadoulet 2010). This is largely due to private investment resulting from improved land management (Sheahan and Barrett 2014). For example, SSA farmers accounted for 86 % of the total agricultural investment[4] from 2005–07 (Lowder et al. 2012).[5]

Donor contribution to SLM expenditure is large. Many SLM initiatives in the past have tended to be heavily based on donor funded projects. For example, the ODA accounts for the largest share of forest investment in most SSA countries (Gondo 2010). Additionally, Table 9.8 shows that donor-funding accounted for more than 70 % of SLM expenditure in several countries. In fact it is common in many SSA countries to use revenue from forest concessions as a source for financing local and central governments (Ibid). In few countries however—including Nigeria, Ghana, and Kenya—donor funding contributes only a small share of total expenditure.

The large share of donor contribution to SLM expenditure poses a concern about the sustainability of investment in SLM practices and questions the countries' commitment to sustainable development stated in their policies. ODA total support to agriculture, water, and the environment both decreased following the Paris Declaration in 2005, but increased beginning in 2007 (Fig. 9.3). This was largely due to the renewed interest of high income countries and transnational companies to invest in agriculture following the food price spike and increasing demand for bioenergy (HLPE 2011). However, ODA support to agriculture as a share of total

[4]Investment is expenditure to build long-term capital (e.g. agricultural machinery, livestock, tree planting, road construction, etc.). It excludes current expenditure—or short-term expenditure normally consumed in the same year.

[5]The investment in agricultural R&D is excluded because sources of funding were not reported.

Table 9.8 Donor contribution to public expenditure on SLM

Countries	Donor contribution to SLM expenditure (%)	Comments	Source
Nigeria	5		Nkonya et al. (2010)
Mali	70		Nkonya et al. (2010)
Uganda	83	2001–05 period	World Bank (2008)
Ethiopia			
Kenya	45	Development expenditure of total budget	Yu (2014)
Seychelles, Sierra Leone, Namibia	<20	Agricultural budget	Benin and Yu (2012)
Senegal, Madagascar	>80	Agricultural budget	Benin and Yu (2012)

support to all sectors has not fully recovered to the level attained in the 1980s (Fig. 9.3).

Allocation of the public agricultural expenditure (PAE) budget across subsectors and functions also reveals some weaknesses that needs attention. Crops and livestock account for 77 % of the SSA PAE, while forestry and fisheries respectively account for 14 and 9 % (Benin and Yu 2012). Crops take the largest share for the budget allocated to crops and livestock even though about 170 million people in SSA are entirely or partially dependent on production (FAO 2006) and livestock occupies a much larger land area than crops. Kamuanga et al. (2008) also estimates that livestock accounts for more than 50 % of capital held by rural households.[6] Additionally, the demand for livestock products is increasing. Despite the livestock's large potential and opportunities, it receives less than 5 % of the government budget (Fig. 9.4).

Analysis of PAE by function also shows limited investment in developing agricultural marketing. For example, total expenditure on marketing, feeder roads, and regulation as percent of total PAE was highest in Mali at only 32 %—the highest in the countries reporting these data (Fig. 9.5). This clearly shows the production orientation of PAE and apparent neglect of market development, which is key to increasing farmer incentives for land investment (Barrett et al. 2010; Barrett 2008). Schmidhuber et al. (2011) estimate that to achieve food security by 2025, 37 % of the additional US$50.2 billion investment required will be for developing rural infrastructure and market access.

[6]For details of role played by livestock, see Chap. 8.

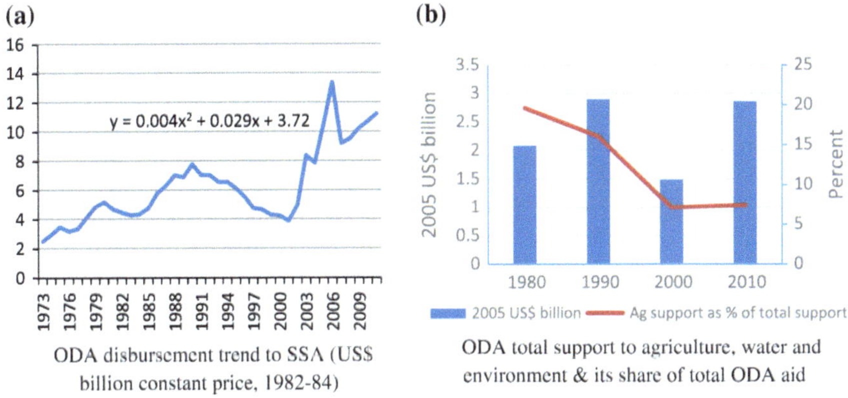

Fig. 9.3 ODA total support trend and allocation to agriculture, water and environment. **a** ODA disbursement trend to SSA (US$ billion constant price, 1982–84). **b** ODA total support to agriculture, water and environment and its share of total ODA aid. *Source* Computed from DAC. http://www.oecd.org/dac/developmentassistancecommitteedac.htm

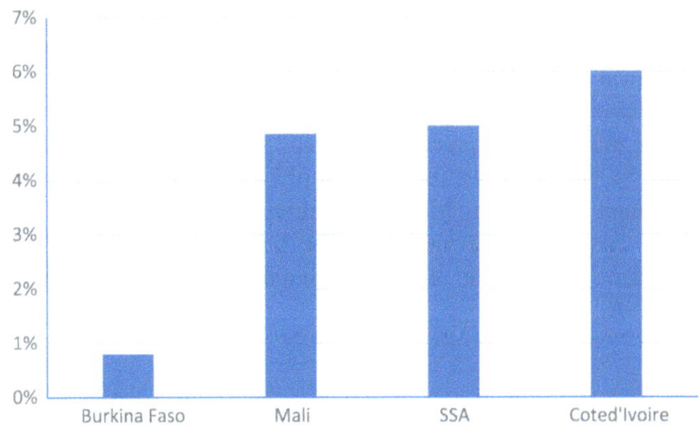

Fig. 9.4 Agricultural budget allocation to livestock as share of total government budget. *Note* Calculated from Kamuanga et al. (2008)

Given the large amount of donor contribution to land-based development, our analysis will examine the impact of donor support on cropland expansion and the cost of land degradation.

Analytical Methods and Data

We analyze the cost of land degradation and drivers of cropland change following the methods discussed in Chaps. 2 (methods) and 6 (cost of land degradation). As discussed in Chap. 6, causes of land degradation are LUCC that replaces high value

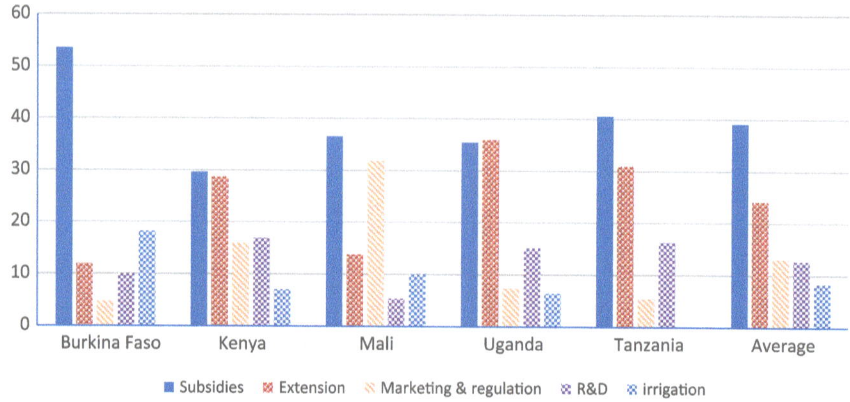

Fig. 9.5 Allocation of agricultural public expenditure by function. *Source* Computed from Benin and Yu (2012)

biomes with low value biomes and use of land degrading management practices on static land use. We cover all biomes when analyzing land degradation due to LUCC and for brevity, we only include cropland and grazing biomes (grassland) for static biomes. Analytical methods that were used without any modification are the same as those for determining the cost of land degradation due to LUCC (Chap. 6) using land degrading management practices on static cropland (Chap. 6) and grazing biomes (Chap. 8). Hereafter, we refer to cost of LUCC-related land degradation as simply cost of land degradation. Methods for drivers of the cost of land degradation and change of cropland were modified. The brief discussion below shows the modifications done to adapt the analysis to biophysical and socio-economic characteristics of SSA.

Drivers of Cropland Change and Cost of Land Degradation

We modify the analytical methods discussed in Chap. 2 by including international aid, which—as seen above contributes the largest source of SLM investment in most countries. We use the following parametric multivariate regression approach to identify the effects of each of the of cropland change and cost of land degradation.

$$\Delta a = \beta_0 \Delta x_1 + \beta_1 \Delta x_1^2 + \beta_2 \Delta x_2 + \beta_3 \Delta x_3 + \beta_4 D + e_i \quad (9.1)$$

where a = cropland area in pixel i, x_1 = vector of variables with quadratic relationship with Δa, which reflect the environmental Kuznet curve (Dinda et al. 2004a, b). These include GDP, which represents economic development and population density, which reflect the Boserupian intensification theory (Boserup 1965); x_2 = a vector of variables with linear relationship with cropland area, namely agricultural export index, access to markets, and government effectiveness and international aid; D a vector of dummy variables representing land tenure; βi = coefficients associated with the corresponding covariate i.

We correct for heteroskedasticity by estimating robust standard errors using White-Huber estimators. To ensure that quadratic terms are validly included in the model and that they are not highly correlated with the error term, we conducted the Wald tests and found that they were valid. However, the quadratic terms lead to serious multicollinearity bias. Given that the quadratic forms are valid and consistent with theory, dropping them to avoid multicollinearity could lead to more biased and inconsistent estimates of parameters than the bias due to multicollinearity (Berry and Feldman 1985). However, to check for robustness of our results, we include the linear model, whose variance inflation factor of all covariates was less than 10 and therefore did not have serious multicollinearity bias (Mukherjee et al. 1998). The discussion however will focus on the model with quadratic terms for reasons discussed above.

Household level characteristics—such as change in livelihoods, level of education, access to credit, etc.—also affect change in cropland extent. However, due to lack of household level panel data for the entire region, our empirical model does not include them. This is a weakness that needs to be taken into account when interpreting our results. Additionally, the country-level case studies used household level data to analyze the drivers of land degradation (Chaps. 11–21).

The same model and data are used to analyze the drivers of the cost of land degradation. So the discussion above and the following discussion on data will refer to cropland only but the same discussion is relevant to the drivers of the cost of land degradation.

Data

LUCC We use MODIS data discussed in Chap. 6 for analyzing the cost of land degradation due to LUCC. Similarly we use the MODIS data to analyze the drivers of the change of cropland.

Road connectivity: We use travel time to the nearest urban area with a population of 50,000 or more. We used UNEP road data (Nelson 2007) and the Global Rural-Urban Mapping Project (GRUMP) population data from the Center for International Earth Science Information Network (CIESIN) to identify the urban areas with 50,000 or more population.[7] A 1 h delay is added for travel across international borders.

[7]http://sedac.ciesin.columbia.edu/plue/gpw.

Land tenure We use tenure security, which is threat or absence of likelihood of land expropriation by government or elites. USAID and ARD (2008) used country-level land policies and past history of land expropriation to give a country level tenure security. The land tenure security is divided into three major groups—(i) Moderately serious concern. This group includes countries where land users/owners have the least concern about expropriation. Examples of such countries include: Mali, Senegal, Tanzania, and Zambia. (ii) Serious concern, which is medium threat of expropriation, examples of which include DRC, Ethiopia, Kenya, and Nigeria. (iii) Extremely serious concern of expropriation. This is the group with the worst land tenure security and includes such countries as Zimbabwe and Sudan. Surprisingly even South Africa and Namibia are included in this group.

Government effectiveness We use the World Bank measure of government effectiveness index, which measures the quality of public services, civil service, and the degree of its independence from political pressures.

Poverty We use infant mortality rate (IMR) to represent poverty. The IMR is a good indicator of poverty and has been used in many poverty studies (e.g. see Dasgupta 2010). We use the IMR to represent the impact of poverty on cropland extent and cost of land degradation. IMR data are at half degree resolution and are obtained from CISIEN.

Table 9.9 summarizes the data used, their sources and baseline and endline periods. As far as possible, the baseline and endline periods of all the covariates were matched with the corresponding periods for cropland area and cost of land degradation. For some variables, data for the baseline period (2001) were not available. Hence, an alternative period which is as close as possible to the 2001 periods was used. These include GEI and population density at half degree resolution.

Extent of Land Degradation in SSA

According to Le et al. (2014) who used Normalized Difference Vegetation Index (NDVI) to determine land degradation in 1982–2006, SSA accounts for 17 % of the global 3.623 billion ha that experienced land degradation in the same period. The Eastern, Central, and Southern African sub-regions experienced the most widespread degradation (Fig. 9.6). However, Western Africa—especially southern Ghana and northern Nigeria—also experienced severe deforestation (Fig. 9.7). At the same time, there was significant land improvement through conversion of low value biomes to forest along the Sahelian zone—an aspect consistent with the regreening of the Sahel (Anyamba et al. 2014). Cropland expansion also occurred throughout the SSA region but was more intense in Western Africa and central Africa (Fig. 9.7). Conversion to grassland also occurred in all sub-regions but was more significant in drier areas (Fig. 9.8). About 40 % of the grasslands experienced degradation—a level that is the highest among the major biomes (Fig. 9.9). The second most

Table 9.9 Summary of data sources, resolution and baseline and endline periods

Data type	Resolution	Baseline and endline periods	Source
Biophysical data: total annual precipitation (mm)	0.540 × 0.540	Baseline: 2001–03	Climate Research Unit (CRU), University of East Anglia www.cru.uea.ac.uk/cru/
		Endline: 2009–11	
Cropland expansion	1 km × 1 km	Baseline: 2001	MODIS data
		Endline: 2009	
Socio-economic data			
Total bilateral aid disbursement to all sectors	Country-level	Baseline: 1973–83	http://www.oecd.org/dac/stats/
		Endline: 1997–2007	
Cattle density	Subnational	Fixed: 2005	FAO http://www.fao.org/ag/aga/glipha/index.jsp. Data exclude land unsuitable for livestock
Road density	0.50 × 0.50	Fixed	Nelson (2007)
IMR (infant mortality rate)	0.50 × 0.50	Single period: 2005	CISIEN (2010) http://sedac.ciesin.columbia.edu/povmap/
Government effectivenessa	Country-level	Baseline: 1996–98	http://info.worldbank.org/governance/wgi/index.asp
		Endline: 2005–12	
Population density	0.50 × 0.50	Baseline: 1990	http://sedac.ciesin.columbia.edu/plue/gpw
		Endline: 2007	
GDP	Country-level	Baseline: 2001–3	IMF: www.imf.org/external/pubs/ft/weo/2010/02/
		Endline: 2009–11	
Agricultural R&D expenditure	Country-level	Baseline: 1973–83	ASTI: http://www.asti.cgiar.org
		Endline: 1997–2007	
Agricultural export quantity index	Country-level	Baseline: 2001–3b	FAOSTAT
		Endline: 2009–11	

Notes A Government effectiveness index (GEI) is based on 17 component sources, measures the quality of public services, the quality of the civil service and the degree of its independence from political pressures, the quality of policy formulation and implementation, and the credibility of the government's commitment to such policies. The index values range from −2.5 (very poor performance) to +2.5 (excellent performance) (Kaufmann et al. 2010)
Source See last column of table
The section below discusses land degradation and improvement in SSA by first examining the land use/cover change (LUCC) and particularly cropland change and their association with land degradation

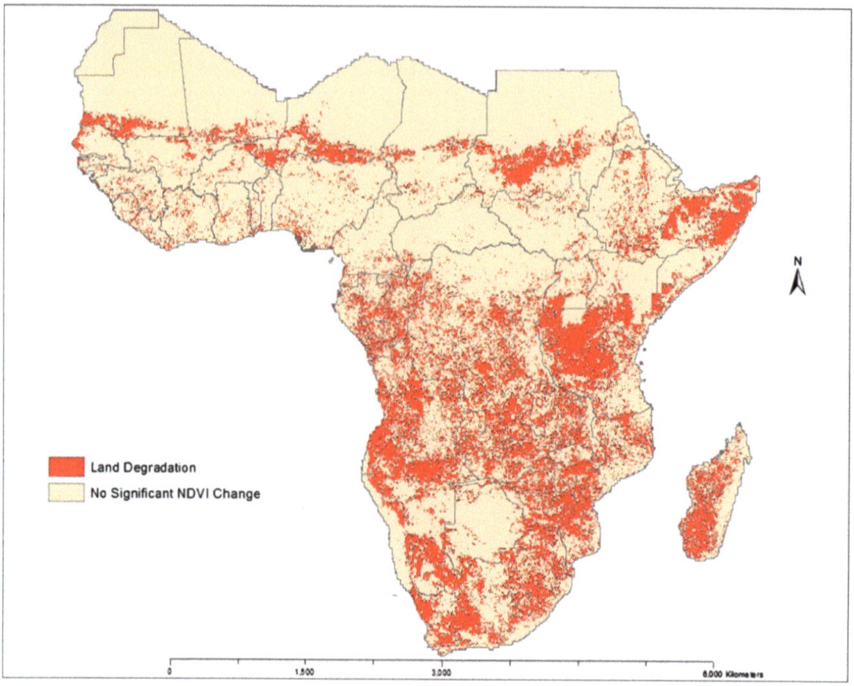

Fig. 9.6 Extent of land degradation in SSA. Note: *Red color* indicates degradation after correction for rainfall variability and carbon fertilization. *Gray color* indicates areas that did not experience degradation after correction for rainfall variability and carbon fertilization. *Source* Le et al. (2014)

degraded area is forest as 26 % of its area from 1982 to 2006 experienced degradation as measured by NDVI (Fig. 9.9).[8]

We overlaid the degraded areas with the major drivers of land degradation, namely, change in population density, government effectiveness, access to markets, and IMR. A significant area in Western Africa with high market access experienced land improvement (Fig. 9.10). This is the area along the Guinea Savanna agroecological zone, where there is active crop and livestock production. The areas of high market access that experienced land degradation are in Eastern and Southern Africa as well as the Sahelian belt in Western Africa.

As shown in Fig. 9.11, a large area experienced land degradation even though population change was only moderate. Conversely and as expected, a large area experienced both land degradation and increase in population. The interesting

[8]It should be noted that NDVI is derived from Advanced Very High Resolution Radiometer (AVHRR) to determine land degradation and the time period is from 1982 to 2006. Figures 9.7 and 9.8 use Moderate Resolution Imaging Spectroradiometer (MODIS) land cover data from 2001 to 2009 to approximate land-cover changes 2001–09 occurring. The differences in data source and time could lead to inconsistent results.

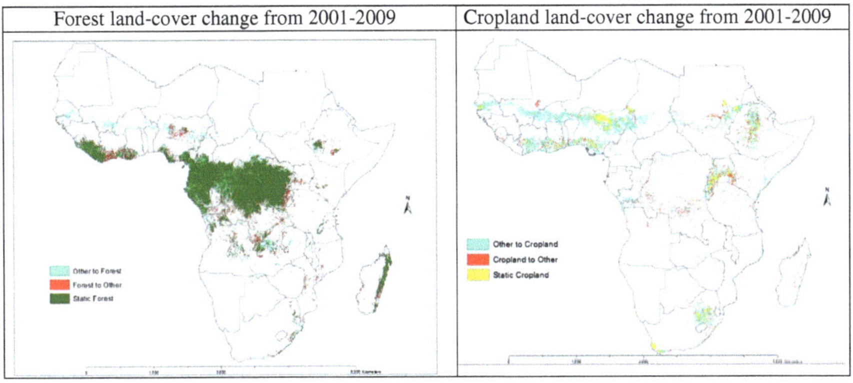

Fig. 9.7 LUCC on forest and cropland biomes. *Sources* Derived from MODIS land cover data

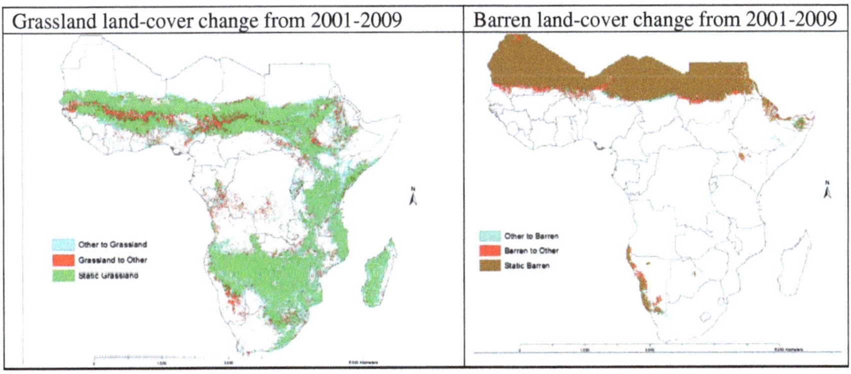

Fig. 9.8 LUCC on grasslands and barren land biomes

results are in Western Africa where there was high population increase but land improvement. As discussed below, improvement of government effectiveness in the area could be the major driver of this favorable pattern.

All possible combinations of weak and strong government effectiveness and land degradation and improvement are observed in Fig. 9.12. Of interest is Western Africa and parts of Southern Sudan, Chad, and Cameroon, where there was improvement in government effectiveness and land—supporting Foster and Rosenzweig (2003) and Esty and Porter (2005) observation of the role played by governance on mediating drivers of land degradation. As expected, a large area experienced land degradation in countries where government effectiveness worsened.

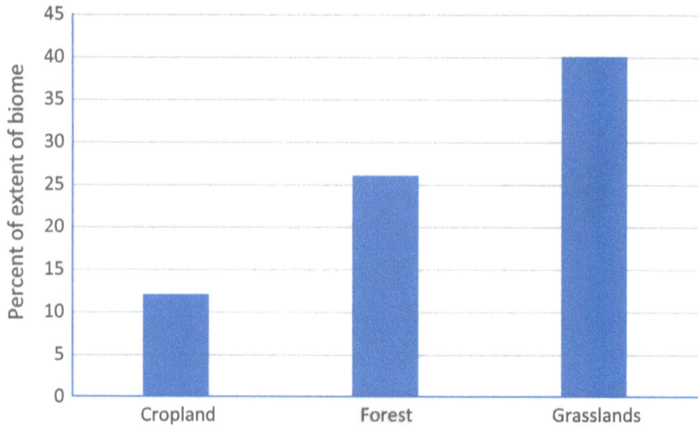

Fig. 9.9 Extent of land degradation for the major biome, 1982–2006. *Source* Computed from Le et al. (2014)

The Western Africa region and Southern Chad again shows a pattern of land improvement combined with high poverty (Fig. 9.13)—an aspect which contradicts the poverty-land degradation spiral (Scherr 2000) and demonstrates that even poor farmers could sustainably use their land resources (Nkonya and Anderson 2015). Swinton et al. (2003) observe both poor and well-off farmers in Latin America degrade their lands and conclude that land policies that provide incentives for environmental stewardship—rather than wealth endowment—are key drivers of land management. Accordingly and consistent with the downward spiral (Scherr 2000), high poverty and degradation are observed in Eastern, Central Africa, Mozambique, and Madagascar—largely due to the weak governance and lack of policies that provide incentives for land improvement.

Cost of Land Degradation Due to LUCC

The annual cost of land degradation is 2007 US$58 billion, which is about 7 % of the region's 2007 GDP of US$879.15 billion (Table 9.10). But if only provisioning services are considered, the annual cost of land degradation is US$29.19 billion or 3.3 % of GDP. As observed in Chap. 6, SSA accounts for 26 % of the global total annual cost of land degradation, though the region's land area and population respectively account for only 18 and 13 % of the global land area and population.[9]

[9]Global and SSA land area is respectively 14.08 and 2.6 billion ha (FAOSTAT). SSA and global population in 2014 was respectively 911 and 7244 million people UNFPA (2014).

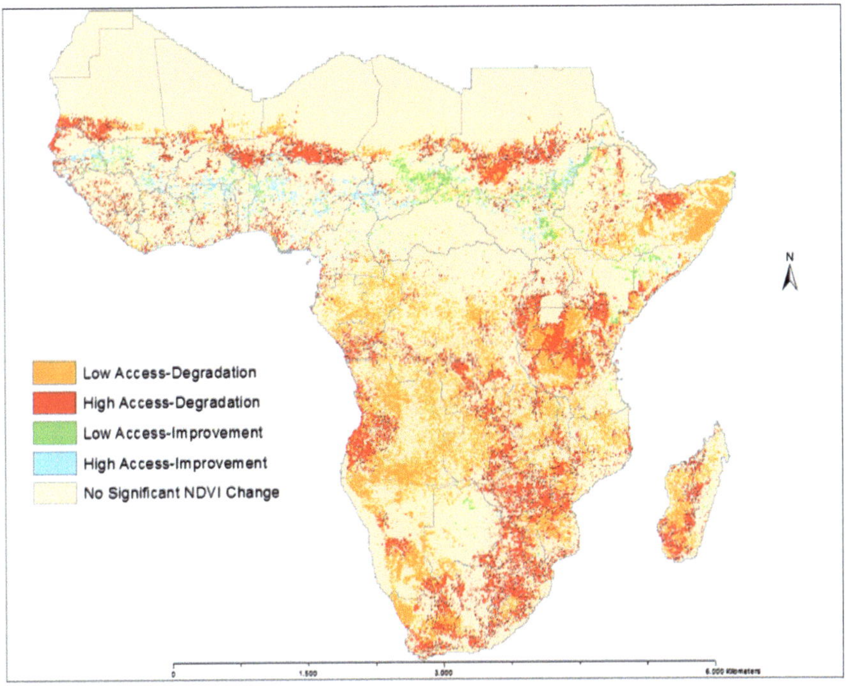

Fig. 9.10 Land degradation and access to market. *Note*

Market access	Minutes to city with population of at least 50,000 people	(%)
High	≤60	12.4
Medium	>60–100	35.6
Low	>100	52.0

The cost of land degradation is highest in Western Africa but commensurate with its area and population. Western Africa accounted for 32 % of the total cost of land degradation and as a sub-region accounts for about a third of SSA's population and land area (Table 9.10). The sub-region that has an unproportionally higher degradation than the corresponding share of its population is Central Africa, whose cost of land degradation is about 20 % of the total cost but its population accounts for only 10 % of SSA's population.

The marginal rate of returns (MRR) for taking action against land degradation is about 4—i.e., land users would receive US$4 for every US$ they invest to address land degradation. Such high returns justifies programs to address land degradation but raises serious questions about the current inaction against land degradation.

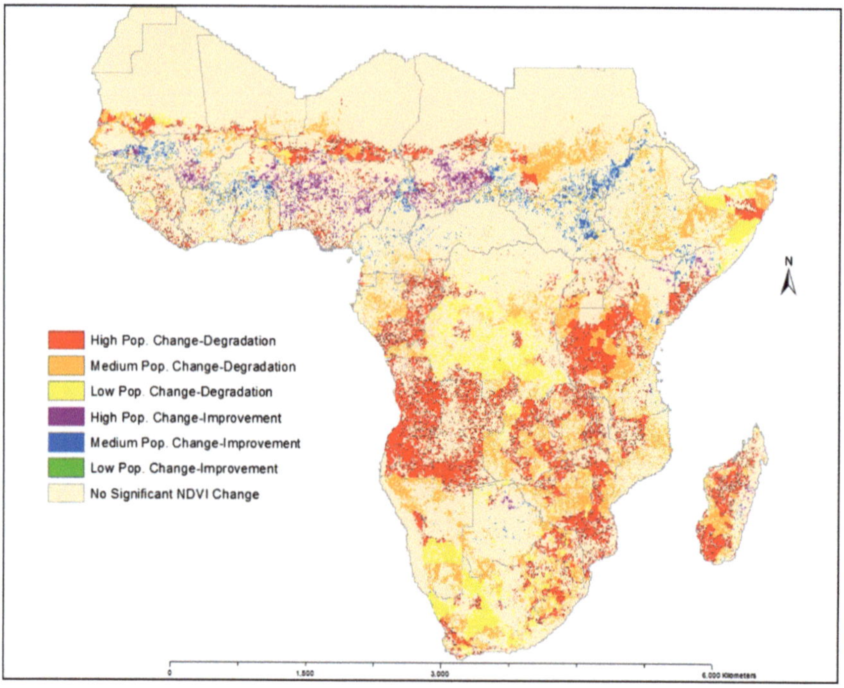

Fig. 9.11 Human population and land degradation

Land Degradation on Static Land—Grazing Biomass

The Eastern Africa sub-region accounts for about 40 % of the livestock population in SSA and it experienced the most severe grazing biomass degradation as 65 % of livestock were grazing on degraded grasslands (Table 9.11). The arid agroecological zone also accounts for the largest livestock population and 65 % of its grazing area experienced degradation.

The cost of land degradation on grazing biomass is about US$1.11 billion (Table 9.12), an amount that is equivalent to about 4 % of the SSA agricultural expenditure of US$20.729 billion in 2010 (Benin and Yu 2012). The Central African region and Eastern sub-regions accounted for more than 60 % of the total cost of land degradation. This is due to the widespread grassland degradation in DRC and Central African Republic (Fig. 9.8).

The high cost of land degradation in the arid areas is a concern given that the majority of the resident people are among the poorest in most of SSA countries (Thornton et al. 2002). Livestock also accounts for the largest wealth endowment and provides security against biophysical and socio-economic shocks. This underscores the need to take action to address land degradation in the grasslands as

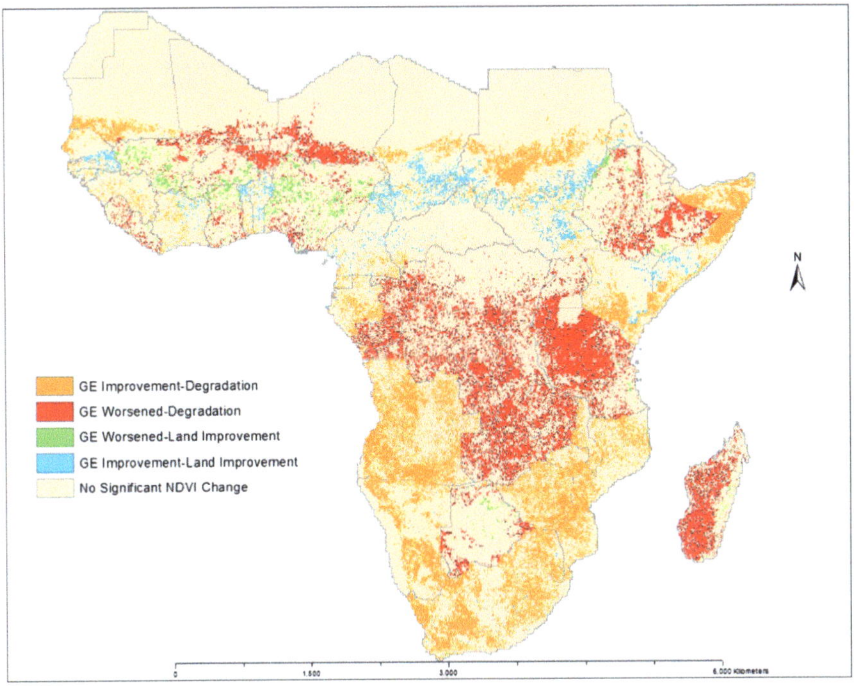

Fig. 9.12 Change in government effectiveness and land degradation

this will have multiplier effects on poverty reduction, food security efforts, and adaptation to climate change (Table 9.13).

On-farm cost of land degradation due to using land degrading management practices on cropland. Based on nationally representative data drawn from agricultural household surveys in six SSA countries only 6 % of households used integrated soil fertility management (ISFM) in SSA. Analysis of profitability of ISFM and selected land degrading management practices show an inverse relationship between adoption and profitability (Fig. 9.14). Given that smallholder farmers respond to price and other market signals (Eriksson 1993; Barrett 2008), the inverse relationship implies that there are constraints which inhibit adoption of profitable land management practices.

Country-level household data from Ethiopia, Kenya, Niger, Senegal, Tanzania, and Malawi (Chaps. 14, 16, 17, 19, and 20) identify such constraints and discuss the factors that affect adoption of ISFM. The discussion below focuses on the cost of land degradation in SSA caused by using land degrading management practices on cropland. As explained in Chap. 6, we focus on maize, rice, and wheat crops which cover only about 19 % of the cropland area in SSA (Table 9.14). Maize is the major staple crop in SSA and it covers about 14 % of the cropland. Its area coverage

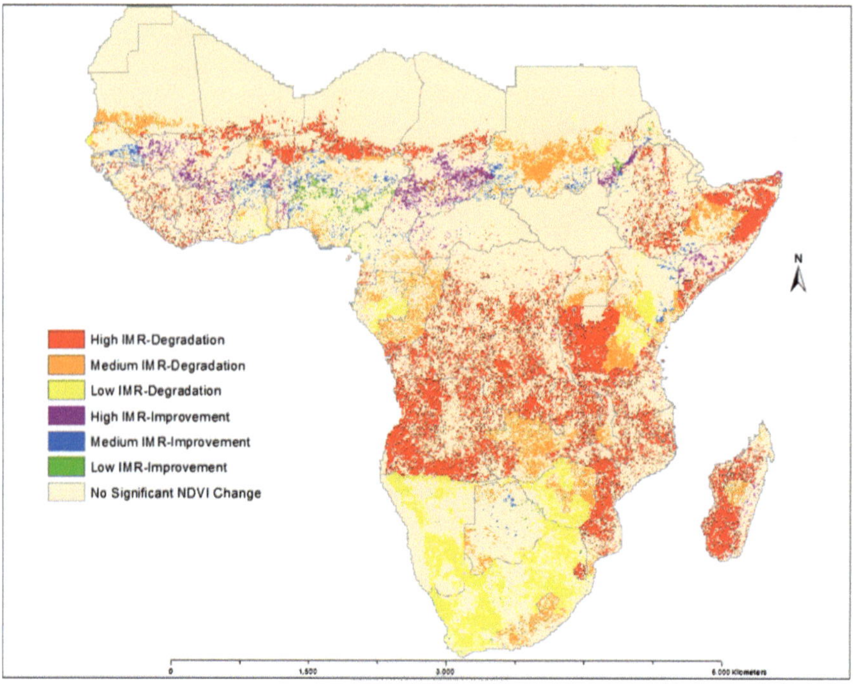

Fig. 9.13 Poverty and land degradation

Table 9.10 Cost of LUCC-related land degradation in SSA

Subregion	Central	Eastern	Indian	Southern	Western	SSA
% of land area	30.5	28.5	2.4	12.5	28.5	
% of population	9.8	33.6	2.5	20.8	33.2	
Cost of land degradation, action and inaction (2007 US$ billion)						
Total cost of land degradation (TEV)	11.09	13.43	1.6	13.38	18.9	58.4
Cost of loss of provisioning services	4.96	7.25	0.8	7.88	8.3	29.19
Cost of action	134.5	182.71	25.62	210.48	205.76	759.07
Opportunity cost	132.34	182.84	25.42	206.92	202.24	749.76
Cost of inaction	552.32	749.83	94.53	828.93	955.84	3181.45
Loss of provisioning services as % of total loss	44.67	54	50.28	58.89	43.91	49.98
MRR of taking action	4.11	4.1	3.69	3.94	4.65	4.19

Sources Population and land area (FAOSTAT). Rest of data (authors)

Table 9.11 Livestock population and percent in degraded grazing lands

Subregion	Hyperarid		Arid		Humid		Temperate		% of total TLU	% in DG
	Thousand in TLU	% in DG	Thousand in TLU	% in DG	Thousand in TLU	% in DG	Thousand in TLU	% in DG		
Central	0		269.8	67	3943.2	43	232.7	26	8.8	44
Eastern	18.1	14	17505.1	65	532.6	64	541.0	85	36.9	65
Indian	24.9	14	2509.3	61	417.7	40	31.6	57	5.9	58
Southern	1.4	97	12415.8	29	1071.4	62	2293.5	41	31.4	33
Western	0.1	62	7261.5	46	1265.9	61	0.1	0	16.9	48
SSA	44.5	16	39961.4	50	7230.9	50	3098.9	48	100.0	50
% of total	0.1	14	79.4	67	14.4	43	6.2	26		

Notes: *DG* livestock in degraded grazing area
Sources Computed from FAO http://www.fao.org/ag/aga/glipha/index.jsp

Table 9.12 On-farm cost of land degradation due to grazing biomass degradation

Sub-region	Milk	Meat	Total	Gross total[a]
	2007 US$ million			
Central Africa	370	14	384	423
East Africa	274	29	303	395
Indian Ocean	28	2	30	49
Southern Africa	161	44	206	289
West Africa	178	16	193	266
Total	1011	98	1110	1422

[a]Includes meat of livestock not sold or slaughtered for home consumption

is largest in Eastern and Southern Africa. Wheat production occupies the smallest area—less than 2 % of total area.

Table 9.15 shows that land degradation due to the most commonly used land management practices is about 2007 US$3.37 billion. Western Africa accounts for the largest cost largely due to the low adoption rate of ISFM. The cost of land degradation due to loss of carbon sequestration accounts for about 76 % of the total cost. This is due to the large soil carbon storage of ISFM (Vanlauwe et al. 2014). Continuous use of ISFM also contributes a large cost of land degradation and is consistent with Nandwa and Bekunda (1998), who used data from a long-term soil fertility experiment in Kenya and observed declining yield even for plots receiving ISFM at recommended rates. This means rotational cropping is necessary even for farmers using ISFM. The results also underscore the large potential of carbon sequestration on agricultural land and the need for finding incentives for using ISFM.

Table 9.13 Adoption and profitability of soil fertility management practices in SSA

Country	ISFM	Fertilizer	Organic inputs	Nothing
	Adoption (%)			
Mali	0	23	11	66
Uganda	0	1	68	31
Kenya	16	17	22	44
Nigeria	1	23	28	47
Malawi	8	52	3	38
Tanzania	1	1	3	95
Mali	18	16	37	27
	Average adoption rate and profit			
Adoption rate (%)	6.2	19.1	24.6	49.8
Profit (US$/ha/year)[a]	36.5	24.6	15.1	10.4

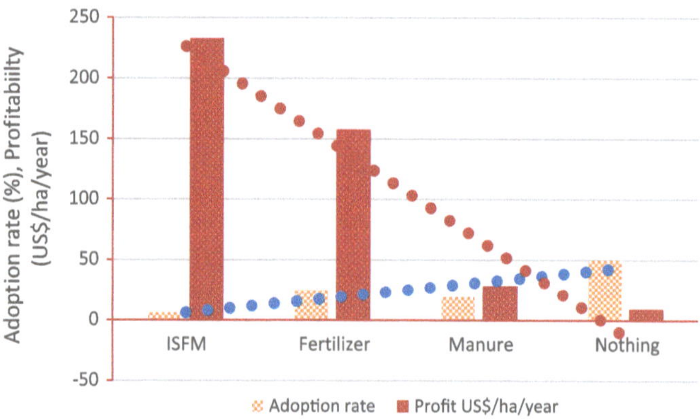

Fig. 9.14 Unholy cross: inverse relationship between adoption rate and profitability. *Sources* Adoption rate of land management practices: Mali (Direction nationale de la Statistique et de l'informatique (DNSI). Recensement general de l'agriculture, 2004/2005); *Uganda* Uganda national panel survey 2009/10 agriculture module; *Kenya* Kenya Agricultural Sector Household Baseline Survey; *Nigeria* Fadama III household survey, 2012; *Malawi* National panel survey, agriculture module, 2010/11. *Note* A returns to maize in Nigeria for the following land management practices: (i) ISFM: 5 tons/ha manure, 80 kgN/ha, 100 % crop residues, (ii) Fertilizer: 80 kgN/ha + 100 % crop residues, (iii) Manure: 5 tons/ha, 100 % crop residues, (iv) Nothing—no manure or fertilizer applied: 100 % crop residues

Econometric Results

Market access and rural population: Controlling for government effectiveness, rural population density, and other covariates, distance to urban areas increases cost of land degradation but reduces cropland expansion (Table 9.16). This suggests greater cropland expansion to meet demand for the urban population. The lower cost of land degradation could be due to stricter enforcement of deforestation in

Table 9.14 Maize, rice, and wheat harvested area and yield across SSA sub-regions

Maize	Eastern Africa	Central Africa	Southern Africa	Western Africa	SSA
Area as % of total cropland area	20.19	13.28	21.81	7.89	13.5
Yield (tons/ha)	1.48	0.97	3.14	1.57	
Rice					
Area as % of total cropland area	3.78	2.40	0.01	5.23	4.0
Yield (tons/ha)	2.23	0.93	2.63	1.76	
Wheat					
Area as % of total cropland area	2.62	0.05	5.29	0.06	1.3
Yield (tons/ha)	1.71	1.34	2.128	1.43	
Total area	26.6	15.7	27.1	13.2	18.8

Source FAOSTAT data

Table 9.15 Cost of land degradation due to using land degrading management practices on cropland

SSA sub-region	Cost of land degradation due to		Cost of loss of CO_2 sequestration due to using		Total cost
	BAU	Continuous ISFM	BAU	Continuous ISFM	
	2007 US$ billion				
Central	0.018	0.002	0.075	0.069	0.164
Eastern	0.127	0.01	0.464	0.053	0.654
Indian Ocean	0.004	0.00	0.021	0.051	0.076
Southern	0.188	0.023	0.741	0.14	1.092
Western	0.352	0.09	0.303	0.635	1.38
Total	0.689	0.126	1.604	0.947	3.367

Notes: *BAU* Business as usual land management practice, i.e., commonly used land management practice in the area. *ISFM* Integrated land management practice—assumed to be sustainable but its yield declines with continuous cultivation

areas closer to cities. For example Banana et al. (2004) found stricter deforestation laws for areas closer to urban areas in Uganda. Rural population density has a U-shaped relationship with cost of land degradation suggesting greater land degradation at high population densities beyond a threshold. Such pattern supports Rockstrom et al. (2009) ecological boundary beyond which an irreversible ecological damage could occur. Cropland expansion has an inverted U-shaped relationship with rural population— implying a potential establishment of non-farm activities or migration to urban area.

Table 9.16 Drivers of cost of land degradation and extent of cropland—robust OLS regression

	Land degradation cost (2007 million US$)		Change of cropland (ha)	
	Structural	Reduced	Structural	Reduced
Market access and population density				
Travel time (minutes) to city with 50 k people	0.01***	0.01***	−19.63***	−15.65***
Δ Rural population (million people)	−0.09***	−0.05***	65.97***	47.98***
(Δ rural population)2	1.49e−5***		−0.01*	
Economic development and international trade and aid				
Δ GDP (2005 million US$)	1.45***	2.20***	4568.98***	1216.77***
Δ GDP2 (2005 million US$)2	0.01***		−42.20***	
Adjusted IMR (of 1000 live births)	−0.49***	−0.38***	−1664.87***	−2181.42***
Δ Ag export index (2004–06 = 100)	0.57***	0.55***	−421.56***	−317.63***
Δ ODA aid (constant price 1982–84 million US$)	−39.78***	−31.81***	27575.18***	−8275.28***
Cattle density 2005	−0.14***	−0.15***	471.42***	471.47***
Governance and land tenure				
Δ Government effectiveness	−32.12***	−34.19***	−217654.10***	−210264.30***
Land Tenure security (cf Secure tenure)				
Moderate concern	212.71***	217.16***	111256.60***	91039.39***
Severe concern	156.51***	162.05***	206836.30***	183099.60***
Extremely severe concern	54.47***	65.97***	−177483.00***	−228307.00***
Precipitation (1982–86)	0.01***	0.01***	−71.21***	−68.44***
Constant	53.97***	37.79***	271117.90***	342259.30***

Note Standard errors are corrected for heteroskedasticity using Huber-White estimators
*, **, and *** respectively mean the corresponding coefficient is significant at $P = 0.10$, 0.05 and 0.01

Economic development, international trade and aid: Change in GDP and cropland is consistent with the environmental Kuznet curve—i.e., a simultaneous increase in cropland and GDP until a GDP threshold is reached, beyond which cropland expansion declines. Some countries have in fact seen decreasing cropland area (e.g. Botswana, Guinea, Senegal, Equatorial Guinea, Congo, and DRC)

(Nkonya et al. 2013). This is consistent with Orubu and Omotor (2011) who observed that African countries are turning the environmental Kuznet curve at a much faster pace and at a lower income level than countries in other regions. The cost of land degradation however has a positive relationship with GDP suggesting increasing degradation beyond the inflection point. This shows the potential for severe degradation even in high incomes that are observed in Chap. 6. Interestingly, severity of poverty, as represented by the infant mortality rate, is negatively related to cost of land degradation and cropland expansion. The results suggest that poor people have the capacity to sustainably manage their land if other mediating factors are taken into account.

Export leads to higher cost of land degradation but reduces cropland expansion. The impact of export on cost of land degradation is consistent with Rudel et al. (2009b) and Foley et al. (2011)—predominantly agricultural export volume. The negative impact of export on cropland expansion is contrary to Lambin and Meyfroidt (2011) and could be explained by the greater intensification of export crops compared to non-export crops (Kelly 2006; Crawford et al. 2003). For example, fertilizer application and use of improved varieties is greater for high-value and export crops than on other crops (Ibid). The contradictory results of higher cost of land degradation and reduced cropland expansion could be explained by the fact that cost of land degradation is a sum of all types of LUCC. It is possible that export crops are planted on a relatively smaller area but are replacing high value biome such as forests. For example, the recent large foreign agricultural investment in SSA with heavy orientation towards meeting food and energy needs of investing countries, rather than for domestic consumption (Anseeuw et al. 2012; World Bank 2011) has triggered cropland expansion into forested areas even when there is intensification (Schoneveld et al. 2011). The expansion into forested area could occupy a smaller but higher value area and could therefore imply reduced cropland expansion but lead to high value LUCC.

As expected, ODA funding reduces cost of land degradation—suggesting a favorable impact of international budget on environmental and agricultural ministries in SSA. Similarly, ODA funding has a negative impact on cropland expansion for the reduced model (Table 9.16). The results suggest that public investment can help efforts to address land degradation.

Cattle density has negative impact on cost of land degradation suggesting that areas with higher cattle density are less degraded than other areas. This supports other findings which have shown that pastoral areas are less degraded than cropland areas in SSA. This is consistent with Nkonya and Anderson (2015) who observed greater propensity to sustainably manage land with greater cattle density and with Bai et al. (2008), who observed greater land improvement in pastureland. The results suggest that there is great potential for rehabilitating the 339.80 million ha of degraded grazing areas (Chap. 8).

Government effectiveness and land tenure: As expected and consistent with Esty and Porter (2005), government effectiveness reduces cost of land degradation and cropland expansion. This further underlines the importance of land management institutions that play key roles in private and collective natural resource management in rural communities (Ostrom 1990). For example, government effectiveness is high in countries which have experienced a decrease in cropland (e.g. Botswana GEI = 0.7). This suggests governance could have also contributed to a decrease in cropland extent by limiting expansion into protected areas. For example, Mbaiwa et al. (2011) observed an effective protection of the Okavango delta using a community-based natural resource management approach.

Consistent with Place and Otsuka (2001), Gavian and Fafchamps (1996), tenure security reduces the cost of land degradation. Similarly, cropland expansion is greater in lands held with moderate to extremely severe security concern compared to lands held with secure tenure. These results imply that in countries with more secure land rights, the cropland expansion is slower. Recent foreign land acquisition in SSA is consistent with these results since such acquisitions have been concentrated in countries with weak tenure security (HLPE 2011). The results further underline the importance of land rights to farmers in SSA. However, land held with extremely severe security concern are less likely to experience cropland expansion than those held with secure tenure. This could be due to the tendency of farmers holding land with secure tenure to do cropland expansion in response to increasing demand for agricultural products.

Summary, Suggested Actions to Address Land Degradation, and Conclusion

LUCC accounts for about 93 % of the total annual cost of land degradation (US$ $62.9 billion) when the total economic value (TEV) of all terrestrial biomes are taken into account and for 94 % when only loss of provisioning services is considered (Fig. 9.15). This means action against land degradation needs to involve more aggressive efforts to address LUCC. What actions could be taken to address LUCC?

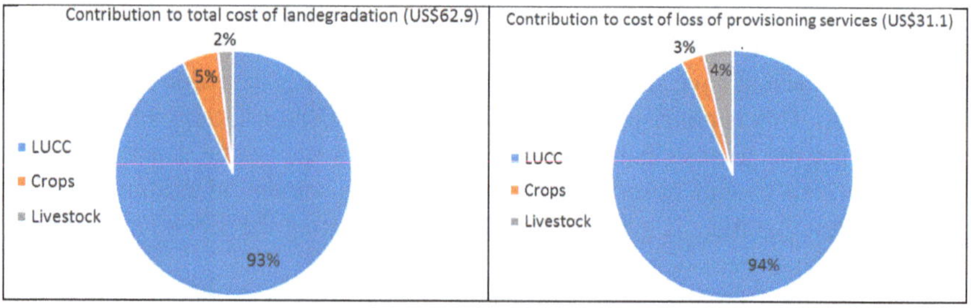

Fig. 9.15 Summary of the annual cost of land degradation

Protection of Grasslands and Forests and Increase Their Productivity

Conversion of grassland to cropland and deforestation are the major factors driving LUCC. One of the major reasons leading farmers to convert grassland to cropland is the low livestock productivity. The increasing demand for livestock products provides an ample opportunity to the value of grasslands and in turn livestock productivity. This will require an increase in the public budget allocation to livestock production, which is currently only about 5 %. Investments in livestock productivity need to be directed to both cost-effective and amenable pasture management practices and breeding programs. There are success stories of livestock systems in SSA which have shown high productivity due to such efforts. The Kenyan dairy programs and Botswana's beef production demonstrate some of the success stories that could be used in other SSA countries (Hazell 2007). The success story for both countries is due to long-term policies for livestock development, which have aimed at; genetic improvement, disease control, strengthening domestic and international markets to allow farmers to address highly seasonal supplies, and health and safety standards (Hazell 2007). Efforts to improve grassland through controlled grazing, planting legumes, and other amenable practices will increase both livestock productivity and carbon sequestration (Henderson et al. 2015).

Our econometric results also show the importance of tenure security and government effectiveness. Such institutional development will help efforts to enforce policies and programs that regulate LUCC. Access to markets will also contribute to reducing the cost of land degradation. Botswana for example has aggressively invested in livestock production and marketing strategies to put the country among the leading exporters of beef in SSA. In Botswana, export policies have been created to establish markets in Europe and other countries (Stevens and Kennan 2005). Sources of land degradation are the most widespread in SSA and this leads to a lower livestock productivity. The major LUCC of SSA involved is the conversion of grassland to other land use types. This is largely a result of the low livestock productivity. Deforestation and conversion of grassland to alternative land uses also means current SSA efforts to strengthen protected areas must increase.

Increase Government and Donor Funding to Support Land-Based Sectors

Econometric analysis showed that donor funding reduces the cost of land degradation. This underscores the role played by investment in land improvement played by donors. It also shows the favorable impact of investment in land improvement. Current public allocation to land based sectors is only about 5 %, a level that is only half of the Maputo declaration of spending 10 % of the government budget on agriculture. This needs to be increased to simultaneously reduce poverty (De Janvry and Sadoulet 2010) and improve natural resources.

Increase Access to Markets

Our econometric analysis also showed that access to market leads to a reduction of the cost of land degradation related to LUCC. This suggests that increasing access to markets could help to create alternative non-farm employment that could reduce pressure on land resources. SSA is currently investing only about 13 % of its agricultural budget on market infrastructure development. Schmidhuber and Bruinsma (2011) have recommended an annual investment of an additional US $50.2 billion of investment to achieve food security by 2025 and 37 % of such investment to be directed to market infrastructure development in developing countries. This is especially high in SSA with the worst market infrastructure in the world. Improvement of market infrastructure will achieve a win-win benefit as it will improve natural resources and reduce poverty. However, improvement of government effectiveness as discussed below is required to mediate the potential degradation that could result from improved market access.

Improve Government Effectiveness and Land Tenure Security

Our econometric analysis showed consistent favorable impact of improvement of government effectiveness on reduction of the cost of land degradation and cropland expansion. This further demonstrates the key role played by governance in mediating the drivers of land degradation (Nkonya and Anderson 2015).

Tenure security also has favorable impact on efforts to prevent land degradation. The recent land grabbing was concentrated on lands held under customary tenure and/or communal lands with no formal tenure (HLPE 2011). Additionally, the prices of land (and shadow prices) are increasing and are expected to increase as the world gets wealthier and more crowded, moving from a population of 7–9 billion in the coming generation. This poses expropriation risks for land held under customary tenure. This means efforts to protect customary tenure systems against arbitrary expropriation requires immediate policy action. Additionally, long-term strategies for enhancing women access to land under customary tenure need to be taken to increase women land acquisition through customary tenure. Short-term strategies for improving women land acquisition include improvement of land markets. It is especially important to legalize land sales in SSA countries where land belongs to the state and where selling and buying land is illegal.

Increase Adoption of ISFM

The current low adoption of ISFM is due to a number of factors discussed above. In addition to these, there is need for enhancing the capacity of agricultural extension services in order to provide ISFM advisory services. This is because studies have shown they have a low capacity to provide advisory services on ISFM and agricultural marketing remains low and weak (AGRA 2014). There is need of retraining agricultural extension service providers on ISFM and agricultural marketing. A pluralistic extension services could be required to achieve this objective since different providers will give complementary advisory services to cover many aspects that the traditional extension services seem to be deficient.

There is also need for finding practical and amenable strategies for incentivizing farmers to use ISFM. For example, conditional fertilizer subsidy could provide incentives for farmers to adopt nitrogen fixing agroforestry trees and improve significantly the current subsidy programs in several SSA countries. Such a strategy will simultaneously reduce the high labor intensity of ISFM and reduce the inorganic fertilizer requirement (Akinnefesi et al. 2010) and thus lower the high cost of subsidies without reducing yield and production. A study conducted in Malawi showed that providing conditional fertilizer subsidies was highly favorable among farmers (Marenya et al. 2014).

Overall, our results show that SSA has the potential to become the breadbasket of the world but it has to significantly improve its market access and government effectiveness to create incentives for land holders to invest in land improvement. The increasing demand for land, urbanization, and other global regional changes are creating a conducive condition for taking action against land degradation. These opportunities should be exploited effectively as they lead to win-win outcomes—reducing poverty and achieving SLM.

References

AGRA (Alliance for a Green Revolution in Africa). (2014). Africa agriculture report 2014. *Climate change and smallholder agriculture in Sub-Saharan Africa.* AGRA, Nairobi. Online at www.agra.org

Akinnifesi, F., Ajayi, O. C., Sileshi, G., Chirwa, P. W., & Chianu, J. (2010). Fertiliser trees for sustainable food security in the maize-based production systems of east and southern Africa a review. *Agronomy for Sustainable Development, 30*, 615–629.

Alexandratos, N., & Bruinsma, J. (2012). *World agriculture towards 2030/2050: The 2012 revision.* ESA Working paper No. 12-03. Rome: FAO.

Andersen, T. B., & Jensen, P. S. (2014). Is Africa's recent growth sustainable? *International Economic Journal, 28*(2), 207–223.

Anseeuw, W., Wily, L. A., Cotula, L., & Taylor, M. (2012). *Land rights and the rush for land: Findings of the global commercial.*

Anyamba, A., Small, J. L., Tucker, C. J., & Pak, E. W. (2014). Thirty-two years of Sahelian zone growing season non-stationary NDVI3g patterns and trends. *Remote Sensing, 6*, 3101–3122.

Aquastat. (2014). Water raw data. available online at http://www.fao.org/nr/water/aquastat/data/query/results.html. Accessed on April 7, 2015.

Arvis, J. F., Mustra, M. A., Ojala, L., Shepherd, B., & Saslavsky, D. (2012). Connecting to compete 2012: Trade logistics in the global economy. World Bank.

AU (African Union). (2014). Malabo declaration on accelerated agricultural growth and transformation for shared prosperity and improved livelihoods. Online at http://www.au.int/en/content/malabo-26-27-June-2014-decisions-declarations-and-resolution-assembly-union-twenty-third-ord. Accessed on January 25, 2015.

Bai, Z. G., Dent, D. L., Olsson, L., & Schaepman, M. E. (2008). *Global assessment of land degradation and improvement. 1. Identification by remote sensing*. GLADA Report 5 (November). Wageningen, The Netherlands.

Banana, A. Y., Vogt, N. D., Gombya-Ssembajjwe, W. S., & Bahati, J. (2004). *Local governance and forest conditions: The case of forests in Mpigi district of Uganda.* Paper presented at the Tenth Biennial Conference of the International Association for the Study of Common Property, Oaxaca, Mexico. August 9–13, 2004.

Barron, J. (2009). Background: The water component of ecosystem services and in human well-being development targets. In J. Barron (Ed.), *Rainwater harvesting: A lifeline for human well-being* (pp. 4–13). New York: United Nations Environment Programme.

Barrett, C. B. (2008). Smallholder market participation: Concepts and evidence from eastern and southern Africa. *Food Policy, 33*(4), 299–317.

Barrett, C. B., Carter, M. R., & Timmer, C. P. (2010). A century-long perspective on agricultural development. *American Journal of Agricultural Economics, 92*(2), 447–468.

Beintema, N., & Stads, G. J. (2014). *Taking stock of national agricultural R&D capacity in Africa South of the Sahara.* ASTI Synthesis Report. Agricultural Science and Technology Indicators report, online at http://www.ifpri.org/sites/default/files/publications/astiafricasynthesis.pdf.

Benin, S., Kennedy, A., Lambert, M., & McBride, L. (2010). *Monitoring African agricultural development processes and performance: A comparative analysis.* ReSAKSS Annual Trends and Outlook Report 2010. International Food Policy Research Institute (IFPRI).

Benin, S., &Yu, B. (2012). *Complying the Maputo declaration target: trends in public agricultural expenditures and implications for pursuit of optimal allocation of public agricultural spending*. ReSAKSS Annual Trends and Outlook Report 2012. International Food Policy Research Institute (IFPRI).

Berry, W., & Feldman, S. (1985). *Multiple regression in practice* (50th ed., pp. 37–50). Thousand Oaks, California: Sage University Paper.

Besley, T. (1995). Property rights and investment incentives: Theory and evidence from Ghana. *Journal of Political Economy, 103*(5), 903–937.

Boserup, E. (1965). *The conditions of agricultural growth.* New York: Aldine.

Bruinsma, J. (2009). *The resource outlook to 2050: How much do land, water and crop yields need to increase by 2050?* Paper presented at the Expert Meeting on How to feed the World in 2050, Rome, Italy, June, 24–26. Rome, Italy: Food and Agriculture Organization of the United Nations. See http://www.fao.org/docrep/fao/ak971e/ak971e00

Bruyninckx, H. (2004). The convention to combat desertification and the role of innovative policy-making discourses: The case of Burkina Faso. *Global Environmental Politics, 4*(3), 107–127.

Burney, J., & Naylor, R. L. (2012). Smallholder irrigation as a poverty alleviation tool in sub-Saharan Africa. *World Development, 40*(1), 110–123.

CAADP (Comprehensive Africa Agriculture Development Program). (2013). Agriculture, Food security and nutrition. 2013 Report. New Partnership for Africa's Development (NEPAD). Pretoria. Retrieved March 21, 2015 from http://www.caadp.net/content/resources

CISIEN. (2010). Poverty map. Online at http://sedac.ciesin.columbia.edu/povmap/methods_global.jsp

CISIEN (Center for International Earth Science Information Network). (2007). Gridded Population of the World (GPW), Version 2. Palisades, NY: CIESIN, Columbia University. http://sedac.ciesin.columbia.edu/plue/gpw

Cotula, L. (2006). Introduction. In Cotula (Ed.), *Changes in "customary" land tenure systems in Africa* (Vol. 38, pp. 1–8). United Nations Food and Agriculture Organization (FAO) Livelihood Support Program (LSP) Working Paper.

Crawford, E., Kelly, V., Jayne, T., & Howard, J. (2003). Input use and market development in sub-Saharan Africa: An overview. *Food Policy, 28*(4), 277–292.

Cropper, M., Puri, J., & Griffiths, C. (2001). Predicting the location of deforestation: The role of roads and protected areas in North Thailand. *Land Economics, 77*(2), 172–186.

Dasgupta, P. (2010). Poverty traps: Exploring the complexity of causation. In J. von Braun, J. R. Vargas Hill & R. Pandya-Lorch (Eds.), *The poorest and hungry assessments, analyses, and actions* (pp. 129–146) Washington, D.C.: International Food Policy Research Institute.

Dc Janvry, A., & Sadoulet, E. (2010). Agricultural growth and poverty reduction: Additional evidence. *World Bank Research Observer, 25*(1), 1–20.

de Soto, H. (2000). *Mystery of capital: Why capitalism triumphs in the west and fails everywhere.* New York: Basic Books.

Deininger, K. (2003). *Land policies for growth and poverty reduction.* World Bank Policy Research Report. 210 p. Washington, D.C.: World Bank.

Dinda, S. (2004a). Environmental Kuznets curve hypothesis: A survey. *Ecological Economics, 49*(4), 431–455.

Dinda, S. (2004b). Environmental Kuznets curve hypothesis: A survey. *Ecological Economics, 49*(4), 431–455.

Doss, C. R., Kovarik, C., Peterman, A., Quisumbing, A. R., & van den Bold, M. (2013). *Gender inequalities in ownership and control of land in Africa: Myth and reality.* IFPRI Discussion Paper Number 1308.

Druilhe, Z., & Barreiro-Hurlé, J. (2012). *Fertilizer subsidies in sub-Saharan Africa. ESA.* Working Paper No. 12-04. Rome: FAO.

ECA (Economic Commission for Africa). (2014). The Africa water vision for 2025: Equitable and sustainable use of water for socioeconomic development. Online at http://www.unwater.org/downloads/African_Water_Vision_2025.pdf. Accessed on April 08, 2015.

Ehrlich, P. (1968). *The population bomb.* New York: Ballantine Books.

Eriksson, G. (1993). *Peasent response to price incentives in Tanzania.* Research Report #91, Nordiska Afrikainstitutet, pp. 5–67.

Esty, D., & Porter, M. (2005). National environmental performance: An empirical analysis of policy results and determinants. *Environment and Development Economics, 10*, 391–434.

Ezeh, A. C., Bongaarts, J., & Mberu, B. (2012). Global population trends and policy options. *Lancet, 380*, 142–148.

FAO. (2006). Afrique de l'Ouest: mobilisation des investissements pour le développement rural et agricole dans la zone CEDEAO, Réunion des ministres des finances de la CEDEAO, mars 2006, Rome: FAO, 53 p.

FAO (Food and Agriculture Organization). (2010). *Global forest resources assessment.* Main report. FAO Forestry Paper 163.

FAO (Food and Agriculture Organization). (2012). State of food and agriculture. Investing in agriculture for a better future. Rome: FAO.

FAOSTAT (Food and Agriculture Organization of the United Nations statistics). (2012). Online at http://faostat.fao.org/site/567/default.aspx#ancor. Accessed May 2012.

Fearnside, P. (2002). Avança brasil: environmental and social consequences of brazil's planned infrastructure in amazonia. *Environmental Management30*(6),0735–0747

Foley, J., Ramankutty, N., Brauman, K. A., Cassidy, E. S., Gerber, J. S., Johnston, M., et al. (2011). Solutions for a cultivated planet. *Nature, 478*, 337–342.

Foster, A., & Rosenzweig, M. (2003). Economic growth and the rise of forests. *Quarterly Journal of Economics, 118*, 601–637.

Foster, V., & Briceno-Garmendia, C. B. (2010). *Africa's infrastructure: A time for transformation*. Paris, Washington: Agence Francaise de Development and World Bank.
Frenken, K. (2005). Irrigation in Africa in figures: AQUASTAT survey (Vol. 29). Food and Agriculture Organization.
Galor, O., & Weil, D. N. (2000). Population, technology, and growth: From Malthusian stagnation to the demographic transition and beyond. *The American Economic Review, 90*(4), 806–828.
Gavian, S., & Fafchamps, M. (1996). Land tenure and allocative efficiency in Niger. *American Journal of Agricultural Economics, 78*(2), 460–471.
Gondo, P. (2010). A review of forest financing in Africa. United Nations Forum on Forests.
Haberl, H., Erb, K. H., Krausmann, F., Gaube, V., Bondeau, A., Plutzar, C., et al. (2004). Quantifying and mapping the human appropriation of net primary production in earth's terrestrial ecosystems. *Proceedings of the National Academy of Sciences, 104*(31), 12942–12947.
Haggblade, S., Hazell, P., & Reardon, T. (2007). The rural Nonfarm economy: Pathway out of poverty or pathway in? In S. Haggblade, P. Hazell, & T. Reardon (Eds.), *Tranforming the rural Nonfarm economy. Opportunities and threats in the developing world* (pp. 254–292). Washington, D.C.: World Bank and IFPRI.
Hatibu, N., Mahoo, H. F., & Kajiru, G. J. (2000). The role of RWH in agriculture and natural resources management: From mitigating droughts to preventing floods. In N. Hatibu & H. F. Mahoo (Eds.), *Rainwater harvesting for natural resources management* (pp. 58–83.). A planning guide for Tanzania. Technical Handbook No. 22. RELMA, Nairobi.
Hazell, P. (2007). All-Africa review of experiences with commercial agriculture. Case study on livestock. Background paper for the Competitive Commercial Agriculture in Sub-Saharan Africa (CCAA) study. Online at http://siteresources.worldbank.org/INTAFRICA/Resources/257994-1215457178567/Ch11_Livestock.pdf
Henderson, B., Gerber, P., Hilinksi, T., Falcucci, A., Ojima, D. S., Salvatore, M., & Conant, R. T. (2015). Greenhouse gas mitigation potential of the world's grazing lands: Modeling soil carbon and nitrogen fluxes of mitigation practices. *Agriculture, Ecosystems and Environment* (Forthcoming).
HLPE (High level Panel of Experts). (2011). *Land tenure and international investments in agriculture*. A Report by the High Level Panel of Experts on Food Security and Nutrition of the Committee on World Food Security, Rome 2011.
Inocencio, A. B. (2007). *Costs and performance of irrigation projects: A comparison of sub-Saharan Africa and other developing regions* (Vol. 109). IWMI.
Jahnke, H. E. (1982). *Livestock production systems and livestock development in tropical Africa*. Kiel, Germany: Kieler Wissenschaftsverlag Vauk. 253 pp.
Jayne, T. S., & Rashid, S. (2013). Input subsidy programs in sub-Saharan Africa: A synthesis of recent evidence. *Agricultural Economics, 44*(6), 547–562.
Kamuanga, M. J. B., Somda, J., Sanon, Y., & Kagoné, H. (2008). Livestock and regional market in the Sahel and West Africa potentials and challenges. Online at http://www.oecd.org/swac/publications/41848366.pdf. Accessed December 31, 2014.
Kaufmann, D., Kraay, A., & Mastruzzi, M. (2010). *The worldwide governance indicators: Methodology and analytical issues*. World Bank Policy Research Working Paper No. 5430.
Kaufmann D., Kraay, A., & Mastruzzi, M. (2012). Worldwide governance indicators. Online at http://info.worldbank.org/governance/wgi/index.aspx#home. Accessed January 13, 2015.
Kellner K., Risoli, C., & Ketz, M. (2011). Terminal evaluation of the UNEP/FAO/GEF project. Land degradation in drylands (LADA). United Nations Environmental Program (UNEP). Online at http://www.unep.org/eou/Portals/52/Reports/DL_LADA_TE_%20FinalReport.pdf. Accessed on January 23, 2015.
Kelly, V. (2006). *Factors affecting demand for fertilizer in sub-Saharan Africa*. World Bank Agriculture and Rural Development Discussion Paper 23. Washington, D.C.
Kelly, V., Crawford, E., & Ricker-Gilbert, J. (2011). The new generation of African fertilizer subsidies: Panacea or Pandora's box? Policy Synthesis for cooperating USAID offices and country missions number 87, May, USAID and MSU.
KNBS (Kenya National Bureau of Statistics). (2014). Statistical abstract. Nairobi Kenya.

Kuriakose, T., & Ahlers, R. (2008). Agricultural water management. Policy Note #3. Online at http://siteresources.worldbank.org/INTGENAGRLIVSOUBOOK/Resources/AWM_Note_3_Policy_Jan08.pdf. Accessed April 08, 2015.

Lambin, E., & Meyfroidt, P. (2011). Global land use change, economic globalization, and the looming land scarcity. *Proceedings of the National Academy of Sciences of the United States of America, 108*(9), 3465–3472.

Lankford, B. (2009). Viewpoint—the right irrigation? Policy directions for agricultural water management in sub-Saharan Africa. *Water Alternatives, 2*(3), 476–480.

Laurance, W., Goosem, M., & Laurance, S. G. (2009). Impacts of roads and linear clearings on tropical forests. *Trends in Ecology evolution, 24*(12), 659–669.

Le, Q. B., Nkonya, E., & Mirzabaev, A. (2014). *Biomass productivity-based mapping of global land degradation hotspots.* ZEF-Discussion Papers on Development Policy No. 193. University of Bonn.

Lobell, D. B., Cassman, K. G., & Field, C. B. (2009). Crop yield gaps: Their importance, magnitudes, and causes. *Annual Review of Environment and Resources, 4*, 179–204.

Lowder, S. K., Carisma, B., & Skoet, J. (2012). *Who invests in agriculture and how much? An empirical review of the relative size of various investments in agriculture in low- and middle-income countries.* FAO ESA Working Paper No. 12-09. Online at http://www.fao.org/3/a-ap854e.pdf. Accessed February 04, 2015.

Lynch, G., & Crawford, G. (2011). Democratization in Africa 1990–2010: An assessment. *Democratization, 18*(2), 275–310.

Malesu, M., Khaka, E., Mati, B., Oduor, A., De Bock, T., Nyabenge, M., & Oduor, V. (2006). Mapping the potentials for rainwater harvesting technologies in Africa. A GIS overview of development domains for the continent and nine selected countries. Technical manual No. 7, Nairobi, Kenya: World Agroforestry Centre (ICRAF), Netherlands Ministry of Foreign Affairs. 120 p.

Marenya, P., Smith, V. H., & Nkonya, E. (2014). Relative preferences for soil conservation incentives among smallholder farmers: Evidence from Malawi. *American Journal of Agricultural Economics, 96*(3), 690–710.

Mbaiwa, J., Stronza, A., & Kreuter, U. (2011). From collaboration to conservation: Insights from the Okavango Delta, Botswana. *Society and Natural Resources: An International Journal, 4*(4), 400–411.

Mugisha, A. R., & Jacobson, S. K. (2004). Threat reduction assessment of conventional and community-based conservation approaches to managing protected areas in Uganda. *Environmental Conservation, 31*(03), 233–241.

Mukherjee, C., White, H., & Wuyts, M. (1998). *Econometric and data analysis for developing countries.* London: Routledge.

Nandwa, & Bekunda, M. A. (1998). Research on nutrient flows and balances in east and southern Africa: State-of-the-art. *Agriculture, Ecosystems and Environment, 71*(1–3), 5–18.

Nelson, A. (2007). Global 1 km accessibility (cost distance) model using publicly available data. Mimeo, Washington, D.C.: World Bank.

Nelson, G. C., & Hellerstein, D. (1997). Do roads cause deforestation? Using satellite images in econometric analysis of land use. *American Journal of Agricultural Economics, 79*(1), 80–88.

Nkonya, E., & Anderson, W. (2015). Exploiting provisions of land economic productivity without degrading its natural capital. *Journal of Arid Environment, 112*, 33–43.

Nkonya, E., Koo, J., Kato, E., & Guo, Z. (2013). *Trends and patterns of land use change and international aid in sub-Saharan Africa.* WIDER Working Paper No. 2013/110.

Nkonya, E., Koo, j., Xie, H., Traore, S., & N'diaye M. K. (2010). Key institutional, financing, and economic elements for scaling up sustainable land and water management in mali. IFPRI Unpublished report.

Nkonya, E., Pender, J., Kaizzi, K. C., Kato, E., Mugarura, S., Ssali, H., & Muwonge, J. (2008). Linkages between land management, land degradation, and poverty in sub-Saharan Africa. The Case of Uganda. IFPRI Research Monograph 159.

Orubu, C. O., & Omotor, D. G. (2011). Environmental quality and economic growth: Searching for environmental Kuznets curves for air and water pollutants in Africa. *Energy Policy, 39*(7), 4178–4188.
Ostrom, E. (1990). *Governing the commons: The evolution of institutions for collection action. Political economy of institutions and decisions*. New York: Cambridge University Press.
Otsuka, K., & F. Place. (2014). *Changes in land tenure and agricultural intensification in sub-Saharan Africa*. WIDER Working Paper 2014/051.
Pahl-Wostl, C., Tabara, D., Bouwen, R., Craps, M., Dewulf, A., Mostert, E., et al. (2008). The importance of social learning and culture for sustainable water management. *Ecological Economics, 64*(3), 484–495.
Peres, C. A. (2001). Paving the way to the future of Amazonia. *Trends in Ecology and Evolution, 16*(5), 217–219.
Pinstrup-Andersen, P. (2014). Contemporary food policy challenges and opportunities. *Australian Journal of Agricultural and Resource Economics, 58*(4), 504–518.
Place, F. (2009). Land tenure and agricultural productivity in Africa: A comparative analysis of the economics literature and recent policy strategies and reforms. *World Development, 37*(8), 1326–1336.
Place, F., & Otsuka, K. (2002). Land tenure systems and their impacts on agricultural investments and productivity in Uganda. *The Journal of Development Studies, 38*(6), 105–128.
Ricker-Gilbert, J., Jayne, T., & Shively, G. (2013). Addressing the "wicked problem" of input subsidy programs in Africa. *Applied Economic Perspectives and Policy, 35*(2), 322–340.
Rockstrom, J., Steffen, W., Noone, K., Persson, A., Chapin, F. S., III, Lambin, E., et al. (2009). Planetary boundaries: Exploring the safe operating space for humanity. *Ecology and Society, 14*(2), 32. [online]. http://www.ecologyandsociety.org/vol14/iss2/art32/
Rosegrant, M. W., Cai, X., & Cline, S. A. (2002). World water and food to 2025: Dealing with scarcity. International Food Policy Research Institute.
Rudel, T. K., Schneider, L., Uriarte, M., Turner, B. L., II, DeFries, R., Lawrence, D., et al. (2009a). Agricultural intensification and changes in cultivated areas, 1970–2005. *Proceedings of the National Academy of Sciences of the United States, 106*(49), 20675–20680.
Rudel, T., Defries, R., Asner, G. P., & Laurance, W. F. (2009b). Changing drivers of deforestation and new opportunities for conservation. *Conservation Biology, 23*(6), 1396–1405.
Scherr, S. (2000). A downward spiral? Research evidence on the relationship between poverty and natural resource degradation. *Food Policy, 25*(4), 479–498.
Schmidhuber, J., Bruinsma, J., & Prakash, A. (2011). Investing towards a world free of hunger: Lowering vulnerability and enhancing resilience. *Safeguarding Food Security in Volatile Global Markets* 543–569.
Schoneveld, G. C., German, L. A., & Nutakor, E. (2011). Land-based investments for rural development? A grounded analysis of the local impacts of biofuel feedstock plantations in Ghana. *Ecology and Society, 16*(4), 10.
Seymour, F., La Vina, T., & Hite, K. (2014). Evidence linking community-level tenure and forest condition: An annotated bibliography. *Climate and Land Use Alliance*. Online at http://www.climateandlandusealliance.org/uploads/PDFs/Community_level_tenure_and_forest_condition_bibliography.pdf. Accessed January 23, 2015.
Sheahan, M., & Barrett, C. B. (2014). *Understanding the agricultural input landscape in sub-Saharan Africa. Recent plot, household, and community-level evidence*. World Bank Policy Research Working Paper 7014.
Smith, P., Gregory, P. J., van Vuuren, D., Obersteiner, M., Havlík, P., Rounsevell, M., et al. (2010). Competition for land. *Transactions of the Royal Society B, 370*(1663), 2941–2957.
Stevens, C., & Kennan, J. (2005). Botswana beef exports and trade policy. Background study to the World Bank-BIDPA Botswana Export diversification study. Institute of Development Studies University of Sussex, Brighton, Online at http://dspace.africaportal.org/jspui/bitstream/123456789/31840/1/theBeefSector.pdf?1. Accessed on February 09, 2015.
Swinton, S., Escobar, G., & Reardon, T. (2003). Poverty and environment in Latin America: Concepts, evidence and policy implications. *World Development, 31*(11), 1865–1872.

TerrAfrica. (2009). Sustainable land management in Africa opportunities for increasing agricultural productivity and greenhouse gas mitigation. TerrAfrica Climate Brief No. 2. Online at http://www.ecoagriculture.org/documents/files/doc_226.pdf. Accessed on January 29, 2015.

Thornton, P. (2010). Livestock production: Recent trends, future prospects. *Philosophical Transactions of the Royal Society B, 365*, 2853–2867.

Thornton, P. K., Kruska, R. L., Henninger, N., Kristjanson, P. M., Reid, R. S., Atieno, F., et al. (2002). *Mapping poverty and livestock in the developing world* (p. 124). Nairobi, Kenya: International Livestock Research Institute.

Turral, H., Svendsen, M., & Faures, J. M. (2010). Investing in irrigation: Reviewing the past and looking to the future. *Agricultural Water Management, 97*(4), 551–560.

UNECA (United Nations Economic Commission for Africa). (2014). MDG 2014 report. *Assessing progress in Africa toward the millennium development goals.* Addis Ababa, Ethiopia.

UNFCCC (United Nations Framework Convention on Climate Change). (2014a). Appendix II—nationally appropriate mitigation actions of developing country parties. http://unfccc.int/meetings/cop_15/copenhagen_accord/items/5265.php

UNFCCC (United Nations Framework Convention on Climate Change). (2014b). Status of negotiations on NAMAs. UNFCCC African Regional Workshop NAMAs, October 1–3, 2014, Windhoek, Namibia. http://unfccc.int/files/focus/mitigation/application/pdf/unfccc-status_of_negotiations-linkages_with_tna.pdf

UNFPA (United Nations Population Fund). Adolescents, youth and the transformation of the future. State of world population 2014. Online at http://www.unfpa.org/swop. Accessed on February 04, 2015.

USAID, & ARD inc. (2008). Land tenure and property rights. Online at: www.usaidlandtenure.net

Wilkie, D., Morelli, G. A., Demmer, J., Starkey, M., Telfer, P., & Steil, M. (2006). Parks and people: Assessing the human welfare effects of establishing protected areas for biodiversity conservation. *Conservation Biology, 20*(1), 247–249.

World Bank. (2008). *Uganda sustainable land management public expenditure (S LM PER).* Report No. 45781-UC. Online at http://wwwwds.worldbank.org/external/default/WDSContentServer/WDSP/IB/2009/01/14/000333038_20090114223841/Rendered/PDF/457810ESW0P105101official0use0only1.pdf

World Bank. (2011). World development report 2011. *Conflict, security, and development.* Washington, D.C.: World Bank.

World Bank. (2014). Africa's pulse: Decades of sustained growth is transforming Africa's economies.

Wuertenberger, L., Koellner, T., & Binder, C. R. (2006). Virtual land use and agricultural trade: Estimating environmental and socio-economic impacts. *Ecological Economics, 57*, 679–697.

WWAP (United Nations World Water Assessment Programme). (2015). The United Nations.

UN (United Nations). (2014). World urbanization prospects: The 2014 revision, highlights. Department of Economic and Social Affairs, Population Division.

Vanlauwe, B., Wendt, J., Giller, K. E., Corbeels, M., Gerard, B., & Nolte, C. (2014). A fourth principle is required to define conservation agriculture in sub-Saharan Africa: The appropriate use of fertilizer to enhance crop productivity. *Field Crops Research, 155*, 10–13.

You, L., Ringler, C., Wood-Sichra, U., Robertson, R., Wood, S., Zhu, T., et al. (2011). What is the irrigation potential for Africa? A combined biophysical and socioeconomic approach. *Food Policy, 36*, 770–782.

Yu, B. (2014). *Public account and coding system in Kenya. The trend and pattern of agricultural expenditure.* IFPRI Discussion Paper 01396.

Chapter 10
Economics of Land Degradation in Central Asia

Alisher Mirzabaev, Jann Goedecke, Olena Dubovyk, Utkur Djanibekov, Quang Bao Le and Aden Aw-Hassan

Abstract Land degradation is a major development challenge in Central Asia, with negative implications on rural livelihoods and food security. We estimate the annual cost of land degradation in the region due to land use and cover change between 2001 and 2009 to be about 6 billion USD, most of which due to rangeland degradation (4.6 billion USD), followed by desertification (0.8 billion USD), deforestation (0.3 billion USD) and abandonment of croplands (0.1 billion USD). The costs of action against land degradation are found to be lower than the costs of

A. Mirzabaev (✉) · J. Goedecke
Center for Development Research, University of Bonn, Walter Flex Str 3, 53113 Bonn, Germany
e-mail: almir@uni-bonn.de

J. Goedecke
e-mail: jann.goedecke@kuleuven.be

J. Goedecke
Faculty of Economics and Business, KU Leuven, Warmoesberg 26, 1000 Brussels, Belgium

O. Dubovyk
Center for Remote Sensing of Land Surfaces (ZFL), University of Bonn, Walter Flex str 3, 53113 Bonn, Germany
e-mail: odubovyk@uni-bonn.de

U. Djanibekov
Production Economics Group, Institute for Food and Resource Economics, University of Bonn, Meckenheimer Allee 174, 53113 Bonn, Germany
e-mail: utkur@uni-bonn.de

Q.B. Le
CGIAR Research Program on Dryland Systems (CRP-DS), International Center for Agricultural Research in the Dry Areas (ICARDA), PO Box 950764, Amman 11195, Jordan
e-mail: q.le@cgiar.org; q.le@alumni.ethz.ch

A. Aw-Hassan
International Center for Agricultural Research in the Dry Areas (ICARDA), Bashir El Kassar Street. Daila Blgn 2nd Floor, Verdun Beirut 1108 2010, Lebanon
e-mail: a.aw-hassan@cgiar.org

E. Nkonya et al. (eds.), *Economics of Land Degradation and Improvement – A Global Assessment for Sustainable Development*,
DOI 10.1007/978-3-319-19168-3_10

inaction in Central Asia by 5 times over a 30-year horizon, meaning that each dollar spent on addressing land degradation is likely to have about 5 dollars of returns. This is a very strong economic justification favoring action versus inaction against land degradation. Specifically, the costs of action were found to equal about 53 billion USD over a 30-year horizon, whereas if nothing is done, the resulting losses may equal almost 288 billion USD during the same period. Better access to markets, extension services, secure land tenure, and livestock ownership among smallholder crop producers are found to be major drivers of SLM adoptions.

Keywords Central Asia · Rangeland degradation · SLM adoptions

Introduction

Central Asia—consisting of Kazakhstan, Kyrgyzstan, Tajikistan, Turkmenistan and Uzbekistan (Fig. 10.1), is strongly affected by land degradation with negative consequences on crop and livestock productivity, agricultural incomes, and rural livelihoods (Pender et al. 2009). The major types of land degradation in the region are secondary salinization in the irrigated lands, soil erosion in the rainfed and mountainous areas, and loss of vegetation, desertification or detrimental change in the vegetation composition in the rangelands (Gupta et al. 2009).

The drivers of land degradation in the region are numerous, highly complex and interrelated (Pender et al. 2009). The major proximate causes include unsustainable

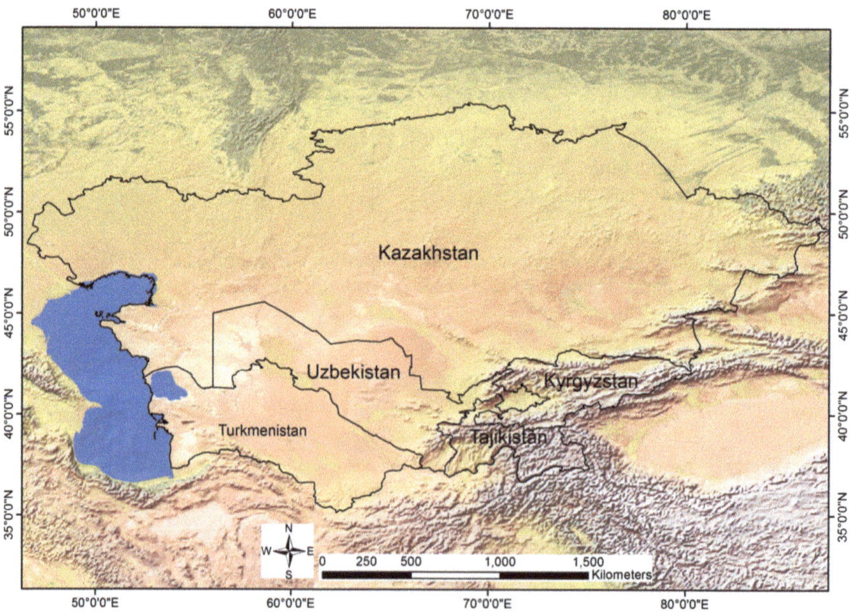

Fig. 10.1 Map of Central Asia. *Source* The authors

agricultural practices, the expansion of crop production to fragile and marginal areas, inadequate maintenance of irrigation and drainage networks, and overgrazing near settlements (Pender et al. 2009; Gupta et al. 2009; Kienzler et al. 2012). However, the underlying drivers of land degradation in the region are likely to be more important in terms of triggering these land degradation trends. The former Soviet policies of cotton and grain self-sufficiency had led to massive expansion of irrigated cotton and rainfed wheat production to marginal areas. Subsequently, there was a lack of resources and incentives to maintain those irrigation and drainage networks and adequately operate the expanded rainfed areas under the conditions of market economy (Gupta et al. 2009). The dismantling of former collective farms into much smaller and fragmented farmer plots has also created a mismatch with the irrigation system planned and operated for large-scale centralized farming and the needs of the new smallholder farmers. This had resulted in an institutional vacuum on sharing the responsibilities for the maintenance of the irrigation and drainage networks (Kazbekov et al. 2007). At the same time, the lack of irrigation water pricing effectively means subsidizing excessive water use by agricultural producers (Pender et al. 2009). A considerable share of previously cultivated rainfed lands, mainly in northern Kazakhstan, has now been abandoned (Propastin et al. 2008). Insufficient development of input and output markets resulted in higher input costs and post-harvest losses of produce. Other key underlying drivers of land degradation in the region are indicated to include land tenure insecurity, breakdown of collective action institutions regulating and facilitating access to common pool rangeland resources (CACILM 2006a, b, c, d, e; Pender et al. 2009; Gupta et al. 2009). The combination of these factors has led to lack of incentives for land users to adopt sustainable land management practices (Pender et al. 2009).

The national governments, research and development organizations, farmer associations and civil society are all well aware of this critical problem of land degradation and have been undertaking various efforts to address it, especially in terms of investments into de-silting and better maintaining drainage and irrigation systems, as well as promoting more sustainable agricultural practices (Pender et al. 2009; Kienzler et al. 2012). These efforts are highly needed and commendable, but could not yet completely address land degradation in the region because they are mainly targeting its proximate causes. On the other hand, there is a need for more efforts directed at addressing the underlying drivers of land degradation. This study aims to draw attention to the economic costs of land degradation in Central Asia and highlight the underlying drivers of land degradation in the region. For achieving these objectives, it seeks to answer the following four research questions:

1. What is the extent of land degradation in Central Asia?
2. What are the major underlying drivers of land degradation in the region?
3. What are the costs of land degradation?
4. How do the costs of inaction against land degradation compare with the costs of actions to address it?

In answering these research questions, the study intends to make the following contributions. Firstly, the latest knowledge on the extent of land degradation in the region is reviewed and discussed. Secondly, using data from nationally representative agricultural household surveys, the study identifies the underlying drivers of land degradation in Central Asia. Being based on actual data, this analysis is a step forward in the current knowledge of the drivers of land degradation in the region, which so far predominantly relied on qualitative analyses and expert opinions. Thirdly, we estimate the total economic costs of land degradation, including the losses in the value of indirect ecosystem services (such as carbon sequestration). Previous studies on the region, in general, have considered the costs of land degradation only associated with reductions in crop yields (see Pender et al. 2009 for a review). Moreover, the extent of adoption of sustainable land management (SLM) practices is identified, together with the drivers and constraints to these SLM adoptions.

Literature Review on Land Degradation in Central Asia

Extent of Land Degradation

Despite the recognized severity of land degradation in Central Asia, there is a lack of published studies identifying the extent of land degradation in the region using observed data at national or regional scales (Ji 2008). Most of the existing studies on the extent of land degradation in Central Asia are based on qualitative expert estimates (Gupta et al. 2009). On the other hand, there are a growing number of localized case studies based on detailed soil surveys or remote sensing data (O'Hara 1997; Buhlmann 2006; Dubovyk et al. 2013; Akramhanov et al. 2011; Akramhanov and Vlek 2012).

Secondary salinization is the major land degradation problem in the irrigated areas in the region, covering an estimated 40–60 % of these irrigated areas (Qadir et al. 2009). The salinization is especially acute in the downstream areas: almost all irrigated areas in Turkmenistan, and the provinces of Uzbekistan and Kazakhstan bordering the Aralkum desert (the former Aral Sea) are affected with secondary salinization (CACILM 2006e; Pender et al. 2009). Farmers commonly try to address salinity by leaching the soil, but the use of increasingly saline irrigation water undermines the effectiveness of leaching, and adds to the problem of excessive water use (Pender et al. 2009).

The main land degradation problems in rainfed croplands of Central Asia are soil erosion and soil fertility depletion. Wind erosion is a major problem in the vast plains of Kazakhstan, while water erosion is a problem in foothill areas (Gupta et al. 2009). Loss of soil fertility is estimated to affect more than 11 million ha in the rainfed steppes of Kazakhstan, with losses of soil organic matter of as much as 40 % (Pender et al. 2009), although there may have been some recovery of carbon in these soils after abandonment from cultivation since early 1990s (De Beurs and Henebry 2004; Schiermeier 2013).

Rangelands are the largest land cover type in the region, occupying 65 % the total land area of Central Asia. Presently, there is a well-established knowledge of strong rangeland degradation close to population settlements (Alimaev 2003;

Gintzburger et al. 2005; Alimaev et al. 2006; Robinson et al. 2010), due to lack of herd mobility (Kerven 2003; Farrington 2005; Bekturova and Romanova 2007).

Mountainous ecosystems in Central Asia occupy about 10 % of the total territory and are ecologically very diverse. In terms of agricultural production, they have irrigated and rainfed crop production and extensive pastoral use of mountain rangelands. In spite of this, land degradation problems in mountainous areas have also their own characteristics. Specifically, soil erosion by water is a key problem in irrigated sloping areas, rather than salinity as in the irrigated areas located in the plains (Gupta et al. 2009).

Mapping Land Degradation Hotspots in Central Asia

Degradation of drylands manifests itself in reduced productive potential (Reynolds et al. 2007), indicated by a gradual loss of vegetation cover over time. Thus, negative vegetation trend over sufficiently long period of time is often related to land degradation. Bai et al. (2008) analyzed land degradation as a negative linear trend in the Normalized Difference Vegetation Index (NDVI) between 1981 and 2003, and found that land degradation ranges from 0.3 % of the territory in Turkmenistan to as much as 17.9 % of the territory in Kazakhstan. However, the NDVI trend can be an indirect indicator of soil degradation or soil improvement if the nutrient source for vegetation/crop growth is solely, or largely, from the soils (i.e., soil-based biomass productivity). In the agricultural areas with intensive application of mineral fertilizers (i.e. fertilizer-based crop productivity), NDVI trend principally cannot be a reliable indicator of soil fertility trend (Le et al. 2012). Moreover, the elevated levels of CO_2 and NO_x in the atmosphere (Reay et al. 2008; World Meteorological Organization 2012) can cause a divergence between Net Primary Productivity (NPP) trend and soil fertility change as the atmospheric fertilization effect has not been substantially mediated through the soil.

Le et al. (2014), in their mapping of land degradation hotspots around the world, account for atmospheric fertilization and delineate areas where chemical fertilizer application may be masking soil degradation processes. Thus, using the same definition of land degradation, Le et al. (2014), in addition, consider land degradation masked by atmospheric fertilization and application of chemical fertilizers. Le et al. (2014) find that relatively higher share of land in the Central Asian countries has been degrading between early 1980s and mid-2000s. The extent of land degradation in Central Asia, according to Le et al. (2014), ranges between 8 % (in Turkmenistan and Uzbekistan) and 60 % of the total area (in Kazakhstan) (Fig. 10.2). Cropland degradation is significant in all five countries, ranging from roughly one fifth of the total cropland in Kyrgyzstan, to 57 % in Kazakhstan. The land degradation hotspots are concentrated in the north of Kazakhstan, and stretch over Eastern Kazakhstan to the southern part of Central Asia, covering Kyrgyzstan, the north-west of Tajikistan and the southern parts of Uzbekistan and Turkmenistan.

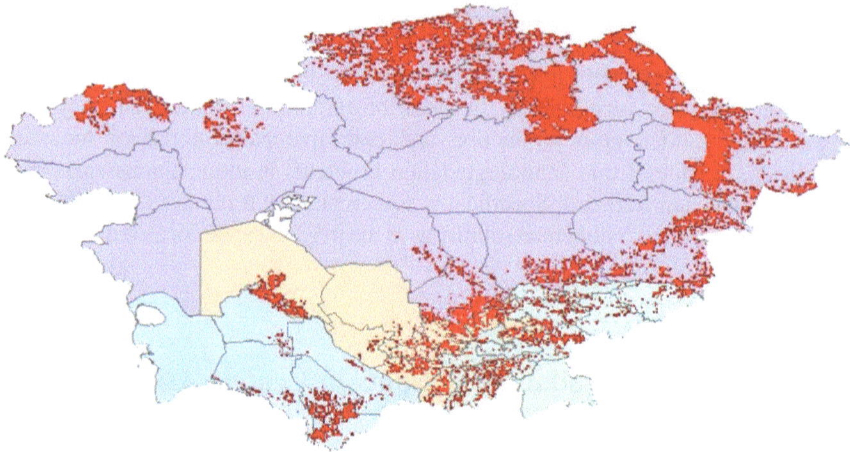

Fig. 10.2 Land degradation hotspots in Central Asia (in *red*), a negative change in NDVI between 1982 and 1984 and 2006. *Source* Adapted from Le et al. (2014)

Despite the advancement in the measurement of land degradation in Le et al. (2014), its definition as a long-term decline in the NDVI still entails some issues, since confounding factors changing over time, such as land use, influence the NDVI. Kazakhstan underwent a considerable transition in agricultural land use in the post-Soviet era, marked by a sharp decline in total rainfed grain area from 25 million ha in 1983 to 14 million ha in 2003, particularly in the country's northern part (De Beurs and Henebry 2004). Today, the area is largely covered by abandoned cropland returning to original land cover types prevalent before their conversion to cultivation (Schierhorn et al. 2013), mainly grassland. Although soil itself might have recovered some of its lost carbon due to abandonment (ibid.), cultivated land may elicit a higher NDVI value than abandoned land with sparser vegetation, leading to an overestimation of inherent soil degradation processes (Klein et al. 2012).

Drivers of Land Degradation in Central Asia

The drivers of land degradation in Central Asia are numerous and interrelated. Here, following the approach by Gupta et al. (2009), they are reviewed by the four major agro-ecological zones.

Irrigated areas. The main proximate causes of salinization are excessive irrigation through poorly constructed and maintained irrigation systems. Drainage systems add to the problem as they fail to drain off the excess water and salts, due to their inappropriate construction and maintenance (ADB 2007). In many upstream areas, drainage water is fed back into the rivers, increasing the salt levels in the rivers and irrigation canals downstream. Some underlying policy factors act through these proximate causes. Irrigated cotton production with inadequate drainage remains promoted (Gupta et al. 2009). Continued subsidies for irrigation create disincentives to economize on water (Pender et al. 2009). Input and output market institutions are underdeveloped or lacking. The interaction of poverty and low access to credit markets may prevent farmers from investing in costly, but in the long-term profitable, SLM technologies. Incomplete land reforms, resulting in continuing land tenure insecurity, are believed to be deterrents to SLM adoptions (Pender et al. 2009).

Rainfed areas. Soil erosion and fertility depletion have been caused by expansion of rainfed wheat production with intensive tillage into marginal rangelands and cultivation on sloping lands with limited soil cover or use of soil and water conservation measures. Soil erosion is particularly severe during summer fallow periods in northern Kazakhstan, when intensive tillage is used to control weeds (Kienzler et al. 2012). Soil fertility depletion also results from insufficient inputs of fertilizers. Underlying these proximate causes are many factors such as lack of farmer awareness or training in the use of appropriate soil conservation practices and lack of access to credit (Gupta et al. 2009).

Rangelands. Rangeland degradation is mainly driven by overgrazing, cutting of shrubs, abandonment, and lack of maintenance of rangeland infrastructure (Pender et al. 2009). Difficult economic, institutional and land tenure conditions for mobile grazing are prevalent (ibid.). On the policy side, effective pasture management mechanisms are often absent and pasture leasing is not clearly regulated in most countries in the region. Institutional mandates are outdated or insufficiently defined (ibid.). In general, institutional mechanisms to sustainably manage rangelands are weak. On the farmers' side, there is a lack of economic and organizational capacity, particularly among individual household pastoralists. Furthermore, the awareness of rangeland degradation issues and approaches is limited (Pender et al. 2009; CACILM 2006a, b, c, d, e).

Mountainous areas. The major drivers of land degradation in mountainous areas in Central Asia are considered to be poverty and low market access; population pressure leading to cultivation of sloping, easily erodible lands without use of sustainable soil conservation technologies, poor extension and institutional limitations (Gupta et al. 2009; Pender et al. 2009).

Past Assessments of the Costs of Land Degradation

There are various estimates of the costs of land degradation in Central Asia. The studies range from the effects of land degradation on certain crops to the effects of land degradation at regional and national scales. To illustrate, the crop specific costs of land degradation were calculated for Uzbekistan by Nkonya et al. (2011) and Djanibekov et al. (2012b). Authors concluded that cultivation of major crops such as cotton and wheat on degraded soils result in profit losses for farmers. At the national scale, according to a World Bank assessment, the annual costs associated with land degradation in Uzbekistan amount to as much as 1 billion USD (Sutton et al. 2007). The costs of desertification in Kazakhstan are estimated to be about 6.2 billion USD (Saigal 2003, citing the National Action Program to Combat Desertification). At the regional scale, one of the widely cited estimates is that land degradation causes annual production losses worth as much as 2 billion USD in Central Asia (World Bank 1998, based on the USAID report). Suzuki (2003), based on the National Action Programs to Combat Desertification and other sources, indicates that desertification costs amount to about 3 % of the total income of Central Asian countries. Based on the ADB (2007) key indicators for the Central Asian countries for 2003, these desertification costs were equivalent to about 1.6 billion USD annually. Hence, the past research related to the national and regional analyses of land degradation underscore the high costs of land degradation in Central Asia. However, these previous studies did not consider the lost value of non-provisional ecosystem services due to land degradation.

Conceptual Framework

This study aims to achieve a more comprehensive estimate of the costs of land degradation in Central Asia by incorporating the value of both direct and indirect ecosystem services. For this purpose, the study is guided by the Total Economic Value (TEV) conceptual framework (Nkonya et al. 2013), presented in detail in Chap. 6 of this volume. The Total Economic Value (TEV) framework seeks to account for the losses of all ecosystem services due to land degradation. TEV framework considers land resources as a natural capital (Daily et al. 2011), yielding a stream of benefits in the form of terrestrial ecosystem goods and services. These ecosystem goods and services include provisional ones, such as food, feed and fiber, but also supporting, regulating and cultural ecosystem services, such as carbon sequestration, soil formation and water purification (Nkonya et al. 2013). The value of provisional ecosystem services and goods are captured by market prices. However, most supporting, regulating and cultural ecosystem services are not traded in the markets and do not have market prices, thus making it much more difficult to valuate them (ibid.). There are several methods of valuation of ecosystem services such as: market price method for those ecosystem services which have a market price (food, fiber, biomass); productivity and hedonic pricing methods which trace the contribution of ecosystem services to the market price of a marketed good (such as locational environmental attributes of land or real estate); travel costs method which infers about the value of ecosystem services in a specific site by asking people's willingness to pay (WTP) to visit that site; replacement cost method which measures the value of an ecosystem service by calculating the costs of substituting it; contingent valuation method which directly asks people about their willingness to pay for non-market ecosystem services; and benefit transfer approach that estimates the values for ecosystem services in one location based on the already existing studies using the above methods in some other location with similar characteristics (cf. Nkonya et al. 2011 for a review). This study, as explained in detail in the methodological section, applies the benefit transfer approach to the valuation of ecosystem services in Central Asia.

The Economics of Land Degradation (ELD) conceptual framework (Chap. 6) also guides the present analysis of the drivers of land degradation in Central Asia. The drivers of land degradation are classified into two categories: proximate and underlying drivers. The proximate drivers include unsustainable land management practices and biophysical factors, such as precipitation, length of growing periods, agro-ecological zones; on the other hand, underlying drivers consist of socio-economic and institutional factors such as poverty, land tenure security, access to credit and extension, and others. The proximate and underlying drivers of land degradation interact with each other to result in different levels of land degradation. As indicated in Chap. 7, the role of proximate drivers in affecting land degradation is well understood and there is a broad consensus in the literature about their causal mechanisms. For example, cultivating steep slopes without soil conservation measures is broadly agreed to lead to land degradation. However, the causal mechanisms of most underlying drivers are still debated (Nkonya et al. 2013), these causal mechanisms may have highly context specific characteristics (Chap. 7). For example, some studies find that poverty may lead to land degradation (Way 2006) due to lack of households' assets to invest into sustainable land management, on the other hand, some other studies find that the poor agricultural households, being more dependent on land for their livelihoods, are inherently more motivated to manage their land sustainably (Nkonya et al. 2008), for example, by applying labor intensive sustainable land management practices. Such opposing findings are prevalent in the literature on the role of most other underlying drivers (Nkonya et al. 2013). The present study studies the impacts of both underlying and proximate factors on land degradation in Central Asia. Among the proximate drivers, the study looks into the effects of annual mean precipitation, agro-ecological zones, length of growing period, temperature and precipitation variability, as well as the frequency of weather shocks. Among the underlying drivers: household characteristics; gender, age and education of the household head, distance to markets, land tenure, farm size, access to extension, and others are investigated for their impact on land degradation. The full list of the studied underlying drivers is given in the data section. The theoretical bases for their identified causal relationships with land degradation are discussed further in detail in the Results section.

Methods and Data Sources

Costs of Land Degradation

This study follows the methodology of estimating the costs of action versus inaction against land degradation described in detail in Chap. 6. First of all, the extent of land use and land cover changes (LUCC) between 2001 and 2009 in Central Asia is identified based on remotely sensed Moderate Resolution Imaging

Spectroradiometer (MODIS) satellite data (Friedl et al. 2010). The MODIS LUCC dataset distinguishes between eight types of biomes: forests, grassland, shrublands, woodlands, croplands, barren lands, urban areas and water bodies (Table 10.1). Following this, the values of ecosystem services of these biomes were estimated for Central Asia based on the benefit transfer approach using the Economics of Ecosystems and Biodiversity (TEEB) database (Van der Ploeg and de Groot 2010). We did not take into account urban areas due to lack of data on ecosystem services produced by urban areas. Moreover, the extent of urban areas in the overall territory of the region is extremely small. The TEEB database contains values of ecosystem services from over 300 case studies from across the world, including from Central Asia (cf. Chap. 6). These values are not only for direct use values, but also include indirect use values (i.e. not only provisional, but also supporting ecosystem services: nutrient cycling, soil formation; regulating: climate regulation, water purification; and cultural: aesthetic and recreational). The benefit transfer approach was employed using data both from the region and from other Asian countries, rather than other regions of the world to limit potential inaccuracies. Moreover, the values of provisional services of croplands are available from statistical databases in Central Asia and hence actual province specific values were used. Furthermore, we also conducted a local contingent valuation of ecosystem services in Uzbekistan (Chap. 21). Interestingly, it was found that the cropland values from statistical sources are very similar to those collected through local contingent valuations (1139 USD/ha from statistical sources versus 1018 USD/ha from contingent valuation). In a similar manner, the values of ecosystem services for grasslands that we estimated for Central Asian countries based on other Asian countries are broadly similar with the results of the grassland ecosystem values obtained directly in Uzbekistan through local contingent valuation (2871 USD/ha vs. 3550 USD/ha, respectively). This difference is also understandable: the regional average values attached to grassland ecosystem services are likely be lower for Central Asia as a whole, compared to only Uzbekistan, since the values attached to rangelands in Kazakhstan are very likely be lower than in Uzbekistan due to relative abundance of rangelands in Kazakhstan. On the other hand, considering that Central Asia is a diverse region, accurate estimates may require doing such contingent valuations at least in several dozens of different locations in the region, which is beyond the

Table 10.1 Land use/cover classification in Central Asia in 2001, in million ha

Land classification	Cropland	Forest	Grassland	Shrublands	Urban	Water	Barren	Total
Kazakhstan	41.3	2.1	187.0	9.2	0.3	5.7	27.8	273.3
Kyrgyzstan	3.0	0.2	10.4	3.0	0.2	0.7	2.4	20.0
Tajikistan	1.7	0.0	4.5	2.0	0.1	0.1	5.8	14.2
Turkmenistan	1.2	0.0	3.5	15.3	0.2	2.2	26.5	49.0
Uzbekistan	5.3	0.0	8.3	7.2	1.0	1.6	21.3	44.7
Total	52.5	2.3	213.0	36.7	1.8	10.4	83.7	400.4

Source Calculated using MODIS data

scope of the present study, but can be a promising topic for future studies. In such a context, using benefit transfer approach, gives first illustrative estimates of the full costs of land degradation in Central Asia. The broad accuracy of these estimates presented here is corroborated by the "ground-truthing" of the ecosystem values through local contingent valuations in Uzbekistan.

To calculate the costs of land degradation due to land use and cover change (LUCC) between 2001 and 2009, the values of ecosystem services provided by these seven biomes[1] (Obtained through benefit transfer approach described above for all except for croplands. For croplands, the province-specific values of provisional ecosystem goods were obtained from statistical databases) were multiplied by the extent of the biome in 2001 and 2009. This multiplication gives the total value of ecosystem services provided by these biomes in 2001 and 2009. Following this, changes in the area from a higher value biome to a lower value biome were used to calculate the total costs of land degradation during this period. Finally, to have the average annual change during this period, the obtained costs of land degradation were divided by eight.

In calculating the costs of action to address land degradation, three types of costs are considered: re-establishment costs from the degraded lower value biome to a higher value biome, maintenance costs and opportunity costs of the lower value biome. More formal and detailed presentation of the calculation process is given in Chap. 6.

Drivers of Sustainable Land Management

Land degradation usually occurs due to lack of use of sustainable land management practices. Those factors preventing households from adopting SLM practices also serve as drivers of land degradation, i.e. identifying the determinants of SLM adoption methodologically would also allow for identifying the drivers of land degradation. The following econometric model is applied to nationally representative agricultural household survey data from the Central Asian countries:

$$\mathbf{A} = \beta_0 + \beta_1 x_1 + \beta_2 x_2 + \beta_3 x_3 + \beta_4 x_4 + \beta_5 z_i + \varepsilon_i \quad (10.1)$$

where,

A Adoption of SLM technologies

x_1 a vector of biophysical factors (e.g. climate conditions, agro-ecological zones, etc.);

[1]Forests, woodlands, shrublands, grasslands, croplands, barren land, water bodies. Urban areas were excluded from the analysis as there are no data on the ecosystem services provided by them. Moreover, their area is very limited in the overall territory of the region. The following values were attached to each ha of these biomes: forests—5264 USD/ha, grasslands—2871 USD/ha, shrublands and woodlands—1588 USD/ha, barren lands—160 USD/ha, water bodies—8498 USD/ha, croplands—varies depending on the location, from 138 USD/ha to 4535 USD/ha.

x_2 a vector of policy-related and institutional factors (e.g. market access, land tenure, etc.);
x_3 a vector of variables representing access to rural services (e.g. access to extension);
x_4 vector of variables representing rural household level capital endowment, level of education, household size, dependency ratio, etc.;
z_i vector of country fixed effects

The dependent variable, A, is the number of sustainable land management technologies adopted by agricultural households in the region, as compiled through the agricultural household surveys, described below. In the survey, the households were asked to indicate the SLM technologies they use. They were given an open-ended list of about 30 SLM technologies[2] to choose from. Having this dependent variable allows to see not only the impact on the adoption of SLM (yes or no categories), but also the effect on the number of adopted SLM technologies.

Data

The MODIS satellite dataset is used to identify the shifts in the land use and land cover change (LUCC) in the region between 2001 and 2009 (Friedl et al. 2010). The MODIS dataset is groundtruthed and quality controlled (ibid.), with overall accuracy of land use classification at 75 % (ibid.).

The dataset used for the analysis of the drivers of land degradation comes from nationally representative agricultural household surveys carried out during 2009–2010 in Central Asia, except Turkmenistan.[3] The multi-stage survey sampling was conducted in a way to ensure representativeness of the sample with the overall population of agricultural producers across different agro-ecologies in each country (Mirzabaev 2013). The confidence interval of 95 % was used to calculate the sample size. The sample size varied between 380 and 385 respondents between the countries. To compensate for any missing or failed cases, the sample size for each country was determined to be 400 respondents, i.e. 1600 respondents in total.

[2]Bench terraces, stone bunds, mulching/surface cover, trash line, log line, grass strips, hedge rows (shrubs), minimum tillage, infiltration ditches, ridge and furrow, fallowing, improved fallowing, composting, farm yard manure application, green manure application, fertilizer (inorganic straight), fertilizer (inorganic compound), agroforestry, cover crops, crop rotation, enclosure of the land, restriction on livestock numbers (destocking), removal of unwanted bush, periodic resting of the rangeland, cattle routing, common watering points, supplementary fodder production, intercropping.

[3]The surveys were conducted by the International Center for Agricultural Research in the Dry Areas (ICARDA) and national partners under the Asian Development Bank (ADB)-funded project on climate change in the region. We are grateful to ADB for funding the surveys and to ICARDA for allowing the use of these datasets.

Uzbekistan and Kazakhstan (countries bigger in size) were first divided into major agro-ecological zones—west, south, center and east for Uzbekistan, north, center, west, south and east for Kazakhstan. Then in each zone, one province was randomly selected. In the case of Tajikistan and Kyrgyzstan (countries smaller in size) all provinces were selected for further sampling of villages in each of them. The number of respondents was allocated to each province depending on the share of the agro-ecological zone (or province, in the cases of Tajikistan and Kyrgyzstan) in the value of the national agricultural production. Following this, the total list of villages was obtained for each province selected. The villages in each province were numbered, and the corresponding numbers for the selected villages were randomly drawn using the Excel software function "RAND" (35 villages in Kazakhstan, 22 in Kyrgyzstan, 25 in Tajikistan, 25 in Uzbekistan) (Mirzabaev 2013). The number of respondents per village was evenly distributed within each province. At the village level, the list of all agricultural producers, including household producers, were obtained from the local administrations; agricultural producers were numbered, and then from this numbered list, respondents were randomly selected. Due to civil unrest during 2010 in southern Kyrgyzstan, it was impossible to include the three provinces in the south of Kyrgyzstan in the sampling. Similarly, Gorno-Badahshan autonomous province of Tajikistan was also excluded from sampling due to its very small share in agricultural production and population, as well as extremely high surveying costs due to its location in high altitude areas with difficult access (Mirzabaev 2013). In summary, in spite of these geographical gaps, the selected samples are expected to be well representative of the key areas in the region in terms of their share in the overall agricultural production and population (Fig. 10.3).

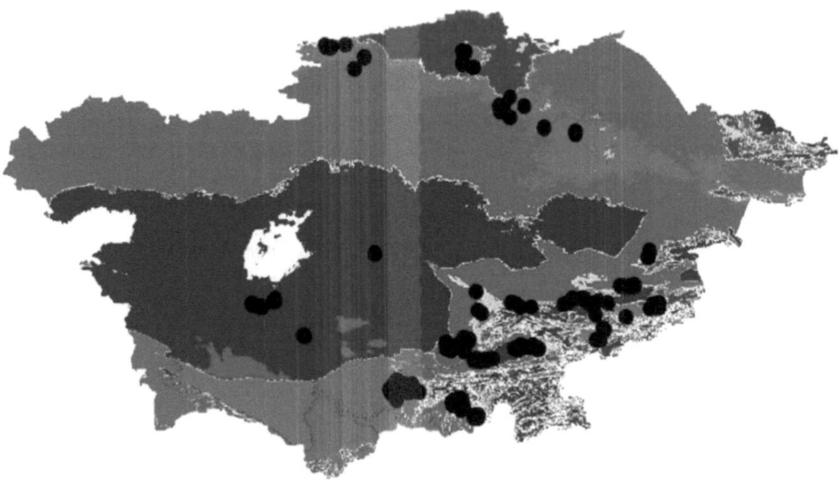

Fig. 10.3 Location of surveyed households across agro-ecological zones in Central Asia. *Source* Mirzabaev (2013)

Results

Land Use and Land Cover Dynamics in the Region

Central Asia has been experiencing dynamic land use and land cover changes (LUCC) over the last decade. Tables 10.1 and 10.2 present these changes over the period of 2001 and 2009, using the data from MODIS satellite datasets. These changes can be summarized into four sources: (1) abandonment of massive areas formerly under rainfed crop production in Kazakhstan, (2) continued desiccation of the Aral Sea, (3) conversion of a sizable share of barren lands into other land uses, mainly shrublands and grasslands, (4) increases in the forested area across the region, but especially in Kazakhstan.

The results show considerable reductions in the cropped area and similarly big increases in grasslands, both mainly in Kazakhstan. This is related to the discontinuation of rainfed crop production in vast areas in northern Kazakhstan, where abandoned croplands shifted back to their natural state of grasslands (Schierhorn et al. 2013). These grasslands were brought under cultivation in 1950s through the so-called "Virgin Lands" program to achieve grain self-sufficiency for the former Soviet Union (De Beurs and Henebry 2004).

However, the crop yields were low and unstable, and after the dissolution of the Soviet Union and institution of market-based mechanisms, crop production in many of those areas has become unprofitable. Similar shifts from croplands to grasslands and shrublands have been observed in other countries of the region, though in much smaller scales. At the same time, Turkmenistan and Uzbekistan had net gains in cropped areas over the last decade by converting grasslands and shrublands into croplands. The second major change is the decrease in the area of barren lands by 19.6 million, mainly shifting to grassland and shrublands: in Kazakhstan mostly to grasslands, whereas in more arid desertic areas of Uzbekistan and Turkmenistan to shrublands. The reasons behind this shift are not fully clear. In the case of desert biomes, Liobimtseva (2007) associates this "greening" to elevated levels of atmospheric fertilization, increasing the photosynthetic rate among desert mosses and higher forms of vegetation. The role of human management, if any, in this shift

Table 10.2 Land use/cover change in Central Asia in 2009 relative to 2001, in million ha

Land classification	Cropland	Forest	Grassland	Shrublands	Urban	Water	Barren
Kazakhstan	−10.0	1.5	19.0	1.4	0	−0.4	−12.3
Kyrgyzstan	−0.8	0.4	1.7	−0.9	0	0.0	−0.4
Tajikistan	−0.4	0.2	−0.5	0.2	0	0.0	0.5
Turkmenistan	0.6	0.0	−1.1	2.7	0	0.0	−2.3
Uzbekistan	0.4	0.1	0.4	4.3	0	−0.4	−5.1
Total	−10.3	2.2	20.0	7.6	0.0	−0.8	−19.6

Source Calculated using MODIS data

is not yet studied. The third major change includes doubling of forested areas, although from a very low base of 2.3 million to 4.5 million ha, mainly through shifts from woodlands and grasslands to forests in Kazakhstan (Almaty and Eastern Kazakhstan provinces). The fourth major land use change is associated with the continued desiccation of the water bodies, principally, the Aral Sea, where about 0.4 million ha in Kazakhstan and Uzbekistan each have shifted from being under water to barren land since 2001. Although the magnitude of this shift is dwarfed in terms of area by other major land use changes in the region, however, the socio-economic, environmental and symbolic importance of this land use change is, arguably, the most widely felt and studied in the region.

Economic Impacts of Land Degradation

Costs of Land Degradation

The results show that the total annual costs of land degradation in Central Asia due to land use change only (i.e. without the costs of land degradation due to lower soil and land productivity within the same land use), are about 5.85 billion USD between 2001 and 2009 (Table 10.3).

Most of these costs, about 4.6 billion USD are related with shifts from grasslands to lower value shrublands and barren lands: in total, about 14 million ha grasslands have shifted to shrublands and barren lands in the region between 2001 and 2009, highlighting the massive problem of rangeland degradation. Another 0.75 billion USD were due to shifts from shrublands to barren lands, especially in the parts of the region near the Aral Sea, highlighting the growing problem of desertification. Deforestation has led to about 0.32 billion USD in losses, whereas the abandonment of croplands has resulted in about 110 million USD of losses, annually. The latter figure does not comprise the losses in crop yields in those croplands that continue to

Table 10.3 The costs of land degradation in Central Asia through land use and cover change

Country	Annual cost of land degradation in 2009, in billion USD	Annual cost of land degradation per capita, in USD	GDP in 2009, current billion USD	The cost of land degradation as a share of GDP (%)
Kazakhstan	3.06	1782	115	3
Kyrgyzstan	0.55	822	5	11
Tajikistan	0.50	609	5	10
Turkmenistan	0.87	1083	20	4
Uzbekistan	0.83	237	33	3
Total	5.85	769	178	3

Source The authors' calculations using MODIS and TEEB datasets

be cultivated but with lower economic returns due to land degradation. Presently, there are no comprehensive and reliable databases to estimate the costs of land degradation due to lower productivity of degraded croplands in all Central Asia. The estimates presented in Chap. 6 indicate at about 330 million USD of annual losses for three crops—wheat, rice and maize, with most of the costs coming through loss of soil carbon storage potential due to land degradation, rather than actual losses due to lower yields under land degrading agricultural practices. Hence, the estimates of 5.85 billion USD of annual costs due to LUCC and potentially another 0.33 billion from lower crop productivity and loss of carbon sequestration in degraded croplands from growing wheat, maize and rice, are conservative estimates of land degradation costs. The actual costs are likely to be higher. Similarly, the cost figures for other land uses are also underestimated as they do not include losses in productivity without land use change (for example, grasslands providing lower vegetation for livestock grazing, etc.). Finally, calculated land degradation costs per capita also vary among countries: the highest in Kazakhstan (about 1800 USD annually) and lowest in Uzbekistan (about 250 USD annually).

However, along with land degradation, there is also land improvement happening in the region through land use change. In fact, the annual monetary amount of land improvement is around 13 billion USD, exceeding land degradation through land use change (Table 10.4). This amount also does not include potential improvements in soil fertility due to application of SLM practices, when land use does not change. The major contributors to this land improvement is the transition of low productive croplands in northern Kazakhstan to grasslands, including the improved provision of ecosystem services (about 10 billion USD): a seemingly very contradictory finding given that many land degradation mapping exercises, including both by Bai et al. (2008) and Le et al. (2014) indicate massive land degradation in the area. However, there is nothing surprising if we take into account that this area of abandoned cropland is returning to original land cover types prevalent before their conversion to cultivation (Schierhorn et al. 2013): although soil itself might have recovered some of its lost carbon due to abandonment (ibid.), and is providing higher levels of ecosystem services in terms of carbon sequestration, nutrient cycling, etc., i.e. may have higher Total Economic Values, the

Table 10.4 Total economic value (TEV) of land ecosystems and GDP in Central Asia, in billion USD, constant for 2007

Country	TEV 2001	TEV 2009	GDP in 2009	Value of ecosystems per capita, in USD	GDP/TEV (%)
Kazakhstan	577	639	115	55,169	18
Kyrgyzstan	40	45	5	14,620	11
Tajikistan	20	19	5	6261	27
Turkmenistan	40	42	20	13,795	48
Uzbekistan	44	53	33	3 481	63
Total	720	797	178	22,935	20

Source The authors' calculations using MODIS and TEEB datasets

cultivated land may elicit a higher NDVI value than abandoned land with sparser vegetation, leading to mapping this area as degraded. From the economic perspective, these areas in northern Kazakhstan had very low crop productivity and extremely low profitability, in fact, periodically even leading to economic losses during often recurring drought years. However, especially during good rainfall years and extensive operation, they would also generate tangible local benefits in terms of provisional goods (grain). As grasslands, they may have larger global benefits (generating higher levels of supporting and regulating ecosystem services) than as croplands, however, these global benefits are not internalized locally. Other major sources of land improvement include afforestation on additional 2.2 million ha (about 1.4 billion USD) and conversion of shrublands to grasslands and croplands (1.6 billion USD).

The total economic value of ecosystem goods and services is estimated to equal about 800 billion USD in the region, exceeding the conventional GDP by 5 times. The relative value of ecosystems per capita depends on the territory, land use/cover characteristics and population. In this regard, Kazakhstan with its huge territory, most of it under higher valued grasslands, and relatively smaller population has the highest per capita value of ecosystems in the region. In contrast, Uzbekistan with the biggest population in the region and almost half of its territory consisting of barren deserts, has the lowest per capita monetary value of ecosystems. From another perspective, if in Kyrgyzstan: the share of GDP in the Total Economic Value is just 11 %, this number is 48 % in Turkmenistan and 63 % in Uzbekistan, implying that population pressure on ecosystems is much higher in Uzbekistan and Turkmenistan.

Cost of Action to Address Land Degradation

The results of the analysis of the costs of action are given in Table 10.5. The results show that the costs of action against land degradation are lower than the costs of inaction in Central Asia by more than 5 times over a 30-year horizon, meaning that each dollar spent on addressing land degradation is likely to have about 5 dollars of returns. This is a strong economic justification favoring action versus inaction. Thus, the costs of action were found to equal about 53 billion USD over a 30-year horizon, whereas if nothing is done, the resulting losses may equal almost 288 billion USD during the same period. Almost 98 % of the costs of action are made up of the opportunity costs of action, for example, the value of new shrublands in areas where the original grasslands are being restored, whereas the actual implementation costs were found to be relatively smaller.

The costs of actions, however, do not include the potential transaction costs of implementing SLM-oriented reforms at the national level, or of transaction costs of adopting SLM technologies at the landusers level, as presently, there are no data available on these transaction costs.

Table 10.5 Costs of action versus inaction in Central Asia

Country	Annual TEV cost of land degradation in 2009, in billion USD	Annual provisional cost of land degradation in 2009, in billion USD	Cost of action (6 years), in billion USD	Cost of action (30 years), in billion USD	Of which, the opportunity cost of action, in billion USD	Cost of inaction (6 years), in billion USD	Cost of inaction (30 years), in billion USD	Ratio of cost of inaction/action
Kazakhstan	24	11	22	22	21	102	138	6
Kyrgyzstan	4	2	6	6	6	22	29	5
Tajikistan	4	2	4	4	4	17	24	6
Turkmenistan	7	3	10	10	9	35	48	5
Uzbekistan	7	3	11	11	11	36	49	5
Central Asia	47	20	53	53	51	213	288	6

Drivers of Land Degradation

Data Descriptives

Table 10.6 reports descriptive statistics for the variables of interest for the analysis of SLM adoption for each country. In the analysis, to ensure that results are not driven by a small amount of large outliers, log transformations have been applied where appropriate. Table 10.6 reports all the variables in their level form for more convenient understanding and comparisons.

The distribution of the number of SLM technologies adopted by the respondents is quite dispersed, ranging from 0 to 15 (Fig. 10.4). About 39 % of the surveyed agricultural households in the region did not use any SLM technology, while the remaining 61 % used at least one SLM technology. Among the most frequent used SLM technologies are the integrated soil fertility management by applying varying levels of fertilizers and manure, as well as more efficient irrigation techniques such as drip irrigation, or the use of portable chutes for irrigation, especially in sloping areas.

Moreover, if the use of SLM practices is taken by country, the conditional variance of the distribution is higher in all cases than conditional mean (Fig. 10.5). The number of adopted SLM technologies varies among the countries of the region, with higher number of adoptions among the surveyed agricultural households in

Table 10.6 Data descriptives

Variables	Kazakhstan	Kyrgyzstan	Tajikistan	Uzbekistan
Number of SLM technologies used	2.8	0.2	4.4	4.9
Household size	6	6	8	6
Dependency ratio	0.7	0.7	0.7	0.8
Average age of household head	51	50	52	47
Length of growing periods	97	102	131	92
Number of crops grown	0.99	1.03	2.12	3.21
Annual precipitation	402	448	486	289
Mean annual temperature	7.0	5.7	14.4	14.4
Frequency of weather shocks	2.7	0.4	1.1	1.4
Land tenure (0—not private, 1—private)	0.63	0.90	0.73	0.60
Farm size	194	5	4	28
Access to extension (0—no, 1—yes)	0.1	0.2	0.7	0.7
Value of livestock (in USD)	5255	8998	869	6796
Distance to markets (in min)	133	150	59	75
Value of total assets (in USD)	83,123	20,727	7407	34,939

Source The survey

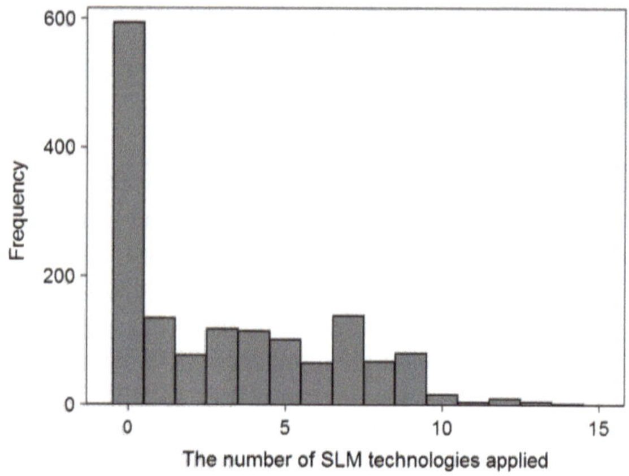

Fig. 10.4 The distribution of the number of SLM technologies used among households in Central Asia. *Source* The survey

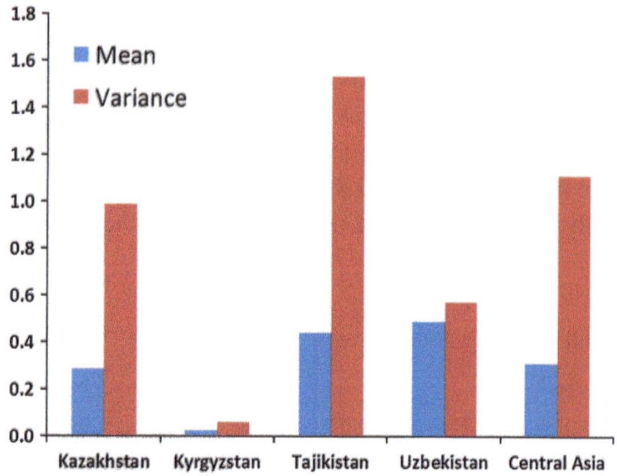

Fig. 10.5 The mean and variance of the number of SLM technologies used. *Source* The survey

Tajikistan and Uzbekistan. On the other hand, the variance of the number of adopted technologies is higher in Tajikistan and Kazakhstan, meaning that in these two countries there are bigger differences among households in the number of the SLM technologies they adopt.

Furthermore, the dependent variable on the number of SLM technologies used is a count variable. Such a nature of the dependent variable requires the application of negative binomial regression, which is a generalization of Poisson regression for count dependent variables with dispersed distribution (Hilbe 2011). Figure 10.6 gives the information on the spatial distribution of adoption of SLM technologies in land degradation hotspots (for hotspots of land degradation see Fig. 10.2 and Chap. 4). Based on this overlay, it seems that higher SLM adoption rates are more closely associated with areas with more land degradation hotspots, i.e. SLM technologies are applied more in areas with higher land degradation.

The results of the regression on the determinants of the number of SLM technologies used by households are given in Table 10.7. The overall test of model fit

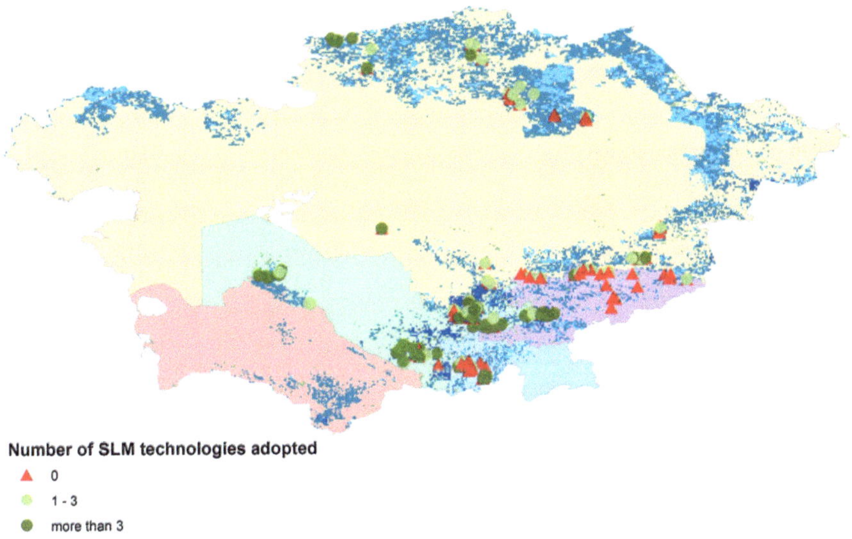

Fig. 10.6 Spatial distribution of SLM adoption. *Note* The hotspots of land degradation are given *blue colors*, for more spatial information on land degradation see Fig. 10.2. *Source* The survey

Table 10.7 Drivers of sustainable land management in Central Asia

Variables	Coefficient	(95 % confidence interval)	
Distance to markets (log)	−0.0565**	−0.11	−0.01
Household size	−0.0149**	−0.03	0.00
Dependency ratio	−0.0619**	−0.11	−0.01
Education (base—Primary education only)			
Middle school	0.0452	−0.15	0.24
High school	−0.00,909	−0.21	0.20
College	0.0421	−0.16	0.24
University degree	0.0691	−0.13	0.27
Ph.D.	0.598*	−0.08	1.28
Country			
Kyrgyzstan	−2.642***	−2.94	−2.34
Tajikistan	−0.0634	−0.34	0.22
Uzbekistan	0.102	−0.10	0.30
Gender (base—Female)	−0.0737	−0.18	0.03
Age	0.00281	0.00	0.01
Agroecological zone (base—Arid)			
Semiarid	−0.770***	−0.97	−0.57
Sub-humid	−1.060***	−1.35	−0.77

(continued)

Table 10.7 (continued)

Variables	Coefficient	(95 % confidence interval)	
Humid	−1.269***	−1.92	−0.62
Length of the growing period	0.00900***	0.00	0.01
Number of crops grown	0.00198	−0.03	0.03
Annual precipitation	0.000404	0.00	0.00
Mean annual temperature	0.0106	−0.01	0.03
Variance of temperature	−0.137***	−0.20	−0.08
Variance of precipitation	−0.00308***	0.00	0.00
Frequency of weather shocks	0.0217***	0.01	0.03
Farm size (log)	0.0110	−0.03	0.05
Private land ownership	−0.0624	−0.20	0.08
Interaction of private land ownership and farm size	−0.0573**	−0.10	−0.01
Access to extension	0.115**	0.02	0.21
Knowledge of SLM technologies	0.0895***	0.08	0.10
Source of SLM knowledge: other farmers	0.0771***	0.07	0.09
Source of SLM knowledge: farmers' association	−0.0796***	−0.09	−0.07
Source of SLM knowledge: media	0.0650***	0.03	0.10
Value of livestock (log)	−1.54e−05**	0.00	0.00
Interaction of crop producer and value of livestock	2.21e−05***	0.00	0.00
Value of total assets	−2.10e−07	0.00	0.00
Constant	0.590**	0.04	1.14
Observations	1519		

*** means statistically significant p-values <0.01, ** p-values < 0.05, * p-values <0.1

shows that the model is statistically significant at 1 % (LR $chi^2(34) = 1681.75$, Prob > $chi^2 = 0.0000$, and Pseudo $R^2 = 0.2460$). The likelihood ratio test comparing this negative binomial model to the Poisson model is statistically significant at 1 %, suggesting that the negative binomial model fits the data better than the Poisson model.

The regression results point at several variables which have statistically significant relationship with the number of SLM technologies adopted by households. For example, one percent increase in the distance to markets could decrease the log count of the number of SLM technologies adopted by 0.0565. Similarly, one unit increase in household size could decrease the log count of the number of SLM technologies adopted by 0.0149.

In this manner, the results of the model show that the key underlying factors positively associated with SLM adoptions in Central Asia are better market access, access to extension, learning about SLM from other farmers, private land tenure among smallholder farmers, livestock ownership among crop producers, lower household sizes and lower dependency ratios.

The distance to markets variable shows the time it takes for the household to reach the nearest urban market with at least 50,000 residents (Nelson 2008). The results show that the households with better market access are likely to adopt higher number of SLM practices, as the better market access is likely to provide with more incentives for increased production and productivity, making the opportunity cost of foregone benefits due to land degradation much higher. Similarly, access to extension is found to increase the number of SLM adoptions, by increasing farmers' knowledge about SLM practices and their awareness about the benefits of SLM. The more number of SLM technologies farmers know, the more SLM technologies they adopt. What is interesting, farmers adopt more SLM practices when they learn about them from their peers—other farmers: this is probably due to the fact that farmers trust more the successful experiences of other farmers. On the contrary, when the source of knowledge are the farmers' association, a more institutionalized, and often state-operated organizations, there is a statistically significant negative association with the number of SLM technologies used, highlighting the need for increasing the relevance and demand orientation of the farmer training courses conducted by the farmers' associations.

These estimates cannot tell much about the impact of private land tenure on SLM adoptions in general, however, the results show that among smallholder farmers having private land tenure has positive influence on SLM adoptions (the interaction of private land tenure and farm size). This may be due to the fact that smaller sizes combined with the incentives coming from private land tenure may allow for more flexibility in farming operations. Specifically, smaller scale farmers are usually specialized in the production of vegetables and fruits in the region, which are considered to be as higher value cash crops, compared to grains. Moreover, in Uzbekistan, small household farms are also exempt from growing two State-mandated crops (where the State regulates both the production process and the marketing of the produce): cotton and wheat, and can sell the vegetables and fruits they produce directly in the market. More detailed information on the institutional aspects of agriculture and of agricultural reforms in the Central Asian countries can be found in Pomfret (2008), Petrick et al. (2013), and OECD (2013).

Owning livestock is expected to provide with savings mechanism for flexible capital which can be invested into SLM technology adoptions. The findings here corroborate this point for crop producing farmers in the sample. Higher livestock ownership among crop producers is associated with larger number of technologies adopted. However, higher livestock values, in general, are negatively associated with the number of SLM technologies adopted. This is not very surprising given that the pastoralist households in the sample have naturally much higher values for livestock ownership, but they apply fewer SLM technologies (the presented list of SLM options includes pastoralists-oriented practices, such as rotational grazing, enclosures, etc.).

Most household characteristics, such as gender, education, and age of the household head, are not significant in the sample. However, household size and dependency ratio are inversely related to the number of SLM technology adoptions. In the case of dependency ratio, it could be due to higher risk aversion among households with higher dependency ratios, whereas the negative impact of larger household size on adoption is somewhat surprising since larger households could provide with more family labor making the adoption of labor intensive SLM technologies easier.

Among significant proximate drivers positively influencing SLM adoptions are being in more arid agro-ecological zones, longer growing period for crops, lower variance in annual precipitation and temperature, more experiences of past weather shocks. More arid agro—ecologies in Central Asia are associated with more intensive agricultural production through application of irrigation and the related higher productivity, making the value of agricultural lands in these areas much higher, thus increasing the opportunity costs of losses due to land degradation and providing with higher incentives for SLM adoptions. The same mechanism explains the significant positive coefficient of the length of growing periods. The higher variability of long-term (30 years) rainfall and precipitation has negative association with SLM adoption. Most agricultural technologies do not perform equally well, for example, under drought and flooding, or under frosts and heatwaves. Higher climate variability leads to inconsistent performance and returns from a given SLM technology, consequently reducing the likelihood of its being adopted. However, past own experiences of short-term weather shocks (as opposed to climate variability) are found to have positive relationship with SLM adoption, as farmers having more experiences of weather shocks may seek ways on how to minimize their impacts by trying out various SLM technologies.

Discussion

SLM technologies are usually innovative approaches that are aimed to reduce the pressure of conventional unsustainable practices. Yet, such technologies are also accompanied by high uncertainty in their economic and environmental performance. Land users may not adopt these options unless they observe their costs and benefits. Accordingly, the dissemination of information on SLM technologies is necessary to tackle the problems of land degradation. This was also confirmed in this study, where it was shown that access to extension plays a vital role in adopting SLM by rural households. Development of extension services may accelerate the process of SLM adoption. Observing the performance of technologies will lead to learning effect and will further boost the expansion of SLM technologies. However, even if sufficient information is available about the SLM practices the lack of private/secure land tenure can be one of the major barriers for investments into such practices in the region. In most of the Central Asian countries farmers have usufruct rights for land. When farmers are uncertain if they will be allowed to continue using this land in the future, as rational decision makers they would rather maximize their immediate returns, and avoid making any costly long-term investments, thus effectively “mining” the land. Therefore, transparent and objective implementation of inalienable user rights to land for a long and secure time horizon would be a vital option to promote longer term SLM investments by farmers. On the other hand, the experiences from the region show that private and even secure, land tenure do not automatically lead to wide-scale adoption of SLM technologies. Some, but not all, SLM technologies may require sizable upfront investments and take several years before these investments are recovered through increased returns (e.g., drip irrigation). There is a need for a wider package of measures to accompany land tenure security for it to be effective in terms of addressing land degradation. Most of the SLM practices require initial investments and generate full benefits only after some time. Thus, farmers, especially poorest, may not have sufficient funds to cover costs of SLM while considering that its benefits would be generated in long-term and especially when there are often high and immediate opportunity costs. Therefore, measures in the form of fiscal and credit incentives to farmers would be important to reduce the burden of high initial costs and provide financial incentives to invest into the SLM. The land tenure is often connected to the state procurement policies, mandating cultivation of certain crops. Failure to accomplish this policy often leads to the expropriation of farmland (Djanibekov et al. 2012a). Abolishing the State quota system, notably for cotton and wheat, is often considered to increase crop diversification and consequently agricultural production and rural livelihoods (e.g. Djanibekov et al. 2013).

The findings of this study show that the costs of actions to address land degradation are only a fraction of the costs of inaction. The question is then why the action undertaken so far was not sufficient to address land degradation if the economic returns from sustainable land management are so high. This analysis is conducted from the social perspectives taking into account both provisional and non-provisional ecosystem services lost due to land degradation (i.e. both private and global public goods). However, rational private landusers would usually include only the private costs of land degradation in their decision making framework because they cannot internalize the benefits from safeguarding or restoring the non-provisional ecosystem services of land (such as for example, climate regulation, nutrient cycling). Since many of these non-provisional ecosystem services of land are global public goods, even national Governments are less likely to incorporate the full value of the lost land ecosystem services into their calculations, since they as well cannot internalize fully the benefits of SLM within the country. Thus, a wider use of payment for ecosystem services (PES) approaches through international investments could potentially help in reducing this lack of incentives to invest into SLM. Finally, this analysis does not include all the potential costs of action to address land degradation. Specifically, transaction costs of implementing SLM-oriented reforms at the national level, or of transaction costs of adopting SLM technologies at the landusers level, are not included, as presently, there are no data available on these transaction costs. Moreover, even when the land users would decide to take action (often the losses of provisional services alone may be more than the costs of action, thus justifying it from private perspectives as well), they may be constrained by lack of information about available SLM options, lack of access to markets and credit, with often long-term nature of investments and high upfront costs, etc.—the conditions which are prevalent across the region, which were, among other factors, also shown in the drivers analysis above as constraining factors for SLM adoptions in Central Asia. Finally, even under ideal conditions for SLM investments, landusers may still decide not to invest in land if the opportunity costs of other investment options available to them are higher than the benefits from sustainable land management (e.g. investing in their children's education and health, with potential longer-term higher returns, rather than in SLM).

Conclusions

Central Asia has four major agro-ecological regions: irrigated, rainfed, rangeland and mountainous areas. The nature of land degradation problems in the region can be best illustrated along these four major agro-ecological regions. The major land use changes in the region over the last decade, which have triggered land degradation processes in the region, can be summarized into four sources: (1) abandonment of massive areas formerly under rainfed crop production in Kazakhstan, (2) continued desiccation of the Aral Sea, (3) conversion of a sizable share of barren lands into other land uses, mainly shrublands and grasslands, (4) increases in the forested area across the region, but especially in Kazakhstan. The main areas affected by land degradation is concentrated in the north of Kazakhstan, and stretches over Eastern Kazakhstan to the southern part of Central Asia, covering Kyrgyzstan, the north-west of Tajikistan and the southern parts of Uzbekistan and Turkmenistan.

The estimates show that the annual cost of land degradation in the region due to land use change is about 6 billion USD, most which due to rangeland degradation (4.6 billion USD), followed by desertification (0.8 billion USD), deforestation (0.3 billion USD) and abandonment of croplands (0.1 billion USD). The costs of action against land degradation are lower than the costs of inaction in Central Asia by more than 5 times over a 30-year horizon, meaning that each dollar spent on addressing land degradation is likely to have about 5 dollars of returns. This is a very strong economic justification favoring action vs. inaction against land degradation. Thus, the costs of action were found to equal about 53 billion USD over a 30-year horizon, whereas if nothing is done, the resulting losses may equal almost 288 billion USD during the same period.

The key underlying factors conducive to SLM adoptions in Central Asia are found to be better market access, access to extension, learning about SLM from other farmers, private land tenure among smallholder farmers, livestock ownership among crop producers, lower household sizes and lower dependency ratios. Among significant proximate drivers positively influencing SLM adoptions are being in more arid agro-ecological zones, longer growing period for crops, lower variance in annual precipitation and temperature, more experiences of past weather shocks.

References

ADB. (2007). *Key indicators 2007* (Vol. 38). Manila, Philippines.

Akramhanov, A., & Vlek, P. L. G. (2012). The assessment of spatial distribution of soil salinity risk using neural network. *Environmental Monitoring and Assessment, 184*(4), 2475–2485.

Akramkhanov, A., Martius, C., Park, S. J., & Hendrickx, J. M. H. (2011). Environmental factors of spatial distribution of soil salinity on flat irrigated terrain. *Geoderma, 163*, 55–62.

Alimaev, I. (2003). Transhumant ecosystems: Fluctuations in seasonal pasture productivity. In C. Kerven (Ed.) *Prospects for Pastoralism in Kazakhstan and Turkmenistan: From State Farms to Private Flocks*. RoutledgeCurzon: London and New York.

Alimaev, I., Torekhanov, A., Smailov, V. K., Yurchenka, V., Sisatov, Zh, & Shanbev, K. (2006). South Kazakhstan pasture use results. Paper prepared for the advanced research workshop on the socio-economic causes and consequences of desertification in Central Asia, Bishkek, Kyrgyzstan May 30–June 1. In R. H. Behnke, L. Alibekov, & I. I. Alimaev (Eds.), *The human causes and consequences of desertification (Forthcoming)*. Dordrecht: Springer.

Bai, Z. G., Dent, D. L., Olsson, L., & Schaepman, M. E. (2008). *Global assessment of land degradation and improvement 1: Identification by remote sensing*. Report 2008/01, FAO/ISRIC, Rome/Wageningen.

Bekturova, G., & Romanova, N. (2007). Traditional land management knowledge in Central Asia: Resource pack. S-Print: Almaty, 86 p.

Buhlmann, E. (2006). *Assessing soil erosion and conservation in the loess area of Faizabad, Western Tajikistan*. Diploma Thesis. Faculty of Natural Sciences. University of Bern. 91 p.

Central Asian Countries Initiative for Land Management (CACILM) (2006a). *Republic of Kazakhstan National Programming Framework*. Prepared by UNCCD National Working Group of the Republic of Kazakhstan. Draft, 01 February 2006. http://www.adb.org/Projects/CACILM/documents.asp

CACILM. (2006b). *Republic of Kyrgyzstan National Programming Framework*. Prepared by UNCCD National Working Group of the Kyrgyz Republic. Draft, February 01, 2006. http://www.adb.org/Projects/CACILM/documents.asp

CACILM. (2006c). *Republic of Tajikistan National Programming Framework*. Prepared by UNCCD National Working Group of the Republic of Tajikistan. Draft, March 14, 2006. http://www.adb.org/Projects/CACILM/documents.asp

CACILM. (2006d). *Turkmenistan National Programming Framework*. Prepared by Turkmenistan UNCCD National Working Group. February 28, 2006. http://www.adb.org/Projects/CACILM/documents.asp

CACILM. (2006e). *Republic of Uzbekistan National Programming Framework*. Prepared by Republic of Uzbekistan UNCCD National Working Group. Draft, February 28, 2006. http://www.adb.org/Projects/CACILM/documents.asp

Daily, G. C., Kareiva, P. M., Polasky, S., Ricketts, T. H., & Tallis, H. (2011). Mainstreaming natural capital into decisions. In *Natural capital: theory and practice of mapping ecosystem services* (pp. 3–14).

De Beurs, K. M., & Henebry, G. M. (2004). Land surface phenology, climatic variation, and institutional change: Analyzing agricultural land cover change in Kazakhstan. *Remote Sensing of Environment, 89*, 497–509.

Djanibekov, U., Khamzina, A., Djanibekov, N., & Lamers, J. P. A. (2012a). How attractive are short-term CDM forestations in arid regions? The case of irrigated croplands in Uzbekistan. *Forest Policy and Economics, 21*, 108–117.

Djanibekov, N., Sommer, R., & Djanibekov, U. (2013). Evaluation of effects of cotton policy changes on land and water use in Uzbekistan: Application of a bio-economic farm model at the level of a water users association. *Agricultural Systems, 118*, 1–13.

Djanibekov, N., Van Assche, K., Bobojonov, I., & Lamers, J. P. A. (2012b). Farm restructuring and land consolidation in Uzbekistan: new farms with old barriers. *Europe-Asia Studies, 64*(6), 1101–1126.

Dubovyk, O., Menz, G., Conrad, C., Kan, E., Machwitz, M., & Khamzina, A. (2013). Spatio-temporal analyses of cropland degradation in the irrigated lowlands of Uzbekistan using remote-sensing and logistic regression modeling. *Environmental Monitoring and Assessment, 185*, 4775–4790.

Farrington, J. D. (2005). De-development in Eastern Kyrgyzstan and persistence of semi-nomadic livestock herding. *Nomadic Peoples, 9*(1&2), 171–196.

Friedl, M. A., Sulla-Menashe, D., Tan, B., Schneider, A., Ramankutty, N., Sibley, A., & Huang, X. (2010). MODIS collection 5 global land cover: Algorithm refinements and characterization of new datasets. *Remote Sensing of Environment, 114*(1), 168–182.

Gintzburger, G., Saidi, S., & Soti, V., (2005). *Rangelands of the Ravnina region in the Karakum desert (Turkmenistan): Current condition and utilization.* INCO-COPERNICUS/RTD Project: ICA2-CT-2000–10015. Montpellier: Centre de coopération internationale en recherche agronomique pour le développement (Cirad).

Gupta, R., Kienzler, K., Mirzabaev, A., Martius, C., de Pauw, E., Shideed, K., Oweis, T., Thomas, R., Qadir, M., Sayre, K., Carli, C., Saparov, A., Bekenov, M., Sanginov, S., Nepesov, M., & Ikramov, R. (2009). *Research prospectus: A vision for sustainable land management research in Central Asia.* ICARDA Central Asia and Caucasus Program. Sustainable Agriculture in Central Asia and the Caucasus Series No. 1. CGIAR-PFU, Tashkent, Uzbekistan. 84 pp.

Hilbe, J. (2011). *Negative binomial regression*. Cambridge: Cambridge University Press.

Ji, C. (2008). *Central Asian Countries initiative for land management multicountry partnership framework support project.* Tashkent: ADB.

Kazbekov, J., Abdullaev, I., Anarbekov, O., & Jumaboev, K. (2007). *Improved water management through effective water users associations in Central Asia: Case of Kyrgyzstan* (No. H040650). International Water Management Institute.

Kerven, C. (Ed). (2003). *Prospects for Pastoralism in Kazakhstan and Turkmenistan: From State farms to Private flocks*. London: Routledge Curzon, 276 p.

Kienzler, K. M., Lamers, J. P. A., McDonald, A., Mirzabaev, A., Ibragimov, N., Egamberdiev, O., et al. (2012). Conservation agriculture in Central Asia—What do we know and where do we go from here? *Field Crops Research, 132*, 95–105.

Klein, I., Gessner, U., & Kuenzer, C. (2012). Regional land cover mapping and change detection in Central Asia using MODIS time-series. *Applied Geography, 35*, 219–234. doi:10.1016/j.apgeog.2012.06.016.

Le, Q. B., Nkonya, E., & Mirzabaev, A. (2014). *Biomass productivity-based mapping of global land degradation hotspots*. ZEF-Discussion Papers on Development Policy, (193). Bonn, Germany.

Le, Q. B., Tamene, L., & Vlek, P. L. G. (2012). Multi-pronged assessment of land degradation in West Africa to assess the importance of atmospheric fertilization in masking the processes involved. *Global and Planetary Change, 92–93*, 71–81.

Liobimtseva, E. (2007). Possible changes in the carbon budget of arid and semi-arid Central Asia inferred from land-use/landcover analyses during 1981–2001. In *Climate change and terrestrial carbon sequestration in Central Asia* (pp. 441–452). London: Taylor & Francis.

Mirzabaev, A. (2013). *Climate volatility and change in Central Asia: Economic impacts and adaptation*. PhD thesis at Agricultural Faculty, University of Bonn. urn:nbn:de:hbz:5n-3238

Nelson, A. (2008). *Accessibility model and population estimates*. Background paper for the World Bank's World Development Report 2009.

Nkonya, E., Gerber, N., Baumgartner, P., von Braun, J., De Pinto, A., Graw, V., Kato, E., Kloos, J., Walter, T. (2011). *The economics of desertification, land degradation, and drought:*

Towards an integrated global assessment. ZEF-Discussion Papers on Development Policy No. 150, Center for Development Research, Bonn, pp. 184.

Nkonya, E., Pender, J., Kaizzi, K., Kato, E., Mugarura, S., Ssali, H., & Muwonge, J. (2008). *Linkages between land management, land degradation, and poverty in Sub-Saharan Africa: The case of Uganda*. IFPRI Research Report 159, Washington D.C., USA.

Nkonya, E., Von Braun, J., Mirzabaev, A., Le, Q. B., Kwon, H. Y., & Kirui, O. (2013). *Economics of land degradation initiative: Methods and approach for global and national assessments*. ZEF-Discussion Papers on Development Policy (183).

O'Hara, S. L. (1997). Irrigation and land degradation: Implications for agriculture in Turkmenistan, Central Asia. *Journal of Arid Environments, 37*, 165–179.

OECD. (2013). *OECD review of agricultural policies: Kazakhstan 2013*. Paris: OECD Publishing.

Pender, J., Mirzabaev, A., & Kato, E. (2009). *Economic analysis of sustainable land management options in Central Asia* (Vol. 168). Final report for the ADB. IFPRI/ICARDA.

Petrick, M., Wandel, J., & Karsten, K. (2013). Rediscovering the virgin lands: Agricultural investment and rural livelihoods in a Eurasian frontier area. *World Development, 43*, 164–179.

Pomfret, R. (2008). Tajikistan, Turkmenistan, and Uzbekistan. In K. Anderson & J. F. M. Swinnen (Eds.), *Distortions to agricultural incentives in Europe's transition economies* (pp. 297–338). Washington, D.C.: World Bank.

Propastin, P. A., Kappas, M., & Muratova, N. R. (2008). Inter-annual changes in vegetation activities and their relationship to temperature and precipitation in Central Asia from 1982 to 2003. *Journal of Environmental Informatics, 12*, 75–87.

Qadir, M., Noble, A. D., Qureshi, A. S., Gupta, R. K., Yuldashev, T., & Karimov, A. (2009, May). Salt-induced land and water degradation in the Aral Sea basin: A challenge to sustainable agriculture in Central Asia. In *Natural Resources Forum* (Vol. 33, No. 2, pp. 134–149). New York: Blackwell Publishing Ltd.

Reay, D. S., Dentener, F., Smith, P., Grace, J., & Feely, R. (2008). Global nitrogen deposition and carbon sinks. *Nature Geoscience, 1*, 430–437.

Reynolds, J. F., Smith, D. M. S., Lambin, E. F., Turner, B. L., Mortimore, M., Batterbury, S. P., & Walker, B. (2007). Global desertification: Building a science for dryland development. *Science, 316*(5826), 847–851.

Robinson, S., Whitton, M., Biber-Klemm, S., & Muzofirshoev, N. (2010). The impact of land-reform legislation on pasture tenure in Gorno-Badakhshan: From common resource to private property? *Mountain Research and Development, 30*(1), 4–13.

Saigal, S. (2003). *Kazakhstan: Issues and approaches to combat desertification*. ADB and The Global Mechanism.

Schierhorn, F., Müller, D., Beringer, T., Prishchepov, A. V., Kuemmerle, T., & Balmann, A. (2013). Post-Soviet cropland abandonment and carbon sequestration in European Russia, Ukraine, and Belarus. *Global Biogeochemical Cycles, 27*(4), 1175–1185.

Schiermeier, Q. (2013). Renewable power: Germany's energy gamble. *Nature, 496*(7444), 156–158.

Sutton, W., Whitford, P., Stephens, E. M., Galinato, S. P., Nevel, B., Plonka, B., & Karamete, E. (2007). *Integrating environment into agriculture and forestry. Progress and prospects in Eastern Europe and Central Asia*. Kosovo: World Bank.

Suzuki, K., (2003). *Sustainable and environmentally sound land use in rural areas with special attention to land degradation*. Issue Paper. Asia-Pacific Forum for Environment and Development Expert Meeting. January 23, 2003. Guilin, People's Republic of China.

Van der Ploeg, S. & de Groot, R. S. (2010). The TEEB valuation database—A searchable database of 1310 estimates of monetary values of ecosystem services. Foundation for Sustainable Development, Wageningen, the Netherlands.

Way, S. A. (2006). Examining the links between poverty and land degradation: From blaming the poor toward recognizing the rights of the poor. In P. Johnson, K. Mayrand, & M. Paquin

(Eds.), *Governing global desertification: Linking environmental degradation, poverty, and participation* (pp. 27–41). Burlington, VT: Ashgate.
World Bank. (1998). *Aral Sea Basin program (Kazakhstan, Kyrgyz Republic, Tajikistan, Turkmenistan and Uzbekistan): Water and Environmental Management Project* (pp. 55). Project Document. Washington DC, USA, Global Environment Division, World Bank.
World Meteorological Organization. (2012). WMO greenhouse gases bulletin: the state of greenhouse gases in the atmosphere using global observations through 2011. In *WMO Greenhouse Gas Bulletin*, Switzerland.

Chapter 11
Economics of Land Degradation in Argentina

Mariana E. Bouza, Adriana Aranda-Rickert, María Magdalena Brizuela, Marcelo G. Wilson, Maria Carolina Sasal, Silvana M.J. Sione, Stella Beghetto, Emmanuel A. Gabioud, José D. Oszust, Donaldo E. Bran, Virginia Velazco, Juan J. Gaitán, Juan C. Silenzi, Nora E. Echeverría, Martín P. De Lucia, Daniel E. Iurman, Juan I. Vanzolini, Federico J. Castoldi, Joaquin Etorena Hormaeche, Timothy Johnson, Stefan Meyer and Ephraim Nkonya

Abstract Argentina is one of the countries with a vibrant agricultural sector, which provides both economic development opportunities and environmental challenges. Argentina was selected as a case study due to its rich land degradation data, its diverse agroecological systems, and rapid poverty reduction. The country also represents high human development index countries. This study reports the cost of

M.E. Bouza · J.C. Silenzi · N.E. Echeverría · M.P. De Lucia
Departamento de Agricultura, Universidad Nacional del Sur, San Andrés 800, Bahía Blanca, Province of Buenos Aires, Argentina

A. Aranda-Rickert · M.M. Brizuela
Centro Regional de Investigaciones Científicas y Transferencia Tecnológica (CRILAR)/ Consejo Nacional de Investigaciones Científicas y Técnicas (COCINET), Entre Ríos y Mendoza s/n, 5301 Anillaco, La Rioja, Argentina

M.G. Wilson
Instituto Nacional de Tecnologia Agropecuria (INTA)—La Paz E. Rios, Ituzaingo 1055 (3190), La Paz, Entre Ríos, Argentina

M.C. Sasal · E.A. Gabioud
Instituto Nacional de Tecnologia Agropecuria (INTA), Ruta Provincial no. 11 km 12.5 (3101), Oro Verde, Paraná, Entre Ríos, Argentina

S.M.J. Sione
Facultad de Ciencias Agropecuarias, Cátedra de Ecología, Universidad Nacional de Entre Ríos, Ruta 11 km 10.5 (3101), Oro Verde, Entre Ríos, Argentina

S. Beghetto
Instituto Nacional de Tecnologia Agropecuria (INTA), Almafuerte 998 y Ruta Nacional 131 (3116), Crespo, Entre Ríos, Argentina

J.D. Oszust
Agricultural Science Faculty, National University of Entre Ríos, Paraná, Entre Ríos, Argentina

E. Nkonya et al. (eds.), *Economics of Land Degradation and Improvement – A Global Assessment for Sustainable Development*,
DOI 10.1007/978-3-319-19168-3_11

land degradation, the cost of inaction and cost and benefits of taking action against land degradation. The total loss of ecosystem services due to land-use/cover change (LUCC), wetlands degradation and use of land degrading management practices on grazing lands and selected croplands is about 2007 US$75 billion, which is about 16 % of the country's GDP. LUCC accounts for 94 % of the loss, underscoring the need for developing more effective land use planning and incentives land users to protect high value biomes. The returns to taking action against land degradation is about US$4 per US$ invested—justifying the need to take action to improve human welfare and environmental protection. The actions against land degradation include investment in restoration of degraded lands and prevention of land degradation through stricter regulation of agricultural expansion into forests and other higher value biomes. They also include reforestation and other restoration efforts; protection wetlands and restoration of degraded wetlands. The excessive use of agrochemicals also require action to regulate their potential off-site effects. Case studies also show that promotion of rotational grazing, extending conservation agriculture beyond soybean; tillage method and crop-livestock production systems offer promising strategies for addressing land degradation. The world has a lot to learn from Argentina—given its rapid poverty reduction and successful adoption rate of conservation agriculture using public-private partnership. If Argentina aims at maintaining its economic and social development, it will need to work harder to address its growth-related environmental challenges that affect the poor the most. Argentina is better prepared to face these challenges. This study will contribute to informing policy makers on the best strategies for taking action against land degradation and the returns to such actions.

D.E. Bran
Instituto Nacional de Tecnologia Agropecuria (INTA), Agencia de Extensión Rural, Av. Roca esquina Seler (8418), Ingeniero Jacobacci, Río Negro, Argentina

V. Velazco
Instituto Nacional de Tecnologia Agropecuria (INTA), Estacion Experimental Agropecuaria, Jacobacci, Argentina

D.E. Iurman · J.I. Vanzolini · F.J. Castoldi
Instituto Nacional de Tecnologia Agropecuria (INTA), Agencia de Extensión Rural, Hilario Ascasubi Ruta 3 Km 794 (8142), Partido de Villarino, Provincia de Buenos Aires, Argentina

J.E. Hormaeche
Secretaría de Ambiente y Desarrollo, San Martin 451, Ciudad Autonoma de Buenos Aires, Argentina

T. Johnson · E. Nkonya
International Food Policy Research Institute, 2033 K Street, Washington, DC, NW 20006, USA
e-mail: e.nkonya@cgiar.org

J.J. Gaitán
Instituto Nacional de Tecnologia Agropecuria (INTA), Agencia de Extensión Rural, Modesta Victoria 4450 (8400), San Carlos de Bariloche, Río Negro, Argentina

S. Meyer
International Food Policy Research Institute IFPRI Malawi office, Lilongwe 3, Malawi

Keywords Argentina • Land degradation • Land-Use/cover change • Wetlands • Cropland

Introduction

With a GDP of US$ billion 475.502 in 2012, Argentina is the 26th largest economy in the world (World Bank 2014). Argentina has made significant economic progress in the past three decades. between 2000 and 2011, the country's middle income class increased from 34 to 53 % of the population of 41.8 million and people below the international poverty line (US$1.25 per capita per day) fell from 12.6 % in 2002 to only 0.92 % in 2010 (World Bank 2014). In three decades, the country's GDP per capita increased by about 40 % from 2005 US$4628 in 1981–90 to 2005 US$ 6388 in 2001–13 (World Bank 2014). What is even more interesting is that Argentina's "Doubly Green Revolution" (Conway 1997), seen from an on-farm-perspective, achieved higher agricultural productivity at lower energy and less pollution, compared to other countries using more intensive agricultural production technologies. A study by Viglizzo et al. (2011) of 1197 different farming systems ecological and environmental performance—which is quantified as the stocks and fluxes of soil carbon, nitrogen and phosphorous on water pollution, soil erosion, habitat intervention and greenhouse gas (GHG) emissions per hectare—showed significant increase in agricultural productivity but a negative impact on habitats and GHG emission. Due to widespread adoption of conservation agriculture (CA)—which in 2013 accounted for 64 % of cropland (AQUASTAT 2013)—and application of less aggressive pesticides, soil erosion, nutrient balance, and energy use per hectare were significantly less than other countries with intensive agricultural production, such as East Asia, West Europe, and the USA (Ibid). Another study showed that use of round-up ready herbicide—or glyphosate—which WHO puts in class IV of lowest toxicity level, led to a consumer surplus of US$ million 335.0 compared to a conventional tillage method and use of more aggressive pesticides (Qaim and Traxler 2005). However, recent experimental evidence show that glyphosate probably has carcinogenic characteristics—i.e. genotoxicity and pro-oxidant activities both in vitro and in vivo (IARC 2014). Consequently, the WHO has put glyphosate into a 2A class—i.e. "probably carcinogenic to humans" (IARC 2014).

As is the case with other middle income countries however, Argentinais experiencing environmental challenges as its economy grows. As the demand for soybean and livestock production increased, large-scale farmers have been acquiring more land—leading to migration of small farmers to urban areas (Paula and Oscar 2012). For example, Altieri and Pengue (2006) estimated that about a quarter of small farms in Argentina were acquired by large-scale farmers in 1998–2002 alone. The fast expansion of soybean, other crops, and pasture has led to deforestation and other land use/cover change (LUCC) that have led to a loss of ecosystem services.

Use of agrochemicals (measured in kg/ha) in Argentina has increased by 1000 % in the last 20 years, and glyphosate accounts for 75 % of the use in 2006 compared with only 50.1 % in 1991. Such large increase in herbicide use poses a concern for the ecosystems in the soybean farming area. It is for this and other reasons that Argentina is debating the overall social and environmental costsand benefits of GMO-based crop production.

While case-studies from the scientific sector are increasingly warning about harmful effects of glyphosate (Paganelli et al. 2010) on human health and the environment, other studies stress the benefits of conservation agriculture (CA) derived from the use of glyphosate and other herbicides, along with Argentina's comparative advantage of soybean production and its role in the modern global economy.

This study was conducted to analyze the economics of land degradation in Argentina as a case study. Argentina was selected as a case study to represent Latin American countries, specifically those that are middle income countries and those which experienced rapid economic growth. Argentina was also deemed an ideal case study since it is one of the Food and Agriculture Organization's (FAO) case study countries of the Global Land Degradation Assessment (GLADA). Argentina is also a good case study because it represents major agroecological zones in Latin America. The country spans from humid pampas and sub-tropical rainforest in the north to the Patagonia desert and additional arid areas in the north-west (Chap. 2).

The study was conducted in collaboration with the National University of Arturo Jauretche and a number of other national institutions such as the National Secretariat for Environment and Sustainable Development, the National Institute for Agricultural Technology, other National Universities, and local experts and technicians from the field. Four case studies in Argentina were conducted by the collaborating institutions to provide strong ground-validation and varying examples and land degradation.

The next section discusses the major natural resource management policies in Argentina. This is followed by discussion of the analytical approaches and data. The national level and four case study results are then discussed. The last section of the chapter discusses the major conclusions and their policy implications.

Natural Resource Management Policies in Argentina

The discussion below focuses on Argentina's policies on sustainable development and its implications on land management and decentralization of natural resource management. The discussion largely dwells on how such policies have been implemented.

Sustainable Land Management Enshrined in Argentina's Goal of Achieving Sustainable Development

Argentinasustainable development has achievement and challenges. The country's per capita CO_2 emission and withdrawal of water as percent of total renewable freshwater are both lower than the very high human development group to which Argentina belongs (Fig. 11.1). However, Argentina has higher depletion of natural resources as percent of gross national income (GNI) than countries with very high human development but lower than in LAC. Additionally, Argentina's deforestation rate is higher than the average in LAC. Forest cover in very high human development countries has actually increased—suggesting Argentina has a big challenge in matching such environmental achievement.

To address such challenges, Argentina has been increasingly formulating policies to address deforestation and other types of land degradation. As of 2009, the Minimum Standard Natural Forest Protection Law was setup to combat deforestation. It is the first federal compensation scheme in which provinces receive payment protecting forest through territorial planning and enforcement. About US$ 100 million have been paid out through the Minimum Standard Natural Forest Protection Law. About 19 % of the natural forest (916,255 ha) is under protection. The Minimum Standard Law requires provincial governments to implement comprehensive and participatory Land Use Planning Processes (LUPPs) to protect native forests (Seghezzo et al. 2011). The law established a moratorium on forest concessions, until each Province drafts a LUPP that comply with the Native Forests environmental criteria (Regúnaga and Rodriguez 2015). The forest law also requires provinces to perform environmental impact assessment and holding public hearing before any forest concessions are issued. Additionally, the forest law requires provinces to respect the rights of indigenous communities (Ibid). The Minimum Standard Law is under the mandate of the National Secretariat for

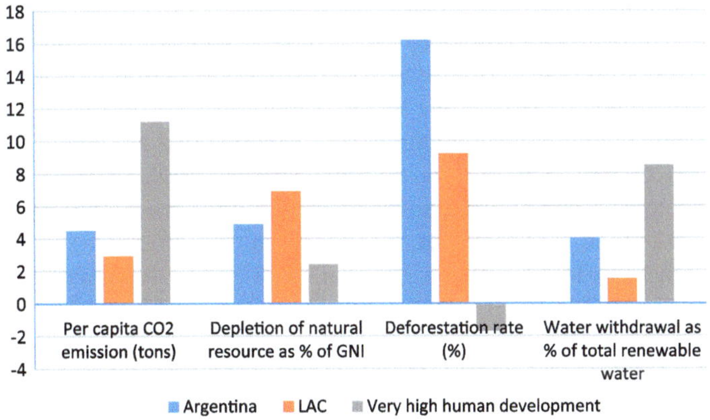

Fig. 11.1 Argentina's sustainable development achievement and challenges. *Source* Calculated from UNDP (2014)

Environment Sustainable Development, which coordinates a number of ministries and departments.

Likewise, the Environmental Report 2012 of the National Secretary of Environment and Sustainable Development of Argentina recognizes that land degradation is a major challenge in Argentina. Accordingly, Argentina ratified the United Nations Convention to combat Desertification (UNCCD) in 1996. In order to implement the UNCCD objectives, the Secretary for Environment and Sustainable Development prepared the National Action Plan (NAP) to coordinate all major sustainable land management (SLM) projects and programs. Argentina was one of FAO's six case study countries selected for studying Land Degradation Assessment in Drylands (LADA). As a follow-up to LADA, Argentina established the National land Degradation Observatory whose objectives are to monitor and assess land degradation and improvement in order to help formulate policies and strategies for controlling and mitigating land degradation and desertification. Seventeen representative land degradation and improvement observatory field sites have been identified for regular data collection. The National Land Degradation Observatory also facilitates exchange of information among ministries, departments, and other institutions that are directly and indirectly involved in land management.

The effect of foreign direct investment on the environment has also been a major concern since it increased significantly in the early 2000s. For example, in 2003 transnational corporations (TNC) accounted for more than 80 % of the value added generated by the 500 largest companies in Argentina (Chudnovsky and López 2008). About 5.9 % of the rural land area in Argentina is owned by foreigners. To address this problem, the Argentine Government passed a National Law on Land Grabbing in 2012 which limits foreign land acquisition to a maximum of 15 % per Federal State. It also creates a National Registry of Rural Land which monitors land acquisitions.

Argentina is also grappling with degradation of wetlands. Argentina ratified the RAMSAR Convention in 1991 and the country has 21 registered wetlands covering about 5 million ha.[1] Nonetheless, there is an increasing pressure on urban and peri-urban costal-wetlands, mainly as the result of urban and agriculture expansion and cattle ranching.

Given that agriculture contributes 56 % of Argentina's total value of exports (Regúnaga and Rodriguez 2015), the country has invested significantly to sustainably increase productivity in the sector. The Ministry of Agriculture promotes sustainable agricultural production through its Program of Agricultural Services in Provinces (PROSAP). The general objective of the PROSAP is to sustainably increase productivity and market participation at the provincial level. On average a total of 373.4 million is allocated to agriculture annually to support (with share of support in brackets) INTA (40 %), National Food Safety and Quality Service or SENASA[2] (39 %), PROSAP (10 %) and the remaining 11 % was allocated to family farming and regional development (Regúnaga and Rodriguez 2015).

[1]RAMSAR Argentina: http://www.ambiente.gov.ar/?idarticulo=1832.

[2]SENASA = Servicio Nacional de Sanidad y Calidad Agroalimentaria.

Decentralized Natural Resource Management

Natural resource management in Argentina is highly decentralized. According to article 121 and Article 124 of the constitutional amendment, provinces "... have original ownership of natural resources existing in their territory." (República de Argentina 1994). The Federal Government holds mandate to influence the Natural Resource Management policies by setting guidelines and directives for provincial level environmental policy and institutional formulation. For example, the Federal government sets legal minimum environmental standards frameworks. National level economic policies and regulations also dictate the corresponding policies and regulations at provincial level that the provincial governments could formulate. For example, Argentina is a signatory of the Convention on International Trade in Endangered Species of Wild Fauna and Flora (CITES). This means provincial governments cannot be engaged in selling endangered species. The Federal government also has subsidy and tax regulations that apply to the entire country.

Research and extension services are also decentralized and operated by National Council of Scientific and Technical Research (CONICET), dedicated to the promotion of science and technology in Argentina, and the National Institute of Agricultural Technology (INTA). Nationwide, INTA has 15 regional centers, 5 research institutes, 50 experimental field-sites and more than 300 extension units. Since 1956 INTA has been conducting research activities and technological innovation that are specific to regions and agroecological zones. The research and extension services have focused on simultaneously increasing productivity and competitiveness and enhancing sustainable development. INTA also has public-private partnership that engages the private sector in provision of research and extension services as well as direct assistance to farmers. For example, PROHUERTA Program—a public policy implemented through the INTA—provides technical services and agricultural input support programs to family farms in peri-urban, urban, and rural areas. PROHUERTA also promotes marketing services to family-based agricultural production. More than three million people have participated in family farming through PROHUERTA.[3]

Analytical Approach

We briefly discuss the analytical approach used in this chapter.[4] As discussed in Chap. 6, we divide the causes of land degradation into two major groups and evaluate the cost for each:

[3]PROHUERTA: http://prohuerta.inta.gov.ar/.

[4]For details of the analytical approach, see Chap. 6.

(i) Loss of ecosystem services due to LUCC that replaces biomes that have higher ecosystem value with those that have lower value. For example, change from one hectare of forest to one hectare of cropland could lead to a loss of ecosystem services since the total economic value (TEV) of a forest is usually higher than the value of cropland. We focus on five major land use types: cropland, grassland, forest, woodland, shrublands and barren land. We do not include wetlands because of their small extent (5 %).

(ii) Using land degrading management practices on a static land use, i.e. land use did not change from the baseline to endline period. Due to lack of data and other constraints, we focus on cropland only.

The approach used for cost of land degradation due to LUCC and use of land degrading management practices on static cropland is discussed in detail in Chap. 6. The approach for determining the cost of action for degradation due to LUCC is also discussed in Chap. 6. Analytical methods for cost of land degradation on static grazing are discussed in Chap. 8.

For analysis of cost of land degradation due to use of land degrading management practices on static cropland, we focus on four major crops: maize, rice, soybean and wheat, which in total cover about 67 % of cropland Argentina (Table 11.1).

Maize, wheat and rice yields have been increasing in most countries despite land degradation. As Fig. 11.2 shows, this is the case for all four crops considered. Use of improved seeds and higher fertilizer application rates account for the yield increase. Nitrogen fertilizer rate increased significantly over the past two decades from 12 to 21 kg/ha (FAOSTAT).

We also use some case studies to illustrate the cost of land degradation for crops and livestock for selected sites. The analytical methods used for each case study are discussed briefly in the case study section.

Table 11.1 Cultivated area of the three most important crops in Argentina

Crop	Area (million ha)	% of total
Soybeans	15.44	44.1
Wheat	4.93	14.1
Maize	3.00	8.6
Rice	0.18	0.5
Total	23.55	67.3

Source FAOSTAT (2015)

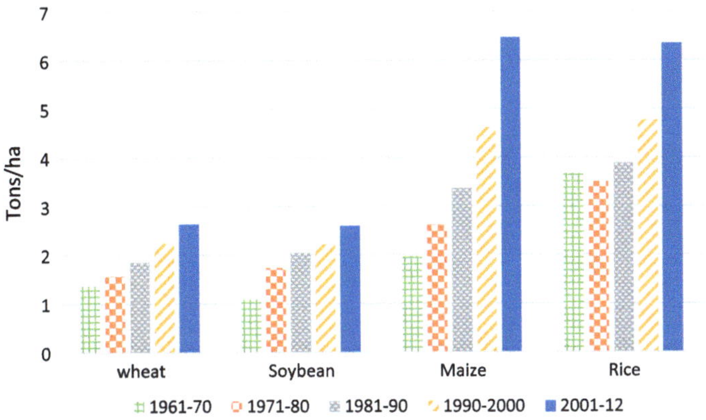

Fig. 11.2 Crop yield trend of wheat, soybean, maize and rice in Argentina, 1961–2012

Data

LUCC

We use the Moderate Resolution Imaging Spectroradiometer (MODIS) landcover data to analyze land-use and land-cover change (LUCC). MODIS data are collected by NASA's two satellites (Terra (EOS AM) and Aqua (EOS PM)) and have three levels of resolutions (250, 500, and 1000 m) (NASA 2014) and were launched in December 1999. For our study we use the 500 m spatial resolution land cover data that matches the International Geosphere-Biosphere Program (IGBP) land cover classification scheme. The MODIS land cover data are quality controlled and ground-truthed (Friedl et al. 2010). The overall accuracy of land use classification is about 75 % (Friedl et al. 2010).

Total Economic Value Data

We derive the TEV from the economics of ecosystems and biodiversity (TEEB) database, which is based on a number of case studies in Latin America and Caribbean (LAC) countries shown in Fig. 11.3. Unlike the approach used in Chap. 6, we include inland wetlands. It is clear that the studies are well-distributed in LAC.

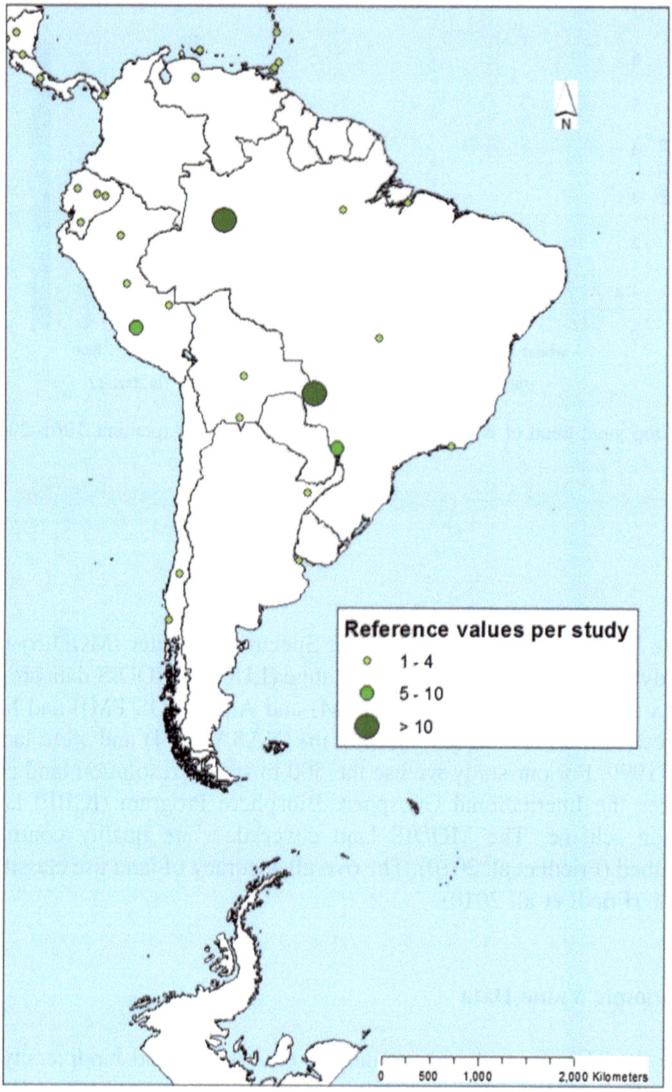

Fig. 11.3 Location of TEEB database of terrestrial ecosystem service valuation studies in LAC. *Source* Derived from TEEB database, the TEV of the five major biomes is shown below

Land Degradation on Static Cropland

DSSAT Crop Simulation

The DSSAT crop simulation baseline land management practices were based on a compilation of global dataset and literature reviews. Given that there is a large difference between irrigated and rainfed land management practices, both the baseline and ISFM scenarios for irrigated and rainfed systems are simulated separately. In the irrigated simulation, a water management scenario is only applied to areas where water management is practiced.

We face a challenge to determine the adoption rate of ISFM in Argentina, a country that has not done an agricultural survey. We use adoption of CA as an indicator of ISFM and assume the 64 % adoption rate for maize, wheat and rice and 100 % for soybean.

Land Degradation on Static Grasslands

Details of data used for calculation of cost of land degradation on static grasslands are given in Chap. 8.

Land-Use/Cover Change in Argentina

About 43 % of Argentina's land was covered with grasslands (pampas) in 2001 (Fig. 11.4). Pampas covers most of the Buenos Aires, La Pampa, Santa Fe, Entre Ríos and Córdoba provinces. Croplands is the second largest biome accounting for about 18 % of the land area (Fig. 11.4). As Fig. 11.5 shows however, significant land-use/cover change (LUCC) has occurred.

About 10 % of forested area in 2001 was cleared and the clearance was most significant in the humid area in northwestern Argentina (Table 11.2). This is also consistent with Volante et al. (2012) who used MODIS data to calculate changes. Land clearing was done mainly for crop production and ranching (Ibid).

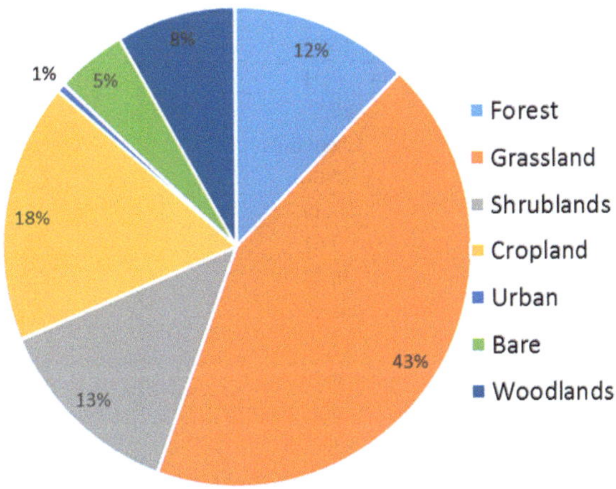

Fig. 11.4 Argentina land use type, 2001

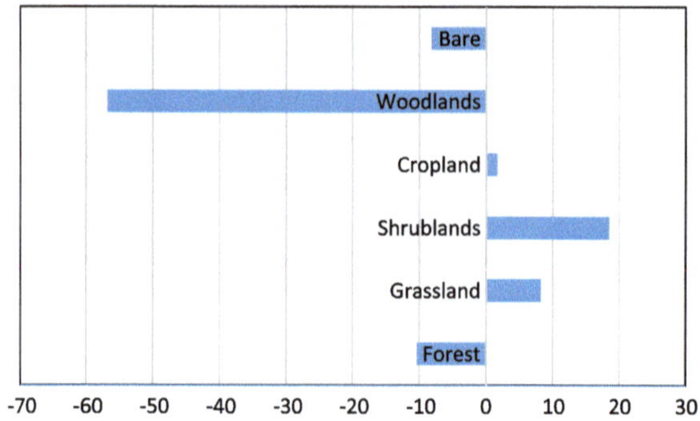

Fig. 11.5 LUCC in Argentina, 2001–09

Table 11.2 Landuse/cover change (LUCC) in Argentina, 2001–09

Agroclimatic zone	Area (million ha), 2001	Loss	Gain	Change (%)
	Forests			
ASAL	10.73	1.3	3.1	17
Sub-humid	17.74	7.4	4.1	-19
Humid	5.25	2.5	0.6	-36
Total	33.71	11.2	7.7	-10
	Grasslands			
ASAL	114.51	10.3	6.3	-3
Sub-humid	4.35	7.5	16.6	209
Humid	0.23	0.9	5.6	2043
Total	119.09	18.7	28.5	8
	Shrublands			
ASAL	14.83	8.1	13.5	36
Sub-humid	14.8	1.9	3.1	8
Humid	6.6	0.2	0.3	2
Total	36.23	10.1	16.8	18
	Woodlands			
ASAL	4.16	3.7	1.4	-55
Sub-humid	15.03	12.5	3.7	-59
Humid	3.31	2.8	1.1	-51
Total	22.5	19	6.2	-57
	Croplands			
ASAL	5.09	1.9	1.9	0
Sub-humid	39.48	7	8.9	5
Humid	3.61	2	0.9	-30
Total	48.17	10.9	11.7	2
	Bare			
ASAL	13.13	3	2.1	-7
Sub-humid	0.2	0.1	0	-50
Humid	0.07	0	0	0
Total	13.4	3.2	2.1	-8

Notes ASAL (<700 mm/year); Sub-humid (700–1200 mm/year); Humid (>1200 mm/year)

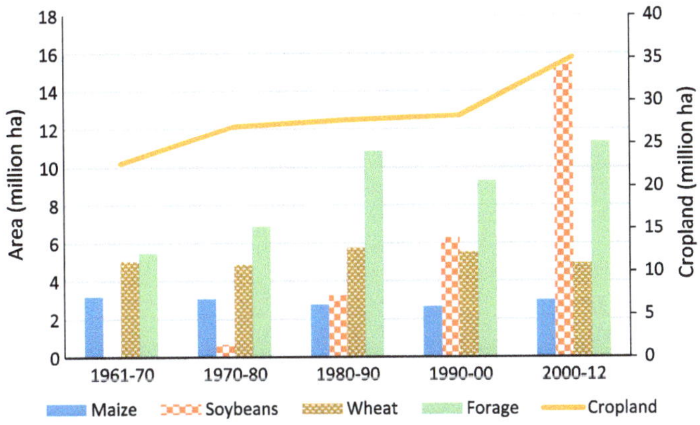

Fig. 11.6 Decadal trend of harvested area of major crops and forage, Argentina

Producing about 49.3 million tons of soybean in 2013, Argentina is the third largest soybean producer in the world—after USA and Brazil (FAOSTAT 2015). Argentina's soybean processing industry in Rosario region is the largest in the world (Altieri and Pengue 2006). The increasing demand for soybean is driven by the increasing demand for animal feeds and biodiesel (Tomei and Upham 2011). Currently, soybean accounts for about 44 % of cropland in Argentina (Fig. 11.6). On the positive note however, use of CA has increased Argentina's agricultural energy use efficiency (Friedrich et al. 2009; Viglizzo et al. 2011). The rapid adoption of CA in Argentina was a result of close collaboration of private companies selling agrochemicals,—particularly herbicides and GM seeds—agricultural extension service providers, and agricultural ministries and department. Such public-private partnership underscores the importance of collaborative efforts for promoting new technologies..

Results

Land Degradation Due to LUCC

Argentina loses about US$70 billion ecosystem services due to LUCC-related land degradation (Table 11.3), an amount which is equivalent to 27 % of its GDP or 12 % of the total value of its ecosystem services (Fig. 11.7). Considering only provisioning services that are locally tangible, cost of land degradation as share of GDP is 12 %. This underscores the high cost of land degradation and the need for the government to take action. The losses were highest in the subhumid zone, which accounted for 82 % of cropland area in 2001 (Fig. 11.6). Grassland area in the subhumid zone more

Table 11.3 Cost of land degradation due to LUCC

	ASAL	Sub-humid	Humid	Argentina
TEV 2001	418.9	180.4	46.5	645.8
Annual cost of land degradation	2007 US$ billion			
– All ecosystem services (ES)	22.0	38.6	9.0	69.7
– Provisioning services only	12.9	15.7	3.3	31.9
Cost action 30 years	36.6	67.7	19.1	123.4
Opportunity cost of taking action	35.7	66.5	18.9	121.1
Cost of inaction, 30 years	163.6	259.5	63.8	486.9
MRR of taking action	4.5	3.8	3.3	3.9

Note: *ASAL* Arid and semi-arid lands

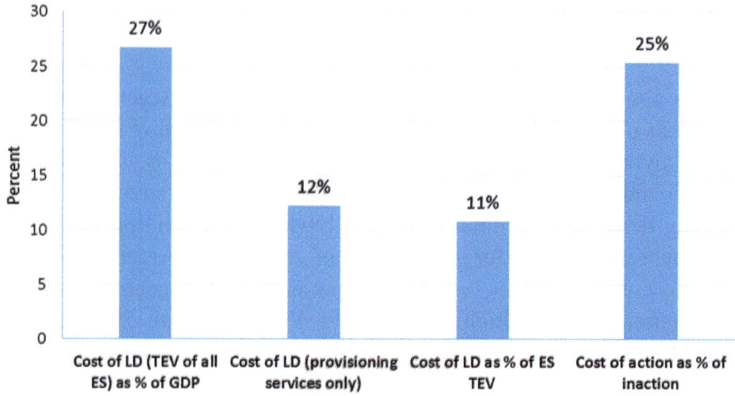

Fig. 11.7 Cost of land degradation as percent of GDP and ecosystem service TEV

than doubled while cropland area increased by about 3 million ha between 2001 and 2009 (Table 11.2). The ecosystem losses in the subhumid area accounted for about 55 % of the total value of land degradation (Table 11.3). Similarly there was a net loss of about 2 million ha of forest area in the humid zone. This is consistent with Altieri and Pengue (2006) and confirms the loss of biodiversity and ecosystem services in pristine forests due to expansion of crop and livestock production.

Using a 30 year planning horizon, the cost of inaction against land degradationis about half a billion 2007 US dollars. Taking action against land degradation over the same period 30 years will cost only 2007 US$123.4 Billion or 25 % of the cost of inaction. The marginal rate of returns (MRR) for taking action against land degradation is about 4, which indicates high pay-off for taking action to prevent LUCC-related land degradation or restore higher value biomes. This further provides empirical evidence for taking action to prevent land degradation or rehabilitate degraded lands in Argentina. Action would include strict protection of forest area and prevention of LUCC that replaces high value biomes with low value biomes. Regulating crop-landexpansion is also required to ensure the country keeps its rich biomes.

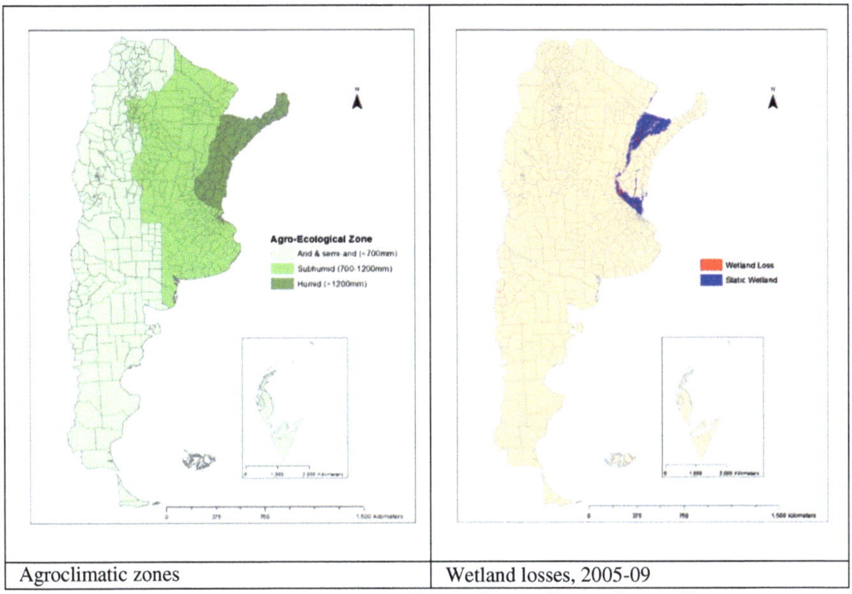

	Area (million km)	Land area	Forest	Grass-lands	Shrub-lands	Crop-lands	Urban	Bare	Wood-lands
	Percent of national total								
Arid & semi-arid (<700 mm)	1.64	59	32	96	41	11	38	98	18
Subhumid (700-1200 mm)	0.95	34	53	4	41	82	55	1	67
Humid (>1200 mm)	0.20	7	16	0	18	7	7	1	15

Fig. 11.8 Agroclimatic zones and extent of wetlands loss

Land Degradation Due to Loss of Wetlands

Wetlands covered about 6.4 million ha in 2005 or 2.3 % of the land (Table 11.5). Even though Argentina is a signatory of the RAMSAR convention—whose mission is "conservation and wise use of all wetlands through local and national actions and international cooperation, as a contribution towards achieving sustainable development throughout the world"—the country lost about 750,000 ha of wetlands in only five years (Table 11.5). In an attempt to understand the nature of loss and their relationship to MODIS land use types used in the cost of land degradation discussed above, we overlaid the GlobCover, which defines wetlands in more detail in Argentina than MODIS. Results show that about a third of the wetlands lost were located in the grasslands and 29 % were located in areas which MODIS classifies as permanent wetlands (Table 11.4 and Fig. 11.7). During field visits of the ELD team in Patagonia, ranchers and INTA scientists explained that the loss of wetlands in grasslands was mainly due to overgrazing—which forms gullies that lead to

Table 11.4 Loss of wetlands and their relationship with MODIS land use types

MODIS land use type	GlobCover wetland area (000 ha)				% of total loss
	2005	2009	Loss	% loss	
Forest	467.5	384.9	82.7	17.7	11.0
Shrublands	976.1	854.8	121.3	12.3	16.2
Grasslands	2952.3	2703.7	248.7	8.4	33.2
Wetlands/natural vegetation	1632.5	1412.6	219.9	13.5	29.3
Cropland	326.9	253.6	73.3	22.4	9.8
Urban	15.3	12.2	3.1	20.4	0.4
Barren	2.3	1.5	0.8	35.87	0.1
Total	6373.0	5623.2	749.7	11.8	

drainage of the wetlands. For example, Molihue wetlands has drained because overgrazing occurred upstream and soil erosion occurred forming gullies that drained the wetlands in the grasslands. Loss of wetlands leads to lower livestock productivity since they serve as grazing areas during the dry season (Fig. 11.8).

In highly populated rural areas, wetlands have been drained by construction of canals connecting inland wetlandswith rivers, valleys and other natural drainage systems (de Prada et al. 2014). This was done in response to sporadic flooding, which prompted farmers and rural communities to ask local and federal governments to construct canals. The wetland draining canals—or locally known as canalization—increased from 97 km in 1975 to 504 km in 2001. The canalization changed hydrologic systems and led to stronger runoff (Ibid). The rural canalization and poor construction of drainage systems in urban areas has resulted in even more flooding and sedimentation (de Prada et al. 2014; Tucci 2007). For example, Buenos Aires has suffered frequent flooding due to its location along the River Plata, unplanned settlement in wetlands, and other low-lying areas and poor drainage systems (Tucci 2007).

Discussion with scientists during a field trip of the authors also revealed that about 20 % of Buenos Aires wetlands have been lost due to mining soils for making bricks and building houses on wetlands. Drainage of wetlands for brick making has also occurred in other countries. For example, the extent of Uganda's wetlands decreased from 32,000 km^2 in 1964 to 26,308 km^2 in 2005, or about a 20 % loss, where brick making was one of the leading drivers of such loss (Aryamanya-Mugisha 2011). Brick making is a lucrative business in urban areas since natural gas and oil used is subsidized at a rate of about 65 %. This leads to overuse of oil and gas for brick making.

Loss of wetlands leads to high costs since they provide a number of ecosystem services and their total economic value (TEV) is second only to coral reefs. The TEV of wetlands is about 2007 US$25,682/ha (De Groot et al. 2010). Table 11.5 shows that in 2005–09, about 12 % of wetlands in Argentina was lost. The TEV of the lost wetlands is about 2007 US$3.85 billion or 1.5 % of the 2007 GDP. The losses of provisioning services of other biomes is high. For example,

Table 11.5 Wetland loss in Argentina

Class	2005	2009	% loss
	000 ha		
Closed to open (>15 %) broadleaved forest regularly flooded (semi-permanently or temporarily)—fresh or brackish water	11.2	11.2	0 %
Closed (>40 %) broadleaved forest or shrubland permanently flooded—saline or brackish water	0.2	0.2	0 %
Closed to open (>15 %) grassland or woody vegetation on regularly flooded or waterlogged soil—fresh, brackish or saline water	6366.3	5615.9	11.8 %
Cost of loss (US$ million)			19,271.78
Cost of loss per year (US$ million)			3854.36
Loss as % of GDP (2007 US$260.769)			1.5 %

Notes One hectare of inland wetlands is worth about US$25,682/ha (de Groot et al. 2010)
Other types of wetlands identified by the GLC2000 are closed to open (>15 %) broadleaved forest regularly flooded (semi-permanently or temporarily)—fresh or brackish water, which covers 11,150 ha. The second category is Closed (>40 %) broadleaved forest or shrubland permanently flooded—saline or brackish water, which covers only 175 ha
Sources GlobCover (2005, 2009)

de Prada et al. (2014) estimated that the annual cost on cropland due to wetland degradation is about $128/ha.

Weak enforcement of environmental laws is the major reason behind wetland degradation, soil mining for brick making, and poor zoning of house construction (de Prada et al. 2014). In general, it seems that proper land-use-planning is the solution to this problem. In order to protect the country's most important and most affected wetland areas, coordinating between different stakeholders and federal jurisdiction, the national Government created the Plan for Integral Strategic Planning for Conservation and Sustainable Development of the Paraná Delta Region (PIECAS—DP). Its main objective is to set up a territorial land-use which enables the maintenance of the ecosystem services provided by the Paraná wetlands to more than 15 million people.[5]

Land Degradation Due to Use of Land Degrading Practices on Soybean Maize, Rice and Wheat

Land degradation due to using land degrading management practices in Argentina is about US$81 million, which is largely due to use of inorganic fertilizer only on the three crops.

---

[5]See this program: http://obio.ambiente.gob.ar/plan-integral-estrategico-para-la-conservacion-y-el-desarrollo-sustentable-en-la-region-delta-del-parana—piecas-dp_p339.

The loss is not including the environmental degradation due to overuse of agrochemicals (Jergentz et al. 2005). As discussed, agrochemical use increased tenfold in the last 20 years. This leads to air pollution that in turn causes loss of pollinators and other fauna and contamination of water resources. Both types of externalities affect people's health (Tomei and Upham 2009).

A study conducted by the National Institute for Agricultural Technology (Cruzate and Casas 2009)[6] on soil depletion due to excessive nutrient extraction on the main mono-cultivars (wheat, maize and sunflower), had alarming results, showing that nutrient balance is −60 %. The study also ranked the crops by soil nutrient mined per unit quantity harvested and found that soybean is a leading nutrient mining crop followed by sunflower and maize. In 2006/07 alone, about 2.3 million tons of soil nutrients were mined without replenishment.

Land Degradation on Static Grasslands

Argentina loses about 2007 US$0.6 billion per year due to degradation of grazing lands. This is equivalent to about 11 % of livestock GDP of US$5490 in 2005 (FAO 2005). The loss is largest in the subtropic-warm/semi-arid, arid, and humid areas (Table 11.6). This is not surprising given that the subtropic humid areas have

Table 11.6 Cost of grazing land degradation in Argentina

AEZ	Milk	Meat	Total
	Cost of land degradation (2007 US$ million)		
Boreal	0.973	1.006	1.979
Subtropic-cool/semi-arid	8.215	0.797	9.012
Subtropic-cool/arid	20.67	1.501	22.172
Subtropic-cool/sub-humid	0.152	0.035	0.187
Subtropic-warm/semi-arid	141.17	6.413	147.583
Subtropic-warm/arid	154.892	8.852	163.744
Subtropic-warm/humid	167.65	10.386	178.036
Subtropic-warm/sub-humid	28.976	1.205	30.181
Temperate/semi-arid	0.393	0.02	0.413
Temperate/arid	19.101	12.049	31.151
Temperate/sub-humid	0.137	0.012	0.149
Tropic-cool/semi-arid	0.708	0.054	0.762
Tropic-cool/arid	0.35	0.022	0.372
Tropic-warm/semi-arid	0.028	0.001	0.029
Total	543.415	42.354	585.769

[6]See report: http://inta.gob.ar/documentos/extraccion-de-nutrientes-en-la-agricultura-argentina/at_multi_download/file/Extraccion_de_nutrientes.pdf.

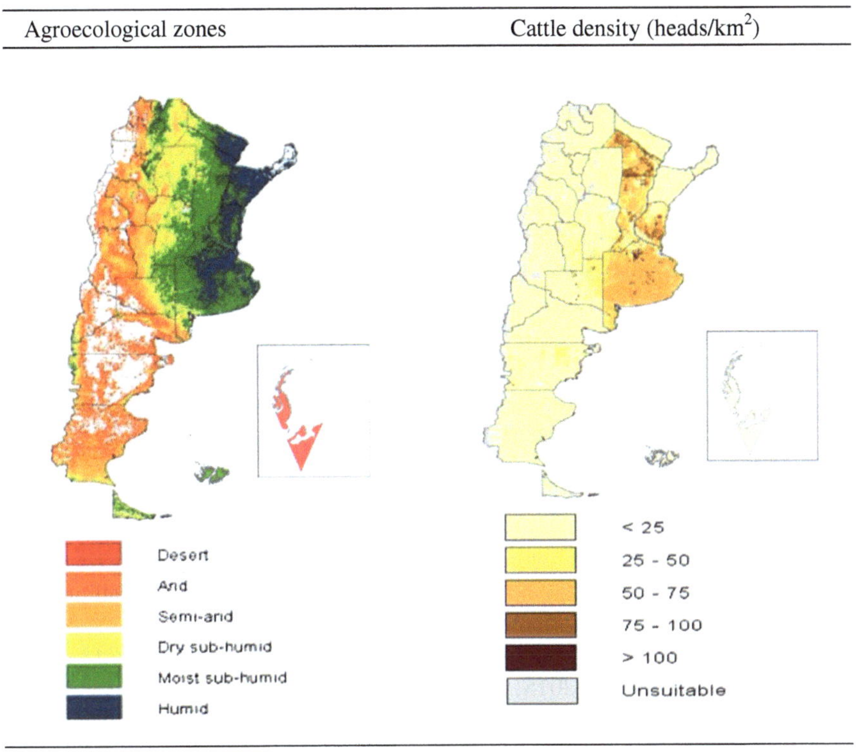

Fig. 11.9 Agroecological zones and corresponding cattle density, 2000. *Source* Extracted from FAO (2005)

the highest concentration of livestock(Fig. 11.9). The losses arising from reduced milk production account for over 90 % of loss. This shows the milk production sensitivity to biomass production.

Case Studies

Patagonia Rangelands and Merino Wool Production

The wool production in Argentina is predominant in the Patagonia steppe, an area which covers about 800,000 km^2 (Ares 2007). The pastoral communities in Patagonia have raised their sheep using a traditional extensive and continuous grazing practice in which grazing is done with minimal human control of livestock movement (Ares 2007; Oliva 2012). Because sheep are highly selective grazing herbivores (Cibils et al. 2001), continuous grazing has led to depletion of preferred forage, such that even after fallowing, palatable forage does not fully recover

(Ares 2007). For example, long-term studies have shown that full recovery of preferred forage required two to three decades of resting in eastern Patagonia (Bertiller et al. 2002).

Rotational grazing has been shown to sustainably keep the preferred forage productivity. The recommended rotational grazing requires putting sheep in the wetlands (malines) during the dry season and in the highlands during the spring season (Golluscio et al. 1998). A special type of rotational grazing has been developed by the Rangeland Research Program at the national research institute—INTA. The recommendation is called a low input management technology (Tecnología de Manejo Extensivo—TME)—appropriately nicknamed "take half leave half". TME is a grazing plan developed after remote sensing assessment is done to determine the carrying capacity. The farmer is advised to manage grazing such that half of aboveground biomass preferred forage is left before animals are moved to another paddock (Anderson et al. 2011).

As discussed above, there has been degradation of wetlands in Patagonia, which has also affected grassland productivity. Additionally, climate change has further reduced the carrying capacity of pasture in Patagonia. The recent volcanic eruption in Chile also deposited ash on pasture, causing significant loss of merino wool production (Easdale et al. 2014). Worse still, wool prices have been falling since World War II largely due to increased used of synthetic fiber (Jones 2004). As a result, sheep population in Argentina fell from about 50 million in 1961 to 15 million heads in 2013 (FAOSTAT 2015).

Despite the decrease in sheep population however, rangeland degradation has continued to occur due to continuous grazing. According to Golluscio et al. (1998) widespread adoption of rotational grazing is constrained by three major challenges: (i) slower recovery of preferred forage due to the fact that fallowing should occur during pasture growth, which is in the spring and early summer period when there is ideal precipitation and temperature. In drier areas, livestock movement during this time is harder (ii) animal movement increases mortality of lambs and therefore is not preferable to farmers (iii) a cultural system of uncontrolled grazing is the major constraint to adoption of rotational grazing. For example, due to the strongly held traditional continuous grazing systems, only 6 % of sheep farmers in southern Patagonia have adopted TME (Anderson et al. 2011). Below, we discuss a case study in Jacobacci to better understand the impact of land degradationand climate change. This study illustrate the steps that the federal and provincial government have done to help farmers cope with land degradation, climate change, and volcanic ash deposition.

Starting with the case study in Jacobacci, following are four case studies highlighting different issues of land degradation in Argentina. Figure 11.10 highlights these areas which are discussed below.

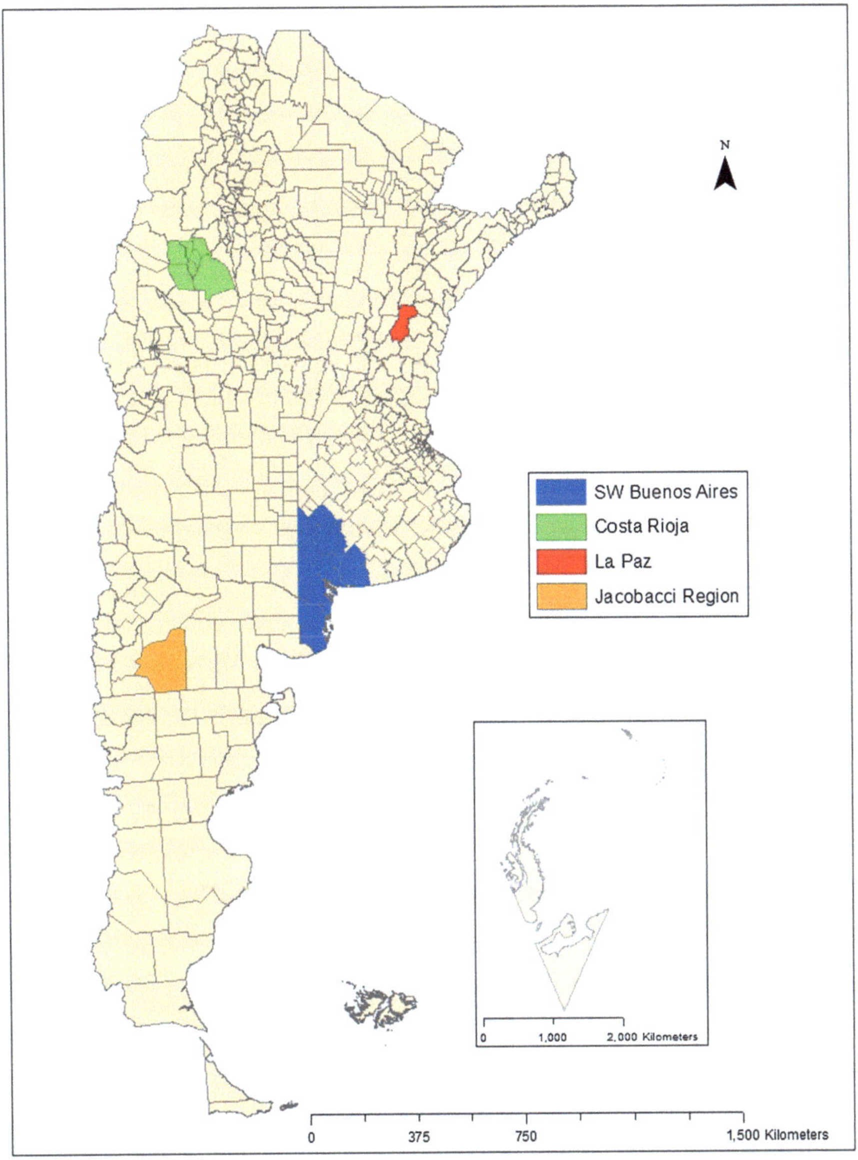

Fig. 11.10 Case study locations of land degradation

Jacobacci Patagonia Case Study

Jacobacci is located in the southwest of the Rio Negro province (Fig. 11.10) and has predominantly semi-shrubby-grass steppe vegetation and Aridisoles and Entisoles soils. There are about 900 farms practicing extensive sheep and goat rearing for wool. About 54 % of farms have fewer than 2500 ha and the remaining share of farmers have larger farms.

As is the case for other areas in Patagonia, overgrazing is a common problem in Jacobacci (Ares 1990). This has resulted in a loss of vegetation and consequently accelerated water and wind erosion (Rostagno and Degorgue 2011). However, the sheep population has declined from more than 750,000 heads in 1930 to the current population of fewer than 350,000 heads. The falling wool price has been the major driver of the declining sheep population. Climate change, which has led to a longer dry season and deposition of volcanic ash from the eruption of mount Puyehue volcano-Caulle in 2011 have also contributed to falling sheep population. This has led to migration of some sheep farmers to urban areas and job losses of farm workers. To address land degradation, the TME recommendation has been given but its adoption rate remains low (Anderson et al. 2011). Diversification to wool and mutton (meat sheep) has also been one of the strategies to address the falling wool price. The sheep farmers also have received from federal and provincial programs compensation for the losses caused by volcanic ash deposition. Other programs include subsidies and low or zero interest loans. Some investments have also been made to improve sheep production. They include construction of shearing and calving sheds, paddock construction with electric fencing to help adoption of rotational grazing and TME, and improving access to drinking water, etc. Strengthening of local institutions have also been promoted through sheep producer organizations and cooperatives. In the past 5 years a range of grants from the National Institute of Indigenous Affairs was also established. The farmer groups and cooperatives have received a variety of assistance in the form of subsidies and zero or low interest rates, etc.

Crop and Livestock Production in La Paz

The La Paz case study lies in the humid agroecological zone with an annual precipitation of 1100 mm and temperatures below 20 °C, it covers an area of 74,691.30 ha (Fig. 11.10). The major economic activity in La Paz is crop and livestock production, but cattle production accounts for the largest land area. Compared to Patagonia however, farmers in La Paz have smaller farms as 72 % of the area is occupied by farmers with smaller than 100 ha lot sizes. The type of land tenure is leasehold, sharecropping and renting.

Land degradation processes. Social and Economic Impacts: Anthropogenic activities in La Paz have resulted in reduced vegetation cover but with increasing heterogeneity (Secretaría de Ambiente y Desarrollo Sustentable de la Nación 2007). The extent of native forests is 42,726.91 ha, of which 59.1 % has not experienced LUCC. The disturbed forest are replaced by succession forests—trees and shrubs that grow on a recently disturbed area—whose dominant trees are exotic species such as Gleditsia triacanthos, Melia azedarach, Morus alba and Ligustrum lucidum (Sabattini et al., In review).

Agricultural expansion is the main driver of LUCC in La Paz (Wilson 2007). The extent of native forest decreased by 19.3 % in 2011 compared to 1991. This suggests an annual deforestation rate of 1.12 % (Sabattini et al. in press). Given that forests provide a variety of ecosystem services, deforestation is causing significant losses that affect both local people and the rest of the world (Zaccagnini et al. 2014). The soybean monoculture has increased the risk of soil erosion and water contamination due to use of herbicides (Wilson 2007).

Efforts to prevent and reverse land degradation processes are being made. They include land use planning to develop more diversified and integrated land use/cover. A watershed approach is promoted to ensure that the planned land use/cover is supported by the natural capacity of the watershed and is consistent with the socio-cultural characteristics of the resident communities (Wilson and Sabattini 2001). In this regard, a number of institutions are conducting evaluation of LUCC, habitat fragmentation, soil and water quality, soil erosion, and other ecosystem indicators in the basin of Arroyo. The institutions include INTA EEA Paraná and FCA UNER with CONICET and SAyDS[7] of Argentina. Furthermore, indicators are seeking to determine the impact of the changes on social issues related to education, health, state assistance, housing quality, land tenure, profitability of agricultural enterprises, and household income.

Thus, it is possible to have scientific technical elements useful in assessing and monitoring, to generate early warnings of degradation processes of natural resources, and from this information, implement appropriate planning of land use policies. This initiative is important in demonstrating Argentina's resolve to develop a monitoring and evaluation of land degradation and improvement as well as developing land use planning based on an ecosystem approach. This is consistent with the country's M&E of land degradation at a country level that follows the LADA case study.

Land Degradation in Southwest of Buenos Aires Province

The case study is located in the Southwest, covering 25 % of the Province of Buenos Aires, is an area with three major agroecological zones (sub-humid, semiarid and arid) and with average rainfall ranging from 300 to 700 mm (Fig. 11.11). The major farming system is rainfed wheat and extensive cattle ranching.

About 30 % of the case study area suffers some form of land degradation. Degradation is especially severe due to the El Nino Southern Oscillation phenomenon which comes up with long cycles of droughts and floods. The Mollisols soil types—which cover 74 % of the land area of southwest Buenos Aires province—are highly susceptible to water, wind erosion, and compaction (Silenzi et al. 2010).

[7]At the National level, SayDS—the Secretariat of Environment and Sustainable Development (SayDS)—is mandated to make environmental policy.

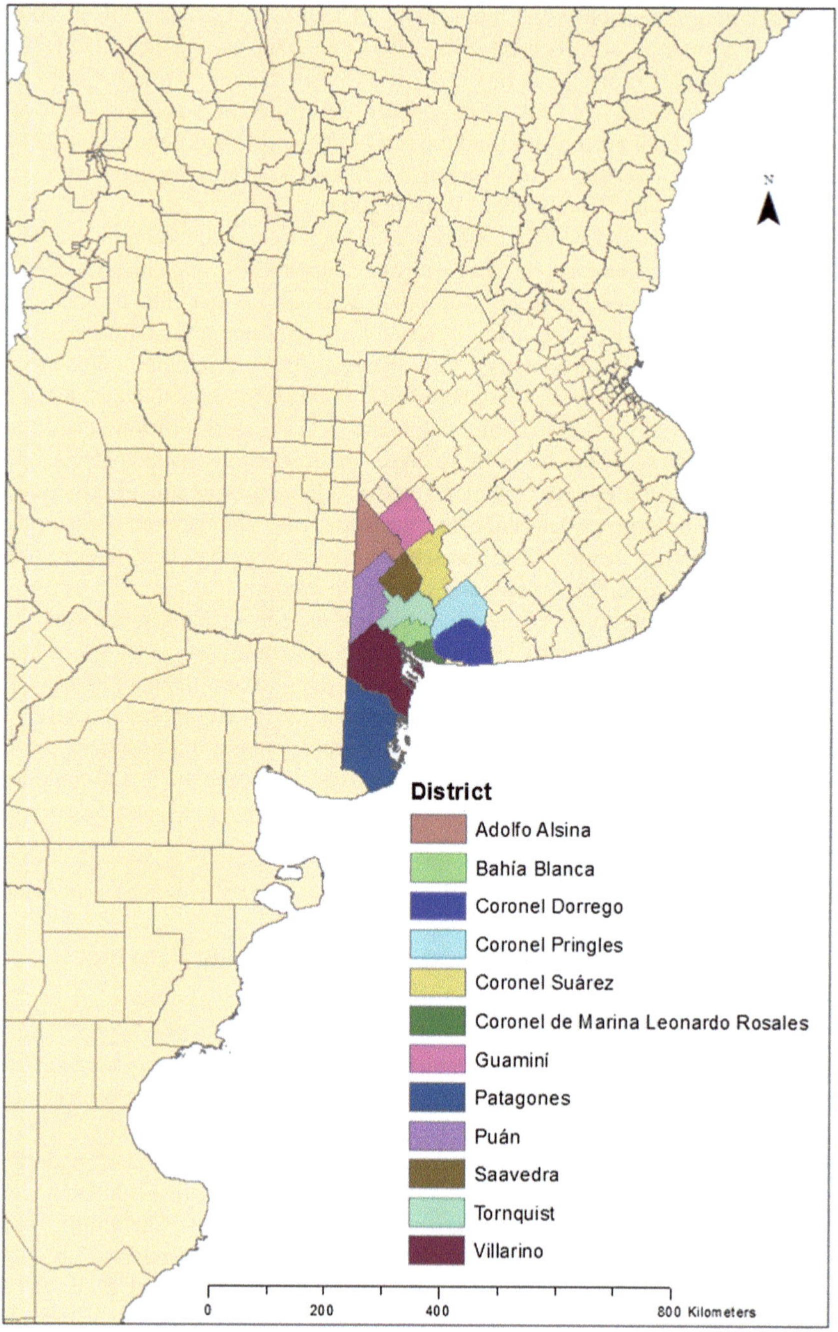

Fig. 11.11 Districts of Southwestern Buenos Aires

Climate change—which has prolonged the dry period—has worsened susceptibility to soil erosion and other forms of land degradation (Silenzi 2011). Given that severe droughts follow the El Niño Southern Oscillation (ENSO) (Glave 2006), its occurrence to some degree is predictable.

As part of efforts to understand the most effective methods of controlling soil erosion, studies have been done to determine the impact of land cover and soil productivity on wind erosion. An inverse linear relationship between wind Erosion Risk (WER) and soil productivity index (PI) was established:

$$\mathrm{WER} = 95.23 - 2.09 * \mathrm{PI}$$
$$\mathrm{R}^2 = 66\ \%.$$

The equation suggests that WER increases as PI declines. A large proportion of wheat is planted on land affected by moderate wind erosion (Silenzi et al. 2010). Table 11.7 reports results used in the equation to determine the cost of land degradation due to wind erosion. Similarly on grazing lands in the arid zone of Caldenal, vegetation cover was less than 50 % and soil compaction was high on areas with high livestock density (Echeverría 2014).

Research by Bouza (2014) and Bouza et al. (2009, 2012), observed that soil loss for each wind storm reached up to 22 t/ha on bare soils. They also found an inverse relationship between vegetation cover and soil erosion. For example Bouza (2012) showed that 30 % of vegetation cover reduces wind erosion by 80 %—underlying the importance of promoting conservation agriculture and other practices that enhance vegetation cover.

An evaluation of the impact of soil erosion on wheat production showed that the loss of wheat production due to soil erosion was 319,859 million tons per year (Silenzi et al. 2009), which is worth 2007 US$ 86 million (Table 11.7 and Fig. 11.11).

In the last 50–75 years, wind erosion in some arid or semiarid areas has exceeded the regenerative capacity of land, i.e., the tolerance level (T) according to the criteria established by the American Society of Agronomy and Soil Science Society.

As for livestock production, loss of vegetation cover has exposed land to serious soil erosion and compaction and consequently loss of livestock productivity. In 34 years (1975–2009) native forest cover decreased by 32 or 9.5 % per year due to agricultural land expansion in the Southwest of the Provinces of Buenos Aires and Northeast Rio Negro. A study was done to evaluate the grassland productivity with and without land degradation arising from soil compaction due to excessive trampling and overgrazing (Silenzi et al. 2014). The results show that rangeland productivity fell by 40–51 % during spring, summer and autumn but surprisingly increased by 84 % during winter season (Table 11.8). The increase in winter could be due to increased unpalatable species that are better adapted to cold seasons.

Table 11.7 Economic cost of soil erosion on wheat production, Southwestern Buenos Aires Province

District	Area					Loss of production due to soil erosion (1000 t/year)	Cost of land degradation (Million US$)	I (t/ha/year)	C (%)	WER (t/ha/year)	PI (%)
	Total (1000 ha)	Harvested area (1000 ha)	% of total area	Wheat area eroded (1000 ha)	(%)						
Adolfo Alsina	587.5	92.4	15.7	58.2	63	29.1	7.86	64.2	42	27	31
Bahía Blanca	230	46	20	37.7	82	18.9	5.10	39.3	57	22.4	34
Cnel Dorrego	586.5	234.1	39.9	65.6	28	32.8	8.86	53.1	35	18.6	46
Cnel Pringles	524.5	115.7	22.1	24.3	21	12.2	3.30	32.2	14	4.5	43
Cnel Rosales	129.5	41.5	32	27.8	67	13.9	3.75	87.6	55	48.2	32
Cnel Suárez	598.5	128.1	21.4	5.1	4	2.6	0.70	30.2	7	2.1	48
Guaminí	484	39.5	8.2	33.6	85	16.8	4.54	59.6	5	3	10
Patagones	1360	222.6	16.4	153.6	69	76.8	20.74	87.2	120	104.6	10
Puan	638.5	120.3	18.8	69.8	58	34.9	9.42	67.9	18	12.2	32
Saavedra	350	92.6	26.4	56.5	61	28.2	7.61	34.9	7	2.4	42
Tornquist	418.3	90.2	21.6	32.5	36	16.2	4.37	32.2	21	6.8	39
Villarino	1140	110.5	9.7	75.1	68	37.6	10.15	85.7	37	31.7	16
Total	7047.3	1 333.5	19	639.8	48	319.9	86.4	56.2	34.8	23.6	31.92

Key Area: total harvested wheat area eroded by wind per year; annual decrease in production wheat due to wind erosion. Wind erodibility of soils (“I”), aggressiveness climate (“C”), risk of wind erosion (WER) and Productivity Index (PI)

Table 11.8 Impact of land degradation on grazing biomass productivity

	Coppice (Caldenal) species	Degraded forests (scrub)—Fachinal	% loss of productivity
	Dry matter productivity (tons/ha/year)		
Spring	1.5	0.86	42.7
Summer	1.0	0.33	67.0
Autumn	1.3	0.64	50.8
Winter	0.5	0.92	−84.0

Source Silenzi et al. (2012)

Table 11.9 Impact of tillage methods on soil fertility, Southeast Bonaerense

Tillage method	Soil cover (%)	Water content in 0–60 cm layer (mm)	Soil bulk density (15 cm depth, tons/m^3)	Root density (m/m^3)	Wheat yield (tons/ha)
Vertical plowing (vertical chisel) VP	19	72		7000	2.5
Conventional tillage (CT)	16	72	1.29	6500	2.15
No Tillage (NT)	96	75	1.22	6000	2.5

NB Bonaerense; *SO* Sud Oeste—or southeast. *Source* Silenzi et al. (2011)

The same study showed disappearance of palatable forage species. Consequently, beef production has fallen by 35 % between 2002 and 2009. As is the case for Patagonia, livestock population and number of farmers have also been falling. The number of farmers decreased by 19 % in 2002 compared to 1988 but the grazing area increased by 22 % during the same period. This is a reflection of land degradation which leads to expansion of grazing lands.

Land management practice for addressing land degradation

Tillage methods: A tillage experiment conducted in the SW of Buenos Aires province have shown that No tillage (NT) is more sustainable than the Conventional tillage (CT). NT used less energy, N and P to achieve the zero net balance of both nutrients. Conventional tillage (CT) also showed to have greater erosion risk than NT. However, CT showed lower risk of pesticide contamination than NT (Silenzi et al. 2004). Soil water content was comparable across all tillage method (Table 11.9). Wheat yield was slightly higher for the VT and NT than the conventional method.

Adoption of NT is higher in the subhumid region than in arid and semiarid areas. One of the challenges of widespread adoption of NT is its difficulty to integrate into a mixed system agricultural livestock. The crop-livestock systems have been shown to be suited to climatic and market risks as they provide greater flexibility and stability to the local system than specialized crop or livestock production systems. Additionally, livestock-crop production systems increase demand for labor, and enable more efficient land use, thus contributing to economic and social development

(Iurman 2010). However, in the southern region, an area of adverse and changing conditions, a pure livestock system is recommended due to the predominantly permanent pasture and low rainfall that is unfit for rainfed crop production (Iurman et al. 2012).

Conventional crop-livestock production versus sustainable livestock production systems: This cost-benefit analysis was done to compare the traditional wheat dominated crop-livestock production systems—business as usual (BAU) and sustainable systems of intensive cattle-ranching. The BAU scenario consists of mixed crop and livestock production while the intensive cattle-ranching scenario involved planted gramine (PG) and natural regeneration rangelands (NR) and reduced crop production. Using a 500 ha farm as a case study, the BAU and the alternative production systems (PG and NR) were compared in terms of productivity, gross-benefits and sustainable stocking rates (Fig. 11.13). As reported in Fig. 11.12, wheat is a dominant crop and pasture management is not practiced in the BAU, while pasture management dominates in the alternative scenario. The results show that the alternative pasture management increased the sustainable stocking rate by 54 % and livestock productivity by 64 % (Fig. 11.13).

The cost of production is lower for the BAU but both the profit and marginal rate of return (MRR) for the alternative production system (PN and PG) is more than five times higher (Fig. 11.14 and Table 11.10).

The results suggest that livestock production using PN and NR is much more profitable and sustainable than the BAU.

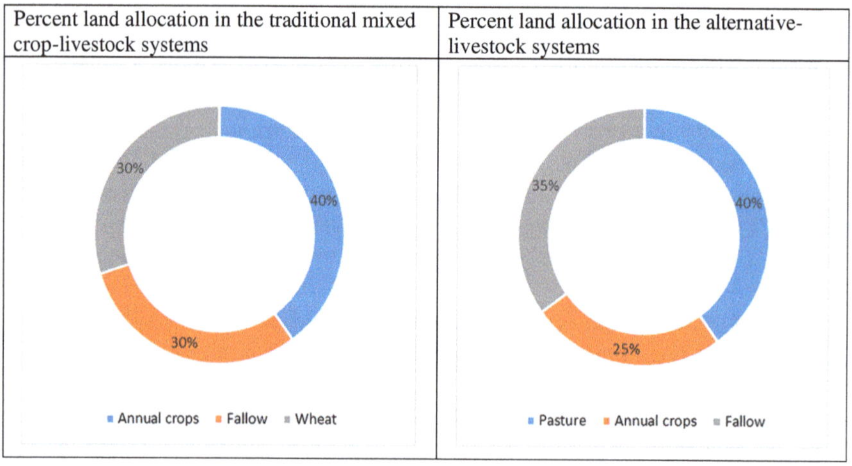

Fig. 11.12 Land allocation to crops and pasture in the traditional and alternative management practices

Fig. 11.13 Sustainable stocking rate and beef productivity in the BAU and alternative systems

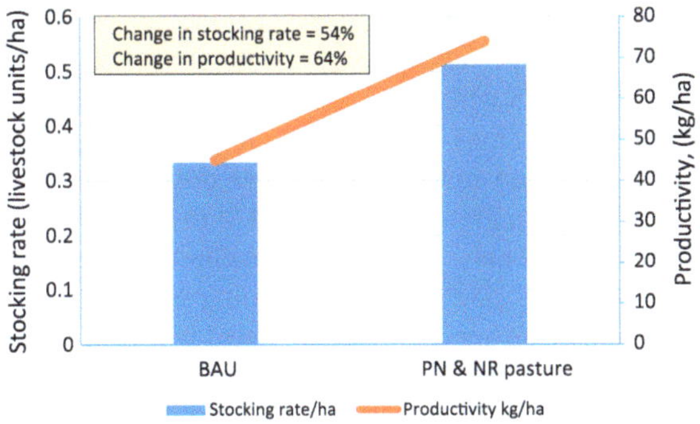

Fig. 11.14 Returns to investments, BAU and PN and NR

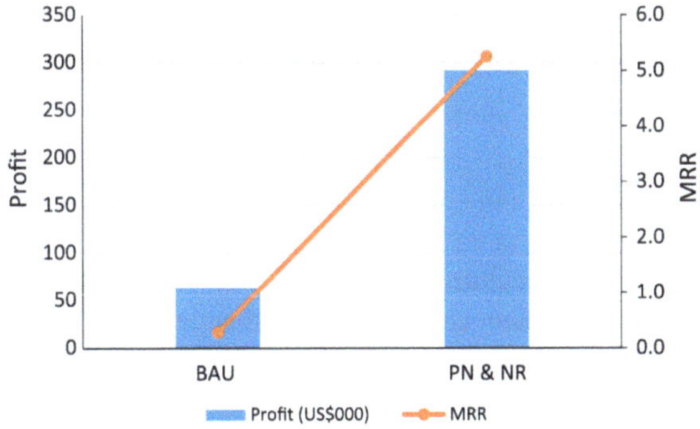

Table 11.10 Production and revenue of BAU and PN and NR

	Enterprise	BAU	PN & NR
		US$ (thousands)	
Production cost	Crops	128.16	0.00
	Livestock	92.46	55.51
Revenue	Crops	132.77	0.00
	Livestock	151.19	347.33

La Rioja Case Study

The arid valleys of La Rioja province occupy the northern portion of the Monte Desert biome in northwest Argentina—regarded as the driest region in Argentina (Abraham et al. 2009). Climate is arid with an average annual rainfall of 270 mm and an average annual temperature of 16 °C. The vegetation is an open shrubland dominated by "jarilla" (Larrea cuneifolia), Bulnesia broom, Fabaceae shrubs and cacti. Woodlands are open and marginal with azonal vegetation, i.e., with plant communities that are influenced more by edaphic factors than climatic factors. The case study has seven villages with population that range from 180 to 1300 inhabitants, located on the eastern slopes of the Sierra de Velasco mountain range.

About 77 % of the 556 farms included in the case study are smallholder farmers with an average farm size of 2.4 ha (Lossino et al. 2002). There is considerable flood irrigation which draws water from the permanent rivers that are recharged on the high elevations of the mountains. Only large holdings of vineyards have sufficient irrigation investment and use drip irrigation. Some large holdings also use groundwater, pumped from up to 300 m deep. Of a total of 867 ha, 255 ha use drip irrigation, and only 7 of the 429 smallholder farmers use groundwater for irrigation (Lossino et al. 2002). Rainfed farming use summer rainfall and grow corn, squash and forage—an ancient practice started by pre-Hispanic inhabitants. Other land uses are extensive grazing of goats and cattle. Hunting is also a traditional livelihood but is prohibited by provincial law.

Land Degradation Processes and Impacts on Ecosystem Services

Deforestation and continuous grazing are among the major land degradation types in the case study area. Since 1988, approximately 5000 ha of forests have been converted to agriculture, while additional 19,000 ha have been acquired by the government. In many cases, due to inadequate planning, degraded lands are abandoned.

The Fifth Assessment Report of the Intergovernmental Panel on Climate Change (Pachauri et al. 2014) estimates that by 2020/2029, precipitation in northwest Argentina will decrease by 2–12 % and temperature will increase by 1–1.4 °C. Given that deserts are fragile ecosystems that are not easily restored once altered (Yanelli et al. 2014), the consequences of climate change, coupled with land degradation by anthropogenic causes, could have irreversible effects on population who heavily depend on natural resources. This could lead to much more severe shortages and consequent conflicts among land users.

Strategies for Addressing Land Degradation

The provincial and Federal governments are implementing a number of strategies to address land degradation in the arid valleys of La Rioja. The Regional Center for Scientific and Technological Research of La Rioja (CRILAR)—which belongs to the CONICET—is monitoring land degradation and improvement. This will help to design appropriate interventions and policies of land use that could lead to socially and environmentally sustainable management practices.

An environmental education to primary school children through CONICET Programs such as “Scientists go to schools” is promoting conservation of biodiversity. The Pro-Huerta Program of INTA and the Ministry of Social Development also promote organic agricultural practices to local farmers. Additionally, the CRILAR participates in the provincial technical board which was created for land use planning, protection and enforcement of compliance with Minimum Standards for environmental Protection Act of the Native Forests of the Province of La Rioja.

Fuel-efficient cook stoves, heating systems and alternative energy are also being promoted to reduce native forest harvesting for fuelwood. A project implemented by INTA is also promoting conservation of agricultural water resources in the Catamarca-La Rioja region. The project aims to improve the use of surface and groundwater resources for irrigation through the provision of appropriate technologies.

Conclusions and Policy Implications

Argentina's economy has grown significantly in the past decade and this has significantly reduced the number of people below the international poverty line (US $1.25/day/capita) from 12.6 % in 2002 to only 0.92 % in 2010 (World Bank 2014). Argentina's adoption of conservation agriculture (CA) is also the highest in the world. Such high CA rate of adoption and other environmental achievements have improved the country's ecological and environmental performance to a higher level than most other countries using intensive agricultural production technologies (Viglizzo et al. 2011). The high adoption of CA in Argentina has demonstrated the effectiveness of public-private partnership in agricultural development but has also highlighted the potential environmental impacts of such partnership. The seemingly "doubly green revolution" has come at an ecological cost due to the rapid expansion of croplandand pasture production into forest and other higher value biomes. Our study shows that the loss of ecosystem services due to land-use/cover change (LUCC) is 2007 US$70 billion or 26 % of the country's 2007 GDP. Considering only provisioning services with tangible local benefits, land degradation due to LUCC is about 12 % of the GDP. Wetland degradation also coststhe country 2007 US$3.8 billion or 1.5 % of the 2007 GDP. The major drivers of wetland degradation are human settlement and mining soil for brick making. Gully formation due to soil erosion in the grasslands in Patagonia and other areas has also drained water from wetlands. A crop simulation model that only considers soil fertility mining shows that land degradation in wheat, maize and rice farms costs about US$81 million per year.

Cost of land degradation on grazing land on milk and meat production is about 2007 US$586 million or 11 % of the livestock GDP. Such high losses require immediate action given the increasing demand for livestock products and its potential to simultaneously increase farmer income, sequester carbon, reduce soil erosion, and other ecosystem service benefits.

The high cost of land degradation calls for action to address it. Our study shows that the returns to taking action against land degradation is about US$4 per US$ invested. The high returns to taking action against land degradation strongly justify investment in restoration of degraded lands and prevention of land degradation. Action against land degradation will require stricter regulation of agricultural expansion into forests and other higher value biomes. This also requires reforestation and other restoration efforts. Argentina faces great challenges ahead regarding the protection of wetlands, addressing the ecological imbalance caused by wetland degradation through LUCC, especially urbanization and waste-disposal of coastal cities.

The case studies also revealed the potential of promising strategies that could achieve sustainable land management. Sheep production in Patagonia is experiencing land degradation but the rotational grazing system designed by INTA (TME) has been shown to be sustainable but its adoption rate is low. Increasing its adoption would require concerted efforts to provide extension services, incentives, and support that could help ranchers to overcome the high upfront costs. The incentives and material support could be justified by the ecosystem benefits that result from rangeland management.

The case studies in La Paz, and La Rioja also reveal that diversified crop-livestock systems are more sustainable and profitable and reduce production risks than specialized production systems. In the case of the SW Buenos Aires Province however, specialized pasture management does offer more sustainable and profitable production systems crop production. But farmers practice mixed systems as a strategy to contend with production and market risks.

Conservation agriculture also need to extend beyond the soybean production. This is especially important in dry areas affected by wind erosion. For example the study in Buenos Aires showed that 30 % of vegetation cover reduces wind erosion by 80 %. This will simultaneously increase agricultural productivity and reduce dust storms in cities and other heavily populated areas.

Argentina has laid out elaborate land use planning strategies, land degradation and improvement monitoring that informs policy formulation. This was a result of political efforts which were strongly backed by FAO's land degradation assessment (LADA) that was completed in 6 different countries. The countries could learn from Argentina's groundbreaking initiative of establishing an elaborate monitoring and evaluation of land degradation and improvement. It is therefore that Argentina started to share its knowledge in this field through its Technical Cooperation Facility of the Ministry of Foreign Affairs ((FOAR), through which LADA experts of the Secretary of Environment and Sustainable Development gave training to institutions and farmers in other Latin-American countries.

The world has a lot to learn from Argentina given its rapid poverty reduction and successful adoption rate of CA using public-private partnership. For Argentina to maintain its economic and social development, it will need to work harder to address its growth-related environmental challenges that affect the poor the most. Argentina of today is much better prepared to face these challenges and take advantage of the emerging opportunities. This study will provide policy makers with empirical evidence to take action against land degradation.

References

Abraham, E., del Valle, H. F., Roig, F., Torres, L., Ares, J. O., Coronato, F., & Godagnone, R. (2009). Overview of the geography of the Monte Desert biome (Argentina). *Journal of Arid Environments, 73*, 144–153.

Altieri, M., & Pengue, W. (2006). GM soybean: Latin America's new colonizer. Seedling January 2006. Online at http://www.grain.org/es/article/entries/588-gm-soybean-latin-america-s-new-colonizer. Accessed 25 Sept 2014.

Anderson, D. L., Bonvissuto, G. L., Brizuela, M. A., Chiossone, G., Cibils, A. F., Cid, M. S., et al. (2011). Perspectives on rangeland management education and research in Argentina. *Rangelands, 33*(1), 2–12.

Aquastat. (2013). Aquastat database. Online at http://www.fao.org/nr/water/aquastat/data/query/index.html?lang=en. Accessed 14 April 2015.

Ares, J. O. (2007). Systems valuing of natural capital and investment in extensive pastoral systems: Lessons from the Patagonian case. *Ecological Economics, 62*(1), 162–173.

Ares, J., Beeskow, A. M., Bertiller, M., Rostagno, M., Irisarri, M., Anchorena, J., et al. (1990). Structural and dynamic characteristics of overgrazed lands of northern Patagonia, Argentina. *Ecosystems of the World, 17*, 149–175.

Aryamanya-Mugisha, H. (2011). *20 years of wetlands conservation in Uganda—have Uganda's wetlands become wastelands again?* Paper presented at the WORLD WETLANDS DAY, February 2, 2011, Kamapal Uganda. Online at http://www.natureuganda.org/downloads/presentations/WETLANDS%20STATUS.pdf. Accessed 25 Sept 2014.

Bertiller, M. B., Ares, J. O., & Bisigato, A. J. (2002). Multiscale indicators of land degradation in the Patagonian Monte, Argentina. *Environmental Management, 30*(5), 0704–0715.

Bouza, M. E. (2014). Estudio del proceso de erosión eólica en el Sudoeste Bonaerense. Validación de un modelo predictivo. Tesis Magister en Ciencias Agrarias de la UNS, 156 pp. Bratislava, EAAP.

Bouza, M. E., Silenzi, J. C., Echeverría, N. E., & De Lucia, M. P. (2012). Analysis of erosive events for a soil in the southwest of Buenos Aires Province, Argentina. *Aeolian Research, 3*, 427–435.

Bouza, M. E., Silenzi, J. C., Echeverría, N. E., & De Lucía, M. P. (2009). Monitor station of wind erosion in south west of Buenos Aires province. Drylands Science for Development (DSD). United Nations Convention to Combat Desertification (UNCCD). First Scientific Conference: Understanding Desertification and Land Degradation Trends. Poster Session at the UNCCD COP-9. Buenos Aires. http://dsd-consortium.jrc.ec.europa.eu/documents/Poster_Session_Abstract_Book.pdf

Chudnovsky, D., & López, A. (2008). *Foreign investment and sustainable development in Argentina*. Working Group on Development and Environment in the Americas. Discussion Paper Number 12.

Cibils, A. F., Coughenour, M. B., & Gallegos, S. C. (2001). Impact of grazing management on the productivity of cold temperate grasslands of Southern Patagonia-a critical assessment. In *Proceedings of the XIX International Grassland Congress* (pp. 807–811). Sao Pablo, Brazil.

Conway, G. (1997). *The doubly green revolution: Food for all in the twenty-first century* (335 pp). New York (USA): Penguin Books.

Cruzate, G. A., & Casas, R. (2009). Extraccion de nutrients en la agricultura Argentina. Mimeo Inta. Online at http://inta.gob.ar/documentos/extraccion-de-nutrientes-en-la-agricultura-argentina/at_multi_download/file/Extraccion_de_nutrientes.pdf. Accessed 13 Jan 2015.

de Groot, R., Brander, L., van der Ploeg, S., Costanza, R., Bernard, F., Braat, L., et al. (2010). Benefits of investing in ecosystem restoration. *Conservation Biology, 27*(6), 1286–1293.

De Prada, J. D., Shah, F., Degioanni, A. J., Cisneros, J. M., & Cantero, A. (2014). The external impact of agriculture on inland wetlands: A case study from Argentina. *European Scientific Journal, 10*(17), 1857–7881.

Easdale, M. H., Sacchero, D., Vigna, M., & Willems, P. (2014). Assessing the magnitude of impact of volcanic ash deposits on Merino wool production and fibre traits in the context of a drought in North-west Patagonia, Argentina. *The Rangeland Journal, 36*(2), 143–149.

Echeverría, N. E. (2014). Incidencia de disturbios antropogénicos sobre el escurrimiento y erosión hídrica en el sur de la Región Semiárida Pampeana. Tesis Magister en Ciencias Agrarias de la UNS, 166 pp.

FAO. (2005). Livestock sector brief. Argentina.

FAO. (2006). Fertilizer use by crop. FAO Fertilizer and Plant Nutrition Bulletin No. 17. Online at ftp://ftp.fao.org/agl/agll/docs/fpnb17.pdf. Accessed February 2, 2015.

FAOSTAT. (2015). Online agricultural database. http://faostat3.fao.org/faostat-gateway/go/to/home/E. Accessed 23 Jan 2015.

Friedl, M., Sulla-Menashe, D., Tan, B., Schneider, A., Ramankutty, N., Sibley, A., & Huang, X. (2010). MODIS global land cover: Algorithm refinements and characterization of new datasets. *Remote Sensing of Environment, 114*(1), 168–182.

Friedrich, T., Kassam, A., & Taher, F. (2009). Adoption of conservation agriculture and the role of policy and institutional support. Invited paper for the International Consultation on "No-Till with Soil Cover and Crop Rotation: A Basis for Policy Support to Conservation Agriculture for Sustainable Production Intensification", Astana & Shortandy, Kazakhstan, 8–10 July 2009.

Glave, A. (2006). La Influencia climática en el Sudoeste Bonaerense y el Sudeste Pampeano en: Revista Producción. *Animal, 31*, 18–23.

Globcover. (2005). Global land cover 2005. http://due.esrin.esa.int/page_globcover.php. Accessed 13 Jan 2015.

Globcover. (2009). Global land cover 2009. Online at http://www.gelib.com/globcover-2009.htm. Accessed 13 Jan 2015.

Golluscio, R. A., Deregibus, V. A., & Paruelo, J. M. (1998). Sustainability and range management in the Patagonian steppes. *Ecología Austral, 8*(2), 265–284.

IARC (International Agency for Research on Cancer). (2014). Monographs on the Evaluation of Carcinogenic Risks to Humans. World Health Organization (WHO), Internal Report 14/002.

Lossino, B. N., Heredia, O. S., Sainato, C. M., Giuffré, L., & Galindo, G. (2002). Potential impact of irrigation with groundwater on soils of Pergamino stream basin, Buenos Aires Province, Argentina. Impacto potencial del riego con agua subterránea sobre los suelos en la cuenca del arroyo Pergamino, Provincia de Buenos Aires, Argentina. *Ecología Austral, 12*, 55-63

Iurman, D. (2010). Sistemas agropecuarios de Villarino y Patagones. Análisis y propuestas. Boletín técnico INTA Ascasubi. http://inta.gob.ar/documentos/sistemas-agropecuarios-de-villarino-y-patagones.-analisis-y-propuestas/

Iurman, D., Larreguy, V., Demarchi, R. (2012). Evaluación económica de un sistema ganadero en Levalle, partido de Villarino. No publicado.

Jergentz, S., Mugni, H., Bonetto, C., & Schulz, R. (2005). Assessment of insecticide contamination in runoff and stream water of small agricultural streams in the main soybean area of Argentina. *Chemosphere, 61*(6), 817–826.

Jones, K. G. (2004). *Trends in the US sheep industry*. Washington, DC: USDA Economic Research Service.

NASA (National Aerospace Authority). (2014). Moderate-resolution imaging spectroradiometer (MODIS). Online at http://modis.gsfc.nasa.gov/about/media/modis_brochure.pdf. Accessed 27 May 2014.

Oliva, G., Ferrante, D., Puig, S., & Williams, M. (2012). Sustainable sheep management using continuous grazing and variable stocking rates in Patagonia: A case study. *The Rangeland Journal, 34*(3), 285–295.

Pachauri, R. K., Allen, M. R., Barros, V. R., Broome, J., Cramer, W., Christ, R., et al. (2014). Climate change 2014: Synthesis report. In R. Pachauri, & L. Meyer (Eds.), Contribution of Working Groups I, II and III to the Fifth Assessment Report of the Intergovernmental Panel on Climate Change, Geneva, Switzerland, IPCC, 151 pp. ISBN: 978-92-9169-143-2.

Paganelli, A., Gnazzo, V., Acosta, H., López, S. L., & Carrasco, A. E. (2010). Glyphosate-based herbicides produce teratogenic effects on vertebrates by impairing retinoic acid signaling. *Chemical Research in Toxicology, 23*(10), 1586–1595.

Paula, B. M., & Oscar, M. N. (2012). Land-use planning based on ecosystem service assessment: A case study in the Southeast Pampas of Argentina. *Agriculture, Ecosystems & Environment, 154*, 34–43.

Qaim, M., & Traxler, G. (2005). Roundup ready soybeans in Argentina: Farm level and aggregate welfare effects. *Agricultural Economics, 32*, 73–86.

Regúnaga, M., & Rodriguez, A. T. (2015). Argentina's agricultural policies, trade, and sustainable development objectives. Online at http://www.ictsd.org/sites/default/files/research/Argentina%20Agricultural%20Trade%20Policy%20and%20Sustainable%20Development.pdf. Accessed 23 Jan 2015.

República de Argentina. (1994). Constitución de 1994. Online at http://pdba.georgetown.edu/Constitutions/Argentina/argen94_c.html. Accessed 23 Jan 2015.

Rostagno, C. M., & Degorgue, G. (2011). Desert pavements as indicators of soil erosion on aridic soils in north-east Patagonia (Argentina). *Geomorphology, 134*(3), 224–231.

Secretaría de Ambiente y Desarrollo Sustentable de la Nación. (2007). Primer Inventario Nacional de Bosques Nativos. 2da. Etapa: Inventario de campo de la Región del Espinal (Distritos del Caldén y del Ñandubay). BIRF 4085 AR. 236 p y un Anexo.

Seghezzo, L., Volante, J. N., Paruelo, J. M., Somma, D. J., Buliubasich, E. C., Rodríguez, H. E., et al. (2011). Native forests and agriculture in Salta (Argentina): Conflicting visions of development. The Journal of Environment & Development, 1070496511416915.

Silenzi, J. C., Echeverría, N. E., Bouza, M. E., & De Lucia, M. P. (2011). Degradación de suelos del SO Bonaerense y su recuperación. Academia Nacional de Agronomía y Veterinaria. Jornada sobre: "Evolución y Futuro del Desarrollo de Producciones Agrícolas y Ganaderas en el SO Bonaerense". Tomo LXV, pp. 382–404. ISSN: 0327-8093.

Silenzi, J. C., Echeverría, N. E., Bouza, M. E., & DeLucía, M. P. (2009). The wind erosion cost in the south west of Buenos Aires province. Drylands Science for Development (DSD). United Nations Convention to Combat Desertification (UNCCD). First Scientific Conference: Understanding Desertification and Land Degradation Trends. Poster Session at the UNCCD COP-9. Buenos Aires.

Silenzi, J. C., Echeverría, N. E., Bouza, M. E., & De Lucía, M. P. (2014). Incidencia del manejo sobre el ambiente de montes del Caldenal semiárido y árido. Inédito.

Silenzi, J. C., Echeverría, N. E., Vallejos, A. G., Bouza, M. E., & De Lucia, M. P. (2010). Wind erosion risk for soils of Buenos Aires southwest province and its relationship to the productivity index. In International Conference on Aeolian Research (ICAR VII) Santa Rosa, Julio de 2010. Trabajo en Actas: Technical session 6, p. 130.

Silenzi, J. C., Echeverría, N. E., Vallejos, A. G., Bouza, M.E., & De Lucia, M. P. (2012). Wind erosion risk in the southwest of Buenos Aires Province, Argentina and its relationship to the productivity index. *Aeolian Research, 3*, 419–425.

Silenzi, J. C, Vallejos, A. G., Echeverría, N. E., De Lucía, M. P. (2004). Análisis de la gestión ambiental en la producción de trigo mediante labranza convencional y siembra directa. Indicadores de sustentabilidad 8 a 12. VI Congreso Nacional de Trigo y IV Simposio Nacional de Siembra Otoño Invernal. 20 al 22 de Octubre de 2004. Universidad Nacional del Sur.

Tomei, J., & Upham, P. (2009). Argentinean soy-based biodiesel: An introduction to production and impacts. *Energy Policy, 37*(10), 3890–3898.

Tomei, J., & Upham, P. (2011). Argentine clustering of soy biodiesel production: The role of international networks and the global soy oil and meal markets. *The Open Geography Journal, 4*, 45–54.

Tucci, C. (2007). Urban flood management. Online at http://www.gwp.org/Global/GWP-SAm_Files/Publicaciones/Gesti%C3%B3n%20de%20Inundaciones/Gestion-de-inundaciones-urbanas-ing.pdf. Accessed 25 Sept 2014.

UNDP (United Nations Development Program). Human Development Report. (2014). *Sustaining human progress: Reducing vulnerabilities and building resilience* (p. 212).

Viglizzo, E. F., Frank, F. C., Carreno, L. V., Jobbagy, E. G., Pereyra, H., Clatt, J., et al. (2011). Ecological and environmental footprint of 50 years of agricultural expansion in Argentina. *Global Change Biology, 17*(2), 959–973.

Volante, J. N., Alcaraz-Segura, D., Mosciaro, M. J., Viglizzo, E. F., & Paruelo, J. M. (2012). Ecosystem functional changes associated with land clearing in NW Argentina. *Agriculture, Ecosystems & Environment, 154*, 12–22.

Wilson, M. G. (2007). Uso de la Tierra en el área de bosques nativos de Entre Ríos, Argentina. Tesis Doctoral. Universidad de la Coruña, España. 277 pp.

Wilson, M., & Sabattini, R. (2001). Sustentabilidad de los agroecosistemas de bosques de Entre Ríos: Revisión crítica y modelo conceptual. *Revista Facultad de Agronomía, 21*(2), 117–128.

World Bank. (2014). Country database. Online at http://www.worldbank.org/en/country/argentina

Yanelli, F. A., Tabeni, S., Mastrantonio, L. E., & Vezzani, N. (2014). Assessing degradation of abandoned farmlands for conservation of the Monte Desert biome in Argentina. *Environmental Management, 53*, 231–239.

Zaccagnini, M. E., Wilson, M. G., & Oszust, J. D. (2014). Manual de buenas prácticas para la conservación del suelo, la biodiversidad y sus servicios ecosistémicos. Área piloto Aldea Santa María. 1ª. Edición. Buenos Aires. ISBN 978-987-1560-55-4. Programa Naciones Unidas para el Desarrollo—PNUD. Secretaría de Ambiente y Desarrollo Sustentable de la Nación; INTA. Bs. As. 95 pp.

Chapter 12
Economics of Land Degradation and Improvement in Bhutan

Ephraim Nkonya, Raghavan Srinivasan, Weston Anderson and Edward Kato

Abstract This study was conducted with the objective of determining the returns to sustainable land management (SLM) at the national level in Bhutan. The study first uses satellite data on land change (Landsat) to examine land use change in 1990–2010 and its impact on sediment loading in hydroelectric power plants. The study then uses the Soil and Water Assessment Tool (SWAT) model to analyze the impact of land use change and land management on sediment loading. The results from the land use change and SWAT analyses are used to assess the economic benefits of SLM. We estimate the benefits and costs of SLM practices and compare them with the land-degrading practices that are most prevalent in Bhutan—that is, business as usual. An analysis of the drivers of adoption of SLM practices is also done to draw conclusions about strategies that Bhutan could use to enhance adoption of SLM practices. The land cover change results show that the vast majority of forested areas remained as such between 1994 and 2010. SWAT results show that with long-term SLM practices such as contouring, increased forested cover and density, terracing, and other SLM practices, soil erosion from forested area could be reduced by 50 %. Analysis of returns to SLM practices showed that citrus orchards are the most profitable enterprises in 13 of the 20 districts (dzongkhag), but they require farmers to wait for at least six years before the first harvest. Improved pasture management is the second most profitable enterprise—underscoring the potential role it can play to meet the growing demand for livestock products as household incomes increase. Returns to community forest management are low but profitable at a 10 % discount rate. Considering the drivers of SLM

E. Nkonya (✉) · E. Kato
International Food Policy Research Institute, 2033 K Street NW,
Washington DC 20006, USA
e-mail: e.nkonya@cgiar.org

R. Srinivasan
Departments of Ecosystem Sciences and Management and Biological and Agricultural Engineering, Texas A&M University, College Station, Texas, TX 77843, USA

W. Anderson
Department of Earth & Environmental Science Lamont-Doherty Earth Observatory, Columbia University, 61 Route 9W, Palisades, NY 10964, USA

E. Nkonya et al. (eds.), *Economics of Land Degradation and Improvement – A Global Assessment for Sustainable Development*,
DOI 10.1007/978-3-319-19168-3_12

adoption, our research shows an inverse relationship between returns to land management and their corresponding adoption rates. The factors that increase adoption of SLM were land security, access to extension services, and roads. In summary, Bhutan's policies and its cultural and historical background have set the country on the path to becoming a global green growth success story. Results of this study vindicate the country's efforts to invest in sustainable land and forest management and highlight the additional policies and strategies that will enhance achievement of Bhutan's SLM objectives.

Keywords Sustainable land management · Bhutan · Soil and water assessment tool · Hydroelectric power · Sediment

Introduction and Context

Bhutan's economy is dominated by hydroelectric power (HEP) generation—a sector that contributes about 22 % of the country's gross domestic product (GDP), which makes HEP the largest sector (NSB 2009). Sediment loading leads to significant cost for most HEP plants in the world (IPCC 2012), relating to power generation loss, reduction of turbine efficiency and lifetime, and increased repair costs (Lysne et al. 2003). This underscores the role played by sustainable land management (SLM) in Bhutan, whose economy heavily depends on the HEP sector. In addition, about 69.1 % of the population of 733,033 live in rural areas and depends on agriculture—a sector that contributed only 17 % of the GDP in 2013 (NSB 2013). Crops—excluding horticultural crops—account for only 7.7 % of the land area, whereas pasture and horticulture, respectively, account for 3.9 and 0.1 % (Ministry of Agriculture 1995; currently Ministry of Agriculture and Forests [MoAF]).

Forests—which cover 70 % of the land area—contributed only about 6.9 % of Bhutan's GDP in 2010, but this contribution was from only timber and paper products (Food and Agriculture Organization of the United Nations [FAO] 2011). The value of non-timber forest products (NTFP)—including regulating and supporting ecosystem services—is much greater. Unlike in other countries, Forest and Nature Conservation Acts and Rules (NCD 2003) allow communities currently living in protected areas (PAs) to continue living in PAs on the condition that they observe key rules and regulations (Choden et al. 2010; Phuntsho et al. 2011). Our study estimates that at least 25 % of Bhutan's population lives in PAs. The PAs comprise 19,751 km^2, which is more than 51 % of the land area of 38,394 km^2, a level that only a few countries have achieved (MoAF 2010). This suggests that the PAs provide abundant ecosystem services to the population living both inside and outside PAs. The PAs also serve as the catchment and source of rivers supplying water to HEP plants. Out of the four major HEP plants of Bhutan, the sources of water for Chhukha, Kurichhu, and Tala HEP come from the PAs.

This study was undertaken with the objective of assessing the economic benefits of SLM in clear monetary terms and conducting a national-level cost-benefit assessment of investments into SLM. Results of the study will be used to design Bhutan's SLM strategies to achieve its 2020 Vision of Peace, Prosperity and Happiness of the Bhutanese people by enhancing their traditional values and improving their standard of living and environmental sustainability (RGoB 2002). Based on the economic analysis, the study would also identify priority investments with the highest economic benefits for the country. Furthermore, the analysis will allow the Royal Government of Bhutan (RGoB) to mainstream SLM in its five-year plan's programs and provide budgetary support on a priority basis.

The next section summarizes Bhutan's opportunities and challenges related to SLM. A brief discussion about the study background and approach is provided to set the stage for subsequent sections. This is followed by a discussion of Bhutan's land cover change trends and major biophysical characteristics. Analysis of soil erosion using the SWAT model follows the Land Use Change section. Using data collected by the renewable natural resource (RNR) household survey conducted in 2009, the study then analyzes land management practices and the drivers of adoption of SLM practices. This is followed by the economic analysis of the SLM practices at a national level. The final section concludes the study and gives policy implications.

Bhutan's Opportunities and Challenges Related to Sustainable Land Management

Opportunities

- Bhutan's mountains provide immense opportunities for HEP. The HEP sector currently accounts for up to 40 % of government revenue (DGPC 2009) and has the potential to grow. Owing to the large quantity of suitable terrain, the currently installed capacity of 1488 mw is only about 5 % of the estimated total HEP potential. Bhutan's vision is to achieve 10,000 mw installed capacity by 2020 (DGPC 2009).
- The large area under cover provides local benefits—including serving as a source of water used for HEP generation—and global benefits of carbon sequestration, biodiversity, genetic information, and other forest ecosystems. Such services provide opportunities for Bhutan to derive payment for ecosystem services from the global community.
- Bhutan's deep-rooted traditions and its cultural values of Mahayana Buddhism serve as a robust cultural foundation for realizing the benefits of sustainable development. It is these cultural values, which stress the co-existence of people with nature and the sanctity of life, compassion for others, and happiness in general, that led Bhutan to adopt the Gross National Happiness measure instead of the traditional GDP. However, given that Bhutan's economy is heavily

dependent on natural resources, these cultural values also have been contributing to the long-term economic welfare of the Bhutanese people by encouraging sustainable development as Bhutan works toward its 2020 Vision of Peace, Prosperity and Happiness.

Challenges

- Only 30 % of the population uses inorganic fertilizer, and 60 % uses manure. As a result of this and other challenges, yields of maize and rice are only about 67 and 50 % of the potential yield (Chetri et al. 2003).
- Bhutan's forest development policy from 1961 to the 1980s followed centrally managed and industrial forest harvesting, which eroded community responsibility for forest management and subsequently led to forest degradation (Gyamtsho et al. 2006). In response to this, a royal decree in 1979 and the Forest and Nature Conservation Act in 1995, among other statutes, gave communities a mandate to practice CFM) (Gyamtsho et al. 2006; Phuntsho et al. 2011). In 2010, fewer than 300 CFM systems existed, and it is expected that the total number of community forests (CFs) will reach only 400 by 2013, covering a negligible 4 % of the total forest area. The total forest area appropriate for CFM is 2380 km^2, or 20 % of forest area managed by the central government (Phuntsho et al. 2011). The slow pace of CFM adoption poses a challenge to ensuring sustainable forest management (SFM).
- Significant soil erosion leads to high repair costs of HEP plants. DGPC spends US$16 million each year to repair turbines and other underwater structures due to sediment loading. About 60 % of such cost is associated with sediment loading.
- Bhutan's topography makes land management and transportation infrastructure development a challenge. Road and other market infrastructure development is costlier and could trigger more severe soil erosion than is the case in flatter landscapes. About 30 % of Bhutan's population lives in areas from which it takes more than three hours to walk to the nearest motor-road (RGoB, MoAF 2010a, b).

Study Background and Approach

There are many definitions of SLM, and each emphasizes some elements of two key issues: long-term maintenance of ecosystem services and provision of ecosystem services desired by people (Winslow et al. 2011). The World Overview of Conservation Approaches and Technologies (WOCAT) defines SLM as the use of land resources for the production of goods and services to meet changing human needs while simultaneously ensuring the long-term productive potential of land resources and the maintenance of their environmental functions (WOCAT 2007). However, the United Nations Convention to Combat Desertification (UNCCD) defines SLM as “land managed in such a way as to maintain or improve ecosystem services for human wellbeing, as negotiated by all stakeholders” (Winslow et al. 2011). The element of desired functions is context specific since human needs differ significantly. One type of land management practice may be viewed as land degrading in one part of the world but as SLM in another. So our working definition will be in the context of Bhutan’s needs according to 2020 Vision: “Peace, Prosperity and Happiness of the Bhutanese people by enhancing their traditional values, improving their standard of living and environmental sustainability” (RGoB 2002). For RGoB to be able to achieve such a goal, our analysis will look at both on-farm and off-site benefits of SLM practices and the costs and benefits of land-degrading management practices. In this study, the primary off-site benefit of SLM considered is the reduction of sediment, which has large benefits to HEP plants. The SWAT model results will be used to determine the impact of SLM on sediment loading.

SLM—as used in this study—does not necessarily mean complete prevention of land degradation or complete rehabilitation of degraded lands. A land management practice will be regarded as SLM if it completely or partially prevents or reduces land degradation. This could apply to land management that may still be causing a reduced form of land degradation but is better than the prevailing land-degrading practices. For example, the amount of chemical fertilizer applied may be less than the amount required to fully replenish soil nutrients taken up by crops but is regarded as SLM if it is better than the prevailing land-degrading practice. However, to ensure that we reflect Bhutan’s desired function and needs, a land management practice is regarded as sustainable if it is undertaken according to the country’s recommended practices. For cropland, the recommended soil fertility management practices and crop varieties will be regarded as SLM. Improved pasture management is regarded as SLM for livestock management. Likewise, the country’s effort to promote CFM is regarded as SLM for the relevant and available forested area.

Responding to Bhutan’s desired functions, our SLM analysis will focus on HEP, forest, livestock, and agricultural land management. Given the large data needs required for determining the on-farm and off-farm benefits of SLM, our study will rely heavily on existing data and studies. The study will also use the SWAT simulation model to assess the short- and long-term impacts of management practices on the watersheds. This approach will allow us to determine the off-site impact of upstream SLM practices on sediment loading in HEP.

The study was motivated by an SLM project that was funded by the Global Environment Facility (GEF) under the World Bank’s administration. The main objective of the SLM project—which ended in June 2013—was to protect vulnerable land and to rehabilitate degraded lands. Table 12.1 summarizes SLM project’s major activities and their expected outcomes.

Table 12.1 Prevention of land degradation and rehabilitation of degraded lands by sustainable land management project

Sustainable land management project	Area covered (ha)	Expected major outcome
Protection of vulnerable lands	2410	
• Bamboo plantation	296	Bamboo planted in rills gullies to reduce gully formation
• Community and private forest	1422	Sustainable timber production, protection and use of natural forests and water resources, and rehabilitation of barren area through plantation
• Check dams	937[a]	Water conservation and availability through water source protection
• Planting leguminous crops	141	Improved soil fertility through nitrogen fixation
• Other	17	
• Stonewalling/bunding		Prevention/reduction of soil erosion
• Rehabilitation of degraded lands	2573	Conversion of slash-and-burn agriculture practice (ex-*tseri* land) to more sustainable land use
• Dryland terracing	45	This involves conversion of steep-sloped land to terraced land that is used for irrigated crops (*chhuzhing*) if irrigation water is available
• Wetland terracing	49	Terracing irrigated areas (wetlands) to reduce soil erosion
• Contour	157	Reduced soil erosion
• Hedgerow	326	Reduced soil erosion
• Agroforestry	39	Reduced soil erosion, nitrogen fixation
• Orchard plantation	833	Planting of fruit trees on steep dry land previously used as *tseri* or allowed to lie fallow, generate income for fruit sales
• Annual crops	1126	Income generation
• Manure shed construction		Reduction of forest degradation and soil erosion by reducing number of stray grazing animals, increase crop yield through use of farm yard manure, increase milk production

Source GEF (2012)
Note: *tseri* shifting cultivation/slash-and-burn cultivation; *chhuzhing* wetlands
[a]Number of check dams constructed

Just as in the SLM project, our study will focus on land management practices that prevent land degradation and those that rehabilitate degraded lands. However, our study was conducted at a national level and will move beyond SLM project's focus on agricultural land. The focus will be on the three land use types—forests, cropland, and grazing lands. We will focus on selected land management practices that are the most commonly used. The discussion for each of the major land use types gives its corresponding economic importance and land area coverage.

Forest

Forest contributed about 24 % of the agricultural GDP in 2000–2009 and grew at a modest average of 1.7 % during the same time (Christensen et al. 2012). About 70.5 % of the land area in Bhutan is covered with forests (RGoB, MoAF 2010a, b), and the constitution states that forest cover should be at least 60 % of the total land area (RGoB 2008). The small contribution of forest to GDP is due to the nonvaluation of other ecosystem services provided by forests. As discussed earlier, rivers supplying HEP originate from forests, but the water catchment, prevention of soil erosion, and other roles of the forests are not taken into account when computing GDP.

The RGoB has realized the importance of decentralizing forest management and has encouraged communities to manage the forest resources to meet their forest needs. As of 2012, 21,723 rural households—or 24 % of all rural households—managed CF, which covered 62,237 ha or 1.8 % of forested area (Dukra 2013). There are two ways that more households could participate in CF programs: (1) converting centrally managed government forest reserve to CF and (2) converting unused lands to CF. As shown in Table 12.2, only about 4000 km^2 is available for CF. The government had estimated that the CF area would account for 4 % of the total forested area by 2013 (RGoB, MoAF 2010a, b), but only 1.8 % of the forested area was CF by 2012 (Dukra 2013).

SFM can be achieved in part by reforesting cleared lands and by increasing forest density of degraded forests. As shown below, only a small area experienced deforestation. But there is large potential for improvement of forest density through better management, which could be achieved through decentralization of public forest to CF management.

Table 12.2 Available area for community forest in Bhutan

Sustainable land management project	Area (km^2)	Estimated impact on forest ecosystem services (% change)
Convert centrally managed non–protected area forests to community forests	3974.3[a]	25
Convert unused lands to community forest (km^2)	2.4[b]	

Source Ministry of Agriculture and Forests data (2010)
Note: *km*^{2} square kilometers. [a]Total forest area (27,053.0 km^2)—protected area (19,751.0 km^2)—community forests (622.4 km^2)—government forest reserve (2705.3 km^2) = 3974.3 km^2. [b]Unused land: agriculture to fallow, bushland, or bare land (2.17) + unused land (0.17) + deforested area (0.02) = 2.36 km^2

Crops and Citrus

The contribution of the major cereal crops (rice, maize, barley, and wheat) to the agricultural GDP has declined significantly since 2007 (Christensen et al. 2012). One of the reasons for such decline is land degradation. We focus our analysis on maize and rice, which, respectively, account for 42 and 52 % of the cultivated crop area. We also analyze fruit crops, which occupy a small land area yet form the largest cash income of the rural households and dominate the commercial agriculture for both domestic and export markets. Thirteen out of 20 districts (dzongkhag) are major growers of citrus (mainly mandarin orange) (MoAF 2011).

Maize Maize contributed 17 % of the crop GDP in 2009 (Christensen et al. 2012), but 69 % of farmers in BhutanBhutan grow maize, and the crop accounts for 49 % of the food basket and 42 % of the cultivated area (Tobgay and McCullough 2008). Cultivated mainly in the eastern region of the country, maize is the second most important food crop in Bhutan after rice (Tobgay and McCullough 2008).

Rice Paddy rice contributed 23.3 % of the crop GDP in 2009 (Christensen et al. 2012)—the largest contribution, shared with citrus. Rice production occupied 59,609 ha or 52 % of the cultivated area of 112,550 ha in 2010 (RGoB, MoAF 2012). The crop is mainly irrigated and grown in the warmer areas in the mid-altitude and low-altitude areas. Rice is an important staple crop, and its demand is growing, putting pressure on domestic production.

Fruit and horticultural crops Citrus production contributed 73.6 % of the crop GDP growth in 2000–2009 (Christensen et al. 2012) and 66 % of the household cash income. Fruit production has increased faster than production of cereals due to fruit's high returns and increasing demand. Fruit and horticultural crops are grown mainly during the summer period and are grown in the following agroecological zones (AEZs): warm temperate, dry subtropical, humid subtropical, and wet subtropical.

The SLM practice to be analyzed for maize and rice production is integrated soil fertility management (ISFM), which entails the use of organic inputs, judicious amounts of chemical fertilizer, and improved seeds (Vanlauwe and Giller 2006). The ISM matches the manure shed construction done by the SLM project to increase the production and use of farm yard manure. Studies in Bhutan have shown that ISFM significantly increases yields of rice and maize (Chetri et al. 2003). ISFM is used since it performs better than the use of mineral fertilizer or organic input alone (Vanlauwe and Giller 2006; Nandwa and Bekunda 1998).

Livestock

Livestock accounted for about 28 % of the agricultural GDP from 2000 to 2009 and grew at an average of 2.7 % during the same period (Christensen et al. 2012).

Two-thirds of rural households own cattle; most have two or more head of cattle (NSB and AsDB 2013). Livestock ownership is inversely related to consumption quintile. About 78 % of households in the poorest quintile and 18 % of the richest quintile own cattle (NSB and AsDB 2013). However, in the rural areas, 82 % of the poorest quintile and 44 % of the richest quintile own cattle (NSB and AsDB 2013).

The grazing area covers 11 % of the land area (Wangdi 2006), which is greater than the cropland area. The SLM practice that will be used is improved pasture, which could lead to both prevention of soil erosion and greater livestock productivity. Improved pasture includes planting leguminous seeds, improved grasses such as cocksfoot, and Italian rye and lotus (Samdup et al. 2013; Dorji 1993). Improved pasture also includes rotational grazing on rangelands, which allows pasture to recover (Chophyel 2009). Rearing of few improved breeds in lieu of large numbers of local breeds to reduce pressure on resources is encouraged.

Methodological Analysis and Data

To achieve a national-level SLM analysis, we will rely heavily on existing data and on simulation modeling to analyze SLM and its economic impact. The first aspect to analyze is land use change, which will help determine the potential impact on sediment loading. The effect of land use change on sediment loading will be analyzed using SWAT model simulation. The SWAT modeling will also include SLM practices beyond land use changes, including those that could affect sediment loading, for example, using SWM practices on cropland to reduce soil erosion. The economic analysis will include all results to determine the returns to all SLM practices.

Land Use Change

To measure the accuracy of and consistency between records of land cover, we use two datasets to analyze land use change:

Landsat Land Cover Dataset, Covering the 1990–2010 Period

The 30 meter (m) 30–m resolution data were derived from Landsat ETM + Satellite imagery and evaluated using Advanced Land Observation Satellite imagery and Google Earth. The data were harmonized and standardized by the International Center for Integrated Mountain Development in collaboration with the Bhutanese Ministry of Agriculture and Forests.

Bhutan Land Cover Assessment, Covering the 1994–2010 Period

The data sources, classification, and methods differed between the data collected in 1994 and that collected in 2010, which makes computation of land use change less reliable. The 1994 data were obtained from Panchromatic (black-and-white photographic film) images and were processed manually to delineate land use types. The 2010 data were obtained from Advanced Land Observation Satellite (AVNIR-2) images with a 10-m resolution. Unlike the 1994 dataset, the 2010 dataset was rigorously conducted with extensive ground truthing, an aspect missing from the Landsat dataset.

An analysis of the 2010 Landsat and 2010 national land cover datasets demonstrated that they compare favorably in their classification of agriculture, urban area, forested area, shrubland, and grassland. The comparison lends considerable credibility to the Landsat dataset, which was not ground-thruthed in the same rigorous manner as was the national land cover dataset. The moderate differences in the grassland/shrubland classes and more pronounced differences in snow cover and barren land may be explained in part by seasonality. The season in which the satellite images were taken will strongly influence the advance/retreat of the snowpack, grassland, and shrubland in the northern regions of Bhutan.

The decision about which land cover dataset—if not both—to use in the land cover change detection was based on the intended purpose of each dataset. The documentation for the national land cover dataset states explicitly that the dataset is not intended to be used in a change analysis given the methodological advances between the two datasets. But the Landsat-derived dataset produced all three years of coverage simultaneously with the express purpose of maintaining consistency in the methodology. While the Landsat dataset does have validation shortcomings (discussed previously), the consistency between years makes it ideal for land cover change analysis. In the case of pastureland, however, the Landsat dataset does not distinguish between grassland/shrubland and pastureland. For calculation of pastureland expansion and contraction the national dataset was used. These results should be interpreted keeping in mind the change in classification methods between 1994 and 2010.

Soil Erosion Analysis

Study Area

The total drainage area of the 11 river basins in Bhutan is approximately 47,541 km^2. The northern region of Bhutan consists of glaciated mountain peaks, with the highest elevations more than 7000 m above sea level. In the south, the southern foothills are covered with dense, deciduous forests; alluvial lowland river valleys; and mountains up to 1500 m above sea level (Fig. 12.1).

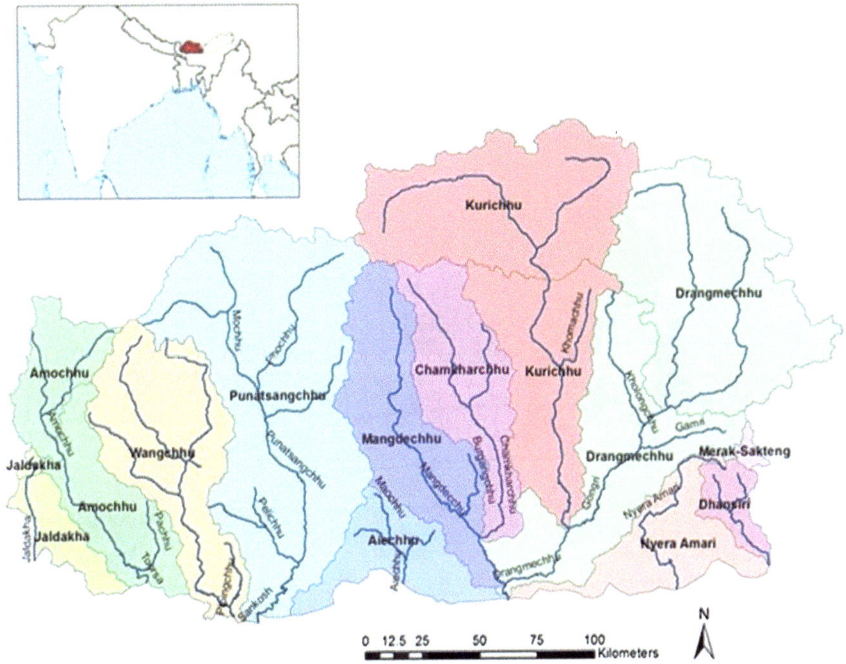

Fig. 12.1 Main rivers and major river basins. *Source* Ministry of Agriculture and Forests data (2013)

According to the United Nations Environment Programme (2009), Bhutan can be divided into three climatic zones: subtropical zone in the southern foothills with high humidity and heavy rainfall between 2500 and 5550 mm per year; temperate zone in the highlands with cool winters and hot summers, rising to 3000 m; and alpine climate zone under perpetual snow, with elevations up to 7550 m and average annual precipitation of 400 mm. Bhutan's water resources are confined to four major river basins: Amo Chhu, Wang Chhu, Puna-Tsang Chhu, and Manas Chhu. They all originate from the high-altitude alpine area and from the perpetual snow cover in the north and flow into the Brahmaputra River in the Indian plains.

SWAT

SWAT (Arnold et al. 1998) is a physically based, continuous simulation model developed to assess the short- and long-term impacts of management practices on large watersheds. The model requires extensive input data, which can be supplemented using internal model databases and algorithms for generating synthetic weather data (Luzio et al. 2002). The model divides watersheds into a number of sub-basins and adopts the concept of the hydrologic response unit (HRU), which is delineated according to a number of key parameters, such as land use, soil, and

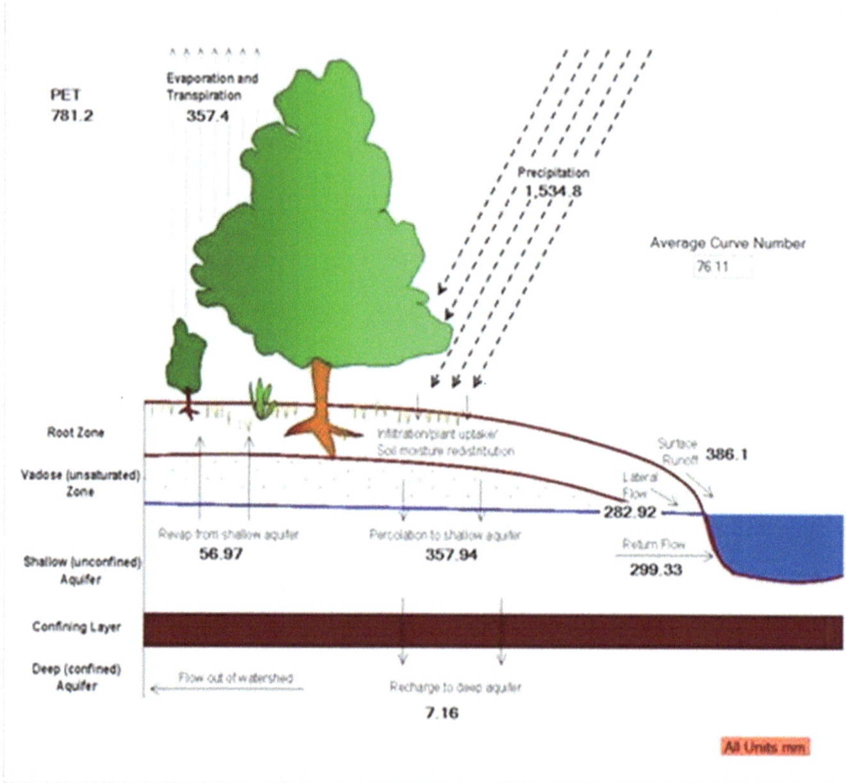

Fig. 12.2 Hydrologic budget of the basin from SWAT-check. *Source* Authors. Note: *SWAT* soil and water assessment tool; *PET* potential evapotranspiration; *mm* millimeters

slope. SWAT is able to simulate rainfall-runoff based on separate HRUs, which are aggregated to generate output from each sub-basin. SWAT is a combination of modules for water flow and balance, sediment transport, vegetation growth, nutrient cycling, and weather generation. SWAT can establish various scenarios detailed by different climate, soil, and land cover as well as the schedule of agricultural activities including crop planting, tillage, and best management practices (Flay 2001). A schematic presentation of SWAT hydrological modeling is presented in Fig. 12.2.

In summary, the benefits of using SWAT for this project are that, first, SWAT offers finer spatial and temporal scales, which allow the user to observe an output at a particular sub-basin on a particular day. Second, it considers comprehensive hydrological processes, estimating not only surface runoff with associated sediment and nutrients but also groundwater flow and channel processes within each sub-basin and at the watershed scale. However, nutrients were not modeled as part of this study. Third, on completion of this study, the calibrated model can be developed to further analyze scenarios such as best management practices, land use changes, climate change, and more.

Data Required for SWAT Analysis

Elevation (digital elevation model DEM) The National Soil Services Center (NSSC) provided DEM data with 10-meter resolution. The DEM was used to automatically delineate watershed boundaries and channel networks. Elevation ranges from 22 to 7456 m (Fig. 12.3). Steep area (slope of more than 63 %) accounts for 42.9 % of the area, whereas less than 6 % of the area is flat with slopes of 0–2 %.

Land use NSSC provided the land cover dataset created in 2010 (Fig. 12.4). Percentages of each land cover are summarized in Table 12.3. However, as seen above, Landsat land cover datasets were also used to analyze land use change. For 2010, land use types consist primarily of pine (55.35 %) and cool-season grass (17.91 %). Concerning land use change, there are more than 600 glaciers in Bhutan with an area of approximately 1300 km^2 (Beldring and Voksø 2011). There is an increasing tendency to go for cash crops such as apples in the temperate north and oranges in the subtropical south (Wangdi 2006).

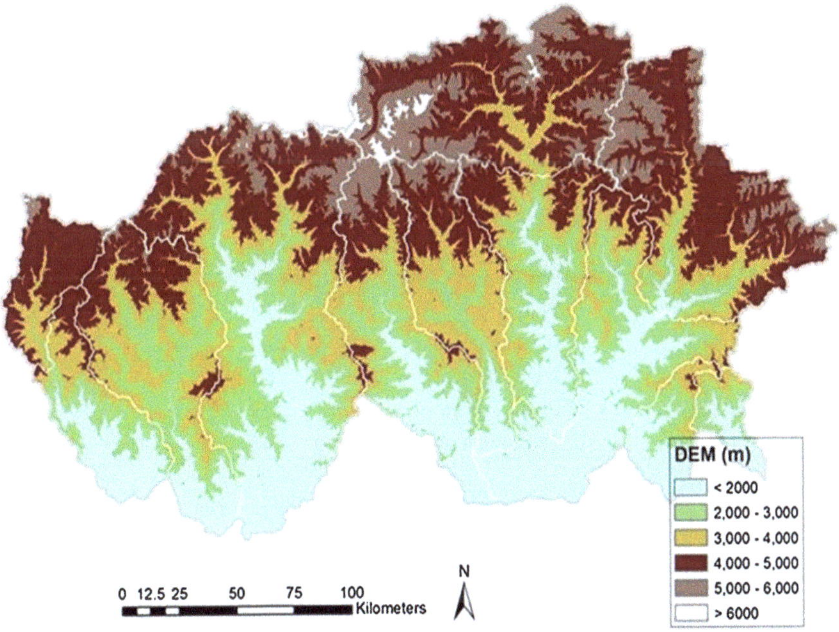

Fig. 12.3 DEM of for the country of Bhutan at 10-meter resolution. *Source* National Soil Services Center data (2013). Note: *DEM* digital elevation model; *m* meters

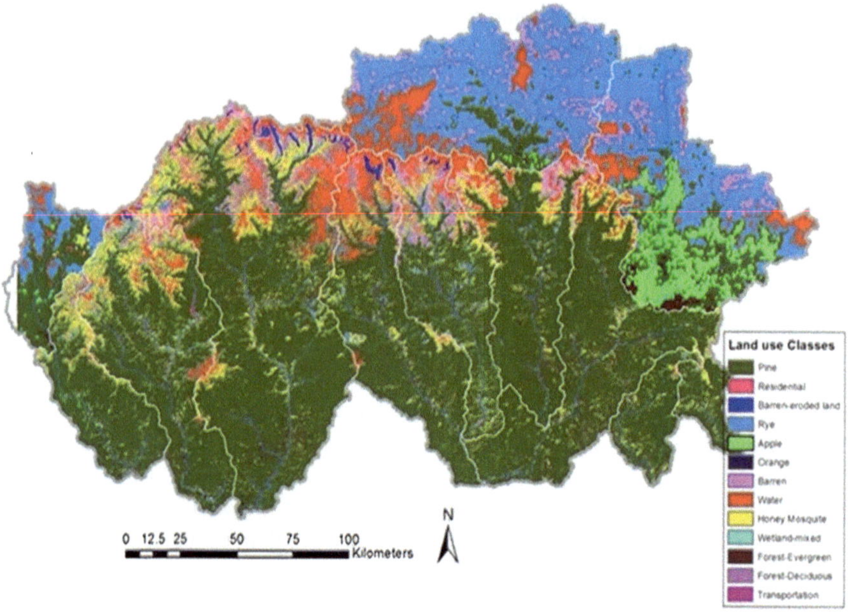

Fig. 12.4 Bhutan national land cover dataset (30-meter resolution) created in 2010. *Source* National Soil Services Center data (2010)

Table 12.3 Land use categories determined by the national land cover dataset (2010)

Land use type	Percentage of watershed area
Pine	55.35
Residential	0.08
Barren-eroded land	0.38
Natural grassland	17.91
Apple	2.56
Orange	0.08
Barren	4.31
Water	10.03
Honey mesquite	8.42
Wetlands-mixed	0.01
Forest-evergreen	0.39
Transportation	0.48
Total	100.00

Source National Soil Services Center data (2010)

Soil FAO/UNESCO provided soil data in shape file format and converted it to GRID format at a 1:5,000,000 scale (Fig. 12.5). The FAO/UNESCO soil map (FAO/UNESCO 1977) classified about 27 % of Bhutan as having either cambisols

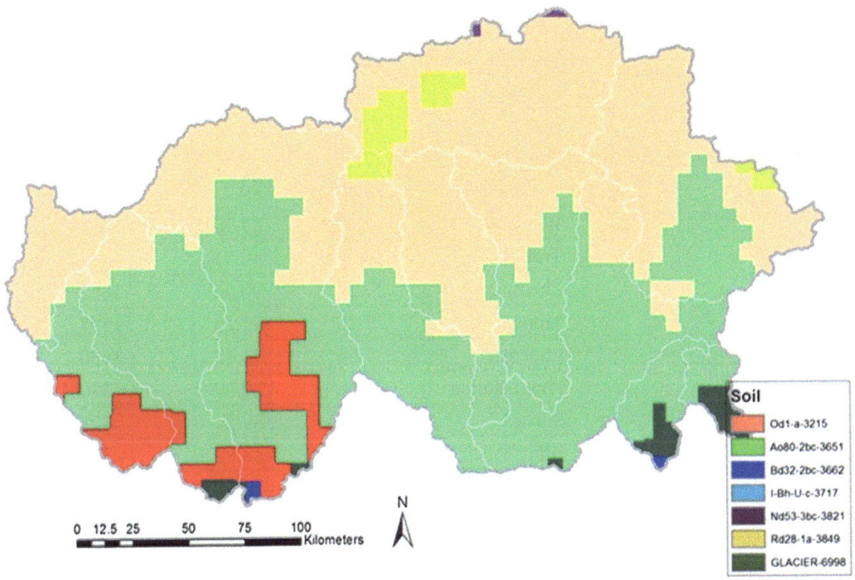

Fig. 12.5 FAO/UNESCO soil map of Bhutan. *Source* FAO/UNESCO (1977). *Note* Legend references FAO soil type codes. Od1-a-3215: Dystric Histosols, Ao80-2bc-3651: Orthic Acrisols, Bd32-2bc-3662: Dystric Cambisols, I-Bh-U-c-3717: Lithosols—Humic Cambisols—Rankers, Nd53-3bc-3821: Dystric Nitosols, Rd28-1a-3849: Dystric Regosols, GLACIER-6998: Glacier

or fluvisols (cambisols are most common in the medium-altitude zone, and fluvisols mostly occur in the southern belt). Less fertile acrisols, ferrasols, and podzols were estimated to cover 45 % of the country. The same study also reports that 21 % of the soil-covered area suffers from shallow depth with mostly lithosol occurring on steep slopes (Roder et al. 2001).

Weather stations The Hydromet department provided daily precipitation and temperature (minimum and maximum) data within and near the watershed from 1996 to 2012 (Table 12.4 and Fig. 12.6). A total of 20 local weather stations were used in this study (Fig. 12.7). The National Centers for Environmental Prediction's Climate Forecast System Reanalysis provided daily wind speed, relative humidity, and solar data in SWAT file format with ~31 km horizontal and ~35 km vertical resolution from 1979 through 2010.

Streamflow gauging stations Hydromet provided flow data at stream gauging stations, 24 of which were available in the basin (Fig. 12.8). Of those stations, 20 were used for modeling. All other stations were eliminated either because they had too much missing data or the gauging stations were located in a minor tributary and could not be analyzed. Table 12.5 summarizes the available gauging stations.

Table 12.4 Local precipitation and temperature stations throughout and near the basin

Name	Latitude	Longitude	Elevation
Simtokha	27.44	89.68	2310
Paro	27.38	89.42	2406
Haa	27.39	89.28	2711
Punakha	27.58	89.86	1239
Gasakhatey	27.96	89.73	2760
Wangdue	27.49	89.90	1214
Trongsa	27.50	90.51	2195
Zhemgang	27.22	90.66	1862
Mongar	27.28	91.26	1597
Lhuentse	27.66	91.18	1430
Phuntsholing	26.86	89.39	280
Sipsu	28.51	89.54	423
Bhur	28.27	88.87	377
Damphu	27.50	90.55	1564
Dagana	27.96	89.86	1865
Deothang	26.86	91.46	861
PemaGatshel	27.34	91.43	1723
TrashiYangtse	27.61	91.50	1839
Kanglung	27.28	91.52	2005
Bumthang	27.55	90.72	3032

Source Hydromet data (2013)

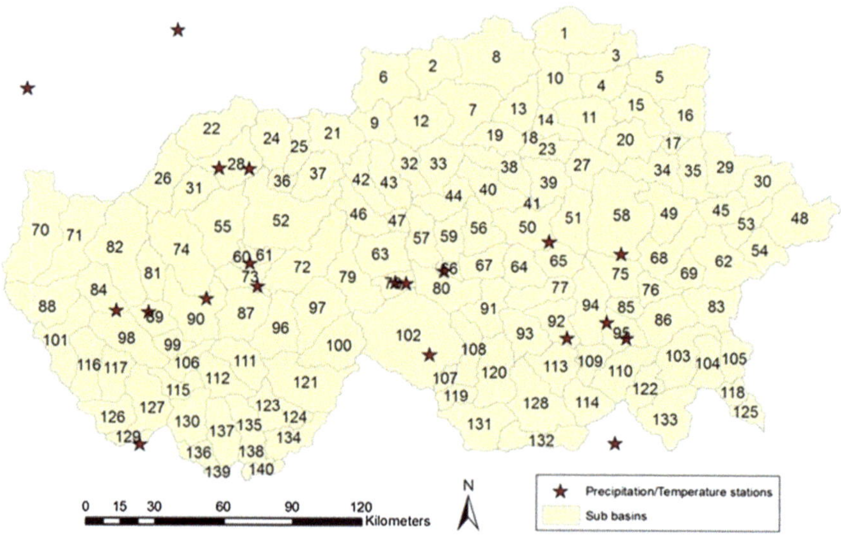

Fig. 12.6 Local precipitation and temperature stations throughout and near the basin. *Source* Hydromet data (2013)

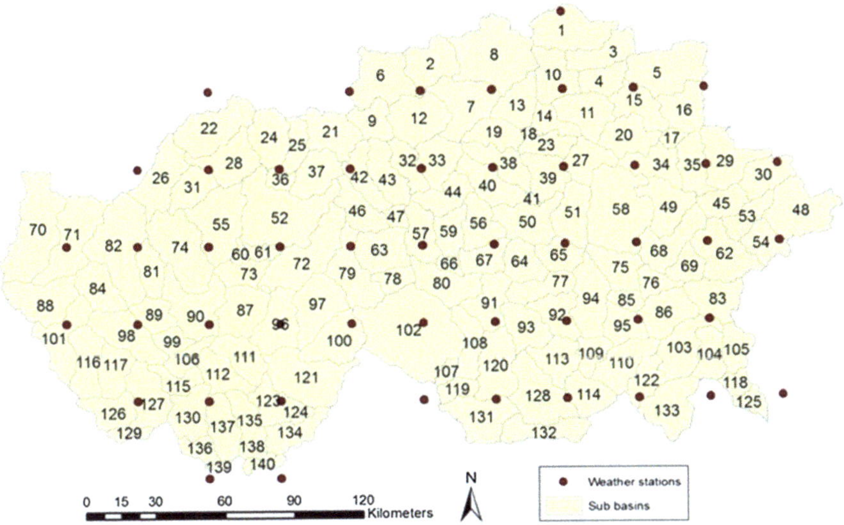

Fig. 12.7 Weather stations used in this project. *Source* Hydromet data (2013)

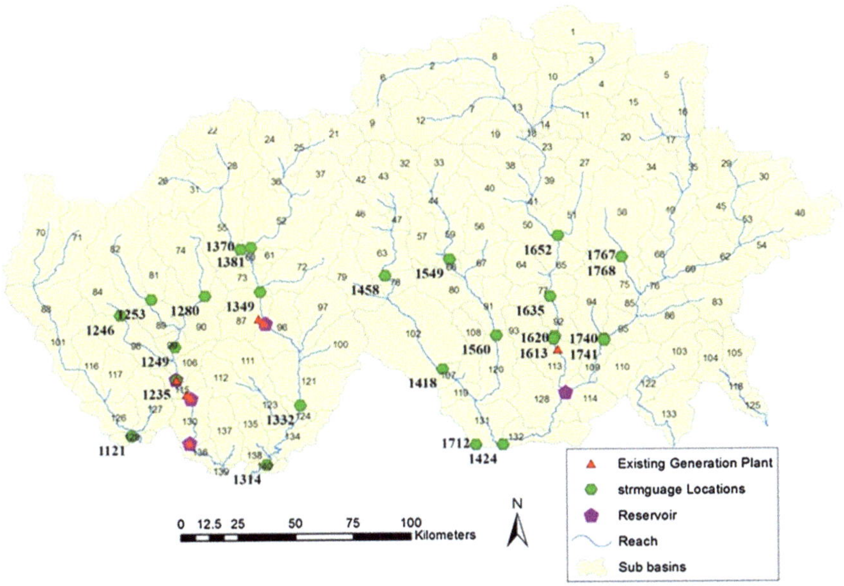

Fig. 12.8 Stream gauging stations available in the basin. *Source* Hydromet data (2013). Note: *strmguage* stream gauge

Table 12.5 List of available gauging stations

Station ID	Name	Sub-basin	Elevation (meters above sea level)	Drainage area (km^2)	Latitude	Longitude
1121	Doyagang on Amochhu	129	355	3650	26.89	89.34
1235	Chimakoti Dam on Wangchhu	106	1820	3550	27.11	89.53
1246	Hachhu	84	2700	320	27.37	89.29
1249	Damchhu on Wanchhu	99	1990	2520	27.24	89.53
1253	Parochhu	82	2255	1049	27.43	89.43
1280	Lungtenphug on Wangchhu	74	2260	663	27.45	89.66
1314	Kerabari on Sankosh	138	150	10,355	26.77	89.93
1332	Turitar on Sankosh	121	320	8593	27.01	90.08
1349	Wangdirapids on Phochhu + Mochhu	73	1190	6271	27.46	89.90
1370	Yebesa on Mochhu	55	1230	2320	27.63	89.82
1381	Samdingkha on Pho chhu	52	1220	1284	27.64	89.86
1418	Tingtibi on Mangdechhu Down Stream	102	530	3322	27.15	90.70
1424	Tingtibi on Dakpichhu	132	580	122	26.84	90.96
1458	Bjizam on Mangdechhu	63	1848	1390	27.52	90.45
1549	Kurjey on Chamkharchhu	59	2600	1350	27.59	90.74
1560	Bemethang on Chamkharchhu (Singkhar)	91	320	–	27.28	90.94
1613	Lingmethang on Maurichhu	93	565	284	27.26	91.19
1620	Kurizampa on Kurichhu	92	519	8600	27.27	91.19
1635	Autsho on Kurichhu	77	814	8453	27.43	91.18
1652	Sumpa on Kurichhu	50	1170	–	27.68	91.22
1712	Panbang on Dangmechhu		136	20,925	26.84	90.84
1740	Uzorong on Gongri	95	554	8560	27.26	91.41

(continued)

Table 12.5 (continued)

Station ID	Name	Sub-basin	Elevation (meters above sea level)	Drainage area (km^2)	Latitude	Longitude
1741	Sherichhu on Sherichhu	94	542	437	27.25	91.41
1767	Muktirap on Kholong Chhu	58	1640	905	27.59	91.49

Source Hydromet data (2013)
Note Sub-basin numbers indicate the contributing sub-basins for each gauging station. Dashes indicate no data

Project Setup

Watershed delineation The basin was delineated using a DEM in SWAT. The maximum drainage area threshold was 22,500 ha. When a gauging station was available for calibration, an outlet was inserted manually, splitting the sub-basin in two, with a gauged upper half and non-gauged lower half.

Automatic sub-basin delineation, based on given threshold areas and manual input of sub-basin outlets, generated 140 sub-basins (Fig. 12.9). SWAT then divided each sub-basin into more detailed HRUs. HRUs represent unique combinations of land use, soil type, and slope. SWAT delineates HRUs with user-defined thresholds represented as percentages of each land use, soil type, and slope. In this project, land use and soil type thresholds were set at 2 %, meaning that any land use covering more than 2 % of a sub-basin was considered an HRU, and from that

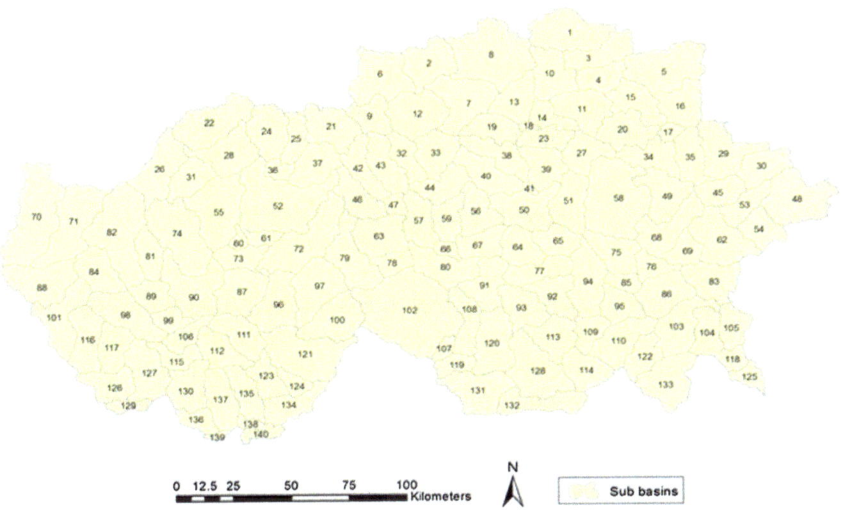

Fig. 12.9 Map of the basin showing sub-basin delineation. *Source* Hydromet data (2013)

portion of land use, any soil type covering more than 2 % was considered an HRU. These thresholds were chosen to avoid creating too many HRUs, which would make analyses too complicated and time consuming for the model process.

Based on the thresholds selected, there were a total of 4508 HRUs in the basin. These HRUs can be used for analyses on a particular land use or soil type.

HEP plant and reservoirs: All of the hydroelectric plants in this study generate power through run-of-the-river hydroelectricity. Five reservoirs were modeled at sub-basins 87, 106, 113, 115, and 130 (Fig. 12.8). The Tala Hydropower plant located at Wangchu contains a 92-m-high concrete dam and underground powerhouse. The Kurichhu Hydropower plant—located on Kurichhu river in the Mongar District—consists of a dam and has a 1-million-cubic-meter capacity cement reservoir and four turbines. The plant became operational on a staggered basis between April 2001 and May 2002. The list of the dams and HEP plants are summarized in Table 12.6.

Point sources: This study did not include any point sources, but they were set up in most modeled sub-basins for future use. All outputs from point sources were set to zero in this project. There is no wastewater treatment in Bhutan.

Model Calibration and Validation

Monthly streamflows were simulated against gauging station data; however, time periods with available data varied by gauging station (Table 12.7).

For statistical analyses of the calibration and validation, coefficient of determination (R^2), Nash-Sutcliffe model efficiency (NSE; Nash and Sutcliffe 1970), and percent bias (PBIAS) were examined. R^2 can range from 0.0 to 1.0, with higher values' indicating better model performance in predicting the variations of observed data. NSE indicates how well the plot of observed versus simulated data fits the 1:1 line. NSE ranges from $-\infty$ to 1.0; 1.0 indicates a perfect fit, and negative values indicate that average values of observed data are more reliable than the model predictions. Positive values show a better match of observed data and predicted values. NSE is calculated with Eq. 12.1:

$$NSE = 1 - \frac{\sum_{i=1}^{n}(O_i - P_i)^2}{\sum_{i=1}^{n}(O_i - \bar{O})^2} \qquad (12.1)$$

where O is the observed statistic for month *i*, P is the SWAT-simulated statistic for the same month i, and = the average of all the monthly observation data.

PBIAS measures the average tendency of the simulated data to be larger or smaller than their observed counterparts (Gupta et al. 1999). The optimal value of PBIAS is 0.0, with low values' indicating accurate model simulation in term of magnitude. Positive values indicate model underestimation bias, and negative values indicate model overestimation bias (Gupta, et al. 1999). It is calculated as

Table 12.6 SWAT input information used in the watershed

HEP Plant name	Location	River	Design capacity (mw)	Year commissioned	Component	Comments
KuriChu[a]	Gyelposhing	Mongar	60	2001	Dam + PH	Capacity of main reservoir: 15.7
						Height: 55 m
						Crest length: 285 m
BasoChhu[a]	Wangduephodrang	BasoChhu	40	2002	PH	Height: 4.5 m
Tala[a]	Wangkha	Chukha	1020	2007	Dam + PH	Reservoir surface area: 0.75 km^2
						Capacity of main reservoir: 9.8 million m^3
						Height: 92 m
Chhukha[b]	Tsimakhoti	Chukha	336	1988	Dam	Catchment area: 3108 km^2
						Height: 43 m

Source [a]Raw data obtained from Tala powerhouse. [b]GlobalEnergyObservatory.org (2013)
Note: *SWAT* Soil and Water Assessment Tool; *HEP* Hydroelectric power; *mw* megawatts; *m* meters; km^2 square kilometers; m^3 cubic meters

Table 12.7 Comparison statistics of simulated and actual monthly streamflow at 20 monitoring sites

Station ID	Sub-basin number	R^2	NSE	PBIAS	Station ID	Sub-basin number	R^2	NSE	PBIAS
1121	129	0.87	0.74	+1.80	1418	102	0.94	0.81	+13.03
1246	84	0.89	0.56	−33.89	1424	132	0.93	0.84	+4.04
1249	99	0.90	0.79	+9.10	1458	63	0.86	0.75	+1.28
1253	82	0.90	0.77	−2.39	1549	59	0.94	0.87	+1.81
1280	74	0.92	0.83	+13.00	1560	91	0.93	0.81	+14.00
1314	138	0.91	0.44	+44.17	1620	92	0.80	0.15	+28.84
1332	121	0.89	0.37	+49.67	1635	77	0.77	−0.80	−56.80
1349	73	0.89	−40.86	+37.20	1652	50	0.70	−1.61	−61.66
1370	55	0.85	0.46	−1.61	1740	95	0.88	0.82	+6.16
1381	52	0.79	−0.05	+1.40	1767	58	0.83	0.19	+45.75

Source Hydromet raw data
Note: *NSE* Nash-Sutcliffe model efficiency; *PBIAS* percent bias

$$\boldsymbol{PBIAS} = \left[\frac{\sum_{i=1}^{n}(\boldsymbol{O}_i - \boldsymbol{P}_i) * 100}{\sum_{i=1}^{n}\boldsymbol{O}_i}\right] \tag{12.2}$$

P = SWAT prediction. All other variables are as defined in Eq. 12.1.

According to Moriasi et al. (2007), model predictions can be classified as satisfactory if 0.5 < NSE ≤ 0.65 while ± 15 % ≤ PBIAS < ±25 %, good if 0.65 < NSE ≤ 0.75 while ±10 % ≤ PBIAS < ±15 %, and very good if 0.75 < NSE ≤ 1.00 while PBIAS ≤ ±10 %. Model performance is unsatisfactory if NSE ≤ 0.5 and PBIAS ≥ ±25 %.

Tables 12.7 and 12.8 include statistical comparisons of long-term means, standard deviations, R^2, NSE, and PBIAS. Model performance statistics used to assess calibration efforts indicate that SWAT model estimates are satisfactory with a range of 0.70–0.94 for R^2 and an NSE value greater than 0.50 for 11 gauged subwatersheds and unsatisfactory with an NSE value less than 0.50 for 9 subwatersheds. Differences between observed and modeled monthly streamflow, averaged over the entire simulation period at each gauging station, range from 1.45 to 61.67 % with an average difference of +3.92 % (Table 12.7). Table 12.9 presents predicted average monthly outflow from sub-basins for the relevant simulation period. Average monthly and annual basin values are presented in Table 12.10 and Table 12.11, respectively. According to the model outputs, 70 % of fallen snow is melted or evaporated, and only 5 % of total precipitation remains on the ground and is added to the snowpack each year.

Overall, the model compared well at a monthly temporal scale across 11 monitoring sites, given the input data developed in this study, while predicted flow from gauging stations on the Kurichhu (1620, 1635, 1652) and Puntasangchhu (1381, 1349, 1370) was not satisfactory. The main reason for poor results in these stations could be associated with the large gaps in precipitation data at these regions.

Table 12.8 Multiyear average and standard deviation of monthly streamflow

Station ID	Sub-basin number	Monthly average flow (cm)		Standard deviation		Simulation period
		Observed	Simulated	Observed	Simulated	
1121	129	182.39	179.74	169.45	125.00	2006–2012
1246	84	5.75	7.70	4.44	4.81	2000–2012
1249	99	65.84	59.85	60.34	57.27	2002–2012
1253	82	25.51	25.96	25.17	26.52	1997–2012
1280	74	22.77	19.81	22.02	21.47	1997–2012
1314	138	454.01	256.35	409.39	217.69	2007–2012
1332	121	359.47	180.90	315.62	147.77	2006–2012
1349	73	296.69	186.32	256.57	158.73	2003–2012
1370	55	113.49	111.44	105.50	90.34	2005–2012
1381	52	43.06	42.45	31.61	41.40	2008–2012
1418	102	147.76	128.50	121.49	89.04	2005–2012
1424	132	723.80	694.53	695.11	552.31	2011–2012
1458	63	59.78	58.25	52.02	51.86	2003–2012
1549	59	53.64	52.31	46.87	47.23	1997–2012
1560	91	97.06	83.46	82.72	63.54	2009–2012
1620	92	272.16	332.13	222.86	320.57	2006–2012
1635	77	223.39	329.42	178.59	318.37	2006–2012
1652	50	176.39	285.16	149.86	291.83	2007–2012
1740	95	304.89	286.11	236.06	205.83	1997–2012
1767	58	64.96	35.14	53.57	20.76	2001–2012

Source Soil and Water Assessment Tool results (2013)

Considerable uncertainty has been reported for the variations of precipitation with elevation in the mountainous terrain of Bhutan as well. For further improvements in monthly streamflow, more detailed information (for example, reservoirs, dams, and irrigation) needs to be collected.

To save space, six gauges—two in the west (1249 and 1121), one in the northwestern mountains (1370), two in the lower middle (1418 and 1549), and one in the east of the basin (1740)—were used to graphically illustrate simulated and observed streamflow. The simulated and observed streamflow at these gauges is shown in Fig. 12.10. Flow time series curves show the model captured well seasonal variation in streamflow, snowmelt, and evapotranspiration, although peaks are not always perfectly simulated. The hydrological regime of the rivers in this region is characterized by low flow in the cold dry winter, resulting in accumulation of snow at high altitudes, and high flow during summer caused by monsoon precipitation and melting of glacier ice and snow.

Snow season in the mountain area elevation of 3000 m often starts from late autumn to the next early summer. In the pre-monsoon and early monsoon season (May to July), snowmelt from all subwatersheds contributes significantly to river

Table 12.9 Average monthly streamflow from sub-basins

Reach number	Area (km^2)	Flow (cm)	Sub-basin number	Area (km^2)	Flow (cm)	Sub-basin number	Area (km^2)	Flow (cm)
1	546.30	4.22	48	594.90	21.90	95	8304.00	289.30
2	1166.00	41.11	49	2686.00	92.39	96	6492.00	157.60
3	865.60	8.86	50	7280.00	167.90	97	480.20	6.62
4	234.20	2.09	51	659.00	14.11	98	778.60	14.50
5	619.80	20.14	52	2342.00	42.54	99	2605.00	59.96
6	766.90	11.51	53	1213.00	46.46	100	441.20	15.35
7	983.80	30.17	54	843.90	33.39	101	2352.00	102.10
8	2017.00	52.45	55	2301.00	87.43	102	3319.00	149.10
9	243.30	1.34	56	310.10	13.15	103	418.10	10.18
10	1474.00	17.42	57	306.20	9.11	104	260.00	5.79
11	387.00	5.13	58	882.50	37.59	105	225.60	5.14
12	469.60	23.05	59	1378.00	52.94	106	3558.00	76.67
13	3311.00	91.41	60	2361.00	87.81	107	3393.00	150.80
14	2043.00	26.51	61	2438.00	43.39	108	281.70	9.72
15	321.00	5.67	62	2556.00	99.87	109	8942.00	310.20
16	957.30	29.86	63	1388.00	76.59	110	386.30	7.10
17	737.50	16.24	64	274.70	8.26	111	321.50	3.44
18	5384.00	118.70	65	8175.00	185.60	112	283.40	1.64
19	258.80	5.82	66	1451.00	53.54	113	9664.00	205.80
20	343.50	7.17	67	557.00	15.77	114	9624.00	348.40
21	397.50	3.47	68	3094.00	108.10	115	3739.00	98.68
22	537.70	21.78	69	2747.00	103.90	116	2724.00	105.90
23	5850.00	129.30	70	816.80	42.12	117	276.50	3.22
24	374.20	4.10	71	612.50	31.52	118	600.60	13.08
25	594.00	8.06	72	638.30	15.29	119	3817.00	163.80
26	461.00	23.16	73	5662.00	148.20	120	3177.00	88.56
27	287.60	5.58	74	663.40	19.94	121	8064.00	186.00
28	953.00	39.25	75	1196.00	45.51	122	650.00	14.24
29	452.20	18.55	76	6003.00	215.30	123	831.10	6.43
30	303.70	7.97	77	8722.00	196.70	124	8175.00	186.50
31	738.20	35.00	78	1541.00	80.34	125	727.80	26.47
32	226.50	9.40	79	454.50	18.75	126	3280.00	141.60
33	330.10	14.80	80	2390.00	73.26	127	412.10	48.67
34	304.90	14.28	81	232.50	5.12	128	19,850.00	559.10
35	2000.00	60.71	82	808.40	26.11	129	3785.00	200.90
36	1070.00	17.22	83	359.50	11.39	130	4078.00	141.30
37	338.90	5.02	84	323.50	7.69	131	7445.00	262.50
38	312.00	8.08	85	7313.00	265.20	132	20,170.00	593.10
39	6160.00	136.00	86	743.10	19.74	133	1103.00	62.98

(continued)

Table 12.9 (continued)

Reach number	Area (km^2)	Flow (cm)	Sub-basin number	Area (km^2)	Flow (cm)	Sub-basin number	Area (km^2)	Flow (cm)
40	353.20	9.56	87	6072.00	153.00	134	9289.00	223.20
41	6497.00	144.50	88	1914.00	91.20	135	270.10	29.25
42	281.00	15.50	89	1266.00	32.36	136	4227.00	160.90
43	328.20	19.13	90	1191.00	26.85	137	332.40	38.98
44	838.70	38.41	91	2721.00	76.84	138	9627.00	260.10
45	993.20	38.39	92	9017.00	199.20	139	4590.00	203.30
46	301.30	22.53	93	323.40	4.07	140	9718.00	270.50
47	694.90	39.00	94	448.40	19.55			

Source Soil and Water Assessment Tool results (2013)
Note: km^2 square kilometers; *cm* centimeters

Table 12.10 Average monthly basin values (millimeters)

Month	Rain	Snow fall	Surface runoff	Lateral flow	Water yield	Evapotranspiration
1	18.61	11.95	0.37	0.69	25.60	15.25
2	34.97	19.53	1.10	1.71	22.23	23.17
3	63.76	27.75	4.09	4.65	25.72	34.46
4	119.23	34.62	15.15	14.92	43.59	40.32
5	155.05	28.12	35.78	25.86	75.14	45.94
6	252.00	25.29	80.70	47.86	144.27	36.97
7	308.85	31.15	97.25	67.94	188.66	29.74
8	269.82	32.49	79.12	60.51	171.30	29.26
9	188.69	26.95	49.55	43.57	129.29	30.24
10	95.04	23.11	21.55	17.80	77.46	32.20
11	17.45	9.77	0.91	1.97	36.04	23.47
12	12.20	7.45	0.30	0.69	30.31	16.83

Source Soil and water assessment tool results (2013)

Table 12.11 Average annual basin values (millimeters)

Precipitation	1534.80	Groundwater	56.74
Snow fall	277.70	Deep aquifer discharge	7.06
Snow melt	173.54	Total aquifer discharge	353.20
Sublimation	22.26	Total water yield	969.03
Surface runoff	385.85	Percolation out of soil	353.19
Lateral soil flow	288.14	Evapotranspiration	357.20
Shallow aquifer percolation	295.05	Potential evapotranspiration	781.20

Source Soil and water assessment tool results (2013)

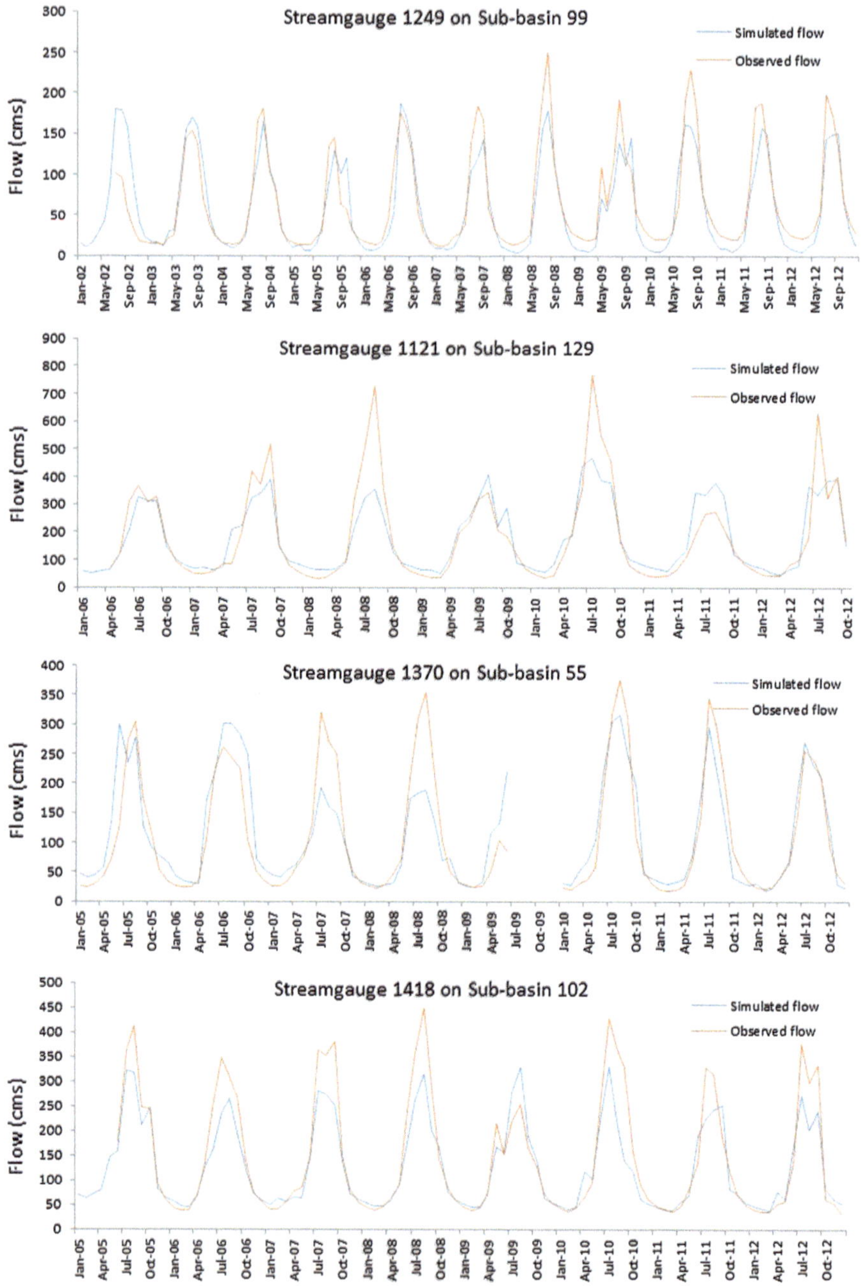

Fig. 12.10 Observed and simulated monthly streamflow (m^3/sec) at selected gauges. *Source* Authors. Note: *cms* centimeters; *Jan* January; *Sep* September; *Apr* April; *Jul* July; *Oct* October. Gauges 1249 and 1121 in the west; 1370 in the northwestern mountains; 1418 and 1549 in the lower middle, and 1740 in the east of the basin

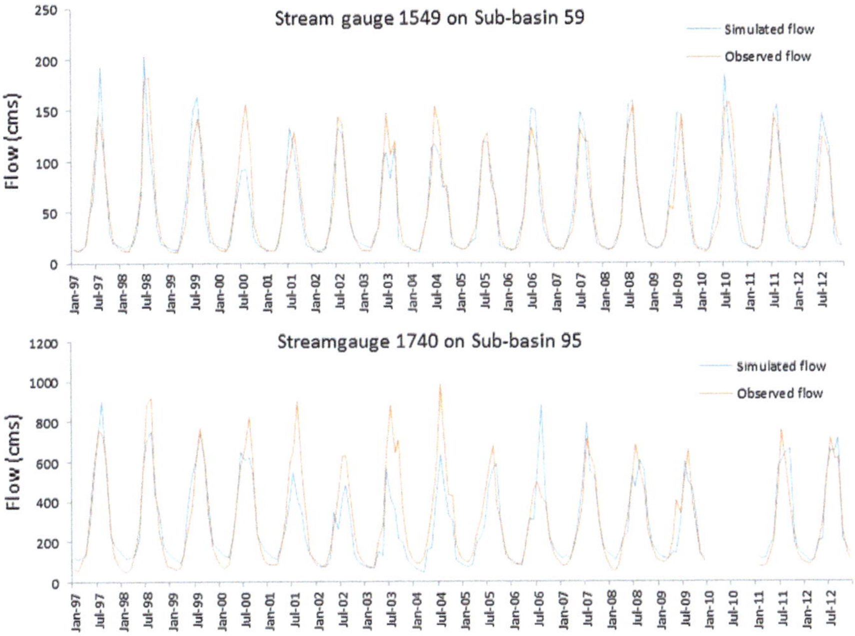

Fig. 12.10 (continued)

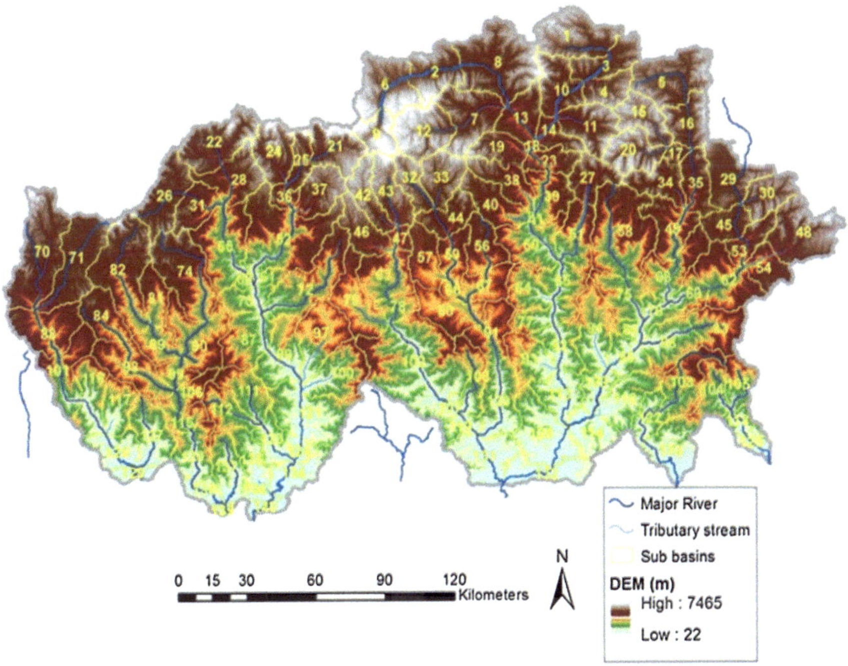

Fig. 12.11 Topographic situation of subwatersheds and gauging stations. *Source* National Soil Services Center data (2013). Note: *DEM* digital elevation model; *m* meters

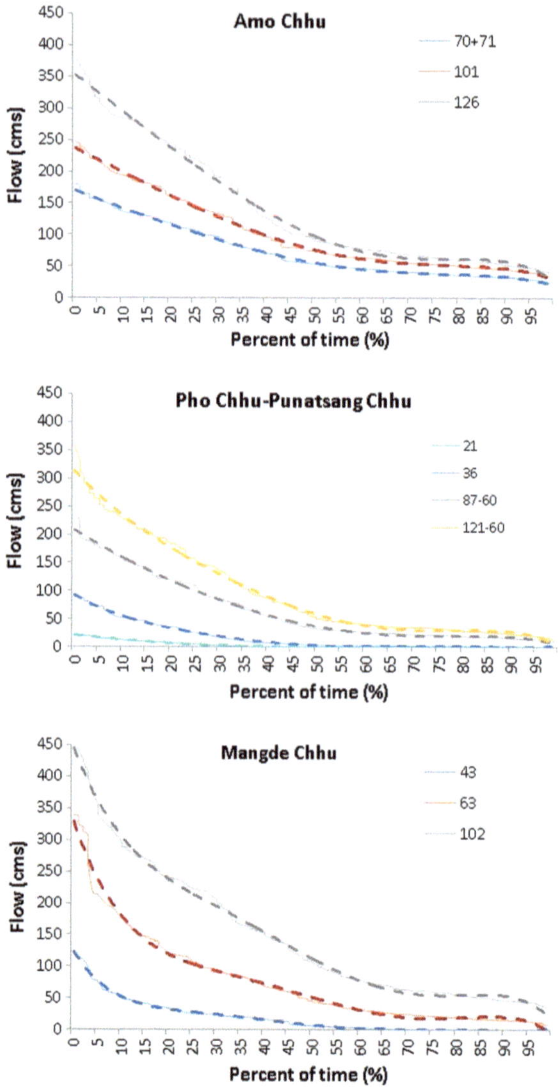

Fig. 12.11 (continued)

discharges. Every June to September is wet season, with frequent showers and night rainfalls. There is permanent snow cover in the area of elevation of 6000 meters. Sub-basins delineated by elevation is depicted in Fig. 12.11.

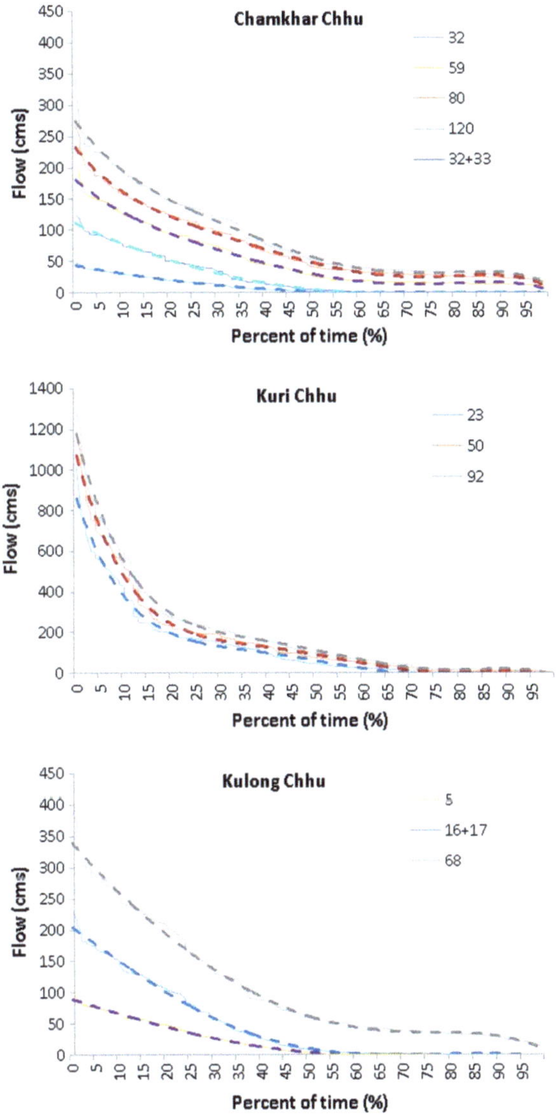

Fig. 12.11 (continued)

Spatial Distribution of Hydrologic Components by Subwatersheds

In southern subwatersheds with the elevation of 1500 m, there are frequent heavy rains during summer and stream contribution dominated by rainfall (Fig. 12.13). Snowmelt from higher-elevation ranges contributes more water to discharge despite lower rainfall in these subwatersheds. Figure 12.14 shows the spatial distribution of

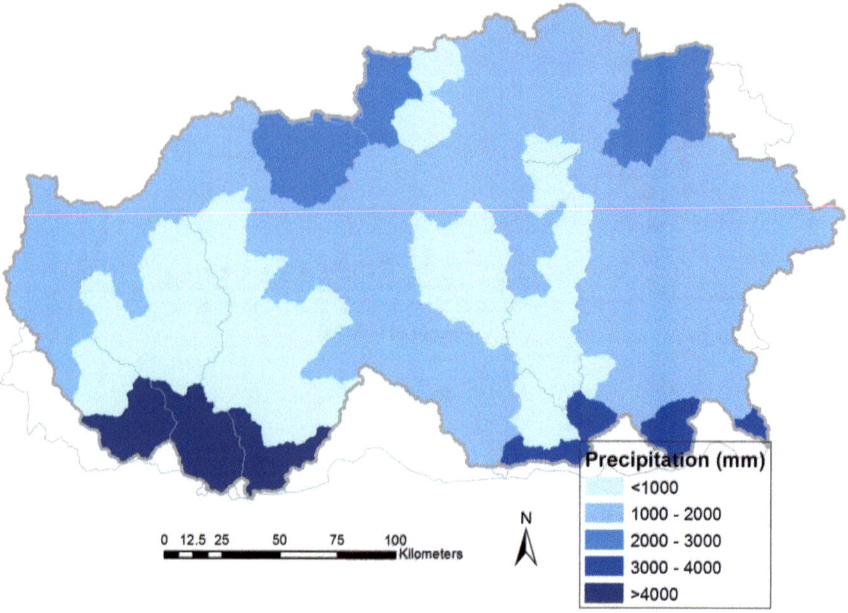

Fig. 12.12 Spatial distribution of average annual precipitation. *Source* Hydromet data (2013). Note: *mm* millimeters

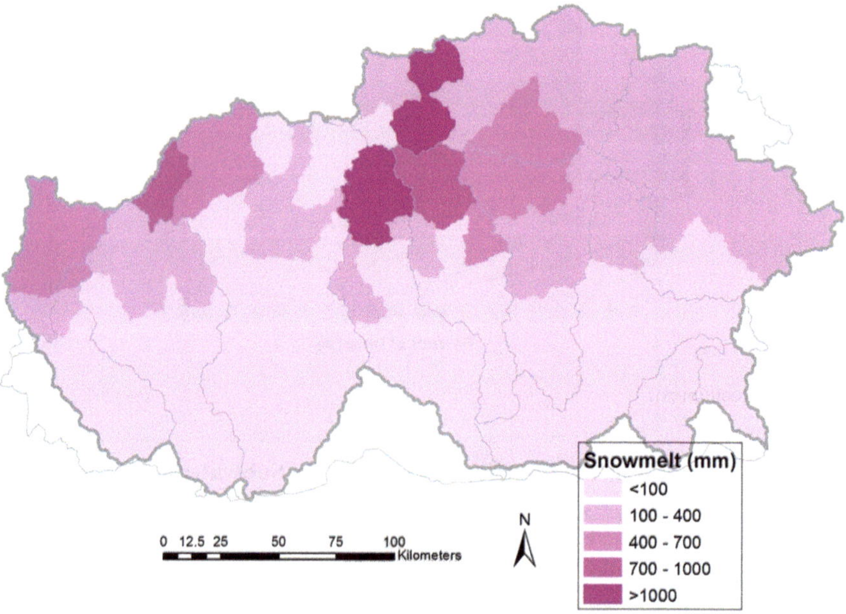

Fig. 12.13 Spatial distribution of average annual snowmelt. *Source* Hydromet data (2013). Note: *mm* millimeters

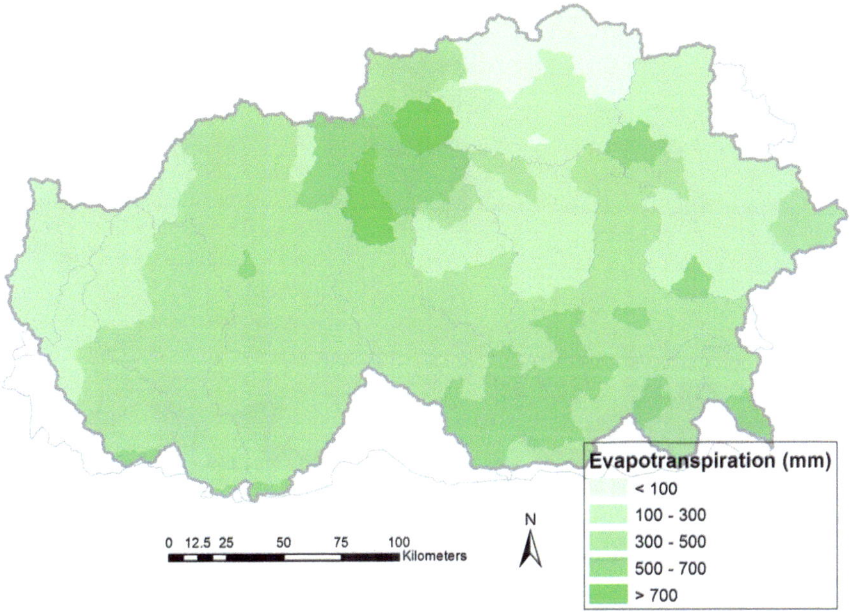

Fig. 12.14 Spatial distribution of average annual evapotranspiration. *Source* Hydromet data (2013). Note: *mm* millimeters

annual snowmelt. Note the high percentages derived from snowmelt in the upper central subwatersheds as well as in the high elevations (subwatersheds 42, 43, 48, 2, and 12). The frontal areas are dominated by rainfall and thus have a low snowmelt contribution. Figure 12.14 shows the evapotranspiration by sub-basin. Figure 12.15 shows the spatial distribution of surface runoff, which is highly dominated by rainfall contribution at the south and snowmelt contribution at mountainous sub-watersheds (Fig. 12.12).

Economic Analysis of SLM

To assess the economic benefits of SLM, we estimate the benefits and costs of SLM practices and compare them with practices that are most prevalent in Bhutan—that is, business as usual (BAU). Since land degradation, SLM investments, and their returns are long-term processes, time series data are required to determine the impact of SLM on land productivity. For example, greater yield due to terraces built in one year to prevent soil erosion may prevail over many years. Similarly, plants established to fix nitrogen may take years to show significant impact on crop yield, but once well established, nitrogen fixation and consequent higher crop yield could continue until when the leguminous tree is cut. As mentioned earlier, our analysis will include both on-farm and off-farm costs of land degradation and benefits of

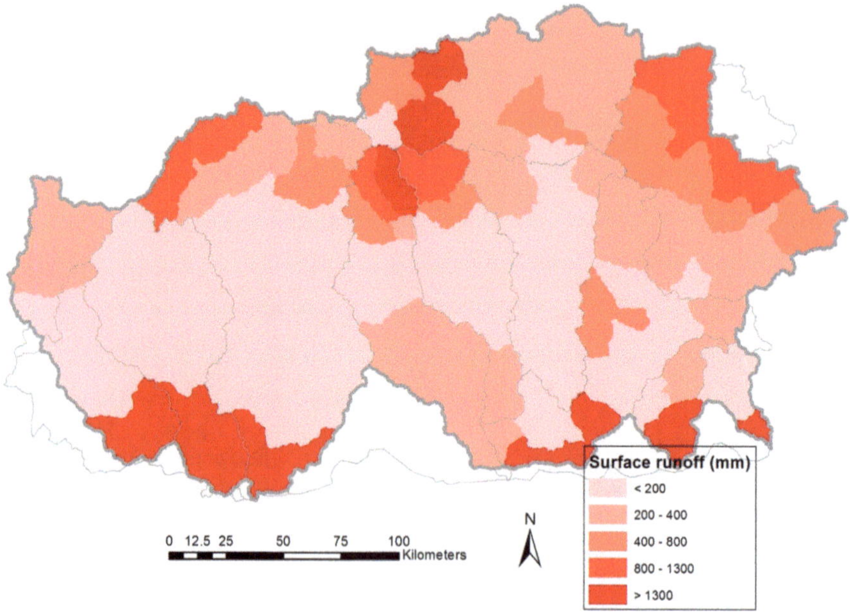

Fig. 12.15 Spatial distribution of average annual surface runoff. *Source* Hydromet data (2013). Note: *mm* millimeters

SLM. Assessment of the off-farm costs and benefits is complicated and difficult to measure (Berry et al. 2003; Hein 2006). Hence there has been a limited number of studies that have assessed the on-farm and off-site costs and benefits of land degradation and SLM investment. As mentioned earlier, the off-site benefits of SLM considered in this study are reductions in sediment loading. Accordingly, the off-site costs of land degradation are higher sediment loadings due to use of land-degrading practices. This study will use fairly simple methods and approaches that can be easily replicated in other studies. The approach compares profit of land productivity with and without SLM practices and includes both on-farm and off-site benefits and costs of management practices.

The returns to SLM investment (profit) analysis will be on a per-hectare basis for each of the major AEZs. However, for livestock production, the unit of analysis will be at the household level—the livestock production per household using SLM practices (that is, improved pasture management). To obtain national-level results, the results under each AEZ will be extrapolated to the relevant AEZ (Table 12.12).

Factors Influencing Adoption of SLM Practices

We analyze the drivers of adoption of SLM practices using the RNR 2009 data. Such analysis will help to determine the policies and strategies that could be used to achieve Bhutan's objectives of SLM stated in its 2020 Vision and other policies.

Table 12.12 Agroecological zones and the corresponding agricultural enterprises

Agroecological zone	Altitude (meters above sea level)	Annual rainfall (mm)	Major enterprises
Alpine	3600–4600	<650	Yak herding by nomadic communities, dairy products, barley, buckwheat, mustard, and vegetables
Cool temperate	2600–3600	650–850	Yak, cattle, sheep, horses, dairy products, barley, wheatand potatoes on dryland, buckwheat and mustard under shifting cultivation
Warm temperate	1800–2600	650–850	Rice on irrigated land, double cropped with wheat and mustard; barley and potatoes on dryland; temperate fruit trees; vegetables; cattle
Dry subtropical	1200–1800	850–1200	Maize, rice, millet, pulses, fruit trees and vegetables, wild lemon grass, cattle, pigs and poultry
Humid subtropical	600–1200	1200–2500	Irrigated rice rotated with mustard, wheat, pulses, and vegetables; tropical fruit trees
Wet subtropical	150–600	2500–5500	Irrigated rice rotated with mustard, wheat, pulses, and vegetables; tropical fruit trees

Source Tobgay (2005)
Note: *mm* millimeters

Understanding of the factors influencing adoption of SLM practices will help the government to design strategies that will enhance adoption of SLM practices. The focus of the discussion will be on factors that have policy relevancy. These include farmer access to rural services (extension services and rural roads), land tenure security, and household physical capital endowment (land area and livestock) and human capital (sex and age of household head) (Barrett et al. 2002).

We use a nonlinear bivariate Probit model as specified below:

$$P(\mathbf{y} = 1|\mathbf{x_i}) = f(\beta_0 + \beta_i x_i + e_i),$$

where f(z) is normally distributed with a probability density function of the following:

$$\frac{1}{\sigma\sqrt{2\pi}} exp\left(\frac{(x_i - \mu)^2}{2\sigma^2}\right)$$

where P = probability that the household uses SLM practices. P = 1 if the household uses SLM; P = 0 otherwise.

$$\mathbf{x_i} = \mathbf{x_1} + \mathbf{x_2} + \mathbf{x_3},$$

where $\mathbf{x_1}$ = the vector of the household capital endowment—which includes human capital (age and sex household head); $\mathbf{x_2}$ = vector of land rights, method of acquisition (own land, renting, leasehold, and unused land—fallow), or both; $\mathbf{x_3}$ = ownership of physical capital (livestock used as an indicator of physical capital); and $\mathbf{z}$ = vector of access to rural services (time to nearest road and access to extension services) and

β_i = coefficients associated with the corresponding covariate *i*.

The choice of covariates to include in the model was dictated by data availability. Some important variables—such as the level of education of the household head or other family members and total farm area—were not collected.

We do not include prices of commodities in this model since this is a generalized model that explains the adoption of any type of SLM practice—regardless of the type of land use (cropland, livestock, or forests). The next section on benefits-costs analysis of SLM will address price aspects.

Multicollinearity was not a serious problem since the average variance inflation factor was 2.28 and the largest variance inflation factor only 6.41, less than 10—a level deemed the threshold for serious bias due to multicollinearity (Mukherjee et al. 1998). We corrected for heteroskedasticity by estimating robust standard errors.

Returns to SLM Practices

Profit with SLM Practices

The general model for returns to SLM practices for all land use types (forest, cropland, and livestock) is given in Eq. 12.1, and the corresponding model for land-degrading practices is given in Eq. 12.2

$$\pi_t^c = p_t y_t^c - z_t^c - \lambda_t \tag{12.3}$$

where π_t^c = profit per hectare or household with SLM practices in year *t*. For brevity, we will simply refer to returns per hectare, but this also means returns per household for livestock production land management practices

y_t^c Production per hectare with SLM practices in year *t*,

P_t a constant price of output in year t.

This will be the social price, that is, price that excludes market failures or policy-induced distortions—including subsidies and taxes.

z_t^c social cost of production using SLM practices per hectare in year *t*

λ_t external (off-site) costs or benefit of SLM practice per hectare—for example, clearing forest area for crop production could lead to greater sediment loading in HEP dams. If >0, then off-site impact is a benefit to society, and if $\lambda t < 0$, then off-site effect is a cost.

Profit with Land-degrading Practices (BAU)

$$\pi_t^d = p_t y_t^d - z_t^d - \tau_t \tag{12.4}$$

where

- y_t^d production per hectare with BAU in year t,
- π_t^d profit with BAU per hectare in year t
- P_t social price of one unit of output in year t. A specific price will be applied for each enterprise analyzed (maize, rice, forest livestock products, and so forth). A private price is important to analyze since it determines farmers' choices to use SLM practices. However, we did not use it in this study since we used market prices that are not affected by government failure, subsidies, or taxes
- z_t^d social cost of production of per hectare using land-degrading practices
- τ_t external (off-site) costs or benefit of land-degrading management practice per hectare, for example, sedimentation.

The decision by a landowner to use SLM will depend on the marginal rate of returns (MRR), which is defined as the returns per unit of investment. Holding all else constant, the higher the MRR, the greater is the uptake of SLM. For example, Heisey and Mwangi (1998) observed adoption of fertilizer among smallholder farmers in Africa south of the Sahara requires an MRR of at least 100 %; that is, for every unit of currency (for example, Bhutanese ngultrum) invested, one or more additional units are obtained.

MRR analysis will help to determine the attractiveness of SLM practices over time. MRR is given by

$$MRR_t = \frac{\pi_t^c - \pi_t^d}{z_t^c + \lambda_t^c - z_t^d - \lambda_t^d} \tag{12.5}$$

However, MRR_t is given at one point in time, that is, MRR_t in year t. This could differ for each planning horizon. An analysis that looks at the streams of benefits of SLM and associated costs is the net present value (NPV). NPV is summed over the planning horizon and therefore reflects the benefits and costs of investment during the entire planning horizon (Gardner and Barrows 1985). The social NPV (NPV^S) of adopting SLM practices is therefore given by

$$NPV = \rho^t \left\{ \sum_{t=1}^{T} (\pi_t^c - \pi_t^d) \right\} \tag{12.6}$$

where

- T farmer's planning horizon
- ρ^t farmers' discount factor, where r is the farmer's discount rate

Discounting the future value is an integral part of farmers' decisionmaking processes (Duquette et al. 2011) as it reveals farmers' time preferences and risk attitudes. The discount rate varies widely even among poor farmers. Recent social experiments have elicited valuable information about farmer discount rates (Duflo et al. 2004; Duquette et al. 2011; D'Exelle et al. 2012). Using experimental evidence from American farmers, one study showed an annual discount rate of 28 % (Duquette et al. 2011). Lower discount rates have also been used (for example, Pagiola 1996 used a 10 % discount rate for SLM practices in Kenya). Based on this, we use a discount rate of 25 %. But we also conduct sensitivity analysis of NPV and internal rate of return (IRR) by using discount rates of 10, 25, and 30 % to determine robustness of the results. The sensitivity analysis of MRR is not conducted since this is not affected by the discount factor given that MRR is a ratio of net benefits and costs, both of which are discounted, hence canceling out the effect of the discount factor.

Farmers find it profitable to adopt an SLM practice if NPV > 0. However, a given farmer's decision to adopt SLM practices typically does not take into account the off-site costs and benefits that result from adoption or nonadoption of SLM practices. The literature on these issues establishes that a positive NPV may be far from sufficient to induce investment (for example, Pender 1996; Dixit and Pindyck 1994; Fafchamps and Pender 1997). Hence, the MRR trend over the planning horizon will also be used to evaluate the change in attractiveness of SLM practices over time. For example, this analysis is likely to show a negative or small MRR at the beginning, after the initial large fixed costs of SLM are incurred. The MRR will improve over time as the large initial overhead investments decrease and their returns become more significant. Robustness of the MRR to the discount factor also will be computed using the three levels used for NPV, that is, $r = 10$, 25, and 30 %.

Economic Data Used

Returns to SLM Practices

For all three land use types (forests, croplands, and grazing lands), we assume that the land management practices recommended by the Ministry of Agriculture and Forests lead to SLM. So we use experimental results to determine the land production per hectare when farmers use or do not use SLM. We discuss each of the data sources under each land use type and corresponding to the six AEZs (Table 12.12). Other studies (for example, United Nations Environment Programme 2009) divide Bhutan into only three major agroclimatic zones, which are largely determined by altitude: (1) alpine zone (>4000 m)—the alpine zone, where glaciers and glacial lakes are located, account for 10 % of the total land area of Bhutan (Choden, et al. 2010); (2) temperate zone (1000–4000 m)—this zone lies in the middle belt; and (3) subtropical zone (200–1000 m)—this zone lies in the southern part (Choden et al. 2010). We will use the six AEZs (Table 12.12) since this reflects well the forest ecosystem that occupies the largest land area.

Cropland

As discussed earlier, we focus only on maize, rice, and citrus. Data required for conducting returns to SLM practices are SLM practices and their impact on crop yield—that is, yield with and without SLM practices. We use experimental results from the Bhutan Overview of Conservation Approaches and Technologies (WOCAT) conducted by NSSC in collaboration with WOCAT to identify the SLM practices and their impact on maize and rice yields—that is, yield with SLM practices. The literature of past soil fertility studies also is used to determine crop yield with SLM practices. Yield obtained by farmers (BAU) was obtained from the 2011 RNR household survey data. Table 12.13 reports the SLM and yield under BAU.

Maize

For the major maize-growing zone—the dry subtropical zone, which runs from central to eastern Bhutan—the recommended SLM practices are ISFM with nitrogen, phosphorus, and potassium per hectare of 100, 80, and 60, respectively, plus 7 tons/ha farm yard manure (Chetri et al. 2003). With these inputs, the maize yield potential for improved varieties is 4.15 tons/ha (Chetri et al. 2003), while the farmer yield is only 2.79 tons/ha (RGoB and and MoA2011) or 67 % of the yield potential. For a given crop, yield potential is the maximum yield of a crop under given agroecological characteristics (solar radiation, temperatures, soil characteristics, and so forth) and varietal characteristics (fraction of photosynthetic efficiency of converting biomass into economically important yield) (FAO 1996). Yield potential is used in studies determining yield gap and associated production constraints such as land degradation (for example, Licker et al. 2010).

Rice

Irrigated rice is grown in the humid (wet) and subhumid subtropics. ISFM is also recommended for irrigated rice with 7 tons/ha of farm yard manure and 17 kg of phosphorus/ha (Chetri et al. 2003). With ISFM and improved seeds, irrigated rice yield potential is 7 tons/ha (Chetri et al. 2003), but farmer yield is only 3.5 tons/ha (RGoB and MoA2009).

Citrus

The SLM practice used for oranges is to plant on fallow land, ex-tseri land (i.e. slash and burn) and on cropland where there is high risk of land degradation through soil and water erosion. About 23 % of rural households reported that they had left their land fallow in the 2009 RNR survey (Christensen et al. 2012). Such land could be used for citrus production, and this could greatly contribute to reducing poverty since—as will be seen later—citrus is among the most profitable crops and, as discussed earlier, orchard production contributed 73.6 % of crop GDP growth in 2000–2009 (Christensen et al. 2012) and 66 % of household cash income. Planting pure stand citrus trees could be a challenge due to their long gestation period (six years), which investment smallholder farmers may not be able to afford. Using the farmer practice, oranges yield 10.7 tons/ha (FAOSTAT 2013).

Table 12.13 Enterprises and their potential and actual yield

Enterprise	Location	Price or value per unit (US$)	Yield potential	Farmer yield/farmer practice	Input recommended	Inputs farmer practice	Source
Maize	Eastern regions	231.21/ton	4.15	2.79	kg of N,P, and K per ha = 100, 80, and 60 plus 7 tons/ha FYM	6.7 kg N/ha, 1.9 kg P_2O_5/ha, 1.3 K_2O/ha	RNR 2011 NSSC (211), FAOSTAT 2013
Paddy rice	Humid subtropics and humid tropics	662/ton	7 tons/ha	3.5 tons/ha	7 tons/ha FYM + 17 kg P/ha		Chetri, Ghimiray, and Floyd (2003)
Oranges		754/ton	10.17 tons/ha	Fallow land	Plantation		FAOSTAT
Livestock	Cool and warm temperate, humid, and dry subtropical zones						
	Milk[a]	55.96/ton	0.96 tons/cow/year[b]	2.5 liters/cow/day, 240 lactation days = 0.6 tons/year/cow	Improved pasture	No pasture improvement	
	Meat	120/ton	1.54 tons/year/household	0.8775 tons/year	As above	As above	NSSC (2011)

(continued)

Table 12.13 (continued)

Enterprise	Location	Price or value per unit (US$)	Yield potential	Farmer yield/farmer practice	Input recommended	Inputs farmer practice	Source
Private forest (value per ha)[c]							
	Alpine—cool conifers		Plant or protect trees, adopt sustainable annual harvest limit = 26 % of forest value	Unsustainable tree harvesting and forest grazing	Observe sustainable AHL	Land & labor input	NSSC (2011)
	WFP[d]	41,918/ha					
	NWFP[d]	419/ha	Tree density in the Himalayan region = 1900 trees/ha (Kharkwal and Rawat 2010)	As above	As above		
	Broadleaf trees—humid deciduous temperate				As above		
	WFP	26,108/ha	As above				
	NWFP	261/ha					
	CFM*	1231/ha					

Source [a]Gyaltsen and Bhattarai (2002). [b]Delgado et al. (2002). [c]Chiabai et al. (2011), Phuntsho et al. (2011). Note this is total value including unused value. AHL will involve harvesting 26 % of the forest value. [d]Source food prices: numbeo.com (2014). [e]Brooks (2010)

Note: *kg* kilograms; *FYM* farm yard manure; *RNR* Renewable natural resources; *NSSC* National Soil Services Center; *FAOSTAT* Food and Agriculture Organization Corporate Statistical Database; AHL = annual harvest limit; WFP = wood forest product; NWFP = non-wood forest product; CFM = community forest management. *Zhasela community CFM—with 15 households participating—is used as an example. The community CFM has 33.9 ha. AHL = 36 mature trees (>50 cm dbh = diameter at breast height or drashing size trees). NWFP from CFM includes mushrooms, wild asparagus, and bedding material. Sexual maturity of the *Pinus roxburghii*—the most common tree in the Zhasela CFM—is 12 to 14 years (Sharma et al. 2012). The tree can live up to 120 years—rotation period (Sharma et al. 2012). The value of US$1231 includes timber harvest of 26 % of AHL (Phuntsho et al. 2011)

Forest

Forest plantations span all zones in Bhutan, and their productivity and value vary accordingly. Converting centrally managed non-PA forests to CFs and converting unused lands to CFs are the major SLM practices proposed to reduce soil erosion in HEP plants. A review by Bowler et al. (2010) showed that tree density under community-managed forests (CF) improved as compared to density under government management. For example, Agarwal (2009)'s study showed the forest density of CFs improved from the condition of CFs before in Nepal and India by 50 % and 36 %, respectively. The SWAT model results reflect the benefit of reduction of soil erosion due to planting trees on unused lands and increase in forest density. The value of other forest ecosystem services—timber, NTFP, and so forth—will also increase accordingly. To ensure that the forest value is relevant to the local economy, we will consider only ecosystem services that are felt at the national level. This includes water catchment, regulating services, timber and NTFP, and medicinal plants. It is well documented that the value of a forest differs depending on its use (for example, see Secretariat of the Convention on Biological Diversity 2001). Holding all else constant, forests closer to high population density have greater value than forests in remote areas (Pearce 2001). Forests used for tourism or those with rich biodiversity and other ecosystem values have higher values than those with lower ecosystem values (Secretariat of the Convention on Biological Diversity 2001). The private forests considered in this study are closer to human population and will have relatively higher values.

NTFP that are harvested from the forest include mushrooms, bamboo shoots, herbs, medicinal plants, canes, fodder, and loppings. For timber products, SLM is achieved when harvesting does not exceed the regeneration rate. The Ministry of Agriculture and Forests gives the annual harvest limit for each type of forest. For forest products, the sustainable annual harvest limit is determined using guidelines given by the Ministry of Agriculture and Forests.

Grazing Land (Livestock Production)

SLM for grazing land is improved pasture management—which includes planting leguminous seeds and improved grasses such as cocksfoot, Italian rye, and lotus (Samdup et al. 2013; Dorji 1993). It also includes rotational grazing on rangelands, which allows pasture to recover (Chophyel 2009). Improved pasture management could increase total digestible nutrient fivefold from 0.654 tons/ha for traditional pasture management (Dorji 1993) to 4.0 tons/ha (Roder et al. 2001). Improved pasture management can increase the live weight of livestock by up to 100 %. For example, a study in Australia showed that sowing pasture using improved pasture management increased cattle live weight 2.3 fold (Alcock and Hegarty 2006). NSSC (2011) showed that improved pasture management can increase livestock productivity between 50 and 100 %. We assume a minimum increase of 50 % of livestock productivity if a farmer uses improved pasture management. Only 12 % of farmers reported to have improved pastures.

Meat production is about 51,000 mt and 0.6 mt per cow per year of milk (Wangdi 2012). This suggests each of the 58,120 households that own cattle (NSB and AsDB 2013) produce 0.8775 tons/year. Hence, with a 50 % increase in livestock productivity, this will translate to 0.96 tons per cow/year of milk and 1.54 tons/year of beef per household.

Due to lack of livestock management data, a farmer was deemed to be using SLM if he or she reported use of improved pasture management. We use data from past studies to determine the different values of forest ecosystem services.

The next section discusses the results, starting with the land use change descriptive analysis, which reveals a 20-year pattern ranging from 1990 to 2010. This is followed by results on soil erosion analysis using SWAT modeling. The third section uses the results from the land use change analysis and the SWAT results to analyze the economic returns to SLM investments to address land degradation.

Results

Land Use Change

Land Cover Change Classes

We focus on four major land use types: forest, agricultural, pasture, and barren land. Table 12.14 describes the classification system used in this analysis and the interpretation of each class: deforestation and agricultural expansion. Two datasets were used to assess land cover change: The national land cover dataset was used to assess changes in pastureland, and an independently produced classified Landsat dataset was used to analyze other land cover changes. While methodological changes in the classification system between 1994 and 2010 precluded use of the

Table 12.14 Land cover change classes

Deforestation	Agriculture Expansion	Agriculture Contraction
• Forest to grassland or shrub	• Barren land to agriculture	• Agriculture to unused land
• Forest to bare land	• Grassland or shrubland to agriculture	• Agriculture to forest
• Forest to urban area	• Forest to agriculture	• Agriculture to urban area
• Forest to agriculture		
Land Clearing	*Pasture Expansion*	*Pasture Contraction*
Agriculture, shrubland, or grassland to barren land	• Forest to pasture	• Pasture to forest
	• Grassland, shrubland, or barren area to pasture	• Pasture to grass, shrubland, or barren land
	• Agriculture to pasture	• Pasture to agriculture

Source Authors

national land cover dataset in much of the land cover change analysis, it was considered more reliable for static analyses and for diagnosing changes in pastureland, which is not separated from other grasslands in the Landsat data.

The vast majority of forested area remained as such between 1990 and 2010. The minor deforestation that was present primarily consisted of a conversion from forest to grassland/shrubland or agriculture. Despite agriculture's being a primary player in the minor deforestation, as a whole, agricultural expansion occurred mostly in barren land, grassland, or shrubland. In fact, nearly as much agriculture was converted back to forested land as forest was to agriculture. For the time period analyzed, there was a net expansion in agriculture.

According to the land use change analysis conducted on the national dataset to assess pastureland expansion and contraction, pastureland as a whole is in slight decline. Although the dataset indicates a substantial conversion from agricultural land to pasture, it also demonstrates that twice as much pasture was converted to forested land. These conversions may be real observed trends, but they may also be spurious artifacts of the difference in methods between the 1994 dataset and the 2010 dataset. To assess the validity of the observed decline, independent land cover assessments were analyzed. FAO data indicate a stagnation in permanent meadows and pastureland while classified Landsat data from 1990 and 2010—produced independently from the national land cover dataset—indicate a significant decline in grasslands. While not all grasslands can be assumed to be pasture, the decline in grasslands in combination with the FAO data lends credence to the observed trend in the national land cover data.

Impact of Land Use Change and Land Management on Soil Erosion

Sediment Results

Using the SWAT model sediment algorithms, the landscape total sediment yield for BAU was calculated for each sub-basin, and the average annual result is presented in Fig. 12.16. Rainfall and runoff, drive the sediment process, it is obvious that higher sediment was observed at these high rainfall/runoff regions. However, land cover, slope, and soil erodibility factors play major roles in the sediment yield potential. In this case, Table 12.15 provides the distribution of hydrology and sediment yield by land use and corresponding slope and slope length combined factors. Most of the sediment was coming from higher elevations in the north of the country including the Chinese part of the watershed but also from the southernmost part of the watershed draining into India. In the northern part of the basins, sediment delivery is mainly due to high snowfall and snowmelt processes with steeper slopes. However, due to lack of quality soils data and poor soil scale (1: 1,000,000 scale) maps, the simulated outputs may contain large uncertainity. The sedimentation process has been going on for thousands of years, and most of the soils may have

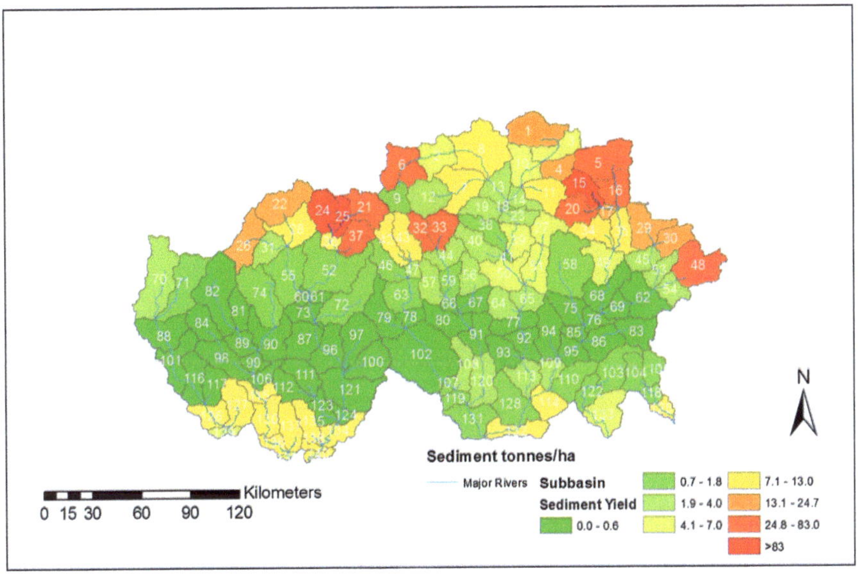

Fig. 12.16 Average annual (1997–2012) sediment load (tons per hectare) from each sub-basin. *Source* Hydromet data (1997–2010) and Author's calculation using Soil and water assessment tool results

been eroded already. But the sedimentary rocks in the higher altitudes with steep slopes can contribute to the sediment yields slowly over many years to come. The high volume of snow and runoff process due to glacier lake breaks, heavy boulders, rocks, and large aggregates may contribute to the sediment process. It is unlikely that small suspended particles are seen from these area, which is also evident from the observed sediment data collected by the Hydromet department.

During the field visit it was clear that there were several boulders and rocks removed from the river bottoms and stored on the side of the stream as protection from additional stream bank erosion in the large river sections and flat areas. The southern part of the watershed experiences very high rainfall during the monsoon season from June through October. The main sources of sediment are highly managed agriculture and urban development including road construction between various small to medium towns and across international trade. These exist along with a high slope area with barren and erodible land, and they contribute significant sediment loading to the rivers. The middle part of the watershed, where the rainfall is low and of less intensity, contributes little or no sediment and is also well covered by forest and grass on the ground to protect from any sediment contribution. Figure 12.17 shows the average annual sediment load from the entire basin simulation as 9.39 tons/ha/year during the simulation period f 2007–2012. It also shows that as the sediment reaches the flat areas, some of the sediment—up to 14 %—may get deposited into the channels and river network, resulting in only about 8

Table 12.15 Average basin hydrology and sediment results from SWAT (1997–2012) by land use

Land use	Area[a] (2010)	Area[a] (2000)	Slope and slope length factor	Precipitation[b]	Runoff[b]	GW[b]	Actual evapotrans-piration[b]	Sediment (t/ha)	Sediment (t/ha)
Pine	26.312	26.312	11.50	1548	365.48	752.04	329.42	3.50	3.50
Grassland	8.515	8.821	10.02	1516	614.24	284.51	126.46	5.41	5.52
Barren	2.051	1.743	10.96	1535	716.49	229.48	130.74	116.75	114.46
Water/Snow	4.770	4.770	0.18	1582	0.00	0.00	1153.54	0.00	0.00
Evergreen forest/shrubland	4.190	4.190	11.32	1395	390.46	643.43	239.35	4.74	4.74
Cropland	1.217	1.217	0.37	1565	355.66	892.01	231.27	5.93	5.93
Erodible land	0.179	0.179	9.32	2097	925.06	130.07	185.63	223.8	223.8
Urban	0.040	0.040	0.83	1469	711.61	391.7	394.61	0.84	0.84
Wetland	0.003	0.003	0.18	972	232.33	99.53	537.32	0.63	0.63
Roads	0.226	0.226	11.10	1456	1017.19	94.24	348.67	6.03	6.03
Oranges/Orchards	0.039	0.039	11.38	3015	1409.88	813.06	667.39	5.96	5.96

Source Soil and water assessment tool results (2013)

Note: *GW* Ground Water; *km*^{2} square kilometers; *mm* millimeters; *t/ha* tons per hectare. [a]In thousand km^2. [b]In mm

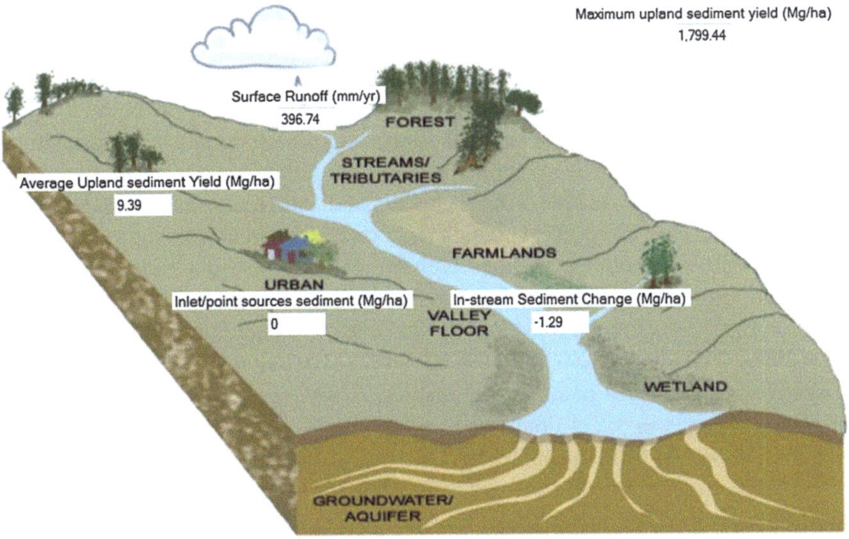

Fig. 12.17 Average sub-basin sediment load from the entire basin and sediment deposition in the stream for the entire period of the simulation (1997–2012). *Source* Authors. Note: *Mg/ha* megagram (ton) per hectare; *mm/yr* millimeters per year

tons/ha/year of sediment leaving the watershed. However, the sediment delivery varies by each major river basin.

In addition, the land use change data between 2000 and 2010 were used in the model. The major changes observed were from grassland to brushland and barren land. Also in 2000 the percentage of barren land was less compared to 2010 by almost 10 %, with more grassland. With these changes the model predicted 8.61 tons/year, that is, about 8.3 % less sediment in 2000 than the current land use based on 2010 data. This is mainly because there was less barren and highly erodible land in 2000 than now and these lands were covered by grassland that protected the soil surface. The overall 2000 land use area and corresponding sediment yield per ha is shown in Table 12.16. There were some landuse changes between 2000 and 2010 in the water/glacier/snow area. Most of this area was either grassland or barren land. Even though there was more water/glacier/snow area in 2000 than in 2010, this

Table 12.16 Basinwide annual average of sediment under sustainable land management program

Land use	Area (in km^2)	Sediment under SLM (t/ha)	Baseline sediment (t/ha)	Percentage change
High altitude forestland	26,311.71	1.75	3.50	50
Cropland	1216.65	4.58	5.93	23
Oranges/orchards	38.64	2.98	5.96	50

Source Soil and water assessment toolmodel results (year?)
Note: *SLM* Sustainable Land Management; km^2 square kilometers; *t/ha* tons per hectare

could be due to the various remote sensing scenes used for classification that may be from the winter or spring seasons' snapshots. So this change was not included in the simulation.

With proper land management techniques such as contouring, increased forested cover and selection of proper plants, and terracing where possible for agricultural land, the SLM techniques were applied to only needle leaf forested land, cropland, and orange landscapes in the SWAT model, and the results are summarized in Table 12.16 and Fig. 12.18. Even though the expected reduction seems to be high—as much as 50 % erosion reduction—with the combination of various SLM techniques and long-term maintenance or caretaking, one can reach the reduction goal. However, the range of reduction certainly varies based on rainfall, intensity, landuse, slope, and soil condition from as low as 12–70 %. Also it is assumed all eligible land areas have adopted SLM practices. In practice, however, the adoption rate is lower and varies across space and time. What is reported in Table 12.16 is the potential impact of SLM that Bhutan can achieve if it fully implements its 2020 Vision.

It is important to compare our results with the results of other studies done in areas with comparable topography. Ziadat and Taimeh (2013) published results from field studies in arid regions where the steep slope, soil moisture, and land management can account for as much as 90 % of the land degradation. Such land erosion can be avoided by as much as 50–60 % using proper land management techniques and preserving soil moisture with vegetation or ground cover. This is an arid region with less rain, but the intensity is high; it can be compared to humid,

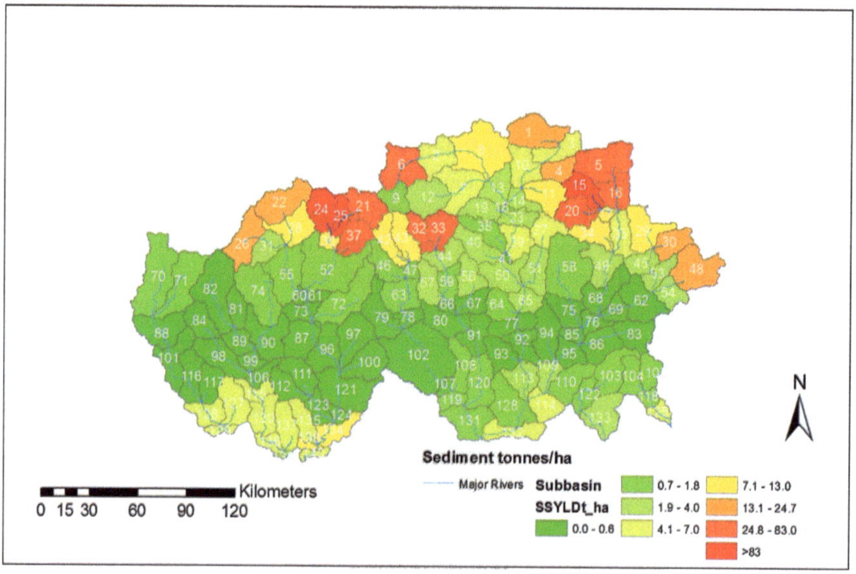

Fig. 12.18 Average annual (1997–2012) sediment load (t/ha) from each sub-basin under SLM scenarios. *Source* Author's calculation using the Soil and water assessment tool model results. Note: *t/ha* tons per hectare; *SLM* Sustainable Land Management; *SSYLDt_ha* sediment load (t/ha)

high-rainfall regions with soil moisture near saturation all the time, leading to similar outcomes. In addition, Ziadat et al. (2012) have published a technical report to show various agricultural land management measures in steep slopes and annual precipitation of about 700 to 1000 mm in Syria. The soil and water conservation practices used were stone bunds, stone walls, intercultivation, and other SLM techniques. The authors showed in real field measurements that the erosion can be reduced by as much as 55–60 % during a sustained long period with proper SLM techniques (Ziadat et al. 2012). Appendix 1 of the paper reports actual SLM practices and their impact on reducing soil erosion. The watershed where these were practiced is smaller, but the practices are promising. All these SLM techniques are documented qualitatively and in a simple way to understand by WOCAT and can be accessed at http://qt.wocat.net/qt_report.php.

The three SLM projects demonstrated are similar to what is experienced in Bhutan: high slopes, high rainfall, and forest degradation. Most of the benefits from the SLM techniques will be in the lower part of the watershed where agriculture is present, and improved land management will help greatly since this is where the rainfall is also high. Appropriate pine plantation management may also be helpful; however, pine plantations above the tree line, such as at 3800 m or above, will be not be beneficial.

Economic Analysis of SLM

Use and Drivers of Adoption of SLM Practices

The discussion below analyzes returns to SLM by focusing on three land use types: forest, grazing lands, and croplands. We focus this portion of our analysis on the interaction of livestock, fertilizer, and roads. To understand current SLM practices among land users, we analyze the 2009 RNR survey data.

Descriptive statistics and an econometric analysis of the data reveal that access to roads and livestock ownership significantly increase the quantity and type of fertilizer (inorganic or manure) applied by farmers (Tables 12.18 and 12.19). An analysis of the RNR survey data shows that only 31 % of crop farmers use inorganic fertilizer and that it is the farmers closer to roads who are more likely to apply inorganic fertilizer. This result, which is robust across both the descriptive statistics and the econometric analysis, highlights the importance of roads in the delivery and use of inorganic fertilizer. Econometric results also show that farmers closer to roads have a higher propensity to use manure than those farther away from roads. No farmer reported to have used both inorganic fertilizer and manure—suggesting that farmers substitute inorganic fertilizer with manure or vice versa. It could also mean that farmers who do not own livestock can apply only inorganic fertilizer and that farmers do not see the need to apply both manure and inorganic fertilizer. As expected, livestock ownership increases propensity to use manure (Table 12.18). In addition, livestock and land ownership both increase the propensity to use all four

Table 12.17 Share (percentage) of farmers who used inorganic and organic inputs

Category	Use inorganic fertilizer	Use manure	Have private forest	Have improved pastures
Nationally (*N* = 57,705)	30.9	59.6	3.6	12.0
Distance to road				
0	19.2	69.2	0.0	0.0
Less than 1 h	38.3	59.5	4.3	13.1
1–3 h	29.9	68.0	3.1	9.4
3–6 h	27.1	62.5	2.6	13
6 h–1 day	17.5	57.5	2.1	13
>1 day	7.0	43.8	2.9	9.3
Land owned				
Land-poor tercile	35.7	57.9	3.1	9.8
Land-rich tercile	25.9	61.4	4.2	14.3

Source RNR household survey (2009)

Table 12.18 Drivers of propensity to use sustainable land management practices (marginal effects)

Driver	Manure	Urea	Private Forest	Improved Pasture
Land tenure/method of acquisition (cf. renting)				
- Own land	0.025***	0.002***	0.008***	0.012***
- Leased out land	−0.028***	−0.003**	0.021**	0.001
- Leased in land	0.009***	0.000	−0.002	−0.017**
- Fallow land	−0.014***	0.000	0.007*	0.009***
Own livestock cattle	1.363***	0.119***	0.259***	0.992***
Own donkey	0.246**	0.006	0.423***	0.220*
Own horse	0.006	0.000	−0.012	0.249***
Age of respondent	0.000	−0.000***	0.002***	0.001
Male respondent sex	−0.006	−0.010***	0.094***	0.096***
Time to Road (cf. more than one day)				
- Less than one hour	0.268***	0.128***	0.160***	0.344***
- One to three hours	0.359***	0.085***	0.038	0.140***
- Three to six hours	0.344***	0.082***	−0.087*	0.244***
- Six hours to one day	0.305***	0.034***	−0.152***	0.313***
Time to extension services (cf. more than one day)				
- Less than one hour	−0.273***	0.089***	0.151**	0.330***
- One to three hours	−0.147***	0.064***	0.135**	0.289***
- Three to six hours	−0.149***	0.064***	0.092	0.277***
- Six hours to one day	−0.228***	0.021**	0.016	0.148***
Constant	−0.845***	0.426***	−2.379***	−1.590***

Source Computed from RNR survey data (2009)
Note: Dash in the "Driver" column indicates that the variable is part of a multi-part variable. *p = 0.10. **p = 0.05. ***p = 0.01

Table 12.19 Returns to sustainable land management practices

	Internal rate of return			BCR	30-year total NPV (US dollars) per hectare		
Enterprise	*r* = 10 %	*r* = 25 %	*r* = 30 %		*r* = 10 %	*r* = 25 %	*r* = 30 %
Maize—ISFM	2.52	2.10	1.98	2.05	3578.47	1406.86	1159.54
Rice—ISFM	0.80	0.59	0.53	4.12	7916.75	2860.29	2322.90
Citrus orchard	0.27	0.12	0.08	66.33	32,520.38	4935.72	2718.17
Community forest	0.23	0.08	0.04	22.20	24,404.28	3711.01	1915.71
Cool broadleaf forest	0.01	−0.13	−0.16	2.40	299.42	−609.51	−562.69
Warm broadleaf	−0.02	−0.13	–	2.30	209.35	−626.57	−574.00
Mixed conifer forest	0.00	−0.12	−0.15	2.93	822.91	−510.33	−496.94
Chir pine (*Pinus roxburghii*)	0.00	−0.12	−0.15	3.00	887.45	−498.10	−488.84
Blue pine forest	0.01	−0.11	−0.15	3.24	1124.53	−453.19	−459.06
Improved pasture	1.36	1.08	1.00	35.46	13,845.97	5173.27	4143.95

Source Author's calculations
Note: *NPV* net present value; *BCR* 30-year average benefit-cost ratio; *ISFM* integrated soil fertility management (combination of inorganic fertilizer and organic inputs)

SLM practices reported (manure, urea, private forest, and improved pasture). With the exception of manure use, access to extension services also increases the propensity to use all SLM practices—as expected. The results underscore the importance of rural services in enhancing SLM practices in Bhutan (Table 12.17).

Constraints to access to rural services and other important drivers of adoption of SLM could lead to unexpected farmer behavior. We examined the relationship between profitability and returns to land management practices.

Returns to SLM Practices

Equation 12.4 summarizes the returns to SLM for the enterprises considered. To check robustness of results to farmer discount factor, NPV and IRR are reported at discount factors of 10, 25, and 30 %. NPV > 0 and IRR ≥ 0.12 are considered the minimum requirements for adoption of SLM.

Results show that a citrus orchard is the most profitable enterprise, but it requires farmers to wait for at least six years before the first harvest. Such a prolonged period of time could be a challenge for smallholder farmers to be engaged in citrus production on a large scale. An amenable approach could be producing citrus on a small piece of land or planting trees in annual crops and planting them on fallow land. Profitability of citrus is robust across all three discount factors since both NPV and IRR remain higher or closer to the minimum level deemed economically desirable for farmers to grow citrus. Given this profitability, it is not surprising to see that the production of citrus and other horticultural crops and their contribution to household income has been increasing tremendously while the contribution of cereal crops to household cash income has been declining. Improved pasture management is the second most profitable enterprise—underscoring the potential role it can play in meeting the growing demand for livestock products as household income increases. Both NPV and IRR are robust across the three discount factors and significantly greater than their corresponding minimum levels. This suggests that adoption of improved pasture is an attractive SLM practice, and its adoption is enhanced by access to rural services (roads and extension services), secure land tenure, and number of livestock owned. Likewise, NPV and IRR for maize and rice are robust across the discount factor and greater than the minimum level, suggesting ISFM is an attractive SLM practice for two crops. NPV and IRR for private forests under CFM are both positive, but IRR for $r = 25$ % and $r = 30$ % are both below the minimum IRR of 12 %—suggesting that CFM may not compete favorably with other enterprises. However, CFM remains attractive for areas unfavorable to crop or livestock production. NPV for $r = 10$ % for publicly owned pine and broadleaf forests is greater than zero, but the corresponding IRR is about zero—hence not likely to attract private investment to increase forest density or replant deforested areas. NPV and IRR for $r = 25$ % and $r = 30$ % are negative, suggesting private investment in enhancement of pine and broadleaf forests is not economically attractive and will require payment for ecosystem services to motivate communities to engage in improvement of forest resources.

The Unholy Cross

We analyzed the relationship between the adoption of land management practices (Table 12.17) and their returns (Table 12.19). The results show an inverse relationship—that is, the greater the returns to land management, the lower is the corresponding adoption rate. Such an “unholy cross” is due to constraints to adoption of high returns. For example, farmers away from roads may not be able to adopt inorganic fertilizer even when their returns are higher than nonuse of fertilizer. Likewise, the negative relationship between manure application and access to extension suggests lack of or limited advisory services on organic soil fertility management practices. This could mean that extension agents do not advise farmers to use organic soil fertility management in combination with inorganic fertilizers (ISFM), which has greater returns than use of fertilizer alone.

We now turn our analysis to the national level by extrapolating the per-hectare results to each zone and consequently to the whole country. When calculating

Table 12.20 On-farm and off-farm benefits of action and cost of inaction against land degradation in Bhutan

Land Type	Annual (in NPV USdollars per hectare)	Area (in thousands of hectares)	Total benefit/loss (in million US dollars)
Forest			
On-farm benefits (millions of US dollars) of SLM			
- Cool broadleaf forest	9.98	34.80	0.35
- Warm broadleaf	6.98	1685.00	11.76
- Mixed conifer forest	27.43	612.90	16.81
- Chir pine (*Pinus roxburghii*) and fir pine	29.58	294.10	8.70
- Blue pine forest	37.48	78.30	2.94
- Total on-farm direct benefit from forests[a]			40.56
Loss due to deforestation and reduced forest density (25 % of on-farm benefit)			10.14
Off-site benefit—50 % reduction of sediment loading[b]			7.80
Cropland			
- Maize	119.28	28,641	3.42
- Rice	263.89	24,357	6.43
-Off-site benefit—sediment reduction due to SLM on cropland and grassland			0.15
Benefits of SLM on livestock production			17.85
Total benefit of SLM			
- On-farm			37.83
- Off-site			7.95
Change in GDP due to SLM			2.5 %

Source Author's calculations
Note: *SLM* sustainable land management; *GDP* gross domestic product. [a]Forest contributed 24 % of the agricultural GDP—which was US$284.73 million in 2012. This means the value of harvesting considered in the GDP calculation (US$68.33 million) was greater than our estimates. [b]See Table 6.3. Druk Green Power Company spends US$16 million each year to repair turbines and other underwater structures due to sediment loading. About 60 % of such cost is associated with sediment loading

national scale returns, however, it is important to account for both on-site and off-site benefits. The results from the land use analysis and SWAT are also used to compute the off-site values of both forests and crops reported in Table 12.20. The computations are according to Eq. 12.6 and corresponding extrapolation to the national level. The calculations are done assuming $r = 10\ \%$ since the national-level social planning discount factor is lower than the private discount factor (Rambaud and Torrecillas 2007). The results assessing returns to SLM at a national scale show that adopting SLM could increase Bhutan's GDP by at least 2.5 %, a level that can be achieved if certain socioeconomic conditions are taken into account. However, it is important to note that a significant portion of the benefits accrue off-site, particularly for SFM. This is unsurprising given the role that forests play in reducing sediment loading to rivers and therefore HEP plants (Table 12.20).

Study Limitations and Gaps

Due to the short time and small budget of the project, we heavily relied on existing data. This was especially crucial given the national-level analysis done in this study. The heavy reliance on secondary data led to using second-best secondary data. We benefited from a large database from a number of institutions discussed in the Methodological Analysis and Data section, yet there were some key data gaps that hampered analysis. For example, the RNR household survey did not collect some important data required to determine the farmer land management practices and household-level characteristics. For the land use analysis, the data for the Bhutan Land Cover Assessment covering the 1994–2010 period had several issues. The data sources, classification, and methods differed between the data collected in 1994 and that collected in 2010, and this made computation of land use change less reliable. Unlike the 1994 dataset, the 2010 dataset was rigorously conducted with extensive ground truthing, an aspect missing from the Landsat dataset. This led to heavy reliance on Landsat data, which were consistently collected between the two time periods but were not ground-truthed.

For the SWAT modeling data, the elevation data at 10 m has lots of noise including a high unrealistic slope estimation due to a high difference in adjacent pixels. Slope is an important and significant factor in estimating sediment. In addition, land use is based on broad categories such as pine and broadleaf areas, but no data exist about the density or age of these plantations, which can also affect the sediment loads from these lands. In several areas there have been mudslides, forest fires, and so forth; these were not captured in the landuse map. Also, the landuse map was created using 2010 satellite images, which were run from 1997 to 2012, so the map may not represent landuse in the watershed for the entire time period of the simulation. There was concern about the impact of road construction on sediment loading, but no data were collected to measure such impact. This hampered inclusion of soil erosion due to road, house, and other types of construction.

Soils have significant limitations; for example, the scale of FAO soils data is 1:1,000,000, and its parameters are not measured—just estimated based on global soil properties and pedo-transfer functions—which may not capture the local metamorphism and erodibility factors properly. Finally, most of the rainfall and temperature gauge data were gathered in the lower altitudes, typically less than 3000 m. However, much of the watershed covers higher than 3000 m of elevation, even though elevation correction for temperature and precipitation was used as an input to the model; the spatial variability of these parameters is not captured due to lack of any knowledge or field data. In addition, there are many months and years of data that were missing in the precipitation gauges, and those were estimated with SWAT's built-in weather generator using the historical statistics generated by Climate Forecast System Reanalysis global weather data. Despite these limitations and gaps, this study provides empirical evidence that has important policy implications. The next section summarizes the policy implications of the study.

Implications of the Results

Bhutan's economy is heavily dependent on generation of HEP, and the country's efforts to achieve SLM are justified by our findings, which show that the adoption of SFM could reduce the cost of sediment loading by 50 %.

Results show that a citrus orchard is the most profitable enterprise, but its long gestation period is a hindrance to large-scale investment. Given the growing demand for citrus and horticultural crops, there is need of increasing efforts to promote citrus and horticultural crop production in a manner that is amenable among smallholder farmers. Producing citrus fruits on a small piece of land or planting citrus trees in annual crops could lead to significant production that does not burden farmers to set a large piece of land and wait for six years before the first harvest. The increasing production of fruits and horticultural crops could be accelerated by enhancing nurseries and extension services that provide both production and marketing advisory services.

Returns to CFM are low but profitable at a lower discount rate. This means CFM may not compete with annual crops or livestock but is still favorable for abandoned areas. Likewise, investment in pine and broadleaf forests is profitable at high discount factors, which suggests the importance of enhancing incentives of communities to engage in CF programs by payment for ecosystem services. As our results show, SFM can reduce sediment loading to rivers serving HEP plants by 50 %. This justifies improvement of the current payment for ecosystem services program in which DGPC pays about 1 % of its revenue to the government to encourage farmers to adopt SLM and SFM. Because such money is given to the government, which in turn uses the money to provide advisory services, it is hard for farmers to connect DGPC payments and the DGPC-funded advisory services provided by the government. There is great need for designing a policy that will give DGPC a mandate to interact directly with land users. DGPC has actually requested RGoB's permission to work with farmers directly, but this has not yet been approved. This could be enhanced under a CF program by allocating the forest currently under government control to communities, which in turn will increase forest density and contribute to reducing sediment loading. Instead DGPC is currently implementing corporate responsibility programs such as planting trees and supporting communities to take up environmentally friendly practices. For example, tree planting is done between Paro and Chhukha dam. In addition, around each of the HEP plants, DGPC is supporting green and clean programs.

Considering the drivers of SLM, we see that land security, access to extension services, and roads will enhance SLM and will have multiplier effects. RGoB has already started investing heavily in improving rural roads. However, road construction has contributed to increasing sediment loading. This suggests the need for adopting sustainable road construction that minimizes soil erosion.

In summary, Bhutan's policies and its cultural and historical background have set the country on the path to becoming a global green growth success story. Results of this study vindicate the country's efforts to invest in sustainable land and forest management.

References

Agarwal, B. (2009). Gender and forest conservation: The impact of women's participation in community forest governance. *Ecological Economics, 68*, 2785–2799.

Alcock, D., & Hegarty, R. S. (2006). Effects of pasture improvement on productivity, gross margin and methane emissions of a grazing sheep enterprise. *International Congress Series, 1293*, 103–106.

Arnold, J. G., Srinivasan, R., Muttiah, R. S., & Williams, J. R. (1998). Large-area hydrologic modeling and assessment: Part I. model development. *Journal of American Water Resources Association, 34*(1), 73–89.

Barrett, C. B., Place, F., & Aboud, A. (2002). The challenges of stimulating adoption of improved natural resource management practices in African agriculture. In C. B. Barrett, F. Place, & A. A. Aboud (Eds.), *Natural resources management in African agriculture* (pp. 1–22). Nairobi, Kenya: World Agroforestry Centreand CAB International.

Beldring, S., & Voksø, A. (2011). *Report No. 4—2011: Climate change impacts on the flow regimes of rivers in Bhutan and possible consequences for hydropower development.* Oslo, Norway: Norwegian Water Resources and Energy Directorate. ISSN: 1502-3540.

Berry, L., Olson, J., & Campbell, D. (2003). *Assessing the extent, cost and impact of land degradation at the national level: Finding and lessons learned from seven pilot case studies.* New York: Global Mechanism, United Nations.

Bowler, D., Buyung-Ali, L., Healey, J. R., Jones, J. P. G., Knight, T., & Pullin, A. S. (2010). *The evidence base for community forest management as a mechanism for supplying global environmental benefits and improving local welfare.* CEE Review 08-011. Bangor, UK:Centre for Evidence-Based Conservation.

Brooks, J. S. (2010). The Buddha mushroom: Conservation behavior and the development of institutions in Bhutan. *Ecological Economics, 69*, 779–795.

Chetri, G. B., Ghimiray, M., & Floyd, C. N. (2003). Effects of farmyard manure, fertilizers and green manuring in rice-wheat systems in Bhutan: Results from a long-term experiment. *Experimental Agriculture, 39*, 129–144.

Chiabai, A., Travisi, C. M., Markandya, A., Ding, H., & Nunes, P. A. L. D. (2011). Economic assessment of forest ecosystem services losses: Cost of policy inaction. *Environmental & Resource Economics, 50*, 405–445.

Choden, S., Tashi, S., & Dhendup, N. (2010). *Analysis of the contributions of protected areas to the social and economic development of Bhutan at national level*. Thimphu, Bhutan: Ministry of Agriculture and Forests, Royal Government of Bhutan.
Chophyel, P. (2009). *Rangeland management in Bhutan: A consultancy report*. Thimphu, Bhutan: Royal Government of Bhutan, Ministry of Agriculture.
Christensen, G., Fileccia, T., & Gulliver, A. (2012). *Bhutan. Agricultural sector review*, Vol. 1, Issues, Institutions and Policies. Rome: FAO; Washington, DC: World Bank.
D'Exelle, B., van Campenhout, B., & Lecoutere, E. (2012). Modernisation and time preferences in Tanzania: Evidence from a large-scale elicitation exercise. *Journal of Development Studies, 48* (4), 564–580.
Delgado, C., Narrod, C., & Tiongco, M. (2002). *Policy, technical, and environmental determinants and implications of the scaling-up of livestock production in four fast-growing developing countries: A synthesis*. FAO: Final Research Report of Phase II. Rome.
DGPC (Drik Green Power Coroporation). (2009). *Druk green power limited*. Thimphu: Brochure.
Dixit, A. K., & Pindyck, R. S. (1994). *Investment under uncertainty*. Princeton, NJ: Princeton UniversityPress.
Dorji, J. (1993). *Estimation of grazing animal feed requirement in the kingdom of Bhutan*. Thimphu, Bhutan: Royal Government of Bhutan, National Environment Commission.
Duflo, E., Mullainathan, S., & Bertrand, M. (2004). How much should we trust difference-in-difference estimates? *Quarterly Journal of Economics, 119*(1), 249–275.
Dukra, K. (2013). *Bhutan RNR statistics 2012*. Thimphu, Bhutan: Royal Government of Bhutan, Ministry of Agriculture and Forests.
Duquette, E., Higgins, N., & Horowitz, J. (2011). Farmer discount rates: Experimental evidence. *American Journal of Agricultural Economics, 94*(2), 451–456.
Fafchamps, M., & Pender, J. (1997). Precautionary saving, credit constraints, and irreversible investment: Theory and evidence from semiarid India. *Journal of Business and Economic Statistics, 15*(2), 180–194.
FAO (Food and Agriculture Organization of the United Nations). (1996). *Agro-ecological zoning guidelines*. FAO Soils Bulletin 73. Rome. www.fao.org/docrep/w2962e/w2962e00.htm#P-2
FAO (Food and Agriculture Organization of the United Nations). (2011). State of the world's forests food. Accessed 21 Mar 2014. www.fao.org/forestry
FAO (Food and Agriculture Organization of the United Nations). (2013). FAOSTAT database. Accessed 21 Mar 2014. http://faostat3.fao.org/faostat-gateway/go/to/home/E
FAO/UNESCO. (1977). *Soil Map of the world* (Vol. VI). Paris: Africa. Unesco.
Flay, R. B. (2001). Modeling nitrates and phosphates in agricultural watersheds with the soil and water assessment tool. Accessed 22 2006. www.waterscape.org/pubs/tech_swat/SWAT_Review.doc
Gardner, K., & Barrows, R. (1985). The impact of soil conservation investments on land prices. *American Journal of Agricultural Economics, 67*(5), 943–947.
GEF (Global Environment Facility). (2012). Bhutan sustainable land management. Accessed 15 Jan 2014. www.thegef.org/gef/greenline/january-2012/bhutan-sustainable-land-management
Gupta, H. V., Sorooshian, S., & Yapo, P. O. (1999). Status of automatic calibration for hydrologic models: Comparison with multilevel expert calibration. *Journal of Hydrologic Engineering, 4*(2), 135–143.
Gyaltsen, T., & Bhattarai, B. N. (2002). *Cattle migration system of western Bhutan: A case study*. Rome: FAO. www.fao.org/ag/agp/AGPC/doc/pasture/peshawarproceedings/cattlemigration.pdf
Gyamtsho, P., Singh, B. K., & Rasul, G. (2006). *Capitalisation and sharing of experiences on the interaction between forest policies and land use patterns in Asia: Linking people with resources*. Technical Paper. Kathmandu, Nepal: International Centre for Integrated Mountain Development.
Hein, L. (2006). *Environmental economics tool kit: Analyzing the economic costs of land degradation and the benefits of sustainable land management*. Wageningen, The Netherlands: United Nations and Global Environment Fund.

Heisey, P. W., & Mwangi, W. (1998). *Fertilizer use and maize production in Sub-Saharan Africa.* CIMMYT Economics Working Paper 96-01. Mexico City, Mexico: International Maize and Wheat Improvement Center.

Hydromet. Various years. Hydrological and meteorological raw data. Accessed 30 June 2014. www.moea.gov.bt/departments/department.php?id=4

IPCC (Intergovernmental Panel on Climate Change). (2012). *Renewable energy sources and climate change mitigation special report of the intergovernmental panel on climate change.* Cambridge, UK: Cambridge University Press.

Licker, R. M., Johnston, J. A., Foley, C., Barford, C. J., Kucharik, C., & Monfreda, Ramankutty N. (2010). Mind the gap: How do climate and agricultural management explain the 'yield gap' of croplands around the world? *Global Ecology and Biogeography, 19*(6), 769–782.

Luzio, M., Srinivasan, R., & Arnold, J. G. (2002). Integration of watershed tools and SWAT model into BASINS. *Journal of American Water Resource Association, 38*(4), 1127–1141.

Lysne, D., Glover, B., Stole, H., & Tesakar, E. (2003). *Hydraulic design*. Publication No. 8. Trondheim. Norway: Norwegian Institute of Technology.

MoAF. (2011). *Agriculture survey 2011 Dzongkhag level statistics* (Vol. 1). Thimphu, Bhutan: Ministry of Agriculture and Forests.

MoAF (Ministry of Agriculture and Forests). (2010). Bhutan land cover mapping. Online at http://www.rspnbhutan.org/news-and-events/news/301-bhutans-land-cover-maps-updated.html. Accessed 28 July 2014.

Moriasi, D. N., Arnold, J. G., Van Liew, M. W., Bingner, R. L., Harmel, R. D., & Veith, T. L. (2007). Model evaluation guidelines for systematic quantification of accuracy in watershed simulations. *ASABE, 50*(3), 885–900.

Mukherjee, C., White, H., & Wuyts, M. (1998). *Econometrics and data analysis for developing countries*. London: Routledge.

Nandwa, S. M., & Bekunda, M. A. (1998). Research on nutrient flows and balances in East and Southern Africa: State-of-the-art. *Agriculture, Ecosystems & Environment, 71*, 5–18.

Nash, J. E., & Sutcliffe, J. V. (1970). River flow forecasting through conceptual models: Part I. A discussion of principles. *Journal of Hydrology, 10*(3), 190–282.

National Statistical Bureau (NSB). (2009). National accounts statistics: 2000–2008. National Statistical Bureau. ThimphuNational Statistical Bureau (NSB). 2012. National Accounts Statistics. National Statistical Bureau. Thimphu.

National Statistical Bureau and Asian Development Bank. (2013). *Bhutan living standards survey 2012 report.*www.nsb.gov.bt/publication/files/pub1tm2120wp.pdf

NSSC (National Soil Services Center). (2011). *BHUCAT. Bhutan catalogue of soil and water conservation approaches and technologies. Best practices and guidelines from Bhutan for sustainable land management on steep to very steep slopes.* Thimphu, Bhutan: Department of Agriculture, Ministry of Agriculture and Forests, Royal Government of Bhutan. www.nssc.gov.bt

Numbeo.com. (2014). *Food prices in Bhutan*. www.numbeo.com/food-prices/country_result.jsp?country=Bhutan. Accessed 15 May 2014.

Pagiola, S. (1996). Price policy and returns to soil conservation in semi-arid Kenya. *Environmental & Resource Economics, 8*, 255–271.

Pearce, D. W. (2001). The economic value of forest ecosystems. *Ecosystem health, 7*(4), 284–296.

Pender, J. (1996). Discount rates and credit markets: Theory and evidence from rural India. *Journal of Development Economics, 50*, 257–296.

Phuntsho, S., Schmidt, K., Kuyakanon, R., & Temphel, K. J. (Eds.). (2011). *Community forestry in Bhutan: Putting people at the heart of poverty reduction*. Thimphu, Bhutan: Ministry of Agriculture and Forests.

Rambaud, S. C., & Torrecillas, M. J. (2007). Some considerations on the social discount rate. *Environmental Science & Policy, 8*(4), 343–355.

RGoB (Royal Government of Bhutan). (2002). *Bhutan 2020: A vision for peace*. Thimphu, Bhutan: Prosperity and Happiness.

RGoB (Royal Government of Bhutan). (2008). *Constitution of the kingdom of Bhutan*. Thimphu, Bhutan: Constitution Drafting Committee.
RGoB, MoA (Royal Government of Bhutan, Ministry of Agriculture). (1995). *LUPP Dzongkhag data sheets for Bhutan*. Thimphu, Bhutan: Land Use Planning Project.
RGoB, MoAF (Royal Government of Bhutan, Ministry of Agriculture and Forests). (2010a). *National forest policy of Bhutan 2010*. Bhutan: Thimphu.
RGoB, MoAF (Royal Government of Bhutan, Ministry of Agriculture and Forests). (2010b). Bhutan renewable natural resources census 2009. Thimphu, Bhutan.
RGoB, MoAF (Royal Government of Bhutan, Ministry of Agriculture and Forests). (2012). Agriculture survey 2011, Vol. I. Dzongkhag level statistics. Thimphu, Bhutan.
Roder, W., Wangdi, K., Gyamtsho, P., Dorji, K. (2001). *Feeding the herds: Improving fodder resources in Bhutan*. Kathmandu, Nepal: ICIMOD. ISBN: 92-9115-409-1. http://books.icimod.org/index.php/search/publication/109
Samdup, T., Udo, H. M. J., Viets, T. C., & van der Zijpp, A. J. (2013). Livestock intensification and use of natural resources in smallholder mixed farming systems of Bhutan. *Livestock Research for Rural Development*, *25*(7), article 114.
SCBD (Secretariat of the Convention on Biological Diversity). (2001). *The value of forest ecosystems.*CBD Technical Series No. 4. Montreal, Canada.
Sharma, C. M., Khanduri, V. P., & Ghildiyal, S. K. (2012). Reproductive ecology of male and female strobili and mating system in two different populations of pinus Roxburghii. *Scientific World Journal, 2012*, 1–13.
Tobgay, S. (2005). *Small farmers and the food system in Bhutan*. Thimphu, Bhutan: Royal Government of Bhutan, Ministry of Agriculture.
Tobgay, S., & McCullough, E. (2008). Linking smallholder farmers in Bhutan with markets: The importance of access to roads. In E. McCullough, P. Pingali, & K. Stamoulis (Eds.), *Transformation of agri-food systems: Globalization, supply chains and smallholder farmers* (pp. 259–278). London: Earthscan.
UNEP (United Nations Environment Programme). (2009). *Strategizing climate change for Bhutan.* National Environment Commission, Royal Government of Bhutan and UNEP Report. www.rrcap.unep.org/nsds/uploadedfiles/file/bhutan.pdf
Vanlauwe, B., & Giller, K. E. (2006). Popular myths around soil fertility management in Sub-Saharan Africa. *Agriculture, Ecosystem and Environment, 116*, 34–46.
Wangdi, K. (2006). *Country pasture/forage resource profiles for Bhutan.* Thimphu, Bhutan: FAO. www.fao.org/ag/AGP/agpc/doc/Proceedings/Tapafon02/tapafon8.htm
Wangdi, K. (2012). *Bhutan country pasture profile.* www.fao.org/ag/agp/AGPC/doc/pasture/forage.htm
Winslow, M., Sommer, S., Bigas, H., Martius, C., Vogt, J., Akhtar-Schuster, M., Thomas, R. (Eds.). (2011). Understanding desertification and land degradation trends. In *Proceedings of the UNCCD First Scientific Conference, during the UNCCD Ninth Conference of Parties, Buenos Aires, Argentina*. 22–24 Sept 2009. Luxembourg: Office for Official Publications of the European Communities. doi:10.2788/62563
WOCAT (World Overview of Conservation Approaches and Technologies). (2007). *Where the land is greener: Case studies and analysis of soil and water conservation initiatives worldwide.* www.wocat.net/fileadmin/user_upload/documents/Books/WOOK_PART1.pdf
Ziadat, F. M., Oweis, T., Al-Wadaey, A., Aw Hassan, A., Sakai, H., van der Zanden, E., et al. (2012). *Soil conservation and water harvesting to improve community livelihoods and fight land degradation in the mountains of Syria.* ICARDA working paper 9. Beirut, Lebanon: ICARDA.
Ziadat, F. M., & Taimeh, A. Y. (2013). Effect of rainfall intensity, slope, land use and antecedent soil moisture on soil erosion in an arid environment. *Land Degradation and Development, 24*, 582–590.

Chapter 13
Economics of Land Degradation in China

Xiangzheng Deng and Zhihui Li

Abstract Land degradation is a complex process that involves both the natural ecosystem and the socioeconomic system, among which climate and land use changes are the two predominant driving factors. We reviewed the status of degradation in grasslands, forests and cultivated lands in China, as well as the major drivers of land degradation in the North China Plain. The previous research shows that an increase in rainfall and temperature would significantly and positively contribute to land improvement. The conversion from cultivated land to grassland and forest land showed positive relationship with land improvement, while conversion to built-up area is associated with land degradation. In addition, human agricultural intensification may help improve the land quality. The overall economic development may exert positive impacts on land quality, while the increased agricultural production may exert negative impacts on land. Infrastructure construction would modify the land surface and further result in land degradation. Finally, our analysis of the costs of actions to address land degradation in China shows that the annual costs of land degradation due to land use and cover change (LUCC) is equal to about 24.5 billion USD. In addition, the cost of grassland degradation, without shifts in LUCC, is estimated to equal about 0.49 billion USD due to losses in livestock productivity resulting from grassland degradation. Moreover, the costs of cropland degradation for three crops: wheat, maize and rice, is estimated to be about 12 billion USD annually. The total cost of land degradation due to LUCC and using land degrading management practices on cropland and grazing land is 2007 US$37 billion or 1 % of China's 2007 GDP. Finally, the analysis shows that the costs of the rehabilitation of the lands degraded due to LUCC are significantly lower than the costs of inaction, with the returns of up to 4.7 times for every yuan invested over a 30-year period. This underscores the need to take action against land degradation. This is particularly important given China's

X. Deng (✉) · Z. Li
Institute of Geographic Sciences and Natural Resources Research, Chinse Academy of Sciences, No. 11A, Datun Road, Chaoyang District, Beijing 100101, China
e-mail: dengxz.ccap@igsnrr.ac.cn

Z. Li
e-mail: lizh.12b@igsnrr.ac.cn

E. Nkonya et al. (eds.), *Economics of Land Degradation and Improvement – A Global Assessment for Sustainable Development*,
DOI 10.1007/978-3-319-19168-3_13

new sustainable development and green economy approach reflected in its five year plan (2011–15) and other environmental policies. Results of this study will inform policy makers on the key areas for addressing land degradation.

Keywords Land degradation · Land use change · Climate change · NDVI · China

Introduction

Land degradation means a significant reduction of the productive capacity of land. It is a complex process involving various causal factors, among which climate changes, land use/cover changes and human dominated land management play a dominant role (Barbier 1997; Sivakumar and Ndiang'Ui 2007; Symeonakis et al. 2007; Bajocco et al. 2012). There are two interlocking complex systems involved in the land degradation process, i.e. the natural ecosystem and the human social system, and both changes in biophysical natural ecosystem and socioeconomic conditions will affect the land degradation process (MEA 2005). Natural forces affect land degradation through periodic stresses exerted by extreme and persistent climatic events, while human activities contribute to land degradation through (1) deforestation, removal of natural vegetation and urban sprawl which lead to land use/cover changes, (2) unsustainable agricultural land management practices, such as use and abuse of fertilizers, pesticides and heavy machinery, (3) and overgrazing, improper crop rotation and poor irrigation practices etc. (Sivakumar and Ndiang'Ui 2007).

In comparison to other regions, land degradation afflicts China more seriously in terms of the extent, intensity, socio-economic impacts and the number of affected population (Bai and Dent 2009). With just 7.2 % of the world's cultivated land area, China needs to feed 22 % of the world's population, thus agricultural production is a critical issue related with national economy and livelihood of its citizens in China (Deng et al. 2008). However, rapid population growth and urbanization, unreasonable human utilization and influence of natural factors, have caused degradation of 5.392 million km^2 land, accounting for about 56.2 % of the total national area, among which the area of land degradation resulting from soil erosion and water loss, desertification, soil salinization, pasture degradation and soil pollution is 1.80, 0.334, 0.9913, 2.00 and 0.267 million km^2, respectively (Long 2013). The suitable land for agricultural production is only about 1.3 million km^2, accounting for 14 % of the total land area in China. In addition, more than 50 % of the total cultivated land has experienced land degradation, which further exerts more pressure on the economic benefits of agricultural production and food security. Besides, as cultivated land degradation will directly affect the potential land productivity, more inputs such as fertilizer and irrigation water will be needed in order to get the same production and yield level, which will increase the production costs (Li et al. 2011). In addition, the land use structural change and pattern succession resulting from land conversions will definitely affect the suitability and quality of land and directly influence land productivity (Deng et al. 2006). Hence, for the long-term sustainable development of agricultural economy, it's critical to take sustainable productive land management measures.

China is a large country with significant spatial variation of natural/climatic conditions and diverse socioeconomic characteristics. For example, the eastern, central and western parts of China have different population densities, industrial structure, per capita incomes, etc. The difference among regions will affect land use, leading to differences in the ways and extent of economic use of land resources. In this chapter, we review three types of land degradation, including grassland degradation, forest degradation and cultivated land degradation, and also assessment of the driving causes of land degradation. Finally, we estimate the costs of land degradation in China and compare them with the costs of inaction.

Review of Land Degradation Assessments in China

Distribution of ecosystems and their total economic value (TEV) is shown in Fig. 13.1. The highest TEV is in the northeastern area, where about 29 % of forest cover is located (Deng et al. 2010) and the south-western region, which is also endowed with both natural and planted forests.

The northwestern area is endowed with grasslands—which also have high value, while the densely populated and urbanized eastern region has the lowest TEV. As it will be seen in the cost of land degradation section, the highest cost of land degradation is found in areas with highest TEV.

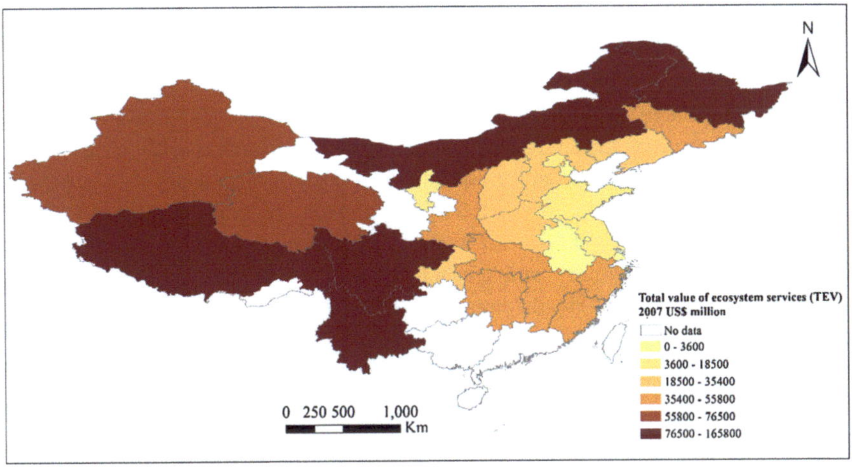

Fig. 13.1 Total economic value of ecosystem services of major biomes, 2001. *Source* Authors' data

Land degradation in China is an increasingly serious economic, social and environmental problem. With the continuously serious land degradation leading to the reduction of agricultural yields, China may face critical food security problems. To clarify the conditions of land degradation in China, it is necessary to carry out comprehensive analyses of the differences among regions and the heterogeneity of different types of land degradation in different regions considering the environmental, social and economic conditions. A comprehensive analysis of the typical spectral characteristics of various types of land degradation can be conducted on the basis of previous studies, field investigations, and remote sensing data of a variety of spatial and temporal resolutions in combination with the application of the RS and GIS techniques.

Grassland degradation indicates the deterioration of ecological function of grassland ecosystem. It is a process accompanied by the decline of grass quality and primary productivity, the loss of bio-diversity and complexity, and the deterioration of resilience and recovery functions (Yang et al. 2007; Jiang et al. 2011). The grassland, with an area of 400 million km^2 and covering more than 40 % of China (Ren et al. 2008), supports the development of animal husbandry, is one of the most important terrestrial ecosystems in China. Grassland ecosystem can provide significant ecological benefits and economic benefits for humans, including forage, milk, meat, wool and pelts etc. However, with grassland degradation, the average grassland productivity level of China is much lower than that of other parts in the world.

There have been many studies to identify and assess grassland degradation in China. With assistance of RS and GIS, the vegetation pattern is regarded as a good indicator to monitor vegetation dynamics and assess grassland degradation (Li et al. 2012). Based on a landscape-scale approach, Tong et al. (2004) combined the field survey data, vegetation maps, and RS data to assess the degradation degree of different steppe communities at the local scale and analyze the spatial pattern at the landscape scale. Further, a steppe degradation index (SDI) that integrates the spatial extent and steppe degradation severity information was developed to quantify the spatio-temporal grassland ecosystem degradation. Similarly, with Landsat Thematic Mapper (TM) image conjunct with 1 m^2 plot sampled percent grass cover and proportion (by weight) of unpalatable grasses (PUG) information, Liu et al. (2004) assessed the grassland degradation and conducted regression analyses, the results showed that NDVI is the most reliable indicator of grass cover and PUG. Furthermore, Liu et al. (2008) used Multispectral Scanner Sensor (MSS) images and TM images to spatially and temporally analyze the grassland degradation degree in the Three-River Headwaters Region. Also, Li et al. (2012) estimated the regional vegetation fractional coverage (VFC) based on the Gutman model (Gutman 1987), which is one of the most widely used models to estimate VFC based on NDVI.

Grassland has a wide distribution in China and shows significant regional heterogeneity. The NPP in the eastern China was higher than that in the western region, and with higher value in the southern region than in the northern region. Overall, from northwest to southeast China, except the Tibetan Plateau, the NPP showed an increasing trend with some fluctuations, and reached the highest value in the southwest karst area with a value of 1000 gC/m^2 in 2010 (Wu et al. 2013).

Researchers have identified many causes of grassland degradation, including overgrazing, improper cultivation methods, unreasonable harvest of herbs for medicine, and damages induced by rodent activities. Besides, there have been many studies showing that climate changes have great impacts on the grassland productivity, especially in the arid and semi-arid regions (Baldocchi 2011; Qi et al. 2012). In addition, a key issue is how natural and anthropogenic causes influence grassland degradation. Li et al. (2012) carried out an in-depth empirical analyses on the natural and anthropogenic drivers and mechanisms of grassland degradation, ten biophysical and socioeconomic factors, including precipitation, temperature, population density, sheep unit density, etc., were chosen to analyze the impacts on the observed patterns of steppe degradation on the basis of econometric analysis. Their results show that the higher altitude, rainfall amounts, distance to markets and sustainable land management measures, such as fencing, are associated with less grassland degradation (ibid.).

Wu et al. (2013) also find that the climate factors and geographical factors have great impacts on grassland productivity. The precipitation and temperature play a more important role than sunshine duration. The soil phosphorus has significant positive effects on net primary productivity (NPP), indicating that the increase of soil nitrogen and phosphorus will improve the grassland productivity (ibid). Moreover, Wu et al. (2013) find that elevation exerts significantly negative impacts on NPP, while the percentage of plain area plays a positive role in NPP. As to the socioeconomic factors, both the population and the demand for meat show significantly positive relationship with NPP. The higher share of agricultural production in the total GDP has been found to have negative effects on NPP, indicating that the expansion of the agricultural production will exert more pressure on the grassland and further result in the decline of grassland productivity (ibid.). The population shows significantly positive impacts on NPP. Wu et al. (2013) find that when population increases by ten thousand, the grassland NPP would increase by 0.03 %. With the growth of population, more labor inputs might be devoted into the sustainable grassland production and management (ibid.).

Deforestation is a complicated transformation process with temporal dynamics and spatial heterogeneity. The current studies of land degradation in China mainly focus on grassland productivity and cropland degradation. However, research on deforestation began late and mainly focuses on the soil fertility decline caused by continuous crop production in deforested areas. There is still no general consensus on how to correctly assess deforestation, which is a complex process, and there are many difficulties to overcome, such as how to define deforestation, how to improve the reliability and availability of the deforestation data, how to deal with the limited time-series data, and how to map deforestation with higher spatial resolution satellite images at the global level, and, how to identify the particular drivers of deforestation dynamics. It is still a challenge to get reliable estimates of forest degradation in China (Gao et al. 2011), and there is a lot yet to be advanced on the assessment method of deforestation.

Jiang et al. (2011) study deforestation in Northeast China, which accounts for 28.9 % of the total forest land area in China (Deng et al. 2010), and the forest stock accounts for 27.8 % of the national total (SFA 2005). This makes the Northeast China an important forest production base and plays an important role in sustaining the ecological and socio-economic development in China. Jiang et al. (2011) find that due to the long-term exploitation, the forests in Northeast China have shrunk dramatically, with monotonous and juvenile forest age structures and less forest resources to be exploited. According to the national forest resources survey, the ripe forests decreased by 49 % during 1981–1988, and 0.61 million ha of forests continually disappeared in the next decade (Xiao et al. 2002). Although the complementation of the Grain for Green Project, the Logging Ban Program, and other ecological restoration projects have made some achievements in the Northeast China, the forest shrinkage and degradation still continue (Wang et al. 2003; Zhao et al. 2006; Shen et al. 2006; Peng et al. 2007).

The analysis by Jiang et al. (2011) shows that the average slope and elevation has significant impacts on forestry production and forest conversion, with higher forest coverage in the areas with steeper slopes and higher elevation. Besides, in the regions with habitats where crop cultivation is forbidden and the urbanization and industrialization levels are low, the open forests and other land uses are converted to the closed forest to some extent. As to the climate change impacts on the forestry area, the estimation results by Jiang et al. (2011) show that temperature and precipitation only have significant impacts on the forestry production, but not on the forest conversion. The distance to the nearest water area is found to be positively associated with forest production (ibid.). The socioeconomic factors are the major factors that affect forest production and the spatial pattern of forest coverage. With more dense populations, there might be more damages to the forests, which leads to a relatively lower gross output value of forest production and constraints land use conversions to the closed forest (ibid.). However, with the increase in agricultural population, the conversion amount from other land uses into the closed forest may increase (ibid.). The increase in gross output value of forestry sector may stimulate the expansion of the closed forest (ibid.).

Cropland degradation is an important problem in China. With a large population and relatively limited cultivated land, food security is always an important issue concerning the economic development and citizens' livelihood (Deng et al. 2008). Along with rapid population growth and urbanization, the cultivated land degradation due to unreasonable utilization and conversion from cultivated land to other lands exerts more pressure on the economic benefits of agricultural production and food security. Besides, as the cultivated land degradation directly affects the potential land productivity, more inputs such as fertilizer and irrigation water will be needed in order to get the same production and yield level, which will increase the production cost (Li et al. 2011).

In the analysis of cropland degradation in the North China Plain, Li et al. (2015) find that higher temperature and rainfall are positively related with increases in cropland NDVI. Moreover, the agricultural intensification proxied by fertilizer utilization, is significantly positively related with land improvement, as fertilizer application will make soil carbon increase (Vlek et al. 2004), which further lead to an increase in NDVI. In addition, increases in the share of the primary industry (Agriculture, Animal, Husbandry and Fishery) in GDP are associated with lower NDVI values. In addition, geographic and topographic factors were also found to affect land degradation (Li et al. 2015). Steeper slopes are found to lead to land degradation, as steep slope regions are more vulnerable to severe water-induced soil erosion (ibid.). Besides, the distances to highways are significantly positively related with land improvement, which suggest that larger distances to a road network means there is less human disturbance, less infrastructure development and fewer land use changes, which will exert less impacts on the land degradation (ibid).

Cost of Land Degradation and Cost of Action and Inaction Against Land Degradation Due to Land Use/Cover Change in China

We follow the methods discussed in Chap. 6 to determine the cost of land degradation and the cost of action and inaction against land degradation.

To take action to control land degradation, the awareness about urgent conditions in regard of the loss of economic opportunities and livelihoods should be raised, then an assessment of the economic consequences of land degradation and the costs of related inaction, compared against the costs of action for sustainable land use, is required. In this section, we aim to assess the cost of land degradation due to land use/cover changes, and compare the cost of action and inaction.

Land use/cover changes (LUCC) are a major driver of land degradation, which replace the high value biomes with low value biomes (Nkonya et al. 2014). In this section, we used the 1-km resolution Moderate Resolution Imaging Spectroradiometer (MODIS) land cover data to analyze LUCC (Fig. 13.2). Accordingly, the grasslands covered about 8.37 % of land area in China in 2001, then decreased to 5.88 % in 2009. Shrublands and woodlands covered about 21.25 and 9.23 % respectively of land area in 2001, and the extent of shrublands and woodlands increased to 23.62 and 9.51 % respectively in 2009. Forestland covered only 14.60 % of land area in 2001 and its extent increased to 16.20 % of the land area in 2009. The increase was mainly due to the Grain for Green Project in China, which was launched in 1999. Cropland area increased from 18.52 to 18.91 %.

The costs related to land degradation as a result of LUCC for China are shown in Table 13.1. Based on the MODIS land use data of year 2001 and year 2009, along with the application of the total economic value (TEV) approach (see Chap. 6), the total cost of land degradation due to LUCC for the period between 2001 and 2009 is

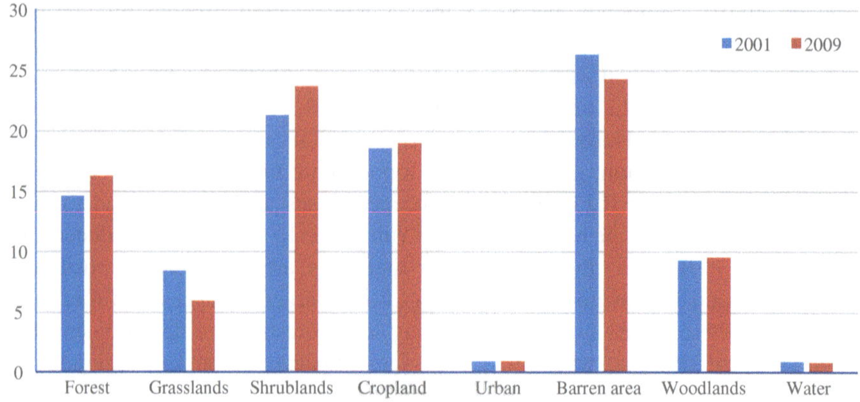

Fig. 13.2 Extent of land uses in China, 2001 and 2009

Table 13.1 The cost of land degradation due to LUCC for the period of 2001–2009 and cost of action and inaction in China across degraded biomes

	Agroecological zone			Total
	Arid and semi-arid	Sub-humid	Humid	
	2007 US$ billion			
Cost of land degradation				
• TEV	103.37	24.94	67.44	195.75
• Provisioning services	49.91	9.12	25.63	84.66
• Loss of provisioning services as % of TEV	48.28	36.57	38.01	43.25
Cost of restoration of degraded biomes				
• Forest	25.55	21.71	64.59	111.85
• Grassland	68.08	5.64	7.71	81.43
• Shrublands	12.70	4.22	7.49	24.41
• Woodlands	4.33	9.92	23.51	37.76
Total cost of				
• Action	110.66	41.50	103.29	255.45
• Inaction	608.57	175.55	423.95	1208.08
MRR of taking action	5.5	4.2	4.1	4.7

Note: *MRR* Marginal rate of return
Source Authors' data

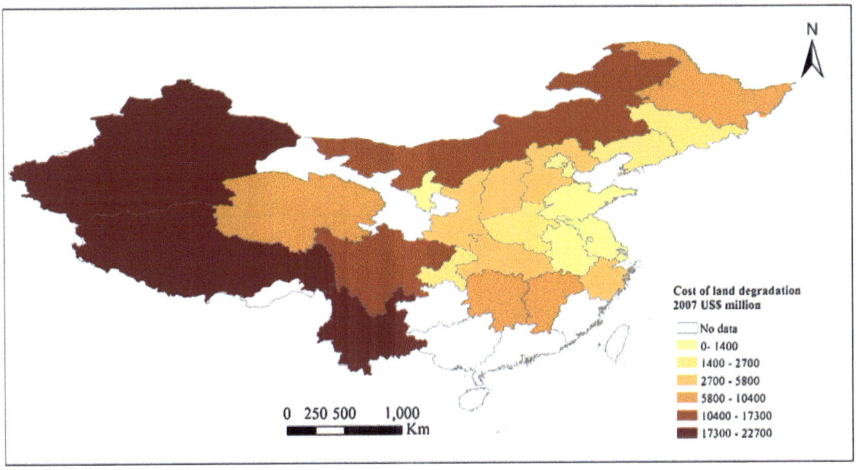

Fig. 13.3 Cost of land degradation due to LUCC for the period of 2001–2009 (million US$). *Source* Authors' data

estimated to be about 2007 US$ 195.747 billion,[1] which is about 5.4 % of Chinese 2007 GDP. This means that annually between 2001 and 2009, the costs of land degradation due to LUCC in China were about 24.5 billion USD. The cost is highest in the arid and semi-arid area (Table 13.1; Fig. 13.3). We calculated the cost of taking action against land degradation, the cost of establishing and maintaining degraded biomes. The results showed that in order to completely rehabilitate the land degraded due to LUCC between 2001 and 2009 in China, a total amount of US $ 255.45 billion will be required during a 30 year period (Table 13.1). While, if action is not taken to rehabilitate these degraded lands, China will incur a loss of US $ 1208.08 billion during the same period. The marginal rate of return for investment in restoration of degraded land is above 4—suggesting very high payoff for taking action. Restoration of degraded forest accounts for the largest cost. This is followed by restoration of degraded grasslands—especially in the arid and semi-arid areas in northwestern China.

China is has already started a reforestation program and has been the world's leading country in afforestation and reforestation programs that involved payment for ecosystem (PES) or other strategies (FAO 2010). For example in 2005, China accounted for 90 % of the global afforested area of 4.9 million ha (Ibid).[2]

[1]These costs do not include the losses due to land degradation on static land use, such as croplands and grazing lands—which are discussed below.

[2]Afforestation is planting of forest on an area previously under non-forest biome.

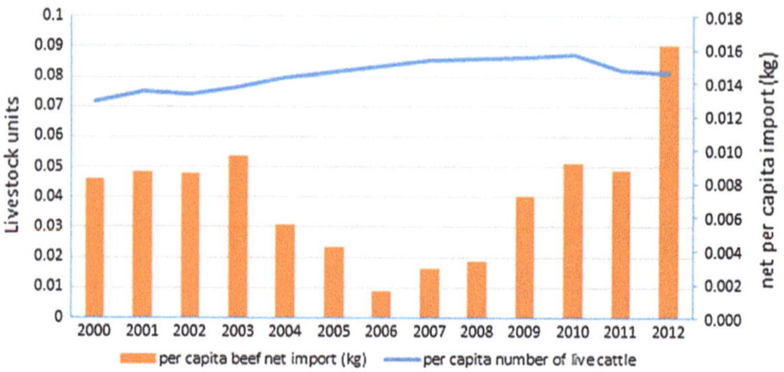

Fig. 13.4 China's growing demand for livestock products. *Source* Calculated from FAOSTAT (2012)

Cost of Land Degradation on Grazing Land

The livestock sector accounted for 34 % of the agricultural sector, which in turn accounted for 14 % of the China's GDP in 2005 (FAO 2005). The livestock sector has been growing with growing income and change in consumer tastes and preferences (Ibid). Consequently, per capita number of livestock increased by 21 % from 0.071 in 2000 to 0.087 in 2010 (FAOSTAT 2012). Net import per capita of beef doubled from 0.008 kg in 2000 to 0.016 kg in 2012 (Fig. 13.4).

The increasing livestock population density and over-exploitation of grazing resources in response to the increasing demand for livestock products has resulted in land degradation. Following analytical approaches discussed in Chap. 8, the cost of land degradation on static grazing lands was US$491 million (Table 13.2).

Table 13.2 Cost of land degradation on grazing land (2007 US$ million)

AEZ	Milk loss cost	Meat loss cost	Total cost	Percent of total cost
Subtropic-cool/semi-arid	20.59	21.74	42.33	8.6
Subtropic-cool/arid	10.53	11.55	22.08	4.5
Subtropic-cool/humid	0.12	0.04	0.16	0.0
Subtropic-cool/sub-humid	10.01	5.05	15.06	3.1
Temperate/semi-arid	33.26	33.48	66.75	13.6
Temperate/arid	100.56	230.03	330.59	67.3
Temperate/sub-humid	0.43	0.40	0.83	0.2
Tropic-cool/sub-humid	0.91	0.12	1.03	0.2
Tropic-warm/humid	5.61	0.86	6.46	1.3
Tropic-warm/sub-humid	5.09	0.63	5.72	1.2
Total	187.11	303.90	491.00	

The loss accounts for only milk and meat production. This suggests other losses—especially carbon sequestration, are not taken into account. The temperate arid area in the northwestern region accounted for two thirds of the loss. Meat loss also accounted for 62 % of the loss. This is due to the fact that livestock production in temperate rangeland in the northwestern China is largely for meat production.

The high cost of degradation on grazing lands coupled with the increasing demand for livestock products underscores the need to take action to address land degradation on grazing lands.

Land Degradation on Static Cropland

Crop production accounted for 12.3 % of China's GDP in 2004 (CNBS 2010). The number of farmers in China is aging and rapidly dropping with growing urbanization. For example, the share of rural population as the share of total population dropped from about 82 % in 1978 to about 47 % in 2012 (Yang 2013). Yet China still has a large number of crop farmers and therefore need to address cropland degradation. China is among the countries that uses the highest rate of fertilizer in the world. China accounts for a third of the global consumption of inorganic nitrogen fertilizer (Kahrl et al. 2012), though its cropland area accounts for only about 8 % of the global cropland (FAOSTAT 2013). The high rate of inorganic fertilizer application is leading to eutrophication and other environment consequences. For example, concentration of nitrate in groundwater in northern China was about 30 times U.S. EPA-allowed levels (Kahrl et al. 2012). Adoption rate of organic inputs and integrated soil fertility management (ISFM) is limited. Using analytical methods discussed in Chap. 6 and focusing on maize, rice and wheat only, the cost of land degradation on static cropland is about US$12 billion. Due to limited use of organic inputs and continuous cropping, loss of carbon sequestration accounts for the largest share of total cost (Fig. 13.5).

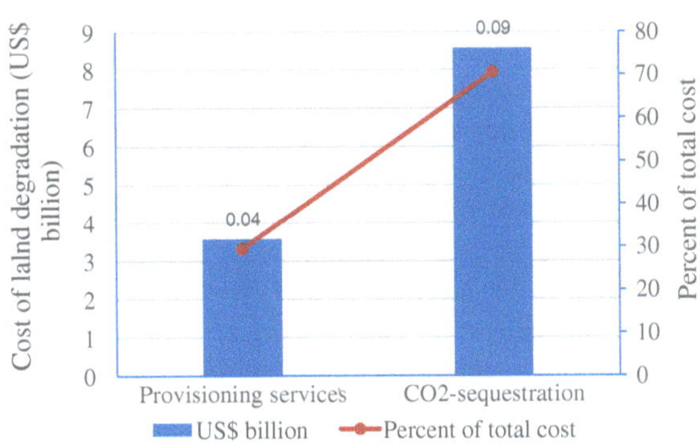

Fig. 13.5 Cost of land degradation due to using land degrading management practices on cropland

Table 13.3 The annual cost of land degradation due to LUCC and land degrading management practices on static cropland and grazing lands

Type of land degradation	Total cost (TEV)	Provisioning services	Cost of land degradation as % of GDP of 2007 US$3494.06 billion	
	2007 US$ billion		Total cost (TEV)	Provisioning services
LUCC	24.46	10.58	0.70	0.30
Livestock	0.49	0.49	0.01	0.01
Cropland	12.13	3.57	0.35	0.10
Total annual cost	37.09	14.64	1.06	0.42

Summary

The total annual cost of land degradation reported in Table 13.3 is US$ 37.09 billion in China or about 1 % of China's GDP in 2007. This is an enormous loss that calls for action—especially given that the returns to taking action are high and China's new sustainable development and green economy approach reflected in its five year plan (2011–15) and other environmental policies (He et al. 2012). The rapid economic development and the consequent natural resource degradation is posing a challenge in the country's human health and welfare in general. The results of this study will inform policy makers on the key areas for addressing land degradation.

Conclusions and Policy Implications

Land degradation is a serious potential threat to food production and rural livelihoods. Land degradation or improvement is an outcome of many proximate and underlying causes. The changes of land quality are the result of many highly inter-linked factors including natural, socioeconomic and also policy and related agricultural practices. In China, many types of land degradation are occurring, such as grassland degradation, deforestation, and cultivated land degradation. In this chapter, we conduct a revisit to the researches on the assessment and driving mechanism of degradation in grasslands, forests and cultivated lands in China and the North China Plain. The results show that degraded areas have been expanding in the northern part of the North China Plain, while many parts of the North China Plain show land improvement, and the increases in temperature and rainfall corresponded to the increase in NDVI in most parts of the North China Plain, agricultural intensification and soil organic matter will benefit the land quality, while rural economic and agricultural development may lead to land degradation. As the rural economic and agricultural production growth exerted negative impacts on land quality, which means the development of rural economy and agricultural production led to land degradation. The increases in rural farmers' per capita income and primary production value ratio did not result in the improvement of land quality, which may be due to the overexploitation of land with insufficient investment into the land conservation. In this regard, an effective response to land degradation calls for increasing the incentives of farmers to conserve their cultivated land and improving their access to the knowledge and inputs required for proper conservation. Promotion of such land improvements should be a development policy priority. During the process to promote rural economic development, the governments should also focus on the monitoring and assessment of land quality and make measures to improve land quality, and such improvement measures should be designed together with farmers to meet their prior needs and use appropriate techniques according to the local economic and social conditions. In addition, access to infrastructures may also have negative effects on land quality. Infrastructure development is the basis for regional prosperity, and a booming economy will result in more construction of infrastructure such as new commercial and industrial buildings. The expansion of basic transport infrastructure such as roads, railways and airports can further occupy land resources and further lead to land overexploitation and degradation. Soil sealing resulted from the urban development and infrastructure construction means the soil surface being covered by impervious materials. If the impervious surfaces replace the natural, semi-natural and cultivated land, this will degrade soil functions or cause their loss. To reduce the impacts of infrastructure construction on land quality, the local government should take the assessment of land degradation into consideration during the construction of infrastructures.

Further, the cost of land degradation due to land use/cover changes, and cost of action and inaction were computed. The results show that, in China, the cost of taking action against land degradation is lower than the cost of inaction even just considering the first 6 years of rehabilitation. The opportunity cost of taking action accounts for the largest share of the cost.

Based on the above analysis results, to achieve sustainable land management, climate changes should be monitored so as to make adaptation measures to mitigate the impacts of climate changes on land quality. Along with the socioeconomic development, investments and better land management for improving land quality should be encouraged through appropriate policy measures. Human activities that change the land surface, such as infrastructure constructions, should be regulated on the basis of the assessment of impacts on land quality, and corresponding land conservation measures should be taken during the construction process. Government strategies should be developed that give incentives to take positive action to manage lands sustainably.

References

Bai, Z. G., & Dent, D. (2009). Recent land degradation and improvement in China. *AMBIO: A Journal of the Human Environment, 38*(3), 150–156.

Bajocco, S., De Angelis, A., Perini, L., Ferrara, A., & Salvati, L. (2012). The impact of land use/land cover changes on land degradation dynamics: A Mediterranean case study. *Environmental Management, 49*(5), 980–989.

Baldocchi, D. (2011). Global change: The grass response. *Nature, 476*(7359), 160–161.

Barbier, E. B. (1997). The economic determinants of land degradation in developing countries. *Philosophical Transactions of the Royal Society of London. Series B, Biological Sciences, 352* (1356), 891–899.

CNBS. (2010). China National Bureau of Statistics raw data.

Deng, X. Z., Huang, J. K., Rozelle, S., & Uchida, E. (2006). Cultivated land conversion and potential agricultural productivity in China. *Land Use Policy, 23*(4), 372–384.

Deng, X. Z., Huang, J. K., Rozelle, S., & Uchida, E. (2008). Growth, population and industrialization, and urban land expansion of China. *Journal of Urban Economics, 63*(1), 96–115.

Deng, X. Z., Jiang, Q. O., Su, H. B., & Wu, F. (2010). Trace forest conversions in Northeast China with a 1-km area percentage data model. *Journal of Applied Remote Sensing*. doi:10.1117/1.3491193

FAO. (2005). China livestock sector brief.

FAO. (2010). *Global forest resources assessment 2010.* Main Report. Forestry Paper 163.

FAOSTAT. (2012). FAO statistical Yearbook 2012.

FAOSTAT. (2013). FAO statistical Yearbook 2012.

Gao, Y., Skutsch, M., Drigo, R., Pacheco, P., & Masera, O. (2011). Assessing deforestation from biofuels: methodological challenges. *Applied Geography, 31*(2), 508–518.

Gutman, G. (1987). The derivation of vegetation indices from AVHRR data. *International Journal of Remote Sensing, 8*, 1235–1242.

He, G., Lu, Y., Mol, A. P., & Beckers, T. (2012). Changes and challenges: China's environmental management in transition. *Environmental Development, 3*, 25–38.

Jiang, Q. O., Deng, X. Z., Zhan, J. Y., & He, S. J. (2011). Estimation of land production and its response to cultivated land conversion in North China Plain. *Chinese Geographical Science, 21* (6), 685–694.

Kahrl, F., Yunju, L., Roland-Holst, D., Jianchu, X., & Zilberman, D. (2012). *Toward sustainable use of nitrogen fertilizers in China.* Giannini Foundation of Agricultural Economics University of California. Online at http://giannini.ucop.edu/media/are-update/files/articles/v14n2_2.pdf. Accessed June 24, 2015.

Li, Z. H., Deng, X. Z., Yin, F., Yang, C. Y. (2015). Analysis of climate and land use changes impacts on land degradation in the North China Plain. *Advances in Meteorology*. doi:10.1155/2015/976370

Li, H. J., Liu, Z. J., Zheng, L., & Lei, Y. P. (2011). Resilience analysis for agricultural systems of north China plain based on a dynamic system model. *Scientia Agricola, 68*(1), 8–17.

Li, S., Verburg, P. H., Lv, S. H., Wu, J. L., & Li, X. B. (2012). Spatial analysis of the driving factors of grassland degradation under conditions of climate change and intensive use in Inner Mongolia, China. *Regional Environmental Change, 12*(3), 461–474.

Liu, J. Y., Xu, X. L., & Shao, Q. Q. (2008). The spatial and temporal characteristics of grassland degradation in the three-river headwaters region in Qinghai Province. *Acta Geographica Sinica, 4*, 009.

Liu, Y., Zha, Y., Gao, J., & Ni, S. (2004). Assessment of grassland degradation near Lake Qinghai, West China, using Landsat TM and in situ reflectance spectra data. *International Journal of Remote Sensing, 25*(20), 4177–4189.

Long, F. (2013). *Introduction to the resources status in China-Land resources*, Jingchengnew.cn. http://www.jingchengw.cn/new/20130411/4927.htm. Accessed September 9, 2014 (in Chinese).

MEA. (2005). *Ecosystems and human well-being: Synthesis*. Washington, DC: Island Press.

Nkonya, E., Anderson, W., Kato, E., Koo, J., Mirzabaev, A., von Braun, J., & Meyer, S. (2014). *Global cost of land degradation*. Berlin, Heidelberg: Springer. (Forthcoming).

Peng, H., Cheng, G., Xu, Z., Yin, Y., & Xu, W. (2007). Social, economic, and ecological impacts of the "Grain for Green" project in China: A preliminary case in Zhangye, Northwest China. *Journal of Environmental Management, 85*(3), 774–784.

Qi, J. G., Chen, J. Q., Wan, S. Q., & Ai, L. K. (2012). Understanding the coupled natural and human systems in Dryland East Asia. *Environmental Research Letters, 7*(1), 015202.

Ren, J. Z., Hu, Z. Z., Zhao, J., Zhang, D. G., Hou, F. J., Lin, H. L., et al. (2008). A grassland classification system and its application in China. *The Rangeland Journal, 30*(2), 199–209.

SFA. (2005). *Statistics on the national forest resources (the 6th National Forest Inventory 1999–2003)*. Beijing: State Forestry Administration. (in Chinese).

Shen, Y. Q., Liao, X. C., & Yin, R. S. (2006). Measuring the socioeconomic impacts of China's Natural Forest Protection program. *Environment and Development Economics, 11*(06), 769–788.

Sivakumar, M. V., & Ndiang'Ui, N. (2007). *Climate and land degradation*. Berlin, Heidelberg: Springer.

Symeonakis, E., Calvo-Cases, A., & Arnau-Rosalen, E. (2007). Land use change and land degradation in southeastern Mediterranean Spain. *Environmental Management, 40*(1), 80–94.

Tong, C., Wu, J., Yong, S. P., Yang, J., & Yong, W. (2004). A landscape-scale assessment of steppe degradation in the Xilin River Basin, Inner Mongolia, China. *Journal of Arid Environments, 59*(1), 133–149.

Vlek, P. G., Rodríguez-Kuhl, G., & Sommer, R. (2004). Energy use and CO_2 production in tropical agriculture and means and strategies for reduction or mitigation. *Environment, Development and Sustainability, 6*(1–2), 213–233.

Wang, T. M., Wang, X. C., Guo, Q. X., Sun, L., & Gui, G. D. (2003). Forest landscape diversity changes in Heilongjiang Province. *Chinese Biodiversity, 12*(4), 396–402.

Wu, F., Deng, X. Z., Yin, F., & Yuan, Y. W. (2013). Projected changes of grassland productivity along the representative concentration pathways during 2010–2050 in China. *Advances in Meteorology*. doi:10.1155/2013/812723

Xiao, X. M., Boles, S., Liu, J. Y., Zhuang, D. F., & Liu, M. L. (2002). Characterization of forest types in Northeastern China, using multi-temporal SPOT-4 VEGETATION sensor data. *Remote Sensing of Environment, 82*(2), 335–348.

Yang, Z. (2013). Demographic changes in China's farmers: The future of farming in China. *Asian Social Science, 9*(7), 136–143.

Yang, X., Ding, Z., Fan, X., Zhou, Z., & Ma, N. (2007). Processes and mechanisms of desertification in northern China during the last 30 years, with a special reference to the Hunshandake Sandy Land, eastern Inner Mongolia. *Catena, 71*(1), 2–12.

Zhao, B. Z., Jia, W. W., & Li, F. R. (2006). Effect evaluation of natural forest protection project for forestry enterprises in Daxing'anling of Inner Mongolia. *Journal of Northeast Forestry University, 34*(2), 84.

Chapter 14
Economics of Land Degradation and Improvement in Ethiopia

Samuel Gebreselassie, Oliver K. Kirui and Alisher Mirzabaev

Abstract Land degradation is an important problem in Ethiopia, with more than 85 % of the land degraded to various degrees. Recent estimates using satellite imagery show that land degradation hotspots over the last three decades cover about 23 % of the land area in the country. The assessment of nationally representative household survey shows that important drivers of sustainable land management in Ethiopia are biophysical, regional and socio-economic determinants. Specifically, access to agricultural extension services and markets and secure land tenure are important incentives to adoption of sustainable land management practices. Thus, policies and strategies relating to securing tenure rights, building the capacity of land users through access to extension services, and improving access to input, output and financial markets should be considered in order to incentivize sustainable land management. Important local level initiatives and institutions to manage grazing lands and forests through collective action should also be encouraged. We use the Total Economic Value approach (TEV) to estimate the cost of land degradation in Ethiopia. The annual cost of land degradation associated with land use and cover change in Ethiopia is estimated to be about $4.3 billion. Only about 51 % of this cost of land degradation represents the provisioning ecosystem services. The remaining 49 % represent the loss of supporting and regulatory and cultural ecosystem services. Use of land degrading practices in maize and wheat farms resulted in losses amounting to $162 million—representing 2 % equivalent of the GDP in 2007. The costs of action to rehabilitate lands degraded during the 2001–2009 period through land use and cover change were found to equal about $54 billion over a 30-year horizon, whereas if nothing is done, the resulting losses may equal almost $228 billion during the same period. Thus, the costs of action against land degradation are lower than the costs of inaction by about 4.4 times over

O.K. Kirui (✉) · A. Mirzabaev
Center for Development Research (ZEF), University of Bonn, Walter-Flex Str. 3, 53115 Bonn, Germany
e-mail: okirui@uni-bonn.de; oliverkk@yahoo.com

S. Gebreselassie
Ethiopian Economic Policy Research Institute (EEPRI), Ethiopian Economic Association, Yeka, Addis Ababa, Ethiopia

E. Nkonya et al. (eds.), *Economics of Land Degradation and Improvement – A Global Assessment for Sustainable Development*,
DOI 10.1007/978-3-319-19168-3_14

the 30 year horizon; implying that a dollar spent to rehabilitate degraded lands returns about 4.4 dollars in Ethiopia.

Keywords Economics of land degradation · Drivers of land degradation · Sustainable land management · Cost of land degradation

Introduction

Ethiopia is one of the most highly populated countries in Africa with about 92 million people (United Nations, 2012, cited by World Bank 2013). Rain-fed agriculture employs 80 % of the population, forming the basis of Ethiopia's economy. Despite a consistent, relatively high growth over the past decade (CSA 2013), the agricultural sector is still characterized by subsistence nature and low productivity. The reasons for this low productivity are many and complex. Environmental degradation, as exhibited in land and water resources' degradation together biodiversity loss, remains a key development challenge for the Ethiopian agriculture.

Ethiopia experiences several types of land degradation ranging from water and wind erosion; salinization (and recently acidification); and physical and biological soil degradation. The Global Mechanism (2007) estimated that over 85 % of the land in Ethiopia is moderately to very severely degraded, and about 75 % is affected by desertification. Soil erosion, with its associated loss of fertility and rooting depth, water resource degradation and loss of bio-diversity (Eyasu 2003), is a key problem that undermines land productivity in the highlands of Ethiopia. Soil erosion is particularly serious in the high and low potential cereal zones of the north-central highlands. In regions such as Wolo, Tigray and Harerge, 50 % of the agricultural lands have soils with depths less than 10 cm, which make them unsuitable for farming (Eyasu 2003; Kidane 2008).

The costs of land degradation, which has been going on for centuries in Ethiopia (Kidane 2008), are substantial and include both direct and indirect costs, such as on-farm soil nutrient loss (direct) and other indirect losses, such as lower food security and higher poverty (Berry 2003).

Farmers in different parts of the country realize soil erosion as an immediate threat to their livelihood and apply different traditional soil and water conservation practices. Despite some positive progress over time, the impact of investments in remedial actions is either hard to quantify (or less researched), but seems to be of scale smaller than the scope and the complexity of the problem. Under the prevailing natural and socio-economic conditions, farmers in most parts of the country cannot cope with the rapid rate of soil erosion and nutrient mining. With a continued population growth, the problem is likely to persist in the future (Shiferaw and Holden 1999).

Most studies conducted on the cost of land degradation in Ethiopia indicate that land degradation is one of the most serious problems facing the country's agriculture and food security. Some authors (von Braun et al. 2013, 2014) even warn that 'eradicating extreme poverty without adequately addressing land degradation is highly unlikely'. The proximate drivers of land degradation in Ethiopia include forest clearance and soil surface exposure (high removal of vegetative cover); detrimental cultivation practices with emphasis on small-seed crops that require a fine tillage; and overgrazing. Due to land shortage and lack of alternative livelihoods, farmers cultivate lands that have slopes more than 60 % with shallow and stony soils prone to erosion. Slopes more than 30 % should not normally be used for agricultural purposes, but rather allocated to natural vegetation or forestry. However, in Ethiopia there is no land use policy that prohibits farmers from using such lands and thus, more and more marginal lands are cultivated (Eyasu 2003). Several factors including poverty, land fragmentation and high human and livestock population pressure act more indirectly as driving forces for land degradation. Pressure from human and livestock leads huge removal of vegetation cover to meet increasing crops, grazing and fuel wood demand.

Despite a vast accumulation of knowledge and evidence on the impacts of land degradation and a well-documented database of its proximate and underlying causes, progress to address the problem is at best mixed. The Ethiopian government reaffirms its commitment to address the problem in its official policies, stated in the Growth and Transformation Plan (GTP) yet the undertaking and investments to halt the problem are far lower than the scope and the complexity of the problem. Natural resource management and conservation has been taken up as an important intervention in all parts of Ethiopia. The overwhelming proportion of these activities is accomplished through popular participation (mass mobilization). But it is not clear to what extent these initiatives are based on evidence on the ground. In addition, these interventions are yet to deliver results.

Most of the prescriptions to tackle the problem such as the numerous conservation programs financed through food/cash aid projects, for instance, focus excessively on technical solutions, to the negligence (or inadequate attention) to policy and institutional factors. Genanew and Alemu (2012) indicate that "policies and programs were adopted based on incorrect assumptions and little understanding of the incentives and constraints related to land conservation—which could be misleading". These problems are compounded by little previous research (Shiferaw and Holden 1999). As time passes, the dynamics and complexity of the problem have been increasing due to a host of factors such as population growth, poverty effects, climate effects, etc.

Mitigating land degradation and fostering sustainable land management practices needs a suitable policy framework that sufficiently accounts for the interest of present and future generations in a dynamic and evolving environment. Consequently, actions to prevent and reverse the problem should consistently be based on context specific and continuous research findings. Recognizing the extent of land degradation and its impact on rural food security and livelihoods of rural people, the Ethiopian Government, with aid from several international agencies, initiated a massive program of soil conservation and rehabilitation in the worst affected areas since early 1980s (Eyasu 2003). Since then both the government and donors initiated large-scale soil conservation programs that implement a variety of conservation measures (terraces, bunds, tree planting, and closure of grazing areas etc.). There exists little information on the impact of these actions. The efforts to address the problem become more complicated because there is not sufficient emphasis on institutional and participation issues (Berry 2003). It is, therefore, important to study the role of such factors as well as the political economy of implementing technical remedies (or the transaction costs of policy and institutional reforms required to implement identified technical remedies).

Given the extent of the land degradation problem and a limited impact of interventions so far made both by the government and the international community, the country needs to revisit shortcomings (in existing strategies, projects and programs) that hamper sustainable land management and development. Efforts should be made to identify gaps and opportunities in existing (technical) knowledge as well as in policy and institutional factors that hamper or facilitate the implementation of technical remedies.

Many of the land ecosystems services are not transacted in markets, thus different actors do not pay for negative or positive effects on those ecosystems. Thus, farmers do not consider the value of these externalities their land-use decision. This eventually leads to an undervaluation of land and its provision of ecosystem services (Nkonya et al. 2013). On the other hand, institutional issues like communal or public ownership of farm lands as well as high poverty/food insecurity level make efforts to address land degradation difficult and complex.

The present study aims to contribute to the knowledge and on-going discussions on addressing land degradation in Ethiopia by it analysis of key proximate and underlying drivers of land degradation and sustainable land management (SLM) in in the country and by estimating and comparing the costs and benefits of action versus costs of inaction against land degradation in Ethiopia.

Literature Review

Land Degradation in Ethiopia

The most common form of land degradation in Ethiopia is soil erosion by water. Soil erosion is indeed considered the most significant environmental challenge to the food security of the population and future development prospects of the country (Wagayehu 2003). A considerable volume of information has been produced since the mid-1980s regarding soil erosion in Ethiopia (Barbier 1989, 2000; FAO 1986; Hurni 1993 among others, all cited Eyasu 2003). But there is a lack of reliable and consistent data on the extent and rate of soil loss (tones/ha/year). Different data sources report different estimates on the amount of soil loss from arable land. As shown below in Table 14.1, the current rates of soil erosion in Ethiopia are estimated to vary between 42 and 300 tones/ha/year.

The wide range of estimates in soil erosion rate is indicative of the complex patterns of spatial and temporal variations and conceptual and methodological difficulties inherent in making such estimates. Obviously there is considerable

Table 14.1 Estimates of rates of soil loss on croplands in Ethiopia

Author	Estimates of annual soil loss from arable land (t/ha/year)	Method used
FAO/EHRS 1986	130	USLE: universal soil loss equation and guess estimates
Hurni 1988: soil conservation research project	42	Measurement from runoff plots from eight stations across the country
Belay Tegene 1992	75	Measurement from runoff plots
Azene Bekele 1997	100	Guess estimate
Tamire Hawndo 1996	300	Secondary data and estimates

Source Eyasu (2003)

variability of erosion rates over time and place depending on agro-ecological zone and soil type. Soil erosion occurs at varying rates and with varying degrees in different parts of the country. Deforestation, forest burning and expansion of cultivated lands to marginal lands have also contributed to the widespread problem of land degradation in the country. 'About 70 % of Ethiopia's highland population and an area of over 40 million ha are affected by land degradation' (Melaku 2013), indicating the scale and extent of the problem confronting the country.

Economic Studies of Land Degradation in Ethiopia

Land degradation has high economic costs in Ethiopia. There exist several studies dealing with land degradation at the national level in Ethiopia. Some of these studies include; the Highlands Reclamation Study by FAO in 1986; the Ethiopian Forestry Action Plan (1993), the National Conservation Strategy Secretariat (Sutcliffe 1993), the Effect of Soil Degradation on Agricultural Productivity in Ethiopia by Keyser and Sonneveld in 2001 (see Berry 2003; Eyasu 2003) and the Economics of Soil and Water Conservation by Wagayehu (2003). These studies investigate a wide range of issues ranging from the causes, nature, extent and economic cost of the land degradation problem to the potential remedial actions necessary to tackle the problem.

Though the conclusions from these studies vary in detail, many of the authors argued on the following few silent points. First, many argue that Ethiopia has a long history of widespread and serious land degradation in all of its regions. Second, the 'problem of land degradation attracted the attention of policy-makers only after the consequences became felt during recent decades' (Wagayehu 2003; Shiferaw and Holden 1999; Shibru and Kifle 1998 cited by Kidane 2008) when the Ethiopian Government, with aid from the international agencies, initiated a massive program of soil conservation and rehabilitation in the worst affected areas. Third, most of the remedial measures focused largely on physical structures including terracing, bunds, tree planting and, to some extent, closure of grazing areas, as well as increased use of chemical fertilizers and relatively high negligence of policy and institutional issues (Berry 2003; Eyasu 2003; The Global Mechanism 2007), which has greatly reduced the impact as well as sustainability of investments on SLM. Despite all the extension efforts, there is a steadily increasing rate of land degradation.

Based on findings of previous studies, the next section tries to identify and examine the drivers of land degradation in Ethiopia and its impacts on rural livelihoods and food security. It also reviews the stock of knowledge on sustainably managing agricultural land and preventing and mitigating the impacts of land degradation. It also tries to identify gaps in knowledge for future studies.

Drivers of Land Degradation in Ethiopia

Poor land-use practices and population pressure are the major drivers of land degradation in Ethiopia (Genanew and Alemu 2012; Berry 2003). High population pressure, especially in the highland, has led to a decline in arable area, which in turn led to agricultural encroachment onto marginal areas. Several other factors contribute to the unsustainable land management in Ethiopia. The patterns of land ownership and government control, low levels of investment in agriculture and animal husbandry, poor rural infrastructure and markets and low levels of technology are cited as the underlying causes of land degradation by Berry (2003). Policy failures and lack of capacity to implement government interventions also contribute to land and other resource degradation (The Global Mechanism 2007; Wagayehu 2003).

The less-than-desired and largely unsustainable impact of series of conservation measures usually involving physical structures such as terraces, bunds and tree planting, among others, is explained by lack of policy action or framework that is essential to address (or minimize the effect of) the externalities of benefits or costs associated with participation or lack of participation in such programs (by farmers). This problem is attributed to the relative negligence of policy and institutional factors in the numerous conservation programs financed through food/cash aid projects (Berry 2003; Eyasu 2003). This problem is compounded by little evidence-based and action-oriented research (Shiferaw and Holden 1999; von Braun et al. 2013).

Another key driver of the problem is a lack of capacity and/or commitment to address the problem appropriately. Inconsistent, partial or insufficient interventions reinforce the problem while eroding the capacity of farmers/the real victims/and local authorities to deal with the problem fundamentally. Most interventions focus on addressing the symptoms of the problem (i.e. reducing the human cost of the problem, distress sales of assets) at the expense of long-term and long-lasting solutions. In other words, by focusing on short-term solutions, such interventions encourage inaction or the postponement of real-actions (i.e. actions by beneficiaries and authorities to address the root cause of the problem).

A review to document various proximate and underlying drivers of land degradation in Eastern Africa, including Ethiopia, has been carried out by Kirui and

Table 14.2 Proximate and underlying drivers of land degradation in Ethiopia

Proximate drivers	Underlying drivers	References
Topography, unsustainable agriculture, fuel wood consumption, conversion of forests, woodlands, shrub-lands to new agricultural land (deforestation)	Weak regulatory environment and institutions, demographic growth, unclear user rights, low empowerment of local communities, poverty, infrastructural development, population density	Pender et al. (2001), Jagger and Pender (2003), Holden et al. (2004), Rudel et al. (2009), Bai et al. (2008), Belay et al. (2014), Tesfa and Mekuriae (2014)

Source Kirui and Mirzabaev (2014)

Mirzabaev (2014). A summary for Ethiopia is presented in Table 14.2. Important proximate drivers of land degradation include; topography, unsustainable agricultural practices, and land cover change (forests, woodlands, and shrub-land conversion to new agricultural land uses). Similarly, the pertinent underlying drivers of land degradation include weak policy and regulatory environment and institutions, poverty, demographic growth, low empowerment of local communities, infrastructural development and unclear user rights (especially land tenure).

Impacts of Land Degradation on Rural Livelihoods and Food Security

Land degradation has a negative implication to household food security status and contributes directly to the reduction in livelihoods among the rural communities in Ethiopia. The immediate consequence of land degradation is lower crop yields, leading to higher poverty rates among agricultural households. Based on a review of recent studies conducted by a range of institutions and scientists, the Global Mechanism to Combat of Desertification of the UN (UNCCD) shows that the country loses about 30,000 ha of agricultural land annually due to water erosion, and more than 2 million ha are degraded (National Review Report 2002). Based on experts' opinion, Dregne (1991) recounted an irreversible soil productivity loss in about 20 % of Ethiopia agricultural land due to water erosion. Ethiopia loses an estimated 1 billion tons of topsoil annually as a result of soil erosion alone (Berry 2003). Further losses of about $23 million of forest as a result of deforestation and $10 million of livestock capacity are also reported annually (Yesuf et al. 2005).

In addition to these estimates on the rate and extent of land degradation via soil erosion, deforestation, over-grazing etc., many other studies provide quantitative estimates on the cost of land degradation. A study by Teketay (2001), for instance, estimates that "reduced soil depth caused by erosion resulted in a grain production loss of 57,000 (at 3.5 mm soil loss) to 128,000 tons (at 8 mm soil depth) in 1990 alone. It has been estimated that the grain production lost due to land degradation in 1990 would have been sufficient to feed more than four million people" (Teketay 2001). Similarly, Berry (2003) estimates that land degradation and other unsustainable land management practices cost the country (via loss of soil and essential nutrients) about three percent of its agricultural Gross Domestic Product (GDP) or $106 million (1994$). Bojö and Cassells (1995) also estimate that Ethiopia loses about 3 % of the agricultural gross domestic production due to soil erosion and nutrient loss. While modelling the impact of water erosion on food production in Ethiopia, Sonneveld (2002) reported a range of potential reduction in production of 10–30 % by 2030.

The most critical and urgent on-site impact of soil erosion to the farmers are decline in both the current and potential crop and livestock yields—which translate into income loses. The consequences of soil erosion may also be viewed in the need to use more inputs to maintain soil productivity so as to attain the same level of yield (Wagayehu 2003). The impact of land degradation on agricultural productivity represents an on-site cost. However, soil erosion from agricultural fields has also serious external or off-site effects, which indirectly affect the rest of society. The external effects of soil erosion are caused by sedimentation of hydroelectric dams, pollution of municipal water reservoirs, ponds, etc. For instance, the hydroelectric generation capacity of the Koka dam, one of the major dams in Ethiopia, is severely affected by sedimentation. It is estimated that about 30 % of the total storage volume of the reservoir has already been lost to sedimentation (EEPC 2002, cited by Eyasu 2003), which had a negative impact on the annual energy generation from the plant. The effect of land use change (such as expansion of the agricultural frontier and the migration of households and communities towards pastoral land, fragile ecosystem) is another off-site (or on-site) effect of soil erosion (Kirui and Mirzabaev 2014).

Other off-site environmental effect of land degradation due to soil erosion and deforestation include its effect on the biodiversity of the country and many ecosystem services (e.g. nutrient cycling, soil formation), regulating (e.g. flood regulation, water purification), cultural, spiritual and recreational services for the present and future generations (Nkonya et al. 2011).

Methods and Data

The empirical approaches used to estimate the determinants of SLM adoption and the number of SLM technologies adopted are discussed in detail in this section. These methods are based on the methodological Chap. 2, and are consistently applied throughout several case studies in this volume, specifically, in Chaps. 16 and 20.

Determinants of SLM Adoption: Logit Regression Model

Land degradation usually occurs due to lack of sustainable land management practices. Factors preventing households from adopting SLM practices are also likely to cause land degradation. Therefore, analyzing the drivers of SLM is similar in its implications as analyzing the drivers of land degradation. The adoption of SLM technologies/practices in this study refers to use of one or more SLM technologies in a given plot.

The adoption of SLM technology/practice in a farm plot was measured as a binary dummy variable (1 = adopted SLM in a farm plot, 0 = otherwise). The two appropriate approaches to estimate such binary dummy dependent variable regression models are the logit and the probit regression models. Here we use the logit model.

The reduced form of the logit model applied to nationally representative agricultural household survey data from Ethiopia is presented as:

$$\mathrm{A} - \beta_0 + \beta_1 x_1 + \beta_2 x_2 + \beta_3 x_3 + \beta_4 x_4 + \beta_5 z_i + \varepsilon_i \quad (14.1)$$

where, A = Adoption of SLM technologies; x_1 = a vector of biophysical factors (climate conditions, agro-ecological zones); x_2 = a vector of demographic characteristics factors (level of education, age, gender of the household head); x_3 = a vector of farm-level variables (access to extension, market access, distance to market, distance to market); x_4 = vector of socio-economic and institutional characteristics (access to extension, market access, land tenure, land tenure); z_i = vector of country fixed effects; and is the error term.

Robust checks are carried out to check these misspecifications. Further, assessment beyond adoption to intensity (number) of SLM adoption can also counter such inherent weakness. We explore this option in our study.

Determinants of Number of SLM Technologies Adopted: Poisson Model

The number of SLM technologies and the corresponding proportion of plots in which these technologies were applied are as presented in Table 14.8. The number of SLM technologies is thus a count variable (ranging from 0 to 6 in our case). Thus the assessment of the determinants of the number of SLM technologies adopted requires models that accounts for count variables. For this reason, here we apply the Poisson regression model (PRM). The reduced form of the Poisson regression is presented as follows:

$$\mathrm{A} = \beta_0 + \beta_1 x_1 + \beta_2 x_2 + \beta_3 x_3 + \beta_4 x_4 + \beta_5 z_i + \varepsilon_i \quad (14.2)$$

where, A = Number of SLM technologies adopted; and the vector of explanatory variables x_i are similar to those used in Eq. 14.1; (i.e. x_1 = a vector of biophysical factors (climate conditions, agro-ecological zones); x_2 = a vector of demographic characteristics factors (level of education, age, gender of the household head); x_3 = a vector of farm-level variables (access to extension, market access, distance to market, distance to market); x_4 = vector of socio-economic and institutional characteristics (access to extension, market access, land tenure, land tenure); z_i = vector of country fixed effects; and is the error term).

Cost of Action Verses Inaction Against Degradation

Refer to Chap. 6 of this volume for a comprehensive discussion on the empirical strategy to estimate the costs of land degradation (due to LUCC and due to use of land degrading practices) and also the empirical strategy to estimate the costs of taking action against land degradation.

Data and Sampling Procedure

This study uses the Ethiopia Rural Socioeconomic Survey (ERSS) data collected during the period October 2011–March 2012 by the Central Statistical Agency (CSA) in Ethiopia. The ERSS sample is designed to be representative of rural and small town areas of Ethiopia. Based on population estimates from the 2007 Population Census, the CSA categorizes a town with a population of less than 10,000 inhabitants as small. The ERSS rural sample is a sub-sample of the Annual Agricultural Sample Survey (AgSS) while the small town sample comes from the collection of small town Enumeration Areas (EAs).

The sample is a two-stage probability sample. The first stage of sampling entailed selecting primary sampling units—the CSA's enumeration areas (EAs). For the rural sample, 290 enumeration areas were selected from the AgSS enumeration areas based on probability proportional to size of the total enumeration areas in each region. For small town EAs, a total of 43 EAs were selected. The second stage involved a random selection of households to be interviewed in each EAs. For rural EAs, a total of 12 households were sampled in each EA. Of these, 10 households were randomly selected from the sample of 30 AgSS households.

The AgSS households are households which are involved in farming or livestock activities. Another 2 households were randomly selected from all other households in the rural EA (those not involved in agriculture or livestock production). In some EAs, there is only one or no such households, in which case, less than two non-agricultural households were surveyed and more agricultural households were interviewed instead so that the total number of households per EA remains the same. In the small town EAs, 12 households are selected randomly from the listing of each EA, with no stratification as to whether the household is engaged in agriculture/livestock. Households were not selected using replacement. The sample covers a total of 3969 households (24,954 farm plots).

Choice of Independent Variables for Econometric Estimations

The choice of relevant independent variables is based on economic theory, empirical review of previous literature, and data availability. These variables have been grouped as biophysical, demographic, plot, and socio-economic variables. Brief descriptions alongside the direction of the hypothesized effects of these variables on SLM adoption are presented in Table 14.3. The positive sign means a positive relationship is expected, while the minus sign means that a negative relationship is expected. When both plus and minus signs are given, there are no specific theory-based expectations made, but the relationship is considered a matter of empirical investigation.

Table 14.3 Definitions of hypothesized explanatory variables

Variable	Definition	Hypothesized effect on SLM adoption
Temperature	Annual mean temperature (°C)	+/−
Rainfall	Annual mean rainfall (mm)	+/−
Land cover	Land cover type	+/−
Soils	Soil rooting conditions, soil type	+/−
AEZ	Agro-ecological zone	+/−
Slope	Slope elevation (SRTM)	+/−
Age	Age of household head (years)	+/−
Gender	Gender of household head	+
Education	Years of formal education of HH head	+
Family size	Size of household (adult equivalent)	+/−
Tenure	Land tenure status of the plot	+
Soil type	Soil type of the plot	+/−
Extension	Access to agricultural extension	+/−
Market dist.	Distance from plot from the market	−
Assets value	Value of household assets	+
Plot size	Size of the plot	+
Credit access	Amount of credit accessed	+
Group membership	Membership in cooperatives/SACCOs	+
Irrigation	Access to irrigation water	+

Source Authors' compilation

Results and Discussion

Extent and Trends of Land Degradation in Ethiopia

The use of satellite–based imagery and remote sensing techniques to identify the magnitude and processes of land degradation at different levels has increased recently. This involves the use of Normalized Difference Vegetation Index (NDVI) derived from Advanced Very High-Resolution Radiometer (AVHRR) data. This approach was previously used by Evans and Geerken (2004), Bai et al. (2008), Hellden and Tottrup (2008), and Vlek et al. (2010). Using this technique, Bai et al. (2008) estimated that about 26 % of Ethiopian territory was experiencing land degradation processes between the periods 1981–2003; affecting about 30 % of the population over the same period (Table 14.4).

More recently, Le et al. (2014), Chap. 4, carried out an assessment using improved techniques which correct for the effect of atmospheric and chemical fertilizations, and rainfall factors. Unlike the study by Bai et al. (2008), their estimation also considers the major land use/cover types of every country covered in their study. The results for Ethiopia (Fig. 14.1) show that land degradation occurred in about 228,160 km^2 (or 23 % of total land area) between 1982 and 2006. A look at land use land cover types shows that the areas that experienced much degradation include sparse vegetation (32 %), mosaic forest-shrub/grass (27 %), shrub-land (20 %) and mosaic vegetation-crop (19 %). These degradation and improvement hotspots are depicted in Fig. 14.1.

Land degradation can occur in two ways—either through productivity decline as a result of such factors as soil erosion, nutrient depletion and mining or changes in land use/land cover (from more economically and environmentally productive land

Table 14.4 Statistics of degrading areas for Ethiopia (1981–2003)

Degraded area			Population affected		Total NPP loss
Km^2	% territory (of the country)	% of global degraded area	Number	% of total population	(ton C/23 years)
296,812	26.3 %	0.84 %	20,650,316	29.1 %	14,276,065

Source Adapted from Bai et al. (2008)

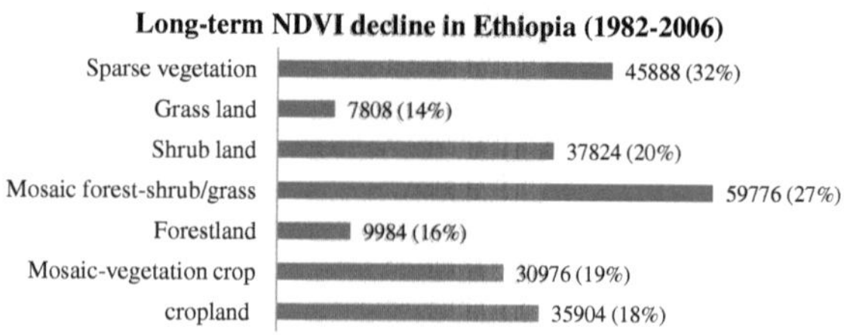

Fig. 14.1 Long-term NDVI decline in Ethiopia (1982–2006)–Area in km^2 and %. *Source* Calculated from Le et al. (2014)

uses/covers to a less economically and environmentally one). Based on high quality satellite data from Moderate Resolution Imaging Spectroradiometer (MODIS), the next section discuss changes in land use and cover for Ethiopia during the 2001 and 2009 period.

Land Degradation as a Result of Land Use Change

Results from our assessment presents a dynamic land use and land cover changes in Ethiopia over the 2001–2009 periods. Table 14.5 presents the different shares of land use land cover types for the period 2001 and 2009. For example, in 2001 there were about 8.5 million ha of cropland, 5.5 million ha of forest land and about 29 million ha of grassland. In 2009 however, cropland increased to 11.3 million while forests and grasslands decreased to 4.1 and 25.5 million ha respectively. The detailed land use and land cover (LULC) change by region is presented in Table 14.5.

Table 14.6 presents percentage change in LULC change by region and nationally; with year 2001 as a baseline. Nationally, results show significant increases in the cropped area (33 %) and shrublands (7 %). Significant losses were reported in forests (26 %), grasslands (11 %), and water (8 %). About 12 % of barren land was also brought into use during this period. There was no significant change in the urban land. There are variations however by region as described below.

While substantial increases are reported for cropped land in Harari (750 %), Gambela (101 %), Addis Ababa (55 %), Amhara (54 %) and Tigray (48 %); significant decreases were reported in Benshangul (65 %), Afar (36 %) and Somali (29 %) regions. These changes may be associated to the conversion of forests and grasslands to cropland.

Table 14.5 Changes in land use land cover classification in Ethiopia between 2001 and 2009 (million ha)

Land use/cover	2001	2009	Percentage change (%)
Cropland	8.51	11.30	32.7
Forest	5.49	4.07	−25.9
Grassland	28.50	25.50	−10.5
Shrublands	41.80	44.60	6.7
Woodland	22.40	22.00	−1.8
Urban	0.07	0.07	0.1
Barren	5.65	4.96	−12.2
Water	0.64	0.59	−7.8
Total	113.06	113.08	–

Source Calculated based on Nkonya et al. (2014), using MODIS data

Table 14.6 Change in land use land cover in Ethiopia in 2009 relative to 2001 (%)

Region	Cropland	Forest	Grassland	Shrublands	Woodland	Urban	Barren	Water
Addis Ababa	54.8	−82.6	−13.5	134.6	−60.1	0.0	0.0	0.0
Afar	−36.3	3.5	−23.5	44.8	−77.8	0.0	−22.5	−28.9
Amhara	53.9	−72.9	6.5	−6.6	−47.2	1.1	−7.7	−2.1
Benshangul	−64.7	−89.5	−1.3	658.3	3.6	0.0	0.0	0.0
Dire Dawa	7.8	−100	−69.7	114.3	−1.7	0.0	0.0	0.0
Gambela	101.1	31.6	−60.4	1622.2	34.3	0.0	−53.3	26.5
Harari	750.0	−89.8	−43.2	49.8	−57.1	0.0	0.0	0.0
Oromia	21.4	−30.5	−11.2	2.2	13.5	0.0	−1.6	−8.1
Somali	−29.4	−90.3	−45.7	70.0	−15.9	0.0	0.0	0.0
Southern	31.9	−15.9	−8.5	0.4	5.8	0.0	−59.5	−11.7
Tigray	48.0	−95.8	−24.7	61.6	−55.6	0.0	−25.3	−36.6
Total	32.9	−25.8	−10.5	6.7	−1.8	0.1	−12.3	−7.8

Source Calculated based on Nkonya et al. (2014), using MODIS data

A closer look in the table shows that forests decreased in all the regions (shift to cropland and shrublands) ranging from (16–100 %) except in Afar and Gambela where it increased by 4 % and 32 % respectively. Similarly, grasslands decreased in all regions by about 9–70 % except only in Amhara region where it increased by about 7 %. The other important LULC change is the decrease of woodlands (shift to cropland and shrublands) in all regions except some reported increase in Southern (6 %), Oromia (14 %) and Gambela (34 %) regions.

Economic Costs of Land Degradation

As discussed earlier, several studies have previously tried to impute the costs and consequences of land degradation in Ethiopia. However, most of these studies estimated the cost of degradation via proxies such as productivity losses, cost of siltation to dams, the additional costs of increased input usage (especially fertilizer etc.). In this study, we estimate the costs of land degradation associated with LULC change following the TEV framework. Total Economic Value (TEV) refers to the total value of ecosystem services. TEV of the ecosystem is reported as the sum of use values and non-use values of the ecosystem services, both market and non-market ecosystem services. Further description of the TEV framework is presented by Nkonya et al. (2011), Kumar (2010) and Chap. 6 of this book.

A summary of the TEV for Ethiopia as well as its relationship to GDP are presented in Table 14.7. Our results show that there was a decline in the TEV between 2001 and 2009 of about 5 % due to LULC change. Highest losses were recorded in Harari (30 %), Addis Ababa (24 %), Dire Dawa (23 %), and Tigray

Table 14.7 The total economic value (TEV) of land ecosystem services in Ethiopia

Region	TEV 2001 (million USD)	TEV 2009 (million USD)	Change in TEV (%)
Addis Ababa	72	55	−23.65
Afar	11,700	12,600	7.69
Amhara	34,300	33,100	−3.50
Benshangul	10,600	10,400	−1.89
Dire Dawa	240	185	−22.92
Gambela	6090	5620	−7.72
Harari	<1	69	−29.35
Oromia	73,800	68,400	−7.32
Somali	49,200	48,200	−2.03
Southern	28,500	26,800	−5.96
Tigray	11,000	9730	−11.55
Total	226,000	215,000	−4.87

Source Calculated based on Nkonya et al. (2014), using MODIS data

(12 %) regions. It is notable that increase in TEV was reported in one region—Afar region by about 8 %.

Cost of Land Degradation

Cost of Land Degradation Due to Land Use Cover Change (LUCC)

The total terrestrial ecosystem value and the loss of ecosystems values due to land use and cover change (LUCC) are reported in Table 14.8. The total TEV for Ethiopia in 2007 is estimated at US$206 billion (based on the constant 2007 USD values). The GDP value for Ethiopia was US$19 billion in 2007. Similarly, based on TEV framework, the total cost of land degradation due to LUCC in Ethiopia was $35 billion (based on the constant 2007 USD values); translating to annual costs of about $4.3 billion. When computed as a percentage of GDP and TEV, the average annual costs of land degradation is 22.5 and 2.1 % respectively.

Table 14.8 Terrestrial ecosystem value and cost of land degradation due to LUCC

GDP 2007	TEV 2007	Costs of land degradation due to LUCC for the period of 2001–2009	Cost of LD as % of 2007 GDP	Cost of LD as % of TEV of ES
US$ billion				
19.3	206	34.8	22.5 %	2.1 %

Source TEV and Land Degradation—Authors' compilation; GDP—World Bank data

Cost of Land Degradation Due to Use of Land Degrading Practices

Table 14.9 shows the simulated results of rain-fed maize yield under business-as-usual (BAU) and ISFM scenarios for a period of forty years. Results further show that average maize yield are higher under ISFM—2.8 tons/ha (baseline) and 2.4 tons/ha (end-line) as compared with the BAU scenario—2.4 tons/ha (baseline) and 1.8 tons/ha (end-line) periods. However, there is a yield decline between the end-line and baseline periods for both ISFM and BAU scenarios. Under ISFM, yield end-line yield declined by about 13 % while under BAU scenario, yield declined by about 25 %. Overall, the yield decline due to use of land management practices in maize plots is about 36 %. Similarly, simulation analysis show that the yield of wheat declined by about 25 % due to use of land degrading management practices on rain-fed wheat as compared to yield in the previous 30 years. Under ISFM, yield declined by about 8 % while under BAU yield declined by about 20 %.

The annually cost of land degradation for the two crops is about $162 million (or about 2 % of the GDP). Following FAOSTAT (2013) these three cereals (maize, rice and wheat) account for about 40 % of the cropland globally. While assuming similar levels of land degradation is analogous to that happening on the entire cropland, thus the overall cost of land degradation on entire cropland is about 3.8 % of GDP in Ethiopia (Table 14.10).

Table 14.9 Change in maize and wheat yields under BAU and ISFM

Crop	BAU		ISFM		Yield Change (%)		Change due to land degradation
	Baseline	End-line	Baseline	End-line	BAU	ISFM	
	Yield (tons/ha)		Yield (tons/ha)		Percent		
Maize	2.39	1.79	2.79	2.44	−25.1	−12.6	36.0
Wheat	1.67	1.33	1.80	1.66	−20.4	−7.9	24.7

Source Authors' compilation

Table 14.10 Cost of soil fertility mining on maize, rice and wheat cropland in Ethiopia

Cost of land degradation (soil fertility mining)	Cost as % of GDP	Cost of cropland degradation as % GDP
2007 US$ million	(%)	(%)
305	1.58	3.75

Source Authors' compilation

Cost of Loss of Milk and Meat Production Due to Land Degradation in Grazing Lands

Table 14.11 shows the simulated results of costs of loss of milk, meat, and costs associated with weight loss of animals not slaughtered or sold associated with land degradation in grazing biomass. Chapter 8 of this volume presents a comprehensive approach to modelling these costs. The results shows that land degradation in rangelands had a negligible effect on milk and meat production. The total annual costs of milk and meat production losses were about $38 million and $2.4 million respectively. The bigger proportion of milk and meat losses is experienced in warm semi-arid ($10.8 million), and warm sub-humid ($8.5 million). The total annual gross loss was about $52 million. The bigger proportion of the total gross losses is consequently experienced in warm semi-arid ($14 million), warm sub-humid ($11.2 million) and cool sub-humid ($10.4 million) agro-ecologies.

Cost of Action and Inaction Against Land Degradation Due to LUCC

Results of the assessment of the costs of action against land degradation which help in determining whether the action against land degradation could be justified economically are presented in Table 14.12. As Nkonya et al. (2013) note, an action against land degradation will be taken if the cost of inaction is greater than the cost

Table 14.11 Cost of milk and meat production loss due to degradation of rangelands

Agro-ecological zones	Milk	Meat	Total loss (Milk and Meat)	Total gross loss—includes weight loss of animals not slaughtered
	2007 US$ million			
Tropic-cool semi-arid	4.535	0.338	4.873	6.194
Tropic-cool arid	0.003	0.003	0.006	0.004
Tropic-cool humid	0.145	0.005	0.150	0.198
Tropic-cool sub-humid	7.640	0.315	7.945	10.435
Tropic-warm semi-arid	10.262	0.507	10.769	14.016
Tropic-warm arid	7.087	0.922	8.009	9.680
Tropic-warm sub-humid	8.177	0.327	8.504	11.168
Total	37.849	2.417	40.266	51.696

Source Authors' compilation

Table 14.12 Cost of action and inaction against land degradation in Ethiopia ($ billion)

Region	Total costs of land degradation (for 2001–2009)	Total costs of land degradation in terms of provisional ES only	Cost of action (6 yrs)	Cost of action (30 yrs)	Opportunity cost of action	Cost of inaction (6 years)	Cost of inaction (30 years)	Ratio of cost of action: cost of inaction (30 years) (%)
Addis Ababa	0.03	0.01	0.045	0.045	0.088	0.135	0.182	24.8
Afar	5.49	2.77	8.578	8.595	8.635	26.331	35.641	24.1
Amhara	2.53	1.49	4.504	4.514	4.222	13.234	17.913	25.2
Benshangul	1.66	0.96	2.685	2.693	2.501	8.588	11.625	23.2
Dire Dawa	7.36	3.26	9.836	9.863	7.387	31.973	43.278	22.8
Gambela	0.86	0.62	1.870	1.873	1.833	5.189	7.024	26.7
Harari	0.07	0.05	0.151	0.151	0.199	0.419	0.567	26.7
Oromia	1.03	0.79	2.381	2.385	2.91	6.489	8.783	27.2
Somali	0.04	0.02	0.051	0.052	0.151	0.168	0.227	22.7
Southern	13.18	6.95	21.256	21.301	19.246	64.619	87.468	24.4
Tigray	2.58	1.12	2.691	2.702	3.619	11.532	15.609	17.3
Total	34.8	18.0	54.05	54.17	50.98	168.67	228.32	24.8

Source Calculated based on Nkonya et al. (2014), using MODIS data

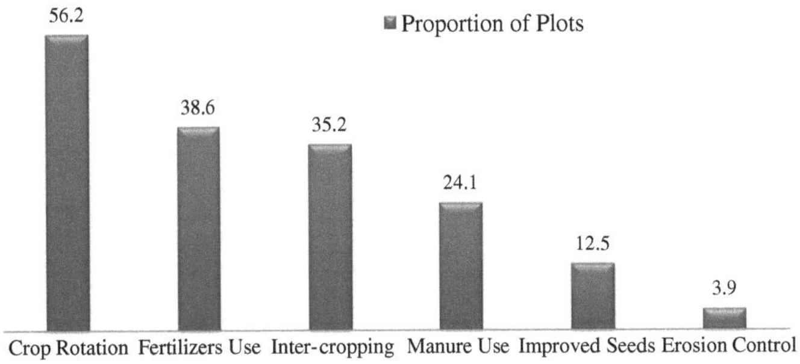

Fig. 14.2 The type of SLM technologies adopted in Ethiopia. *Source* Kirui (in press) unpublished Ph.D. thesis

of taking action. The total cost of land degradation is about 34 billion USD (translating to about 4.3 billion USD annually). Half (51 %) of this cost, or $18 billion of this cost represent the loss of provisional ecosystem services. The other (about 49 %) represents the supporting and regulatory and cultural ecosystem services.

In a 6-year period, the total cost of action to about $54 billion while the cost of inaction summed to about $169 billion. In a 30-year horizon, the costs of action were about $54 billion. However, the cost of inaction (if nothing is done to address land degradation) the resulting losses may equal almost $228 billion during the same period. The implications is that, the costs of action against land degradation are lower than the costs of inaction by about 4.4 times over the 30 year horizon; i.e. the ratio of action to cost of inaction is 24 %. This implies that each dollar spent on addressing land degradation is likely to have about 4.4 dollars of returns.

Adoption of SLM Practices/Technologies in Ethiopia

Based on farmers' responses, six SLM practices were considered including crop rotation, intercropping, improved seeds,[1] use of manure, use of chemical fertilizers, and soil erosion control (such as soil bunds, stone bunds, gabions, grass strips, terraces among others) were selected as major SLM technologies/practices adopted by small farmers in Ethiopia.

As shown in Fig. 14.2 below crop rotation, chemical fertilizer use and inter-cropping are the most common SLM practices adopted by most farmers. Crop rotation was practiced in about 56 % of the plots while fertilizer was used in about 39 % of the plots (Fig. 14.2).

[1]We consider improved seeds as SLM technology following the definition by Liniger (2011) and Liniger et al. (2011). The adoption of a new technology, such as improved seeds, is usually a choice between traditional and new technology. Farmers' decision to adopt or not to adopt is, thus, based on the profitability of the technology.

Table 14.13 Number of SLM technologies/practices adopted

Number of SLM technologies applied (on a given plot)	Proportion of plots (where the technology applied)
0	14.8
1	33.5
2	26.8
3	17.2
4	7.1
5	0.7
6	0.0

Source Kirui (in press) unpublished Ph.D. thesis

We present the distribution of the number of SLM practices/technologies used in farm plots in Table 14.13. The distribution ranged from 0 to 6. About 15 % of the surveyed households did not apply any SLM technologies in their farm plots. Further, our assessments show that only one SLM technology was used in about 33 % of the plots. Similarly, two SLM technologies were applied in about 27 % of the plots. Fewer plots applied more than two SLM technologies simultaneously in one plot. In total, about 17 and 7 % of the plots applied three and four SLM technologies in one plot in the region. Very few plots applied five SLM technologies (0.7 %) (Table 14.13).

Determinants of SLM Adoption: Logit Model

The results of the Logit regression model on the determinants of adoption of SLM technologies are presented in Table 14.14. An adopter was defined as an individual using at least one SLM technology. The assessment is done at plot level. The model fit the data well; it is statistically significant at 1 % with a log likelihood ratio (Chi^2 (30)) of 1649 and Pseudo $R^2 = 0.1387$ (Table 14.14).

The proximate factors that significantly determine the likelihood of adopting SLM technology include temperature, rainfall, and agro-ecological zonal characteristics. Both rainfall and temperature positively influence the probability of using SLM technologies. However, plots located in warm humid/sub-humid, cool arid semi-arid agro-ecological zones or cool humid/sub-humid are less likely to adopt SLM technologies compared to those located in warm arid/semi-arid agro-ecology.

The adoption of SLM technologies is also significantly influenced by household-level variables such as age, gender and education level of the household head, and family size. Age variable is positively significant while age squared was negatively significant indicating that adoption increase with age but at a decreasing rate. Male-headed households are also more likely to adopt SLM technologies compared to their counterparts. Education and the abundance of labor supply through larger bigger family size positively influence the adoption of SLM technologies.

Table 14.14 Drivers of adoption and number of SLM adopted: logit and poisson results

Variable	Logit		Poisson	
	Coefficient	Std. Err.	Coefficient	Std. Err.
Annual mean temperature (°C)	0.134***	0.013	0.024***	0.004
Annual mean temperature square	−0.000***	0.000	−0.000***	0.000
Annual mean rainfall (mm)	0.005***	0.001	0.001***	0.000
Annual mean rainfall square	−0.000***	0.000	−0.000***	0.000
Temperature × rainfall	0.000	0.000	0.000***	0.000
Elevation (meters above sea level)	0.000	0.000	0.000***	0.000
AEZ (1 = warm humid/sub-humid, 0 = No)	−0.648***	0.250	−0.159*	0.089
AEZ (1 = cool arid/semiarid, 0 = No)	−1.094***	0.201	−0.126*	0.068
AEZ (1 = cool humid/sub-humid, 0 = No)	−0.663***	0.228	−0.006	0.075
Age of household head (years)	0.027***	0.010	0.002	0.003
Age of household head square	−0.000***	0.000	0.000	0.000
Gender of household head (1 = Male, 0 = No)	0.189***	0.071	−0.002	0.019
Years of education of household head	−0.025	0.023	0.011*	0.006
Size of household (adult equivalent)	0.036***	0.014	0.018***	0.003
Slope of the plot	0.083**	0.039	−0.003	0.010
Land tenure status of the plot	−0.063	0.061	0.033**	0.014
Size of the plot (ha)	0.008	0.038	−0.017*	0.009
Access to extension (1 = Yes, 0 = No)	1.039***	0.080	0.189***	0.015
Distance to plot from home (km)	0.000	0.000	0.000	0.000
Distance from plot to market (km)	−0.014***	0.002	−0.003***	0.001
Membership farmer groups (1 = Yes 0 = No)	0.070	0.072	0.007	0.016
Access to credit (1 = Yes, 0 = No)	0.160**	0.064	0.027*	0.015
Amount of credit accessed (USD)	0.000	0.000	0.000*	0.000
Value of household assets (USD)	0.000	0.000	0.000	0.000
Use of irrigation (1 = Yes, 0 = No)	0.971***	0.153	0.380***	0.034
Constant	−5.49	4.836	3.77***	1.294
Model characteristics	No. of obs. = 14,170		No. of obs. = 14,170	
	LR $Chi^2(30)$ = 1649		LR $Chi^2(30)$ = 1537	
	Prob > chi^2 = 0.000		Prob > chi^2 = 0.000	
	Pseudo R^2 = 0.1837		Pseudo R^2 = 0.135	

***, **, and *Denotes significance at 1, 5 and 10 % respectively
Source Kirui (in press) unpublished Ph.D. thesis

The effect of plot level characteristics on the adoption of SLM technologies is also evident in our analysis. Steeper slopes have a positive relationship with the adoption of SLM technologies. Similarly access to extension services positively influence the adoption of SLM technologies. Market access also acts as a significant determinant of SLM technologies. This is shown by the negative significant relationship between the distance from the plot to the market and the adoption of SLM technologies. The number of SLM technologies adopted is also significantly incentivized by such socio economic variables such as access to credit and the household per capita expenditure. While access to credit positively influences the adoption of SLM technologies, the relationship between household per capita expenditure and adoption of SLM technologies is however negative.

Determinants of Number of SLM Practices Adopted: Poisson Regression

The results of the Poisson regression on the determinants of the number of SLM technologies used by households are also presented in Table 14.14. The assessment is also done at plot level. The model fits the data well–it is statistically significant at 1 % with a log likelihood ratio (Chi^2 (30)) of 1537 and Pseudo $R^2 = 0.305$. There was no evidence of dispersion (over-dispersion and under-dispersion). We estimated the corresponding negative binomial regressions and all the likelihood ratio tests (comparing the negative binomial model to the Poisson model) were not statistically significant—suggesting that the Poisson model was best fit for our study objective. Results show that several proximate and underlying factors significantly determine the number of SLM technologies adopted (Table 14.14).

Among the proximate biophysical factors that significantly determine the number of SLM adopted include temperature, rainfall elevation, latitude and longitude positions, and agro-ecological zonal characteristics. The relationships between these factors and number of SLM technologies adopted are mixed. For example, the proximate biophysical factors that positively influence the number of SLM technologies adopted include temperature, rainfall and elevation. However, being in warm humid/sub-humid or in cool arid semi-arid agro-ecological zones (as compared to warm arid/semi-arid) has a negative significant influence on the number of SLM technologies adopted. The number of SLM technologies adopted has a negative relationship with latitude and longitude but a positive relationship with the interaction of latitude and longitude.

Among the household-level variables, only education level of the household head and family size were significant in influencing the number of technologies adopted. Education and the abundance of labor supply through larger bigger family size positively influence the adoption of more SLM technologies.

We also assessed the effect of plot level characteristics on the number of SLM technologies adopted. The ownership of land title (deed) is an incentive to investment on several SLM technologies. Similarly access to extension services positively influence the adoption of several SLM technologies.

Market access also acts as a significant determinant of the number of SLM technologies. The farther away from the market, the less the number of SLM technologies adopted. We also find a negative significant effect between the size of the farm and the number of SLM technologies used. The number of SLM technologies adopted is also significantly incentivized by such socio-economic variables such as access to and amount of credit accessed.

Local and Community-Level Initiatives to Address Land Degradation in Ethiopia

The actions that the communities take to address loss of ecosystem services or enhance or maintain ecosystem services improvement are presented in Table 14.15. For example, afforestation is one key action taken to address loss of forests' ecosystem services and to enhance ecosystem services improvement within forest ecosystems in Kemona, Ifabas, Jogo and Garambabo communities. To further curtail deforestation, area closures and stricter enforcement of existing bylaws and enacting new laws were some of the approaches taken by local communities in Kemona, Ifabas and Koka Negewo. The bylaws constitute community sanctions and fines and imprisonment with the help of government law enforcement agencies.

The most common approach applied to maintain or address the deterioration in the quality of cropland was soil fertility management (use organic and inorganic fertilizer). Other SLM practices such as crop rotation and use of soil and water conservation measures (such as crop and fallow rotations, soil and stone bunds, and terracing).

Likewise, area closure, controlled grazing and community sanctions for over-grazing were the most common approaches used to maintain the quality and address decline in grassland ecosystem service values. Area closures (zoning)—when

Table 14.15 Actions taken to maintain and/or address the loss of ecosystem services

District	Village	Actions in cropland	Actions in forest	Actions in grassland
Guba Goricha	Kemona	Fertilizer, composting, soil and stone bands	Afforestation, protection of the existing forest	Area closures Soil and stone bunds, planting of trees
Tulo	Ifabas	Fertilizer, compost, soil and stone bands, terracing	Area closure, afforestation, watershed management	None
Becho	Mande Tufisa	Fertilizer, composting	None	Terracing, stone and soil bunds
Lume	Jogo	Fertilizer, soil and stone bunds	Afforestation	Area closures
Nonsebo	Gara-mbabo	None	Afforestation, watershed management	Water and soil conservation
Lume	Koka Negewo	Fertilizer, composting, crop rotation	Protected forests	None

Source Kirui (in press) unpublished Ph.D. thesis

accompanied by community bylaws to sanction and punish offenders—were a particularly successful way to address degraded community grasslands.

Conclusions

The solutions to land degradation need to be based on through addressing their local drivers. Better understanding of households' behavior about land management as well as policy and institutional factors that affect such decisions are crucial, but usually underestimated in most measures to address land degradation in Ethiopia.

Many forms of land degradation occur in Ethiopia: water and wind erosion; salinization and acidification, and both physical and biological degradation of soils. More than 85 % of the land in Ethiopia is estimated to be moderately to very severely degraded, and about 75 % is affected by desertification. Recent estimates using satellite imagery show that land degradation hotspots over the last three decades cover about 23 % of land area in Ethiopia.

The analysis of nationally representative household surveys shows that the key drivers of SLM in Ethiopia are biophysical, demographic, regional and socio-economic determinants. Access to agricultural extension services, secure land tenure as proxied by ownership of land title deed and market access are important incentives to the adoption of SLM and the number of SLM technologies adopted. Thus, policies and strategies relating to securing tenure rights, building the capacity of land users through access to extension services, and access to financial and physical assets may incentivize SLM uptake. The local institutions to manage grazing lands and forests through collective action need to be encouraged.

The total value of land ecosystem services for Ethiopia is estimated to be about US$206 billion. The annual cost of land degradation is about $4.3 billion. Only about $2.2 billion (51 %) of this cost of land degradation represent the provisional ecosystem services. The other (49 %) represents the supporting and regulatory and cultural ecosystem services. Use of land degrading practices in croplands (maize and wheat) was estimated to result in losses amounting to US$162 million—representing 2 % of GDP. The costs of land degradation on static grazing land (loss of milk, meat and the cost of weight loss of animals not slaughtered or sold) were estimated to amount to $52 million.

The costs of action to rehabilitate lands degraded between 2001 and 2009 due to land use and land cover change were found to equal about US$54 billion over a 30-year horizon, whereas if nothing is done, the resulting losses may equal almost US$228 billion during the same period. This implies that the costs of action against land degradation are lower than the costs of inaction by about 4.4 times over the 30 year horizon; i.e. the ratio of action to cost of inaction is 23 %. This implies that each dollar spent on rehabilitating degraded lands in Ethiopia may return about 4.4 dollars.

Annex

See Tables A.1, A.2 and A.3.

Table A.1 Land use land cover classification in Ethiopia in 2001 (million ha)

Region	Cropland	Forest	Grassland	Shrublands	Woodland	Urban	Barren	Water
Addis Ababa	0.014	0.003	0.009	0.002	0.010	0.017	–	–
Afar	0.482	0.009	1.444	3.557	0.226	0.001	3.935	0.063
Amhara	3.067	0.195	7.272	0.632	4.085	0.008	0.009	0.298
Benshangul	0.044	0.058	1.968	0.000	2.894	0.001	–	–
Dire Dawa	0.004	0.000	0.061	0.037	0.002	0.002	–	–
Gambela	0.014	0.230	0.930	0.000	1.378	0.000	0.000	0.001
Harari	0.001	0.002	0.027	0.006	0.001	0.000	–	–
Oromia	3.041	3.011	9.829	7.144	9.077	0.032	0.102	0.188
Somali	0.050	0.007	1.082	28.700	0.082	0.004	1.535	–
Southern	1.192	1.905	3.237	0.590	4.159	0.005	0.063	0.086
Tigray	0.597	0.063	2.676	1.130	0.466	0.002	0.008	0.001
Total	8.51	5.49	28.50	41.80	22.40	0.07	5.65	0.64

Source Calculated based on Nkonya et al. (2014), using MODIS data

Table A.2 Land use land cover classification in Ethiopia in 2009 (million ha)

Region	Cropland	Forest	Grassland	Shrublands	Woodland	Urban	Barren	Water
Addis Ababa	0.021	0.001	0.008	0.004	0.004	0.017	–	–
Afar	0.307	0.009	1.105	5.153	0.050	0.001	3.048	0.045
Amhara	4.719	0.053	7.742	0.590	2.155	0.008	0.009	0.291
Benshangul	0.016	0.006	1.943	0.001	2.999	0.001	–	–
Dire Dawa	0.004	–	0.018	0.080	0.002	0.002	–	–
Gambela	0.027	0.303	0.368	0.002	1.851	0.000	0.000	0.001
Harari	0.012	0.000	0.015	0.010	0.000	0.000	–	–
Oromia	3.692	2.094	8.731	7.299	10.300	0.032	0.100	0.173
Somali	0.035	0.001	0.587	29.000	0.069	0.004	1.768	–
Southern	1.573	1.602	2.966	0.593	4.400	0.005	0.026	0.076
Tigray	0.883	0.003	2.015	1.826	0.207	0.002	0.006	0.001
Total	11.30	4.07	25.50	44.60	22.00	0.07	4.96	0.59

Source Calculated based on Nkonya et al. (2014), using MODIS data

Table A.3 Major issues and priority areas in combating land degradation and poverty

Important issues/factors	Main problems; why it is an issue?	Desired situation (objective, aim)	Measures to be taken (strategy)	Responsible body
Participation	Lack of an enabling environment Lack of awareness Misconception of partnership	Enhancing enabling environment – Enhancing partnership – Devolution of power	Awareness creation Clear definition of partnership Empower local governance	GOs, NGOs, International partners
Land tenure	Insecurity of tenure	Ensure long term use through issuing a sort of title deed	Proper land use policy and legislation Promote proper indigenous practices	Federal and regional governments
Inappropriate land use system	Steep slope farming Deforestation No or short fallowing period Lack of modern technologies Lack of know-how Overgrazing Population pressure	In place land use and ownership policy Forest policy Availability of modern know-how and technology Grazing management policy and legislation population policy (in place)	Issues appropriate policies and legislation on land use, forest, SWC and grazing management Educate the public Implement population policy Make available modern technology through research	Federal and regional governments NGOs/CBOs development partners
Livestock population	Overgrazing/uncontrolled grazing Quantity valued than quality	Livestock number balanced to the available feed resources	Increase off-take rate Change the mgt system from open to zero grazing	Govt's, NGOs/CBOs, communities
Population pressure	Man to land ratio incompatible Uncontrolled growth Women not educated and empowered to control their own fertility	Population growth balanced to economic growth Family planning exercised Women empowered	Proper implementation of the population policy (family planning) Alternative employment opportunity created Resettlement Educate and empower women	Governments NGOs/CBOs Development partners

(continued)

Table A.3 (continued)

Important issues/factors	Main problems; why it is an issue?	Desired situation (objective, aim)	Measures to be taken (strategy)	Responsible body
Poverty	Unbalanced population growth vis-à-vis economic growth High unemployment rate Low productivity (land/man) Lack of poverty reduction strategy Inequitable share and distribution of resources and services Hunger, illiteracy, etc. Deprivation of basic needs (food, shelter, cloth)	Economic growth balanced to population growth Access to basic needs Access to social services Equitable sharing and distribution to resources and services	Integrate economic development with population controlled strategy Encourage labor intensive investment Improve the quality of the population through education, knowledge and skill Promote equitable share and distribution of resources and services	Governments NGOs/CBOs Development partners Population
Institutional failures	Institutional instability Overlapping of mandates Shortage resources Integration and coordination problem Lack of a common forum	Stable with clear mandates institutions Adequate resources Clear mechanism of integration and coordination Established M&E	Establish institution with clear mandate and empowerment Secure appropriate resources Create a mechanism where institutions integrate and coordinate their activities Established MandE	– Federal Govt's – Regional States – NGOs – Development partners
Investment	Conflict with NR conservation measures Low investment on off-farm activities	Proper EIA Labor intensive investment promoted	EPA should be empowered Labor intensive investments should be encouraged	Governments Private investors Development partners

(continued)

Table A.3 (continued)

Important issues/factors	Main problems; why it is an issue?	Desired situation (objective, aim)	Measures to be taken (strategy)	Responsible body
Infrastructure and market failures	Lack of access to market Lack of access to services (school, light, clinic, water grinding mill, communication, extension and family planning services	Access to services Access to markets	Improve rural infrastructure and services Promote appropriate energy saving technology Develop alternative renewable energy system	Federal and Regional Governments NGOs/CBOs Development partners

Source MeKonen (2002) (cited by Berry 2003)

References

Bai, Z. G., Dent, D. L., Olsson, L., & Schaepman, M. E. (2008). Global assessment of land degradation and improvement. 1. Identification by remote sensing. Wageningen, The Netherlands: International Soil Reference and Information Centre (ISRIC).

Barbier, E. B. (1989). Sustaining agriculture on marginal land: A policy framework. *Environment Science and Policy for Sustainable Development, 31*(9), 12–40.

Barbier, E. B. (2000). The economic linkages between rural poverty and land degradation: Some evidence from Africa. *Agriculture, Ecosystems & Environment, 82*(1), 355–370.

Belay, K. T., Van Rompaey, A., Poesen, J., Van Bruyssel, S., Deckers, J., & Amare, K. (2014). Spatial analysis of land cover changes in eastern Tigray (Ethiopia) from 1965 to 2007: Are there signs of a forest transition? Land Degradation and Development. doi:10.1002/ldr.2275

Berry, L. (2003). Land degradation in Ethiopia: Its extent and impact. A study commissioned by the GM with WB support.

Bojö, J., & Cassells, D. (1995). Land degradation and rehabilitation in Ethiopia: A reassessment. Working Paper No. 17, World Bank, 1995, pp. 36.

CSA. (2013). *Agriculture in figures: Key findings of the 2012/2013 (2005 EC) crop year*. Ethiopia: Addis Ababa.

Dregne, H. E. (1991). Human activities and soil degradation. *Semiarid Lands and Deserts: Soil Resource and Reclamation, 19*, 335.

EEPC. (2002). *Koka dam sedimentation study: recommendations report*. Ethiopian Electric Power Corporation. Ethiopia: Addis Ababa.

Evans, J., & Geerken, R. (2004). Discrimination between climate and human-induced dryland degradation. *Journal of Arid Environments, 57*(4), 535–554.

Eyasu, E. (2003). *National assessment on environmental roles of agriculture in Ethiopia*. Unpublished Research Report Submitted to EEA, Addis Ababa.

FAO. (1986). *Highlands reclamation study ethiopia final report* (Vol. I & II). Italy: Rome.

Genanew, B. W., & Alemu, M. (2012). Investments in land conservation in the Ethiopian highlands: A household plot-level analysis of the roles of poverty, tenure security, and market incentives. *International Journal of Economics and Finance, 4*(6). URL: http://dx.doi.org/10.5539/ijef.v4n6p32. Accessed 31 May 2015.

Helldén, U., & Tottrup, C. (2008). Regional desertification: A global synthesis. *Global and Planetary Change, 64*(3), 169–176.

Holden, S., Shiferaw, B., & Pender, J. (2004). Non-farm income, household welfare, and sustainable land management in a less-favoured area in the Ethiopian highlands. *Food Policy, 29*, 369–392.

Hurni, H. 1993. Land degradation, famines and resources scenarios. In D. Pimental, *World soil erosion and conservation* (pp. 27–62). Cambridge: Cambridge University Press.

Jagger, P., & Pender, J. (2003). The role of trees for sustainable management of less-favored lands: The case of eucalyptus in Ethiopia. *Forest Policy and Economics, 3*(1), 83–95.

Kidane, T. (2008). *Determinants of physical soil and water conservation practices: The case of Bati District, Oromia Zone, Amhara Region*. Unpublished M.Sc. Thesis, Haramaya University, Ethiopia.

Kirui, O. K., & Mirzabaev, A. (2014). Economics of land degradation in Eastern Africa (No. 128). ZEF Working Paper Series. Center for Development Research (ZEF), University of Bonn, Germany.

Kumar, P. (Ed.). (2010). *The economics of ecosystems and biodiversity: Ecological and economic foundations*. London, Hardback: UNEP/Earthprint.

Le, B. Q., Nkonya, E., & Mirzabaev, A. (2014). *Biomass productivity-based mapping of global land degradation hotspots*. ZEF-Discussion Papers on Development Policy No. 185, Bonn, Germany.

Liniger, H. (2011). *Sustainable land management in practice*. United Nations: FAO (Food and Agriculture Organization).

Liniger, H. P., Mekdaschi, R., Studer, C. H., & Gurtner, M. (2011). Sustainable land management in practice—guidelines and best practices for Sub-Saharan Africa. TerrAfrica, World Overview of Conservation Approaches and Technologies (WOCAT) and Food and Agriculture Organization of the United Nations (FAO).

MeKonen, G. (2002). *Country partnership framework to combat land degradation & poverty*. Ethiopia: Global Mechanism.

Melaku, T. (2013). Sustainable land management program in Ethiopia: Linking Local REDD+ projects to national REDD+ strategies and initiatives. PowerPoint Presentation Made by National Program Coordinator of SLMP. April 29–May 1, 2013, Hawassa, Ethiopia.

National Review Report (2002). Government of Ethiopia, Addis Ababa.

Nkonya, E., Gerber, N., Baumgartner, P., von Braun, J., De Pinto, A., Graw, V., et al. (2011). The economics of land degradation: Toward an integrated global assessment. In F. Heidhues, J. von Braun, & M. Zeller (Eds.), *Development economics and policy series* (vol. 66). Frankfurt A.M., Peter Lang GmbH.

Nkonya, E., Von Braun, J., Alisher, M., Bao Le, Q., Ho Young, K., Kirui, O., et al. (2013). *Economics of land degradation initiative: Methods and approach for global and national assessments*. ZEF-Discussion Papers on Development policy No. 183, Bonn, Germany.

Nkonya, E., von Braun, J., Mirzabaev, A., Le, B. Q., Young, K. H., Kato, E., et al. (2014). *Economics of land degradation initiative: Methods and approach for global and national assessments (basic standards for comparable assessments). Draft for discussion*. Center for Development Research (ZEF), University of Bonn.

Pender, J., Gebremedhin, B., Benin, S., & Ehui, S. (2001). Strategies for sustainable development in the Ethiopian highlands. *American Journal of Agricultural Economics, 83*(5), 1231–1240.

Rudel, T. K., Schneider, L., Uriarte, M., Turner, B. L., DeFries, R., Lawrence, D., & Grau, R. (2009). Agricultural intensification and changes in cultivated areas, 1970–2005. *Proceedings of the National Academy of Sciences, 106*(49), 20675–20680.

Shibru, T. & Kifle, L. (1998). *Environmental management in ethiopia: have the national conservation plans worked?* Organization for Social Science Research in Eastern and Southern Africa (OSSRIA) Environmental Forum Publications Series No. 1, Addis Ababa.

Shiferaw, B., & Holden, S. T. (1999). Soil erosion and smallholders' conservation decisions in the highlands of Ethiopia. *World Development, 27*(4), 739–752.

Sonneveld, B. S. (2002). *Land under pressure: The impact of water erosion on food production in Ethiopia*. Netherlands: Shaker Publishing.

Sutcliffe, J. P. (1993). Economic assessment of land degradation in the Ethiopian highlands: A case study. Addis Ababa, Ethiopia: National Conservation Strategy Secretariat, Ministry of Planning and Economic Development. Addis Ababa, Ethiopia.

Teketay, D. (2001). Deforestation, wood famine, and environmental degradation in Ethiopia's highland ecosystems: Urgent need for action. *Northeast African Studies, 8*(1), 53–76.

Tesfa, A., & Mekuriaw, S. (2014). The effect of land degradation on farm size dynamics and crop livestock farming system in Ethiopia: A review. *Open Journal of Soil Science, 4*, 1.

The Global Mechanism. (2007). Increasing finance for sustainable land management. The Global Mechanism of the UNCCD—Via Paolo di Dono 44—00142 Rome, Italy. Available online at www.global-mechanism.org. Accessed 31 May 2015.

The World Bank. (2013). Ethiopia overview: First economic update. 1818 H Street NW, Washington DC 20433, USA.

Vlek, P., Le, Q. B., & Tamene, L. (2010). Assessment of land degradation, its possible causes and threat to food security in Sub-Saharan Africa. In R. Lal & B. A. Stewart (Eds.), *Food security and soil quality* (pp. 57–86). Boca Raton, Florida: CRC Press.

von Braun, J., Algieri, B., & Kalkuhl, M. (2014). World food system disruptions in the early 2000s: Causes, impacts and cures. *World Food Policy, 1*(1), 1–22.

von Braun, J., Gerber, N., Mirzabaev, A., & Nkonya, E. M. (2013). *The economics of land degradation (No. 147910)*. Bonn, Germany: University of Bonn, Center for Development Research (ZEF).

Wagayehu, B. (2003). *Economics of soil and water conservation: Theory and empirical application to subsistence farming in the eastern Ethiopian highlands*. Doctoral thesis, Swedish University of Agricultural Sciences, Uppsala, Sweden.

Yesuf, M., Mekonnen, A., Kassie, M., & Pender, J. (2005). *Cost of land degradation in Ethiopia: A critical review of past studies*. http://www.efdinitiative.org/sites/default/files/costs_of_land_degradation_in_ethiopia_v2_final.pdf.. Accessed 11 Sep 2015.

Chapter 15
Economics of Land Degradation in India

Gurumurthy Mythili and Jann Goedecke

Abstract Land degradation is increasingly becoming a major concern for Indian agriculture on which two-third of the population depend for their livelihood. Many policies and programs have been initiated in the last two decades to address this problem but the results are meager. Analysis of causes of land degradation and their extents is very important to design suitable policies to overcome the degradation problem. It is in this context, this paper identifies the major socio-economic variables that explain land degradation. It also finds economic and social costs of land degradation and the net benefits from taking up conservation activities and finally draws some lessons on what are the right policy instruments to promote sustainable land management practices. The Total Economic Value (TEV) concept has been used in deriving the costs and benefits. Our findings from state level analysis suggest that 'input subsidies' and 'decreasing land-man ratio' are two major determining factors that increase land degradation. Rationalizing input subsidies will go a long way in improving the management of land resources. At the household level, the number of crops grown and the operating area are significantly influencing land degradation. The analysis of the costs of action versus inaction against land degradation shows that costs of inaction are higher than the costs of action, indicating the benefits that will accrue if sufficient conservation practices are undertaken. Institutions and incentive mechanisms play important roles in changing the behavior of farmers to act in a resource conservative way.

Keywords Total economic value · Costs of inaction · Drivers of land degradation · Land policies

G. Mythili (✉)
Indira Gandhi Institute of Development Research, Film City Road, Santosh Nagar, Goregaon (East), Mumbai 400065, India
e-mail: mythili@igidr.ac.in

J. Goedecke
Center for Development Research, University of Bonn, Walter-Flex-Straße 3, 53113 Bonn, Germany

J. Goedecke
Faculty of Economics and Business, KU Leuven, Warmoesberg 26, 1000 Brussels, Belgium

E. Nkonya et al. (eds.), *Economics of Land Degradation and Improvement – A Global Assessment for Sustainable Development*,
DOI 10.1007/978-3-319-19168-3_15

Introduction

Land degradation poses a considerable challenge to agricultural growth and poverty reduction in India. It is officially estimated that about 44 % of India's land area is degraded. The causes of land degradation are numerous and complex. Proximate factors include the extension of crop cultivation to marginal and low potential lands or to lands vulnerable to natural hazards,[1] improper crop rotations, overuse of agrochemicals, and mismanagement of the irrigation system. Moreover, "shifting cultivation" practiced in many parts of the country is responsible for deforestation and the expansion of agriculture to less productive lands. However, the underlying causes are believed to be poverty among agricultural households, land fragmentation, insecure land tenure, open access nature of some resources, and policy and institutional failures.

To illustrate one of these drivers in more detail, India supports 18 % of the world human population, 15 % of the global livestock population, but endowed with only 2.4 % of world land area. Moreover, the average size of land holdings in agriculture declined from 2.30 to 1.16 ha during 1970–2010 due to increasing population pressure. About 60 % of the land is rainfed and low in productivity, leading to high inter-annual fluctuations in agricultural output. About 200 million rural poor depend on these rainfed areas for their livelihoods.

Intensive farming practices, particularly with wheat and rice, initiated during the Green Revolution in 1970s, have mined nutrients from the soil. Soil degradation is limiting gains in agricultural output and forest production. Land degradation is a big challenge to policy makers who need to balance the multiple goals of poverty eradication, food security and sustainable land management.

The major objective of this study is to scientifically support policy actions in India on sustainable land management, through finding answers to the three research questions below:

- (i) What are key causes of land degradation across typical agro-ecological regions of India?
- (ii) What are the economic, social and environmental costs of land degradation and net benefits resulting from taking actions against degradation compared to inaction?
- (iii) What are the feasible policy and development strategies that enable and catalyze sustainable land management (SLM) actions?

This Economics of Land Degradation (ELD) research seeks to test two hypotheses. Firstly, we test which factors, such as climate and agricultural practices, population density, poverty, absence of secure land tenure, lack of market access and others, are significant causes of land degradation. Secondly, we also

[1]Steep slopes, shallow and sandy soils, fragile arid and semi-arid lands bordering deserts.

hypothesize that the benefit of taking action against land degradation through SLM measures is greater than the costs of inaction.

The chapter begins with a brief introduction to Conceptual Framework and followed by Land use, land degradation status, trend and classifications. The following section focuses on land policies and their influences on land degradation. This is followed by the impacts of land degradation where the survey of past studies, the methodology adopted for our own estimates and the estimates of costs of action vs inaction are highlighted. Then we move to the drivers of land degradation which contains state level and household level analysis. Finally we draw inferences from the findings and policy implications.

ELD Conceptual Framework

The conceptual framework used in the India case study of Economics of Land Degradation broadly follows the ELD framework presented in von Braun et al. (2013). The causes of land degradation are divided into proximate and underlying, which interact with each other to result in different levels of land degradation. The level of land degradation determines its outcomes or effects—whether on-site or offsite—on the provision of ecosystem services and the benefits humans derive from those services. Actors can then take action to control the causes of land degradation, its level, or its effects (ibid.).

Many of the services provided by ecosystems are not transacted through the markets, so different agents do not take into account negative or positive effects on those ecosystems. Since the external costs or benefits are not accounted for in the farmer's land use decision, this leads to an undervaluation of land and its provision of ecosystem services (ibid.). The failure to capture these values causes higher rates of land degradation. To adequately account for ecosystem services in decision making, the economic values of those services have to be determined (Nkonya et al. 2011). Attributing economic values to ecosystem services is challenging, due to measurement problems. As economic values are linked to the number of (human) beneficiaries and the socioeconomic context, these services depend on local or regional conditions (ibid.). As TEEB (2010) indicates, a global framework that identifies a set of key attributes and then monitors these by building on national indicators could help answering this challenge.

It is also crucial to identify and understand institutional arrangements affecting land management, in order to devise sustainable and efficient policies to combat land degradation. For example, if farmers use excessive water or fertilizer, leading to some forms of land degradation, it must be understood why they do so. Missing or very low prices of irrigation water or fertilizer provide incentives to degrade land and soils in a misleading institutional setup.

The Extent and Types of Land Degradation in India

Cultivable lands (175 million ha) make up almost 60 % of the total Indian territory, 80 % of which is under crops (141 million ha), and another 6 % (10 million ha) is under rangelands (Table A.1 in the Annex and Fig. 15.1). The remaining arable lands are not cultivated. Forests (70 million ha) are the second most important land cover category, making up about a quarter of the total area.

The land use dynamics over the last four decades between 1970s and 2010, point at increasing share of croplands at the expense of rangelands and wastelands,

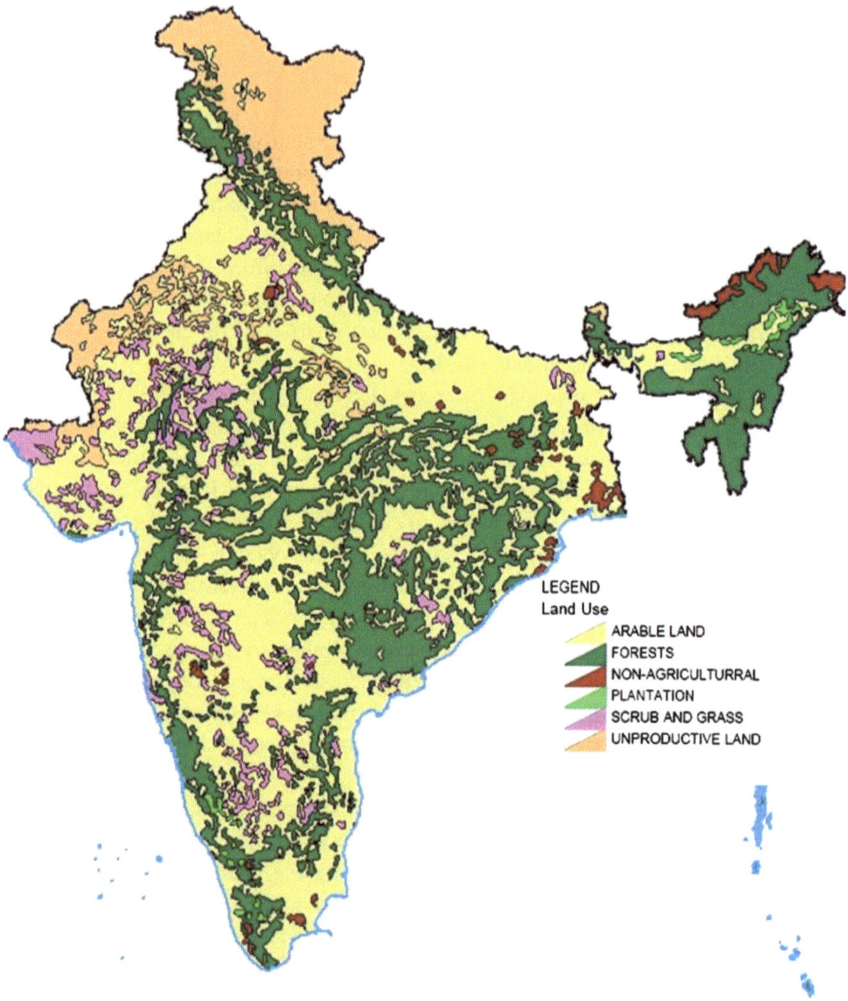

Fig. 15.1 Land use and land cover in India. *Source* National Institute of Hydrology (2009), Accessed from IndiaWaterPortal.org

rapidly growing urbanization and a slight extension in the forest cover (Table A.1 in the Annex). However, the analysis of more recent MODIS satellite data shows that between 2001 and 2009, the forest cover declined all across India by a total of 2.8 million ha, of which the largest shares are in Kerala, Madhya Pradesh, and Andhra Pradesh (Table 15.1).

Similarly, the areas under woodlands and barren lands have also decreased by 3.2 million ha each. On the other hand, the biggest land use change was the increase

Table 15.1 Land use change between 2001 and 2009 in Indian states (without Union territories), in thousand ha

Location	Forest	Shrub	Grassland	Cropland	Wood	Barren	Water
Andhra Pradesh	−324	85	1418	1230	−2330	−48	−32
Arunachal Pradesh	265	−141	80	−5	−41	−144	−13
Assam	−200	−68	−138	19	409	−49	27
Bihar	−148	−221	−115	725	−216	−13	−12
Chhattisgarh	−123	26	−69	521	−358	5	−3
Goa	−1	−8	−14	−7	32	−3	0
Gujarat	10	−787	−105	1331	30	−597	116
Haryana	3	−143	−11	155	0	−5	0
Jammu & Kashmir	427	−253	−595	130	−64	387	−32
Jharkhand	−237	99	−1	472	−332	0	0
Karnataka	−118	−81	1347	−1524	379	−9	6
Kerala	−945	−16	−11	172	820	−1	−19
Madhya Pradesh	−452	−152	481	372	−312	12	51
Maharashtra	−35	−413	473	227	−256	−10	15
Manipur	−123	−25	3	58	88	0	−1
Meghalaya	−110	2	−24	−1	134	0	−1
Mizoram	−291	−2	−15	−25	332	0	0
Nagaland	36	−2	−14	−16	−3	0	−1
Orissa	−268	62	62	772	−599	−19	−10
Punjab	7	−18	−17	24	5	0	−1
Rajasthan	−16	4893	−770	−1400	107	−2815	1
Sikkim	19	−4	15	0	−17	−10	−2
Tamil Nadu	−159	−210	325	774	−736	5	2
Tripura	−240	−7	−29	−14	291	0	−2
Uttar Pradesh	−104	−145	−108	528	−151	−7	−14
Uttarakhand	234	−178	−77	104	−153	80	−10
West Bengal	43	−42	−43	390	−283	−29	−34
India	**−2848**	**2252**	**2048**	**5010**	**−3222**	**−3271**	**32**

Source MODIS land cover

Note "urban" was left out since no change is reported in the considered time period

of the cropped areas by 5 million ha between 2001 and 2009, and increase of 2.2 and 2 million ha of shrublands and grasslands, respectively. These overall figures hide significant regional differences. For example, even though the overall cropland area has increased in India, such states as Karnataka, Rajasthan, have lost about 1.5 million ha of croplands each; whereas such other states as Gujarat, Andhra Pradesh have gained about 1.3 million ha of croplands each. Table 15.1 shows these regional differences in detail.

Geographically, India is divided into six zones: North, South, East, North East, West, Central, and Union territories. The land degradation data (Table 15.2) show that soil erosion due to water and wind occupy more than 70 % of the total degraded area. The water induced soil erosion is the single largest contributor to land degradation, i.e. about two-third of the total, followed by salinity, about 15 %, which is a common problem in the irrigated lands in the country. Region-wise statistics show that central region is the worst affected of all (59 % of its total area), followed by North-Eastern and Southern regions.

Land degradation statistics vary depending on the source and estimation method. One estimate is based on universal soil loss function, as applied in the NBSS and the other, on National Remote Sensing Agency (NRSA). NRSA bases its estimates on remotely sensed satellite data. NRSA estimates are lower than the former estimates by NBSS&LUP-ICAR-2005 and are expected to be more accurate and to give more detailed information.

Table 15.3 provides trends on land degradation using the former method. The NRSA estimates are given in Table 15.4. The trend shows that land degradation declined after 1996. There is a need to evaluate the reasons behind this decline. One potential cause could be the increased public investments to address degradation after 1996. The most important type of land degradation in India is soil erosion (both by wind and water) (on 119 million ha), followed by shifting cultivation, waterlogging and salinity.

According to the NRSA estimates only about 20 % of the territory in India, i.e. 65 million ha of land are considered as wastelands. However, it should be noted that these two estimates do not necessarily contradict each other as they measure different things.

More recent estimates by Le et al. (2014), using remotely sensed NDVI data, show that about 16 % of the Indian territory, i.e. about 47 million ha, showed declining NDVI trends between 1982 and 2006 (Fig. 15.2), of which 29 million ha in croplands and 12 million ha in forested areas.

The levels of soil erosion are classified by the degree of severity in Table 15.5. It shows that moderate erosion of 5–10 tons per ha (per year) is the largest category affecting 43 % of the total area affected by soil erosion. About 1.4 billion tons of soils are lost annually due to moderate erosion, and 1.6 billion tons due to high erosion. The total annual soil losses are estimated at about 5 billion tons.

While water erosion prevails across the country, wind erosion is dominant in the western part of the country, particularly in the state of Rajasthan. Singh et al. (1990) estimated that the annual erosion rate varies from below 5 tons/ha for dense forests, snow-clad cold deserts, and arid regions of western Rajasthan to above 80 tons/ha

Table 15.2 The classification of land degradation in India, by types and regions (in 1000 ha)

Region	Water erosion	Wind erosion	Water logging	Salinity/alkalinity	Several degradation types combined	Total degraded area	Area	Degraded area (%)
North	23,449	9040	4396	3342	335	40,562	101,061	40
North East	4136	–	522	5534	2422	12,614	26,219	48
Central	17,883	–	359	6842	1126	26,210	44,345	59
East	9249	–	3392	2322	194	15,157	41,833	36
West	16,446	443	599	1869	1993	21,350	50,743	42
South	22,330	–	5031	1902	1302	30,565	63,576	48
Union Territories	187	–	–	9	9	205	825	25
INDIA	93,680 (64 %)	9483 (6 %)	14,299 (10 %)	21,820 (15 %)	7381 (5 %)	146,663 (100 %)	328,602	45

Note Figures in parentheses are percentages to total degraded area. States in each region: North: Delhi, Jammu and Kashmir, Himachal Pradesh, Punjab, Haryana, Uttarakhand, Uttar Pradesh. North East: Assam, Sikkim, Nagaland, Meghalaya, Manipur, Mizoram, Tripura, Arunachal Pradesh. Central: Madhya Pradesh, Chhattisgarh. East: Bihar, Orissa, Jharkhand, West Bengal. West: Rajasthan, Gujarat, Goa, Maharashtra. South: Andhra Pradesh, Kerala, Karnataka, Tamil Nadu

Source NBSS&LUP-ICAR-2005 on the Scale of 1:250,000

Table 15.3 Trend in land degradation in India (area in million hectares)

Type	Ministry of agriculture and co-operation		Sehgal and Abrol		NBSS&LUP
	1980	1985	1994	1997	2005
Soil erosion[a]	150.0	141.2	162.4	167.0	119.19
Saline and alkaline soil	8.0	9.4	10.1	11.0	5.95
Water logging[b]	6.0	8.5	11.6	13.0	14.3
Shifting cultivation	4.4	4.9		9.0	7.38
Total degradation	168.4	175.1	175.0	187.8	146.82

Source As in column titles

[a]This includes both wind and water erosion, but water erosion accounts for more than 90 %

[b]Canal areas account for about 50 % of the total water logged area

Table 15.4 Category wise wastelands of India in 1999–2000 (estimated by NRSA)

Category	% of total geographical area
Gullied/or Ravenous land	0.65
Land with or without scrub	6.13
Water logged and marshy land	0.52
Land affected by salinity/alkalinity coastal/inland	0.65
Shifting cultivation area	1.11
Underutilized/degraded notified forest land	4.44
Degraded pastures/grazing land	0.82
Degraded land under plantation crop	0.18
Sands—Inland/coastal	1.58
Mining/industrial waste land	0.04
Barren rocky/stony waste/sheet rock area	2.04
Steep sloping area	0.24
Snow covered and/or glacial area	1.76
Total waste land area	20.17

Source NRSA

in the Shiwalik hills. Severe wind erosion is recorded mostly in the extreme western parts of the country. Almost one-third of the area under soil erosion suffers from low productivity. The topsoil erosion depletes the nutrient content of the soil (State of the Environment 2001).

Statistics from The National Bureau of Soil Survey and Land Use Planning (Sehgal and Abrol 1994) reveal that about 3.7 million ha suffer from nutrient loss and/or depletion of organic matter. Nutrient depletion is fairly widespread in the cultivated areas of the subtropical region. Estimates of loss of nutrients, using the annual soil specific erosion rates provided by the Central Soil and Water Conservation Research and Training Institute, ICAR, show that nearly 74 million tons of major nutrients is lost due to erosion annually in India. On an average, every

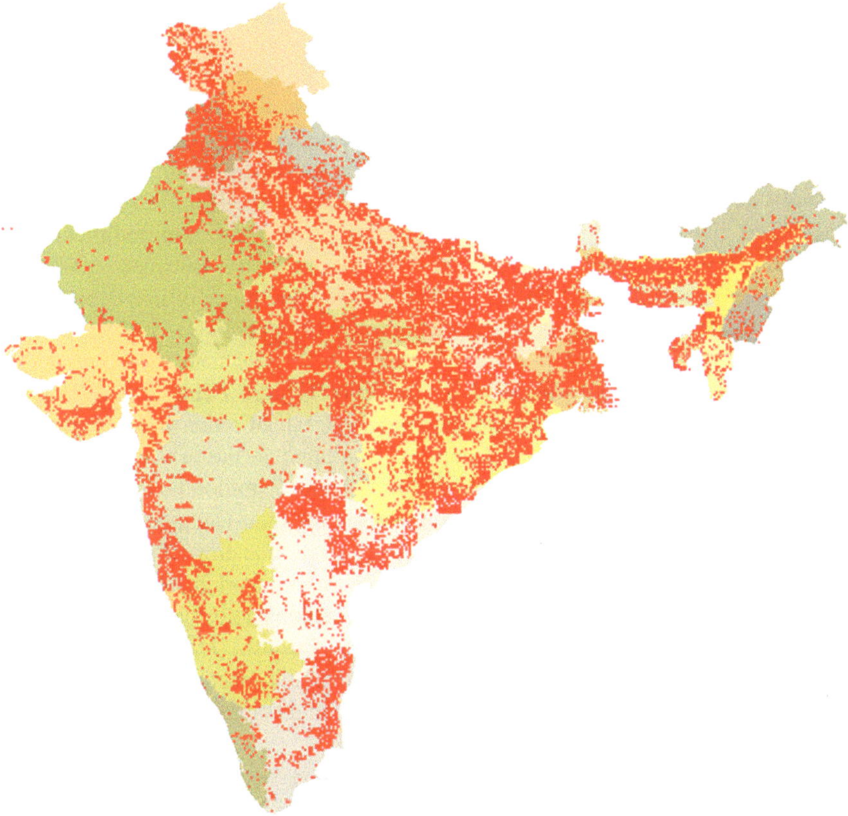

Fig. 15.2 Land degradation hotspots in India. *Source* Le et al. (2014). *Note* Land degradation hotspots are colored in *red*

Table 15.5 Levels of soil erosion of varying severity for India

Severity of erosion	Annual soil loss range (ton/ha)	The share of the total affected area (%)	Annual loss of soil (million tons)
Slight	≤5	24	401
Moderate	5–10	43	1406
High	10–20	24	1610
Very high	20–40	5	640
Severe	40–80	3	666
Very severe	≥80	1	255
Total			4978

Source Singh et al. (1990)

year, the country loses 0.8 million tons of nitrogen, 1.8 million tons of phosphorus, and 26.3 million tons of potassium (State of the Environment 2001). The offsite effect of erosion is the siltation in the reservoirs. Many reservoirs have suffered from reduced storage capacity due to increasing erosion and deposition. Siltation of major river courses due to excessive silt deposits is observed widely in Bihar and Uttar Pradesh since many rivers in these regions are flood-prone. The total area affected due to this problem is about 2.73 million ha (Das 1977; Mukherjee et al. 1985). The rivers Ganga and Brahmaputra carry the maximum sediment load annually, about 586 and 470 million tons, respectively. Between 6000 and 12,000 million tons of fertile soil are eroded annually and much of it is deposited in the reservoirs leading to a reduction in their storage capacity by 1–2 % (State of the Environment 2001).

Salt-affected soils are widespread in the different agro climatic zones of the Indo-Gangetic Plain. Areas with a mean annual rainfall of more than 600 mm are mostly of alkali soils, while saline soils are dominant in the arid, semiarid, and coastal regions (State of the Environment 2001). About 7 million ha is salt-affected, of which 2.5 million ha represents the alkali soils in the Indo-Gangetic Plain. Nearly 50 % of the canal-irrigated area is affected by salinization and/or alkalisation due to inadequate drainage, inefficient water management and distorted subsidized energy pricing (State of the Environment 2001). The regions affected by salinization caused by the rise in ground water are Uttar Pradesh, Haryana, Rajasthan, Maharashtra, and Karnataka. Inadequate planning and management of surface irrigation systems is the major cause of salinity of canal command area (State of the Environment 2001).

Evolution of Land Policies

The land policy is one major factor in the societal efforts to conserve land resources. Looking back, the pre-independence period was characterized by Zamindari and Ryotwari systems where the main motive was collecting land revenue or tax from the users of the land. In this system many non-cultivating intermediaries emerged and the government did not make any effort to abolish the intermediaries. Hence at the time of independence, the major challenge was to reform the agrarian structure and this brought about land reforms in the country. Various programs and policies that have bearing on land resources is given in Annex Table A.2.

In the subsequent Five Year Plans, land Policy was one of the major components. It broadly consists of (1) abolition of intermediaries, tenancy Reform and Redistribution of land (1950–72), (2) Bringing uncultivated land under cultivation (1972–85), (3) Water and Soil Conservation efforts (1985–95), and (4) Improve land revenue administration and land entitlement (1995 till date) (Deshpande 2003). The issues in various plan period and policy focus is given in the Annex Table A.3.

Secured land rights gives the cultivator incentives to use the land in such a way that the long term interest is protected. However the tenancy laws did not meet with success in India as it helped tenants acquire ownership right of only a very small percentage of the cultivated area. There were many forms of concealed tenancy which were difficult to break. If we go through the statistics provided by National Sample Survey, there was a very sharp reduction in tenancy over time. One factor responsible for reduction in tenancy was that many land owners evicted their tenants in response to the tenancy legislation (Deshpande 2003). Even though reduction in tenancy is likely to help reduce land degradation, there is no sufficient information available to conclude if the land vacated by tenants is put to productive use by the land owner or left as fallow land.

In recent land policies, attention was drawn to loss of micronutrient due to irrational and imbalanced use of fertiliser. Rationalising fertiliser subsidies is being considered as one of the objectives in the current policies (Annex Table A.3).

The Impact of Land Degradation

A Survey of Past Studies

In the literature on the costs of land degradation in India, soil loss has been valued using productivity approach, preventive cost approach, and replacement cost approach. The productivity approach basically attempts to value through impacts, viz. through productivity loss. Preventive measures are practices such as conservation agriculture. The replacement cost is cost of restoration of soil to its original state (Mythili 2003).

Econometric techniques have been utilized in a few studies (e.g. Parikh 1989; Parikh and Ghosh 1991) to estimate soil loss by having the yield function as separable in input response function and soil quality multiplier function. Given a measurable soil quality multiplier, potential yield value foregone as a result of decline in soil quality for a given input bundle can be determined.[2] Few studies estimate benefits from soil conservation through watershed development program in terms of productivity gains (e.g. Ninan 2002). This method is known as preventive method. However loss of productivity is widely used in the Indian context to measure the impact (Mythili 2003).

Most of the studies which attempted valuation of degradation failed to recognize the regional level diversities. According to soil types, black and red soils are more vulnerable to land degradation (Sehgal and Abrol 1994). Loss estimates of some major studies are presented in Table 15.6.

Table 15.7 presents state wise estimates of losses due to different types of land degradation based on soil loss, extracted from the study by Vasisht et al. (2003). About 8 states reported more than 20 % loss in the production due to degradation.

[2]The farmers' adaptation mechanism for alteration in the soil quality can also be dealt within the model.

Table 15.6 Impact of soil erosion, salinity and water logging in India—a review

Study	Data period	Type	Loss	Remark
Narayana and Ram Babu (1983)	1976	Soil erosion (water induced)	Annual loss of soil 16.4 tons/ha	
Singh et al. (1990)	1970s	Soil erosion (water induced)	Annual loss of soil 15.2 tons/ha	
Bansil (1990)	1986	Soil erosion (water induced)	Annual loss in production of major crops 13.5 million tons (3.1 % of total production)	Cover agricultural land, other non-wasteland and non-forest land
UNDP, FAO and UNEP (1993)	1993	Soil erosion (water induced)	Annual loss in production 8.2 million tons (1.7 % of total production)	Only agricultural land
Sehgal and Abrol (1994)	1990s	Soil erosion (water induced)	Soil productivity decline ranges from 12 % in deep soil to 73 % in shallow soil	Loss is more in red and black soil as compared to alluvium derived soil
Brandon et al. (1996)	1990s	Soil erosion	Annual loss of 4–6.3 % agricultural production	
UNDP, FAO and UNEP (1993)	1993	Salinity	6.2 million tons of Production loss	As per FAO data
Singh (1994)	1990s	Salinity	About 50 % of canal irrigated area is affected by salinity	
Singh (1994)	1990s	Waterlogging	Productivity loss ranging from 40 % for paddy to 80 % for potato	
Reddy (2003)	1989	Soil erosion	Loss in terms of replacement cost range from 1 to 1.7 % of GDP based on various data estimates. In terms of production loss it is 4 times higher	Erosion data of NRSA and ARPU and Sehgal and Abrol (1994) are used to find cost of erosion

(continued)

Table 15.6 (continued)

Study	Data period	Type	Loss	Remark
Reddy (2003)	1989	Salinity and Alkalinity	Loss of production to the tune of 0.67 million tons which is 0.2 % of GDP	Based on NRSA estimates of area affected
	1994	Salinity and Alkalinity	Loss of production is 3.80 million tonnes equal to 0.3 % of GDP	Based on the degradation area data of Sehgal and Abrol (1994)
Reddy (2003)	1989	Water logging	Production loss of 0.85 mt equal to 0.25 % of GDP	Based on NRSA estimates
	1994	Water logging	Production loss of 8.72 m equal to 0.8 % of GDP	Based on Sehgal and Abrol (1994) estimates
Vasisht et al. (2003)	1994–96	All types	Production loss of 12 % of total value of production	Statewise estimates also computed

Source For some studies: Reddy (2003) and TERI (1998). Others were extracted from the respective studies

Table 15.7 State-wise estimates of economic losses of land degradation in India

State	Degraded land area[a] (1000 ha)	Losses due to degradation as % to total value of production
Andhra Pradesh	15,662	20
Assam	2807	25
Bihar	6291	14
Gujarat	10,336	22
Himachal Pradesh	3008	27
Haryana	1384	15
Jammu & Kashmir	2225	17
Karnataka	7681	18
Kerala	2608	24
Maharashtra	13,328	22
Madhya Pradesh	26,209	20
Orissa	6121	19
Rajasthan	13,586	17
Tamil Nadu	5273	21
Uttar Pradesh	15,253	13
West Bengal	2752	10
Punjab	896	19
All India[b]	187,770	12

Source Vasisht et al. (2003)
[a]Based on the estimate of Sehgal and Abrol (1994)
[b]National Bureau of Soil Survey and Land Use Planning

Methodology of Deriving Costs of Land Degradation

In the present study, the economic impacts of land degradation are calculated using the Total Economic Value (TEV) Framework (MEA 2005). TEV approach captures the total costs of land degradation more comprehensively (Nkonya et al. 2013). We use the data from TEEB database, based on more than 300 case studies around the world, and use value transfer approach to cover the areas for which the data is lacking (Nkonya et al. 2013). The values of the ecosystem services thus obtained were used in calculating the Total Economic Value of the economic impacts of land degradation.

Cost of Inaction Versus Cost of Action

The calculation of costs of inaction and the costs of action against land degradation follows the methodology described in detail in Chap. 6 of this volume. The methodology to assess the cost of inaction is based on the fact that land degradation mainly occurs in two forms (Nkonya et al. 2013). Costs of inaction arise if land use changes from more economically and environmentally productive (considering its ecosystem functions) land uses to those with less productivity. The cost of action against degradation due to land use and land cover change are incurred by re-establishing the high value biome and the opportunity cost, since the benefits given by the biome that is being replaced have to be taken account of.

Estimates of Cost

Our estimates using the TEV approach presented in the methodology section are given in Table 15.8. The total annual costs of land degradation by land use and cover change in 2009 as compared to 2001 in India are estimated to be about 5.35 billion USD.

The biggest share of these costs are occurring in Kerala, Rajasthan, Andhra Pradesh, Orissa and Madhya Pradesh, whereas the lowest land degradation by land use change are in Haryana, Punjab and Goa (Fig. 15.3). These land degradation costs estimates are only due to land use and cover change, and do not yet account for costs of land degradation when land use did not change, i.e. when cropland stayed as cropland between 2001 and 2009, but crop yields were negatively affected by land degradation. As for the per capita costs of land degradation, the highest per capita costs are observed in Mizoram and Arunachal Pradesh and the lowest per capita costs again in Haryana and Punjab. The reason for such low figures for Haryana and Punjab is that there has been very little land use change in these two States. However, these estimates exclude the costs of land degradation other than land use change, which are expected to be more prevalent in these states.

The share of LD in the regional GDP shows that the share is significant in the Northern and North-eastern regions of India (Fig. 15.4).

The estimates in Table 15.9 confirm that the cost of inaction exceeds cost of action in every state. The ratio of action over inaction is in the range 20–40 % in humid regions in general and above 40 % in sub humid and arid regions. Further cost of action for crop and grassland are more or less similar to cost of taking action against deforestation. However when it comes to inaction there are wide variations between the two. Cost of inaction against deforestation, is consistently higher in all the states. Cost of inaction in crop and grass lands is the highest in Madhya Pradesh which is a relatively backward region and the smallest in Punjab & Haryana province. In this region, the land use change is much less and the land degradations mainly occur in the form of loss of productivity due to salinity. This region exposes

Table 15.8 Total economic cost of land degradation in India

State	Gross regional product (GRP) in 2009, in billion USD	GRP per capita, in USD	Annual costs of land degradation, in million USD	Annual per capita cost of land degradation, in USD	The share of land degradation costs in GRP (%)
Andhra Pradesh	102.6	1056	335.0	4.0	<1
Arunachal Pradesh	1.5	973	106.0	76.6	7
Assam	19.4	549	268.3	8.6	1
Bihar	37.1	341	126.1	1.2	<1
Chhattisgarh	20.8	702	255.2	10.0	1
Goa	6.2	2963	9.3	6.4	<1
Gujarat	89.4	1271	201.4	3.3	<1
Haryana	46.5	1615	4.8	0.2	<1
Jammu & Kashmir	10.1	673	250.9	20.0	2
Jharkhand	20.2	543	218.7	6.6	1
Karnataka	72.2	1044	244.4	4.0	<1
Kerala	48.6	1205	517.8	15.5	1
Madhya Pradesh	47.5	571	325.5	4.5	1
Maharashtra	188.6	1481	158.1	1.4	<1
Manipur	1.7	547	122.3	47.6	7
Meghalaya	2.8	900	126.2	42.5	5
Mizoram	1.1	869	193.3	176.1	17
Nagaland	2.1	989	92.8	46.9	4
Orissa	34.3	687	333.3	7.9	1
Punjab	41.9	1252	7.5	0.3	<1
Rajasthan	55.1	681	405.3	5.9	1
Sikkim	1.0	1375	28.7	47.0	3
Tamil Nadu	99.1	1271	254.1	3.5	<1
Tripura	3.2	799	147.3	40.1	5
Uttar Pradesh	109.2	468	130.1	0.7	<1
Uttarakhand	13.9	1186	205.1	20.3	1
West Bengal	84.8	837	84.9	0.9	<1
Total	1224.3	922	5351.3	4.4	<1

Source Authors' calculation based on the data extracted from Government of Punjab, Department of Planning (2014); Indian Ministry of Statistics and Programme Implementation (2014); TEEB dataset; Modis land cover dataset

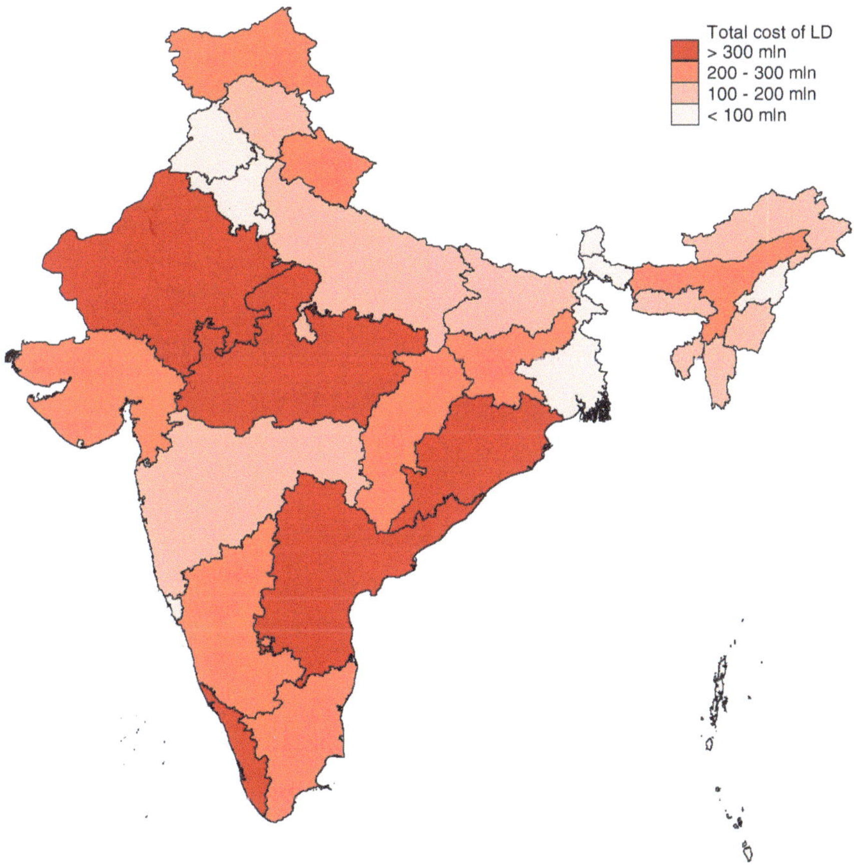

Fig. 15.3 Annual costs of land degradation, in million USD. *Source* Government of Punjab, Department of Planning (2014); Indian Ministry of Statistics and Programme Implementation (2014); TEEB dataset; Modis land cover dataset

a high level of irrigation and fertiliser use. Since this analysis takes into account only land use cover changes, Punjab and Haryana show much less costs of inaction. Goa also shows smaller units of costs of inaction but it has much less activity under crop and grass lands and it mainly derives its income from tourism.

Loss Due to Rangeland Degradation

With regard to Biomass decline of grazing land for livestock, it is estimated by Kwon et al. (Chap. 8 of the book) that 7.70 US million dollars of value (at 2007 prices) is lost in milk and meat production due to decline in grass biomass from

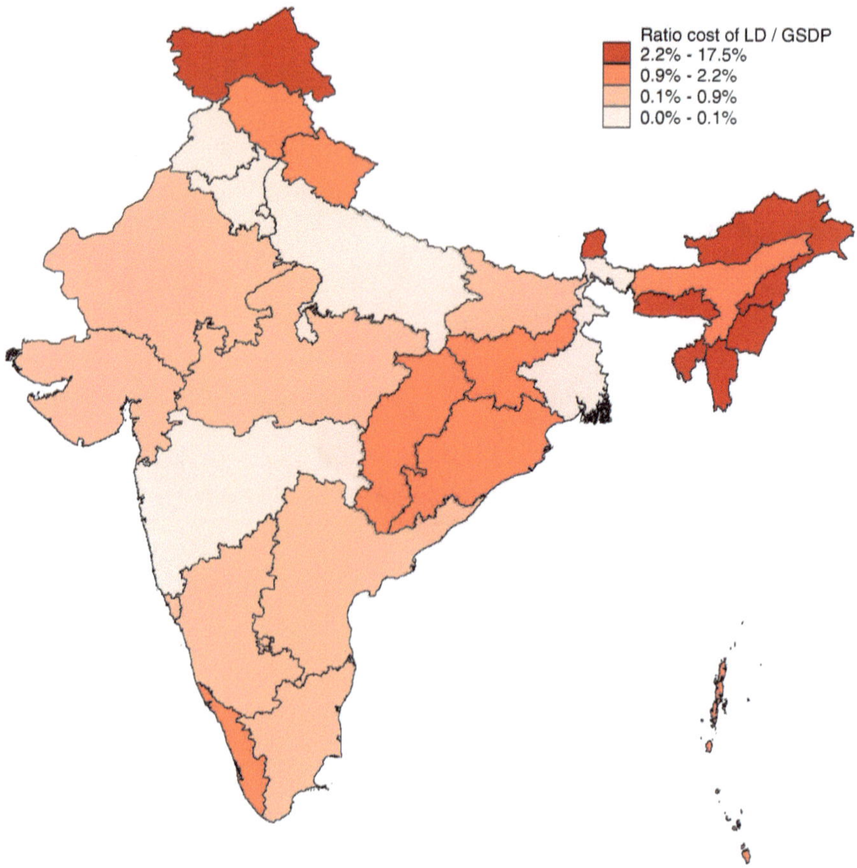

Fig. 15.4 The share of annual land degradation costs in regional GDP (thresholds according to quartiles). *Source* Indian Ministry of Statistics and Programme Implementation; simulations based on TEEB and MODIS land cover datasets, agroecological zones defined according to IISD (2015)

rangeland degradation.[3] Almost 80 % of this decline constitutes loss of milk production as meat consumption is low in India.

This estimate of total loss of livestock products for India by this study is much less in comparison with smaller African countries like Ethiopia and Kenya. However this study did not consider the forest lands which are widely used for grazing in India. In India, about 60 % of livestock grazing area is forest area (Kapur et al. 2010). The loss of rangeland value significantly varies between studies due to varying methodologies. Mani et al. (2012) reported 3–4 billion dollars of livestock value loss at 2010 prices due to grassland degradation.

[3]Only cattle, buffalo, sheep and goat are considered in this study.

Table 15.9 Cost of action and inaction against land degradation, by state (in billion USD)

State	Annual costs of LD, in million USD	Annual costs of LD in terms of provisional ecosystem services only	Cost of action (6 years)	Cost of action (30 years)	Of which, opportunity cost of action	Cost of inaction (6 years)	Cost of inaction (30 years)	Ratio cost of action/inaction (%)	Agro-ecological zone
Andhra Pradesh	334.96	2.29	20.02	20.05	19.88	28.41	38.46	52	Subhumid
Arunachal Pradesh	106.02	0.39	1.46	1.46	1.45	4.09	5.54	26	Humid
Assam	268.28	1.2	5.4	5.41	5.36	12.06	16.33	33	Humid
Bihar	126.14	0.74	4.75	4.76	4.72	7.97	10.79	44	Humid
Chhattisgarh	255.19	1.31	8.89	8.9	8.83	15.11	20.45	43	Subhumid
Goa	9.35	0.04	0.15	0.15	0.15	0.39	0.53	28	Humid
Gujarat	201.42	1.78	11.94	11.96	11.83	18.18	24.61	49	A&S
Haryana	4.75	0.07	0.9	0.9	0.89	1.03	1.39	65	A&S
Jammu & Kashmir	250.94	1.14	2.89	2.9	2.85	9.47	12.82	23	A&S
Jharkhand	218.66	1.07	6.68	6.69	6.63	12.01	16.25	41	Subhumid
Karnataka	244.4	1.34	9.08	9.1	9.02	15.22	20.6	44	Subhumid
Kerala	517.78	1.87	6.1	6.11	6.06	18.34	24.82	25	Humid
Madhya Pradesh	325.53	1.94	15.49	15.51	15.38	23.52	31.84	49	Subhumid
Maharashtra	158.15	1.22	11.77	11.78	11.69	15.81	21.4	55	Subhumid
Manipur	122.34	0.45	1.63	1.64	1.62	4.53	6.14	27	Humid
Meghalaya	126.21	0.46	1.49	1.49	1.48	4.52	6.12	24	Humid
Mizoram	193.25	0.67	2.01	2.01	2.0	6.57	8.9	23	Humid

(continued)

Table 15.9 (continued)

State	Annual costs of LD, in million USD	Annual costs of LD in terms of provisional ecosystem services only	Cost of action (6 years)	Cost of action (30 years)	Of which, opportunity cost of action	Cost of inaction (6 years)	Cost of inaction (30 years)	Ratio cost of action/inaction (%)	Agro-ecological zone
Nagaland	92.82	0.33	1.03	1.03	1.02	3.23	4.37	24	Humid
Orissa	333.26	1.68	11.84	11.86	11.76	19.88	26.91	44	Subhumid
Punjab	7.49	0.05	0.32	0.32	0.32	0.52	0.71	45	A&S
Rajasthan	405.34	2.95	13.78	13.81	13.63	26.3	35.6	39	A&S
Sikkim	28.71	0.11	0.31	0.31	0.3	1.03	1.39	22	Humid
Tamil Nadu	254.08	1.61	10.1	10.12	10.02	16.84	22.79	44	Subhumid
Tripura	147.25	0.53	1.68	1.69	1.67	5.19	7.03	24	Humid
Uttar Pradesh	130.13	0.73	4.25	4.26	4.22	7.57	10.24	42	Subhumid
Uttarakhand	205.11	0.87	3.17	3.18	3.14	8.35	11.3	28	Subhumid
West Bengal	84.89	0.55	4.22	4.22	4.19	6.36	8.61	49	Humid
Total	5152.46	27.38	161.36	161.6	160.11	292.51	395.95	41	

Source Authors' calculation based on the data extracted from Indian Ministry of Statistics and Programme Implementation; simulations based on TEEB and MODIS land cover datasets, agroecological zones defined according to IISD (2015). *Notes* A&S means arid and semi-arid

Focus Group Discussions

Focus Group Discussions were conducted in 8 villages from 2 districts. Ahmednagar in the western Maharashtra and Karnal in eastern part of Haryana were chosen. They both fall in the Hot semi-arid ecological zone. Six villages were selected from Ahmednagar and two were selected from Karnal for ground truthing exercise. The villages are depicted in Fig. 15.5. Table 15.10 presents the basic statistics of the village economy for the year 2013.

The FGD uncovered the following results. As for LUCC, the shrub land and grass land have come down in Hivare bazar of Ahmednagar, the grass land has increased in Karnal in both the villages. The major drivers of land use change are cited as infrastructure development, income increase, easier access to information technology and policies. For Hivare bazar livestock is as important as crops. Livestock population has drastically increased in this region in the last decade and that could be one reason that the grass land has been over exploited which led to its fall. This village also actively engaged in non-farm activities. As against this, villages in Haryana mainly depend on agriculture, uses machinery intensively on farm and as a result, the grassland has not witnessed a fall. About 50 % of the sample villages witnessed moderate to severe deforestation due to expansion of cropland. Almost 75 % perceived change in attitude towards higher interest in preserving cultural heritage.

The off-site eco system valuation from the perception of focal group participants of the village revealed that the benefits far exceed the costs. It was felt that community awareness, governmental policies would help contributing towards conservation of ecosystem. Many have revealed that they would be willing to contribute towards provision of any service that would improve their soil quality.

Drivers of Land Degradation

Survey of Literature

In mid-sixties, before the start of the Green revolution, increases in agricultural production in India were mainly achieved through expansion of the cultivated area, usually at the expense of community lands and forests. Since much of the area was brought under cultivation, or subject to grazing pressure, soil erosion and degradation had been substantial. The later advancements of Green revolution were mostly land saving. Therefore, it was believed that technological innovations will reduce pressure on marginal and sub-marginal lands, and thus, reduce further land degradation. However, the technological innovations were also capital intensive and not sufficiently labor-absorbing. Moreover, in many states, real wages either remained stagnant or declined between mid-1950s and mid-1970s, leading to lack

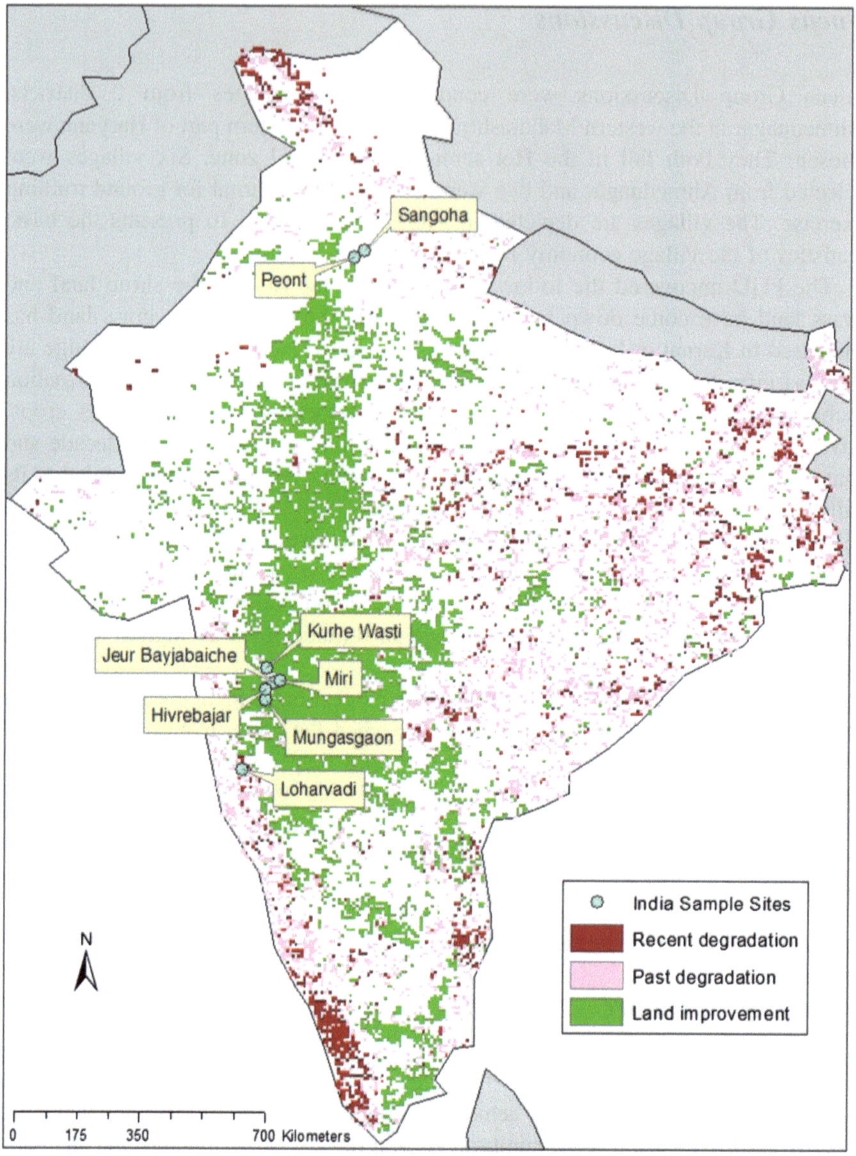

Fig. 15.5 Selected groundtruthing cites. *Source* FGD. Note: *Dark red* indicates pixels that demonstrate both long-term degradation as well as degradation in recent (2000–2006) years, *green pixels* indicate sites with improved land

of substantial increase in the incomes of the poor agricultural households, who continued exploiting forest resources (Hanumantha Rao 1994).

On the investment front, rising demand was not matched with adequate investment to augment the yield potential of the land resources. Degradation could

Table 15.10 Status of the villages in 2013

District	Villages in Ahmed Nagar district						Villages in Karnal district	
Particulars	Loharwadi	Mungusgaon	Hivare Bazar	Miri	Jeur	Pimpri-Gouli	Peont	Sangoha
No. of Households	1500	1450	1350	2000	1200	972	775	1065
Villagers engaged in								
Agriculture (%)	80	95	100	98	80	100	100	100
Crop (%)	80	100	100	98	100	100	100	100
Livestock (%)	5	10	100	90	70	50	50	100
Forest (%)	0	5	75	5	0	20	0	0
Fisheries (%)	0	0	0	0	0	0	0	0
Non-agriculture (%)	0	7	100	10	0	70	0	0

Source Focus group discussions

be perceived as a consequence of the failure to cope with the rising demand for food, fodder, fuel wood and other forest products through necessary investment in technological change and institutional arrangement for managing the resources. The agrarian change in India is different in different regions and hence problem of degradation is different. The regions with intensive cultivation which caused land degradation problems are, Punjab, Haryana, West Uttar Pradesh, and the deltaic regions of Andhra Pradesh and Tamil Nadu. This region is characterised by more intensive application of inputs, irrigation, fertiliser and pesticide, HYV seeds and mechanisation. Increasing demand for labour has resulted in higher wages and hence lower poverty. The other extreme is the region with more extension of area to ecologically fragile lands ranging from arid and semi-arid zones with low and uncertain rainfall, to hilly areas with assured rainfall. They have comparative advantage in animal husbandry, forestry and horticulture. They are characterised by increasing poverty and pressure for land under cultivation. In between these two types lies the majority of area. The progress of irrigation and land augmenting technological change is slow. Expansion of area under cultivation is moderate and mechanisation is slow. They exert pressure on common lands.

The existing studies on the link between land degradation and socioeconomic variables are very few. In fact there is only one systematic attempt on the determinants of land degradation in India (Reddy 2003). But this study deals only with district level and state level data and not at the household level. Some empirical studies have rejected the direct relation between poverty and resource degradation (Nadkarni 1990; Jodha 1986; Reddy 1999). These studies argue that the poor have greater motivation to conserve the resource because their livelihood depends on it; they are often victims of degradation and not the cause of degradation.

Reddy (2003) has conducted an empirical exercise using a regression technique to find the determinants of degradation at the district level and at the state level. The proportion of area degraded under various components to the total geographical area of the region (Source: NRSA) is the dependent variable. The regressors consist of: Socioeconomic, demographic, technological, institutional and climatic factors. At the district level, the period of analysis is 1986–93, while at the state level, the analysis was conducted for the 3 periods, 1981–82, 1988–89 and 1986–93. The state-wise analysis reveals that land-man ratio (defined as rural population per hectare of net sown area) exerts significantly positive influence on degradation, meaning that higher population pressure on agricultural land is not the cause of land degradation. The regions of intensive cultivation are actually less prone to degradation. In the district level analysis, there were 3 different regressions, one each for total degraded, salt affected and water logged area. For the salt affected land, percentage of irrigated area and population density, as expected, imposed a significantly positive influence; output per hectare imposed a negative influence.

From Reddy's (2003) analysis it appeared that better carrying capacity of lands support higher population densities. Hence no direct relationship was revealed between poverty and degradation. Per capita income does not exert any influence on degradation. Output per hectare is inversely related to land degradation indicating that regions with higher productive land are less prone to degradation. Rainfall does not have any bearing on degradation. Even the variable on availability of institutional credit has no impact on extent of degradation.

From a case study of Maharashtra, Joshi et al. (1996) has found that the investment for the mitigation of land degradation always gets the last priority. Farmers are enthusiastically willing to spend family labour time for conservation activities. It has been found that farmers are rational in following soil conservation methods. Absence of direct economic benefit results in non-adoption (Chopra 1996). The solution here would be the creation of incentives by the state. Most of the conservation technologies are capital intensive and hence needs support from the state.

Various programs initiated by the government over time have impacted land management directly and indirectly (Annex Table A.3) and studies on impact of programs on land management have shown that programs such as Wasteland Development Programs and Watershed Development Programs have mitigated degradation.

Empirical Analysis of Drivers of Land Degradation

We analyse the drivers of land degradation both on the macro (comparing states) as well as on the micro (comparing households) level. As the results of existing state-level analyses were based on the data for the period before 2000, it is hence proposed to update the analysis using the data of post 2000 periods. For this purpose, we have selected 13 states[4] of India which have significant land degradation due to soil erosion and the time periods are 2000, 2005, 2007 and 2010, the years for which data are available for soil erosion. The model to estimate follows a panel design and is given by

$$Y_{s,t} = \alpha_s + \beta_1 x_{s,t} + \beta_1 z_{s,t} + \varepsilon_{s,t} \tag{15.1}$$

where s denotes the observed state and t is the year of observation. Our dependent variable Y is 'waste land' which is the area affected by soil erosion. We regressed this with the host of influencing agricultural variables captured by the vector x, such as number of cultivators per unit of area, cropping intensity, fertiliser consumption or fertiliser subsidy, percentage of irrigated area, and yield. We control for a state-dependent characteristics, GDP, population density, poverty ratio and literacy rate. All the variables except the dummies have been used in logarithmic form in the estimation.

Additionally to the state-level analysis, we also perform an analysis of drivers of land degradation at household level. More specifically, the unit of observation is a

[4]The selected states are: Andhra Pradesh, Bihar, Gujarat, Haryana, Karnataka, Madhya Pradesh (including Chattisgarh), Maharashtra, Orissa, Punjab, Rajasthan, Tamilnadu, Uttar Pradesh and West Bengal.

plot cultivated by a household, where households may own more than one plot. To achieve this, the Cost of Cultivation Survey (CCS)[5] dataset is employed, which is conducted annually, covering 19 Indian states. The dependent variable is the plot level of soil erosion perceived by farmers themselves, serving as a proxy for land degradation, with 4 possible states in ranked order (none, sheet erosion, small gullies, large gullies). For this reason we regress soil erosion on household characteristics and plot specific information in an ordered probit regression framework:

$$Pr(LD_{ij}^{t+1} = k) = \Phi(\mu_k - \beta \mathbf{X}_{ij}^t) - \Phi(\mu_{k-1} - \beta' \mathbf{X}_{ij}^t) \quad (15.2)$$

where

$i = 1,\ldots, N$	households
$j = 1,\ldots, M_i$	plots for the ith households
$k = 1,\ldots, 4$	ordered outcomes
$t = 2005$	the base year
$\mu_{-1} = -\infty$	and $\mu_4 = \infty$

Vector X_{ij} contains socio-demographic characteristics of the household and plot-specific information, which is further explained in the next section.

Data and Variables

For the state-level analysis, information on the extent of wastelands per state was obtained from various sources, and is measured in 1000 ha.[6] The variables considered independent for our purposes can be summarized as follows:

Gross agricultural State Domestic Product per capita: The Gross state Domestic Product from agriculture and allied activities was considered at the constant prices of 1999–2000 for this variable. Since the 2010 GSDP was available only at 2004–05 prices, it was converted at 1999–2000 prices using an implicit price deflator.
Number of Cultivators per cultivated area: The Number of cultivators per unit of cultivated area measures the density of farm holdings in the available area. This is measured in number of cultivators per 1000 ha.

[5]Indian Commission for Agricultural Costs and Prices (CACP), Comprehensive Cost of Cultivation scheme for the year 2005–06 and 2006–07, Indian directorate of economics and statistics, Ministry of Agriculture.

[6]Degraded and wastelands of India, status and spatial distribution, ICAR, 2010; Wastelands Atlas of India by National remote sensing agency, 2000; *Degraded and Wastelands of India—Status and Spatial Distribution*, Indian Council of Agricultural Research and National Academy of Agricultural Sciences, New Delhi, June 2010, website (http://www.icar.org.in/files/Degraded-and-Wastelands.pdf). Wasteland atlas of India by National remote sensing agency, 2005; Statistics released by ministry of rural development, Govt. of India.

Fertiliser subsidy: The fertiliser subsidy was available at the national level and it was allocated using the weights of fertiliser consumption share of the state to the all India consumption.
Cropping Intensity: The cropping intensity, measured as ratio of gross cropped area over net sown area, was collected from the database available at Ministry of agriculture, Government of India.
Population density: The population density is measured as population in 1000 km^{-2} of geographical area of the state.
Rural Poverty ratio and the literacy rates: The poverty ratios and the literacy rates have been interpolated for the study years from the available years. Poverty ratio was available for the years 1996–97, 2001–02, 2006–07 and 2011–12 whereas literacy rates were available on the decadal basis for the years 1991, 2001 and 2011. The data were taken from Ministry of Statistics and Programme Implementation and Rural development statistics, National Institute of Rural Development.
Yield: The yield of major food grains is the value added in agriculture per hectare of cultivated area.
Percentage of Irrigated area: The percentage of irrigated area has been calculated by dividing the net irrigated area by net sown area.

To account for spatial differences, dummy variables are used for each region, North, West, East while keeping South as the reference category. Data for all described variables were compiled from different sources.[7]

For the micro level analysis, several items asked for in the CCS are considered as explanatory for the extent of soil erosion. Household demographics include highest education completed, age, time available for work (all given for head of household), a dummy denoting if the head of household is female, size of the household as well as proxies for the household's wealth: the log value of livestock, the number of livestock and the log value of physical assets. Plot specific information entails quality of drainage, the number of different crops grown on the plot, the number of seasons where crops are grown and the total area of the plot, as well as dummies for irrigation, property of land and land use. While those variables are cross sectional as of 2005, the CCS data also includes monthly data on crop inputs between 2005 and 2006, where the intensity in the application of organic manure, chemical fertilizers, and pesticides are of interest. Data on agricultural extension, and sources of farmer's information, were not available in the data. To account for correlation in the dependent variable within villages, standard errors are clustered on the village level.

---

[7]Source: Yield, The Gross State Domestic Product, Percentage of Irrigated area for the year 2010, Number of Cultivators, Cultivated area and fertiliser consumption has been collected from The Agriculture statistics at a glance, 2003; 2007, 2010 and 2013. The Irrigated area and the net sown area for the years 2000, 2005 and 2007 has been taken from Ministry of agriculture, Govt. of India. Whereas the fertiliser subsidy has been taken from: Lok Sabha Unstarred Question No. 2623, dated 23.07.2009, the statistics released by: Lok Sabha Starred Question No. 121, dated on 11.3.2005, statistics released by: Lok sabha Unstarred Question No. 2484, dated 10.03.2011 and Unstarred question no. 1810, dated 01.12.2011.

Estimation

State Level Analysis

This section reviews the results of the econometric estimation, starting with the state-level panel regression. Table 15.11 presents the basic statistics of the variables considered for the regression.

Since panel methodology has been used to find the estimates, the Hausman test was conducted first to decide if the model follows Fixed Effect or Random Effect model. The Hausman test for testing fixed effect vs random effect did not reject the random effects model. Hence we ran the panel model of random effects with wasteland as the dependent variable and the results are presented in Table 15.12.

Fertiliser subsidy turns out be a major determinant of land degradation. This has also been a talking point recently in the academic literature as well as policy forums and reports and action is being proposed in the plan documents for a phase wise withdrawal of input subsidies. However due to political pressure, lobbying by farmers' group, government is not able to cut down subsidies on fertilizer in a desirable manner. According to the coefficient, a 1 % reduction in subsidy is likely to reduce land degradation by nearly 3 %. Population density and poverty ratio, coefficients of both are statistically significant but signs are other than expected. They show that these two variables cannot be held as reasons for land degradation. The results of poverty ratio-land degradation link also corroborates the results of other studies (e.g. Reddy 2003), that poor are victims rather than a cause of land degradation.

A negative coefficient for yield negates the prevailing argument that more intensive application of inputs in search of better yield in the short run results in soil degradation. The coefficient indicates that efforts to bring in 1 % more yield can in

Table 15.11 Basic statistics for state level variables

Variable	Mean	Std. Dev.	Min	Max
Waste lands	3186	4242	1	15,887
Yield	2062	895	757	4280
GSDP	6112	2626	2496	12,905
Fertiliser subsidy	2584	2136	265	10,104
Density of Cultivators per unit of cultivated area	785	416	96	1850
Irrigated area (%)	51	23	20	98
Cropping intensity	152	39	111	267
Population density	27,831	18,395	5122	70,923
Rural Poverty ratio (%)	24	11	6	48
Rural Literacy rate (%)	63	7	44	77

Source The authors

Table 15.12 Estimates of random effect model

Explanatory variables	Coefficient	Z value
Yield	−0.8765*	−2.68
Fertiliser subsidy	2.937*	8.73
Population density	−3.5083*	−5.11
Sectoral GDP from agriculture per capita	0.5786	0.63
Density of cultivators	0.9026*	2.22
Cropping intensity	1.3688	1.56
% of irrigated area	0.9326	1.03
Poverty ratio	−0.4795	−1.16
Literacy rate	3.9741*	2.02
Dummy variables		
Northern	0.1914	0.28
Eastern	1.8706*	2.86
Western	−0.8709	−1.54
Constant	−6.7865	−0.69
Wald Chi^2	153.23*	
Observations	52	

Source The authors
Note The dependent variable is area affected by soil erosion. All the variables except dummies are expressed in logarithm. Hence the coefficients directly measure elasticities
*Indicates significance at 5 % level

fact reduce soil degradation by about 0.9 %. Inclusion of cropping intensity as a variable has helped in holding the intensity of application constant. Hence the other factors which help in increasing the yield, namely soil conservation measures, better irrigation system, etc. gives a negative coefficient for this variable. The number of cultivators per unit of cultivated area which is a measure of land scarcity, as expected, shows a positive relation. It indicates that a 1 % increase in this measure will lead to nearly 0.9 % increase in soil degradation. The rural literacy rate has given a wrong sign as the increase in literacy leads to increased degradation. However this measure is debatable since quality of education in rural areas varies substantially and is not accounted for in this simple measure of literacy. Variables such as Agriculture value added per capita, cropping intensity, percentage of irrigated area did not give statistically significant coefficients even though they all have their expected sign. The agricultural GDP per capita is an indicator for rural growth. Growth versus resource degradation literature debates on Environmental Kuznets curve (EKC) theory that in the phase of initial growth, more environmental harm will take place which will slowly decline along the growth path and once the threshold level is reached, further growth will be environmental friendly. Hence we can say that the income per capita is yet to reach the threshold level.

The coefficients of regional dummies indicate that, as compared to the southern region, the northern and eastern regions suffer from more degradation, holding everything else constant, and the western region is subject to less land degradation. The northern region allots a larger percentage of land to cereal crops due to which it is likely that over-application of fertilizer and water causes more degradation. Some parts of the eastern region receive a maximum quantum of rainfall. Hence the possibility of water induced soil erosion is higher in this region if the rainfall is not scattered across region or time.

The Household Plot Level Analysis

This section presents the analysis of drivers of land degradation on the household level as described in the methodology. Since soil erosion induced by water is unambiguously the major symptom of land degradation in India, as shown in Table 15.2, it is regarded as a suitable proxy for land degradation in a broader sense. Table 15.13 displays descriptive statistics of all the variables used in the analysis.

The main results are depicted in Table 15.14, first column. They show that the higher the frequency of application of organic manure, as well as chemical fertilizers, the lower the likelihood of soil erosion, given equal characteristics, where the effects are significant at 1 %. The use of pesticides, in contrast, is found to increase the occurrence of soil erosion. The number of different crops grown within the time span of the monthly survey also significantly ($p < 0.001$) drives the extent of soil erosion. The quality of drainage exposes a U-shaped influence on erosion, where a good drainage system fosters erosion and a mediocre one works against it, compared to bad quality drainage. Erosion is rather present on large fields, as shown by the positive significant coefficient of the plot area. Other variables that are negatively associated with erosion are the education dummies (relative to the category "illiterate") and the time of the household head devoted to work on the parcel. Interestingly, land property is positively associated with soil erosion, which might hint at a certain degree of insecurity in land tenure.

The second column of Table 15.14 displays results with state fixed effects, which account for some variation. While some variables display lower coefficients, the main explanatory variables, namely application of manure and fertilizer, respectively, remain significant in their explanatory power. The last two columns run a usual probit, where erosion is measured with two outcomes, "yes" or "no", regardless of the extent. The results are qualitatively similar, with the coefficients for use of manure and fertilizer still on a high level, while use of pesticides does not significantly explain erosion. The positive effect of organic manure application than the effect of fertilizer application is stronger in all four specifications. Thus, the application of manure seems to be more sustainable way in terms of land conservation compared to the utilization of chemical fertilizer or pesticides.

Table 15.13 Descriptive statistics of variables from CACP household survey

Variable	Observations	Mean	Std. Dev.	Min	Max
Erosion					
None	21,044	0.747	0.435		
Sheet erosion	21,044	0.187	0.390	0	1
Small gullies	21,044	0.057	0.232	0	1
Large gullies	21,044	0.009	0.093	0	1
Land use					
Crops	23,139	0.903	0.295	0	1
Fallows	23,139	0.015	0.123	0	1
Other	23,139	0.081	0.273		
Drainage					
Poor	22,263	0.192	0.394		
Middling	22,263	0.327	0.469	0	1
Good	22,263	0.481	0.500	0	1
Education					
Illiterate	22,409	0.196	0.397		
Up to primary	22,409	0.264	0.441	0	1
Up to secondary	22,409	0.279	0.449	0	1
Secondary	22,409	0.140	0.347	0	1
Post-secondary	22,409	0.121	0.326	0	1
Frequency of manure applied	19,891	0.688	1.261	0	32
Frequency of fertilizer applied	19,891	4.399	4.442	0	60
Frequency of pesticides applied	19,891	1.221	2.647	0	50
Total area	22,391	1.034	1.241	0	42
Time available to work	22,424	65.181	35.271	0	101
Female head	22,424	0.033	0.180	0	1
Plot irrigated	22,387	0.566	0.496	0	1
Land owned and managed	22,391	0.976	0.153	0	1
Household size	22,424	6.847	3.597	1	40
Age of household head	22,424	52.616	13.685	0	105
Livestock value (log)	23,129	7.901	3.806	0	12.60
Asset value (log)	23,139	10.059	2.113	0	15.26
Livestock present	23,139	0.182	0.386	0	1
# of crops grown	20,096	1.852	1.265	1	13
# of cropping seasons	20,096	1.583	0.680	1	4

Overall, it emerges that agricultural industry on a larger scale seems to drive land degradation. The larger the cultivated area, and the more crops are grown on it, the more a plot is affected by soil erosion. Sustainable land management practices help to work against this kind of degradation, such as feeding the soil with organic

Table 15.14 Estimation results from the ordered probit model

	(1) Ordered probit	(2) Ordered probit, state FE	(3) Ordinary probit	(4) Ordinary probit, state FE
# of times manure applied	−0.087***	−0.097***	−0.098***	−0.105***
	(−4.629)	(−4.648)	(−4.735)	(−4.495)
# of times fertilizer applied	−0.052***	−0.026***	−0.047***	−0.020*
	(−7.258)	(−3.433)	(−6.304)	(−2.564)
# of times pesticides applied	0.024*	0.016	0.028*	0.017
	(2.455)	(1.623)	(2.441)	(1.412)
Irrigation: plot irrigated	−0.09	−0.05	−0.076	−0.024
	(−1.807)	(−0.943)	(−1.408)	(−0.406)
Tenure: land owned and managed	0.338**	0.038	0.299*	−0.044
	(2.786)	(0.301)	(2.267)	(−0.297)
Land use: crops	0.083	−0.345	0.25	−0.27
	(0.217)	(−0.938)	(0.735)	(−0.801)
Land use: fallows	0.145	−0.235	0.431	0.009
	(0.315)	(−0.534)	(0.933)	(0.019)
Drainage: middling	0.154*	0.147*	0.146	0.154
	(2.230)	(1.968)	(1.886)	(1.768)
Drainage: good	−0.174**	−0.147*	−0.201**	−0.155
	(−2.729)	(−2.091)	(−2.792)	(−1.863)
Education: up to primary	−0.150**	−0.142*	−0.137*	−0.150*
	(−2.776)	(−2.502)	(−2.457)	(−2.514)
Education: up to secondary	−0.04	0.026	−0.027	0.027
	(−0.691)	(0.425)	(−0.428)	(0.420)
Education: secondary	−0.167*	−0.146	−0.154	−0.152
	(−2.276)	(−1.893)	(−1.958)	(−1.826)
Education: post-secondary	−0.154*	−0.115	−0.098	−0.081
	(−2.167)	(−1.518)	(−1.274)	(−1.000)
Total area	0.051***	0.012	0.046**	−0.002
	(3.452)	(0.739)	(2.882)	(−0.095)
Time available to work	−0.003***	−0.001	−0.003***	−0.001
	(−4.751)	(−1.922)	(−4.287)	(−1.467)
Female head	−0.098	−0.211	−0.144	−0.307*
	(−0.848)	(−1.731)	(−1.301)	(−2.497)
Household size	0.001	0.005	0.000	0.004
	(0.183)	(0.677)	(−0.054)	(0.498)
Age (head)	−0.002	−0.001	0.000	0.000
	(−1.044)	(−0.642)	(−0.289)	(0.029)
Livestock value	−0.062*	−0.027	−0.072*	−0.028
	(−2.201)	(−0.941)	(−2.336)	(−0.904)

(continued)

Table 15.14 (continued)

	(1) Ordered probit	(2) Ordered probit, state FE	(3) Ordinary probit	(4) Ordinary probit, state FE
Asset value	0.036*	−0.002	0.044**	0.011
	(2.304)	(−0.122)	(2.624)	(0.584)
Livestock present	−0.549*	−0.269	−0.621*	−0.276
	(−2.049)	(−0.998)	(−2.113)	(−0.934)
# of crops grown	0.100***	0.075***	0.093***	0.086***
	(6.294)	(4.532)	(5.159)	(4.617)
# of cropping seasons	−0.041	−0.028	−0.033	−0.022
	(−1.138)	(−0.717)	(−0.830)	(−0.479)
Constant			−0.528	−0.248
			(−1.092)	(−0.430)
μ_1	0.345	−0.25		
	(0.700)	(−0.423)		
μ_2	1.289**	0.759		
	(2.614)	(1.277)		
μ_3	2.252***	1.746**		
	(4.540)	(2.949)		
State fixed effects	No	Yes	No	Yes
Observations	16,649	16,649	16,649	16,649
Pseudo R-squared	0.041	0.100	0.048	0.135

Source CACP, calculation by the authors
t-statistics shown in parentheses
$^*p < 0.05$, $^{**}p < 0.01$, $^{***}p < 0.001$. Standard errors clustered on the village level

manure, or usage of a well-working drainage system, which prevents loss of water and increases water use efficiency. If livestock is held on a plot, this likewise seems to help the soil recover, possibly because the area is then cultivated less intensively. Some of the results' magnitude shrink considerably when controlling for state effects, which points at systematic differences in the surrounding conditions and agriculture practices across regions. For instance, land tenure exhibits no meaningful influence on soil erosion, once state fixed effects are included. This may hint at different legislations regarding land tenure security between states. No effect can be attributed to irrigation, which means that neither rainfed nor irrigated plots are stronger affected per se, and sustainable land management practices are expected to have a desired outcome in both.

Concluding Remarks

Understanding the major causes of land degradation is important for finding solution to mitigate the problem. Our analysis on drivers of land degradation shows that fertiliser subsidy and decreasing land-man ratio are important reasons for increasing land degradation. At the household level, the quality of the drainage system, as well as application of organic manure may significantly reduce soil erosion. A larger operated area, and a higher number of different crops grown, both increase degradation. This hints at sustainable land management practices reducing erosion.

While access to irrigation checks degradation, poor management of irrigation water itself contributes to degradation. Proper management of irrigation water will go a long way in controlling degradation. If wastage of water is tackled, it would help in reducing water logging and salinity problems. Judicious management of forests through the right kind of institutional mechanism would help in checking water and wind erosion, which forms a major share of total degradation.

Water and energy are underpriced which leads to inefficient use of land and water. However, energy pricing is a political pursuit in India. Unless the scarcity of the resource is reflected in pricing, overutilization of the resource continues to occur which in turn increases degradation. Agricultural extension services is another factor that needs to be strengthened for training the users of the land for the adoption of resource conserving technologies.

Creating awareness and ownership rights for cultivators are important steps in the challenge of mitigating land degradation. The solution lies in changing the behaviour of the farmer through the right set of institutional arrangements and market based instruments. Identifying all the stakeholders of land improvement, viz. farmers, farm labour, industries and institutions and how they are impacted by the policies related to the improvement would help in finding a comprehensive solution. This awaits further analysis.

Acknowledgments We are thankful to Dr. Vijaylaxmi Pandey, IGIDR for useful discussions on an earlier draft, Dr. Nandan Nawn, Indian Society for Ecological Economics and Teri University for helping us in gathering data of Cost of Cultivation Scheme and Ms. Arpita Nehra, former Intern, IGIDR for her help in collecting data for the state level analysis.

Annex

(See Tables A.1, A.2 and A.3).

Table A.1 Land use dynamics in India

Classification	Area in million hectares					
	1970–71	1980–81	1990–91	2000–01	2010–11	% Change from 1970–71 to 2010–11
Geographical area (reported)	303.76	304.15	304.86	305.12	305.9	
	(100)					
1. Forest	63.91	67.47	67.8	69.53	70	9.53
	(21.04)					
2. Not available for cultivation	44.64	39.62	40.48	41.48	43.56	−2.42
	(14.7)					
(a) Non Agricultural uses	16.48	19.66	21.09	23.86	26.51	60.86
	(5.43)					
(b) Barren and uncultivable land	28.16	19.66	19.39	17.6	17.05	−39.45
	(9.27)					
3. Other uncultivated land total	35.06	32.31	30.22	27.5	26.17	−25.36
(Excluding fallow land)	(11.54)					
(a) Permanent pastures and other grazing land	13.26	11.97	11.4	10.66	10.3	−22.32
	(4.37)					
(b) Land under Miscellaneous tree crops and groves not included in net area sown	4.3	3.6	3.82	3.46	3.21	−25.35
	(1.42)					
(c) Cultivable Waste land	17.5	16.74	15	13.63	12.66	−−27.66
	(5.76)					
4. Fallow land total	19.88	24.75	23.36	27.73	26.17	31.64
	(6.54)					
(a) Fallow land other than Current fallows	8.76	9.92	9.66	10.27	10.32	17.81
	(2.88)					
(b) Current Fallows	11.12	14.83	13.7	14.78	14.26	28.24
	(3.66)					
5. Net area sown (6–7)	140.27	140	143	141.34	141.58	0.93
	(46.18)					
6. Gross cropped area	165.79	172.63	185.74	185.34	198.97	20.01
	(54.58)					
7. Area sown more than once	25.52	32.63	42.74	44	57.39	124.88
	(8.4)					

Source Indiastat.com. *Note* Figures in the parentheses are percentages to geographical area

Table A.2 Policies/programs that have a bearing on Land Resource

Year	Programs/policies	Specific features
1977–78	Desert Development Program	Restoration of ecological balance by harnessing, conserving and developing natural resources
1980–81	Integrated watershed management in the catchment of flood-prone rivers	Enhance the productivity and tackle menace of floods
1985	National Land Use and Wasteland Development Council	Policy planning concerning the scientific management of the country's land resources development of wasteland
1985	National Land Use and Conservation Board	Formulate a national policy and perspective plan for conservation, management and development of land resources of the country Review of Progress of implementation of ongoing schemes and programs connected with conservation and development of land resources and soils
1985	National Wastelands Development Board	Formulate a perspective plan for the management and development of wastelands in the country Identify the waste land and assess the progress of programs and schemes for the development of wasteland Create a reliable data base and documentation centre for waste land development
1985–86	National Watershed Development Project for Rainfed Areas	Area approach to watershed development improve crop productivity Restore ecological balance
1985–86	Reclamation & development of Alkali & Acid soil	Reclamation of soil
1988	National Land Use Policy	To devise an effective administrative procedures for regulating land use To prevent further deterioration of land resources Restore the productivity of degraded lands Allocate land for different uses based on land capability, productivity and goals
1989–90	Integrated Wastelands Development Project	Adopt soil and moisture conservation measures such as terracing, bunding etc… To enhance people's participation in wasteland development programs
1992	Constitution (74th Amendment) Act, 1992	Regulation of land use and urban planning brought under the domain of urban self-governing bodies

(continued)

Table A.2 (continued)

Year	Programs/policies	Specific features
1992	Policy statement of Abatement of Pollution	Advocate use of mix of policy instruments in the form of legislation, regulation and fiscal incentives
1999	Department of Land Resources	Formulation of Integrated Land Resource Management Policies Implementation of land based development programs
2006	National Rainfed Area Authority	Sustainable and holistic development of rainfed areas

Source http://envfor.nic.in/

Table A.3 Land policy formulation through planning period

Plan period	Issues	Policy focus
First 1951–56	To increase area under cultivation	Land reform for efficient use of land and tenancy rights to cultivate land and abolition of intermediaries
Second 1956–61	Low productivity in dry land	Soil conservation, irrigation development, strengthen extension services
Third 1961–66	Food security, reclaiming cultiwable waste land and ways to tackle low growth regions to increase the growth	Intensive area development program, conducting soil surveys
Fourth 1969–74	Food security, ways to shifting land towards food crops, tackle allocation and technical inefficiency in production	Focus on soil and water conservation in dry regions, technological change, land ceiling Act, institutional changes
Fifth 1974–79	Irrigated land management, Drought-prone areas	Drought prone area and desert area development programs, focus on dry farming
Sixth 1980–85	Underutilisation of land resources	Land and water management programs
Seventh 1985–90	Soil erosion and land degradation, deforestation, degradation of forest land	Specific attention to soil and water conservation
Eighth 1992–97	Dryland and rainfed areas, importance of peoples participation in land management in villages recognised	Soil conservation integrated with watershed programs. Agroclimatic regional planning approach
Ninth 1997–2002	Faster rate of land degradation, revisit of Land reforms, tackling technical inefficiency, long term policy needed	Maintenance of village commons, Decentralised land management, Panchayat Raj institutions

(continued)

Table A.3 (continued)

Plan period	Issues	Policy focus
Tenth 2002–2007	Groundwater depletion and water logging	Rainwater harvesting, groundwater recharging measures and controlling groundwater exploitation, treatment of waterlogged areas
Eleventh 2007–2012	In addition to erosion, salinity and alkalinity, soils losing soil carbon and micronutrients due to irrational and unbalanced fertilizer use	Rationalise subsidies across nutrients, reform delivery method of subsidies, agriculture extension

Source Deshpande (2003) and five year plan documents

References

Bansil, P. C. (1990). *Agricultural statistical compendium* (Vol. 1). New Delhi: Techno-economic Research Institute.

Brandon, C. & Hommann, K. (1996). The cost of inaction: valuing the economy-wide cost of environmental degradation in India, UNU/IAS Working paper No. 9.

Chopra, K. (1996). The management of degraded land: issues and an analysis of technological and institutional solutions. *Indian Journal of Agricultural Economics, 51*, 1–2.

Das, D. C. (1977). Soil conservation practices and erosion control in India—a case study. *FAO Soils Bulletin, 33*, 11–50.

Deshpande, R. S. (2003). Current land policy Issues in India. In *Land Reform: Land Settlement and Cooperatives*. Rural Development Division, FAO.

Government of Punjab, Department of Planning (2014). State-wise statistics 2009–2011. http://pbplanning.gov.in/pdf/Statewise%20GSDP%20PCI%20and%20G.R.pdf. Accessed December 2014.

Hanumantha Rao, C. H. (1994). *Agricultural growth, rural poverty and environmental degradation in India*. Oxford: Oxford University Press.

IISD. (2015). Arid and semi-arid lands: Characteristics and importance. http://www.iisd.org/casl/asalprojectdetails/asal.htm. Accessed December 2014.

Indian Ministry of Statistics and Programme Implementation (2014). Gross state domestic products. http://mospi.nic.in/Mospi_New/upload/State_wise_SDP_2004-05_14mar12.pdf. Accessed December 2014.

Jodha, N. S. (1986). Common property resources and rural poor in dry regions of India. *Economic and Political Weekly, 21*(27), 1169–1181.

Joshi, P. K., Wani, S. P., Chopde, V. K., & Foster, J. (1996). Farmers' perception of land degradation: A case study. *Economic and Political Weekly, 31*(26), A89–A92.

Kapur, D., Ravindranath, D., Kishore, K., Sandeep, K., Priyadarshini, P., Kavoori, P. S., & Sinha, S. (2010). A commons story. The Rain Shadow of Green Revolution. FES.

Le Q. B., Nkonya, E., & Mirzabaev, A. (2014). Biomass productivity-based mapping of global land degradation hotspots, ZEF Discussion Paper on Development Policy No. 193, Centre for Development Research, University of Bonn.

Mani, M., Markandya, A, Sagar, A., & Strukova, E. (2012). An analysis of physical and monetary losses of environmental health and natural resources in India, Policy Research Working Paper No. 6219. The World Bank.

MEA (Millenium Ecosystem Assessment). (2005). Dryland Systems. In R. Hassan, R. Scholes, & N. Ash (Eds.), *Ecosystem and well-being: Current state and trends* (pp. 623–662). Washington, DC: Island Press.

Mukherjee, B. K., Das, D. C., Singh, Shamsher, Prasad, C. S., & Samuel, J. C. (1985). *Statistics: Soil and water conservation-watershed management, land resources and land Reclamation-soil and water conservation division*. GOI, New Delhi: Ministry of Agriculture and Rural Development.

Mythili, G. (2003). Land degradation due to agriculture. In *Envisage Newsletter,* Environmental Economics Node, Madras School of Economics, 2(1), 1–7.

Nadkarni, M. V. (1990). Use and management of Common lands: Towards an Environmentally Sound Strategy. In C. J. Saldanha (Ed.), *Karnataka: State of the Environment Report IV,* centre for Taxonomic Studies, Bangalore.

Narayana, V. V. D., & Babu, Ram. (1983). Estimation of soil erosion in India. *Journal of Irrigation and Drainage Engineering, 109*(4), 419–434.

Ninan, K. N. (2002). Watershed development programs in India: A review. Paper Presented at the 12th ISCO Conference, Beijing, 2002.

Nkonya, E., Gerber, N., Von Braun J., & De Pinto, A. (2011). Economics of land degradation: The costs of action versus inaction. *International Food Policy Research Institute Brief 68*, IFPRI and ZEF, Bonn.

Nkonya, E., von Braun, J., Mirzabaev, A., Le, Q. B. Kwon H. Y. & Kirui, O. (2013). Economics of land degradation initiative: Methods and approach for global and national assessments. ZEF Discussion Papers 183.

Parikh, K. S. (1989). An operational measureable definition of sustainable development, Indira Gandhi Institute of Development Research, Discussion paper No. 21.

Parikh, K. S. & Ghosh, U. (1991). Natural resource accounting for soils: Towards an empirical estimate of costs of soil degradation in India. Indira Gandhi Institute of Development Research Discussion Paper No. 48.

Ratna, Reddy V. (1999). Valuation of renewable natural resource: User perspective. *Economic and Political Weekly, 34*(23), 1435–1444.

Reddy, V. R. (2003). Land degradation in India: Extent, costs and determinants. *Economic and Political Weekly, 38*(44), 4700–4713.

Sehgal, J., & Abrol, I. P. (1994). *Soil degradation in India: Status and impact*. Oxford: Oxford and IBH.

Singh, N. T. (1994). Land degradation and remedial measures with reference to salinity, alkalinity, waterlogging and acidity. In D. L. Deb (Ed.), *Natural resource management for sustainable agriculture and environment* (pp. 109–142), Noida, India.

Singh, G., Babu, R., Bhushan, N., & Abrol, I. P. (1990). Soil erosion rates in India. *Journal of Soil and Water Conservation, 47*(1), 97–99.

State of the Environment India. (2001). Land degradation, Part III http://envfor.nic.in/sites/default/files/soer/2001/soer.html. Accessed February 2014.

TEEB (The Economics of Ecosystems and Biodiversity). (2010). *Mainstreaming the economics of nature: A synthesis of the approach*. Malta: Conclusions and Recommendations of TEEB.

TERI. (1998). *Green India 2047: Looking Back to Think Ahead.* In R. K. Pachauri, & P. V. Sridharan (Eds.), Tata energy research Institute, New Delhi.

UNDP, FAO and UNEP. (1993). Land degradation in South Asia: Its severity, causes and effects upon the people. Rome: FAO, World Soil Research Report No. 78.

Vasisht, A. K., Singh, R. P., & Mathur, V. C. (2003). Economic implications of land degradation on sustainability and food security in India. *Agropedology, 13*(2), 19–27.

von Braun, J., Gerber, N., Mirzabaev, A., & Nkonya, E. (2013). The economics of land degradation. An Issue Paper for Global Soil Week. Berlin, Germany 08–22 November, 2012.

Chapter 16
Economics of Land Degradation and Improvement in Kenya

Wellington Mulinge, Patrick Gicheru, Festus Murithi, Peter Maingi, Evelyne Kihiu, Oliver K. Kirui and Alisher Mirzabaev

Abstract Kenya is an agricultural nation, with over 12 million people residing in areas with degraded lands. Unfortunately, the food crop productivity growth in the country has failed to exceed the population growth. The growth of agricultural output in Kenya is constrained by many challenges including soil erosion, low productivity, agro-biodiversity loss, and soil nutrient depletion. Land exploitation devoid of proper compensating investments in soil and water conservation will lead to severe land degradation. This will translate to loss of rural livelihoods, diminished water supplies and threaten the wildlife habitat. This study explores the causes, extent and impacts of land degradation in Kenya, discusses the costs of action versus inaction in rehabilitating degraded lands, and proposes policy options for promoting sustainable land management (SLM). In order to appropriately support SLM, there is a need to account for the total economic value (TEV) of land degradation, i.e. including the value of both provisioning and indirect ecosystem services of land. Using such a TEV approach, findings show that the costs of land degradation due to land use and land cover changes (LUCC) in Kenya reach the equivalent of 1.3 billion USD annually between 2001 and 2009. Moreover, the costs of rangeland degradation calculated through losses in milk and meat production, as well as in livestock live weight decreases reach about 80 million USD annually. Furthermore, the costs of "soil nutrient mining" leading to lower yields for three crops, namely wheat, maize and rice in Kenya were estimated at about 270 million USD annually. The cost of taking action

W. Mulinge (✉) · P. Gicheru · F. Murithi · P. Maingi
Kenya Agricultural and Livestock Research Organization (KALRO), KALRO Headquarters, Kaptagat Road, Off Waiyaki Way, P.O. Box 57811–00200 Nairobi, Kenya
e-mail: wellington.mulinge@kalro.org

E. Kihiu · O.K. Kirui · A. Mirzabaev
Center for Development Research, University of Bonn, Walter Flex Str 3, 53113 Bonn, Germany
e-mail: evelynenyathira@yahoo.com

O.K. Kirui
e-mail: okirui@uni-bonn.de

A. Mirzabaev
e-mail: almir@uni-bonn.de

E. Nkonya et al. (eds.), *Economics of Land Degradation and Improvement – A Global Assessment for Sustainable Development*,
DOI 10.1007/978-3-319-19168-3_16

to rehabilitate lands degraded through LUCC is found to be lower than the cost of inaction by 4 times over a 30 year period, i.e. each dollar invested in land rehabilitation is likely to yield four dollars of returns. This may strongly justify the urgent need for taking action against land degradation. Addressing land degradation involves investments in SLM. Our econometric results show that improving access to information on SLM and to the markets (input, output, financial) may likely stimulate investments into SLM by agricultural households.

Keywords Economics of land degradation · Drivers of land degradation · Sustainable land management · Cost of land degradation · Kenya

Introduction

Land degradation is a multi-faceted and complex phenomenon (Mbow et al. 2015). The United Nations Convention to Combat Desertification, (UNCCD) defines land itself as "the terrestrial bio-productive system that comprises soil, vegetation, other biota, and the ecological and hydrological processes that operate within the system." It further defines land degradation as a "reduction or loss in arid, semi-arid, and dry sub-humid areas, of the biological or economic productivity and complexity of rain-fed cropland, irrigated cropland, or range, pasture, forest, and woodlands resulting from land uses or from a process or combination of processes, including processes arising from human activities and habitation patterns, such as: (i) soil erosion caused by wind and/or water; (ii) deterioration of the physical, chemical, and biological or economic properties of soil; and (iii) long-term loss of natural vegetation" (UNCCD 2013). On the other hand, the Global Environment Facility (GEF) further describes land degradation as "any form of deterioration of the natural potential of land that affects ecosystem integrity either in terms of reducing its sustainable ecological productivity or in terms of its native biological richness and maintenance of resilience" (UNCCD 2013). Muchena et al. (2005a, b) define land degradation as a "loss in productivity of the land and its ability to provide quantitative or qualitative goods or services as a result of natural and human- induced changes in physical, chemical and biological processes". Land degradation is also defined as "reduction of the current or future capacity of land to produce" (Oluwole and Sikhalazo 2008). All these definitions imply that the costs of land degradation are manifested not only through the losses in tangible goods and services derived from land, such as food or feed, but also include the non-provisional ecosystem services, such as carbon sequestration, water purification, etc. (Nkonya et al. 2011), thus necessitating Total Economic Value approaches (Chap. 2) to comprehensively evaluate these losses.

It is widely acknowledged that land degradation remains an important problem affecting the sustainable development of many regions in the globe, especially Sub-Saharan Africa (Nkonya et al. 2011; Lal et al. 2013; von Braun et al. 2013).

Land degradation is complex and varies from place to place and over time. Thus, its exact measurements are difficult (Waswa 2012). The importance of land will remain critical in the years to come (Eswaran and Lal 2001). Moreover, land degradation is poised to diminish land productivity, especially in dry areas. Land degradation can also lead to loss of vegetation cover and thus make them susceptible to climatic hazards like droughts. Without sustainable use and management of land and soil resources, global sustainable development and environmental sustainability are unlikely to be attained (Lal et al. 2012; EAA 2005).

Land degradation is threatening the livelihoods of millions of people, who depend on land ecosystem goods and services the world over for their livelihoods, including in the dry lands of Kenya (Muia and Ndunda 2013). Kenya is an agricultural nation, with over 12 million people residing in areas with degraded lands (Bai et al. 2008; Le et al. 2014). Unfortunately, the food crop productivity growth in the country has over the last decades failed to exceed population growth (Waswa 2012). On average, the productivity of the major cereal—maize—is less than 1 metric ton per ha on most smallholder plots (Muasya and Diallo 2001; cited by Waswa 2012). Land degradation and the associated "nutrient mining" have also lead to this outcome, with significant impacts on rural livelihoods and the overall economy (Maitima et al. 2009; Henao and Baanante 2006).

The rural poor primarily depend on natural resources (especially land) for their livelihoods. Degradation of these productive resources will thus affect them disproportionately higher (Nkonya et al. 2008a, b). For example, in Kenya, the yield of most smallholder maize farmers in Kisii County was less than 2 tons/ha as compared to on-station yields of about 9 tons/ha (Nzabi et al. 2000). These low harvests are attributed to deteriorating soil fertility as a result of continuous cropping, soil erosion, non-use or inadequate use of both organic and inorganic fertilizers (Kamoni and Makhoha 2010).

Unfortunately, there exists no sufficient monitoring of land degradation issues both at national and local scales in Kenya (Waswa 2012). The growth of agricultural output in Kenya is constrained by many challenges including soil erosion, low productivity, agro-biodiversity loss, and soil nutrient depletion (GoK 2007). Land exploitation devoid of proper compensating investments in soil and water conservation will lead to severe land degradation (GoK 2013a).

This study seeks to explore the causes, extent and impacts of land degradation in Kenya, evaluate the costs of action versus inaction in rehabilitating degraded lands, and propose policy measures that can be instituted to address land degradation. In doing so, the study seeks to find answers to three research questions, namely: (1) What are the key causes of land degradation in Kenya? (2) What are the economic costs of land degradation and net benefits resulting from taking actions against land degradation? (3) What are the feasible policy and development strategies that can enable and catalyze sustainable land management (SLM)?

Literature Review

Extent of Land Degradation in Kenya

The major land degradation problems of Kenya are the loss of soil fertility through so called "soil nutrient mining", wind and water erosion of the soils, rangeland degradation, deforestation and desertification. The loss of soil by water erosion in Kenya was some time ago estimated at 72 tons per hectare per year (de Graff 1993). An even earlier study by Dregne (1990) reported a permanent reduction of soil productivity from water erosion in about 20 % of the Kenyan territory. Soil erosion is often manifest on the slopes near water streams, riparian areas, and in the marginal lands.

Salinization is believed to occur in 30 % of the irrigated lands in Kenya (Liniger et al. 2011). Resources degradation (resulting from soil and water) has both onsite and many offsite costs. It also impacts on food prices, food security and ecosystem service provision in downstream locations, beyond the source of the degradation.

It is notable that no single and comprehensive approach can map patterns, the status, and quantify the extent of land degradation in Kenya (Waswa 2012). The processes of land degradation are complex process, thus a variety of approaches are needed to adequately assess it. The types of soil and land degradation often found in Kenya are soil erosion, increased sediment loading of water bodies, such as Lake Olbollosat, the Winam Gulf and lake Baringo, loss of soil fertility, salinity, reduced ground cover, and the reduced carrying capacity of pastures, such as Amboseli National Park (FAO n.d).

The estimates of the extent of land degradation in Kenya vary depending on the source and methodologies of calculation. The potential areas of land degradation, defined as "places where both net primary productivity and rain-use efficiency (the ratio of net primary productivity to precipitation)" were found to be declining, stretching to 17 % of the country and 30 % of its cropland (Bai and Dent 2006). In these areas, land degradation was especially due to the expansion of cropping into marginal lands (for example, in the drylands around Lake Turkana and marginal croplands in Eastern Province) (ibid).

Land degradation is more pronounced in the Eastern parts and North Eastern parts of Kenya (as shown in Fig. 16.1), where 12.3 % of the land suffers from severe degradation, 52 % from moderate degradation and 33 % is vulnerable to land degradation (Muchena 2008; UNEP 2009). Bai et al. (2008) depicts that in about 64 % of Kenya's total land area was subject to moderate land degradation and about 23 % to very severe degradation problems in 1997. The latter had increased to nearly 30 % in the early 2000s (Bai et al. 2008). More recently, Le et al. (2014) estimated that the total of 22 % of the Kenyan land area has degraded between 1982 and 2006, including 31 % of croplands, 46 % of forested land, 42 % of shrub lands, and 18 % of grasslands.

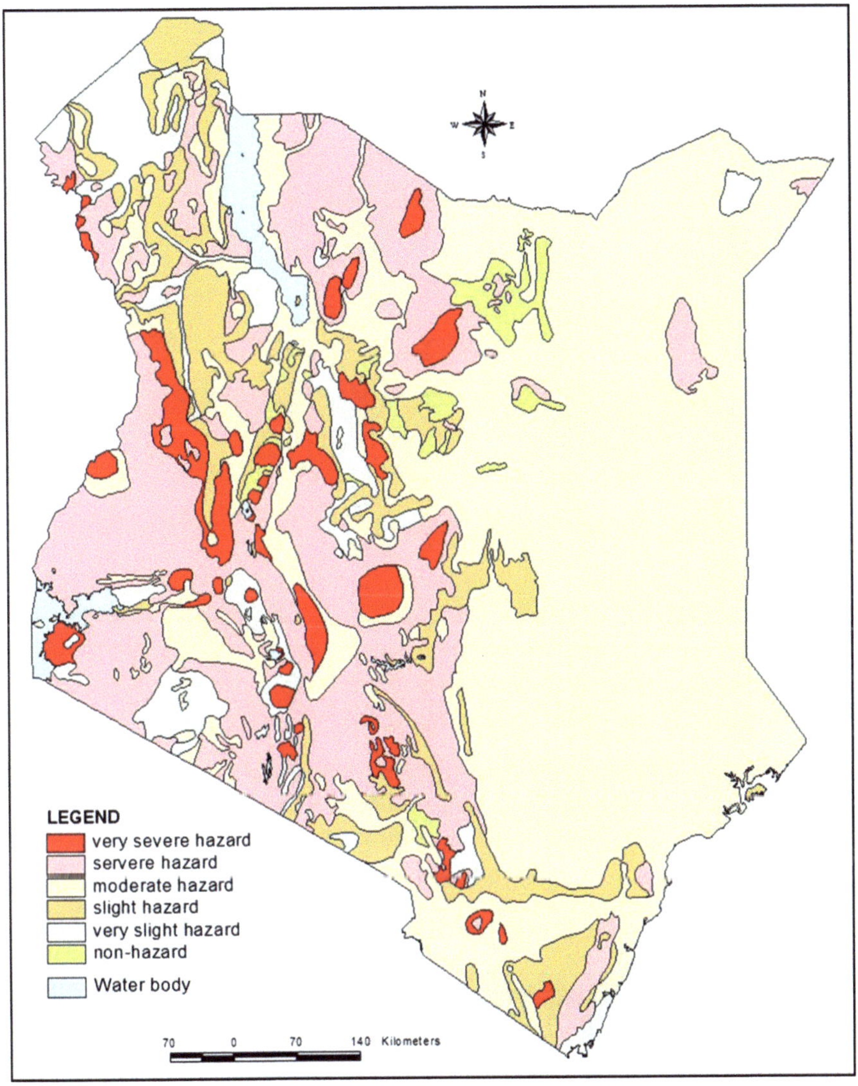

Fig. 16.1 Land degradation hazard areas in Kenya. *Source* Based on Kenya soil survey

Land Use and Cover Changes

Kenya has been undergoing dynamic land use and land cover changes over the last decade. The Moderate Resolution Imaging Spectroradiometer (MODIS) remotely sensed datasets that over the period of 2001 and 2009 present these dynamic changes for Kenya (Friedl et al. 2010) as shown in Tables 16.1 and 16.2.

Table 16.1 Land use and land cover in Kenya in 2001 (hectares)

Regions	Forests	Shrublands	Cropland	Grassland	Woodland	Barren	Water	Urban
Central	289,779	22,343	64,720	623,424	327,469	0	68	2583
Coast	131,067	2,686,984	381,133	4,677,692	467787	4947	19146	5644
Eastern	139,430	8,195,093	210,396	5,775,804	623,438	390,549	392,982	3471
Nairobi	4619	150	3362	44,823	3006	27	0	17,820
N/Eastern	60,908	9,384,587	61,413	2,879,600	212,486	15,305	55	5371
Nyanza	51,109	27,686	477,134	506,488	194,530	11,055	346,628	1804
Rift Valley	892,199	4,920,953	730,303	7,282,204	1,752,859	1,647,729	340,711	8459
Western	63,108	19,692	374,164	131,326	239,558	260	13,392	342
Total	1,632,219	25,300,000	2,302,625	21,900,000	3,821,133	2,069,873	1,112,981	45,493

Source Calculated by authors using MODIS data

Table 16.2 Land use and land cover change in Kenya between 2001 and 2009 (hectares)

Regions	Forests	Shrub-land	Cropland	Grassland	Woodland	Barren	Water	Urban
Central	−11,288	19,979	46,955	−57,095	1312	0	137	0
Coast	−28,438	−1,568,715	315,416	1,170,308	121,036	−2173	−7174	−123
Eastern	9252	−1,494,510	−67,932	1,887,028	−287,087	−27,126	−16,973	0
Nairobi	−2624	96	−1736	−492	4728	27	0	0
North-Eastern	−36,077	−2,326,594	152,238	2,175,877	37,348	−12,736	−55	0
Nyanza	−16,112	−16,002	−125,368	17,683	150,609	1462	−11,165	0
Rift Valley	−285,269	−677,471	−143,256	1,878,062	−123,510	−626,977	−19,829	0
Western	−765	−6259	−177,243	−35,052	220,604	519	−1613	0
Total	−371,322	−6,100,000	9074	7,100,000	125,040	−667,004	−56,672	−123

Source Calculated by the authors using MODIS data

These changes can be summarized into four major categories at the national level:

- Deforestation, especially in the Rift valley (mainly encroachment of water towers like Mau forest/escarpment) (Baker and Miller 2013; Kiage et al. 2007).
- Massive shift from shrublands, barren lands, and in some areas, from croplands to grasslands. Studies in the country indicate an overall decline in shrublands and grasslands with subsequent increases in croplands and built-up lands (Were et al. 2013; Kioko and Okello 2011; Maitima et al. 2009; Serneels and Lambin 2001). However, the distinction between grasslands and croplands may be compounded by the fact that at different time periods, crop areas maybe left fallow for long periods and thus some parcels drifting into grasslands and vice versa (Kiage et al. 2007). This may explain the increased area under grasslands as shown using MODIS data.
- Human movement and settlement in arid ASAL areas (low lands) as population pressure mounts in the high potential highlands (Kameri-Mbote 2007).
- Considerable reductions in the cropped area in Nyanza, Rift Valley, Western and Eastern provinces and big increases in the cropped area in Coastal (new settlements), North-Eastern and Central provinces. This in support of literature on land use/land cover in the country indicating that the area under crop cultivation has more than doubled over the last few decades (Maitima et al. 2009).
- Reductions in the extent of water bodies (frequent droughts in recent past, but with increased rains the reservoirs are presently recharging) (Kiage et al. 2007).

Drivers and Impacts of Land Degradation in Kenya

The last century has seen an increase in land degradation and desertification (UNCCD 2013). As described in Chap. 2 of this volume, the causes of land degradation are grouped into two, namely; proximate (biophysical) and underlying (socioeconomic) causes. These causes interact together to determine the rates of degradation. Biophysical causes are factors relating to unsustainable agronomic practices, and land physical conditions, rainfall and pest and diseases.

The large share of the documented unsustainable management practices in Kenya in the literature relate to land use/land cover changes experienced in significant environments of the country (Kiage et al. 2007; Maitima et al. 2009). The land use/land cover changes are often associated with deforestation, loss of natural vegetation, biodiversity loss and land degradation (Kiage et al. 2007; Maitima et al. 2009). The drivers linked to the land use/land cover changes include unsustainable fuel wood extraction, logging for charcoal and commercial timber, and land clearing for purposes of agriculture (Kiage et al. 2007; Mundia and Aniya 2006; UNEP 2002; Serneels and Lambin 2001). Specific drivers of forest degradation include illegal logging for commercial timber and for domestic demand for wood and charcoal (in west Pokot, Turkana and Marakwet), illegal growing of bhang in forests (such as Mount Kenya), considerable excisions of protected forests (such as Mau and Abadares) and forest fires (as reported in Mt. Elgon). With regard to clearing native vegetation for purposes of agriculture, Serneels and Lambin (2001) identify accessibility as a key driver in some parts of the country. Accessible areas, were found to be more prone to conversions to mechanized and smallholder agriculture. Whereas the productivity of not so fertile land, such as range lands, can be improved by use of fertilizers and other modern technology, accessible areas characterized by factors such as distance to the markets and low altitude plains emerge as important factors determining whether a parcel is modified or not.

The other documented unsustainable management practices include water pollution, soil nutrient mining, overgrazing, and cultivation on steep slopes. 'Soil nutrient mining' in croplands is an important driver of cropland degradation in Kenya. According to Blum (2006) soil is a limited resource and could be considered a non-renewable resource (Bai et al. 2008). Areas with poor soil fertility and with poor management practices tend to suffer from soil nutrient depletion. Fertilizer application rates in much of Kenya remain low (Table 16.3), resulting in "soil nutrient mining", when crop producers remove more nutrients from the soils than they apply. This process is not sustainable.

The underlying drivers of land degradation are manifold. Increasing human population pressure subjects land to intense pressure leading to degradation (Maitima et al. 2009; King 2008; Kiage et al. 2007; Mundia and Aniya 2006; Serneels and Lambin 2001). High population growth rates in Kenya have increased the demand for ecosystem services. The high population pressure fuels expansion of agricultural area to meet food demands and also for economic development of the rural populations (Maitima et al. 2009).

This has led to expansion of cropland into marginal areas, pastureland and forest lands and steep slopes. The pressure on fragile ecosystems has led to increased land degradation. The growth of the pastoralist population and subsequent increase of the livestock population have also led to extension of grazing activity into semi-arid marginal lands and forests, causing severe degradation and reduced livestock productivity.

Table 16.3 Fertilizer dose rate (Kgs/acre)

Agro ecological zone	1997	2000	2004	2007
Marginal rain shadow	26.1	31.7	33.4	28.6
Central highlands	105.9	121.4	103.2	96.1
Western highlands	30.4	44.5	51.1	46.7
High potential maize zone	63.4	62.8	66.9	70.9
Western transitional	37.4	69.8	51.6	54.4
Western lowlands	59.3	42.5	9.8	18.7
Eastern lowlands	27.5	13.8	11.0	16.5
Coastal lowlands	18.1	2.3	4.5	5.6
Overall sample	64.8	72.1	64.8	63.2

Source Tegemeo survey data

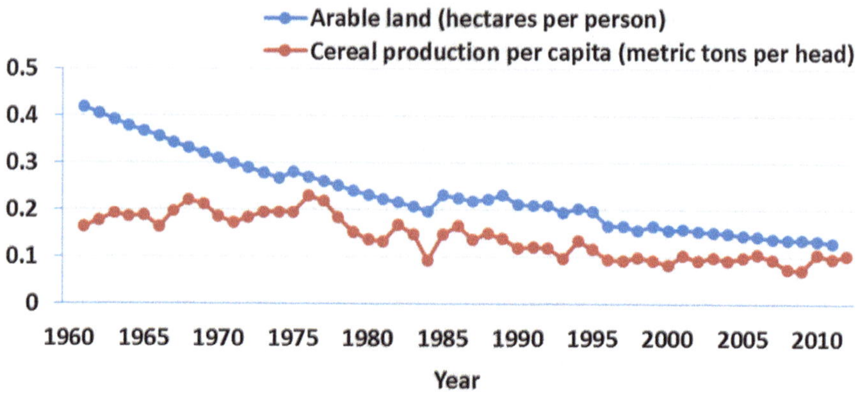

Fig. 16.2 Arable land and cereal production per capita in Kenya. *Source* The Authors

Over the period 1981–2003, the productivity declined across 40 % of croplands in the country—a critical situation in the context of a doubling of the human population over the same period in the country (Bai and Dent 2008; Fig. 16.2).

Other than modifications for agricultural purposes, unplanned growths of built-up areas are observed to be on the increase and are observed to contribute to the degradation processes (Maitima et al. 2009; Mundia and Aniya 2006; Were et al. 2013; Mireri 2005). The rising conversion of agricultural lands into industrial and residential lands especially with the increasing urbanization has also led to an increased pressure on initially productive lands. A case in point is the ongoing development of a techno-city on over 2000 acres of prime agricultural land in Machakos County, Kenya. The story is similar in other counties like Narok, Kiambu and Nakuru that are rapidly urbanizing. The construction of infrastructure such as roads on steep slopes without proper barriers, buildings without proper water drainage systems are also contributing factors to soil degradation and to making water in rivers less fit for human consumption. These developments certainly contribute to direct and indirect land degradation leading to a reduction in ecosystem balance and production of goods and services.

Investment in soil and water conservation is also incentivized by secure land tenure and land rights. There are various tenure regimes in Kenya with varying degrees of tenure security. Insecure land tenure can lead to the adoption of unsustainable land management practices.

As for the economic impacts of land degradation, IMF (2010) estimates that land degradation has huge economic costs in Kenya—about USD 390 million or (about 3 % of GDP) annually. These costs are associated to the decline in the quality of land as a result of the impact of unsustainable farming practices, the impacts of climate change, soil erosion, pollution and toxicity from agro-chemicals and alien and invasive species (such as *Ipomea kituiensils, Prosopis juliflora*, and water hyacinth).

Dregne (1990) reported that irreversible productivity losses due to soil erosion occurred in about 20 % over the last century in large parts of Ethiopia and Kenya.

Further, high percentage (27 %) of high value irrigated land was lost due to salinization over the last century in Kenya (Tiffen et al. 1994).

Land degradation in the country has been linked to increased sedimentation of water bodies from soil erosion, as it is the case in Lake Baringo, reducing their surface areas (Kiage et al. 2007). A study by Nkonya et al. (2008a, b) in Sasumua Dam Water Treatment estimated the cost of potable water production at KES 14.77 million, of which KES 9.91 million was the cost attributable to soil erosion. About 20 % of portable water supply to Nairobi city originates from the Sasumua Water Treatment Plant. The method used in the study involved comparing of estimated cost of water treatment and purification during both the wet and the dry seasons. The dry season was used as the proxy for the water treatment costs with effective control measures of soil erosion/land degradation whereas the wet/rainy season water treatment cost reflected the without effective control measures of soil erosion/land degradation scenario. The difference in costs between the two scenarios arises from the use of extra alum (aluminum sulphate), a coagulant to remove silt and other solid waste and chlorine to disinfect the water. The cost of extra use of alum and chlorine and the subsequent cost of de-silting the dam during the rainy season was estimated at KES 9.91 million.

On the other hand, deforestation is observed to decreases infiltration rates of the land, and has also led to reduced water quality and ability of catchment areas to support flow of rivers especially in the dry season (Were et al. 2013; Kiage et al. 2007).

Land use/land cover changes in rangelands has led to friction between people, livestock and wildlife over the scarce rangeland resources, with the intensity of the friction increasing over the years (Maitima et al. 2009; Campbell et al. 2003). Among the resulting effects has been the strong decline of wildlife in the rangelands (Maitima et al. 2009) which impact negatively the tourism sector of the country. Land use/land cover changes is also associated with decline in bird species, loss in plant biodiversity, and decline in soil productivity (Maitima et al. 2009).

Policy, Legal and Institutional Framework Addressing Land Degradation in Kenya

Kenya is currently having very comprehensive Sustainable Land Management (SLM) policy documents which are intended to provide guidelines on land use management and administration. The period before 2009 was characterized by land use policy scattered in bits and pieces in many national and sector policy documents (Gok 2009). The period was marred by poor coordination, lack of transparency, conflicting policies, institutions and legal framework leading to a very complicated land use management and administration system (GoK 2009). The National Land Policy (NLP) (Sessional Paper No. 3 of 2009) ensures that all land policy is unified after a thorough consultative process used in developing the policy. The vision of the policy as spelled out in the policy document is “To guide the country towards efficient, sustainable and equitable use of land for prosperity and posterity”. The vision sums up the key principles of Land Use Planning, Sustainable Production and Environmental Management used to guide the policy formulation. The most important aspects in the policy relevant to land degradation are spelled out in Chap. 3 section Improving Resource Allocation, or “L4 Actions”. The rationale is to restore the environmental integrity of land and facilitate sustainable management of land based resources. The policy proposes the following measures: Development of an incentive structure to catalyze development and adoption of technologies and methods for soil conservation; Mainstreaming use of appropriate land conservation methods; Developing and implementing measures to control land degradation associated with inappropriate land use practice and misuse of inputs; and establishing institutional mechanisms for land quality conservation for environmental preservation purposes. The main sector policy strengthening sustainable land use and conservation of natural resources is the draft National Environment Policy 2013 as provided in Chap. 4 on Management of Ecosystems and Sustainable Use of Natural Resources (GoK 2013b). Other relevant sector policies supporting the Sustainable land use policy framework in Kenya include National Water Policy 1999, National Water Management Strategy (GoK 2010a), National Climate Change Response Strategy (GoK 2010b), the Agriculture Sector Development Strategy (ASDS) (GoK 2010c), National Land Reclamation Policy (GoK 2013c) and National Environment Change Action Plan 2013–2017 (GoK 2013d).

To improve the institutional framework to implement the NLP, parliament enacted the National Land Commission Act in 2012 (GoK 2012a), which formed the National Land Commission (NLC) in 2013. The act mandates the NLC as the lead agency in land matters, functioning with the Ministry of Lands, Housing and Urban Development (MLHUD) and other regional and county institutions. Subsequently, the Commission developed a five-year National Strategic Plan to guide implementation of the NLP (GoK 2013e). The MLHUD on the other hand is responsible for policy formulation, coordination, and mobilization of resources. To support administration and management of land, the following institutions including; the local authorities, land property tribunals, district land tribunals and Land Courts play a major role. The National Environment Management Authority (NEMA), is established under the Environmental Management and Co-ordination Act No. 8 of 1999 (EMCA) as the principal instrument of Government for the implementation of all policies relating to environment. NEMA is one of the most important institutions in land management ensuring environmental capacity development and enforcement of environmental regulations. Currently many actors, both in the public and private sector play a role in land reclamation, albeit in an un-coordinated manner. The lack of a regulatory framework to drive the process and ensure consistency and quality standards indicates a responsive institutional mechanism is necessary. This is exemplified by constant turf wars between MLHUD and NLC which have ended in High Court for interpretation.

The land management and administration legal framework supportive of SLM is composed of the Constitution of Kenya, 2010. The supreme law has provisions on land; which is operationalized by the new legislations on land including the Land Act, Land Registration Act and the National Land Commission Act as well as the continuing legal reforms in the land sector. The legal framework address critical issues related to land degradation such as land administration, access to land, land use planning and environmental degradation. Environmental Management and Coordination Act (EMCA), 1999 established NEMA which has the mandate to develop the Integrated National Land Use Guidelines (INLUG).

Other sector laws supportive of SLM include; the Environment and Land Court Act, the Land Act, the Crops Act, and the Fisheries Act, the Agriculture, Fisheries And Food Authority (AFFA) Act No. 13 of 2013 the Kenya Agricultural and Livestock Research (KALR) Act No. 17 of 2013, Crop Act No. 16 of 2013 and Water Act 2002. The KALR act mandates the Kenya Agricultural and Livestock Research Organization (KALRO) to develop and promote SLM technologies and methodologies for the agricultural sector. The necessary policies and laws are largely in place. However serious cases of underfunding, political will and vested interests inhibit efficient and effective implementation of Sustainable land use policies as spelled out in the various sector and policy documents.

Methods and Data

Conceptual Framework

The conceptual framework applied in this study follows the ELD framework presented in Nkonya et al. (2014) and elaborated in Chap. 2 of this volume. The framework groups the causes of land degradation in two categories; proximate biophysical causes and underlying causes. These two categories act together hence resulting in different levels of land degradation—which in turn determines the effects (on-site or off-site), on the ecosystem services and the benefits humans derive from those services. Actors could take action to control the causes, levels and effects of land degradation. For a further comprehensive discussion on the conceptual framework, refer to Chap. 2 of this volume.

Empirical Strategy

The empirical approaches used to estimate the determinants of SLM adoption and the number of SLM technologies adopted are discussed in detail in this section. These methods are based on the methodological Chap. 2, and are consistently applied throughout several case studies in this volume, including in Chaps. 14 and 20. The variables used in these chapters are measured in exactly the same way but for different countries.

Drivers of Number of Sustainable Land Management Practices Adopted

Land degradation usually occurs due to lack of use of sustainable land management practices. Those factors preventing households from adopting SLM practices are also likely to lead land degradation. Therefore, analyzing the drivers of SLM is similar in its implications as analyzing the drivers of land degradation. The number of SLM technologies adopted by agricultural households is a count variable (ranging from 0 to 12 in our case). Thus the assessment of the determinants of the number of SLM technologies adopted needs to be conducted by Poisson regression model (Xiang and Lee 2005; Greene 2003). Poisson regression model (PRM) is normally the first step for most count data analyses. Thus in this study, we apply PRM to the following reduced form econometric model using nationally representative agricultural household survey data from Kenya.

$$A = \beta_0 + \beta_1 x_1 + \beta_2 x_2 + \beta_3 x_3 + \beta_4 x_4 + \beta_5 z_i + \varepsilon_i \tag{16.1}$$

where A = number of SLM technologies; x_1 = a vector of biophysical factors (e.g. climate conditions, agro-ecological zones, etc.); x_2 = a vector of policy-related and institutional factors (e.g. market access, land tenure, etc.); x_3 = a vector of variables representing access to rural services (e.g. access to extension); x_4 = vector of variables representing rural household level capital endowment, level of education, household size, dependency ratio, etc.; and z_i = vector of country fixed effects.

Costs of Action and Inaction Against Land Degradation Due to LUCC

The approach for determining the for degradation due to LUCC considers the cost of reestablishing the high value biome lost and the opportunity cost of foregoing the benefits drawn from the lower value biome that is being replaced (Chap. 6). The cost of inaction on the other hand is the sum of annual losses due to land degradation. In this study, two time horizons are presumed; 6 year period—a planning horizon typical for small holder farmers in cropland biomes, and 30 year period—a typical planning horizon for afforestation program in forests, woodlands, and shrub-lands biomes. The rational land user will take action against land degradation if costs of taking action are less than the costs of inaction (Chap. 6).

Refer to Chaps. 2 and 6 of this volume for an in-depth and comprehensive discussion on the methods, formulae and datasets used to estimate the costs of land degradation and also the empirical strategy to estimate the costs of taking action (versus inaction) against land degradation.

Cost of Land Degradation Due to Use of Land Degrading Management Practices

We use Decision Support System for Agro-technology Transfer (DSSAT) crop simulation model to determine the impact of SLM practices on crop yield and soil carbon. DSSAT combines crop, soil, and weather databases for access by a suite of crop models enclosed under one system. Two crop simulation scenarios are considered, namely; (i) Integrated soil fertility management (ISFM)—combined use of organic inputs, recommended amount of chemical fertilizer and improved seeds, and (ii) Business as usual (BAU)—reflecting the current management practices practiced by majority of farmers. Refer to Chap. 6 of this volume for a comprehensive description of DSSAT simulation model.

Cost of Land Degradation on Static Rangelands (Grasslands)

Static rangeland (grazing land) degradation is analyzed for the entire rangelands at pixel level. The total costs of static rangeland degradation are divided into three: costs due to loss of milk production, costs due to loss of meat production, and costs due to loss of live weight of livestock not slaughtered or sold. An elaborate presentation and explanation of the analytical approach used to estimate static rangeland degradation provided for in Chap. 8 of this volume. Some aspects not captured in this methodology due to data limitations include the costs associated to land degradation on livestock health, parturition, and mortality rates. Also some other costs such as loss of carbon sequestration and the loss of other ecosystem services provided by grasslands are not included.

Data

The Kenya case study is based on spatial GIS data and existing household surveys (Agricultural Sector Development Support Programme (ASDSP)). The ASDSP national survey covered all the 47 counties, with the overall sample consisting of 12,651 agricultural households. The sample size for each county was determined using the proportionate to population size (PPS) sampling technique, based on total number of farming households in each county. Additional data sources include: The Economics of Ecosystems and Biodiversity (TEEB) database on the value of ecosystem services, MODIS LUCC datasets (cf. Chap. 6 for more details), Tegemeo Panel data: 2000–2004, 2011; and secondary statistics at district level.

Results and Discussion

Drivers of Sustainable Land Management: Adoption of Improved SLM-Friendly Technologies

The analysis of the 2013 country wide ASDSP baseline survey data shows that only about 40 % of surveyed households have applied some practices that could be considered as SLM practices. The most common SLM practices include: cutoff drains and drainage trenches, terraces planted with fodder species such as Napier grass, contour ploughing, use of stone bounds and trash lines, and tree planting, use of manure, inorganic fertilizer and compost and agricultural lime. The remaining 60 % households having no adoption of any improved technologies (Fig. 16.3).

The major source of knowledge and extension on these technologies came from agro-dealers, followed by government extension offices, and then private companies. The role of local and international NGOs was relatively low (Fig. 16.4).

The most important constraint against using these technologies were cited to be their high costs and lack of information and expertise in their proper application (Fig. 16.5).

The distribution of the number of SLM technologies used is quite dispersed, ranging from 0 to 12 (Fig. 16.4). Moreover, if we analyze by county, the conditional variance of the distribution is higher in all cases than the conditional mean. Furthermore, our dependent variable on the number of SLM technologies used is a counting variable. Such a nature of the dependent variable requires the application of negative binomial regression, which is a generalization of Poisson regression for a count dependent variable with dispersed distribution.

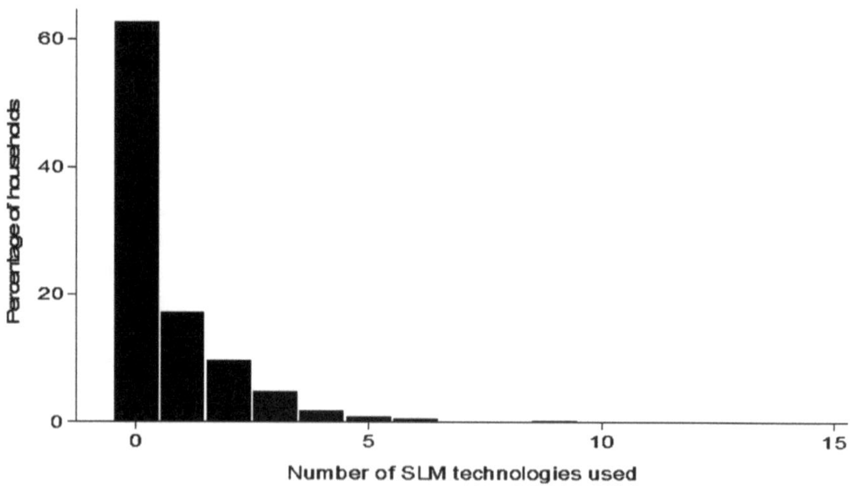

Fig. 16.3 Adoption of improved SLM-friendly technologies. *Source* Calculated by authors using initial data from ASDSP household survey data

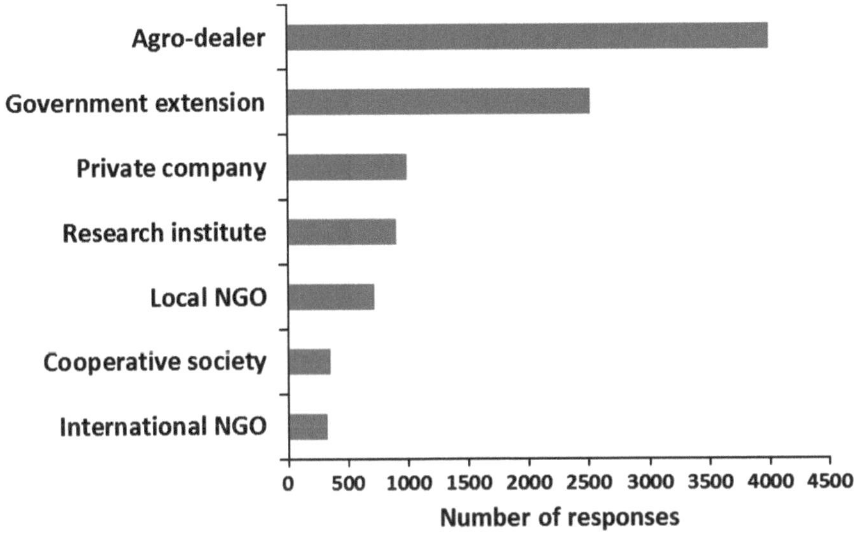

Fig. 16.4 The role of different organizations in catalyzing adoption of SLM practices. *Source* Authors' compilation

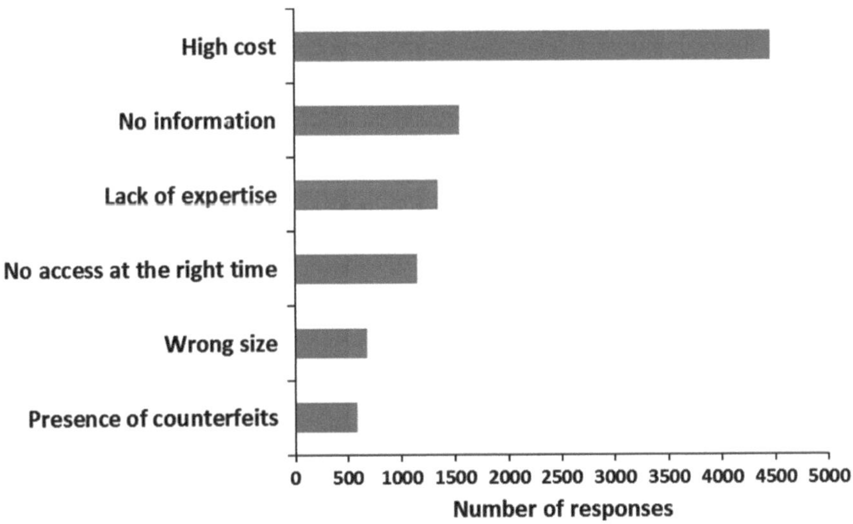

Fig. 16.5 Constraints in using the SLM technologies. *Source* Authors' compilation

The results of the regression on the determinants of the number of SLM technologies used by households are given in Table 16.4. The overall test of model fit shows that the model is statistically significant at 1 % (LR chi^2 (84) = 10,901.84, Prob > $chi^2 = 0.0000$, and Pseudo $R^2 = 0.359$). The likelihood ratio test comparing this negative binomial model to the Poisson model is statistically significant at 1 %, suggesting that the negative binomial model fits the data better than the Poisson model.

Robust checks on the model show no evidence of multicollinearity, heteroscedasticity and omitted variables. Ramsey RESET test (ovitest) was not significant; showing no evidence of omitted variables while the Breusch-Pagan/Cook-Weisberg test (hettest) showed no evidence of heteroscedasticity. We however, report robust standard errors. Further, the VIF test was less than 10 showing no evidence of multicollinearity.

The regression results point at several variables which have statistically significant relationships with the number of SLM technologies adopted by households. Particularly, access to information through various means (including extension officers, research institution, cooperatives and local NGOs) increased the log count of the number of SLM technologies adopted. For example, farmers with access to government extension officers increased the log count of the number of SLM technologies adopted by 43.7 % while those with access to agricultural cooperatives increased the log count of the number of SLM technologies adopted by 21.5 %, ceteris paribus. Similar to previous studies (such as Nhemachena and Hassan 2007; Teklewold et al. 2013) this finding points to the importance of agricultural extension services when making farm decisions and in influencing farmers' technology adoption behavior.

Access to market information, agricultural dealers and access to credit facilities facilitates the adoption of more SLM technologies. Farmers with access to market information increased the log count of the number of SLM technologies adopted by 12.3 %, holding other factors constant. Agricultural dealers play an important role in delivering information on various and emerging SLM technologies besides supplying some of the SLM (such as seed and fertilizers). Where government extension services are scarce, the local NGOs serve as focal points for information and technology dissemination among the rural population. Access to a local NGO increased the log count of the number of SLM technologies adopted by 33.2 % ceteris paribus. This corroborates earlier studies on the important role played by the NGOs in disseminating agricultural information in rural agricultural communities (Amr and Richiedei 2000; Wattenbach et al. 2005; Molua 2014; Schipper et al. 2014).

Further, access to markets (input and output) significantly influences the number of SLM technologies adopted. Increase in distance to these markets reduces the the log count of the number of SLM technologies adopted by about 5.5 % holding other factors constant. This finding may suggests that proximity to markets represents reductions in transaction costs related to access to both inputs and outputs, increased availability of information, financial and credit organizations, and technology accessibility. All these factors are important in enhancing technology adoption decisions. (Pender et al. 2006; von Braun et al. 2012).

Household characteristics, such as gender, education, and age of the household head, household size, and dependency ratio are not significant in the sample. Similarly capacity and socio-economic variables such as total cultivated land,

Table 16.4 The drivers of number of SLM technologies adopted in Kenya

Variables	Coefficient	Standard error	z-value	Confidence interval (lower, upper)
Extension (dummy)	0.052*	0.029	1.799	−0.005, 0.108
Distance to extension	−0.001	0.001	−1.036	−0.003, 0.001
Extension by agrodealers	0.771***	0.028	27.695	0.717, 0.826
Extension by research orgs	0.250***	0.037	6.715	0.177, 0.323
Extension by Govt org	0.437***	0.033	13.165	0.372, 0.502
Extension by cooperatives	0.215***	0.052	4.174	0.114, 0.317
Extension by local NGO	0.332***	0.041	8.042	0.251, 0.413
No. of SLM extension sources	0.418***	0.010	41.245	0.398, 0.438
Education some schooling	0.009	0.028	0.304	−0.047, 0.064
Education completed school	0.033	0.063	0.530	−0.090, 0.157
Education university	0.025	0.047	0.543	−0.066, 0.117
Land tenure—owns, but no title	0.010	0.026	0.399	−0.041, 0.062
Land tenure—lease-rented in	−0.106	0.101	−1.052	−0.304, 0.091
Land tenure—communal rights	0.008	0.062	0.123	−0.114, 0.129
Land tenure-squats	−0.081	0.097	−0.830	−0.272, 0.110
Distance to road	−0.001	0.001	−0.849	−0.002, 0.001
Access to weather information	0.033	0.032	1.045	−0.029, 0.096
Savings	0.000	0.000	0.178	−0.000, 0.000
Amount borrowed	−0.000*	0.000	−1.684	−0.000, 0.000
Savings#Amout borrowed	0.000***	0.000	2.938	0.000, 0.000
Input#output market distances	−0.055**	0.027	−2.064	−0.107, −0.003
Access to market information	0.123***	0.026	4.769	0.072, 0.173
Gender of household head	−0.024	0.033	−0.722	−0.087, 0.040
Age of household head	0.002	0.005	0.478	−0.007, 0.012
Age of household head, sq.	0.000	0.000	−0.376	−0.000, 0.000
Family size	−0.006	0.005	−1.242	−0.016, 0.004
Dependency ratio	0.001	0.014	0.063	−0.027, 0.029
Total cropped area	0.000	0.000	−0.264	−0.000, 0.000
Perception of land degradation	−0.027	0.024	−1.132	−0.074, 0.020
Total assets value	−0.000**	0.000	−2.555	−0.000, −0.000
Membership in association	0.004	0.031	0.133	−0.056, 0.064
Agricultural income	0.000	0.000	0.134	−0.000, 0.000
Off-farm income	0.000	0.000	−0.342	−0.000, 0.000
Livestock value	0.000	0.000	0.410	−0.000, 0.000
County dummies (47)	Yes	Yes	Yes	Yes
Constant	−1.438***	0.167	−8.628	−1.764, −1.111
lnalpha_constant	−2.522***	0.109	−23.187	−2.736, −2.309
Model characteristics	No. of obs. = 12,651		Chi^2 = 10,901.84	
	p-value = 0.000		Pseudo R^2 = 0.359	

Source Authors' compilation

***, **, and * denotes significance at 1%, 5% and 10% significance level respectively

income, land tenure, and value of livestock are not significant in influencing the adoption of SLM technologies. However, contrary to expectations, the value of total household assets showed a negative relationship with the number of the number of SLM technologies adopted. This is contrary to the expectation that wealthier households are deemed able to adopt several SLM technologies because of their ability to better access such technologies as improved seeds, inorganic fertilizers, irrigation equipment and soil and water conservation measures (McCarthy 2011).

Costs of Action and Inaction Against Land Degradation Due to LUCC

The results show that the costs of land degradation, using land use change as a measure and the Total Economic Values framework accounting for the losses of ecosystem services, were about 10.6 billion USD for the period 2001–2009 (expressed in constant 2007 USD). This translated to about 1.3 billion USD annually, or about a 4.9 % equivalent of the Kenyan GDP (Table 16.5). The biggest losses in terms of magnitudes have occurred in the Rift Valley (452 million USD), the Coastal (290 million USD) and Eastern (214 million USD) provinces.

In terms of per capita costs of land degradation, the biggest negative impacts have occurred in the Coastal ($680) and North-Eastern ($640) provinces, followed by the Rift Valley ($352). These losses are mostly related to deforestation. The areas with net improvements are the Rift Valley, North-Eastern, Coastal, Eastern and Western province. The major driver of this improvement was the massive shift from shrub lands and barren lands to grasslands in these provinces.

Table 16.5 The costs of land degradation in Kenya through land use change (LUCC)

Regions	Cost of land degradation between 2001 and 2009 (million USD)	Annual cost of land degradation expressed in 2007 constant USD (million USD)	Annual cost of land degradation per capita, in USD
Central	647.4	80.9	144
Coast	2321.5	290.2	680
Eastern	1713.7	214.2	296
Nairobi	18.5	2.3	8
North-Eastern	1502.8	187.8	640
Nyanza	577.1	72.1	104
Rift Valley	3616.6	452.1	352
Western	247.7	31.0	56
Total	10,645.2	1330.6	272

Source Calculated by the authors

Table 16.6 Total economic value (TEV) of land ecosystems and GDP in Kenya, $ billion

Region	TEV/GDP ratio	Annual TEV 2001	Annual TEV 2009	TEV per capita 2009
Central	1.1	4	4	857
Coast	8.1	20	21	6200
Eastern	8.6	35	37	6582
Nairobi	0.1	0	0	48
North-Eastern	14.9	24	26	11,426
Nyanza	1.3	5	5	983
Rift Valley	5.5	40	42	4208
Western	0.5	1	2	367
Total	4.72	129	137	3343

Source Calculated by the authors

However, there have also been improvements in land use of about 19 billion USD equivalent, making the net change in the Total Economic Value of land ecosystems in the country positive by about 8 billion USD in 2009 as compared to 2001 (Table 16.6).

The results on costs of taking action verses inaction against land degradation are presented in Table 16.7. Results show that the costs of action against land degradation are lower than the costs of inaction in Kenya by about 4 times over the 30 year horizon. The costs of action were found to equal about 18 billion USD over a 30-year horizon, whereas if nothing is done, the resulting losses may equal to almost 75 billion USD during the same period. The implications is that each dollar spent on addressing land degradation is likely to have about 4 dollars of returns. This is a very strong economic justification favoring action as opposed to taking no action.

Table 16.7 Costs of action verses inaction in Kenya

Provinces	GDP 2007	Annual costs of land degradation	Annual costs in terms of provisional ecosystem services	Cost of action (6 years)	Cost of action (30 years)	Cost of inaction (6 years)	Cost of inaction (30 years)	Ratio of cost of action: inaction 30 years
	Billion	Million		Billion				%
Central	3.37	80.9	35.691	1.08	1.08	3.24	4.38	25
Coast	2.55	290.2	128.895	3.34	3.35	11.28	15.27	22
Eastern	4.35	214.2	125.718	2.99	3.00	9.35	12.66	24
Nairobi	2.41	2.3	1.050	0.04	0.04	0.10	0.13	28
N/Eastern	1.77	187.8	110.820	2.81	2.82	8.37	11.33	25
Nyanza	4.18	72.1	30.206	0.81	0.82	2.75	3.73	22
R/Valley	7.69	452.1	219.726	6.53	6.55	18.96	25.66	26
Western	3.33	31.0	14.043	0.41	0.42	1.27	1.72	24
Total	29.65	1330.6	666.15	18.03	18.07	55.33	74.89	24

Source Calculated by the authors

Cost of Land Degradation Due to Use of Land Degrading Practices

We present the simulated results of rain-fed maize yield under business-as-usual (BAU) and integrated soil fertility management (ISFM) scenarios for a period of forty years in Kenya in Table 16.8. The average maize yields are higher under ISFM—1.84 tons/ha (baseline) and 1.79 tons/ha (end-line) as compared with the BAU scenario—1.63 tons/ha (baseline) and 1.35 tons/ha (end-line) periods. However, there is a yield decline between the end-line and baseline periods for both ISFM and BAU scenarios. Under ISFM, yield end-line yield declined by about 2.5 % while under BAU scenario, yield declined by about 17.1 %. Overall, the yield decline due to use of land management practices in maize plots is about 32 %. Similarly, simulation analysis show that the use of land degrading management practices on rain-fed wheat leads to a decline of about 32 % as compared to yield in the previous 40 years. Under ISFM, yield declined is negligible (about 0.3 %) while under BAU yield declined by about 15.6 %. Similarly, the use of land degrading management practices on irrigated rice leads to a decline of about 31.6 % as compared to yield in the previous 40 years. Under ISFM, yield declined by about 3 % while under BAU yield declined by about 9.4 %.

The cost of land degradation for the three crops is about $270 million. When these losses are expressed as percent of GDP, Kenya loses about 1 % of the GDP annually as a result of cropland (maize, wheat and rice) degradation. Statistics show that the three crops (maize, wheat and rice) account for about 40 % of the cropland globally. Assuming that the levels of degradation is comparable to that occurring on the two major crops, then the total cost of land degradation on cropland is about 2.4 % of GDP in Kenya. On per hectare basis, use of degrading practices on cropland leads to losses amounting to about $117 annually in Kenya (Table 16.9).

Table 16.8 Change in maize and wheat yields under BAU and ISFM in Kenya

Crop	BAU		ISFM		Yield change (%)		Change due to land degradation
	Baseline	End-line	Baseline	End-line	BAU	ISFM	
	Yield (tons/ha)		Yield (tons/ha)		Percent		
Maize	1.63	1.35	1.84	1.79	−17.1	−2.5	32.4
Wheat	2.77	2.34	3.09	3.08	−15.6	−0.3	32.0
Rice	3.55	3.21	4.36	4.23	−9.4	−3.0	31.6

Source Kirui O.K. (Unpublished Ph.D. Thesis)

Table 16.9 Cost of soil fertility mining on maize, rice and wheat cropland in Kenya

Cost of land degradation (soil fertility mining)	Cost as % of GDP	Cost of cropland degradation as % GDP	Annual cost of land degradation (per ha)
2007 US$ million	(%)	(%)	(US$/ha)
269.77	0.99	2.36	116.70

Source Authors' compilation

Land Degradation on Static Grasslands

Livestock production is mainly concentrated in the arid and semi-arid lands (ASALs) parts of the country which cover above 80 % of total land area and supports approximately 70 % of the country's livestock (GoK 2012a). Livestock production plays a crucial role not only in sustaining livelihoods but plays a significant role in national development by contributing about $4.54 billion US dollars to agricultural GDP (GoK 2012b; Behnke and Muthami 2011). Livestock production is however hampered by reduced grazing biomass productivity brought about by degraded lands, translating to high costs to the nation as a whole.

Table 16.10 shows the simulated results of costs of loss of milk, meat, and costs associated with weight loss of animals not slaughtered or sold due to land degradation in grazing biomass. A detailed methodological approach is presented in Chap. 6 of this volume. Results show that land degradation in grazing biomass had a huge impact on milk production in Kenya. The total costs of milk and meat production losses were about $49.5 million and $8.7 million respectively. The bigger proportion of milk and meat losses is experienced in warm arid ($24 million), warm semi-arid ($16 million) and cool sub-humid ($10 million) agro-ecologies.

Table 16.10 Cost of loss of milk and meat production due to land degradation of grazing biomass

Agro-ecological zones	Milk	Meat	Total loss (milk and meat)	Total gross loss—includes weight loss of animals not slaughtered/sold
	2007 US$ million			
Tropic-cool semi-arid	4.056	0.874	4.930	6.383
Tropic-cool arid	1.152	0.095	1.247	1.813
Tropic-cool humid	0.820	0.069	0.889	1.291
Tropic-cool sub-humid	9.027	1.109	10.137	14.207
Tropic-warm semi-arid	13.393	2.666	16.059	21.078
Tropic-warm arid	20.551	3.873	24.424	32.343
Tropic-warm sub-humid	0.508	0.036	0.544	0.799
Total	49.507	8.723	58.23	77.914

Source Authors' compilation

The total gross loss—cost of milk, meat and cost of weight loss of animals not slaughtered or sold—in Kenya was about $78 million. The bigger proportion of the total gross losses is consequently experienced in warm arid ($32 million), warm semi-arid ($21 million) and cool sub-humid ($14 million) agro-ecologies.

Conclusion

This study investigated the causes, extent and impacts of land degradation in Kenya It also evaluated the costs of action versus inaction in rehabilitating degraded lands, and proposed policy measures that can be instituted to address land degradation. Our results indicate that land degradation is a serious problem in Kenya especially in the ASALs. About 30 % of the Kenya's landmass is subject to severe land degradation. This trend of land use changes is expected to become more serious as population pressure increases.

The analysis of nationally representative data showed that access to information through various means (including extension officers, research institution, cooperatives and local NGOs) facilitated the adoption of SLM technologies. Agricultural dealers play an important role in delivering information on various and emerging SLM technologies besides supplying some of the SLM sources (such as seed and fertilizers). Where government extension services are scarce, the local NGOs serve as focal points for information and technology dissemination among the rural population. Policies and strategies relating to agricultural extension, information and market access could be prioritized to boost SLM adoption and thus address land degradation, especially in croplands. Equipping the agro-dealers with relevant and credible SLM information will enhance their capacity to disseminate timely and important information to benefit the farmers.

Using the Total Economic Values framework, it was estimated that the economic costs emanating from land degradation due to land use and land cover change at the national scale amount to about out 1.3 billion USD annually, or about a 4.9 % equivalent of the Kenyan GDP in 2007. The annual costs of land degradation on static cropland amounted to 270 million USD while the annual costs of rangeland (static) degradation amounted to 80 million USD. This estimate is significantly higher than the previous estimate of land degradation by IMF (2010) of USD 390 million. Further analysis indicated that the cost of taking action against land degradation is lower than the cost of inaction both in a shorter term of six years and a longer term of 30 years. The returns to investment in action against land degradation are about four times the costs of inaction in the first six years. This provides a justification for taking action against land degradation.

Recommendations

To reverse the trends in land degradation, actions on land rehabilitation and reclamation are recommended. First, increased support for research and extension to increase crop yields is crucial to meeting the needs of a growing human population for food, biomass energy, fiber, and timber. Secondly, there is a need to increase support to biodiversity preservation by alleviating pressure to convert remaining natural habitat to croplands. This can be achieved partly by establishing linkages to carbon markets to make the cost benefit ratios favorable for adoption SLM practices. And third, there is a need for more public investments to support SLM to slow land degradation and reclamation of already degraded lands. Land is often a limiting factor of economic output, and thus its degradation may further undermine the prospects of economic growth in the poor areas of Kenya.

References

Amr, H., & Richiedei, S. (2000). *Sahel NGO population network case study*. Washington, DC: Policy Project USAID.

Bai, Z. G. & Dent, D. L. (2006). *Global assessment of land degradation and improvement: pilot study in Kenya*. Report 2006/01. Wageningen: ISRIC—World Soil Information.

Bai, Z., & Dent, D. (2008). *Land degradation and improvement in Argentina. 1. Identification by remote sensing* (p. 149). Wageningen, The Netherlands: International Soil Reference Information Center—World Soil Information.

Bai, Z. G., Dent, D.L., Olsson, L., & Schaepman, M. E. (2008). *Global assessment of land degradation and improvement 1: Identification by remote sensing*. Report 2008/01. Rome/Wageningen: FAO/ISRIC.

Baker, T. J., & Miller, S. N. (2013). Using the soil and water assessment tool (SWAT) to assess land use impact on water resources in an East African watershed. *Journal of Hydrology, 486*, 100–111.

Behnke, R., & Muthami, D. (2011). *The contribution of livestock to the Kenyan economy*. IGAD Livestock Policy Initiative Working Paper, 03–11.

Blum, W. E. H. (2006). Soil Resources-The basis of human society and the environment. *BODENKULTUR-WIEN AND MUNCHEN-, 57*(1/4), 197.

Campbell, D., Gichohi, H., Reid, R., Mwangi, A., Chege, L., & Sawin, T. (2003). *Interactions between people and wildlife in Southeast Kajiado District, Kenya*. LUCID Working paper No. 18. Nairobi: Int. Livestock Res. Institute.

de Graff, J. (1993). *Soil conservation and sustainable land use: An economic approach*. Amsterdam, The Netherlands: Royal Tropical Institute.

Dregne, H. E. (1990). Erosion and soil productivity in Africa. *Journal of Soil and Water Conservation, 45*(4), 431–436.

Eswaran, H., Lal, R. & Reich. P. F. (2001). Land degradation: an overview. In *Responses to land Degradation. Proceedings of 2nd International Conference on Land Degradation and desertification, Khon Kaen, Thailand. Oxford Press, New Delhi, India.*

European Environment Agency (EAA). (2005). *Sustainable use and management of natural resources*. EEA Report No 9/2005.

FAO (United Nations Food and Agriculture Organization). (n.d). *Land degradation estimates in Kenya: Chapter 4*. Rome, Italy.

Friedl, M. A., Sulla-Menashe, D., Tan, B., Schneider, A., Ramankutty, N., Sibley, A., & Huang, X. (2010). MODIS collection 5 global land cover: Algorithm refinements and characterization of new datasets. *Remote Sensing of Environment, 114*(1), 168–182.

Government of Kenya (GoK). (2007). *Kenya vision 2030: A globally competitive and prosperous Kenya*. Nairobi: Government of Kenya (GoK).

Government of Kenya (GoK). (2009). Sessional Paper No. 3 of 2009 on the National Land Policy August 2009.

Government of Kenya (GoK). (2010a). Agricultural Sector Development Strategy 2010–2020.

Government of Kenya (GoK). (2010b). National Climate Change Response Strategy, April 2010.

Government of Kenya (GoK). (2010c). The Constitution of Kenya, 2010.

Government of Kenya (GoK). (2012a). Sessional Paper No. 8 of 2012 on *National Policy for the Sustainable Development of Northern Kenya and Other Arid Lands.* Ministry of State for Development of Northern Kenya and Other Arid Lands, Nairobi. Retrieved September 17, 2015. http://www.adaconsortium.org/images/publications/Sessional-Paper-on-National-policy-for-development-of-ASALs.pdf

Government of Kenya (GoK). (2012b). Land Registration Act (Number 3 of 2012).

Government of Kenya (GoK). (2012c). The National Land Commission Act (Number 5 of 2012).

Government of Kenya (GoK). (2013a). Agriculture, Fisheries and Food Authority Act (Number 13 of 2013).

Government of Kenya (GoK). (2013b). National Environment Policy Final Draft, February 2013.

Government of Kenya (GoK). (2013c). National Land Reclamation Policy Final Draft, February 2013.

Government of Kenya (GoK). (2013d). National Environment Change Action Plan 2013–2017.

Government of Kenya (GoK). (2013e). Kenya Agricultural and Livestock Research Act (Number 17 of 2013).

Greene, H. W. (2003). Econometric Analysis: Pearson Education, Inc., Upper Saddle River, New Jersey, USA.

International Monetary Fund (IMF). (2010). Kenya: Poverty Reduction Strategy Paper MF Country Report No. 10/224 July 2010. Washington, D.C.

Henao, J.& Baanante, C. (2006). Agricultural Production and Soil Nutrient Mining in Africa: Implications for Resource Conservation and Policy Development: International Center for Soil Fertility and Agricultural Development (IFDC) Muscle Shoals, Alabama 35662, U.S.A. www.ifdc.org March 2006.

Kameri-Mbote, P. (2007). *Land tenure, land use and sustainability in Kenya: Towards innovative use of property rights in wildlife management: Land Use for Sustainable Development*. New York: Cambridge University Press.

Kamoni, P. T. & Makokha, S. N. (2010). Influence of land use practices and socio-economic factors on land degradation and environmental sustainability in Gucha district, Kenya. In *The 12th Kari Biennial Scientific Conference,* Nairobi, Kenya.

Kiage, L. M., Liu, K. B., Walker, N. D., Lam, N., & Huh, O. K. (2007). Recent land-cover/use change associated with land degradation in the Lake Baringo catchment, Kenya, East Africa: evidence from Landsat TM and ETM+. *International Journal of Remote Sensing, 28*(19), 4285–4309.

King, E. G. (2008). Facilitative effects of Aloe secundiflora shrubs in degraded semi-arid rangelands in Kenya. *Journal of Arid Environments, 72*(4), 358–369.

Kioko, J., & Okello, M. (2011). Land use cover and environmental changes in a semiarid rangeland, Southern Kenya. *Journal of Geography and Regional Planning, 3*(11), 322–326.

Lal, R., Lorenz, K., Hüttl, R. F., Schneider, B. U., & von Braun, J. (Eds.). (2013). *Ecosystem services and carbon sequestration in the biosphere*. New York: Springer Science.

Lal, R., Safriel, U. & Boer, B. (2012). Zero net land degradation: A new sustainable development goal for Rio+ 2: A report prepared for the Secretariat of the United Nations Convention to combat Desertification.

Le, Q. B., Nkonya, E., & Mirzabaev, A. (2014). Biomass productivity-based mapping of global land degradation hotspots. *ZEF-Discussion Papers on Development Policy*, 193.

Liniger, H. P., Studer, R. M., Hauert, C., & Gurtner, M. (2011). *Sustainable land management in practice—Guidelines and best practices for Sub-Saharan Africa*. TerrAfrica, World overview of conservation approaches and technologies (WOCAT) and food and agriculture organization of the United Nations (FAO).

Maitima, J. M., Mugatha, S. M., Reid, R. S., Gachimbi, L. N., Majule, A., & Lyaruu, H. et al. (2009). The linkages between land use change, land degradation and biodiversity across East Africa. *African Journal of Environmental Science and Technology, 3*(10), 310–325.

Mbow, C., Brandt, M., Ouedraogo, I., de Leeuw, J. & Marshall,M. (2015). What four decades of earth observation tell us about land degradation in the Sahel? *Remote Sensing* 7, 4048–4067 (ISSN 2072-4292).

McCarthy, N. (2011). *Understanding agricultural households' adaptation to climate change and implications for mitigation: land management and investment options. Living Standards Measurement Study—Integrated Surveys on Agriculture*. Washington, D.C., USA: LEAD Analytics Inc.

Mireri, C. (2005). Challenges facing the conservation of Lake Naivasha, Kenya. *FWU Topics of Integrated Watershed Management-Proceedings, 3*, 89–98.

Molua, E. L. (2014). Climate change perception and farmers' adoption of sustainable land management for robust adaptation in Cameroon. *Journal of Agricultural Science, 6*(12), 202.

Muasya, W. N. P., & Diallo, A. O. (2001). Development of early and extra early drought and low nitrogen-tolerant varieties using exotic and local germplasm for the dry mid-altitude ecology. In D. K. Friesen & A. F. E. Palmer (Eds.), Integrated *approaches to higher maize productivity in the New Millennium. Proceedings of the Seventh Eastern and Southern Africa Regional Maize Conference*, February 5–11, 2001, Nairobi, Kenya: CIMMYT and KARI, pp. 253–259.

Muchena, F. N. (2008). *Indicators for sustainable land management in Kenya's context. GEF land degradation focal area indicators*. East Africa, Nairobi: ETC.

Muchena, F., Onduru, D., Gachini, G., & de Jager, A. (2005a). Turning the tides of soil degradation in Africa: Capturing the reality and exploring opportunities. *Land Use Policy, 22*, 23–31.

Muchena, F. N., Onduru, D. D., Gachini, G. N., & De Jager, A. (2005b). Turning the tides of soil degradation in Africa: Capturing the reality and exploring opportunities. *Land Use Policy, 22*(1), 23–31.

Muia, V. K., & Ndunda, E. (2013). *Evaluating the impact of direct anthropogenic activities on land degradation in arid and semi-arid regions in Kenya*. Nairobi, Kenya: Kenyatta University.

Mundia, C. N., & Aniya, M. (2006). Dynamics of landuse/cover changes and degradation of Nairobi City. *Kenya. Land Degradation & Development, 17*(1), 97–108.

Nhemachena, C., & Hassan, R. (2007). Micro-level analysis of farmers' adaption to climate change in Southern Africa. IFPRI. Washington DC.

Nkonya, E., Gerber, N., Baumgartner, P., Von Braun, J., De Pinto, A., & Graw, V. et al. (2011). The Economics of Desertification, Land Degradation, and Drought: Toward an Integrated Global Assessment. IFPRI Discussion Paper 01086.

Nkonya, E., Gicheru, P., Woelcke, J., Okoba, B., Kilambya, D. & Gachimbi, L. N. (2008a). On-site and off-site long-term economic impacts of soil fertility management practices: *The case of maize-based cropping systems in Kenya*. International Food Policy Research Institute (IFPRI) IFPRI Discussion Paper 00778, July 2008.

Nkonya, E., Pender, J., Kato, E., Mugarura, S. & Muwonge, J. (2008b). Who cares? The determination of awareness, enactment and compliance with Natural Resource Management Regulations in Uganda

Nkonya, E., von Braun, J., Mirzabaev, A., Le, B. Q., Young, K. H., Kato, E., Kirui, O. K., & Gerber, N. (2014). Economics of land degradation initiative: Methods and approach for global and national assessments (Basic standards for comparable assessments). Draft for Discussion. Center for Development Research (ZEF), University of Bonn.

Nzabi, A. W., Tana, P., Masinde, A., Gesare, M., Ngoti, B., & Mwangi, G. (2000). On-farm erosion control experiment using exotic grasses and locally available materials in Nyamonyo and Kamingusa villages of southwest Kenya. In J. G. Mureithi, C. W. Mwendia, F. N. Muyekho, M. A. Anyango & S. N. Maobe (Eds.), *Participatory technology development for soil management by smallholders in Kenya. A Compilation of Selected Papers Presented at the Soil Management and Legume Research Network Projects Conference*, Kanamai, Mombasa, Kenya on March 24–26, 1997 (pp. 39–44).

Oluwole, F. A., & Sikhalazo, D. (2008). Land degradation evaluation in a game reserve in Eastern Cape of South Africa: soil properties and vegetation cover. *Scientific Research and Essays, 3*(3), 111–119.

Pender, J., Ehui, S., & Place, F. (2006). Conceptual framework and hypotheses. Strategies for sustainable land management in the East African highlands, 31.

Schipper, E. L. F., Ayers, J., Reid, H., Huq, S., & Rahman, A. (Eds.). (2014). *Community-based adaptation to climate change: Scaling it up*. Routledge

Serneels, S., & Lambin, E. F. (2001). Proximate causes of land-use change in Narok District, Kenya: A spatial statistical model. *Agriculture, Ecosystems & Environment, 85*(1), 65–81.

Sinange, R. (2007). *Environmental and Natural Resources as a Core Asset in the IGAD Region for Wealth creation, poverty Reduction, and sustainable Development: Kenya Nation Situation Report*. Nairobi, Kenya: IUCN.

Teklewold, H., Kassie, M., & Shiferaw, B. (2013). Adoption of multiple sustainable agricultural practices in rural Ethiopia. *Journal of Agricultural Economics, 64*(3), 597–623.

Tiffen, M., Mortimore, M., & Gichuki, F. (1994). *More people, less erosion: Environmental recovery in Kenya*. Overseas Development Institute, London: John Wiley & Sons Ltd.

UNCCD. (2013). Background Document, The Economics of Desertification, Land Degradation and Drought: Methodologies and Analysis for Decision-Making. In *2nd Scientific Conference on Economic Assessment of Desertification, Sustainable Land Management and Resilience of Arid, Semi-Arid and Dry Sub-Humid Areas*. April 9–12, 2013—Bonn, Germany.

UNEP. (2002). African Environment Outlook: GEO-4, United Nations Environment Programme Nairobi.

UNEP. (2009). *Kenya: Atlas of our changing Environment*. Nairobi: United Nations Environment Programme (UNEP).

von Braun, J., Gerber, N., Mirzabaev, A., & Nkonya, E. (2012). *The Economics of Land Degradation*. An Issue Paper for Global Soil Week, 08–22 November, 2012. Berlin, Germany.

von Braun, J., Gerber, N., Mirzabaev, A., & Nkonya, E. (2013). *The economics of land degradation*. ZEF Working Paper Series, 109.

Waswa, B. S. (2012). Assessment of Land Degradation Patterns in Western Kenya: Implications for Restoration and Rehabilitation. ZEF. University of Bonn, Germany.

Wattenbach, H., Bishop-Sambrook, C., & Dixon, J. (2005). Improving information flows to the rural community. *Agricultural Management, Marketing and Finance Occasional Paper (FAO)*

Were, K. O., Dick, Ø. B., & Singh, B. R. (2013). Remotely sensing the spatial and temporal land cover changes in Eastern Mau forest reserve and Lake Nakuru drainage basin, Kenya. *Applied Geography, 41*, 75–86.

Xiang, L., & Lee, A. H. (2005). Sensitivity of test for overdispersion in Poisson regression. Biometrical Journal, *47*(2), 167–176.

Chapter 17
Economics of Land Degradation and Improvement in Niger

Bokar Moussa, Ephraim Nkonya, Stefan Meyer, Edward Kato, Timothy Johnson and James Hawkins

Abstract Niger's colonial and post-independence natural resource management policies contributed to land degradation. The country also experienced a prolonged drought that amplified the suffering of the people who are heavily dependent on natural resources. The country learnt hard lessons from its past mistakes and changed its policies and strategies. This study shows a strong association of the policy changes and improved human welfare demonstrating that even poor countries could achieve sustainable development. Enhancing government effectiveness by giving communities mandate to manage natural resources and by giving incentives to land users to benefit from their investment played a key role in realizing simultaneous improvement in land management and human welfare in Niger. Given these achievements, Niger was picked as a case study to showcase its achievement and what other countries could learn from the country's mistakes and achievements. The analytical approach used focuses on estimation of cost of land degradation, ground-truthing of satellite data and drivers of adoption of sustainable land management practices. Land use/cover change (LUCC) analysis shows that a total of 6.12 million ha experienced LUCC and shrublands and grassland accounted for the largest change. Excluding the desert, 19 % of the land area experienced LUCC. Cropland expansion accounted for about 57 % of deforestation followed by grassland expansion. The cost of land degradation due to LUCC is about 2007 US$0.75 billion, which is 11 % of the 2007 GDP of US$6.773 billion and 1 % of the 2001 value of ecosystem services (ES) in Niger. Every US dollar invested in taking action returns about $6—a level that is quite attractive. Ground-truthing showed high level of agreement between satellite data and communities perception on degraded lands but poor agreement in areas for which satellite data showed land improvement.

B. Moussa (✉)
INRAN/NIGER, BP 429, Niamey, Niger
e-mail: bokarmoussa@gmail.com

E. Nkonya · E. Kato · T. Johnson · J. Hawkins
International Food Policy Research Institute, 2033 K Street NW, Washington, DC 20006, USA

S. Meyer
International Food Policy Research Institute, Lilongwe 3, Lilongwe 31666, Malawi

E. Nkonya et al. (eds.), *Economics of Land Degradation and Improvement – A Global Assessment for Sustainable Development*,
DOI 10.1007/978-3-319-19168-3_17

Communities also reported that tree planting and protection were the most common actions against land degradation. Tree planting was done mainly on bare lands to fix sand dunes. In summary, this study shows that severe land degradation and the consequent negative impacts on human welfare is a low-hanging fruit that needs to be utilized by countries as they address land degradation. This implies that instead of abandoning severely degraded lands, strategies should be used to rehabilitate such lands using low-cost organic soil fertility management practices and progressively followed by using high cost inputs as soil fertility improves. Improvement of access to rural services and facilitation of non-farm activities will also lead to faster and greater impacts on adoption of SLM practices and increasing resilience to agricultural production shocks in Niger. As Niger continues to improve sustainable land management, it faces daunting challenges to alleviate the high cost of land degradation. Niger serves as a success story to the world in addressing land degradation. Both the national and international communities need to learn from the achievement of Niger and help land users to sustainably manage their natural resources.

Keywords Niger · Land degradation · Livestock · Land use/land cover change · Pasture management practices · Grazing biomass productivity

Introduction

With a population of only 18 million people over a land area of 1.27 million km^2, Niger's population density of 14 people per km^2 is one of the 30 most sparsely populated countries in the world. About 77 % of the land area is in the Sahara desert, where rainfall is only 150 mm per year (CNEDD 2005). The remaining 23 % of the land area in the Southern part of the country is home to a majority of the people, 87 % of whom depend on rainfed agriculture. The arid and semiarid lands (ASAL) under which the farmers live are prone to drought risks which lead to calamities. The drought in 1977–1985 led to loss of 50 % of the livestock population (RoN 2006). Since 1900, there have been 13 drought events, each leading to death of about 6500 people and affecting more than 2 million people (CRED 2014). About 60 % of the population live below the poverty line and since the 1990s Niger has been classified among the poorest countries in the world. Its human development index—an index of measuring longevity and healthy life, knowledge and a decent standard of living has been below 0.4 (UNDP 2014).[1]

Despite this gloomy picture, the sun is rising in Niger! The country has made significant progress in reducing poverty and deprivation. The country has also witnessed an improvement in governance and more sustainable management of its natural resources, upon which the majority of the poor depend. This chapter discusses land

[1]HDI ranges from 0 to 1, with HDI = 1 being the highest level of development and 0 as the lowest level.

degradation and improvement and the government land-based policies and strategies implemented with an objective of reducing rural poverty and improve human welfare. The country's significant achievement in addressing land degradation serves as a good example for other low income countries. The chapter first begins with discussion of the natural resource management policies and strategies and their impacts on human welfare. To set the stage for land degradation and improvement analysis, this section is followed by a discussion on land management practices and productivity. This is followed by a discussion on methodological approach used in the study. A discussion on the economics of land degradation then follows. The chapter ends with lessons learnt and policy implications for Niger's natural resource policies and their impacts on human development.

Historical Context of Nigerien Natural Resource Management Policies

Niger's economic development serves a powerful case study on how policies and institutions[2] could lead to land degradation and how they could incentivize farmers to practice sustainable land management (SLM). Our definition of SLM has been contested (e.g. see Kaphengst 2014). For the purpose of this study, we define SLM as land management that maintains or improves ecosystem services for human wellbeing, as negotiated by all stakeholders (Winslow et al. 2011). However, we will refer to land management as SLM if it is an improvement over the commonly used land degrading management practices even when such practice does not maintain or improve terrestrial ecosystems. Before colonialism, Niger had customary unwritten right of axe law—which stipulated that a farmer who clears land owns it (Gnoumou and Bloch 2003). The Law of the Axe was made worse by the French colonial laws 'Aubreville Decree' of 1935, which made all vegetation the property of the government and farmers were required to purchase permits to cut and use wood—even when such trees were on their own farms (Brough and Kimenyi 2002; Montagne and Amadou 2012). Another decree given in the same year stipulated that all lands not occupied or used for more than 10 years becomes state property—even when such land belonged to a farmer but lying fallow (Boffa 1999). Both laws served as disincentives for farmers to invest in tree planting or protection. After independence in 1960, the Nigerien government slightly changed the French law as it maintained ownership of most economically valuable tree species on both protected areas and private lands (Boffa 1999). For example, its 1974 Forest code listed most economically valuable trees as 'protected species' (Boffa 1999; Rinaudo 2005). Due to weak enforcement of the forest code, naturally occurring trees were cut without replacement and this led to severe loss of tree cover.

[2]According to North (1991), institutions are formal and informal regulations that structure political, economic and social interaction. They include laws, statutes, taboos, code of conduct, etc.

Matters were made worse by the prolonged drought that led to loss of vegetation and decimated over 50 % of the existing livestock (RoN 2006). Firewood collection —done mainly by women—became a one day task. The natural resource scarcity also led to intensification of conflicts between transhumant pastoralists and sedentary farmers over water and terrestrial biomes (trees, croplands, and grazing lands). Tree scarcity and the massive loss of livestock and other impacts of land degradation required the Nigerien government to reconsider its natural resource management policies and strategies. The section below discusses the policy reforms.

Natural Resources and Agricultural Policy Reforms

Consistent with Cooke et al. (2008), the dire scarcity of trees and tree products changed the community's perception from tree cutting to clear land to tree planting and protection. The tree scarcity also affected the livestock sector, especially in the central part of Niger, where trees are used as fodder during the dry season. The government also responded to this land degradation by promoting tree planting. As part of the decentralization process in the 1990s (Mohamadou 2009), the Nigerien government passed the Rural Code (Principe d'Orientational du Code Rural Ordinance) in 1993. This law was developed after a consultative process initiated in 1986, and was intended to establish a framework for synthesizing and ultimately replacing the complex and sometimes overlapping set of tenure rights existing under customary, Islamic, colonial and state laws and rules (Toulmin and Quan 2000). The goal of the Rural Code was to integrate customary systems into formal law, drawing upon in-depth studies of local farming, pastoral and forestry practices (Lavigne et al. 2002). It sought to provide land tenure security, to organize and manage rural lands, and to plan and manage natural resources (Gnoumou and Bloch 2003). The Rural Code recognized private land rights only when they are acquired through customary law or written contracts (République du Niger 2003). The Rural Code also gives customary leaders the role of resolving land conflicts and enacting natural resource management (NRM) by-laws (Toulmin and Quan 2000; Lavigne and Delville 2002).

The Rural Code addressed four main issues: protection of the rights of rural operators, conservation and management of natural resources, organization of rural peoples (farmers, herders) and regional land use planning. To complement the Rural Code, the 2004 forestry law also gave tree tenure—i.e., a farmer who plants trees or protects trees on her farm owns it and could use it in any way she wanted (Adam et al. 2006; Stickler 2012).

The Nigerien institutional changes implemented in the 1990s to 2011 had a favorable impact of government effectiveness—quality of public services, civil service and the degree of its independence from political pressures, the quality of policy formulation and implementation, and the credibility of the government's

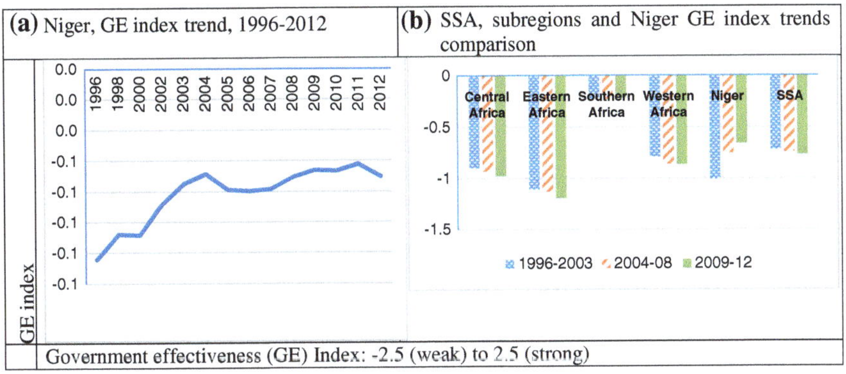

Fig. 17.1 Trend of government effectiveness, SSA and Niger. *Source* Calculated from http://data.worldbank.org/data-catalog/worldwide-governance-indicators

commitment to such policies (Kaufman et al. 2010). Figure 17.1 shows that the government effectiveness (GE) index rose in Niger by about 43 % while it fell in SSA and Western Africa sub-region. The Nigerien GE index in 2009–12 period was greater than the corresponding average in both SSA and Western Africa. This reveals the significant progress the country made in the two decades.

Improvement in government effectiveness and community perception of natural resources showed a significant impact on natural resources. In addition to allowing communities to own and benefit from trees—thus incentivizing them to plant and protect trees—the Rural Code and other institutional reforms received strong support of civil society that provided significant technical support (Sendzimir et al. 2011). In collaboration with NGOs and international donors, the government initiated tree planting and protection (Reij et al. 2009). Since then, communities and farmers felt much greater ownership over the trees on their land. It is estimated that at least 3 million hectares of land has been reforested since the early 1980s in Niger, largely as a result of community tree planting and natural regeneration of trees (Adam et al. 2006). This is about 2.5 times the forest area of 1.2 million ha in 2012 (FAOSTAT 2014). The tree planting and protection programs contributed to what is known as the regreening of the Sahel (Anyamba et al. 2014; Sendzimir et al. 2011). There was significant increase in rainfall in the Sahelian region that explained the increased vegetation from 1994 to 2012 (Anyamba et al. 2014). However, after controlling for wetter conditions, Herrmann et al. (2005) observed residual increase in greenness that was not explained by increased precipitation. The residual greenness was concentrated in the Projet Intégré Keita (PIK), and where other tree planting and protection programs operated (Reij et al. 2009; Pender et al. 2009).

As Fig. 17.2 shows, the Nigerien forest area declined rapidly in the 1990s, but the rate of loss slowed down beginning in 2001. Such a slowdown could be linked to the lagged impact of the policy changes discussed above.

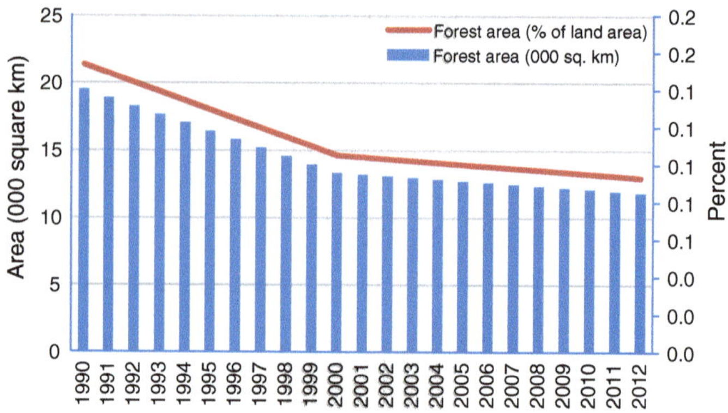

Fig. 17.2 Niger forest area trend, *Note* FAO's forest data available only from 1990. *Source* FAO (2012)

Illustrating the Nigerien success story that resulted from policy and institutional changes that provided incentives for land operators to plant and protect trees, the area of planted forest as a percent of the total forest area in Niger was greater than the corresponding percent in three other countries (Fig. 17.3).

A large area of degraded land has been rehabilitated through a presidential program on land rehabilitation and several donor funded projects. According to Adam et al. (2006), at least 250,000 ha of land have been rehabilitated using tree planting and soil and water conservation (SWC) measures since the mid-1980s. The rehabilitated land is about 16 % of the 16 million ha cropland in 2012 (FAOSTAT 2014).

The 1997 Memorandum for Orientation for Livestock Policy, and the 1998 Strategic Orientation Document (DOS) for the agricultural sector specify that sustainable land management (SLM) is a precondition for sustainable agricultural

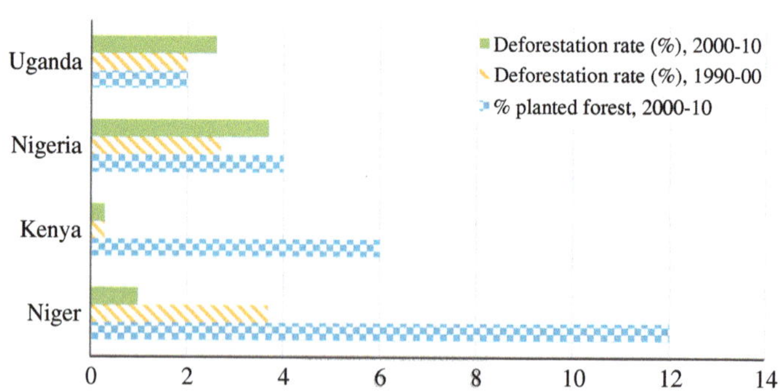

Fig. 17.3 Deforestation rate and planted forest as share of total forest area in selected countries. *Source* Calculated from FAO (2012)

development. This policy framework gives a clear mandate for mainstreaming SLM in all ministries that affect land management significantly. Niger is also one of the 37 countries in the world that have revised their national forest policy (NFP) to include sustainable forest management (SFM) (FAO 2014). Niger's NFP also specifically links SFM and ecosystem services (Ibid).

Consistent with DOS, Niger formulated its Poverty Reduction Strategy (PRS) in 2002, in which SLM is one of the key strategies for poverty reduction. To address risky production in the mainly rainfed agriculture, the PRS promotes diversification and intensification as key elements of agricultural development. The PRS is supported by the 2003 Rural Development Strategy (RDS), in which promotion of sustainable natural resource management, profitable agricultural production and food security are among its main objectives (République du Niger 2003). To achieve its goals sustainably, the RDS aims at decentralization of natural resource management (NRM) by building the capacity of the rural institutions to manage natural resources and rural development in general.

Niger has ratified all three Earth Summit conventions—United Nations Convention to Combat Desertification (UNCCD), Convention on Biological Diversity (CBD) and Framework Convention on Climate Change (UNFCC). Accordingly, Niger created Termit and Tin Toumma National Nature and Cultural Reserve in 2007, which covers 97,000 km^2 or 14 % of the land area (Sahara Conservation Fund 2007). To address desertification and land degradation in general, the government adopted the UNCCD convention in 2000 and prepared its national Action Plan (NAP). The NAP sets short-term and long-term plans to address land degradation through promotion of sustainable pasture management, water harvesting, tree planting, developing livestock markets, and other strategies.

Niger designed the national adaptation plan of action (NAPA) in 2006, which identified 14 climate change adaptation action strategies with the broad objectives of food security, sustainable resource management, and poverty reduction. The 14 strategic activities are achieved through the following broad activities: (1) pasture and rangeland improvement; (2) increasing livestock productivity by improving local livestock breeds; (3) development and protection of water resources for domestic use, irrigation, and livestock; (4) promotion of sustainable land and water management (SLWM) practices that enhance adaptation to climate change; (5) promoting peri-urban agriculture and nonfarm activities; (6) building the capacity and organizational skills of rural community development groups; (7) preventing and fighting against climate-related pests and diseases; and (8) dissemination of climate information.

As is the case in other countries however, the total budget set for Niger's NAPA is small and its implementation is short-term (two to three years). Investment in the NAPA has also been largely funded by donors, with limited contribution by the government. This reveals the weak political will of the government to put the NAPA into the sustainable and long-term operation required for effectiveness. However, NAPA has spurred country-level policy awareness of climate change and the need to design policies and strategies to enhance adaptation and mitigation.

Niger has formulated a national plan on soil fertility and water management, whose objective is to promote the use of appropriate technologies for SLWM (RoN 2006). This policy further shows government's sustainable development and its commitment to SLWM. In 2006, the government also adopted a national strategy for sustainable input supply to farmers (SIAD). The inputs being promoted under the SIAD include seed, fertilizers, pesticides, feed, and others. The objectives of SIAD are to ensure regular access to agricultural inputs at a competitive price; to regulate production, marketing and use of agricultural inputs and to strengthen the capacity of farmer organizations to produce and market their products. It is too early to evaluate the SIAD performance. However, if fully implemented SIAD will help in increasing agricultural productivity and will support the national plan on soil fertility and water management and other NRM and agricultural policies. The policy also sets a stage for supporting the growth of the private input sector, which is weak.

Niger subsidizes fertilizer and some donors distribute fertilizer as part of the emergency aid. The government does not involve the private sector in the distribution of donor fertilizer. Instead, it distributes the donated fertilizer through the "central d'approvisionement", the National government agency for input distribution. The government has justified its participation in input distribution as necessary because of the weak private input marketing sector and to ensure regional equity.[3] However, this approach works against other efforts to promote growth of the private sector. For example, the "IARBIC project" and other projects are helping to establish a private sector for fertilizers and other input distribution. These efforts are being undermined by the free fertilizer distribution.

After trade liberalization in Niger, the government removed most imports and exports taxes on agricultural input and output. The move was aimed at facilitating food imports to address the food deficiency that affects the country frequently.[4] The move was also aimed at increasing domestic production. This made Niger one of the most liberalized economies in West Africa. Niger is also one of the West African Monetary and Economic Union (UMEOA) and the Economic Community of West African States (ECOWAS). The objective of both economic unions is to remove all tax and barriers among member states. Niger agricultural exports go mainly within the region (ECOWAS and UMEOA).

The discussion reveals that Niger has designed a number of policies aimed at correcting the old programs that contributed to land degradation and to respond to new global and national changes. The section below discusses the trends and patterns of human welfare in order to understand the potential impact which such changes could have made. The discussion is not meant to attribute the changes directly to policy changes, but rather to establish an association that could help to better understand the environment-human welfare linkage (Reynolds et al. 2011).

[3]Discussion with some government officials and researchers in Niger also revealed that the government uses the free distribution of fertilizer to gain political credit during election seasons.

[4]Only imported rice is taxed.

Trends of Human Welfare Indicators and Their Relationship with Policy and Institutional Changes

The Nigerien human development index (HDI)—a statistical indicator of a country's social and economic development that is calculated using life expectancy at birth, mean years of schooling, expected years of schooling and gross national income per capita—has been improving in the past three decades along with other low human development countries (Fig. 17.4). Despite this development however, Niger remains well below the average of the HDI of other low development index countries.

The Nigerien HDI improvement is strongly correlated with the agricultural sector development and important rural development programs. Microdosing—which involves placing seeds in planting basin systems, i.e., planting holes made to harvest water, in which a small amount of organic inputs and inorganic fertilizer are placed (Tabo et al. 2009)[5]—has been increasing in Niger due to promotion by government extension agents, international research organizations, and civil societies (Pender et al. 2009). Accordingly, the rate of nitrogen fertilizer application rate in Niger increased by over 60 % from its average level 2002–05 to 2009–12 (Fig. 17.5). This was the largest increase in West Africa—though the average application rate in Niger is lower than the rate in Western Africa and SSA. The low application rate in Niger is due to the semi-arid conditions, high cost of fertilizer and limited access to credit (Pender et al. 2008). Accordingly, increase in inorganic fertilizer application in Niger is strongly associated with an exponential increase in the crop production index from 1996 to 2012 (Fig. 17.5b). Milk and beef production per capita also increased significantly after the devastating decline during prolonged drought in 1977–1985 (Fig. 17.6). The regreening of the Sahel could have improved pasture and consequently livestock productivity.

Figure 17.7 shows that the percent of the population with malnutrition in 2012–14 Niger fell by about 60 % compared to its level in 1990–92. The corresponding change in Western Africa and SSA was 43 and 25 % respectively. Accordingly, the global hunger index (GHI)—a multidimensional statistical index depicting severity of hunger in a country (Von Grebmer et al. 2013) and infant mortality rate (IMR)—number of children under five years who die per 1000 live births (WHO 2014) have both been falling (Fig. 17.7).

Even though there may be no direct connection between the improving human development indicators and the government policy and institutional changes, the two have a strong correlation that suggest a causal relationship. Indeed, the sun is rising in Niger.

To set the stage for the methodological analysis of the economics of land degradation, the next section discusses land degradation and improvement and livestock and crop productivity in Niger.

[5]Microdosing is also referred to as precision conservation agriculture (PCA) (Twomlow et al. 2009).

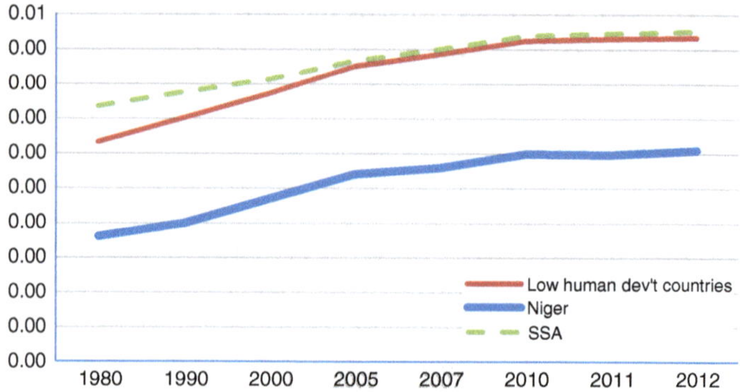

Fig. 17.4 Nigerien human development index trend, 1980–2012, *Note* HDI ranges from 0 = lowest human development to 1 = highest human development. *Source* UNDP (2013)

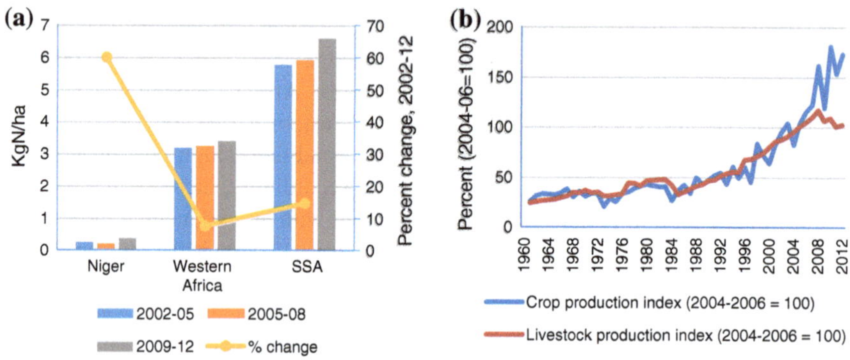

Fig. 17.5 Trend of Nitrogen fertilizer application rates and agricultural, 1990–2012, **a** Fertilizer application rate. **b** Trend of agricultural productivity, Niger. *Note* Percent N application rate calculated as follows: $\Delta\% = \frac{y_2 - y_1}{y_1} \times 100$, where y_1 = average application rate, 2002–05, y_2 = average application rate, 2009–12. *Source* Calculated from FAOSTAT (2014)

Land Use/Cover Change, Livestock and Cropland Management and Production in Niger

As noted in the analytical methods in Chap. 2 and cost of land degradation in Chap. 6, our analysis will examine the change in the ecosystem services due to land use/cover change (LUCC) and use of land degrading or improving management practices on static cropland and grazing lands (grasslands).

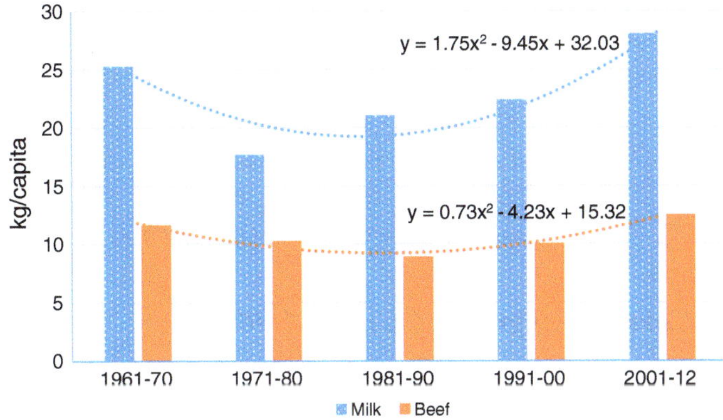

Fig. 17.6 Per capita milk and beef production in Niger

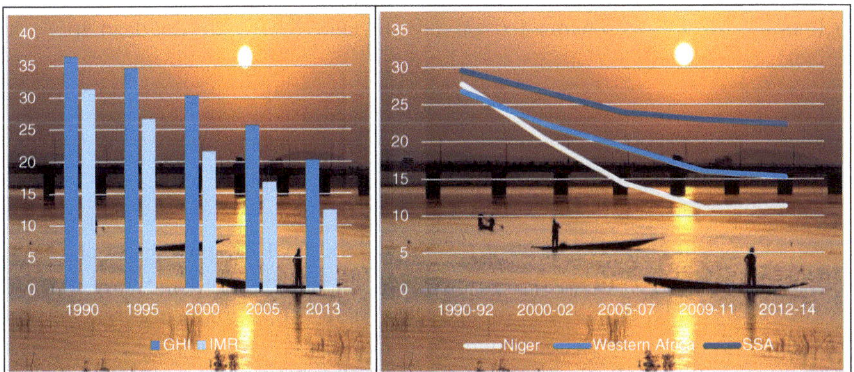

GHI and IMR	Percent of population with malnutrition

Change of malnutrition

Region/subregion	2000-02	2005-07	2009-11	2012-14
		Percent change		
Niger	25.99	48.01	60.29	59.21
Western Africa	16.27	28.19	40.43	42.84
SSA	9.52	19.41	22.60	24.64

Fig. 17.7 The sun is rising in Niger: trend of infant mortality rate, hunger, and population with malnutrition, Percent change $= \frac{y_2 - y_1}{y_1} * 100$, where y_2 = Percent of population with malnutrition in year i, i = 2000–02, 2005–07 to 2012–14, y_1 = percent of population with malnutrition in year 1990–92. *Sources* Malnutrition and IMR: World Bank poverty database http://data.worldbank.org/topic/poverty; GHI: Grebmer et al. (2013). *Photo credit* © iStockphoto.com Jamie Geysbeek "Niger River in the Morning"

Table 17.1 Change of biome extent, 2001–09, Niger

Biome	2001–05	2006–09	Change	% change
Million ha				
Pasture	25.08	28.78	3.70	14.8
Forest	1.29	1.24	−0.056	−4.3
Cropland	14.09	14.80	0.71	5.1
Total	26.37	30.02	3.65	13.8

Source Calculated from FAOSTAT (2014)

Land Use/Cover Change (LUCC), 2001–09

Using year 2001–05 and 2006–09 as baseline and endline respectively, average cropland area increased by 5 % while grazing lands increased by 15 % (Table 17.1). The large increase of the pasture is also due to the regreening of the Sahel (Ouedraogo et al. 2013). Forest extent fell by 56,000 ha or 4.3 %. This is not contrary to the tree planting and protection success story discussed earlier because such programs were implemented on private lands that may not lead to forest biomes.

Livestock Production

Livestock contributes 35 % of Nigerien agricultural GDP (Kamuanga et al. 2008). Niger has a population of 9.214 million heads of cattle or about one head of cattle for each two people. A livestock production system is predominantly pastoral with 26 and 38 % of the household engaged in pastoral and agropastoral production systems respectively (Table 17.2). The average herdsize is 11 and the maximum size is 122. Cows account for 40 % of the herdsize. However, livestock productivity is low. The average daily milk production per cow in Niger is only 1.4 l, a level which is comparable with overall average of 1.6 l per day per local breed cow in the Sahelian region (Desta 2002).[6] This is due to the low rainfall, poor rangeland management, and poor livestock breeds. Only about 4 % used improved pasture management—suggesting that degraded grasslands dominate the production systems. Milk off-take per lactation is 185 kg in the ASAL and 750 kg in the sub-humid and humid areas (Otte and Chilonda 2002). As individual animal productivity has remained unchanged, changes in production over time has largely been determined by livestock density, as observed by Otte and Chilonda (2011).

[6]Milk off-take for local breeds is 524 kg per lactation period, which lasts 329 days (Desta 2002). This translates to 1.6 l per cow per lactation day.

Table 17.2 Livelihoods of rural communities, adoption of pasture management and breeds, productivity and composition of livestock

Household characteristics	Statistic
Own livestock (%)	97
Practice rotational grazing (%)	2.24
Milk production per day per cow (liters), 3 months after calving	1.4
- Own cross-bred cattle (%)	2.1
Household production systems (% of households)	
Crop production only	37
Agropastoral	38
Pastoral	26
Households using improved pasture management (%)[a]	4
Shoats (goats and sheep) herd size	16
Cattle herd size (number of heads)	13
Cattle off-take (head of cattle)	0.16
Herd composition of cattle (%)[b]	
Ox	3
Bull	15
Cow	40
Young Bull/Young	12
Heifer	12
Calf	19
Milking cows	19
Adult cattle	58
Improved breeds (cross-breed or exotic breeds)	11

Notes [a]Improved pasture management include rotational grazing and managed natural regeneration. No farmer reported planted pasture
[b]Calves = <1 year, young males and heifers = 1–3 years, males = >3 years (not specified whether bulls or oxen), cows = >3 years
Source Extracted from INS (2012)

Cropland

Millet, cowpeas and sorghum are the three most important crops accounting for 94 % of cropland area (Table 17.3). Other crops, namely maize and rice are not widely grown due to their high water requirements. However, maize and rice consumption and consequently net import have been increasing. For example, per capita net rice import increased from 8 kg in 2000 to 11 kg in 2011 (FAOSTAT 2014). Actual yield achieved by farmers is quite low—especially for cowpea, sorghum and maize, whose farmer yields are less than 50 % of the potential (Table 17.3). This shows the large potential that Niger enjoys in increasing yield and food security. Microdosing and moisture conservation technologies are among the agronomic practices that could be used to simultaneously increase yield and reduce high risk production in the Sahelian region (Tabo et al. 2009).

Table 17.3 Cultivated area and actual and potential yield of major crops in Niger

	Cropland area (000 ha)	Share of total cropland (%)	Actual yield (Tons/ha)	Yield potential (Tons/ha)	Actual yield as % of potential (%)
Millet	7100	44.4	0.5	1.0	50
Cowpeas	4900	30.6	0.2	0.8	25
Sorghum	3100	19.4	0.3	1.0	30
Rice	13	0.1	1.9	3.0	63
Maize	13	0.1	0.9	2.0	45
Total	15126.5	94.5			
Total cropland area	16,000	100			

Sources Calculated from FAOSTAT (2014): farmer yield, cropland area; ILO JASPA (1981): Yield potential millet, rice and rice; Tabo et al. (2009) yield potential sorghum

Building on the discussion above and on Chaps. 2 and 6, the discussion below focuses on the analytical approach. The discussion gives more details on aspects that are specific to Niger and to data used in this chapter.

Analytical Approach

Our analytical approach focuses on estimation of cost of land degradation, groundtruthing of satellite data and drivers of adoption of sustainable land management practices. To take into account the high production risks in Niger, we also estimate the Just-Pope mean-variance model to determine the land management practices that farmers could use to reduce production risks (Just and Pope 1979, 2003).

Cost of Land Degradation

The approach used for assessing land degradation is discussed in Chap. 6. There few differences in the approach, which are briefly discussed below.

Land Degradation on Static Cropland

We add millet—the most important staple crop in Niger and drop wheat, which is not a common crop in the country. However, we use the same crop simulation approach to determine the impact of land degradation on static cropland.

Land Degradation on Grazing Lands

Impact of Land Degradation or Improvement on Livestock Productivity

We assess livestock productivity using beef and milk offtake only. This approach ignores other effects of pasture degradation such as parturition and mortality rate. Parturition could increase while mortality rate could fall due to better pasture intake. Rufino et al. (2009) find that adding supplements to diets increases calving rate among smallholder Kenyan dairy farms. Huttner et al. (2001) reports that malnutrition is a major factor predisposing cattle to poor health among Malawian smallholders. Like the case for crops, we estimate the impact of grazing biomass change on livestock productivity using two scenarios:

Business as usual (BAU)—Continuous grazing and improved pasture management —rotational grazing which allows natural regeneration of grasslands. Choice of rotational grazing as an improved forage management is done due to the observation that a number of farmers reported to have used it.

Consistent with Havlic et al. (2014), forage productivity under continuous and rotational grazing was estimated using EPIC model estimated in Sokoto Nigeria by Izzaraulde (2010). The biophysical and socio-economic characteristics of the sites selected in Sokoto were comparable with those selected in Southern Niger (Nkonya et al. 2015). Grazing biomass productivity under BAU and rotational grazing was simulated with the EPIC model, establishing a generic, perennial C4 species and grazing regime during the rainy season (June 1–October 31) and a livestock density of 1 TLU/ha. Continuous grazing was set such that animals could continue grazing until biomass reduces to a minimum amount of plant dry matter of 0.1 Mg/ha. Rotational grazing scenario allowed 15-day resting periods in-between to allow for grass natural regeneration.

It is important to establish the feed requirement of grazing animals and match this with available pasture. The feed requirement will provide the potential productivity of livestock. Assuming the animals feed on forage with specific nutrient properties, the quantity of feed intake will vary depending on the characteristics of the animal. Specifically, the body weight, growth rate, milk production, and activity level of the animal will jointly determine the level of intake required. Stéphenne and Lambin (2001) estimated the DM biomass consumption per TLULivestock in the Sahelian zone to be 4.6 tons/year based on the following:

- Average daily dietary requirements are 6.25 kg DM per TLU (Houérou and Hoste 1977; Behnke and Scoones 1993; Leeuw and Tothill 1993).
- Consumable forage of grasses is only one-third of the above-ground biomass (Penning de Vries and Djitèye 1982; Leeuw and Tothill 1993). This means requirement must be multiplied by a factor of 3 to account for this.
- Shrubs, trees and crops residues contribute 33 % of livestock biomass requirements (Houérou and Hoste 1977; Pieri 1989).

This translates to 6.25 kg * 365 * 3 * 2/3 = 4.6 tons/year/TLU. The feed requirement was used to determine the cost of land degradation in the areas experiencing overgrazing but not practicing rotational grazing. The feed requirement was also used to determine the grazing area experiencing overgrazing. Overgrazing occurs when

$$ovr = TLU\ density > \frac{biom}{4.6}$$

where ovr = overgrazing; TLU density is the TLU density per ha; biom = grazing biomass productivity (tons of dry matter per ha per year).

Given that the TLU density data are available for only 2005, we extrapolated it over nine periods using the FAOSTAT national livestock population data and assumed the livestock distribution remained unchanged.

Impact of Forage Intake on Milk Production

Consistent with NRC (2001) and Muia (2000), we estimate the response of milk production to dry matter intake using a linear equation:

$$y_i = a + bx, \tag{17.3}$$

where y_i = daily milk offtake of cow i, x = dry matter intake (DMI) per day. To determine the impact of feeding practices only, this equation assumes all other cow nutritional and health requirements are fixed at optimal levels. Table 17.4 reports some results of the impact of dry matter intake (DMI) on milk off-take in Kenya and USA. The study by Muia (2000) is appealing since the constant and coefficient of the equation were determined under controlled experiments in SSA. However, Muia (2000) determined the impact of feed intake on milk yield using zero-grazed Friesian cows in Kenya—an aspect that requires calibrating the model to fit the predominantly local cows raised by farmers in Niger. Dairy cows were fed with

Table 17.4 Linear regression coefficients of dry matter intake impact on daily milk off-take per cow

	Constant term	Coefficient	Study country	Comments
NRC (2001)	–	2.17	USA	Weight of cow 450 kg
Muia (2000)	0.18	0.77	Kenya	Friesian cow weighing 450 kg. Napier and Leucaena
Muia (2000)	0.98	0.87	Kenya	As above, but cows fed with Napier and concentrate

Napier grass supplemented with Leucaena legume. However, the added supplement had only a marginal impact on milk productivity since the slope of the equation with Napier grass, Leucaena and concentrates is 0.87 (Table 17.4).

Muia (2000) used Napier grass (Pennisetum purpureum)—which is tropical grass suitable in tropical humid environment, which is not widely distributed in Niger. Additionally he used improved breeds, which account for only 2.1 % of cattle in Niger. This suggests the need to test the model and modify it to take these challenges into account. We evaluated the model performance in predicting milk yield after feeding on the common forage in Southern Niger. To address the different offtake of local and improved breeds, we introduce a technology scalar, which is a ratio of milk production for local and cross-bred cows. Given the above, the loss of milk production due to land degradation is given by the following model

$$m_t = \sum_{t=4}^{T} a[0.18 + 0.77(DMI_t^c - DMI_t^d)]x_t \tag{17.4}$$

where m_i = total milk production in year t, DM I_t^c = dry matter biomass intake (kg/head per day) for cows grazing under rotational grazing; DMI_t^d = dry matter biomass intake (kg/head per day) for cows grazing under continuous grazing; t = year, t = 4…0.9; a = technology coefficient given by $a = \frac{m_l}{m_e}$, where m_l = daily milk production of one local cow; and m_e = daily milk production of one exotic cow used by Muia (2000) and x_t = number of milking cows in year in overgrazed grasslands in t.

We start to detect the impact of improved pasture management in the fourth year (t = 4) because we assume that grassland biomass increase due to rotational grazing will reach an equilibrium in year 3. The annual biomass productivity per ha in Niger ranges from 0.21 to 2.02 tons DM/ha with an average of 0.63 tons DM/ha (Havlic et al. 2014). Based on LSMS household survey data collected in 2012, the daily milk offtake per local cow ranges from 0.5 to 4 l with an average of 1.4 kg. Muia et al. (2000)'s one Friesian cow fed with 12.2 kg DM of Napier grass per day and supplemented with sunflower produces 11.7 kg of milk. Using these data to calibrate Muia's model shows that the average milk production is overestimated by only 10 % (Table 17.5)—suggesting that the technology factor a = 0.90.

Table 17.5 Calibration of the Muia (2000) model to local cow breeds

Biomass productivity statistics	Annual biomass (tons/ha)	Equivalent daily DMI (kg/cow)	Milk offtake per cow (kg/day)	% of actual milk offtake of local cows
Average	0.63	1.8	1.6	110
	1.00	2.7	2.3	160
Maximum	2.02	5.5	4.4	317
	5.50	15.1	11.8	840

To determine milk production during the reference period, we compute the cow herd growth model proposed by Upton (1989):

$$x_{t+1} = (1 + \beta - \omega)x_t - \tau x_t, \tag{17.5}$$

where x_t = cow herd in year t; β = growth rate of heifer into cows; ω = cow mortality rate; τ = cow offtake rate.

We set the growth rate of cow herd to reach an equilibrium that matches the average herd size, i.e.,

$$x_{t+1} \leq \bar{x},$$

where $\bar{x}$ = average cow herd. Since we estimate cow herd growth rate at national level, we do not include stolen cows since we assume such theft is a transfer within Niger.

Impact of Forage Intake on Beef Production

We compute the impact of land degradation or improvement using the meat off-take only and ignoring the change in weight for livestock which were not sold or slaughtered. Based on Blench (1999), the feed conversion ratio (kg grazed dry matter per change (kg) in live weight) is 7:1 for cattle and 10:1 for sheep and goats (shoats). This suggests the extra 100 kg of forage due to improved pasture management (e.g. rotational grazing) would convert in gains of 14 kg of live weight for cattle and 10 of live weight for shoats. However, these comparisons should be taken with caution since they apply mostly to European breeds, which may have different behavior from indigenous cattle breeds in Niger.

Based on the discussion of milk and meat offtake changes due to feed intake, we estimate the cost of land degradation from 2001 to 09 on overgrazed grassland using the following model:

$$CLD_{grass} = \sum_{t=4}^{T} [m_t p_m + off(b^c - b^d)p_b + \tau \Delta CO_2 a] \tag{17.6}$$

where CLD_{grass} = Cost of land degradation in Niger; m_t = as defined in Eq. (17.5), b^c and b^d = meat production under improved and unimproved pasture management; P_b = price of beef per kg; P_m = price of milk per kg; off = livestock offtake rate (slaughter and sales of live animals); ΔCO_2 = change in the amount of carbon sequestered under SLM and BAU and τ = price of CO_2 in the global carbon market and a = area being overgrazed.

Table 17.6 Land status and primary economic activities in the selected communities, 2013

Community	KoneBeri	Tiguey	Bazaga	Babaye	Djibiri	Bla Birin
Population	2734	1616	1712	1061	37	84
Land status	Degraded	Degraded	Improved	Degraded	Improved	Degraded
Primary activities of households						
Crop production	80	80	90	80	30	10
Livestock		10	7		17	
Crop/livestock	15			15	20	70
Forest			3		3	
Fisheries					15	
Non-farm	5	10		5	15	20

Source Authors

Groundtruthing and Focus Group Discussion

Focus Group Discussions (FGD) were conducted in seven Nigerien communities shown in Fig. 17.9. The communities were selected to cover AEZ and to represent areas that Le et al. (2014) showed land improvement or land degradation in each AEZ (see Table 17.6). All seven communities fell into one agroecological zone—the arid and semiarid land (ASAL), i.e., with rainfall below 700 mm/year. Approximately 10–20 community members participated in the FGD. KoneBeri, Tiguey, Bazaga, and Babaye are predominantly crop producers while Djibiri and Bla Birin are pastoral and agropastoral communities. Le et al. (2014) classify Bazaga and Djibiri as having experienced land improvement while the rest of the communities experienced land degradation (Fig. 17.8).

Participants were purposely selected to represent old people who could give informed perception on land use change over the 30 year reference period; women, the youth, local government leaders, crop producers, livestock producers, people who earn their livelihoods from forest and other non-agricultural terrestrial biomes, and customary leaders. Such a diverse groups afforded a rich discussion on ecosystem value and their change from 1982 to 2012.

Groundtruthing remote sensing data was done by asking FGD members to show the LUCC and land degradation or improvement of the major biomes which have occurred in the community over a 30 year period (1982–2012). Groundtruthing helps to determine reliability of the satellite data used in this report. Results of the groundtruthing are reported in Chap. 5 of this book.

Drivers of Adoption of SLM and Risk Reducing Land Management Practices

Drivers of adoption of SLM: We estimate the drivers of adoption of ISFM, inorganic fertilizer, organic inputs and crop rotation using a Probit model specified as follows:

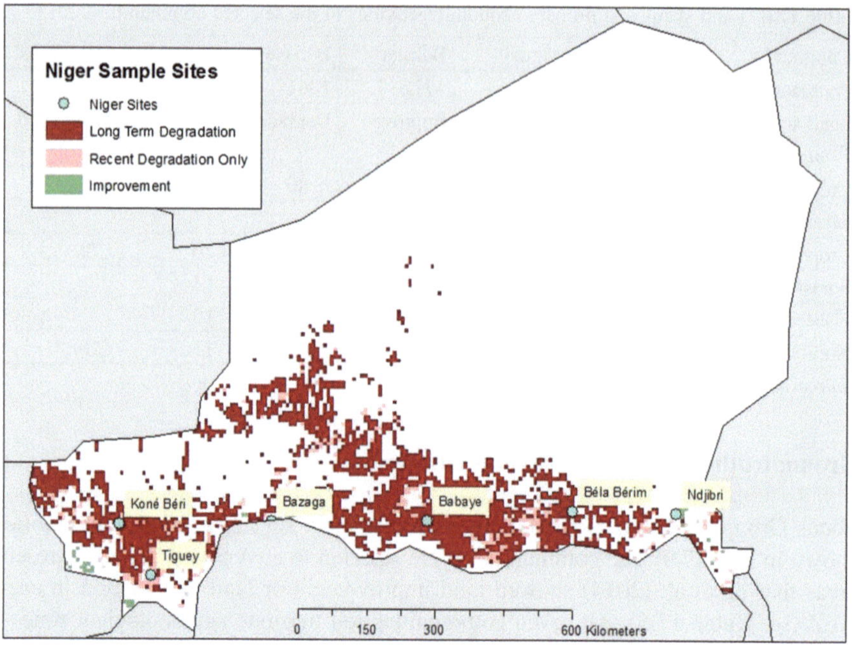

Fig. 17.8 Case study communities selected for FGD and groundtruthing

$$Y^* = \Phi - 1(Y) = X\beta + \varepsilon,$$

where Y* is a latent variable, such that

$$Y = \begin{cases} 0 & \text{if } Y^* \leq 0 \\ 1 & \text{if } Y^* \geq 1 \end{cases},$$

Φ is a cumulative normal distribution with Z-distribution, i.e., $\Phi(Z)\epsilon(0,1)$, X is a vector of covariates of drivers of adoption of land management practices and β is a vector of the associated coefficients. $X\beta \sim N(0, 1)$; ε is an error term with normal distribution, i.e., $\varepsilon \sim N(0, 1)$.

Choice of the elements of the X vector in the empirical model is guided by literature[7] and data availability. We include some variables that are potentially endogenous. To address the endogeneity bias, we estimate a reduced form model and an instrumental variable linear probability model (IV-LPM) (Horace and Oaxaca 2006). The LPM has two major problems: (i) some estimates of probability are above 1 and are meaningless. The farther away from 0 to 1 interval, the more biased and inconsistent the estimates are (Ibid) and (ii) violation of

[7]See Chap. 7 for details.

homoscedasticity and normality assumptions. The dependent variable as dichotomous variable cannot yield a homoscedastic error term, unless the odds of p = 1 for all observations are the same and that the error term is not normally distributed, given that there are only two values (0 and 1). Following Horace and Oaxaca (2006), it is possible to address both problems by dropping values that lead to coefficients outside the 0 to 1 interval. Estimates are unbiased and are consistent if they lie within the unit interval (ibid). To check robustness of the coefficients, we estimate the structural model and the corresponding IV-LPM and the reduced Probit model.

Impacts of land management on production risks: Given that the land management practices that affect yield also influence risk (variance), we use the Just-Pope mean-variance model:

$$Y = f(X, C) = p(X, C) + \sqrt{\varphi(X, C)e(\xi)}$$

where Y = yield which is affected by a deterministic production function P(·) and a stochastic risk function $\varphi(\cdot)$ with an error term of unknown random effects $(e(\xi))$ determined by rainfall and other risks and stressors that affect Y. Drivers of $e(\xi)$ are unknown to farmers when they make production decisions.

C and X are respectively covariates of land management practices and other covariates, which simultaneously affect P(·) and $\varphi(\cdot)$.

$$\frac{\partial var(Y)}{\partial C} > 0 \rightarrow \text{Risk-increasing land management practice},$$
$$\frac{\partial var(Y)}{\partial C} < 0 \rightarrow \text{Risk reducing land management practice}.$$

The following section discusses the results of the study, starting with the cost of land degradation due to LUCC.

Cost of Land Degradation Due to LUCC and Community Restoration Efforts

According to Table 17.7, desert or barren land accounts for about 72 % of the land area. However, excluding the desert, grasslands and shrublands respectively account for 76 and 23 % of the land area. A total of 6.12 million ha experienced LUCC and shrublands and grassland accounted for the largest change (Fig. 17.9 and Table 17.7). Excluding the desert, 19 % of the land area experienced LUCC. Cropland expansion accounted for about 57 % of deforestation followed by grassland expansion (Fig. 17.10). This is consistent with Gibbs et al. (2010) who

Table 17.7 Extent of major biomes and LUCC in Niger, 2001

Biome	Area	Percent of total area		LUCC to other biome(s)
	(million ha)	Excluding the desert	Including the desert	(million ha)
Forest	0.01	0.03	0.01	–
Shrublands	7.55	23.09	6.38	3.40
Grasslands	24.71	75.58	20.88	2.51
Cropland	0.32	0.99	0.27	0.15
Urban	0.04	0.14	0.04	–
Woodlands	0.06	0.17	0.05	0.04
Desert/barren	85.65	–	72.38	–

Note Change in forest area excluded since it is too small
Source MODIS data

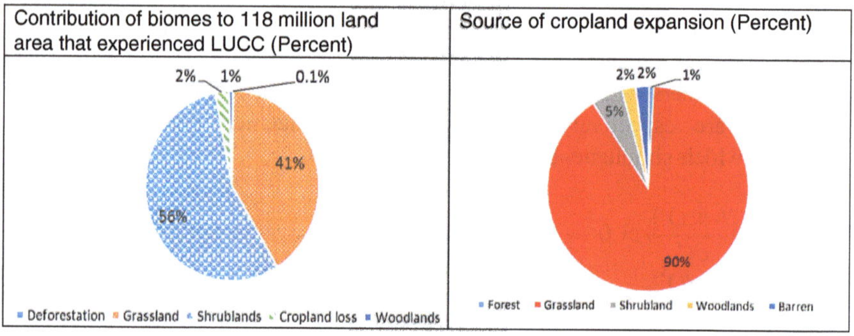

Fig. 17.9 Contribution of major biomes to LUCC and to cropland expansion

also observed forest contributing the largest share of cropland expansion in SSA. However, grasslands accounted for about 90 % of cropland expansion (Fig. 17.9). The changes from high to low value biome leads to land degradation and are considered in the cost of land degradation discussed below.

Cost of land degradation due to LUCC is about 2007 US$0.75 billion, which is 11 % of the 2007 GDP of US$6.773 billion and 1 % of the 2001 value of ecosystem services (ES) in Niger (Fig. 17.11).

The cost of action to address land degradation is US$5 billion while the cost of inaction is about US$30 billion over the 30 year planning horizon. As expected the returns for taking action are quite high. Every US dollar invested in taking action returns about $6—a level that is quite attractive.

In the section below, we examine the perceptions of farmers on land degradation to verify the satellite data results discussed above.

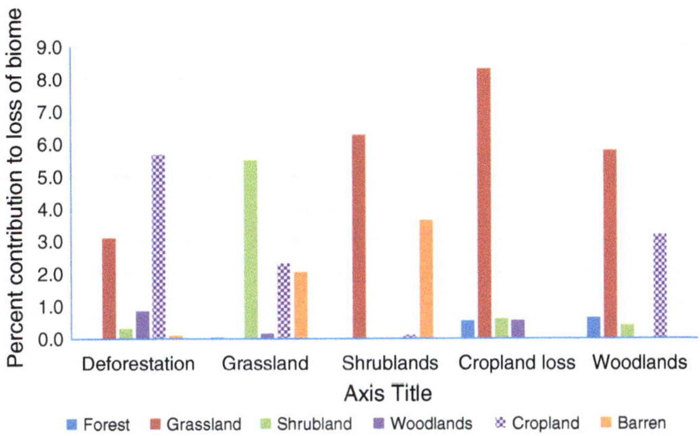

Fig. 17.10 Source of loss of biome extent and destination biome in the LUCCC, Niger

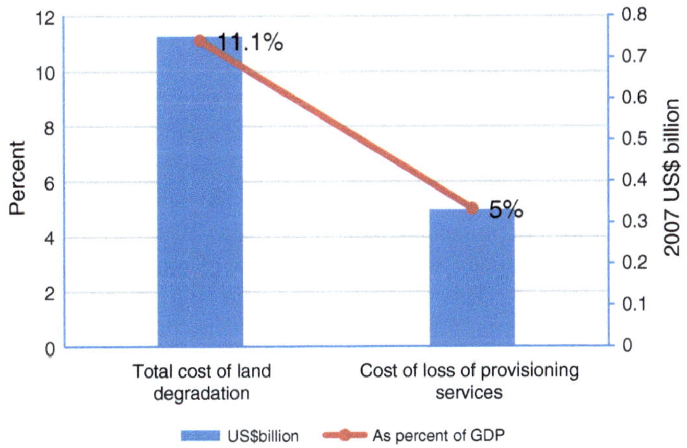

Fig. 17.11 Cost of land degradation due to LUCC, Niger

Focus Group Discussion Results

Trend of Importance of Ecosystem Services

Consistent with the MODIS data results, communities perceived that importance of provisioning services fell for both degraded and improved lands. In both cases, the fall in importance—ranked from not important = 1, somehow important = 2 and very important = 3 fell by over 40 % (Fig. 17.12). In the last 30 years, Niger was affected by several severe droughts, locust pests and floods. The events caused a lot of stress for the ecosystem and the farmer's production systems (World Bank 2011)

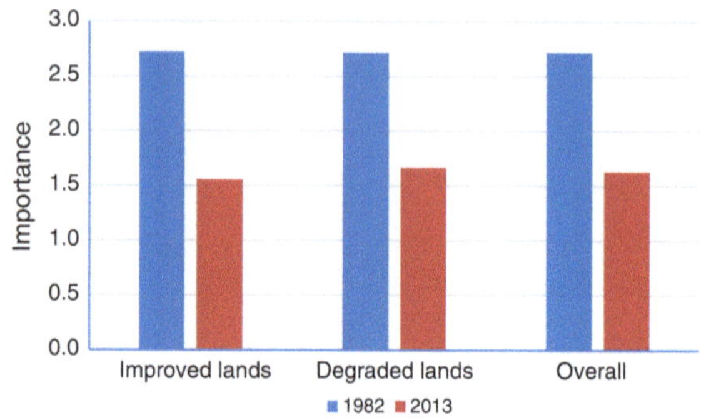

Fig. 17.12 Importance of provisioning services, Niger, *Note* Importance of ecosystem services: *1* Not Important; *2* Somehow important; *3* Very important; *4* Don't know). *Source* Authors

and had generally a negative impact on the supply of provisioning, regulating and supporting as well as cultural services. Regulation of air quality, pollination, waste treatment, nutrient cycling and other regulating and supporting systems were affected by these events. Importance of regulating services fell by 52 % the steepest decline of all the ecosystem services.

Detailed analysis of the trends of ecosystem services show that importance of provisioning services declined in both communities with degraded and improved NDVI (Fig. 17.13). However, a look at the specific services in detail reveals that perceptions of the importance of crops were rated the same over the time period from communities with improved lands. In one village (Bazaga), where 90 % of the households primarily produce crops, the importance of provisioning services from crops actually increased. This is consistent with Fig. 17.14—which reports increasing crop productivity. The farmers reported that this increase results from infrastructure development.

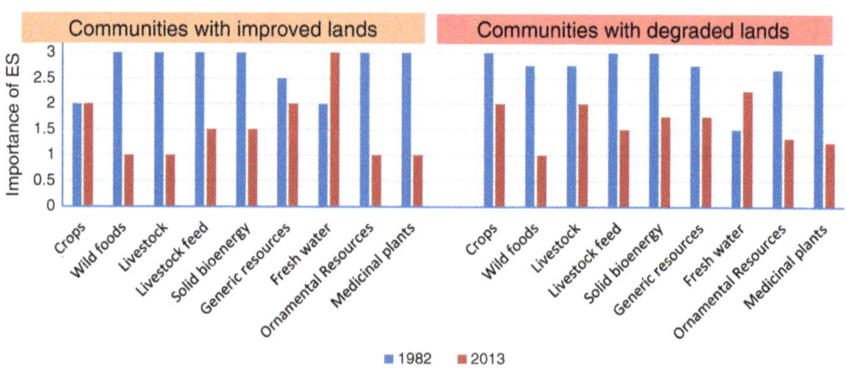

Fig. 17.13 Detailed listing of provisioning services' importance in communities with degraded and improved lands, Niger, *Note* Importance of ecosystem services (ES): *1* Not Important; *2* Somehow important; *3* Very important), *Source* Authors

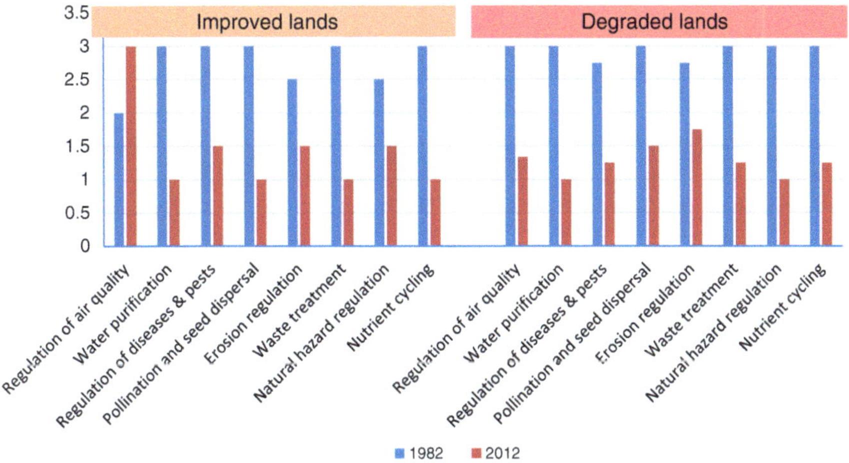

Fig. 17.14 Detailed listing of regulating and supporting services importance, Niger, *Notes* Importance of ecosystem services in 1982 and 2013: *1* Not Important; *2* Somehow important; *3* Very important); *Source* FGD

Additionally, a majority of villages stated that they have better access to fresh water in 2012 than was the case in 1982. Publicly financed wells were constructed in the villages. This positive development is mostly due to a transferring of responsibilities for water supply from the national government to local authorities (AMCOW 2011).

Importance of regulating and supporting systems declined in communities with decreased NDVI but increased in villages which experienced higher NDVI (see Fig. 17.15). In villages with an improved NDVI, cleaning of the air is functioning better in 2013 compared to 1982. The participants, who were situated in predominantly crop producing areas, specified that this is a consequence of land improvement. The promotion of improved production technologies increased the soil quality of cropland. For instance, leaving millet stumps after the harvest on the fields, which reduces wind erosion in the dry season, is a successfully applied approach in Niger (Hayashi et al. 2010).

Cultural services were generally declining in importance in nearly all villages. One of the factors driving this change is erosion of traditional values among the youth (Blum 2007). Additionally, a shift from traditional beliefs to Islam is also contributing to movement from traditional spiritual services that nurture nature. Only one village reported that cultural services are improving. The farmers in the community who reported improvement in cultural services attributed the improvement to government promotion of trees, which significantly increased the ability to rest and recover during field work.

Land degradation is the most important reason for the decline of all three types of ecosystem services (see Fig. 17.15). The FGD participants reported that wind

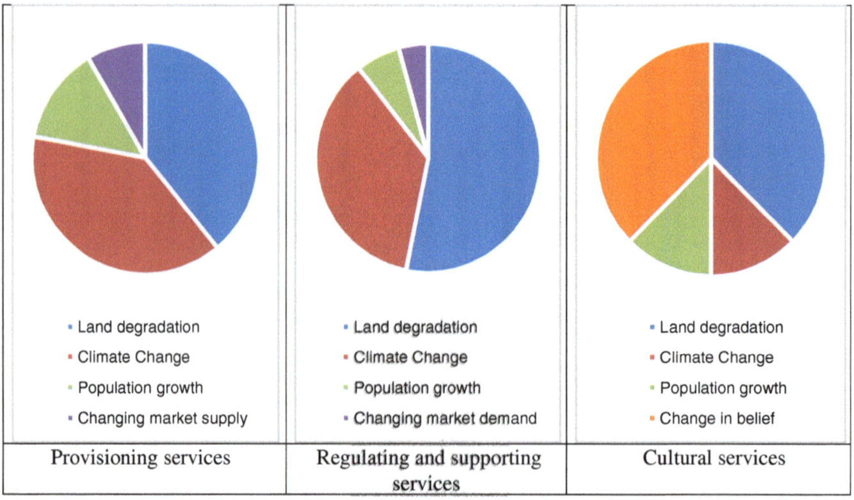

Fig. 17.15 Reasons for the fall in importance of ecosystem services, Niger, *Source* FGD

and water erosion as well as loss of soil fertility are a consequence of deforestation, poor agricultural techniques and overgrazing. In general, rates of sustainably managed natural resources are still low in Niger, as can be seen by the low fertilizer application rates in Fig. 17.5 or the low application rates of rotational grazing in Table 17.2. Climate Change, especially reduced precipitation, is also an important reason for a decline of provisioning as well as regulating and supporting services.

In general there is a strong agreement between FGD and the MODIS data on land degradation. Chapter 5 reports further on the groundtruthing of satellite data with community perception. The discussion below examines the community response to land degradation.

Restoration of Degraded Lands

Communities were asked to mention the three most important actions they have taken to address land degradation for each of the major biomes. Communities reported to have taken actions on cropland, grasslands and bare lands only. There were no actions mentioned to address land degradation on forests and shrublands. About 40 % of the communities that reported land degradation on cropland adopted SLWM practices and 13 % passed byelaws to address it (Fig. 17.17). The SLWM practices used include promotion of improved agricultural technologies, application of organic and inorganic fertilizers and other management practices. Other actions taken to address land degradation on cropland include shifting cultivation, tree planting, postharvest handling and other actions.[8] Tree planting was the most common strategy used to restore bare lands. Tree planting was done mainly on bare lands to fix sand dunes. As discussed earlier, this is in line with Niger's tree planting programs that have shown significant impacts.

For grazing land, farmers reported mixed results of the activities reported as other in Fig. 17.17. In Bazaga, farmers received credits for livestock. The larger herd sizes increased the demand for fodder and this led to overgrazing. In contrast, in Babaye the distribution of animals improved grazing land. Vulnerable women received goats, which used to be a traditional income source for female villagers. In Babaye women were not only given access to animals adopted to the irregular precipitation, but also awareness for the changing climate and its consequences, as well as trainings including sustainable fodder production and rotational grazing were provided by an NGO. A similar project was conducted by CBA (2010) in other parts of Niger.

Land Degradation on Static Land Use

The discussion below focuses on cropland and grazing lands that did not undergo LUCC. As discussed earlier, only 19 % of land south of the Sahara desert experienced LUCC and the remaining land (81 %) maintained the same biome in 2001 and 2009. We start our discussion with adoption and profit of cropland SLM practices.

Land Degradation on Static Grasslands

Livestock production is mainly concentrated in the southern part of the country and its density increases towards the Nigerian border (Fig. 17.16). Grazing land pressure has been increasing and this has led to reduced biomass productivity. Controlling for rainfall, a long-term experiment of rangeland productivity in Niger showed an annual decrease of 5 % from 1994 to 2006 and the causes of decrease included decreasing soil fertility and increased grazing pressure (Hiernaux et al. 2014).

The increasing grazing pressure suggests some level of overgrazing. The average carrying capacity in the Sahelian region varies from 10 to 3.5 ha/TLU—depending on the precipitation of each year (Boudet 1975; Penning de Vries and Djitèye 1982). The carrying capacity of livestock in Niger is between 5 and 7 ha per tropical livestock unit (TLU) (Kamuanga et al. 2008). Results of biomass productivity in Niger done by Havlic et al. (2014) show that the average productivity of grazing

[8]These prayers and rituals.

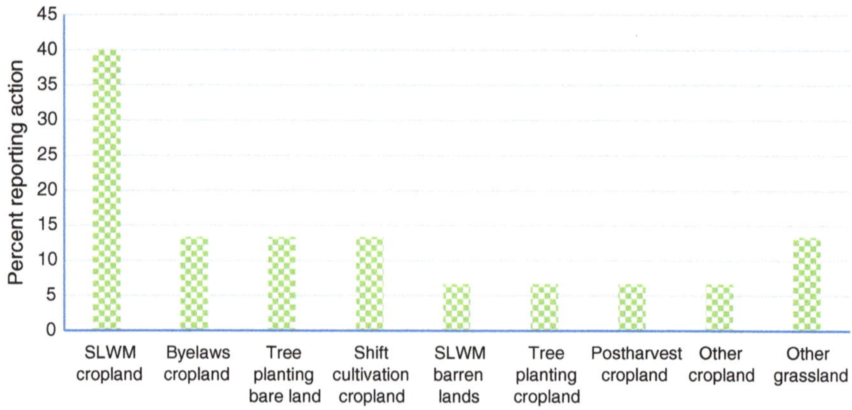

Fig. 17.16 Action taken to address land degradation on major biomes

biomass in Niger is 0.634 tons DM/ha/year. Stéphenne and Lambin (2001) also show that feed requirement per TLU in the Sahelian region is 4.6 tons of dry matter (DM) per year. This translates to a carrying capacity of 7.25 ha per TLU. Based on this, we overlaid the grazing biomass productivity and livestock density and determined that more than 75 % of the grazing lands are experiencing overgrazing. This partly explains the low livestock productivity in the country—an aspect that leads to high cost of land degradation.

Only about 4 % of the households with livestock practice improved pasture management (Table 17.8). The improved pasture management include different forms of rotational grazing and restricted movement of livestock. Based on EPIC simulation discussed earlier, the cost of land degradation due to loss of milk and beef offtake is US$152 million, which is about 2.2 % of the GDP. Loss of milk production accounts for 88 % of total on-farm loss. Loss of beef offtake is small due to the small offtake rate and the small gain in weight due to rotational grazing (Table 17.9).

Table 17.8 Adoption of pasture management practices and impacts on grazing biomass productivity

Pasture management	Adoption rate (%)
Rotational grazing	0.4
Restricted grazing	0.4
Resting of grazing land	2.5
Improved pasture management	3.64
Pasture management impact on grassland productivity (EPIC simulation results)	
Biomass with rotational grazing (dry matter tons/ha)	0.69
Continuous grazing (dry matter tons/ha)	0.55
Gain (dry matter tons/ha)	0.14

Table 17.9 Cost of land degradation due to overgrazing

	Continuous grazing	Rotational grazing
Mean milk production per cow per day (l)	1.7	2.1
Beef offtake (kg per head sold/slaughtered)	0.272	0.267
	Without carbon	With carbon
National level cost of land degradation due to loss of:		
Milk production	133	
Beef	17.8	
Gain in CO_2-equiv sequestration (tons/ha)		1.29
Cost of land degradation due to loss of CO_2 sequestration (US$ million)	691.71	
Total cost of land degradation	843.33	
Off-farm cost of land degradation as % of total cost	82 %	
Total on-farm cost of land degradation as % of GDP	2.2 %	

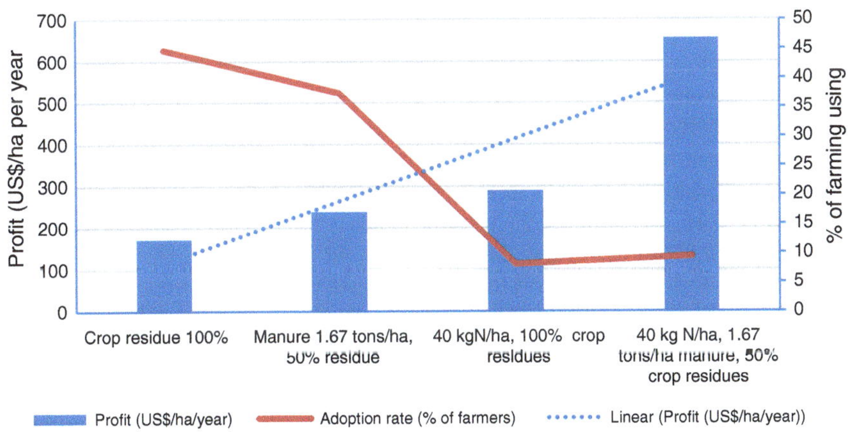

Fig. 17.17 The unholy cross: Inverse relationship between profit and adoption rate of soil fertility management practices on millet plots, Niger

Adoption Rates and Profit of Cropland SLM Practices

Figure 17.17 shows that while only 9 % of plots received the most profitable practice—integrated soil fertility management (ISFM), i.e., a practice that combines judicious quantities of chemical fertilizer with organic inputs and improved germplasm (Vanlauwe and Giller 2006), about half of the plots did not receive any external inputs—the least profitable management practice. Table 17.10 gives details of adoption rate of the three soil fertility management practices for the four major crops and all consistently show the same pattern—lowest adoption rate for ISFM and inorganic fertilizer and highest use for the least profitable soil fertility

Table 17.10 Adoption rate of soil fertility management practices for major crops in Niger

Crop	ISFM	Fertilizer only	Organic only	No inputs
	% of plots with SLM practice			
Millet (n = 2174)	9.4	8.0	72.0	10.6
Groundnuts (n = 459)	14.4	7.2	72.0	6.4
Sorghum (n = 1253)	11.1	6.5	72.0	10.4
Cowpea (n = 1121)	12.3	9.3	72.0	6.4
All crops	8.9	9.3	33.7	8.5
	Mean yields (kg/ha)			
Millet	521	423	477	340
Groundnuts	907	697	349	525
Sorghum	515	349	411	348
Cowpea	565	205	300	259

A Includes: manure, crop rotation, agroforestry

management practices. The inverse relationship between profitability and adoption rate of land management suggests there are challenges which hamper farmers from adopting the most profitable land management practices. We look at these in the section addressing drivers of adoption of soil fertility management practices.

Millet accounts for 42 % of cropland in Niger (FAOSTAT 2014) but its yield is much lower than the potential yield. Literature estimates of the low, medium and high yield of pearl millet yield in Eastern and Southern Africa is estimated to be respectively 0.16, 0.72 and 1.93 tons/ha (Tittonell and Giller 2013). However, LSMS household survey show the average yield is 0.92 tons/ha. A long-term experiment in Sadore Niger showed that millet-cowpea rotation improves nitrogen use efficiency from 20 % to 28 % and increased grain yield from 0.516 tons/ha to 1.200 tons/ha—a 57 % increase on plots that did not receive any external inputs (Bationo and Ntare 2000). However household survey data show that 36 % increase in millet-cowpea yield and 72 % of households practiced millet-cowpea rotational cropping (Pender 2009).

We analyze the cost of land degradation due to use of land degrading management practices on maize, rice and millet plots. We use DSSAT results for non-adoption of ISFM and long-term soil fertility experiments on millet-cowpea rotational cropping vs. millet-millet continuous cropping.

DSSAT results on ISFM and non-use of inorganic and fertilizer on maize, rice and millet plots. Table 17.11 summarizes the DSSAT results for all three crops and shows that the total cost of land degradation is US77.44 million. Despite the high adoption rate of rotational cropping, the cost of land degradation due to millet-millet continuous cropping is much larger (US$154.68 million) due to the large area covered by millet (Table 17.12). The summary of on-farm cost of land degradation on crops covered is US$318.74 million or 2.5 % of the GDP (Table 17.13).

Table 17.11 Grain yield and carbon sequestration (CO_2-equiv)

Management practice	Maize—rainfed		Rice—irrigated		Millet-rainfed	
	Grain yield	CO_2-equiv	Grain yield	CO_2-equiv	Grain yield	CO_2-equiv
	Tons/ha					
ISFM: 40 kgN/ha, 1.67 tons organic inputs/ha and/or crop rotation						
ISFM 1st 10	2.5	144.32	1.7	360.7	1.3	343.0
ISFM last 10	2.1	133.50	1.3	271.3	1.3	327.4
Change (%)	−15.6	−7.49	−23.1	−24.8	−0.7	−4.5
BAU: no inorganic fertilizer, organic inputs or crop rotation						
Control 1st 10	1.8	140.73	1.5	359.6	1.2	340.8
Control last 10	1.2	125.89	0.93	269.6	1.0	318.2
Change (%)	−29.5	−10.55	−36.6	−25.1	−16.7	−6.6
Cost of land degradation (US$ million)	2.75	4.24	1.61	3.48	21.30	77.44

Table 17.12 Cost of land degradation due to millet-millet continuous cropping

Management practice	Statistics
Adoption rate millet-cowpea rotation cropping	72 %
Area under BAU (000 ha)	1164.36
Grain yield (tons/ha)	
SLM	1.20
BAU	0.52
CO_2-equiv (tons/ha)	
SLM	7.93
BAU	5.95
Cost of land degradation (US$) due to:	
Grain yield loss	143.61
CO_2-sequestration loss—only millet aboveground dry matter	11.07
Total cost of land degradation	154.68

Assume producer price of millet of US$431
Source Bationo and Ntare (2000). Converted from aboveground dry matter using the following formula: DM = C/0.45 (Steeg et al. 2013); CO_2 = 3.67C—Price of CO_2 = US$20/ton

Drivers of Adoption Rate of SLM Practices on Cropland

Results across the three models (structural, reduced and LPM-IV) are consistent suggesting they are robust. Additionally, all coefficients of the LPM are below 1 implying that they are less biased and are consistent (Horace and Oaxaca 2006). Results also show consistent relationships between adoption of management practices that involve purchased inputs (inorganic fertilizer and ISFM) and organic soil fertility practices (organic inputs, and rotational cropping) which are produced

Table 17.13 Summary of cost of land degradation

Crop	Grain yield loss	CO_2 sequestration	Total	Cost of land degradation as % of GDP	
	2007 US$ million			Total cost	Grain yield loss
Maize	2.75	4.24	6.99	0.10	0.04
Rice	1.61	3.48	5.09	0.08	0.02
Millet—ISFM	21.30	77.44	98.74	1.46	0.31
MM—CC[a]	143.61	11.07	154	2.28	2.12
Total	318.74	107.76	426.5	3.92	2.50
% of GDP	2.50	1.42	3.92		

Notes [a]MM-CC = millet-millet continuous cropping

on-farm or don't go through the market. Accordingly, our discussion will follow this pattern by referring adoption of inorganic fertilizer and ISFM as land management practices that involve purchased inputs and non-purchased inputs.

Endowment of family male labor has favorable influence on adoption of all four soil fertility management practices while female labor has negative impact on ISFM and inorganic fertilizer—both of which include purchased inputs (Table 17.14). This is consistent with past studies showing favorable impact of male labor on adoption of purchased inputs (e.g. see Peterman et al. 2014). Consistent with Nkonya et al. (2008) and Kaizzi (2002), farmers are more likely to use organic soil fertility management practices and less likely to apply inorganic fertilizer on sandy soils. Farmers tend to avoid using purchased inputs on less fertile soils to avoid losses but tend to use non-purchased organic inputs to rehabilitate degraded soil or those naturally low fertility (e.g. sandy soils). Similarly and by design, zai and demi-lunes are associated with adoption of organic inputs—partly because organic inputs are added into constructed SWC structures—and with less likelihood to use purchased inputs.

Non-farm activities increase the propensity to use purchased inputs (inorganic fertilizer and ISFM). This shows the synergistic relationship between non-farm and farm activities. Contrary to expectation however, remittances and value of assets negative impact on adoption of management practices that involve purchased inputs. The results could be explained by tendency of farmers to focus less on agricultural activities when they become wealthier or when they have alternative sources of income such as remittances. However, values of assets have a favorable impact on adoption of crop rotation. Consistent with the fertility gradient reported by Zingore et al. (2007), plots closer to home are likely to receive both organic inputs and inorganic fertilizer.

Risks and Land Management Practices

As expected, crop rotation, stone bunds and demi-lunes are risk-reducing land management practices (Table 17.15). This is consistent with recent studies which

Table 17.14 Drivers of adoption of soil fertility management practices, Niger

	ISFM			Fertilizer			Organic			Crop rotation		
	Structutral	Reduced	IV-LPM	Structural	Reduced	IV-LPM	Structural	Reduced	IV-LPM	Structural	Reduced	IV-LPM
Human capital endowment[a]												
Male labor	0.007***	0.007***	0.001**	0.007***	0.007***	0.001**	0.008***	0.008***	0.002**	0.004	0.004	0.002*
Female labor	−0.014**	−0.014**	−0.001*	−0.014**	−0.014**	−0.001*	0.003	0.003	0.001	0.018*	0.018*	0.001
Age of hhd	0.052	0.063	0.032	0.052	0.063	0.032	−0.087	−0.111	0	0.063	0.06	−0.051
FHH	0.032	0.042	0.001	0.032	0.042	0.001	−0.367**	−0.372**	−0.048	−0.488***	−0.545***	−0.290***
Education of household head (cf no formal education)[b]												
– Primary	0.179*	0.179*	0.048	0.179*	0.179*	0.048	0.167*	0.162*	0.078**	0.038	0.026	−0.018
– Secondary	0.208*	0.214*	0.067	0.208*	0.214*	0.067	0.227*	0.218*	0.114**	0.211	0.194	0.008
– Koranic	−0.05	−0.06	−0.027	−0.05	−0.06	−0.027	0.066	0.085	−0.016	−0.016	−0.005	0.088
– Literacy ed[b]	0.188**	0.182**	0.029	0.188**	0.182**	0.029	0.503***	0.515***	0.191***	0.320***	0.293***	0.109***
Soil texture (cf loamy)												
– Sandy	−0.260**	−0.262**	−0.066*	−0.260**	−0.262**	−0.066*	0.493***	0.490***	0.154***	0.478***	0.501***	0.196***
– Clay	−0.213	−0.216	−0.053	−0.213	−0.216	−0.053	−0.156	−0.154	−0.085	−0.293**	−0.267**	−0.056
– Sandy and clay	−0.249*	−0.252*	−0.067	−0.249*	−0.252*	−0.067	0.289**	0.290**	0.072	0.310***	0.332***	0.157***
– Other	−0.407*	−0.412*	−0.1	−0.407*	−0.412*	−0.1	0.498**	0.498**	0.144*	0.446**	0.473**	0.213**
Method of land acquisition (cf leasehold)												
– Customary	0.017	0.011	−0.001	0.017	0.011	−0.001	0.204**	0.209**	0.061*	0.496***	0.498***	0.201***
– Purchased	0.308**	0.301*	0.088*	0.308**	0.301*	0.088*	0.218	0.225	0.055	0.468***	0.482***	0.221***
– Other	0.157	0.146	0.028	0.157	0.146	0.028	−0.244	−0.231	−0.096	0.377***	0.370**	0.180***
Long-term land investments[c]												
– Stone bunds	0.066	0.056	−0.002	0.066	0.056	−0.002	0.159	0.177	0.01	0.289**	0.311**	0.189**
– Zai	0.1	0.102	0.024	0.1	0.102	0.024	0.429***	0.429***	0.158***	0.076	0.071	0.02
– Demi-Lunes	−0.537***	−0.532***	−0.111*	−0.537***	−0.532***	−0.111*	0.380***	0.362***	0.183**	0.414**	0.385**	−0.012
Assets (CFA)	−0.011*	−0.012*	−0.004**	−0.011*	−0.012*	−0.004**	0	0.001	0	0.026***	0.025***	0.010***
Farm area (ha)	−0.024	−0.02	0.001	−0.024	−0.02	0.001	0.023	0.016	0.024	−0.093***	−0.097***	−0.064***
Non-farm	0.229***	0.226***	0.048***	0.229***	0.226***	0.048***	0.090*	0.096*	0.028	0.165***	0.162***	0.065***

(continued)

Table 17.14 (continued)

	ISFM			Fertilizer			Organic			Crop rotation		
	Structutral	Reduced	IV-LPM	Structural	Reduced	IV-LPM	Structural	Reduced	IV-LPM	Structural	Reduced	IV-LPM
Access to rural services												
Remittances	−0.011*	−0.012**	−0.004*	−0.01*	−0.01**	−0.01*	−0.02***	−0.02***	−0.01***	−0.006	−0.006	0.002
Credit dummy	−0.056		0.125	−0.056		0.125	0.117**		0.157	−0.056		−0.383*
Distance (km) to plot	−0.262***	−0.261***	−0.061***	−0.262***	−0.261***	−0.06***	−0.24***	−0.24***	−0.08***	0.052	0.051	0.012
Member to farmer group	0.066		−0.049	0.066		−0.049	−0.106*		−0.336	−0.137**		0.591
Constant	−0.723	−0.758*	0.14	−0.723	−0.758*	0.140	−0.427	−0.331	0.296	−0.792*	−0.855**	0.433**

Notes
[a]hhd = household head; FHH = female-headed household
[b]Literacy ed = Adult literacy education
[c]Demi-lunes: Half-moon shaped earthen ridges for water harvesting. Demi-lunes have a diameter of about 4 m
Zai: Improved planting pits for water harvesting and breaking hard surface crust. Organic inputs are placed in the planting pits
Stone bunds: rows of stones placed along the contour line—to prevent soil erosion and for water harvesting

Table 17.15 Drivers of deviation from conditional mean yield (log value of production/ha)

Variable	Coefficient
Land management practices and long-term investments	
Organic inputs	0.452***
Inorganic fertilizer	0.275***
Crop rotation	−0.421***
Stone bunds	−0.642***
Zai	0.287**
Demi-lunes	−0.579**
Human capital endowment	
Male family labor	0.001
Female family labor	−0.024***
Age of household head	0.873***
Female-headed household	1.427***
Have non-farm income	−0.234***
Education of household head	
Primary	0.066
Secondary	−0.077
Koranic education	0.273***
Literacy adult education	0.086
Physical and biophysical capital endowment	
Value of productive assets (CFA)	0.039***
Farm area (ha)	0.153***
Soil texture	
Sandy	0.137
Clay	0.613***
Sandy and clay	0.374**
Other soil texture	−0.093
Method of land acquisition (cf leasehold)	
Customary (inherit)	−0.889***
Purchased	−0.749***
Other	−1.632***
Access to rural services	
Received remittances	−0.004
Distance to plot from homestead (km)	−0.164**
Received credit	−0.054
Member to farmer organization	−0.015
Constant	17.225***

have demonstrated that water harvesting, and farmer management natural regeneration (FMNR) can both increase agricultural productivity and reduce climate-related risks (AGRA 2014; Garrity et al. 2010; Bayala et al. 2014; Reij et al. 2009; Place and Binam 2013). The results underscores the importance of promoting these practices to increase farmers' resilience to the high production risks in the

Sahelian zone. Contrary to other studies (e.g. Cooper et al. 2009; Cooper and Coe 2011) however, zai and organic inputs increase yield variance. Likewise, inorganic fertilizers increase yield variance. This could be due to their likely impact in yield variability across relevant but excluded land management and/or soil characteristics. For example response of an inorganic fertilizer to improved crop varieties is greater than is the case for unimproved varieties.

With a number of female household members having non-farm activities, customary land tenure and proximity of plot to home also reduce production risks. The results further underscore the importance of non-farm activities and the role that female household members play in enhancing resilience of households to shocks. The results also show that the plots held under customary tenure are likely to have greater resilience to production risks than those held under leasehold. Proximity of plots to homestead could be a result of better soil fertility management reported by Zingore et al. (2007), which in turn reduces variance (Nkonya et al. 2015). However, female-headed households experience greater yield variance, probably due to their failure to adopt the risk reducing management practices discussed above.

Conclusions and Policy Implications

Recent policy changes in Niger and their strong association with improved human welfare demonstrate that even poor countries could achieve sustainable development enshrined in the United Nations Green Economy initiative (UNEP 2011). Enhancing government effectiveness by giving communities a mandate to manage natural resources, and by giving incentives to land users to benefit from their investment, played a key role in realizing simultaneous improvement in land management and human welfare in Niger. The country also learned hard lessons from its past mistakes that involved policies which provided disincentive to land investment and the consequent land degradation that was amplified by prolonged drought. The results further suggest that severe land degradation and the consequent negative impacts on human welfare is low-hanging fruit that needs to be utilized by countries as they address land degradation. This suggests instead of abandoning severely degraded lands, strategies should be used to rehabilitate such lands using low-cost organic soil fertility management practices and progressively followed by using high cost inputs as soil fertility improve. Improvement of access to rural services and facilitation of non-farm activities will also lead to faster and greater impacts on adoption of SLM practices and increasing resilience to production in Niger.

As Niger continues to improve sustainable land management, it faces daunting challenges to alleviate the high cost of land degradation. Niger serves as a success story to the world in addressing land degradation. Both the national and international community need to learn from the achievement of Niger and help land users to sustainably management their natural resources.

References

Adam, T., Reij, C., Abdoulaye, T., Larwanou, M., & Tappan, G. (2006). *Impacts des Investissements dans la Gestion des Resources Naturalles (GRN) au Niger: Rapport de Synthese*. Niamey, Niger: Centre Régional d'Enseignement Specialise en Agriculture.

AGRA (Alliance for a Green Revolution in Africa). (2014). Africa Agriculture Report 2014. Climate change and smallholder agriculture in Sub-Saharan Africa. AGRA, Nairobi. Online at www.agra.org.

AMCOW (African Ministers Council on Water). (2011). Water Supply and Sanitation in Niger. AMCOW Country Status Overview.

Anyamba, A., Small, J. L., Tucker, C. J., & Pak, E. W. (2014). Thirty-two years of Sahelian Zone growing season non-stationary NDVI3g patterns and trends. *Remote Sensing, 6*, 3101–3122.

Bationo, A., & Ntare, B. R. (2000). Rotation and nitrogen fertilizer effects on pearl millet, cowpea and groundnut yield and soil chemical properties in a sandy soil in the semi-arid tropics, Africa. *Journal of Agricultural Sciences, 134*(3), 277–284.

Bayala J. J. B., Teklehaimanot, Z., Kalinganire, A., & Ouèdraogo, S. J. (2014). Parklands for buffering climate risk and sustaining agricultural production in the Sahel of West Africa. *Current Opinion in Environmental Sustainability, 6*, 28–34.

Behnke, R. H., & Scoones, I. (1993). Rethinking range ecology: Implications for rangeland management in Africa. In R. H. Behnke, I. Scoones, & C. Kerven (Eds.), *Range ecology at disequilibrium* (pp. 1–30). London: Overseas Development Institute.

Blench, R. (1999). Traditional livestock breeds: Geographical distribution and dynamics in relation to the Ecology of West Africa. Working Paper 122, Overseas Development Institute, Portland House, Stag Place, London. (http://www.odi.org.uk/resources/download/2041.pdf). Accessed on June 1, 2014.

Blum, R. W. (2007). Youth in Sub-Saharan Africa. *Journal of Adolescent Health, 41*(3), 230–238.

Boffa, J. M. (1999). Agroforestry parklands in Sub-Saharan Africa. FAO Conservation Guide 34. Rome: Food and Agriculture Organization of the United Nations (FAO). http://www.fao.org/docrep/005/X3940e/X3940e07.htm.

Boudet, G. (1975). *Manuel sur les pâturages tropicaux et les cultures fourragères. Coll Manuels et Précis D'élevages* (IEMVT ed.). Paris: du Ministère de la Coopération.

Brough, W. & Kimeny, M. (2002). "Desertification" of the Sahel—exploring the role of property rights. Bozeman, Mt: Property and environment resource Center. Retrieved from http://www.perc.org/perc.php?id=142.

CBA (Community-Based Adaptation Programme) (2010). Niger-Fast facts. CBA: New York.

CNEDD. (2005). *Programme d'Action National pour l'Adaptation.* Communautés et Zones Vulnérables: Identification et Hiérarchisation des Secteurs.

Cooke, P., Köhlin, G., & Hyde, W. F. (2008). Fuelwood, forests and community management—evidence from household studies. *Environment and Development Economics, 13*(1), 103–135.

Cooper, P. J. M., Rao, K. P. C., Singh, P., Dimes, J., Traore, P. S., Rao, K., et al. (2009). Farming with current and future climate risk: Advancing a 'Hypothesis of Hope' for rainfed agriculture in the semi-arid tropics. *Journal of SAT Agricultural Research, 7*, 1–19.

Cooper, P. J. M., & Coe, R. (2011). Assessing and addressing climate-induced risk in Sub-Saharan Rainfed agriculture foreword to a special issue of experimental agriculture. *Experimental Agriculture, 47*(2), 179–184.

CRED (Center for Research on the Epidemiology of Disasters). (2014). International Disaster Database. http://www.emdat.be/result-country-profile. Accessed September 30, 2014.

de Leeuw, P. N., & Tothill, J. C. (1993). The concept of rangeland carrying capacity in Sub-Saharan Africa—myth or reality. In R. H. Behnke Jr, I. Scoones, & C. Kerven (Eds.), *Range ecology at disequilibrium. New models of natural variability and pastoral adaptation in African Savannas* (pp. 77–88). London: IIED, Overseas Development Institute.

Desta K. B (2002). Analyses of Dairy Cattle Breeding Practices in Selected Areas of Ethiopia. PhD Dissertation submitted to zur Erlangung des akademischen Grades doctor rerum agriculturarum, Berlin. Humboldt University.

FAO. (2014). State of the World's Forests. Enhancing the socioeconomic benefits from forests.

FAO (Food and Agriculture organization). (2012). *State of the World's Forests*. Rome: FAO.

FAOSTAT. (2014). Food and agriculture Organization corporate database. Available at http://faostat3.fao.org/faostat-gateway/go/to/home/E. Accessed August 12, 2014.

Garrity, D. P., Akinnifesi, F.K., Ajayi, O. C., Weldesemayat, S.G., Mowo, J.G., Kalinganire, A., Larwanou, M., & Bayala, J. (2010). Evergreen agriculture: A robust approach to sustainable food security in Africa. *Food Security, 2*, 197–214.

Gibbs, H. K., Ruesch, A. S., Achard, F., Clayton, M. K., Holmgren, P., Ramankutty, N., & Foley, J. A. (2010). Tropical forests were the primary sources of new agricultural land in the 1980s and 1990s. *Proceedings of the National Academy of Sciences of the United States, 107*(38), 16732–16737.

Gnoumou Y., & Bloch, P. (2003). Niger country brief: Property rights and land markets.

Havlík, P., Valin, H., Herrero, M., Obersteiner, M., Schmid, E., Rufino, M. C., et al. (2014). Climate change mitigation through livestock system transitions. *Proceedings of the National Academy of Science, 111*(10), 3709–3714.

Hayashi, K., Matsumoto, N., Tobita, S., Shinjo, H., Tanaka, U., Boubachar, I., & Tabo, R. (2010). Technology development of soil fertility management based on understanding local agricultural systems of the Sahel in Niger, West Africa. Presented at the 19th World Congress of Soil Sciences, Soil Solutions for a Changing World.

Herrmann, S. M., Anyamba, A., & Tucker, C. J. (2005). Recent trends in vegetation dynamics in the African Sahel and their relationship to climate. *Global Environmental Change, 15*, 394–404.

Hiernaux, P., Ayantunde, A., Kalilou, A., Mougin, E., Gérard, B., Baup, F., et al. (2014). Trends in productivity of crops, fallow and rangelands in Southwest Niger: Impact of land use, management and variable rainfall. *Journal of Hydrology, 375*(1–2), 65–77.

Horace, W., & Oaxaca, (2006). Results on the bias and inconsistency of ordinary least squares for the linear probability model. *Economics Letters, 90*(3), 321–327.

Houérou, H. N. Le, & Hoste, H. (1977). Rangeland production and Annual rainfall relations in the mediterranean basin and in the African Sahelo-Sudanian zone. *Journal of Range Management, 30*(3), 181–189.

Hüttner, K., Leidl, K., Pfeiffer, D. U., Kasambara, D., & Jere, F. B. D. (2001). The effect of a community-based animal health service programme on livestock mortality, off-take and selected husbandry applications: A field study in Northern Malawi. *Livestock Production Science, 72*(3), 263–278.

INS (Institut National de la Statistique). (2012). Living standards measurement survey (LSMS) Agriculture household survey, 2012.

Izzaurralde, R. C. (2010). *Nigeria. Simulation of sustainable land management practices*. Mimeo: IFPRI.

Jaspa, I. L. O. (1981). *First things first: Meeting the basic needs people of Nigeria*. Geneva: ILO.

Just, R., & Pope, R. D. (1979). Production function estimation and related risk considerations. *American Journal of Agricultural Economics, 61*(2), 276–284.

Just, R., & Pope, R. D. (2003). Agricultural risk analysis: Adequacy of models, data, and issues. *American Journal of Agricultural Economics, 85*(5), 1249–1256.

Kaizzi, C. K. (2002). The potential benefit of green manures and inorganic fertilizers in cereal production on contrasting soils in eastern Uganda. Ph.D. Dissertation., University of Bonn and German Center for Development Research (ZEF), Germany, pp. 64–69.

Kamuanga, M., Somda, J., Sanon, Y., & Kagoné, H. (2008). The future of livestock in the Sahel and West Africa: Potentials and challenges for strengthening the regional market. OECD. http://www.oecd.org/swac/publications/38402714.pdf. Accessed October 8, 2014.
Kaphengst, T. (2014). Towards a definition of global sustainable land use? A discussion on theory, concepts and implications for governance. Discussion paper produced within the research project "GLOBALANDS—Global Land Use and Sustainability". http://www.ecologic.eu/globalands/about.
Kaufmann, D., Kraay, A., & Mastruzzi, M. (2010). The Worldwide Governance indicators: Methodology and analytical issues. World Bank Policy Research Working Paper No. 5430.
Lavigne-Delville, P., Ouedraogo, H., & Toulmin, C. (2002). Land tenure dynamics and state intervention: Challenges, ongoing experience and current debates on land tenure in West Africa. In Making land rights more secure', conclusions of a seminar held in Ouagadougou, Burkina Faso, 19–21 March, 2002.
Lavigne-Delville, P., Toulmin, C., Colin, J. P., & Chauveau, J. P. (2002). Negotiating access to land in West Africa: A synthesis of findings from research on derived rights to land. Land Tenure and Resource Access in West Africa series, IIED, London.
Le Bao, Q. B., Nkonya, E., & Mirzabaev, A. (2014). Biomass productivity-based mapping of global land degradation hotspots. *ZEF-Discussion Papers on Development Policy*, (193). University of Bonn.
Mohamadou, A. (2009). Decentralisation and local power in Niger. IIED Issue paper no. 150. Online at http://pubs.iied.org/pdfs/12557IIED.pdf. Accessed October 3, 2014.
Montagne, P., & Amadou, O. (2012). Rural districts and community forest management and the fight against poverty in Niger. Field actions Sciences reports. Special issue 6. Online at http://factsreports.revues.org/1473. Accessed January 12, 2015.
Muia J. M. (2000). Use of Napier grass to improve smallholder milk production in Kenya. PhD Thesis Wageningen University, Wageningen, The Netherlands.
Muia, J. M., Tamminga, S., & Mbugua, P. N. (2000). Effect of supplementing napier grass (Pennisetum purpureum) with sunflower meal or poultry litter-based concentrates on feed intake, live-weight changes and economics of milk production in Friesian cows. *Livestock Production Science, 67*, 89–99.
Nkonya, E., Pender, J., Kaizzi, K., Kato, E., Mugarura, S., Ssali, H., & Muwonge. J. (2008). Linkages between land management, land degradation, and poverty in Sub-Saharan Africa: The case of Uganda. IFPRI Research Report #159, Washington, D.C.
Nkonya, E., Place, F., Kato, E., & Mwanjololo, M. (2015). Climate risk management through sustainable land management in Sub-Saharan Africa. In R. Lal B. Singh, D. Mwaseba, D. Kraybill, D. Hansen, & L. Eik, (eds.), Sustainable intensification to advance food security and enhance climate resilience in Africa, Springer International Publishing, Switzerland, pp. 75–112. doi:10.1007/978-3-319-09360-4_5.
North, D. (1991). Institutions. *Journal of Economic Perspectives, 5*(1), 97–112.
NRC (National Research Council). (2001). *Nutrient Requirements of Dairy Cattle* (7th ed.). Washington, D.C.: National Academy Press.
Otte, M. J., & Chilonda, P. (2002). *Cattle and small ruminant production systems in sub-Saharan Africa*. Food and Agriculture Organization (FAO), Rome: A Systematic Review.
Otte, J., & Chilonda, P. (2011). Spatial livestock production modelling. In Robinson, T., & P. Thornton, (Eds.), Global mapping of agricultural production systems. Pro-poor Livestock Policy Initiative Meeting Report, Bangkok, Thailand, 4–6 April 2006.
Ouedraogo, I., Runge, J., Eisenberg, J., Barron, J., & Sawadogo-Kaboré, S. (2013). The re-greening of the Sahel: Natural cyclicity or human-induced change? *Land, 3*, 1075–1090.
Pender, J. (2009). Impacts of sustainable land management programs on land management and poverty in Niger. World Bank Report No.: 48230-NE.
Pender, J., Abdoulaye, T., Ndjeunga, J., Gerard, B. & Kato, E. (2008). Impacts of inventory credit, input supply shops, and fertilizer micro-dosing in the Drylands of Niger. IFPRI Discussion Paper No. 763. Washington, D.C.: International Food Policy Research Institute.

Penning de Vries, F. W. T., & Djitèye, M. A. (1982). *La Productivité des Pâturages Sahéliens, une Étude des Sols, des Végétations et de L'exploitation de Cette Ressources Naturelle*. Wageningen: Centre for Agricultural Publishing and Documentation.

Peterman, A., Behrman, J.A. & Quisumbing, A.R. (2014). A review of empirical evidence on gender differences in nonland agricultural inputs, technology, and services in developing countries. In A.R. Quisumbing, R. Meinzen-Dick, T. L. Raney, A. Croppenstedt, J.A. Behrman, & A. Peterman (Eds.), Gender in agriculture Springer Netherlands, pp. 145–186.

Pieri, C. (1989). Fertilité des terres de savanes. Bilan de trente ans de recherche et de développement agricole au sud du Sahara. Ministère de la Coopération/CIRAD/IRAT, Paris.

Place, F. & Binam, J.N. (2013). Economic impacts of farmer managed natural regeneration in the Sahel. End of project technical report for the Free University Amsterdam and IFAD. Nairobi, World Agroforestry Centre.

Reij, C., Tappan, G., & Smale, M. (2009). Re-Greening the Sahel: Farmer-led innovation in Burkina Faso and Niger. In D. Spielman & R. Pandya-Lorch (Eds.), *Millions Fed. Proven Successes in Agricultural Development* (pp. 53–58). Washington, DC: IFPRI.

République du Niger. (2003). *Strategie de Developpement Rural*. Niamey, Niger: Cabinet du Premier Ministre, Secretariat Permanent de la SRP.

Reynolds, J. F., Grainger, A., Stafford Smith, D. M., Bastin, G., Garcia-Barrios, L., Fernández, R. J., et al. (2011). Scientific concepts for an integrated analysis of desertification. *Land Degradation and Development, 22*, 166–183.

Rinaudo, T. (2005). *Uncovering the underground Forest: A short History and description of Farmer managed natural regeneration*. Melbourne: World Vision.

RoN (Republic of Niger). (2006). National adaptation programme of action.

Rufino, M. C., Herrero, M., Van Wijk, M. T., Hemerik, L., De Ridder, N., & Giller, K. E. (2009). Lifetime productivity of dairy cows in smallholder farming systems of the central highlands of Kenya. *Animal, 3*(07), 1044–1056.

Sahara Conservation Fund. (2007). Niger creates the largest protected area in Africa. http://www.saharaconservation.org/?Niger-creates-the-largest.

Steeg, J. van de, M. Herrero, & Notenbaert, A. (2013). Supporting the vulnerable: Increasing adaptive capacities of agropastoralists to climate change in West and southern Africa using a transdisciplinary research approach. Nairobi, Kenya: International Livestock Research Institute (ILRI).

Sendzimir, J., Reij, C. P., & Magnuszewski, P. (2011). Rebuilding resilience in the Sahel: Regreening in the Maradi and Zinder regions of Niger. *Ecology and Society, 16*(3), 1.

Stéphenne, N., & Lambin, E. F. (2001). A dynamic simulation model of land-use changes in Sudano-sahelian countries of Africa (SALU). *Agriculture, Ecosystems and Environment, 85*, 145–161.

Stickler, M. (2012). Rights to trees and livelihoods in Niger. Focus on land in Africa. Placing land rights at the heart of development. Brief. www.focusonland.com/download/51c49667b7626/.

Tabo, R., Bationo, A., Hassane, O., Amadou, B., Fosu, M., Sawadogo-Kabore, S., Fatondji, D., Korodjouma, O., Abdou, A., & Koala, S. (2009). Fertilizer microdosing for the prosperity of resource poor farmers: A success story. In: Humphreys, E. & R.S. Bayot (Eds.), (2009). Increasing the productivity and sustainability of rainfed cropping systems of poor smallholder farmers. In *Proceedings of the CGIAR Challenge Program on Water and Food International Workshop on Rainfed Cropping Systems*, Tamale, Ghana, 22–25 September 2008. The CGIAR Challenge Program on Water and Food, Colombo, Sri Lanka.

Tittonell, P., & Giller, K. E. (2013). When yield gaps are poverty traps: The paradigm of ecological intensification in African smallholder agriculture. *Field Crops Research, 143*, 76–90.

Toulmin, C., & Quan, J. (2000). Evolving land rights, policy and tenure in Africa. International Inst. for Environment and Development, London. 336 pp.

Twomlow, S., Hove, L., Mupangwa, W., Masikati, P., & Mashingaidze, N. (2009). Precision conservation agriculture for vulnerable farmers in low potential zones. In: Humphreys, E. & R. S. Bayot, (Eds.), *Increasing the productivity and sustainability of rainfed cropping systems of poor smallholder farmers. Proceedings of the CGIAR Challenge Program on Water and Food*

International Workshop on Rainfed Cropping Systems, Tamale, Ghana, 22–25 September 2008. The CGIAR Challenge Program on Water and Food, Colombo, Sri Lanka.
UNDP. (2014). Human Development Report 2014. Sustaining Human Progress: Reducing Vulnerabilities and Building Resilience. http://hdr.undp.org/sites/default/files/hdr14-report-en-1.pdf. Accessed September 30, 2014.
UNDP (United Nations Development Program). (2013). Human Development Report. The Rise of the South: Human Progress in a Diverse World. New York, pp 203.
Upton, M. (1989). Livestock productivity assessment and herd growth models. *Agricultural Systems*, *29*(2), 149–164.
WHO (World Health Organization) (2014). World Health Statistics. http://apps.who.int/iris/bitstream/10665/112738/1/9789240692671_eng.pdf?ua=1. Accessed October 6, 2014.
World Bank. (2011). Africa emergency locust project. Online at http://www-wds.worldbank.org/external/default/WDSContentServer/WDSP/IB/2012/01/11/000333037_20120111005226/Rendered/PDF/ICR15530P092570IC0disclosed01090120.pdf. Accessed June 12, 2014.
Vanlauwe, B., & Giller, K. E. (2006). Popular myths around soil fertility management in sub-Saharan Africa. *Agriculture, Ecosystems and Environment, 116*(1), 34–46.
Von Grebmer, K., Headey, D., Olofinbiyi, T., Wiesmann, D., Fritschel, H., Yin, S., & Yohannes, Y. (2013). Global hunger index the challenge of hunger: Building resilience to achieve food and nutrition security. IFPRI. http://www.ifpri.org/publication/2013-global-hunger-index.
Winslow, M. D., Vogt, J. V., Thomas, R. J., Sommer, S., Martius, C., & Akhtar-Schuster, M. (2011). Science for improving the monitoring and assessment of dryland degradation. *Land Degradation & Development*, *22*(2), 145–149.
Zingore, S., Murwira, H. K., Delve, R. J., & Giller, K. E. (2007). Influence of nutrient management strategies on variability of soil fertility, crop yields and nutrient balances on smallholder farms in Zimbabwe. *Agriculture, Ecosystems and Environment, 119*, 112–126.

Chapter 18
The Economics of Land Degradation in Russia

Alexey Sorokin, Aleksey Bryzzhev, Anton Strokov, Alisher Mirzabaev, Timothy Johnson and Sergey V. Kiselev

Abstract The analysis of the costs for action versus inaction in addressing land degradation at national and sub-national (regional and district) levels in Russia showed that the total annual costs of land degradation due to land use and cover change only are about 189 billion USD in 2009 as compared with 2001, i.e. about 23.6 billion USD annually, or about 2 % of Russia's Gross Domestic Product (GDP) in 2010. These land use and land cover changes occurred in the area of 130 million ha. The area of arable lands decreased by 25 % during the period of the economic reforms between 1990 and 2009. The total economic value of ecosystem goods and services is estimated to equal about 3700 billion USD in Russia, exceeding the conventional GDP by 3 times. The costs of action against land degradation are lower than the costs of inaction in Russia by 5–6 times over a 30-year horizon. Almost 92 % of the costs of action are made up of the opportunity costs of action. The methodology of the economics of land degradation can be successfully applied in peculiar socioeconomic conditions of Russia, but the lack of harmonization of methods and indicators brings uncertainty to quantitative assessments.

Keywords Rostov region · Soil maps · Land use maps · Remote sensing data

The study was performed with a financial support of the Russian Scientific Fund (project no. 14-38-00023).

A. Bryzzhev
Russian Academy of Sciences, V.V. Dokuchaev Soil Science Institute, Moscow, Russia

A. Mirzabaev
Center for Development Research (ZEF), University of Bonn, Bonn, Germany

T. Johnson
International Food Policy Research Institute (IFPRI), Washington, D.C., USA

A. Sorokin (✉) · A. Strokov · S.V. Kiselev
Eurasian Center for Food Security (ECFS), Lomonosov Moscow State University, Flat22, Building 1134, Filaretovskaya Str, Zelenograd, Moscow, Russia
e-mail: alexey.sorokin@ecfs.msu.ru

E. Nkonya et al. (eds.), *Economics of Land Degradation and Improvement – A Global Assessment for Sustainable Development*,
DOI 10.1007/978-3-319-19168-3_18

Introduction

Russia stretches over a large part of Eastern Europe and Northern Asia. The total area of Russia is more than 17 million km^2 (Rudneva 2001). The vastness of the territory of the country inevitably leads to a diversity of natural conditions that causes the development of multiple economic uses of land resources. Climatic conditions have direct and indirect impacts on biological components of natural landscapes and soil forming processes. In their turn, the biophysical conditions determine the shape of agricultural development of the territory, with various land-use systems and with different major degradation processes. Figure 18.1 illustrates the nine major and accompanying processes of degradation of arable lands in Russia.

The increasing degradation of land resources in many parts of Russia, manifested in numerous forms such as desertification, soil erosion, secondary salinization, waterlogging, and overgrazing, to name a few, considerably limits land productivity and the ability of land to provide ecosystem services (Table 18.1). Swamping and erosion result in the biggest affected areas. Salinization processes are most characteristic of the southern part of Volga Federal district (FD) (the Caspian depression, etc.). The major drivers of degradation include: climatic change, unsustainable agricultural practices, industrial and mining activities, expansion of crop production to fragile and marginal areas, inadequate maintenance of irrigation and drainage networks, and overgrazing.

Socioeconomic characteristics of the regions of Russia are extremely heterogeneous. The population in each region of Russia varies in density and per capita income. Actually in rural areas the income is 40 % of the average income in cities (Nefedova 2013). The regions differ in terms of transportation networks, access to

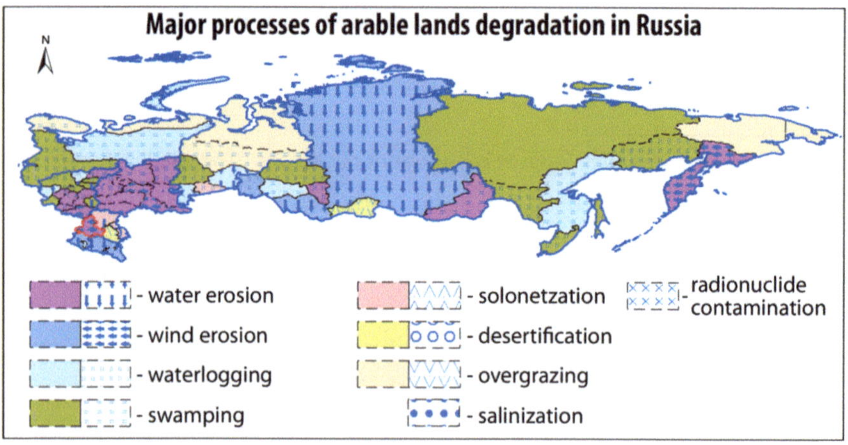

Fig. 18.1 Major processes of arable lands degradation in Russia with legend. Note: *Color*—the basic processes, *mark*—accompanying processes, *blue polygons*—borders of Federal districts, *red polygon*—boarder of Rostov region. *Source* Vandysheva and Gurov (2011). Reproduced with permission

Table 18.1 Major processes of arable lands degradation in Russia by federal districts (areas of basic and accompanying processes)

Federal districts	Units	Total area	Water erosion	Wind erosion	Waterlogging	Swamping	Solonetzation	Desertification	Overgrazing	Salinization	Radionuclide contamination
Type			Basic	Basic	Basic	Basic	Basic	Basic	Basic	Accompanying	Accompanying
Central	km^2	647,694	313,318	–	85,956	248,420	–	–	–	–	–
	%	100	48.37	–	13.27	38.35	–	–	–	–	–
Northern-West	km^2	1,862,379	–	–	1,021,812	518,855	–	–	321,712	–	–
	%	100	–	–	54.87	27.86	–	–	17.27	–	–
Southern	km^2	420,876	100,967	75,485	7792	–	161,901	74,731	–	–	–
	%	100	23.99	17.94	1.85	–	38.47	17.76	–	–	–
North Caucasian	km^2	170,439	7987	143,177	–	–	–	–	–	101,240	–
	%	100	4.69	84.00	–	–	–	–	–	9.76	–
Volga	km^2	1,036,975	1,036,975	–	–	–	–	–	–	–	88,529
	%	100	100.00	–	–	–	–	–	–	–	4.87
Ural	km^2	1,818,497	–	–	248 651	194,307	71,488	–	1,304,051	–	–
	%	100	–	–	13.67	10.69	3.93	–	71.71	–	–
Siberian	km^2	5,144,953	527,617	3,956,585	177 756	314,391	–	168,604	–	–	–
	%	100	10.26	76.90	3.45	6.11	–	3.28	–	–	–
Far Eastern	km^2	6,169,329	464,275	–	823 899	4,159,674	–	–	721,481	101,250	138,873
	%	100	7.53	–	13.35	67.43	–	–	11.69	0.59	0.80
Russia (total)	km^2	17,271,142	2,451,334	4,175,426	2,365,966	5,435,797	233,431	243,356	2,347,345	–	50,331
	%	100	14.19	24.18	13.70	31.47	1.35	1.41	13.59	–	7.77

Source Based on Vandysheva and Gurov (2011)

infrastructure, and the provision of social services. All these differences affect the ways and extent of the economic use of lands, but are also conditioned by them.

The natural conditions and socio-economic factors determine the structure and the principles of land use in Russia. In the recent history in Russia, there was a rapid transition from state and collective farms formed under conditions of a planned centralized economy to private farms of various forms and sizes operating under market conditions. Such changes resulted in changes in land use, including of arable lands. Between 1990 and 2002, the economic reforms resulted in a drastic reduction in arable lands and cultivated areas. Since 2002, the area of arable lands in Russia has stabilized (Nefedova 2013). The State land records show that during the period from 1990 to 2001, the area of arable land has decreased by 8.5 million ha. During the period 2001–2006 the rate of land abandonment has decreased resulting in the decline of 1.9 million ha. In general for the period from 1990 to 2006 the area of arable land has decreased by 10.7 million ha (Federal State Statistics Service 2014a). Most of the abandoned lands were located in the regions with severe climate and poor soils; however, the biophysical conditions in the abandoned areas were not restrictive for agricultural production. Also, the reduction of the area of arable land was partly due to the formal transfer of the land from one category to another during the inventory undertaken by the legislation (Shoba et al. 2010). Following these reductions in the size of arable lands, the pressure on the fields remaining under use has increased, thus leading to more intensive use and creating conditions for the degradation of these most productive soils. Land degradation is a major challenge for the agriculture in the country, which is not properly addressed until now. We need deeper understanding of both the socioeconomic and biophysical drivers of land degradation in the Russian Federation. We have to estimate the cost of land degradation in Russia using a Total Economic Value (TEV) framework. The latter estimates tangible economic losses due to land degradation, such as the decline in the productivity of crops, together with the losses in non-market values of the ecosystem services, also essential for human and social well-being.

The aim of this study is to estimate the extent and the effect of land degradation on the agricultural economy of Russia. The research questions were:

1. What are the major drivers of land degradation in various zones of Russia with differing levels of socio-economic development, bioclimatic conditions, and resource potentials?
2. What is the total economic cost of land degradation in large (Federal district level) and small (region level) administrative-territorial units of Russia?
3. What is the value of potential benefits from sustainable land management in Russia?

Thus, the first section of this chapter analyses the degradation and improvement of the land resources on a national scale with an emphasis on the period of economic reforms from 1990 to 2009 in Russia, where the area of arable lands decreased by 25 %. We provide an estimation of the costs of the measures for controlling land degradation and then compare this cost with potential losses of land value if no land protection or remediation action was taken. The main causes and drivers of these processes, both natural and socioeconomic, and the global consequences of these land use changes are discussed. The total economic costs of land degradation are estimated, including the losses in the value of non-marketed ecosystem services. The study also estimates the value of benefits from land improvement. Both land degradation costs and benefits from land improvement are estimated for the period of 2001–2009 at the Federal districts level in Russia.

The second section presents a case study of the state of agricultural production and land degradation in the Azov district of Rostov region in the southern part of European Russia. The analysis is done on the basis of accessible information on the socioeconomic characteristics of the district, the state of agricultural sector, maps and the reports on the land resources of the district. The latter group of data sources includes three land use maps of the district for 1990, 2000, and 2010, the map of the land planning of the district, and soil maps in both raster (scale 1:10,000) and vector formats (scales 1:50,000 and 1:300,000). Other available remote sensing data have also been used. Three maps showing land-use change for three time periods were developed: 1990–2000, 2000–2010 and 1990–2010. We estimate the total economic costs of land degradation, including the losses in the value of non-marketed ecosystem services. The study also estimated the value of benefits from land improvement. Both land degradation costs and benefits from land improvement were estimated for the periods of 1990–2000, 2000–2010 and 1990–2010.

Methodology

In this chapter a multiscale approach was used to estimate the economic effect of land degradation in Russia on the national, regional, and farm scale. The methodology used in the study follows the approaches proposed by von Braun et al. (2013) and Nkonya et al. (2014), and is based on the comparative evaluation of the cost of action and the cost of inaction. Following Nkonya et al. (2014), we calculated the costs of land degradation due to land-use and land-cover change (LUCC) through:

$$C_{LUCC} = \sum_{i}^{K} (\Delta a_1 * p_1 - \Delta a_1 * p_2) \qquad (18.1)$$

where CLUCC = cost of land degradation due to LUCC; a_1 = land area of biome 1 being replaced by biome 2; P_1 and P_2 are the total economic value (TEV) of biomes 1 and 2, respectively.

By definition of land degradation, $P_1 > P_2$. In cases where $P_1 < P_2$, LUCC is not regarded as land degradation, but as land improvement (Nkonya et al. 2014).

The cost of taking action against land degradation due to LUCC is given by:

$$CTA_i = A_i \frac{1}{\rho^t} \left\{ z_i + \sum_{t=1}^{T} (x_i + p_j x_j) \right\} \quad (18.2)$$

where CTA_i = cost of restoring high value biome i; ρ^t = discount factor of land user; A_i = area of high value biome i that was replaced by low value biome j; z_i = cost of establishing high value biome I; x_i = maintenance cost of high value biome i until it reaches maturity; x_j = productivity of low value biome j per ha; p_j = price of low value biome j per unit (e.g. ton); t = time in years and T = planning horizon of taking action against land degradation. The term $p_j x_j$ represents the opportunity cost of foregoing production of the low value biome j being replaced.

The cost of inaction will be the sum of annual losses due to land degradation:

$$CI_i = \sum_{t=1}^{T} C_{LUCC} \quad (18.3)$$

where CI_i = cost of not taking action against degradation of biome i. Given that the benefit of restoring degraded land goes beyond the maturity period of biome i, we have to use the planning horizon of the land user. Poor farmers tend to have a shorter planning horizon while better off farmers tend to have a longer planning horizon (Pannell et al. 2014). The planning horizon also depends on the type of investment. For example, tree planting requires a longer planning horizon than annual cropland management. We will assume a 30 year planning horizon for the afforestation program to redress deforestation and loss of woodlands and shrublands. We will use a 6 year planning horizon for grassland and croplands—majority of which are annual crops. As Nkonya et al. (2013) notes, land users will take action against land degradation if $CTA_i < CI_i$.

Data and Materials

First Level Analysis—8 Federal Districts of Russian Federation

Moderate Resolution Imaging Spectroradiometer (MODIS) remotely sensed datasets on land cover were used to identify the shifts in the land use and land cover in the region between 2001 and 2009 at the level of Federal districts of the Russian Federation. These included forests, grassland, cropland, shrublands (including woodlands), urban areas, barren lands, and water bodies. The MODIS land cover dataset is groundtruthed and quality controlled (Friedl et al. 2010), with overall accuracy of land use classification at 75 %. Following this analysis of the land-use and land-cover change, total economic values were assigned to each land use using the data from TEEB (The Economics of Ecosystems and Biodiversity) (van der Ploeg and de Groot 2010), using the benefit transfer approach.

Table 18.2 Data used for the evaluation of the land degradation at the district level (Azov district of Rostov region of Russian Federation)

Data	Year	Spatial resolution, m	Links
Base data			
Landsat 5 TM	1990	30	usgs.gov
Landsat 7 ETM+	2000	15	usgs.gov
IRS	2007	6	Commercial data
Navteq maps		0.6	navteq.com
Panchromatic images		From 1 to 2	http://gptl.ru/
References purposes data			
Landsat 2	1975, 1976	60	usgs.gov
Landsat 3	1979	60	usgs.gov
Landsat 5	1984, 1986 and 2011	30	usgs.gov
Landsat 7	1999	15	usgs.gov
Spot	2010	2.5	Commercial data
Interpretation of soil and land cover data			
TDM		30 and 90	
SRTM		90	maps-for-free.com
SRTM (alternative palette)		90	maps-for-free.com
ASTER DEM		30–70	maps-for-free.com

Source The authors

Second Level Analysis—Azov District (Rostov Region, Southern FD of Russian Federation)

The following data sources and materials have been used for the evaluation of land degradation at the district level (Table 18.2).

A Review of the State and Current Tendencies in Russian Agriculture

The size of agricultural lands in Russia is similar to Brazil and Canada. Since the late 1980s, the rural population of Russia declined sharply from almost 60 to 20 million people by 2010 (Federal State Statistics Service 2014b). Official statistics of Russia show that the density of rural population is about 2.2 persons/km^2, the area of arable land is 122 million ha (about 23 % of the land fund of Russia). The area of arable land per rural person is 3.2 ha, and the share of the population employed in agriculture and forestry is 15.6 % (Federal State Statistics Service 2014a). It should be noted that the value for the average

Table 18.3 Some characteristics of rural lands and agriculture of Federal districts of Russia and European countries with respectively similar bioclimatic conditions

Federal districts of Russia and European countries	Rural population density, person/km^2	Area of arable lands, million ha	Share of arable lands in the territory (%)	Availability of arable lands, ha/person	Share of employment in agriculture of rural population (%)
Northern FD	1.4	2.4	1.6	1.2	18.9
Finland	5.8	2.3	6.7	1.1	6.0
Central FD	11.0	20.1	32.0	2.9	18.7
Poland	45.6	12.5	38.6	0.8	15.8
Southern FD	16.7	20.4	35.0	2.1	16.7
France	26.0	18.5	33.6	1.3	5.4

Source Based on Nefedova (2013)

availability of cropland per one rural inhabitant is deceptive, because of the uneven development of the territory. In the share of employment in agriculture (15.6 %) Russia is comparable with other developing countries (Nefedova 2013).

Since the territory of Russia developed unevenly, it is more informative to compare other countries with macro-regions of Russia, such as the federal districts (there are eight of them as of 2014), with similar agro-climatic conditions. For example, we can compare the Northern, Central, and Southern Federal districts with the countries of Northern, Central and Southern Europe, respectively (Table 18.3). The comparison shows that at a much lower population density (1.4, 11.0, 16.7 persons/km^2, in the Northern, Central, and Southern Federal districts, respectively) and higher availability of land (1.2, 2.9, 2.1 ha/person, respectively), the Russian regions stand out with the higher employment in agriculture (18.9, 18.7, 16.7 %, respectively) than in the European countries with similar bioclimatic conditions (Nefedova 2013).

The claim that Russia has a lot of land should be considered as a relative one. The areas with optimal heat and moisture for agriculture in Russia occupy 14 % of the territory that is inhabited by 58 % of the rural population. Only in 1 % of the territory of the country there is a combination of sufficient heat with satisfactory humidity.[1]

The yield of the main crops in Russia is not high compared to other countries with rainfed agricultural production, and only Kazakhstan and Australia are surpassed by Russia. It means that the productivity of the Russian lands is not high and the gross volume of production is obtained through enormous use of land resources (Federal State Statistics Service 2014c). The yield of grain crops in Russia is far behind that of most Western countries. The average yield of grain crop is within 2100–2300 kg/ha, while in the US it is above 6500 kg/ha.

[1]Considering that for the majority of crops the sum of active temperatures (above 10 °C) should exceed 2500 °C, and the ratio of annual precipitation to potential evaporation should be over 0.75 (Shoba et al. 2010).

Table 18.4 The percentage of livestock for different categories of land tenure

Russia and Federal districts	Agricultural organizations (%)		Households (%)		Farms (%)	
	1990s	2000s	1990s	2000s	1990s	2000s
Russia	69.8	54.8	28.7	42.0	1.4	3.2
Central	81.5	73.8	17.8	24.7	0.7	1.5
Northern-West	78.4	73.5	20.2	23.4	1.4	3.1
Southern	66.9	44.3	30.6	49.5	2.5	6.2
North Caucasian	36.9	16.9	58.6	75.8	4.5	7.3
Volga	70.9	58.4	28.2	39.1	0.9	2.5
Ural	63.0	50.3	35.3	47.2	1.7	2.5
Siberian	62.6	48.8	35.5	48.6	1.9	2.6
Far Eastern	53.9	27.3	40.4	60.4	5.7	12.3

Mean values for 1990s and 2000s by the end of each year, the share of livestock to all categories
Source Based on Federal State Statistics Service (2014a)

Table 18.4 shows the structure of livestock for different categories of land tenure: agricultural organizations, households and farms. The share of livestock in agricultural organizations decreases in 2000s compared with other market players (households and farms). These results can be explained by the fact that since the reforms of the 1990s the demonopolization of the agricultural sector has occurred.

Since the 1990s the application of water for irrigation, fertilizers, and other ameliorative facilities for intensification of land productivity in Russia has decreased in most Federal districts. These results can be explained by several facts. Overall, there was a reorganization of the agricultural organizations. Many unprofitable farms were closed and many lands were abandoned due to unfavorable performance. At the same time, due to lack of funding, the landlords began to invest less money in fertilizer and water for irrigation.

Russia is far behind Europe in the density of paved roads. The total road density is below 50 km/1000 km^2. The western part of Russia has a relatively high density of paved roads, but density falls gradually or abruptly from about 600 km/1000 km^2 in the Moscow region to about 60 km/1000 km^2 in the Novosibirsk region (the equivalent distance between Mexico and Canada). This gradient is similar to the yield of crops and many other agricultural indicators (Nefedova 2013).

Agricultural production remains an important factor of regional development in Russia. Its share in gross domestic product in 2010 on average was 8 %, but in many regions, such as the Belgorod and Orel regions, agricultural production was about 30 % of the gross regional product (GRP). In the southern region of the Russian Plain it was from 20 to 30 % (Federal State Statistics Service 2014a). Unlike Western countries, where the agro-industrial complex (AIC) is dominated by manufacturing and services associated with the processing of agricultural raw material (feedstock), marketing, and supply and maintenance of agricultural production, in Russia it is dominated by raw agricultural products.

Table 18.5 Application of water for irrigation, fertilizers, and other ameliorative facilities for intensification of land productivity in Russia (the mean values for 1990s and 2000s)

Russia and its Federal districts	Water for irrigation, million m^3		Mineral fertilizers, kg/ha		Organic fertilizers, kg/ha		Lime application, 1000 ha		Phosphate application, 1000 ha	
	90s	00s	90s	00s	90s	00s	90s	00s	90s	00s
Russia	11,562	9,413	52.6	26.4	2500	0.9	493.0	362.8	91.4	40.9
Central	705	272	90.3	42.8	3700	1.2	79.5	101.2	22.0	18.2
Northern-West	90	37	90.4	30.9	6700	2.5	8.8	15.3	0.3	1.1
Southern	4899	4464	51.1	37.9	2000	0.8	263.4	0.2	4.6	0.0
North Caucasian	3373	3617	64.0	33.2	1700	1.1	0.0	0.3	0.0	0.0
Volga	1440	436	49.0	23.9	2500	1.0	126.2	240.6	47.3	15.8
Ural	137	54	35.5	15.5	1900	0.6	7.7	2.8	15.7	3.3
Siberian	821	433	21.5	6.3	1200	0.5	5.5	0.8	0.1	0.0
Far Eastern	98	101	52.8	19.8	1800	0.2	2.0	1.8	1.5	2.5

Source Based on Federal State Statistics Service (2014a)

Table 18.6 Socio-economic characteristics of Russia

Federal districts	Area, 1000 km^2	GRP per capita, RUB		Population, 1000 ppl		Poverty (%)		Investment per capita, RUB		Employment in agriculture, in %		Density of roads, km/1000 km^2		Density of railways, km/10000 km^2	
Period		90s	00s	90s	00s	90s	00s	90s	00s	90s	00s	90s	00s	90s	00s
Central	650.2	14505.2	153571.2	38119.3	38171.5	35.7	15.6	1982.9	25257.6	9.7	8.7	167.2	193.8	269.6	263.1
Northern-West	1687	13497.1	120532.3	15058.7	13795.2	32.2	14.2	1681.3	33433.1	6.2	7	36.4	41.2	77.6	77.3
Southern	420.9	8544.5	67237.7	14895.1	13884.2	38.2	19.2	1183.1	19718.9	20.4	18.6	97.2	110.8	162.7	160
North Caucasian	170.4	3578.7	38583.8	8138	9023.8	54	20.2	1080.2	11011.4	21.3	20.8	174.3	199.6	131.6	128.3
Volga	1037	12447.4	87178.3	31933	30569.5	37.8	17.3	1769.7	20445.1	14.8	13.5	105.4	128	146	143.2
Ural	1818.5	23513.2	211311.1	12678.6	12183.5	30.9	13.6	4562	54152.8	8.8	7.6	17	20.7	48	47.6
Siberian	5145	13258.6	91954	21023	19507.3	41.6	18.6	1670.5	18873.3	13.1	12.5	16.2	18.7	29.8	28.9
Far Eastern	6169.3	16073.8	120303	7746.8	6507.6	42.9	21.1	2058.3	38357.9	9.5	9.5	4.9	5.6	13.4	13
Total	17098.3	20785.9	138764.2	148172.6	143742.6	29	14.9	1971.9	25796.3	14.7	11.5	28	33.1	50.6	50

Source Based on Federal State Statistics Service (2014b)

The average annual salary in the agricultural sector in 2010 was 3500 USD with the average indicators in all the sectors of economy 6970 USD. In 1989 the wage in this industry reached the national average wage, so with this in mind we have to admit that agriculture and rural areas have greatly suffered (Federal State Statistics Service 2014a). Other socio-economic characteristics of Russia are shown in Table 18.6. The important outcomes of the reforms are: (1) double decrease in percentage of population living under the poverty level; (2) the increase of investments per capita; (3) slight increase in road density. The negative outcomes are: (1) decrease of population; (2) decrease of share of employments in agriculture, which, at the same time, could have a positive impact if the modernization of agricultural industry occurs.

Some experts (Nefedova 2013) distinguish 5 zones with different types of land development in Russia: 1—low level of land reclamation and land without reclamation in the North and East of the country (47 % of the total area of Russia): this group is characterized by small centers of agriculture, low population density, seasonal population migration, weak access to information, and traditional economy of indigenous peoples; 2—Forest area with mining of mineral resources, sparse (a few percent of territory) settlements and agriculture (22 % of the Russia's territory): characterized by suburban agriculture, a small part of rural population, poor access to information, and the crisis of agricultural enterprises; 3—Forest agricultural area (13 % of the area of Russia and 30 % of the rural population): characterized by a developed industry, a big heterogeneity of land reclamation (from suburbs to the periphery), low density of rural population, and the decline of agriculture; 4—Mostly agricultural area (12 % of the area of Russia and 58 % of the rural population) characterized by good land reclamation, with problems of over-plowed soils and aridity of some territories. These problems can be resolved within the framework of sustainable (rational) natural resource management; 5—Mountain pastoral area (6 % of the area of Russia, 8 % of the rural population) (Table 18.5).

In Russia 70 % of the territory is characterized by sparse population, complexity of management and natural conditions, and sparse networks of paved roads.

Soil Resources

Soil resources are basic for sustainable agricultural production. To a great extent soils determine the agricultural practices and application of fertilizers. The Chernozem zone is the main base of grain production in Russia. Within this zone there are 85–90 % of lands that are under cultivation. Though it occupies about 12 % of the country's area, more than 50 % of arable lands of Russia are concentrated here (Shoba et al. 2010). More than half of the arable lands of the country is represented by the Chernozem zone, 15 % are represented by the Albeluvisol/Phaeozem zone, and the extension of the Kastanozem zone is more than 10 % (Ministry of Natural Resources and Environment of the Russian Federation 2013).

The Reforms of 1990s

The agricultural sector was faced with several challenges at the very beginning: dramatic reduction of State support; the rudimentary state of market relations; the struggle for ownership; lack of coordination of government entities; the impact of the international market; the imperfection of the law and ignorance of the law; and the lack of feedback between society and the State.

The reforms have resulted in several changes: the elimination of state monopoly on land (more than 85 % of lands were transferred to the ownership of individuals); the creation of an administrative land market (prices were established depending on the quality and location of the plot, with annual indexation); the population had the opportunity to purchase and sell land; and the account of unclaimed land and their transfer to municipal ownership was simplified.

According to the Federal State Statistics Service (2014a) the share of loss-making enterprises reached a maximum in 1998 and amounted up to 88 % of the total. In 2010 unprofitable enterprises were only 28 % of large and medium-sized agricultural organizations. The share of all loss-making enterprises in the Russian Federation is 30 %. The decrease in the share of unprofitable enterprises was not only due to their coping with the crisis, but also due to the closure of non-viable ones. Employment in enterprises has also dropped from 8.3 million in 1990 to 2 million in 2010. Average acreage of enterprises decreased from 2.9 to 2.3 thousand ha. Catastrophic changes have occurred with an average number of cattle, which decreased from 1800 heads in 1990 to 130 heads in 2010.

As stated earlier, a lot of land became unused, which led, on the one hand to a significant reduction of degradation processes in agricultural areas, but, on the other hand, on those lands that remained agricultural (usually the most fertile lands), the intensification of production was observed.

A Review of the State and Tendencies of Land Degradation in Russia

Land degradation can be classified into physical, chemical, and biological types. These types do not necessarily occur individually; spiral feedbacks between processes are often present (Katyal and Vlek 2000). Physical land degradation refers to erosion; changes in the soil physical structure, such as compaction or crusting and waterlogging. Chemical degradation, on the other hand, includes leaching, salinization, acidification, nutrient imbalances, and fertility depletion, soil organic carbon loss. Biological degradation includes rangeland degradation, deforestation, and loss in biodiversity, involving loss of soil organic matter or of flora and fauna populations or species in the soil (Scherr 1999).

Causes of land degradation are classified into proximate and underlying. Proximate causes of land degradation are those that have a direct effect on the terrestrial ecosystem. The proximate causes are further divided into biophysical proximate causes (natural) and unsustainable land management practices (anthropogenic). The underlying causes of land degradation are those that indirectly affect the proximate causes of land degradation (von Braun et al. 2013).

The negative processes related to development of land degradation have reached alarming proportions at the beginning of 2000s in the Russian Federation. More than 20 types of land degradation processes can be identified, which lead to a deterioration in the quality of land, reversible and irreversible transfers of land from one category to another. In arable land, most degradation is caused by the development of processes of erosion and deflation, secondary salinization, reduction of humus, phosphorus and potassium content, and adverse values of pH. The reversible transfer of lands from one category to another is related to the covering with shrubs and woodland, the flooding of the floodplain meadows by water in reservoirs and clogging by the stones. Long-term and irreversible losses of arable land is due to factors such as the contamination by radioactive substances, the extraction of minerals, development of gully systems, subsidence effects associated with waterlogging of soil, and construction of residential and industrial buildings on lands suitable for farming (Kashtanov 2001; Dobrovolski 2002).

The Federal program "Preservation and restoration of soil fertility of agricultural lands and agricultural landscapes as a national treasure of Russia in 2006–2010 and for the period till 2013" established indicators for restoration and rehabilitation of agricultural lands for 2010. These target indicators were exceeded by 2010; however, the rate of rehabilitation of degraded agricultural land is insufficient in comparison to the scale of land degradation in Russia. The area protected from water erosion, inundation and flooding, wind erosion and desertification constituted approximately 0.4 % of lands of Russia. The decrease in the degree of acidity of the soil was approximately 0.6 %, which equates to 0.06 % of the amelioration of solonetzic soils of all agricultural lands (Ministry of Agriculture 2011).

According to estimates at the present time, the total expected yield of eroded and deflated arable land is about 25 % less than of areas not affected by erosion. It means that the loss is 400 kg per ha in the equivalent for grain, and for the entire country it is about 14 billion kg, even taking into account the actual low crop yields and low productivity of natural grasslands. The shortage of products from degraded grasslands is about 100 kg per ha of hay, which gives 1400 million kg loss for the total area of the country (Ministry of Natural Resources and Environment of the Russian Federation 2013).

Erosion is evident in areas with hilly terrain. About 20 % of agricultural lands in Russia are on slopes steeper than 20 %. Under these conditions, water flow, resulting from intensive snowmelt or precipitation of heavy rainfalls, lead to the development of gully erosion. The total area of the gullies is 2.4 million ha (0.14 % of the total land area of the Russian Federation). The main part of the gullies are located on agricultural lands (0.6 million ha), forest (1.1 million ha) and protected environmental lands. Every year the area of ravines grows with devastating speed up to 180–200 thousand ha. The growth of gullies leads to the complete withdrawal of productive land or transforms it into other categories such as pasture or unused land. The land area affected by gully erosion is 2.5–3 times larger than the area of the gullies, because of the difficulties for operation of agricultural machinery. Due to production conditions they have low productivity and are eventually transformed into low productive grazing lands. The annual loss of production from these lands is estimated at 1200 million kg of grain (Ministry of Natural Resources and Environment of the Russian Federation 2013).

Soil compaction leads to the loss of tillage performance by up to 5–10 %. Costs for fertilizer increase approximately by 1.5 times, as low-degraded lands require higher doses of fertilizers by 10 %, medium-degraded by 30 % and high-degraded 1.5–2 times (Gordeeva and Romanenko 2008). On heavily compacted soils yield reduction reaches 50 %. Low-compacted soils occupy 17 million ha; medium-compacted—69 million ha, and high-compacted—49 million ha of arable lands. Loss of fertility is 5–10, 20–30 and 50–60 %, respectively. Humus content is decreasing, the environmental condition of the soil is deteriorating, and more recently, the stability of the soils is decreasing. Humus storage in Chernozems is reduced annually by 0.62 t/ha over the last 15–25 years. Losses from the presence of acidic soils are 15–16 billion kg of agricultural products in terms of grain per year (Gordeeva and Romanenko 2008) (Table 18.7).

As it was mentioned above, it is more useful to take into analysis the macro-regions of Russia, such as the federal districts, because they are more homogenous in climatic conditions, economic development, and land-use practices. We have taken into consideration eight Federal districts—Central, North-Western, Southern, North Caucasian, Volga, Ural, Siberian, and Far Eastern.

Following Nkonya et al. (2011) we compare the changes in NDVI between 1981 and 2006 and some key biophysical and socioeconomic variables, such as precipitation, population density, government effectiveness, agricultural intensification, and Gross Domestic Product (GDP) (Figs. 18.2, 18.3, 18.4 and 18.5). Since such relationships could differ across the country, we disaggregate the analysis across the eight Federal districts of Russia. The analysis showed a positive correlation between changes in key biophysical and socioeconomic variables with NDVI in most of the Federal districts of Russia. The exceptions are the FD with large and more heterogeneous territory such as Siberian and Far Eastern FDs. The most positive results were in the Chernozem Agro-ecological zone—the southern part of Russia.

Table 18.7 Dynamics of agrochemicals application and land improvement in Russia (on average)

Indicators	1991–1995	2003–2007
Application of organic fertilizers, billion kg (kg/ha)	150.1 (1700)	51.8 (900)
Supply of mineral fertilizers, billion kg	4.5	1.5
Application of mineral fertilizers, kg/ha	35	28
Melioration of acidic soils, thousand ha	2733	314
Application of phosphorous fertilizers, thousand ha	1021	39.1
Melioration of Solonetz, thousand ha	66.2	3.2
Processing of Solonetz, thousand ha	84	10.1

Source Gordeeva and Romanenko (2008)

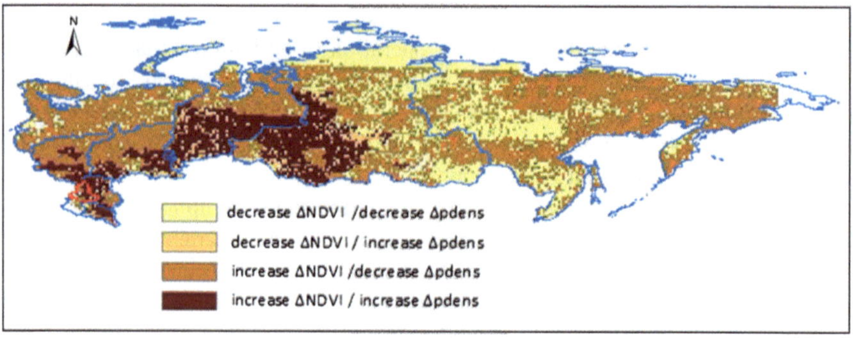

Fig. 18.2 Relationship between change in NDVI and population density. *Source* Based on Nkonya et al. (2011)

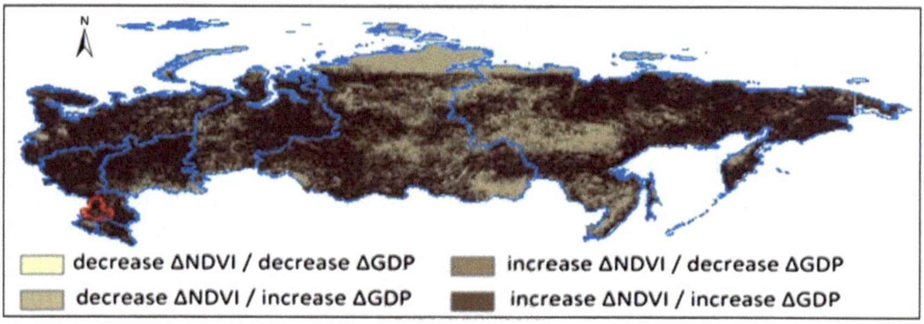

Fig. 18.3 Relationship between GDP and NDVI. *Source* Based on Nkonya et al. (2011)

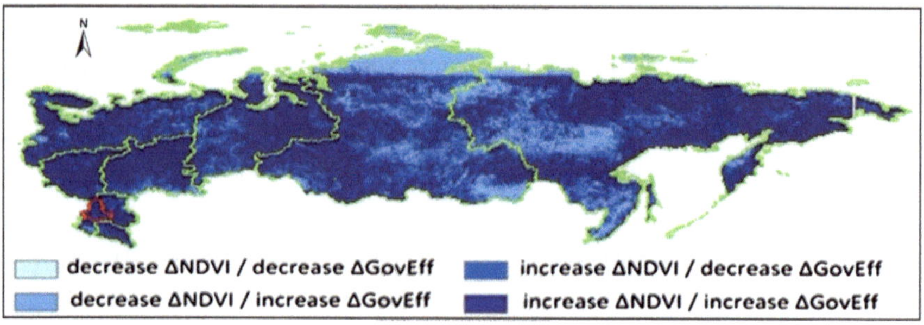

Fig. 18.4 Relationship between government effectiveness and NDVI. *Source* Based on Nkonya et al. (2011)

Le et al. (2014) used 7 broad land use/cover classes (see Fig. 18.6) aggregated from 23 classes of the Globcover 2005–2006 data (Bicheron et al. 2008). Figure 18.6 shows the main land-cover/land-use changes compared to long term NDVI (1982–2006). The NDVI layer corrects for AF (atmospheric fertilization),

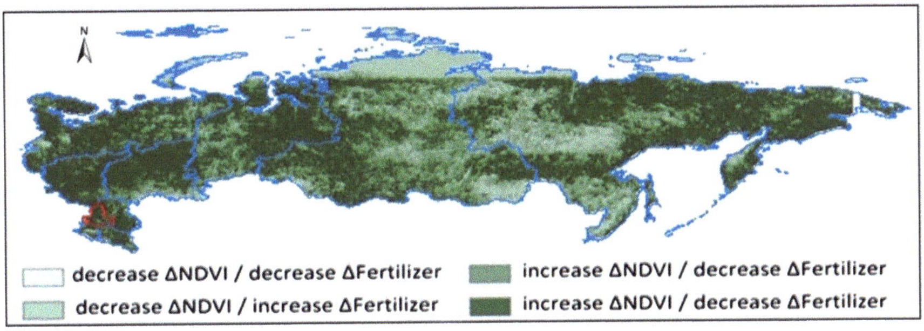

Fig. 18.5 Relationship between fertilizer application and NDVI. *Source* Based on Nkonya et al. (2011)

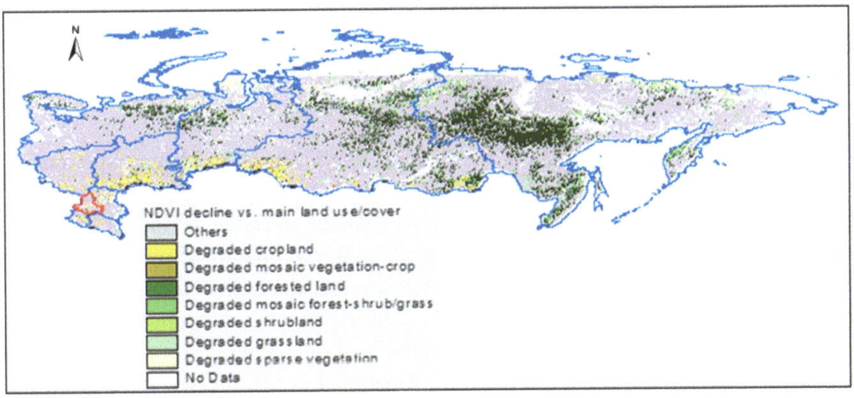

Fig. 18.6 Areas of long-term (1982–2006) NDVI decline (with correction of RF and AF effects and masking saturated NDVI zones) versus main land cover/use types of the Russian Federation. *Source* Based on Le et al. (2014). Note: *Blue color*—boundaries of Federal districts, *red color*—boundaries of Rostov region. "*Others*" means not degraded areas

areas with a high positive correlation with RF (rainfall), and saturated areas of NDVI (see Chap. 5). The related statistics for Russia are shown in Table 18.8. Figure 18.6 shows that land degradation hotspots in Russia are mainly on forested areas, croplands and areas with sparse vegetation. These are areas affected by forest fires (Sakha Republic, Krasnoyarskiy territory, etc.) and crop land degradation (Saratov, Omsk, Tyumen, Kurgan regions, etc.), due to processes such as salinization, degradation of irrigated lands, and desertification. In the case study of the Rostov region, we can also see the manifestation of cropland degradation processes.

Table 18.8 shows that close to 20 % or more (except shrub-land) of each main land cover/use types were affected by degradation processes. Croplands, especially in the southern part of Russia, where the agricultural industry is more risky due to drought, wind erosion, and problems with moral obsolescence of the irrigation system, have the biggest percentage of degradation in Russia (27 %).

Table 18.8 Value for Areas of long-term (1982–2006) NDVI decline (with correction of RF and AF effects and masking saturated NDVI zones) versus main land cover/use types of the Russian Federation in km^2 and in percentages for the corresponding land cover

NDVI decline versus main land use/cover	Value (km^2)	Percentage (%)
Degraded cropland	562,048	27
Degraded mosaic vegetation-crop	183,296	27
Degraded forest land	4,074,176	24
Degraded mosaic forest land	482,944	22
Degraded shrub-land	116,416	6
Degraded grassland	162,176	17
Degraded sparse vegetation	1,401,792	19
Total	6,982,848	43

Source Le et al. (2014)

Identification of Land Degradation Trends and Hotpots in Federal Districts of Russia

Our analysis shows that Russia at the Federal district level has been experiencing dynamic land-use and land-cover changes (LUCC) over the last decade (2001–2009). Tables 18.9 and 18.10 present these changes over the period of 2001 and 2009, using the data from the Moderate Resolution Imaging Spectroradiometer (MODIS) remotely sensed datasets. We can see that the largest areas of croplands are in Siberian and Volga FD (Fig. 18.7). But the bioclimatic conditions of these FDs are far from the optimum. Arable lands of the Volga FD are affected by salinization and water erosion and of the Siberian FD are affected by erosion and desertification.

Table 18.10 shows that Siberian, Far Eastern, and Ural FDs lost vast areas of grassland (66 million ha) and shrublands (55 million ha), which were almost totally converted into forestland (Fig. 18.8). The total addition to forests over the last

Table 18.9 Land use/cover classification in Federal districts of Russia in 2001, in million ha

Federal districts	Cropland	Forest	Grassland	Shrublands	Urban	Water	Barren
Central	31.1	25.8	5.7	1.6	0.6	0.4	0.0
Southern	22.8	2.4	14.0	1.6	0.7	0.4	0.1
Northwestern	3.4	83.5	8.4	58.0	8.1	0.1	5.3
Far Eastern	10.8	147.0	59.8	388.0	6.3	0.3	2.6
Siberian	50.2	188.0	43.5	213.8	9.0	0.6	4.3
Ural	12.9	47.3	10.2	96.7	5.2	0.1	0.2
Volga	53.8	38.7	6.2	3.2	1.4	0.3	0.0
North Caucasian	7.9	1.8	4.9	1.5	0.1	0.3	0.3
Total	193	535	153	765	32	3	13

Source Calculated using MODIS data

Table 18.10 Land use/cover change in Federal districts of Russia in 2009 relative to 2001, in million ha

Federal districts	Cropland	Forest	Grassland	Shrublands	Urban	Water	Barren
Central	0	4	−3	−1	0	0	0
Southern	−2	0	2	−1	0	0	0
Northwestern	−1	8	1	−7	−2	0	1
Far Eastern	1	44	−40	−3	−2	0	0
Siberian	−1	49	−22	−27	−1	0	3
Ural	3	14	−4	−13	0	0	0
Volga	−4	6	0	−2	0	0	0
North Caucasian	0	0	0	0	0	0	0
Total	−4	125	−66	−55	−6	0	4

Source Calculated using MODIS data

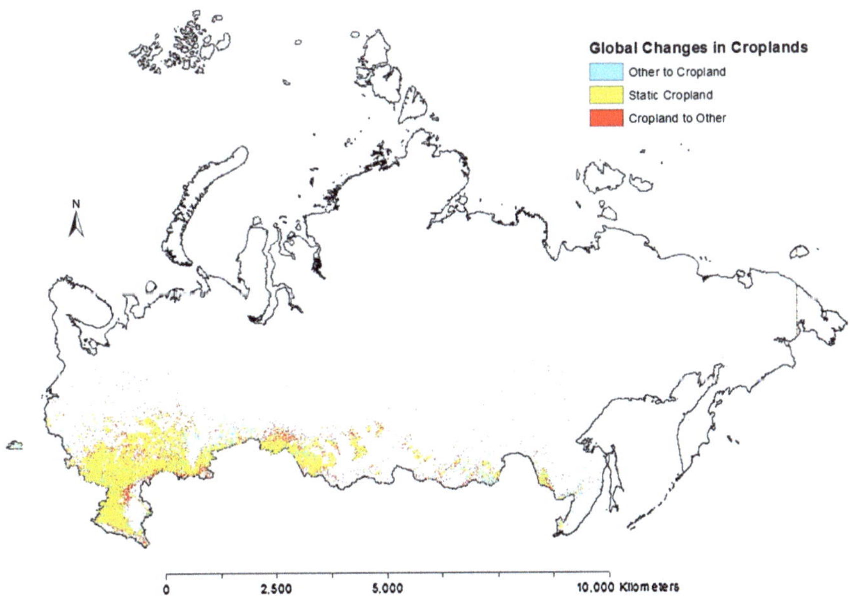

Fig. 18.7 Global changes in croplands in Russia in 2009 relative to 2001. *Source* Based on MODIS data

period was 125 million ha. This conversion can be explained by land abandonment and reduction of the number of cattle over the last twenty years. The reduction of croplands still takes place in most of the territory. In some respects, this may be a beneficial change since ecological functions provided by forests are larger than grasslands and shrublands. Another positive impact is that Russia did not have a desiccation of the water bodies. The increase of barren lands by 4 million ha can be

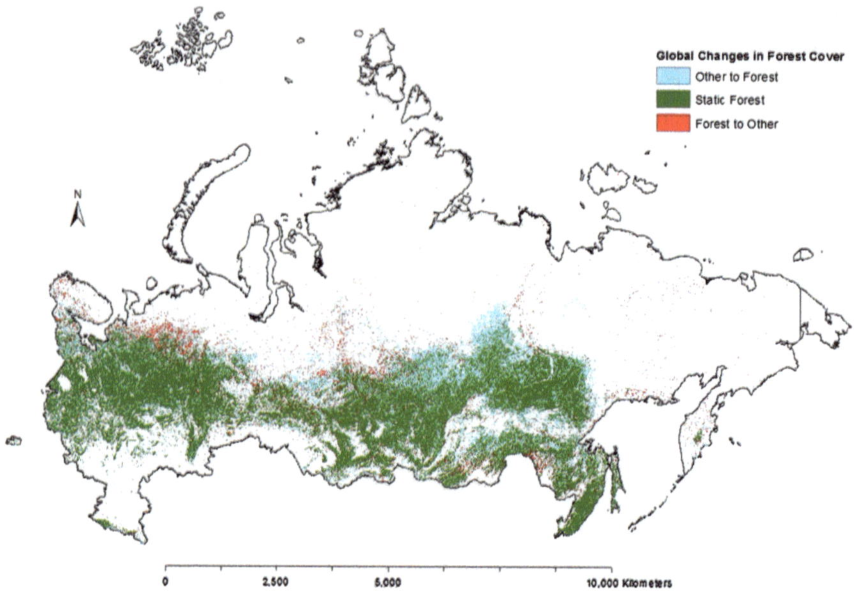

Fig. 18.8 Global changes in forest cover in Russia in 2009 relative to 2001. *Source* Based on MODIS data

explained by intensive developing of mineral resources, industrial construction, and manifestation of degradation processes in the southern part of the country such as desertification and salinization.

Economic Impacts of Land Degradation

We have calculated the costs of land degradation in Russia using the approach described in detail in the methodological chapter of this book. The results show that the total costs of land degradation due to land-use change only (i.e. without the costs of land degradation due to lower soil and land productivity within the same land use), are about 189 billion USD during the period of 2001–2009 (Table 18.11), i.e. about 23.6 billion USD annually, or about 2 % of Russia's Gross Domestic Product (GDP) in 2010. Most of these costs, about two thirds, are related to land-cover change in Siberian and Far Eastern districts. Land degradation costs per capita also vary among Federal districts: the highest in Far Eastern (1460 USD annually) and lowest in Southern, Central and Volga (18, 20 and 21 USD annually, respectively).

The Total Economic Value of ecosystem goods and services is estimated to equal about 3700 billion USD in Russia, exceeding the GDP by 3 times. The relative value of ecosystems per capita depends on the territory, land use/cover characteristics, and 0. In this regard, the Far Eastern district with its huge territory,

Table 18.11 The costs of land degradation in Federal districts of Russia through land-use change, including TEV values

Federal district	Costs of land degradation (2001–2009)	Annual costs of land degradation, in billion USD	Annual cost of land degradation per capita, in USD	GDPin 2010, current billion USD	Land degradation as a share of GDP (%), annually
Central	6	0.8	20	434	0.2
Southern	2	0.3	18	75	0.4
Northwestern	17	2.1	154	127	1.7
Far Eastern	76	9.5	1460	68	14.0
Siberian	61	7.6	389	133	5.7
Ural	18	2.3	185	165	1.4
Volga	5	0.6	21	184	0.3
North Caucasian	3	0.4	42	29	1.4
Total	189	23.6	164	1216	1.9

Source Calculated by authors using initial data from Nkonya et al. (2014), based on LUCC during the period of 2001–2009

most of it under higher valued shrublands, forest lands, and grasslands, and relatively smaller population, has the highest per capita value of ecosystems in Russia. Whereas, for example the Central district, with the biggest population in the region and almost half of its territory consisting of croplands, has one of the lowest value of ecosystems. From another perspective, in the Far Eastern district the share of GDP of the Total Economic Value is just 5 %, this number is 334 % in the Central district and between 90 % and 97 % in the Southern, Volga and North Caucasian districts. This implies that population pressure on ecosystems is much higher in these four districts (Table 18.12).

Table 18.12 Total Economic Value (TEV) of Land Ecosystems and GDP in Federal districts of Russia, billion USD

Federal district	TEV 2001	TEV 2009	GDP in 2009	Value of ecosystems per capita, in USD	GDP/TEV (%)
Central	129	130	434	3406	334
Southern	76	80	75	5762	94
Northwestern	441	439	127	31,823	29
Far Eastern	1300	1290	68	198,229	5
Siberian	1150	1180	133	60,182	11
Ural	381	394	165	32,339	42
Volga	199	208	184	6804	88
North Caucasian	30	30	29	3325	97
Total	3700	3750	1216	26,088	32

Source Calculated by authors using initial data from Nkonya et al. (2014)

Cost of Actions

The results of the analysis of the costs of action, following the methodology presented earlier, are given in Table 18.13. The results show that the costs of action against land degradation are lower than the costs of inaction in Russia by 5–6 times over the 30 year horizon, meaning that each dollar spent on addressing land degradation is likely to have about 5–6 dollars of returns. The costs of action were found to equal about 702 billion USD over the 30-year horizon (Fig. 18.9), whereas if nothing is done, the resulting losses may equal almost 3663 billion USD during the same period. Almost 92 % of the costs of action are made up of the opportunity costs of action. This is one of the key barriers for actions against land degradation, as the costs are tangible and may need to be borne by landusers, as well as regional and federal budgets, however, the benefits of action are not fully internalized by landusers and often not even locally, as they represent global benefits from additional ecosystem services enjoyed by the whole world. At the same time, it is also true that these restored ecosystem services and goods would benefit first and foremost the people living in these degraded areas and Russian society as whole.

Figure 18.10 showed the map with several layers: costs of action over the 30-year horizon in US dollars shown per hectare and land degradation hotspots. For example, we will look at the European part of Russia. This region should show the most accurate results because of the data used and benefit transfer approach. Three categories of lands might be distinguished: the first category—the degraded lands with high costs of actions; the second category—the improved lands with low costs of actions; and third category—cross-matches of the first and second categories. The cost of action of this category is from 2 to 11 thousand US dollars per ha. The areas are mostly concentrated in the southern part of Russia: the dig cluster consists of Astrakhan, Volgograd, Saratov, Orenburg regions. These regions are affected by soil salinity and alkalinity problems; the other cluster consists of Caucasia regions, which are affected by moderate and serve water erosion; the third cluster is Chernozem zone, where there is an intensive agricultural activity (the lands basically change into croplands); and last cluster is northern part (mainly Komi Republic)—the area of rivers and swamps. The degraded area is situated in the basin of Pechora and Usa rivers. We link these results with hydrological conditions and type of rivers dietary habits—mainly snow, which is not stable from year to year. It was shown that different sources come to the same results, so we can talk about land degradation in these regions with a big share of confidence. The cost of action of the second category is from 0.1 to 2 thousand US dollars per ha. The area is mainly the northern border of Central Chernozem zone, where many croplands, due to different reasons, which were described in the first part of the chapter, were changed to other categories (Fig. 18.7) and so land improvements occurred. It should be also taken into account that this area is less eroded and not affected by salinity and alkalinity as was the case in the southern part of Russia. The third category needs additional analyses on land degradation and improvement.

Table 18.13 Costs of action versus inaction in Federal districts of Russia, in billion USD

Federal districts	Costs of land degradation (2001–2009)	Of which, the costs of provisional ecosystem services	Cost of action (6 years)	Cost of action (30 years)	Opportunity cost of action	Cost of inaction (6 years)	Cost of inaction (30 years)	Proportion of cost of action/inaction (30 years) (%)
Central	6	2	14	14	13	43	93	14
Southern	2	0	5	5	5	15	32	16
Northwestern	17	16	81	82	75	161	348	22
Far Eastern	76	60	279	283	263	720	1558	17
Siberian	61	44	217	220	201	530	1147	18
Ural	18	12	77	77	71	164	355	20
Volga	5	2	14	14	12	39	85	15
North Caucasian	3	1	7	7	6	21	46	14
Total	189	136	694	702	647	1693	3663	18

Source Calculated by authors using initial data from Nkonya et al. (2014)

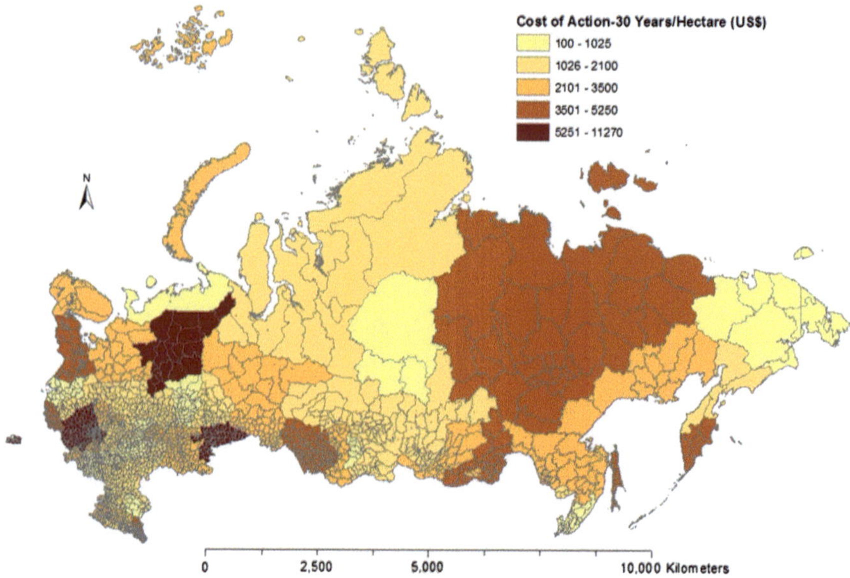

Fig. 18.9 Costs of action over the 30-year horizon in US dollars shown per hectare. *Source* Image was prepared by authors using initial data from Nkonya et al. (2014)

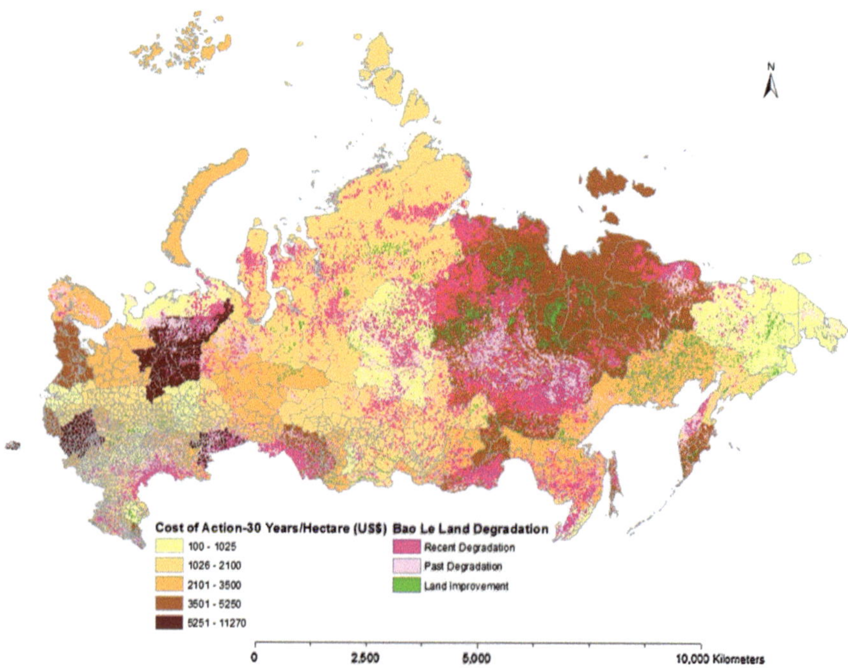

Fig. 18.10 Costs of action over the 30-year horizon in USD shown per hectare with land degradation hotspots. *Source* Image was prepared by authors using initial data from Nkonya et al. (2014) and Le et al. (2014)

Fig. 18.11 Map of the subjects of Russian Federation. *Source* https://commons.wikimedia.org/wiki/File%3ARostov_in_Russia.svg. Note: *Red color*—Rostov region, *light-green color* marked with *arrowhead*—Azov district

A Detailed Study of the Issues Related to Agriculture and Land Degradation in the Azov District of the Rostov Region

The Azov district is a very favorable economic and geographical area of the Rostov region. Transportation infrastructure, skilled manpower, and lack of social tensions has historically defined the area as one of the largest centers of diversified industries, developed agriculture, science, and culture in the Southern part of Russia (Fig. 18.11).

General Information About the Azov District of the Rostov Region

The Azov district is located in the South-Western part of the Rostov region. The total area of the district is 286.2 thousand ha. The Azov district has the largest population in the area. According to statistics, the population of the district is 90,642 people (Federal State Statistics Service 2014b). The demographic situation in the region continues to be adverse due to the natural decrease of population. Migration remains the main source of replenishment of the population. The agricultural lands occupy up to 73.9 % of the total area of the district, and the arable lands constitute 85.7 % of the agricultural land. The agricultural specialization of the Azov district is crop production, though livestock production also present.

The main crops grown in the area are: winter wheat, spring barley, sunflower, corn, annual and perennial herbs, vegetables, and fruits. Agricultural production in the area is based on 26 large and medium-sized farms, 108 small farms, 107 individual entrepreneurs, 62 horticultural and 5 suburban associations, and a total of 33,892 households. The share of the State sector in the total number of registered entities is 5.9 %, and of private individuals is 94.1 % (Federal State Statistics Service 2014a, b, c). The structure of agricultural land use is: 210.4 thousand ha of agricultural land, including 182.5 thousand ha of arable land, 4.0 thousand ha of hayfields, 21.1 thousand ha of pasture, and 1.5 thousand ha of perennial plants. More than 25 % of the agricultural undertakings in the region have a positive profit margin. The gross grain harvest in 2010 was 353,300 thousand kg, with the average yield of 3900 kg/ha. The volatility of the yields of crops depends not only on fluctuations in the weather, but also from insufficient application of fertilizers and violation of farming system methods. At the same period of time in the seed-growing farms the yield was 4350 kg/ha. This fact indicates the presence of some reserves to improve crop yields in the district. However, there are issues related to losses of water, nutrients and carbon storage, and degradation processes.

Large losses of water are found during the process of transporting of up to 40 % (instead of the projected 22 %) on water supply networks. Mostly from irrigation channels due to their physical and moral wear and tear. Burning stubble in the fields of agricultural enterprises is unauthorized but yet takes place in almost all territories of the region. Intensive development of negative processes and phenomena, such as water and wind erosion, loss of humus, waterlogging, salinity, alkalinity, soil pollution with toxic substances continues to take place. The region is affected by erosion, on more than 35 % of agricultural land. For combating erosion, it has been planned to plant windbreaks and to stabilize gullies by planting trees however only 10–20 % of the planned work has been performed. Desertification is the most important environmental and socio-economic problem of the region (Ministry of Natural Resources and Environment of the Russian Federation 2013). Natural soil fertility has to be maintained by application of fertilizers: organic and nitrogen fertilizers are applied in almost sufficient doses, while phosphate and potash fertilization is not enough (Table 18.14).

In spite of the fact that the Azov district is in a zone of strong wind erosion and moderate water erosion, there is not enough attention aimed at the conservation of crops and lands from erosion on farms. The development of the erosion processes is

Table 18.14 Mean application of fertilizers (for 5 years) and qualitative assessment of deviation from norm (regarding the data from experimental farms, which was adopted as a norm)

Fertilizer application	Mean for 5 years, kg/ha	Variation from norm
Organic	2900	Almost enough
Nitrogen	28.2	Almost enough
Phosphate	18.4	Not enough
Potash	2.4	Not enough

Source Based on Federal State Statistics Service (2014a)

insufficiently monitored in the region. Old soil survey materials do not reflect the processes of wind erosion. There are no ongoing works on reclamation of saline soils, while there are about 24,967 ha of soils with various degree of salinization in the district. The formation of saline soils in the district mainly occurs because of improper or excessive irrigation. Such phenomena occur in areas with shallow saline groundwater or saline deposits. Many farms do not comply with the recommendations (Ministry of Agriculture of Russian SFSR 1978).

The climate of the Azov district is moderately continental with the average amplitude of temperatures 28.1 °C and the ratio of annual precipitation to potential evaporation of 0.7–0.8. According to the agro-climatic zoning of the Rostov region, the Azov district belongs to the dry zone. In general, the climatic conditions are quite favorable for the development of agricultural production, but some climatc features such as drought, strong winds and strong fluctuations in other climatic indexes over the years, require a strict adherence of agricultural technology for the accumulation and preservation of moisture in the soil and protection of soil from wind and water erosion. In general, flat topography creates favorable conditions for soil management, plant care, and harvesting.

The Azov district belongs to the soil province of Ciscaucasia Chernozems. The main features of the district's soil cover are homogeneity caused by flat steppe conditions, as well as deep topsoil (humus accumulative horizon) and the accumulation of a large number of shallow carbonate salts. Also hydromorphic Chernozems, Luvisols, and wetlands soils with various degree of salinization are formed in this district territory. Ministry of Agriculture of Russian SFSR (1978) shows that in the Azov district 214,149 ha or 70.6 % of its territory is formed by Chernozems, among which 15,198 ha or 5 % of the soils are exposed to water erosion, and 23,074 ha or 7.6 % are exposed to wind erosion. Within the district there are 2657 ha of nitric soils, 2346 ha of sodic soils, 18,505 ha of saline soils (mostly floodplain), and 16.775 ha of wetland soils.

Soil data analysis shows that in the district's soil cover, potentially rich soils predominate. A high percentage of saline (6.1 %) and wetland (7.7 %) soils occur in the floodplains. The presence of eroded soils in watersheds indicates that after their improvement (melioration) and cultivation, there are additional opportunities for further development of agriculture and animal husbandry at the expense of not yet productive and sometimes unproductive land use. It is important to emphasize the necessity of sustainable use of cultivated soils and maintenance of their fertility.

In accordance with the old system having been used in the Soviet Union, the agricultural lands of a farm are divided into agroindustrial groups. The last report of Ministry of Agriculture of Russian SFSR (1978) said that all soil types that are allocated in the Azov district are combined in 25 land management groups by taking into account their genesis, physic-chemical properties, water-air regime, geology, relief, etc. The first group included the best arable soils with no limitations for producing zonal crops. In the case of the Pobeda farm the soils of the 1st agroindustrial group included Chernozems and Gleyic Chernozems, and the recommended crops were winter wheat, corn, barley, millet, beans, and sunflower (Ministry of Agriculture of Russian SFSR 1978). It was recommended to cultivate sugar beet, and upland vegetable cultures in depressions. The complex of agrotechnical measures had to be directed on moisture accumulation in soil. Other groups included areas with weak development of wind and water erosional processes. They are also suitable to cultivate general crops. The complex of agrotechnical measures had to be directed on prevention of further erosion and moisture containment. The worst soils were included in the other agroindustrial groups: each of the groups had certain limitations in soil use and required special measures for soil protection. For example, sodification, salinity and severe erosion. It is not completely clear, if these recommendations are still followed at the Azov farms.

Identification of the Causes and Extent of Land Degradation in the Azov District of the Rostov Region

The Choice of the Model Object

The Southern Federal district is the most intensive agricultural region of the Russian Federation. The level of tilled lands in this region exceeds 80 %. Obviously, land-use change studies require spatially distributed research, which is time-consuming, even on the level of data collection. The compromise was to study one administrative district, the Azov district of the Rostov region (Fig. 18.12). The time interval for the study (1990–2010) was identified by the availability and accuracy of the data used. Multi-temporal maps were made to assess the variability of land use in the area (Bryzzhev and Ruhovich 2013).

Figure 18.13 shows the plots where at least once during the analyzed period (1990–2010) the agricultural processing was not performed, was difficult, or did not give the intended outcome (harvest).

The total studied area is 292,478 ha. Agricultural lands, i.e. lands that were processed at any given time (arable land, including irrigated areas, garden areas, etc.), take up 193,261 ha (66 %) of the resulting data. The territory was subjected to different land-use changes. From 1990 to 2000, 10,355 ha (5.35 %) had changed, from 2000 to 2010, 5450 ha (3.5 %) changed. Bryzzhev and Ruhovich (2013) showed that despite the relative homogeneity of the district in climatic, geological, and topographical terms, for 20 years (from 1990 to 2010), more than 8 % of the territory ware affected by land-use change.

The main trends of land-use changes are:

- The withdrawal of lands from agricultural use to under buildings—2584 ha. This process is controlled exclusively by the administration of the Azov district. Most often it does not depend on soil characteristics, so sometimes the best soils were removed from agricultural land.
- Agricultural activity, which was not previously active (fallow)—1535 ha.

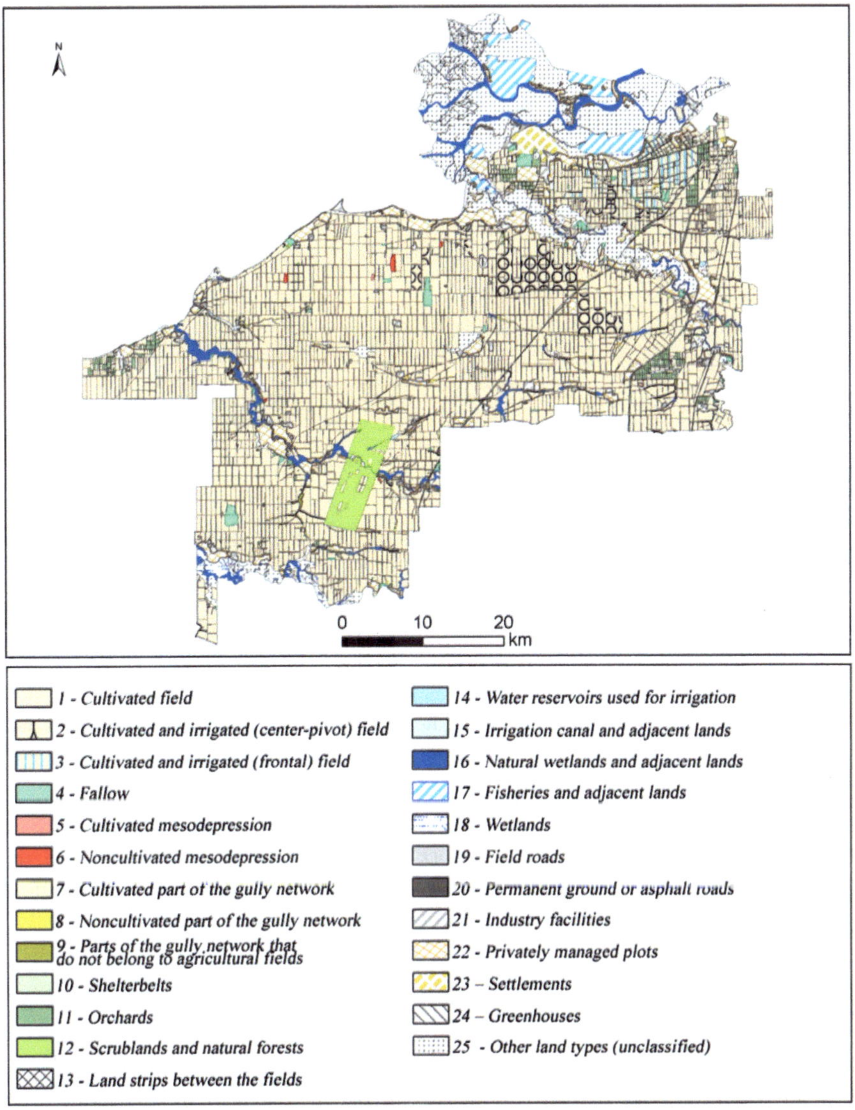

Fig. 18.12 Map of land use of the Azov district of the Rostov region. *Source* The authors

- Termination of agricultural fields (deposits)—1210 ha. Processes related to the improvement/degradation of soil characteristics, as a result of climate change, land improvement, melioration, etc.
- The irrigation (of various types) of previously rain-fed agricultural fields—4136 ha. Irrigation was introduced on agricultural fields, mainly occupying automorphic areas.

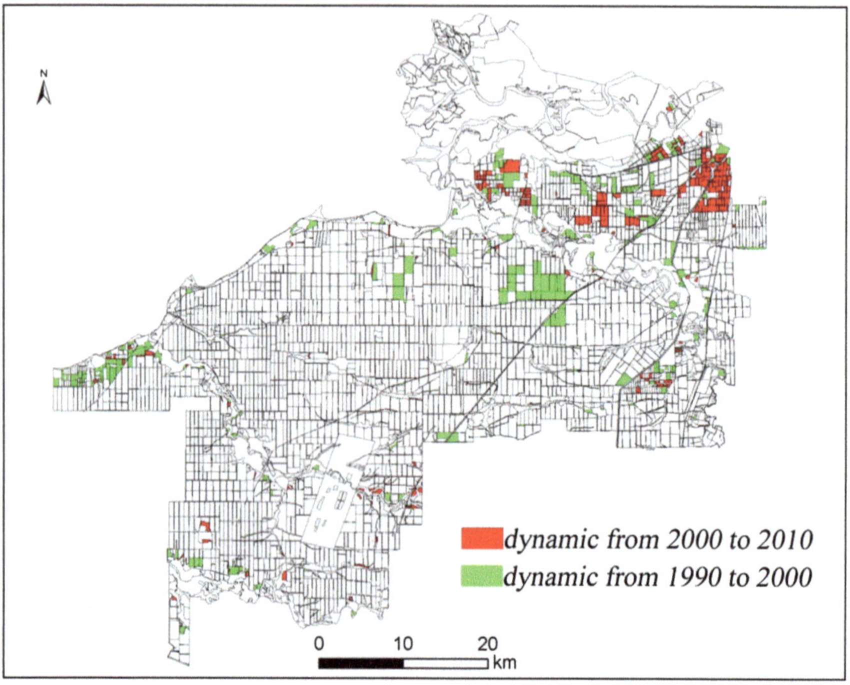

Fig. 18.13 Map of land use change on plots of the Azov district of Rostov region (1990–2000 and 2000–2010). *Source* The authors. *Note* The *colors* refer to any land-use change occurring between each date

- The development of a gully network—738 ha. The process leading to the increase in the area occupied by eroded soils. This is a process that is difficult to reverse, it is necessary to conduct special anti-erosion measures.

One of the leading negative soil processes of the district is the process of soil salinization. Moreover, this process was exacerbated mainly due to improper planning of agricultural lands. The establishment of agricultural fields in the majority of cases is conducted by planting forest belts and roads along the fields. As a result saline soils were involved in tillage lands. The area of the saline soils occupies about 11 % of the total area of the Azov district, but it occupies about 2 % of arable land, i.e. there is not a specific need to use these lands for agriculture. But saline soils exist as fragments of many fields due to the rectangular cut of the fields bordered by forest belts and roads. Moreover forest belts and roads violate the original hydrological regime of the landscape, leading to the gradual spread of saline soils or increase of the degree of salinization. Agriculture in saline soils is unsustainable. Table 18.15 shows that the share of the shift to other land uses of non-saline soils was 7.2 %, but the same for saline soils was 17.3 % (2.4 times higher for the period of 20 years (Ruhovich et al. in press). It should be noted that the land-use changes of non-saline soils was mostly from building construction, the

Table 18.15 Dynamics of the territory of the Azov district, Rostov region including non-saline and saline soils

Soils	Total area (ha)	Agricultural area (ha)	Area of dynamics 1990–2000 (ha)	Dynamics 1990–2000 (%)	Area of dynamics 2000–2010 (ha)	Dynamics 2000–2010 (%)
Total	292,478	193,261	10,355	5.36	5450	2.82
Non-saline	260,812	189,295	9838	5.20	5271	2.78
Saline	31,666	3966	517	13.02	179	4.53

Source The authors

uprooting of orchards, etc. and in saline soils the changes were only due to the absence of harvest, due to salt regime. In addition, saline soils often hinder the passage of agricultural machinery, which leads to the fragmentation of fields and serves as a source of weeds.

The Evaluation of the Potential Cost of Land Degradation

Our analysis shows that the Azov district has been experiencing dynamic land-use and land-cover changes over the last two decades: in 2000 relative to 1990 and in 2010 relative to 2000 (Table 18.16).

Table 18.16 shows that Azov district totally lost areas of shrublands (4122 ha), which were converted mainly into croplands and urban territories. The total increase in croplands over the last period 2000–2010 was 2908 ha. This conversion can be explained by liquidation of orchard areas over the last ten years. The reduction of croplands in 2000 relative to 1990 can be explained by termination of processing of agricultural fields with subsequent construction of household outbuildings (including roads) or residential housings. The increase of grasslands by 235 ha, as it was mentioned before, can be explained by termination of processing of agricultural fields due to erosion or degradation of soil agronomy quality.

The time period of 2000–2010 was chosen for economics of land degradation analysis due to the availability and accuracy of the data used. Our analysis shows that Azov district has been experiencing dynamic land use and land cover changes (LUCC) over the 2000s.

Table 18.16 Land use/cover change in the Azov district of the Rostov region in 2000 relative to 1990, in 2010 relative to 2000 and total change, ha

Period	Cropland	Forest	Grassland	Shrublands	Urban	Water	Barren
2000–1990	−1566.59	3.79	233.80	−1200.79	2529.79	0	0
2010–2000	2908.19	−2.66	1.05	−2921.60	15.02	0	0
Total	1341.60	1.13	234.85	−4122.39	2544.81	0	0

Source Using land-use monitoring datasets

Table 18.17 The costs of land degradation in the Azov district of the Rostov region of Russia through land use change in 2010 relative to 2000

Annual cost of land degradation in 2010 as compared with 2000, in million USD	Annual cost of land degradation per capita including the value lost ecosystem services, in USD	Total agricultural production (TAP) in 2010, current million USD	Land degradation as a share of TAP (%), annually
0.3	3.6	242.5	0.1

Source Authors calculations using data of ROSSTAT, World Bank and initial data from Nkonya et al. (2014)

Table 18.18 Total Economic Value (TEV) of Land Ecosystems and TAP in Azov district of Rostov region of Russia, million USD

TEV 2000	TEV 2010	Total agricultural production (TAP) in 2010	Value of ecosystems per capita, in USD	TAP/TEV
505	503	242.5	52.5	48.1 %

Source Authors calculations using data of ROSSTAT, World Bank and initial data from Nkonya et al. (2014)

We have calculated the cost of land degradation in the region using the approach described in detail in the methodological chapter of this book. The results in Table 18.17 show that annual cost of degradation on the sample period due to land use change only, i.e. without the costs of land degradation due to soil-ecological conditions and productivity within the same land use, are 0.3 in 2010 as compared with 2000, in million USD. The land use shift happened because of favorable conditions for growing crops in Azov region.

The Russian attitude to ecosystem value is rather low—52.5 USD per capita,[2] which is ten times lower than in the developed countries. The total economic value of ecosystem goods and services is estimated to equal about 503 million USD in Azov district, doubling the TAP. The TAP/TEV estimation 48.1 % for Azov district shows us that there's much else to do in economic activities besides agriculture (Table 18.18).

Cost of Actions

Cost of action and inaction, presented in Table 18.19. The results show that the cost of action against land degradation in the Azov district will be 12.65 million dollars in a 6 year time period. For example the planned volume of financial support for the

[2]Estimation taken from TEEB website.

Table 18.19 Costs of action vs inaction in Azov district of Rostov region of Russia, in million USD

District	TAP in 2010	Annual TEV cost of land degradation in 2010 as compared with 2000, in million USD	Cost of action (6 years)	Cost of action (30 years)	Cost of inaction (6 years)	Cost of inaction (30 years)	Ratio of cost of action/inaction in 30 years (%)	Ratio (USD)
Azov	242.5	0.3	12.55	23.53	13.37	25.08	94	1.07

Source Authors calculations using data of ROSSTAT, World Bank and initial data from Nkonya et al. (2014)

Russian Federal program for Melioration in 2014–2020 is 4012 million USD.[3] The ratio of cost of action/inaction in a 30 years period is 94 %: 23.53–25.08 million USD, respectively. In other words every invested dollar against land degradation in this area will give back 1.07 dollars. We have to take this result as being critical, because the TEV used for these calculations are suitable for Russia as a whole, but in the Azov district more precise values might be different.

Conclusions

The vastness of the territory of the Russian Federation inevitably leads to a diversity of natural conditions that causes the development of multiple approaches to the economic use of land resources. Climatic conditions have a direct and indirect impact on biological components of natural landscapes and soil forming processes. In their turn the biophysical conditions determine the shape of agricultural development of the territory, with various land-use systems and with different major degradation processes. The major drivers of degradation include climatic change, unsustainable agricultural practices, industrial and mining activities, expansion of crop production to fragile and marginal areas, inadequate maintenance of irrigation and drainage networks, and overgrazing.

The calculations show that the total land use/cover dynamic changes are about 130 million ha, and the total annual costs of land degradation due to land-use change only, i.e. without the costs of land degradation due to soil-ecological conditions and productivity within the same land use, are about 189 billion USD for the period of 2001–2009. i.e. 23.6 billion USD annually. The total economic value of ecosystem goods and services is estimated to equal about 3700 billion USD in Russia, exceeding the GDP by 3 times. The costs of action against land degradation are lower than the costs of inaction in Russia by 5–6 times over the 30 year horizon, meaning that each dollar spent on addressing land degradation is likely to have about 5–6 dollars of returns. In our opinion this is a significant economic justification to favor rational agricultural and sustainable land use practices and also actions against degradation. Almost 92 % of the costs of action are made up of the opportunity costs of action. On the other hand, at the level of Azov district, Rostov province, we have found that the cost of action against land degradation is 1.07 times higher than cost of inaction.

We recommend raising awareness on the ELD in Russia for improving the effectiveness of agricultural production, however we have to mention that the average TEV used in these calculations should be corrected in future work, with reference to Russian local surveys and data.

---

[3]Ratio RUB to USD equal to 0.022.

References

Bicheron, P., Defourny, P., Brockmann, C., Schouten, L., Vancutsem, C., Huc, M., et al. (2008). GLOBCOVER: products description and validation report. http://due.esrin.esa.int/globcover/LandCover_V2.2/GLOBCOVER_Products_Description_Validation_Report_I2.1.pdf. ESA Globcover Project, led by MEDIAS-France/POSTEL.

Bryzzhev, A. V., & Ruhovich, D. I. (2013). Organization of retrospective monitoring soil and land cover of Azov district of Rostov region. *Eurasian Soil Science., 11*, 1294–1315.

Dobrovolski, G. V. (Ed.). (2002). *Soil degradation and preservation*. Moscow: Moscow University publishing house. (in Russian).

Federal State Statistics Service. (2014a). Official statistics. Entrepreneurship. Agriculture, hunting and forestry. http://www.gks.ru/. (in Russian).

Federal State Statistics Service. (2014b). Official statistics. Publications. Catalogue of publications. Demographic Yearbook of Russia. http://www.gks.ru/. (in Russian).

Federal State Statistics Service. (2014c). Official statistics. Publications. Catalogue of publications. Russia and foreign countries. http://www.gks.ru/. (in Russian).

Friedl, M. A., Sulla-Menashe, D., Tan, B., Schneider, A., Ramankutty, N., Sibley, A., & Huang, X. (2010). MODIS Collection 5 global land cover: Algorithm refinements and characterization of new datasets. *Remote Sensing of Environment, 114*, 168–182.

Gordeeva, A. V., & Romanenko, G.A. (Eds.). (2008). *Issues of degradation and productivity restoration of agricultural lands in Russia*. Moscow: Rosinformagroteh. (in Russian).

Kashtanov, A. N. (2001). Concept of sustainable development of agriculture of Russia in XXI century. *Pochvovedenie, 3*, 263–265. (in Russian).

Katyal, J. C., & Vlek, P. L. (2000). *Desertification: Concept, causes, and amelioration*. Bonn, Germany: Center for Development Research.

Le, Q. B., Nkonya, E., & Mirzabaev, A. (2014). *Biomass productivity-based mapping of global land degradation hotspots*. ZEF—Discussion Papers on Development Policy No. 193, 1-57.

Ministry of Agriculture of Russian Federation. (2011). *Report on the state and use of agricultural lands*. Moscow: FGBNU Rosinformagroteh. (in Russian).

Ministry of Agriculture of Russian SFSR. (1978). *Soils of Azov district of Rostov region and their land-use*. Roszemproekt, Yujgiprozem: Rostov-na-Donu. (in Russian).

Ministry of Natural Resources and Environment of the Russian Federation. (2013). Government report "On state and on environment protection in Russian Federation in 2012". http://www.mnr.gov.ru. (in Russian).

Nefedova, T. G. (2013). *Ten topical issues about rural Russia: A geographer's viewpoint*. Moscow: LENAND. (in Russian).

Nkonya, E., Anderson, W., Kato, E., Koo, J., Mirzabaev, A., von Braun, J., & Meyer, S. (2014). Global cost of land degradation. In E. Nkonya, A. Mirzabaev & J. von Braun (Eds.), *Economics of land degradation and improvement*. Netherlands: Springer.

Nkonya, E., Gerber, N., Baumgartner, P., von Braun, J., De Pinto, A., Graw, V., et al. (2011). *The economics of land degradation—towards an integrated global assessment*. Germany: Peter Lang.

Nkonya, E., von Braun, J., Mirzabaev, A., Bao Le, Q., Kwon, H. Y., & Kirui, O. (2013). *Economics of land degradation initiative: Methods and approach for global and national assessments*. ZEF-Discussion Papers on Development Policy No. 183.

Pannell, D. J., Llewellyn, R. S., & Corbeels, M. (2014). The farm-level economics of conservation agriculture for resource-poor farmers. *Agriculture, Ecosystems and Environment, 187*, 52–64.

Rudneva, E. N. (2001). Soil map content and principals of soil cover mapping. In *Soil cover and land resources of Russian Federation* (pp. 4–98). Moscow. (in Russian).

Ruhovich, D. I., Simakova, M. S., & Bryzzhev, A. V. (in press). Influence of saline soils on the variability of land-use types.

Scherr, S. (1999). *Soil degradation: A threat to developing-country food security by 2020, food, agriculture and the environment*. Washington, D.C., USA: International Food Policy Research Institute.

Shoba, S. A., Alyabina, I. O., Kolesnikova, V. M., Molchanov, E. N., Rojkov, V. A., Stolbovoi, V. S., et al. (2010). *Soil resources of Russia. Soil-geographic data base*. Moscow: GEOS. (in Russian).

Van der Ploeg, S., & de Groot, R. S. (2010). The TEEB valuation database—a searchable database of 1310 estimates of monetary values of ecosystem services. Foundation for Sustainable Development, Wageningen, The Netherlands.

Vandysheva, N. M., & Gurov, A. F. (2011). Predominant negative processes on agricultural lands. In S. A. Shoba (Ed.), *National atlas of soils in Russian federation* (pp. 266–267). Moscow, Astrel: ACT. (in Russian).

von Braun, J., Gerber, N., Mirzabaev, A., & Nkonya, E. (2013). *The economics of land degradation*. ZEF Working paper 109. Bonn, Germany.

Chapter 19
Cost, Drivers and Action Against Land Degradation in Senegal

Samba Sow, Ephraim Nkonya, Stefan Meyer and Edward Kato

Abstract Senegal is facing a major land degradation challenge that poses threat to livelihoods of the rural poor. This study was done to inform policy makers on the cost of inaction and the costs and benefits of taking action against land degradation. The study shows that the annual cost of land degradation on rice, millet and maize —which account for 45 % of cropland area—is US$103 million, or 2 % of the country's GDP. The on-farm cost of grazing land degradation is about US$9 million or 0.1 % of the GDP. The low cost of grazing degradation is a reflection of the low livestock productivity. The cost of land degradation due to Land Use/Cover Change (LUCC) is about US$0.412 billion or about 4 % of the GDP. This shows that LUCC accounts for the largest cost of land degradation. The marginal rate of return to investment in restoration of degraded lands is greater than 4—suggesting high returns to taking action against land degradation. Action against land degradation will have far-reaching benefits for the rural poor who heavily depend on natural resources. Senegal has great potential for successfully addressing land degradation. For example, the large number of agricultural extension agents from public and private providers, promoting Integrated Soil Fertility Management (ISFM) practices, Community-Based Forest Management (CBFM) and strengthening public-private partnership could help increase adoption of sustainable land management (SLM) practices. The Dankou Classified Forest investment in awareness creation of ecosystem services led to effective participation of the communities and their participation in protecting it. This demonstrates that awareness creation is a key strategy for ensuring community involvement in protecting natural resources.

Keywords Groundthruthing of remote sensing data · Economics of land degradation · Cost of land degradation · Benefits of taking action · Sustainable land management

S. Sow (✉)
Institut National de Pedologie, Dakar, Senegal
e-mail: samba_sow@hotmail.fr

E. Nkonya · S. Meyer · E. Kato
International Food Policy Research Institute, Washington, DC, USA

E. Nkonya et al. (eds.), *Economics of Land Degradation and Improvement – A Global Assessment for Sustainable Development*,
DOI 10.1007/978-3-319-19168-3_19

Introduction

Senegal is one of the countries in sub-Saharan Africa (SSA) that have seen large changes in its economy in the past decade. The country's Gross Domestic Product (GDP) per capita declined from 1982 and bottomed out in 1994 to continue rising through 2012 (World Bank 2012). Between 2003 and 2010, Senegal's expenditure on agriculture increased by 7 % annually. It is one of the 13 SSA countries which have surpassed the Comprehensive Africa Agricultural Development Policy (CAADP) target to spend 10 % of total public expenditure on agriculture (Agriculture for Impact 2014). One of the drivers of such growth has been the political stability of the country and its policies that have been aimed at reducing rural poverty. The strong orientation to agricultural development is explained by the sector's large contribution to the economy and rural employment. The agricultural area (including cropland, forestry) accounts for 49.4 % of the land area and employs 81 % of the rural population (World Bank 2012; DPS 2004). However, the country is facing a major challenge of land degradation. In order to inform policy makers on the costs and benefits of taking action against land degradation, this chapter examines the economics of land degradation. The results will help the country to design appropriate and cost effective approaches to addressing land degradation.

The rest of the report is organized as follows. The next section discusses the severity of land degradation in Senegal. This is followed by key policies and strategies that the country has put in place to achieve its objective of rural development. This is then followed by results based on focus group discussion and other sources of data. The study concludes with policy implications of the results and the way forward for achieving Senegal's objective of preventing and/or reducing land degradation and to restore degraded lands, which is stated in its national action plan that it prepared when it ratified the United Nations Convention to Combat Desertification (UNCCD) in 1995 and more recently (2012) in the National Strategic Investment Framework for SLM.

Extent and Severity of Land Degradation in Senegal

About 22.2 % of Senegal's population of 13 million live in degraded areas (Le et al. 2014). This is comparable to the share of SSA population affected by land degradation (Ibid). About 9280 ha or 13 % of the agricultural area is degraded (Ibid). However, the Senegal Country Environmental Assessment (World Bank 2008) reports that nearly 65 % of the agricultural land is degraded (Table 19.1). The difference could be due to the type of data used to compute land degradation. Le et al. (2014) use the Normalized Difference Vegetation Index (NDVI)—a vegetation cover index—which may not capture degradation due to soil erosion, salinity and other forms of land degradation that are not well reflected by vegetation cover.

Table 19.1 Type and extent of land degradation in Senegal, 2001

	Share of total land area (%)
Water-erosion	50.30
Wind-erosion	1.94
Chemical degradation (e.g. Salinization)	5.80
Anthropogenic erosion	7.15
Non-degraded Soils	34.59

Note There are no reliable recent studies on the severity of land degradation in Senegal. The degradation of land in Senegal increased within the last 30 years. So the actual figures are even worse (World Bank 2008)
Source DAT/USAID/RSI (1985)

Grassland and sparse vegetation were most affected by land degradation (Le et al. 2014). Between 1982 and 2006, 20 % of the grassland area experienced degradation while the sparse vegetation was reduced by 36 % (Ibid). Such loss of vegetation exposes soil to water- and wind-erosion. Additionally, grassland, which covers 12.3 % of the Senegalese land area experiences annual bush fires, a problem, which is common in the bushlands of the Sudanian zones of West Africa (Savadogo et al. 2007). It is estimated that 25 %—50 % of the Sudanian zone burn every year (Delmas et al. 1991). In Senegal, the area burnt in the period 1997–2012 was 3,141,537 ha, which corresponds to an average of 196,000 ha/year (Centre de Suivi Ecologique 2013).

Land Use/Cover Change (LUCC) is the leading cause of land degradation in SSA since high value biomes are replaced with low value biomes (Nkonya et al. 2015). For example, replacing grasslands with cropland could lead to loss of greater value of ecosystem services. Using classified land use types—could help determine the extent of LUCC-related land degradation. We used the Moderate Resolution Imaging Spectroradiometer (MODIS) landcover data to analyze LUCC. MODIS data used in this study have a resolution of 1 km, which matches the International Geosphere-Biosphere Program (IGBP) land cover classification. Grasslands covered about 72 % of land area in Senegal (see Fig. 19.1) but its extent fell by 21 % in 2009. Shrublands and woodlands covered about 11 and 10 % respectively of land area but the extent of shrublands fell by 32 % while that of woodlands increased by 18 % in 2009.

Forest covered only 0.2 % of land area but its extent increased to a little over 1 % of the land area. The increase occurred mainly in the subhumid area and in the arid and semi-arid zones. Even though MODIS shows an increase in forestand woodlands area, Food and Agriculture Organization (FAO) show moderate deforestation. About 45,000 ha of forest was lost annually in 1990–2000 and about 43,000 ha were lost annually in 2000–2010 (FAO 2011). This is about 0.5 % deforestation rate in both decades, which is the average in SSA (Ibid). The difference between MODIS and FAO forest data is due to the differences in forest definition. FAO defines forest as an area with a minimum coverage of 1 ha, with at least 10 % crown cover and with mature trees at least 2 m tall (Ibid). The definition explicitly includes

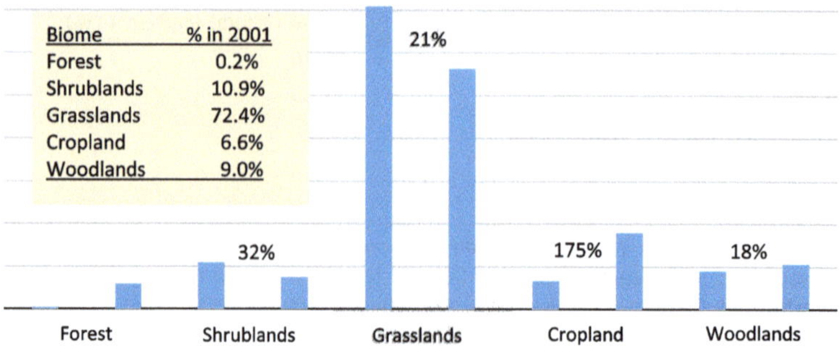

Fig. 19.1 Extent of major biomes in Senegal, 2001 and 2009. *Note* Definition of forest used by Woody vegetation with height >2 m and covering at least 60 % of land area. FAO defines forests as an area with a minimum coverage of 1 ha, with at least 10 % crown cover and with mature trees at least 2 m tall (FAO 2011). The definition explicitly includes open woodlands, such as those found in the African Sahel and differs from IGBP's definition. *Source* MODIS data 2010

open woodlands, such as those found in the Sahelian region. This differs from IGBP's (and MODIS) definition that requires a 60 % canopy coverage.

Charcoal burning has contributed to deforestation since local councils lack capacity and legitimacy to enforce tree cutting regulations (Post and Snel 2003). Elite capture by the merchants and village chiefs, circumvent the local governments and operate charcoal production and marketing—leading to land degradation (Ibid). Despite the Decentralization Law of 1996 (see Appendix), which transferred natural resource management to local communities, the central government owns 100 % of forested area (FAO 2005). Such public ownership could be one of the drivers of deforestation. The primary function of forest could also cause deforestation. About 60 % of the total forest area of 8.7 million ha is designed for production and only 18 % is for protection or conservation and the remaining share (22 %) for multi-purpose use (FAO 2005).

Cropland area increased by 175 % in 2009 from its level in 2001. The increase occurred mainly in the groundnut production areas in the arid and semi-arid and subhumid zones. Cropland expansion replaced mainly grasslands and shrublands—a change that amounts to land degradation due to the low ecosystem value of crops compared to grasslands and shrublands (Nkonya et al. 2015).

In addition to land degradation arising from LUCC, Senegal experiences severe salinity problem. It is estimated that 645,000 ha is affected by salinity (DPS 2004). This is about 6.8 % of 9.5 million ha agricultural land (World Bank 2012). Senegal's downstream position of several large rivers and deltas and its largely flat topography leads to poor drainage, which in turn causes salinity (average altitude is less than 50 m above sea level) (INP 2012) (Fig. 19.2). High seawater tides flood in the coastal area flood, depositing salts on the coastal belt.

Additionally, irrigated areas are poorly drained and this leads to water logging and consequently salinity. The high temperatures for most of the year leads to evaporation—which also contributes to salinity.

Fig. 19.2 Saline pond in Simal valley (Fatick region). *Source* Milo Mitchell 2013

Anthropogenic soil erosion was reported to have affected 7.15 % of the total land area and according to Table 19.1 it is the second largest form of land degradation. In the large agricultural areas, like the groundnut basin and Casamance, soil nutrient mining was a major cause of land degradation (World Bank 2008). The application rate of fertilizer in Senegal is among the lowest in SSA. About 1.7 kgN/ha is applied, a level which is 21 % of the SSA's application rate of 8 kgN/ha (FAOSTAT 2014). The soil nutrient mining in Senegal is estimated at 41 kgNPK/ha (Henao and Baanante 2006).

Due to land degradation discussed above and other factors, agricultural value added per worker has remained flat since 1990 (Fig. 19.3) and agricultural production index remained flat since 1990 but grew modestly from 2007 to 2010 and this increase could be attributed to the implementation of special programs to boost production.[1] The Total Factor Productivity (TFP) grew to the highest level in 1991 and then fell dramatically. Recent recovery of TFP has not yet fully reached its peak in 1991 (Fig. 19.3).

[1]In response to the food crisis of 2008, the government initiated GOANA (Great Push Forward for Agriculture, Food, and Abundance) which corresponded to the integration of special programs (Maize Program, Sesame Program etc.) and National Self-Sufficiency Program.

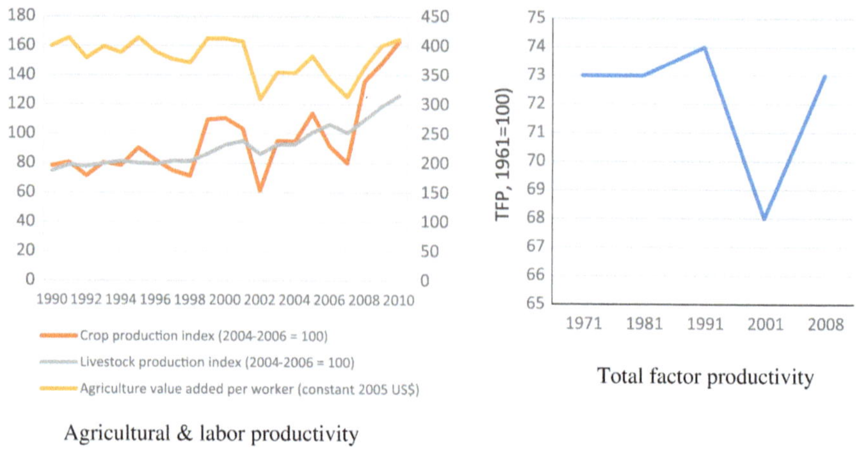

Fig. 19.3 Agricultural and labor productivity and total factor productivity trends in Senegal

Review of Senegal's Natural Resource and Rural Development Policies and Strategies

Compared to other SSA countries, Senegal has made significant progress in rural service development and provision. There is a total of 731 agricultural extension service providers of which 68 % were affiliated with NGOs or were private providers.[2] This puts Senegal among the countries with the smallest number of agricultural households per agricultural extension agent in SSA. On average, each agricultural extension worker served 794 rural households. The corresponding average number of rural household per extension agent in SSA is over 1000 (Davis et al. 2010). DPS (2004) estimated that 58 % of rural households take a maximum of 15 min to reach a public transportation service. This reflects the significant infrastructure development in Senegal, which ranks the second country in SSA—after South Africa—with high infrastructure development (Fig. 19.4).

However, the country's investment in agricultural research and development as percent of agricultural GDP remains below the New Partnership for Africa's Development (NEPAD) target of 1 % (Beintema and Stads 2011) but its public expenditure in the agriculture sector as percent of total public expenditure exceeded the Maputo declaration target of 10 % (Benin and Yu 2012). As noted earlier however, the country's total factor productivity declined in 2001 and has not yet reached its peak, which it achieved in 1991 (Fig. 19.3).

The government of Senegal has designed a number of policies to prevent land degradation and rehabilitate degraded lands and enhance land productivity.[3]

[2]Raw data from the National Agency for Agricultural and Rural Council.

[3]See a summary of policies in Appendix.

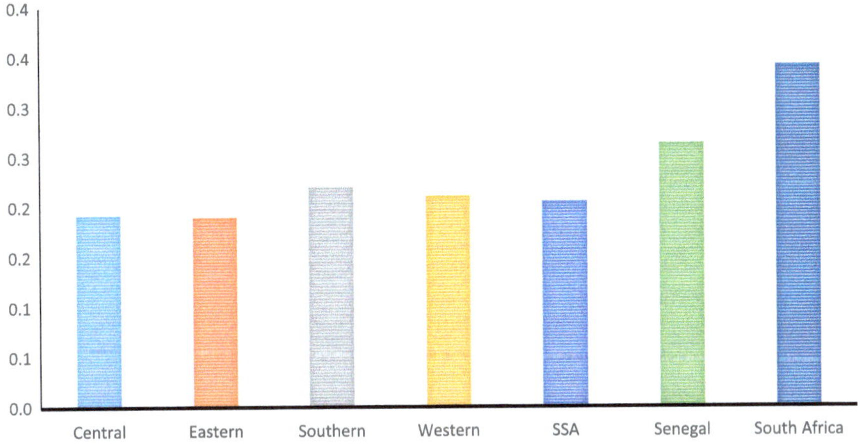

Fig. 19.4 Infrastructure development index. *Note* Infrastructure development index: 1 = Poorest, 5 = Best. *Source* Calculated from http://data.worldbank.org/indicator/LP.LPI.INFR.XQ/; http://www.doingbusiness.org/rankings

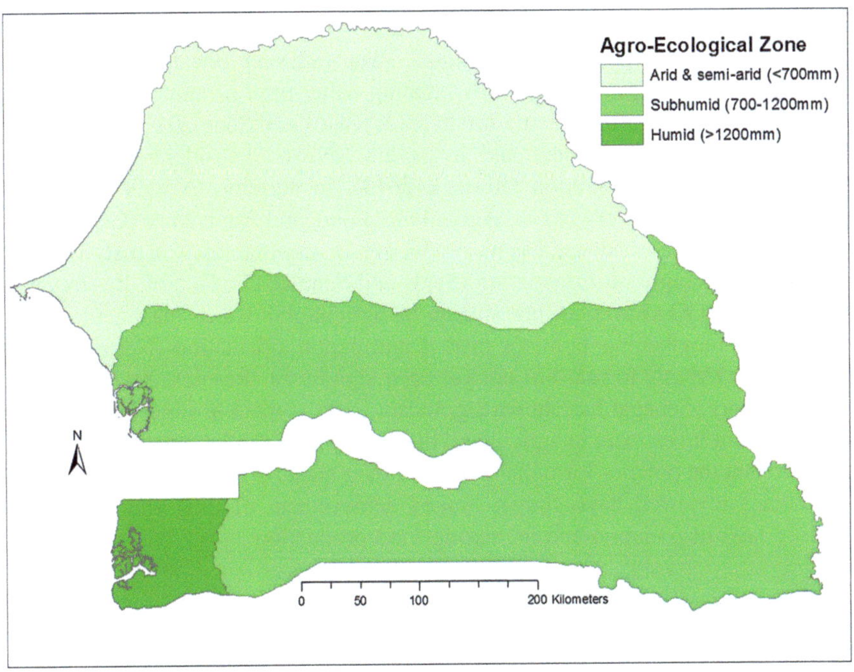

Fig. 19.5 Agroecological zones of Senegal. *Source* Authors using rainfall data available at Climate Research Unit (CRU), University of East Anglia www.cru.uea.ac.uk/cru/data/precip/

Senegal ratified the United Nations Convention to Combat Desertification (UNCCD) in 1995 and has implemented a number of land rehabilitation activities as part of its National Action Plan (NAP). However, the country has been facing challenges in implementing some of NAP activities due to budget constraints.

Senegal enacted the decentralization of natural resource management and other forms of devolution in 1996. Land administration and management was transferred to local governments. As mentioned earlier however, the central government still owns 100 % of the forest resources. As in other countries, the low local capacity of human resource and limited financial resources has contributed to poor performance in land management.

Senegal enacted the Agriculture, Forestry, and Livestock Act (LOASP) in 2004 with an objective of increasing private agricultural investment and to ensure SLM. Despite its good intentions however, implementation of LOASP contributed to land grabbing and deforestation (Stads and Sène 2011). In collaboration with the World Bank, Senegal also implemented the National Framework for Investment into Sustainable Land Management (CNIS/SLM) in 2009. Likewise, the National Institute of Pedology (INP) developed a strategy to coordinate investment to SLM from 2009 to 2012. The project addressed the different forms of land degradation in Senegal by collecting evidence for the severity of soil fertility losses. Best practices were highlighted and a favorable environment implemented for scaling up best management practices (INP 2012).

Through the "Return to Agriculture" Plan (REVA), the government has responded to rural-urban migration by creating better rural economic environment attractive to the youth in rural and urban areas (Stads and Sène 2011). REVA also attracted funding from donors and its review showed considerable impact on reducing rural-urban migration (Resnick 2013). In addition to REVA, Senegal started the Great Push Forward for Agriculture, Food, and Abundance (GOANA) in 2008 with an objective of increasing production of staple foods—namely rice and millet and reducing food importation (Stads and Sène 2011). One of the strategies to implement GOANA was investment in agricultural water management and inputs and strengthening farmer's market and export orientation (Ndione 2009). However, GOANA's impact has not yet been significant (Resnick 2013).

In summary, Senegal has shown significant improvement in rural infrastructure and significant investment in agricultural development. Yet a lot remains to be done to ensure that the policies formulated achieve their stated goals. As of now, most of the policies reviewed have shown limited achievement of their stated goals of reducing land degradation and increasing food production.

Analytical Methods and Data

Our analytical approach focuses on estimation of cost of land degradation, groundtruthing of satellite data and drivers of adoption of sustainable land management practices.

Cost of Land Degradation

We use the approach discussed in detail in Chap. 6, which divides the causes of land degradation into two major groups.

Land Degradation Due to LUCC

The cost of land degradation due to LUCC is given by

$$C_{LUCC} = \sum_{i}^{K} (\Delta a_1 * p_1 - \Delta a_1 * p_2) \tag{19.1}$$

where C_{LUCC} = cost of land degradation due to LUCC; a_1 = land area of biome 1 being replaced by biome 2; p_1 and p_2 are the Total Economic Value (TEV) of biome 1 and 2, respectively, per unit of area. By definition of land degradation, $p_1 > p_2$. This means, LUCC that does not lead to lower TEV is not regarded as land degradation but rather as land improvement or restoration. To obtain the net loss of ecosystem value, the second term in the equation nets out the value of the biome 1 replacing the high value. i = biome i, i == 1, 2, … k.

Land Degradation Due to Use of Land Degrading Management Practices on a Static Cropland

We focus on millet, maize and rice to determine the impacts of cropland degradation. Choice of millet is dictated by its extent in Senegal. Millet and cowpeas accounts for 34 and 5 % of cropland area, respectively (FAOSTAT 2014). Millet is grown throughout the country but the crop is predominantly planted on sandy and phosphorus deficient soils (Directorate for Agriculture 2001; Ndiaye 1999) and this results in very low yields. However rotation cropping significantly improves millet yield even on sandy soils. We use DSSAT-CENTURY (Decision Support System for Agrotechnology Transfer) crop simulation model (Gijsman et al. 2002) to determine the impact of SLM practices on crop yield and soil carbon. To capture the long-term impacts of soil fertility management, we simulate the yield for 30 years. We also use results from long-term soil fertility experiments conducted in Senegal to determine the impacts of millet-cowpea rotation versus continuous millet-millet cropping and salinity controlling management practices versus management practices that lead to salinity.

We use two crop simulation scenarios:

- SLM practices: We consider three types of SLM practices—(a) Integrated Soil Fertility Management (ISFM)—combined use of organic inputs, judicious amount of chemical fertilizer and improved seeds (Vanlauwe and Giller 2006) (b) Millet-cowpea rotation and/or intercropping (c) salinity controlling management practices. The choice of the three SLM practices is largely dictated by empirical evidence of their effectiveness, the type of crops grown in Senegal and the main type of cropland degradation and data availability. Long-term soil fertility experiments have shown that ISFM performs better than the use of fertilizer or organic input alone (Vanlauwe and Giller 2006; Nandwa and Bekunda 1998). Millet-cowpea rotational cropping and intercropping significantly increase crop yield. A long-term experiment conducted in Senegal by Bagayoko et al. (1996) compared different cropping systems of millet and cowpeas between 1991 and 1995 and found that millet yields increased by 24 % and by 26 % for millet and cowpea intercrop and millet-cowpea rotation cropping respectively.
- Business as usual (BAU). The BAU scenario reflects the current management practices practiced by majority of farmers. These could be land degrading management practices or those which are not significantly different from the performance of ISFM.

The cost of land degradation will be determined by comparing the yield differences between the two scenarios. Additionally, long-term soil fertility experiments have shown that, even when using ISFM at recommended levels, yields decline due to decrease of soil organic matter (Nandwa and Bekunda 1998). This is also an indication of land degradation that will be taken into account as shown below.

$$\mathbf{CLD} = \left(y^c - y^d\right)\boldsymbol{P} * (\boldsymbol{A} - \boldsymbol{A}^c) + \left(y_1^c - y_2^c\right) * \boldsymbol{A}^c\big)\boldsymbol{P} - \tau\Delta \boldsymbol{CO}_2 \tag{19.2}$$

where CLD = cost of land degradation on cropland, y^c = yield with SLM (namely ISFM, crop rotation or salinity-controlling land management), y^d yield with BAU, A = total area that remained under cropland in baseline and endline periods, A^c = cropland area under SLM. P = price of crop i; y_1^c, y_2^c are yield under SLM in period 1 and 2, respectively; ΔCO_2 = change in the amount of carbon sequestered under SLM and BAU and τ = price of CO_2 in the global carbon market.

We compute the net carbon sequestration after considering the amount of CO_2 emission from nitrogen fertilization and from manure application. Manufacturing, transportation and application one kg of Nitrogen leads to an emission of 9.3 kg of CO_2-equivalent (Vlek et al. 2004).

Land Degradation Due to Use of Land Degrading Management Practices on Static Grazing Lands

We briefly discuss the approach used to assess livestock productivity using beef and milk offtake only. Detailed approach of the analysis is given in Chap. 8. This approach ignores other effects of pasture degradation such as parturition and mortality rate. We also ignore the off-farm impact of grassland degradation such as loss of carbon sequestration and other environmental and ecological services provided by grassland. This means our estimates are conservative.

To determine the anthropogenic land degradation, we identified land degradation as areas where the inter annual mean NDVI has declined over the historical period of 2001 to 2011—after netting out the impact of rainfall on NDVI change. Aboveground biomass productivity of grazing lands is then estimated using statistical models which use NDVI to estimate biomass productivity. The cost of land degradation on grasslands is estimated by treating grassland biomass productivity in 2001 and 2011 as baseline and endline, respectively. For details of the approach, please see Chap. 8.

Drivers of Adoption of SLM Practices

We estimate the drivers of adoption of ISFM, inorganic fertilizer and organic inputs using a probit model specified as follows:

$$\mathbf{Y}^* = \Phi - 1(\mathbf{Y}) = \mathbf{X}\beta + \varepsilon \tag{19.3}$$

where Y* is a latent variable, such that

$$Y = \begin{cases} 0 & \mathit{if}\ Y^* \leq 0 \\ 1 & \mathit{if}\ Y^* \geq 1 \end{cases},$$

Φ is a cumulative normal distribution with Z-distribution, i.e. $\Phi(Z) \in (0, 1)$.

X is a vector of covariates of drivers of adoption of land management practices and β is a vector of the associated coefficients. Xβ ~ N(0, 1); ε is an error term with normal distribution, i.e., ε ~ N(0, 1).

Choice of the elements of the X vector in the empirical model is guided by literature and data availability. We use an agricultural household survey conducted in 2011/12.

Cost of Cropland Degradation

In this section, we estimate the cost of land degradation of major crops in Senegal. As is the case in other SSA countries, adoption rate of SLM practices is low. Figure 19.6 shows that while only 2.5 % of parcels received the most profitable

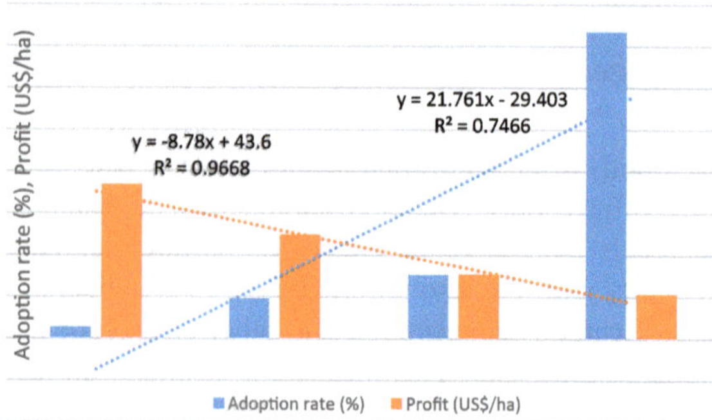

Fig. 19.6 The unholy cross: inverse relationship between profit and adoption rate of soil fertility management practices. *Source* Authors

practice—ISFM, i.e., a practice that combines judicious quantities of chemical fertilizer with organic inputs and improved germplasm (Vanlauwe and Giller 2006), about three quarters of parcels did not receive any external inputs—the least profitable management practice. Table 19.2 gives details of adoption rate of the

Table 19.2 Adoption rate of soil fertility management practices in Senegal, 2011/12

	Sample size	Manure only	Fertilizer only	No inputs	ISFM
Arid and semi-arid	16,971	15.3	9.5	72.5	2.6
Humid and sub-humid	6620	14.1	8.8	74.8	2.3
Irrigated rice					
Arid and semi-arid	315	7.6	86.0	2.5	3.8
Humid and sub-humid	22	4.6	18.2	77.3	0.0
Rainfed rice					
Arid and semi-arid	43	16.3	13.9	55.8	13.9
Humid and sub-humid	2001	21.9	4.5	72.4	1.2
Groundnuts					
Arid and semi-arid	6935	11.7	8.1	78.7	1.6
Humid and sub-humid	1643	4.2	10.2	84.2	1.3
Millet					
Arid and semi-arid	5527	21.2	8.0	67.8	3.0
Humid and sub-humid	933	13.7	7.9	76.4	1.9
Sorghum					
Arid and semi-arid	1057	8.8	3.2	87.3	0.7
Humid and sub-humid	711	9.7	4.8	84.4	1.1
Maize					
Arid and semi-arid	922	24.1	18.1	48.1	9.8
Humid and sub-humid	818	18.7	14.8	60.5	6.0
Cowpea					
Arid and semi-arid	1363	14.7	1.6	83.4	0.4
Humid and sub-humid	112	7.1	2.7	90.2	0.0

Sources Adoption rates: Computed from raw data of the Agricultural survey (Enquête Agricole) (2011/12)

three management practices across agroecological zones (AEZ) (Fig. 19.5) and crops and all consistently show the same pattern—lowest adoption rate for the most profitable and highest adoption for the least profitable land management. The inverse relationship between profitability and adoption rate of land management suggests there are challenges which hamper farmers from adopting the most profitable land management practices. Of interest is the greater adoption of ISFM in arid and semi-arid lands (ASAL) than in humid and sub-humid zone for almost all crops. This could be an attempt of farmers in the ASAL to increase soil carbon and consequently reduce production risks.

The low adoption of sustainable land management practices lead to land degradation. DSSAT simulation results show that cost of land degradation for maize and rice, which respectively account for only 5 and 6 % of the cropland of 2.6 million ha of cropland (FAOSTAT 2014) is about 2007 US$114.52 million (Table 19.3) or 1 % of the 2007 GDP of US$ 11.285 billion (World Bank 2013). The results have important implications on rice, a crop that is currently receiving significant attention as its consumption is increasing—leading to large importation. To contribute to country's goal of food self-sufficiency, steps need to be taken to address land degradation on rice and other crops.

Cowpea-millet rotation increased millet yields by 24 % and by 26 % for millet and cowpea intercrop-cowpea rotation (Table 19.4). Crop rotation improves soil fertility through symbiotic nitrogen fixation. Additionally cowpea does not mine soil phosphorus reserves. Thus, after cowpea cultivation, soils have amounts of nitrogen and phosphorus that leads to higher millet yield. According to recent work at the Center for Studies and Research (CERAAS), high nitrogen content in the soil also promotes good soil moisture. The results are consistent with Gueye (1992) who

Table 19.3 Cost of cropland degradation due to use of soil fertility mining practices

Crop	Technology	Average yield		Percent change	ISFM adoption rate (%)	Cost of land degradation (US$ million)
		First 10 years	Last 10 years			
Irrigated rice	ISFM	7.5	6.2	17.4	3.8	12.45
	BAU	6.7	5.1	24.6		
Rainfed rice	ISFM	7.8	4.9	21.4	13.9	48.53
	BAU	7.7	4.8	35.0		
Rainfed maize	ISFM	2.4	1.9	36.9	9.8	41.78
	BAU	1.9	1.3	38.1		
Total cost						102.76
Total cost of rice and maize cropland degradation as % of GDP						1 %

Notes Percent change = $\frac{y_1 - y_2}{y_1} * 100$

BAU Business as usual—farmer practice

Average harvested area of crops are (with corresponding area in brackets): Rice (116,226 ha) and maize (154,347 ha) (*Source* FAOSTAT 2014). Crop prices: Rice (US$656/ton) and maize US $543/ton; *Source* Calculated from DSSAT simulation results (see Nkonya et al. 2015). Adoption rate of soil fertility management practices: Agricultural survey (2011/12)

Table 19.4 Impact of millet-cowpea cropping systems on millet yield in Senegal

	1991	1992	1993	1994	1995	Average	% change
	Millet yield (tons/ha)						
Cowpea-pearl millet rotation	1.4	2.4	1.4	1.6	2.1	1.8	24
Intercrop-pearl millet rotation	1.2	2.2	1.2	1.3	1.6	1.5	4
Continuous pearl millet—control	1.1	2.0	1.1	1.3	1.6	1.4	
Continuous intercrop	0.8	1.5	0.9	1.0	1.4	1.1	−20
Pearl Millet-Intercrop Rotation	1.4	2.4	1.4	1.6	2.1	1.8	26

Source Bagayoko et al. (1996)

found greater millet yield in cowpea-millet rotation cropping. Based on Bagayoko et al. (1996) results, Table 19.5 shows that millet continuous cropping leads to a national loss of about US$ 77 million per year.

Salinity affects mainly rice production in the Sine-saloum and Casamance river basins. The recommended practice for addressing salinity is flushing and good drainage. Demonstration plots showing the proper management practices for addressing salinity was carried out by the Project to Support Local Small-Scale Irrigation (PAPIL). The long-term PAPIL demonstration included one treatments that included the recommended practice of addressing salinity—flushing salinity and proper drainage and a control treatment, which was the farmer practice of poor drainage and no flushing. The yield of treatment plots was 2.8 tons/ha while the yield on control plots was only 1.4 tons in the arid and semi-arid zone (Table 19.5). The corresponding cost of salinity is about US$22 million per year (Table 19.5).

Table 19.5 Cost of continuous cropping and salinity on millet and rice cropland

	BAU Yield (t/ha)	SLM Yield (t/ha)	Cost of land degradation, US$/ha	Total area affected by salinity (ha)	Total cost of land degradation (US$ million)
Cereal-legume cropping system	Continuous millet cropping	Millet-cowpea rotation			
Millet	1.43	1.78	258	402,813	77.39
Salinity—rice	With salinity	Without salinity			
Humid and subhumid zone	1.8	2.7	591	7384	4.37
Arid and semi-arid zone	1.4	2.8	834	20,982	17.49
Total Cost of LD					99.25

Source Authors

Cost of Land Degradation on Grasslands

While pasture covers 56,500 km^2 or 69.3 % of Senegalese land area, it accounts for only 14.8 % of the Senegal's GDP and 37.3 % of the agricultural GDP (FAO 2005). This is due to the low livestock productivity in the country. Senegal lost about 2007 US$ 9 million annually due to degradation grazing biomass or about 0.1 % of the 2007 GDP (Table 19.6). While the small cost of land degradation underscores the low livestock productivity, it signifies the need to address degradation of grazing lands to take advantage of the increasing national and international demand for livestock products.

Cost of Land Degradation Due to Land Use/Cover Change

The costs related to land degradation as a result of LUCC for Senegal are reported in Table 19.7. The LUCC data used in the analysis is reported in Fig. 19.7. Using the TEV approach (see Nkonya et al. 2015), the annual cost of land degradation due to LUCC is estimated to be about US$0.733 billion. The cost is highest in the subhumid area—which experienced the largest cropland expansion into grasslands and shrublands (Fig. 19.7). However if we only consider the provisioning services and other local benefits, the cost of land degradation is US$0.412 billion or about 4 % of the GDP. Table 19.8 summarizes the annual cost of land degradation for LUCC and cropland. Land degradation due to LUCC is about 7 % of the GDP and the cost of salinity, continuous cropping and soil fertility mining for the selected crops (maize, rice and millet) is only about 2 % of the GDP. The cost of grazing biomass degradation is US$9 billion or 0.1 % of the GDP. The low cost of grazing biomass degradation is largely due to the low livestock productivity. However, the local impact of land degradation on cropland on human welfare of the Senegalese population is much greater than its small value shown since crops provide provisioning services that directly affect welfare.

As expected the cost of action to address LUCC-related land degradation is much smaller than the cost of inaction. Over the 30 year planning horizon, the cost of action as percent of cost of inaction ranges from 22 % in the humid areas to 25 % in the ASAL (Table 19.7). Accordingly, the returns to taking action against

Table 19.6 On-farm cost of land degradation on grasslands in Senegal

AEZ	Milk	Meat	Total cost
	2007 US$ million		
Tropic-warm/semi-arid	0.141	0.008	0.149
Tropic-warm/arid	0.153	0.012	0.165
Tropic-warm/sub-humid	8.554	0.566	9.120
Total	8.847	0.586	9.434
Percent of 2007 GDP	0.08	0.01	0.08

Source Authors

Table 19.7 Cost of land degradation due to LUCC, action and inaction in Senegal

	Arid and semi-arid	Sub-humid	Humid	Total
	2007 US$ billion			
Total annual cost of land degradation	0.238	0.482	0.013	0.733
Total annual cost—local ES loss only	0.122	0.285	0.006	0.412
Cost of action 1st 6 years	3.30	6.67	0.23	10.19
Cost of action 30 years	3.32	6.70	0.23	10.24
Opportunity cost	3.22	6.55	0.22	9.99
Cost of inaction	14.57	30.32	0.91	45.80
Marginal rate of returns to action against LUCC land degradation	4.4	4.5	4.0	4.5
	Percent			
Zonal contribution to cost of land degradation as % of total	32	66	2	100
Opportunity cost as % of cost of action	97	98	98	98
Cost of action as % of cost of inaction	23	22	25	22

Source Authors

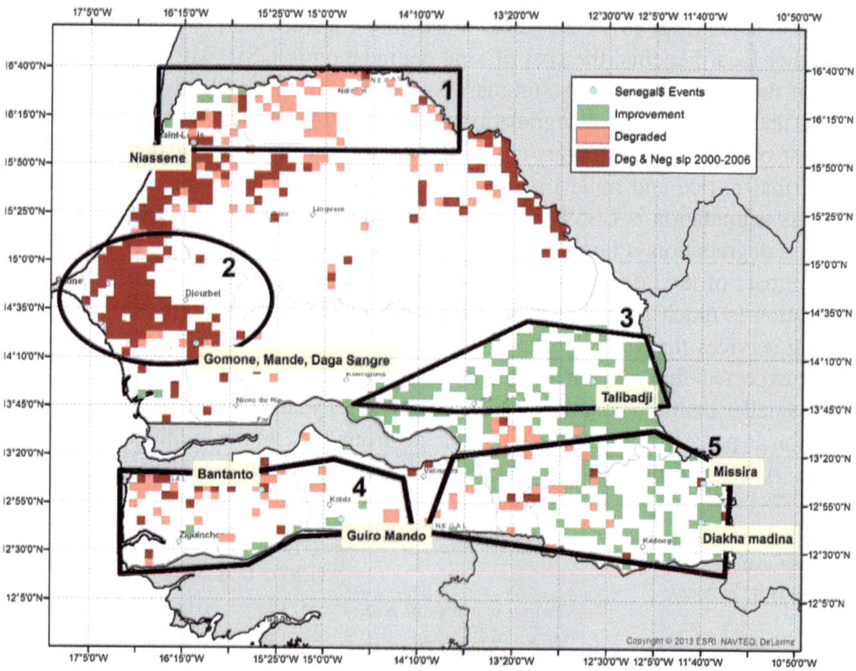

Fig. 19.7 Case study communities selected for FGD and groundtruthing

Table 19.8 Summary of annual cost of land degradation

Type of land degradation	Source	Annual cost (US$ million)	% of GDP
LUCC	Table 19.5	733	6.5
LUCC—local tangible benefits	Table 19.5	412	3.7
Soil fertility mining—maize and rice	Table 19.2	103	0.9
Salinity—irrigated rice	Table 19.5	22	0.2
Continuous cropping—millet	Table 19.5	77	0.7
Degradation of grazing biomass	Table 19.6	9	0.1
Gross total		944	8.4
Total—local ES loss only		623	5.5

Source Authors

LUCC-related land degradation is high. The returns for every dollar invested to rehabilitate LUCC-related land degradation is about US$4. However, given that a large share of the benefits of rehabilitation of LUCC-related are off-site, land users may not take action since their decision making is driven by on-farm benefits. Thus, an important question is to examine the perception of land users on LUCC and other forms of land degradation and to analyze their response to land degradation. We use Focus Group Discussions (FGD) to examine the community perception on land degradation and steps they take to address it.

Focus Group Discussion Results

FGD were conducted in seven Senegalese communities shown in Fig. 19.7. The communities were selected to cover AEZ and to represent areas that Le et al. (2014) showed land improvement or land degradation in each AEZ (see Table 19.9). Approximately 10–20 community members participated in the FGD.

Participants were purposively selected to represent old people who could give informed perception on land use change over the 30 year reference period; women, the youth, local government leaders, crop producers, livestock producers, people

Table 19.9 Names, agroecological zone and status of land degradation or improvement of the selected communities

Community	Agroecological zone	Status of land degradation and improvement
Diakha Madina	Sub-humid	Improvement
Missira	Sub-humid	Improvement
Guiro Mandou	Subhumid	Degradation
Bantanto	Semi-arid	Degradation
Gomone	Semi-arid	Severe degradation
Niassene	Arid	Severe degradation
Talibadji	Semi-arid	Improvement

who earn their livelihoods from forest and other non-agricultural terrestrial biomes, and customary leaders. Such a diverse groups afforded a rich discussion on ecosystem value and their change from 1982 to 2012.

Groundtruthing remote sensing data was done by asking FGD members to show the LUCC and land degradation or improvement of the major biomes which have occurred in the community over a 30 year period (1982–2012). Groundtruthing helps to determine reliability of the satellite data used in this report.

Change in the Importance of Ecosystem Services and Drivers of Change

The members of the FGD's stated their perception of the importance of ecosystem services provided by different biomes in 1982 and in 2012. Figure 19.8 summarizes the trend of importance and the communities' awareness of the ecosystem services. As expected, awareness of the provisioning is the highest followed by that of cultural services. Awareness of the regulating and support services is the lowest. The degree of awareness implies the priority that the ecosystem services receive from communities in their decision making process. Communities perceived that importance of all three major types of ecosystem services in 2012 decreased from their levels in 1982 (Fig. 19.8). Importance of the regulating and support services experienced the steepest decline while that of cultural services experienced the smallest loss. The major reason driving the decline in importance of the regulating services is climate change, which was mentioned by four of the six communities.

Soil erosion was mentioned by three of the six communities as the driver of declining regulating services. The communities argued that soil erosion decreased nature's capacity to fight pests and diseases as well as water quality. Change in spiritual values was the major driver of declining cultural values of ecosystem services. Such trend is expected as modernism among young people erodes cultural

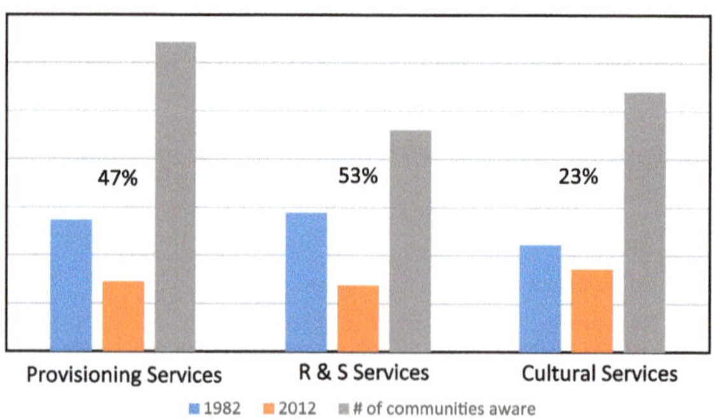

Fig. 19.8 Awareness of ecosystem services and summary of trend of their importance. *Notes* Ecosystem importance index: 1 = Not important, 2 = Important, 3 = Very important. Percentage above histograms show the % loss of Ecosystem Services

values (Inglehart and Welzel 2005). Three communities reported an increase in importance of ecotourism and other three reported a fall. The driver of increase in importance of ecotourism was promotion of tourism by the government. Land degradation and changing cultural beliefs were cited as the major cause of falling importance of ecotourism.

A detailed analysis of trend of importance of specific ecosystem services is given in Fig. 19.9. With the exception of two cultural services (ecotourism and knowledge), importance of all other types of ecosystem services declined in 2012 from their levels in 1982 (Fig. 19.9). Six out of the seven communities reported a declining importance for crop provisioning services. Six communities reported land degradation as the major driver of declining importance of the crop provisioning services. Figure 19.9 shows that importance of provisioning services changed from very important in 1982 to not important in 2012. Increasing salinity and declining soil fertility were explicitly mentioned in Bantanto as drivers of such fall in importance.

The provisioning services from livestock shows an interesting pattern. Three of the seven communities reported increasing importance of provisioning services from livestock (Table 19.10). All three communities (Gomone, Niassene and Talibadji) are in the ASAL zone (Table 19.9), where livestock production is an important sector. Consistent with Kearney (2010), increasing demand for livestock products is reported as the major driver of the increasing importance of livestock provisioning services. The increasing importance of livestock provisioning services reflects farmers' response to market signals. The results are also supported by the increasing livestock population and production of animal products in Senegal (FAO 2005). Accordingly, consumption of animal products has increased (FAO 2005).

The government livestock development program in Gomone could have contributed to increasing importance of livestock since community members reported that the intervention contributed to higher livestock productivity. Theft and diseases

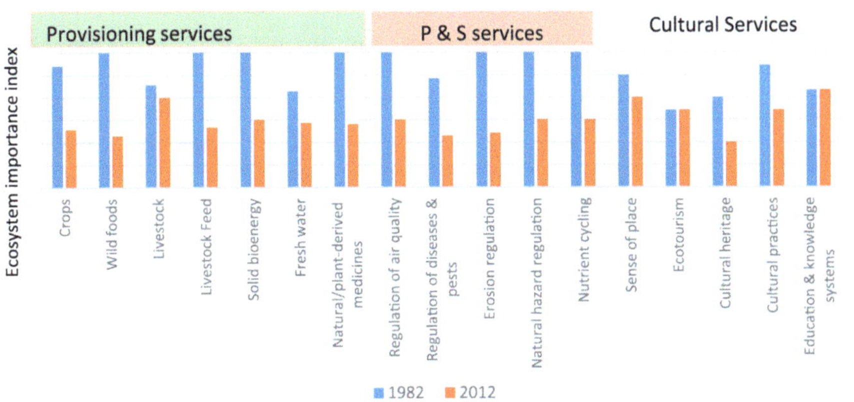

Fig. 19.9 Ecosystem services and trend of their importance. *Notes* Ecosystem importance index: 1 = Not important 2 = Important 3 = Very important. R & S services = regulating and support services

Table 19.10 Trend of importance of provisioning services from livestock

Community	Trend	Reasons of trend		
Bantanto	Decrease	Theft	Diseases	
Diakha Madina	Decrease	Diseases		
Gomone	Increase	Livestock development project		
Guiro Mandou	Decrease	Theft		
Missira	Decrease	Less extension services		
Niassene	Increase	Greater demand of livestock products	Greater awareness of livestock importance	Greater income
Talibaldji	Increase	Changing market supply	Greater awareness of livestock importance	

Source Focus Group Discussion 2014

were the two major causes of decreasing importance of livestock provisioning services. Cattle theft remains a major problem in Senegal and the "safeguard livestock operations" is among government efforts to address it (Stads and Sène 2011). Contrary to MODIS data, which shows an increase in forest area, forest area decreased in six of the seven communities (Fig. 19.10). Diakha Madina and Talibadji, both of which have the largest areas under forest, forested areas declined in all villages. This explains the corresponding reduction in importance of forest product provisioning services (e.g. solid bioenergy) reported in Fig. 19.9.

A follow up question on trend of importance of ecosystem services was on how the communities were responding to unfavorable and favorable trends. The section below reports actions taken by communities in response to changes in ecosystem services. Emphasis is placed on actions that have been successful and those which have not worked and the reasons behind success or failure.

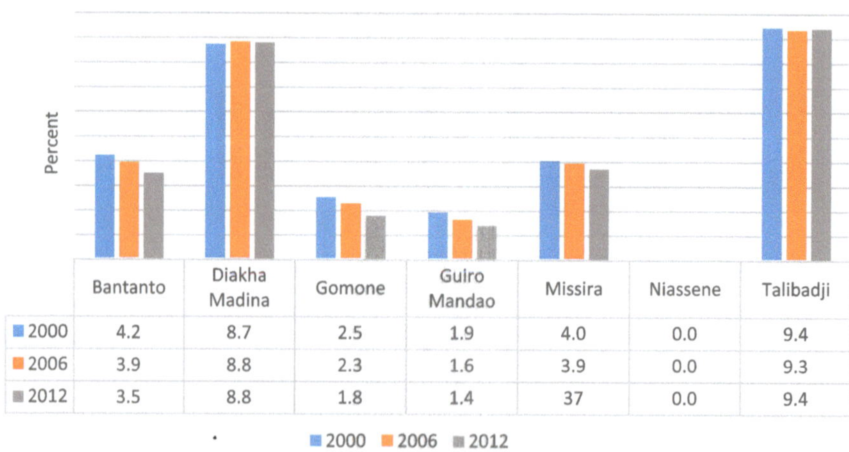

Fig. 19.10 Trend of forested area in case study villages. *Source* Focus Group Discussion 2014

Actions Taken to Address Declining Importance of Ecosystem Service

In order to maintain or restore the quality of cropland, the most common approaches taken were fertility management, expansion of cropland area and control of livestock movement. Only Guiro Mandou community reported to have seen successful implementation of all three actions (Table 19.11). Limited production of manure and high cost of inorganic inputs were the major reasons behind failure of action to address declining soil fertility. Restriction of movement of animals was also not successful due to deep culture of feeding on crop residues by livestock keepers during dry season.

For forests, firewall, zoning, stricter enforcement of existing byelaws and enacting new ones were the most common approaches taken to address deforestation. Their implementation was successful in five of the seven communities

Table 19.11 Action taken to address decreasing ecosystem services of major biomes

	Cropland	Forest	Grazing lands	Has it worked? Yes = +, No = −		
				Cropland	Forests	Grazing land
Diakha Madina	Fertilizer application	Firewall, collective protection and byelaws	Firewalls, collective action to control bush burning	−	+	+
Missira	ISFM, rudimentary dam	Reduce forest harvesting	Increase advisory services on better pasture management	−	+	+
Guiro Mandou	Zero grazing animals, cropland expansion	Firefighting committee	Improved grassland management	+	+	+
Bantanto	Use manure, cropland expansion	Committee against bush fires, enforcement of zonation	Firewalls, committee against cattle theft	−	+	+
Gomone	Cropland expansion, ISFM	Byelaws, zoning	Transhumance, use of crop residues	−	−	+
Niassene	Change crop type, zero grazing, zoning	Zoning, promotion of modern houses		−	−	−
Talibadji	Manure, control of livestock movement	Nothing done	Use crop residues, common penning area	−	+	+

Source Focus Group Discussion 2014

suggesting that the collective action of enacting byelaws and enforcing them appear to be most effective. This is consistent with Nkonya et al. (2008) who observed greater compliance with byelaws enacted by local council than those enacted by higher legislative bodies. Likewise, collective action on community pasture management, committees against cattle theft and advisory services on improved pasture management were the most common approaches used and they worked in six of the seven communities.

A clear pattern is seen in the successful action to improve resource management. The cropland management approaches used are done at household level and remain hampered by resource scarcity of farmers. Most communities reported success in improving forest and grazing land biome largely through participatory involvement of the communities. This underscores the importance of the collective management and byelaws that tend to be more effective when enacted and enforced at community level the community. To illustrate the importance of community participation in decision making and collective management of resources, we give a case study of a successful participatory forestmanagement, which is being implemented under collaboration between communities surrounding the forest and the government. The case study illustrates the key features required for successful government collaboration with communities surrounding forests.

Initiated in 2006, Dankou Forest in the region of Kaffrine is implemented using participatory forest management approach. With an area of 10 ha, Dankou forest was replanted by the participating communities after it experienced complete deforestation. A total of 16 surrounding villages are involved in planning, monitoring and evaluation of the forestdevelopment. Additionally, the communities are responsible for protecting and managing the forest. The routine forest management activities include fire control and guarding against illegal forest product harvesting (Käser 2003; Gill 2013). The participating communities have enacted a number of byelaws and have formed committees to enforce them in collaboration with the department of water and forestry and the local government, which—according the Decentralization Act of 1996—has the land administration mandate. To incentivize communities to participate in forest management, they are allowed to harvest firewood and other non-timber forest products but the harvesting is regulated to ensure it is sustainable. The net profit that communities have obtained in the past eight years is estimated to be US$103, 580 and the cost of afforestation program during the same period was US$49,560. Table 19.12 reveals a detailed overview of the afforestation and maintenance costs of Dankou forest.

Establishing the forest at the beginning is the largest share of the cost (Fig. 19.11). The protection, which involves pecuniary and non-pecuniary costs, is just around one third of the total cost.

However, of particular importance is the investment that the government put in information and awareness creation on CBFM. The major objectives of information and awareness creation are to build local capacity to sustainably manage forest resources and to educate community members on the importance of their participation in the CBFM. The information and awareness effort also involved discussion on sharing the benefits and the community responsibility of forest protection,

Table 19.12 Cost of afforestation of 10 ha forest, Senegal

Type of operation	Total cost (US$)
Establishment	
Setting boundary markers	123.88
Establishing and maintaining plant nursery	12.39
Planting material	665.49
Transportation of plants	51.19
Small planting material	102.38
Fencing	20.48
Digging holes	133.10
Planting	133.10
Maintenance	
Maintenance	225.24
Support and supervision	22.52
Other	45.97
Total	1535.75

Source Calculated using data obtained from Development and sylvo-pastoral management plan of the Dankou classified forest

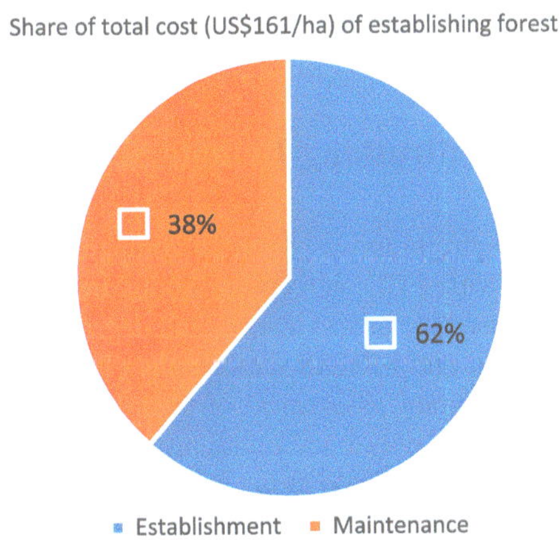

Fig. 19.11 Cost of protection of Dankou classified forest. *Source* Calculated using data obtained from development and sylvo-pastoral management plan of the Dankou classified forest

management, monitoring and evaluation and sustainable forest harvesting. Interestingly, the information and awareness creation was the largest cost item after the replanting and establishment activities ended in 2009, when trees reached biological maturity (Fig. 19.12). The information and awareness campaign might be the main driver of the long-run success of the project and could even help communities to realize the local and global ecosystem benefits of the forests. Additionally, by using the channels of the information campaign other integrated agro-forestry-pastoral activities were promoted, such as assisted natural regeneration of important tree species on farmland, cereal-legume intercropping, plant

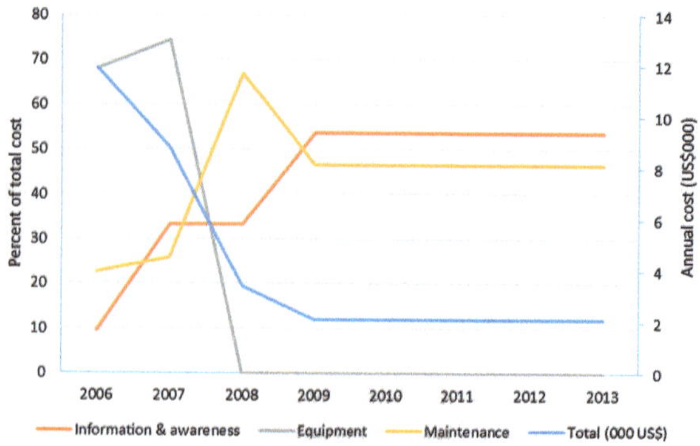

Fig. 19.12 Trend of cost of protection of Dankou classified forest. *Source* Calculated using data obtained from the development and sylvo-pastoral management plan of the Dankou classified forest

windbreaks, diversification of agricultural production, application manure from livestock and promoting intensive farming. As a result of the positive outcome of Dankou Forest, there were six new registrations for CBFM in the neighboring region of Kaolack within the Regional Forest Action Plan. This shows that the Dankou CBFM could be scaled-up.

Groundtruthing Remote Sensing Data

Groundtruthing was done by comparing the Le et al. (2014), Landsat and MODIS data with FGD perception about trend of land cover change.[4] FGD results in villages which experienced land degradation showed high degree of agreement with Landsat and MODIS data results (Table 19.13). Bantanto, Gomone, and Niassene communities' assessment of land degradation was consistent with all three satellite data while only one community which remote sensing data showed improvement (Diakha Madina) was perceived by FGD participants to have improved (Table 19.13). As Anderson and Johnson (2014) argue, the inability of satellite data to capture specific type of land degradation is complemented by the its ability to reflect the reduced vegetative health of plants growing on saline soils, eroded soils and other forms of non-vegetative cover land degradation. However, the inability of satellite data to capture some form of land degradation is revealed in sites that experienced improvement. For example, FGD at Dakha Madina, observed a decrease in crop value due to soil erosion. There may, in fact, be a number of competing processes at work as increasing cropland area is causing deforestation, but regeneration of fallowed fields increases natural vegetation cover. Similarly the site has experienced water erosion and a perceived decrease in crop values but also reports an increased yields in recent years.

[4]For more details on the methodology, see Anderson and Johnson (2014).

Table 19.13 Groundtruthing of satellite-derived data using FGD

Site	Bao Le assessment	FGD assessment	Change in landsat NDVI	MODIS Land cover change	Agreement
Talibdji	Improved	Degraded	Degraded	Improved	2/4
Niassene	Degraded	Degraded	Degraded	Degraded	4/4
Missira	Degraded	Degraded	Improved	Mixed	2.5/4
Guiro Yoro Mandou	Improved	Degraded	Degraded	Mixed	2.5/4
Gomone	Degraded	Degraded	Degraded	Degraded	4/4
Diakha Madina	Improved	Mixed	Improved	Improved	3.5/4
Bantanto	Degraded	Degraded	Degraded	Degraded	4/4

Source Anderson and Johnson (2014)

Talibadji showed the lowest consistency, which could be due to MODIS land cover classes that dominate Talibadji have poor user accuracy (many below 50 %, i.e., misclassifications are likely (Friedl et al. 2010). The FGD, meanwhile, revealed that erosion has decreased yields and therefore the value of crops, which would not have shown up in the NDVI analysis.

Drivers of Adoption of Sustainable Land Management Practices

As expected physical capital endowment increases the propensity to adopt all types of SLM practices considered (Table 19.14). Surprisingly, farmers in the arid and semi-arid areas are more likely to adopt SLM practices than those in the humid areas. This could be due to the better soil fertility (e.g. high soil carbon) in the humid area that does not require significant soil improvement investment. Similar pattern has been observed in Nigeria where farmers in drier northern Nigeria apply more fertilizer and organic inputs than those in the humid southern zone (Nkonya et al. 2010).

Human capital endowment have ambiguous impact on adoption of SLM practices. While household size increases the probability to adopt ISFM and fertilizer, it reduces the propensity to adopt manure. Female managed plots are less likely to receive any of the three SLM practices while number of adult males increases the likelihood of using manure and fertilizer. These results are consistent with other studies which have shown that women-operated plots are less likely to use improved land management practices due to the resource constraints they face (Peterman et al. 2014).

Having non-farm income increases the likelihood to use manure and fertilizer but has no significant impact on using ISFM. This is consistent with Moussa et al. (2015) who observed similar results in Niger. The results underscore the synergistic role played that non-farm and farm activities play in rural economic activities.

Consistent with Boserupian theory (Boserup 1965), high population density increases the propensity to use ISFM. Market access increases the likelihood to use

Table 19.14 Drivers of adoption of SLM practices in Senegal

	Manure only	Fertilizer only	ISFM
Human capital endowment			
Household size	−0.021***	0.022***	0.028**
Female headed household	0.05	−0.21	0.154
Number adult females	0.041**	0.044**	−0.019
Number adult males	0.012	−0.025	−0.016
Female Managed plot	−0.529***	−0.410***	−0.290*
Has nonfarm income	0.143***	0.161***	−0.073
Physical capital endowment			
TLU	0.020***	−0.050***	−0.014
Own radio	0.122**	0.157**	0.388***
Own mobile phone	0.086	−0.017	0.107
Own bicycle	0.361***	0.131	0.452**
Plot area (ha)	0.108***	0.185***	0.194***
Arid and semi arid (cf humid and subhumid)	0.398***	0.328***	0.413*
Access to rural services			
High population density (cf low density)	−0.328***	0.186**	0.825***
High market access (cf low market)	1.262***	−1.424***	0.340**
Use improved seed	−0.097	0.353***	0.465***
Received ag extension services	−0.34	−1.023***	−0.862**
Land tenure/method of acquisition (cf customary)			
Sharecropping	−0.284	0.454	−0.768
Loaned	−0.343***	0.348***	0.182
Leasehold	−0.005	1.385***	1.726***
Other method of land tenure	−0.075	0.834***	−13.246***
Constant	−2.599***	−1.003***	−3.202***

*statistically significant at 10 %; **statistically significant at 5 %; ***statistically significant at 1 %

Source Agricultural survey (Enquête Agricole) (2011/12), Direction de l'analyse de la prevision et des statistiques (DAPS)

manure and ISFM but surprisingly reduces the propensity to use fertilizer. Consistent with Nkonya et al. (1997) farmers who use improved seeds are more likely to use fertilizer and ISFM. This demonstrates farmers' effort to increase returns to their investments by simultaneously adopting synergistic technologies. Access to extension services has either a negative or non-significant impact on SLM adoption—underlining the weak extension services in the country.

Farmers who hold their land under leasehold are more likely to use fertilizer and ISFM than those who acquired their land under customary tenure—inheritance. However, plots under customary tenure are more likely to receive ISFM than those under other types of land tenure. Similarly plots held under customary tenure are more likely to receive manure than those loaned. Overall, the results on land tenure and method of land acquisition are ambiguous and further research is required to draw robust results.

Conclusions and Policy Implications

Senegal has invested significantly in agricultural and rural development and it is one of the countries with highest rural development infrastructure and access to agricultural extension services. Public expenditure on agriculture grew by 7 % annually from 2003 to 2010, making Senegal one of the 13 SSA countries to achieve the Maputo Declaration target of spending at least 10 % of government budget on agriculture. The country has also enjoyed robust political stability and democracy that has given investment confidence to both domestic and foreign investors. Despite these impressive achievements, the country is facing a major challenge of land degradation, which has contributed to the almost stagnant agricultural productivity. About 22.2 % of Senegal's population of 13 million live in degraded areas. Groundthruthing of the remote sensing data used in this study showed that communities' assessment of land degradation was consistent with the satellite data while improvement measured by remote sensing was only confirmed by one community. Focus group discussion results also showed that communities perceived decreasing ecosystem services largely due to land degradation and climate change. This suggests greater reliability of remote sensing data showing land degradation but lower reliability for satellite data showing improvement.

Our study shows that the annual cost of land degradation on rice, millet and maize—which account for 45 % of cropland area—is US103 million, or 2 % of the country's GDP. The on-farm cost of grassland degradation is about 9 million or 0.1 % of the GDP. The low cost of grassland degradation is a reflection of the low livestock productivity. This calls for the need to increase livestock productivity by addressing grassland degradation, improving the livestock genetic resources through breeding and pasture management. Such investment will have large returns given that the national and international demand for livestock products is increasing. Investment in improving livestock will also simultaneously address severe land degradation and achieve poverty reduction objectives.

Considering only local tangible benefits, the cost of land degradation due to LUCC is about US$0.412 billion or 4 % of the GDP. This shows the large cost of land degradation and the need for taking effective strategies to address this challenge. Returns to taking action against land degradation are high and investment in restoration of degraded lands will be of greater benefit to the rural poor who heavily depend on natural resources. The current rural development investments that Senegal has put in place provide great potential for successfully addressing land degradation. For example, the large number of agricultural extension agents from NGOs and other private providers creates an ideal environment for addressing the "unholy cross"—which portrays an inverse relationship between adoption rate and profitability of SLM practices. Extension messages promoting ISFM practices and strengthened public-private partnerships could help increase adoption of ISFM and other SLM practices. Having non-farm activities and higher market access increase the propensity to use SLM practices. Additionally physical endowment increases the likelihood to adopt SLM practices. These results underscore the importance of improving access to market and enhancing non-farm activities which appear to provide synergistic support to farm activities.

The success story of Dankou CBFM also offers lessons for addressing LUCC related land degradation in Senegal and other SSA countries. Strong local governments and community participation in natural resource management that was successfully implemented in the Dankou CBFM and the significant investment in awareness creation and information sharing offers an important lesson for building land users knowledge on ecosystem services and their capacity to sustainably manage natural resources.

Appendix

Policies related to land management.

Period	Title of taken agricultural policy measure	Content of the policy	Expected impacts on land	Real impacts on land
1964	Law No. 64-46 of 17 June 1964 on the national domain	Abolition of customary land rights	Repeal of customary rules on land	Insufficient law enforcement
		Integration into the regime of national domain of about 95 % of the land of the country	Limitation of private land ownership	Persistence of customary practices
		The state now owns land in the national domain	Prohibition of land transaction	Tenure insecurity unfavorable to private investment
			Substitution of the usage right to the right of land ownership with an obligation of development	
			Free access to land (no tax is levied on the occupation and use of land in the national domain)	
			Decentralization of land management to local communities that are emanations of populations	

(continued)

(continued)

Period	Title of taken agricultural policy measure	Content of the policy	Expected impacts on land	Real impacts on land
1995	Ratification by Senegal of the United Nations Convention to Combat Desertification (UNCCD)	Creation of a legal and institutional environment for the full participation of populations and local communities to all action against desertification and the adverse effects of drought	Prevent and/or reduce land degradation	Poor integration of priorities for fight against desertification in national budgets
			Restore potentially degraded land and desertified land	Weakness funding allocated to the fight against desertification
				Weak harmonization of interventions
				Lack of relevant indicators for monitoring activities against desertification…
1996	Laws no. 96-06 and 96-07 of 22 May 1996 on decentralization	New areas of competence of the State, including natural resources transferred to local communities	Transfer of new land powers to local authorities	On the lands of interest for economic and social development, reduction of central state land powers for the benefit of local communities
		Possibility of the State to transfer all or part of its prerogatives on national domain land, to local communities	Facilitate access to land for private investors	Inadequate implementation of transferred due competencies:
				- Lack of human resources in local communities
				- Weakness of instruments of land management (land registry, land etc. development plans.)
2004	Law of Agro-Silvo-Pastoral Orientation	Improvement of living conditions in rural areas	Modernization of the family farm	Delay in the publication of implementing decrees
		Environmental protection and sustainable land management	Securing the productive base by promoting private investment	The development of agro-business
		Incentives for private investment in agriculture and rural areas		Trend of land grabbing by foreign capital
				Deforestation

(continued)

(continued)

Period	Title of taken agricultural policy measure	Content of the policy	Expected impacts on land	Real impacts on land
2004	Decree No. 2004-802 of 28 June 2004 establishing the National Institute of Pedology of Senegal	Creation of a national structure to coordinate sustainable land management in Senegal	Improve knowledge on soil resources of the country	Increased awareness of stakeholders in the sustainable land management
			Develop rehabilitation activities and land reclamation	Strategic planning of investments in sustainable land management
			Promoting regional and international cooperation in the field of soil science	Establishment of a technical package of proven SLM in different pedo-climatic zones of the country

References

Agricultural survey (Enquête Agricole). (2011/12). Direction de l'analyse de la prevision et des statistiques (DAPS). Raw data.

Agriculture for Impact. (2014). Small and growing entrepreneurship in African agriculture. A Montpellier Panel Report.

Anderson, W., & Johnson, T. (2014). Evaluating global land degradation mapping using ground-based measurements and remote sensing. In E. Nkonya, A. Mirzabaev & J. von Braun (Eds.), *Global assessment of the economics of land degradation and improvement*. Springer (Forthcoming).

Bagayoko, M., Mason, S. C., Traore, S., & Eskridge, K. M. (1996). Pearl millet/cowpea cropping system yields and soil nutrient levels. *Afr Crop Sci J, 4*, 453–462.

Beintema, N., & Stads, G.J. (2011). African agricultural R&D in the new millennium. Progress for some, challenges for many. International Food Policy Research Institute. Food Policy Report 24.

Benin, S., & Yu, B. (2012). Complying the Maputo declaration target: Trends in public agricultural expenditures and implications for pursuit of optimal allocation of public agricultural spending. ReSAKSS Annual Trends and Outlook Report 2012. International Food Policy Research Institute (IFPRI).

Boserup, E. (1965). *The conditions of agricultural growth*. London: Allen and Unwin.

Centre de Suivi Ecologique. (2013). Annuaire sur l'environnement et les resources naturelles du Sénégal (3rd edn).

DAT/USAID/RSI. (1985). Mapping and remote sensing of the resources of the Republic of Senegal—A study of the geology, hydrology, soils, vegetation and land use potential, Brookings, South Dakota.

Davis, K., Nkonya, E., Kato, E., Mekonnen, D. A., Odendo, M., & Miiro, R. (2010). Impact of farmer field schools on agricultural productivity and poverty in East Africa. International Food Policy Research Institute.

Delmas, R.A., Loudjani, P., Podaire, A., & Menaut, J. (1991). Biomass burning in Africa: An assessment of annually burned biomass. In S. J. Levine (Ed.), *Global biomass burning. Atmospheric, climatic and biospheric implications* (pp. 126–132). Cambridge, Massachusetts: The MIT Press.

Directorate of Agriculture. (2001). The cultivation and production of millet and sorghum in Senegal: Diagnostic assessment and perspectives. Dakar.

DPS (Direction de la Prévision et de la Statistique). (2004). Deuxième Enquête Sénégalaise Auprès des Ménages (ESAM-II), 2004, Dakar, rapport, p. 260.

FAO. (2005). Senegal livestock brief. http://www.fao.org/ag/againfo/resources/en/publications/sector_briefs/lsb_SEN.pdf. Accessed 3 Aug 2014.

FAO. (2011). *State of the world's forests 2011*. Rome: Italy.

FAOSTAT. (2014). Online agricultural database. http://faostat3.fao.org/faostat-gateway/go/to/home/E. Accessed 2 Sept 2014.

Friedl, M., Sulla-Menashe, D., Tan, B., Schneider, A., Ramankutty, N., Sibley, A., & Huang, X. (2010). MODIS global land cover: Algorithm refinements and characterization of new datasets. *Remote Sensing of Environment, 114*(1), 168–182.

Gijsman, A. J., Hoogenboom, G., Parton, W. J., & Kerridge, P. C. (2002). Modifying DSSAT crop models for low-input agricultural systems using a soil organic matter–residue module from CENTURY. *Agronomy Journal, 94*(3), 462–474.

Gill, P. (2013). *Working with local people to identify tree services, deforestation trends, and strategies to combat deforestation: A case study from Senegal's Peanut Basin*. Thesis of Master Forest Resources: Washington University.

Guèye, M. (1992). *Rapports d'activités analytiques 1989*. Tambacounda: ISRA. http://depts.washington.edu/sefspcmi/wordpress/wp-content/uploads/2014/07/Gill-Final-paper1.pdf. Accessed 14 Sept 2014.

Henao, J., & Baanante, C. (2006). Agricultural production and soil nutrient mining in Africa: Implications for resource conservation and policy development. Technical Bulletin IFDC T-72.

Inglehart, R., & Welzel, C. (2005). *Modernization, cultural change, and democracy: The human development sequence*. Cambridge University Press, 333 p.

INP. (2012). *Cadre National d'Investissement Strategique pour la Gestion Durable des Terres (CNIS/GDT)*. Dakar: Rapport Final.

Käser, M. (2003). Perception of the forest as a "Green Bank" evolved among rural population in the test zone of Dankou, Sénégal. Presented at the Tropentag 2003. Göttingen.

Kearney, J. (2010). Food consumption trends and drivers. *Philosophical Transactions of the Royal Society B, 365*, 2793–2807.

Le, Q. B., Nkonya, E. & Mirzabaev, A. (2014). Biomass productivity-based mapping of global land degradation hotspots. ZEF-Discussion Papers on Development Policy No. 193. University of Bonn.

Moussa, B., Nkonya, E., Meyer, S., Kato,E., Johnson, T., & Hawkins, J. (2015). Economics of land degradation and improvement in Niger. In E. Nkonya, A. Mirzabaev & J. von Braun (Eds.), *Economics of Land Degradation and Improvement – A Global Assessment for Sustainable Development*. Springer (This volume).

Nandwa, S., & Bekunda, M. A. (1998). Research on nutrient flows and balances in East and Southern Africa: State-of-the-art. *Agriculture, ecosystems & environment, 71*(1), 5–18.

Ndione, Y. C. (2009). *Impact des politiques agricoles sur la sécurité alimentaire au Sénégal*. Mémoire de maîtrise: Universite Cheikh Anta Diop de Dakar.

Ndiaye, J. P. (1999). Recapitalization of phosphate reserves of Senegal soils: interest and limits. ISRA (Institut sénégalais de recherches agricoles)

Nkonya, E., Schroeder, T., & Norman, D. W. (1997). Factors affecting adoption of improved maize seed & fertilizer in Northern Tanzania. *Journal of Agricultural Economics, 48*, 1–12.

Nkonya, E., Pender, J., & Kato, E. (2008). Who knows who cares? Determinants of enactment, awareness and compliance with community natural resource management regulations in Uganda. *Environment and Development Economics, 13*(1), 79–109.

Nkonya, E., Phillip, D., Mogues, T., Pender, J., & Kato, E. (2010). *From the Ground up: Impact of a pro-poor community driven development project in Nigeria* (p. 93). Washington DC: International Food Policy Research Institute Research Monograph.

Nkonya, E., Anderson, W., Kato, E., Koo, J., Mirzabaev, A., von Braun, J., & Meyer, S. (2015). Global cost of land degradation. Springer (chapter 6).

Peterman, A., Behrman, J. A., & Quisumbing, A. R. (2014). A review of empirical evidence on gender differences in nonland agricultural inputs, technology, and services in developing countries. In A. R. Quisumbing, R. Meinzen-Dick, T.L. Raney, A. Croppenstedt, J.A. Behrman & A. Peterman (Eds.), *Gender in Agriculture* (pp. 145–186). Netherlands: Springer.

Post, J., & Snel, M. (2003). The impact of decentralised forest management on charcoal production practices in Eastern Senegal. *Geoforum, 34*(1), 85–98.

Resnick, D. (2013). The political economy of food price policy in Senegal. Policy Brief No. 7. UNU-WIDER. Helsinki.

Savadogo, P., Sawadogo, L., & Tiveau, D. (2007). Effects of grazing intensity and prescribed fire on soil physical and hydrological properties and pasture yield in the savanna woodlands of Burkina Faso agriculture. *Ecosystems and Environment, 118*(1–4), 80–92.

Stads, G. J., & Sène, L. (2011). Private-sector agricultural research and innovation in Senegal. Recent Policy, Investment, and Capacity Trends. http://www.ifpri.org/sites/default/files/publications/senegal-ps-note-full.pdf. Accessed 3 Aug 2014.

Vanlauwe, B., & Giller, K. E. (2006). Popular myths around soil fertility management in sub-Saharan Africa. *Agriculture, Ecosystems & Environment, 116*, 34–46.

Vlek, P., Rodríguez-Kuhl, G., & Sommer, R. (2004). Energy use and CO_2 production in tropical agriculture and means and strategies for reduction or mitigation. *Environment, Development and Sustainability, 6*, 213–233.

World Bank. (2008). Senegal—country environmental analysis. Report No. 48804-SN. Sustainable Development Department Africa Region. Washington.

World Bank. (2012). Agriculture and rural development data. http://data.worldbank.org/topic/agriculture-and-rural-development. Accessed 13 Jan 2015.

World Bank. (2013). Senegal country at a glance. Available at http://www.worldbank.org/en/country/senegal. Accessed 13 Jan 2015.

Chapter 20
Economics of Land Degradation and Improvement in Tanzania and Malawi

Oliver K. Kirui

Abstract Land degradation is a serious impediment to improving rural livelihoods in Tanzania and Malawi. This paper identifies major land degradation patterns and causes, and analyzes the determinants of soil erosion and sustainable land management (SLM) in these two countries. The results show that land degradation hotspots cover about 51 and 41 % of the terrestrial areas in Tanzania and Malawi, respectively. The analysis of nationally representative household surveys shows that the key drivers of SLM in these countries are biophysical, demographic, regional and socio-economic determinants. Secure land tenure, access to markets and extension services are major factors incentivizing SLM adoption. The implications of this study are that policies and strategies that facilitate secure land tenure and access to SLM information are likely to stimulate investments in SLM. Local institutions providing credit services, inputs such as seed and fertilizers, and extension services must be included in the development policies. Following a Total Economic Value approach, we find that the annual cost of land degradation due to land use and land cover change during the 2001–2009 period is about $244 million in Malawi and $2.3 billion in Tanzania (expressed in constant 2007 USD). These represent about 6.8 and 13.7 % of GDP in Malawi and Tanzania, respectively. Use of land degrading practices in croplands (maize, rice and wheat) resulted in losses amounting to $5.7 million in Malawi and $1.8 million in Tanzania. Consequently, we conclude that the costs of action against land degradation are lower than the costs of inaction by about 4.3 times in Malawi and 3.8 times in Tanzania over the 30 year horizon. This implies that a dollar spent to restore/rehabilitate degraded lands returns about 4.3 dollars in Malawi and 3.8 dollars in Tanzania, respectively. Some of the actions taken by communities to address the loss of ecosystem services or enhance or maintain ecosystem services improvement include afforestation programs, enacting of bylaws to protect existing forests, area closures and controlled grazing, community sanctions for overgrazing, and integrated soil fertility management in croplands.

O.K. Kirui (✉)
Center for Development Research (ZEF), University of Bonn,
Walter-Flex Street 3, 53113 Bonn, Germany
e-mail: okirui@uni-bonn.de; oliverkk@yahoo.com

E. Nkonya et al. (eds.), *Economics of Land Degradation and Improvement – A Global Assessment for Sustainable Development*,
DOI 10.1007/978-3-319-19168-3_20

Keywords Economics of land degradation · Causes of land degradation · Sustainable land management · Cost of land degradation · Tanzania · Malawi

Introduction

Land degradation is a major problem in Tanzania and Malawi. A recent assessment shows that 'land degradation hotspots' cover about 51 and 41 % of land area in Tanzania and Malawi, respectively (Le et al. 2014; Fig. 20.1). Figure 20.1 shows a depiction of land degradation and improvement 'hotspots' in Africa.[1] A country-specific hotspot map for Malawi and Tanzania is also presented alongside the African map. In Tanzania, land degradation has been ranked as the top environmental problem for more than 60 years (Assey et al. 2007). Soil erosion is reportedly affecting about 61 % of the entire land area in this country (ibid). Chemical land degradation, including soil pollution and salinization/alkalinisation, has led to 15 % loss in the arable land in Malawi in the last decade alone (Chabala et al. 2012).

Investments in sustainable land management (SLM) are an economically sensible way to address land degradation (MEA 2005; Akhtar-Schuster et al. 2011; FAO 2011; ELD Initiative 2013). SLM, also referred to as 'ecosystem approach', ensures long-term conservation of the productive capacity of lands and the sustainable use of natural ecosystems. However, available estimates show that the adoption of SLM practices in sub-Saharan Africa, including Tanzania and Malawi, is low—just on about 3 % of total cropland (WB 2010). Several factors limit the adoption of SLM in the region, including: lack of local-level capacities, knowledge gaps on specific land degradation and SLM issues, poor monitoring and evaluation of land degradation and its accompanying impacts, inappropriate incentive structure (such as, inappropriate land tenure and user rights), market and infrastructure constraints (such as, insecure prices of agricultural products, increasing input costs, inaccessible markets), and policy and institutional bottlenecks (such as, difficulty and costly enforcement of existing laws that favor SLM) (Thompson et al. 2009; Chasek et al. 2011; Akhtar-Schuster et al. 2011; Reed et al. 2011; ELD Initiative 2013).

Despite on-going land degradation and the urgent need for action to prevent and reverse land degradation, the problem has yet to be appropriately addressed, especially in the developing countries, including in Tanzania and Malawi. Adequately strong policy action for SLM is missing, and a coherent and evidence-based policy framework addressing it is still lacking (Nkonya et al. 2013). Identifying drivers of land degradation and the determinants of SLM adoption is a step towards addressing them (von Braun et al. 2012).

The assessment of relevant drivers of land degradation by robust techniques at farm level is still lacking in Tanzania and Malawi. There is a need for evidence-based economic evaluations, using more data and robust economic tools,

[1]See Chap. 4 of this volume for a global 'hotspots' maps.

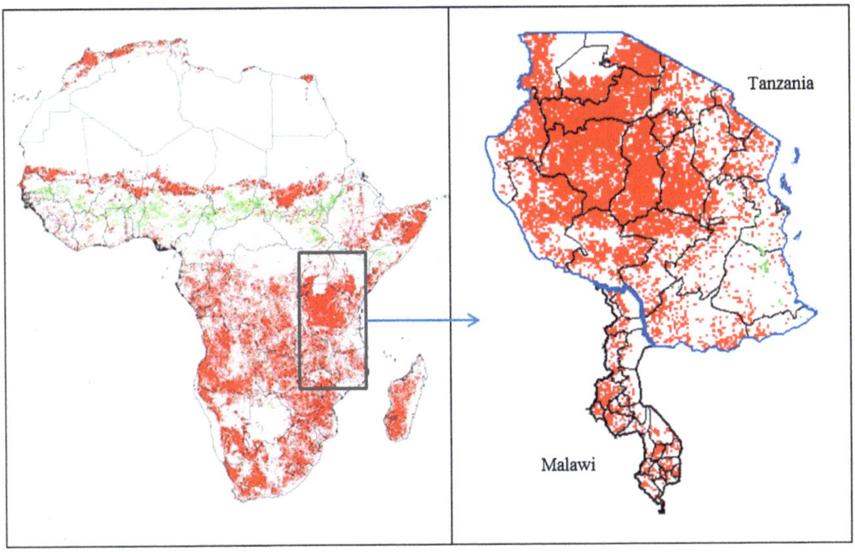

Fig. 20.1 Biomass productivity decline (*Note* The geographic spread of the area subject to human-induced degradation processes among the different climatic zones of SSA and selected countries in Eastern Africa. The red spots show the pixels with significantly declining NDVI while the green spots show the pixels with significantly improving NDVI.) in Malawi and Tanzania for 1982–2006. *Source* Adapted from Le et al. (2014)

to identify the determinants of adoption as well as economic returns from SLM. The objectives of this paper are thus two-fold; (i) to assess the determinants of SLM adoption in Malawi and Tanzania, and (ii) to examine the costs and benefits of action versus of inaction against land degradation in Malawi and Tanzania.

The rest of this paper is organized as follows: see section "Relevant Literature" provides a brief review of key studies on the extent, drivers of land degradation and determinants of SLM adoption in Tanzania and Malawi; see section "Land Management Policy Frameworks in Malawi and Tanzania" presents the policy frameworks in Malawi and Tanzania; see section "Conceptual Framework and Empirical Strategy" presents the study methods and the empirical strategy; see section "Data, Sampling Procedure and Variables for Estimations" outlines the data, study area and sampling procedure; see section "Results and Discussions" discusses the findings of the study; see section "Conclusions and Policy Implications" concludes.

Relevant Literature

Drivers of land degradation can be grouped into two categories, namely; proximate and underlying causes (Lambin and Geist 2006; Lal and Stewart 2010; Belay et al. 2014; Pingali et al. 2014). Proximate causes are those that have a direct effect on the terrestrial ecosystem. These include biophysical (natural) conditions related to climatic conditions and extreme weather events such as droughts and coastal surges.

Key proximate drivers include; climatic conditions, topography, unsuitable land uses and inappropriate land management practices (such as slash and burn agriculture, timber and charcoal extraction, deforestation, overgrazing) and uncontrolled fires. The dry aid and semi-arid arid lands are prone to fires which may lead to serious soil erosion (Voortman et al. 2000; D'Odorico et al. 2013). The erratic rainfall in these areas may also be thought to induce salinization of the soil (Safriel and Adeel 2005; Wale and Dejenie 2013). Similarly, practicing unsustainable agriculture such as land clearing, overstocking of herds, charcoal and wood extraction, cultivation on steep slopes, bush burning, pollution of land and water sources, and soil nutrient mining (Eswaran et al. 2001; Lal 1995; Dregne 2002). Most deforestation exercises are associated with the continued demand for agricultural land, fuel-wood, charcoal, construction materials, large-scale and resettlement of people in forested areas. This often happens at the backdrop of ineffective institutional mechanisms to preserve forests. Grazing pressure and reduction of the tree cover continue to diminish rangelands productivity (Hein and de Ridder 2006; Waters et al. 2013).

Important underlying drivers of land degradation include land tenure, poverty, population density and weak policy and regulatory environment in the agricultural and environmental sectors (Table 20.1). Insecure land tenure may act as a disincentive to investment in sustainable agricultural practices and Technologies (Kabubo-Mariara 2007). Similarly, a growing population without proper land management will exhaust the capacity of land to provide ecosystem services (Tiffen et al. 1994). It is also argued that population pressure leads to expansion of agriculture into fragile areas and reduction of fallow periods in the cultivated plots.

Table 20.1 Empirical review of proximate and underlying causes of land degradation

Country	Proximate drivers	Underlying drivers	References
Malawi	Charcoal and wood fuel (for domestic and commercial), timber production; unsustainable agric. Methods (slash and burn with shorter rotations), mining	Development processes in energy, forestry, agriculture and water sectors; poverty; lack of alternative energy sources; weak policy environment, lack of planning; insecure land tenure	Pender et al. (2004a), Lambin and Meyfroidt (2010), Rademaekers et al. (2010), Kiage (2013), Thierfelder et al. (2013), Harris et al. (2014)
Tanzania	Topography, climate change, settlement and agricultural expansion, overgrazing, fuelwood and timber extraction, uncontrolled fires	Market and institutional failures, rapid population growth, rural poverty, insecure tenure, and absence of land use planning, development of infrastructure	Pender et al. (2004b), de Fries et al. (2010), Fisher et al. (2010), Wasige et al. (2013), Ligonja and Shrestha (2013), Heckmann (2014)

Source Kirui and Mirzabaev (2014)

However, this is not always the case. Population pressure has been found to increase agricultural intensification and higher land productivity as well as technological and institutional innovation that reduce natural resource degradation (Tiffen et al. 1994; Nkonya et al. 2008).

Empirical review of literature on adoption of production–related technologies dates back to Feder et al. (1985) which summarizes that the adoption of new technology may be constrained by many factors such as lack of credit, inadequate and unstable supply of complementary inputs, uncertainty and risks. A comprehensive review of literature shows several factors determining investment in sustainable land management practices. These include; household and farm characteristics, technology attributes, perception of land degradation problem, profitability of the technology/practice, institutional factors, such as, land tenure, access to credit, information and markets and risks and uncertainty (Ervin and Ervin 1982; Norris and Batie 1987; Pagiola 1996; Shiferaw and Holden 1998; Kazianga and Masters 2002; Shively 2001; Bamire et al. 2002; Barrett et al. 2001; Gebremedhin and Swinton 2003; Habron 2004; Kim et al. 2005; Park and Lohr 2005; Pender et al. 2006; Gillespie et al. 2007; Prokopy et al. 2008).

Detailed empirical studies in developing countries include that of Pagiola (1996) in Kenya, Nakhumwa and Hassan (2012) in Malawi, Shiferaw and Holden (1998), Gebremedhin and Swinton (2003) and Bekele and Drake (2003) in Ethiopia. All these studies highlighted the direction as well as the magnitude of factors hypothesized to condition the adoption of SLM.

In summary, these factors are largely area specific and their importance is varied between and within agro-ecological zones and across countries. Thus, caution should be exercised in attempting to generalize such individual constraints across regions and countries.

Important contributions have been made by these previous studies on identifying the determinants of adoption of SLM practices, however, a number of limitations are evident. Despite the fact that a long list of explanatory variables is used, most of the statistical estimations used by these studies have lower explanatory power (Ghadim and Pannell 1999). The results from different studies are often contradictory regarding any given variable (ibid).

Lindner (1987) and Ghadim et al. (2005) point out that the inconsistency results in most empirical studies could be explained by four shortcomings, namely; poorly specified models, inability to account for the dynamic adoption learning process, omitted variable biases, and poorly related hypotheses to the conceptual frameworks.

Land Management Policy Frameworks in Malawi and Tanzania

To counter the challenges of low input use, rising food and fertilizer prices, fertilizer subsidies have become a common policy response to increase fertilizer use and improve food production. Use of inorganic fertilizer is considered one of the agricultural technologies that have the potential to increase productivity of small-scale agriculture, increase incomes, expand assets base of the poor farmers and break the poverty cycle. In recent years Malawi and Tanzania have used subsidies in order to increase fertilizer application at farm level. Subsequently, there has been a substantial increase in public investment reported in the subsidies in these countries. Malawi, for instance, used about 72 % of the agricultural budget in 2008/09 period on the subsidies (Dorward and Chirwa 2009) while Tanzania spent about 50 % of its agricultural budget on the subsidy program (URT 2008; cited from Marenya et al. 2012).

At the end of the 1990s, there was widespread perception in Malawi that reduction in fertilizer subsidies was leading to falling in the production of maize and thus to a food and political crisis (Chinsinga 2008). In response the government of Malawi implemented three programs of fertilizer subsidies: the Starter Pack (SP), the Targeted Input Program (TIP) (later changed to the Extended Targeted Input program-ETIP), and the Agricultural Input Subsidy Program (AISP). The AISP program was launched in 1998 and was mainly supported by the UK Department for International Development (DFID) (Chinsinga 2008). The program targeted an estimated 2.86 million rural farming households and consisted of delivering free inputs to these farmers. The package consisted of 15 kg of fertilizer, 2 kg of hybrid maize seed, and 1 kg legume seed (Morris et al. 2007; Chinsinga 2008; Levy and Barahona 2002).

The second program implemented was the Targeted Input Program (TIP). TIP was introduced during the 2000–2001 growing season as a gradual exit strategy decided to scale down the SP and for purposes of sustainability with a target of 1.5 million farmers (Chinsinga 2008). Moreover, it also delivered a smaller quantity of fertilizer (10 kg) per beneficiary, replaced hybrid maize seeds with OPV maize seeds (which were considered more sustainable), and targeted the poorest households in the community (Levy and Barahona 2002). Later TIP was phased out and reconfigured as the Extended Targeted Input program (ETIP) with increased number of targeted beneficiaries of 2.8 million farmers and increased the provision of fertilizer to 26 kg and seeds to 5 kg per beneficiary. This third and much larger fertilizer subsidy program was the Agricultural Input Subsidy Program (AISP) and started in 2005. The AISP provided about 50 % of farm households (around 1.5 million of households) with 100 kg fertilizer vouchers and smaller quantities of maize seed. Since 2005, the program has been repeated on a similar scale, enabling beneficiaries to purchase the same amounts of fertilizer (Denning et al. 2009).

Following the successes of the input subsidy program in Malawi in terms of higher crop productivity, other countries, namely Tanzania, have also started a voucher-based fertilizer subsidies program named National Agricultural Input Voucher System (NAIVS) (URT 2005). With NAIVS the Tanzanian government used to subsidize ensured delivery of fertilizer to remote areas. The program was redesigned in 2008 into a voucher-based subsidy. This subsidy involved delivery of 100 kg of fertilizer, seeds, seedlings, and agrochemicals. These were exchangeable at any private agro-input dealer across the country. In this respect, the Tanzania voucher program is considered more successful in enhancing and facilitating the development of a private distribution network (Zorya 2009; Minot and Benson 2009). NAIVS the subsidy program is progressive type of transfer that targets the smallholder farmers. It covers a large fraction of agricultural households—2.5 million in 2011. The program design includes rationing with a set a ceiling of subsidized volumes per beneficiary of 1 acre and is geared towards staple crops, primarily maize. The subsidy program focus is on national and also household food security and explicitly includes poverty reduction in its objectives (Zorya 2009).

The other alternative that can be considered as an alternative to straight subsidies is the payments for environmental services (PES) model. The State of Food and Agriculture 2007 published by FAO (2007) highlighted the potential of PES in agriculture to contribute to the provision of ecosystem services that are not usually tradeable in the market. Future studies must explore the contributions of the PES options to soil fertility management (Marenya et al. 2012).

Conceptual Framework and Empirical Strategy

The conceptual framework used in this study broadly follows the ELD framework presented in Nkonya et al. (2013). 'The causes of land degradation are divided into two broad categories; proximate and underlying causes, which interact with each other to result in different levels of land degradation. The level of land degradation determines its outcomes or effects—whether on-site or off-site, on the provision of ecosystem services and the benefits humans derive from those services. Actors (including land users, policy makers etc.) can then take action to control the causes of land degradation, its level, or its effects'. 'There also exists institutional arrangements that determine whether actors choose to act against land degradation and whether the level or type of action undertaken will effectively reduce or halt land degradation' (Nkonya et al. 2013). For a comprehensive discussion on the conceptual framework, refer to Chap. 2 of this volume.

Empirical Strategy

Determinants of SLM Adoption: Logit Regression Model

Land degradation occurs as a result of lack of use of SLM. The determinants inhibiting the adoption of SLM practices are also possible to promote land degradation. The assessment of the determinants of SLM has the same implications as the assessment of the determinants of land degradation. The adoption of SLM technologies/practices in this study refers to use of one or more SLM technologies in a given plot. The adoption was of SLM technology/practice in a farm plot was measured as a binary dummy variable (1 = adopted SLM in a farm plot, 0 = otherwise). The two appropriate methods to estimate such binary dummy dependent variable regression models are the logit and the probit regression models. Here, we used the logit model.

The reduced form of the logit model applied to nationally representative agricultural household survey data from Tanzania and Malawi is presented as:

$$\mathrm{A} = \beta_0 + \beta_1 x_1 + \beta_2 x_2 + \beta_3 x_3 + \beta_4 x_4 + \beta_5 z_i + \varepsilon_i \tag{20.1}$$

where, A = Adoption of SLM technologies; x_1 = a vector of biophysical factors (climate conditions, agro-ecological zones); x_2 = a vector of demographic characteristics factors (age, gender, and level of education of the household head); x_3 = a vector of farm-level variables (access to extension, market access, distance to market, distance to market); x_4 = vector of socio-economic and institutional characteristics (access to extension, market access, land tenure, land tenure); z_i = vector of country fixed effects; and ε_i is the error term.

Adoption studies using dichotomous adoption decisions models have inherent weakness (Dimara and Skuras 2003). The single stage decision making process characterized by a dichotomous adoption decision models is a direct consequence of the full information assumption entrenched in the definition of adoption, that is, individual adoption is defined as 'the degree of use of a technology in the long run equilibrium when the farmer has full information about the new technology and its potential' (Dimara and Skuras 2003). This assumption of full information is usually violated and hence use of logit or probit models in modeling adoption decision may lead to model misspecification. Robust checks tare carried out to check these misspecifications. Further, assessment beyond adoption to intensity (number) of SLM adoption can also counter such inherent weakness. We explore this option in our study.

Determinants of Number of SLM Technologies Adopted: Poisson Regression Model

The number of SLM technologies and the corresponding proportion of plots in which these technologies were applied are as presented in Table 20.8. The number of SLM technologies is thus a count variable (ranging from 0 to 6 in our case). Thus the assessment of the determinants number of SLM technologies adopted requires models that accounts for count variables. Poisson regression model (PRM) is typically the initial step for most count data analyses (Areal et al. 2008). PRM is preferred because it takes considers the non-negative and binary nature of the data (Winkelmann and Zimmermann 1995). The assumption of equality of the variance and conditional mean in PRM also accounts for the inherent heteroscedasticity and skewed distribution of nonnegative data (ibid). PRM is further preferred because the log-linear model allows for treatment of zeros (ibid). The reduced form of the Poisson regression is presented as follows:

$$A = \beta_0 + \beta_1 x_1 + \beta_2 x_2 + \beta_3 x_3 + \beta_4 x_4 + \beta_5 z_i + \varepsilon_i \quad (20.2)$$

where, A = Number of SLM technologies adopted; and the vector of explanatory variables xi are similar to those used in Eq. 20.1; (i.e. x1 = a vector of biophysical factors (climate conditions, agro-ecological zones); x2 = a vector of demographic characteristics factors (level of education, age, gender of the household head); x3 = a vector of farm-level variables (access to extension, market access, distance to market, distance to market); x4 = vector of socio-economic and institutional characteristics (access to extension, market access, land tenure, land tenure); zi = vector of country fixed effects; and ε_i is the error term).

Some of the limitations of PRM in empirical work relates to the restrictions imposed by the model on the conditional mean and the variance of the dependent variable. This violation leads to under-dispersion or over-dispersion. Overdispersion refers to excess variation when the systematic structure of the model is correct (Berk 2007). Overdispersion means that to variance of the coefficient estimates are larger than anticipated mean—which results in inefficient, potentially biased parameter estimates and spuriously small standard errors (Xiang and Lee 2005). Under dispersion on the other hand refers to a situation in which the variance of the dependent is less than its conditional mean. In presence of under- or over-dispersion, though still consistent, the estimates of the PRM are inefficient and biased and may lead to misleading inference (Famoye et al. 2005; Greene 2012). Our tests showed no evidence of under- or over-dispersion. Moreover, the conditional mean of the distribution of SLM technologies was similar to the conditional variance. Thus PRM was appropriately applied.

Cost of Action Verses Inaction Against Degradation

This study utilizes the Total Economic Value (TEV) approach–that captures the comprehensive definition of land degradation to estimate the costs of land degradation. TEV is broadly sub-divided into two categories; use and non-use values. The use value comprises of direct and indirect use. The direct use includes marketed outputs involving priced consumption (such as crop production, fisheries, tourism) as well as un-priced benefits (such as local culture and recreation value). The indirect use value consists of un-priced ecosystem functions such as water purification, carbon sequestration among others. The non-use value is divided into three categories namely; bequest, altruistic and existence values. All these three benefits are un-priced. In between these two major categories, there is the option value, which includes both marketable outputs and ecosystem services for future direct or indirect use. TEV analytical approach, thus, assigns value to both tradable and non-tradable ecosystem services.

Refer to Chaps. 2 and 6 of this volume for a comprehensive discussion on the empirical strategy to estimate the costs of land degradation (due to LUCC and due to use of land degrading practices in croplands and rangelands) and also the empirical strategy to estimate the costs of taking action against land degradation.

Data, Sampling Procedure and Variables for Estimations

Data and Sampling Procedure

The data used for this study is based on household surveys in two countries; Malawi and Tanzania conducted over time periods. The surveys were supported by the Living Standards Measurement Study—Integrated Surveys on Agriculture (LSMS-ISA) project undertaken by the Development Research Group at the World Bank.[2] The surveys under the LSMS-ISA project are modeled on the multi-topic integrated household survey design of the LSMS; household, agriculture, and community questionnaires, are each an integral part of every survey. We describe the sampling procedure in each of the two countries below.

Tanzania

The 2010–2011 Tanzania National Panel Survey data was collected during a twelve-month period from September 2010 to September 2011 by the Tanzania National Bureau of Statistics (NBS). In order to produce nationally representative statistics, the TNPS is based on a stratified multi-stage cluster sample design. The sampling frame used the National Master Sample Frame (2002 Population and Housing Census) which is a list of all populated enumeration areas in the country. 'In the first stage stratification was done along two dimensions; (i) eight administrative zones (seven on Mainland Tanzania plus Zanzibar as an eighth zone), and (ii) rural versus urban clusters within each administrative zone. The combination of these two dimensions yields 16 strata. Within each stratum, clusters were then randomly selected as the primary sampling units, with the probability of selection proportional to their population size'. In rural areas a cluster was defined as an entire village while in urban areas a cluster was defined as a census enumeration area (2002 Population and Housing Census). In the last stage, 8 households were randomly chosen in each cluster. Overall, 409 clusters and 3924 households (6038 farm plots) were selected.

---

[2]Funded by the Bill and Melinda Gates Foundation.

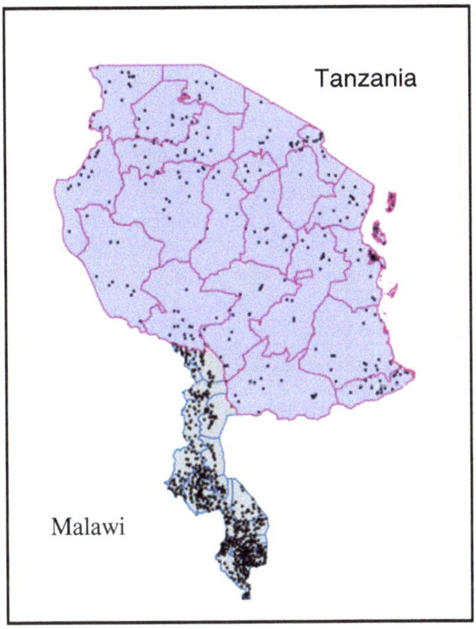

Fig. 20.2 Distribution of sampled households. *Source* Authors

Malawi

The Malawi 2010–2011 Integrated Household Survey (IHS) is a national-wide survey collected during the period March 2010–March 2011 by the National Statistics Office (NSO). The sampling frame for the IHS is based on the listing information from the 2008 Malawi Population and Housing Census. The IHS followed a stratified two-stage sample design. The first stage involved selection of the primary sampling units following proportionate to size sampling procedure. These include the census enumerations areas (EAs) defined for the 2008 Malawi Population and Housing Census. An enumerations area was the smallest operational area established for the census with well-defined boundaries and with an average of about 235 households. A total of 768 EAs (average of 24 EAs in each of the 31 districts) were selected across the country. In the second stage, 16 households were randomly selected for interviews in each EA. In total 12,271 households (18,329 farm plots) were interviewed. The distribution of this representative data is also depicted in Fig. 20.2.

Variables Used in the Econometric Estimations

Dependent Variables

In the empirical estimation of the determinants of adoption of SLM practices, the dependent variable is the choice of SLM option(s) from the set of SLM practices

Table 20.2 Dependent variables

Variable	Malawi (n = 18,162)	Tanzania (n = 5614)	Total (n = 239,776)
Adoption of SLM practices (% of plots)			
Inorganic fertilizers use	63.6	12.4	46.7
Modern seeds varieties	58.0	24.4	36.0
Manure application	10.6	8.6	15.3
Intercropping	35.1	32.5	34.8
Crop rotation	10.6	14.8	23.5
Soil erosion control	41.0	8.6	22.4
Used at least one SLM practice	89.4	68.5	84.5

Source Authors' compilation

applied in the farm plots as enumerated by the respondents. The list of the specific SLM practices is also presented in Table 20.2. They include six practices namely; soil and water conservation measures (especially those aimed at soil erosion control), manure application, modern crop seeds, inorganic fertilizers application, crop rotation (cereal-legume), and intercropping (cereal-legume).

Soil-water conservation practices include soil erosion conservation measures such as terraces, grass strips and gabions. They also include tillage practices that entail minimized soil disturbance (reduced tillage, zero tillage) and crop residue retention for better improved soil fertility and soil aeration (Delgado et al. 2011; Triboi and Triboi-Blondel 2014; Teklewold et al. 2013). Crop rotation and intercropping systems are considered as temporal diversifications aimed at maintaining farm productivity (Deressa et al. 2009; Kassie et al. 2013; Lin and Chen 2014). The application of manure (farm yard and/or animal manure) on the farm plots aids the long-term maintenance of soil fertility and supply of nutrients in the soil (Diacono and Montemurro 2010; Shakeel et al. 2014). The use of modern seed varieties and inorganic fertilizers (NPK) has the potential to spur productivity and hence improving the household food security situation and income (Asfaw et al. 2012; Folberth et al. 2013).

We considered six SLM practices. In organic fertilizers were applied in about 47 % of the plots while improved seed varieties were used in about 36 % of the plots. Manure use is low—average of 15 % of the plots. Crop rotation and cereal-legume intercropping was practiced in about 24 and 35 % of the plots respectively. Soil erosion control measure comprising of soil bunds, stone bunds terraces, plant barriers and check dams were used in about 22 % of the plots. The variations in application of these practices are presented in Table 20.2.

Independent Variables

The choice of relevant explanatory variables is based on economic theory, empirical review of previous literature, and data availability. Thus, we have utilized a total of 29 variables for the empirical estimations in this chapter. These can be grouped as biophysical, demographic, plot, and socio-economic variables. Brief descriptions alongside the direction of the hypothesized effects of these variables on land degradation and on SLM adoption are presented in Table 20.3 and discussed below.

The relevant biophysical variables included are temperature, rainfall, soil properties (rooting condition) and agro-ecological zonal classification. Adequate and timely rainfall, optimal temperature and favorable soil conditions are some of

Table 20.3 Definitions of hypothesized explanatory variables

Variable	Definition	Hypothesized effect on SLM adoption
Temperature	Annual mean temperature (°C)	+/−
Rainfall	Annual mean rainfall (mm)	+/−
Land cover	Land cover type	+/−
Elevation	The plot altitude	+/−
Soils quality	Soil rooting conditions	+/−
Soil type	The type of soil in the plot	
aez	Agro-ecological zone	+/−
Slope	Slope elevation (SRTM)	+/−
Age	Age of household head (years)	+/−
Gender	Gender of household head	+
Education	Years of formal education of HH head	+
Family size	Size of household (adult equivalent)	+/−
Plot slope	Slope of the plot (SRTM)	+
Tenure	Land tenure status of the plot	+
Soil type	Soil type of the plot	+/−
Extension	Access to agricultural extension	+/−
Home distance	Distance to plot from the farmer's home	−
Market distance	Distance from plot from the market	−
Assets value	Value of household assets	+
Plot size	Size of the plot	+
Credit access	Access to credit accessed	+
Credit amount	Amount of credit accessed	+
Group membership	Membership in cooperatives/SACCOs	+
Irrigation	Access to irrigation water	+

Source Authors' compilation

the biophysical factors needed for agricultural production to thrive. Favorable rainfall, temperature and soil conditions are hypothesized to positively influence adoption of improved seed varieties and use of fertilizers (Belay and Bewket 2013; Kassie et al. 2013). On the contrary, inadequate rainfall, increasing temperatures are thus hypothesized to positively influence the adoption of such SLM practices as conservation tillage, use of manure and intercropping (Yu et al. 2008). High rainfall is hypothesized to negatively influence adoption of such SLM as conservation tillage practices because it may encourage weed growth and also cause water logging (Jansen et al. 2006).

Our analyses also include such standard household level variables as age, gender, and education level of the household head and household size (adult equivalent) and household size. Household demographic characteristics have been found to affect the adoption of SLM practices (Pender and Gebremedhin 2008; Bluffstone and Köhlin 2011; Belay and Bewket 2013; Kassie et al. 2013; Genius et al. 2014). We hypothesize that higher level of education of the household decision maker/head is associated with adoption of SLM practices and technologies. Previous studies show a positive relationship between the education level of the household decision maker and the adoption of improved technologies and land management (Maddison 2006; Marenya and Barrett 2007; Kassie et al. 2011; Arslan et al. 2013; Teklewold et al. 2013). Households with more education may have greater access to productivity enhancing inputs as a result of access to non-farm income (Kassie et al. 2011). Such households may also be more aware of the benefits of SLM strategies due to their ability to search, decode and apply new information and knowledge pertaining SLM (Kassie et al. 2011; Kirui and Njiraini 2013).

The hypothesized effect of age on SLM adoption is thus indeterminate. Gender of the household decision maker plays a critical role in SLM adoption. Existing cultural and social setups that dictate access to and control over farm resources (especially land) and other external inputs (fertilizer and seeds) are deemed to discriminate against women (de Groote and Coulibaly 1998; Gebreselassie et al. 2013).We thus hypothesize that male-headed households are more likely to invest in land conservation measures than their counterparts. Household size may affect SLM adoption in two ways; larger household sizes may be associated with higher labor endowment, thus, in peak times such households are not limited with labor supply requirement and are more likely to adopt SLM practices (Burger and Zaal 2012; Belay and Bewket 2013; Kassie et al. 2013). On the other hand, higher consumption pressure occasioned by increased household size may lead to diversion of labor to non-farm/off-farm activities (Yirga 2007; Pender and Gebremedhin 2008; Fentie et al. 2013).

Relevant plot level characteristics identified from previous literature that determine SLM adoption include; plot tenure, plot size, and distance from the plot to the markets. Distance from the plot to market represents the transaction costs related to output and input markets, availability of information, financial and credit organizations, and technology accessibility. Previous studies do not find a consistent relationship between market access and land degradation. Good access to markets is associated with increased opportunity costs of labor as a result of benefits accrued from alternative opportunities; thus discouraging the adoption of labor-intensive SLM practices such as conservation farming (von Braun et al. 2012). However, better market access may act as an incentive to land users to invest in SLM practices because of a reduction in transaction costs of access to inputs such as improved seed and fertilizers (Pender et al. 2006) and improved access to output markets (von Braun et al. 2012). We hypothesize that the further away the plot is from markets, the smaller the likelihood of adoption of new seed varieties and fertilizers. However, we hypothesize also that the further away the plot is from the markets the bigger the likelihood of adoption of alternative SLM practices such as conservation farming, crop rotation and manure application.

Results and Discussions

Descriptive Statistics of the Independent Variables

We discuss the results of the descriptive analysis on this section. Table 20.4 presents the results of the mean and standard deviation of all the independent variables used in the regression models. Results show substantial differences in the mean values of the biophysical, demographic, plot-level, and socioeconomic characteristics by country (Table 20.4).

Among the biophysical characteristics, notable differences are reported in such variables as mean annual rainfall, elevation and agro-ecological classification. For example, the mean annual rainfall ranged from as low as 1080 mm per annum in Malawi to as high as 1227 mm per annum in Tanzania; with the average for the two countries being about 1085 mm per annum. Regarding elevation, the average plot elevation for the region was 900 m above sea level. This was not much varied between the two countries. The mean value of plot elevation in Malawi was 890 m above sea level but as high as 931 mm above sea level in Tanzania.

Similarly considerable differences is notable across countries with regards to agro-ecological classification; a larger proportion (46 %) of Malawi is classified as warm arid/semiarid, while in Tanzania a bigger proportion (55 %) is classified as warm humid/sub-humid environment.

Regarding demographic characteristics, no considerable change was reported with regard to such variables as average age of the household head (45 years) and average family size (4.3 adults). However, there seems to be a marginal difference in the education level of the household head; as low as about 2.7 years in Malawi and as high as 4.9 years in Tanzania. The households were predominantly male-head; 78 % in Malawi, and 79 % in Tanzania.

Plot characteristics also differed by country. For instance, ownership of the plots (possession of a plot title-deed) was least in Tanzania (11 %) but higher in Malawi (79 %). On average, distance from the farm plot to the farmer's house was closer in

Table 20.4 Descriptive statistics of explanatory variables (country and regional level)

Variable	Description	Malawi (N = 18,162)		Tanzania (N = 5614)		Total (N = 37,946)	
		Mean	Std. dev	Mean	Std. dev	Mean	Std. dev
Biophysical characteristics							
temperature	Annual mean temperature (°C × 10)	216.811	19.097	225.374	26.590	218.833	21.418
rainfall	Annual mean rainfall (mm)	1079.455	253.774	1104.054	320.785	1085.263	271.289
terr_hlands	Terrain (1 = Highlands, 0 = Otherwise)	0.085	0.345	0.112	0.232	0.092	0.289
terr_plains	Terrain (1 = Plains and lowlands, 0 = Otherwise)	0.463	0.499	0.438	0.496	0.457	0.498
terr_plateaus	Terrain (1 = Plateaus, 0 = Otherwise)	0.452	0.498	0.450	0.498	0.451	0.498
elevation	Topography—meters above sea level (m)	890.515	348.654	931.311	556.612	900.148	407.799
aeztwa	AEZ (1 = warm arid/semiarid, 0 = Otherwise)	0.464	0.499	0.073	0.261	0.372	0.483
aeztwh	AEZ (1 = warm humid/sub humid, 0 = Otherwise)	0.327	0.469	0.550	0.497	0.380	0.485
aeztca	AEZ (1 = cool arid/semiarid, 0 = Otherwise)	0.123	0.329	0.029	0.168	0.101	0.301
aeztch	AEZ (1 = cool humid/sub-humid, 0 = Otherwise)	0.086	0.213	0.338	0.311	0.148	0.355
Demographic characteristics							
age	Age of household head (years)	43.295	15.928	49.298	15.525	44.712	16.037
age^2	Squared age of household head (years × years)	2128.095	1596.439	2671.268	1668.311	2176.209	1178.32
sex	Sex of household head (1 = Male, 0 = Otherwise)	0.780	0.414	0.788	0.409	0.782	0.413
education	Years of formal education of head (years)	2.704	4.865	4.995	3.921	3.245	4.760
$education^2$	Squared value of years of formal education	30.980	61.053	40.315	49.963	34.992	40.488
familysize	Size of household (adult equivalent)	4.166	1.876	4.863	2.779	4.331	2.145
Plot characteristics							
plotslope	Slope of the plot (SRTM)	1.459	0.556	1.552	0.566	1.481	0.560
tittledeed	Possess plot title deed (1 = Yes, 0 = Otherwise)	0.786	0.410	0.105	0.306	0.625	0.484
sandy	Soil type (Sandy soils = Yes, 0 = Otherwise)	0.189	0.392	0.161	0.368	0.183	0.386

(continued)

Table 20.4 (continued)

Variable	Description	Malawi (N = 18,162)		Tanzania (N = 5614)		Total (N = 37,946)	
		Mean	Std. dev	Mean	Std. dev	Mean	Std. dev
loam	Soil type (Loam soils = Yes, 0 = Otherwise)	0.625	0.484	0.508	0.500	0.598	0.490
clay	Soil type (Clay soils = Yes, 0 = Otherwise)	0.184	0.387	0.145	0.352	0.174	0.379
soilquality	Soil quality (1 = Poor, 2 = Fair, 3 = Good)	0.890	0.313	0.768	0.422	0.861	0.345
plot_dist	Distance from plot to farmer's home (km)	0.766	1.174	5.442	23.723	1.870	11.741
market_dist	Distance from plot from the market (km)	9.761	10.403	2.363	4.348	8.014	9.849
Socio-economic characteristics							
plotsize	Size of the plot (acres)	1.025	0.929	2.536	6.335	1.382	3.248
extension	Access to extension services (1 = Yes, 0 = No)	0.032	0.176	0.158	0.365	0.062	0.241
group	Membership in farmer groups (1 = Yes, 0 = No)	0.118	0.323	0.213	0.410	0.141	0.348
credit_access	Access to credit (1 = Yes, 0 = Otherwise)	0.143	0.350	0.086	0.280	0.129	0.336
credit_amount[a]	Amount of credit accessed (USD)	13.699	148.374	28.605	213.204	17.219	166.097
assets[a]	Value of household assets (USD)	172.35	793.105	114.346	370.743	158.654	716.619

[a]We use the natural log form for these variables in our econometric analysis in the next sections
[2] Describes mean values
Source Authors' compilation

Malawi (0.8 km) as compared to Tanzania (5.4 km). Similarly, the distance to the market from the plots varied substantially between the two countries; from 2.4 km in Tanzania to about 10 km in Malawi. Loam soils were predominant soil type in both Malawi (63 % of plots) and Tanzania (50 % of the plots).

The average size of the plots was 1.4 acres. This ranged from an average of 1.0 acre in Malawi to 2.5 acres in Tanzania. About 18 % of the sampled farmers were involved in social capital formation as shown by participation in collective action groups (farmer groups and cooperatives). The average proportion of sampled farmers with access to credit financial services was 13 % (ranging from as low as 9 % in Tanzania to 14 % in Malawi). The average household assets were about 158 USD. This varied substantially by country—171 USD in Malawi and 114 USD in Tanzania.

Adoption of SLM Technologies/Practices

We examine the proportion of plots that adopted at least one SLM practice in Fig. 20.3. Results indicate that about 85 % of plots were under at least one of the six SLM practices. This was varied across countries ranging from 68 % in Tanzania to 89 % in Malawi.

We also present the proportion of plots in which the various SLM practices/technologies were used in Fig. 20.4. Overall, inorganic fertilizers, improved seeds, manure application was used in about 51, 32 and 10 % of the farm plots. Intercropping, crop rotation and use of soil erosion control measure were applied in about 35, 14 and 33 % respectively. The adoptions of these technologies/practices were varied between the two countries. For example, the use of inorganic fertilizers was highest in Malawi (64 %) and lowest in Tanzania (12 %). Improved seeds were used in about 34 % of the plots in Malawi and in about 24 % of plots in Tanzania.

The application of manure was quite low; about 11 % in Malawi and 9 % in Tanzania. Intercropping was similar in both countries; about 35 % of plots in Malawi and about 32 % in Tanzania. Crop rotation was practiced in about 12 % of plots in Malawi and about 15 % of plots in Tanzania. The use of soil erosion control measures ranged from 9 % in Tanzania to 41 % in Malawi.

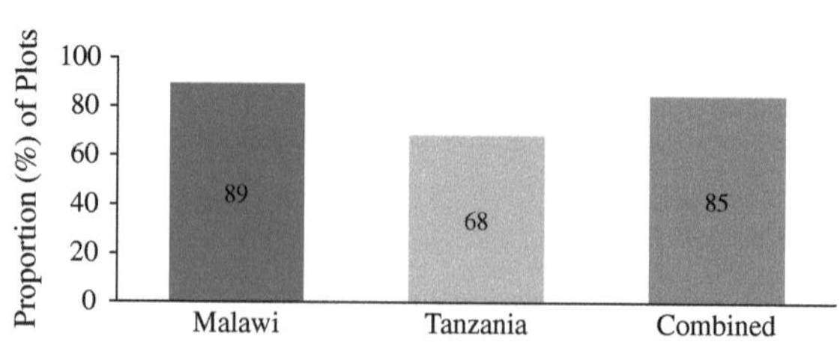

Fig. 20.3 The adoption of SLM technologies in Malawi and Tanzania. *Source* Authors' compilation

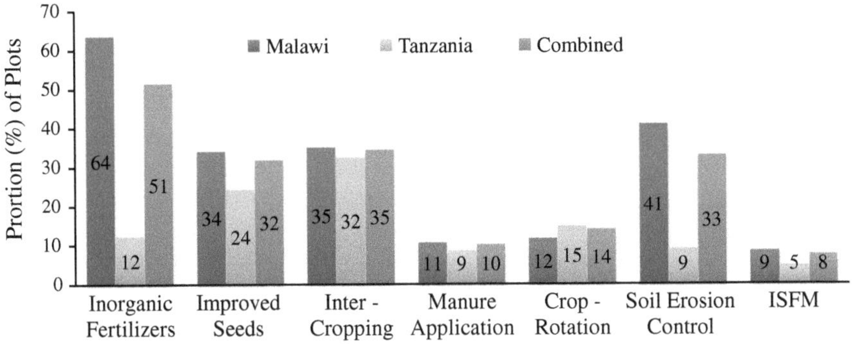

Fig. 20.4 The distribution of different SLM technologies adopted in Malawi and Tanzania. *Source* Authors' compilation

We also assessed the adoption of Integrated Soil Fertility Management (ISFM) practices (use of inorganic fertilizers and organic inputs) in the case study countries. Overall, ISFM was used in about 8 % of plots (about 9 % in Malawi and only 5 % in Tanzania). We further present the distribution of the number of SLM practices/technologies used in farm plots in Fig. 20.5. The distribution ranged from 0 to 6. On average, about 16 % of the surveyed households did not apply any SLM technologies in their farm plots in the two countries. About 33, 28 and 18 % applied 1, 2, and 3 technologies respectively. While about 5 and 1 % applied 4 and 5 technologies respectively.

At country-level, 11 and 32 % of the plots were not under any SLM technology in Malawi and Tanzania respectively. Further, our assessments show the proportion of plots with only one SLM technology was about 29 and 45 % in Malawi and Tanzania respectively. Similarly, two SLM technologies were applied in about 32

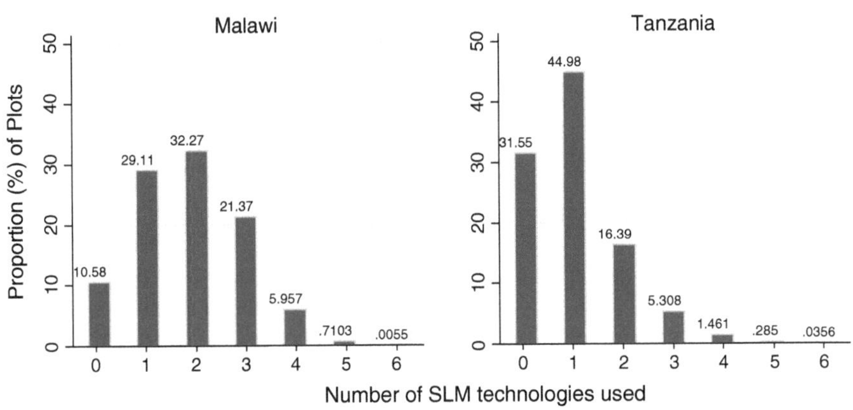

Fig. 20.5 The distribution of number SLM technologies used in Malawi and Tanzania. *Source* Authors' compilation

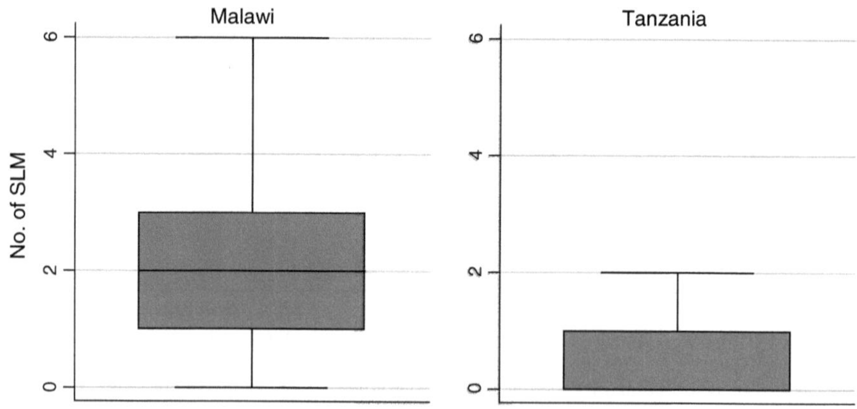

Fig. 20.6 The mean number of SLM technologies adopted by households, by country. *Source* Authors' compilation

and 16 % in Malawi and Tanzania respectively. Fewer plots applied more than two SLM technologies simultaneously in one plot respectively in the two countries. Three SLM technologies were applied in about 21 and 5 % in Malawi and Tanzania respectively while four SLM technologies were applied in about 6 and 2 % in Malawi and Tanzania respectively. Even fewer plots applied 5 SLM technologies in the region; about 0.7 and 0.3 % in Malawi and Tanzania respectively (Fig. 20.5).

Figure 20.6 presents the plot of the mean number of SLM technologies applied by country. The average number SLM technologies applied per plot were 1.7. This also varied across the countries; 1.9 in Malawi and 0.8 in Tanzania.

Determinants of SLM Adoption: Logit Model

The results of the logit regression models on the determinants of adoption of SLM technologies are presented in Table 20.5. An adopter was defined as an individual using at least one SLM technology. The assessment was carried out using plot level data. The logit models fit the data well (Table 20.5). All the F-test showed that the models were statistically significant at the 1 % level. The Wald tests of the hypothesis that all regression coefficients in are jointly equal to zero were rejected in all the equations [(All-countries (joint model): Wald Chi^2 (35) = 2452.2, *p*-value = 0.000), (Malawi: Wald Chi^2 (34) = 1742.6, *p*-value = 0.000), (Tanzania: Wald Chi^2 (34) = 239.5, *p*-value = 0.000)]. The results (marginal effects) suggest that biophysical, demographic, plot-level, and socioeconomic characteristics significantly influence SLM adoption. We discuss significant factors for each country model in the subsequent section.

Results show that several biophysical, socioeconomic, demographic, institutional and regional characteristics dictate the adoption of SLM practices

Table 20.5 Drivers of adoption of SLM practices in Eastern Africa: logit regression results

Variables	Combined (n = 23,776)		Malawi (n = 18,162)		Tanzania (n = 5614)	
	Coef.	Std. err.	Coef.	Std. err.	Coef.	Std. err.
rainfall (log)	0.481***	0.114	2.110***	0.203	−0.802***	0.155
rainfall^2 (log)	0.003	0.011	−0.084	0.762	−0.207	0.036
remperature (log)	0.107	0.556	6.643***	1.030	−0.025	0.719
temperature^2 (log)	0.000	0.103	0.000	0.120	0.000	0.004
temp#rainfall (log)	0.000	0.455	0.000	2.829	0.000	0.085
terrain_plateaus	0.112**	0.044	0.223***	0.056	0.020	0.074
terainr_hills	0.168**	0.085	0.687***	0.146	−0.049	0.131
elevation	0.001***	0.000	0.002***	0.000	0.000	0.000
warm_humid aez	0.470***	0.055	0.936***	0.085	0.346**	0.144
cool_arid aez	0.076	0.084	0.295***	0.093	0.175	0.223
cool_humid aez	0.173**	0.083	0.570***	0.153	0.584***	0.163
age	−0.008	0.007	−0.006	0.010	−0.015	0.013
age^2	0.000	0.000	0.000	0.000	0.000	0.000
sex	−0.110**	0.051	−0.111*	0.067	−0.070	0.085
education	0.133***	0.016	0.050*	0.027	0.031*	0.022
education^2	0.011	0.001	−0.004	0.002	0.004	0.002
family_size	0.046***	0.011	0.014*	0.019	0.032**	0.013
plots_lope	0.468***	0.042	0.565***	0.056	0.353***	0.068
tittledeed	0.293***	0.044	0.204***	0.062	0.345***	0.111
sandy	−0.001	0.054	0.005	0.068	−0.078	0.095
clay	−1.043***	0.113	1.998***	0.499	−0.257	0.162
soil_quality	−0.211***	0.071	−0.305***	0.089	0.179	0.132
plot_distance (log)	−0.182***	0.028	−0.077	0.065	0.068*	0.036
market_distance (log)	−0.638**	0.018	−0.770***	0.024	−0.751***	0.046
extension	0.137*	0.076	0.202***	0.299	0.140**	0.089
plot_size	0.002	0.005	0.340***	0.049	0.002*	0.004
group	0.072**	0.057	0.185**	0.084	0.098**	0.082
credit_access	0.042**	0.060	0.027*	0.074	0.075*	0.116
credit_amount (log)	0.008	0.037	0.172***	0.051	0.084	0.065
assets (log)	0.199***	0.015	0.165***	0.022	0.067***	0.023
irrigation	0.167	0.188	−0.879*	0.254	0.472*	0.270
constant	−3.876	3.373	−52.556*	5.989	5.098	4.459
Tanzania	0.144***	0.334				
Model characteristics	No of obs. = 23,776		No. of obs. = 18,162		No. of obs. = 5614	
	LR Chi^2(35) = 2452.2		LR Chi^2(34) = 1742.6		LR Chi^2(34) = 239.5	
	Prob > chi^2 = 0.000		Prob > chi^2 = 0.000		Prob > chi^2 = 0.000	
	Pseudo R^2 = 0.169		Pseudo R^2 = 0.187		Pseudo R^2 = 0.165	

***, **, and *Denotes significance at 1, 5 and 10 % respectively

[2] Describes mean values

Source Authors' compilation

(Table 20.5). Among the proximate biophysical factors that significantly determine the probability of adopting SLM technology, we include temperature, rainfall and agro-ecological zonal characteristics. Temperature positively influences the probability of using SLM technologies in Malawi. For every 1 % increase in mean annual temperature (°C * 10), we expect 6.6 %, increase in probability of SLM adoption holding other factors constant.

Rainfall on the other hand showed varied effect on the probability of adopting SLM technologies; positive in Malawi and the joint model but negative in Tanzania. For every 1 % increase in mean annual rainfall, we expect 0.48 and 2.1 % increase in probability of adopting SLM technology in the joint model and in Malawi respectively, but a decrease of 0.8 % in Tanzania holding other factors constant. The interaction between rainfall and temperature did not yield any significant effects.

Our results also suggest that terrain is critical in determining SLM adoption in the case study countries. While taking lowlands as the base terrain, results show that SLM is more likely to occur in both the plateaus and the hilly terrains in both Malawi and in the joint model but insignificant in Tanzania. The probability of SLM adoption is 22.3 and 11.2 % more for plots located in the plateaus of Malawi and in the joint model respectively, ceteris paribus. Similarly, SLM adoption is 68.7 and 16.8 % more likely to be adopted in the hills of Malawi and the combined model holding other factors constant.

The adoption of SLM technologies is also significantly influenced by such household-level variables as sex and education level of the household head, and family size. Male-headed households are less likely to adopt SLM technologies by about 11 % in Malawi and also by about 10 % in the joint model than their female counterparts, holding other factors constant. Education and the abundance of labor supply through larger bigger family size positively influence the adoption of SLM technologies both in Malawi and Tanzania and in the joint model. For instance increase in education by 1 year of formal learning increases the probability of SLM adoption by about 5 and 3 % in Malawi and Tanzania respectively, ceteris paribus.

We also assessed the effect of plot level characteristics on the adoption of SLM technologies. Plots with steeper slopes have a positive relationship with the adoption of SLM technologies in all cases. 1 % increase in the slope of the plot increases SLM adoption by about 56.5 and 35.3 % in Malawi and Tanzania respectively. Similarly secure land tenure through ownership of title deed positively influences the adoption of SLM technologies.

Holding other factors constant, ownership of title deed increased the probability of SLM adoption by about 20 and 35 % in Malawi and Tanzania respectively. Market accessed or proximity to markets (shown by distance to the market from the plot) has negative significant influence on the probability of SLM adoption in Malawi and Tanzania and in the joint models. One kilometer increase in distance to market reduced the probability of SLM adoption by 0.64, 0.77 and 0.75 % in the joint model, Malawi and Tanzania respectively, holding other factors constant.

Important socio-economic variables including access to agricultural extension services and credit access are also significant determinants of SLM technologies. Access to extension increased probability SLM adoption by 13.7, 20.2 and 14 % in the joint model, Malawi and Tanzania respectively, while membership in farmer organizations increased probability of SLM adoption by 7.2, 18.5 and 9.8 % in the joint model, Malawi and Tanzania respectively, ceteris paribus. Further, credit access increased probability LM adoption by 7.2, 18.5 and 9.8 % in the joint model, Malawi and Tanzania respectively, ceteris paribus. The adoption of SLM technologies was significantly higher in Tanzania by about 14 % than in Malawi.

Determinants of Number of SLM Practices Adopted: Poisson Regression

Results of the Poisson regression on the determinants of the number of SLM technologies used by households are presented in Table 20.6. The assessment is done at plot level in each of the case study countries and a joint model is also estimated for all the countries. The models fit the data well. All the models are statistically significant at 1 % [(All-countries (joint model): Wald Chi^2 (35) = 2335.6, p-value = 0.000), (Malawi: Wald Chi^2 (34) = 1649.2, p-value = 0.000), (Tanzania: Wald Chi^2 (34) = 349.1, p-value = 0.000)]. There was no evidence of dispersion (over-dispersion and under-dispersion). We estimated the corresponding negative binomial regressions and all the likelihood ratio tests (comparing the negative binomial model to the Poisson model) were not statistically significant—suggesting that the Poisson model was best fit for our study assessments.

Results (Table 20.6) show that biophysical, plot-level, demographic, socio-economic and regional factors significantly determine the number of SLM technologies adopted. Among the proximate biophysical factors that significantly determine the number of SLM technologies adopted include temperature, rainfall, elevation and agro-ecological zonal characteristics. For example, a 1 % increase in temperature (°C * 10) increases the number of SLM technologies by 0.3 % in Malawi but reduces number of SLM technologies by 0.5 % in Tanzania holding other factors constant. Similarly, a 1 % increase in rainfall increased the number of SLM technologies adopted by 0.3 % in Malawi but reduces the number of SLM technologies by 0.2 % in Tanzania ceteris paribus. Like in the probability of SLM adoption technologies, the interaction between rainfall and temperature did not yield any significant effects. Our results also suggest that terrain is an important determinant of the number of SLM technologies adopted in Malawi. Lowlands were selected as the base terrain. Results show that the number of SLM technologies adopted was about 10 and 13 % more in Malawian plateaus and hills respectively, *ceteris paribus*.

Table 20.6 Drivers of number of SLM technologies adopted: poisson regression

Variables	All (n = 23,776)		Malawi (n = 18,162)		Tanzania (n = 5614)	
	Coef.	Std. Err.	Coef.	Std. Err.	Coef.	Std. Err.
rainfall (log)	0.312***	0.023	0.423***	0.025	−0.224***	0.061
rainfall^2 (log)	0.000	0.031	0.000	0.082	0.007	0.011
temperature (log)	−0.389***	0.121	0.280*	0.149	−0.531**	0.255
temperature^2 (log)	−0.243	0.672	−0.137	0.327	−0.536	0.863
tempe#rainfall (log)	0.118	0.002	0.009	0.001	0.022	0.000
terrain_plateaus	0.080***	0.010	0.100***	0.010	0.003	0.029
terainr_hills	0.078***	0.015	0.129***	0.015	−0.073	0.048
elevation	0.000*	0.000	0.000***	0.000	0.000**	0.000
warm_humid aez	0.092***	0.012	0.148***	0.013	−0.030	0.060
cool_arid aez	−0.063***	0.016	−0.016	0.016	0.151*	0.084
cool_humid aez	0.013	0.017	0.070***	0.018	0.106	0.065
age	0.002	0.001	0.002	0.002	0.006	0.005
age^2	0.000	0.000	0.000	0.000	0.000	0.000
sex (male = 1)	−0.034***	0.011	−0.025**	0.011	−0.002	0.033
education	0.129***	0.003	0.111***	0.004	0.172**	0.008
education^2	0.002	0.000	−0.001	0.000	0.002	0.001
family_size	−0.010***	0.002	−0.001	0.003	−0.016**	0.005
plots_lope	0.151***	0.008	0.148***	0.008	0.146***	0.025
tittle_deed (1 = yes)	0.233***	0.011	0.210***	0.011	0.235***	0.038
sandy (1 = yes)	−0.016	0.011	−0.028**	0.012	−0.011	0.037
clay (1 = yes)	−0.596*	0.032	−0.500	0.172	−0.272	0.064
soil_quality	−0.041*	0.014	−0.035	0.014	0.113	0.053
plot_distance (log)	−0.111	0.009	−0.056*	0.012	−0.004	0.014
market_distance (log)	−0.112***	0.004	−0.142***	0.004	−0.054***	0.018
extension (1 = yes)	0.120**	0.019	0.159***	0.019	0.174**	0.035
plot_size	0.002*	0.001	0.023***	0.005	0.002**	0.001
group	0.036***	0.012	0.056***	0.012	0.060**	0.030
credit_access (1 = yes)	0.029**	0.012	0.010**	0.012	0.045***	0.040
credit_amount (log)	0.014*	0.008	0.018**	0.008	0.055**	0.026
assets (log)	0.246***	0.003	0.428***	0.004	0.830***	0.009
irrigation (1 = yes)	−0.030	0.055	0.198*	0.076	0.192*	0.086
constant	0.050	0.722	4.576***	0.858	3.504**	1.634
Malawi	−0.071***	0.029	–			
Model Characteristics	No of obs. = 23,776		No. of obs. = 18,162		No. of obs. = 5614	
	LR Chi^2(34) = 2335.6		LR Chi^2(34) = 1649.2		LR Chi^2(36) = 394.1	
	Prob > chi^2 = 0.0000		Prob > chi^2 = 0.0000		Prob > chi^2 = 0.0000	
	Pseudo R^2 = 0.1697		Pseudo R^2 = 0.1874		Pseudo R^2 = 0.1657	

***, **, and *Denotes significance at 1, 5 and 10 % respectively

[2] Describes mean values

Source Authors' compilation

The number of SLM technologies adopted is also significantly determined by such household-level variables as sex and education level of the household head and family size. Male-headed households are less likely to adopt SLM technologies by about 2.5 % in Malawi and by about 3.4 % in the joint model than their female counterparts, holding other factors constant. Education level of the household head positively influenced the number of SLM technologies adopted both in Malawi and Tanzania and in the joint model. A unit increase in education by 1 year of formal learning increases the number of SLM technologies adopted by about 12.9, 11.1 and 17.2 % in the joint model, Malawi and Tanzania respectively, ceteris paribus. In contrast, an additional family member (in adult equivalent) reduced the number of SLM technologies adopted by about 1 and 1.6 % in Tanzania and the joint model respectively, holding other factors constant.

The number of SLM technologies adopted is also significantly determined by such slope, tenure status, soil type, and market access from the plot. The number of SLM technologies adopted is positively related to slope of the plot. A 1 % increase in the slope of the plot increases the number of SLM technologies adopted by about 15.5, 14.8 and 14.6 % in joint model, Malawi and Tanzania respectively, ceteris paribus.

Similarly secure land tenure through ownership of title deed positively influences the number of SLM technologies adopted. Ownership of title deed increased the probability of number of SLM technologies adopted by about 23, 21 and 23 % in the joint model, Malawi and Tanzania respectively ceteris paribus. Our assessment further shows that proximity to markets (distance to the market) from the plot has negative significant influence on the probability of SLM adoption in Malawi and Tanzania and in the joint models. One kilometer increase in distance to market reduced the probability of SLM adoption by 0.11, 0.14 and 0.05 % in the joint model, Malawi and Tanzania respectively, holding other factors constant.

Our results further show that socio-economic variables including access to agricultural extension services, access to credit services and household assets also determine the number of SLM technologies adopted. Access to extension increased the number of SLM technologies adopted by 12, 16 and 17 % in the joint model, Malawi and Tanzania respectively, while membership in farmer organizations increased the number of SLM technologies adopted by 3.6, 5.6 and 6 % in the joint model, Malawi and Tanzania respectively, ceteris paribus. Further, credit access increased number of SLM technologies adopted by 2.9, 1 and 4.5 % in the joint model, Malawi and Tanzania respectively, ceteris paribus. A 1 % increase in household assets increased the number of SLM technologies adopted by 0.25, 0.43 and 0.83 % in the joint model, Malawi and Tanzania respectively, ceteris paribus. The adoption of SLM technologies was significantly higher in Malawi by about 7.1 % than in Tanzania.

Robust checks show no evidence of multicollinearity, heteroscedasticity and omitted variables. Ramsey RESET test (ovitest) was not significant, showing no evidence of omitted variable, while the Breusch-Pagan/Cook-Weisberg test (hettest) showed no evidence of heteroscedasticity. We report robust standard errors. Further, the VIF test was less than 10, showing no evidence of multicollinearity.

Cost of Action and Inaction Against Land Degradation Due to LUCC

The results of cost of action and costs of inaction against land degradation in Malawi and Tanzania are discussed in this section. In Malawi, results show that the average annual cost of land degradation during 2000–2009 periods was about 244 million USD (Table 20.7). Only about 153 million USD (62 %) of this cost represent the provisional ecosystem services. The other (about 38 %) represents the supporting and regulatory and cultural ecosystem services. Most of these costs were experienced in Mangochi (27 million USD), Nkhata Bay (24 million USD), and Nkhotakota district (20 million USD). Priority action is thus needed in these regions.

The costs of action over a 30-year horizon were about 4.1 billion USD, as opposed to inaction costs of about 15.6 billion USD if nothing is done over the same time period (30 years). Similarly, over a shorter time period of 6 years, the cost of action sums to about 4 billion USD as opposed to of inaction of about 11.5 billion USD. This implies that the costs of action against land degradation are about 4.3 times lower than the costs of inaction over the 30 year horizon. The implications is that; each dollar spent on addressing land degradation is likely to yield about 4.3 dollars of returns.

In Tanzania, results show that the annual cost of land degradation between 2000 and 2009 periods was about 2.3 billion USD (Table 20.8). Only about 1.3 billion USD (57 %) of this cost of land degradation represent the provisional ecosystem services. The other (about 43 %) represents the supporting and regulatory and cultural ecosystem services. Most of these costs were experienced in Morogoro region (297 million USD), Ruvuma region (214 million USD), and Rukwa region (193 million USD). These areas can be considered areas where priority action is needed. The results further show the costs of action against land degradation in a 30-year horizon is about 36.3 billion USD but the resulting losses (costs) may equal almost 138.8 billion USD during the same period if nothing is done. Similarly, over a shorter time period of 6 years, the cost of action sums to about 36.2 billion USD as opposed to costs of inaction of about 102.6 billion USD. This suggests that the costs of action against land degradation are 3.8 times lower than the costs of inaction over the 30 year horizon. For every dollar spent to address land degradation, the returns are about 3.8 dollars. Taking action against land degradation in both short and long-term periods is thus more favorable than inaction.

Cost of Land Degradation Due to Use of Land Degrading Practices on Cropland

Table 20.9 shows the simulated results of rain-fed maize and wheat and irrigated rice yields under business-as-usual and ISFM scenarios for a period of forty years.

Table 20.7 Cost of action and inaction against land degradation in Malawi (million USD)

District	Annual costs of land degradation (for period 2001–2009)	Annual costs of land degradation in terms of provisional ES only	Cost of action (6 years)	Cost of action (30 years)	Of which, the opportunity cost of action	Cost of inaction (6 years)	Cost of inaction (30 years)	Ratio of cost of action: cost of inaction (30 years) (%)
Balaka	0.75	0.50	0.04	0.04	12.49	36.06	48.81	0.1
Lilongwe	9.97	7.02	175.69	176.04	173.66	485.47	657.13	26.8
Machinga	11.03	7.08	196.24	196.59	194.18	524.73	710.28	27.7
Mangochi	27.30	14.97	401.96	402.72	397.52	1169.47	1583.00	25.4
Mchinji	5.59	4.30	103.94	104.15	102.72	283.75	384.09	27.1
Mulanje	6.61	4.02	1.77	1.78	110.24	307.52	416.26	0.4
Mwanza	6.25	4.27	111.01	111.22	109.80	301.10	407.57	27.3
Mzimba	19.64	13.03	366.46	367.12	362.62	961.42	1301.38	28.2
Nkhata Bay	24.38	9.22	414.18	414.72	411.53	1030.70	1395.15	29.7
Nkhotakota	19.99	11.71	335.94	336.54	332.99	916.37	1240.40	27.1
Nsanje	4.22	2.87	79.28	79.43	78.41	209.90	284.12	27.9
Blantyre	1.93	1.28	34.85	34.91	34.45	94.70	128.19	27.2
Ntcheu	4.38	3.13	85.44	85.60	84.51	223.65	302.73	28.3
Ntchisi	5.56	4.00	102.23	102.43	101.10	275.38	372.75	27.5
Phalombe	3.95	2.74	71.50	71.64	70.81	194.85	263.74	27.2
Rumphi	19.57	12.28	329.90	330.51	326.34	907.73	1228.70	26.9
Salima	5.02	2.83	6.56	6.58	74.49	226.63	306.77	2.2
Thyolo	4.66	3.05	80.88	81.05	80.08	225.99	305.90	26.5
Zomba	4.67	2.74	82.79	82.95	82.05	222.02	300.53	27.6
Chikwawa	8.78	6.03	154.40	154.71	152.59	428.35	579.82	26.7

(continued)

Table 20.7 (continued)

District	Annual costs of land degradation (for period 2001–2009)	Annual costs of land degradation in terms of provisional ES only	Cost of action (6 years)	Cost of action (30 years)	Of which, the opportunity cost of action	Cost of inaction (6 years)	Cost of inaction (30 years)	Ratio of cost of action: cost of inaction (30 years) (%)
Chiradzulu	0.87	0.59	15.53	15.56	15.38	43.06	58.29	26.7
Chitipa	9.25	6.72	173.04	173.38	171.02	468.54	634.22	27.3
Dedza	7.44	5.23	134.31	134.58	132.74	368.57	498.90	26.9
Dowa	4.89	3.39	86.12	86.31	85.05	242.27	327.94	26.3
Karonga	12.39	7.90	205.06	205.47	202.67	579.33	784.18	26.2
Kasungu	15.32	12.21	294.73	295.33	291.25	797.38	1079.34	27.4
Total	244.40	153.11	4043.9	4051.4	4190.7	11,524.9	15,600.2	25.9

Source Calculated based on Nkonya et al. (in press) using MODIS data

Table 20.8 Cost of action and inaction against land degradation in Tanzania (million USD)

Region	Annual costs of land degradation (for period 2001–2009)	Annual costs of land degradation in terms of provisional ES only	Cost of action (6 years)	Cost of action (30 years)	Of which, the opportunity cost of action	Cost of inaction (6 years)	Cost of inaction (30 years)	Ratio of cost of action: cost of inaction (30 years) (%)
Arusha	56.0	30.3	880.1	881.8	868.7	2479.3	3356.0	26.3
Pemba South	7.3	2.0	46.0	46.1	45.3	223.1	302.0	15.3
Lindi	122.9	69.6	2351.8	2355.7	2332.9	5934.7	8033.3	29.3
Manyara	60.6	41.2	1108.3	1110.5	1093.7	2987.2	4043.5	27.5
Mara	42.1	14.8	415.8	416.8	409.7	1522.6	2061.0	20.2
Mbeya	160.7	116.8	2912.3	2918.2	2878.0	8003.1	10,833.0	26.9
Morogoro	297.4	171.1	5186.4	5194.9	5136.2	13,621.3	18,437.8	28.2
Mtwara	15.2	6.3	180.7	181.2	178.3	596.3	807.1	22.4
Mwanza	70.8	24.0	549.0	550.7	539.4	2386.7	3230.7	17.1
Pwani	129.5	62.9	2135.0	2138.6	2113.9	5711.5	7731.1	27.7
Rukwa	192.8	122.2	3076.6	3082.7	3041.1	8789.6	11,897.6	25.9
Dar-Es-Salaam	6.4	2.7	5.6	5.6	68.4	245.7	332.6	1.7
Ruvuma	214.4	144.5	3584.9	3591.7	3545.1	10,002.2	13,538.9	26.5
Shinyang	44.9	20.8	503.1	504.3	496.1	1737.3	2351.7	21.5
Singida	55.6	29.4	1054.8	1056.5	1043.0	2643.5	3578.3	29.5
Tabora	100.6	73.5	1834.9	1838.6	1813.2	5036.5	6817.4	26.9
Tanga	161.9	88.4	2536.1	2540.8	2508.9	7113.2	9628.4	26.4
Zanzibar South	9.2	3.1	2.2	2.2	122.4	347.1	469.9	0.5
Zanzibar West	3.2	0.9	37.9	38.0	37.6	116.2	157.3	24.1
Dodoma	32.0	18.2	475.4	476.5	468.4	1418.6	1920.2	24.8

(continued)

Table 20.8 (continued)

Region	Annual costs of land degradation (for period 2001–2009)	Annual costs of land degradation in terms of provisional ES only	Cost of action (6 years)	Cost of action (30 years)	Of which, the opportunity cost of action	Cost of inaction (6 years)	Cost of inaction (30 years)	Ratio of cost of action: cost of inaction (30 years) (%)
Iringa	144.6	85.8	2447.3	2451.7	2421.7	6631.4	8976.2	27.3
Kagera	157.5	85.3	2246.8	2251.4	2220.0	6735.5	9117.2	24.7
Pemba North	8.6	2.4	2.7	2.7	63.0	272.6	369.1	0.7
Unguja North	6.7	2.1	1.3	1.3	66.9	233.4	315.9	0.4
Kigoma	157.6	79.5	2009.9	2013.4	1989.2	6139.7	8310.7	24.2
Kilimanjaro	36.7	20.3	597.5	598.6	590.4	1634.2	2212.1	27.1
Total	2295.05	1318.00	36,182	36,250	36,092	102,563	138,829	26.1

Source Calculated based on Nkonya et al. (in press) using MODIS data

Table 20.9 Change in maize, rice and wheat yields under BAU and ISFM—DSSAT results

Country	BAU		ISFM		Yield change (%)		Change due to land degradation
	Baseline	End-line	Baseline	End-line	BAU	ISFM	Percent
	Yield (tons/ha)		Yield (tons/ha)		$\%\Delta y = \frac{y_2 - y_1}{y_1} * 100$		$\%D = \frac{y_2^c - y_2^d}{y_2^d} * 100$
Maize							
Malawi	2.37	1.57	2.51	1.92	−33.5	−23.3	22.0
Tanzania	2.14	1.57	2.29	1.92	−26.6	−16.0	22.3
Rice							
Malawi	6.06	4.04	6.61	4.68	−33.3	−29.2	15.9
Tanzania	5.88	4.17	6.16	4.51	−29.0	−26.8	8.0
Wheat							
Malawi	0.55	0.52	0.53	0.52	−6.4	−2.1	0.2
Tanzania	0.66	0.64	0.67	0.68	−3.5	0.6	5.9

Note y_1 = Baseline yield (average first 10 years); y_2 = Yield end-line period (average last 10 years). y_2^c = ISFM yield in the last 10 years; y_2^d = BAU yield, last 10 years
Source Authors' compilation

The average maize yield in Malawi is 2.4 tons/ha (baseline) and 1.6 tons/ha (end-line) under the BAU scenario. This implies that the use of land degrading management practices on rain-fed maize leads to a 34 % fall in yield compared to yield in the past 30 years. In Tanzania, the average maize yield under the BAU scenario is 2.1 tons/ha (baseline) and 1.6 tons/ha (end-line)—implying 34 % fall in yield compared to yield in the past 30 years as a result of use of land-degrading management practices. Results further show that average maize yield are higher under ISFM—2.5 tons/ha (baseline) and 1.9 tons/ha (end-line) periods in Ethiopia and 2.3 tons/ha (baseline) and 1.9 tons/ha (end-line) periods in Tanzania. This represents a decline of about 23 and 16 % in Malawi and Tanzania respectively compared to yield in the past 30 years.

Irrigated rice yield declines under BAU scenario are 33 % in Malawi and 29 % in Tanzania and about 29 % in Malawi and 27 % in Tanzania under ISFM. On the other hand, wheat yield declines under BAU scenario are 6 % in Malawi and 4 % in Tanzania and about 2 % in Malawi and 0.6 % in Tanzania under ISFM.

On average the use of land degrading management practices on rain-fed maize leads to a 22 % decline in yield as compared to yield the previous 30 years in each of the two countries. Similarly, analysis show that the use of land degrading management practices on irrigated rice leads to a 16 % decline in yield in Malawi and 8 % in Tanzania. Further, the use of land degrading management practices on rain-fed wheat leads to a 6 % decline in yield Tanzania and about 0.2 % decline in Malawi as compared to yield the previous 30 years.

The cost of land degradation for the three crops is about $277 million per year (Table 20.10); $114 million in Malawi and $162 million in Tanzania. When these losses are expressed as percent of GDP, the two countries lose about 1.3 % of the GDP annually as a result of cropland (maize, rice and wheat) degradation. At

Table 20.10 Cost of soil fertility mining on static maize, rice and wheat cropland

Country	Cost of land degradation (soil fertility mining) 2007 $ million	Cost as % of GDP (%)	Cost of all cropland degradation as % GDP (%)
Malawi	114.09	3.1	7.4
Tanzania	161.94	1.0	2.3
Total	276.94	1.3	3.2

Source Authors' compilation

country level Malawi is the most severely affect by cropland degradation – loses about 3 % of its GDP annually while in Tanzania the losses amount to about 1 % of GDP. Statistics show that the three crops (maize, rice and wheat) account for about 42 % of the cropland globally (Nkonya et al. in press). Assuming that the levels of degradation is comparable to that occurring on the three major crops, then the total cost of land degradation on cropland is about 3.2 % of GDP in the two countries—ranging from 2.3 % in Tanzania to 7.4 % in Malawi (Table 20.10).

The costs of land degradation due to soil fertility mining reported in Table 20.10 are conservative. Other aspects of land degradation common on a static biome (cropland) including soil erosion and salinity, and offside costs of pesticide use are not considered because of lack of data. The DSSAT data used in this study also assumes higher BAU fertilizer application rates—this reduces the actual costs of land degradation.

Cost of Loss of Milk and Meat Production Due to Land Degradation of Rangelands

Table 20.11 shows the simulated results of the costs of losses of milk, meat, and costs associated with weight loss of animals not slaughtered or sold associated with land degradation in rangelands. Computations were done by agro-ecological zone for an in-depth depiction and discussions of these costs. Chapter 8 of this volume presents a comprehensive analytical approach on how each of these components are computed.

Results shows that land degradation in grazing biomass had a significant impact on milk production both in Malawi and Tanzania. In Tanzania, the total costs of milk and meat production losses were about $53 and $3.3 respectively. The bigger proportion of milk and meat losses is experienced in the warm sub-humid ($26 million), cool sub-humid ($19 million) and cool semi-arid ($9 million) agro-ecologies.

When the cost of weight loss of animals not slaughtered or sold is considered, the total costs of grassland degradation increases to about $74 million in Tanzania. The bigger proportion of the total gross losses is experienced in the warm sub-humid ($33 million), cool sub-humid ($25 million) and cool semi-arid ($12 million) agro-ecologies.

Table 20.11 Annual cost of milk and meat production loss due to degradation of grazing biomass

Agro-ecological zones	Milk	Meat	Total loss (milk and meat)	Total gross loss—includes weight loss of animals not slaughtered/sold
	2007 $ million			
Tanzania				
Tropic-cool semi-arid	8.304	0.425	8.729	11.700
Tropic-cool sub-humid	17.862	0.837	18.699	25.166
Tropic-warm semi-arid	2.797	0.131	2.928	3.941
Tropic-warm arid	0.167	0.013	0.180	0.235
Tropic-warm sub-humid	23.652	1.934	25.586	33.324
Total	52.781	3.34	56.122	74.366
Malawi				
Tropic-cool semi-arid	0.138	0.008	0.146	0.200
Tropic-cool sub-humid	0.183	0.034	0.217	0.265
Tropic-warm semi-arid	1.128	0.09	1.218	1.634
Tropic-warm sub-humid	0.106	0.009	0.114	0.153
Total	1.555	0.141	1.696	2.253

Source Authors' compilation

In Malawi, the total costs of milk is about $1.5 million while the cost of meat production losses is about $0.14 million. The biggest losses are experienced in the warm semi-arid ($0.22 million), cool sub-humid ($0.22 million) and cool semi-arid ($0.15 million) agro-ecologies. The total gross loss—cost of milk, meant and cost of weight loss of animals not slaughtered or sold—in Malawi was about $2.3 million. The bigger proportion of the total gross losses is consequently experienced in warm semi-arid ($1.6 million), cool sub-humid ($0.27 million) and cool semi-arid ($0.2 million) agro-ecologies.

Actions Taken to Address ES Loss and Enhance ES Improvement

Given the above big losses as a result of land degradation, we present the results of the assessment of the perception of trend in value of ES for major land use types for eight local communities in Tanzania (Table 20.12). From the community perspective, results show that the ES value of cropland is decreasing in all districts except one (Mufindi). Similarly, the value of forest ES is all decreasing in all cases except in Mufindi district. On the other hand the trend in value of grassland is mixed. Two districts reported an increase (Sejeli and Zuzu communities), while two districts reported a decline (Dakawa and Mazingira).

The actions that the communities take to address loss of ES or enhance or maintain ES improvement are presented in Table 20.13. For example, in forest

Table 20.12 Perceptions of trend in value of ecosystem services by biomes in Tanzania

District	Village	Trend of ES value of cropland	Trend of ES value of forest	Trend of ES value grassland	Trend of ES value shrub-land
Kilosa	Zombo	Decreasing	Decreasing	N/A	N/A
Morogoro	Dakawa	Decreasing	Decreasing	Decreasing	N/A
Mufindi	Mtili	Increasing	Increasing	N/A	N/A
Kongwa	Sejeli	Decreasing	N/A	Increasing	Increasing
Dodoma	Zuzu	Decreasing	N/A	Increasing	N/A
Bahi	Maya	Decreasing	Decreasing	N/A	Decreasing
Manyoni	Mamba	Decreasing	N/A	N/A	Decreasing
Handeni	Mazingira	Decreasing	Decreasing	Decreasing	N/A

Source Authors' compilation

Table 20.13 Actions taken to address ES loss and enhance ES improvement in Tanzania

District	Village	Actions for cropland	Actions for forest	Actions for grassland
Kilosa	Zombo	Use tractors to break land, crop and fallow rotations, fertilizer use	Afforestation, bylaw for protection of the existing forest	
Morogoro	Dakawa	Use of inorganic fertilizer, promotion of SLM	Strongly enforced bylaws; fines for illegal logging	Area closure for rehabilitation; controlled grazing
Mufindi	Mtili	Use of inorganic fertilizers	Bylaw for protection of the existing forest —protected areas	
Kongwa	Sejeli	Leave land fallow, mulching, crop rotation		Protected areas; Bylaws and community fines and sanctions
Dodoma	Zuzu	Organic manure application		They burn dried grasses that green grass can re-grow
Bahi	Maya	Apply organic manure	Protected forest Bylaw and punishment (fine imprisonment)	
Manyoni	Mamba	Apply organic manure SLM practices		
Handeni	Mazingira	Use new seed varieties	Development of bylaws	

Source Authors' compilation

biomes, some of the actions taken to address loss of ES or enhance ES improvement include; afforestation programs (Zombo community), bylaws to protect existing forests (Zombo, Dakawa, and Mtili villages). Some actions taken in grasslands include area closure and controlled grazing (in Dakawa village) to community sanctions for overgrazing in Sejeli village.

Conclusions and Policy Implications

Land degradation is increasingly becoming an important subject due to the increasing number of causes as well as its effects. Recent assessments show that land degradation affected 51 and 41 % in Tanzania, Malawi respectively. The adoption of sustainable land management practices as well as the number of SLM technologies adopted is critical in addressing land degradation in Malawi and Tanzania. Securing land tenure and access to relevant agricultural information pertaining to SLM will play an important role in enhancing SLM adoption. This implies that policies and strategies that facilities use to secure land tenure is likely to incentivize investments in SLM in the long-run since benefits accrue over time. There is a need to improve the capacity of land users through education and extension as well as improve access to financial and social capital to enhance SLM uptake. Local institutions providing credit services, inputs such as seed and fertilizers, and extension services must not be ignored in the development policies. The important role of rainfall and agro-ecological classification on adoption of and number of SLM technologies adopted suggests the need for proper geographical planning and targeting of SLM practices by stakeholders.

Losses due to land degradation are substantial. The annual costs of land degradation due to LUCC between 2001 and 2009 period based on TEV framework amount to about $244 million in Malawi and $2.3 billion in Tanzania—representing about 6.8 and 13.7 % of GDP in 2007 in Malawi and Tanzania, respectively. It is worthwhile to take action against land degradation. The TEV computation points to lower costs of action ($4.05 billion in Malawi and $36.3 billion in Tanzania) as compared to costs of inaction ($15.6 billion in Malawi and $138.8 billion in Tanzania) by about 4.3 times and 3.8 times over a 30-year horizon in Malawi and Tanzania, respectively. This implies that for each dollar spent to rehabilitate/restore degraded lands, it returns about 4.3 dollars and 3.8 dollars in Malawi and Tanzania, respectively. The use of land degrading practices in croplands (maize, rice and wheat) resulted in losses amounting to $5.7 million in Malawi and $1.8 million in Tanzania—0.2 % of GDP in Malawi and 0.01 % of GDP in Tanzania. These costs are, however, conservative. We consider only three crops, other aspects of land degradation common on a static biome (cropland) including soil erosion and salinity, and offside costs of pesticide use are not considered because of lack of data. The results further show that the of land degradation on static grazing biomass (loss of milk, meat and the cost of weight loss of animals not slaughtered or sold) amounted to $74 million in Tanzania and $2.3 million in Malawi.

Some of the local level initiatives taken by local communities address loss of ecosystem services or enhance/maintain ecosystem services improvement such as afforestation programs, enacting of bylaws to protect existing forests, area closures and controlled grazing, community sanctions for overgrazing, and use of ISFM in croplands ought to be out-scaled and backed by formal laws.

References

Akhtar-Schuster, M., Thomas, R. J., Stringer, L. C., Chasek, P., & Seely, M. (2011). Improving the enabling environment to combat land degradation: Institutional, financial, legal and science-policy challenges and solutions. *Land Degradation and Development, 22*(2), 299–312.

Areal, F. J., Touza, J., McLeod, A., Dehnen-Schmutz, K., Perrings, C., Palmieri, M. G., & Spence, N. J. (2008). Integrating drivers influencing the detection of plant pests carried in the international cut flower trade. *Journal of Environmental Management, 89*, 300–307.

Arslan, A., McCarthy, N., Lipper, L., Asfaw, S., & Cattaneo, A. (2013). Adoption and intensity of adoption of conservation farming practices in Zambia. *Agriculture, Ecosystems & Environment, 187*, 72–86.

Asfaw, S., Shiferaw, B., Simtowe, F., & Lipper, L. (2012). Impact of modern agricultural technologies on smallholder welfare: Evidence from Tanzania and Ethiopia. *Food Policy, 37* (3), 283–295.

Assey, P. (2007). Environment at the Heart of Tanzania's development: Lessons from Tanzania's National Strategy for Growth and Reduction of Poverty, MKUKUTA (No. 6). IIED.

Bamire, A. S., Fabiyi, Y. L., & Manyong, V. M. (2002). Adoption pattern of fertiliser technology among farmers in the ecological zones of south-western Nigeria: A Tobit analysis. *Crop and Pasture Science, 53*(8), 901–910.

Barrett, C. B., Bezuneh, M., & Aboud, A. (2001). Income diversification, poverty traps and policy shocks in Côte d'Ivoire and Kenya. *Food Policy, 26*(4), 367–384.

Bekele, W., & Drake, L. (2003). Soil and water conservation decision behavior of subsistence farmers in the eastern highlands of Ethiopia: A case study of the Hunde-Lafto area. *Ecological Economics, 46*, 437–451.

Belay, M., & Bewket, W. (2013). Farmers' livelihood assets and adoption of sustainable land management practices in north-western highlands of Ethiopia. *International Journal of Environmental Studies, 70*(2), 284–301.

Belay, K. T., Van Rompaey, A., Poesen, J., Van Bruyssel, S., Deckers, J., & Amare, K. (2014). Spatial analysis of land cover changes in eastern Tigray (Ethiopia) from 1965 to 2007: Are there signs of a forest transition? Land Degrad. Dev. doi:10.1002/ldr.2275

Berk, R. (2007). Overdispersion and poisson regression ensemble methods for data analysis in the behavioral, social and economic sciences. pp. 1–24. http://www.udel.edu/soc/faculty/parker/SOCI836_S08_files/Berk%26MacDonald_JQCF.pdf

Bluffstone, R. A., & Köhlin, G. (2011). *Agricultural investments, Livelihoods and Sustainability in East African Agriculture*. Oxford, UK: RFF Press/Earthscan.

Burger, K., & Zaal, F. (Eds.). (2012). *Sustainable land management in the tropics: Explaining the miracle*. Farnham, Surrey, UK: Ashgate Publishing, Ltd.

Chabala, L.M., Kuntashula, E., Hamukwala, P., Chishala, B.H., & Phiri, E. (2012). Assessing the value of land and costs of land degradation in Zambia: First draft report. University of Zambia, the Global Mechanism United Nations Convention to Combat Desertification and the Stockholm Environment Institute. pp. 1–93. http://www.theoslo.net/wp-content/uploads/2012/04/EVS_Zambia_Final_Report_Feb2012_EDITED.pdf. Accessed 01 May 2015.

Chasek, P., Essahli, W., Akhtar-Schuster, M., Stringer, L. C., & Thomas, R. (2011). Integrated land degradation monitoring and assessment: Horizontal knowledge management at the national and international levels. *Land Degradation and Development, 22*(2), 272–284.

Chinsinga, B. (2008). *Reclaiming policy space: Lessons from Malawi's 2005/2006 fertilizer subsidy programme future agricultures*. Brighton, UK: Institute of Development Studies.

D'Odorico, P., Bhattachan, A., Davis, K. F., Ravi, S., & Runyan, C. W. (2013). Global desertification: Drivers and feedbacks. *Advances in Water Resources, 51*, 326–344.

de Fries, R. S., Rudel, T., Uriarte, M., & Hansen, M. (2010). Deforestation driven by urban population growth and agricultural trade in the twenty-first century. *Nature Geoscience, 3*, 178–181.

de Groote, H., & Coulibaly, N. G. (1998). Gender and generation: an intra-household analysis on access to resources in Southern Mali. *African Crop Science Journal, 6*(1), 79–95.

Delgado, J. A., Groffman, P. M., Nearing, M. A., Goddard, T., Reicosky, D., Lal, R., et al. (2011). Conservation practices to mitigate and adapt to climate change. *Journal of Soil and Water Conservation, 66*(2011), 118–129.

Denning, G., Kabambe, P., Sanchez, P., Malik, A., Flor, R., Harawa, R., et al. (2009). Input subsidies to improve smallholder maize productivity in Malawi: Toward an African green revolution. *PLoS Biology, 7*(1), 2–10.

Deressa, T., Hassan, R.M., & Ringler, C. (2009). Assessing household vulnerability to climate change. IFPRI discussion paper 00935. Intl Food Policy Res Inst. Washington D.C. USA.

Diacono, M., & Montemurro, F. (2010). Long-term effects of organic amendments on soil fertility. A review. *Agronomy for Sustainable Development, 30*(2), 401–422.

Dimara, E., & Skuras, D. (2003). Adoption of agricultural innovations as a two-stage partial observability process. *Agricultural Economics, 28*(3), 187–196.

Dorward, A., & Chirwa, E. (2009). *The agricultural input subsidy programme 2005 to 2008: Further Analysis*. Mimeo.

Dregne, H. E. (2002). Land degradation in the drylands. *Arid land research and management, 16*(2), 99–132.

Ervin, C. A., & Ervin, D. E. (1982). Factors affecting the use of soil conservation practices: Hypotheses, evidence, and policy implications. Land economics, pp. 277–292.

Eswaran, H., Lal, R., & Reich, P. F. (2001). Land degradation: An overview. Responses to Land degradation, pp. 20–35.

Famoye, F., Wulu, J. T., & Singh, K. P. (2005). On the generalized poisson regression model with an application to accident data. *Journal of Data Science, 2*(2004), 287–295.

FAO. (2007). *Paying farmers for environmental services, state of food and agriculture 2007, Rome: FAO*. Rome: Italy.

FAO. (2011). *Sustainable land management in practice guidelines and best practices for Sub-Saharan Africa*. Rome.

Feder, G., Just, R. E., & Zilberman, D. (1985). Adoption of agricultural innovations in developing countries: A survey. *Economic Development and Cultural Change, 33*(2), 255–298.

Fentie, D., Fufa, B., & Bekele, W. (2013). Determinants of the use of soil conservation technologies by smallholder farmers: The Case of Hulet Eju Enesie District, East Gojjam Zone, Ethiopia. *Asian Journal of Agriculture and Food Sciences, 1*(04). ISSN: 2321–1571.

Fisher, M., Chaudhury, M., & McCusker, B. (2010). Do forests help rural households adapt to climate variability? Evidence from Southern Malawi. *World Development, 38*(9), 1241–1250.

Folberth, C., Yang, H., Gaiser, T., Abbaspour, K. C., & Schulin, R. (2013). Modelling maize yield responses to improvement in nutrient, water and cultivar inputs in sub-Saharan Africa. *Agricultural Systems, 119*, 22–34.

Gebremedhin, B., & Swinton, S. M. (2003). Investment in soil conservation in northern Ethiopia: the role of land tenure security and public programs. *Agricultural Economics, 29*(1), 69–84.

Gebreselassie, K., De Groote, H., & Friesen, D. (2013). Gender analysis and approaches to gender responsive extension to promote quality protein maize (QPM) in Ethiopia. In *Invited paper presented at the 4th International Conference of the African Association of Agricultural Economists*, 22–25 Sept 2013, Hammamet, Tunisia.

Genius, M., Koundouri, P., Nauges, C., & Tzouvelekas, V. (2014). Information transmission in irrigation technology adoption and diffusion: Social learning, extension services, and spatial effects. *American Journal of Agricultural Economics, 96*(1), 328–344.

Ghadim, A. A. K., & Pannell, D. J. (1999). A conceptual framework of adoption of an agricultural innovation. *Agricultural Economics, 21*(2), 145–154.

Ghadim, A. K. A., Pannell, D. J., & Burton, M. P. (2005). Risk, uncertainty, and learning in adoption of a crop innovation. *Agricultural Economics, 33*(1), 1–9.

Gillespie, J., Kim, S., & Paudel, K. (2007). Why don't producers adopt best management practices? An analysis of the beef cattle industry. *Agricultural Economics, 36*(1), 89–102.

Greene, W. H. (2012). *Econometric analysis* (7th ed.). Boston, USA: Prentice Hall.

Habron, G. B. (2004). Adoption of conservation practices by agricultural landowners in three Oregon watersheds. *Journal of Soil and Water Conservation, 59*(3), 109–115.

Harris, A., Carr, A. S., & Dash, J. (2014). Remote sensing of vegetation cover dynamics and resilience across southern Africa. *International Journal of Applied Earth Observation and Geoinformation, 28*, 131–139.

Heckmann, M. (2014). Farmers, smelters and caravans: Two thousand years of land use and soil erosion in North Pare, NE Tanzania. *Catena, 113*, 187–201.

Hein, L., & De Ridder, N. (2006). Desertification in the Sahel: a reinterpretation. *Global Change Biology, 12*(5), 751–758.

ELD Initiative. (2013). *The rewards of investing in sustainable land management.* Interim report for the economics of land degradation initiative: A global strategy for sustainable land management. Available at: www.eld-initiative.org/

Jansen, H. G. P., Pender, J., Damon, A., Wielemaker, W., & Schipper, R. (2006). Policies for sustainable development in the hillside areas of Honduras: A quantitative livelihoods approach. *Agricultural Economics, 34*, 141–153.

Kabubo-Mariara, J. (2007). Land conservation and tenure security in Kenya: Boserup's hypothesis revisited. *Ecological Economics, 64*, 25–35.

Kassie, M., Jaleta, M., Shiferaw, B., Mmbando, F., & Mekuria, M. (2013). Adoption of interrelated sustainable agricultural practices in smallholder systems: evidence from rural Tanzania. *Technological Forecasting and Social Change, 80*(3), 525–540.

Kassie, M., Shiferaw, B., & Muricho, G. (2011). Agricultural technology, crop income, and poverty alleviation in Uganda. *World Development, 39*(10), 1784–1795.

Kazianga, H., & Masters, W. A. (2002). Investing in soils: Field bunds and microcatchments in Burkina Faso. *Environment and Development Economics, 7*(03), 571–591.

Kiage, L. M. (2013). Perspectives on the assumed causes of land degradation in the rangelands of Sub-Saharan Africa. *Progress in Physical Geography, 37*(5), 664–684.

Kim, S., Gillespie, J. M., & Paudel, K. P. (2005). The effect of socioeconomic factors on the adoption of best management practices in beef cattle production. *Journal of Soil and Water Conservation, 60*(3), 111–120.

Kirui, O. K., & Mirzabaev, A. (2014). Economics of land degradation in Eastern Africa (No. 128). ZEF Working Paper Series. Center for Development Research (ZEF), University of Bonn, Germany.

Kirui, O. K., & Njiraini, G. W. (2013). Determinants of agricultural commercialization among the rural poor: Role of ICT and Collective Action Initiatives and gender perspective in Kenya. In *African Association of Agricultural Economists (AAAE) 2013 Fourth International Conference*, 22–25 Sept 2013. Hammamet, Tunisia.

Lal, R. (1995). Erosion-crop productivity relationships for soils of Africa. *Soil Science Society of America Journal, 59*(3), 661–667.

Lal, R., & Stewart, B. A. (2010). Food security and soil quality. Advances in soil science. http://library.wur.nl/WebQuery/clc/1945402. Accessed 30 May 2015.

Lambin, E. F., & Geist, H. (Eds.). (2006). *Land-use and land-cover change local processes and global impacts*. Berlin: Springer.

Lambin, E. F., & Meyfroidt, P. (2010). Land use transitions: Socio-ecological feedback versus socio-economic change. *Land use policy, 27*(2), 108–118.

Le, Q. B., Nkonya, E., & Mirzabaev, A. (2014). Biomass productivity-based mapping of global land degradation hotspots. *ZEF-discussion papers on development policy, 193*.

Levy, S., & Barahona, C. (2002). *2001–2002 targeted input programme*. Lilongwe, Malawi: Main Report of the Evaluation Programme.

Ligonja, P. J., & Shrestha, R. P. (2013). Soil erosion assessment in Kondoa Eroded area in Tanzania using universal soil loss equation, geographic information systems and socioeconomic approach. Land degradation and development. Wiley Online Library. doi:10.1002/ldr.2215, online first.

Lin, R., & Chen, C. (2014). Tillage, crop rotation, and nitrogen management strategies for wheat in central Montana. *Agronomy Journal, 106*(2), 475–485.

Lindner, R. K. (1987). Adoption and diffusion of technology: An overview. In ACIAR proceedings series.

Maddison, D. (2006). The perception of and adaptation to climate change in Africa. CEEPA. Discussion Paper No. 10. Centre for Environmental Economics and Policy in Africa. University of Pretoria, Pretoria, South Africa.

Marenya, P. P., & Barrett, C. B. (2007). Household-level determinants of adoption of improved natural resources management practices among smallholder farmers in western Kenya. *Food Policy, 32*(4), 515–536.

Marenya, P., Nkonya, E., Xiong, W., Deustua, J., & Kato, E. (2012). Which policy would work better for improved soil fertility management in sub-Saharan Africa, fertilizer subsidies or carbon credits? *Agricultural Systems, 110*, 162–172.

MEA (Millennium Ecosystem Assessment). (2005). Dryland Systems. In R. Hassan, R. Scholes, & N. Ash (Eds.), *Ecosystem and well-being: Current state and trends* (pp. 623–662). Washington, DC: Island Press.

Minot, N., & Benson, T. (2009). Fertilizer subsidies in Africa: Are vouchers the answer? (No. 60). International Food Policy Research Institute (IFPRI).

Morris, M., Valerie, A. K., Kopicki, Ron J., & Byerlee, D. (2007). *Fertilizer use in African agriculture: Lessons learned and good practice guidelines*. Washington, D.C.: The World Bank.

Nakhumwa, T. O., & Hassan, R. M. (2012). Optimal management of soil quality stocks and long-term consequences of land degradation for smallholder farmers in Malawi. *Environmental & Resource Economics, 52*(3), 415–433.

Nkonya, E., Mirzabaev, A., & von Braun, J. (in press) Economics of land degradation and improvement—A global assessment for sustainable development. Springer International Publishing. doi:10.1007/978-3-319-19168-3_20

Nkonya, E. M., Pender, J. L., Kaizzi, K. C., Kato, E., Mugarura, S., Ssali, H., & Muwonge, J. (2008). Linkages between land management, land degradation, and poverty in Sub-Saharan Africa: The case of Uganda (No. 159). International Food Policy Research Institute (IFPRI).

Nkonya, E., Von Braun, J., Alisher, M., Bao Le, Q., Ho Young, K., Kirui, O., & Edward, K. (2013). Economics of land degradation initiative: Methods and approach for global and national assessments. ZEF—discussion papers on development policy no. 183, Bonn, Germany.

Norris, E., & Batie, S. (1987). Virginia farmers' soil conservation decisions: an application of Tobit analysis. *Southern Journal of Agricultural Economics, 19*(1), 89–97.

Pagiola, S. (1996). Price policy and returns to soil conservation in semi-arid Kenya. *Environmental & Resource Economics, 8*(3), 225–271.

Park, T. A., & Lohr, L. (2005). Organic pest management decisions: A systems approach to technology adoption. *Agricultural Economics, 33*(s3), 467–478.

Pender, J., & Gebremedhin, B. (2008). Determinants of agricultural and land management practices and impacts on crop production and household income in the highlands of Tigray, Ethiopia. *Journal of African Economies, 17*(3), 395–450.
Pender, J., Jagger, P., Nkonya, E., & Sserunkuuma, D. (2004a). Development pathways and land management in Uganda. *World Development, 32*(5), 767–792.
Pender, J., Nkonya, E., Jagger, P., Sserunkuuma, D., & Ssali, H. (2004b). Strategies to increase agricultural productivity and reduce land degradation: evidence from Uganda. *Agricultural Economics, 31*(2–3), 181–195.
Pender, J., Nkonya, E., Jagger, P., Sserunkuuma, D., & Ssali, H. (2006). Strategies to increase agricultural productivity and reduce land degradation in Uganda: An econometric analysis. Strategies for sustainable land management in the east African Highlands. International Food Policy Research Institute, Washington, DC, USA, pp. 165–190.
Pingali, P., Schneider, K., & Zurek, M. (2014). Poverty, agriculture and the environment: The case of Sub-Saharan Africa. In Marginality (pp. 151–168). Netherlands: Springer.
Prokopy, L. S., Floress, K., Klotthor-Weinkauf, D., & Baumgart-Getz, A. (2008). Determinants of agricultural best management practice adoption: Evidence from the literature. *Journal of Soil and Water Conservation, 63*(5), 300–311.
Rademaekers, K., Eichler, L., Berg, J., Obersteiner, M., & Havlik, P. (2010). Study on the evolution of some deforestation drivers and their potential impacts on the costs of an avoiding deforestation scheme. European Commission Directorate-General for environment. Rotterdam. The Netherlands.
Reed, M. S., Buenemann, M., Atlhopheng, J., Akhtar-Schuster, M., Bachmann, F., Bastin, et al. (2011). Cross-scale monitoring and assessment of land degradation and sustainable land management: A methodological framework for knowledge management. *Land Degradation and Development*, *22*(2), 261–271.
Safriel, U. N., & Adeel, Z. (2005). Dryland systems.‖ In R. Hassan, R. Scholes & N. Ash (Eds.), *Ecosystems and human well-being: Current state and trends* (Vol. 1, pp. 623–662).
Shakeel, S., Akhtar, S., & Fatima, S. A. (2014). A review on the usage, suitability and efficiency of animal manures for soil fertility in developing countries. *Continental Journal of Agronomy*, *7*(1).
Shiferaw, B., & Holden, S. (1998). Resource degradation and adoption of land conservation technologies in the Ethiopian highlands: case study in Andit Tid. *North Shewa. Agricultural Economics, 27*(4), 739–752.
Shively, G. E. (2001). Agricultural change, rural labor markets, and forest clearing: An illustrative case from the Philippines. *Land Economics, 77*(2), 268–284.
Teklewold, H., Kassie, M., & Shiferaw, B. (2013). Adoption of multiple sustainable agricultural practices in rural Ethiopia. *Journal of Agricultural Economics, 64*(3), 597–623.
Thierfelder, C., Chisui, J. L., Gama, M., Cheesman, S., Jere, Z. D., Bunderson, Trent, et al. (2013). Maize-based conservation agriculture systems in Malawi: Long-term trends in productivity. *Field Crops Research, 142*, 47–57.
Thompson, A., Kotoglou, K., & Deepayan, B. R. (2009). *Financing sources for sustainable land management*. United Kingdom: Oxford Policy Management London.
Tiffen, M., Mortimore, M., & Gichuki, F. (1994). *More people, less erosion: Environmental recovery in Kenya*. Overseas Development Institute, London: John Wiley & Sons Ltd.
Triboi, E., & Triboi-Blondel, A. M. (2014). Towards sustainable, self-supporting agriculture: Biological nitrogen factories as a key for future cropping systems. In *Soil as world heritage* (pp. 329–342). The Netherlands: Springer.
United Republic of Tanzania (URT). (2005). National strategy for growth and reduction of poverty, Vice Presidents' Office, June.
United Republic of Tanzania (URT). (2008). Progress in millennium development goals: Mid way assessment, December.
von Braun, J., Gerber, N., Mirzabaev, A., & Nkonya, E. (2012). The economics of land degradation. An Issue Paper for Global Soil Week, 08–22 Nov 2012. Berlin, Germany.

Voortman, R. L., Sonneveld, B. G., & Keyzer, M. A. (2000). African land ecology: Opportunities and constraints for agricultural development. Center for International Development Working Paper 37. Harvard University, Cambridge, Mass., USA.

Wale, H. A., & Dejenie, T. (2013). Dryland ecosystems: Their features, constraints, potentials and managements. *Research Journal of Agricultural and Environmental Management, 2*(10), 277–288.

Wasige, J. E., Groen, T. A., Smaling, E., & Jetten, V. (2013). Monitoring basin-scale land cover changes in Kagera Basin of Lake Victoria using ancillary data and remote sensing. *International Journal of Applied Earth Observation and Geoinformation, 21*, 32–42.

Waters, C. M., Penman, T. D., Hacker, R. B., Law, B., Kavanagh, R. P., Lemckert, F., & Alemseged, Y. (2013). Balancing trade-offs between biodiversity and production in the re-design of rangeland landscapes. *The Rangeland Journal, 35*(2), 143–154.

Winkelmann, R., & Zimmermann, K. F. (1995). Recent developments in count data modelling: Theory and application. *Journal of economic surveys, 9*(1), 1–24.

World Bank (WB). (2010). Managing land in a changing climate: An operational perspective for Sub-Saharan Africa. Draft version Report No.: 54134-AFR. WB, Washington D.C.

Xiang, L., & Lee, A. H. (2005). Sensitivity of test for overdispersion in poisson regression. *Biometrical Journal, 47*, 167–176.

Yirga, C. T. (2007). The dynamics of soil degradation and incentives for optimal management in Central Highlands of Ethiopia. Ph.D. Thesis, Department of Agricultural Economics, Extension and Rural Development. University of Pretoria, South Africa.

Yu, L., Hurley, T., Kliebenstein, J., & Orazen, P. (2008). Testing for complementarity and substitutability among multiple technologies: The case of U.S. hog farms, working paper, no. 08026, Iowa State University, Department of Economics, Ames, IA, USA.

Zorya S. (2009). National agricultural input voucher scheme in Tanzania. In *Presentation prepared for the Common Market for Eastern and Southern Africa workshop Input Market Development*, 15–16 June, Livingstone, Zambia.

Chapter 21
Economics of Land Degradation and Improvement in Uzbekistan

Aden Aw-Hassan, Vitalii Korol, Nariman Nishanov, Utkur Djanibekov, Olena Dubovyk and Alisher Mirzabaev

Abstract Land degradation is a major challenge for agricultural and rural development in Uzbekistan. Our research findings indicate that the costs of land degradation in Uzbekistan are substantial; reaching about 0.85 billion USD annually resulting from the loss of valuable land ecosystem services due to land use and land cover changes alone between 2001 and 2009. On the other hand, economic simulations also show that the returns from actions to address land degradation can be four times higher their costs over a 30-year planning horizon, i.e. every dollar invested into land rehabilitation can yield 4 dollars of returns over this period. The

A. Aw-Hassan (✉)
Economic and Policy Research Program, International Center for Agricultural Research in the Dry Areas (ICARDA), Daila Blgn 2nd Floor, Bashir El Kassar Street, Verdun, Beirut 1108-2010, Lebanon
e-mail: a.aw-hassan@cgiar.org

V. Korol
Sustainable Resource Management M.Sc. Program, Technische Universität München, Arcisstraße 21, 80333 Munich, Germany
e-mail: vitalii.korol@tum.de

N. Nishanov
Regional office of the International Center for Agricultural Research in the Dry Areas (ICARDA) for Central Asia and Caucasus, P.O. Box 4375, Tashkent 100000, Uzbekistan
e-mail: n.nishanov@cgiar.org

U. Djanibekov
Production Economics Group, Institute for Food and Resource Economics, University of Bonn, Meckenheimer Allee 174, 53115 Bonn, Germany
e-mail: utkur@uni-bonn.de

O. Dubovyk
Center for Remote Sensing of Land Surfaces (ZFL), University of Bonn, Walter Flex str 3, 53113 Bonn, Germany
e-mail: odubovyk@uni-bonn.de

A. Mirzabaev
Center for Development Research (ZEF), University of Bonn, Walter Flex Str 3, 53115 Bonn, Germany
e-mail: almir@uni-bonn.de

E. Nkonya et al. (eds.), *Economics of Land Degradation and Improvement – A Global Assessment for Sustainable Development*,
DOI 10.1007/978-3-319-19168-3_21

priority geographic locations for actions against land degradation are suggested to be Karakalpakstan, Buhoro and Syrdaryo provinces of Uzbekistan, where the returns from actions are the biggest. The econometric analysis of a nationally representative survey of agricultural producers shows that national policies could enhance the uptake of sustainable land management practices by increasing crop diversification, securing land tenure and creating non-farm jobs in rural areas.

Keywords Uzbekistan · Land tenure security · Crop diversification · Costs of land degradation

Introduction

Land degradation is a severe economic and environmental challenge for Uzbekistan. It occurs in many agro-ecological zones of the country, leading to negative consequences on crop and livestock production, agricultural incomes, and rural livelihoods (Pender et al. 2009). The major types of land degradation in Uzbekistan are secondary salinization, soil erosion and desertification (Gupta et al. 2009). Due to the arid climate, agricultural production in most of the country is possible only with irrigation. Presently, the irrigated areas extend to about 4.3 million ha (CACILM 2006), whereas the rainfed arable lands occupy 0.8 mln ha, or only about a fifth of the irrigated lands (ICARDA 2003). The rangelands are the biggest land cover type in the country, stretching to about 24 mln ha (CACILM 2006), more than a half of the total territory of Uzbekistan. The latest estimates indicate that about 26 % of croplands and 17 % of rangelands have experienced considerable degradation during the last three decades (Le et al. 2014).

Land degradation is acknowledged as one of the major problems for the sustainable development in Uzbekistan, and the Central Asian region, as a whole. In this context, there have been numerous efforts to address land degradation, especially in terms of investments in repair and better maintenance of drainage and irrigation systems, and promoting more sustainable agricultural practices (Gupta et al. 2009; Pender et al. 2009; Kienzler et al. 2012). For example, within the next five years till 2020, the government of Uzbekistan is planning to allocate more than 1 billion USD for maintenance and modernization of the irrigation and drainage system in the country (ICTSD 2014). Despite the wide and growing publicity about land degradation in the country, as well as a long history of rich qualitative and expert-opinion based research on economic aspects of land degradation, there are not many quantitative studies assessing the costs and drivers of land degradation in the country. To fill this gap, and to scientifically support the national investments and policy actions to combat land degradation, this study seeks to find answers to the following three research questions:

1. What are the key causes of land degradation in Uzbekistan?
2. What are the economic costs of land degradation and net benefits of actions against degradation compared to inaction?
3. What are the feasible policy and development strategies that enable and catalyze sustainable land management (SLM) in the country?

This research on Economics of Land Degradation (ELD) in Uzbekistan seeks to test two hypotheses. Firstly, we test which factors, such as climate and agricultural practices, population density, income levels, land tenure, market access and others, are significantly influencing land degradation and adoption of sustainable land management practices. Secondly, we also hypothesize that benefit of taking action against land degradation through sustainable land management (SLM) measures is greater than the costs of inaction. The rest of the chapter is structured in the following way: first, we review the literature and present the background information on the extent, types, drivers and impacts of land degradation in Uzbekistan. Secondly, we provide an overview of the conceptual framework and the methodologies applied in this study, without, however, being detailed as the study follows the same concepts and methods already presented thoroughly in Chaps. 2, 6 and 7 of this volume. We dwell more on those aspects of the methodology which are unique to this chapter. Thirdly, we describe the data used in the study. Finally, we present the results and conclude.

Literature Review and Background Information on Land Degradation in Uzbekistan

In Uzbekistan, agriculture accounts for about 20 % of the gross domestic product (GDP) and employs one third of the active labor force (Sutton et al. 2007). However, land degradation has been a crucial factor negatively affecting rural living standards (CACILM 2006). The annual costs associated with land degradation in Uzbekistan are estimated to amount to about 1 billion USD (Sutton et al. 2007). Most degraded areas are concentrated in the lowlands of the Amudarya river (Horazm and Karakalpakstan) and in Bukhara, Navoi, Kashkadarya and Fergana provinces (Fig. 21.1).

Figure 21.1 shows the land degradation hotspot areas (in red) in Uzbekistan based on the change in the surface vegetation between 1982 and 1984 (baseline) and 2006 (endline) (Le et al. 2014, Chap. 4). As indicated earlier, these land degradation hotspots cover about 26 % of the area of croplands and 17 % of rangelands in Uzbekistan (Le et al. 2014).

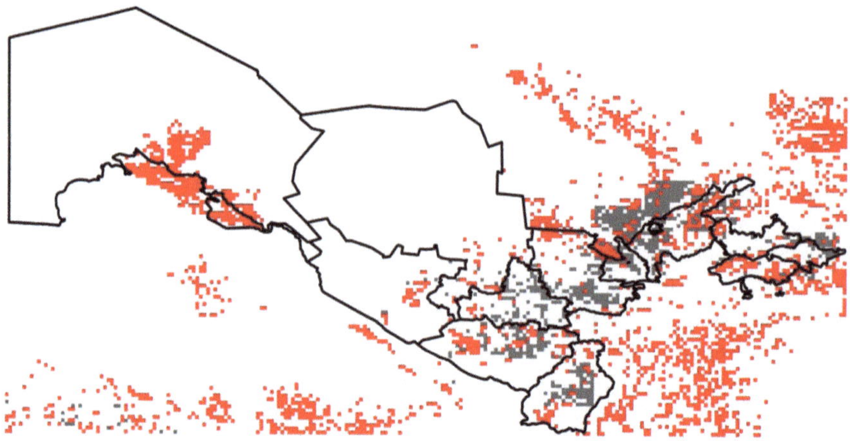

Fig. 21.1 Biomass-based identification of land degradation hotspots in Uzbekistan (*in red*). *Source* Le et al. (2014)

Types of Land Degradation

In Uzbekistan, land degradation occurs mostly as secondary salinization, rangeland degradation and desertification, as well as soil erosion (Gupta et al. 2009). Negative environmental impacts due to land degradation include the drying up of the Aral Sea, water and air pollution caused by salinization and erosion, which result in the loss of biodiversity and reduction of land ecosystem services (Nkonya et al. 2011).

Soil Erosion

Soil erosion due to poor agricultural practices are estimated to be occurring in about 800,000 ha of irrigated croplands, with annual soil losses of up to 80 tons per ha of fertile topsoil (CACILM 2006; Pender et al. 2009). More than 50 % of farmlands in Uzbekistan are estimated to be affected, to different degrees, by wind erosion (CACILM 2006; Pender et al. 2009). About 19 % of the irrigated area of Uzbekistan is affected by water erosion (Bucknall et al. 2003). Strong wind activity, ploughing of sloping lands, inappropriate irrigation and livestock grazing practices have resulted in a vast erosion of soils (ICARDA 2003). Common cropping practices: usually leaving open the soil between rows of cotton or wheat and involving intensive tillage, expose the soil to significant erosion (Nkonya et al. 2011). Furrow irrigation may result in soil erosion in areas with inadequate land leveling (World Bank 2003).

Salinization

In the irrigated cropland areas of Uzbekistan, salinity is a major problem (Pender et al. 2009). Reportedly, up to 53 % of irrigated lands are exposed to varying degrees of soil salinity in the country, leading to low or no profits from annual crops (Djanibekov et al. 2012b; Table 21.1). Each year, waterlogging and salinization result in a loss of about 30,000 ha of land in Uzbekistan (Bucknall et al. 2003; Pender et al. 2009). In the areas near the former Aral Sea: 90–94 % of the irrigated lands in Karakalpakstan, Horazm and Bukhara provinces of Uzbekistan are salinized (Bucknall, et al. 2003; Pender et al. 2009).

Inappropriate irrigation practices are the major cause of secondary soil salinization (ICARDA 2003). The presence of shallow groundwater tables is another major factor contributing to the salinization of irrigated lands. This leads to wide spread waterlogging and salinity problems. Moreover, the existence of shallow groundwater tables due to malfunctioning of surface and subsurface drainage systems makes this leaching practice more unsustainable (Abdullaev 2005).

Overgrazing

The area of pastures in Uzbekistan is about half of the country's total territory (24 million ha) (ICARDA 2003). Most of the rangelands are located in Kashkadarya, Samarkand and Jizzah provinces (ibid.). In Uzbekistan, during the past decades, there has been an extensive degradation of pasture lands, due to unsustainable use of pastures for livestock grazing, lack of maintenance of pastures and other human activities (ibid.). About 10 million ha (42 %) of rangelands have been estimated by to be degraded (CACILM 2006). However, the analysis of the remotely sensed satellite data shows only 17 % of rangelands in the country have shown a vegetation decline between 1982 and 2006 (Le et al. 2014). Overgrazing is one of the major causes of rangeland degradation in the country. The area of rainfed rangelands has considerably decreased due to overgrazing and deforestation. The National Programming Frameworks for the Central Asian countries (CACILM 2006)

Table 21.1 Extent of salinized irrigated areas in Uzbekistan (mln ha)

Category	Years			In 2001 as % of 1990
	1990	2000	2001	
Low saline lands	1.029	1.317	1.258	122.3
Medium saline lands	0.602	0.665	0.720	119.6
High saline lands	0.206	0.416	0.467	226.7
Total saline lands	1.837	2.398	2.445	133.1

Source Khusanov (2009)

provide a comprehensive list of causes of rangeland degradation, including among others "overgrazing, cutting of shrubs, land abandonment, overstocking, lack of maintenance of rangeland infrastructure, lack of economic and organizational capacity among farmers, and limited awareness of rangeland degradation issues and approaches" (Pender et al. 2009).

Spatial Assessments of Land Degradation in Uzbekistan

Despite the recognized severity of land degradation in Uzbekistan, there are few published studies on spatial assessment of this problem (Ji 2008). Kharin et al. (1999 cited in Ji 2008) created a land degradation map of 4 by 4 arc-minutes based on expert opinions and existing soil maps. It shows that land degradation is generally present throughout Uzbekistan, and that it is differentiated by land-use type and degradation cause. Based on these data, desertification is mainly characterized by vegetation cover degradation in rangelands and meadows. Given the fact that this map is partly based on expert opinion, objective and updated assessment is necessary. The spatial assessment of land degradation was also performed by Dubovyk et al. (2013b, c) for Khorezm, one of the most land degradation affected regions of Uzbekistan. The authors find that land productivity decline, calculated from the 250 m Moderate Resolution Imaging Spectroradiometer (MODIS) satellite data on normalized difference vegetation index (NDVI) time series for the monitoring period between 2000 and 2010, affects 23 % (94,835 ha) of the arable area in the study region. Le et al. (2014) have indicated a similar number of 26 % of croplands being degraded in Uzbekistan based on the trend analysis of 8 km Advanced Very High Resolution Radiometer (AVHRR) satellite data series for 1982–2006. Moreover, Dubovyk et al. (2013a) conducted a spatial logistic regression modeling to determine main factors of distribution of degraded croplands in Khorezm region. The results of the statistical modeling suggest that the degradation processes were mainly determined by groundwater table and groundwater salinity, land use, slope, and irrigation water availability.

There have been more studies on land use and cover changes (LUCC) in the region. For example, Chen et al. (2013) assessed changes in LUCC and ecosystem services in Central Asia during 1990–2009. Klein et al. (2012) presented a classification approach for regional land-cover mapping of Central Asia. Spatial analyses on the aeolian geomorphic processes of the Central Asia were conducted by Maman et al. (2011). Kariyeva and Van Leeuwen (2011) studied environmental drivers of vegetation phenology in Central Asia based on the normalized difference vegetation index (NDVI) calculated from the AQUA/TERRA-MODIS NDVI and NOAA-AVHRR NDVI time series (1981–2008). Spatial cropping patterns were observed in the Horazm region in Uzbekistan (Conrad et al. 2011, 2014). Inter-annual changes in vegetation activities and their relationship to temperature and precipitation in Central Asia from 1982 to 2003 were analyzed by Propastin et al. (2008). Yet cropland degradation per se and the relevant aspects for assessing, for instance, relations between the degradation and their possible drivers have not been studied within quantitative data-based frameworks in Uzbekistan.

Drivers of Land Degradation

The major reasons of land degradation, especially soil salinization in the country, are thought to be outdated drainage systems and excessive irrigation application in crop production couple with inadequate agronomic practices (Abdullaev et al. 2005). Leaching of salts from crop fields is not providing with a sustainable solution as it exacerbates the problem of water scarcity (Abdullaev et al. 2005). Using water resources more efficiently is constrained by existing agricultural policies limiting crop choice and diversification (Djanibekov et al. 2013a; Bobojonov et al. 2012). Akramkhanov et al. (2011) found a correlation with distance to drainage collectors and the groundwater parameters. Dubovyk et al. (2013a) found that cropland degradation is mainly linked to the level of the groundwater table, land-use intensity, low soil quality, slope, and salinity of the groundwater. The previous studies above have thus mostly concentrated on proximate drivers of land degradation, whereas there have been very little actual data based analyses of the effects of underlying drivers of land degradation, such as the role of access to markets, land tenure security, the availability of extension services and others. This is the gap that we intend to fill in the present study.

Impacts of Land Degradation and Sustainable Land Management

Very few studies have so far attempted to estimate the economic costs of land degradation in Uzbekistan. For instance, the Project Document of the GEF/World Bank Aral Sea Basin Program calculates the costs due to salinization in Uzbekistan at US$ 250/ha (ICARDA 2003).[1] According to the World Bank, inadequate irrigation and drainage systems, and the resulting soil salinization are leading to about 1 billion USD of losses annually in the country (ICARDA 2003).[2] Another back of the envelope calculation, based on Khusanov (2009), indicates that the reduction in soil quality between 1990 and 2005 resulted in lower cotton and wheat yields equivalent to annual losses of 130–140 mln USD. Gupta et al. (2009) review that the annual losses in agricultural production due to soil salinization might be about US$ 31 million, and economic losses due to land abandonment at US$ 12 million.

---

[1]GEF, *Water and Environment Management Project*, May 1998, p. 7, footnote 11.

[2]The World Bank, *Project Concept Document*, Uzbekistan Drainage Project, December 2, 1999.

Nkonya et al. (2011) assessed the economic impact of soil salinity and soil erosion on wheat and cotton production. The authors conclude that the same level of salinity has a greater economic impact on wheat than on cotton. Nkonya et al. (2011) estimated that the annual economic loss of salinity for wheat and cotton alone is $13.29 million. From their simulations, the authors conclude that the most pressing issue is salinity on wheat and that resources should first be devoted to the affected lands where these two strategically and economically important crops are cultivated usually in rotation.

In addition to national level studies, there have been studies looking at the impacts of land degradation in the specific regions of the country. Djanibekov et al. (2012b) concluded that cultivation of major crops such as cotton and wheat on degraded soils in Khorezm province result in profit losses for farmers. ICARDA has evaluated the impact of salinity on rural livelihoods in Syrdarya province, Uzbekistan (ICARDA 2007). The salinity was found to have had a noticeable impact on the agricultural productivity in the area. All other factors being equal, with the price of raw cotton at around 300 USD/t, farmers in the high and medium salinity zones lost on average 116 USD/ha and 77 USD/ha, respectively, as compared to farmers operating land with low salinity. In the case of wheat, at a price of 100 USD/t, farmers in the high and medium salinity zones lost on average 149 USD/ha and 66 USD/ha as compared to low salinity group farmers because of salinity.

The above literature review on the impacts of land degradation indicates that most previous studies were estimating only the losses in provisional and market-priced ecosystem goods and services, while ignoring the non-provisional, indirect ecosystems services of land reduced due to land degradation, such as, for example, carbon sequestration. In the present, we seek to fill this gap by including the value of both direct and indirect ecosystem services into our analyses.

Land Policies in Uzbekistan

After becoming independent in 1991, Uzbekistan started reforming its national economy and agriculture. It was a challenging issue due to the need to completely change from the centrally planned to the market oriented economy. Given that a larger part of the population in the country is rural, reforms in the agricultural sector were the most complicated. Former collective farms had been transformed to cooperatives and joint-stock companies by 1994 (Khan 1996). In addition, there were individual farming units consisting of farmer enterprises (legal entities) and household plots (Bloch 2002). Uzbekistan has not introduced private ownership for agricultural land (Akramov and Omuraliev 2009), but since 1994, land was leased for long periods of time to individual farming enterprises (Republic of Uzbekistan 1994) through dismantlement of cooperatives and joint-stock companies. By 1997, there were nearly 20,000 individual farmers, with an average landholding of 16 ha (Spoor 1999). Their number peaked at 217,000 farms, but later the state farm optimization program led to a consolidation of farmlands with about 70,000 farmers with an average 30 ha of cropland as of year 2014. Presently, there are two major types of agricultural producers in the country: farmers and household plot owners. The land operated by farmers is leased from the State for a certain period of time, whereas the land under household plots (much smaller than the lands operated by farmers, usually less than a hectare) is given for indefinite use with the right to bequeath to children, so enjoys a higher level of tenure security. Cotton and wheat (two major crops, occupying most of the cropped area) in Uzbekistan are mostly produced in individual farming enterprises (all cooperatives and joint stock companies in crop production have been dismantled), whereas the bulk of fruits and vegetables are produced by rural households in their household plots. The Government regulates and controls the production and marketing for cotton and wheat, whereas the production of other crops, mainly fruits and vegetables by the rural population in their household plots are based on free market mechanisms.

Conceptual Basis

The conceptual framework of the case study follows the Economics of Land Degradation (ELD) conceptual framework presented in Chap. 2 and in Nkonya et al. (2013). The major characteristic of this framework is that it seeks to apply the Total Economic Value (TEV) approach in the assessment of the costs of land degradation, which implies that the ELD conceptual framework seeks to incorporate the value of not only provisional ecosystem goods and services into its analysis (e.g. crop yields and livestock products), but also of the value of indirect ecosystem services such as supporting, regulating and cultural services (e.g. carbon sequestration, nutrient cycling), option values, as well as non-use values. The elements of this conceptual framework are described in detail in Chap. 2. The ELD conceptual framework divides the causes of land degradation into proximate and underlying, which interact with each other to result in different levels of land degradation. Proximate causes include biophysical factors and unsustainable land management practices, whereas underlying causes include socio-economic and institutional factors such as land tenure security, access to markets, population density, poverty and others (Chaps. 2 and 7).

Methodology and Data Sources

The economic impacts of land degradation are calculated using the Total Economic Value (TEV) Framework (MEA 2005). TEV approach captures the total costs of land degradation more comprehensively (Nkonya et al. 2011), by incorporating the values of both direct and indirect ecosystem services.

Cost of Inaction

The methodology applied recognizes that land degradation occurs in two ways (Chap. 6). First, through shifts in land use/cover from more economically and environmentally productive (in terms of provision of ecosystem services) land uses/covers to those which have lower economic and environmental productivity. For example, from croplands to barren lands, or from forests to shrublands. The second, and more widely associated mechanism of land degradation, is when land use itself does not change, but the productivity of that land use decreases due to soil and land degradation. For example, secondary salinization leads to lower crop yields in irrigated croplands, even if these croplands do not shift to any other land use/cover.

Cost of Action

The approach for determining the cost of action for degradation due to land use and cover change (LUCC) has to consider the cost of reestablishing the high value biome lost and the opportunity cost of foregoing the benefits drawn from the lower value biome that is being replaced. For example, if a forest was replaced with cropland, the cost of planting trees or allowing natural regeneration (if still feasible) and cost of maintaining the new plantation or protecting the trees until they reach maturity has to be taken into account. Additionally, the opportunity cost of the crops being foregone to replant trees or allow natural regeneration has to be also taken into account. A detailed elaboration of the methodologies for calculating the costs of action versus in action applied in this study is given in Chap. 6.

Drivers of Sustainable Land Management

Land degradation usually occurs due to lack of use of sustainable land management (SLM) practices. Those factors preventing households from adopting SLM practices are also likely to cause land degradation. Therefore, analyzing the drivers of SLM is similar in its implications as analyzing the drivers of land degradation. In our empirical approach we apply the following reduced form econometric model to a nationally representative agricultural household survey data from Uzbekistan.

$$\mathbf{A} = \beta_0 + \beta_1 x_1 + \beta_2 x_2 + \beta_3 x_3 + \beta_4 x_4 + \beta_5 z_i + \varepsilon_i \qquad (21.1)$$

where,, etc.);

A the number of adopted SLM technologies

x_1

a vector of biophysical factors (e.g. climate conditions, agro-ecological zones, etc.);

x_2 a vector of policy-related and institutional factors (e.g. market access, land tenure

x_3 a vector of variables representing access to rural services (e.g. access to extension);

x_4 vector of variables representing rural household level capital endowment, level of education, household size, dependency ratio, etc.;

z_i vector of country fixed effects.

The dependent variable, A, is the number of sustainable land management technologies adopted by agricultural households in the country, as compiled through the agricultural household surveys, described below. In the survey, the households were asked to indicate the SLM technologies they use. They were given an open-ended list of about 30 SLM technologies, including such options as mulching, terracing, applying manure, planting cover crops, minimum or zero tillage, rotational grazing of livestock, etc., with the last option to add any others they use but not listed. We check the robustness of our findings on the role of various factors in affecting sustainable land management through different models in addition to the one elaborated above (Table 21.2). The explanatory variables in all of these models are the same as in model specification formula 21.1, however, the dependent variable and the estimation approaches do change (Table 21.2).

In Model 1, the distribution of the number of SLM technologies used is quite dispersed, ranging from 0 to 12 (Fig. 21.2). However, if we look at individual provinces, the conditional variance of the distribution is smaller in all cases than the conditional mean (Table 21.3). Furthermore, the dependent variable on the number of SLM technologies used is a count variable. Such a nature of the dependent variable requires the application of Poisson regression.

Model 2 uses the land degradation dummy indicator based on Le et al. (2014), who use the time series of GIMMS NDVI, to identify the hotspots of land degradation. In doing so, they also account for the masking effects of rainfall dynamics and

Table 21.2 The models used for the analysis of SLM drivers in Uzbekistan

Model	Type	Left hand side (LHS) variable	Nature of LHS variable
1	Poisson regression	The number of SLM technologies adopted by farmers	Count
2	Logistic	NDVI-based indicator of land degradation	Categorical dichotomous
3	Stereotype logit	Farmers' perceptions of soil erosion on their plots	Categorical ordinal
4	OLS regression	Cotton yields	Continuous

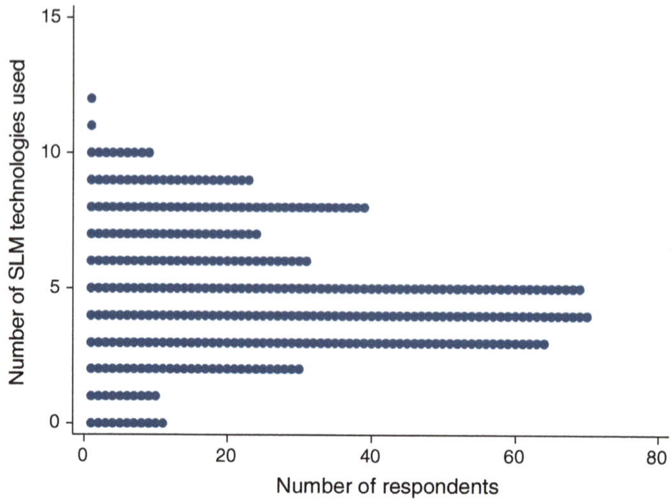

Fig. 21.2 The frequency of SLM technologies use among respondents

Table 21.3 The conditional mean and conditional variance of the number of SLM technologies used

Province	Conditional mean	Conditional variance
Andijon	4.48	1.84
Karakalpakstan	3.27	1.02
Kashkadarya	5.30	2.51
Tashkent	5.61	2.64
Total	4.90	2.39

atmospheric fertilization (Chap. 4). This variable shows the areas with negative difference in the NDVI, i.e. areas with NDVI decline between the baseline of 1982–84 and the end line of 2006. As we can see from the distribution, over 40 % of land plots were degraded and none of the households had improvement on their land plots in the period between 1982 and 2006 (Fig. 21.3). Bivariate choice nature of the dependent variable leads us to the use of logistic regression as the estimation method.

In Model 3, plot-level soil fertility as perceived by farmers themselves is taken as the explained variable. In the household survey analyzed, the respondents were asked to rate their land plots into three categories: 1-very fertile, 2-moderate, 3-poor (Fig. 21.4). Distribution shows that most of the farmers (66 %) rate their land plots to be moderately fertile. The dependent variable is a categorical ordinal variable where the ordering of ranks is uncertain. For this nature of variable, stereotype logistic regression needs to be used (Mirzabaev 2013).

Model 4 employs cotton yields as its dependent variable. The cotton yields were reported separately for each plot. Average yields weighted by plot size are used as the left-hand side variable (Fig. 21.5). The limitation of this model is the reduced sample size as only 135 of the 400 respondents grow cotton.

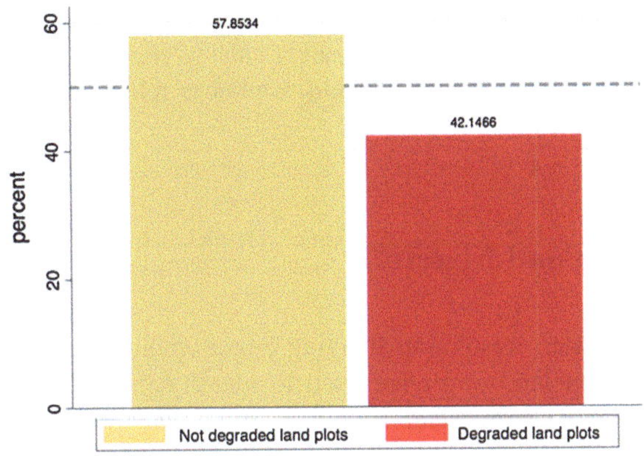

Fig. 21.3 The distribution of the land degradation indicator among households in Uzbekistan

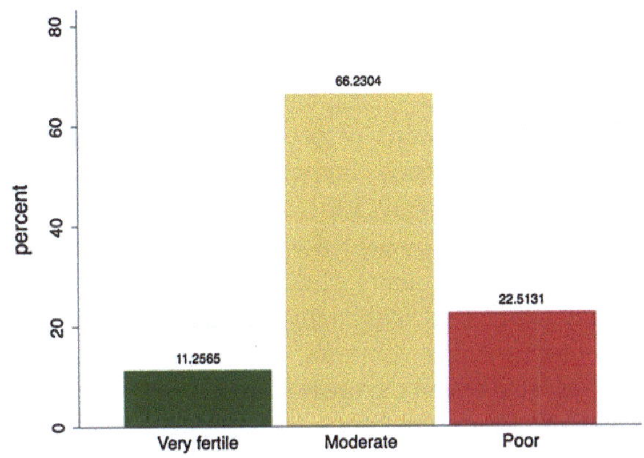

Fig. 21.4 The distribution of the index of soil fertility based on farmer's perception

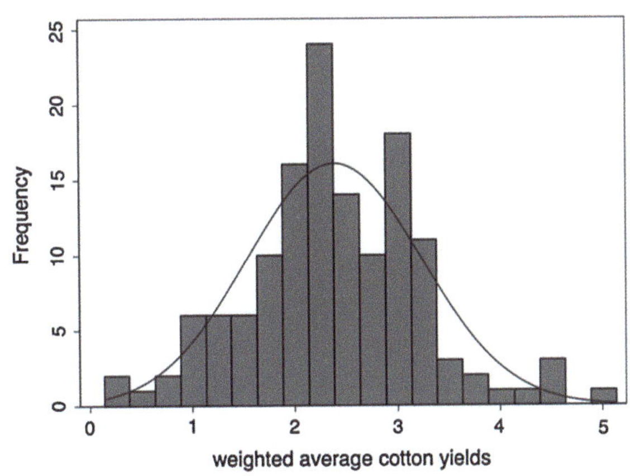

Fig. 21.5 The distribution of cotton yields among 135 large farms in Uzbekistan

In all of the models, the choice of explanatory variables is based on theoretical grounds and previous research, such as those indicated in Chaps. 2 and 7. Various appropriate interactions and nonlinear relationships among specific variables are also tested.

Data and Materials

Moderate Resolution Imaging Spectroradiometer (MODIS) remotely sensed datasets on land cover are used to identify the shifts in land use and land cover in Uzbekistan between 2001 and 2009. These include forests, grassland, cropland, shrublands (including woodlands), urban areas, barren land, and water bodies. The MODIS land cover dataset is ground truthed and quality controlled (Friedl et al. 2010), with overall accuracy of land use classification at 75 % (ibid.).

Following this analysis of land-use and land-cover change, total economic values are assigned to each land use and land cover using our own local contingent valuation of the value of ecosystem services in Uzbekistan through community focus group discussions and also using the data on the value of ecosystem services compiled from about 300 case studies in the Economics of Ecosystems and Biodiversity (TEEB) database (Van der Ploeg and de Groot 2010), as computed in Chap. 6 for each country of the world using the benefit transfer approach, whereby missing values of ecosystem services for Uzbekistan were imputed from other neighboring Asian countries. The communities for the focus group discussions were selected from both areas shown to have experienced NDVI declines during the last three decades and those which have experienced NDVI improvements during the same period (Le et al. 2014). Moreover, the selection of the communities also strived to capture all major land use/land cover categories in the country. The relevant data for Uzbekistan on the costs of action for re-establishing the higher value biomes is also obtained from the global level database on the costs of action developed in Chap. 6 of this volume.

Local Contingent Valuation

Focus Group Discussions (FGD) with stakeholders on the community level were organized in 6 specifically selected communities. Four stratified polygons were allocated across Uzbekistan based on agro-ecological zones—Toshkent region, Qashqadariya region, Karakalpakstan region, the Fergana Valley, from which the sites for FGDs were selected. The sites were allocated based on land degradation hotspots database by Le et al. (2014), also presented in Chap. 4. The main criteria that were followed for choosing the sites are given below. The locations of the sites are indicated in Fig. 21.6.

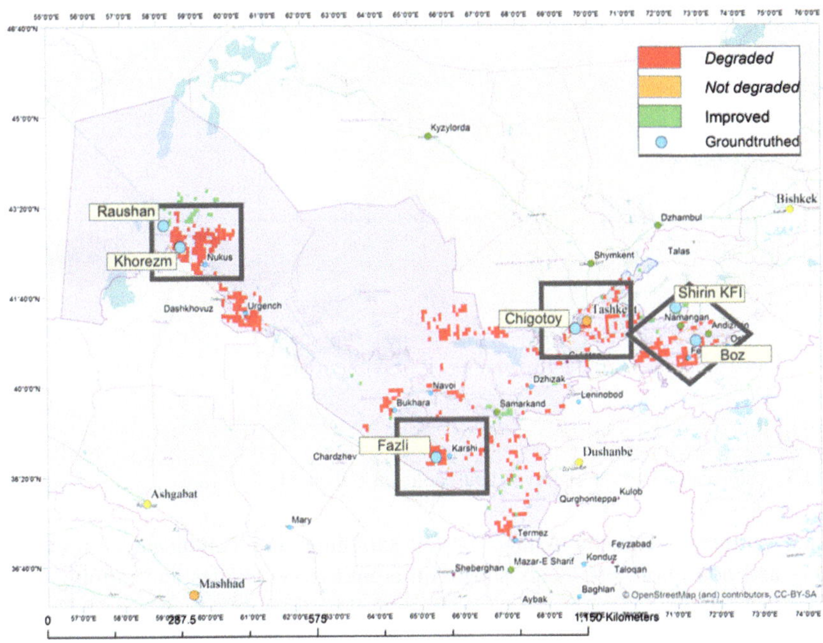

Fig. 21.6 The location of communities where focus group discussions were held

1. Choose sites both from areas with land degradation and land improvement
2. Select communities (or groups of communities) that span at least 8 km^2
3. Allocate at least one site from each polygon.

As a result, two communities with improved land, one community without change and four communities with degraded land plots were selected for Focus Group Discussions (FGD). The focus group discussions also sought to find out about land use changes in the past 30 years, actions taken to address ecosystem services loss and enhance ecosystem services improvement, off-site ecosystem services benefits and costs, as well as the perception about Payments for Ecosystem Services (PES). The information was collected both on provisional services (crop yields), but also on the values the communities attach to supporting, regulating, and cultural ecosystem services provided by land and soils.

Agricultural Survey Dataset

The dataset used for the analysis of the drivers of the adoption of sustainable land management practices comes from a nationally representative agricultural household survey in the country carried out during the 2009–2010 cropping season by the International Center for Agricultural Research in the Dry Areas (ICARDA) and

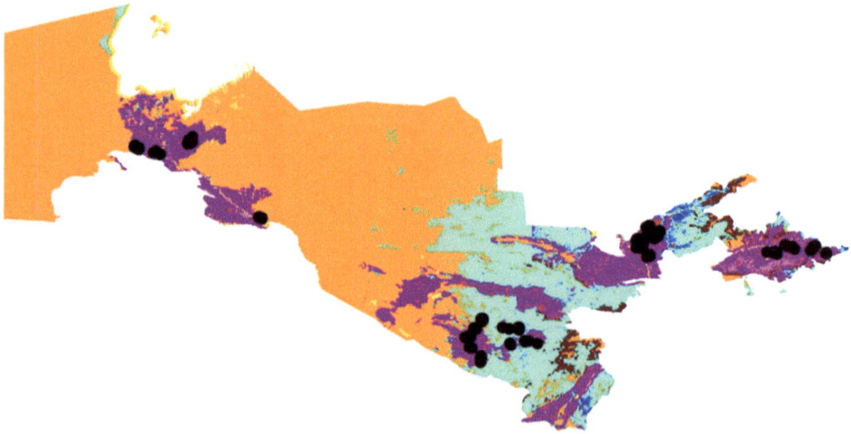

Fig. 21.7 The locations of the surveyed households in Uzbekistan

national partners.[3] The multi-stage survey sampling was conducted comprising farmers and household producers across different agro-ecologies and farming systems in the country (Mirzabaev 2013). With the confidence interval of 95 %, the sample size was set at 400 respondents. Uzbekistan was first divided into major agro-ecological zones—west, south, center and east for Uzbekistan. Then in each zone, one province was randomly selected (ibid.). The number of respondents was allocated to each province depending on the share of the agro-ecological zone in the value of the national agricultural production. Following this, the total list of villages was obtained for each province selected. The villages in each province were numbered, and the corresponding numbers for the selected villages were randomly drawn using the Excel software function "RAND" (25 villages) (ibid.). The number of respondents per village was evenly distributed within each province. At the village level, the list of all agricultural producers, including household producers, were obtained from the local administrations; agricultural producers were numbered, and then from this numbered list, respondents were randomly selected (Mirzabaev 2013; Fig. 21.7).

Results

Land Use and Land Cover Changes

Remotely sensed datasets on land cover from Moderate Resolution Imaging Spectroradiometer (MODIS) were analyzed to identify the shifts in the land use and land cover in Uzbekistan between 2001 and 2009 (Tables 21.4 and 21.5).

[3]We thank the Asian Development Bank for funding the surveys.

Table 21.4 Land use/cover classification in Uzbekistan in 2001, thousand ha

Province	Cropland	Forest	Grassland	Shrublands	Urban	Water	Barren
Andijon	292	0	39	15	97	0	0
Buhoro	316	2	262	465	72	34	2890
Farg'ona	295	0	127	46	163	0	9
Horazm	289	0	38	120	53	1	228
Jizzah	532	12	771	614	29	143	19
Karakalpakstan	408	4	1238	572	84	1320	12,800
Kashkadarya	647	1	569	1469	51	8	67
Namangan	303	0	314	35	80	0	16
Navoi	185	4	3478	2315	73	107	5048
Samarkand	372	0	183	723	142	2	10
Surhandaryo	434	1	712	663	35	2	143
Sirdaryo	428	0	21	12	29	0	0
Toshkent	757	2	537	112	114	4	13
Total	5258	27	8289	7161	1020	1622	21,243

Source Based on MODIS database

Table 21.5 Land use/cover change in Uzbekistan in 2009 relative to 2001, in thousand ha

Province	Cropland	Forest	Grassland	Shrublands	Urban	Water	Barren
Andijon	−15.7	0	26	−10.8	0	0	1
Buhoro	19	3	−155.6	186	0	0	−54.7
Farg'ona	6	1	−25.9	22	0	0	−3.3
Horazm	28	1	−13.2	15	0	1	−35.1
Jizzah	72	40	44	−170.9	0	17	−4.2
Karakalpakstan	250	24	892	296	0	−439.6	−1400.0
Kashkadarya	89	2	−40.5	−188.2	0	1	137
Namangan	−27.9	1	10	27	0	0	−10.0
Navoi	0	9	−294.6	3926	0	13	−3654.9
Samarkand	48	0	−52.4	−15.3	0	0	19
Surhandaryo	9	4	−135.8	171	0	1	−49.6
Sirdaryo	10	1	−5.4	−5.0	0	0	0
Toshkent	−130.9	12	146	−27.1	0	2	−3.8
Total	357	98	395	4227	0	−401.4	−5059.9

Source Based on MODIS database

The analysis shows that the major land use and land cover shifts in the country in this period were: (1) a 5 mln ha shift from barren areas (including deserts and desertic rangelands) mainly to shrublands (about 4 mln ha, almost all of which in the Navoi province) and to a lesser degree to grasslands (especially in Karakalpakstan: 0.8 mln ha, and Tashkent province 0.1 mln ha), (2) increase the in area of croplands by 0.3 mln ha (here important to note an increase of 0.25 mln ha in Karakalpakstan and a decrease of 0.13 mln ha in Tashkent province), (3) continued desiccation of the Aral Sea.

Drivers of Sustainable Land Management

As described in the conceptual framework, land degradation is a complex problem where numerous proximate and underlying factors influence the state of land degradation. The following set of variables was used (Table 21.6) to determine the most influential drivers of sustainable land management in the country.

These explanatory variables can be divided into proximate and underlying drivers of land degradation as explained in the conceptual framework. Among proximate drivers, agro-ecological zones, length of growing period, frequency of

Table 21.6 Descriptive statistics of variables included in the models

Variables	Mean	Min	Max
Dependent variables (in 4 models):			
Number of SLM technologies used	4.90	0	12
NDVI-based indicator of land degradation	0.58	0	1
Famer's perception of soil fertility (log)	−0.40	−5.30	4.99
Cotton yields	2.39	0.14	4.99
Independent (similar in all models):			
Age of household head (years)	47.29	20	80
Annual mean temperature (in °C)	14.40	11.95	16.48
Annual precipitation (in mm)	288.80	108.60	497.00
Crop producer (no-0, yes-1)	0.85	0	1
Distance to markets (in minutes)	74.83	3	336
Extension services availability (no-0, yes-1)	0.70	0	1
Frequency of weather shocks	1.41	0	5
Gender of household head (female-0, male-1)	0.94	0	1
Household members of working age	4	1	10
Household size	6	1	17
Length of the growing period (days)	91.64	34	137
Night time lighting intensity (NTLI)[a]	12.42	0	63
Livestock value	6.99	0	13.68
Distance to markets-NTLI interaction	556	0	2086
Net agricultural trading position (0-net buyer, 1-net seller)	0.51	0	1
Number of crops grown	3.21	0	8
Total assets	34,939	0	954.1
Total farm size (ha)	27.66	0.01	268.9

[a]Remotely sensed intensity of night time lighting (i.e. at the basic level shows the availability of electricity during the night time. Should not be confounded with natural day time brightness). Here used as a proxy for broad socio-economic development and availability of non-farm sector

weather shocks, annual temperature and precipitation, land slope are used. There is no firm theoretical basis for the relationship between these variables and land degradation and sustainable land management, and the nature of the influence of these variables on sustainable land management is empirical. However, there are some expectations regarding the influence of underlying drivers of sustainable land management. For example, closer distance to markets, private land tenure, higher livestock and other assets ownership, access to extension are expected to positively contribute to sustainable land management. The role of demographic variables such as gender, age and education of the household head, family size need to be empirically examined.

Following the analytical approach described in the methodology section, four different models were used to analyze the drivers of land degradation in Uzbekistan. The results of the econometric analyses on the household level are given in Table 21.7.

Key Common Insights from the Models

Regional differences The level of SLM adoptions seems to be lower in Karakalpakstan province of the country which, as we shall see later, is also located near the Aral Sea and in areas with highest negative TEV impacts of land degradation. This highlights that, in case of prioritization of SLM investments and actions, that region could be among the top provinces where there is a high need to address land degradation and the consequences of the drying up of the Aral Sea. The soil fertility perception and NDVI-based land degradation models also agree that land degradation problems are the most severe in Karakalpakstan province, even if the impact on cotton yields does not seem to be statistically significant.

Institutional and market characteristics Among institutional and market-related variables, only the number of crops grown, i.e. the higher level of crop diversification, was found to be positively associated with the number of SLM technology adoptions. The effect of other variables such as distance to markets, share of household plots with high tenure security in the total operated land, asset ownership, etc. were not statistically significant in this sample. Larger samples of households are normally needed to identify the direction of their impact. However, given the very small confidence intervals of most of these variables around zero, their impact on SLM adoptions seems low. The positive association between crop diversification and sustainable land management calls for increased efforts for reducing the mono-cropping practices (where mainly cotton and wheat are planted), and transiting to more diverse crop rotations. Specifically, experiences from the region indicate that including legumes to existing crop rotations can both help in improving soil fertility and increasing farmers' profitability (Pender et al. 2009). Moreover, several of the institutional and market-related variables were found to have statistically significant associations with NDVI-based land degradation

Table 21.7 Drivers of sustainable land management in Uzbekistan

Variables	Model 1: number of SLM technologies used	Model 2: NDVI (odds)	Model 3: farmer's perception of land fertility	Model 4: cotton yields (tons/ha)
	Count variable	0—degraded; 1—not degraded	1—very fertile; 2—moderate; 3—poor	
Provinces (base—Andijon)				
Karakalpakstan	−0.406**	−9.033***	−5.455*	−0.3
Kashkadarya	0.2	1.5	13.66***	−0.8
Tashkent	0.2	2.698**	10.11***	−1.049**
Annual precipitation	0.0	−0.0218***	−0.0466***	0.0
Annual mean temperature	−0.152**	−1.507***	−3.587***	0.2
Agroecological zone (base—Arid)				
Semiarid	−0.667***	0.9	−5.717***	0.657**
Length of the growing period	0.00768*	−0.0579*	0.0951**	0.0
Slope of the land	−0.241***	2.075***	1.4	−0.2
Farmers' perception of soil fertility (base—very fertile)				
Moderate	0.1	0.5	0.0	−0.560*
Poor	0.1	0.5	0.0	−0.658*
Frequency of weather shocks	0.0	0.481*	0.5	0.0
Household size	0.0	0.0	−0.2	0.0
Dependency ratio	0.0	−0.2	−0.2	0.0
Education of the household (HH) head (base—primary school)				
Middle school	0.2	−0.7	−0.4	0.0
High school	0.0	−1.3	−4.5	−1.352*
College	0.0	−2.0	−6.124**	−1.403**
University degree	0.0	−2.1	−4.4	−1.447**
Ph.D.	0.829**	0.0	0.0	0.0
Gender of HH head (base—female)				
Male	0.0	0.3	0.3	0.0
Age of HH head	0.0	0.0	−0.3	0.0
Age of HH head, squared	0.0	0.0	0.0	0.0
Total farm size ha	0.0	0.0212***	0.0	0.0
Leased/owned (household plot) land ratio	−0.1	1.599**	−2.593*	−0.2

(continued)

Table 21.7 (continued)

Variables	Model 1: number of SLM technologies used	Model 2: NDVI (odds)	Model 3: farmer's perception of land fertility	Model 4: cotton yields (tons/ha)
	Count variable	0—degraded; 1—not degraded	1—very fertile; 2—moderate; 3—poor	
Access to extension	−0.1	−1.787***	0.6	0.526**
The value of total assets	0.0	−8.38e−06**	1.77e−05**	2.23e−06*
Number of crops grown	0.0462**	−0.1	−0.3	0.115*
Livestock value (log)	0.0	0.0	0.0	0.0
Distance to markets	0.0	0.0187***	0.0489***	−0.0034*
Lights intensity at night time	0.0	0.112**	0.0	0.0
Distance to markets + Lights intensity	0.0	−0.00224**	−0.005***	0.0
Net position (base—net food buyer)				
Net food seller	0.0	−0.1	−1.473*	0.0
Number of SLM technologies known	0.0486***	−0.1	0.0	0.0
Number of SLM technologies used	0.0	0.2	0.0	0.0
Observations	378	377	378	135

*p-values<0.1; **p-values<0.05; ***means statistically significant p-values<0.01

measurement. Specifically, bigger farms sizes, the higher share of household plots with high tenure security in the total operated land, longer distance to markets, and stronger night-time lighting intensity as measured from the satellite were found to be associated with less land degradation. On the other hand, higher total assets and access to extension were associated with more land degradation, which is a surprising finding. Bigger farm sizes could allow for the adoption of scale-sensitive SLM measures in the country, such as for example, laser land leveling. Moreover, bigger farms usually have preferential access to Government subsidized fertilizer and other inputs. Operating household plots with high tenure security provides with more incentives for the adoption of sustainable land management practices as it allows for fuller internalization of often long-term benefits of sustainable land management. Higher night time lighting intensity is used as a proxy for the availability of a dynamic non-farm sector. Availability of non-farm jobs may allow for positive spillovers between farm and non-farm sectors (financial, technological) and also serve as a source of off-farm income which could be invested in adopting sustainable land management practices.

Greater distances to markets were positively associated with perceptions of soil fertility (consistent with the finding on NVDI-based measure). Several of the institutional and market-related variables also had a statistically significant effect on cotton yields. Namely, households with access to extension, higher total assets, higher crop diversity, and closer to markets reported higher cotton yields.

Focus Group Discussions

The results of the focus group discussion indicated that the values of almost all ecosystem services, such as provisional, regulating, supporting and cultural, have increased between 1982 to 2013 and it happens on both types of selected sites—degraded and improved. Among the main reasons for the increase in the values of ecosystem services, land degradation and the effects of climate change are named most frequently. The promotion of SLM was not always successful, reportedly due to the lack of financial resources for its implementation. There were also differences observed between the regions. A general increase of degradation and desertification processes was observed on all areas, although with a different rate. Karakalpakstan is reportedly the most affected region.

Values of Provisioning Ecosystem Services

FGDs showed that there was a tendency to an increase in the share of livestock and mixed farming systems in all of the studied regions in Uzbekistan. The monetary value of provisioning ecosystem services (ES) has greatly changed over the last 25 years in Uzbekistan with an increase of its value near the big cities (Tashkent) and a great decrease of ES value in remote areas (Karakalpakstan) that do not have access to big markets. One of the surveyed locations in Karakalpakstan region (Raushan), which borders with desert, also has a very high value of livestock per household, suggesting higher dependency on livestock products.

Indirect and Cultural Values of Ecosystem Services

ES values such as air quality regulation and water purification are given a significant value only in the region of Karakalpakstan, where reportedly the effect of a dried up Aral Sea has influenced the quality of the ecosystem services. Other indirect ecosystem services such as pollination, waste treatment, natural hazard regulation etc. as well as cultural ecosystem services were not given a significant value in any other surveyed site.

Costs of Land Degradation

Our estimation of the costs of land degradation in Uzbekistan following the Total Economic Value (TEV) framework described in the methodological section is given in Table 21.8. This valuation includes both direct and indirect ecosystem services, namely, the value of provisional, supporting, regulating and cultural ecosystem services. These cost estimates are based only on changes in the values of ecosystem services due to land use/cover change, and do not include the costs of land degradation when land use/cover did not change, i.e. it does not include the of land degradation when cropland remained cropland but yields have declined due to land degradation.

The results show that, in total, the economic value of land degradation costs, including the costs of lost ecosystem services, in Uzbekistan in 2009 as compared to 2001 was 0.838 billion USD, i.e. about 4 % equivalent of the Gross Domestic Product (GDP) in 2007 (all USD values are given in constant 2007 terms).

The highest costs of land degradation are occurring in Karakalpakstan and Navoi provinces of the country. Specifically for these two provinces: the major reason for elevated costs of land degradation in Karakalpakstan is due to the continued desiccation of the Aral Sea, and for Navoi province is due to grassland degradation,

Table 21.8 The costs of land degradation in Uzbekistan through land use change

Provinces	Annual cost of and degradation between 2001 and 2009, in mln USD	Per capita annual cost of land degradation, in USD	Land degradation costs as a share of GDP in 2007 (%), annually
Andijon	2	1	0
Buhoro	93	58	6
Fergana	12	4	1
Khorezm	12	8	2
Jizzah	68	62	11
Karakalpakstan	160	99	20
Kashkadarya	81	31	4
Namangan	11	5	1
Navoi	303	359	20
Samarkand	24	8	2
Surhandaryo	54	26	6
Syrdarya	5	7	1
Tashkent	17	7	1
Total	838	30	4

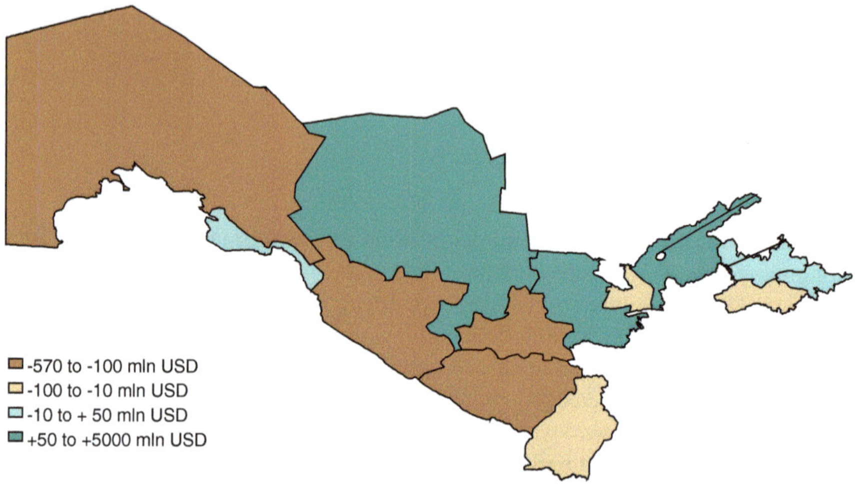

Fig. 21.8 Net changes in the TEV of ecosystems in Uzbekistan between 2001 and 2009

whereby grasslands are shifting to less fertile shrublands. If we look at the net change in the total economic value of ecosystems in the country, the overall figure for Uzbekistan is positive by about 4.4 billion USD, i.e. the Total Economic Value of Ecosystems has increased between 2001 and 2009. However, this overall figure masks sharp regional differences. Most of this increase is due to land improvement in Navoi province, where significant area of formerly barren lands has also shifted to shrublands (about 3.4 mln ha), with shrublands ecosystem functions having higher economic values than barren lands, potentially due to elevated levels of atmospheric fertilization, increasing the photosynthetic rate among desert mosses and higher forms of vegetation (Liobimtseva 2007). The major areas with net negative change are Karakalpakstan, Kashkadarya, Buhoro, Samarkand, Surhandaryo, Farg'ona and Sirdaryo provinces (Fig. 21.8 and Table 21.9).

Actions Against Land Degradation

The results show that the costs of action against land degradation are lower than the costs of inaction in Uzbekistan by more than 4 times over the 30 year horizon, meaning that each dollar spent on restoring lands degraded through shifts to lower value biomes is likely to have about 4.3 dollars of returns. Thus, the costs of action were found to equal about 11 billion USD over a 30-year horizon, whereas if nothing is done, the resulting losses may equal almost 50 billion USD during the same period. Almost 98 % of the costs of action are made up of the opportunity costs of action, for example, the value of new shrublands in areas where the original

Table 21.9 The net change in total economic value of land ecosystems in Uzbekistan

Provinces	Total economic value of ecosystems in 2001, in mln USD	Total economic value of ecosystems in 2009, in mln USD	Difference between 2001 and 2009, in mln USD
Andijon	722	748	27
Buhoro	2785	2679	−106
Farg'ona	831	803	−28
Horazm	657	708	50
Jizzah	4755	5013	258
Karakalpakstan	17,989	17,423	−566
Kashkadarya	4560	4255	−305
Namangan	1362	1399	37
Navoi	15,635	20,602	4968
Samarkand	2256	2162	−94
Surhandaryo	3701	3614	−87
Sirdaryo	371	360	−11
Toshkent	2729	3021	292
Total	58,353	62,787	4434

grasslands are being restored, whereas the actual implementation costs are found to be relatively smaller.

These estimates of the costs of actions are from the global social perspective, including the value of many global public goods such as carbon sequestration or nutrient cycling. As shown in Table 21.10, more than half of the costs of land degradation belong to the losses of indirect ecosystem services. However, private land users may include only the losses in provisional ecosystem services of land due to degradation in their decision making because they cannot fully internalize the benefits from safeguarding or restoring the non-provisional ecosystem services of land (such as for example, climate regulation, nutrient cycling). Since many of these non-provisional ecosystem services of land are global public goods, even the national Government is less likely to incorporate the full value of the lost land ecosystem services into their calculations, since they as well cannot internalize fully the benefits of SLM within the country. Thus, a wider use of payment for ecosystem services (PES) approaches through international investments could potentially help in reducing this lack of incentives to invest into SLM (Chap. 10).

The calculations of the costs of action vs inaction against land degradation presented above are based on land degradation due to land use and cover change (LUCC). Although these calculations are able to capture the effect of extreme forms of cropland or rangeland degradation when these croplands and rangelands shift to barren lands, these calculations do not include the costs of land degradation associated with lower crop yields and lower grassland productivity due to degradation but without land use and cover change. Chapter 8 calculates that the costs of productivity decline in rangelands through lower meat, milk and live weight loss among livestock in Uzbekistan are about 6 million USD annually. However, this

Table 21.10 Costs of action versus inaction in Uzbekistan, in mln USD

Provinces	Land degradation costs for the entire 2001–2009 period	Annual costs of land degradation in terms of provisional ecosystem services only	Cost of action (6 years)	Cost of action (30 years)	Of which, the opportunity cost of action	Cost of inaction (6 years)	Cost of inaction (30 years)	Ratio of cost of inaction/action
Andijon	16	7	51	51	50	112	152	2.9
Buhoro	742	298	535	536	523	2942	3982	7.7
Farg'ona	96	26	248	249	244	622	841	3.3
Horazm	98	3	183	183	179	519	703	3.8
Jizzah	546	242	831	834	814	2769	3748	4.5
Karakalpakstan	1282	495	1164	1169	1131	5441	7366	6.3
Kashkadarya	648	141	849	853	829	3074	4161	5.0
Namangan	92	35	206	206	203	563	762	3.7
Navoi	2425	1812	5375	5388	5286	15,185	20,554	3.8
Samarkand	191	13	630	631	621	1372	1857	2.9
Surhandaryo	425	230	1011	1014	995	2685	3635	3.6
Sirdaryo	41	8	39	39	38	170	231	5.9
Toshkent	138	18	286	286	281	796	1078	3.7
Tashkent city	0	0	1	1	1	1	2	2.0
Total	6741	3314	11,408	11,442	11,197	36,251	49,070	4.3

figure is likely underestimating the impact of land degradation on livestock productivity in the country since the major share of the livestock in Uzbekistan is reared through stable feeding of forage crops grown in cropped areas and not through open grazing in rangelands. The estimates on the impacts of cropland degradation on the yields of wheat, maize and rice for the whole Central Asian region in Chap. 6 point to about 300 million USD of losses. However, it is difficult to disaggregate meaningfully these losses for Uzbekistan alone. Besides, this figure does not include cotton—a major crop in Uzbekistan. ICARDA (2007) evaluated the impact of salinity on rural livelihoods in Syrdarya province of Uzbekistan. With the price of raw cotton at around 300 USD/t, farmers in the high and medium salinity zones were found to lose on average 116 USD/ha and 77 USD/ha in, respectively, as compared to farmers operating land with low salinity. In the case of wheat, at a price of 100 USD/t, farmers in the high and medium salinity zones lost on average 149 USD/ha and 66 USD/ha as compared to low salinity group farmers because of salinity. Gupta et al. (2009) review that the annual losses in agricultural production due to soil salinization might be about US$ 31 million, and economic losses due to land abandonment at 12 million USD. Nkonya et al. (2011) estimated that the annual economic loss of salinity for wheat and cotton alone is 13.29 million USD. Despite these available estimates, there is a lack of quantitative studies assessing the costs of land degradation through lower crop yields and livestock productivity with nationally representative data samples. Hence, more research is required in this area in the future.

Technological Options for Sustainable Land Management

Over the past five years, the Government of Uzbekistan has taken many steps to improve irrigation and drainage infrastructure to reduce water losses and mitigate soil salinization. The government has planned to rehabilitate 10,000–15,000 ha of abandoned land annually through reconstruction of irrigation and drainage infrastructure. The construction of such facilities is estimated to cost 2000 USD per ha. This approach will require massive financial and technical support from government as individual farmers are unable to bear these costs. In addition to this, there are also cost-effective interventions that can be undertaken by farmers to compliment state efforts in mitigating salinization problems. Below we review some of such technological options for sustainable land management which may be undertaken as part of action programs to address land degradation.

For rehabilitating desert rangelands, planting salt and drought tolerant species in rangelands such as salt tolerant alfalfa varieties has shown promising results in trials in the Kyzylkum desert in Uzbekistan, where introduced varieties significantly outperformed local varieties. Reseeding with native drought and salt tolerant legumes such as Acacia, Astralagus, Alhagi, Glycyrrhiza, Melilotus, Cicer, Vicia, and Lathyrus also shows promise, and these are capable of sustaining relatively heavy grazing (Pender et al. 2009; Toderich et al. 2008a, b).

Moreover, nitrogen fixing forage crops can play a crucial role in saving fertilizer and improving soil fertility when added to crop rotations. In this respect, the creation of highly productive fodder systems through the establishment of palatable halophytes in saline areas has been shown to remediate saline soils as well as provide an income to resource poor farmers (Toderich et al. 2002, 2008a, b). In 2000–2004, the use of licorice (*Glycyrrhiza glabra*) to reclaim abandoned saline areas was studied in Syrdarya province. After 4 years of licorice cultivation, cotton yields in these formerly highly saline areas recovered from initial 0.87–2.42 t/ha (Kushiev et al. 2005).

Contour irrigation with plastic chutes in Uzbekistan reduced soil erosion to 0.1 t/ha from 4.5 to 8.2 t/ha using conventional practices (Pender et al. 2009). Since poor drainage is a major problem in irrigated areas of Central Asia, research is needed to adapt and test conservation tillage options for irrigated agriculture in this region, including minimum as well as zero tillage options (Gupta et al. 2009).

An experiment in the wheat—fallow system in Uzbekistan demonstrated the advantages of zero or minimum tillage in improving soil conditions (ICARDA 2007). The level of soil organic matter was highest in the zero tillage treatment and lowest with conventional tillage during summer fallow. Although soil bulk density was slightly greater under no till, soil moisture was greater with no till, especially in the driest year.

Tree plantations in degraded croplands may help in rehabilitating degraded soils and restoring some part of their provisional services (Khamzina et al. 2008). Afforestation of abandoned croplands due to their degradation in Uzbekistan can allow for provisioning of tree products for income generation (Lamers et al. 2008; Djanibekov et al. 2013b). However, insecure farmland tenure restrains Uzbek farmers from investing into long-term land use activities (Djanibekov et al. 2012a). In such conditions a short-rotation forestry might be a more appropriate option to encourage farmers' towards agroforestry practices (Djanibekov et al. 2012b).

Needless to say that only the application of technological solutions may not be enough to address land degradation in a sustainable manner. The application of these technological options need to go hand in hand with institutional and socio-economic policies conducive to sustainable land management, such as, as we have seen in the analysis earlier, information and knowledge dissemination, access to high quality extension services, land tenure security, non-agricultural rural development and crop diversification.

Conclusions

The research findings indicate that the costs of land degradation in Uzbekistan are substantial reaching as high as about 0.85 billion USD annually between 2001 and 2009 only due to land use and land cover changes (LUCC). These figures do not include the costs of land degradation on a static land use. Addressing land degradation has significant economic returns. Every dollar invested into land rehabilitation can yield about 4 dollars of returns over a 30-year planning horizon in the country. The highest returns from actions against land degradation due to LUCC are estimated for Karakalpakstan, Buhoro, and Syrdaryo provinces of Uzbekistan. The major factors associated with sustainable land management are found to be crop diversification, more secure land tenure and availability of non-farm jobs in rural areas.

References

Abdullaev, I., Giordano, M., & Rasulov, A. (2005). Cotton in Uzbekistan: Water and welfare. In *Conference on "Cotton Sector in Central Asia: Economic Policy and Development Challenges"*. University of London: The School of Oriental and African Studies, 3–4 Nov 2005.

Akramkhanov, A., Martius, C., Park, S. J., & Hendrickx, J. M. H. (2011). Environmental factors of spatial distribution of soil salinity on flat irrigated terrain. *Geoderma, 163*(1–2), 55–62.

Akramkhanov, A., & Vlek, P. (2011). The assessment of spatial distribution of soil salinity risk using neural network. *Environmental Monitoring and Assessment, 184*(4), 1–11.

Akramov, K., & Omuraliev, N. (2009). Institutional change, rural services, and agricultural performance in Kyrgyzstan. IFPRI Discussion Paper 00904. Washington DC, USA.

Bloch, P. (2002). Agrarian reform in Uzbekistan and other Central Asian countries. Working paper, no. 49, Land Tenure Center, University of Wisconsin–Madison, USA.

Bobojonov, I., Lamers, J. P. A., Djanibekov, N., Ibragimov, N., Begdullaeva, T., Ergashev, A., et al. (2012). Crop diversification in support of sustainable agriculture in Khorezm. In C. Martius, I. Rudenko, J. P. A. Lamers, & P. L. G. Vlek (Eds.), *Cotton, water, salts and soums—economic and ecological restructuring in Khorezm, Uzbekistan* (pp. 219–233). Dordrecht/Heidelberg/London/New York: Springer.

Bucknall, J., Klytchnikova, I., Lampietti, J., Lundell, M., Scatasta, M., & Thurman, M. (2003). *Irrigation in Central Asia: Social, economic and environmental considerations*. Washington, USA: World Bank.

CACILM. (2006). Country pilot partnerships on sustainable land management. CACILM Multicountry Partnership Framework. Executive Summary. Tashkent, ADB.

Chen, X., Bai, J., Li, X., Luo, G., Li, J., & Li, B. L. (2013). Changes in land use/land cover and ecosystem services in Central Asia during 1990–2009. *Current Opinion in Environmental Sustainability, 5*, 116–127.

Conrad, C., Colditz, R. R., Dech, S., Klein, D., & Vlek, P. L. G. (2011). Temporal segmentation of MODIS time series for improving crop classification in Central Asian irrigation systems. *International Journal of Remote Sensing, 32*, 1–16.

Conrad, C., Dech, S., Dubovyk, O., Fritsch, S., Klein, D., Löw, F., et al. (2014). Derivation of temporal windows for accurate crop discrimination in heterogeneous croplands of Uzbekistan using multitemporal rapid eye images. *Computers and Electronics in Agriculture, 103*, 63–74.

Djanibekov, N., Sommer, R., & Djanibekov, U. (2013b). Evaluation of effects of cotton policy changes on land and water use in Uzbekistan: Application of a bio-economic farm model at the level of a water users association. *Agricultural Systems, 118*, 1–13.

Djanibekov, N., Van Assche, K., Bobojonov, I., & Lamers, J. P. A. (2012b). Farm restructuring and land consolidation in Uzbekistan: New farms with old barriers. *Europe-Asia Studies, 64*(6), 1101–1126.

Djanibekov, U., Djanibekov, N., Khamzina, A., Bhaduri, A., Lamers, J. P. A., & Berg, E. (2013a). Impacts of innovative forestry land use on rural livelihood in a bimodal agricultural system in irrigated drylands. *Land Use Policy, 35*, 95–106.

Djanibekov, U., Khamzina, A., Djanibekov, N., & Lamers, J. P. A. (2012a). How attractive are short-term CDM forestations in arid regions? The case of irrigated croplands in Uzbekistan. *Forest Policy and Economics, 21*, 108–117.

Dubovyk, O., Menz, G., Conrad, C., Kan, E., Machwitz, M., & Khamzina, A. (2013a). Spatio-temporal analyses of cropland degradation in the irrigated lowlands of Uzbekistan using remote-sensing and logistic regression modeling. *Environmental Monitoring and Assessment, 185*, 4775–4790.

Dubovyk, O., Menz, G., Conrad, C., Lamers, J., Lee, A., & Khamzina, A. (2013b). Spatial targeting of land rehabilitation: A relational analysis of cropland productivity decline in arid Uzbekistan. *Erdkunde, 67*, 167–181.

Dubovyk, O., Menz, G., Conrad, C., Thonfeld, F., & Khamzina, A. (2013c). Object-based identification of vegetation cover decline in irrigated agro-ecosystems in Uzbekistan. *Quaternary International, 311*, 163–174.

Friedl, M. A., Sulla-Menashe, D., Tan, B., Schneider, A., Ramankutty, N., Sibley, A., & Huang, X. (2010). MODIS Collection 5 global land cover: Algorithm refinements and characterization of new datasets. *Remote Sensing of Environment, 114*(1), 168–182.

Gupta, R., Kienzler, K., Mirzabaev, A., Martius, C., de Pauw, E., Shideed, K. et al. (2009). Research prospectus: A vision for sustainable land management research in Central Asia. ICARDA Central Asia and Caucasus Program. Sustainable Agriculture in Central Asia and the Caucasus Series No. 1. CGIAR-PFU, Tashkent, Uzbekistan. 84pp.

ICARDA. (2003). On-Farm Soil and Water Management for Sustainable Agricultural Systems in Central Asia. Final Report (Funded By The Asian Development Bank) November.

ICARDA. (2007). Improving Rural Livelihoods Through Efficient On-Farm Water and Soil Fertility Management in Central Asia Project Funded By Adb Under Reta 6136 Project Report 2004–2007.

ICTSD (International Center for Trade and Sustainable Development). (2014). The problem of water resources in Central Asia (in Russian). http://ictsd.org/i/news/mosty-blog/187411/#sthash.bZ4pi386.dpuf. Accessed 22 April 2014.

IWMI-ICARDA-ICBA. (2008). Enabling Communities in the Aral Sea Basin to Combat Land and Water Resource Degradation Through the Creation of Bright Spots. Project Report. The ADB supported project: RETA 6208 (2005–2008).

Ji, C. (2008). *Central Asian countries initiative for land management multicountry partnership framework support project*. Tashkent: ADB.

Kariyeva, J., & Van Leeuwen, W. J. D. (2011). Environmental drivers of NDVI-based vegetation phenology in Central Asia. *Remote Sensing, 3*, 203–246.

Khamzina, A., Lamers, J. P. A., & Vlek, P. L. G. (2008). Tree establishment under deficit irrigation on degraded land in the lower Amu Darya River region, Aral Sea Basin. *Forest Ecology and Management, 255*(1), 168–178.

Khan, A. R. (1996). The transition to a market economy in agriculture. In *Social policy and economic transformation in Uzbekistan* (pp. 65–92). Geneva: ILO.

Kharin, N. G., Tateishi, R., & Harahsheh, H. (1999). *Degradation of the drylands of Asia. Center for environmental remote sensing*. Japan: Chiba University.

Khusanov, R. (2009). *IFPRI-ICARDA project on "Economic Evaluation of Sustainable Land Management Options in Central Asia" Uzbekistan Report*. Uzbekistan: Tashkent.

Kienzler, K. M., Lamers, J. P. A., McDonald, A., Mirzabaev, A., Ibragimov, N., Egamberdiev, O., et al. (2012). Conservation agriculture in Central Asia—what do we know and where do we go from here? *Field Crops Research, 132*, 95–105.

Klein, I., Gessner, U., & Kuenzer, C. (2012). Regional land cover mapping and change detection in Central Asia using MODIS time-series. *Applied Geography, 35*, 219–234.

Kushiev, H., Noble, A. D., Abdullaev, I., & Toshbekov, U. (2005). Remediation of abandoned saline soils using Glycyrrhiza glabra: A study from the hungry steppes of Central Asia. *International Journal of Agricultural Sustainability, 3*(2), 102–113.

Lamers, J. P. A., Bobojonov, I., Khamzina, A., & Franz, J. S. (2008). Financial analysis of small-scale forests in the Amu Darya lowlands of rural Uzbekistan. *Forests, Trees and Livelihoods, 18*(4), 375–382.

Le, Q. B., Nkonya, E., & Mirzabaev, A. (2014). Biomass productivity-based mapping of global land degradation hotspots. ZEF-Discussion Papers on Development Policy (p. 193). Bonn, Germany.

Liobimtseva, E. (2007). Possible changes in the carbon budget of arid and semi-arid Central Asia inferred from land-use/landcover analyses during 1981–2001. In Climate change and terrestrial carbon sequestration in Central Asia (pp. 441–452). London: Taylor & Francis.

Maman, S., Blumberg, D. G., Tsoar, H., Mamedov, B., & Porat, N. (2011). The Central Asian ergs: A study by remote sensing and geographic information systems. *Aeolian Research, 3*, 353–366.

MEA (Millenium Ecosystem Assessment). (2005). Dryland Systems. Ecosystem and Well-Being: Current State and Trends. In R. Hassan, R. Scholes, & N. Ash (Eds.), (pp. 623–662). Washington, DC: Island Press.

Mirzabaev, A. (2013). Climate Volatility and Change in Central Asia: Economic Impacts and Adaptation. PhD thesis at Agricultural Faculty, University of Bonn. urn:nbn:de:hbz:5n-3238.

Nkonya, E., Gerber, N., Baumgartner, P., Von Braun, J., De Pinto, A., Graw, V., et al. (2011). The Economics of Desertification Land Degradation, and Drought IFPRI Discussion Paper. IFPRI: Washington DC.

Nkonya, E., Von Braun, J., Mirzabaev, A., Le, Q. B., Kwon, H. Y., & Kirui, O. (2013). Economics of land degradation initiative: Methods and approach for global and national assessments. ZEF-Discussion Papers on Development Policy, (183). Center for Development Research, Bonn, Germany.

Pender, J., Mirzabaev, A., & Kato, E. (2009). *Economic analysis of sustainable land management options in Central Asia*. Washington, DC, USA: Final Report submitted to ADB.

Propastin, P. A., Kappas, M., & Muratova, N. R. (2008). Inter-annual changes in vegetation activities and their relationship to temperature and precipitation in Central Asia from 1982 to 2003. *Journal of Environmental Informatics, 12*, 75–87.

Republic of Uzbekistan. (1994). *Decrees and resolutions: On measures for intensification of economic reforms, protection of private property and promotion of entrepreneurship*. Tashkent: Uzbekistan Publishing House.

Spoor, M. (1999). Agrarian transition in former soviet Central Asia: A comparative study of Kazakhstan, Kyrgyzsrtan and Uzbekistan. Working Paper 298, Centre for the Study of Transition and Development [CESTRAD], ISS, Rotterdam, Netherlands.

Sutton, W., Whitford, P., Stephens, E. M., Galinato, S. P., Nevel, B., Plonka, B., & Karamete, E. (2007). *Integrating environment into agriculture and forestry. Progress and prospects in Eastern Europe and Central Asia*. Kosovo: World Bank.

Toderich, K., Shoaib, I., Juylova, E., Rabbimov, A., Bekchanov, B., Shuyskaya, E., et al. (2008a). New approaches for biosaline agriculture development, management and conservation of sandy desert ecosystems. In C. Abdelly, M. Ozturk, M. Ashraf, & K. Grignon (Eds.), *Biosaline agriculture and high salinity tolerance*. Switzerland: Birkhauser Verlag.

Toderich, K., Tsukatani, T., Mardonov, B., Gintzburger, G., Zemtsova, O., Tsukervanik, E., & Shuyskaya, E. (2002). Water quality, cropping and small ruminants: A challenge for the future agriculture in dry areas of Uzbekistan. Discussion Paper No. 553. Kyoto Institute of Economic Research. Kyoto University.

Toderich, K., Tsukatani, T., Shoaib, I., Massino, I., Wilhelm, M., Yusupov, S., et al. (2008b). *Extent of salt-affected land in Central Asia: Biosaline agriculture and utilization of salt-affected resources*. Discussion paper No. 648. Kier Discussion paper series. Kyoto Institute of Economic Research.

Van der Ploeg, S., & de Groot, R. S. (2010). *The TEEB valuation database—a searchable database of 1310 estimates of monetary values of ecosystem services*. Wageningen, the Netherlands: Foundation for Sustainable Development.

World Bank. (2003). Assessment of irrigation and drainage infrastructure in Uzbekistan (Russian). Report (108 pp). Tashkent, Uzbekistan: World Bank.

Index

E. Nkonya et al. (eds.), *Economics of Land Degradation and Improvement – A Global Assessment for Sustainable Development*,
DOI 10.1007/978-3-319-19168-3

MIX
Papier aus verantwortungsvollen Quellen
Paper from responsible sources
FSC® C105338

If you have any concerns about our products,
you can contact us on
ProductSafety@springernature.com

In case Publisher is established outside the EU,
the EU authorized representative is:
Springer Nature Customer Service Center GmbH
Europaplatz 3, 69115 Heidelberg, Germany

Printed by Libri Plureos GmbH
in Hamburg, Germany